ISBN: 9781314619270

Published by:
HardPress Publishing
8345 NW 66TH ST #2561
MIAMI FL 33166-2626

Email: info@hardpress.net
Web: http://www.hardpress.net

# ALBERT R. MANN LIBRARY
## Cornell University

# Gift of
# Thomas Bass

From *Home Bakings*, by Edna Evans
San Francisco, 1912.

# The Picayune's Creole Cook Book

― FOURTH EDITION ―

THE Question of "a good cook" is now becoming a very vexing problem. The only remedy for this state of things is for the ladies of the present day to do as their grandmothers did, acquaint themselves thoroughly with the art of cooking in all its important and minutest details, and learn how to properly apply them. To assist the good housewives of the present day in this, to preserve to future generations the many excellent and matchless recipes of our New Orleans cuisine, to gather these up from the lips of the old Creole negro cooks and the grand old housekeepers who still survive, ere they, too, pass away, and Creole Cookery, with all its delightful combinations and possibilities, will have become a lost art, is, in a measure, the object of this book. :: :: :: :: ::

Retail Price at Picayune Office, - $1.00

By Registered Mail, - - $1.25

Copyright 1901, 1906 and 1910 by
THE PICAYUNE, - NEW ORLEANS, LA.

PICAYUNE JOB PRINT

# The PICAYUNE'S CREOLE COOK BOOK

## INTRODUCTION.

**T**HE universal favor with which the first editions of THE PICAYUNE'S CREOLE COOK BOOK were received throughout the United States, the remarkably short time in which they were exhausted, and the numerous demands for copies that are continually coming in from all sections, has impelled the publishers to issue a Fourth Edition of this work.

The Revised Edition has been prepared with great care. Each recipe that has been added has been tried and tested and is given as the result of personal practical experience and success in the Creole Kitchen. The topics have been more conveniently and systematically classified and arranged, the methods of preparation and manipulation in many instances simplified, and the edition, in its entirety, will therefore be found far more complete, comprehensive and valuable than the first.

With these explanations THE PICAYUNE sends forth the Creole Cook Book. Its name tells its story and bespeaks its value. It is

**THE ONLY BOOK OF THE KIND.**

 I'm the Picayune's Weather Prophet,
It's Froggie so faithful and true;
"Tante Zoe" has asked me to help her
In serving so nicely to you,
The dishes The Picayune bade her
Prepare as a Creole cook can,
That men might grow wiser and better,
And happiness reign in the land.

# INTRODUCTION

## TO THE FIRST EDITION

IN PRESENTING to the public this Creole Cook Book, *The Picayune* is actuated by the desire to fill a want that has long been felt, not only in New Orleans, where the art of good cooking was long ago reduced to a positive science, but in many sections of the country where the fame of our Creole cuisine has spread, and with slight modification incident to local supplies of food articles, many of our most delightful recipes may be adapted by the intelligent housekeeper with profit and pleasure.

Time was when the question of a Creole Cook Book would have been, as far as New Orleans is concerned, as useless an addition to our local literature as it is now a necessity, for the Creole negro cooks of nearly two hundred years ago, carefully instructed and directed by their white Creole mistresses, who received their inheritance of gastronomic lore from France, where the art of good cooking first had birth, faithfully transmitted their knowledge to their progeny, and these, quick to appreciate and understand, and with a keen intelligence and zeal born of the desire to please, improvised and improved upon the products of the cuisine of Louisiana's mother country; then came the Spanish domination, with its influx of rich and stately dishes, brought over by the grand dames of Spain of a century and a half ago; after that came the gradual amalgamation of the two races on Louisiana soil; and with this was evolved a new school of cookery, partaking of the best elements of the French and Spanish cuisines, and yet peculiarly distinct from either, a system of cookery that has held its own through succeeding generations and which drew from even such a learned authority as Thackeray, that noted tribute to New Orleans, "the old Franco-Spanish city on the banks of the Mississippi, where, of all the cities in the world, you can eat the most and suffer the least, where claret is as good as at Bordeaux, and where a 'ragout' and a 'bouillabaisse' can be had, the like of which was never eaten in Marseilles or Paris."

But the Civil War, with its vast upheaval of social conditions, wrought great changes in the household economy of New Orleans, as it did throughout the South; here, as elsewhere, she who had ruled as the mistress of yesterday, became her own cook of to-day; in nine cases out of ten the younger darkies accepted their freedom with alacrity, but in many ancient families the older Creole "negresse," as they were called, were slow to leave the haunts of the old cuisine and the families of which they felt themselves an integral part, Many lingered on, and the young girls who grew up after that period had opportunities that will never again come to the Creole girls of New Orleans. For one of the most significant changes and one of the saddest, too, in this old city, is the passing of the faithful old negro cooks—the "mammies," who felt it a pride and honor, even in poverty, to cling to the fortunes of their former masters and mistresses, and out of the scant family allowance to be still able to prepare for their "ole Miss'" table a "ragout" from a piece of neck meat, or a "pot-au-poivre" from many mixturees that might grace the dining of a king.

But the "bandana and tignon" are fast disappearing from our kitchens. Soon will the last of the olden negro cooks of ante-bellum days have passed away and their places will not be supplied, for in New Orleans, as in other cities of the South, there is "a new colored woman" as well as a new white. The question of "a good cook" is now becoming a very vexing problem , and the only remedy for this state of things is for the ladies of the present day to do as their grandmothers did, acquaint themselves thoroughly with the art of cooking in all its important and minutest details, and learn how to properly apply them. To assist them in this, to preserve to future generations the many excellent and matchless recipes of our New Orleans cuisine, to gather these up from the lips of the Old Creole negro cooks and the grand old housekeepers who still survive, ere they too, pass away, and Creole cookery, with all its delightful combinations and possibilities, will have become a lost art, is, in a measure, the object of this book.

But far and above this, *The Picayune*, in compiling this book, has been animated by the laudable desire to teach the great mass of the public how to live cheaply and well. The moral influences of good cooking cannot be too forcibly insisted upon. There is an old saying that "the way to a man's heart is through his stomach." Every housewife knows the importance of setting a well-cooked meal before her husband if she wishes him to preserve his equanimity of temper. Every mother should know the importance of preparing good, nutritious dishes for her children in the most palatable and appetizing manner, if she would give them that most precious of all gifts "a healthy mind in a healthy body." People are the better, the happier and the longer lived for the good, wholesome, well-cooked daily meal.

The introduction, then, of the art of good cooking into every household and a general, intelligent knowledge of the nutritive qualities of food substances, are ends greatly to be desired, for the best food often loses half its value through the faults displayed in preparation, while, on the other hand, simple and plain dishes may be so cooked that they will acquire a flavor and a nutritive value through special combinations that will please the most delicate appetities. Among all classes to-day there is a deplorable and constant waste. Among the rich, the sole aim, of what appears to be good cookery, seems rather an effort to tempt by a succession of highly-seasoned and savory food and to consume to excess; while among the poor and middle classes living and cooking seem to go on as best they may, with little variety from day to day, and still less care and preparation, indeed, the food is often cooked in such a way that ready digestion becomes an impossibility, and a large portion of the nutriment is either wasted or destroyed utterly.

It is proposed in this book to assist the housekeepers generally to set a dainty and appetizing table at a moderate outlay; to give recipes clearly and accurately with simplicity and exactness, so that the problem of "how to live," may become easier of solution and even the most ignorant and inexperienced cook may be able to prepare a toothsome and nutritious meal with success. The housekeeper is not told "to take some of this, a little of that," and "a pinch" of some other ingredient; she is not left to the chance of guessing accidentally at the proper proportions of component parts of any dish, but the relative proportions of all ingredients are given with accuracy, the proper length of time required for cooking different dishes. *In all the recipes the quantities are given for a family of six. The intelligent housekeeper will thus be able to form a happy medium and increase or reduce proportionately according to the size of her family, the number of invited guests, etc.*

The Picayune's Creole Cook Book is not designed for chefs of cuisines; it has been prepared with special appreciation of the wants of the household and of that immense class of housekeepers who, thrown upon their own resources and anxious to learn, are yet ignorant of the simplest details of good cooking; for young housekeepers who are left to "experience" for a teacher, and who often learn only after many disheartening failures and a great outlay and waste of good material, and for the public generally, who, as a rule, have yet to learn that in a well-regulated kitchen nothing is ever wasted, but with careful preparation even the "rough-ends" of a beef steak may be made into a wholesome, tender and appetizing dish; that "stale bread" may be used in the most delicious "desserts" and "farcies," and "left-over" food from the day before need not be thrown in the trash-box, but may be made into an endless variety of wholesome and nutritious dishes.

Hence, especial care has been taken to rescue from oblivion many fine old-fashioned dishes, and bring them back into general use—dishes whose places can never be equaled by elegant novelties or fancifully extravagant recipes; special attention has been given to the simple, every-day home dishes of the Creole household, while those that tempted the gourmet and epicureans in the palmiest days of old Creole cookery have not been omitted. The *Picayune* points with pride to the famous "soupes," "gumbos," "ragouts," "entremets," "hors d'oeuvres," "jambalayas" and "desserts," that in turn receive particular attention. A special chapter has been devoted to the science of making good coffee "a la Creole," and one to the modes of cooking Louisiana rice. The consumption of rice has increased enormously of late, and it will continue to become more and more popular as an article of food when the people in the North and West learn how to cook it, and understand how largely it enters into a variety of delightful and dainty combinations. Our "Calas," our "Pralines," and "Pacane Amandes," our "Marrons Glaces," and Ices, and our "Meringues," and our delicious ways of serving Louisiana oranges peculiar to ourselves alone, are given in respective order. The history of many dishes is also given, thus affording a glimpse into old Creole hospitality, customs and traditions. Commendable features are the series of menus for holidays and daily suggestions for the table, as also the thoroughly classified list of seasonable foods.

Throughout this work *The Picayune* has had but one desire at heart, and that is to reach the wants of every household in our cosmopolitan community; to show the earnest houskeeper how the best food may be prepared at the least cost, and how it is possible for every family, from the palace to the cottage, to keep a good table and at the same time an economical one.

"Whatever is worth doing at all is worth doing well." If this is true of other things, how much more of cooking, upon which the life and health of the family depend. The kitchen should not be looked upon as a place of drudgery; a poet once sung of

> "Making drudgery divine;
> Who sweeps a room as to God's laws,
> Makes that and the action fine."

The benefits that will ultimately accrue to every family, morally and physically, from paying greater attention to the proper preparation of food cannot be overestimated; the fact that good cooking operates to the greatest extent in the preservation of the domestic peace and happiness of a family cannot be gainsaid. That this Creole Cook Book may find its way to many hearths and homes, and that the life of the household may be the better, healthier and happier for its advent, is the wish of

THE PICAYUNE.

# The Picayune's Creole Cook Book.

(Fourth Edition)

## CHAPTER I.
### CREOLE COFFEE.

Café à la Créole.

A good cup of Creole Coffee.

Is there anything in the whole range of food substances to be compared with it? And is there any city in the world where coffee is so delightfully concocted as in New Orleans? Travelers the world over unite in praise of Creole Coffee, or "Café à la Créole," as they are fond of putting it. The Creole cuisinieres succeeded far beyond even the famous chefs of France in discovering the secret of good coffee-making, and they have never yielded the palm of victory. There is no place in the world in which the use of coffee is more general than in the old Creole city of New Orleans, where, from the famous French Market, with its world-renowned coffee stands, to the olden homes on the Bayou St. John, from Lake Pontchartrain to the verge of Southport, the cup of "Café Noir," or "Café au Lait," at morning, at noon and at night, has become a necessary and delightful part of the life of the people, and the wonder and the joy of visitors.

The morning cup of Café Noir is an integral part of the life of a Creole household. The Creoles hold as a physiological fact that this custom contributes to longevity, and point, day after day, to examples of old men and women of fourscore, and over, who attest to the powerful aid they have received through life from a good, fragrant cup of coffee in the early morning. The ancient residents hold, too, that, after a hearty meal, a cup of "Café Noir," or black coffee, will relieve the sense of oppression so apt to be experienced, and enables the stomach to perform its functions with greater facility. Café Noir is known, too, as one of the best preventives of infectious diseases, and the ancient Creole physicians never used any other deodorizer than passing a chafing dish with burning grains of coffee through the room. As an antidote for poison the uses of coffee are too well known to be dilated upon.

Coffee is also the greatest brain food and stimulant known. Men of science, poets and scholars and journalists, have testified to its beneficial effects. Coffee supported the old age of Voltaire, and enabled Fontenelle to reach his one hundredth birthday. Charles Gayarre, the illustrious Louisiana historian, at the advanced age of eighty, paid tribute to the Creole cup of "Café Noir." Among advanced scientists it is rapidly taking the place of digitalis in the treatment of certain cardiac affections, and the basis of black coffee, "caffeine," enters largely into medicinal compositions. Coffee is now classed by physicians as an auxiliary food substance, as retarding the waste of nerve tissue and acting with peculiarly strengthening effect upon the nervous and vascular system.

How important, then, is the art of making good coffee, entering, as it does, so largely into the daily life of the American people. There is no reason why the secret should be confined to any section or city; but, with a little care and attention, every household in the land may enjoy its morning or after-dinner cup of coffee with as much real pleasure as the Creoles of New Orleans and the thousands of visitors who yearly migrate to this old Franco-Spanish city.

It is, therefore, with pardonable pride that the Picayune begins this Creole Cook Book by introducing its readers into a typical Creole kitchen where "Tante Zoé," in the early morning hour, in her quaint, guinea-blue dress and bandana "tignon," is carefully concocting the morning cup of

### CAFÉ NOIR.

And the first she will tell you, this old Créole Négresse, as she busies herself parching to a beautiful brown the morning portion of green coffee, that the secret of good coffee lies in having

### The Best Ingredients and in the Proper Making.

By the best ingredients she means those delightful coffees grown on well-watered mountain slopes, such as the famous Java and Mocha coffees. It must be of the best quality, the Mocha and Java mixed producing a concoction of a most delightful aroma and stimulating effect. She will tell you, too, that one of the first essentials is to "Parch the Coffee Grains Just Before Making the Coffee," because coffee that has been long parched and left standing loses its flavor and strength. The coffee grains should "Be Roasted to a Rich Brown," and never allowed to scorch or burn, otherwise the flavor of the coffee is at once affected or destroyed. Good coffee should never be boiled. Bear this in mind, that the GOOD CREOLE COOK NEVER BOILS COFFEE; but insists on dripping it in a covered strainer, slowly, slowly—DRIP, DRIP, DRIP—till all the flavor is extracted.

To reach this desired end, immediately after the coffee has been roasted and allowed to cool in a covered dish, so that none of the flavor will escape, the coffee is ground—neither too fine, for that will make the coffee dreggy; nor too coarse, for that prevents the escape of the full strength of the coffee juice—but a careful medium proportion, which will not allow the hot water pouring to run rapidly through, but which will admit of the water percolating slowly through and through the grounds, extracting every bit of the strength and aroma, and falling steadily with "a drip! drip!" into the coffee pot.

To make good coffee, the water must be "freshly boiled," and must never be poured upon the grounds until it has reached the good boiling point, otherwise the flavor is destroyed, and subsequent pourings of boiling water can never quite succeed in extracting the superb strength and aroma which distinguish the good cup of coffee.

It is of the greatest importance that "The Coffee Pot Be Kept Perfectly Clean," and the good cook will bear in mind that absolute cleanliness is as necessary for the "interior" of the coffee pot as for the shining "exterior." This fact is one too commonly overlooked, and yet the coffee pot requires more than ordinary care, for the reason that the chemical action of the coffee upon the tin or agate tends to create a substance which collects and clings to every crevice and seam, and, naturally, in the course of time will affect the flavor of the coffee most peculiarly and unpleasantly. Very often the fact that the coffee tastes bitter or muddy arises from this fact. The "inside" of the coffee pot should, therefore, be washed as carefully "every day" as the outside.

Having observed these conditions, proceed to make the coffee according to the following unfailing

### Creole Rule.

Have the water heated to a good boil. Set the coffee pot in front of the stove; never on top, as the coffee will boil, and then the taste is destroyed.

Allow one cup, or the ordinary mill, of coffee to make four good cups of the liquid; ground and put in the strainer, being careful to keep both the strainer and the spout of the coffee pot covered; to prevent the flavor from escaping. Pour, first, about two tablespoonfuls of the boiling water on the coffee grounds, or, according to the quantity of coffee used, just sufficient to settle the grounds. Wait about five minutes; then pour a little more water, and allow it to drip slowly through, but never pour water the second time) until the grounds have ceased to puff or bubble, as this is an indication that the grounds have settled. Keep pouring slowly, at intervals, a little boiling water at a time, until the delightful aroma of the coffee begins to escape from the closed spout of the coffee pot. If the coffee dyes the cup, it is a little too strong; but do not go far beyond this, or the coffee will be too weak. When you have produced a rich, fragrant concoction, whose delightful aroma, filling the room, is a constant, tempting invitation to taste it, serve in fine china cups, using in preference loaf sugar for sweetening. You have then a real cup of the famous Creole Café Noir, so extensively used at morning dawn, at breakfast, and as the "afterdinner cup."

If the coffee appears muddy, or not clear, some of the old Creoles drop a piece of charcoal an inch thick into the water, which settles it, and at once makes it clear. Demonstrations prove that strength remains in the coffee grounds. A matter of economy in making coffee is to save the grounds from the meal or day before and boil these in a half gallon of water. Settle the grounds by dropping two or three drops of cold water in, and pour the water over the fresh grounds. This is a suggestion that rich and poor might heed with profit.

### CAFÉ AU LAIT.

Proceed in the same manner as in the making of "Café Noir," allowing the usual quantity of boiling water to the amount of coffee used. When made, pour the coffee into delicate china cups, allowing a half cup of coffee to each cup. Serve, at the same time, a small pitcher of very sweet and fresh cream, allowing a half cup of cream to a half cup of coffee. The milk should always be boiled, and the cream very hot. If the cream is not fresh and sweet, it will curdle the coffee, by reason of the heat. Café au Lait is a great breakfast drink in New Orleans, while Café Noir is more generally the early morning and the afternoon drink.

Having thus bid its readers "Good morning," and drank with them a cup of Café Noir, the Picayune will proceed to discuss Creole Cookery in all its forms, from soup "à la Créole," to "pacandes amandes" and "pralines."

## CHAPTER II.

### SOUPS.

General Directions for Making Soup—The Pot-au-Feu, the Bouillon and the Consommé.

Uncooked meat is the base of all soups, except such as the Creoles call "Maigre;" or fast-day soups. These delightful Cream Soups, or Purées, will be specially treated later. They enter largely into the domestic life of New Orleans, as also more particularly the Pot-au-Feu, the Bouillon and the Consommé. These three are the "mother-soups," for upon their careful preparation, depend, taste, flavor and the entire problem of good soup-making.

The ancient Creoles preserved with few modifications many of the customs of their French ancestors. Among these was the daily plate of soup.

In France soup enters far more largely into the life of the people than in this old French city of New Orleans. The morning cup of bouillon is served in the most exclusive homes. A cup of claret and a plate of good soup is the essential morning portion of the peasantry. Soup is always served at dinner from palace to hovel. Again, the "déliceuse" cup of cold soup is served at teas and soirees in old France just as served to-day in its ancient colony on the banks of the Mississippi. The Creoles relegated the morning cup of bouillon, but retained the daily serving of soup at dinner, in time introducing, as a frequent substitute that exclusive Creole conception, Gumbo. No dinner is considered complete without either. The custom has been sustained and adopted by American residents of New Orleans. The Creole housewife lays the greatest stress upon two great essentials in the making of good soup; in the first place, the soup must never stop boiling one instant until done; secondly, once the soup is started, water must never be added. Neither, on the other hand, must the soup be allowed to boil rapidly, or it will be muddy and lose much of its flavor and strength by evaporation. The "soup bone," or "bouilli," as we call it down here in New Orleans, must be put on in cold water, without salt, and must heat slowly. The pot must be kept well covered, and no salt must be added until the meat is thoroughly cooked, as the addition of salt tends to harden the fibers of the meat and prevents the free flow of the juices. At no stage of the proceeding must the soup be allowed to boil fast. If the bone has been fractured every inch of its length, the soup will be all the stronger and more nutritious. The beef should be selected for its quality, as freshly killed as possible, and preferably of the cut known by butchers as "The Horseshoe." To be most nutritious the soup should boil a long time. The Creoles never serve soup that has been cooking less than five or seven hours, according to the quantity to be served. In a well-regulated household, the soup is put on at breakfast time, in the rear of the stove, and allowed to cook slowly for four or five hours, until the time comes for putting on the dinner proper. In the meantime, the fire has been replenished slowly from time to time, so that when the moment for adding the vegetables or other ingredients arrives, the strength of the meat has been nearly or quite extracted.

The two suggestions, "Never allow the soup to cease boiling when once it has begun, and never to add water after the ingredients are once put together and begin to boil," have been called the "Golden Rule" of soup-making. The housekeeper should take them to heart, for upon their strict observance depends that boon to poor, suffering humanity—a good plate of soup. If these rules are learned and reliably followed, the first step has been taken towards setting a good dinner.

It might be added here that while soup stock is of general use in colder climates, and can be made and kept for several days, the warm tropical climate of New Orleans precludes this, as the stock would become sour; the soup broth must, therefore, be prepared fresh every day.

Rice flour, arrowroot or cornstarch mixed with a little water are often used to thicken soups; but every good Creole cook knows that the soup that is properly made needs no thickening. Salt should be used sparingly, as also spices, which should always be used whole.

To be palatable, soup must be served very hot.

It is generally estimated that in preparing soups a pound of meat should be allowed for every quart of water. In the following recipes the ingredients must be increased proportionately, according to the number of persons to be served. The intelligent housekeeper can readily determine the exact measurements needed in her family, increasing proportions when guests are expected at the family table.

### The Every-Day Pot-au-Feu, or Simple Bouillon.

The Pot-au-Feu, or Bouillon, is made by boiling a good soup bone which has been carefully selected for its nutritive qualities in water a certain length of time, by means of which the nutriment is extracted. Bouillon of the best quality can only be made from good meat, which should be chosen from the fleshy, juicy part of the thigh. Meat from the breast or lower ribs makes good Pot-au-Feu, but of a lighter quality, and is preferred by some Creole cuisinières.

The vegetables used are found in the "soup bunch" sold by every New Orleans butcher, and carefully arranged. The bunch comprises pieces of cabbage, a turnip or two, carrots, parsley, celery and onion. Many of the most famous Creole cooks add garlic and cloves, thyme, bay leaf and allspice. But this is a matter of taste. The every day Bouillon is made by boiling the soup bone for four or five hours, skimming carefully as the scum rises, and adding, as it starts boiling well, the vegetables contained in the "soup bunch." If vermicelli, macaroni or other soup is desired, such as can be made from the simple Bouillon, or Pot-au-Feu, these ingredients are added in the proportions mentioned in the special receipt for these soups, and the soup is boiled an hour or so longer.

### The Herb Bouquet.

Every good Creole cook keeps on hand an "herb bouquet," made of a spray of parsley, a sprig of thyme, celery, parsley and bay leaf. These are tied together, and constitute the "bouquet." It will flavor a gallon of soup, if cooked for an hour.

### POT-AU-FEU A LA CRÉOLE.

4 Pounds of Lean Beef.
6 Quarts of Cold Water.
2 Small Turnips.   2 Onions.   2 Carrots.
1 Parsnip.   1 Cup of Cut-up Tomatoes.
2 Whole Cloves.
1 Bay Leaf.   1 Clove of Garlic.   5 Allspice.
2 Irish Potatoes.
Small Piece of Lemon Peel.
Small Piece of Red Pepper Pod.
Bunch of Celery Leaves (Chopped.)
Bunch of Parsley (Chopped.)
Pinch of Salt.   Pinch of Black Pepper.
Sprig of Cabbage.

This Pot-au-Feu, properly made, is truly delicious, savory and delicately odorous. The best cut for this is from the round lower end of the beef. It is important to have good beef, and that it be as freshly killed as can be had. Many of the Creoles add the beef spleen or brisket to the soup. This is rich and juicy, and gives nutritive value to the dish. If delicacy is preferred to richness in the soup, the marrow bone is omitted. Put the meat into cold water, heating by slow degrees in order that it may gradually penetrate the meat, softening it and dissolving the non-nutritive portion, which rises to the top of the liquid as a scum. As the scum becomes thicker remove it. After having skimmed well, set the soup back where it can be kept on a gentle but steady boil; when the soup is well skimmed, add the vegetables, which have been cut to proper fineness, and a little salt to suit the taste, and let the soup continue to boil from five to six hours, remembering strictly the two essential rules given. By following this recipe you will have an excellent soup for family use.

The Creoles often serve the Pot-au-Feu with small squares of dry or toasted bread, put into the tureen, and the hot soup is poured over them at the moment of serving.

Should the flavor of the garlic, allspice, cloves or bay leaf be disagreeable, they may be omitted. But they are essential ingredients of the Creole Pot-au-Feu.

A particularly delicate flavor is often obtained by adding to the beef some pieces of raw fowl, or the remains of a cooked fowl, more especially the carcass. But never add remains of mutton, pork or veal, as these meats impart an acrid odor, detracting from the perfection of the Pot-au-Feu.

### BOUILLON.

To make a good Bouillon is an art in itself. It is the soup that most frequently, after the Pot-au-Feu, enters into the economy of the Creole household. It is not only used in the daily menu, but on occasions of family reunions and soirées, is served cold or warm in cups. It is always prepared in a concentrated form for the use of invalids. In illness, where the quantity administered is required to be as nutritious as possible, the round steak should always be chosen for the Bouillon, and it is decidedly better not to clear the soup, as the process of clearing not only destroys a great deal of the delicate flavor, but also of the nutriment contained in the Bouillon.

Select good fresh beef, and where intended for an invalid allow two pounds of beef to every quart of water. The Bouillon should always boil from six to seven hours. For dinners, luncheons, etc., the following proportions may be used:

6 Pounds of Beef, without Bone or Fat.
6 Quarts of Cold Water.
4 Cloves.  6 Allspice.
A Small Cup of Fresh or Canned Tomatoes.
1 Teaspoon of Salt.
1 Spoon of Celery Seed.
1 Bay Leaf.
A Piece of Red Pepper Pod, without Seeds. (Omit for the Sick.)
1 Clove of Garlic (omit for the Sick.)

Put these ingredients into the soup kettle, after the Bouillon has been brought to a boil. Then set aside and let it simmer gently, but never allow the soup to rack. After two and a half hours add

A Sprig of Thyme.
1 Onion cut in pieces.
1 Small Bunch of Celery, if you have not used the seed.
1 Medium-Sized Carrot, chopped fine.

Replace the cover and let the Bouillon boil gently for two and one-half hours more, making five hours of actual boiling when not intended for invalid use. At this stage, from the quantity of ingredients used in the above recipe, the Bouillon will measure about three quarts for family use. If you decide not to clarify the soup, set it aside and let it settle, then carefully pour off the upper portion, but do not shake the bowl or disturb the sediment. The Creoles then add about a tablespoonful of celery and a little cayenne. This soup requires no artificial coloring, its own strength and long boiling producing a beautiful tint. Should a greater quantity be required, the housekeeper will guide herself according to the proportions given in this receipt.

### To Clarify Bouillon.

To clarify Bouillon, remove the fat and pour the broth into a clear kettle. Add the crushed shells of two eggs. Stir this into the cold soup until well mixed. Set it on the fire, and from the moment it begins to boil let it cook steadily ten minutes longer. Set it back on the stove or hearth for four or five minutes to settle. Then strain it through a towel. Allow the Bouillon to drip, remembering never to squeeze the bag. A very clear soup is never a very nutritious one.

### CONSOMMÉ.

6 Pounds of Lean Beef.
2 Large-Sized Onions.
2 Carrots.  2 Stalks Celery.
1 Piece of Cabbage.
Salt and Cayenne to Taste.

A Consommé is a clear soup.

Select six pounds of lean beef, rump of beef and some bones, and cut the meat into small pieces, the bones also being mashed. Put this on in about six quarts of cold water, and, when it comes to a boil, skim well. Then add a teaspoonful of salt to help the scum rise more thoroughly, and skim as it rises. Take two large sized onions, two carrots, a piece of cabbage and two pieces of celery; chop fine and add to the soup, and let it boil six hours, or until the broth is reduced about one-half the quantity. By this time the meat should be cooked into rags. Pass all through a colander and then strain through a coarse flannel cloth. Season highly with Cayenne pepper and salt to the taste. If the meat is good, the soup will be perfectly clear. If it is cloudy or muddy before straining, crush the shells of two eggs and put them into the soup and let it come to a good boil. Set it back about ten minutes and then strain. Add vermicelli, or macaroni, or pâtés, according to taste. This soup will require no artificial coloring.

### Colorings for Soup.

Having given the recipes for the "mother soups," which are the bases of all soups, a word must be said about colorings for soup. While colorings have been extensively used in New Orleans, the good old Creoles long ago found out that coloring matter, whether in liquid form or in balls or tablets, detracted from the good flavor of the soup, and that a properly made soup needed no coloring. The good Bouillon has a color peculiar to itself—a reddish yellow, which comes from the juice of the meat. The absence of natural color in the soup indicates that too small an amount of meat has been used in proportion to the water, a poor quality of meat, or there has been a too rapid process of boiling. Still, if colorings are desired, the following recipe, which is free from the deleterious compounds sold in stores, has long been used by the Creoles for coloring gravies, and may be used with good effect in soups. It is called by the Creoles

### Caramel.

Take about a half pint of brown sugar, put it in a pan, on a slow fire, and let it burn or parch, slowly stirring all the time. When it turns a dark brown, add two pints of water and stir well, and then bottle. Put it away and use a few drops at a time to color and thicken gravies and soup broths. Or, take a large raw onion, skin and all, and thrust into the burning coals. When it begins to brown well, take out of the coals, dust off all the ashes and throw into the soup or gravy. This will give all the coloring that is needed.

More simple or satisfactory recipes cannot be found. Nevertheless, the Creoles maintain and demonstrate that the best coloring for soups is that produced by good material and long boiling.

## CHAPTER III.
## MEAT SOUPS.

### Julienne Soup.
Potage à la Julienne.

5 Pounds of Lean Beef.  5 Quarts of Water.
2 Turnips.  2 Carrots.  2 Onions.
2 Leeks.  A Small Stalk of Celery.
3 Tomatoes.
A Small Half-Head of White Cabbage.
1 Gill of Green Peas.

The shin of the beef is the best to make a good Julienne soup. Set the beef and water in a close vessel where they will heat gradually. After boiling five or six hours add the following vegetables, which have been carefully prepared according to these directions: Cut the vegetables into long, thin shreds. Take a tablespoonful of lard, heat and add the vegetables, letting them fry or smother until a golden brown. Then add to the boiling broth. If fresh peas are used they must be boiled apart. If canned peas, simply add to the broth, after throwing in the vegetables. Let them cook in the broth one hour longer and serve hot with the vegetables.

### Vermicelli Soup.
Consommé, ou Potage au Vermicelle.

½ Pint of Broth to Each Person.
1 Ounce of Vermicelli to Each Person.

Prepare a good Bouillon, or Pot-au-Feu, or Consommé, according to the taste of the household, the simple Pot-au-Feu being most generally used. A half hour before serving add the vermicelli to the broth, and serve hot.

### Macaroni Soup.
Potage au Macaroni.

2 Quarts of Broth.
¼ Pound of Macaroni.

Prepare a good Pot-au-Feu, or Bouillon, according to directions given, and allowing a quarter of a pound of macaroni to two quarts of broth. Break the macaroni into two-inch length pieces and add to the boiling broth about a half hour or so before serving. Some housekeepers cook the macaroni seperately in salted boiling water about ten or fifteen minutes draining thoroughly, and dropping into the boiling broth about fifteen minutes before serving. The soup is often served with Parmesan cheese, grated. But this is not necessary.

### Tapioca Soup.
Potage au Tapioca.

4 Ounces of Tapioca.  3 Quarts of Broth.

To three quarts of broth add, about forty minutes before serving, four ounces of tapioca. The tapioca should be previously soaked a few hours. Stir frequently in the broth while boiling, and serve hot.

### Sago Soup.
#### Potage au Sago.
3 Pints of Broth.
2 Ounces of Sago.

The sago should always be soaked overnight. Allow two ounces to every three pints of broth or Consommé. Boil for one hour before serving, stirring occasionally.

### Rice Soup.
#### Potage au Riz.
1 Half Cup of Rice.
3 Pints of Broth or Consomme.

Prepare the clear Pot-au-Feu or Consommé. When nearly done add one half cupful of rice, which has been thoroughly washed and dried. Cook for about twenty-five minutes longer, or until done, and serve.

Barley soup is prepared after the same style, using a clear Bouillon or Consommé.

### Okra Soup.
#### Potage au Févi.
2 Pounds of Beef without fat or bone.
2 Cups of Okra, chopped fine.
¼ Pound of Butter.   4 Quarts of Cold Water.
1 Onion, sliced and chopped.
Salt and Pepper.

Cut the beef into small pieces, and season well with butter, pepper and salt. Fry it in the soup kettle with the onion and butter until very brown. Then add the cold water and let it simmer for an hour and a half. Add the okra and let it simmer gently for three or four hours longer.

### Ox-Tail Soup.
#### Soupe de Queue de Boeuf.
1 Ox Tail.
A Bunch of Soup Herbs. 1 Head of Celery.
4 Quarts of Boiling Water. 1 Large Onion.
2 Carrots.   3 Cloves.
A Sprig of Parsley.
A Small Slice of Lean Ham or Beef.
Salt and Pepper.

Cut the tail in pieces from the joint, and then cut again into the size of a peanut, or one inch and a half in length. Chop the onions very fine. Put the onion and a tablespoonful of lard into a frying pan and add the ox tail. Cook slowly until it begins to brown, then add the carrot, cut in pieces about the size of a green pea, and about a square inch of ham, chopped very fine. Let this brown, and, when it begins to brown nicely, add the thyme, bay leaf, three cloves, one clove of garlic, all chopped very fine. Let this continue to brown, being careful not to burn, and then add one tablespoonful of flour, dredged in lightly and stirred, and when all is nicely browned, add about five quarts of Consommé, if you have it; if not, five quarts of boiling water and three tablespoonfuls of barley. Let it cook together about four hours, simmering gently, seasoning with salt, pepper and cayenne to taste, and when ready to serve, add two tablespoonfuls of sherry wine. Serve one joint to each person. Wine may be omitted.

### Noodle Soup.
#### Potage au Nouilles.
3 Quarts of Good Bouillon or Consomme.
The Yolks of 3 Eggs.
The Whites of 2 Eggs.
1 Cup of Flour.  ½ Tablespoonful of Salt.

Prepare a good Bouillon or Consommé. To a quart of the soup, add noodles made as follows: Beat the yolks of three eggs, and the white of two together until very light; add one cup of flour, one half teaspoon of salt, and mix with cold water; making a stiff paste; roll very thin; then roll each strip to form a tube; cut in strips, grease and simmer a few at a time in boiling salt water for about twenty minutes. Simmer the noodles in the soup about fifteen minutes.

### Mushroom Soup.
#### Potage au Champignons.
¼ Pound of Good Macaroni.
¼ Pound of Fresh Mushrooms or a Half Can of Mushrooms.
½ Carrot and Onion.
3 Tablespoonfuls of Butter.
2 Pints of Consomme or Bouillon.
1 Pint of Cream.
2 Tablespoonfuls of Flour.
Salt and Pepper to Taste.

Break the macaroni into pieces of about three inches; wash and put into a stewpan, with two quarts of boiling water; add three teaspoonfuls of salt. Let the macaroni boil half an hour, and meanwhile make a sauce. Put the butter and flour in a small stewpan and beat to a cream. Then add the chopped onion, carrot and pepper, and remaining salt and broth, and heat slowly. When the sauce begins to boil, set it back, where it will only simmer, for about twenty minutes. At the end of that time, add the cream and then strain the sauce. Pour the water from the macaroni, and in its place put the sauce and mushrooms; cook for five minutes, and serve hot.

The Creole housekeeper never uses any but a silver spoon in cooking fresh mushrooms. If the spoon is darkened, the mushrooms are not good. This is an infallible test in using fresh mushrooms. The canned French mushrooms are not only the best, but the safest.

### Potage Croupe-au-Pot.

3 Quarts of Good Consomme.
10 Pieces of Dried Toast. 1 Carrot, cut fine.
1 Head of Celery, cut fine.
1 Turnip, cut fine.

Potage Croute-au-pot is one of the most popular and excellent Creole soups. Prepare a good consommé. In the meantime, parboil the vegetables in salted boiling water. When tender, drain off the water, and add to them about two and one-half quarts of the boiling consommé. Let them simmer until they are very tender. Prepare the toasts and put them into a saucepan with enough consommé to cover them. Simmer gently until the toasts have absorbed all the consommé and show signs of drying up. Then add a little hot consommé, detach them from the saucepan, lay them in the tureen and pour the soup with the vegetables very gently over them. Serve immediately..

### Savory Soup.

Potage à la Bonne Ménagère.
4 Pounds of Lean Beef. 4 Quarts of Water.
1 Onion, chopped fine.
3 Sprigs of Parsley. 1 Bay Leaf.
1 Sprig of Thyme. ½ Cup of Rice.
3 Tablespoonfuls of Oatmeal.
1 Tablespoonful of Salt. ¼ Teaspoonful of Pepper.

Put the meat in four quarts of cold water and let it simmer for three hours.

One hour before serving, add one-half cup of rice, which has been soaked in water until soft, and three tablespoonfuls of oatmeal, one tablespoonful of salt and one-fourth teaspoonful of pepper. Add parsley, sprig of thyme and one onion, chopped fine. Boil an hour longer and serve, very hot. This makes a delicious soup.

### Corn Soup.

Soupe au Maï Tendre.
6 Pounds of the Lower Ribs of Beef.
6 Quarts of Cold Water.
1 Quart of Sliced Fresh Tomatoes.
1 Quart of Corn, sliced from the cob.
1 Tablespoonful of Butter.
1 Tablespoonful of Flour.
One Pod of Cayenne Pepper, without seeds.
Salt and Black Pepper to Taste.

Corn soup is one of the most popular Creole summer soups. At this season, when corn and tomatoes are plentiful, the following will be found not only a delicious, but a highly nutritive soup:

Take six pounds of the lower ribs of the beef, a quart of sliced fresh tomatoes, a quart of corn sliced from the cob, six quarts of water, one tablespoonful of butter, one of flour, and salt and pepper to suit the taste.

Put the meat and water into a soup pot, and as soon as the scum begins to rise, skim carefully. Then add the tomatoes and the corncobs. Cook for four hours or so longer; then take out the corncobs, and add the corn, cut fine, salt and pepper to suit the taste, adding a pod of Cayenne pepper, without the seeds; cook one hour longer and then serve with slices of toast bread.

### Tomato Consommé.

Consommé de Tomates.

A Shin of Veal.
3 Pounds of Shin of Beef.
8 Quarts of Water. 1 Cup of Tomatoes.
A Handful of Sorrel (if tomatoes are not used.)
Salt and Pepper. 3 Onions. 3 Leeks.
10 Allspice 6 Cloves. 3 Large Carrots.
1 Head of Celery. 1 Bunch of Parsley.
A Chicken may be substituted for the Shin of Veal.

Put the meat and chicken (the latter cut up) into a large soup kettle and let it come slowly to a boil. Then draw it forward, and as it begins to boil more rapidly skim as the scum rises. After another hour add the pepper, salt and vegetables. The soup should boil incessantly, but gently, for about eight hours, requiring in all about nine hours of good cooking. It should, therefore, be put on very early in the morning, and, if required, for luncheon, should be made the day before. When the soup has boiled gently for the prescribed time take it off, strain into a large bowl and set it away in the ice box until the next day, if not for immediate use. Then remove the fat from the surface, and pour off all the clear part into a saucepan and boil again for one or two hours. Then remove it from the fire. This will make a stiff jelly, which will keep in winter for several days in the ice box. It also serves to make a beautiful Sauce Espagnole, or Spanish Sauce. The best way to keep it is in earthern pitchers holding from one to two quarts, allowing a certain quantity for each day.

This soup requires no artificial coloring. Use the thick part of the soup with vegetables or other purée.

### Mock-Turtle Soup.

Soupe à la Tortue.

1 Calf's Head. ¼ Pound of Calf's Liver.
5 Quarts of Cold Water.
Bunch of Soup Herbs. 2 Hard-Boiled Eggs.
2 Tablespoonfuls of Butter.
1 Gill of Sherry. 1 Bay Leaf. 12 Cloves.
1 Onion. 1 Lemon.
4 Level Teaspoonfuls of Flour.
1 Turnip.
1 Level Teaspoonful Mushroom Catsup.
1 Carrot.
1 Level Teaspoonful Worcestershire Sauce.
Salt and Pepper to Suit Taste.

Select a fine calf's head, not too large. If large, reserve half and the tongue and brains to make another dish. Get the butcher to crack the head well and remove the brains. Wash the head thoroughly in cold water, and then be careful to pour boiling water through the nose and throat passages until they are perfectly clean, and scrape out the ears thoroughly, washing very clean. Rinse all well in cold water, and be very sure that the head is very sweet and clean before attempting to cook it. Put the head in a kettle with five quarts of cold water, and set it over a moderate fire. When it begins to boil well, skim thoroughly, till every particle of scum has been taken off. Then set it back and let it simmer until the meat is quite tender. This will require about two hours and a half. Then remove the head; take the meat from the bones; skin the tongue, and set away to cool. Return the bones to the kettle, with the vegetables, which have been washed and cut fine; as, also, the spices and the liver. Simmer gently again for two hours, and when cool, strain. Set aside to cool, and when the soup is cold, remove all the fat. Put the butter in a saucepan and melt, adding the flour until nicely browned, but be careful not to burn it. Then add by degrees the boiling soup, stirring constantly. Boil, keeping up a gentle stir, for about five minutes. Then add the meat of the head and the liver, having first cut them into dice, and bring to a boil at once. Take the saucepan from the fire, and add the catsup, salt, pepper and wine. Slice the hard-boiled eggs and the lemon and place them in the tureen, and pour the soup over them and serve.

If force-meat balls are desired for the soup, prepare them as follows:

### Forcé-Meat Balls.

Chop a half of a pound of beef or veal and chopped chicken about an inch in thickness; add a little of the liver and tongue of the calf, a half dozen small onions, one tablespoonful of sweet marjoram, one grated nutmeg, a teaspoonful each of powdered black pepper and mace, and a half teaspoonful of cloves (powdered), three eggs, three grated crackers (sifted), half a gill of good sherry wine, a tablespoonful of butter and two teaspoonfuls of salt; chop up and mix thoroughly together. Then roll in balls and fry slowly in lard or butter. Serve with the soup.

### Mutton Broth.

Soupe de Mouton.

8 Pounds of the Neck of the Mutton.
4 Quarts of Cold Water. ½ Cup of Rice.
1 Onion. 1 Bay Leaf.
2 Large Turnips. Salt and Pepper to Taste.

Wash the neck of the mutton, or wipe it with a damp towel, and put it into the kettle with the cold water. Let it come to a slow boil and skim carefully. Cover well and let it simmer for about four hours. Then remove from the stove and pour into an earthern vessel to cool. When cold, remove all the fat from the surface, or, better still, remove all the fat before boiling. Return to the kettle and add the rice, the sliced turnip and the bay leaf, and season to taste, or prepare as in Oxtail Soup.

### Chicken Broth.

Bouillon de Volaille.

To make a good chicken broth for invalids, take one good large chicken; clean carefully and cut up, being careful to mash all the bones with an ax. Place in a saucepan of cold water, and let it simmer gently for four or five hours, until it is boiled down to about two cups of broth. It will have a rich, strong color, and this broth, seasoned with a little salt and pepper, omitting all vegetables, can be taken by the most delicate stomachs.

### Chicken Consommé.

Consommé de Volaille.

1 Large Chicken Cut in Pieces.
1 Onion. 3 Quarts of Cold Water.
1 Small Stalk of Celery.
1 Carrot. 1 Turnip.
Salt and Pepper.

Put the chicken into the salt and water and let it simmer gently until the scum begins to rise; then skim. Add the other ingredients. Boil gently for two hours, and serve, with slices of toast. The chicken left over will serve to make croquettes, or chicken salad. Nothing is ever wasted in a well regulated household.

### Gilt-Edged Consommé.

Consommé Doré.

1 Fine Chicken. 1 Good Soup Bone.
1 Slice of Fine Ham.
1 Gallon of Water.
2 Eggs, whites and shells.
2 Sprigs of Parsley.
½ Each of Small Parsnip, Carrot and Head of Celery.
1 Onion. 3 Cloves. Salt and Pepper.

Have the fowl thorouhly cleaned, and put the chicken, beef and ham into a kettle of cold water of the quantity mentioned in the above, and boil slowly for five hours, being careful to keep the pot well covered. Chop the onion and vegetables and fry them in a little butter, and add all the seasonings to the soup. Boil two hours longer, and set away overnight in an ice box. The next day remove all the fat; from the top take out the jelly, leaving the thickest part of the sediment, which is good to put into a thick soup. Mix in the shells and the whites of eggs and boil quickly for about ten minutes. Then set it on the hearth to settle. Pour the soup through a thin bag without squeezing; if it does not come out perfectly clear, pass it through again. It should then be a beautiful golden-brown color. Only the brightest and cleanest of kettles should be used, and the sieve should be scalded each time to keep the particles from washing back into the soup. This is a delightful soup for luncheons and dinner parties. It may be garnished according to taste, serving with "Croutons," or Querelles. No artificial coloring should ever be used in making the Consommé Doré. Depend upon the natural ingredients for the golden-brown color so much admired by all chefs.

**Consommé With Poached Eggs.**

Consommé aux Oeufs Pochés.

6 Eggs.
3 Quarts of Consomme or Bouillon.

Break the eggs and drop them one by one into boiling salted water, being careful not to allow the water to boil when once the eggs are in it; but have the frying pan, which is always best for poaching eggs, to one side of the stove, and cook slowly until the eggs are firm. When firm, carefully remove with a spoon or perforated skimmer, the latter being best, and lay in cold water for a moment, until the edges are trimmed evenly. The boiling water tends to make the edges ragged, and eggs served in this slovenly manner are not tempting. Transfer to the tureen and pour the boiling soup very gently into the tureen and serve. One egg and about a half pint of broth should be allowed to each person.

**Queen Soup.**

Potage à la Reine.
1 Chicken. ¼ Pound of Rice.
½ Pint of Cream.
¼ Blade of Mace. 1 Sprig of Thyme.
4 Sprigs of Parsley.
2 Quarts of White Veal Broth.
Salt and Pepper.

Take a fine large chicken, clean it nicely and put it whole into a pot containing about five quarts of water. Add chopped onion, thyme, bay leaf, one carrot, a small bunch of celery, and one cup of rice. Let the chicken simmer well for about four hours, and, when well cooked, take out the chicken from the broth. Cut off the white meat and cut it into pieces about the size of dice. Then strain the broth, mashing the rice well. Make a purée by taking another saucepan, putting in one tablespoonful of butter and one of flour, letting it melt together without browning. Moisten this well with the soup and a glass of milk, and season with salt and pepper, and one-quarter of a grated nutmeg, and add to the broth. Then add the chicken, which has been cut up. Put in the tureen little dice of croutons of bread fried in butter. Pour the soup over and serve hot. The remainder of the chicken is used to make Chicken Croquettes, Chicken Salad, etc.

**Giblet Soup.**

Potage à l'Essence de Gesier.
1 Hard-Boiled Yolk for Each Person.
2 Cups of Chicken Broth.
3 Quarts of Boiling Water or Broth.
1 Onion, Carrot and ½ Turnip, chopped.
2 Tablespoonfuls of Port or Madeira Wine.
Parsley.
Juice of 1 Lemon.
1 Leaf Each of Sage and Bay.
1 Tablespoonful of Flour and 1 of Butter.
The Giblets, Heart, Liver, etc., of Two Turkeys or Four Chickens.

Chop the onion fine and put it into the stewpan with the butter; let it brown, and then add the chopped vegetables, whole giblets, etc.; fry until nicely browned, but do not let it burn. Then slit the giblets with a knife, that the juices may run out in boiling, and put all into the soup kettle, with pepper, salt, sage, parsley, and the three quarts of consommé or boiling water. Add bones or lean meat, cooked or raw, that are left, preferably the meat of the chicken, and let all simmer for five hours. Then strain. Mash one liver fine and add it to the broth; season with Cayenne pepper, lemon juice to taste, and two tablespoonfuls of Madeira or Port wine. Boil three minutes, and have in the tureen one hard-boiled yolk of an egg for each person. Pour the soup over it and serve hot.

**Rabbit Soup.**

Potage de Lapin.

2 Young Rabbits.
2 Quarts of Cold Water. 1 Onion.
1 Bay Leaf.
1 Blade of Mace. 1 Tablespoonful of Butter.
½ Cup of Rice.
Cayenne Pepper, ½ Pod. Salt to the Taste.

This is a famous Creole soup. The rabbits should be well skinned and singed. Wash thoroughly in warm water; this is very important. Then cut the meat into small pieces and put into the soup pot, with the quantity of water given. Chop the onion, mace and bay leaf and add. Place on a very moderate fire, and let it simmer gently until the meat has grown very tender. This will require about two hours or less. Add the salt, pepper and rice, and simmer for an hour longer. Pour into the tureen over croutons and serve. The Creoles add two tablespoonfuls of sherry or port wine, thus increasing the delicacy of the flavor.

### Squirrel Soup.

Potage d'Ecureil.

When squirrels are used the gray Louisiana squirrel is best. Venison may be substituted for squirrels. Prepare as for Rabbit Soup.

### Pepper Pot.

Pot de Poivres.

4 Pound of Plain Tripe.  2 Potatoes.
1 Pound of Honeycomb Tripe.
Sprig of Parsley.  1 Knuckle of Veal.
3 Quarts of Cold Water.

1 Herb Bouquet.  1 Onion.
2 Teaspoonfuls of Flour.
2 Tablespoonfuls of Butter.
Cayenne to Suit the Taste.
Salt and Pepper.

The knuckle of the veal is best for this. Wash and put into the soup kettle, covering with water and bring it to a slow boil. Carefully skim off the scum. Let it simmer gently for three hours. The tripe should be prepared the day before. Wash it thoroughly in cold water and boil for about seven hours. Put away in the ice box till needed. Chop the parsley and herbs fine and one-half of the red pepper pod, and add to the boiling knuckle of veal, and also the potatoes, which have been cut into dice. Cut up the tripe into pieces of about one inch square. Take out the knuckle of veal and cut up meat into small pieces, and add all with the tripe to the soup. At the boiling point, season with salt and pepper.

The Creoles serve this soup with Croutons. Throw them into the soup; let it simmer for about ten minutes more and serve.

~~~~~~~

## CHAPTER IV.

### FISH SOUPS.

Soupes de Poissons.

Under this heading come some of the most delightful Creole soups, such as Green Turtle Soup, Oyster Soup, Crawfish Bisque, etc. These not only serve as fast-day soups, but are considered elegant introductions to the most recherché feast.

### Fish Soup.

Bouillon de Poisson.

6 Slices of Fish of Almost Any Variety.
4 Onions, Chopped Fine.
6 Tomatoes, Chopped Fine.
1 Herb Bouquet.  Sprig of Parsley.
1 Glass of White Wine.
4 Tablespoonfuls of Salad Oil.
4 Tablespoonfuls of Flour.
3 Pints of Water.

Chop the onions and fry them in the salad oil. Cut the tomatoes fine and add onions, and put in all the other ingredients, except the fish, adding the flour to make a good roux. When brown add the water, and, after it has boiled about a half hour, add the slices of fish. When they are firm remove the herb bouquet, add Cayenne pepper, and salt and pepper to taste, and serve the fish soup in a tureen, pouring it over crusts of dried toast.

### Green Turtle Soup.

Soupe à la Tortue.

2 Pounds of Turtle Meat, or a 2-Pound Turtle.
2 Fine Large Onions.  6 Cloves.
1 Square inch of Ham.  6 Allspice.
2 Cloves of Garlic.
2 Tablespoonfuls of Flour.
¼ of a Small Lemon.  2 Hard-Boiled Eggs.
1 Glass of Sherry Wine.
Parsley, Thyme, Bay Leaf.
Salt, Pepper and Cayenne to Taste.

The Creoles pride themselves upon their famous "Soupe à la Tortue," and justly; the old saying that only a good Creole cook knows how to make a good Turtle Soup being testified to by epicurean visitors from every country.

The following is one of the simplest and best ways of making Turtle Soup—a recipe that may always be relied upon and one that has been used from generation to generation in the most aristocratic Creole homes: In making Turtle Soup, remember that Green Turtle is always the best for this purpose. Select two pounds of fine Green Turtle meat, if the turtle is not bought whole. This amount will make a soup for six persons. Increase proportionately. If the turtle is bought whole, first cut off the head. To do this properly, the turtle should be hung with the head downwards, and a very sharp knife should be used to cut off the head as close as possible. Often for hours after this operation is performed, the turtle will exhibit extraordinary signs of life, the flesh quivering constantly. The old Creole cooks say that a turtle never dies, but this is a darky tradition. To remove the shells, first separate the upper from the lower shell, always being exceedingly careful to avoid touching the gall bladder, which is very large. If this bladder is penetrated, the contents running over the turtle meat would render it utterly unfit for use.

Clean the turtle and the entrails by cutting open and washing thoroughly in cold water. Then put the meat and entrails into a saucepan and parboil about ten minutes. Be careful to save this stock of water. Chop an onion very fine, and the ham into very fine pieces. Cut the turtle meat into one-inch pieces, mash the cloves and the allspice very fine and chop the thyme and bay leaf. Brown the onions in a tablespoonful of butter or lard, and add immediately the turtle meat. Brown together slightly and after minutes add the chopped ham. Let this continue browning and then add two cloves of garlic, chopped fine, and the thyme, bay leaf (minced fine), cloves and allspice (ground), all mixed together, and lay on the turtle. Stir this almost constantly to prevent burning, and add two tablespoonfuls of flour that has been well rubbed, stirring constantly all the time. Then dissolve the meat with the water in which the turtle was parboiled, adding gradually until a certain consistency is reached. About three quarts of water will be the required amount. Season this with salt, black pepper and Cayenne to taste, and boil slowly for fully an hour, stirring almost constantly. After cooking one hour taste, and if not seasoned sufficiently, season again and taste. Then chop one-quarter of a small lemon and put it in the soup. Let it continue to cook, and when well done—that is, when no blood exudes from the turtle after sticking it with a fork—pour into the tureen. Add the whites and yolks of two hard-boiled eggs, chopped fine, and one good glass of Sherry wine, and the soup is ready to serve. This is a dish fit for a king and is most highly recommended as a genuine Creole Turtle Soup.

If Quenelles or Forcemeat Balls are desired, they may be prepared according to the recipe given under the heading "Quenelles." (See recipe, under chapter "Stuffings and Dressings," etc.)

### Turtle Soup No. 2.

Soupe à la Tortue.
2 Pounds of Turtle Meat.
½ Tablespoonful of Lard.
½ Tablespoonful of Butter.
2 Tablespoonfuls of Flour.
2 Tomatoes.   1 Large Onion.
1 Sprig of Thyme.   2 Sprigs of Parsley.
1 Bay Leaf.   1 Clove of Garlic.
1 Square Inch of Ham.
1 Dozen Cloves Tied in Muslin.
6 Allspice Mashed Fine.
3 Quarts of Water.   2 Hard-Boiled Eggs.
1 Glass of Sherry or White Wine.
Salt and Cayenne to Taste.

Clean the turtle and entrails by cutting open the latter and washing thoroughly in cold water. Then put the meat and entrails into a saucepan and parboil them for ten minutes. Carefully save this stock of water. Chop the onion very fine, and cut the ham into very fine pieces. Cut the turtle meat into one-inch pieces; mash the allspice very fine, and mince the parsley, thyme and bay leaf. Then brown the onions in the lard and butter mixed, and almost immediately add the turtle meat. Brown together for ten minutes and add the finely chopped ham. As this continues to brown, add the cloves of garlic (minced fine), the thyme and bay leaf and the ground allspice. Mix all together, stirring almost constantly to prevent burning. Then add the well-rubbed tablespoonfuls of flour, stirring constantly. Scald and skin the tomatoes and chop them fine, and add to the turtle meat. When well-browned, pour over three quarts of the water in which the turtle was parboiled, season with salt and pepper and Cayenne to taste, and let it boil slowly for fully an hour, stirring frequently. After one hour, taste the soup, and, if not sufficiently seasoned, add seasoning of salt, pepper and Cayenne again, according to taste. Let it cook for an hour longer and then take off the stove if the turtle is thoroughly done. This may be ascertained by sticking it with a fork. If no blood exudes, the soup is ready to serve. Take off the stove and strain through a colander into the tureen. Add the whites and yolks of two hard-boiled eggs, chopped fine, and one good glass of Sherry or White Wine. Slice a lemon fine and add to the soup and serve hot.

### How to Serve Turtle Soup.

Great care should be taken in serving the soup. It should be borne in mind that boiling the soup a second time, or warming it over, deprives it of much of its delicious flavor. To avoid this, fill two tureens with boiling water; let them stand a few minutes, then dry the inside thoroughly and place the tureens in a "bain-marie," or a hot-water bath. Fill the tureens with the soup and cover tightly. Bring them to the table as needed, throwing in just before serving, some dainty slices of lemon. If the meat is served, use only the most delicate portions.

### Mock Eggs for Turtle Soup.

Should the turtle possess no eggs, the following method of making mock eggs is often used. Break and beat thoroughly one fresh egg; then take the yolks of three hard-boiled eggs, and rub them into a fine paste with about a teaspoonful of butter. Mix this with the raw egg and roll into pellets of the identical size and shape of the turtle eggs, let them lie in boiling water about two minutes, and then drop into the soup.

### Terrapin Soup.

Soupe à la Tortue.

1 Two-Pound Diamond-Back Terrapin.
2 Fine Large Onions.    6 Cloves.
1 Square Inch of Ham.   6 Allspice.
¼ of a Small Lemon.   2 Hard-Boiled Eggs.
1 Glass of Sherry Wine.
Parsley, Thyme and Bay Leaf.
Salt, Pepper and Cayenne to Taste.

Remember always that the land terrapin is unfit to eat. The fresh-water terrapin can be made into a most relishable article of food if cooked according to Creole methods. The diamond-back terrapin is the best and the females make the finest and daintiest food, the males being not only of inferior size, but of far less delicate flavor. Terrapins must always be bought alive. They are in season from November till March, and, like all other fish, should not be eaten out of season. The red leg or fresh-water terrapin, or the terrapin of common variety, called "Gopher," are eschewed by the Creoles, but are good to eat. To have a good terrapin soup the diamond back must be used.

To make the soup, clean the terrapin as you would a turtle. Then place in a kettle and boil till tender. Take out and cut into small pieces, saving the water. Proceed as for Turtle Soup. When it boils up take from the fire, add a grated nutmeg, a glass of Sherry or Madeira wine and serve. The farci or forcemeat balls is made in exactly the same manner as for Turtle Soup. Serve with green pickle and delicate slices of fried toast.

### Crawfish Bisque.

Potage à la Bisque d'Ecrevisse.
8 Dozen Fine Large Crawfish.
3 Onions.   1 Carrot.   1 Bunch of Celery.
2 Sprigs of Thyme.      2 Bay Leaves.
4 Sprigs of Parsley.    6 Cloves.
2 Blades of Mace.       1 Clove of Garlic.
2 Tablespoonfuls of Butter.
2 Quarts of Oyster Liquor.
A Dash of Cayenne. 1 Seedless Cayenne Pod.
Salt and Pepper to Taste.

Crawfish Bisque is a distinctive Creole luxury. It is prepared as follows:

Take about eight dozen fine, large crawfish and wash thoroughly, being careful to cleanse of every particle of dust or sand. Set to boil in about a gallon of water. When boiled, take the fish out of the water; save the water. Pick out two dozen of the largest crawfish; pick out the inside of the tails and save the heads, cleansing them of every particle of meat. Set this meat to one side with the shells of the head. Pick the meat from the rest of the crawfish, saving all the shells. Take one large onion, a carrot, a bunch of celery, a sprig of thyme, one bay leaf, three sprigs of parsley, six cloves and two blades of mace, one clove of garlic; chop all very fine and put into the pot of water in which the crawfish were boiled. Add all the picked meat, except the reserved tails, and all the shells of the bodies and heads, except the reserved heads. Add one cup of rice and let it all boil till the mixture becomes thick and mushy. When it is well cooked, take it off the fire and mash the shells thoroughly, and the meat also, and strain all through a sieve. Take about a tablespoonful of butter and two quarts of oyster liquor and add this to the soup, seasoning to taste with Cayenne, salt and black pepper. Set to boil slowly. In the meantime, take the reserved crawfish meat and make a stuffing as follows for the reserve heads; chop an onion very fine and let it brown in a tablespoonful of butter. Squeeze thoroughly a cup of bread wet with water. When well squeezed, mix with a little milk, sufficient to make a paste, season to taste and mix with the well-seasoned crawfish meat. Chop another onion and put in melted butter, and add the crawfish stuffing, letting all fry about ten minutes, adding, in the meantime, a finely-chopped sprig each of thyme and parsley and a bay leaf, and mixing thoroughly. Take off the fire and stuff the reserved head of crawfish. Put on every stuffed head a dot of butter, and set in the oven and bake ten minutes. Place the stuffed heads in the tureen and pour the soup over. Serve hot with Croûtons of buttered toast, passing the latter in a separate dish.

### Crawfish Soup.

Potage d'Écrevisses.

50 Fine, Large Crawfish.
1½ Pounds of a Fillet of Veal.
1 Slice of Ham.
1 Herb Bouquet. 1 Half Can of Mushrooms.
2 Tablespoonfuls of Flour.
2 Carrots. 1 Tablespoonful of Butter.
1 Clove of Garlic. 1 Large Onion. 1 Parsnip.
1 Dozen Almonds. 1 Dozen Allspice.
4 Shallots. 6 Tomatoes or a Half Can.
Croutons.

Wash the crawfish thoroughly over and over again to take away every particle of dust. Then boil them in plain water. Save the water. Take out the crawfish and take off all the shells, putting the meat aside. Pound the shells fine; pound one dozen almonds fine and mix thoroughly with the meat of the crawfish and pound this in a mortar. In the meanwhile, take one pound and a half of a filet of veal and a slice of ham, and cut in small pieces. Cut up the onion, carrots and parsnips. Put one tablespoonful of lard in a kettle, and when it begins to heat, add the herb bouquet (sweet basil, parsley, bay leaf), the onions, parsnip, shallots, clove of garlic, chopped fine; as these brown, add the veal and ham. Add two tablespoonfuls of flour and butter, rubbed, and the mushrooms, chopped finely. Let these simmer for about five minutes and then add the tomatoes, allspice and cloves. After ten minutes, when the mixture is well browned, add the pounded crawfish shells and the pounded meat and almonds. Pour over all the water from the boiled crawfish and set it back on the stove and let it simmer for about two hours. Skim off all the grease when near time for serving. Then strain through a sieve, and serve with Croutons of toast, cut in slices, placed in the bottom of the tureen.

On fast days, instead of the veal and ham, substitute butter and lard, making a Roux (see recipe), and moistening a little with the stock of the crawfish. Then proceed as above.

Rice or Crouton Soup is rendered delicious by introducing a small quantity of the broth of the crawfish. The broth is also used extensively by the Creoles in seasoning ragoûts on fast days, and hot pies, such as pâtés de foies gras; also such entrémets as cauliflower, artichokes, etc. The chief essential in making the broth is to have it of the right consistency, and to skim carefully of all the grease before straining. Good judgment must be the guide of the cook in seeking the proper consistency.

### Oyster Soup.

Soupe aux Huitres.

4 Dozen Large, Fresh Oysters.
1 Quart of Rich Milk. The Oyster Liquor.
1 Tablespoonful of Butter.
3 Sprigs of Parsley, Chopped Fine.
1 Dozen Pepper Corns.
Salt and Pepper to Taste.

In purchasing the oysters always be careful to make the vendor add the oyster juice when intended for soup. In making good oyster soup the Creoles never use any water, but the liquor from the oysters. Drain the oysters through a colander and set them over the ice box to keep fresh and cold. Strain the liquor, and put it into a soup kettle, adding the chopped parsley and the pepper corns. Let it come to a boil. In the meantime, boil the milk separately in a saucepan, as boiling the milk and oyster juice together is likely to curdle the milk. When the milk comes to a boil, add to the oyster juice and put in the tablespoonful of butter. Some thicken the soup by adding a tablespoonful of corn starch, rubbing it into the flour before putting it in the soup. But this is a matter of taste. If the milk is rich and good, the soup will require no thickening, and is far daintier without it. Stir the soup constantly at this point, throwing in the oysters and continuing to stir until it comes to a boil again. Under no circumstances allow the oysters to boil, as that destroys their flavor and makes them tough and indigestible. But one must be also careful to see that they are steamed through and through; and then they are delightful and palatable. The crowning triumph in making oyster soup is to have the oysters cooked just enough. The ruffling of the edges indicates the right condition; at this point the soup must be served immediately. Serve with sliced lemon and oyster or water crackers. Some add a little nutmeg and mace, and, still again, some Creoles place chopped celery in exceedingly small quantities, and a herb bouquet into the oyster juice, being careful to allow it to give just the desired flavor; and taking it out before adding the milk. But this, too, is a matter of taste. Made according to the above formula, oyster soup is a most delightful dish and can be eaten and relished by the most delicate stomachs.

### Oyster Soup Without Milk.

Soupe aux Huitres à la Créole.

The Creoles have another delightful method of preparing oyster soup, a method evolved by the old negro cooks of ante-bellum days, and still in vogue in the ancient families.

It is a soup made without milk and is prepared as follows: Take

4 Dozen Bayou Cook Oysters.
The Oyster Liquor.
1 Large Onion. 1 Tablespoonful of Lard.
2 Tablespoonfuls of Sifted Flour.
4 Sprigs of Parsley. 1 Tablespoonful of Butter.
1 Quart of Boiling Water.

Put the tablespoonful of lard into the soup kettle. Have ready one onion, some parsley, chopped very fine. When the lard is hot, stir in two tablespoonfuls of sifted flour, and make a Brown Roux (see recipe), stirring constantly to prevent burning. When the Roux is of a light brown color, add the chopped onions and parsley, continuing to stir, being exceedingly careful to avoid the semblance of burning. Strain the oyster juice of about four dozen oysters into the Roux, mixing thoroughly, to avoid bits of shell; mix with about a quart of boiling water and pour When it shows signs of coming to a boil, add the oysters and a teaspoonful of butter. At the boiling point remove from the stove and serve with oyster soda crackers or dry toast, the oyster crackers being always preferable.

This form of soup may be improved by using the milk instead of the hot water, but either way is very palatable and a great favorite as a fast-day soup.

### Crab Soup.

Potage de Crabes.

1 Dozen Fine Crabs. 6 Ripe Tomatoes.
1 Sprig of Thyme. 3 Sprigs of Parsley.
1 of Sweet Marjoram.
1 Large Onion. 1 Clove of Garlic.
1 Teaspoonful of Butter.
2 Tablespoonfuls (level) of Lard.
1 Lemon.
Salt, Pepper and Cayenne.

Cleanse the crabs thoroughly and extract all the meat from the body and claws; scald and skin the tomatoes, and squeeze the pulp from the seeds and juice; chop very fine. Pour boiling water over the seed and juice and strain. Chop the onion and garlic and stew with the tablespoonful of butter and lard. As they begin to brown, add the tomatoes, cover, and, after simmering a few minutes, add the well-seasoned meat of the crab. Sift over this some grated bread or crackers and season with Cayenne, sweet marjoram and thyme. Pour in tomato water and add about a quart or more of water, and let it boil moderately for about an hour. Add the juice of two lemons and serve.

## CHAPTER V.

### LENTEN SOUPS.

Potages Maigres.

The Creoles excel in the preparation of soups without meat, or fast-day soups, as they are called. The ingenuity of the cooks from generation to generation have been taxed in the preparation of these soups, which are in great vogue during the Lenten season. But many of them, such as "Cream of Asparagus Soup," "Cream of Celery Soup," have entered into the daily life of the city, and, like the famous Creole Gumbos, are held as dainty and elegant introductions to the most distinguished feasts.

The nutritive value of the soups without meat cannot be overestimated especially those made with red or white beans, lentils, corn and other vegetables, whose health-giving properties are beyond dispute. To the poor especially they are recommended, not only on the score of economy, but of health as well.

### Fast-Day Broth.

Bouillon Maigre.

6 Fine Carrots. 6 Large White Onions.
6 Turnips.
½ Pound of Beans or Dried Split Peas.
1 Small Head of Cabbage. 1 Parsnip.
1 Stalk of Celery.
4 Sprigs of Parsley.
¼ Pound of Butter, or 1 Large Tablespoonful of Lard.
3 Quarts of Water.
1 Red Pepper Pod, Without the Seed.
Salt and Pepper to Taste.

Peel and cut into fine, thin slices the carrots, turnips and parsnips; cut and chop fine the cabbage, celery and onions; put all in a saucepan and add one glass of water, and a quarter of a pound of butter, using the butter preferably to the lard; add the parsley, chopped very fine. Let all boil till the water has evaporated, and then add one pint of red or white beans or split peas, which have been soaked overnight; add three quarts of water and the pepper pod, and let all simmer well for three hours. Then if the beans are perfectly tender at this point, drain or press through a colander; return to the fire and add the seasonings. Let all boil up once and then serve with Croûtons. Stale bread may be utilized in preparing the Croûtons. A more nutritious soup than this cannot be prepared.

### A Summer Fast-Day Soup.

Potage Maigre d'Été.

The Hearts of 6 Lettuce Cut in Pieces.
2 Large Onions.
2 Cucumbers, Pared and Sliced.
4 Pints of Young Green Peas.
Chopped Parsley.
3 Lumps of Crushed Sugar.
½ Pound of Butter.
Salt and Pepper to Taste.

Chop the vegetables fine and stew all together, except the young peas. After one hour add the young peas. Press them through a sieve and return all into the water in which they have been boiled. Add to this the vegetables that have been stewed in the butter and simmer about an hour and a half. A sprig of mint is added just before the soup is taken off the fire. This is a most excellent and nourishing soup and is recommended to the families of the poor.

### A Winter Fast-Day Soup.

Potage Maigre d'Hiver.

1 Quart of Dried Peas.
3 Quarts of Water. 1 Lettuce, Sliced.
1 Head of Celery.
1 Carrot. 2 Turnips. 2 Large Onions.
Handful of Spinach.
Sprig Each of Mint, Thyme and Parsley.
1 Bay Leaf.
A Tablespoonful of Butter.

Stew all the vegetables, except the lettuce, together, after having chopped fine, until they are perfectly soft. Then return to the fire with the chopped lettuce, butter and sugar. Boil quickly about twenty minutes, and serve with Croûtons.

### Vegetable Soup Without Meat.

Purée de Légumes.

1 Sweet Potato. 1 Bunch of Celery Leaves.
1 Turnip. 1 Parsnip.
1 Carrot. 1 Bay Leaf. 2 Onions.
Sprig of Parsley and Thyme.
1 Irish Potato.
2 Tablespoonfuls of Flour.
1 Large Tablespoonful of Butter.
3½ Quarts of Cold Water.
Salt and Pepper to Taste.

Cut the vegetables into dice and boil until thoroughly tender in about three and a half quarts of water; this will require about two hours. Then press the whole through a sieve; add the remaining water and bring to a boil. Then add the butter, rubbed smooth with the flour in a little rich cream, or a little of the hot soup. A gill of cream or milk added just before serving increases the flavor. Boil and stir about two or three minutes more and serve.

### Lentil Soup.

Potage à Purée de Lentilles.

1 Pint of Lentils. 2 Quarts of Water.
1 Onion. 1 Small Bunch of Parsley.
1 Bay Leaf. 1 Sprig of Thyme.
1 Tablespoonful of Butter or Lard.
1 Pod of Red Pepper, Without the Seeds.
1 Stalk of Celery, Chopped Fine.
Salt and Pepper to Taste.

Wash the lentils, and, if dried, soak them over night. Drain off the water and put them in a saucepan with the cold water. Allow them to come gradually to a boil. Then set them back on the stove and let them simmer gently for about two hours. Melt the butter in the saucepan and fry in it the minced onion, celery, parsley, thyme and bay leaf, and let these brown; then add them to the lentils; boil about an hour longer, and, if particularly tender, press all through a colander. Return to the fire and add the seasonings. Let them boil up once and serve with Croûtons.

Lentils are used constantly by the poorer class of Creoles, but they ought to be more generally used by all classes of people. The above soup is very palatable and most nourishing. As an illustration of the nutritive value of "légumes," as lentils, beans and peas are generally called, during the Franco-Prussian war the Germans, who learned much from the French as regards food values, supplied the German soldiers with a kind of sausage called "Erbswurst;" this was made of peasmeal and lentils, or the condensed soup mixed with a certain proportion of lard or bacon, onions, etc., and dried so as to be portable. Each sausage was a pound in weight, and one constituted the ration of a soldier. It was easily cooked by boiling in water, or it could be eaten cold. This instance is given in the hope that, through this Cook Book, people may learn how to cook not only palatably and well, but also how to live, selecting such foods as will give the greatest amount of nutriment in proportion to the quantity consumed. Lentils, peas and beans have been found by scientific experiment to possess a greater nutritive value than all other vegetable foods, since they contain more nitrogen than any of the cereals and are as rich in carbon as wheaten flour.

### Red Bean Soup.
#### Purée à la Condé.

1 Pint of Red Beans.
2 Quarts of Cold Water.
1 Minced Onion.
1 Tablespoonful of Butter.
1 Bay Leaf.
Bunch of Parsley.   Sprig of Thyme.
Salt and Pepper.

Wash the beans and soak them overnight in lukewarm water. Drain and put them in a saucepan with the cold water. Allow them to come gradually to a boil; then set them back, and let them simmer gently for about two hours. Melt the butter in a saucepan and fry in it the onion, parsley, thyme and bay leaf until brown. Add these to the beans and boil about an hour and a half longer. If the beans are perfectly tender at this point, press the whole through a colander. Return to the fire, and add the seasonings. Let them boil up once and serve with the Croûtons. Some think that the flavor is enhanced by beating up an egg in the tureen and pouring the boiling soup gradually over it, stirring constantly. This soup should always be served with Croûtons.

### White Bean Soup.
#### Potage à la Purée d'Haricots.

1 Pint of White Beans.
2 Quarts of Cold Water.
1 Minced Onion.   1 Tablespoonful of Butter.
1 Bay Leaf.   Bunch of Parsley.
Sprig of Thyme.
Salt and Pepper.

Wash the beans and soak them overnight in lukewarm water. Drain and put them in a saucepan with the cold water. Allow them to come gradually to a boil; then set them back and let them simmer gently for about two hours. Melt the butter in a saucepan and fry in it the onion, parsley, thyme and bay leaf until brown. Add these to the beans and boil about an hour and a half longer. If the beans are perfectly tender at this point, press the whole through a colander. Return to the fire and add the seasonings. Let them boil up once and then serve with the Croûtons. As in Red Bean Soup, a beaten egg may be added when about to pour into the tureen. First beat up the egg and pour the boiling soup gradually over, stirring all the while.

### Dried or Split Pea Soup.
#### Potage à la Purée de Pois Secs.

1 Pint of Dried or Split Peas.
1 Quart of Boiling Water.
1 Small Bunch of Celery. 1Bunch of Parsley.
1 Quart of Good Milk or Cream.
2 Onions.
Salt and Pepper to Taste.

It is always best to soak the peas overnight, after washing them in cold water and rejecting all that float. In the morning drain off the water and cover the peas again with one quart of boiling water, setting them back on the stove and letting them cook slowly until tender. Cut up the onion and parsley and celery into fine pieces and add to the boiling peas. When perfectly tender remove from the stove and press through a sieve or colander and add the salt and pepper. Then return the soup to the fire and let it boil up once; just before serving add the rich cream or milk, stirring well. The soup should be served with Croûtons or Oyster Crackers. White Bean Soup may be made in exactly the same manner. When not intended for fast days, the addition of a ham bone adds greatly to the flavor.

### Purée of Green Peas.
#### Purée de Pois Verts.

1 Quart of Young Green Peas.
Bunch of Parsley.   2 Young Onions.
2 Quarts of Good Milk or Broth.
Pepper and Salt.

Cut the onions and parsley fine, and boil with the peas until all are quite tender, in boiling water, for about a half hour. Then drain. Rub all through a sieve or colander, and add them to the boiling broth or milk. Do not allow this to boil after adding the peas. Season and serve with dainty Croûtons. To keep hot, stand the soup on a "bain-marie," or kettle of boiling water.

### Sorrel Soup.
#### Potage à la "Bonne Femme," ou Soupe à l'Oiselle.

A Small Bunch of Fresh Sorrel.
3 Quarts of Boiling Water.
1 Cup of Cream or Rich Milk.
1 Cup of Mashed Potatoes.
4 Eggs.   3 Sprigs of Parsley.
3 Leaves of Lettuce.   1 Onion.
1 Tablespoonful of Butter.
2 Tablespoonfuls of Flour. A Pinch of Nutmeg.
Pepper and Salt to Taste.

Sorrel Soup, or Soupe à l'Oiselle, is a popular Creole soup much prized for its cooling properties. The Indians gather near Bayou Lacombe the sorrel and bring it to New Orleans and sell it in the French Market. It is also grown in the home garden by many Creoles. The leaves only are used in making soup or purées.

Wash the leaves and stem them, the entire length of the leaf. Then chop them fine until you have a quantity equal to a pint or two teacupfuls. Chop the other vegetables and put these and the sorrel into a saucepan with the butter; cover and let them stew gently for ten minutes; and then add the flour, which has been well mixed with a little water. Pour gradually, stirring always, into the three quarts of boiling water. Beat the yolks of the eggs and mix with a little cream or milk in a tureen. Rub the rest of the cream of milk smooth with the mashed potato and put into the soup; add the seasonings. Prepare toast in the form of dice, rubbing them first with the raw onion, and pour some of the boiling soup over the eggs in the tureen and mix very carefully. Put in the pieces of toast, and then add the remainder of the soup. Cover and stand five minutes in a warm oven, and serve hot.

### Potato Soup.
Potage Parmentier.

8 Potatoes. 2 Onions, Cut Fine.
1 Cup of Cream or Rich Milk.
1 Pinch of Grated Nutmeg.
1 Tablespoonful of Butter. Pepper and Salt.

After washing and peeling the potatoes, put them into a saucepan with the onions and add about two quarts of cold water. Bring to a boil. After allowing to cook about forty minutes, if the vegetables are then very tender, mash and pass all through a sieve, and, returning to the fire, add the seasoning and butter. Bring to a boil, and add the cream and a beaten egg, serving immediately with Croûtons.

### Carrot Soup.
Potage Crecy.

4 Large Carrots (the redder the better).
2 Large Onions, Cut Fine.
1 Quart of New Milk. 1 Turnip.
1 Teaspoon of Corn Starch.
2 Sticks of Celery. 1 Bay Leaf.
Sprig of Thyme. Sprig of Parsley.
3 Cloves.
1 Large Teaspoonful of Butter.
Salt and Pepper and Sugar to Taste.

Wash the vegetables thoroughly, cutting them fine and boiling until tender in three pints of water. When very soft, mash them and press through a sieve. The carrots must be mashed very fine. Then return to the fire, and, adding about two quarts of boiling water, cover and simmer gently for a while, adding one teaspoonful of cornstarch that has been blended well with a little milk. Add the boiling milk and cook for about two minutes more, and serve with Croûtons. (See recipe.)

### Lettuce Soup.
Potage de Laitues.

1 Large Head of Lettuce.
1 Spoon of French Vinegar. 1 Egg.
1 Tablespoonful of Butter. 1 Gill of Cream.
1 Teaspoonful of Flour.
Dices of Stale Bread. 1 Pinch of Sugar.
3 Quarts of Broth.

Prepare a good broth and cook till it is reduced to three pints; this will serve six persons. Chop the lettuce fine and stew it with a tablespoonful of butter, adding the pinch of sugar and one spoon of French vinegar. Keep stirring constantly, so that it will not burn. Then add the flour (which has been rolled smoothly in butter), the pepper and salt, throw in a dash of Cayenne pepper. Break in the egg and stir thoroughly. Then pour on the broth. Place the dice of bread in the tureen, and add the gill of cream to the soup before pouring over the bread.

### Okra Soup.
Potage de Févi.

2 Pints of Okra, or Fifty Counted.
6 Fresh Tomatoes. 2 Onions Chopped Fine.
2 Tablespoonfuls of Butter.
3 Sprigs of Parsley.
2 Sprigs of Thyme. 1 Bay Leaf.
3 Quarts of Water. Salt and Pepper to Taste.
A Red Pepper Pod, Without the Seed.

Wash and stem the okra and then slice it very fine. Chop the tomatoes fine, being careful to preserve the juice. Chop the onions fine and fry them in the butter. Then add the chopped thyme, bay leaf, parsley and tomatoes and the pepper pod, and, after letting it stew about five minutes, add the okra, stirring constantly almost, as it burns quickly. When well browned, add the juice of the tomatoes. Then add the hot water, and set on the back of the stove and let it simmer well for about an hour and a half. Season to taste and serve hot, with Croûtons.

N. B.—The housekeeper should always remember that okra must be cooked in a porcelain-lined pot, as iron or other metal tends to blacken it.

### Winter Okra Soup.
Potage Févi d'Hiver.

1 Can of Good New Orleans Okra.
1 Can of Tomatoes. 2 Onions Chopped Fine.
2 Tablespoonfuls of Butter.
2 Dozen Oysters. 3 Tablespoonfuls of Rice.
A Red Pepper Pod, Without the Seed.

Chop the onions fine and fry them in the butter. Wash the rice well, then stew the onions, tomatoes and pepper together in about three quarts of water and one pint of oyster water for about three hours, stirring frequently. Ten minutes before serving add the okra and let it come to a boil. Then drop in the oysters. Boil up once and serve.

### Onion Soup.
Potage à l'Ognon.

3 Large Onions, Sliced Very Thin or Chopped.
½ Cup of Flour.
1 Large Spoon of Butter.
1 Quart of Milk.
2 Large Potatoes, Mashed Fine.
Dice of Bread or Toast.
Salt and Pepper.

Fry the onions in the butter, until reddish brown. Then add the flour and stir until browned, gently; do not burn. Put the boiling water in gradually, stirring perfectly smooth, and adding the salt and pepper; mix well and boil one minute. Then pour it into the kettle and set back. Before serving, add the milk warmed, and rubbed with mashed potatoes until they are a smooth paste. Simmer a few moments. Have the pieces of toast ready in the tureen and pour in the hot soup. A purée of onions is made by pressing the ingredients through a sieve and returning to the fire for a few moments. Serve hot.

### Cream of Onion Soup.

#### Purée d'Ognons.

6 Onions. ½ Ounce of Butter.
1½ Pints of Cream. 2 Ounces of Flour.
2 Pints of Boiling Water.
Pepper. Nutmeg.

Peel the onions and boil in salted water until very tender; then drain and dry well with a cloth; put them on the fire in a saucepan, with one ounce of butter; add the other ingredients, except the remaining half ounce of butter. When the soup comes to a boil, press through the sieve, and return to the fire; add the remainder of the butter and serve. This is a very delicately flavored soup for fast days.

### Cream of Tomato Soup.

#### Potage aux Tomates.

2 Quarts of Pure Tomato Juice.
1 Gill of Rice. 3 Onions. 8 Allspice.
4 Cloves. A Sprig of Thyme.
A Pinch of Sugar to Taste.
Pepper and Salt.

Stew the Tomatoes for about two hours, and then extract the juice. Add the other ingredients, and boil for about an hour and a half; then strain. The rice, being creamy, should now make the soup as thick as cream. Serve with Croûtons or Quenelles. (See recipe.)

In the summertime, when tomatoes are so plentiful in New Orleans, this is not only one of the most delightful but one of the least extravagant cream soups that can be made.

### Cream of Celery Soup.

#### Potage à la Crème de Celeri.

Celery Stalks. 2 Quarts of Milk or Cream.
2 Tablespoonfuls of Flour.
1 Pint of Water. 1 Tablespoonful of Butter.
½ Small Onion.
Salt and Pepper to Taste.

Wash the celery and onion and cut into fine pieces. Then place them in a porcelain-lined saucepan and let boil for about a half hour. Take off and mash, and press through a colander. Set the milk to boil in a farina boiler, and as it heats well, add to it the water and celery that have been pressed. Rub smoothly together the flour and butter, and then stir into the boiling soup, stirring constantly till it thickens to a cream of the right consistency. Add salt and pepper to taste and serve hot. It is very delicious served with slices of delicately toasted and buttered Croûtons. Serve on a separate dish and garnish with sprigs of parsley and slices of hard-boiled eggs.

### Cream of Corn Soup.

#### Potage à la Crème de Mais.

2 Pints of Grated Corn.
4 Quarts of Boiling Water.
1 Pint of Hot Milk or Cream.
3 Tablespoonfuls of Butter.
2 Level Tablespoonfuls of Flour.
The Yolks of 2 Eggs.
Salt and Pepper to Taste.

Slit the corn in two and grate from the cobs. Put the cobs into the boiling water and let them boil slowly about an hour, till the water is reduced to three quarts. Then take the cobs out and drain over the kettle. Add the corn and let it boil till very soft. This will require about thirty minutes. Take the soup off and press all through a sieve. Season highly and set back to simmer gently, adding, in the meanwhile, the flour and butter, thoroughly rubbed together. Stir constantly till the soup thickens, and then add the boiling milk. Cook a moment only, take off the fire, stir in the beaten yolks and serve hot, with buttered toast cut in dice shape.

### Cream of Asparagus Soup.

#### Crème d'Asperges.

1 Large Bunch of Asparagus.
1 Tablespoonful of Butter. 1 Quart of Milk.
3 Tablespoonfuls of Rich Cream.
2 Even Tablespoonfuls of Flour or Corn Starch.
Salt and Pepper to Taste.

Wash the Asparagus, tie it in a bunch and put in a saucepan of boiling water. Let it boil gently for about three-quarters of an hour, or until perfectly tender. Take it from the water, cut off the tips or points and put them aside until wanted. Put the milk on to boil in a farina boiler. Press the Asparagus stalks through a colander, and add them to the milk. Rub the butter and cornstarch or flour together until perfectly smooth, and add to the boiling milk, stirring constantly till it thickens. Now add the Asparagus tops, salt and pepper, and serve, without Croûtons, as the Asparagus tips form a beautiful garnish.

### Cream of Spinach Soup.
Potage à la Crême d'Epinards.

Half a Peck or Four Pints of Spinach.
2 Ounces of Fresh Butter.
Two Quarts of Oyster Water.
1 Teaspoonful of Salt.
1 Teaspoonful of Granulated Sugar.
¼ of a Grated Nutmeg.

Wash and boil one-half peck, or four pints of Spinach; this quantity will measure about one pint when cooked, chopped and pounded into a fine paste. Then put it into a stew pan with four ounces of fresh butter, the grated nutmeg and a teaspoonful of salt. Let it cook for ten minutes, stirring constantly. Add to this two quarts of oyster juice (on other than fast days consommé may be used, or good bouillon). Let all boil up, and then press through a strainer. Set it over the fire again and just at the boiling point, mix with it a tablespoonful of butter, and a teaspoonful of granulated sugar. Serve hot with Croûtons.

### Cream of Barley Soup.
Purée d'Orge.

3 Tablespoonfuls of Barley, or a Half Cup.
1 Pint of Cream or Milk.
The Yolks of 2 Eggs    3 Quarts of Water
(boiling).
Salt and Pepper to Taste.

Scald the barley and then put into a kettle with three quarts of boiling water and let it boil about three hours. Take it off and mash thoroughly, and strain through a sieve. Add the hot milk to the stock of the barley, season with salt and pepper, and let it come to a boil. Take off and add the yolks of two eggs.

### Cream of Rice Soup.
Crême de Riz.

1 Cup of Rice.    3 Quarts of Water.
1 Pint of Milk.    The Yolks of 2 Eggs.
1 Tablespoonful of Butter.
Pepper and Salt to Taste.

Wash the Rice thoroughly, rubbing dry. Put it into a saucepan with one quart of cold water; when swelled add one quart of boiling water, and when it begins to get very tender add the remaining quart of boiling water. Then add the pepper and salt. Take from the fire, mash the rice well and rub all through a sieve. Beat up the yolks of the eggs well with a few tablespoonfuls of cream. When quite smooth stir in carefully a few spoons of the boiling rice water, and then pour the eggs and cream or milk into the saucepan with the rice, which you will have returned to the stove. Mix briskly and then draw aside and stir for two or three minutes, being very careful not to allow the mixture to boil when once the eggs will have been added. Serve hot with Croûtons or Crackers.

On other than fast days this is most delicious made with Chicken Consommé.

### Rice Soup, Without Meat.
Riz au Maigre.

1 Cup of Rice.    The Yolks of 2 Eggs.
3 Quarts of Water.    1 Spoon of Butter.
1 Pint of Milk.    Pepper and Salt.

Wash the rice thoroughly, rubbing dry. Put it in a saucepan with one pint of cold water; when swelled, add one pint of boiling water; and when it begins to get very tender, add the remaining pint of boiling water. Add the pepper and salt. Beat up the yolks of the eggs with a few tablespoonfuls of cream. When quite smooth, stir in carefully a few spoonfuls of the boiling rice water, and then pour the eggs and cream into the saucepan, stirring very briskly. Draw aside and stir for two or three minutes, but do not allow the soup to boil when once the eggs are added.

### Cocoanut Soup.
Potage de Cocoa.

6 or 8 Calves' Feet.
½ Pound of Grated Cocoanut.
1 Gallon of Water.
1 Pint of Ceam or Rich Milk.
1 Tablespoonful of Flour or Arrowroot.
3 Ounces of Fresh Butter.
6 Blades of Mace.
The Grated Rind of 1 Lemon.

Scald the calves' feet, and scrape thoroughly without skinning; put them into the soup kettle with a gallon of cold water, and cover the kettle well. Let the feet come to a slow boil and skim carefully. Then add the blades of mace and let the soup boil slowly till the meat is reduced to rags and has fallen from the bones. Then strain into a white porcelain dish or pan, and set it away to cool. After it has congealed, scrape off fat and sediment, and a beautiful jelly will remain. Cut up this cake of jelly and put it into a thoroughly cleansed, white porcelain soup kettle. In the meantime grate the cocoanut very fine, till about a half pound is on hand. Mix this with the pint of rich cream or milk, and add the butter which has been rolled smoothly in the arrowroot or flour. Mix this carefully and gradually with the calves' feet stock or soup, and season with a grated nutmeg. The soup should then be set back on the fire and allowed to boil slowly for about fifteen minutes, stirring almost constantly. Pour into the tureen and serve with French rolls, or milk biscuit, made very light and thin. On fast days omit the calves' feet, using another ounce of butter instead.

The Creoles often serve powdered white sugar in small plates or in salt cellars for those of the company who prefer more sweetening.

### Chestnut Soup.

Potage à la Purée de Marrons.

3 Quarts of Oyster Water, or
A Good Round of Beef or Veal.
1 Quart of Chestnuts.   1 Herb Bouquet.
Cayenne Pepper.

Make a good broth of the veal or beef; season with the Cayenne pepper and salt. Follow the rule given for making soups, by allowing a pound of meat to each quart of water. Skim and boil till the meat falls into rags; then strain and put in a clean porcelain pot. In the meantime, shell the chestnuts and throw them into boiling water until the skin comes off easily. Put them into a saucepan with some of the soup water, and boil about thirty minutes, till quite soft. Press through a colander; add butter, pepper and salt. Then add to the soup. Make dumplings the size of a marble with fresh butter rolled in flour, and add. (See recipe for Dumplings.) Boil the soup about fifteen minutes longer and serve. Some prefer the soup without dumplings, thinking it gives more of the flavor of the chestnuts. On fast days use the oyster water instead of the beef broth, following the recipe in all other particulars, and adding a half tablespoonful of butter to the purée before pressing through the colander.

## CHAPTER VI.

### THE BOUILLI.

"Le Bouilli."

Before leaving the subejct of soups it has been thought advisable to devote a short chapter to the "Bouilli," or the boiled meat that is usually thrown away by other nationalities than the Creole and French when the "Pot-au-Feu," the "Consommé" or the "Bouillon" has been completed.

The Creoles long ago discovered or rather brought over with them from the mother country, France, the delightful possibilities for a good entrée that lurked within the generally despised and cast aside Bouilli, and these possibilities they improved upon in their own unique and palatable styles of cuisine preparations.

In France the "Bouilli" is always served at the home dinner, and so with the new France, New Orleans. Far from rejecting the "Bouilli" as unpalatable and unfit for food, the Creoles discovered many delightful ways of serving it, and their theories of the nutrition that still remained in the boiled beef have been sustained by medical science. The most eminent scientists have found by experiment that while heat coagulates the nutritious substances of the beef, only a small amount is dissolved when the water is heated gradually, and that the "Bouilli" is still valuable as an article of food.

The pleasant ways that the Creoles have of preparing it restores its flavor and makes it a delightful accompaniment to even the most aristocratic dinners. For breakfast the boiled beef left over is utilized in various ways.

The Picayune has selected from among many the following recipes which need only to be tried to be repeated often, or perhaps daily, in one form or the other.

The recipes for the sauces mentioned will be found in the chapter especially devoted to "Creole Sauces."

### Mirontons.
The Left-Over Bouilli.

3 Large Onions.   6 Shallots.
1 Clove of Garlic.   1 Sprig of Thyme.
1 Bay Leaf.   2 Pickles.
1 Tablespoonful of Flour.
1 Tablespoonful of Butter.
Salt, Pepper and Cayenne to Taste.

This is a favorite way the Creoles have of serving the cold bouilli that has been saved from the preceding day:

Slice the onions fine; brown in one tablespoonful of butter. Chop the shallots and add to the onions, then add the garlic, thyme and bay leaf, all chopped very fine, and season with salt, Cayenne and black pepper to taste. When the whole is browning nicely, add a tablespoonful of flour and water, or left-over broth, sufficient to cover. Season this to taste and then take two pickles, about one finger long, slice very fine, and add. Let all boil about fifteen minutes and then lay the cold bouilli, which has been thickly sliced, in the sauce.

Set it to bake in the oven about twenty minutes. Garnish with buttered toast and serve hot.

### Boiled Beef Sauté à la Lyonnaise.
Bouilli Sauté à la Lyonnaise.

The Bouilli. 3 Onions.
1 Tablespoonful of Lard.
1 Tablespoonful of Olive Oil.
1 Tablespoonful of Chili Vinegar.
The Peel of One Lemon.

Slice the onions and brown them in lard, using about one tablespoonful. Skim the lard off the onions and put the beef in the pan. Stir up and smother. Add the oil, the peel of a lemon, cut fine, and the Chili vinegar. Serve hot.

### Boiled Beef à la Bordelaise.
Bouilli à la Bordelaise.

The Bouilli.
½ Dozen Shallots.
1 Glass of White Wine.
2 Teaspoonfuls of Sauce Espagnole.

Slice the left-over beef. Then hash the shallots into very fine pieces; add a glass of white wine, pepper and salt to taste, and boil to half the quantity over a brisk fire. Then add the mashed beef marrow from the bone and two teaspoonfuls of "Sauce Espagnole" (see recipe), first melting the marrow in a little bouillon. Stir rapidly over the fire, and as soon as it begins to bubble, withdraw it and set it back on the stove, letting it simmer gently for a quarter of an hour. Add the sliced beef for about ten minutes and then serve with Croûtons or fried crusts.

### Boiled Beef à la Paysanne.
Bouilli à la Paysanne.

The Bouilli.
5 Large Onions.
1 Tablespoonful of Butter.
1 Teaspoonful of Flour.
1 Wineglassful of Claret.
A Dash of Mustard and Vinegar.

Hash the left-over beef, and then chop five large onions very fine and cook them to a golden brown in butter. When nearly done, dust over them a teaspoonful of flour and moisten with a little red wine. Cook the onions till done and then put in the cold hashed beef, adding a dash of French vinegar and a little mustard and serve.

### Boiled Beef à l'Indienne.
Bouilli à l'Indienne.

The Bouilli.
1 Teaspoonful of Powdered Saffron.
2 Cayenne Pepper Pods.
1 Tablespoonful of Butter.
½ Cup of Bouillon.

This is a dinner dish. Crush the pods of two Cayenne peppers and a teaspoonful of powdered saffron and heat and brown in butter. Then moisten with a little bouillon. Boil the sauce down, and when nearly ready to serve, thicken with a little butter. Serve in a gravy dish with the "Bouilli," which has been nicely and tastefully garnished with lettuce leaves on a parsley bed.

### Boiled Beef With Tomatoes.
Bouilli aux Tomates.

The Bouilli.
½ Dozen Tomatoes.
2 Cups of Bouillon.
½ Teaspoonful of Flour.
1 Clove of Garlic.
1 Sprig Each of Thyme and Parsley.
1 Bay Leaf.

Take a half dozen fine, ripe tomatoes, and parboil them in butter, being careful not to let them burn. Add a pinch of flour and two good cups of bouillon, a little salt and pepper, a clove of garlic, a sprig of parsley, thyme and bay leaf. After two hours, take out the tomatoes and allow the beef to cook a few minutes in the sauce. Then serve on a flat dish, arranging the tomatoes around the beef and under each tomato put a nice piece of buttered toast.

### Boiled Beef à la Bruxelloise.
Bouilli à la Bruxelloise.

The Bouilli.
1 Dozen Brussels Sprouts.
4 Tablespoonfuls of Butter.
3 Sprigs of Parsley.
Salt and Pepper to Taste.

Take about a dozen Brussels sprouts and blanch them in boiling water. Drain thoroughly and stew in butter with chopped parsley. After they have cooked ten minutes, take them out of the pan and parboil them in fresh butter, which has been melted before the stove. Salt and pepper to taste and garnish nicely around the bouilli and serve.

### Boiled Beef en Papillottes.
Bouilli en Papillottes.

The Bouilli.
2 Tablespoonfuls of Butter.
6 Sausages. (Chaurice.)
2 Eggs. 1 Cup Bread Crumbs.
4 Sprigs of Parsley.
Salt and Pepper to Taste.

This is a nice breakfast dish. Take the left-over bouilli cut in slices and parboil slightly in butter. Make a forcemeat or quenelle of pork sausage, garlic, parsley and moistened bread crumbs, add two eggs, salt and pepper. Put a layer of this "farci" between each layer of sliced beef, and then add the bread crumbs, mixed with chopped parsley. Put the beef in oiled paper, folded as tightly as possible, cook a quarter of an hour in the oven and serve in the pappillottes (paper.).

### Boiled Beef With Carrot Sauce.
Bouilli à la Crécy.

The Bouilli.
4 Carrots. 2 Onions.
1 Gill of Cream.
2 Sticks of Celery.
3 Sprigs of Parsley. 1 Sprig of Thyme.
1 Tablespoonful of Butter.
Salt and Pepper to Taste.

Make a good purée of fine, red carrots (see recipe), and then strain in butter. Add a gill of rich cream and salt and pepper to the taste. Put the bouilli in the platter and pour the sauce around it, serving hot just after the soup.

### Boiled Beef With Lettuce.
Bouilli à la Laitue.

The Bouilli.
6 Head of Lettuce. 2 Hard-Boiled Eggs.
12 Sausages. (Chaurice.)
1½ Cups Bread Crumbs.
Salt and Pepper to Taste.

Take six fine, firm heads of lettuce, strip off all the green leaves, wash thoroughly and soak and blanch in boiling water. Then throw them into cold water. When very cold squeeze in a towel till they are thoroughly dry and cut off the stalks from below without injuring the heart. Fill this open place with forcemeat balls, made from the bouilli after the recipe already given in Boiled Beef en Papillottes, that is, fry them in lard, with fresh bread crumbs soaked in bouillon and worked into the meat. Chop up with pepper, salt and garlic, and add one or two hard-boiled eggs. Tie the balls up and cook without adding water and fill the heart of the lettuce. This may be served around the body of the bouilli and makes a beautiful garnish.

### Boiled Beef à la Lyonnaise.
Bouilli à la Lyonnaise.

The Bouilli.
6 Sausages. (Chaurice.)
1 Clove of Garlic. 3 Sprigs of Parsley.
1 Sprig of Thyme.
2 Eggs. Bread Crumbs.
The Juice of 1 Lemon.

Make sausage meat of the bouilli, adding the pork sausage, garlic, parsley and thyme. Moisten some bread crumbs in water and dissolve over them two eggs, salt and pepper. Chop the whole and tie it tightly in a cabbage leaf. An hour before serving take out the remaining bouilli and the farci or stuffed cabbage leaf. Let them cool and cut them into slices and roll these in beaten eggs, and then in bread crumbs, and fry in butter. Throw over them a dash of powdered parsley and squeeze over all the juice of a lemon.

### Boiled Beef With Egg Toast.
Bouilli au "Pain Perdu."

6 Slices of Bouilli.
6 Slices of Stale Bread.
2 Eggs. 1 Pint of Milk.
2 Tablespoonfuls of Butter.
Parsley and Lettuce Leaves to Garnish.

Take left-over or stale bread, slice it thickly and dip in cream or milk. Then dip it in the beaten whites and yolks of egg and fry in butter. Cut the bouilli into slices to match the bread, dip it in the egg and fry also. Serve on a dish with chopped parsley dashed over it and a garnish of parsley or lettuce leaves.

### Boiled Beef Sauté With Onions.
Bouilli Sauté aux Ognons.

The Bouilli.
3 Large Onions.
2 Tablespoonfuls of Butter.
1. Clove of Garlic. 3 Sprigs of Parsley.
The Juice of 1 Lemon.

Take three fine onions and parboil them in butter over a slow fire. When a rich, creamy brown, add clove garlic and Cayenne pepper. Cut the bouillon in thin slices and add, shaking the pan until browned. Place in the platter and serve with chopped parsley dusted over, and the juice of a lemon squeezed over it.

### Boiled Beef à la Marseillaise.
Bouilli à la Marseillaise.

The Bouilli.
1 Dozen Small Onions.
½ Cup Claret. ½ Cup Meat Gravy.
¼ Can of Mushrooms.
1 Herb Bouquet. ⅛ of a Grated Nutmeg.
Salt and Pepper to Taste.

Slice the bouilli into thin, fine slices. Take a dozen onions, the smallest kind, and dust over with sugar, and bake in the oven. When a good color, put a little of the bouillon in the stewing pan and boil down one half. Moisten with a cup of red wine and thick meat sauce, allowing half and half in proportion. Then add the beef, the mushrooms, the bouquet garni, salt, pepper and a little nutmeg, and serve very hot.

### Boiled Beef Sausage.
Saucisse de Bouilli.

The Bouilli.
1 Pound of Pork. 3 Sprigs of Parsley.
1 Clove of Garlic.
6 Allspice. 3 Truffles.
A Dash of Cayenne.
1 Wineglass of Madeira.
½ Cup of Bouillon.

Take the bouilli of the day before, mince and add chopped parsley, a few spices, salt and Cayenne pepper, and a little beef extract saved from the bouillon. Take a pound of pork and add, mixing thoroughly. When the whole is well mixed, add a few truffles and a little Madeira. Fill some entrails that have been thoroughly cleansed with this meat and shape the sausage as one desires. Boil in butter and serve alone. This makes an excel.ent breakfast dish.

### Beef Croquettes.

Croquettes de Boeuf.

The Bouilli.
1 Pound of Pork or Sausage Meat.
1 Clove of Garlic.
2 Onions.   Whites of 3 Eggs.
3 Sprigs of Parsley.
1 Cup of Bread Crumbs.
Salt and Pepper.

Mince the beef with sausage meat and add garlic, parsley, pepper, salt and onions, and bread crumbs soaked in water. Add the whites of two eggs beaten to a froth. Make into balls and roll in the beaten white of an egg, and fry, being careful not to cook too rapidly. When sufficiently browned, pile in a pyramid shape on a dish, garnish with parsley sprigs and serve.

### Boiled Beef Gros Sel.

Bouilli Gros Sel.

The Bouilli.
1 Bunch of Parsley.   1 Head of Lettuce.
A French Dressing.

This is the simplest way of serving the bouilli, and the one most used by the Creoles as a daily dish. Take the bouilli from the bouillon, and serve on a platter, laying the whole on a bed of parsley and lettuce. Serve with salt or French dressing.

### A Good Every-Day Hash.

Hachis.

1 Quart of Chopped Soup Meat.
1 Onion.   2 Potatoes.
2 Hard-Boiled Eggs.
1 Tablespoonful of Butter.
½ Pint of Water.
Salt and Pepper to Taste.
A Dash of Cayenne.

Chop the left-over bouilli fine in dice shapes, and to every quart of the meat allow one onion, a tablespoonful of butter, two hard-boiled eggs, two cold (left-over) potatoes, a half pint of water, and salt and pepper to taste. Chop the potatoes, onions and eggs fine and put them into the stewing pan with the meat, adding by degrees the butter, salt and pepper with a little dash of Cayenne. Stew very slowly for about fifteen or twenty minutes and serve hot.

## CHAPTER VII.

### CREOLE GUMBO.

Gombo à la Créole.

Gumbo, of all other products of the New Orleans cuisine, represents a most distinctive type of the evolution of good cookery under the hands of the famous Creole cuisiniéres of old New Orleans. Indeed, the word "evolution" fails to apply when speaking of Gumbo, for it is an original conception, a something sui generis in cooking, peculiar to this ancient Creole city alone, and to the manor born. With equal ability the olden Creole cooks saw the possibilities of exquisite and delicious combinations in making Gumbo and hence we have many varieties, till the occult science of making a good "Gombo à la Créole" seems to the Picayune too fine an inheritance of gastronomic lore to remain forever hidden away in the cuisines of this old Southern metropolis. The following recipes, gathered with care from the best Creole housekeepers of New Orleans, have been handed down from generation to generation by the old negro cooks, and preserved in all their delightful combinations by their white Creole mistresses. They need only to be tried to prove thier perfect claim to the admiration of the many distinguished visitors and epicures who have paid tribute to our Creole Gumbo:

### Gumbo Filé.

Gombo Filé.

First, it will be necessary to explain here, for the benefit of many, that "Filé" is a powder manufactured by the remaining tribe of Choctaw Indians in Louisiana, from the young and tender leaves of the sassafras. The Indian squaws gather the leaves and spread them out on a stone mortar to dry. When thoroughly dried, they pound them into a fine powder, pass them through a hair sieve, and then bring the Filé to New Orleans to sell, coming twice a week to the French Market, from the old reservation set aside for their home on Bayou Lacombe, near Mandeville, La. The Indians used sassafras leaves and the sassafras for many medicinal purposes, and still sell bunches of the dried roots in the French Market. The Creoles, quick to discover and apply, found the possibilities of the powdered sassafras, or "Filé," and originated the well-known dish, "Gumbo Filé."

To make a good "Gumbo Filé," use the following ingredients:

1 Large Tender Chicken.
2 Large Slices or ½ Pound Lean Ham.
2 Tableapoofuls of Butter or 1 of Lard.
1 Bay Leaf.   3 Sprigs of Parsley.
3 Dozen Oysters.
1 Large Onion.   1 Sprig of Thyme.
2 Quarts of Oyster Water.
2 Quarts of Boiling Water.
1 Half Pod of Red Pepper, Without the Seeds.
Salt and Pepper and Cayenne to Taste.

Clean and cut up the chicken as for a fricassée. Dredge with salt and black pepper, judging according to taste. Cut the ham into dice shapes and chop the onion, parsley and thyme very fine. Put the lard or butter into the soup kettle or deep stewing pot, and when hot, put in the ham and chicken. Cover closely and fry for about five or ten minutes. Then add the onion and parsley and thyme, stirring occasionally to prevent burning. When nicely browned add the boiling water and throw in the oyster stock, which has been thoroughly heated. Add the bay leaf chopped very fine, and the pepper pod, cut in two, and set the gumbo back to simmer for about an hour longer. When nearly ready to serve dinner, and while the Gumbo is boiling, add the fresh oysters. Let the gumbo remain on the stove for about three minutes longer, and then remove the pot from the fire. Have ready the tureens, set in a "bain-marie" or hot water bath, for once the Filé is added the gumbo must never be warmed over. Take two tablespoonfuls of the Filé and drop gradually into the pot of boiling hot Gumbo, stirring slowly to mix thoroughly; pour into the tureen, or tureens, if there should be a second demand and serve with boiled rice. (See recipe.) The rice, it should be remarked, must be boiled so that the grains stand quite apart, and brought to the table in a separate dish, covered. Serve about two spoonfuls of rice to one plate of gumbo.

The above recipe is for a family of six. Increased quantities in proportion as required. Never boil the gumbo with the rice, and never add the Filé while the gumbo is on the fire, as boiling after the file is added tends to make the gumbo stringy and unfit for use, else the Filé is precipitated to the bottom of the pot, which is equally to be avoided.

Where families cannot afford a fowl, a good gumbo may be made by substituting the round of the beef for the chicken.

### Turkey Gumbo.

Gombo de Dinde.

The Remains of a Turkey.
½ Pound of Lean Ham.
2 Tablespoons of Butter or 1 of Lard.
1 Bay Leaf.   3 Sprigs of Parsley.
3 Dozen Oysters.
1 Large Onion.   1 Sprig of Thyme.
2 Quarts of Oyster Water.
½ Pod of Red Pepper, Without the Seeds.
Salt, Pepper and Cayenne to Taste.

Nothing is ever lost in a well-regulated Creole kitchen. When turkey is served one day, the remains or "left-over" are saved and made into that most excellent dish—a Turkey Gumbo. It is made in the same manner as Chicken Gumbo, only instead of the chicken, the turkey meat, black and white, that is left over, is stripped from the bones and carcass. Chop fine and add to the hot lard, and then put in the ham, cut fine into dice shapes. Proceed exactly as in the recipe above, only after adding the boiling water, throw in the bones and carcass of the turkey. At the proper time remove the carcass and bones, add the oysters, and then remove the pot and "Filé" the gumbo. Serve with boiled rice. Turkey Gumbo, when made from the remains of wild turkey, has a delicious flavor.

### Squirrel or Rabbit Gumbo.

Gombo d'Ecureil ou de Lapin.

These are famous Creole Gumbos. The following ingredients are used:

1 Fine Squirrel or Rabbit.
2 Slices or ½ Pound of Lean Ham.
3 Sprigs of Parsley.   1 Sprig of Thyme.
1 Bay Leaf.   1 Large Onion.
3 Dozen Oysters.
2 Quarts of Oyster Water.
½ Pod of Red Pepper, Without the Seed.
A Dash of Cayenne.
Salt and Pepper to Taste.

Skin, clean and cut up the squirrel or rabbit, as for a fricassé. Dredge well with salt and black pepper. Cut the ham into dice shapes, and chop the onion, parsley and thyme very fine. Put the lard or butter into a deep stew pot and, when hot, put in the squirrel or rabbit. Cover closely and fry for about eight or ten minutes. Then proceed in exactly the same manner as for Chicken Gumbo; add the "filé" at the time indicated, and serve with boiled Louisiana rice. (See recipe.)

### Okra Gumbo.
#### Gombo Févi.

1 Chicken.    1 Onion.
6 Large Fresh Tomatoes.
2 Pints of Okra, or Fifty Counted.
½ Pod of Red Pepper, Without the Seeds.
2 Large Slices of Ham.
1 Bay Leaf.    1 Sprig of Thyme or Parsley.
1 Tablespoonful of Lard or Two Level Spoons of Butter.
Salt and Cayenne to Taste.

Clean and cut up the chicken. Cut the ham into small squares or dice and chop the onions, parsley and thyme. Skin the tomatoes, and chop fine, saving the juice. Wash and stem the okras and slice into thin layers of one-half inch each. Put the lard or butter into the soup kettle, and when hot add the chicken and the ham. Cover closely and let it simmer for about ten minutes. Then add the chopped onions, parsley, thyme and tomatoes, stirring frequently to prevent scorching. Then add the okras, and, when well-browned, add the juice of the tomatoes, which imparts a superior flavor. The okra is very delicate and is liable to scorch quickly if not stirred frequently. For this reason many Creole cooks fry the okra separately in a frying pan, seasoning with the pepper, Cayenne and salt, and then add to the chicken. But equally good results may be obtained with less trouble by simply adding the okra to the frying chicken, and watching constantly to prevent scorching. The least taste of a "scorch" spoils the flavor of the gumbo. When well fried and browned, add the boiling water (about three quarts) and set on the back of the stove, letting it simmer gently for about an hour longer. Serve hot, with nicely boiled rice. The remains of turkey may be utilized in the gumbo, instead of using chicken.

In families where it is not possible to procure a fowl, use a round steak of beef or veal, instead of the chicken, and chop fine. But it must always be borne in mind that the Chicken Gumbo has the best flavor. Much, however, depends upon the seasoning, which is always high, and thus cooked, the Meat Gumbo makes a most nutritious and excellent dish.

#### Crab Gumbo.
#### Gombo aux Crabes.

1 Dozen Hard-Shell or Soft-Shell Crabs.
1 Onion.
6 Large Fresh Tomatoes.
2 Pints of Okra, or Fifty Counted.
½ Pod of Red Pepper, Without the Seeds.
1 Bay Leaf.    1 Sprig of Thyme or Parsley.
1 Tablespoonful of Lard or Two Level Spoons of Butter.
Salt and Cayenne to Taste.

This is a great fast-day or "maigre" dish with the Creoles. Hard or soft-shelled crabs may be used, though more frequently the former, as they are always procurable and far cheaper than the latter article, which is considered a luxury. Crabs are always sold alive. Scald the hard-shell crabs and clean according to recipe already given, "taking off the dead man's fingers" and the spongy substances, and being careful to see that the sandbags on the under part are removed. Then cut off the claws, crack and cut the body of the crab in quarters. Season nicely with salt and pepper. Put the lard into the pot, and when hot throw in the bodies and claws. Cover closely, and, after five or ten minutes add the skinned tomatoes, chopped onions, thyme and parsley, stirring occassionally to prevent scorching. After five minutes add the okras, sliced fine, and when well-browned, without the semblance of scorching, add the bay leaf, chopped fine, and the juice of the tomatoes. Pour over about two quarts and a half of boiling water, and set back on the stove and let it simmer well for about an hour, having thrown in the pepper pod. When nearly ready to serve, season according to taste with Cayenne and added salt; pour into a tureen and serve with boiled rice. This quantity will allow two soft-shell crabs or two bodies of hard-shelled crabs to each person. The soft-shell crab is simply the hard-shelled crab that has shed its shell. In three or four days the shell begins to harden again, hence the supply is never as generous as the hard-shelled crabs, which are always to be found in the New Orleans markets.

#### Oyster Gumbo.
#### Gombo aux Huîtres.

4 Dozen Oysters.
2 Quarts of Oyster Liquor.
1 Tablespoonful of Lard or Butter.
1 Quart of Hot Water.
2 Tablespoonfuls of Flour.
1 Large White Onion.
Parsley, Thyme and Bay Leaf.
Salt and Pepper to Taste.

Put the lard into a kettle, and when hot add the flour, making a brown roux. When quite brown without burning, add the chopped onions and parsley. Fry these, and when brown, add the chopped bay leaf; pour in the hot oyster liquor and then add the hot water. When it comes to a good boil, just before serving, add the oysters which have been well drained, without pouring water over them, however. Cook for about three minutes longer and take off the stove and stir gradually two tablespoonfuls of Filé into the boiling hot gumbo. Have the tureen ready in a "bain-marie," or hot-water bath, and pour in the gumbo and cover. Bring to the table immediately and serve with boiled rice, allowing about six or eight oysters to each person.

**Shrimp Gumbo.**
Gombo aux Chevrettes.

Lake shrimps are always used in making this gumbo, the river shrimp being too small and delicate. Purchase always about 100 shrimps, or a small basketfull, for there are always smaller shrimps in the pile which, when cooked, amount to little or nothing. In making Shrimp Gumbo, either "Filé or Okra may be used in the combination, but it must be borne in mind that, while the "Filé" is frequently used, shrimp are far more delicious for gumbo purposes when used with okra. The shrimp should always be scalded or boiled before putting in the gumbo. (See recipe for "Boiling Shrimp.")

**Shrimp Gumbo Filé.**
Gombo Filé aux Chevrettes.
50 Fine Lake Shrimp.
2 Quarts of Oyster Liquor.
1 Quart of Hot Water.
1 Large White Onion. 1 Bay Leaf.
3 Sprigs of Parsley. 1 Sprig of Thyme.
1 Tablespoonful of Lard or Butter.
1 Tablespoonful of Flour.
A Dash of Cayenne.
Salt and Black Pepper to Taste.

Scald and shell the shrimp, seasoning highly with the boiling water. Put the lard into a kettle, and, when hot, add the flour, making a brown roux. When quite brown, without a semblance of burning, add the chopped onion and the parsley. Fry these, and when brown, add the chopped bay leaf; pour in the hot oyster liquor and the hot water, or use the carefully strained liquor in which the shrimp have been boiled. When it comes to a good boil, and about five minutes before serving, add the shrimp to the gumbo and take off the stove. Then add to the boiling hot liquid about two tablespoonfuls of the "Filé," thickening according to taste. Season again with salt and pepper to taste. Serve immediately, with boiled rice. (See recipe, "Boiled Rice.")

**Green or Herb Gumbo.**
Gombo aux Herbes.
A Veal Brisket.
1 Large Slice of Lean Ham.
Equal Parts of the Leaves of Young Cabbage, Radish, Turnips, Mustard, Spinach, Watercress. Parsley and Green Onions.
1 Large Red or White Onion.
½ Red Pepper Pod.
1 Bay Leaf. 1 Sprig of Thyme.
1 Sprig of Sweet Marjoram.
1 Clove. 9 Allspice.
Cayenne to Taste.

Soak and wash the leaves thoroughly, being careful to wash each leaf separately, to be sure there lurk no insects in the folds or ridges. Then trim by taking off all the coarse midrib of the leaves, which will make the gumbo taste coarse and unpalatable. Boil the leaves together for about two hours and then parboil by adding a teaspoonful of cooking soda. Strain and chop very fine, being careful to save the water in which they were boiled. Cut the brisket of veal and the sliced ham into small pieces and dredge with black pepper and salt, and chop one large white or red onion. Put a heaping teaspoonful of lard into a deep frying pan, and, when hot, add the chopped veal and the ham. Cover and let it simmer for about ten minutes, stirring occasionally to prevent burning. Then add the chopped onion and a little sprig of parsley chopped fine. When it comes to a rich brown, add the greens, and when these are browned, pour over four quarts of the water in which the leaves have been boiled. Throw in the finely chopped bay leaf, thyme, sweet marjoram, and the red pepper pod and the clove and allspice, mashed fine. Set it back on the stove and let it boil for about one hour longer, adding the Cayenne or "hot pepper," and you will have a regular Creole gumbo peculiar to New Orleans alone. Serve with boiled rice.

**Cabbage Gumbo.**

Gombo Choux.
1 Large Head of Cabbage (green and white mixed.)
1 Round Steak.
2 Large Slices of Lean Ham.
2 Pounds of Creole Sausage.
(About ⌢ to Pound.)
1 Pod of Cayenne Pepper, Without the Seeds.
1 Pint of Milk. 1 Tablespoonful of Lard.
Salt and Black Pepper and Cayenne to Taste.

Gombo Choux, or Cabbage Gumbo, is a favorite Creole dish, especially in families where there are children, possessing, as it does, nutritive qualities in the highest degree, and being besides a most palatable and savory way of preparing cabbage.

Shred the cabbage and wash each leaf separately and thoroughly to avoid insects. Then chop the entire head very fine, into pieces about half the size of dice. Cut the steak or brisket into small squares, also the ham, and fry in the deepest kettle you have, putting the meat into the pot when the lard is very hot. When it begins to brown, add a chopped onion and the sausage, and then add the chopped cabbage, stirring and pouring in enough water to prevent it from burning. Throw in the red pepper pod and a dash of Cayenne, and salt to taste. Add a little black pepper. Stir often and allow the ingredients to cook well, gradually adding, if necessary, a little water, and stirring frequently to prevent burning. When thoroughly cooked, make a cream sauce as follows:

Take one pint of new milk and two tablespoonfuls of flour and mix thoroughly, so as not to be lumpy. Stir this into the gumbo while boiling, and continue stirring for five minutes. Serve with boiled rice. If it is not possible to procure milk, almost the same effect may be attained by mixing the flour in cold water of the same measurement and stirring in as already given. The gumbo must not be allowed to stand on the fire after the flour has been boiled on it for five minutes, at it will burn.

Should the recipe prove above the purses of the poor, either the sausage or the round of beef may be omitted. With the ingredients given in this recipe, it should not cost more than the following: Head of cabbage, 5 cents; ham, 5 cents; steak 10 cents; sausage, 10 cents; milk, 5 cents. It may be varied to suit the purses of the rich or poor, and is always a nutritious dish and quite a dinner in itself.

## CHAPTER VIII.

### FISH.

#### Du Poisson.

The Fish Market of New Orleans is famous over the world. No stranger comes to the city without visiting this notable spot, and never thinks of leaving New Orleans without partaking of a "Fish Breakfast," or "Fish Dinner," at one of the Lake resorts.

The perfection and variety of the fish found in the New Orleans market are unsurpassed. We have here all the fish found in the waters of the Gulf of Mexico contiguous to New Orleans, the Mississippi Sound and our own lake shores. These constitute the famous salt-water varieties, such as the Sheepshead, considered by many the best fish in the Gulf; the famous Pompano and Spanish Mackerel, the dainty Croaker, the toothsome Flounder, the Bluefish, the Silver Trout, Tenderloin Trout, Speckled Trout, the Grouper, and the Mullet, the latter, however, being seldom eaten, owing to the softness of its flesh, the number of its bones and the continued presence of the other and finer fish which are to be had for the fishing. Among shell fish we have the Hard-Shell Crab, the Soft-Shell Crab, considered a great luxury in other parts, but always to be found in the New Orleans market; the appetizing Lake Shrimps; that delicious bivalve, the Oyster; the Crawfish, and the famous Green Turtle, so highly prized as a dainty morsel. Again, in the rivers and bayous and small streams of Louisiana we have many delightful varieties of fresh-water fish, such as fresh-water or Green Trout, the Sacalait and a coarse fish called the Buffalo. The River Shrimp of Louisiana are unique in the United States. They are of a far more delicate variety than the Lake Shrimp and much prized as an article of food. Both Lake and River Shrimp are abundant in the summer time and are used alike by rich and poor.

In the following recipes the most delightful methods of preparing these fish are given, methods which may be used by all according to the purse, the conditions of the poorest having been considered as well as the wants of the wealthy. All are equally recommended, being the most perfect preparations of their kind in use among the Creole housekeepers. It might be added here, for the benefit of any Northern housekeepers into whose hands this book may fall, that many of the recipes may be modified according to good judgment in preparing the fish found exclusively in the Northern markets. For instance, in making the famous "Courtbouillon," which is in all respects a distinctive Creole conception, any firm fish, such as the Bass, may be used, though, of course, the flavor of the delicious Red Snapper or Red Fish used by the Creoles to the exclusion of all other fish in making a "Courtbouillon," will be found wanting. With modifications that will suggest themselves to any intelligent housekeeper, they may be used the world over in preparing fish of other varieties than those which are the delight and pride of the New Orleans Fish Market.

#### How to Tell Good Fish.

Unless perfectly fresh, fish is unfit for use. Care should be taken to see that the gills are bright and red, the scales shining, the eyes clear and the flesh very firm and free from any unpleasant odor. In the New Orleans Fish Market the vendors generally clean and scale the fish, if requested to do so; but this cleaning and scaling is not to be entirely depended upon, because it is rarely thorough, only the heavier scales and entrails being removed. On coming home from the market, the fish should be immediately rescaled and thoroughly cleansed and washed without soaking in water; it is far better to let the water run over the fish, for thus the smallest particle of blood is removed. This is very important in order to have a good, wholesome, savory dish. Then sprinkle the fish on the inside with salt, and set in the ice box. If this is wanting, put it in a very cool place, but it is always best for it to remain on ice until ready to use, especially during the summer. The small vendors in the New Orleans private markets frequently oblige their poor customers by placing the fish in their ice boxes until the time for preparation, when it is sent for and is found cold and firm and ready for cooking.

### Methods of Cooking Fish.

Fish may be boiled, broiled, stewed, fried or baked.

Visitors to New Orleans declare that nowhere is fish cooked in such palatable ways as in this old Franco-Spanish city. The experience of generations of fine old cooks has been brought to bear upon the preparation of the fish found in the Louisiana waters and those of the Mexican Gulf, with the result that a Creole code of rules for the cooking of even the smallest and less important fish prevails, and it is considered little short of barbarous to depart from it.

The Creole methods of boiling and baking fish are the perfection of culinary art and unlike any method in vogue elsewhere.

Special recipes are, therefore, given for the boiling and baking of Sheepshead, Redfish, Red Snapper, as, also, for making the world-famous Creole "Courtbouillon" and "Bouillabaise." These rules should be strictly observed in cooking these fish if one would bring out the best flavor of each. But there are other fish, such as Green Trout and Perch, which, when simply boiled and served with appropriate sauces, are known to reserve their best flavor for this species of cooking.

The following general rules for boiling, broiling, baking, stewing and frying fish should be carefully followed wherever indicated in the recipes.

### BOILED FISH.
### Poisson Bouilli.
### General Rule for Boiling Fish.

Clean and wash the fish thoroughly. Make a small letter "S" with knife on the back; pass twine around the body of the fish so as to secure it. Never wrap or tie in a cloth. Have ready a kettle of boiling water and throw in a sprig of onion, thyme and bay leaf, eight or ten cloves, about two dozen allspice, all mashed fine; a bit of lemon peel and a red pepper pod. When the water has boiled long enough to have extracted the flavor of these ingredients, drop the fish in carefully, so as to avoid breaking. Let it boil about ten minutes and then take out carefully. Put into a strainer and drain quickly. Place on a bed of parsley with garnishes of lemon and serve either a Mayonnaise or Genoise Sauce or Sauce Hollandaise. (See recipes.)

The Creoles add a clove of garlic to the boiling water, but this is according to taste.

### BROILED FISH.
### Poisson Grillé.
### General Rules for Broiling Fish.

Always use the double broiler, made of wire, as this allows the cook to turn the fish from side to side without disturbing the body during the process of broiling, and possibly breaking the flesh. Clean the fish, without cutting off the head and tail. When the fish is large, split down the back; else broil whole. Always serve broiled fish whole. Have a clear moderate fire. Expose first the flesh side to the fire, and then the skin, as the latter browns it is liable to burn quickly. Great care must, therefore, be taken not to burn the skin side.

Before placing on the broiler, rub the fish well with salt and pepper, mixed in a little sweet oil or a little butter oil or butter. If the fish is small, broil on a quick, clear fire; if large, as mentioned above, the fire must be moderate, or the outside of the fish will be charred before the inside is done. When the fish is done through and through, which can quickly be determined by the fish parting easily from the bone, remove the gridiron from the fire, and loosen the fins from the broiler with a knife, being careful not to break the flesh. Then place the hot dish over the fish, and, with a dexterous movement, turn the two back again, thus separating the gridiron from the fish and placing the latter in the dish. Butter well, season with a little pepper and salt, if deemed necessary, and pour over a tablespoonful of chopped parsley and lemon juice. Serve with garnishes of sliced lemon and parsley, or garnishes of delicate green lettuce leaves.

Broiling is one of the nicest ways of cooking certain kinds of fish, and cannot be too highly recommended.

## BAKED FISH.
### Poisson au Gratin.
#### General Rule for Baking Fish.

Clean the Fish, cutting off the fins. Make the letter "S" on the sides. Rub well inside and out with pepper and salt. Butter a stewpan and put in one large chopped onion and a wineglassful of white wine. Place the fish in the pan, put in the oven and let it bake about twenty minutes, having been careful to place lumps of butter over it and basting frequently. When done carefully, lift the fish out of the pan and put it into the dish in which it is to be served. Take the gravy in which the fish has been cooked and add about a cup of oyster water, the juice of one lemon, two tablespoonfuls of chopped mushrooms, one tablespoonful of minced parsley, thyme and sweet marjoram, ten allspice, one clove of garlic, a little Cayenne, and salt and pepper to taste. Mix all thoroughly over the stove, adding a little butter if the gravy adheres too much to the pan. Pour over the fish, and garnish with whole mushrooms and slices of lemon laid alternately upon Croûtons or dried toast, cut diamond shape.

## STEWED FISH.
### Poisson en Matelote.
#### General Rule for Stewing Fish.

Clean the fish well and slice and pour over one cup of good, boiling vinegar. Make a roux by putting one tablespoonful of lard into the stewpan, and when hot add gradually two tablespoonfuls of flour rubbed smoothly. When quite brown, take the fish, which has been previously rubbed with salt and pepper, and place in the pot. Let it simmer gently a few minutes, and then add a large chopped onion, parsley, one clove of garlic, one sprig of thyme, a bay leaf, two blades of mace and eight or ten allspice. Let these brown and cover with water sufficient to prevent burning. Put the fish on a slow fire to stew, and when half done, add a little Cayenne, and, if possible, add a pint or glass of Port Wine. When done, place the fish in a dish, pour the gravy over it, and garnish with Croûtons, with alternate slices of lemon and prepared horseradish.

## FRIED FISH.
### Poissons Frits.
#### General Rule for Frying Fish.

Certain of the fish of the Mexican Gulf are always best when fried. Of these are the toothsome Croakers, the delicate Sacalait and Patassas, and also the Speckled Trout when served in tenderloin steaks.

There is an art in knowing how to fry fish properly. Perhaps there is no other method of cooking fish which is more commonly used, and no other which is more generally abused. There are few people who really know how to fry fish properly. The following general rule will give

#### The Secret of Good Frying.

The secret of good frying lies in having the lard heated just to the proper point. If the fish is placed in the boiling lard, it is liable to burn quickly without being cooked through and through. If placed simply in the well-heated lard, it absorbs the fat and is delicate and tender and there is no tax upon the digestive organs. Always have sufficient lard in the pan to fry all the fish that is on hand and never add a lump of cold lard to the heated substance. This checks the cooking of the fish and spoils the taste. If the lard spits and crackles, that is no evidence of boiling. It only means that the lard is throwing off drops of moisture that have crept in. Boiling lard is perfectly still until it begins to smoke, and then it is in danger of burning and must be removed from the fire. To test the lard, drop in a piece of bread. If it begins to color, the lard is ready for frying. When the fish is fried, skim it out, draining off all the fat. Butter is never used in frying fish, as it burns quickly.

### A Short Resume of the Way in Which the Fish of the New Orleans Markets Should Always Be Cooked.

Sheepshead may be boiled, broiled or baked, and is good with any sauce.

Redfish is principally used in making "Courtbouillon," or it is boiled and served with an Hollandaise Sauce, or baked.

Red Snapper should always be boiled or baked. It is delightful served à la Chambord, but it is best à la Créole.

Grouper is served in the same way as Red Snapper.

Flounder should always be baked à la Nouvelle Orléans, or à la Normande, or with a white wine sauce as in Baked Sheepshead or in the famous recipe "Sole à la Orly." (See recipe.)

Pompano should always be broiled and served with Sauce à la Maître d'Hôtel.

Spanish Mackerel should always be broiled in the same manner as Pompano, and served with Sauce à la Maître d'Hôtel.

Bluefish should be cooked and served in the same manner as Pompano and Spanish Mackerel.

Speckled Trout is generally broiled and served in tenderloin, or a Tenderloin Trout, with Sauce à la Tartare.

Green Trout and Perch should be broiled and served with a Sauce à la Maître d'Hôtel, or else boiled and served with a Sauce Genoise, or an Hollandaise or Drawn Butter Sauce.

Croakers are fried and served with garnish of parsley or lemon.

Patassas, Sacalait and other small fish are served in the same manner as Croakers.

Soft-shell crabs may be fried in the same manner as Croakers, or broiled and served on toast.

Shrimp are generally boiled, with plenty of seasoning. The River Shrimp are always served as boiled, shells and all, but the Lake Shrimp enter into many combinations in cooking.

Hard-shelled Crabs may be stuffed, stewed, fried and made into gumbo.

All left-over, broiled, baked or boiled fish should be utilized in making salads, croquettes, etc.

Oysters are served in almost every conceivable way, and enter into the most delightful combinations in cooking.

A fish weighing three pounds, or small fish in quantity sufficient to make three pounds (uncooked), will serve six persons.

### THE SHEEPSHEAD.
Casburgot.

Of all the fish found in the waters of the Gulf of Mexico, the Sheepshead is perhaps the most to be commended for frequent household use, being susceptible of a far greater variety of modes of preparation than any other fish; the flesh being of a less richer fiber than the Redfish, Red Snapper, Pompano and Spanish Mackerel, it may be used from day to day without injury to the stomach. It is good in almost any form and may be boiled, baked or broiled, and served with almost any sauce.

#### Boiled Sheepshead.
Casburgot Bouilli.

A 3-Pound Sheepshead. 1 Sliced Onion.
3 Bay Leaves. 1 Sprig of Thyme. 1 Sprig of Parsley.
1 Sprig of Sweet Marjoram. 1 Tablespoonful French Vinegar.
Salt and Pepper to Taste.
A Cream Sauce.

Wash and thoroughly clean the fish, and then lay on a pan and open the flesh on either side by making the letter "S" with the knife. This is done to prevent the fish from puffing out or drawing up, and to insure thorough cooking and a perfect shape afterwards. Then tie the fish well with cord or twine, wrapping it around the body. Never encase a boiled fish in a cloth; put the fish in a deep saucepan and add boiling water sufficient for the fish to swim in it. Throw in a tablespoonful of spice (well mashed), a sliced onion, three bay leaves, a sprig of parsley (all chopped very fine), a tablespoonful of French vinegar, and salt and pepper to taste. Cover well and let it boil for ten minutes. After ten minutes, the fish is cooked. Prepare a "Cream Sauce" (see recipe) and serve immediately.

#### Sheepshead à la Créole.
Casburgot à la Créole.

A 3-Pound Sheepshead.
2 Onions. 1 Bunch of Parsley.
2 Sprigs of Thyme. 4 Bay Leaves. 1 Sprig of Sweet Marjoram.
1 Quart of Boiled Cream. Yolks of 4 Eggs.
3 Tablespoonfuls of Flour. 2 Tablespoonfuls of Butter.
Bread Crumbs.

Prepare the Sheepshead as for boiling (see recipe Boiled Sheepshead). When quite done, take out of the water and flake off all the flesh from the bones. Have ready a quarter of boiled cream or milk. Beat the yolks of four eggs and mix with the cream. Chop one large onion, a bunch of parsley, a sprig each of thyme and bay leaf, and add to the cream and eggs. Let it boil up once, and while boiling, throw in three tablespoonfuls of flour, rubbed perfectly smooth, in a little cream, and about two tablespoonfuls of butter. Remove from the fire. Have ready a deep dish, well buttered, and put in a layer of fish and then a layer of the sauce, until the dish is full. Sprinkle over with bread crumbs. Place in the oven and bake about a half hour, or until brown. This is a very delightful method of preparing Sheepshead.

#### Baked Sheepshead.
Casburgot au Gratin.

A 3-Pound Sheepshead. 1 Large Onion.
2 Tablespoonfuls of Flour.
2 Tablespoonfuls of Butter. 1 Bay Leaf.
1 Sprig of Thyme. ½ Bottle of White Wine.
6 Fresh Tomatoes. 2 Dozen Lake Shrimp.
1 Dozen Oysters. ½ Can of Mushrooms.
2 Crackers. Dry Toast Cut in Dice Shape.
3 Sprigs Chopped Parsley to Garnish.

Clean and wash the fish; place on a platter; chop one large onion fine, rub the fish first with salt and black pepper, and then take a large and deep kitchen pan, place within a tablespoonful of butter, the chopped onion, bay leaf and thyme. Place the fish on top of this and pour over a half bottle of white wine. Cover with another close pan and put the whole on top of the oven (not on the inside). Bake from the bottom. When it begins to boil from below, turn the fish over carefully without breaking, and let it bake on the other side. Take a saucepan and put within a tablespoonful of butter and mix thoroughly with two tablespoonfuls of flour. Let it brown without burning, and then add six fresh tomatoes, skinned and chopped fine, or a half can. Add two dozen Lake Shrimp that have been cleaned well and scalded, a half can of mushrooms, salt and pepper to taste. Let all cook for about five minutes and then water with the gravy in which the fish is cooking. Mix well and cover the fish with it. Parboil one dozen oysters, and when the fish is cooked, set it in the dish in which it is to be served and place the oysters all around it on small slices of dry toast. Cover the fish alternately with the shrimp and oysters, as a garnish over and around it. Mash two crackers into crumbs and sprinkle over, and place alternately small bits of butter on top of the fish. Place the dish in the oven and bake the fish with a quick fire until brown, and serve immediately.

This preparation is an exclusive conception of our Creole cuisinières and cannot be too highly recommended.

### Baked Sheepshead à la Créole.

Casburgot à la Créole au Gratin.

A 3-Pound Sheepshead.
1 Cup of Stale Bread Crumbs.
1 Onion. 1 Tablespoonful of Chopped Parsley.
1 Tablespoonful of Melted Butter.
1 Tablespoonful of Lard. 1 Pint of White Wine or Boiling Water.
Salt and Pepper and Flour to Dredge.
A Hollandaise, Bechamel or Tomato Sauce.

The following is a more simple manner, where means are limited, of baking Sheepshead for frequent family use. Clean the fish thoroughly, inside and out; wash well and dry thoroughly with a clean towel. Rub it well with salt and pepper, then make a dressing, taking one cup of stale bread crumbs, wet and squeezed thoroughly of all water, one tablespoonful of melted butter, one tablespoonful of chopped parsley, a half teaspoonful of salt and a little black pepper. Mix well and fry in a little lard. One dozen oysters or shrimp, or the yolks of two hard-boiled eggs added and mixed increase the flavor of the dressing, but the dressing can be made very nicely without. After frying the dressing a few minutes take off the stove and stuff the body of the fish and sew up with soft thread or soft yarn. Score or slit the fish on either side, making the scores about an inch apart and lard it either by putting a strip of salt fat in each gash or filling with lard. Grease the bottom of a baking pan put the fish in it and dredge thickly with salt and flour and a little Cayenne. If possible, pour over a half bottle of white wine, otherwise simply cover the bottom of the pan with the grease, add a little boiling water, and put the fish in a hot oven. Baste every ten minutes or so by taking a spoon and pouring the gravy over the fish. Allow about fifteen minutes of baking to every pound of fish, the ordinary sized fish of four pounds requiring about one hour. When brown on one side, turn on the other, and when done carefully, slide the fish into the center of the flat dish in which it is to be served, and garnish nicely with slices of lemon, fried potato balls and chopped parsley. Make the garnish by placing sprigs of parsley between the fried potato balls and laying on the slices of lemon. Serve with Hollandaise Sauce or Bechamel Sauce. (See ceipts.)

Again, where the the fish is not baked in wine and served with separate sauce a good sauce from its own juices may be made. Simply grease and cover the bottom of the pan with boiling water and place in the fish. As it begins to bake well take a half dozen good, fresh tomatoes, or a half can of tomatoes, one onion, one bay leaf, a sprig of thyme and a blade of mace, chop all fine, and mix thoroughly and pour over the baking fish. Add a little butter, salt and pepper, and a very good every-day sauce will be the result. Red Snapper may be baked in this same simple style where the purse will not permit of the more expensive recipe, given further on.

### Red Snapper and Redfish.

Red Snapper et Poisson Rouge.

These are distinctive fish, and form unique and most delightful dishes of the Creole cuisine.

### Courtbouillon à la Créole.

Six Fine Slices of Redfish or Red Snapper (equal to 3 Pounds.)
1 Tablespoonful of Lard. 2 Tablespoonfuls of Flour.
12 Well-Mashed Allspice. 3 Sprigs of Thyme.
3 Sprigs of Parsley. 3 Sprigs of Sweet Marjoram.
3 Bay Leaves.
1 Large Onion. 1 Clove of Garlic.
6 Large Fresh Tomatoes or a Half Can.
1 Quart of Water. 1 Glass of Claret. The Juice of 1 Lemon.
Salt and Cayenne to Taste.

Those kings of the New Orleans French Market, the Red Snapper or the Redfish, are used in making the pride and glory of the New Orleans cuisines, a good "Courtbouillon." More generally and with finer results the Redfish or "Poisson Rouge" is used. This fish may always be known by the single spot on the tail. The old Creole darkies have a tradition that this was the fish which the Apostles brought to the Savior when he performed his great miracle of the loaves and the fishes. They hand down the quaint legend that the Savior took up this fish between his fingers and blessed it, and it was ever after a marked fish in the waters, the imprint of the Lord's fingers having remained on the spot where he held up the fish and blessed it and offered it to His Father. They hold the Redfish in reverent veneration, and never fail to tell the little children when cooking it: "dose am de marks ob de Lord's hand."

To make a real Courtbouillon slice the Redfish in fine, clear-cut pieces, after having thoroughly washed and cleaned it. Make a "Roux" by putting one tablespoonful of lard in a deep can or kettle. When hot add gradually two tablespoonfuls of flour, stirring constantly to prevent burning. Throw in about ten or twelve well-mashed allspice, and three sprigs each of chopped thyme, parsley, bay leaf and sweet marjoram, one clove of garlic and one large onion, chopped very fine. Add six fresh, large tomatoes, chopped fine, or one-half can of tomatoes. Pour in one glass of good claret, add about one quart of water, and let it boil well. Then add salt and Cayenne to taste, and when this has boiled about five minutes add the fish, putting in slice by slice. Add the juice of a lemon, and let all boil about ten minutes. Serve with French fried potatoes, mashed potatoes or potato croquettes.

A Courtbouillon of Red Snapper is made in the same way.

### Spanish Courtbouillon.

Courtbouillon à l'Espagnole.
6 Slices of Redfish or Red Snapper (equal to 3 pounds.)
1 Tablespoonful of Lard. 2 Tablespoonfuls of Flour.
1 Large Onion. 6 Tomatoes. 3 Sprigs of Parsley.
1 Clove of Garlic. 3 Sprigs of Thyme.
1 Sprig of Sweet Basil.
2 Bay Leaves. 1 Cup of White Wine.
2 Pints of Water.

The delightful adaptability of the New Orleans cuisine to the wants of all the people may be seen in the following Courtbouillon, which is in general use among the families of moderate means, and is, indeed, a very pleasing way of cooking Redfish:

Buy in the French Market four or six slices of Redfish. Make a Roux by putting one tablespoonful of lard into the stew pan, and when it is hot, stir in gradually two tablespoonfuls of flour. Add one large chopped onion, six tomatoes (chopped), the chopped parsley, clove of garlic, sweet basil and thyme, all chopped very fine. Add two bay leaves whole. When it browns nicely without burning, pour in about two pints of water and let it come to a boil. Rub the fish well with salt and pepper, and pour over it a cup of boiling vinegar, if you have no white wine. Put the fish slice by slice into the pot and let it simmer for about a half hour, or until the flesh begins to be soft. Then remove from the fire, take out of the pot, and lay the slices in a dish. Take the bay leaves out of the gravy, pour the gravy over the fish, and serve with garnishes of sliced lemon.

Courtbouillon is very palatable served in this way. It is a most economical Friday or fast-day dish in large families when served with boiled rice, or potatoes boiled whole.

### Bouillabaise.

6 Slices of Red Snapper. 6 Slices of Redfish.
½ Bottle of White Wine. ½ Lemon.
6 Large Fresh Tomatoes, or ½ Can.
3 Onions. 1 Herb Bouquet.
3 Cloves of Garlic.
3 Bay Leaves. 3 Sprigs of Thyme.
3 Sprigs of Parsley.
6 Allspices. 2 Tablespoonfuls of Olive Oil.
1 Good Strong Pinch of Saffron.
Salt, Pepper and Cayenne to Taste.

This is the dish that drew from Thackeray that famous tribute to Creole cookery: "In New Orleans you can eat a Bouillabaisse, the like of which was never eaten in Marseilles or Paris."

The reason is clear, for in those old French cities the Bouillabaisse is made from the fish of the waters of the Mediterranean Sea, notably the Sturgeon and the Perch combined, while in New Orleans it is made from those matchless fish of the Gulf of Mexico, the Red Snapper and the Redfish (Poisson Rouge). It will be noticed that it takes two kinds of fish to make a Bouillabaisse. The first Bouillabaisse was made in Marseilles, and the old Creole tradition runs that it was the discovery of two sailor fishermen, who were disputing as they sat in a schooner as to the proper way of cooking a Sturgeon and Perch combined. Both essayed: One succeeded in making a delightful dish that would have gladdened the heart of any old French "bon vivant." The other failed. The successful one enthusiastically offered to teach his friend, and as the latter was following the directions implicitly, and the finishing touches were being given to the dish, the teacher, seeing that the critical and important moment had come when the fish must be taken from the fire, or it would be spoiled if it cooked a moment longer, cried out, bringing down his hand emphatically: "Et quand ça commence a bouillir—Baisse!" Hence the name "Bouillabaisse," which was given to the dish from that moment. From all portions of Europe people go to Marseilles to eat a "Bouillabaisse" on the seashore.

The taste of the Bouillabaisse still lingered in the mouths of the old French Creole settlers of New Orleans. The famous old chefs sought two fish from the water of the Mexican Gulf that might be used in the making of the dish with a reasonable hope of success. They chose the Red Snapper and the Redfish. The result is told in Thackeray's tribute. The Creole Bouillabaisse, with the modifications and improvements that early ingenuity suggested, is a dish that was the standing offering in antebellum days to every distinguished Parisian or foreigner that visited New Orleans. Its reputation is sustained by the Creole cuisinières of our own day. It is made as follows:

First cut off the head of the Red Snapper and boil it in about one and a half quarts of water, so as to make a fish stock. Put one sliced onion and a herb bouquet consisting of thyme, bay leaf and parsley, into the water. When reduced to one pint, take out the head of the fish and the herb bouquet and strain the water and set it aside for use later on.

Take six slices of Redfish and six slices of Red Snapper of equal sizes and rub well with salt and pepper. Mince three sprigs of thyme, three sprigs of parsley, three bay leaves and three cloves of garlic, very, very fine, and take six allspice and grind them very fine, and mix thoroughly with the minced herbs and garlic. Then take each slice of fish and rub well with this mixture till every portion is permeated by the herbs, spice and garlic. They must be, as it were, soaked into the flesh, if you would achieve the success of this dish. Take two tablespoonfuls of fine olive oil and put into a very large pan, so large that each slice of the fish may be put in without one piece overlapping the other. Chop two onions very fine and add them to the heating oil. Lay the fish slice by slice in the pan and cover, and let them "étouffé," or smother for about ten minutes, turning once over so that each side may cook partly. Then take the fish out of the pan and set the slices in a dish. Pour a half bottle of white wine into the pan and stir well. Add a half can of tomatoes, or six large fresh tomatoes sliced fine, and let them boil well. Then add half a lemon, cut in very thin slices, and pour over a pint of the liquor in which the head of the snapper was boiled. Season well to taste with salt, pepper and a dash of Cayenne. Let it boil until very strong and till reduced almost one half; then lay the fish slice by slice, apart one from the other, in the pan, and let boil five minutes. In the meantime have prepared one good pinch of saffron, chopped very fine. Set it in a small deep dish and add a little of the sauce in which the fish is boiling to dissolve well. When well melted, and when the fish has been just five minutes in the pan, spread the saffron over the top of the fish. Take out of the pan, lay each slice on toast, which has been fried in butter; pour the sauce over and serve hot immediately. You will have a dish that Lucullus would have envied.

**Boiled Red Fish or Boiled Red Snapper.**

Poisson Rouge ou Red Snapper Bouilli.

A 3-Pound Redfish or Red Snapper.
1 Sliced Onion.
3 Bay Leaves. 1 Sprig of Thyme.
3 Sprigs of Parsley.
1 Sprig of Sweet Marjoram. 1 Tablespoonful of French Vinegar.
Salt and Pepper to Taste.
An Hollandaise Sauce.

Wash and thoroughly clean the fish, and then lay on a pan and open the flesh on either side by making the letter "S" with the knife. This is done to prevent the fish from puffing out or drawing up, and to insure thorough cooking and a perfect shape afterwards. Then tie the fish well with cord or twine, wrapping it around the body. Never encase a boiled fish in a cloth; put the fish in a deep saucepan and add boiling water sufficient for the fish to swim in it. Throw in a tablespoonful of spice (well mashed), a sliced onion, three bay leaves, a sprig of thyme and sweet marjoram, a sprig of parsley (all chopped very fine), a tablespoonful of French vinegar, and salt and pepper to taste. Cover well and let it boil for ten minutes. After ten minutes, the fish is cooked. Prepare a "Cream Sauce" (see recipe) and serve immediately.

## Baked Red Snapper.

### Red Snapper à la Créole.

A Fine Red Snapper, 3 Pounds in Weight.
2 Dozen Oysters. 2 Dozen Boiled Shrimp.
1 Dozen Boiled Crawfish.
2 Large Onions. 2 Tablespoonfuls of Butter.
1 Cup of Stale Bread Crumbs.
3 Large Tomatoes. ½ Can of Mushrooms.
3 Sprigs Each of Thyme and Parsley.
2 Bay Leaves. 6 Allspice. 3 Cloves. 1 Bottle of White Wine.
Salt and Pepper.

Clean and wash the Red Snapper thoroughly. Make a cut in the shape of the letter "S" on the back and stuff this with spice, thyme, clove and bay leaf, chopped fine. Rub thoroughly inside and out with salt and pepper. Make a good stuffing by taking one dozen oysters, one cup of stale bread crumbs, wet and squeezed of all water, one large onion chopped fine, a half teaspoonful of salt and a little black pepper. Mix well and fry in a pan with a tablespoonful of butter. Stuff the body of the fish and sew up with soft thread. Lard well, that is, rub thoroughly with lard and place in the oven. Pour over immediately a bottle of white wine, and let the fish bake well in the wine. In the meantime, prepare the following sauce: Take one large tablespoonful of butter, one large chopped onion, one sprig of thyme, one of bay leaf. Brown the onions and butter, being careful not to burn, and put in three tomatoes; add the chopped herbs; brown and add a pint of oyster water which has been heated by blanching the oysters. (Blanching means to place the oysters on the fire in their own water and heat thoroughly without boiling.) Season the sauce with pepper and salt to taste. Have ready in another dish one dozen parboiled or blanched oysters and two dozen boiled shrimp. Put the fish in the dish in which it is to be served garnish with the oysters and shrimp, placing them over the fish, and mingle about a half can of mushrooms. Have also ready a dozen nicely boiled crawfish. Garnish the fish with these, placing them all around it in the dish in which it is to be served. Pour the sauce over all and set in the oven and bake a few minutes longer and serve hot.

### A Simple Every-Day Recipe For Baking Red Snapper.

### Red Snapper au Gratin.

1 Fine 3-Pound Red Snapper.
2 Tablespoonfuls of Butter.
1 Large Onion. 3 Sprigs of Parsley.
1 Bay Leaf.
1 Cup of Stale Bread Crumbs.
½ Tea Cup of Water. Salt and Pepper.

Select a fine, large fish, clean and wash thoroughly. Make a dressing by taking one cup of stale bread, wet and squeezed of all water; one large onion and three sprigs of parsley. Chop the onions and parsley fine and mix with the bread crumbs and fry in a spoonful of butter, seasoning well with salt and pepper. Stuff the fish and sew up with a soft thread. Then rub the fish thoroughly with salt and pepper and butter. Put small pieces of butter all over the fish and add a few pieces on the bottom of the baking pan. Pour in water to the depth of two inches, cover the pan and bake on the outside of the oven, about an hour and a half. When the fish is baked in the oven it partakes more of the character of roasted fish.

### Red Snapper à la Chambord.

### Red Snapper à la Chambord.

A Fine Red Snapper, 3 Pounds in Weight.
2 Dozen Oysters. ½ Can Mushrooms.
3 Large Tomatoes. 2 Large Onions.
1 Cup of Stale Bread.
3 Sprigs Each of Thyme and Parsley.
2 Bay Leaves. 6 Allspice. 3 Cloves.
1 Bottle of White Wine.
Salt and Pepper.

Clean and wash the Red Snapper carefully. Cut a space six inches square on the surface of the upper side of the fish, and carefully remove the skin within the enclosed space. Then lard this space closely with very fine larding needles, and fill in with spice, thyme, clove and bay leaf, all minced very fine. Rub thoroughly inside and outside with salt. Make a good stuffing by taking one dozen oysters, one cup of stale bread crumbs, wet and squeezed of all water; one large onion, chopped fine; a half tablespoonful of salt and black pepper to taste. Mix well and fry in a pan with a tablespoonful of butter. Stuff the body of the fish and sew up with soft thread. Lard well and, after rubbing thoroughly with the lard, place in the oven. Pour over immediately a bottle of white wine and let the fish bake well in the wine. In the meantime prepare the following sauce: Take one large tablespoonful of butter, one large chopped onion, one sprig of thyme, one of bay leaf. Brown the onions and butter, being careful not to burn, and put in three large tomatoes. Add the chopped herbs, brown and add the pint of oyster water, which has been heated with blanching the oysters. (Blanching means to place the oysters on the fire in their own water and heat thoroughly without boiling.) Season the sauce with pepper and salt to taste. Put the fish in the dish in which it is to be served, and garnish with the oysters, placing them over the fish and mingling between about a half can of mushrooms. After garnishing the fish nicely, pour the sauce over all and set in the oven a few minutes longer and serve hot.

### Red Snapper With Tomato Sauce.

#### Red Snapper à la Sauce Tomate.

A Fine Red Snapper, 3 Pounds in Weight.
12 Large Tomatoes or a Can.
½ Can of Mushrooms.
2 Large Onions.
3 Sprigs Each of Thyme and Parsley.
2 Bay Leaves.   6 Allspice.   3 Cloves.
½ Inch of Garlic, or 1 Clove.
1 Cup of Stale Bread Crumbs.
1 Bottle of White Wine.
1 Large Tablespoonful of Butter, or Olive Oil.
1 Tablespoonful of Flour.
Salt and Red Pepper.

Prepare the fish, following the directions given in the recipe for Red Snapper à la Créole to the point of larding thoroughly. After larding pour over immediately the bottle of white wine, and let the fish bake well in the wine. If wine is not available, use a cup of warm water instead; but the wine enhances the taste of the dish. When the fish is done, put one tablespoonful of olive oil or one large tablespoonful of butter into a saucepan, and one large chopped onion and let brown; add one tablespoonful of flour, and let the same brown. Then take the sliced and chopped fresh tomatoes, or strain a can of tomatoes in lieu of the former, and add to the sauce. Add immediately a small glass of the best white wine, and a half can of mushrooms chopped fine. Place in the sauce the bouquet of sweet herbs, thyme, bay leaf, and add an inch of garlic, minced very fine. Season with red pepper only. Pour this sauce over the baked fish after placing it in the dish in which it is to be served; set in the oven a few minutes and bring to the table hot.

Redfish, Sheepshead and Grouper may also be cooked according to this recipe.

### A Simple Way of Baking Redfish.

#### Poisson Rouge au Gratin.

6 Slices of Redfish or a Fish Weighing Pounds.
2 Large Onions.   3 Sprigs of Parsley.
2 Tablespoonfuls of Butter.
3 Sprigs of Thyme   1 Bay Leaf.
Salt and Pepper to Taste.
A Hollandaise Sauce.

In families of very moderate means it is more economical to purchase the Redfish or Red Snapper by the slice than to buy a whole fish. The slices vary according to the size of the fish; six medium-sized slices, or four or five large slices, will serve a family of six. Where the Redfish is purchased whole it may be prepared for everyday dinner, according to the recipe given above for baking Red Snapper. When purchased in slices, clean the outer edges well of the fins, wash and then rub the fish well with salt and pepper. Prepare some chopped onion and parsley and lay in a deep baking pan. Place a layer of fish over this and then a layer of small lumps of butter and chopped parsley and onion. Place over this another layer of fish. Cover with another layer of chopped parsley, onions and butter, and place in the oven to bake. Bake about an hour, basting frequently, and serve with a Hollandaise Sauce. (See recipe.)

### Baked Grouper.

#### Grouper au Gratin.

A Fine Grouper (weight 3 pounds.)
2 Dozen Oysters.   2 Dozen Boiled Shrimp.
1 Dozen Boiled Crawfish.
2 Large Onions.   2 Tablespoonfuls of Butter.
1 Cup of Stale Bread.
2 Large Tomatoes.   ½ Can of Mushrooms.
3 Sprigs Each of Thyme and Parsley.
2 Bay Leaves.   6 Allspice.   3 Cloves.
1 Bottle of White Wine.
Salt and Pepper to Taste.

Clean and wash the Grouper thoroughly. Make a cut in the shape of the letter "S" on the back and stuff this with spice, thyme, clove and bay leaf, chopped fine. Rub thoroughly inside and out with salt and pepper. Make a good stuffing by taking one dozen oysters, one cup of stale bread crumbs, wet and squeezed of all water, one large onion, chopped fine, a half teaspoonful of salt and a little black pepper. Mix well and fry in a pan with a tablespoonful of butter. Stuff the body of the fish and sew up with soft thread. Lard well, that is, rub thoroughly with lard and place in the oven. Pour over immediately a bottle of white wine, and let the fish bake well in the wine. In the meantime, prepare the following sauce, à la Chambord: Take one large tablespoonful of butter, one large chopped onion, one sprig of thyme, one of bay leaf. Brown the onions and butter, being careful not to burn, and put in three large tomatoes; add the chopped herbs; brown and add a pint of oyster water, which has been heated by blanching the oysters. (Blanching means to place the oysters on the fire in their own water and heat thoroughly without boiling.) Season the sauce with salt and pepper to taste. Have ready in another dish one dozen parboiled or blanched oysters and two dozen boiled shrimps. Put the fish in the dish in which it is to be served, garnish with the oysters and shrimps placing them over the fish, and mingle between about a half can of mushrooms. Have also ready a dozen nicely boiled crawfish. Garnish the fish with these, placing them all around it in the dish in which it is to be served. Pour the sauce over all and set in the oven and bake a few minutes longer and serve hot. Where economy is desired Grouper may be boiled or baked according to the more simple methods given above for cooking Red Snapper. See recipes "Boiled Red Snapper" and "Red Snapper au Gratin."

## FLOUNDER.
### Sole.

The Creoles gave to the Flounder, one of the finest fish found in the waters of the Mexican Gulf, the French name "Sole," because while the fish was somewhat different in size and shape, they found that the meat of the Flounder was identically the same as that of the "Sole" found in the waters of the Mediterranean Sea. Quick to discover and appreciate, they applied to the Flounder the name "Sole," and adapted it to the French modes of cooking the latter fish, especially applying to it the famous old French recipe "Sole à la Orly." Otherwise in New Orleans the Flounder is always either fried and served with a sauce "à la Tartare," or baked "à la Nouvelle Orléans," or "à la Normande." or served with a white wine sauce as in Baked Sheepshead. (See recipe "Baked Sheepshead," or "Casburgot au Gratin.")

### Flounder à la Orly.
Filets de Sole à la Orly.
6 Filets of Flounder.  A Cup of Milk.
2 Tablespoonfuls of Butter.
1 Egg.  Bread Crumbs.  A Tomato Sauce.
Parsley to Garnish.

Have the fish dealer cut the Flounder in filets and trim, neatly removing all the bones. Beat an egg with milk, and dip in the slices of fish. Roll in bread crumbs and fry in butter. Serve with parsley garnish. with a Tomato Sauce. (See recipe.)

### Flounders à la Tartare.
Soles Frites à la Tartare.
3 Pounds of Flounders.  3 Eggs.
10 Tablespoonfuls of Olive Oil.
A Bunch of Parsley.  1 Sliced Lemon.
A Sauce a la Tartare.

Clean and trim the Flounders. Beat well two or three raw eggs. Have ready a frying pan, with eight or ten tablespoonfuls of olive oil. Place over the fire. When well heated, dip the fish into the eggs, roll well and place in the frying pan. Cook for about five minutes, turn on the other side, and cook about the same period. Then drain by placing on a heated brown paper. Garnish a dish with a bed of fried parsley, lay the Flounders upon it and garnish with sliced lemon. Serve with Sauce à la Tartare. (See recipe.)

### Flounder à la Nouvelle Orleans.
Sole à la Nouvelle Orleans.
A 3-Pound Flounder.
2 Tablespoonfuls of Flour.
1 Tablespoonful of Butter.  6 Allspice.
1 Sprig of Thyme.
2 Sprigs of Parsley.  1 Sprig of Sweet Basil.
1 Can of Mushrooms.  Croutons.
Salt and Pepper to Taste.

Select a fine, fresh Flounder, parboil, by scalding well after it has been cleansed. Slit open in scores on top and put in butter and salt, and set to bake in an oven. When it is two-thirds cooked, take off and pour over a cream sauce made of two tablespoonfuls of flour, one tablespoonful of butter, spice, thyme, parsley, sweet basil and bay leaf, a can of mushrooms, all chopped fine, and cook about five minutes. After pouring this over the fish, put back in the oven and let it bake till done, which will be in about fifteen minutes. Prepare Croûtons, or crusts of bread cut in diamond shape, fry these in butter and use as a garnish for the fish.

### Flounder à la Normande.
Sole à la Normande.
A 3-Pound Flounder.  8 Shallots.
3 Bay Leaves.  3 Sprigs of Thyme.
1 Clove of Garlic.
2 Tablespoonfuls of Butter.
2 Tablespoonfuls of Flour.
2 Cups of Bouillon or Water.
The Yolks of 2 Eggs.  1 Can of Mushrooms.
Salt and Pepper to Taste.
A Dash of Cayenne. Croutons Cut in Dice Shape.

Cut open the Flounder down the back. Dig inside under bone to right and left, without breaking the meat. Chop the bay leaves, thyme and clove of garlic very, very fine and mix with a half teaspoonful of salt and a half teaspoonful of black pepper and a dash of Cayenne. Rub the Flounder all over on the inside and under the cutting and outside with this preparation, seasoning thoroughly. Chop the shallots, green and white, very fine. Put a tablespoonful of butter in a flat saucepan or stewing dish, and put the shallots with the butter. Lay the Flounder on top of the shallots and butter, and let it cook slowly on a slow fire for about ten minutes. Then turn on the other side and cook ten minutes longer. In the meantime take another saucepan and put into it one tablespoonful of butter and two of flour. Dissolve this immediately with two cups of bouillon or water so that the sauce will be white. Let it cook about five minutes, and then add the well-beaten yolks of the eggs, and one can of mushrooms. Let all cook ten minutes longer, and then take the Flounder out of the saucepan in which it has been cooking and lay on a flat silver dish; then mix the sauce in which it has been cooking with the mushroom sauce. Taste the sauce and add salt pepper and Cayenne, according to taste. Pour this sauce over the fish, around which you will have placed Croûtons cut as dice and fried in the dish, and then cover the fish and put it in the bake oven for fifteen minutes. Serve hot in the dish in which it was baked.

### Baked Flounder.
#### Sole au Gratin.

A 3-Pound Flounder.     1 Large Onion.
2 Tablespoonfuls of Butter.
2 Tablespoonfuls of Flour.
1 Bay Leaf.     1 Sprig of Thyme.
3 Sprigs of Parsley.
½ Bottle of White Wine. 6 Fresh Tomatoes.
2 Dozen Lake Shrimp.
1 Dozen Oysters.     ½ Can of Mushrooms.

Clean and wash the fish; place on a platter; chop one large onion fine, 2 Crackers. Dry Toast Cut in Dice Shape. rub the fish first with salt and black pepper, then take a large and deep kitchen pan, place within a tablespoonful of butter, the chopped onion, bay leaf and thyme. Place the fish on top of this and pour over a half bottle of white wine. Cover with another close pan and put the whole on top of the oven (not on the inside). Bake from the bottom. When it begins to boil from below, turn the fish over carefully without breaking, and let it bake on the other side. Take a saucepan and put within a tablespoonful of butter and mix thoroughly with two tablespoonfuls of flour. Let it brown without burning, and then add six fresh tomatoes, skinned and chopped fine, or a half can. Add two dozen Lake Shrimp that have been cleaned well and scalded, a half can of mushrooms, salt and pepper to taste. Let all cook for about five minutes and then water with the gravy in which the fish is cooking. Mix well and cover the fish with it. Parboil one dozen oysters, and when the fish is cooked, set it in the dish in which it is to be served and place the oysters all around it on small slices of dry toast. Cover the fish alternately with the shrimp and oysters, as a garnish over and around it. Mash two crackers into crumbs and sprinkle over it; also some finely-chopped parsley. Place small bits of butter alternately over the fish; set the dish in the oven, and bake with a quick fire until brown. Serve immediately.

### POMPANO.

Pompano is the crowning glory of the fish of the New Orleans market. It is peculiar to the waters of the Gulf of Mexico, Mississippi Sound and the Louisiana Grand Isle shore. The word Pompano is derived from the Spanish **"Pampano," signifying a** peculiar greenish-tinted plant, and the name "Pompano" was given to the fish by the early Spanish fishermen on account of the delicate greenish color which distinguishes it. Nothing to be compared with the Pompano exists in the Northern, Eastern or Western waters, and no stranger leaves New Orleans without having tasted once of this delightful fish. The New Orleans Pompano has a world-wide fame. The Pompano used to come in the early spring and remain but a few weeks, hence the first fish that appeared in the French Market were eagerly sought after as a great luxury. Pompano are more plentiful now and are to be found in the market almost all the year round.

#### Pompano à la Maitre d'Hotel.

A Fine Pompano, or Small Ones in Weight
to Equal Three Pounds.
A Tablespoonful of Olive Oil.
A Tablespoonful of Butter.
The Juice of 1 Lemon.
A Sliced Lemon.     Parsley to Garnish.
Sauce a la Maitre d'Hotel.

There is only one way to cook Pompano and that is to broil it and serve with a Sauce à la Maitre d'Hotel.

To broil the Pompano split the fish in the middle of the back if the fish is large; if small, broil whole. Season well by rubbing with salt and pepper, mixed with a little sweet oil. Put the Pompano on the broiler and see that it is browned well on both sides, using always the double wire broiler. When done, place in a heated dish (heat by placing in a bain-marie or hot water bath and dry thoroughly). Butter the fish nicely and squeeze the juice of a lemon over it. Garnish with parsley and sliced lemon, and serve with a Sauce à la Maitre d'Hotel. (See recipe.) You will have a dish that a king might envy.

### SPANISH MACKEREL.
#### Maquereau Espagnol.

Spanish Mackerel is another delicate and delicious fish, only to be found in the waters of the Gulf of Mexico. The Gulf of Mexico, in early Creole days, a part of the vast expanse known as "The Waters of the Spanish Main." The early Spanish fishermen found here a fish resembling the mackerel, but of a dainty delicacy of flavor far superior to any mackerel yet known to epicures, and they gave to it the name "Spanish Mackerel." It stands on an equal footing with the Pompano in the estimation of epicures. The Spanish Mackerel should always be broiled. It is a splendid breakfast dish and a famous entrée at dinners.

### Broiled Spanish Mackerel.

Maquereau Espagnol Grillé.

A Spanish Mackerel, or 3 Pounds Weight.
1 Tablespoonful of Olive Oil.
1 Tablespoonful of Butter.
The Juice of 1 Lemon.  1 Sliced Lemon.
Parsley to Garnish.
Sauce à la Maitre d'Hotel.

Prepare in the same manner as the Pompano, serving whole. Where the fish is large, split downwards, in the middle of the back, and broil in the same manner as the Pompano and place on a dish garnished with parsley and slices of lemon. Serve with a Sauce à la Maitre d'Hotel. (See recipe.) These are special recipes, used only in broiling Pompano and Spanish Mackerel.

### BLUE FISH.

Le Poisson Bleu.

A Fine Bluefish, or Fish in Quantity to Equal 3 Pounds.
1 Tablespoonful of Olive Oil.
1 Tablespoonful of Butter.
1 Sliced Lemon.   The Juice of 1 Lemon.
Parsley to Garnish.
Sauce a la Maitre d'Hotel.

The Bluefish is a splendid fish of the salt-water variety and much sought after. It should always be broiled. Split the fish in the middle of the back if the fish is large; if small, broil whole. Season well by rubbing with salt and pepper, mixed with a little sweet oil. Put the Pompano on the broiler and see that it is browned well on both sides, using always the double wire broiler. When done, place in a heated dish (heat by placing in a bainmarie or hot-water bath and dry thoroughly). Butter the fish nicely and squeeze the juice of a lemon over it. Garnish with parsley and sliced lemon, and serve with a Sauce à la Maitre d'Hotel. (See recipe.)

### TROUT.

De la Truite.

Of fine and delicate flavor, the Green Trout and Speckled Trout are great favorites in the New Orleans cuisines. Trout is especially recommended as a breakfast dish, nothing being more appetizing than this for a morning portion. It may be broiled or boiled. Tenderloin Trout cut into filets, or cutlets, is also fried and makes a most palatable dish. We have the Salt-Water Trout and the Fresh-Water Trout, and both are excellent.

### Boiled Green Trout.

Truite Verte Bouillie.

6 Medium-Sized Trout, or 3 Large Ones.
A Kettle of Boiling Water.   1 Bay Leaf.
1 Sprig of Thyme. 1 Sprig of Onion.
A Clove of Garlic (if desired.)   10 Cloves.
2 Dozen Allspice.
A Seedless Red Pepper Pod.
A Bit of Lemon Peel.
Parsley and Lemon to Garnish.

Select fine fresh Trout. Clean and wash the fish thoroughly. Make a small letter "S" with knife on the back; pass twine around the body of the fish so as to secure it. Never wrap or tie in a cloth. Have ready a kettle of boiling water and throw in a sprig of onion, thyme and bay leaf, eight or ten cloves, about two dozen allspice, all mashed fine; a bit of lemon peel and a red pepper pod. When the water has boiled long enough to have extracted the flavor of these ingredients, drop the fish in carefully, so as to avoid breaking. Let it boil about ten minutes and then take out carefully. Put into a strainer and drain quickly. Place on a platter on a bed of parsley, with chopped parsley thrown over, and garnish with parsley and sliced lemon. Serve with a drawn butter Hollandaise Sauce, or Sauce Genoise. (See recipe.) If the flavor of the spices is not desired the fish may be boiled simply in the salt and pepper water, with sprigs of parsley.

The Creoles add a clove of garlic to the boiling water, but this is according to taste.

### Broiled Green Trout.

Truite Verte Grillée.

6 Medium-Sized Trout, or 3 Large Ones.
2 Tablespoonfuls of Butter. Juice of 1 Lemon.
1 Sliced Lemon and Parsley to Garnish.

Follow implicitly the directions given under the heading "General Rule for Broiling Fish." (See recipe.) Clean the fish without cutting off the head or tail. Broil whole over a clear, moderate fire. Before placing on the broiler rub the fish well with salt and pepper, mixed in a little sweet oil or a little butter oil. If the fish is small, broil on a quick, clear fire; if large, as mentioned above, the fire must be moderate, or the outside of the fish will be charred before the inside is done. When the fish is done through and through, which can easily be determined by the flesh parting easily from the bone, remove the gridiron from the fire and loosen the fish from the broiler with a knife, being careful not to break the flesh. Then place the hot dish over the fish, and, with a dexterous movement, turn the two back again, thus separating the gridiron from the fish and placing the latter in the dish. Butter well, season with a little pepper and salt, if deemed necessary, and pour over a tablespoonful of chopped parsley and lemon juice. Serve with garnishes of parsley and sliced lemon.

### Speckled Trout.

Truites Grillées.

6 Filets of Speckled Trout.
2 Tablespoonfuls of Butter.
Parsley and Sliced Lemon to Garnish.

The Speckled Trout is usually served in tenderloin steaks or filets. Skin and cut the fish, after cleaning, into filets or square pieces, slicing across the back. Remove all the bones and rub well with pepper and salt, and a little sweet oil mixed with the pepper and salt. Place on the gridiron or double broiler and broil carefully, turning the broiler frequently to prevent the fish being charred before it is done. When nicely browned, place on a bed of parsley and garnish with sliced lemon. Serve with Sauce à la Tartare. (See recipe.)

### Fried Speckled Trout.

Truite Frite.

6 Filets of Speckled Trout.
The Yolks of 2 Eggs.   1 Cup of Milk.
1 Onion.   4 Sprigs of Parsley.
2 Gills of Mustard.
½ Pint of Mayonnaise Dressing.
Parsley and Sliced Lemon to Garnish.

Select fine Spotted Trout. Skin the fish and clean thoroughly. Then cut the Trout into filets or steaks. Take the yolks of two eggs and a little milk and beat together. Add salt and pepper and soak the Trout well in this, rolling over and over. Then take it out of the pan and roll in cracker or bread crumbs. Pat the fish a little all over with your hands and then fry in the same manner as Croakers. Serve on a bed of fried parsley, with garnish of sliced lemon, with the following Sauce à la Tartare: Take one large onion and four or five sprigs of parsley and chop fine. Squeeze the juice out well and parboil, chopping fine and squeezing out the water. Prepare about one-half pint of Mayonnaise Dressing (see recipe) and add about two gills of mustard. Mix well and add to the parsley and onion and juices. Serve the sauce cold.

### Cutlets of Fish.

Filets de Poisson.

6 Tenderloin Trout Cutlets.   1 Cup of Milk.
Salt and Pepper to Taste.
Parsley and Sliced Lemon to Garnish.
A Mayonnaise Sauce, or Sauce a la Tartare.

Cut the fish (Tenderloin Trout) into filets or square pieces; remove all the bones, dip in milk which has been freely salted and peppered, and roll in flour; drop into the well-heated lard so that the filets will swim and fry to a golden brown. When done, drain on a brown paper and serve on a bed of fried parsley, with garnishes of parsley and sliced lemon. With these cutlets serve either a Mayonnaise Sauce, a Sauce à la Tartare or a Tomato Sauce, preferably either of the former. (See recipes for sauces.)

### PERCH.

De la Perche.

The Perch is a fresh-water fish of delightful flavor. It should always be boiled or broiled.

### Boiled Perch.

Perche Bouille.

6 Fine Fresh Perch.   1 Bay Leaf.
1 Sprig of Thyme.   1 Sprig of Onion.
1 Clove of Garlic (if desired). 10 Cloves.
2 Dozen Allspice.   A Bit of Lemon Peel.
1 Red Pepper Pod, Without the Seed.
Parsley and Lemon to Garnish.

Select fine, fresh Perch. Clean and wash the fish well. Make a small letter "S" with a knife on the back. Pass a piece of twine around the body, so as to secure it. Have ready a kettle of boiling water, and throw in a sprig of onion, thyme and bay leaf, the cloves and allspice, mashed fine, a bit of lemon peel and the red pepper pod. When the water has boiled long enough to have fully extracted the flavor of these ingredients, drop the fish in carefully, so as to avoid breaking. Let it boil ten minutes, and then take out carefully and drain quickly in a strainer. Place in a dish on a bed of parsley, sprinkle chopped parsley over it and garnish prettily with parsley and sliced lemon. The spices may be omitted if the flavor is not agreeable to some, and the Perch may be simply boiled in the salt and pepper water with the sprigs of parsley thrown in. Serve with a Drawn Butter Sauce or Sauce Genoise. (See recipes.)

### Broiled Perch.

Perche Grillée.

6 Fine Perch.   2 Tablespoonfuls of Butter.
The Juice of 1 Lemon.
1 Sliced Lemon.   Parsley to Garnish.

Proceed in the same manner indicated under the heading "General

Rule for Broiling Fish." (See recipe.) If large, split the fish down the middle of the back, else broil whole. Serve with garnishes of parsley and sliced lemon. A row of radishes nicely dressed is often added to the garnish when it is made of lettuce leaves, and sliced, hard-boiled eggs.

## CROAKERS.

### Des Grognards.

12 Small or Six Large Croakers.
1 Pint of Milk.
Salt and Pepper to Taste.
Parsley and Sliced Lemon to Garnish.

Croakers are a famous breakfast fish. They are of smaller size than the Trout generally, therefore, no definite rule can be given as to the number required to serve a family of six, all depending upon the size of the fish. They are most delicious when fried. To fry the Croaker properly fill a small pan with milk, and add salt and pepper to taste. Roll the Croakers in the milk and then take out and roll in dry, sifted flour. Have ready a pan of grease that has been heated very hot without boiling. Drop in the Croakers and cook till brown. The fish must swim in the grease. Lift carefully out of the frying pan and serve on a bed of fried parsley, with garnishes of sliced lemon.

Many persons roll the Croakers in cornmeal, but the above recipe is far daintier and more palatable.

### SACALAIT-PATASSAS.

These are delightfully flavored fish of the small variety found in the Louisiana waters. They are excellent either fried, as in recipe for Croakers, or broiled whole.

### FISH BALLS.

### Boulettes de Poisson.

The Remains of Any Fish.   1 Large Onion.
1 Sprig of Thyme.   3 Sprigs of Parsley.
1 Clove of Garlic.
1 Tablespoonful of Butter.
1 Egg.   Bread Crumbs.
A Dash of Cayenne.

Take the remains of any fish, season well with chopped parsley, onions, thyme and Cayenne, and a touch of garlic if the flavor is liked. Then mince all well, adding a tablespoonful of butter and mix with one-third bread crumbs, mashed well. Beat the yolk and white of an egg and roll the balls, shaped in the form of a cake, in this. Pat with bread crumbs and fry in butter to a pale brown.

### Fish Chowder.

### Mélée Créole.

2 Pounds of Fresh Fish, Preferably Redfish or Sheepshead.
3 Medium-Sized Potatoes.   1 Onion.
1 Clove of Garlic.
3 Sprigs Each of Thyme, Parsley and Bay Leaf.
½ Can of Tomatoes.   ½ Cup of Milk.
1 Quart of Boiling Water.
2 Ounces of Salt Pork or Ham Chopped Very Fine.
Grated Oyster Crackers.
Salt, Cayenne and Black Pepper to Taste.

Cut two pounds of fresh fish of any kind, preferably the Redfish or Sheepshead. Take three medium-sized potatoes and one onion and cut into slices. Take two ounces of salt pork, wash well and chop very fine. Put the pork into a frying pan, and when it is hot add the sliced onion. Smother slightly, and add chopped thyme, parsley, bay leaf, one clove of garlic, very fine, and Cayenne and black pepper to taste. Let this simmer for about ten minutes longer. Pour over this one quart of boiling water, and add fish and half a can of tomatoes and the potatoes. Season to taste, and cover the pan and let the contents simmer for half an hour. A half cup of milk may be added, if desired. Take oyster crackers, place in a bowl and pour the chowder over and serve hot.

### LOUISIANA EELS.

### De l'Anguille.

Few of the American residents of New Orleans know the possibilities of preparing a most delightful dish that lurks in the often-rejected eel. But the ancient Creoles inherited the taste of their French ancestors, who considered eels a delicacy, and have evolved from the traditional recipes of old France pleasing and various ways of serving this fish. The most generally used in households is called

### Eels en Matelote,

Or, More Familiarly, Matelote d'Anguille.

2 Pounds of Eel, or a 2-Pound Fish.
1 Large Onion.
* Pint of Button Onions.   1 Clove of Garlic.
1 Tablespoonful of Lard.
2 Tablespoonfuls of Flour.
1 Glass of Good Claret.   1 Can of Mushrooms.
1 Pint of Oyster Water.
1 Bay Leaf.   1 Sprig of Thyme.
Croutons to Garnish.

Matelote d'Anguille is a famous old Creole dish. The following is the old Creole recipe, and when once eaten after this mode of preparation, there is seldom a refusal to give the eel its due credit as a dish fit for the most fastidious gourmet. It should always be remembered that the largest eels are not the best for eating. The Creoles always reject those taken from the river, near the wharves. The eels found in the bay and lakes are the most recherché.

Clean and skin the eel, using about two pounds. Cut in one inch or two-inch pieces, as desired. Take one large onion and a half pint of button onions, or a clove of garlic, and chop fine. Make a roux with one tablespoonful of lard, adding, when hot, the chopped onions and parsley, and gradually adding, when these begin to brown, the two tablespoonfuls of flour. Pour in one good glass of Claret and a can of mushrooms. Add a pint of oyster stock or oyster water, and let cook a while. Season to taste with Cayenne and salt, adding bay leaf and thyme. When it boils, add the eels that have been thoroughly cleansed and placed in cold water and allowed to stand about fifteen minutes. When these are added to the matelote, let it simmer about an hour. Serve with fancy garnish of Croûtons.

### Fried Eels.
#### Anguilles Frites.
A 2-Pound Eel. 2 Eggs.
Mashed Bread Crumbs.
Salt and Pepper to Taste.

Clean and skin the eel and place in boiling water and vinegar till thoroughly disgorged. Cut into lengths of two inches. Wipe dry with a clean towel. Beat two eggs well and add mashed bread crumbs. Roll the eel well in this preparation and fry in hot lard, following implicitly the directions given for frying, and remembering that the fish must always swim in the grease. Drain of all grease and serve on a bed of parsley.

### Broiled Eels.
#### Anguilles Grillées.
2 Pounds of Eel. 1 Sprig of Thyme.
1 Teaspoonful of Black Pepper.
½ Teaspoonful of Salt.
A Drawn Butter Sauce, or Sauce a la Tartare.

Clean and skin the eel as for frying. Cut in two-inch pieces and boil till disgorged. Then roll in oil and pepper and salt. Mix well and broil quickly over a clear fire. Serve with melted or Drawn Butter Sauce and pickles, or a Sauce à la Tartare.

### Eels à la Maître d'Hotel.
#### Anguilles à la Maître d'Hotel.
2 Pounds of Eel. 1 Sprig of Thyme.
1 Bay Leaf. 6 Cloves. 1 Dozen Allspice.
1 Onion Chopped Fine. 1 Clove of Garlic.
A Sauce a la Tartare.
A Half Cup of Lemon or Citron Juice.
Fried Potato Balls.

Cut and clean the eel as directed and boil about twenty minutes in salt and water, putting a great quantity of salt into the kettle, and adding the thyme, bay leaf, cloves, allspice, chopped onion, garlic and a glass of Claret. Remove the eels after cooking twenty minutes and serve on a dish garnished with parsley and fried potato balls. Serve with a Sauce à la Maître d'Hotel (see recipe), only be careful to add about a half cup of citron or lemon juice to the sauce.

### Eels à la Poulette.
#### Anguilles à la Poulette.
2 Pounds of Eel. 1 Cup of Hot Vinegar.
1 Tablespoonful of Butter.
1 Can of Mushrooms.
2 Tablespoonfuls of Flour.
1 Glass of White Wine.
1 Sprig of Thyme. 1 Sprig of Sweet Basil.
2 Sprigs of Parsley.
1 Onion Minced Very Fine.
The Yolks of 3 Eggs. Juice of 2 Lemons.
A Dash of Cayenne. Salt and Pepper to Taste.
Croutons and Sliced Lemon to Garnish.

Clean and skin the eels and put in a pot of boiling water. To be sure that they disgorge thoroughly add a cup of hot vinegar. After boiling fifteen minutes, take them out and cut into three-inch pieces. Take one tablespoonful of butter, put into a frying pan, and add the eels and one can of mushrooms poured over. Add two tablespoonfuls of flour rubbed smoothly in butter as the eels begin to fry. Pour over, when this begins to brown, a glassful of white wine; and add parsley, thyme, bay leaf, sweet basil, and an onion minced like the herbs, very fine. As the grease rises, floating, skim it off. Add a little Cayenne, and salt to taste, if necessary. When quite done, take the yolks of three eggs and mix thoroughly with the juice of two lemons. Take the eels off the fire and add the lemon juice and eggs and be careful not to set back on the fire when once these are added, or the eggs will curdle. Place on a dish and garnish with Croûtons and slices of lemon and serve hot.

### STINGAREE.
#### De la Raie.

The Stingaree is a fish that the Americans laugh at, not dreaming of the possibilities for a delicate dish that lurks within its wings. The Creoles, following in the wake of their French ancestors, who ate the Stingaree found in the waters of the Mediterranean, have evolved a different dish from the old French cuisinières, but one that holds its own even among the many distinguished French critics and gourmets who have visited our shores. It is called Raie au Beurre Noir.

### Stingaree au Beurre Noir.
#### Raie au Beurre Noir.

2 Pounds of Eel.  1 Cup of Hot Vinegar.
1 Tablespoonful of Butter.
1 Can of Mushrooms.
2 Tablespoonfuls of Flour.
1 Glass of White Wine.
1 Sprig of Thyme.  1 Sprig of Sweet Basil.
2 Sprigs of Parsley.
1 Onion Minced Very Fine.
The Yolks of 3 Eggs.  Juice of 2 Lemons.
A Dash of Cayenne, Salt and Pepper to Taste.
Croutons and Sliced Lemon to Garnish.

Take a fine young Stingaree and cut off the tail. Cut the wings from the body and throw away the rest of the fish. Throw the wings into boiling water and parboil them When boiled ten minutes, take them off the water and then take all the skin off. The flesh will then become as white as snow. Put one tablespoonful of butter in a frying pan and let it brown without burning. When a nice coffee color, add a handful of chopped parsley and let it brown for a half minute. Then add the juice of one lemon or a spoonful of French vinegar. Pour this over the fish, salt and pepper to taste, and serve hot. This is a dish much affected by Creole connoisseurs.

### Fried Stingaree.
#### Raie Frite.

A Fine Young Stingaree.
1 Tablespoonful of Butter.
A Handful of Chopped Parsley.
The Juice of 1 Lemon, or 1 Spoon of French Vinegar.
Salt and Pepper to Taste.

Prepare the Stingaree wings as directed in the above recipe. Cut it into square pieces of about three inches, and let these soak in the vinegar which has been charged with the salt and minced parsley. Then roll in egg and bread crumbs and fry in boiling lard. Drain and serve on a bed of fried parsley, with a Sauce à la Poivrade. (See recipe.)

### Stingaree With Caper Sauce.
#### Raie Sauce aux Capres.

A Fine Young Stingaree.
A Pint of French Vinegar.
A Handful of Parsley Minced Very Fine.
A Teaspoonful of Salt.  Parsley to Garnish.
A Sauce Poivrade.

Cut off the tail of the Stingaree. Cut off the wings, and throw the rest of the fish away. Throw the wings into boiling water charged with salt, and parboil them for fifteen or twenty minutes. Then take them out of the water and skin thoroughly. Place in a heated dish and pour over a Caper Sauce. (See recipe.)

### Stingarettes.
#### Raitons.

A Fine Young Stingaree.  A Caper Sauce.
Salt and Boiling Water.

This name is given to the little Stingarees. They are prepared just like the larger ones, the wings only being used. These are soaked in vinegar and a little salt, and then fried, after being rolled in bread crumbs and beaten egg. Place on a bed of fried parsley and serve.

### ROE.
#### Oeufs de Poisson.

1 Dozen Roe.  2 Tablespoonfuls of Butter.
The Juice of a Lemon.
Lemon Sliced in Quarters.

Fish eggs are a great delicacy for the reason that it is not often that sufficient can be bought to supply a dinner or breakfast table. The only eggs of fish that are used as an epicurean dish in New Orleans are the Roe of the Green Trout. These are exceedingly fine and delicate and are prepared after the following manner: First wash the eggs well and cut out fibres; butter a silver dish or, if you have not one, a nice agate, and lay the roe in the dish. Split them open, if large, and put a dot of butter on top of each. Sprinkle nicely with salt and pepper; place in the oven, bake a few minutes, and serve hot with lemon juice.

Roe are also used to garnish a dish of fish whenever the eggs can be obtained in sufficient quantity.

### FROGS.
#### Des Grenouilles.

Like their French ancestors, Frog legs are highly prized as a delicacy by the ancient Creoles. Properly cooked, they are much more delicate than chicken and a great dish at récherché dinners. It must be remembered that only the hind legs of the frogs are used. These are usually sold, cleaned and skinned in the French Market. But if caught by the small boys of the household or the amateur fisherman and brought home to be cleaned, the legs must be first skinned and then thrown into boiling water for five minutes. Then take them out and put in cold water. When cold, take out of the water, and wipe dry, with a clean towel. They are now ready for cooking.

### The Picayune Frog.

When the Picayune Frog first made its advent in New Orleans as the "Weather Prophet" of this old and faithful journal, the enthusiasm throughout the city was very great. "Picayune Teas," "Picayune Souvenir Pins," with the picture of our

Frog in all his various garbs as "Weather Prophet," became the fashion of the hour. No entertainment, no reunion, no fair was considered complete without the presence of the Picayune Frog. The Frog soon became the "Mascot" of every charitable and philanthropic entertainment, the booth at which he was invited to take up his headquarters generally carrying the fair. So great was the enthusiasm that one fair lady originated the "Picayune Frog Lemonade" in his honor, another originated the "Picayune Cake," and so on. At this juncture a famous old chef, residing in the French Quarter, unable to control his enthusiasm for our distinguished little weather prophet, who had left the swamps and bayous of this old Creole State to take up his abode in a great newspaper office, complimented him with an original dish, modeled upon the old French preparation of a century ago, and named it in his honor.

With the dish the old chef sent the following recipe. It has been tried and is acknowledged throughout New Orleans to be the most delightful manner of cooking Frogs:

#### Picayune Frogs à la Créole.

A Half Dozen Picayune Frogs.
3 Eggs.   A Cup of Sifted Bread Crumbs.
1 Tablespoonful of Butter.
1 Tablespoonful of Flour.
2 Gills of Milk or Fresh Cream.
½ Teaspoonful of Salt.
½ of an Onion Chopped Very Fine.
Salt and Pepper to Taste.

Take a half dozen Picayune Frogs, the more delicate the better. Cut off the hind legs and skin. Scald the legs about four minutes in boiling water, adding salt and lemon juice to the water. Then take out and dry with a clean towel. Beat the yolks and whites of two or three eggs, and mix in bread crumbs sifted. Have ready a pot of heated lard. Rub the Frog legs well with pepper and salt, and put into the pot of hot lard. Let them fry to a nice golden brown. Then make a sauce as follows: Take one tablespoonful of flour, one very large tablespoonful of butter, two gills of fresh milk or cream, and a half teaspoonful of salt. Put the butter in a saucepan over the fire. As soon as it melts, add the flour, which as been rubbed smoothly. Stir in gradually, and when blended, add by degrees the boiling milk, stirring constantly to prevent burning. Then take a teaspoonful of chopped parsley and a half of a chopped onion that has been well grated. Have ready two fresh eggs, beaten in a bowl. Warm the Frogs' legs in the sauce, and when it begins to simmer stir the sauce briskly into the eggs. Return to the back of the stove a minute or two, being careful not to let the sauce boil after the eggs have been added, else they will curdle the sauce. Serve hot, with the compliments of the Picayune.

#### Frogs à la Poulette

Grenouilles à la Poulette
6 Frog Legs.
2 Tablespoonfuls of Butter.
½ Can of Mushrooms.   1 Tablespoon Flour.
1 Lemon.   Salt and Pepper to Taste.

Clean and skin the Frogs' legs and cut them in small pieces of about an inch in size. Have ready a stew pot and put in the Frogs' legs, with salt and pepper to taste, and half a lemon cut fine. Cover well with water and let it cook till the meat is tender. When cooked, drain and put the meat aside and make a sauce as follows: Take one tablespoonful of butter, two spoonfuls of flour; rub the flour smoothly and put in a sauce pan with the butter to melt. Add two cups of water and stir well. When it begins to boil well, add a half can of mushrooms. Season with salt and Cayenne. Then add the frogs; season again to taste, and let this boil ten minutes. Beat the yolks of two raw eggs well, take the frogs off the fire and stir in the yolks thoroughly. Add the juice of one-half lemon and serve.

#### Frogs Sauté à la Créole.

Grenouilles Sautées à la Créole.
6 Frog Legs.
2 Tablespoonfuls of Butter.
3 Large Onions.
6 Fresh Tomatoes or a Half Can.
1 Sprig of Thyme.   1 Bay Leaf.
2 Cloves of Garlic.
6 Green Sweet Peppers.
Cup of Consomme or Boiling Water.
Salt and Pepper to Taste.

Wash the Frogs' legs. Put two tablespoonfuls of butter in a saucepan and add the legs. Let this brown well, being careful not to burn. After ten minutes of very slow cooking on a good fire, take three large onions and slice them and let them brown with the frogs. Then add one-half dozen nice large fresh tomatoes, or a half can; cover and let these brown. Cook very slowly, adding salt and pepper to taste, thyme, bay leaf, two cloves of garlic, all chopped very fine indeed. Let the mixture smother slowly over the fire, and, if possible, add one-half dozen green sweet peppers sliced very fine, being careful to extract all the seeds. Stir well and let it smother twenty minutes longer, stirring frequently to prevent burning. When well smothered, that is, when the Frogs' legs are tender, which is easily ascertained by touching with a fork add one cup of broth, if you have it, or consommé; if not, add one cup of boiling water, and let it cook again for half an hour very slowly and well covered. Serve hot.

### Fried Frogs.
### Grenouilles Frites.

6 Frog Legs.
½ Cup of Lemon Juice and a Teaspoon of Salt.
2 Eggs.   1 Cup of Sifted Bread Crumbs.
Parsley, Sliced Lemon and Radishes to Garnish.
Salt and Pepper to Taste.

Scald the Frogs' legs about three minutes in boiling water and add a half cup of lemon juice and salt. Take out of the water and dry with a clean towel. Season with salt and pepper and dip into a batter made of the well beaten yolks and whites of two eggs and sifted bread crumbs. Pat the Frogs well and drop into the lard, heated to a boiling point, and fry to a golden brown. Take them from the lard and drain well by placing on soft brown paper, heated. Place a snow-white folded napkin in a dish, and lay the frogs upon it and garnish with fried parsley and sliced lemon, or place the Frogs in a bed of fried parsley laid in the dish and garnish with decorated radishes and sliced lemons.

### Broiled Frogs.
### Grenouilles Grillées.

6 Frog Legs.
A Cup of Boiling Lemon Juice and Salt.
1 Tablespoonful of Olive Oil.
1 Teaspoonful of Black Pepper.
1 Tablespoonful of Butter.
Salt and Pepper to Taste.
Lettuce Leaves and Parsley, or Sliced Lemons and Olives to Garnish.

Clean and skin the Frogs; scald well in boiling lemon juice and salt. Dry with a clean towel. Mix thoroughly a little black pepper, salt and olive oil, or butter melted, and rub the frogs thoroughly, rolling them over and over. Take out and put on a double wire broiler, being careful to turn frequently to prevent scorching. When done, place in a platter of delicate lettuce leaves or parsley and garnish with sliced lemons and olives.

### Stewed Frogs.
### Grenouilles en Fricassée.

1 Dozen Frog Legs.
1 Tablespoonful of Butter.
1 Tablespoonful of Flour.  ½ Pint of Water.
½ Pint of Oyster Water.
1 Sprig of Thyme.    1 Sprig of Parsley.
1 Bay Leaf.  1 Sprig of Sweet Marjoram.
10 Allspice.         1 Clove.
The Yolk of an Egg.         Croutons.
2 Dozen Oysters.

Take the legs of one dozen frogs and prepare the same as for frying. Take a tablespoonful of butter and put in a frying pan. When it begins to melt, add a tablespoonful of flour and stir constantly. When it begins to brown nicely, add a half pint of water and a pint of oyster water. Throw in the Frog legs as it begins to boil, and add salt and pepper, a little Cayenne, a sprig of thyme, bay leaf and sweet marjoram, eight or ten allspice, one clove. Let it simmer about fifteen minutes and take off the fire. Have ready the yolk of a beaten egg and add, blending well, and serve immediately with garnishes of Croûtons, and fried in a little butter, with oysters laid upon them.

## CHAPTER IX.

### SHELL FISH.

### Des Crustacés.

Under this heading are classed the shell fish found in our Louisiana waters and those of the Mississippi Sound adjacent to New Orleans. Oysters, Shrimp, Crabs, and Crawfish and the famous Green Turtle—these are the delightful varieties that are common articles of food among the people and which are to be had for the fishing.

That delicious bivalve, the Oyster, has its home among us. Everyone who has visited New Orleans in winter has noted the exceptionally palatable oysters that are sold in every restaurant and by the numerous small vendors on almost every other corner or so throughout the lower section of the city. In the cafés, the hotels, the oyster saloons, they are served in every conceivable style known to epicures and caterers. The oyster beds adjacent to New Orleans send to our markets the famous Bayou Cook and Barataria Oysters. eagerly sought and highly prized for exquisite flavor and unsurpassed in quality. The Mississippi Sound is well-nigh stocked with oysters from one end to the other, and millions of cans are shipped yearly from Biloxi and other points to every part of the United States. And so with our celebrated Lake and River Shrimp. No oysters are caught in the Mississippi Sound between May and September, because they are somewhat milky and considered unfit for use, and so strict are the laws governing the uses of dredges in the Sound that a watchman accompanies each dredge boat to see that no attempt is made to use the dredge in less than fourteen feet of water, the idea being that dredges shall not be used where the water is sufficiently shallow to admit of their being dug of tongs. Thus are preserved, in all their splendid flavor and almost inexhaustible supply, our oyster beds, and while the yearly increase in consumption of this delicious bivalve has tended to alarm scientists and to awaken an interest in the question as to whether the American oyster beds may not likely become depleted, scientists acquainted with the oyster beds on our Gulf coast say that for domestic purposes there are sufficient oysters to supply the United States. The railroad facilities for handling oysters can hardly be improved, and fresh and fine and ready to be eaten, they arrive in our markets. The Bayou Cook and Barataria Oysters are with us all summer, and New Orleans is the acknowledged commercial center of the oyster trade on the Gulf Coast.

New Orleans opened the eyes of the United States to the possibilities of the oyster in every variety and form of cooking. Her chefs evolved the most dainty and palatable ways of preparing them, and while raw oysters remained practically an unknown quantity in aristocratic centers in other States of the Union, the Creoles, quick to discover and apply, placed the raw oyster on their table as one of the greatest delicacies that could be offered the most fastidious appetite. In the following recipes are given the most delightful manner of serving

## OYSTERS.

### Huîtres à la Créole.

The Picayune has already given, in the chapter devoted to soups, the several ways that the Creoles have of preparing oysters in this style. (See Oyster Soups.) In a general treatment of oysters, it presents, first, that famous but exceptionally palatable manner in which oysters can be eaten at all hours, day or night, without overloading the stomach or causing the least symptom of indigestion, viz:

### Raw Oysters on Half Shell.

### Huîtres en Coquilles.

6 Oysters to Each Plate. Cracked Ice.
Maunsell White or Black Pepper, Cayenne and Vinegar.
Lemon, Sliced or Cut in Quarters.

Allow six oysters to each person where the bivalve is used to begin the dinner or breakfast. Have the oysters opened in their shell and remove one-half of the shell. Drain the water from the oyster shell. without disturbing the oyster, and place in plates, with cracked ice, sprinkled over with a quarter of a sliced lemon in the center of the plate. Serve with black pepper and Cayenne, if desired, or the famous Maunsell White, sold in all New Orleans oyster saloons. A half cup is given as "lagniappe" by the dealers to their customers.

A more attractive way of serving raw oysters is to remove them from the shell and place in the delicate oyster plates used by the old Creoles garnished with sliced lemon between the little bed that holds each oyster, and placing the Maunsell White or pepper and Cayenne in the little cell in the center of the dish.

Again, where these delicate plates are not in family use, place the oysters in the usual dinner plate in a bed of finely chopped ice, allowing a half dozen oysters for each person. Cut lemon in quarters and hand around with black pepper, salt and pepper vinegar.

Dainty rolls of fresh butter and oyster crackers are served with raw oysters.

A daily sight in our New Orleans streets is to see the negro servants going at lunch or supper time to the nearest oyster saloon with a great salver for oysters on half-shell. They return with the dainty bivalves ranged closely in their open shells on the salver, and with a small glass of Maunsell White, and a plate of "hard-tack" (oyster bread), or crackers.

Worcestershire Sauce is often used instead of the Maunsell White by those who do not like the taste of pepper. But the piquant Maunsell White is essentially Creole, originated in New Orleans, and gives the oyster a toothsome touch that must be tasted in order to be appreciated.

### Oysters Served in a Block of Ice.
#### Huîtres sur la Glace.
6 Oysters to Each Person. A Square Block of Ice.
Black Pepper and Cayenne.
Sprigs of Parsley and Radishes to Garnish.
Lemon Cut in Quarters.

This is one of the prettiest ways of serving oysters at a dinner or luncheon, as well as one of the most recherché. Have your dealer send a square block of ice of the size desired and make a hollow in the center of the block by placing a flat-iron on the top, scooping out with the iron the shape desired. Then place a folded napkin on a platter and stand the block of ice upon it. Pepper the oysters nicely with Cayenne and black pepper, and place in the ice. Then take sprigs of parsley and decorate the platter, placing between decorated radishes, and alternate slices of lemon, and serve the oysters with lemon cut in quarters. The effect of this decoration is very charming. Smilax may be substituted for the parsley or mixed with it. The cavity should be square and deep, leaving walls of ice about two inches in thickness.

### Broiled Oysters.
#### Huîtres sur le Gril.
6 or 8 Oysters to Each Person. Salt and Cayenne to Taste.
Melted Butter and Chopped Parsley.
Sliced Lemon and Sprigs of Parsley to Garnish.

Allow six or eight oysters for each person. The oysters must be large and fat, else they will shrivel to nothing in cooking. Drain the oysters through a colander, lay them on a dish and wipe with a dry, clean towel. Melt butter and dip in the oysters, seasoned well with salt and Cayenne on both sides. Have ready the gridiron ( use always the double wire broiler) and test the heat by dropping a little water on it. If the water hisses, the broiler is quite ready. Place the broiler in a warm place—just over the oven will do. Butter and place the oysters on it. Return to moderate coals. As soon as the oysters are browned on one side, turn on the other and brown. Have ready a heated dish and serve the oysters, pouring over melted butter and chopped parsley (chopped very fine). Garnish with sprigs of parsley and sliced lemon and serve immediately.

### Broiled Oysters on Toast.
#### Huîtres sur Canapés.
6 or 8 Oysters to Each Person. Salt and Pepper to Taste.
6 or 8 Pieces of Buttered Toast or Milk Toast.
2 Tablespoonfuls of Melted Butter.
Chopped Parsley to Garnish.

Broil the oysters according to the recipe given above. Have ready a heated dish; sprinkle the oysters with salt and pepper and pour over melted butter. Serve on small pieces of buttered toast, or milk toast. Sprinkle with finely-chopped parsley.

### Broiled Oysters With Sauce Espaognole.
#### Huîtres Grillées à la Sauce Espagnole.
1 Pint of Oyster Liquor to Every 2 Dozen Oysters.
1 Tablespoonful of Butter. 2 Tablespoonfuls of Sifted Flour.
Salt and Cayenne to Taste. Chopped Parsley.
6 or 8 Squares of Buttered Toast.

Drain the oysters and allow about one pint of the oyster liquor to every two dozen oysters. Have ready a porcelain-lined saucepan and put the liquor on to boil. As the scum rises skim it carefully. Put one tablespoonful of butter into a frying pan, and when it begins to heat, add gradually two tablespoonfuls of sifted flour. Mix well and brown. Pour over this the oyster liquor and stir constantly till it begins to boil, seasoning with salt and pepper (Cayenne) and parsley chopped very fine. Stand the sauce in a vessel in hot water (bain-marie) until wanted, and proceed to broil the oysters in the same manner as in the recipe first given. Place squares of buttered toast in a dish, lay the oysters on top, pour over the sauce, and serve immediately.

### Oysters en Brochettes.
#### Huîtres en Brochettes.
3 Dozen Large, Fat Oysters. Thin Slits of Bacon.
A Tablespoonful of Butter.
1 Tablespoonful of Minced Parsley.
Sliced Lemon and Olives to Garnish.

Have ready a furnace with red hot coals; take fine sliced breakfast bacon and cut into thin slits about the size of the oyster. Drain three dozen large, fat oysters; take a long skewer, of silver or metal that is not dangerous, and string it first with a slit of bacon and then an oyster, alternating this until it is filled, the extreme ends terminating with the bacon. Then hold the oysters over the clear fire and broil until the edges begin to ruffle, when they are done. In the meantime prepare some drawn butter by placing about a tablespoonful in a cup before the fire to melt; place the oysters in a hot dish, alternating with slices of bacon, sprinkle with pepper and salt, and pour over the drawn butter mixed with about one tablespoonful of parsley, chopped fine; garnish with slices of lemons and whole olives, and serve. The oysters and bacon may be served on the skewers, if they are not charred or blackened; but the other is the far daintier method.

### Oysters Broiled In Shells.

Huîtres en Coquilles sur le Gril.

3 Dozen Fine, Fat Oysters.
1 Tablespoonful of Finely Chopped Parsley.
1 Bay Leaf.   Sprigs of Thyme.
1 Sprig of Sweet Basil.  2 Shallots.
1 Tablespoonful of Butter. Grated Bread Crumbs.
Asparagus Tips and Sliced Lemon to Garnish.
* Dozen Well Washed Oyster Shells.

Take three dozen fine oysters; blanch in their own water and drain. Chop a tablespoonful of fine parsley, bay leaf and thyme, using a sprig each of the latter and a sprig of sweet basil. Cut up two nice shallots very fine and add. Place a tablespoonful of butter in a saucepan; add a little oyster juice sauté, or shake the oysters without making a bouillon. When two minutes have passed, take off the stove, place the oysters in the well washed shells, sprinkle over a little bread crumbs, and put on top of each a pinch of butter. Have ready the gridiron or broiler very hot; place the shells between the double broiler, set over the fire to broil for about four or five minutes, and serve with delicate garnishes of asparagus tips and sliced lemon.

### Oysters and Bacon.

Huîtres Bardées.

3 Dozen Oysters. Thin Slices of Breakfast Bacon.
Minced Parsley.    Sauce Piquante.

Wrap each oyster in a very thin slice of breakfast bacon. Lay on a broiler over a baking pan in a hot oven. Remove when the bacon is brown. Each must be fastened with a wooden toothpick. Serve with minced parsley and pepper sauce, or Sauce Piquante. (See recipe.)

### Fried Oysters.

Huîtres Frites.

6 or 8 Oysters to Each Person.
Salt and Pepper.
Finely Grated Bread Crumbs. Parsley to Garnish.
Boiling Lard.

Drain the oysters, allowing about six or eight to each person to be served. Salt and pepper and then roll oysters in bread crumbs, grated very fine. Drop in the frying pan of boiling lard, having sufficient lard to allow the oysters to swim in the grease. Remove when a golden brown and place on brown paper and drain. Serve on a platter garnished with parsley or on a bed of fried parsley. (See recipe for Fried Parsley.)

### Fried Oysters à la Créole.

Huîtres Frites à la Créole.

6 or 8 Oysters to Each Person.
1 Egg.   1 Glass of Milk.
½ Teaspoonful of Salt.  ½ Teaspoonful of Black Pepper.
Grated Cracker or Bread Crumbs. Butter Oil. Parsley.
Sliced Lemon and Pickle to Garnish.

Select the firmest and largest oysters, allowing six or eight to each person. Drain in a colander and dry with a soft linen towel. Beat an egg thoroughly and mix with a glass of milk and a half teaspoonful of salt and pepper. Mash bread crumbs or crackers in another dish. Dip the oysters one by one in the milk and roll gently in the bread crumbs, patting softly with the hands, and drop into a deep frying pan with sufficient lard or butter oil for the oyster to swim in it. In from three to five minutes the oysters will be done. The time given will allow them to fry to a nice golden brown, and it will not be necessary to turn them if the oil in the pan is deep enough. Take them out with a skimmer, being careful not to break, and drain on a piece of soft brown paper. Serve on a bed of fried parsley, with garnishes of sliced lemon and pickle. Bread crumbs are far preferable to crackers. Butter is often used in frying oysters, but the butter oil is found by experience to be better than either lard or butter. Some also use cornmeal instead of the bread crumbs, but there is no comparison as to results.

### Stewed Oysters.

Huîtres en Fricassée.

4 Dozen Large Oysters.
1 Tablespoonful of Flour. 1 Tablespoonful of Butter.
1 Pint of Oyster Liquor.
1 Pint of Rich Cream or Milk.
Salt and Pepper to Taste.

Take about four dozen large oysters, drain in a colander. Mix one tablespoonful of flour and one of butter together. Put one pint of oyster liquor on the fire and add the flour and butter blended. Have ready in another saucepan a pint of rich, hot cream. After five minutes, add this to the oyster liquor, stirring constantly to prevent burning. Salt and pepper to taste. Let it boil up once and then add the oysters. After three minutes serve. This is a very delicate dish.

### Oyster Sautées.
Huîtres Sautées.

6 or 8 Oysters to Each Person.
3 Slices of Fat Bacon.
1 Tablespoonful of Flour. Salt and Pepper to Taste.
6 or 8 Squares of Buttered Toast.
Olives. Pickles and Sliced Lemon to Garnish.

Drain the oysters well and dry with a clean towel. Sprinkle them with pepper and salt, and roll in a little flour. Place the bacon, cut into thin slices, in a frying pan, and let all the fat fry out. Remove the bacon from the pan and place in the oysters, covering the bottom. As they turn a golden brown on one side, turn over on the other. Serve on squares of buttered toast, with garnishes of olives, pickles and sliced lemon.

### Coddled Oysters.
Huîtres Rotie sur Canapés.

6 or 8 Oysters to Each Person.
6 Slices of Bread.
1 Large Tablespoonful of Butter. ½ Teaspoonful of Salt.
½ Teaspoonful of Black Pepper. A Dash of Cayenne.
2 Sprigs of Parsley Chopped Very Fine.
1 Bay Leaf Minced Fine.
3 Cloves. 1 Blade of Mace. 1 Pint of Oyster Liquor.

Toast five or six slices of bread to a nice brown and butter them on both sides. Drain the liquor from the oysters and put it in a saucepan. When hot, add a large lump of butter. Have ready a baking dish and place the toast within; lay the oysters on the toast, having seasoned well with salt, Cayenne pepper. chopped parsley, bay leaf, mace and cloves. Put the liquor of the oysters over the toast until it is well absorbed. Set in an oven and bake for five or six minutes with a quick fire.

### Deviled Oysters.
Huîtres à la Diable.

3 Dozen Oysters. 1 Tablespoonful of Butter.
2 Tablespoonfuls of Flour.
½ Pint of Cream. The Yolks of 2 Eggs.
1 Tablespoonful of Chopped Parsley. 1 Bay Leaf. 1 Blade of Mace.
3 Sprigs of Parsley. Salt and Cayenne to Taste.
Sprigs of Parsley or Asparagus Tips, and Sliced Lemon and Olives to Garnish.

Take three dozen fine, large oysters, drain and chop them into middling fine pieces. Rub together one tablespoonful of butter and two tablespoonfuls of flour, very smoothly. Place in a saucepan one-half pint of cream, and, when it is coming to a boil, stir in the flour and butter. Have ready the yolks of two eggs well beaten, and, as soon as the milk boils, take from the fire and add the eggs, one tablespoonful of parsley chopped fine, one bay leaf chopped fine, mace, and a sprig of finely-chopped thyme. Add salt and Cayenne to taste, and add the oysters. Take the deep shells of the oysters, which have been washed perfectly clean, and fill with this mixture; sprinkle lightly with bread crumbs; put a pinch of butter on top, and set in the baking pan and brown. The oven should be very quick, and only five minutes are needed for the browning. Serve the oysters thus baked in their shells, and garnish the dish with sprigs of parsley or asparagus tips, olives and sliced lemon.

### Curried Oysters.
Huîtres au Kari.

4 Dozen Oysters.
1 Tablespoonful of Butter. 2 Tablespoonfuls Flour.
1 Gill of Rich Cream or 2 Gills of Good Milk.
½ Teaspoonful of Curry Powder.
A Pinch of Corn Starch.
2 Sprigs of Thyme. 1 Bay Leaf. 3 Sprigs of Parsley.
Salt and Cayenne to Taste. The Oyster Water.
1 Cup of Louisiana Rice Boiled a la Creole, for Border.

Take four dozen fine, large oysters and drain the oyster liquor into a saucepan, being careful to extract all pieces of shell, and set it to boil. Wipe the oysters dry with a clean towel. Put in another saucepan one tablespoonful of butter and let it melt; then add two tablespoonfuls of flour, stirring constantly and rubbing smoothly; do not let it brown. Add about one gill of rich cream, or two gills of good milk, to the boiling oyster juice, and stir all this into the flour slowly, avoiding the formation of any lumps, and stirring constantly. Let this boil about two minutes. Take one-half teaspoonful of curry powder and a pinch of cornstarch or flour and rub smoothly with a few drops of cold milk. Stir this into the oyster juice; season à la Créole with Cayenne, salt, chopped thyme, etc., and, as it boils up, drop in the oysters; let them cook about three minutes and serve on a dish with a border of Louisiana Rice, boiled so as to appear like snowflakes, the grains standing apart. Sprinkle chopped parsley over the oysters to form a garnish.

### Oysters à la Poulette.
Huîtres à la Poulette.

4 Dozen Oysters. 1 Gill of Sherry.
The Yolks of 2 Eggs. 2 Tablespoonfuls of Rich Cream.
Toasted and Buttered Croutons.
Sliced Lemon and Parsley Sprigs to Garnish.

Prepare as in the above recipe for

Curried Oysters, using a gill of sherry instead of the milk and cream, and omitting the curry powder. Having dropped the oysters into the boiling oyster juice, remove from the fire after cooking three minutes. Beat well the yolks of two eggs with two tablespoonfuls of rich cream, add to the oysters, and serve with toasted and buttered Croûtons, a garnish of sliced lemons and parsley sprigs.

### Minced Oysters.

Huîtres en Hachis.

4 Dozen Oysters. 1 Gill of Oyster Juice.
A Half Can of Mushrooms.
1 Gill of White Wine. 3 Yolks of Eggs.
1 Tablespoonful of Butter.
1 Gill of Rich Cream. 1 Tablespoonful of Flour.

Parsley and Chives and Thyme, chopped fine.
Scald the oysters in their own water. Drain and mince, but not too fine. Put into the saucepan a tablespoonful of butter, and, when melted, add the parsley (chopped fine), the herbs and the mushrooms. Then add the flour, which has been rubbed smoothly in a gill of oyster juice, and, after it stews about five minutes, add the white wine; if this is not obtainable, add another gill of oyster juice. Mix thoroughly, and then add the minced oysters, and stew gently until the sauce is absorbed and the mince forms a thick batter. Be very careful not to scorch. Remove from the fire and add in the yolks of the eggs, which have been beaten smoothly in the cream. Set it back on the fire and let it remain about one minute, and serve on large toasted and buttered Croûtons, with garnish of lemon and parsley and olives.

### Baked Oysters.

Huîtres au Gratin.

3 Dozen Fine, Large Oysters.
1 Tablespoonful of Butter.
Sauce Piquante. 3 Shallots.
½ Can of Mushrooms.
1 Tablespoonful of Flour. 1 Gill White Wine.
Parsley, Thyme and Bay Leaf, chopped fine.

Boil the oysters about two minutes in their own liquor, dropping them in the liquor as it comes to the boiling point. Pass them through a "Sauce Piquante," rolling nicely. Mix the melted butter and the chopped parsley, thyme, etc., the shallots chopped very fine, and moisten well with a little oyster juice; chop the mushrooms fine and add, pouring in the gill of wine. After it is reduced, being careful to stir constantly, select the finest and largest shells of the oysters, which have been cleaned well, and place in each four or six oysters; pour over each shell the sauce, filling nicely, in pyramidal shape; place on each a bit of butter, and set in the stove for about five minutes, or over a gridiron on a slow fire for about ten minutes. Serve in the shells, with garnish of parsley and lemons, sliced.

### Scalloped Oysters.

Coquilles d'Huîtres.

4 Dozen Fine Oysters. 3 Tablespoonfuls of Butter.
1 Blade of Mace. 4 Cloves. 1 Sprig of Thyme
1 Bay Leaf. 3 Sprigs of Parsley.
½ Cup of Rich Milk or Cream.
½ Cup of Oyster Liquor. Grated Bread Crumbs.

Select about four dozen fine oysters. Have ready a porcelain-lined baking dish, or any good dish that will not darken the oysters. Drain the oysters in a colander, strain the liquor to remove all pieces of shell and save it. Butter the baking dish and place in a layer of oysters, well seasoned, à la Créole, with Cayenne, salt, chopped mace, cloves, thyme, parsley and bay leaf, chopped very fine. Place over a layer of bread crumbs, about a half-inch in thickness. Place here and there little dots of butter and sprinkle with salt and pepper. Add another layer of seasoned oysters, and then another layer of bread crumbs, until the dish is full. Then mix a half cup of rich cream and milk and a half cup of the oyster liquor, and pour over the dish. Sprinkle the last layer with bread crumbs and dot gently with bits of butter. Place in a quick oven and bake about fifteen or twenty minutes, or until a nice brown.

The above is a splendid receipt for family use. Where it is desired to be more fastidious and scalloped oysters are served for luncheon, or when guests are expected, follow the above directions for seasoning and preparing the oysters. Have ready about one dozen of the deep shells which have been thoroughly washed and scalloped nicely, taking off the rough edges and every grain of dust or dirt by scraping well. Have ready a large baking pan. Place the oyster shells within and fill the shells with alternate layers of oysters and crumbs, allowing three or six oysters to each shell; sprinkle with bread crumbs, moisten a little with cream and oyster juice, and bake and serve in their own shells. The flavor of the oyster is highly improved by baking in its own shell, care being taken always not to scrape the inside or blanch with hot water.

### Oysters au Parmesan.
#### Huîtres au Parmesan.
3 Dozen Oysters.
Grated Parmesan Cheese.
1 Cup of Grated Bread Crumbs.
1 Gill of White Wine.
1 Tablespoonful of Chopped Parsley.
1 Tablespoonful of Butter.
Salt, Cayenne.   1 Bay Leaf.
1 Sprig of Thyme.

Brown the bread crumbs in a little butter, and butter a shallow dish and stew with bread crumbs. Drain the oysters and dry with a clean towel; season highly à la Créole; place them, one by one, on the bread crumbs; strew chopped parsley over them, and the grated cheese, using good judgment as to quantity. Sprinkle lightly with bread crumbs again, and pour over all a gill of white wine. Place in the oven, which should be very quick; let them remain about fifteen minutes, till quite brown. Take out and pour over a little drawn butter, and serve with lemon garnish.

### Roasted Oysters.
#### Huîtres Rôties.
3 Dozen Fine, Large, Fat Oysters.
1 Tablespoonful Butter.
Salt and Pepper to Taste.
Buttered Toast.

Clean the oyster shells thoroughly, set them on the top of the stove or place in a baking pan until the shell is easily removed. Remove the flat outer shell. Butter the oyster in the deep shell and serve very hot with salt and pepper. In old Creole families roasting parties were often given and there was always a frolic in the kitchen, the belles and beaux vying with one another in roasting the delicious bivalve. As the shells open put in a little butter. The oysters were sent to the table in their shells; by a quick movement the outer shell was removed, and they were eaten with pepper sauce or pepper, salt and vinegar. There were great frolics in the kitchens in those days roasting oysters as at the famous "Crêpe" or doughnut parties.

The good wife who wishes to delight her husband when he comes home tired of an evening cannot better win her way to his heart than by serving him with roasted or steamed oysters.

### Oyster Pan Roast.
#### Huîtres à la Poêle.
A Tablespoonful of Butter.
1 Tablespoonful of Chopped Parsley.
Salt and Pepper to Taste.
Sliced Lemon and Parsley to Garnish.

The largest and finest oysters are used for this purpose. Drain the oysters, heat a deep frying pan, drop in a generous lump of butter. When it melts, add the oysters, covering and shaking the pan constantly over a hot fire. Have ready a dish well buttered and nicely garnished with parsley and lemon slices. When the oysters are brown, turn quickly into the dish and add salt and pepper and melted butter, into which you have dropped finely chopped parsley, and serve hot.

### Steamed Oysters.
#### Huîtres à la Vapeur.
4 Dozen Oysters.
A Tablespoonful of Butter.
Salt and Pepper to Taste.
A Dash of Cayenne.

This is a favorite way of eating oysters in New Orleans. Have ready a pot of boiling water. Drain the oysters in their shells and put them in a shallow tin pan, the bottom being perforated. Cover and put them over the steamer. Let them stand about ten minutes, put into a hot dish, season with pepper and Cayenne, and serve with drawn butter sauce. If one has not the perforated tin, steam the oysters in their shells. Wash the shells thoroughly on the outside, place the oysters in the steamer and cover, letting them remain about fifteen minutes over the boiling water, or until the shells open easily, and serve. A steamer may be improvised by using a colander and a closely fitting pot lid. The steamed oyster must be eaten when very hot to be appreciated in all its flavor.

### Oyster Fritters.
#### Beignets d'Huîtres.
3 Dozen Oysters.
2 Eggs. 1 Cup of Milk.
2 Cups of Flour. 1 Teaspoonful of Salt.
½ Teaspoonful of Good Baking Powder.
Parsley or Asparagus Tips to Garnish.

Take two dozen large oysters, drain in a colander and remove any pieces of shell or grit that may adhere. Chop the oysters fine. Take two eggs and beat until very light. Then add a cup of milk and rub in smoothly two cupfuls of flour and one teaspoonful of salt. Beat until perfectly smooth. Add one-half teaspoonful of good baking powder. Mix well and then drop in the oysters which must be dry. Then drop into boiling lard or oil. When browned on one side, turn on the other, being careful not to use a fork or to pierce them, as that would render the oysters and fritters heavy. Use a skimmer in removing from the pot, and drain on brown paper. Serve on a dish in which you have placed a folded napkin and garnish with sprigs of parsley or asparagus tips.

## Oyster Croquettes.

Croquettes d'Huîtres.

3 Dozen Oysters. 1 Gill of Rich Cream.
1 Gill of Oyster Liquor.
2 Tablespoonfuls of Flour.
1 Tablespoonful of Butter.
The Yolks of 2 Eggs.
3 Sprigs of Parsley.
Salt and Pepper to Taste.
A Dash of Cayenne. A Well Beaten Egg.
Grated Bread Crumbs. Boiling Lard.

Take two dozen oysters and boil them in their own liquor. Stir constantly and boil for about five minutes. Remove from the fire. Take out the oysters and chop very fine. Put them into a saucepan with about one gill each of rich cream and oyster liquor. Rub together two tablespoonfuls of flour and one of butter. Add this and the oysters to the boiling milk and cream. Stir until it thickens and boils. Then add the yolk of two eggs. Stir this over the fire for about one minute, and then take off and add parsley, chopped fine, salt and Cayenne. Mix well and place in a dish to cool. Then roll in a beaten egg to bind and form into cylinders of about a finger in length. Roll in bread crumbs mashed fine, and fry in boiling lard or oil.

## Oyster Croquettes à la Créole.

Croquettes d'Huîtres à la Créole.

3 Dozen Fine Oysters.
1 Cup of the White Meat of a Chicken Minced.
6 Finely Chopped Mushrooms.
1 Teaspoonful of Onion Juice.
½ Cup of Cream.
2 Tablespoonfuls of Flour.
1 Bay Leaf. 1 Tablespoonful of Parsley.
1 Sprig of Thyme.
Salt and Cayenne Pepper to Taste.

Boil the oysters about three minutes in their own liquor. Drain and chop the oysters fine. Take a half cup of the liquor in which the oysters have been broiled, set it on the fire and add the chopped oysters. Then add the half cup of cream, the chopped mushrooms and the minced chicken. Stir thoroughly into this boiling mixture the butter and flour which have been rubbed smoothly. Add the chopped parsley, onion juice, salt and Cayenne, and mix well. Then add the yolks of the eggs, well beaten. Let it cook about two minutes and turn it out into a dish to cool. When cold, roll into cylinders about two inches in length and one inch in diameter. Pass through bread crumbs and fry in boiling lard. Serve immediately on a bed of fried parsley.

## Oyster Balls.

Boulettes d'Huîtres.

2 Pints of Chopped Oysters.
2 Pints of Chopped Sausage Meat.
1 Egg. Grated Bread Crumbs.

To every pint of chopped oysters add one pint of chopped sausage meat. Roll in bread crumbs; season highly. Add one egg and roll in bread crumbs. Make into small cakes and fry in boiling lard. Serve hot.

## Oyster Patties.

Petites Bouchées d'Huîtres.

4 Dozen Oysters. ½ Can of Mushrooms.
2 Tablespoonfuls of Butter.
1 Small Onion, Grated.
Pepper, Salt, Chopped Parsley and Lemon Juice.

Prepare a puff paste (see recipe) and lay on the ice to cool. Boil the oysters in their own liquor. Drain, put the butter in the saucepan, and when it is heated, add the grated onion and rub in the flour until smooth. Add a gill of mushroom juice and pepper, salt and Cayenne to taste, and the mushrooms chopped in quarters. Then add the oysters and let all stew about five minutes, adding the lemon juice. A tablespoonful of cream will improve the oysters. If this is used, omit the lemon juice. Line the small tins with the puff paste and put in each three or four oysters according to the size of the pâté. Cover with the paste and bake in a quick oven about fifteen minutes.

To make the open pâtés so much used at luncheon and entertainments in New Orleans, cut the puff paste into round cakes. Those intended for the bottom crust should be about a little less than an eigth of an inch thick. Those intended for the upper layers should be a little thicker. Take a small biscuit cutter and remove a round paste from the center of these latter. This will leave a nice ring. Carefully place this upon the bottom crust, then a second ring, until the cavity is deep enough to hold several oysters. Lay the pieces that have been extracted into a pan with these and bake to a fine brown in a quick oven. Then take out and fill the cavities with the oysters prepared as above, fit on the top very lightly, and set in the oven a second or two and serve.

## Oyster Pie.

Vol-au-Vent d'Huîtres.

8 Dozen Large, Fine Oysters.
1 Tablespoonful of Butter.
6 Yolks of Eggs.
Spices, Thyme, Bay Leaf, Parsley.
1 Slice of Grated Bread.

Take an earthen dish which will

hold about three and a half pints and line the sides with rich pie crust. (See recipe for Pie Crust.) Set in the stove and let it bake a few minutes. In the meantime, take about one pint and a half of the oyster liquor and put on the fire, after having drained well. Add the seasonings of chopped herbs and Cayenne. Rub a tablespoonful of flour into the butter and add to the liquor, stirring constantly. Mash the grated crumbs; add to this, and mix well. Chop the hard-boiled eggs fine. Then pour the oysters into the pan of pie crust, sprinkle some of the chopped eggs and grated bread crumbs over, and put a teaspoonful of butter in small bits here and there over this. Then roll out very fine and thin a layer of the pie crust. Place this over the preparation and ornament here and there, all around, with neat notches or designs, which can be easily formed with the end of a spoon or the prongs of a fork. Cut a hole in the center in the shape of the letter X. Set in a moderately quick oven and bake till brown. In the meantime, melt one tablespoonful of butter, add the remaining oyster liquor and season with pepper and salt. When it is about to come to a boil, add one-half cup of rich, hot cream or boiled milk, and when the pie is nearly brown, put a funnel into the opening in the center and pour in as much of the liquor as the pie will hold. Place a delicate garnish of pastry leaves over the whole and bake a minute or so longer. If there is any sauce left over, serve it with the pie.

Great care must be taken not to have the oysters over done. For this reason the upper crust is often baked separately, as the bottom of the pie is filled with the ingredients and the upper crust placed on and served. Else the oysters are laid in layers while raw into the crust. But they are liable to become too dry when used in this way.

### Oyster Salad.

#### Huîtres en Salade.

4 Dozen Large Oysters. 2 Crisp Heads of Lettuce.
The Yolks of Three Eggs. ½ Teaspoonful of Mustard.
¼ Teaspoonful of Salt.
2 Tablespoonfuls of Olive Oil.
1 Tablespoonful of Vinegar.
Pepper and Cayenne to Taste.

Oyster Salad is a favorite lunch dish. Boil about four dozen large oysters in their own liquor, season with salt and pepper. Drain and set aside to cool. Take two crisp heads of lettuce leaves and arrange nicely in the salad bowl. Turn the oysters into the center of the leaves and pour over them the following dressing: Take the yolks of three raw eggs, half a teaspoonful of mustard, and a little salt; beat these together until they begin to thicken, and add gradually olive oil, as in making Mayonnaise, until it begins to thicken. Add a little vinegar to thin and serve with the oysters.

### Pickled Oysters.

#### Huîtres en Marinade.

Huîtres en Marinade.
50 or 100 Large, Fine Oysters.
12 Blades of Mace.
1 Large Tablespoonful of Allspice.
1 Level Tablespoonful of Cloves.
1 Pepper. 2 Sliced Lemons.
½ Pint of White Vinegar.
Salt to Taste.
¼ Dozen Pepper Corns.

Boil the oysters in their own liquor until the edges begin to ruffle. Then take a half pint of white wine vinegar and a half pint of the oyster water and set to boil, adding the blades of mace, cloves, allspice, pepper corns and a dash of Cayenne. Salt to taste. As soon as they come to a good boil, pour the oysters into the boiling liquor. Care must be taken to have the oysters very cold, as they will make the pickles slimy otherwise. After adding the oysters to the boiling liquid, set it aside to cool. Put in a very cool ice box and serve cold. This is a delicious Creole luncheon dish.

### Oyster Loaf.

#### La Médiatrice.

Delicate French Loaves of Bread.
2 Dozen Oysters to a Loaf.
1 Tablespoonful of Melted Butter.

This is called the "famous peacemaker" in New Orleans. Every husband, who is detained down town, laughingly carries home an oyster loaf, or Médiatrice, to make "peace" with his anxiously waiting wife. Right justly is the Oyster Loaf called the "Peacemaker," for, well made, it is enough to bring the smiles to the face of the most disheartened wife.

Take delicate French loaves of bread and cut off, lengthwise, the upper portion. Dig the crumbs out of the center of each piece, leaving the sides and bottom like a square box. Brush each corner of the box and the bottom with melted butter, and place in a quick oven to brown. Fill with broiled or creamed oysters. Cover with each other and serve.

## CHAPTER X.

### SHELL FISH—(Continued.)

#### Des Crustacés

This chapter embraces methods of cooking Shrimp, Crab, Crawfish and Turtle, according to the most approved rules of the Creole Cuisine.

### SHRIMPS.
#### Des Chevrettes.

New Orleans is famous for the exquisite flavor of the River and Lake shrimps which abound in its markets. The River shrimp is the more delicate of the two and is always eaten broiled as a preliminary to dinner or breakfast or luncheon. The Lake shrimp of larger size and firmer qualities is used for cooking purposes, and is served in various delightful ways, known only to our Creole cuisinières. From the Mississippi Sound and the New Orleans shore shrimp are sent deliciously canned to every part of the United States. In our markets they are sold fresh from the waters.

### Boiled Shrimps.
#### Chevrettes Bouillies.

100 Fine River Shrimp.
A Large Bunch of Celery and Celery Tops.
2 Dozen Allspice. 2 Blades of Mace.
1 Dozen Cloves.
4 Sprigs Each of Thyme, Parsley and Bay Leaf. 1 Red Pepper Pod.
Cayenne, Black Pepper, Salt. Parsley Sprigs to Garnish.

Select fine large River shrimp for this purpose. About 100 will serve a family of eight. Into a pot of water put a great quantity of salt, almost enough to make a brine. Pepper a great bunch of celery and celery tops, chopped fine; two dozen allspice, two blades of mace, one dozen cloves, mashed fine; thyme, parsley, bay leaf, chopped fine; Cayenne and a red pepper pod. When this has boiled so that all the flavor of the herbs have been thoroughly extracted, throw in the shrimp. Let them boil ten minutes and then set the pot aside and let the shrimp cool in their own water. Serve in a platter on a bed of cracked ice, and garnish with parsley sprigs. This dish is always served as a preliminary to a meal. A great deal of salt is required in boiling, as the shrimp absorb but little, and no after addition can quite give them the same taste as when boiled in the briny water.

### Stewed Shrimps.
#### Chevrettes à la Créole.

100 Fine Lake Shrimp. 1 Large Onion.
1 Tablespoonful of Butter. 1 Can of Tomatoes or 12 Fresh Ones.
4 Celery Stalks, 1 Clove of Garlic, 1 Sprig of Thyme.
2 Bay Leaves. Salt and Pepper to Taste.
A Dash of Cayenne.

Get about 100 large Lake shrimp for this recipe. Boil the shrimp first according to the recipe given above, and then pick off the shells, leaving the shrimp whole. Place them in a dish. Chop fine one large onion and brown it with a tablespoonful of butter. Add a can of tomatoes or twelve large, ripe tomatoes, chopped fine, in their own liquor. Stir well and brown lightly. Then add three or four stalks of celery, a clove of garlic, a dash of Cayenne, a sprig of thyme, two bay leaves, all chopped finely and seasoned with salt to taste. After this has cooked ten minutes, add the shrimp. Let them cook ten minutes longer and serve. Never pour water into stewed shrimps, as the tomato juice makes gravy enough.

### Fried Shrimps.
#### Chevrettes Frites.

100 Fine Lake Shrimp.
1 Cup of Milk. Grated Bread Crumbs.
Salt and Pepper to Taste. A Dash of Cayenne.
Fried Parsley and Parsley Tips and Olives to Garnish.

Use Fine Lake shrimp for this recipe. Boil first according to the recipe given for Boiled Shrimps. Then take off the fire, pick off shells and season well. Take a pan of milk, season well with salt and pepper. After rolling the shrimp well in this, roll them in grated bread crumbs or yellow cornmeal (the latter being preferable) and fry in boiling lard. The shrimp must swim in the lard. When they are a nice golden brown, skim out with a skimmer and drain on heated brown paper. Serve on a hot dish on a bed of fried parsley and garnish with parsley tips and olives.

### Baked Shrimps.
#### Chevrettes au Gratin.

100 Lake Shrimp. 1 Dozen Tomatoes.
1 Tablespoonful of Butter. 1 Cup of Grated Bread Crumbs or Crackers.

Boil the shrimps according to recipe. Butter a deep dish well and place within a layer of grated bread crumbs or powdered crackers. Pick and clean the shrimp and season well. Stew about a dozen tomatoes in a little butter and season with pepper and salt. Place a layer of the tomatoes in the dish and then a thin layer of crackers or grated bread and over this a layer of shrimp. Continue till you have four or five layers, the last being of the grated bread crumbs. Put little dots of butter here and there; place in the oven and bake till quite brown.

### Shrimp Pie.
#### Vol-au-Vent de Chevrettes.

100 Lake Shrimp.
2 Slices of Stale Bread. 2 Glasses of White Wine.
1 Blade of Mace. 3 Sprigs of Thyme.
¼ of a Ground Nutmeg.
3 Sprigs of Parsley. 1 Tablespoonful of Butter.
5 Tomatoes. ½ of a Celery Stalk.
1 Bay Leaf. ½ Pint of Oyster Liquor.

Boil and pick about 100 shrimp. Take two large slices of stale bread and break off the crusts, grating this fine. Moisten the bread with two glasses of white wine, and season highly with salt, pepper, a dash of Cayenne, ground nutmeg, chopped mace, thyme and parsley. Mix the shrimp with the bread and bake in a dish. Sprinkle over the grated crusts and dotting with butter. Serve this pie with a sauce of dressed shrimp. To make this, take a pint of shrimp, boiled and picked; put a tablespoonful of butter into a saucepan. Add the shrimp and four or five tomatoes, chopped fine; a little celery, thyme, one bay leaf, chopped fine; parsley (chopped) and mix thoroughly. Let it cook for about three or four minutes and add a half pint of oyster stock. This is delicious poured over the sliced pie.

### Shrimps in Tomato Catsup.
#### Chevrettes à la Sauce Tomate.

100 River Shrimp.
2 Tablespoonfuls of Tomato Catsup.
3 Hard-Boiled Eggs. Salt, Pepper and Cayenne to Taste.

Boil the shrimp and pick. Put them into a salad dish. Season well with black pepper and salt and a dash of Cayenne. Then add two tablespoonfuls of tomato catsup to every half pint of shrimps. Garnish with lettuce leaves and hard-boiled egg and serve.

### Shrimp Salad.
#### Mayonnaise de Chevrettes.

100 River or Lake. Shrimp.
1 Small Onion. 1 Bunch of Celery.
3 Hard-Boiled Eggs. Salt and Pepper to Taste.
Sliced Lemons, Beets and Celery Tips to Garnish.

Boil and pick the shrimp, according to the recipe given. If Lake shrimp are used, serve whole; if River shrimp, slice in two, as they will be more dainty, and season well with salt and pepper. Chop celery fine and add a little onion. Place the shrimp in the salad dish and pour over all fine Mayonnaise Sauce (see recipe) and garnish with sliced hard-boiled eggs, sliced lemon, beets and celery tops, making a beautiful and welcome dish at any luncheon, tea or home affair.

### A Shrimp Bush.
#### Buisson de Chevrettes.

100 Lake Shrimp.
Celery Tips. Asparagus Tips.

A Shrimp Bush is a famous Creole hors d'oeuvre, and forms a very handsome table decoration also. Boil the shrimp according to recipe. (See recipe Boiled Shrimps.) Take a glass fruit or cake stand, the fruit stand with several tiers being the prettier. As shrimp are small, they cannot be hung gracefully around the stand as in a Crawfish Bush. (See recipe.) They are, therefore, piled, first, into a small deep dish, and a close cover is put on to press them down. They are then turned over and will be found clinging together in one solid mass. If a cake stand is used, set a glass bowl or goblet on it. Place the shrimp on top of this glass bowl or goblet; then take dainty bits of celery tips and asparagus tips, and heap around as for a border. Another row is formed a little lower, and again intermingled with asparagus tips and celery tops, between which the pink shrimp are gracefully placed and glimmer. The effect is very pretty. The shrimp are served from the bush as an hors d'oeuvre. The effect of the pink against the green looks for all the world like a bush of green and red.

### CRABS.
#### Des Crabes.

New Orleans points with pride, and justly, not only to the splendid supply of crabs that are to be found at all seasons in her markets, but to the various delightful ways that the natives have of serving them. The following are recipes that have been handed down by the Creoles from generation to generation, and no modern innovations of cookery have been able to improve upon them.

### Hard Shell Crabs.
### Crabes Durs.

Many Northerners object to eating hard-shell crabs on account of the difficulty in picking them. Some Northern cooks have gone so far as to declare the hard-shell crab an unpalatable and indigestible article of food on account of its shell. This idea, of course, is very amusing. One Northern authority goes so far as to declare that the crab can never take the place of the aristocratic lobster, the latter being far more digestible. In reality there is no comparison in the delicacy of the meats of these fish, which are, indeed, of the lobster variety, the hard-shell crab being the smaller, and by far the more delicate. And as for the soft shell crab, it is a born aristocrat and is acknowledged as such by the most fastidious epicureans. There is a science in eating the hard-shell crab cooked in its own shell. The Creoles have reduced this to a fine point, and a crab may be eaten without once using the fingers, if one only follows the following simple direction:

### How to Eat a Hard-Shell Crab Cooked In Its Shell.

The shell and claws should be cracked in the kitchen, very gently, before being brought to the table if the crabs are boiled and served whole. By a delicate manipulation of the knife and fork, remove the "apron" or "tablier," which is the small loose shell running to a point about the middle of the under shell. Then cut the crab claws off, still using the knife and fork; and finally cut the crab into parts, and these again in two. Proceed to extract the meat from each quarter with the fork and eat with salt and pepper. It is considered quite "comme il faut" to use the fingers, however, in holding the crabs, extracting the meat with the prongs of the fork.

### Boiled Crabs.
### Crabes Bouillis.

1 Dozen Fine Crabs. 1 Bunch of Celery and Celery Tops.
2 Dozen Allspice. 4 Sprigs of Thyme.
4 Sprigs of Sweet Basil.
4 Sprigs of Sweet Marjoram. 3 Blades of Mace.
3 Bay Leaves. 4 Sprigs of Chives.
A Red Pepper Pod. A Dash of Cayenne.
Black Pepper and Salt Sufficient to Make a Brine.

Proceed in the same manner as for boiling shrimp. Buy fine, large crabs. The livelier they are the better. The crabs must be alive when put into the pot. Have ready a large pot of water. Throw in bunches of celery tops, stalks of celery chopped fine, four or five large sprigs each of thyme, chopped sweet basil, marjoram, chives, two dozen allspice, three blades of mace, three bay leaves, chopped fine; a pod of red pepper, a dash of Cayenne, black pepper and salt enough to make the water briny. When this has boiled long enough to have extracted all the flavor of the herbs, throw in the live crabs and let them boil rapidly for about ten minutes, or until the shells are a bright red, but do not let them boil one minute longer than this, as they will become watery. Let them cool a little in their own water and then take out, strip off the "dead man's fingers," crack the claws, without breaking open, and pile high in a broad platter and serve with salt and pepper.

### Stewed Crabs.
### Crabes à la Créole.

1 Dozen Large Live Crabs.
Tablespoonful of Butter or Lard.
1 Stalk Chopped Celery.
1 Dozen Fresh Tomatoes or 1 Can.
Thyme, Parsley, Bay Leaf, 1 Clove, Garlic.
Salt and Cayenne to Taste.

Boil a dozen fine large crabs about five minutes in order to kill them. Take off the fire and place in a dish. When sufficiently cooled, cut off the claws and crack, separating the joints. Remove the "apron" or "tablier" of the crab and the "dead man's fingers," and take off the spongy substance. These are the portions that are uneatable. Remove the shell, cut the body of the crab into four parts, cutting down the center and across. Chop a large onion very fine and brown with butter or lard, using a tablespoonful of either. Add a dozen fine, large, fresh tomatoes, chopped fine, in their liquor, and brown nicely. Stir in chopped celery, thyme, parsley, one bay leaf, chopped fine; pepper and salt to taste, and a dash of Cayenne pepper. Add one clove of garlic, chopped fine. Taste and add more seasoning if necessary. Let the mixture cook ten minutes, then add the crabs and let them cook ten minutes longer. Never add water to this sauce, as the liquor of the tomatoes is sufficient and makes an excellent sauce. This is a fine fast-day dish. Serve with boiled rice or potatoes boiled whole.

### Fried Crabs.
### Crabes Frits.

1 Dozen Fine Large Crabs.
1 Pint of Milk.
6 Tablespoonfuls of Butter or Lard.
Stale Bread Crumbs, Grated.
Thyme, Parsley, Bay Leaf, Onions.

Boil the crabs according to recipe. Cut off the claws and crack and cut the crabs into quarters as for stewing. Season well with pepper and salt. Have ready a pint of milk. Mix pepper and salt in proprotions of about two teaspoonfuls each. Have ready a pan of boiling lard and a plate of grated bread crumbs. Dip the crabs into the milk and then roll in the bread crumbs and drop into the boiling lard, frying about ten minutes or until a golden brown. Serve on a platter with the claws piled in the center, the bodies of the crabs grouped nicely around, and garnish with sprigs of parsley. This is a delicious way of serving Hard-Shell Crabs.

### Stuffed Crabs.

Crabes Farcis.

1 Dozen Large Fine Crabs.
1 Large Onion.   1 Clove of Garlic.
1 Bay Leaf. 3 Sprigs of Thyme.
3 Sprigs of Parsley.
Hot Pepper.   1 Tablespoonful of Butter.
Salt to Taste.
1 Cup of Wet Bread.

Boil the Crabs according to recipe. Take off the fire and let them cool in their own water. When cool crack the claws and pick out all the meat. In like manner, after having removed the uneatable portions, pick out all the meat from the bodies. Season well with salt and black pepper. Chop the onions and herbs very fine. Put a tablespoonful of butter heaping over into the frying pan. As it melts, add the chopped onion, and when it begins to fry, add the crab meat, which has been thoroughly seasoned with the chopped thyme, bay leaf, parsley and a dash of Cayenne to taste. Let this fry and add a small clove of garlic, chopped very fine, and finally add the bread, which has been wet and thoroughly squeezed of all water. Mix this well with the ingredients in the frying pan and let it fry about five minutes longer. Then take off the fire and let it get cool. Take a dozen of the finest and largest crab shells, or as many as this mixture will fill, and wash and stuff with the mixture, forming it into a rolling lump. Sprinkle this with grated bread crumbs and put a dot of butter on top, or, better still, sprinkle with the melted butter; place in the oven and bake about five minutes, or until a nice brown. Place on a platter and garnish with sprigs of parsley or celery tops. This is an excellent method of preparing stuffed crabs for family use.

### Stuffed Crabs—No. 2.

Crabes Farcis.

2 Dozen Large Fine Crabs.
Grated Bread Crumbs.
Salt and Pepper.   1 Tablespoonful of Butter.
1 Bay Leaf. 2 Hard-Boiled Eggs.
Thyme, Parsley and Onion.
Cayenne to Taste.

Boil the crabs according to recipe. Clean and cut and pick out all the meat. Chop an onion fine; chop the thyme, bay leaf, and parsley and hard-boiled eggs, and mix well with the crab meat. Season highly with hot pepper and salt to taste. Put one tablespoonful heaping over with butter into the frying pan. As it melts, add the onion and fry, being careful not to burn. Then add the crab meat, and, if desired, the very small clove of a garlic, chopped very fine. Let this fry about five minutes, stirring constantly. Mix thoroughly, fry three minutes longer, and then take off the stove. Stuff the crab shells, forming a rolling lump in the middle. Sprinkle lightly with grated bread crumbs, and put a dot of butter on top. Place in a quick oven and let them bake about five minutes, or until a nice brown. The same or even better results are obtained by omitting the egg, many claiming that the delicate flavor of the crab meat is more daintily preserved without this addition. This is a delightful way of serving crabs for luncheons, or where it is not necessary to make, as the Creoles say, " a long family dish."

### Deviled Crabs.

Crabes à le Diable.

1 Dozen Fine Large Crabs.
2 Tablespoonfuls of Flour.
1 Tablespoon of Salt.
1 Tablespoonful of Chopped Parsley.
1 Half Pint of Cream.   ¼ Nutmeg Grated.
1 Tablespoonful of Butter.
The Yolks of 4 Hard-Boiled Eggs.
Salt and Cayenne to Taste.

Boil the crabs according to recipe. Take out and drain after they have cooled in their own water. Break off the claws, separate the shells, remove the spongy portions and the "dead man's fingers," and then pick out the meat. Put the cream on to boil, rub the flour and butter together well and add to the boiling cream. Stir and cook for two minutes. Take from the fire and add the crab meat, the yolks of the hard-boiled eggs, mashed very fine; the chopped parsley, grated nutmeg, salt and Cayenne. Clean the upper shells of the crabs, fill them with the mixture, brush over with a beaten egg, sprinkle with bread crumbs and put in a quick oven to brown;

or, better still, if you have a frying basket, plunge the crabs into the boiling fat or lard until a nice brown. But many prefer them baked.

### Scalloped Crabs.
#### Coquilles de Crabes.

The Meat of 1 Dozen Picked Crabs.
A Dash of Grated Nutmeg.
Bread Crumbs. 1 Egg.
Pepper and Salt to Taste.

Boil and pick the crabs according to recipe given above. Beat an egg thoroughly and add to the meat which has been seasoned highly with Cayenne and salt to taste. Take one clove of garlic, chop fine and add, then sift into this mixture fine grated bread crumbs or cracker crumbs, and mix thoroughly. Beat an egg, roll the crabs into boulets or graceful meat balls, and then bind by rolling lightly in the egg. Roll in the bread crumbs, grated nicely, and then drop into boiling lard, and fry until a pale golden brown, which will generally require about three minutes. The secret is to have them cooked just enough, for, as a rule, they are generally overdone. Wash and clean the shells thoroughly; wipe dry, set a boulet in the center of each and garnish prettily with sprigs of parsley and sliced lemon. This is a dainty dish for breakfast or luncheon. They must be served very hot.

### Crab Croquettes.
#### Crabes en Croquettes.

1 Dozen Crabs.
1 Cup of Wet Bread, Squeezed Well.
1 Onion. 1 Clove of Garlic. 1 Bay Leaf.
1 Sprig of Thyme. 3 Sprigs of Parsley.
1 Tablespoonful of Butter.
Salt and Cayenne to Taste.

Boil the crabs clean and pick. Then season the meat well with salt and pepper. Chop the onion fine, also the herbs. Put a tablespoonful of butter in the frying pan, and as it melts, add the chopped onion. When it begins to fry add the crab meat which has been mixed thoroughly with the chopped thyme, bay leaf, parsley and garlic. Add a dash of Cayenne and put in the frying pan with the onion. Add the bread which has been thoroughly squeezed, and mix all and fry about three minutes. Take off the fire, and when cool form the mixture into cylindrical shapes of about two or three inches in length and one in thickness. Roll in grated bread crumbs and fry in boiling lard. Serve hot on a dish nicely garnished with parsley and sliced lemon.

### Crab Salad.
#### Crabes en Salade.

2 Dozen Fine Large Crabs.
12 Celery Stalks. 1 Dozen Olives.
A Mayonnaise Sauce.

Boil the crabs according to recipe. Clean and pick out all the meat. Season well with salt and pepper and a dash of Cayenne. Chop the celery fine and mix with the crab meat. Place on a dish in pyramidal shape and pour over nicely a Sauce à la Mayonnaise. (See recipe.) Garnish tastefully with sliced hard-boiled eggs, sliced beets, asparagus or celery tips on top and around with sprigs of parsley and asparagus tips, with sliced lemon and sliced hard-boiled egg alternating. This is a delicious salad.

### Crab Salad No. 2.
#### Crabes en Salade.

1 Dozen Large Crabs.
2 Tablespoonfuls of Olive Oil.
1 Tablespoonful of French Vinegar.
1 Saltspoonful Salt. 1 Head Lettuce.
Pepper and Cayenne to Taste.

Pick the boiled crabs carefully, keeping the pieces as large as possible. Lay in a salad bowl. Mix a dressing of two tablespoonfuls of sweet oil, one of French vinegar, one saltspoon of salt, black pepper and Cayenne, according to taste, and pour over the crabs which have been cooled in the ice box. Clean the lettuce well and put a row of crisp leaves around the edge of the salad dish. Garnish nicely with sliced lemon and hard-boiled eggs sliced. This is a delightful and simple way that the Creoles have of making crab salad. The above quantity will serve six persons. Increase in proportion to the number to be served.

### Crab Pie.
#### Vol-au-Vent de Crabes.

1 Dozen Large Crabs.
Sliced Stale Bread.
Butter. Milk. Cayenne.
Salt.

Boil according to recipe one dozen fine large crabs and pick out all the meat. Season nicely with salt, Cayenne and chopped thyme and bay leaf. Take stale bread and slice very thin. Lay in a little milk to moisten. Butter a baking pan and cover the bottom with a layer of bread. Then put in a layer of crab meat and lay over at intervals slices of lemon cut very fine and thin. Dot here and there with bits of butter, and then spread over another layer of bread. Then another layer of crabs, and repeat till the meat is used up. Lay on top a thick sprinkling of bread crumbs, dotted with butter. Place in the oven and bake for about twenty minutes. Serve hot.

### Soft-Shell Crabs.
### Crabes Mous.

The soft-shell crab is greatly affected by epicures, and is a dainty dish that graces the most aristocratic tables.

The soft-shell crab has always been considered a great luxury in New Orleans, where its possibilities as a most delicate and savory dish were first discovered. Northern epicures quick to appreciate the toothsome morsel, returned to their homes loud in their praises of this Creole discovery. The soft-shell crab is now being shipped North, and is a popular feature of the Northern markets, though the prices range very high. It is said that the crab is so delicate that it does not stand shipment very well; sudden stopping of the express car often kills them; a clap of thunder will frighten them to death, while a sunbeam through glass will kill every one it shines upon. The soft-shell crab is found the year round in the New Orleans French Market. This crab is at its best when prepared according to the following Creole methods:

### Fried Soft-Shell Crabs.
### Crabes Mous Frites.

1 Dozen Soft-Shell Crabs.
1 Quart of Milk.   Bread Crumbs.
Salt, Pepper and Cayenne to Taste.

The greatest care must be taken in preparing and cleaning the crab. Wash carefully, removing all sand, but do not scald or blanch them, as this destroys the fine flavor completely. Remove the spongy, feathery substances under the side points. These are called the "man-eaters," and are very irritating and indigestible. Remove also the sand bag or "sand pouch" from under the shells just between the eyes; also remove the "tablier" or "apron." Then wash "tablier" or "apron." Then wash well in cold water and dry with a clean towel. Take a pint of milk and season well with pepper and salt; season the crabs and crack them in the milk, rubbing thoroughly, so that the milk may thoroughly impregnate them. Take out and roll in a little sifted flour. Pat lightly with the hand, shake off superfluous flour and fry in boiling grease, being always careful to have sufficient grease in the pan for the crabs to swim in it. When a delicate golden brown, take out of the grease with a skimmer. Drain on a piece of heated brown paper, and serve on a bed of fried parsley, with garnishes of sliced lemon. Serve with "Sauce à la Tartare." (See recipe.)

Soft-shell Crabs are of too delicate a flavor to be dipped in egg batter or burdened with bread crumbs.

### Broiled Soft-Shell Crabs.
### Crabes à la Créole.

1 Dozen Soft-Shell Crabs.
1 Pint of Milk.
4 Tablespoonfuls of Flour, Sifted.
Butter.   Sliced Lemon.
Parsley Garnish.

It was a celebrated New Orleans chef who first decided to broil the Soft-Shell Crab. His success was great and "Crabes à la Créole" were in great demand at once at the hotels and restaurants. To broil the Soft-Shell Crab always use the double wire broiler. Clean the crab according to the method given above and wash in cold water. Dry with a clean towel and season well. Season a pint of milk with salt and black pepper, and soak the crabs in it so as to thoroughly impregnate them with the milk. Then pat lightly with a little flour and brush over with melted butter. Place between the broiler and broil till a delicate brown over a slow fire. It will generally require about fifteen minutes to cook thoroughly. Serve on a platter, nicely garnished with parsley, sprigs and lemon cut in quarters. Pour over the crabs a little melted butter and chopped parsley, and you will have a famous Creole dish, fit for the table of a king— a dish served at the most aristocratic functions.

### CRAWFISH.
### Des Écrevisses.

Besides the famous Crawfish Bisque (Bisque d'Écrevisses. See recipe) the Creoles have dainty ways of serving this typical Louisiana shell fish. Among the most popular are the following:

### Boiled Crawfish.
### Des Écrevisses Bouillies.

50 Crawfish.   1 Gallon of Water.
1 Herb Bouquet.
Half Gallon of French Vinegar.

Put the water on to boil, adding the chopped herb bouquet, one clove of garlic (chopped fine), one dozen allspice and six cloves. When the water has boiled long enough to have extracted all the juices of the herb bouquet, add white wine or the vinegar and salt—enough to make it almost briny, and Cayenne enough to make it hot. Then throw in the crawfish and let them boil about twenty minutes or until a bright red. Set them to cool in their own water and serve on a platter piled high in pyramidal shape, and garnish nicely with sprigs of parsley and sliced lemon. Serve with salt and pepper, oil and Chili vinegar, each person making the dressing as it suits his taste.

### Crawfish Baked à la Créole.

Écrevisses Gratinées à la Créole.

50 Crawfish.  2 Livers.
½ Can of Mushrooms.
2 Tablespoonfuls of Butter.
1 Bouquet of Fine Herbs.
The Yolks of 2 Eggs.
Salt, Pepper and Cayenne to Taste.

Boil according to recipe fifty large fine crawfish. When cooked, allow them to cool in their own water. Clean them, picking off the shells and leaving the crawfish whole. Take out all the smallest ones, and cut off the tail ends of the largest and place with the small ones; take the remainder of the large crawfish and cut up, and make a dressing with two chopped livers, parsley, the minced contents of one-half can of mushrooms, the bouquet of fine herbs consisting of thyme, bay leaf, sweet marjoram, etc.; chop a half dozen shallots and add to the dressing, and season highly with Cayenne and salt and black pepper to taste. Cut up the yolks of two eggs and mix with a cup of the soft portion of bread, which has been wet and thoroughly squeezed of all water. Place two tablespoonfuls of butter in a frying pan and add the dressing when it begins to heat; cook about ten minutes and then place in the dish in which the crawfish are to be served, making a bed of the dressing. Arrange with symmetry and grace the reserve crawfish upon this bed, cover lightly with the rest of the stuffing, and dot with small bits of butter, after sprinkling with grated bread crumbs. Pour over all a Cream Sauce and the juice of a lemon. Place in the oven and let it bake about ten or fifteen minutes, and serve with Cream Sauce, seasoned with lemon juice. (See recipe Cream Sauce.)

### A Crawfish Bush.

Buisson d'Écrevisses.

100 Fine Crawfish.  Celery Tips.
Asparagus Tips.  Parsley Tips.

This is a celebrated Creole hors d'oeuvre, as also a very handsome and graceful table garnish. Boil the Crawfish according to recipe. (See recipe.) Take a glass fruit or cake stand and place in the center of the table. Set a goblet upon it. Fit the goblet with celery tips and parsley tips, and hang a number of Crawfish gracefully around the goblet from the rim or outer edges. Continue hanging the dish with celery, asparagus and parsley tips, and hanging the Crawfish around the edges of the fruit stand, and in and out amid the greenery. The effect of the red amid the green is very pretty, presenting the appearance of a beautiful bush of red and green. The Crawfish are served from the bush.

### TURTLE.

De la Tortue.

In addition to the delicious soups already given, the Creoles serve turtle after the following manner.

### Green Turtle Steaks.

Filets de Tortue.

2 Pounds of Turtle Steaks.
2 Tablespoonfuls of Butter.
Salt and Pepper to Taste. Sliced Lemon and Parsley to Garnish.
Currant Jelly Sauce or Sauce Poivrade.

Select the female turtle, as the meat is best. If bought alive from the market, clean according to recipe. (See recipe for cleaning turtle. Otherwise the butcher may prepare it as is frequently done in the New Orleans market.) Turtle meat is very irregular, therefore cut the meat into thick slices or steaks, about the size of a filet of beef, and batter down with the hands to make smooth and regular. Then fry in butter. Season well with salt and pepper and garnish with parsley and lemon, and serve with Currant Jelly Sauce or the delightful Sauce Poivrade. (See recipes.)

### Stewed Turtle.

Ragoût de Tortue a la Bourgeoise.

2 Pounds of Turtle Meat. 1 Onion.
1 Tablespoonful of Butter or Lard.
1 Tablespoonful of Flour.
1 Bay Leaf.  1 Clove of Garlic.  1 Sprig of Thyme.
1 Cup of Water.

A Wineglassful of Sherry or Madeira.
Cut the meat of the turtle about an inch in size. Chop an onion and put all into a saucepan, with a tablespoonful of lard to brown. As it begins to brown, add a tablespoonful of flour, one bay leaf, one clove of garlic, and a sprig of thyme, chopped very fine. Mix this thoroughly with the turtle meat, then add a wineglassful of Sherry or Madeira, and a cup of water, and cook for half an hour.

## CHAPTER XI.

### SALT AND CANNED FISH.

#### Poissons Salés.

Halibut, Salmon, Fresh Codfish, Fresh Lobster, Shad and other fish peculiar to the Northern and Eastern waters are rarely seen on New Orleans tables, except in the great hotels and restaurants, which import them. With these fish, in their fresh state, this book will not treat. But the Salt Codfish, Salted Mackerel and Canned Salmon are in general family use. The Salted Mackerel and Codfish, indeed, enter very largely into the daily household economy of New Orleans, especially on fast days, as also sardines. The following recipes are modeled after Creole methods of preparation:

### CODFISH.
#### Salted Codfish.
#### De la Morue.

First, and above all, it is necessary to "dessaler la Morue," as the Creoles put it, or to remove every trace and appearance of the salt in which the fish has been put up. Always soak the codfish at least overnight or twenty-four hours before using in cold water, changing the water as often as possible, to assist in removing the salt; and always boil on a hot fire fifteen or twenty minutes before making into any of the following dishes:

#### Boiled Codfish.
#### La Morue Bouillie.

Codfish. 3 Dozen Oysters.
1 Tablespoonful of Butter. 1 Tablespoonful of Flour.
2 Gills of Fresh Cream or Milk.
The Oyster Water.
Salt and Pepper to Taste.
A Dash of Cayenne.

Boil the Codfish about thirty or forty minutes, after soaking overnight; drain and serve with an Oyster Sauce, or Sauce aux Huîtres, prepared as follows: Make a Cream Sauce (See recipe), only use, in this case, the strained juice of the oyster to blend the flour and butter, and add the rich cream or milk to make up the desired quantity, using always good judgment. Scald the oysters in their own water about three minutes, and then add to the sauce, mixing thoroughly, seasoning with salt, pepper and Cayenne, using preferably celery salt; let it boil up once and serve with the boiled Codfish. Egg Sauce (see recipe) may also be used with Boiled Codfish, but is not to be compared to the Oyster Sauce.

#### Fried Codfish.
#### La Morue Frite.

Codfish. 1 Pint of Milk.
1 Egg. 1 Cup of Grated Bread Crumbs.
Salt and Pepper to Taste.
Parsley and Lemon to Garnish.

Soak the Codfish overnight, and boil twenty minutes, or until very tender; take out and cut into slices of one-inch thickness, and dry with a clean towel; have ready a pint of milk, and season well with pepper only; season the Codfish, rubbing a little black pepper to taste and a dash of Cayenne over it. Soak the fish in the milk, and have ready some crushed bread crumbs and a well-beaten egg; when the fish is well soaked, take out of the milk, and dip each slice first into the egg, and then roll in bread crumbs, patting lightly, and drop in to the boiling lard; the fish must swim in the lard. When fried a golden brown, take out with a skimmer, drain off all fat, and serve hot on a bed of fried parsley, garnished with sliced lemon.

#### Stewed Codfish.
#### Morue Sautée à la Lyonnaise.

1 Dozen Small Potatoes, or Left-Over.
Salt Cod, Enough for Six Persons.
1 Quart of Milk. 1 Dozen White Onions.
3 Tablespoonfuls of Butter.
1 Tablespoonful of Flour Blended With Two of Milk.

If the potatoes are not the leftover from the day before, wash and peel, and also the onion; boil the potatoes till tender; soak the fish overnight, and boil for twenty minutes, or until tender. Then cut the fish into pieces of about two or three inches in length. Put a tablespoonful of lard in the stewpan and lay in the potatoes and then the onions, and the Codfish on top; add enough cold water to cover the whole, and let it simmer until the fish is well cooked. Then take out the fish, and allow the potatoes and onions to simmer on. Remove every piece of bone from the fish, and trim edges nicely. Take another saucepan and dissolve in another stewpan the butter and flour, as directed above; let this simmer gently without browning, and then put in the potatoes, onions and fish in the order given above; pour over this the quart of cream or milk; let it simmer for about ten minutes more till the milk comes to a boil, and serve hot.

### Creamed Codfish.

Morue à la Crème.

3 Cups of Picked Codfish.
1 Pint and a Half of Cream.
The Yolk of 1 Egg.

Soak the codfish overnight, and then let it boil about forty minutes. Then take off scald again and drain, and again scald and drain, allowing it to stand each time about four or five minutes before changing the water. Put one large tablespoonful of butter in the frying pan; when melted add the flour and blend, without browning; then add the milk, stirring constantly until it boils, and then add the fish, seasoning highly with pepper and Cayenne. Let it boil about ten minutes longer, and take off the fire; then add the yolk of an egg which has been beaten thoroughly, and serve hot, with plain boiled potatoes buttered.

### Codfish Balls.

Croquettes de Morue.

2 Cups of Picked Codfish.
2 Cups of Mashed Potatoes.
½ Cup of Cream.
Bread Crumbs.   2 Beaten Eggs.
Pepper and Cayenne to Taste.

Soak the Codfish overnight and boil until tender. Pour off this water, and scald again with hot water; pick fine, scald again and then drain thoroughly, pressing out all the water. Mash the potatoes, and melt about three tablespoonfuls of butter and mix well in the potatoes. Then add the Codfish and mix thoroughly, seasoning with about a teaspoonful of black pepper, and a dash of Cayenne to taste. Add this to the cream, and again mix. Mold the Codfish into round or oval balls; then roll in the egg, which has been well beaten, and pass through the bread crumbs, patting gently, and lay them in a frying basket, if you have one, and sink into the boiling lard. Otherwise drop into the boiling lard, having tested the heat with a bit of bread. The balls must swim in the lard. When a golden brown, lift out the basket, or skim out the balls with a skimmer; drain well of all the fat by laying on a heated brown paper, and then serve hot on a dish garnished with sprigs of parsley. This quantity will make about a dozen and a half balls or croquettes. There is no difference between the preparation of the Codfish Ball and the Codfish Croquette, the only difference being in the form of molding, the croquette being oval or elongated, in cylindrical shapes, and the ball being molded round and a little flattened on top.

### Codfish Bacalao.

Bacalao à la Vizcaina.

1 Pound of Salted Codfish.
1 Large Onion, Chopped Fine.
1 Pint of Rich Tomato Sauce.
2 Cloves of Garlic, Chopped Fine. Croutons.
1 Red Pepper.
2 Tablespoonfuls of Olive Oil.
Pepper to Taste.  6 Tomatoes.
Thyme. Bay Leaf. Parsley.

Soak the Codfish well overnight, and in the morning boil for about forty-five minutes, until very tender. When you set it to boil, put the fish first in cold water. After it has boiled, scald again thoroughly, and pick out all the bones and set away to cool. Then prepare a rich Tomato Sauce, according to the following directions: Take six large fresh tomatoes, or a half can of tomatoes, and add a heaping tablespoonful of butter, four sprigs of parsley, thyme and two bay leaves, all chopped very fine; add two chopped onions and a clove of garlic, chopped fine, and which has been fried in a little butter. Set the saucepan, with the sauce, into boiling water, and add pepper and Cayenne and a pinch of salt to taste. Stew very gently for about two hours or longer, if necessary. Then strain the sauce and make a roux with one tablespoonful of butter and two of flour; stir and let it brown lightly, and stir in the sauce. Boil about four minutes longer until rich and thick. Then fry the remaining large onion and clove of garlic, chopped very fine, in a gill of olive oil, or two tablespoonfuls of butter if the taste of the oil is disliked, and when it browns add this to the sauce and a red sweet pepper, finely chopped. Cut about a dozen Croûtons, in dice or diamond shapes, from the soft part of the bread, and fry in boiling lard. Heat a dish, put the Codfish into it, pour over the Tomato Sauce, border the dish with the fried Croûtons, and set in the oven, allowing it to bake ten or fifteen minutes longer. The Spanish red peppers are the best for this sauce. Black pepper may be added if desired.

## SALT MACKEREL.
### Du Maquereau.

Salt Mackerel is either boiled or broiled, and either method of cooking according to the subjoined recipes makes a most palatable and delicately toothsome dish.

### Boiled Salt Mackerel.
### Maquereau Bouilli.

2 Salt Mackerel.
2 Tablespoonfuls of Butter.
Chopped Parsley and Sliced Lemon to Garnish.

Soak the Mackerel overnight, and in the morning take out of the water, wash thoroughly, taking off every portion of salt, and wash again. Have ready a deep pan of boiling water; place the Mackerel within and let it boil ten or fifteen minutes until done, which can be known by the flesh beginning to part from the bones. Serve whole on a platter garnished with parsley. Pour over the Mackerel melted butter and chopped parsley, and bring to the table very hot.

Mackerel boiled or broiled is a very nice breakfast dish on fast days. Serve with potatoes, boiled whole or made into croquettes.

### Broiled Mackerel.
### Maquereau Grillé.

2 Salt Mackerel. 1 Cup of Milk.
2 Tablespoonfuls of Butter, or a Cream Sauce.
Sliced Lemon, Olives and Parsley Sprigs to Garnish.

Soak the Mackerel and wash thoroughly as directed above, only using boiling water. Have ready some milk, seasoned well with black pepper and soak the Mackerel in the milk until thoroughly impregnated. Take out and wipe dry with a towel. Then dredge the Mackerel with butter, and place between a double broiler, over a slow fire, broiling about fifteen or twenty minutes, the under side being allowed to broil first. When done, take off and pour over melted butter and chopped parsley; garnish the dish with sprigs of parsley, sliced lemons and olives, and serve hot. A Cream Sauce may be also served instead of the butter, and makes a very delicious dish.

### SALMON.
### Mayonnaise de Saumon.

1 Can of Salmon. 2 Heads of Crisp Lettuce.
1 Cup of Milk.
1 Tablespoonful of Butter. 2 Tablespoonfuls of Flour.
1 Tablespoonful of Chopped Parsley.
Salt and Pepper to Taste.
Sauce a la Mayonnaise.

A Mayonnaise of Salmon is a very good luncheon dish, and is frequently served in New Orleans. To one can of Salmon allow two good sized heads of young lettuce. Make a bed of the crisp hearts of the leaves, and tear the other leaves into small pieces with a fork, making very delicate shreds. Drain the oil from the can of Salmon, and separate the fish into flakes. Take a cupful of boiling milk and a tablespoonful of butter and two of flour, and stir over the fire until quite smooth. Add to this a tablespoonful of chopped parsley and the Salmon. Season with pepper and salt, and let it cook about ten minutes. Set away to cool, and then place on the bed of lettuce leaves. Cover with a Sauce à la Mayonnaise (see recipe), and garnish nicely with sliced hard-boiled eggs, celery tips, etc., and serve.

### Salmon Salad.

Saumon en Salade.

1 Can of Salmon.
1-3 the Quantity of Chopped Celery.
2 Hard-Boiled Eggs.
Sliced Lemon.   Olives.   1 Pickled Beet.
A Plain French Dressing.

Canned Salmon may be made into a delightful salad for luncheon or supper. Flake the salmon, heap into a salad bowl, and mix with chopped celery, using one-third of the latter in proportion to the quantity of salmon. Add a Plain French Dressing. (See recipe.) When ready to serve, turn into a salad dish, on which you have arranged a crisp bed of lettuce. Garnish with sliced lemon, olives and hard-boiled eggs, and with one daintily sliced pickled beet.

### HERRINGS.
### Des Harengs.

The Salted Herrings, such as come to New Orleans, must first of all be soaked thoroughly overnight, or longer, to take away all salt. Then they are cleaned nicely and broiled and served with a cream sauce or drawn butter sauce, preferably the former. They are also cut into filets and eaten without further cooking or "Crû," as we say here, and also as an hors d'oeuvre.

### ANCHOVY.
### Des Anchois.

Anchovies are served as a preliminary to the most aristocratic dinners, being drained of the oil which clings to them after being taken from the can. Three or four anchovies are then placed between delicate soda biscuit, and tied with a bit of ribbon in squares, with a dainty bow cut short in the center. The effect is very pretty. The anchovies are also mashed and placed between the crackers, like a sandwich. Either way is excellent and elegant.

### Anchovy Salad.

### Salade d'Anchois.

This salad is a dainty dish for luncheon or supper. Have an oval dish and arrange the anchovies, drained of oil, crosswise on a bed of crisp lettuce, or of chopped watercress. Surround with a border of chopped whites of eggs and a similar border of chopped watercresses, and pour over all a sour French Dressing. (See recipe.) Anchovies are used as an elegant hors d'oeuvre.

## CHAPTER XII.

## MEATS.

### Des Viandes.

Meats are, of course, common to every clime and country, but not every people have the palatable and appetizing methods of preparation that have been handed down to the Creoles of Louisiana by their French and Spanish ancestors and so modified and improved upon that it may be said that they have created a new school of cookery in the choice preparation and serving of beef, veal, mutton, pork and venison. Our "roties," or roasts, our methods of broiling, our delightful "ragouts," our famous "grillades," our unique "daubes," in a word, our dozen and one highly nutritious and eminently agreeable combinations of meats, with vegetables, and our unequaled manner of seasoning, have given to the Creole kitchen a fame that has been as lasting as well deserved.

The Creoles have discovered that almost any portion of the beef from the head to the tail may be delicately and temptingly prepared, so as to please even the most fastidious palates. They have reduced the science of cooking meats to a practical system that works the most beneficial effects in the homes of the poor, and which enables the family of moderate means to live not only economically, but with as much real ease and luxury, even as the wealthy classes.

The secret of cooking meat properly, of course, lies much in the seasoning and the relative time of cooking different varieties; but much indeed, everything depends upon the choice of the meat. The following

### Guides in Choosing Meat

are given, so that the housekeeper may make no mistake in this important choice of the quality of meat which she selects for her family:

Beef, when young, has a fine, open grain and good red color. The fatty part should be a yellowish white, for, when very yellow the meat is seldom of the best. Beef in which the fat is hard and skinny and the lean meat a deep red, with coarse fibers, is of an inferior quality; when the meat is old, it can be told by a line of horny textures running through the meat of the ribs. The lean on the cut surface should show a deep purplish red tint, and the beef should be marbled with fat, which shows the animals have been well fed.

In Mutton the cut surface should have the same purplish tint, but should be quite even in hue throughout. The color of the muscle should be neither too pale nor too dark. If pale and moist, it indicates that the animal was young or diseased; and if dark and livid, it shows that in all probability the animal was slaughtered, but died with the blood in it. Both muscle and fat should be elastic yet firm to the touch, not moist or sodden, and the fat should be free from blood specks.

While the raw fat of beef should be of a light yellow color, like that of suet, the fat of mutton should be white. The quality of meat depends largely upon the free intermixture of streaks of fat with muscular fiber. The muscular fibers should not be large or coarse, nor should there be any gummy or purple-looking fluid in the cellular tissues. The surface of good meat should be perfectly dry, and even the cut surface should scarcely wet the finger.

The muscular fiber of beef in poor condition or wasting from disease is pale in color, and a quantity of watery fat of bad color is mixed up with it. The meat itself is wet, flabby and inelastic and pits when the point of the finger is pressed against it. Such meat, it need hardly be said, is unfit for human food.

The odor of good meat should be slight and not by any means disagreeable. An unpleasant odor indicates that putrefaction has begun or that the meat is diseased. A very good plan to detect any unpleasantness of odor is to thrust a clean knife into the flesh. If any disagreeable odor clings, the meat is unfit for use.

The internal parts, that are so generally used in cooking, such as the heart, liver, kidneys, sweetbreads, should have no unpleasant smell and must be free from spots of congestion or bruises. As these parts decompose much more rapidly than the flesh of the carcass, they should not be kept long before being cooked, and, when cooked, should not be subjected to a very strong or prolonged heat, because it makes them hard and indigestible.

The amount of bone in meat varies considerably, but, on the average, it is not less than 8 per cent. In shins and legs of beef, it amounts to one-third, and sometimes to one-half the total weight, while in the neck and brisket it amounts to about 10 per cent. The most economical parts are the round and thick flank, then the sticking piece and brisket, and lastly the leg. In mutton and pork the leg is the most profitable, and then the shoulder.

Sheep heads make excellent broth, and ox tail a very good soup, but both require longer time to extract the nutriment wholly. If boiled for eight hours, the head of the ox will yield about one fourth of its weight in gelatine, and the cheek will furnish nearly four pounds of good meat. Shins of beef make excellent soup, but, like the ox head, require longer boiling. Even bones, when stripped of the meat, contain a considerable amount of fat and nitrogenous matter, so that six pounds of bones, when broken up and boiled for nine hours, will yield an amount of nitrogen equal to that contained in a pound of meat and twice as much fat. The old Creole cooks always ask the butcher to throw in some bones (cracked) when they purchase meat for soup.

Mutton must be chosen for the firmness and fineness of the grain, its color and the firm, white fat. Good mutton is generally small.

Lamb that has been killed too long can be detected by examination of the veins on the neck. If these are bluish, then the meat is fresh;. if greenish, the meat is stale. In the hind quarter the point to examine is the knuckle, which is not firm when the meat is not perfectly fresh.

The best veal is very firm and of a pinkish white. Never purchase veal that has a bluish tinge. The veal should not be less than six weeks old, nor more than six months. The best season for veal is from April to October; from that time till the next April the meat is not very good and generally stringy. Like all young meats it spoils very quickly, especially in our climate. Veal should always be well cooked. It furnishes an endless variety of dishes.

Mutton is divided into the fore and hind quarters, and these are subdivided into the leg and the loin. The fore quarter is subdivided into the shoulder, breast and neck. A saddle of mutton is two loins. The fatter the mutton the more tender the lean parts, but the mutton must never be overgrown nor over-fat. The leg, shoulder and loins of mutton make nice roasting pieces. The breast and neck are good for soups and stews. The loins are also cut into French chops and loin chops.

Pork, in every form, is indigestible, and should never be eaten by persons of weak digestion, by young children, nor by the old and feeble. In New Orleans it should only be eaten between December and April, when the weather is very cold; never in summer or late spring and autumn. Pork should always be thoroughly cooked. In selecting pork be guided by the grain of the meat. It should always be of a fine grain and the skin smooth. The lean must be of a pale red color, the fat white and the skin smooth and clear. If the flesh is soft, and if the fat is of a yellowish white, or full of small kernels, reject the meat, as it is surely diseased and unfit for food.

Pork is divided into the leg, shoulder, the chine, the spare ribs, middlings, head and feet. The best parts for roasting are the loins and legs. But the nicest roast is always the sucking pig or "cochon de lait," as the Creoles call it. The sucking pig should be no more than four or five weeks old and not less, and should always be roasted the day after it is killed.

Bacon differs from ham and meat in the relatively large proportions of fat and the small proportion of water. It is a great favorite with all classes on account of its flavor, its facilities for cooking, the many combinations into which it enters in preparation of delicate dishes, and because it is easily kept and always handy. As it is rich in carbonaceous food, it forms a suitable adjunct to substances which are rich rabbits, eggs, beans, peas, cabbage, turnips and lentils. Its flavoring qualities can make a dish of the homeliest vegetables palatable as well as nutritious.

With these suggestions as to choosing meat and the relative value of food properties they contain, the Picayune will lay down the following

**Unfailing Rule Which the Creoles Follow**

in cooking meats:

Always remember that Beef and Mutton must be cooked rare, and Pork and Veal well done.

Beef should always be roasted, broiled or smothered.

Mutton may be roasted, broiled boiled or stewed.

Veal may be roasted, stewed, smothered or fried, when cut into chops.

Pork is always roasted or fried.

Ham is broiled, boiled or fried.

Bacon is broiled, fried or boiled, the latter when cooked with vegetables.

Venison is roasted or made into "ragout," like Beef à la Mode, and the cutlets are broiled. The meat of venison should be of fine grain and well covered with fat. If the venison is very young, the hoofs are but slightly opened; if old, the hoofs stand wide apart.

With this preliminary the Picayune will now present the various Creole forms of preparing meats.

**BEEF.**
Du Boeuf.
**Roast Beef.**
Boeuf Roti.

The first four ribs of the beef are always the best for a roast. The tenderloin lies here, and two good ribs or a "full cut," as the butchers term it, should be enough to make a fine roast for a family of six. Always remember that if the roast is cut too thin, the juices dry too rapidly and the exquisite flavor is gone. After the ribs come the sirloin and the spine bone as second and third choice. Have the butcher skewer the roast so that it will have a nice shape when it comes on the table and will retain all the juice of the beef. Leave the bones in the roast, as the meat will be far sweeter than when taken out. Rub the meat well with salt and pepper, dredge slightly with lard and set in a hot oven. The heat of the oven at once coagulates the blood and prevents it from escaping, thus rendering the meat nutritious. Every now and then baste the beef with its own juices and let it cook adding no water, as sufficient fat runs from the beef to baste with. Allow fifteen minutes to every pound of meat if one likes the meat rare, otherwise allow twenty minutes. But the Creoles always roast beef rare. To ascertain the desired state, occasionally stick a needle into the beef. If the blood spurts up, the meat is ready to serve, and, cooked to this point, is a most nutritious dish. Watch carefully and do not let it pass this stage. Serve on a dish in its own gravy. The practice of making a gravy of flour, etc., for roast beef is condemned by the best ethics of Creole cookery.

**Filet of Beef Larded.**
Filet de Boeuf Piqué.
1 Filet of Beef.
Lard Sufficient to Lard Thoroughly.
1 Small Onion. 1 Bay Leaf.
4 Cloves, if desired.
1½ Tablespoonfuls of Butter.
1 Tablespoonful of Glace. (See receipt.)
1 Glass of Madeira or Sherry Wine (or Water).
Salt and Pepper to Taste.

Trim the filet nicely, removing the outer muscular skin. Lard the filet well, using larding needles. The lard must be very thin, like a shoestring. The larding is done by filling the needles with the lard and pushing them through the filet as far as they will go. If the needles are long enough, they will come out on the other side of the filet, leaving the lard within. Repeat this process all down the center and along the sides of the filet, about an inch apart, and have the rows neat and even. If you have not a larding needle, make incisions with a knife, and push the lard in with your finger, but the filet is never as juicy and tender, nor does it look so clean and even when baked. When well larded, dredge well with salt and pepper, rubbing this thoroughly into the beef. Cut up one small onion, one bay leaf, and mash four cloves, and place in the bottom of the baking pan. Lay the larded filet on this bed, the larded side being uppermost. Put small bits of butter equal to a half tablespoonful on top, and bake in a quick oven thirty minutes. This dish is always eaten rare. To ascertain if sufficiently done, stick a fork into the filet; if the blood bubbles out, it is ready to serve. The meat when done is always spongy and elastic to the touch.

In the meantime, prepare the following brown sauce: Take one tablespoonful of butter and one of Glace (see recipe under chapter "Sauces for Meats, Fish, etc."), and three of water; rub smoothly and melt in a saucepan, stirring constantly to prevent burning. When brown, add one glass of Madeira or Sherry wine and add a half cup of water. Season well with salt and pepper. Pour over the filet, which must be placed in a hot dish, and serve.

### Filet of Beef Larded With Mushrooms.

#### Filet de Boeuf Piqué aux Champignons.

1 Filet of Beef.
½ Can of Mushrooms.
Salt and Pepper to Taste.

Trim and lard the beef according to the directions given in the above recipe, and bake in the same manner—rare. When it has cooked for a half hour in a quick oven, it will be done. Then make a sauce as follows: Take one tablespoonful of butter and one of Glace and three of water; melt the butter and add the Glace, browning nicely without burning, and stirring constantly. When brown add one glass of Madeira or Sherry wine, if desired, and one-half pint of water. Season well with salt and pepper. Then add a half can of mushrooms, chopped very fine. Stir well and let it boil about ten minutes, so as not to be too thick nor yet too thin. The intelligent cook will judge by tasting to see that it is seasoned properly. Place the filet in a hot dish and pour the sauce over and serve hot.

### Filet of Beef With Truffles.

#### Filet de Boeuf Piqué aux Truffes ou à la Périgeux.

1 Filet of Beef. ¼ Can of Truffles.
½ Glass of Sherry. 1 Pint of Broth or Water.
Salt and Pepper to Taste.

Proceed in the same manner as in the preparation of Filet of Beef Larded. When it has baked for a half hour, make a sauce as follows: One tablespoonful of butter in a saucepan; add two tablespoonfuls of Glace (see recipe under chapter "Sauces for Meats, Fish, etc.") and add a half wineglass of Sherry and one pint of broth or water. Let it boil slowly for ten minutes, and add one-half can of truffles, chopped very fine, if à la Périgeux; if aux truffes, cut in dice. Let the sauce boil slowly twenty minutes longer, and then pour over the filet, serving hot.

Truffles are always an expensive dish and quite above the means of the great majority of people. The dish should never be attempted by a family who wishes to live economically.

### Broiled Beefsteak.

#### Filet de Boeuf Grillé.

3 Pounds of Steak for Broiling Purposes.
1 Tablespoonful of Butter. The Juice of 1 Lemon.
Chopped Parsley and Lettuce Leaves to Garnish.
Salt and Pepper to Taste.

The cut known as the "Porterhouse Steak," is unquestionably the best for broiling. The next in order is the sirloin, where there are always choice cuts, but the entire sirloin is not profitable for broiling and the coarse ends may be used in making stews, gumbos, etc. The rib steak is very nutritious, as also the round, but the Creoles never broil these. There is an art in broiling a beefsteak properly, and the Creoles have certainly attained this in its perfection. The broiler in a well-regulated household is always put on a furnace of hot charcoals in preference to the open front of the stove. The coals not only render the meat free from any deleterious effects, should, by chance, the meat not be from a perfectly healthy animal, but the broiling over the coals gives the meat a flavor one vainly seeks otherwise. Dredge the meat well with salt and pepper and then brush lightly with butter. Place it on the hot gridiron and let it broil quickly for four minutes; then turn on the other side for four minutes longer. When done take off, place in a hot dish, butter nicely and sprinkle chopped parsley over, and the juice of a lemon, and serve immediately. The great secret of good broiling lies in the proper fire, the clean broiler, the right length of time, the quality of the steak, which should never be tough, and lastly and not the least important of all, eating the steak directly after it comes from the coals.

### Smothered Beefsteak.

#### Filet Braisé.

Braising or smothering meat is a mode of cooking little understood by the Americans, but which has been brought by the Creoles to a high state of perfection. By this process the meat is just covered and no more, with a little water, or with a strong broth made from animal stock or the juices of vegetables. The pot is covered with a closely-fitting lid and is put on a slow fire and allowed to simmer slowly for two or three hours, just short of the boiling point. By this slow process of cooking, tough meats are rendered juicy, tender and very agreeable to the palate, while the covered pot enables the meat to retain all its flavor.

The great secret in smothering meat is to let it cook very slowly, simmering, however, all the time, so that the heat may thoroughly penetrate and render tender and juicy the coarse fiber of the meat. When tender, put the beefsteak into a platter, cover with the onions and gravy, and you will have a delicious and delicately flavored dish.

### Beefsteak Smothered in Onions.
#### Filet Braisé aux Ognons.

3 Pounds of Round Steak.
6 Onions, sliced fine. 1 Tablespoonful of Lard.
1 Tablespoonful of Flour.
2 Tablespoonfuls of Vinegar.
2 Sprigs each of Thyme and Bay Leaf.
3 Sprigs of Parsley.
1 Clove of Garlic.
1 Pint of Water.
Pepper and Salt to Taste.

Beat the round steak well with the rolling pin or steak hammer; cut off the outer skin and press the meat back into shape. Place the tablespoonful of lard in the deep frying pan and let it melt. Then lay in the sliced onions, and over these the beefsteak, which has been well seasoned with salt and pepper and dredged with the flour. Cover closely. Let it simmer over a hot fire for a few minutes and then turn the steak on the other side. After three minutes, add two tablespoonfuls of vinegar, chopped parsley, thyme and bay leaf and a clove of garlic. Turn the steak, letting the flour brown well, and keep the pot closely covered. When brown pour over one cup of water, or a pint, which will be sufficient to cover the meat. Bring this to a brisk boil and set the pot back where it can simmer gently for about two hours.

Filets of beef may be smothered in the same manner, only these will require no beating with the steak hammer.

### Filet of Beef Smothered With Mushrooms or Truffles.

Filet de Boeuf Braisé aux Champignons, ou aux Truffes.
1 Filet of Beef.
1 Can of Mushrooms or ½ Can of Truffles.
6 Onions, sliced fine.
1 Tablespoonful of Lard.
1 Tablespoonful of Flour.
2 Sprigs each of Thyme and Bay Leaf.
1 Clove of Garlic.
1 Pint of Hot Water.
Salt, Pepper and Cayenne to Taste.

Smother the beef, using a filet for this delicious dish according to the recipe given for Smothered Beefsteak. After it has cooked about a half hour add one can of mushrooms and let it continue to simmer gently for an hour and a half longer. When ready to serve, add, if possible, a gill or a small wineglass of Sherry or White Wine; boil ten minutes longer. Put the filet in a dish, place the mushrooms over and around as a garnish, pour over the sauce and serve.

If truffles are used instead of the mushrooms, add one-half can and proceed in exactly the same manner as when using the mushrooms.

### Filet of Beef With Tomatoes.
Filet de Boeuf Braisé aux Tomates.
1 Filet of Beef. 1 Tablespoonful of Lard.
6 Onions, sliced fine. 1 Clove of Garlic.
1 Tablespoonful of Flour.
2 Sprigs each of Thyme and Bay Leaf.
3 Sprigs of Parsley.
½ Can of Tomatoes or 6 Large Fresh Ones.
1 Pint of Hot Water.
Salt, Pepper and Cayenne to Taste.

Smother the filet in exactly the same manner as already described. When cooked for about a half hour, add one-half can of tomatoes and their juice, or six large fresh tomatoes sliced in their juice. Let the mixture simmer for an hour and a half longer, season well and serve, pouring the gravy over the filet.

### Filet of Beef With Stuffed Tomatoes.
Filet Braisé aux Tomates Farcies.
1 Filet of Beef.
1 Dozen Uniform-Sized Tomatoes.
1 Cup of Mushrooms. 1 Clove of Garlic.
½ Cup of Stale Bread Crumbs.
1 Tablespoonful of Butter.
Salt and Cayenne to Taste.

Smother the filet according to the directions given above, adding two chopped tomatoes to the sauce. Take the tomatoes and cut off the stem end, scoop out the soft inside, being careful to retain the skins in proper shape. Then take a half cup of mushrooms, one-half cup of stale bread crumbs, which have been wet and squeezed, one clove of garlic, chopped very fine, and one grated onion, a sprig of chopped parsley. Chop the mushrooms fine, place a tablespoonful of butter into a frying pan, and, when melted, add the bread crumbs which have been seasoned with salt and pepper and Cayenne, and mixed thoroughly with the chopped onion or garlic and the parsley. When these begin to fry, add the chopped mushrooms, stirring constantly for about five or eight minutes. Serve with Stuffed Tomatoes (see recipe.)

### Beef à la Mode.
Daube.

5 Pounds of the Rump or the Round of the Beef.
¼ Pound of Salt Fat.
Large Onions. 2 Turnips. 5 Carrots.
1 Tablespoonful of Lard.
1 Clove of Garlic.
1 Glass of Sherry, Madeira or Claret (if Desired.)
Salt, Pepper and Cayenne to Taste.
2 Bay Leaves.
Sprigs of Thyme and Parsley.

Cut the fat of the salt meat into thin shreds. Chop the onion and bay leaf very fine, as also the garlic, thyme and cloves. Rub the shreds well with salt and pepper. Take the rump of beef and lard thickly by making incisions about three or four inches in length and inserting the pieces of salt fat and spices, onion and thyme and garlic, mixed thoroughly. Take two large onions and cut into quarters and put in a saucepan with one tablespoonful of lard. Let the slices brown and then lay on top the rump of beef, well larded. Cover closely and let it simmer very slowly till well browned. Then add the chopped bay leaf and parsley. When brown add five carrots cut into squares of an inch, and two turnips, cut in the same manner, and two large onions, chopped fine. Let the whole brown, keeping well covered, and cooking slowly over a slow but regular fire. Be always careful to keep the cover very tight on the pot. When it has simmered about ten minutes, turn the daube on the other side, cover closely and let it simmer ten minutes more. Then cover with sufficient boiling water to cover the daube; or, better still, if you have it, use instead of the water, boiling "consommé" or "pot-au-feu," and, if possible, a glass of Sherry or Madeira wine; or, if you have neither of these, which are always to be preferred in cooking meats, a glass of good Claret. Season according to taste with salt, Cayenne and black pepper. Cover the pot tight and set it back on the stove, letting it smother slowly for about three hours, or until tender. Serve hot or cold.

### Cold Daube à la Créole.
### Daube Froide à la Créole.

This is one of the most excellent dishes made by the Creoles, and is always a great standby for luncheons in winter. Take
3 Pounds of the Rump or Round of the Beef.
2 Pounds of Veal Rump.
2 Pigs' Feet. ¼ Pound of Salt Fat Meat.
5 Large Onions. 2 Turnips.
5 Carrots. 2 Cloves of Garlic. 3 Bay Leaves.
1 Tablespoonful of Lard.
1 Glass of Sherry.
3 Sprigs of Thyme and Parsley.
Salt, Pepper and Cayenne to Taste.

Cut the salt meat into shreds, roll well in Cayenne and black pepper. Chop finely several sprigs of thyme and three bay leaves, one clove of garlic, three sprigs of parsley, and mash well three cloves and six allspice. Roll the strips of salt meat, which must be about three inches in length and one-half inch thick, in this. Make incision into the rump of meat and force in the strips of fat meat and the spices. Then rub the whole well with salt and pepper, judging according to taste, and proceed to cook according to the recipe for Beef à la Mode. Let the Daube cook about four hours when you intend to serve it cold.

In the meantime, in another pot, place a veal steak of about two pounds, and two pigs' feet. Season well with salt and pepper and Cayenne, and cover well with four quarts of water, and let them boil. Add one bay leaf, one sprig of thyme, one-half clove of garlic and one onion, all minced very fine, and two cloves mashed into almost a jelly, and one glass of Sherry or Madeira wine. Let these boil well with the veal and pigs' feet. Then, when the veal and pigs' feet are cooked very tender, take them out of the pot and mince the meat of each very fine; return to the sauce, and again season highly, according to taste, for the flavor depends upon the piquant seasoning. After the daube has cooked four or five hours, take off the stove and pour over the sauce and set all in a cool place. Serve the next day—cold, cutting into thin slices. It will all have formed a jelly that is most delicious and appetizing.

Daube Froide à la Créole has only to be tried once to be repeated. It is a standing dish for luncheon in every Creole home during the winter, for it is never essayed in summer, owing to the heated weather that would prevent the jellying of the sauce. Even when put in an ice box it is not the same as when made in winter. It is a dish that may be served with little cost to the most fastidious.

### Beef Marine.
### Boeuf Mariné.

4 Pounds of Beef, from the Round or Shoulder.
4 Tablespoonfuls of Olive Oil.
3 Bay Leaves. 1 Onion. 1 Lemon.
1 Tablespoonful of Vinegar.
½ Teaspoonful each of Ground Cloves, Mace and Allspice.
Salt and Cayenne to Taste.

The "brisket" of the beef is excellent for this, as also the "breast plate." Mix the spices, salt and pepper thoroughly and rub well into both sides of the beef. Chop the onions fine, and cover the meat with them. Then mix the oil and vinegar and the juice of one lemon, and pour this over the meat. Set it in the ice box, or a cool place, and let it stand overnight. Then put it into the stewpan, and be careful to retain all the juices of the spices. Set on the fire and let it simmer ten minutes, adding the bay leaves, chopped very fine. Then add a tablespoonful of flour, rolled smoothly in a half teaspoonful of butter or lard, melted. Let this brown, and then half cover the meat with boiling water, using good judgment. Cover closely and set on the oven, letting the beef cook two hours, and turning once, so that both sides may be well penetrated by the heat. Serve on a hot dish, pouring the gravy over. This is a very old-fashioned dish.

### Fried Meat.
### La Viande Frite.

Frying among the Creoles is done in several ways. The first and the method most generally adopted in households is to put a tablespoonful of lard or an ounce, as the quantity of meat to cook may seem to require, into a frying pan. When the lard has reached the boiling point lay in the meat and cook first on one side then on the other to a nice brown. The second method is that in use among the Creole chefs, restaurateurs, and in the homes of the wealthier classes; the meat is completely immersed in the boiling lard as in frying fish or doughnuts. The intense heat quickly closes up the pores of the meat, and a brown crust is formed; the heat of the lard should be such that a piece of bread dropped into it becomes brown instantly. The lard should never be smoking. This ruins the meat and gives a burnt flavor. As soon as it begins to smoke remove the frying pan to the side of the stove, but still keep it at the boiling point. The half-frying method mentioned above is, however, the one most generally in use, and if followed properly excellent results are obtained; indeed, many Creole chefs prefer it. There is another method that is very generally used, and which imparts a flavor similar to that of broiled meat. This is to lay the meat in a thick-bottomed frying pan with a tablespoonful of butter. Brown the meat quickly first on one side and then on the other; lay in a hot platter and season as you would broiled meat.

In large families where there is a great deal of cooking required, the economical housewife will carefully save all the drippings and the fat remnants of beef, mutton and pork. She will occasionally get a pound or two of suet from the market. These drippings or skimmings may be clarified by boiling them in hot water about twice a week. When the fat is thoroughly melted, strain it with the water and set aside to cool. After a while the hard fat that has been formed on top of the water may be lifted out just as you would a cake of anything; then scrape off all the dark particles from the bottom and melt the fat over again. While it is still very hot strain it into a clean stone jar or tin pail and it is ready for use in cooking. Refined cotton seed oil and butter oil are now being adopted by many professional cooks and in households for culinary purposes. Olive oil has always been in use for this purpose among the Creoles, and is held as a very delicate medium for frying. But many prefer the beef fat or suet for frying, considering it both wholesome and digestible, and more delicate than olive oil or the fat of pork. But the careful housekeeper will always preserve all odds and ends of fat of beef, mutton or pork, and the drippings after frying anything. Set this aside until the fat settles and cools, then pour off carefully so as to clear from the sediment that always settles at the bottom and clarify as above.

### Fried Meat.
### Grillade.

Our "Grillades," or Fried Meat à la Créole are famous, relishable and most digestible dishes, no matter what scientists may say about the non-advisability of eating fried meat. The many octogenarians who walk our streets, and who have been practically raised on "Grillades," for it is a daily dish among the Creoles, are the best refutation of the outcry that is made in the North and West against fried meat. The great truth is that the Creoles know how to fry meat. The round of the meat is always selected for Grillades, and one steak will serve six persons. The steak is cut into pieces of about six or eight squares and each piece is called a "grillade." Season well with salt and pepper, rubbing these into the meat thoroughly and letting it soak well into the fibres. Have ready a hot pan, and place within a tablespoonful of lard, and, when hot, a sliced onion and one clove of garlic, chopped very fine. Let this brown, and then add one chopped tomato. Place the Grillades in this, letting them soak thoroughly. Cover with a tight cover, and set back, letting them fry slowly, so as to absorb all the lard and juices. Serve on a hot dish, when brown, with garnishes of parsley. This is the recipe for making Grillades without gravy. Some also fry simply in the boiling lard, using only a half tablespoonful, and letting it soak and absorb thoroughly after being well seasoned. This is a matter of taste.

Grillades are a favorite dish among the poorer classes of Creoles, especially, being served not only for breakfast, but also at dinner, in the latter instance with gravy and a dish of red beans and boiled rice.

### Grillades With Gravy.
### Grillades à la Sauce.

1 Round Steak.
1 Tomato.   1 Large Onion.
Salt and Pepper.

Select a nice round steak and beat well. Cut into grillades of about four inches square and season highly with salt and pepper and Cayenne. Put a tablespoonful of lard into the frying pan, and when it heats, add a chopped onion, one clove of garlic; and as these brown, add one tablespoonful of flour, making a Brown Roux. (See recipe under chapter "Sauces for Meats, Fish, etc.") Then add two tomatoes, sliced, with their juices, and as this browns lay the grillades upon it. Cover closely, and as it browns on one side, turn on the other. Then add a half tablespoonful of vinegar and a cup of water. Stir well and set back on the stove and let it simmer slowly for about a half hour. This is very nice served with hominy at breakfast, or with red or white beans and boiled rice at dinner.

Again, the Grillades à la Sauce are made by frying the grillades, after seasoning well, simply in half a tablespoonful of boiling lard. The lard must always be boiling, so that the meat juices may at once coagulate. After they are browned nicely on both sides, take the grillades out of the frying pan and set in a hot dish over a pot of boiling water and cover. Have an onion chopped fine, put half a tablespoonful of lard into the frying pan, stirring well to detach all particles of meat that may have adhered. Then add a chopped onion and brown, and a tablespoonful of flour or Glace (see recipe under chapter "Sauces for Meats, Fish, etc.") and let this brown. Pour in a tablespoonful of vinegar and a cup of water, season well with salt, pepper and Cayenne, and let it boil till it reaches a right consistency, which will be in about ten minutes. Pour over the grillades, and serve.

### Grillades Breaded.

#### Grillades Panées.

1 Round of Veal.
1 Tablespoonful of Lard.
1 Beaten Egg. ½ Cup of Bread Crumbs.
Salt, Pepper and Cayenne.

The round of the veal is always used for this. Cut the veal into squares of about four inches; season well with salt, pepper and Cayenne. Beat an egg well and take each grillade and soak it well in the egg, and then roll in bread crumbs grated. Have ready a pan of boiling grease, sufficient for the grillades to swim in it; fry to a nice brown and serve very hot.

### Left-Over Meat.

Left-over meat may be utilized in many delightful ways, such as "Boulettes," "Boulards," "Croquettes," "Rissoles," "Meat Soufflé" and various forms of Hash. The following are the forms of preparation in use among the Creoles:

### Meat Balls.

#### Boulettes.

1 Pound of Raw or Left-Over Meat.
1 Tablespoonful of Butter. 1 Onion.
The Juice of a Lemon.
Salt, Pepper and Cayenne to Taste.

Take one pound of steak from the upper round and mince and chop very fine. Add to it one tablespoonful of lemon juice, one onion (well grated), one tablespoonful of melted butter, and mixed salt, black pepper and Cayenne, seasoning highly; mix all thoroughly. Form the meat into balls, using about two tablespoonfuls for each, which will allow six or eight balls or boulettes. Have ready a deep frying pan of lard, sufficient for the boulettes to swim and fry to a nice brown. Take out and drain of all grease, place on a hot platter and garnish with fried parsley, and serve very hot.

The same directions may be used in making croquettes of meat, only the latter are formed into cylindrical shapes. If fried in butter, the boulettes or croquettes are very delicious, but they are nice either way if well seasoned, for their success depends upon this.

### Meat Balls.

#### Boulards.

Several Slices of Meat (Raw or Cold Cooked).
1 Tomato. 1 Onion. 1 Carrot.
3 Hard-Boiled Eggs.
1 Stalk of Celery. 3 Sprigs of Parsley.
1 Bay Leaf. 1 Sprig of Thyme.
1 Tablespoonful of Butter.
½ Cup of Cracker Crumbs. A Pinch of Ginger.
½ Cup of Water.
Salt and Pepper to Taste.

Select slices of beef cut very thin from the round of the cross rib. Take one tomato, one onion, one carrot, a stalk of celery, several sprigs of parsley, one bay leaf, a sprig of thyme, three hard-boiled eggs, and chop very fine. Mix this with one tablespoonful of butter, a half cup of cracker crumbs and a pinch of ginger. Salt and pepper to taste. Take each slice of meat, and make a roll of it, folding the dressing within and folding over the edges that it may be retained. Tie each with thin twine. Have boiling lard or suet on the fire, drop in the boulards rolled in bread crumbs, set them back on the stove, cover well, and let them simmer gently for about two hours, adding a half cup of water to prevent scorching. Keep the pot covered. After two hours, drain the boulards well by laying them on heated brown paper; place them in a hot dish, garnish it with sliced hard-boiled eggs, parsley and olives, and serve. Each boulard should be about the size of an egg.

## Left-Over Meat.
### Rissoles.

4 Ounces of Cold Roast Beef or Veal, or Left-Over Meat of any Kind.
2 Ounces of Stale Bread, Wet and Squeezed Thoroughly.
½ Teaspoonful of Minced Parsley.
½ Ounce of Flour.
1½ Tablespoonfuls of Milk or Water.
¼ Teaspoonful Each of Salt and Black Pepper.
A Dash of Cayenne.
1 Bay Leaf, Chopped Fine, With Sprigs of Parsley and Thyme.

Mince the meat finely and season well. Mix the ingredients thoroughly with it, adding, if you have it, mince 1 Chaurice or sausage meat, or a little cold ham minced. Form it into balls, using two tablespoonfuls for each ball. Brush lightly with milk, toss in a little flour, pat to get off all superfluous flour, and brown nicely in boiling lard. Drain off all lard and serve on a platter, garnished with parsley sprigs.

### Meat Soufflé.
### Soufflé de Boeuf.

1 Cup of Cold Meat.
2 Tablespoonfuls of Butter.
2 Tablespoonfuls of Flour. 1 Cup of Cold Milk.
2 Eggs.
Salt and Pepper to Taste.

Put two level tablespoonfuls of butter into a frying pan, and when it is hot add two tablespoonfuls of flour, rubbing smoothly and letting it brown. Then add gradually one cup of cold milk. Stir this until it boils. Add one-half teaspoonful of salt; a little pepper and one cupful of chopped meat, or fowl, that has been left over. When this comes to a boil, add the yolk of two beaten eggs. Let it cook a moment longer and set to cool. Then beat the whites of the eggs and when the meat mixture is cold, fold them in carefully. Turn this into a buttered dish and bake in a moderate oven twenty minutes. Serve as soon as removed from the fire. A little grated nutmeg is a great addition.

### Beefsteak Pie.
### Vol-au-Vent de Boeuf.

1 Quart of Cold Cooked Meat.
2 Slices of Breakfast Bacon.
1 Tablespoonful of Butter. ½ Dozen Potatoes.
Thyme, Bay Leaf and Parsley.
Salt, Pepper and Cayenue to Taste.

Make a nice pie crust. (See plain Paste.) Line a baking pan with this, and bake in the oven. Cut the meat very fine, into dice, and season well, rubbing with the minced thyme, parsley, bay leaf, and salt and pepper. Stew the meat as in Ragout de Veau à la Bourgeoise. Place in the pan. Dot the top with bits of butter, and place over all a layer of pie crust, decorating the edges nicely. Bake to a nice brown. Serve in the dish in which it was cooked, with any left-over sauce spread over the slices.

### Potted Beef.
### Terrine de Boeuf.

2 Rounds of Beef.
1 Slice of Suet (Gros de Boeuf).
½ Can Mushrooms.
4 Yolks of Eggs. 1 Dozen Allspice. 4 Cloves.
Salt, Pepper and Cayenne.
1 Glass of Brandy.

Chop the slices of beef very fine with the suet, and season with the mashed spices, the herbs, minced very fine, and mix thoroughly with the beaten yolks of the eggs. Pour over all the brandy and mix. Line the bottom of the baking pan with strips of lean bacon and dot of beef on top with bits of butter. Bake for two hours in a quick oven.

### HASH.
### Hachis.

1 Quart of Cold Meat. 1 Onion.
1 Pint of Chopped Potatoes (Uncooked).
2 Hard-Boiled Eggs. ¼ of a Clove of Garlic.
1 Tablespoonful of Butter or Lard.
Salt, Pepper and Cayenne to Taste.

Take the remains, of cold roast, stew, bouilli, steaks or fowl, and mince very fine. To every quart of meat allow one onion, a quarter of a clove of garlic, chopped fine, and one pint of chopped (uncooked) potatoes, and two hard-boiled eggs, choped fine. Mix all this with the minced meat, add salt, pepper and Cayenne to taste; put into a stew pan with a tablespoonful of butter or lard, and let it simmer gently. After ten minutes add a half pint of hot water. Let it cook ten minutes longer and serve. The egg may be omitted.

### Dry or Baked Hash.
### Hachis Sec.

1 Pint of Chopped Meat, Left-Over.
½ Pint of Water, or Left-Over Broth
1 Pint of Cooked Chopped Tomatoes.
1 Tablespoonful of Melted Butter.
1 Large Onion. 1 Clove of Garlic. 1 Bay Leaf.
1 Sprig of Parsley.

Chop and mince the meat very fine. Chop the potatoes fine, or in square inch pieces. Mince the parsley, bay leaf, onion and garlic fine; mix all together with the meat and potatoes and season highly with pepper and Cayenne, salting to taste. Add the tablespoonful of butter and bake in a moderate oven for about one hour.

### Hash on Toast.
### Hachis sur Canapés.

1 Quart of Cold Meat.
1 Pint of Boiling Water or Milk
2 Tablespoonfuls of Butter.
2 Tablespoonfuls of Flour.
Salt and Pepper to Taste.

Cut the left-over roast, bouilli or

steak into small squares. To each pint of these little squares allow one tablespoonful of butter, one tablespoonful of flour and a half pint of boiling water. Put the butter into a frying pan, and as it melts add the flour, being careful not to let it burn. When browned add the water, or, preferably, milk, and stir until it begins to boil. Then add the hashed and seasoned meat, and season again to taste. Set the hash on a moderate fire and let it simmer for fifteen minutes.

In the meantime, toast slices of bread and butter them. Set them in a hot dish, spread each slice with the hash very thickly and pour the sauce over and serve. The hash may be baked and spread on the toast and served with a sauce à l'Espagnole. (See recipe.)

### Corn Beef.

Boeuf au Mi-Sel.

3 Pounds of Corned Beef.
2 Carrots. 2 Turnips. 1 Stalk of Celery.
2 Onions. 1 Clove of Garlic.

The best cut for this is the lower round of the beef, which is perfectly free from bone. Put the corn beef on to boil in a large pot of cold water. The pot should be well covered. When it begins boiling well, set it back to cook gently, and allow twenty-five minutes to each pound of beef. When within two hours of being cooked, add two carrots, two turnips, a stalk of celery, two onions, one clove of garlic, chopped fine, and let these boil with the beef. Serve with the vegetables ranged whole around the dish. Corn beef is also served with cabbage, but never boil the cabbage in the beef as both will become indigestible. It should be as tender as a spring chicken when done.

### Corn Beef Hash.

Hachis de Boeuf au Mi-Sel.

1 Pint of Corn Beef, Cooked, and 1 Pint of Left-Over Potatoes.
1 Grated Onion. 1 Tablespoonful of Butter.
1 Cup of Broth or Water.
1 Bay Leaf. 1 Sprig of Parsley.
Salt, Pepper and Cayenne to Taste.

Mix the meat thoroughly after mincing fine together with the chopped potatoes. Grate the onion and a half clove of garlic if desired, and chop the herbs fine and mix thoroughly with the beef, seasoning highly. Put the butter into the frying pan, add the meat and the broth or water, and stir constantly till it boils. Spread, after it has cooked for about twenty minutes on slices of buttered toast. Pour over the gravy and garnish with sprigs of parsley and sliced lemon.

### Breaded Ox Tails.

Queues de Boeuf Panées.

2 Ox Tails.
1 Cup of Grated Bread Crumbs.
3 Sprigs of Chopped Parsley.
3 Sprigs of Thyme. 1 Bay Leaf. 1 Egg.
Salt, Pepper and Cayenne to Taste.

Wash the tails and cut them at the joints; then cut again, into two pieces of about four inches in length. Have a pot of boiling water; season this well with chopped parsley, thyme, bay leaf, and salt and pepper and Cayenne to taste. Boil the ox tails til tender; when done, remove from the fire and let them cool in the water in which they were boiled. Beat an egg well, roll the bits of tail in the egg, and then roll in grated bread crumbs. Drop into a pot of boiling grease and fry to a golden brown. Take out and drain and serve with a Sauce à la Tartare, Ravigotte, Tomato, or any sauce. (See recipe.)

### Ox Tails à la Bourgeoise.

Queue de Boeuf à la Bourgeoise.

2 Ox Tails.
2 Onions. 2 Carrots. 1 Turnip.
½ Can of Green Peas.
½ Inch of Ham. 1 Tablespoonful of Butter.
2 Sprigs of Thyme.
1 Bay Leaf. 1 Clove of Garlic.
1 Pint of Consomme or Boiling Water.
1 Glass of Sherry Wine or Water.

Cut the ox tails into pieces of three or four inches in length. Chop two onions fine, and put the whole into a saucepan with a tablespoonful of butter. Let them brown a little and add two large carrots, cut into dice, and one turnip cut the same way. Brown these with the ox tails. Add one-half inch of ham, well chopped and let it brown, and then add two sprigs of thyme and one bay leaf and one clove of garlic, chopped very fine. Let these ingredients all brown about two minutes over a hot fire. Then add one glass of Sherry wine or water. Let all brown two minutes longer, and add one pint of consommé or boiling water. Season again to taste, and add a half can of green peas. Let all boil until the ox tails are tender to the touch, and serve hot.

### Broiled Kidneys.

Brochettes de Rognons.

3 Kidneys.
1 Tablespoonful of Butter.
Lemon Juice. Chopped Parsley.
Salt and Pepper to Taste.

The kidneys must, first of all, be perfectly fresh. Wash them well and slice them; cut into thin pieces of about three inches long and two inches wide. Run a wooden or silver skewer through to hold them together, and season well with salt and pepper. Brush with a little butter, and put on a double broiler and broil for about five minutes, turning over the broiler to alow each side to cook. Place on a platter and pour over melted butter and chopped parsley and lemon juice, and serve hot, as you would broiled steak.

### Stewed Kidneys.
Rognons Sautés à la Créole.

3 Kidneys.  1 Cup of Water.
½ Spoon of Butter.
½ Glass of White Wine.
1 Teaspoonful of Sherry Wine.
Salt and Pepper to Taste.
1 Sprig Each of Chopped Parsley, Thyme and Bay Leaf, Very Fine.

Select perfectly fresh kidneys; wash them well, and then slice very thin. Season well with salt and pepper. Put one and a half tablespoonfuls of butter into the saucepan; when melted and very hot, add the kidneys and chopped herbs, being very careful to stir constantly and very fast, to prevent burning. Add a half glass of White Wine, if possible, and one cup of water or consommé. Let it boil up once, and the kidneys are ready to be served. Kidneys are like eggs—they do not require long to cook, and the more they are cooked the harder they become. Five minutes should be sufficient to cook them well, and at no time should they be allowed to boil. By adding champagne, instead of white wine, you will have Rognons Sauté au Champagne.

### Broiled Liver.
Brochettes de Foie.

1 Pound of Beef's Liver.
Tablespoonful of Melted Butter.
Salt and Pepper to Taste.
Chopped Parsley to Garnish.

Wash and slice the liver into thin pieces of about three inches in length and one-quarter inch in thickness. Run a skewer through to prevent from curling up. Season well with salt and pepper, brush lightly with butter, and place on a double broiler, stringing on the skewer with alternate slices of bacon. Broil as you would a tenderloin steak for about five minutes, and serve with a sauce of melted butter and chopped parsley poured over.

### Fried Liver à la Lyonaise.
Foie Sautées à la Lyonnaise.

1 Pound of Liver of the Beef.
1 Tablespoonful of Butter.
2 Large Onions.
Salt and Pepper to Taste.

Slice the onions nicely. Put one tablespoonful of butter into the frying pan and add the onions. When brown, take the liver which you have cut into slices of about three inches in length and one half inch in thickness, and season well with salt and pepper, and lay it over the onions. Stir well. Cover and let it fry for about three minutes, and then turn over and let it cook three minutes more. Pour a teaspoonful of vinegar on top and again season to taste. Let it simmer three or four minutes longer and serve hot. Liver does not require long to cook.

### Jellied Tongue.
Langue de Boeuf en Genée.

1 Beef Tongue.  2 Calf's Feet.
4 Pints of Strong Consomme.
1 Glass of Sherry Wine.
Spices.

Parboil the tongue and two calf's feet. Then take out of the hot water and skin and clean the tongue well, and take the bones out of the calf's feet. Mince two onions very fine, and fry them in a tablespoonful of butter. Let them brown, and lay on these the well-seasoned tongue and calf's feet. Let them simmer ten minutes, and then add one pint of consommé, and five minutes after, one glass of white wine. Let these smother, keeping well covered, for an hour and a half. Then take the tongue out, and let the calf's feet cook and reduce a half hour longer. After this add the tongue for two minutes longer. Put all into a bowl or dish, and let it cool. You will have a delicious jelly.

### Smothered Tongue.
Langue de Boeuf Braisée.

1 Fresh Tongue of Beef.
1 Pint of Liquor in Which the Tongue Was Boiled.
2 Onions, Minced Very Fine.
3 Sprigs Each of Thyme and Parsley.
1 Bay Leaf.  2 Cloves.
1 Tablespoonful of Butter.
1 Glass of White Wine (if Desired).
Salt and Pepper to Taste.

Parboil the tongue for about ten minutes. Then skin and clean well. Chop an onion very fine, and brown this in a tablespoonful of butter. When brown, add the tongue, which you will have arranged by fastening the thick part to the tip with a skewer, as for roast beef. Let it cook, smothering slowly, for fifteen minutes, and then add another onion sliced nicely. Let this brown, and add one square inch of ham, well chopped, two carrots sliced, and a bay leaf, and two sprigs of thyme, minced fine. Brown again, and add a pint of broth. Season well, and add a glass of white wine, and then let it smother for one hour and a half longer, turning every quarter, so that every part may cook thoroughly. Serve with the sauce in which it was cooked, or with a Sauce Piquante. (See recipe.)

## CHAPTER XIII.

### VEAL.

Du Veau.

The loin, filet, shoulder and breast of the veal are used for roasting. Chops are cut from the loin, and the leg is used for filets and cutlets. The filet of veal is quite different from the filet of beef, and does not, in any manner, correspond to the latter, being a solid piece cut from the legs of the young calf. The knuckle is the lower part of the leg after the cutlets are taken off, and, with the neck, is used extensively for making stews, soups and veal pies. Indeed, as far as stews are concerned, the Creoles never make a "beef stew" or very rarely, the meat of beef being considered too tough. Never buy veal that is very young, for young meats, as a rule, are not nutritious; but properly cooked, as the Creoles know how, they need never be unwholesome or indigestible. A calf should never be killed until it is at least two months old, and then the meat has a pinkish tinge, and is firm and the bones are hard. Calf that has been killed too young may be known by the bluish tinge and the soft, flabby flesh, and small, tender bones.

The Creole cooks always pound the veal almost to a pulp. This renders it very tender and digestible. Veal must always be well cooked, and cooked very slowly, else it will be hard, tough and unfit for food.

Veal furnishes an almost endless variety of delightful dishes. The following are those most important in use in Creole homes:

### Roast Loin of Veal.

Longe de Veau Rotie.

4 Pounds of Veal.
1 Tablespoonful of Butter or Lard.
Salt and Pepper to Taste.
Sprigs of Parsley and Sliced Lemon to Garnish.

Trim and cut the veal nicely of the heavier portion of the fat, leaving enough, however, to render it sweet and juicy. If freshly cut, and not handled too much by the butcher, merely wipe the loin with a damp towel. Then dredge it thickly with salt and pepper, and separate the articulations or joints, that the meat may cook thoroughly. Rub well with a tablespoonful of butter or lard, and place in a very quick oven for about fifteen minutes. Then raise the damper of the stove and cover the veal with a piece of brown buttered paper and let it cook slowly, allowing at least twenty minutes to each pound of veal. Keep the oven at a steady, regular heat. About twenty minutes before serving take off the buttered paper and let the roast brown nicely, augmenting the fire a little. Take out, place on a hot dish, garnish nicely with sprigs of parsley and sliced lemon. Serve with its own gravy. The practice of making a gravy with flour for roast beef and rost veal cannot be too severely condemned. Meat is always best when served in its own juice, if roasted or broiled.

### Roast Veal With Fine Herbs.

Carré de Veau Roti aux Fines Herbes.

A 4-Pound Filet of Veal.
1 Cup of Broth or Water.
1 Tablespoonful of Lard.
1 Onion.   3 Bay Leaves.
2 Sprigs of Sweet Marjoram.
3 Sprigs of Parsley.
3 Sprigs of Thyme.
The Juice of 1 Lemon.
½ Teaspoonful Each of Ground Cloves, Mace and Allspice.

Have the butcher cut the filet of veal square, wipe with a damp towel and then take one tablespoonful of lard and dredge the roast nicely. Season well with salt and Cayenne; mince the onion, bay leaf, marjoram, parsley and thyme, and mix these with the ground spices; add the juice of a lemon, and pour all over the meat. Place in a quick oven for about fifteen minutes. After this, lessen the heat, place on top of the veal a buttered piece of brown paper, and let it roast slowly, allowing twenty minutes for each pound of veal. When almost done, take off the paper and let the roast brown nicely for twenty minutes longer. Then take the roast out of the gravy and place in a hot dish in the oven. Take the gravy, stir well, mixing all the herbs that have run out of the beef. Add one cup of broth or water and the juice of one lemon, and mix this thoroughly. Grate some bread crumbs, beat well in one egg, and pour this over the veal, let it brown nicely and serve with the sauce.

### Filet of Veal With Mushrooms or Truffles.
Filet de Veau aux Champignons ou aux Truffes.

1 Filet of Veal.
½ Can of Mushrooms or Truffles.
1 Small Onion. 1 Bay Leaf.
4 Cloves (if desired).
1½ Tablespoonfuls of Butter.
1 Tablespoonful of Glace (see recipe).
1 Glass of Sherry or Madeira Wine (or water).
Salt and Pepper to Taste.

Proceed in exactly the same manner as for Filet of Beef Larded, with Mushrooms or Truffles, only do not lard the veal. Allow the veal to cook much longer, for it must be well done, twenty minutes to the pound being a good guide always in roasting veal. (See recipe for Filet of Beef Larded, with Mushrooms or Truffles.)

### Stuffed Roast Shoulder or Breast of Veal.
Epaule ou Poitrine de Veau Farcie.
1 Shoulder of Veal. ¼ Pound of Ham.
1 Herb Bouquet.
1 Hard-Boiled Egg. 1 Tablespoonful of Butter.
1 Spoon of Flour.
(If the shoulder of the veal is used, have the butcher remove the bone.)

When ready to cook, wipe well with a damp towel, and then dredge with salt and pepper, seasoning highly. Make a dressing by taking one cup of stale bread, wet and squeezed, one-quarter pound of sliced ham, or salt pork, preferably the ham, and chop very fine. Mix this with the bread and season highly with hot pepper, according to taste; 1 carrot, 1 onion, 1 bay leaf, 1 hard-boiled egg, 1 sprig of thyme, 1 of parsley, all minced very fine. Add one tablespoonful of butter, and place in a frying pan; let it fry for about ten minutes and then add, if you have it, a quarter of a glass of white wine, or two tablespoonfuls, and two tablespoonfuls of beef broth; stir well and cook for five minutes longer. Then stuff the shoulder well and skewer the filet to prevent the dressing from falling out in cooking. It is well to tie the veal at either end with a piece of twine. Take one tablespoonful of lard and dredge roast according to preceding recipes.

If the breast of the veal is used, make long gashes between the ribs and fill with a dressing prepared as above, place in the baking pan and roast slowly, according to directions. When finished cooking, remove the shoulder or breast, and stir the gravy well, adding a cup of broth or water and the juice of one lemon and a teaspoonful of butter, seasoning to taste. Serve with the roast. Some like the addition of a teaspoonful of prepared mustard, but that is a matter of taste.

### Veal Cutlets Breaded.
Cotelettes de Veau Panées.
6 Veal Cutlets.
1 Egg. 1 Cup of Bread Crumbs.
Salt and Pepper to Taste.
Lemon and Parsley to Garnish.
Sauce a la Maitre d'Hotel.

Have the cutlets cut thin. Season well with salt and pepper. Beat an egg well and roll the cutlets in the egg, then roll in bread crumbs. Drop in boiling lard and fry to a nice golden brown. Take out, drain off the lard, place on a heated dish and serve with garnish of parsley and sliced lemon and a Sauce à la Maitre d'Hotel. (See recipe.) The addition of a little lemon juice adds to the flavor when eating the cutlets.

### Veal Cutlets Breaded and Broiled.
Cotelettes de Veau Panées et Grillées.
6 Veal Cutlets. 1 Egg.
1 Cup of Bread Crumbs.
Parsley Sprigs.
Melted Butter or Sauce a la Ravigotte.

Have the cutlets as thin as possible. Season well, after having beat with the rolling-pin, and roll in a well-beaten egg and then in bread crumbs. Pat lightly with the hands and brush with melted butter. Place on a double broiler and broil on a very slow fire till no blood exudes. Serve with drawn butter sauce poured over or a Sauce à la Ravigotte. (See recipe.) Garnish the dish nicely with parsley sprigs.

### Cutlets of Veal à la Milanaise.
Cotelettes de Veau à la Milanaise.
6 Veal Cutlets. 1 Egg.
1 Cup of Bread Crumbs.
1 Tablespoonful of Melted Butter.
A Bed of Macaroni or Spaghetti.
Tomato Sauce.

Prepare as above, and serve the cutlets on a bed of boiled macaroni or spaghetti, and pour over the whole a Tomato Sauce.

### Veal Cutlets en Papillotes.
Cotelettes de Veau en Papillotes.
6 Veal Cutlets.
A Half Pound of Pork Sausage Meat.
½ Can Mushrooms. 1 Tablespoonful Butter.
1 Clove Garlic.
Salt and Pepper to Taste.

Use for this young and tender veal cutlets, cut very thin. Fry the chops, after seasoning well in butter, very slowly, and, when cooked, take out of the frying pan and put in a dish. Take a tablespoonful of butter and put in a frying pan. Add a half pound of sausage meat and a half can of mushrooms, chopped very fine. Mix well, and season with salt and pepper. Add a minced clove of garlic, and let it all cook five minutes. Take pieces of white foolscap paper and cut in cone or pyramidal shapes of the size of the cutlets. Fold the edges over the other very nicely, doubling the paper to form the half diamond or cone. Then oil the paper well with sweet oil. Take the stuffing of sausage meat and put a layer on one side of the fold of each cone. Lay the chop diagonally across this, so that the end reaches the tip of the cone, and spread over this another layer of the stuffing. Fold the paper over neatly around the edges, and then oil well again on the outside. Bake in an oven or lay on top of a gridiron and broil until brown. This will be in about five minutes. They will need no gravy, the oil having slightly permeated, and the chops being kept delicate and juicy by the dressing. Serve hot in the papers or papillotes, the guests removing them at the table. This is a very dainty way of serving veal cutlets, and the only way of serving them in papillotes.

### Veal Cutlets Smothered à la Créole.

Cotelettes de Veau Étouffées ou Braisées à la Créole.

6 Veal Cutlets.
6 Onions, Sliced Fine.
1 Tablespoonful of Lard.
1 Tablespoonful of Flour.
2 Tablespoonfuls of Vinegar.
Pepper and Salt to Taste.

Cut off the outer skin of the cutlets, and season well with salt and pepper. Dredge with flour. Place the tablespoonful of lard in a deep frying pan and let it melt. Then lay in the sliced onions, and over these lay the cutlets. Cover closely. Let them simmer over a hot fire for a few minutes and then turn the cutlets on the other side. After three minutes, add two tablespoonfuls of vinegar, chopped parsley, thyme and bay leaf and a clove of garlic. Turn the veal, letting the flour brown well, and keep the pot closely covered. When brown, pour over one cup of water, or a pint, which will be sufficient to cover the meat. Bring this to a brisk boil and set the pot back, where it can simmer gently for about two hours. Serve with a nice garnish of parsley or radishes.

### Veal Daube à la Créole.

Daube Froide à la Créole.

4 Pounds of Veal Rump.
2 Pig's Feet. ¼ Pound of Salt Fat Meat.
5 Large Onions. 2 Turnips.
5 Carrots. 2 Cloves of Garlic. 3 Bay Leaves.
1 Tablespoonful of Lard.
1 Glass of Sherry.
3 Sprigs of Thyme and Parsley.
Salt, Pepper and Cayenne to Taste.

Cut the salt meat into shreds, roll well in Cayenne and black pepper. Chop finely several sprigs of thyme and three bay leaves, one clove of garlic, three sprigs of parsley, and mash well three cloves and six allspice. Roll the strips of salt meat, which must be about three inches in length and one-half inch thick, in this. Make incisions into the rump of meat and force in the strips of fat meat and the spices. Then rub the whole well with salt and pepper, judging according to taste, and proceed to cook according to the recipe for Beef à la Mode. (See recipe Beef à la Mode.) Let the daube cook about four hours when you intend to serve it cold.

In the meantime, in another pot, place a veal steak of about two pounds and two pigs' feet. Season well with salt and pepper and Cayenne, and cover well with four quarts of water, and let them boil. Add one bay leaf, one sprig of thyme, one-half clove of garlic and one onion, all minced very fine, and two cloves mashed into almost a jelly, and one glass of Sherry or Madeira Wine. Let these boil well with the veal and pigs' feet. Then, when the veal and pigs' feet are cooked very tender, take them out of the pot and mince the meat of each very fine; return to the sauce, and again season highly, according to taste, for the flavor depends upon the piquant seasoning. After the daube has cooked four or five hours, take off the stove and pour over the sauce and set all in a cool place. Serve the next day—cold, cutting into thin slices. It will all have formed a jelly that is most delicious and appetizing.

If the flank is used, have it boned by the butcher, removing the little flat bones and all the gristle. In this case, trim it evenly and make a forcemeat of sausage, 1 cup, grated fine; bread crumbs, 1 cup, wet and squeezed; 1 clove of garlic or 1 grated onion, all minced very fine; 1 hard-boiled egg, 1 sprig of thyme and bay leaf, minced fine. Mix all thoroughly with the sausage meat and the bread; fry in a tablespoonful of butter for about five minutes; add a tablespoonful of Sherry, stir well; stuff the flank of veal, and then proceed in exactly the same manner as above indicated.

### Fricandeau of Veal.

Fricandeau de Veau.

A Rump of Veal of Two Pounds Weight.
1 Pint of Broth.
2 Onions. 2 Carrots.
½ Dozen Slices of Bacon.
½ Can of Green Peas or Mushrooms.
Thyme, Parsley, Bay Leaf.

For this take one whole piece of the rump of the veal, cut about two inches in thickness, and about the size of a large saucepan or frying pan in length and width. Lard the beef well with larding needles, and rub well with salt and pepper. Then slice two onions, two carrots, two sprigs of thyme and two bay leaves, and a half dozen slices of thinly-sliced fat bacon, two inches long and about the thickness of a dollar. Place the bacon in strips in the bottom of the saucepan, and lay over this a layer of the sliced carrots and onions. Put about a dozen little dots of lard over this at intervals, and sprinkle with salt and pepper. Lay the veal on top of this, and then cover up with a layer of the sliced onions and carrots, and lay strips of bacon on top. Cut a piece of paper the size of the saucepan, and cover it up. Place in a good oven, and let it bake three-quarters of an hour longer, slowly. Watch carefully. When done, take out the meat and place it in a dish. Take the sauce and add, if possible, one-half glass of white wine, and let it boil with the vegetables a moment. Then add one pint of broth or water, and let it cook well. Strain after it boils fifteen minutes. It will have become a very fine gravy. Add, if desired, a half can of mushrooms, or a half can of green peas, and let it boil for ten minutes longer. Then add the Fricandeau of Veal and let it warm well for about ten minutes and it is ready for the table. This is a most excellent family dish.

### Stewed Veal.

Ragout de Veau à la Bourgeoise.

3 Pounds of Brisket of Veal. 2 Large Onions.
2 Carrots. 2 Pints of Boiling Water.
½ Can of Tomatoes. 1 Tablespoonful Flour.
1 Tablespoonful of Lard.
1 Clove of Garlic. 1 Bay Leaf.
1 Sprig Each of Thyme and Sweet Marjoram.
Salt and Pepper and Cayenne to Taste.

The brisket of the veal or the neck is best for stews, preferably the brisket. Cut it into pieces of about 1 1-2 inches square, put a tablespoonful of lard in the stew pot, and when hot throw in the veal, which has been well seasoned with salt and black pepper. Let it brown, and then add the onions and carrots, which have been chopped fine, and one clove of garlic, minced very fine. Let this brown, and then add one tablespoonful of flour, sifted well, and let this brown nicely; add two pints of boiling water and 1 can of tomatoes, and a bay leaf, chopped very fine, and salt and pepper again to taste, adding, if desired, a dash of Cayenne. Many of the Creoles add a teaspoonful of vinegar. Set the stew back on the stove and cover closely. Let it simmer slowly for an hour and a half, or until the meat is perfectly tender. Then serve hot.

### Stewed Veal With Potatoes.

Ragout de Veau aux Pommes de Terre.

1 Brisket or Knuckle of Veal.
2 Small Potatoes. 2 Large Onions.
2 Carrots. 1 Tablespoonful of Flour.
1 Tablespoonful of Lard.
1 Clove of Garlic. 1 Bay Leaf.
1 Sprig Each of Thyme, Parsley and Sweet Marjoram.
Salt and Pepper to Taste.

Proceed in the same manner as for Ragoût de Veau à la Bourgeoise. Just before adding the water, add the potatoes, which have been peeled and cut into quarters or halves, according to size. Add the boiling water after they are in the stew about ten minutes, and set back, allowing it to simmer for an hour and a half, or until very tender.

### Stewed Veal With Mushrooms.

Ragoût de Veaux aux Champignons.

3 Pounds of Brisket of Veal. 2 Large Onions.
2 Carrots. 2 Pints of Boiling Water.
1 Can of Mushrooms. 1 Tablespoonful Flour
1 Tablespoonful of Lard.
1 Clove of Garlic. 1 Bay Leaf.
1 Sprig Each of Thyme and Sweet Marjoram.
Salt and Pepper and Cayenne to Taste.
Cut the veal into pieces of about 1 1-2 inches square.

The brisket of the veal or the neck is best for stews, preferably the brisket. Cut it into pieces of about 1 1-2 inches square, put a tablespoonful of lard in the stewpot, and, when hot, throw in the veal, which has been well seasoned with salt and black pepper. Let it brown, and then add the onions and carrots, which have been chopped fine, and 1 clove of garlic, minced very fine. Let this brown, and then add 1 tablespoonful of flour, sifted well, and let this brown nicely; add 2 pints of boiling water and 1 can of mushrooms whole, and a bay leaf, chopped very fine, and salt and pepper again to taste, adding, if desired, a dash of Cayenne. Set the stew back on the stove and cover closely. Let it simmer slowly for an hour and a half, or until the meat is perfectly tender. Then serve hot. This is a very delightful dish.

### Cream of Veal.

Créme de Veau.

3 Cups of Chopped Veal.
1 Cup of Chopped Ham.
Salt, Pepper and Cayenne to Taste.
½ Cup of Cream Sauce.

Utilize in this the left-over filet of veal. Chop very fine and add one cup of minced ham. Prepare a Cream Sauce (see recipe under "Sauces for Meats, Fish, etc.") in the proportions to make just a half cup. Season the chopped veal with this, add a dash of Cayenne and grated nutmeg, spread upon hot buttered toast, and serve at breakfast. Chicken and mutton may be prepared in the same way.

### Veal en Ratatouille.

Ratatouille de Veau à la Créole.

4 Pounds of Brisket of Veal.  ½ Pound of Ham
2 Cloves of Garlic.
½ Can of Tomatoes, or 6 Fresh.
4 Dozen Fresh Okra.   2 Large Onions.
2 Sweet Potatoes.   1 Bay Leaf.
1 Sprig of Thyme.   2 Sprigs of Parsley.
Salt, Pepper and Cayenne.

Cut the veal into pieces of about three inches in length and two in width. Cut the ham into dice shape, and the sweet potatoes, after peeling, into cubes of about one and a half inches. Add a half sweet pepper pod, if possible, being careful to extract all the seeds. Season the veal highly. Put a tablespoonful of lard into the stew pot (butter is nicer, if it can be afforded), add the veal and let it brown nicely; then add the ham, the sweet potatoes and the pepper pod, and let them simmer gently for about fifteen minutes. In the meantime, prepare the following sauce: Place a tablespoonful of butter into a saucepan, and when it melts add the chopped onion, and as they brown nicely, the minced herbs and garlic, and then the tomatoes sliced and chopped, in their own liquor. Let this stew for about fifteen minutes, and then add this to the stewing veal; mix thoroughly and set back on the stove, covering tightly, and let it simmer slowly and constantly, with a regular fire, for about two hours. Then add the okras, which have been tipped and sliced very thinly; let the mixture simmer for a half hour longer, and serve. This is an excellent family dish.

### Veal Patties or Veal Loaf.

Pâté de Veau ou Pain de Veau.

3 Pounds of Veal Cutlets.
3 Yolks of Eggs, beaten light.   6 Crackers.
1 Tablespoonful of Butter.
Chopped Parsley, Thyme and Bay Leaf.
Salt, Pepper and Cayenne to Taste.
1 Pound of Lean Ham. The Juice of 1 Lemon.

Stew the veal, and then powder the crackers very fine. Mince the cutlets, the herbs and the ham very fine. Season well with salt and pepper, and mix with the bread crumbs and beaten eggs. Add a clove of garlic to the taste, if desired; add juice of 1 lemon. With the whole form nice litte oaves of pie shape, smooth over the top with butter, brush with egg, beaten well, sprinkle with crumbs, and bake in a moderate oven, placing a buttered paper over the pâtés. The loaf may be formed whole and cut in thin slices and serve cold.

### Blanquette of Veal.

Blanquette de Veau.

3 Pounds of Veal Brisket.
2 Onions.   1 Carrot.   ½ Can of Mushrooms.
1 Tablespoonful of Butter.
1 Tablespoonful of Flour.
Yolks of 2 Eggs.   Juice of 1 Lemon.
½ Gallon of Water.
Salt and Pepper to Taste.

This is a very cheap and excellent dish and may be made with left-over meat. But the brisket is never expensive, and one may as well have it with the fresh meat. Take a brisket of veal and cut into pieces of two square inches. Put in a stew pot and cover with a half gallon of water, and add salt and pepper and two onions and one carrot, chopped fine. Let it boil till very tender. When it reaches this stage, take the meat out of the saucepan, and keep the water in which it was boiled. Take another saucepan and put a tablespoonful of butter in it, and as it melts add a tablespoonful of flour. Mix well, continuing to dissolve till it becomes a smooth cream; do not let it brown. Add one pint of the water in which the veal was boiled. Stir well, making it very light, and not thick. Add one-half can of mushrooms, and let the whole boil about fifteen minutes, so as to be very light. Then put in the veal, which is already cooked. Let it simmer for about fifteen minutes longer, and take off the fire and add the yolks of two eggs, well beaten, with two tablespoonfuls of the gravy and the juice of one lemon. Serve hot. This is the true Créole Blanquette de Veau, and it is a dish within the reach of all.

### Jellied Veal.

Noix de Veau à la Gelée.

The Filet or Part of Lower Shoulder Blade of Veal.
6 Peppercorns.
2 Calves' Feet.   1 Blade of Mace.
2 Large Onions.   2 Carrots.
1 Gill of French Vinegar.
1 Dozen Cloves Mashed Fine.
4 Allspice Mashed Fine.
3 Quarts of Beef Broth.

Cut the veal into fine pieces, season well, and put it in a kettle with the calves' feet, and season highly with pepper, Cayenne and salt to taste. Add three quarts of beef broth, or "pot-au-feu." Add the minced vegetables, herbs and the peppercorns, and let it boil gently until it forms a jelly, which will be in about two and a half hours. Then take out the veal and calves' feet, and carefuly remove all the bones, if any, and place in a mold. Let the liquor in which it was boiled boil until it is reduced to about a quart, adding, in the meantime, the good vinegar. When reduced, pour over the meat and set it in a cold place over night. When cold, turn out of the mold and garnish nicely with sliced lemon and parsley sprigs and serve in slices.

### Veal With Olives.

Veau aux Olives.

A Flank of Veal.
1 Slice of Cold Boiled Ham.
1 Grated Onion. 1 Hard-Boiled Egg.
1 Lemon. 1 Tablespoonful of Butter.
1 Dozen Stoned Olives.

This is a very old-fashioned Creole dish. Get a flank of veal and cut it into strips of about four inches in length and four in width. Cut off sufficient to make a half cup, and chop this fine, with a slice of cold boiled ham. Make a mince meat, adding chopped herbs, according to taste, 1 grated onion, 1 hard-boiled egg, the juice of 1 lemon and a tablespoonful of butter, with a half cup of bread crumbs. Take the strips of veal, stuff them nicely with this mixture and roll over the ends, tying to prevent the farcie from escaping. Place a tablespoonful of butter in a frying pan, and, when it heats, add the rolls of veal. Let them fry for ten minutes, turning, and then add soup broth sufficient to cover them. Cover closely and set back on the stove, and let them simmer steadily but slowly for an hour longer; then place in a hot dish, pour the gravy over, seasoning highly; add about two dozen stoned olives, and pour over the rolls and serve.

### Veal Pot Pie.

Vol-au-Vent de Veau.

A Veal Brisket.
2 Slices of Breakfast Bacon or Ham.
1 Tablespoonful of Butter. ½ Dozen Potatoes.
Thyme, Bay Leaf and Parsley.
Salt, Pepper and Cayenne to Taste.

This is a famous dish among the Creoles with large families. For a family of six, get a veal brisket, and allow three parts of minced veal to one of ham.

Make a nice pie crust. (See Plain Paste.) Line a baking pan with this, and bake in the oven. Cut the meat very fine, into dice, and season highly, rubbing with the minced thyme, parsley, bay leaf, and salt and pepper and Cayenne. Stew the meat as in Ragoût de Veau à la Bourgeoise. Place in the pan. Dot the top with bits of butter, and place over all a layer of pie crust, decorating the edges nicely. Bake to a nice brown. Serve in the dish in which it was cooked

### Veal Croquettes.

Croquettes de Veau.

3-4 of a Pound of Cold (Cooled) Veal.
1 Small Onion. 1 Bay Leaf.
4 Sprigs of Parsley.
1 Large Tablespoonful of Butter.
1 Onion. 1 Cup of Milk.
1 Teaspoonful of Salt.
Cayenne and Pepper to Taste.

This is an excellent way of utilizing left-over veal. Remove all the tough fibers and nerves. Hash the veal well and season with the minced vegetables and sweet herbs, mixing all thoroughly. Then take a cup of the soft of the bread, wet it and squeeze, and soak in milk, in which you have beaten two eggs. Mix all this with the meat very thoroughly and season to taste. When well mixed, form the meat into cylindrical shapes and brush with a little butter. Then roll in a beaten egg and roll again in powdered bread crumbs. Fry in boiling lard and serve hot on a plate garnished with fried parsley.

If made very carefully, it will be very difficult for anyone to discern the difference between a Chicken Croquette and a Veal Croquette.

### Calf's Head à la Poulette.

Tete de Veau à la Poulette.

1 Calf's Head. Yolk of 1 Egg.
1 Lemon. 2 Tablespoonfuls of Vinegar.
Sauce a la Poulette.

Clean and prepare the calf's head as in the recipe given for "Calf's Head Soup." (See recipe.) Then boil it according to recipe. Cut one lemon fine and add to the boiling calf head, which, it must be remembered, is boiled simply in water, and salt and pepper. Add two tablespoonfuls of good vinegar and let it cook till done. This is either used to make a mock turtle soup or is served with a Sauce à la Poulette. as follows: Make a Sauce à la Poulette (See recipe.) Put the calf's head in the sauce and let it boil for a half hour. Take the yolk of one egg and beat it as you would an omelet. Add to the calf's head and serve. This will give the sauce a fine golden color.

Calf's head may also be served with a Sauce Allemande. (See recipe.)

### Calf's Head à la Tortue.

Tete de Veau à la Tortue.

1 Calf's Head. 2 Large Onions.
½ Can of Mushrooms. 1 Lemon.
Thyme and Bay Leaf.
1 Clove of Garlic. 1 Wineglass of Sherry.
1 Tablespoonful of Butter.
2 Eggs. 1 Pint of Consomme or Water.

Slice the onions and mince the garlic. Put the butter into a stew pot, and as it melts add the onions

Add one tablespoonful of flour, sifted well, and, as this becomes brown, add one pint of consommé or water if you have not the broth. Then add the chopped thyme and bay leaf and the peel of one lemon, cut very fine, and the juice. Let all this simmer for about ten minutes and then cut up the calf's head and add it to the mixture. After fifteen minutes add a half can of mushrooms, and, in a few minutes, one small glass of Sherry wine. Let it all cook about ten minutes, and then season well, according to taste. Let all cook about half an hour longer, and, when ready to serve, place the calf's head in the middle of the dish, pour the gravy over and range the mushrooms around. Garnish them with the pieces of a flat omelet, which you have made from the two eggs and cut into diamond shapes, alternating with toast buttered and cut into diamond-shaped Croûtons.

There are many other ways of serving calf's head, but these are the standing Creole methods. It is well to repeat that a calf's head requires about three hours to boil.

### Calve's Brains Fried.
Cervelles de Veau Marinade.

Calve's Brains.     1 Onion.
2 Sprigs of Parsley.     1 Bay Leaf.
Grated Bread Crumbs.

Plunge the brains into cold water to disgorge them of all blood and remove the fine skin and blood that surrounds them. Then blanch with scalding water. In five minutes take them out of the hot water and put them into a saucepan and cover with cold water. Add a tiny onion, sliced fine; parsley and bay leaf, whole. Let them simmer gently for five minutes. Then take from the fire and drain. When cold, cut into pieces of a square inch and dip in a batter or tomato sauce, and then in grated bread crumbs, patting gently. Drop into boiling lard and fry to a golden brown. Take out and drain of grease and serve on a bed of fried parsley. A garnish of boiled green peas is also very pretty and palatable.

### Calve's Brains, Brown Butter Sauce.
Cervelles de Veau au Beurre Noir.

Calve's Brains.
1 Tablespoonful of Butter.
1 Small Onion.     1 Bay Leaf.
1 Sprig of Thyme.     1 Sprig of Parsley.
Sauce aux Beurre Noir.

Prepare the brains as mentioned above by boiling, and then place in a saucepan, with a tablespoonful of butter. Cut up a tiny onion, and add also a sprig of thyme, bay leaf and parsley, all minced very fine. Add to the butter, and then add the brains cut in slices a half inch thick. Season again to taste. Fry for five minutes, and serve with a Sauce aux Beurre Noir. (See recipe.)

### Calf's Liver Fried.
Foie de Veau Sauté à la Lyonnaise.

1 Pound of Liver     2 Onions.
1 Tablespoonful of Lard or Butter.
Salt and Pepper to Taste.

Slice the liver very fine into pieces of about three inches in length and one in width. Season well with salt and pepper. Slice two onions very fine and take a tablespoonful of lard or butter and put into the frying pan. When it heats, add the onions and, as they brown, place on top the slices of liver. Let them brown on one side about two minutes and a half, and then turn on the other. Let this side brown two minutes and a half longer and serve with the onion sauce, to which add a teaspoonful of vinegar.

### Calve's Liver à la Bourgeoise.
Foie de Veau Sauté à la Bourgeoise.

1 Calf's Liver.  1 Carrot.  1 Onion.
1 Turnip.     1 Tablespoonful of Butter.
1 Bay Leaf.
1 Pint of Broth or Water.
1 Tablespoonful of Flour.
Salt and Pepper to Taste.

Wash the liver and lard it well with needles. Put a tablespoonful of lard of butter into the frying pan, and when hot, add immediately the onion, carrot and turnip, all sliced very fine, and then the fine herbs, nicely minced. Let these brown, and add the liver. Pour over this about two spoons of White Wine or one of Sherry. Add about a pint of consommé or boiling water. Season highly, cover the saucepan well, set back on the fire, and let it simmer for about half an hour, and serve.

### Fried Liver and Bacon.
Foie de Veau Frit au Petit Salé.

1 Pound of Calf's Liver.
½ Pound of Breakfast Bacon.
½ Teaspoonful of Salt.
1 Tablespoonful of Flour.
Black Pepper to Taste.

Slice the liver into pieces of about three inches in length and one-quarter of an inch in thickness; slice the bacon very thin, having as many slices of the bacon as of the liver. Put the bacon in the frying pan and fry brown; then place it in a heated dish and set over a pot of boiling water and cover to keep warm. Dust the liver with flour, after having seasoned well with salt and pepper and fry it in the bacon fat. When it cooks about five minutes, allowing two minutes and a half to each side, take out and arrange on the same dish with the bacon in alternate slices. Garnish nicely with parsley and serve.

### Calf's Feet, Plain.
Pieds de Veau au Naturel.
```
        3 Calf's Feet.
3 Quarts of Cold Water.  1 Gill of Vinegar.
       2 Tablespoonfuls of Flour.
   1 Onion.           1 Carrot.
       12 Whole Pepper Corns.
        2 Tablespoonfuls of Salt.
            1 Herb Bouquet.
```
Split each of the calf's feet in two. Then carefully remove the larger bones, and cut the meat into pieces of about one inch square. Soak well in fresh water for one hour. Then wash and drain thoroughly. Put two tablespoonfuls of flour and three quarts of cold water into a saucepan; stir well, mixing thoroughly; place the feet in the mixture and add one onion (chopped fine), twelve whole peppers, one carrot cut into fine shreds; the herb bouquet and two tablespoonfuls of salt. Let the feet boil briskly for about one hour. Take from the fire and drain well. They are now ready to serve with any sauce that may be desired.

### Calf's Feet à la Poulette.
Pieds de Veau à la Poulette.
```
           Calf's Feet.
     1 Tablespoonful of Butter.
     1 Tablespoonful of Sifted Flour.
1 Pint of Water.  ½ Can of Mushrooms.
   Yolk of 1 Egg.   Juice of 1 Lemon.
```
Boil the calf's feet; then take out the larger bones and cut in pieces of about an inch suare. Prepare a Sauce à la Poulette by putting one tablespoonful of butter in a saucepan, and, as it melts, add two tablespoonfuls of sifted flour; add about one pint of the water in which the calf's feet have been boiled. Stir well and throw in the calf's feet, salt and pepper to taste, and, if desired, about a quarter of a can of chopped mushrooms. Let it boil about five minutes, and then take off the stove and add the yolk of an egg (beaten well), the juice of one lemon, and serve.

### Calf's Feet, Tomato Sauce.
Pieds de Veau, Sauce Tomate.
```
        3 Calf's Feet.
  A Sauce a la Tomate (1 Pint).
```
Prepare the feet as in the recipe "Calf's Feet, Plain," and pour over, when ready to serve, a Sauce à la Tomate. (See recipe.)

### Calf's Feet, Piquant Sauce.
Pieds de Veau, Sauce Piquante.
```
        3 Calf's Feet.
   1 Pint of Sauce Piquante.
```
Prepare the calf's feet as in recipe for "Calf's Feet, Plain," and add, when ready to serve, one pint of Sauce Piquante. (See recipe.)

### Calf's Feet, Sauce Remoulade.
Pieds de Veau à la Sauce Remoulade.
```
        3 Calf's Feet.
    Sauce Remoulade, 1 Pint.
```
Prepare the feet as in the recipe for Calf's Feet Plain, and pour over, when ready to serve, one pint of hot Sauce Remoulade. (See recipe.)

### Calf's Feet, Italian Sauce.
Pieds de Veau à la Sauce Italienne.
```
        3 Calf's Feet.
  1 Pint of Sauce a l'Italienne.
```
Prepare the feet as in the recipe for "Calf's Feet, Plain," and serve with one pint of Sauce à l'Italienne. (See recipe.)

## SWEETBREADS.
Ris de Veau.

Sweetbreads are the glands in the throat of a sucking calf. They are found in the throat of all very young sucking animals, but are more considerable in the throat of the young calf, and even then at the largest are seldom bigger than a man's fist doubled over. The sweetbreads are the glands used by the calf in sucking, and are only found in the young calf during the period when it is fed on its mother's milk. When a calf is turned out to grass, the sweetbreads, or milk glands, begin to grow smaller, and in three or four days disappear, no longer standing out in a mass of delicate flesh, but hanging long and soft and flabby. On account of their delicacy, sweetbreads have always been the object of particular attention of good cuisinières, because, in a fine, fresh state and with proper preparation they can be made not only into a most delightful and palatable dish, but are, perhaps, the most recherché of all meat dishes. At least, the sweetbreads have always been so considered by the French, who set the world the lesson of good eating hundreds of years ago; and the Creole chefs of New Orleans, improving upon old French methods of cooking, as well as originating their own delicious combinations, sustain the verdict of the gourmets of the ancient mother country.

It is surprising what a diversity of definitions of sweetbreads are given by educated people in America. Scarcely one person in ten, if the question is put directly, can tell just what a sweetbread is, and they can scarcely be blamed, for the most distinguished lexicographers, from Webster down to the compiler of the New Century, fail to give the correct definition. Webster defines sweetbreads "as the pancreas of any animal," and defines "pancreas" as "a gland of the body situated between the stomach and the vertebrae of the loïns." The New Century's definition is almost parallel. Every old French dictionary (for it was French cooks who first began to use the sweetbreads in cooking) define sweetbreads as the glands in the throat of any young animal, more generally the sucking calf, as these latter are used exclusively in the preparation of sweetbread dishes. The old Creole gourmets have had infinite amusement over the definitions given by American dictionary makers, and, as for the ancient Creole butchers in the French Market, they curl their lips in scorn and tell you just to come down to the New Orleans Slaughter-House when the calves are being killed, and they will show you the sucking calves, which have sweetbreads, and the calves which have gone out to grass and in whose throats the sweetbreads have disappeared. If you quote Webster and the New Century, they will tell you that a good butcher knows better than the dictionary maker where meats are concerned.

The Picayune feels constrained to give the definition of sweetbreads as a matter of correct information. The custom of calling the panacreas the "sweetbreads" is accounted for by our Creole butchers in this way: The sweetbreads are very expensive, the smallest costing at least 25 cents apiece. To make a dish for six, allowing one apiece, would, therefore, cost $1.50, for sweetbreads alone, without other ingredients. Sweetbreads are not always to be found in the market in quantity to supply the demand. Large canning factories have therefore, made it a practice to take the gland of the stomach of the calf, or pancreas, and prepare it in such a way, by canning, that it partakes somewhat of the nature of a sweetbread; and, as there is such widespread ignorance as to what a sweetbread really is, even among the most fastidious epicureans of the United States, the "pancreas" is passed off as such, and is becoming gradually accepted as such outside of the New Orleans market, where the old French or Gascon butcher scorns to sell you anything but the real sweetbread. He has too much respect for the traditional cooking of his native France and his own reputation as a reliable butcher to do such a thing as this. He laughs at the great big sweetbreads as large as a man's hand, spread out to the full extent and width, that come in cans labeled "Sweetbreads," and will tell you that no sucking calf in the world, unless it had goitre, could have such a gland in the throat. The French, indeed, use the term "Pancreas" in connection with sweetbread; but the word is meant to imply in this signification "toute chair," or "all flesh," and has nothing in common with the pancreas proper, or stomach gland. Hence the very apt name which they have given to the sweetbread, "Ris de Veau"; it implies to all who have a comprehension of this beautiful and expressive language the soft, delicate, milky gland that is so dainty and recherché a dish in the most elegant French and Creole homes.

With this explanation, the Picayune "Cook Book" will now give the most delicious Creole modes of preparing this delectable dish.

### How to Blanch Sweetbreads.

Select three fine pairs of sweetbreads and clean and trim nicely. Soak them for at least two and a half hours in cold fresh water, pouring off the water from time to time till three separate waters have been used. About three-quarters of an hour may be allowed for the first two waters. Add a pinch of salt to each water. After soaking for the time specified, drain the sweetbreads and place them in a saucepan of cold water and set on the fire; add a half teaspoonful of salt, and let them blanch till they come to a boil. Then drain and set them in cold water to freshen. Drain thoroughly, press them into shape and lay on a napkin in a cool place. They are now ready for general use. The sweetbreads should be pressed down gently with a pound weight, in order to flatten well.

### Sweetbreads Larded With Mushroom Sauce.

Ris de Veau Piqué aux Champignons.

6 Sweetbreads. 1 Carrot.
4 Thin Slices of Bacon.
1 Onion. ½ Can of Mushrooms.
1 Tablespoonful of Flour.
1 Tablespoonful of Butter.
1 Whole Sprig of Thyme. 3 Bay Leaves.
1 Wineglass of Madeira or Sherry.
1 Pint of Consomme.
Salt and Pepper. Croutons.

Soak the sweetbreads in clear, cold water as soon as you come from market, for they are so delicate that they spoil very easily. Wash well, to take off all the blood; wash again in a clear cold water, and parboil them for ten minutes. Then drain them of all water, press them into shape and put them on a clean cloth on a table and cover with a plank and put a weight upon them to flatten. When cold, clean with a knife, cutting off all the outside nerves, veins and fibers, without breaking the sweetbreads, however. Cut fat lard into little strips like matches, and, with a larding needle, lard the sweetbreads, slipping the needle in on one side and bringing out on the other. Lard each sweetbread eight times. Then slice one onion and one carrot very fine; mince three bay leaves and a whole sprig of thyme.

Take a very thin slice of very fat bacon, cut it into thin strips and cover the bottom of the saucepan with these. Lay the sweetbreads on top and put on top of these the sliced onion, carrot and finely minced herbs. Salt and pepper by sprinkling nicely. Cover this with a few fine strips of fat bacon. Cover the whole with a brown paper which has been well greased with butter, and put the pan in a slow oven with the paper on top. Let the sweetbreads bake for about twenty minutes, basting occasionally. In the meantime make a Sauce à l'Espagnole as follows: Chop a few pieces of beef very fine, or else use good stock. If meat is used boil in about two pints of water. When it is reduced to about one pint, take off and strain. Take a tablespoonful of butter or lard, and brown lightly with a tablespoonful of flour. Then add the water and dissolve well, stirring constantly to prevent being lumpy. Add to this a half can of mushrooms, and let it simmer a few minutes, and then add a glass of Sherry or Madeira Wine. Let it cook rapidly, for about ten minutes. In the meantime, the sweet breads will have been cooked to a nicety. Take them out of the pan and put one by one into the sauce, and let them cook ten minutes longer. Serve with buttered Croûtons cut in dice shapes. Sweetbreads are always served with fresh young green peas. This is a famous Creole dish.

### Sweetbreads With Green Peas.

Ris de Veau Sauté aux Petit Pois.

3 Pairs of Sweetbreads.
1 Onion. 1 Carrot. 4 Slices of Fat Bacon.
1 Can of French Petit Pois, or 1 Pint
of Fresh Young Green Peas.
3 Bay Leaves.
1 Sprig of Thyme. 3 Cloves.
½ Pint of Fresh Milk. 1 Pint of Consomme.
Salt and Pepper to Taste.
Croutons.

Prepare the Sweetbreads in exactly the same manner as indicated in the above recipe, which is the very nicest way in which they can be served. Make the sauce as indicated, letting it brown slightly, and, instead of the mushrooms, add a can of French Petit Pois or a pint of fresh young green peas that have already been boiled well and drained from all liquor. Place the sweetbreads in one by one and let them cook for ten minutes longer and serve with the sweetbreads placed in the center of the dish, and the green peas around them as a garnish.

### Sweetbreads With Truffles.

Ris de Veau aux Truffes.

3 Pairs of Sweetbreads.
4 Slices of Fat Bacon. ½ Can of Truffles.
1 Onion. 1 Carrot.
1 Glass of Madeira or Sherry Wine.
1 Pint of Consomme or Water.
1 Tablespoonful of Flour.
1 Tablespoonful of Butter.
3 Bay Leaves. 1 Sprig of Thyme.
Salt and Pepper.
Croutons.

Prepare the sweetbreads in exactly the same manner as in the recipe "Sweetbreads with Mushrooms." When making the sauce, add a wineglassful of Madeira or Sherry, and one-half can of truffles cut in halves. Serve with the truffles as a garnish about the sweetbreads. This is a very expensive dish, very récherché and very elegant.

### Sweetbreads à la Crème.

Ris de Veau à la Crème.

3 Pairs of Sweetbreads.
10 Mushrooms. 1½ Tablespoonfuls of Butter.
1½ Tablespoonfuls of Flour.
1 Pint of Cream.

Clean and parboil the sweetbreads for twenty minutes. Then remove all veins and nerves, and chop the meat into pieces of about an inch and a half. Chop the mushrooms very fine indeed. Put the butter in a saucepan, and, when it melts, add the flour, being careful not to let it brown. When perfectly smooth, add the milk and stir constantly until it boils. Then add the chopped mushrooms and let them simmer for five minutes. Season well to taste with salt and white pepper. Then add the sweetbreads and cook for five minutes longer and serve hot. At luncheons and dinners the Sweetbreads à la Crème are served in small silver shells or fancy paper cases.

### Sweetbreads à la Financière.

Ris de Veau à la Financière.

3 Pairs of Sweetbread ½ Pound of Butter.
3 Carrots. 2 Sprigs of Thyme.
3 Bay Leaves.
1 Pint of Beef Consomme or Water.
1 Pint of Rich Chicken Broth or Water.
2 Truffles. 12 Mushrooms. 18 Stoned Olives.
12 Godiveau Quenelles.
2 Blanched Chicken Livers.
A Half Pint of Madeira or Sherry Wine.
A Dash of Cayenne.
Salt and Pepper to Taste.
Croutons Fried in Butter to Garnish.

Select fine, fresh Sweetbreads and prepare as in the recipe for Sweetbreads Larded With Mushrooms. Parboil for twenty minutes; then drain of all water; press them into shape, lay on a clean napkin and cover with a plank and place a weight upon them to press and make solid.

Take a piece of fine salt pork, and cut into little thin strips like matches and lard the Sweetbreads with this, using a very fine larding needle, and following implicitly the direction given in the recipe for Sweetbreads Larded With Mushroom Sauce. Lard each Sweetbread eight times. Then take a shallow saucepan and put within a half pound of butter. When the butter melts, lay in the Sweetbreads, one by one. Season with salt and pepper very lightly, and add the three carrots, sliced fine, and the onion, sliced very fine. Add the finely minced thyme and bay leaves. Butter a piece of brown paper and cover the saucepan; then set in the oven and let the Sweetbreads cook slowly till they are of a bright golden brown. From time to time uncover the saucepan and turn the Sweetbreads, so that all portions of them may be evenly colored. When they have reached this beautiful color add one pint of good beef broth (Consommé or Bouillon), and let them simmer for a half or three-quarters of an hour. When nearly ready to serve, prepare a Sauce à la Financière as follows: Take two tablespoonfuls of butter, melt and remove from the fire, and add gradually a tablespoonful of flour; blend well with a wooden spoon till very smooth, and moisten with one pint of rich chicken broth and set on the fire. Add the truffles, nicely sliced; a dozen and a half stoned olives; the blanched chicken livers, cut in pieces; the mushrooms, nicely chopped; a half pint of Madeira or Sherry Wine, salt and pepper to taste, and a dash of Cayenne or Tabasco. Let the sauce cook for twenty minutes. It should be of the consistency of rich cream. Place the sauce in a round dish, lay the Sweetbreads over it, garnish with the Godiveau Quenelles and Croûtons fried in butter and send to the table hot.

### Sweetbreads à la Poulette.

Ris de Veau à la Poulette.

3 Pairs of Sweetbreads.
The Yolks of 4 Eggs. The Juice of 1 Lemon.
½ Tablespoonful of Butter.
Chopped Parsley to Garnish.
A Sauce a la Poulette.

Parboil the Sweetbreads for about twenty minutes, then make a Sauce à la Poulette (see recipe), adding the juice of one lemon and seasoning to taste. But do not add the eggs till the sauce has been taken from the fire or it will curdle. When the sauce is made, place the sweetbreads in it, one by one, and let it come to the boiling point. Then remove from the fire and stir in the yolks of four eggs that have been well beaten, and a half tablespoonful of butter. Sprinkle with finely-chopped parsley, pour over the sweetbreads and serve.

### Sweetbreads in Casseroles.

Ris de Veau en Casseroles, ou Vol-au-Vent.

3 Pairs of Sweetbreads.
¼ Can of Mushrooms.
2 Dozen Oysters.
1 Glass of Sherry Wine.
A Sauce à la Poulette.

Parboil the Sweetbreads in exactly the same manner as in the above recipe for Sweetbreads à la Poulette. Six sweetbreads will suffice. Cut them into dice pieces after parboiling; add a quarter of a can of finely-chopped mushrooms to the sauce, and a glass of Sherry wine. Take two dozen oysters and cut in pieces, taking off all the hard portions. Add the chopped sweetbreads to the sauce, and, after ten minutes, add the oysters. Let them cook for five minutes, have ready a pan filled with a rich vol-au-vent crust, pour the mixture in and serve. Or make the vol-au-vent crust, which is very difficult (see recipe), into small shells; bake and fill with the sweetbreads. This is an elegant dish for fashionable luncheons, but quite above the ordinary householder's purse. The sweetbreads are generally served in caseroles or fancy cases.

### Sweetbreads Crépinettes.

Crépinettes de Ris de Veau.

3 Pairs of Sweetbreads.
1 Onion. 1 Bay Leaf. 1 Sprig of Thyme.
½ Clove of Garlic.
1 Tablespoonful Butter.
1 Teaspoonful of Prepared Mustard.

Clean and parboil the sweetbreads as already shown in recipe. Chop an onion very fine and place it in a saucepan with a tablespoonful of butter. Let them simmer without browning; add one bay leaf, one sprig of thyme, one-half clove of garlic, a teaspoonful of prepared mustard, and mix well. Then add a pint of water and stir well; then add the sweetbreads which have been chopped very fine and formed into "Crépinettes," or little fringed balls, by patting with the hand; let them simmer for about fifteen minutes longer. Serve with any sauce, preferably a Cream Sauce. (See recipe under chapter "Sauces for Fish, Meats, etc.")

### Fried Sweetbreads Breaded.

Ris de Veau Panées.
3 Pairs of Sweetbreads.
1 Egg.   Grated Bread Crumbs.
A Cream Sauce.

Wash and parboil the sweetbreads

and then trim off all tendons and nerves. Cut into pieces of about two inches long and roll first in a well-beaten egg and then in bread crumbs. Drop into boiling fat and fry till a golden brown. Serve with a Cream Sauce.

### Broiled Sweetbreads.

Ris de Veau Grillées.

3 Pairs of Sweetbreads.
2 Tablespoonfuls of Melted Butter.
Salt and Pepper to Taste.

Parboil the sweetbreads and then remove all nerves. Cut into halves. Brush with melted butter and place on the gridiron. Broil nicely, and, when well colored, take off, pour melted butter over them, season again, and serve very hot. This is a delicious breakfast dish.

### Sweetbreads Smothered.

Ris de Veau Braissés.

3 Pairs of Sweetbreads.
2 Tablespoonfuls of Butter.
1 Carrot. 1 Onion.
2 Sprigs of Thyme. 2 Bay Leaves.
1 Pint of Consomme or Water.
Salt and Pepper to Taste.

Prepare the Sweetbreads as in the recipe for "Sweetbreads Larded With Mushrooms." Put them into a saucepan with two tablespoonfuls of butter, and let them brown slightly. Add a finely-sliced carrot and onion and the minced herbs. Season lightly with salt and pepper. Cover the saucepan with a buttered paper, and then cover closely. Occasionally uncover and turn the Sweetbreads till they are all browned evenly to a nice golden brown. When they have reached this color, add the pint of Consommé or water and cover again and let them simmer for about twenty minutes. They are now ready to serve with any kind of sauce or garnish that may be desired. In serving sweetbreads thus prepared, always place the sauce on the dish, first having the dish very hot; lay the Sweetbreads over the sauce, garnish nicely with fried Croûtons and serve. Sweetbreads thus prepared may be served with a Sauce à l'Oiselle, Sauce Salpicon, Sauce à la Soubise, Sauce à la Bearnaise, Sauce à la Duxelle, Sauce aux Gourmets, with a Purée of Spinach, or with hot Crêpes.

### Observations.

There are many other ways of serving Sweetbreads. We have "Ris de Veau à l'Espagnole," "Ris de Veau en Coquilles," etc., for the Creoles have infinite variety in serving almost every dish. But the above are the recipes in most general use, and the recipes "Sweetbreads Larded with Mushrooms," Sweetbreads with Green Peas" and "Sweetbreads with Truffles" cannot be too highly recommended. These preparations are in a very distinct manner peculiar to New Orleans, and are elegant entrées at the most distinguished feasts.

## TRIPE.

Tripe.

Tripe, which is the large stomach of ruminating animals, is generally cleaned, scraped, bleached and preparde by the butchers before it is sold. It is nutritious and digestible. To prepare the tripe properly for cooking, wash it carefully in several waters. When thoroughly clean, put it in a kettle of cold water; add one tablespoonful of salt and one of vinegar, and let the tripe boil for five hours at least. In the meantime, pared by the butchers before it is always best, if tripe is to be used for breakfast to prepare it and give the long boiling the day before. Drain thoroughly. Then it is ready for preparation according to any of the following recipes:

### Stewed Tripe.

Tripe Sautée.

2 Pounds of Prepared Tripe.
1 Tablespoonful of Butter.
1 Tablespoonful of Flour.
1 Sprig of Parsley. 1 Bay Leaf.
½ Clove of Garlic. ½ Pint of Milk.
Chopped Parsley to Garnish.

Take the prepared tripe and cut into strips of about one finger length and a half inch in width. Put a tablespoonful in a saucepan; add a finely-sliced onion, a sprig of parsley and a bay leaf, minced. Stir in the melted butter without letting it brown, then add a tablespoonful of flour. Stir well and add a pint of milk. Stir constantly till it comes to a boil, seasoning to the taste with salt and pepper. Then add the well-seasoned tripe and let it cook over a moderate fire for about five minutes.

### Stewed Tripe à la Lyonnaise.

Tripe à la Lyonnaise.

2 Pounds of Prepared Tripe.
1 Tablespoonful of Butter.
1 Tablespoonful of Flour.
1 Sprig of Parsley. 1 Bay Leaf.
½ Clove of Garlic.
The Juice of 1 Lemon, or a Teaspoonful of Vinegar.
Chopped Parsley to Garnish.

Place a tablespoonful of butter in a saucepan and add one chopped onion, one carrot, finely sliced; a sprig each of thyme, parsley, bay leaf and salt and pepper. Let it brown slightly and place the tripe on top, and adding a half clove of garlic, minced very fine. Sprinkle with chopped parsley and add the juice of one lemon. Let it all simmer for a few minutes and then add a half cup of broth or hot water. Season to the taste, let it simmer for twenty minutes longer and serve.

### Tripe à la Poulette.

Gras-Double à la Poulette.
2 Pounds of Tripe.
2 Tablespoonfuls of Butter.
1 Tablespoonful of Flour.
1 Sprig of Parsley.   1 Bay Leaf.
The Yolks of 2 Eggs.
A Sauce a la Poulette.

Having prepared the tripe according to the directions given under the heading of "Tripe," make a rich Sauce à la Poulette, always omitting the eggs till later. (See recipe.) Take eight small white onions that have already been boiled in plain water until they are perfectly tender, and add to the sauce. Let them stew for about five minutes. Then add the tripe, which has been cut into pieces of three inches in length, and one-half inch in width, and stew the whole gently for about a half hour. Take off the fire and add the beaten yolks of two eggs, stirring constantly and serve hot.

### Fried Tripe.
Tripe Frite.
2 Pounds of Tripe.
1 Egg.   Grated Bread Crumbs.
Parsley and Lemon to Garnish.

Prepare the tripe, boil well, and cut into pieces of three inches in length and one in width. Roll it in a beaten egg and then roll in grated bread crumbs. Drop in boiling lard and fry to a golden brown. (See directions for frying.) Take off the fire and place on a bed of fried parsley and garnish with sliced lemon. Serve with a Sauce Piquante or a Sauce Poivrade. (See recipe for meat sauces.)

### Tripe à la Créole.
Gras-Double à la Créole.
2 Pounds of Tripe.
12 Tomatoes, or a 2-Pound Can.
2 Onions.   1 Tablespoonful of Butter.
1 Square Inch of Lean Ham.
2 Cloves of Garlic.
3 Sprigs Each of Thyme and Bay Leaf.
Salt and Pepper to Taste.
A Dash of Cayenne.

Clean the tripe well, and boil till tender. Cut it into slices of about two inches long and half an inch wide. Take two onions and slice them fine, and a tablespoonful of butter. Put in a saucepan together and let them smother well. Then chop about one inch sqquare of lean ham very fine, and add. Take two cloves of garlic, chopped fine, with three sprigs each of thyme and bay leaf, minced very fine. Put in a saucepan, and let all brown. Then add about twelve large, fresh tomatoes, or the contents of a two-pound can. Season all to taste with salt and Cayenne pepper. Let it cook for ten minutes, and then add the tripe, and let all smother for twenty-five minutes. Season to taste, and serve hot.

### Tripe à la Mode de Caën.

Gras-Double à la Mode de Caen.

3 Pounds of Tripe. 3 Onions. 3 Carrots.
1 Dozen Whole Bay Leaves.
1 Dozen Whole Cloves.
1 Dozen Whole Allspice.
3 Cloves of Garlic (whole).
1 Ounce of Thyme (whole).
2 Dozen Pieces of Bacon 2 Inches Square.
½ Bottle of White Wine.
1 Cup of Broth or Water.
Salt, Cayenne and Chili Pepper to Taste.

Take three pounds of tripe. Cut the tripe into pieces of about two inches square. Slice three onions and three large carrots very fine. Take one dozen whole bay leaves, one ounce of thyme, whole; one dozen whole cloves, and the same number of allspice, three whole cloves of garlic, two dozen pieces of very thin bacon cut into pieces of two inches square. Have ready a two-gallon earthen jar that can stand baking in an oven. Put in the bottom of the jar a thin layer of butter. Place on top a thin layer of bacon, then a thin layer of onions, carrots, bay leaves, thyme, garlic, spices, dividing into two equal portions the whole amount. Sprinkle over the whole salt, Cayenne and Chili pepper. On top of this lay one-half of the tripe. Over the tripe place a layer of bacon; then vegetables, seasonings, etc. Over this place another layer of tripe, and remnants of thyme, bay leaf, vegetables, bacon, etc., as below, this being the last layer. Pour over all a half bottle of White Wine and one cup of broth or water. Cover the jar closely with a layer of Pie Paste (Paté Brisée—see recipe), set in a very moderate oven, and let it cook slowly for at least five hours of constant, steady cooking. This is a very récherché old-fashioned Creole dish, and very excellent. Some add to the tripe a small quantity of calf's head or feet. In making this dish you will need little else for dinner besides a soup or gumbo.

## CHAPTER XIV.

### MUTTON.

#### Du Mouton

The leg, shoulder and loin of the mutton are used as roasting pieces. The brisket and neck are used for soups and stews, and from the loins are cut the delicate French chops or cutlets of mutton. Mutton is so susceptible of elegant seasoning, and so easily impregnated with the different aromatic herbs used in cooking that it becomes not only most agreeable to the taste, but tender and very easily digested.

**Something to Remember in Cooking Mutton.**

Remember that mutton must never be fried. You will hear of mutton chops breaded, and mutton chops en papilotte, in imitation of the ways of cooking veal chops, but the Creoles very wisely and very sensibly refrain from cooking mutton in any other ways than those given in this book. No good Creole cook will eat a fried mutton chop.

**Roast Leg of Mutton.**

Gigot Roti.

1 Leg of Mutton.
Salt and Pepper to Taste.

Select a fine, tender leg of mutton. Wipe thoroughly with a damp towel and dredge with salt and pepper, thoroughly rubbing, so that the meat may be penetrated by the seasoning. Place the mutton in a baking pan, set in a quick oven and bake, basting every ten minutes or so, allowing twelve minutes to every pound. The mutton must never be overdone but underdone. The Creoles always serve it rare. It will require no larding, for the meat is rich and soon makes sufficient juice to allow frequent basting. To ascertain if done, press with the fingers or stick with a fork; the juice will spurt out, and it is then ready to serve. Decorate the bone with a quilling of white paper, and serve in its own sauce. The dish on which mutton is placed must always be very hot, as also the plates on which it is to be served.

Avoid thickening the gravy with flour. No practice is more reprehensible. If well cooked, the juice will almost spurt from the leg before it is carved. A very nice way to serve it, and one generally used by the Creoles, is to put a circle of nicely boiled and browned turnips around the dish, and serve with the gravy of the mutton.

**Roast Saddle of Mutton.**

Selle de Mouton Rotie.

A Saddle of Mutton.
Salt and Pepper to Taste.
Currant Jelly.

A saddle of mutton is two loins. Proceed to roast in exactly the same manner as for a single leg. Serve with Currant Jelly.

**Roast Loin of Mutton.**

Filet de Mouton Roti.

A Filet of Mutton.
Salt and Pepper to Taste.
Garnish of Green Peas.

The filet of mutton is a square cut from the loin. Proceed to dredge with salt and pepper, and roast in exactly the same manner as leg of mutton. The Creoles serve the filet very often with a garnish of green peas (Petit Pois) piled around.

**Boiled Leg of Mutton, Caper Sauce.**

Gigot de Mouton Bouilli, Sauce aux Câpres.

1 Leg of Mutton. 1 Herb Bouquet.
Salt and Pepper to Taste.
A Caper Sauce.

Rub the leg of mutton well with salt and pepper. Have ready a pot of boiling water, into which you have thrown the herbs, bay leaf, salt and pepper, allowing a teaspoonful each of the two latter ingredients. Put the leg of mutton into the water, being very careful to have it well covered with water, else the meat will blacken. Let it boil gently but steadily, allowing fifteen minutes to every pound of meat. When done, place on a dish and serve with a Caper Sauce. In serving slice nicely and put a few drops of lemon on each slice, and pour over the Caper sauce. (See recipe Caper Sauce.) Mutton thus prepared is also served with a Purée of Turnips.

### Mutton Stew.
Ragoût de Mouton aux Pommes de Terre.

4 Pounds of the Brisket of Mutton.
6 Irish Potatoes.
3 Large Onions.   1 Bay Leaf.
¼ Clove of Garlic.
¼ Tablespoonful of Lard.
2 Quarts of Water.
1 Square Inch of Ham, Chopped Very Fine.
Salt and Pepper to Taste.

Cut the mutton into pieces of about an inch square and season well with salt and pepper. Put one-quarter of a tablespoonful of lard into the stewpot, and when it melts add the thinly sliced onions. Let these brown for a few minutes and then add the mutton and the ham, chopped very fine. Let this continue browning, and when slightly browned, add one tablespoonful of finely sifted flour and stir well. Then add the finely-minced bay leaf and a half clove of garlic, minced fine. Brown lightly, for a mutton stew must never be dark. After twenty minutes, add two quarts of boiling water and let it boil for about ten minutes longer, seasoning to taste. Then add the potatoes, cut into halves, and let the mixture cook for three-quarters of an hour longer, making one hour and a half in all. Let it simmer gently all the time, so that the meat may be perfectly tender.

### Mutton Stew With Turnips.
Ragoûts de Mouton aux Navets.

4 Pounds of the Brisket of Mutton.
6 Turnips.   3 Large Onions.
1 Bay Leaf.   ½ Clove of Garlic.
¼ Tablespoonful of Lard.
2 Quarts of Water.
1 Square Inch of Ham, Chopped Very Fine.
Salt and Pepper to Taste.

Cut the mutton into pieces of about an inch in length and thickness, and season well. Proceed to make the stew as mentioned above, only instead of adding the potatoes, add turnips parboiled, and cut into halves or quarters. This is a very delicious stew. The neck of the mutton may also be used for stews, but preferably the brisket.

### Shoulder of Mutton Smothered With Turnips.
Épaule de Mouton Braisée.

1 Shoulder of Mutton.
1 Carrot.   1 Onion.   ½ Stalk of Celery.
4 Cloves.   1 Bay Leaf.   6 Turnips.

If the mutton does not appear very tender the process of smothering it will make it so. It is well to beat the leg well with a rolling pin, and you will be sure of good and tender eating. Season well. Slice an onion and one carrot very fine; chop fine a half stalk of celery, and put these, with the shoulder of mutton, into a deep baking pot. Cover well and let the mutton juice permeate the vegetables and brown them. Then add the minced bay leaves and cloves; cover and let these brown, and after ten minutes add one quart of boiling water. Season well again and set on a steady fire, allowing fifteen minutes to every pound. An hour before serving add six whole turnips, which have been peeled and parboiled, and let these remain smothered with the mutton. Serve with the turnips as a garnish. This dish is highly recommended.

### Broiled Mutton Chops.
Cotelettes de Mouton Grillées et Panées.

6 Mutton Chops.
Butter.   Salt and Pepper.

In selecting mutton chops for broiling, remember that the smaller French chops, which are cut from the breast of the mutton, are generally served at dinner, and the loin chops for breakfast. The breast chops are daintier in appearance, but the loin chops are sweeter and the meat is more solid. The French chops should always be cut thinner than the loin chops.

Season the chops well with salt and pepper and brush with melted butter and a few bread crumbs. Have the gridiron very hot and place the chops upon it. In a few seconds turn the chop and let this side cook. The blood will be running out, and the chop is done. Place on a platter, butter thickly and sprinkle with chopped parsley and serve very hot.

### Mutton Cutlets.
Cotelettes de Mouton.

4 Mutton Cutlets.
Butter.   Salt and Pepper.

The cutlets are slices from the thick part of the leg of the mutton and are very excellent eating. Trim off the outer skin and broil in the same manner as mutton chops. They are very delicious served for dinner with a garnish of Purée of Spinach. (See recipe.)

### Mutton Chops, Brewer's Style.
Cotelettes de Mouton à la Brasseur.

3 Mutton Chops.   2 Tablespoonfuls of Butter.
Juice of Lemon.
3 Shallots. Chopped Fine.
Salt and Pepper to Taste.

Select six thick chops from the loin of the mutton. Trim neatly and season well with salt and black pepper and a dash of Cayenne. Rub lightly with butter on either side and broil on a hot charcoal fire. Have ready a hot dish and pour over the chops a sauce of melted butter, seasoned nicely with salt and pepper, the juice of one lemon and three minced shallots. Serve hot.

### Mutton Hash.

### Hachis de Mouton.

3 Cups of Hashed Mutton.
6 Potatoes.     1 Herb Bouquet.
Salt and Pepper to Taste.
1 Tablespoonful of Lard or Butter.

This is a splendid way of utilizing the left-over mutton. After having taken off all the rough edges of the roast and cut out the gristle and hard membrane, hash the mutton into pieces of about one inch in size. Take six left-over tomatoes, or freshly boiled, and cut into quarters. Chop fine one herb bouquet. Place a tablespoonful of butter or a half tablespoonful of lard into the stewpot, and as it melts add the mutton seasoned well, and a few minutes later the fine herbs. Mince the clove of garlic if the flavor is liked and add. Stir constantly without browning much, and add a tablespoonful of flour. Let this brown very slightly and then add the tomatoes. Cover and let all simmer for about twenty minutes, and then pour over a pint of boiling water. Season again to taste and set back on the stove and let it simmer gently for about three-quarters of an hour. Cut some Croûtons and fry them in butter; place on a dish and serve with the hash. The Creoles often add several poached eggs if the sauce is not thick enough. It is also a frequent custom to add a quarter or a half can of mushrooms to the hash, but this is always a matter of taste and economy.

### Mutton Feet à la Poulette.

### Pieds de Mouton à la Poulette.

12 Mutton Feet.
A Sauce a la Creme.
The Juice of 1 Lemon.
½ Teaspoonful of French Vinegar.
1 Gill of Water.     The Yolks of 2 Eggs.
½ Can of Mushrooms (if desired.)

This is a famous Creole dish. Scald the mutton feet in boiling water and remove every vestige of wool that may adhere, cleaning and scraping the feet. Then place them in a pot, cover well with boiling water, add half of a lemon (including peel and meat) to the water, and salt well. In the meantime, prepare a Sauce à la Poulette as follows: Make a Cream Sauce (see recipe Meat Sauces) and add the juice of one lemon, or half a tablespoonful of good vinegar. Take the mutton feet out of the water in which they have been boied, take out the big bones from the feet. Put the mutton feet into the Sauce à la Poulette, add a gill of water, let all simmer about five minutes, and then take off the fire and add the yolks of two eggs, beaten well, stirring well into the sauce. Serve hot. Many of the Creoles add a half can of mushrooms to the mutton feet before putting in the sauce. This makes the dish very delicious, increasing the flavor.

### Mutton Feet à la Lyonnaise.

### Pieds de Mouton à la Lyonnaise.

12 Mutton Feet.
2 Onions.     1 Tablespoonful of Butter.
1 Tablespoonful of Flour.
1 Pint of Broth. Salt and Pepper to Taste.
Croutons.

Clean and boil the mutton feet in the same way as indicated in the above recipe. When done take out the large bones and cut the feet into two-inch pieces. Cut two onions very fine, mincing them, and brown in a saucepan with a tablespoonful of butter. When slightly brown, add a tablespoonful of flour. Mix well, making a nice Brown Roux (see recipe under chapter on "Sauces for Meats, Fish, etc.") and then add about a pint of the broth in which the mutton feet have been boiled. As it boils, skim off the grease and let it simmer for about ten minutes. Then add the mutton feet and let them simmer ten minutes longer and serve hot, with Croûtons of bread fried in butter. Mutton feet may also be served with a Purée of Onions. (See recipe.)

### Stuffed Mutton Feet.

### Pieds de Mouton Farcis.

12 Mutton Feet.     ½ Cup of Wet Bread.
1 Hard-Boiled Egg.     1 Spoon of Butter.
1 Tablespoonful of Lard.
3 Thin Slices of Veal.
1 Bay Leaf.     1 Sprig of Thyme.
3 Carrots.     2 Onions.
The Juice of 1 Lemon.
Salt and Pepper to Taste.

Clean the mutton feet well, according to directions given, and boil and take out all the bones. Take a half cup of wet bread and squeeze well. Season well with salt and pepper and fry in a little butter and add a chopped egg. Stuff the feet with this, splitting down the length and sewing up to prevent the dressing escaping. Take a saucepan and put in one tablespoonful of lard and lay over it thin slices of veal, well seasoned, and one bay leaf, one sprig of thyme and geranium (minced very fine), three chopped carrots, and two onions (chopped very fine). Pour over this the juice of a lemon, let it simmer gently for about a half hour, turning the veal, that it may cook well and be thoroughly penetrated by the juices. Put the stuffed mutton feet on top, cover closely, and let all simmer for a half hour longer. Then unsew the mutton feet, lay them on the slices of veal, garnish nicely and serve with a Sauce à l'Espagnole, Sauce aux Tomates, a Sauce aux Ognons, or Sauce à la Provençale. The latter two are highly recommeded.

### Sheep Tongues Smothered.

Langues de Mouton Braisées.

6 Tongues. 1 Large Onion, Cut Fine.
2 Carrots, Cut Fine.
1 Herb Bouquet, Minced Very Fine.
3 Pickles. ¼ of a Cup of Capers.
1 Pint of Boiling Water.
2 Slices of Bacon.

Scald and blanch the tongue removing the skins. Throw them into cold water. Dry and piqué or lard very delicately with larding needles. Season well with salt and pepper. Slice the bacon into fine strips and lay in the bottom of a saucepan; place the lamb tongues over this. Place on top another fine layer of bacon in very fine strips. Add the minced carrots, onion, herbs, and salt and pepper again to taste. Let it simmer for about fifteen minutes and then moisten with about a pint of boiling water or broth. Let it cook over a slow fire about three hours. Then take out the tongues, place them on a hot dish, strain the sauce through a sieve, set back on the stove a few seconds, and add one-quarter of a cup of capers, and three pickles, sliced fine. Stir well and let it boil up once. Pour over the tongues and serve.

Lamb tongues are prepared in the same manner when braised or smothered.

### Sheep Brains.

Cervelles de Mouton.

½ Pound of Brains.
1 Onion. 1 Bay Leaf.
Grated Breadcrumbs.
Parsley to Garnish.

The brains of mutton are prepared in exactly the same manner as calf's brains and served accordingly. (See recipe.) But the brains of mutton are far more delicate, and, consequently, considered a more récherché dish.

Plunge the brains into cold water to disgorge them of all blood and remove the fine skin and blood that surround them. Then blanch with scalding water. In five minutes take them out of the hot water and put them into a saucepan and cover with cold water. Add a tiny onion, sliced fine, parsley and a whole bay leaf. Let them simmer gently for five minutes. Then take from the fire and drain. When cold cut into pieces of a square inch and dip in a batter or tomato sauce, and then in grated bread crumbs, patting gently. Drop into boiling lard and fry to a golden brown. Take out and drain off grease, and serve on a bed of fried parsley. A garnish of boiled green peas is also very pretty and palatable.

### Sheep Brains, Brown Sauce.

Cervelles de Mouton, au Beurre Noir.

Prepare the brains in exactly the same manner as indicated in the above recipe and serve with Brown Butter Sauce. (See recipe.)

### Sheep Kidneys.

Rognons en Brochettes.

6 Kidneys.
1 Tablespoonful of Butter.

Slice the kidneys very thin and wash well, then scald and wipe dry. Pass a skewer through each kidney, after seasoning well, and brush with melted butter. Place on a double broiler and cook for five minutes, allowing two and a half minutes to each side. Place on a hot dish and pour over melted butter and a little lemon juice. Garnish nicely with parsley and serve hot.

## LAMB.

Agneau.

Lamb is in season from April to September. Like very young veal, it is unwholesome and tasteless if eaten too young. A lamb should always be two months old, else it will be what the Creoles call "une viande gélaineuse," or a jelly meat not fit to eat and very difficult to manage. The best way to cook lamb is to roast it or bake it. The loin of the lamb is cut into chops; the brains, tongue, cutlets, tendons and feet are cooked in the same manner as those of sheep, and it would be superfluous to repeat the recipes. Stewed Lambs' Tongues, or "Langues d'Agneau Sauté," served with a Sauce Tomate, or a Sauce à la Tartare, is an excellent entrée, or luncheon dish.

### Roast Lamb, Mint Sauce.

Quartier d'Agneau Roti, Sauce Menthe.

The Hind Quarter of a Lamb.
Salt and Pepper to Taste.
Parsley to Garnish. Mint Sauce.

This is the standing dish for the Easter dinner in New Orleans. Select a fine, fresh, white hind-quarter of lamb. Roast in exactly the same manner as indicated in "Roast Leg of Mutton" (see recipe), only allow about twenty minutes to the pound in cooking. Serve with garnish of parsley and a Mint Sauce. (See recipe.)

Roast Lamb is always served with fresh, young green peas and asparagus tips.

### Roast Lamb à la Béarnaise.
Agneau Roti à la Bearnaise.

The Hind Quarter of a Lamb.
3 Sprigs Each of Thyme, Parsley and Bay Leaf.
6 Minced Shallots.
1 Tablespoonful of Butter.
1 Cup of Grated Bread Crumbs.
The Juice of 1 Lemon.
Parsley and Sliced Lemon to Garnish.

Select a fine, white hind-quarter of the lamb; lard it in the same manner as given for larding "Roast Filet of Beef." (See recipe.) Rub well with butter on top and sprinkle over thickly with the soft of bread crumbs, minced parsley, thyme, bay leaf, salt and pepper and minced shallots. Set in the stove and cover with a buttered brown paper. Let it roast; allowing eighteen or twenty minutes to the pound, in a quick oven, and, when done, take off the paper sprinkle again lightly with grated bread crumbs; let it brown and set in a hot dish; sprinkle over with lemon juice; garnish the dish with sprigs of parsley and sliced lemon, and serve, carving in slices and placing a quarter of a lemon on each plate.

### Filet of Lamb Roasted and Larded.
Filet d'Agneau Roti et Piqué.

A Filet of Lamb.
Lard Sufficient to Lard Thoroughly.
1 Small Onion.      1 Bay Leaf.
4 Cloves, if desired.
1½ Tablespoonfuls of Butter.
1 Tablespoonful of Glace. (See recipe.)
1 Glass of Madeira or Sherry Wine, or Water.
Salt and Pepper to Taste.

Trim the filet nicely, removing the outer muscular skin. Lard the filet well, using larding needles. The lard must be very thin, like a shoestring. The larding is done by filling the needles with the lard and pushing them through the filet as far as they will go. If the needles are long enough they will come out on the other side of the filet, leaving the lard within. Repeat this process all down the center and along the sides of the filet, about an inch apart, and have the rows neat and even. If you have not a larding needle, make incisions with a knife and push the lard in with your finger, but the filet is never as juicy and tender, nor does it look so clean and even when baked. When well larded, dredge well with salt and pepper, rubbing this thoroughly into the beef. Cut up one small onion, one bay leaf, and mash four cloves, and place in the bottom of the baking pan. Lay the larded filet on this bed, the larded side being uppermost. Put small bits of butter equal to a half teaspoonful on top, and bake in a quick oven thirty minutes. This dish is always eaten rare. To ascertain if sufficiently done, stick a fork into the filet; if the blood bubbles out, it is ready to serve. The meat, when done, is always spongy and elastic to the touch.

In the meantime, prepare the following Brown Sauce: Take one tablespoonful of butter and one of Glace (see recipe under chapter "Sauces for Meats, Fish, etc.") and three of water, smoothly rubbed, and melt in a saucepan, stirring constantly to prevent burning. When brown, add one glass of Madeira or Sherry Wine and a half cup of water. Season well with salt and pepper. Pour over the filet, which must be placed in a hot dish, and serve with fresh, young green peas.

### Filet of Lamb à la Bechamel.
Filet d'Agneau à la Bechamel.

A Filet of Lamb.
A Sauce a la Bechamel.

Roast the lamb as in the manner given, and prepare a "Sauce à la Bechamel." (See recipe.) Slice the lamb and pour over the sauce and serve. This is considered an excellent entrée.

### Broiled Lamb Chops.
Cotellettes d'Agneau Grillées.

6 Lamb Chops.
Butter, Salt and Pepper.

Broil in exactly the same manner as Mutton Chops, only let them remain a little longer on the griddle, until the chops are firm under pressure of a fork.

Season the chops well with salt and pepper and brush with melted butter and a few bread crumbs. Have the gridiron hot and place the chops upon it. In a few seconds turn the chops and let the other sides cook. Place on a platter, butter thickly and sprinkle with chopped parsley and serve very hot.

### Smothered Breast of Lamb.
Poitrine d'Agneau Braisée.

Shoulder and Breast of a Lamb.
2 Sprigs of Parsley.
1 Carrot.      2 Onions.
1 Clove of Garlic.    ½ Can of Tomatoes.
A Sprig Each of Thyme and Bay Leaf.
Bread Crumbs.
2 Tablespoonfuls of Butter.
Pepper and Salt to Taste.
1 Pint of Water.

Select nice, fresh breast and shoulder of lamb. Have the butcher remove all the bones; wash or wipe carefully with a damp towel. Take one cup of bread crumbs, which have been wet and squeezed, and season well with one grated onion and clove of garlic, and chopped parsley, thyme and bay leaf, and spices to taste. Put in a frying pan, with one tablespoonful of butter, and fry about five minutes. Place this dressing into the open side of the lamb, and roll it up in its own meat, and tie it securely with thin strips of twine that the dressing may not escape in baking. Slice the carrot, onion and turnip very fine, and fry in a tablespoonful of butter in a deep pan. When brown, add the lamb and cover and let it simmer for about fifteen minutes. Then add the tomatoes and let them brown; then add just enough boiling water to cover the meat (one pint); set the pot back on the stove and let it simmer gently and steadily for about three hours, or according to the size of the roll. Serve with the vegetables dished around and with its own gravy.

### Minced Lamb.
#### Agneau Émincé.

2 Pounds of Cold Minced Lamb.
½ Can of Mushrooms.
4 Ounces of Butter.  ½ Pint of Veal Stock.
1½ Gills of Cream.  Yolks of 2 Eggs.

Place the butter in a frying pan; add one chopped onion and brown slightly; add the mushrooms, and season to taste. Then add the half pint of veal broth, if you have it; if not, boiling water or milk, and let it simmer a few minutes; thicken with a tablespoonful of blended flour; add the minced lamb and a gill and a half of cream; let all simmer, stirring constantly; and when done, which will be in about ten minutes, take off the fire; add the yolks of two eggs, beaten, and stir constantly. Place in a hot dish, garnish with Croûtons (buttered) and serve. This is a very nice breakfast dish from the left-over lamb.

### Epigram of Lamb.
#### Epigramme d'Agneau.

2 Breasts of Lamb.
1 Tablespoonful of Salt.
1 Teaspoonful of Pepper.
3 Tablespoonfuls of Butter or Olive Oil.
Grated Bread Crumbs.

Take two breasts of Lamb; tie them and put them to boil in soup stock for forty-five minutes. Then drain well and extract all the bones. Press them down with a heavy weight on top. When thoroughly cold, cut each breast into three triangular-shaped pieces, dip them in olive oil, or melted lard, or butter, and season with the salt and pepper. Roll each piece in fresh bread crumbs grated, and broil on a slow fire, allowing four minutes to each side. Serve with a pint of hot Macedoine or any garnish that may be desired, arranging the breast over the garnish. The epigram may be served à la Soubise with a hot Soubise sauce, or à la Chicoree with a hot chicory sauce, or à la Louisianaise with a hot Madeira wine sauce, and garnish of fried sweet potatoes.

### Lamb en Blanquette.
#### Blanquette d'Agneau.

3 Pounds of Brisket of Lamb.
1 Onion.  2 Carrots.
½ Dozen Cloves.  1 Leek.
1 Bouquet of Thyme, Parsley and Bay Leaf.
¼ Pound of Butter.  2 Tablespoonfuls Flour.
The Yolks of 2 Eggs.
½ Can of Mushrooms or Green Peas.

The brisket of the lamb is best for this dish. Cut into pieces of two square inches. Put in a stew pot and cover with a half gallon of water, and add salt and pepper and two onions and one carrot, chopped fine. Let it boil till very tender. When it reaches this stage, take the meat out of the saucepan and keep the water in which it was boiled. Take another saucepan and put a tablespoonful of butter in it, and as it melts add a tablespoonful of flour. Let it brown lightly, and add one pint of the water in which the veal was broiled. Stir well, making it very light, and not thick. Add one-half can of mushrooms, and let the whole boil about fifteen minutes, so as to be very light. Then put in the veal, which is already cooked. Let it simmer for about fifteen minutes longer, and take off the fire and add the yolks of two eggs, well beaten, two tablespoonfuls of the gravy, and the juice of one lemon. Serve hot.

### Lamb's Brains.
#### Cervelles d'Agneau.

The recipes given for the preparation of Sheep Brains may be followed in cooking Lamb's Brains. Lamb Brains are a very delicate dish. The following recipe, Lamb's Brains à la Remoulade, however, is a famous Creole dish:

### Lamb's Brains à la Remoulade.
#### Cervelles d'Agneau à la Remoulade.

6 Lamb's Brains.  1 Pint of White Wine.
2 Quarts of Water.  2 Cloves of Garlic.
The Yolks of 4 Eggs.
2 Shallots.  1 Herb Bouquet.  6 Capers.
3 Small Vinegar Pickles.
1 Tablespoonful of Parsley.
4 Tablespoonfuls of Olive Oil.
4 Tablespoonfuls of Vinegar.
1 Tablespoonful of Creole Mustard.
½ Tablespoonful of Chives.
Salt and Pepper to Taste.

Plunge the Lamb's Brains into cold water and let them stand for an hour, changing the water several times. Prepare in exactly the same manner indicated for the preparation of Sheep Brains. After removing from the water and taking off the skin, drain of all water. Have ready a saucepan of boiling water and season it with salt and pepper and an herb bouquet of parsley, bay leaves and thyme. When the herbs begin to boil add a pint of white wine to the water, as it boils up again drop in the brains and let them cook for ten minutes. Remove the herb bouquet and strain the brains through a sieve.

Place on a hot dish and serve with the following sauce: Chop the shallots very fine, mince the garlic and mash the yolks of the eggs. Put the vinegar into a small saucepan and add the shallots, the garlic and let all boil till the vinegar is reduced about one-half. Then mash the yolks of eggs in the sweet oil and cut up the capers and add all to the vinegar. Add the parsley and the vinegar pickles chopped fine and let all come to a boil. Then add the chives and two teaspoonfuls of Creole mustard. Mix well and pour all over the brains and send to the table very hot.

### Lamb's Feet.

Pieds d'Agneau.

The various delightful ways that the Creoles have of serving Mutton Feet may be used in preparing Lamb's Feet, the latter especially making many delightful and récherché entrees. We have "Pieds d'Agneau à la Poulette," etc. (See recipe for cooking Mutton Feet, "Pieds d'Agneau au Blanc," "Pieds d'Agneau à la Bourgeoise," etc.)

### Lamb's Feet, White Sauce.

Pieds d'Agneau, Sauce Blanche.

12 Lamb's Feet.
1 Pint of Broth. The Juice of 1 Lemon.
The Yolk of 1 Egg.
1 Tablespoonful of Butter.

Clean the feet well, and, after boiling, take out all the bones, cut in little pieces of about two inches or less, season nicely and cook in a pint of their own water over a slow fire. Add the juice of a lemon, and then throw in the beaten yolk of an egg to bind nicely, and serve hot.

### Lamb's Feet à la Bourgeoise.

Pieds d'Agneau à la Bourgeoise.

12 Lamb's Feet. 1 Pint of Broth.
1 Tablespoonful of Butter.
1 Tablespoonful of Flour.
2 Sprigs of Parsley. The Juice of 1 Lemon.

Clean the feet well and boil in the manner above indicated. When the water is reduced, take out the feet, cut in pieces, taking out all the bones. Put back in the saucepan, add a tablespoonful of butter blended well with a tablespoonful of flour. Stir well and add two sprigs of parsley, minced very fine, and the juice of one lemon. Let this simmer for ten minutes longer and serve hot.

### Broiled Lamb Kidneys.

Rognons d'Agneau Grillées.

6 Kidneys.
1 Tablespoonful of Butter.
The Juice of 1 Lemon. Parsley to Garnish.

Prepare in exactly the same manner as in the recipe for broiling Sheep Kidneys, and serve with melted butter and lemon juice and chopped parsley, thrown over. In all these recipes, where the skewer is used in broiling to keep the kidneys from separating, the skewer must be drawn out before buttering and serving.

### Stewed Lamb Tongues.

Langues d'Agneau Sautées.

6 Tongues. 1 Onion.
½ of a Small Carrot, Cut Fine.
½ of a Small Turnip. Cut Fine.
1 Pint of Broth or Water.
2 Tablespoonfuls of Butter.
2 Tablespoonfuls of Flour.
1 Bay Leaf. 2 Sprigs of Thyme and Parsley.
Salt and Pepper to Taste.

Clean the tongues; wash well and boil in clear water for an hour and a half. Then throw them into cold water and remove the skins. Cut the vegetables fine, and put them with the butter into a saucepan. Add a pint of broth or water, and then add the finely-minced herbs. Add the tongues and let them simmer gently for two hours. Serve hot, with the gravy poured over.

### Lamb Tongues With Tomato Sauce.

Langues d'Agneau à la Sauce Tomate.

6 Tongues. 1 Onion.
1 Pint of Broth or Water.
2 Tablespoonfuls of Butter.
1 Bay Leaf.
2 Tablespoonfuls of Flour.
2 Sprigs of Thyme.
A Tomato Sauce.

Cook the tongues as in the recipe given above, omitting, of course, the vegetables. When done, place the tongues on a hot dish, pour over a rich Tomato Sauce (see recipe) and serve.

## CHAPTER XV.

### PORK.

#### Du Cochon.

The old Creoles, like their French ancestors, hold that every portion of the hog is good, from the head to the feet, and all portions are utilized in the various dishes which are so delightfully prepared in New Orleans. For roasting, the Creoles always use the delicate "Cochon de Lait," or sucking pig, of not more nor less than four or five weeks old, when the pig is roasted whole; otherwise the best parts of the grown hog for roasting are the loin and the leg. Pork chops or cutlets are taken from the loin. They are used as entrées, as are also slices of cold ham; the kidneys, cooked in wine, and the tails braisées, or smothered.

Pork must always be cooked well done, or else it will be dangerous, unwholesome and indigesible. It must be roasted or fried. The Creoles will never eat a broiled pork chop.

#### Roast Loin of Pork.

#### Longe de Porc Rotie.

A Loin of Pork.
Salt and Pepper to Taste.
Parsley to Garnish.   Apple Sauce.

Score the loin in close lines across and down. The lines should be about a half inch apart. Dredge well with salt and pepper and place in the oven, letting it cook slowly and long, allowing at least twenty-five minutes to every pound, and basting every five minutes for the first half hour and every ten minutes thereafter. Pork must always be well done. When cooked thoroughly, take out of the baking pan, put in a hot serving dish, and garnish nicely with parsley. Serve with Apple Sauce and a little horseradish. (See recipe "Sauces for Meats," etc.)

#### Roast Pork.

#### Porc Roti.

The leg and shoulder may be roasted in the same manner as the loin, allowing from twenty to twenty-five minutes to a pound in cooking.

#### Roast Pig Stuffed.

#### Cochon de Lait Roti et Farci.

1 Pig, Four or Five Weeks Old.
3 Large Onions. 2 Cups of Bread Crumbs.
3 Sprigs of Chopped Parsley.
Salt and Pepper to Taste.
2 Ounces of Butter.
2 Teaspoonfuls of Powdered Sage.
3 Hard-Boiled Eggs.
1 Herb Bouquet.

In New Orleans the pig is always sold killed and cleaned by the butcher. Wash the young pig well, cleaning again, and scraping thoroughly and taking out all remaining hair from the ears and nostrils. Wash again thoroughly in cold water, inside and out, shaking the pig vigorously, head downward. Then turn upwards and pour cold water over it. Wipe dry inside and out with a coarse towel, and then rub well inside with salt and pepper and minced parsley, thyme and bay leaf. Prepare a dressing as follows: Wet the bread crumbs and squeeze thoroughly. Then add the sprigs of minced parsley and hard-boiled eggs and the powdered sage. Mix well. Season all highly with black pepper and salt using about a teaspoonful of salt and a half teaspoonful of black pepper. Place two ounces of butter, which will be equal to two tablespoonfuls, in a frying pan on the stove, and, when it melts, add the minced onions. Let them brown, and then add the dressing, stirring well, and letting it fry for five minutes. Take off and stuff the pig and sew up the opening. Truss the fore legs forward and the hind feet forward, and close under the body. Wipe the pig carefully with a damp towel, and then place a corn cob in its mouth to keep it open. Rub the pig all over the outside with butter, dredging lightly with salt and pepper. Place in a modreate oven, and bake steadily for two and a half or three hours, according to size and age. Baste frequently, and, when half done, rub again with butter until the pan is saturated. Continue basting at intervals. When done, take out of the oven and place on a hot dish. Garnish the dish with parsley. Take the corncob out of the mouth and place instead a nice, rosy apple. Serve very hot, with Apple Sauce. (See recipe "Sauces for Meats," etc.)

Sweet potatoes are a nice vegetable to serve with roast pig. Boil a half dozen first and then peel carefully and place them whole, about fifteen minutes before serving the pig in the pan where it is roasting; let them soak in the gravy, brown nicely and serve on a separate platter or as a garnish.

### Roast Spare Ribs.
Cotelettes de Porc Roti.

Spare Ribs. Salt and Pepper to Taste.
A Garnish of Parsley and Radish.

Dredge the spare ribs lightly with salt and pepper, after having washed well and wiped dry with a coarse towel. Place them in the baking pan and dredge with butter; place them in the oven and cover with a piece of buttered paper. Allow twenty minutes to every pound in cooking. About twenty minutes before serving take off the buttered paper, dredge again, with melted butter, and let it brown nicely. Serve with a garnish of parsley and radishes.

If it is desired to stuff the spare ribs, have the ribs cracked, crosswise, the entire length, in two places. Put a stuffing, as for roast pig, in the center, or a stuffing made of mashed potatoes and three hard-boiled eggs, mixed thoroughly. Close the ends of the ribs over this, tie well and roast as for a roast pig. Serve with an Apple Sauce or a Sauce Piquante. (See recipes "Sauces for Meats," etc.)

### Pork Tenderloins.
Filet de Porc Sauté.

4 Pork Tenderloins.
A Tablespoonful of Lard.
Salt and Pepper to Taste.

Have the tenderloins cut thin and split lengthwise without separating Season well with salt and pepper. Have ready a very hot frying pan, place a tablespoonful of butter or lard within and add the tenderloin. Turn every two minutes, not leaving them very long on either side at a time. Be careful to cook through and through, smothering over a low fire, and serve with Apple Sauce or Currant Jelly. (See recipes "Sauces for Meats," etc.)

### Fried Pork Chops.
Cotelettes de Cochon à la Poele.

6 or 8 Pork Chops.
Grated Bread Crumbs.
Salt and Pepper to Taste.

Wash the pork chops and season well with salt and pepper. Roll in grated bread crumbs and fry in boiling lard twenty-five minutes. This will be when they have reached a rich brown. Take out, place on a platter and serve with pickles or a Sauce aux Cornichons. (See recipe.)

### Pigs' Feet.
Pieds de Cochon.

6 Pigs Feet. 2 Bay Leaves.
3 Blades of Mace. 1 Dozen Whole Cloves.
1 Whole Red Pepper Pod.
1 Pint of Good Cider Vinegar.
Salt, Pepper and Cayenne to Taste.

Select young and tender pigs' feet. Clean and scrape well and soak in cold water several hours. Split and crack the feet in several places; put them in a stewpot; cover with cold water and let them simmer until tender. When done, lay in a crock. Boil the vinegar, mace, cloves and bay leaves and pepper pod together a few minutes. Season the feet with salt and pepper, and pour the spiced vinegar over while boiling hot. Cover the crock and set to cool. The feet will be ready for use in twenty-four hours.

### Pigs' Feet, Sauce Robert.
Pieds de Cochon à la Sauce Robert.

3 Pigs' Feet.
1 Tablespoonful of Butter or Olive Oil.
1 Tablespoonful of Salt.
½ Tablespoonful of Pepper.
Grated Bread Crumbs. ½ Pint of Sauce Robert.

Boil three good-sized Pigs' Feet in a salted water, and when tender, take out of the water and drain thoroughly. Split the feet in two and place in a dish and season well with salt and pepper. Then rub them with the olive oil or butter; roll the feet in grated bread crumbs and put them to broil, allowing four minutes to each side of the feet. Prepare a hot Sauce à la Robert (see recipe), and pour this sauce in a warm dish. Lay the feet nicely over it and send to the table hot.

### Pigs' Feet, Piquant Sauce.
Pieds de Cochon à la Sauce Piquante.

Prepare in exactly the manner directed above, and, after broiling the feet, serve with a half pint of Sauce Piquante. (See recipe.)

### Pigs' Feet, Tomato Sauce.
Pieds de Cochon à la Sauce Tomate.

Boil and prepare the feet as in recipe for "Pigs' Feet, Sauce Robert." and serve with a half pint of hot Tomato Sauce.

### Pig's Feet, Tartar Sauce.
Pieds de Cochon à la Sauce Tartare.

Prepare the feet as indicated in the recipe for "Pig's Feet, Sauce Robert," and serve with a half pint of Sauce à la Tartare. (See recipe.)

### Pig's Feet, St. Hubert Style.
Pieds de Cochon à la St. Hubert.

Prepare the feet as in the recipe for "Pig's Feet, Sauce Robert," and serve with a half pint of hot Piquant Sauce, to which has been added a teaspoonful of Creole mustard, diluted.

### Stuffed Pig's Feet à la Perigueux.
.. Pieds de Cochon à la Perigueux. ..

3 Pigs' Feet. 2 Minced Truffles.
½ Glass of Madeira Wine.
1 Pound of Boned Turkey Forcemeat.
6 Pieces of Crepinette.
1 Egg. 2 Ounces of Butter.
½ Pint of Hot Perigueux Sauce.

Boil the Pig's Feet, and then split them in two; take out the bones, lay the flesh on a dry, clean cloth and wipe well. Make a forcemeat of boned turkey (see recipe under chapter Stuffings for Fowls, etc.); add the truffles, which have been finely minced, and a half glass of Madeira or Sherry Wine. Mix this well together. Crepinette is applied to a skin found in the stomach of the pig. Take six pieces of this crepinette, which you will have secured from the butcher; cut them the size of a man's hand and lay on a clean biscuit board; place on each piece of skin a portion of the forcemeat about the size of a hen's egg and flatten out well. Place one-half of a pig's foot on top of this farcie, and cover with another layer of the stuffing. On either side lay three thin slices of truffles. Wrap the crepinettes up in some fanciful shape, such as an envelope or card case, and dip them separately in a well-beaten egg, and then in grated breadcrumbs. Put two tablespoonfuls of butter in a saucepan or deep frying pan, cover closely, and let the feet cook on a slow fire for twenty-five minutes, allowing twelve minutes and a half to each side. Serve with a pint of hot Perigueux Sauce. (See recipe.) Place the sauce in a dish lay the feet neatly over it and send to the table hot.

### Stuffed Pig's Feet, Madeira Sauce.
Pieds de Cochon à la Sauce Madère.

Prepare the feet in exactly the same manner as indicated in the recipe given above, and serve with a pint of hot Madeira Sauce, instead of the Sauce Perigueux.

### Hogshead Cheese.
Fromage de Cochon.

1 Hog's Head. 1 Lemon.
1 Glass of Sherry or Madeira. 2 Onions.
1 Slice of Ham.
Thyme, Bay Leaf, Spices.

Boil the whole of the hog's head, which has been well cleaned and scraped. Add four teaspoonfuls of salt, and a lemon cut in half. After four hours, when the head will have become very tender, take out of the water and set to cool. Then skin the meat from the head. Preserve the water in which it has been boiled. Cut up the entire head, ears and tongue and two of the feet, if you have boiled them, too, into pieces of about one inch in length. Take two large onions and chop them very fine. Put a tablespoonful of lard and the onions into a pot. Don't let them brown, but slightly smother. Season well with minced thyme, three mashed cloves, a dash of red pepper (Poivre Rouge). Add a teaspoonful of water taken from the reserve in which the head was boiled. Let this simmer gently; then add one pint of the water, the peel of a large lemon, cut fine, and one glass of Sherry or Madeira. Add hot pepper to taste, seasoning highly. Boil well. Then add the head and a slice of ham, cut into pieces of about one inch long and a half inch wide. Season to taste, and add five powdered allspice, one blade of chopped mace and three mashed cloves. Let it boil for a half hour longer, till it comes to the right consistency. When cooked, fill a bowl with the cheese and put a close-fitting dish on top, and then place a piece of plank over this and set a big weight of about fifteen pounds or three or four flatirons on top. When the cheese cools, which will be in about five or six hours, turn out of the bowl. It will have taken the shape of the bowl and become a fine head of cheese, ready to be served. This is the Creole's way of making hogshead cheese, and it cannot be improved upon.

### Salt Meat.
Viande Salée.

Salt pork enters so largely into cooking that it will be unnecessary to devote special attention to it here. It is used in cooking cabbage in pork and beans—a most excellent dish for children—and with nearly all green herbs and vegetables it serves as a delightful flavor. In the the chapter on vegetables, wherever it is advisable to use salt or pickled pork, this subject will be treated.

### Pickled Pork.
Petit Salé.

Coarse Salt Sufficient to make a Brine.
12 Bay Leaves. 2 Dozen Onions.
25 Pounds of Pork. 1 Ounce of Saltpetre.
12 Cloves. 6 Allspice.

Pork should be pickled about twenty hours after killing. It is pickled always in sufficient quantity to last for some time, for, if proper care is taken, it will keep one year after pickling; but it may also be pickled in smaller quantities, of three or four pounds at a time, reducing other ingredients in the recipe according to quantity of pork used. To twenty-five pounds of pork, allow one ounce of saltpetre. Pulverize thoroughly and mix with a sufficient quantity of salt to thoroughly salt the pork. Cut the pork into pieces of about two pounds, and slash each piece through the skin, and then rub thoroughly with the salt and saltpetre mixture till the meat is thoroughly penetrated through and through. Mash the cloves very fine and ground the allspice. Chop the onions. Take a small barrel and place at the bottom a layer of salt, then a layer of coarsely chopped onions, and sprinkle over this a layer of the spices and minced bay leaves. Place on this a layer of the pork; pack tightly; then place above this a layer of the salt and seasonings and continue with alternate layers of pork and seasonings till all the pork is used up. Conclude with a layer of the minced herbs and spices and have a layer of salt on top. Cover the preparation with a board on which a heavy weight must be placed to press down the meat. It will be ready for use in about ten or twelve days.

### HAM.
Jambon.

Ham is one of the most useful articles of supply that can be kept in any household. The Creoles generally keep a nicely boiled ham on hand. In case of unexpected company for lunch or supper, the ham is always ready and sure to be appetizing. It forms combinations in many dishes, and is in itself a delightful breakfast dish and dinner entrée.

### Boiled Ham.
Jambon Bouilli.

A Ham. 2 Blades of Mace.
1 Dozen Cloves. 4 Bay Leaves.
Black Pepper and Parsley to Garnish.

Wash the ham well in cold water, scraping off all portions of mold or salt. Have a large boiler of water on the stove; or, better still, the furnace. Throw in two blades of mace, a dozen cloves and three or four bay leaves. Put the ham in the water and let the fire be slow, allowing the water to heat gradually. Do not permit it to come to a good boil for two hours at least, and be careful to skim carefully, so that all rejected substances may not impregnate the ham. Keep it simmering gently, allowing twenty minutes to every pound. When done, let the ham cool in its own liquor, and then put the ham on a board, cover with another board, and lay a weight over. Leave under weight several hours. This will enable you to cut the ham in thin slices after removing the weight. Then carefully remove the skin without taking off the fat. Sprinkle it in patches with black pepper and ornament the shank bone with quilled paper, or a paper frill. Serve it cold with a garnish of parsley. Cold boiled ham should be sliced very thin and served with pickles and mustard.

### Fried Ham.
Jambon Frit.

8 Thin Slices of Ham.
Pepper to Taste.
Parsley to Garnish.

Slice the ham thin. Heat the frying pan very hot. Lay in the ham in its own fat and fry over a quick fire. The Creoles serve eggs nicely fried, with ham. Allow an egg to every slice of ham. After taking the ham out of the pan, drop in the eggs. If you do not like eggs fried on both sides (many prefer them so), baste the eggs with the hot grease, and be sure to cook the yolks whole. When they are well set, without being hard, take the eggs out and lay one on each slice of ham. Garnish with parsley. Sprinkle the eggs with salt and pepper very lightly and serve. This is a very popular Creole breakfast dish.

If eggs are not served with the fried ham, and a gravy is desired, make one as follows: Take one tablespoonful of flour and add to the remaining fat in the pan. Mix well until smooth. Add a half pint of milk and stir until it boils; throw in a dash of black pepper, pour over the ham and send to the table hot.

### Broiled Ham.
Jambon Grillé.

6 or 8 Thin Slices of Boiled Ham.
6 or 8 Slices of Buttered Toast.

Always use boiled ham for broiling. Slice it about a half inch thick, according to the number to be served, and trim off the rough edges. Have the broiler very hot, lay the slices of ham upon it and brown well. Serve with buttered toast.

### Broiled Ham With Cucumber Garnish.
Jambon Grillé aux Concombres.

6 or 8 Slices of Boiled Ham.
Pepper. Cucumbers.

Cut thin as many slices of ham as desired and broil evenly over hot coals. When well brown butter, add pepper, sprinkling, and serve with slices of cucumber that have been steeped in salted vinegar several hours ranged around it.

### Ham Croquettes.
#### Croquettes de Jambon.
2 Cups of Finely Chopped Boiled Ham.
2 Cups of Mashed Potatoes.
The Yolks of 3 Eggs.
2 Tablespoonfuls of Cream.
2 Tablespoonfuls of Butter.
A Dash of Cayenne.

Chop the ham fine and add to the mashed potatoes. Then add the cream and butter and the yolks of two eggs, beaten well. Beat all together until smooth, then add a dash of Cayenne. Mold the ham into cylinder shapes of about a finger in length and roll in the beaten egg that remains. Then roll in bread crumbs grated and fry in the boiling fat.

Ham puffs are made in the same way, only the potatoes are omitted, and a stiff batter is used instead, made of one pint of flour and one of water, three eggs and four ounces of finely chopped ham. The ham is placed in the batter and fried in boiling lard to a golden brown.

### Ham Soufflé.
#### Soufflé de Jambon.
1 Cup of Minced Ham.
3 Eggs, Beaten With he Whites and Yolks Separate.
1 Tesspoonful of Finely Chopped Parsley.
Pepper to Taste.

Mix together the chopped parsley, ham and yolks of eggs and a dash of Cayenne pepper. Beat all very hard till it becomes light. Then add the whites of the eggs, which have been beaten to a froth. Beat together sufficiently to mix well. Fill a dish and bake in an oven for eight or ten minutes and serve with a Cream Sauce. (See recipe.)

### Boiled Bacon.
#### Petit Salé Bouilli.
Proceed in exactly the same manner as for boiled ham.

### Fried Bacon.
#### Petit Salé Frit.
Cut into very thin slices, put in the frying pan and fry to a nice golden brown. This is a fine breakfast dish.

### Creole Sausage.
#### Saucisses à la Créole.
It has been said by visitors to New Orleans that the Creoles excell all other cooks in preparing appetizing sausages. From the old Creole negresses, who go about the streets in the early morning crying out "Belles Saucisses!" "Belle Chaurice!" to the "Boudins" and "Saucissons" so temptingly prepared by the Creole butchers in the French Market, the Creole sausage enters largely into domestic cookery and forms a delightful flavor for many dainty dishes, especially of the vegetable order, while in the preparation of the famous "Jambalaya," the "Chaurice," is one of the most necessary and indispensible ingredients. Though sausages of any of these varieties may be bought in the French Market and other stalls daily, many of the ancient housewives and cooks prefer to prepare their own sausages, and the following are the carefully compiled recipes.

In making sausage, the Creole housewife generally prepares a sufficient quantity to last several days.

### Chaurice.
4 Pounds of Lean, Fresh Pork.
2 Pounds of Fat Fresh Pork.
2 Large Onions, Minced Very Fine.
1 Clove of Garlic, Minced Very Fine.
1 Teaspoonful of Cayenne Pepper and Chili Pepper (very hot.)
1 Teaspoonful of Red Pepper.
3 Teaspoonfuls of Salt.
2 Teaspoonfuls Finely Ground Black Pepper.
1 Sprig of Thyme, Well Minced.
3 Sprigs of Parsley, Finely Minced.
2 Bay Leaves, Chopped or Minced Very Fine.
½ Teaspoonful of Allspice, Very Fine.

Hash the pork as fine as possible—fat and lean—and mix together. Then season highly with the salt and black pepper and Cayenne, Chili and red pepper (pimento). This high seasoning distinguishes the Creole sausage from all others. Chaurice must be seasoned very hot, so do not fear to have too much red pepper. Mince the onion and garlic as fine as possible, then add to the Chaurice. Mince the herbs as fine as possible, and add, and then mix the finely ground spices thoroughly with the Chaurice. Hash all together, and when well mixed, take the casings (the Creoles always use the entrails of the sheep for this purpose) that have been well cleaned by the butcher. Scald them and wash thoroughly again. Dry them and fill with the mixture, tying them in the lengths you desire.

Chaurice is fried in boiling lard for breakfast, always having sufficient to have the sausage swim in it, and served, after draining of all grease, on a hot dish with minced parsley thrown over as a garnish. It is used most extensively in making "Jambalaya," and a few Chaurice thrown into the pot of boiling cabbage or beans add greatly to the flavor. This is a distinctive Creole sausage and the very nicest and most highly flavored that can be eaten.

### Chaurice With Purée of Potatoes.
Chaurice à la Purée de Pommes de Terre.

2 Pounds of Chaurice.
4 Irish Potatoes. 1 Egg, Well Beaten.

Prick the sausages and lay them in the bottom of a pan. Make a soft Purée of Potatoes (see recipe) and pour this over the sausage. Then spread a beaten egg very evenly on top, sprinkle with bread crumbs, and place in the oven and let it bake a half hour. This is a nice breakfast or luncheon dish.

### Chaurice With Creole Sauce.
Chaurice, Sauce à la Créole.

2 Pounds of Chaurice (about 6 to a pound.)
1 Clove of Minced Garlic.
½ Can of tomatoes. 1 Teaspoonful of Salt.
1 Teaspoonful of Black Pepper.
1 Large Onion. ½ Spoon of Lard.

Place a half teaspoonful of lard in the frying pan or stewpan, and when it heats, add the chopped onion. Let this brown slightly and then add the minced garlic. Then add the half can of tomatoes. As this browns, put in the sausage which you have pricked gently. Cover and let them simmer for about five minutes, then add the seasonings to taste. Add about a half cup of boiling water. Cover well and let all simmer for twenty minutes longer. This is very nice for breakfast.

### Saucisses.

Saucisses, unlike Chaurice, are made from pork and beef mixed. Take

2 Pounds of Lean Beef.
2 Pounds of Lean Pork.
1 Pound of Lean Veal. 1 Pound of Fat Pork.
2 Large Onions Minced Very Fine.
2 Cloves of Garlic.
1 Teaspoonful of Cayenne Pepper.
1 Tablespoonful Black Pepper.
3 Tablespoonfuls of Salt.
3 Bay Leaves, Minced Very Fine.
½ Spoon Each of Ground Cloves, Mace, Allspice and Grated Nutmeg.
1 Teaspoonful Each of Minced Thyme and Sweet Marjoram.

Chop and hash the meat (fat and lean) very fine, mincing it, and then season highly with salt and pepper and Cayenne, mixing well. Add the minced onion and garlic, mix well. and then add the finely minced herbs and spices. Mix thoroughly and fill the casings which you have gotten from the butcher and washed again thoroughly. Fill them with the mixture, in lengths of about two feet or one foot and a half, stuffing tightly. Tie at both ends and let them stand overnight in a deep brine. If used for breakfast, take out as much as desired, wipe dry and cut into slices and fry, or fry the sausage, the whole length, in boiling lard, and then slice nicely. Garnish with chopped parsley and serve.

### Saucissons.

Saucissons are sausage made from the lean, fine flesh of the pork and the filet of beef. Take

2 Pounds of Fresh Pork, Very Lean.
1 Pound of Fat.
2 Pounds of Filet of Beef. 1 Large Onion.
1 Teaspoonful of Cayenne Pepper.
1 Teaspoonful of Black Pepper.
3 Teaspoonfuls of Salt.
1 Bay Leaf, Chopped Fine.
¼ Teaspoonful Each of Ground Allspice, Cloves, and ½ Nutmeg.
½ Teaspoonful Each of Fine Herbs.
1 Clove of Garlic.

Mince and hash the meat very fine, mixing the beef and pork and fat. Then season highly with the Cayenne, salt and pepper, mixing thoroughly. Season next with the minced onion and garlic; mix well, and then with the minced herbs and spices, mixing all thoroughly. Fill the casings, which are never very large for Saucissons. Tie them in sausages of about a finger in length, or three inches, and they are ready to be cooked. Saucissons are always fried in boiling lard and served whole, placing several on each plate.

### Boudins.

Boudins are blood sausages and are much affected by the Creoles. Take

1 Pound of Hog or Beef Blood (1 pint.)
½ Pound of Hog Fat. 2 Onions.
Salt, Pepper and Cayenne to Season Highly.
½ Clove of Garlic.

Mince the onions fine and fry them slightly in a small piece of the hog fat. Add the minced garlic. Hash and mince the remaining fat very fine, and mix it thoroughly with the beef blood. Mix the onions, and then season highly, adding of allspice, mace, clove and nutmeg a half teaspoonful each, finely ground, and a half teaspoonful each of fine herbs. When all mixed, take the prepared casings or entrails and fill with the mixture, being careful to tie the sausage casing at the further end before attempting to fill. Then tie the other end, making the sausage into strings of about two feet. Wash them thoroughly on the outside after filling, and then tie again in spaces of three inches or less in length, being careful not to make too long. Place them to cook in a pot of tepid water, never letting them boil, as that would curdle the blood. Let them remain on the slow fire till you can pick the sausage with a needle and no blood will exude. Then take them out, let them dry and cool.

Boudins are always fried in boiling lard. Some broil them, however.

### Boudin Blanc.

1 Pound of the White Meat of Fowl (left over.)
1 Pound of Lean Pork. 1 Pound of Fat Pork.
1 Pint of Cream.
½ Cup of Soft of Bread.
The Yolks of 2 Eggs.
¼ Teaspoon of Ground Spices.
½ Clove of Garlic.
1 Onion. 1 Teaspoonful Cayenne.
Salt and Pepper, 1 Teaspoonful Each.

Cut the meat and mince. Season highly with the salt and pepper and Cayenne. Add the minced onion and garlic. Mix well with half a cup of the soft of bread, wet and squeezed well. Cook all for about fifteen minutes in one pint of cream. When reduced take off the stove, add the beaten yolks of two eggs, stir well and cool. Fill the prepared entrails and tie either end, and place them in a pot containing half milk and half water. Boil them for about twenty minutes and then prick gently, place in buttered papers and broil gently. The left-over of rabbit, chicken, turkey, partridge and other birds may be prepared in this manner, as also the left-over of crawfish or crabs. This is a Creole hors d'oeuvre.

### Chitterlings.
### Andouilles.

2 Pounds of Fat Pork. 2 Pounds of Lean Pork
1 Pound of Inner Lining of Stomach of Hog.
2 Cloves of Garlic. 3 Bay Leaves. 2 Large Onions.
1 Tablespoonful Each of Salt and Pepper.
1 Teaspoonful of Cayenne. 1 Teaspoonful of Chili Pepper.
½ Teaspoonful Each of Mace, Cloves and Allspice, ground fine.
1 Tablespoonful Each of Minced Thyme, Sweet Marjoram and Parsley.

Select the largest intestines of the hog, wash clean, disgorge and thoroughly cleanse, and let soak for twenty four hours in fresh water, changing the water frequently. Then drain and dry well. Cut them into threadlike pieces of about one inch in length, and hash the pork, lean and fat, together; mix thoroughly with the threads of intestines or inner stomach of the hog, and season highly with the salt, pepper and Cayenne and Chili pepper. Mince the onion and garlic and herbs as fine as possible and add to the meat. Add the ground spices, and mix and hash all together very fine. Take six or eight of the largs intestines that have been thoroughly soaked and disgorged and fill these casings with the preparation, after scalding and drying the casings thoroughly. Tie into the desired lengths and use as desired. This is a very fat sausage and entirely too rich for delicate stomachs. When tied into large sausages about the size of the hand they are called "Andouilles." When tied into small sausages they are styled "Andouillettes." The latter are the more delicate. This sausage is generally served with mashed potatoes, a purée of peas or lentils. The chitterlings are first boiled in an aromatic water, with an herb bouquet, or in milk; they are then broiled, or baked in the oven for eight or ten minutes.

---

## CHAPTER XVI.

### POULTRY.

### De la Volaille.

Poultry of all kinds, especially chicken, furnishes the good cook with an infinite variety of delightful dishes, which are, besides dishes that may grace the table of the people from the simple farmer or the Creole in his humble home, to the rich banker who can afford to serve them with truffles and mushrooms.

Roast chicken, roast turkey, roast goose, roast duck are welcome dishes on every table. The entrées that are made from poultry are various, such as Turkey Daube, Fricassees of Chicken, with truffles, mushrooms, green peas, rice; Ragouts of Ducks, Chapons au Gros Sel, Poulardes à la Sauce Tartare, Poulet Sauté à la Créole, all manner of croquettes and salads, and goose entire à la Chipolata. Full-grown poultry always has the best flavor.

### Guides in Buying Poultry.

In purchasing turkeys, if intended to roast, select always a young gobbler or a young turkey hen, the latter being far preferable, as the meat is more tender and delicate. The turkey should always be fat, the flesh firm, the breast broad and flat and the skin fine and white. Turkey gobblers and hens that are not so young, may be cooked nicely in daube but roasting is the proper way to cook a turkey if you wish to bring out its flavor. The left-over turkey is always used by the Creoles in making Turkey Gumbo. (See recipe Gumbo Dinde.) The shorter the neck the better will be the turkey. An old turkey hen always has purplish legs, and the gobbler, if young, will have black legs and small spurs. But a gobbler is always larger than a turkey hen of the same age. In an old gobbler the flesh is tough and strong in fiber. An old gobbler can easily be told by its long spurs and purplish legs. In general, old turkeys have long hairs, and the flesh is always purplish where it shows under the skin on the legs or back. These are infallible guides. In following them the young housekeeper need never be imposed upon. About the month of March turkeys begin to deterloate in quality.

Purchase chickens that are fat, with firm, fresh-looking flesh, fine skin and yellowish in color. A young rooster has small spurs, an old rooster large ones, and both the young rooster and young hen have smooth, soft legs and tender skin. The breast is soft and pliable and full, the feet moist and limber, the eyes full and bright. Old chickens are known by the opposite characteristics.

A capon is always larger and fatter than the ordinary fowl, but it also makes far more delicate eating. For this reason the capon is always given the preference at fashionable feasts. A duck, to be good, must be young and fat, with light semi-transparent soft breastbone; the breast should be plump as well as fat. In the young duck one always finds that the under bill will break easily, and that the lower part of the legs and the webbing of the feet are soft and fresh colored, and that the windpipe breaks when pressed between the fingers. Ducks are best in fall and winter.

Geese live to be very old. The greatest care must, therefore, be taken in buying a goose. Look for the same characteristics as in the young duck. A goose, to be fit for eating, must never be over three years old. The year-old goose is always the best. To positively determine the young goose examine the legs. They will be covered with a soft down and the flesh will be soft and yellow. As the goose grows older the legs turn reddish or purplish in color, like those of the turkey.

Guinea fowl, when young, make most delicious dishes either in Fricassée or as Pintarde Sautée. The French discovered the value of the young guinea fowl and the Creoles have improved on their methods of preparing it, making most delicious dishes à la Créole.

Young pigeon or squab are prepared in a variety of delightful ways by Creole cuisinières, and are welcome dishes at the most récherché feast, especially when prepared as Pigeons à la Crapaudine, in which the pigeon is so arranged as to represent a young frog. The young pigeon is easily known by the tender touch.

### How to Clean Poultry.

Cut off the head at the joint. To avoid needless pain, hang the turkey or chicken, or other fowl, up by the feet. The blood will then flow more freely and the fowl will die easier and quicker.

Scalding is largely a matter of option with the cook. An old fowl will pick much more easily and it does not injure the meat to scald an old turkey or chicken, but geese should never be scalded nor a turkey that you intend to bone. Young spring chickens are completely spoiled by having the flesh scalded or blanched. As soon as the fowl is dead pick off the feathers with a quick, steady jerk towards the tail. If you pull backwards you will be apt to tear the skin. After picking well and taking out all of the pin feathers, singe the fowl by putting paper in the fire and letting it blaze up. Pass the fowl backward and forward over the blaze and over and around, being careful not to burn the skin.

Then proceed to clean the fowl, cutting off first the feet at the first joint, detaching the skin at the neck without breaking it, and drawing out whole the craw of the fowl. Cut off the bleeding end of the neck and draw the skin over.

Make a slit under the rump of the chicken just large enough for you to draw out easily all the internal organs, being careful to feel your way, and very, very careful, indeed, not to break the gallbag or any of the entrails. The contents of either render the chicken most unpalatable if spilled over it. In this case be careful to wash the chicken immediately and thoroughly before the gall has time to penetrate far. After cleanig out the chicken, rinse it inside and out and set it in a cool place. Proceed to clean the giblets, cut the outer coat of the gizzard and draw off unbroken the inner lining, containing the sand. Cut the gallbag from the liver, being very careful not to break it; if you do, throw the liver away. Cut open the heart and remove all clotted blood.

Geese, pigeons and birds of all kinds are cleaned in the same manner.

Poultry should never be cooked until five or six hours after it has been killed, but it should be picked and drawn as soon as possible. Soda, being cleansing, acts as a corrective and destroys that unpleasant taste which is frequently experienced in dressing when a fowl has been killed some time and allowed to remain with the intestines undrawn, as often happens with fowl or game purchased in city markets or stores. The flavor diffuses itself through the meat and renders it distasteful. In this case, after taking out the intestines, rinse the fowl inside and out in several waters. Then add a teaspoonful of baking soda to a quart of water and rinse again thoroughly. This process will neutralize all sourness and unpleasant taste.

Having prepared your fowl, cook according to any of the following directions:

### TURKEY.
### Dinde.

The turkey hen is called "dinde," the turkey gobbler "dindon." The preference in eating is always given to the "dinde," as the "dindons" never make quite such excellent dishes.

Turkey may be roasted, stewed or made into gumbo. Only a very old and lean turkey is ever stewed. It is utilized in this way as a home dish, never on the company table. The boned turkey is the triumph of the New Orleans cuisine when serving cold turkey. No great reception or buffet luncheon is complete without it. It is the standing dish on New Year's day, when the Creole ladies receive their gentlemen friends, and, on occasions of marriages in the family, every father will insist that there shall be a boned turkey for the wedding feast.

### Roast Turkey.
### Dinde Rotie.

1 Turkey. 2 Tablespoonfuls of Butter, Salt and Pepper to Taste.
Dressing According to Taste.

A hen turkey is always best for roasting. Clean and prepare the turkey according to the directions given. Make a nice stuffing either of oysters, egg, truffles or chestnuts (see Dressings for Fowls.) Rub the turkey well with salt and pepper inside and out, and then rub the inside with butter, using about a half tablespoonful. Stuff first the space from which you took out the craw and then sew up the slit in the skin, fastening the skin by a piece of thread tied around the neck or folding it over and fastening with a small skewer. Then stuff the body of the turkey. Push the legs under the skin near the rump, cross them and fasten them with a small skewer or tie with a piece of twine. Turn the wings back, under the body of the fowl. Rub the turkey all over with butter or lard, and place in the baking pan that has been greased lightly. Bake the turkey in a quick oven, allowing about fifteen minutes to every pound. Baste every ten minutes or so with its own drippings. When done, remove the twine and the skewer and place on a hot dish, garnished nicely with parsley, and serve. The turkey breast should always be carved in delicate slices.

In making the dressing of any kind, always take up the liver and heart, which you have seasoned well and minced very fine, and add to the turkey, dressing and mixing thoroughly.

### Roast Turkey With Truffles.
### Dinde Truffée Rotie.

1 Fine Young Hen Turkey.
1 Pound of Lean Ham, Cut into Dice.
2 Pounds of Truffles. ¼ Nutmeg.
¼ of a Teaspoonful of Pepper.
1 Bay Leaf, Minced Fine.

Clean and prepare the turkey for roasting as directed in the above recipe. Put a saucepan on the fire and put in the ham cut into dice. When hot add two pounds of the very best truffles and the grated nutmeg, the pepper and a minced bay leaf. Stir over the fire for about fifteen minutes. Then take off and let cool. When it is cold stuff the place at the neck of the turkey whence you take the craw, and sew up and arrange as indicated in the directions for dressing a turkey. Stuff the body of the turkey with the remainder of the truffles and sew it up and truss it. Set it in the oven and roast according to the above recipe, serving with a Sauce aux Truffles. This is a very expensive dish.

### Roast Turkey With Mushrooms.

Dinde Rotie Farcie aux Champignons.

Proceed in the above manner, substituting mushrooms instead.

### Turkey With Chestnuts or Oysters.

Dinde Rotie Farcie aux Marrons ou aux Huîtres.

Prepare the turkey in the manner indicated in "Roast Turkey;" stuff according to taste with either a Chestnut or Oyster Dressing (see recipes under chapter "Stuffings and Dressings for Poultry, Game, etc.") and cook as in recipe for "Roast Turkey." Chestnut and Oyster Stuffings are favorite Creole dressings for turkeys.

### Turkey en Daube.
### Dinde en Daube.

1 Large Turkey.
1 Bunch Each of Parsley, Thyme and Small Celery Leaves.
Large Slice of Salt Pork.
2 Onions and 2 Carrots, Sliced.
10 Cloves. ½ Calfs Foot.
1 Clove of Garlic. Bouquet of Sweet Herbs.
1½ Pints of Broth or Boiling Water.
2 Spoonfuls of Brandy.
1 Pint of White Wine.

Clean and prepare the turkey as in the above directions, then stuff either with egg dressing or oyster stuffing. Rub well with salt and pepper. Place at the bottom of a deep pot slender strips of salt pork and half of a calf's foot, well prepared. Place on top of this the slices of onions, carrots, fine herbs, minced nicely; garlic, minced, celery, parsley, etc., and lay the turkey on this bed. Pour over it one pint of white wine and two tablespoonfuls of brandy, and one pint and a half of good broth or boiling water. Season well to taste and cover tightly. Set on the stove to simmer very slowly for at least five hours if the turkey is old. Turn it once very carefully when half done cooking. After five hours, lift the turkey out of the sauce, place on a hot dish. Strain the sauce through a sieve, and if the turkey is served at once, serve hot in a separate dish. If not, pour it over the turkey and set it away to cool. It will become quite jellied and makes an excellent luncheon dish.

### Boned Turkey.
### Gelatine Truffée à la Gelée.

1 Young Turkey Hen.
2 Pounds of Young Veal.
1 Pound of Fat Fresh Pork
1 Pound of Lean Fresh Pork.
¼ Pound of Cooper's Gelatine.
¼ Can of Truffles.
1 Tablespoonful Each of Minced Parsley, and Thyme.
3 Minced Bay Leaves. 1 Lemon.
3 Sprigs Each of Thyme and Bay Leaf.
1 Glass of Brandy.
1 Wineglass of Sherry. 2 Carrots.
1 Turnip. 1 Stalk of Celery.
2 Gallons of Water.
½ Teaspoonful Each of Grated Cinnamon and Allspice.

For this highly-prized dish, select a young hen turkey. It must be hand-picked—that is, it must not be scalded, or it will be unfit for the purpose of boning. Clean it thoroughly, and, when well cleansed, place the turkey on the table, with the breast down, and take a sharp penknife, or a very sharp-pointed knife, and cut the turkey open from the neck to the rump, down the backbone. Then, with great care, run the knife between the bones and the flesh to the wings, and, on reaching the joints, unjoint and separate the bones from the body without breaking the flesh; in like manner remove each bone as you reach the joint, except the small bone in the tips of the wings, which cannot be taken out easily and which are generally left on. Carefully slit out the bones of the leg, and then run the knife between the bones and flesh till you come to the breast bone. Skillfully separate the flesh from the bone by running the knife between, being careful to pull it out without breaking the flesh of the turkey. After removing the carcass, spread out the turkey, which will be whole, and wipe inside and out with a damp towel, and rub well with salt and pepper, inside and out. Set aside in a cool place and prepare the following dressing or stuffing: Take two pounds of young veal, one pound of young, fat, fresh pork, and one pound of lean fresh pork. Mince these as fine as possible, and then season as follows: One-half of a nutmeg, finely grated; one tablespoonful of minced parsley; one of minced thyme, three of minced bay leaves, one teaspoonful of salt and one of black pepper, a teaspoonful of grated cinnamon, one-quarter teaspoonful of grated allspice and the juice of one onion. Mix all this thoroughly in the stuffing. Add two raw eggs, beaten well; one wineglass full of Sherry and one of Brandy; stir well. When well mixed add one-quarter of a box of truffles, chopped, but not too fine. Take the turkey, lay it open and carefully cut a layer of meat in nice slices from the inner part. Then put in a thick layer of the stuffing, and lay over this a layer of the meat, using the whole liver, sliced in strips, also as alternate layers; then put in the rest of the stuffing as a layer, and bring the turkey nicely together and sew up so that it will retain its original shape. Have ready a nice, clean towel; roll the turkey in the towel, and tie it securely at both ends and around the middle in a solid way. Take all the bones of the turkey, the skinned feet, cleaned head and all, and place in a large pot. Add two pounds of veal, cut in pieces, and two calves' feet. Put in two carrots, one turnip, several sprigs of thyme and parsley, three bay leaves and a large piece of celery. Add two gallons of water, and let this boil very hard for an hour. Then add the turkey which you will have tied in the towel and let it boil for two hours. After two hours, take the turkey out of the towel. It will have shrunken up by this time and the towel will be crinkled greatly. Roll the towel out very smoothly again, and place the turkey back in it while hot, and roll carefully again. Tie it at both ends and across the middle, and then place on a table and put a board or plank on top, and over this a fifteen-pound weight. Leave it in a cool place, but not in the ice box, as it must cool gradually and naturally. After it has cooled five or six hours you may put it in the ice box.

In the meantime you will have left on the fire the pot with the water, bones, etc., in which the turkey has been boiled. Let it boil for two hours longer, with the bones and all. Then take off and drain the whole through a strainer, first letting the juice fall in another pan; then strain this through a towel, for there must be no pieces of cinnamon or herbs or dregs in this jelly. Skim off all the grease that floats on top, being careful not to leave a particle. Put it on the fire again, and let it simmer. Add to the boiling mixture one lemon and skin, cut in four or five pieces, and season with salt to taste. Put in a bowl one-quarter of a pound of Cooper's gelatine, and add one pint of water in which the turkey has been boiled; stir well and let the gelatine melt. When well melted, pour into the boiling mixture and beat it as you would a cake, mixing thoroughly. Take another bowl, and break three raw eggs in it, and mash the shells and add; add one small wineglass of water and beat well again, as you would a cake. Prepare a flannel bag of size sufficient to hold a half gallon. Then pour the eggs into the broth beating very thoroughly and rapidly through and through for ten minutes, while it remains on the fire. The moment it begins to boil up it will curdle; then take the mixture off and strain in the flannel bag. Let this fall into a few tin cups or cans, for they are best, and set on ice. The next morning it will be hard. Then unroll the turkey and put it in a dish; cut the jelly from the can into fancy shapes and ornament the turkey with it, placing a fancy border around the dish. You will have a dish that a king might envy.

Boned chicken may be prepared in exactly the same way.

## CHICKEN.

### Poulet.

Chickens may be broiled, boiled, fried, stewed, baked or smothered. For broiling, always purchase spring chickens. For baking, the chicken must be young and tender. For invalids, a delicately boiled spring chicken, with Drawn Butter Sauce, is a most nutritious and easily digestible dish.

### Broiled Chicken.
#### Poulet Grillé.

A Spring Chicken. Melted Butter.
Salt and Pepper to Taste.

Select spring chickens for broiling. For a family of six several will be required. Clean the chickens nicely, singe, and then split down the middle of the back, laying the chicken open. Break the breastbone with a mallet and flatten out the chicken. Season well with salt and pepper, and brush with melted butter. Have the broiler ready over a moderate fire, and place the chicken between (the double broiler is best) and let the fowl broil slowly for about a half hour, if the chicken is very tender, otherwise three-quarters of an hour. It is well to keep a plate over it all the time, as it will retain its flavor better. Turn the chicken frequently, so that it may be broiled through and through. It should be slightly browned on the skin side. When done, place in a heated dish, pour over melted butter and garnish with chopped parsley and serve hot. A garnish of cresses is very pretty. The dish is then called "Poulet Grillé aux Cressons."

### Boiled Chicken.
#### Poulet Bouilli.

A Spring Chicken. Drawn Butter Sauce.
Salt and Pepper to Taste.

Select a nice spring chicken, clean and singe and split down the middle of the back. Season with salt and pepper, rubbing well on the inside of the chicken. Place in a saucepan and cover well with water and let it simmer well for one hour if the chicken is young. If the chicken is a year old and over, let it simmer for two hours, according to age. When done take out of the water and place in a heated dish. Pour over a Drawn Butter Sauce (see recipe) and garnish with chopped parsley.

### Creamed Chicken.
#### Poulet à la Crème.

1 Chicken. Salt and Pepper to Taste.
A Cream Sauce.

Select a fine one-year-old chicken and clean, singe and boil according to the above recipe, first having cut in joints, however. In boiling always simply cover the chicken with water, otherwise you will have chicken soup, all the nutriment of the chicken being absorbed by the soup. When cooked for an hour or longer, if the chicken is now very tender, take out of the saucepan and place in a dish and pour over a Cream Sauce (see recipe), and serve.

### Deviled Chicken.
#### Poulet à la Diable.

1 Chicken. 1 Tablespoonful of Butter.
1 Tablespoonful of Flour.
1 Onion. 1 Bay Leaf. 1 Sprig of Parsley.
½ of a Clove of Garlic.
1 Glass of White Wine.
1 Pint of Water.
1 Teaspoonful of Prepared Mustard.
Salt and Pepper. A Dash of Cayenne.

Boil the chicken according to the above recipe. Mince the meat fine. Make a sauce by putting into a saucepan one tablespoonful of butter, and as it melts add one onion, minced very fine; a sprig of minced parsley, one minced bay leaf, and a half clove of minced garlic. Let it simmer gently without browning and then add one tablespoonful of flour, well sifted. Mix thoroughly, and add three tablespoonfuls of vinegar or a wineglass of White Wine. Stir well and add one pint of the water in which the chicken was boiled. Season with salt and pepper to taste and a slight dash of Cayenne. Then add one teaspoonful of prepared mustard. Let it simmer three minutes longer, and as it comes to a ball pour over the chicken and serve. Any remains of cold chicken are very delicious served with this "Sauce à la Diable." (See recipe "Meat Sauces.")

### Chicken à la Tartare.
#### Poulet à la Tartare.

1 Spring Chicken.
1 Tablespoonful of Butter.
1 Tablespoonful of Chopped Parsley.
1 Tablespoonful of Thyme.
1 Bay Leaf, Minced Fine.
1 Chopped Onion.
Salt and Pepper to Taste.

Boil the chicken according to the above recipe, adding the chopped vegetables and herbs. Season to taste. When done, place on a hot dish, butter nicely and serve with a Sauce à la Tartare. (See recipe.) A broiled chicken may be served in the same manner, but either broiled or boiled, the chicken must be cooked whole, splitting down the back.

### Stewed Chicken, Brown Sauce.
#### Fricassée de Volaille, Sauce Brune.

1 Chicken. 1 Onion.
1 Tablespoonful of Lard.
1 Tablespoonful of Flour.
1 Sprig Each of Thyme, Parsley and Bay Leaf.
Salt and Pepper to Taste.

Clean and cut the chicken into pieces at the joints. Season well with salt and black pepper. Chop the onions fine. Put a tablespoonful of lard into the stewpot, and, when hot, add the onion. Let it brown slightly and then add the flour, which has been well sifted. Let this brown and add the chicken. Let all simmer a few minutes and then add the chopped thyme, parsley and bay leaf. The latter must be minced very fine. Stir well and often. When every piece is nicely browned, add one pint and a half of boiling water or soup broth. Stir until it begins to boil. Season again to taste. Cover and let it simmer gently for an hour, or until tender. In making a fricassée, the liver, heart and gizzard of the chicken are all thrown into the stew. Dish up the chicken, pour over the hot sauce and serve hot. This dish is very nice with boiled rice or potatoes. It is a simple, elegant dish, within the means of everyone. This is a plain fricassée.

### Stewed Chicken, White Sauce.
#### Fricassée de Volaille, Sauce Blanche.

1 Chicken. 1 Onion.
1 Tablespoonful of Butter.
2 Tablespoonfuls Flour. 1 Pint Fresh Milk.
Salt and Pepper to Taste.

Clean and cut the chicken into joints and clean the gizzard, liver and open the heart. Season well with salt and pepper, and put all into a stewpan on a moderate fire. Cover well with boiling water. Let simmer for an hour and a half or quarter if the chicken is very young; longer if the chicken is old. Add the juice of two large onions. Cook until tender. This is the unvarying rule in stewing or cooking chickens, as one may be tender and the other quite tough, though of the same age. When the chicken is done, blend together one large tablespoonful of butter and of flour in a frying pan without browning; add a pint of milk and mix well. Add this to the chicken, mixing and stirring constantly till it boils. Salt and pepper to taste. Take from the fire and add the beaten yolks of two eggs and a little chopped parsley. Serve hot.

### Chicken Sauté à la Créole.
#### Poulet Sauté à la Créole.

2 Fine Spring Chickens.
2 Tablespoonfuls of Butter.
2 Tablespoonfuls of Flour.
6 Large Fresh Tomatoes, or ½ Can.
6 Fresh, Sweet Green Peppers.
2 Cloves of Garlic.
3 Large Onions.
3 Sprigs Each of Thyme and Parsley.
2 Bay Leaves.
1 Pint of Consomme or Boiling Water.
Salt and Pepper to Taste.

Take two spring chickens and clean nicely and cut into pieces at the joints. Season well with salt and pepper. Put two tablespoonfuls of butter into a stewpan, and, when it melts, add the chicken. Let this brown slowly for a good five minutes. Have ready three large onions sliced. Add these to the chickens and let them brown. Every Inch must be nicely browned, but not in the slightest degree burned. Add two tablespoonfuls of flour; let this brown. Then add a half dozen large, fresh tomatoes nicely sliced, or a half can of tomatoes, and let these brown. Cook very slowly, allowing the mixture to simply simmer. Add chopped parsley, thyme and bay leaf, and two cloves of garlic finely minced. Let all brown without burning. Cover and let it smother over a slow but steady fire. The tomato juice will make sufficient gravy as yet. If you have sweet green peppers, add a half dozen, taking the seeds out before adding and slicing the peppers very fine. Stir well. Let all smother steadily for twenty minutes at least, keeping well covered and stirring occasionally. When well smothered, add one cup of Consommé, if you have it; if not, one cup of boiling water. Let it cook again for a full half hour, very, very slowly over a very steady fire, and season again to taste. Cook ten minutes more, and serve hot. You will then have a dish for which any old Creole would go on foot from Carrollton to the Barracks, a distance of fifteen miles, merely to get a taste of.

### Chicken With Mushrooms.

Poulet Sauté aux Champignons.

1 Fine Spring Chicken. ½ Can of Mushrooms.
2 Tablespoonfuls of Butter.
2 Chopped Onions. 1 Clove of Garlic.
1 Glass of Madeira or Sherry Wine.
½ Square Inch of Ham to Season.
Thyme, Parsley, Bay Leaf.

Cut into joints and season a nicely cleaned chicken. Put it in a saucepan with two tablespoonfuls of butter, and let it simmer for about ten minutes, browning slightly. A mushroom sauce is never dark. Add two nicely-chopped onions, and let these brown slightly; then add one-half of a square inch of ham, chopped very fine indeed. Add thyme, parsley and bay leaf, following carefully the order given in adding the ingredients. A minute later add the garlic, which has been minced very fine. Let all brown together for ten minutes. Cut the mushrooms into halves, put them with their water, into the pot, stirring well. Let them simmer five minutes. Then add a wineglass of Sherry or Madeira, stir and cover the pot closely, so that it can smother well. If the sauce appears too thick add about a half cup of broth or boiling water. Season to taste, and let all cook very slowly for an hour longer over a steady fire. The secret in smothering chicken is to let it cook slowly, so that the seasoning may permeate the flesh and the heat by slow degrees render it tender and most palatable.

### Chicken With Truffles.

Poulet Sauté aux Truffes.

Proceed in exactly the same manner as in the above recipe, only add a half can of truffles instead of the mushrooms. This is an expensive dish.

### Chicken and Rice.

Poulet au Riz.

1 Fine Chicken.
½ Square Inch of Ham.
2 Small Turnips. 2 Carrots. 2 Onions.
1 Small Piece Lemon Peel.
1 Clove of Garlic.
1 Small Piece of Red Pepper Pod.
1 Bay Leaf.
2 Whole Cloves, Without the Seed.
3 Sliced Tomatoes.
3 Sprigs Each of Thyme and Parsley.
2 Quarts of Water. 2 Tablespoonfuls Butter.
Salt and Pepper to Taste.

Clean and cut and season the chicken well with salt and pepper. Put the butter into the saucepan and let it melt, and add the seasoned chicken. Let it brown well, and add the vegetables, all chopped very fine. Then add the minced herbs and garlic, and after this the spices. Let all simmer gently for ten minutes, and pour over two quarts of boiling water. Stir and season again to taste and set back on the stove and let it simmer steadily and slowly for three-quarters of an hour. When two-thirds cooked, add one cup of well-washed rice, stir well, seasoning again to taste. Do not let the rice become mushy. Let the grains stand out. Let all cook for twenty minutes longer and serve, taking out first the pieces of chicken and ranging the rice around as a garnish. Serve with the sauce poured over.

### Chicken Stewed With Green Peas.

Poulet Sauté aux Petit Pois.

1 Nice Chicken of a Year Old.
1 Pint of Green Peas.
2 Tablespoonfuls of Butter.
2 Chopped Onions. 1 Clove of Garlic.
1 Pint of Fresh Milk. ½ Square Inch of Ham.
1 Tablespoonful of Flour.
Thyme, Parsley and Bay Leaf.

Cut and season the chicken nicely. Put it in a saucepan with two tablespoonfuls of butter, and let it simmer nicely for about ten minutes without browning. Add two nicely-chopped onions and let these brown slightly. Then add a square inch of ham, chopped very fine, and minced thyme, parsley and bay leaf, one sprig each. Add the garlic, nicely minced. Let all brown together, slightly simmering all the time. Then pour in one pint of boiling water, and set back on the stove and let simmer gently for an hour and a quarter. About twenty minutes before serving add one pint of milk, and let all cook for twenty minutes. Serve with the green peas heaped around the chicken, which should be placed in the center of the dish. Pour the gravy over, and bring to the table.

### Chicken With Dumplings.
#### Poulet aux Échaudés.
1 Fine Year Old Chicken.
1 Tablespoonful of Lard.
1 Tablespoonful of Flour.
1 Sprig Each of Thyme, Parsley and Bay Leaf.
2 Dozen Small Dumplings.

Prepare a Plain Fricassée, Brown or White Gravy, and, about twelve minutes before serving, add the dumplings, dropping them in lightly and bring the chicken to a brisk boil. (See recipe for Dumplings.) Place the chicken and dumplings in the dish, pour the hot gravy over and serve.

### Chicken à la Jardinière.
#### Poulet à la Jardinière.
1 Fine Chicken.
6 Small Onions.   1 Tablespoonful of Lard.
1 Tablespoonful of Flour.
1 Sprig Each of Thyme, Parsley and Bay Leaf.
½ Head of Cauliflower.
½ Cup of Green Peas
3 Small Artichokes.
¼ Can of Mushrooms.

Cut and stew the chicken as in Fricassée Brown Gravy. After adding the water, add a half dozen small onions, and let it simmer for an hour, or until tender. Then add one-quarter can of mushrooms, a small half head of cauliflower (nicely chopped), a half cup of green peas and several cooked artichokes. Set upon a quick fire, mix well and add a pint of good broth or water; let all cook for twenty minutes longer and serve hot.

### Smothered Chicken.
#### Poulet Braisé.
1 Chicken.   1 Tablespoonful of Lard.

This is a most delicate and palatable way of cooking chickens. After cleaning the young chicken, split down the back and dredge with salt and pepper. Put a tablespoonful of lard into the frying pan, and, when it is hot, add the chicken. Let it simmer gently for about fifteen minutes, then add a half cup of water, and set back on the stove, and let it simmer gently and steadily for about an hour. Serve with a garnish of chopped parsley. Some smother the chicken in butter, but this is ac-according to taste. Butter always makes a greasier dish than lard when frying or smothering meats.

### Breasts of Chicken Louisiana Style.
#### Suprême de Volaille à la Louisianaise.
The Filets of 2 Chickens.
4 Tablespoonfuls of Butter.
1 Small Onion, sliced.   1 Minced Bay Leaf.
1 Blade of Mace.   4 Cloves.
Salt and Pepper to Taste.

The filets are the white meat on either side of the breast bone. In one chicken you will have four filets. Form this white meat neatly into filets by patting and flattening. Then season well with salt and pepper. Put the butter into the stewpan and add the sliced onion, the bay leaf (whole) and the spices. Let all simmer without browning. Then lay in the filets of chicken, being careful not to let them brown. Let them simmer gently and add one cup of the water in which you have broiled the dark meat of the chicken. Let all simmer gently for an hour. When done, arrange the filets tastefully on a dish, garnish with parsley sprigs and Croûtons of bread nicely shaped in diamond form and fried in butter. The dark meat may be utilized in making salads, croquettes or boudins.

### Breasts of Chicken, Queen Style.
#### Suprême de Volaille à la Reine.
6 or 8 Breasts of Chicken.   2 Truffles.
4 Mushrooms.
2 Ounces of Chicken Forcemeat.
1 Tablespoonful of Butter.
1 Gill of Madeira Wine.
2 Tablespoonfuls of Mushroom Liquor.
1 Pint of Hot Sauce a la Reine.

Under the breast of each chicken is found a small filet. Carefully remove this, and set aside on a dish for further use. Take a small, sharp knife and make an incision three inches long and one inch deep in the inner side of each breast; season lightly with salt and pepper, and then stuff each breast in the incision made, using two ounces of chicken forcemeat (see recipe), mixed with two truffles and four mushrooms, all finely minced. Put a tablespoonful of butter in a stewpan; lay the breasts in gently. Take each small filet, press gently into shape, and flatten; make several small incisions and place within a fine slice of truffle, about an inch in diameter. Carefully lay on top of each breast lengthwise. Brush lightly with melted butter. Pour into the pan, but not over the breasts, the wine and mushroom liquor. Cover tightly and set in the oven for fifteen minutes. Send to the table hot.

### Smothered Chicken.
#### Poularde Etouffé.
1 Young Hen.   ¼ Pound of Nice Bacon.
1 Lemon.   2 Carrots.   2 Onions.
1 Herb Bouquet.   1½ Cups Broth.
Salt and Pepper to Taste.

This is a nice way to utilize young hens. Clean and singe the chicken nicely, and, after taking out the entrails, truss it as in roasting turkey. Place in the frying pan small pieces of fat bacon, cut in very slender strips of about the size of your finger. Place over this slices of lemon, very fine, and cover again with slender bits of bacon. Moisten this with a half cup of water and lay over two carrots, cut in thin slices, and two onions, cut likewise, and a teaspoonful each of thyme, parsley and one bay leaf, minced fine. Place on top of this the chicken and cover closely. Let it cook on a good fire for three-quarters of an hour, or a half hour, if the chicken is exceedingly tender. When done, take out the chicken, add one-half cup of broth to the liquor in which it has been boiling. Stir well and season highly, and pour over the chicken and serve. A sauce of tomatoes may also be made and served with this dish.

### Fried Chicken.
Poulet Frit.

1 Spring Chicken.
3 Tablespoonfuls of Lard. 2 Eggs.
4 Tablespoonfuls of Flour.
Salt and Pepper to Taste.

Clean and cut the chicken into joints. Dredge well with salt and pepper. Make a nice batter with the eggs and flour and roll the chicken in this, patting lightly. Place in the hot lard in the frying pan and let it cook for about three-quarters of an hour, watching carefully that it may not burn. Serve on a platter garnished with chopped parsley and cresses.

### Fried Chicken, Cream Sauce.
Poulet Frit à la Crème.

1 Spring Chicken.
3 Tablespoonfuls of Lard.
Salt and Pepper. 1 Tablespoonful of Flour.
½ Pint of Milk.

Clean and cut the chicken at the joints. Dredge well with salt and pepper, and a little flour. Put the lard into the frying pan, and, when hot, add the chicken, letting it fry slowly for three-quarters of an hour until done. Be careful not to burn. When done, arrange the pieces on a hot dish. Pour off all the fat that remains in the frying pan but one tablespoonful. Add to this a tablespoonful of sifted flour. Mix thoroughly and then pour in a half pint of rich cream or milk. Season well with salt and pepper, let it come to a slight boil and pour over the chicken and serve.

### Roast Chicken.
Poulet Roti.

1 Chicken.   ½ Tablespoonful Butter.
Salt and Pepper to Taste.

Proceed in exactly the same manned as for roasting a turkey. (See recipe.) The chicken must bake in a quick oven, allowing fifteen minutes to every pound. A roasted chicken may be stuffed or not, according to taste, with a stuffing of oysters, eggs or truffles (see Dressings for Fowls) in exactly the same manner as turkey.

### Chicken à la Reine.
Poulet à la Reine.

2 Chickens of 1 Year Old.
¼ Pound of Nice Bacon. 1 Carrot, cut fine.
1 Onion., cut fine
1 Quart of Broth or Water.
1 Herb Bouquet.

Clean the chickens and truss as for roasting. Then dredge inside and out with salt and pepper. Cut the bacon into very thin strips, about the width of a match, and cover the bottom of the stewpan. Lay over this the carrots and onions, sliced fine, and put another layer of salt meat in delicate strips. Put the chickens in this and cover well and set inside of a hot oven. After twenty minutes add the boiling broth or water and the bunch of sweet herbs. Let the chickens cook for two hours, turning them at the end of one hour and basting occasionally. Put the chicken in a hot dish, boil the gravy down to a half quart, skim off all the grease and pass through a sieve and pour over the chickens and serve.

### Casserole of Chicken.
Casserole de Volaille.

½ Cup of Cream.
3 Quarts of Cold Water.
1 Tablespoonful of Salt.
1 Tablespoonful of Butter.
2 Cups of Louisiana Rice.
Salt and Pepper to Taste.
A White Fricassee of Chicken.

Make a Fricassée of Chicken, White Gravy. Boil the rice according to recipe (see Boiled Rice) and then mash the rice thoroughly and add the butter and season with salt and pepper. Take a raised pie pan or casserole and press the rice into this, and set away to cool. When cool, cut out the center of the rice and fill the wall and bottom with the white fricassée of chicken. Cover the top with the rice which you have cut out, laying on lightly, so as not to press the chicken sauce through. Beat an egg well and brush over this. Set in the oven and bake. Serve with Mushroom Sauce.

### Chicken Soufflé.
Soufflé de Poulet.

1 Pint of Chopped Left-Over Chicken.
1 Tablespoonful of Chopped Parsley.
1 Pint of Milk. 1 Tablespoonful of Flour.
3 Fresh Eggs.
½ Cup of Stale Bread.
Salt, Pepper and Cayenne to Taste.

Melt the butter in a saucepan and add the flour, and mix nicely without browning. Then add the milk and stir constantly till it boils. Add the bread crumbs and cook for one minute longer. Then take from the fire and add the chicken, which has been hashed very fine and seasoned well with salt, pepper and Cayenne, judging according to the taste. Beat the yolks of the eggs and add, mixing thoroughly. Then beat the whites to a stiff froth and stir very carefully into the mixture. Grease the bottom of a baking dish with butter and put the mixture in this, baking for twenty minutes in a quick oven. Serve immediately while hot, or it will fall. This is a very delicate dish.

### Chicken Pie.
Vol-au-Vent de Volaille.

1 Chicken. 1 Onion.
1 Tablespoonful of Lard.
1 Tablespoonful of Flour.
1 Sprig Each of Thyme, Bay Leaf and Parsley.
Pie Paste.

Clean and cut the chicken into small pieces of about two inches in length and make a plain fricassée. (See Fricassee Brown Gravy.) Prepare a Vol-au-Vent Paste (see recipe), and fill a tin pan of about two quarts with the Paste. Pour in the chicken and gravy, and let it bake in the oven till the top crust is nicely browned. Always bake the under crust first. This is a delightful entrée at any feast. Vol-au-Vent of pigeons, young veal and frog legs are made in the same manner. A Vol-au-Vent of Frogs is called "Grenouilles à la Poulet." The Vol-au-Vent paste is difficult to make.

### Chicken Patties, Queen Style.
Petites Bouchées, à la Reine.

1 Small Young Chicken.
12 Rounds of Puff Paste.
1 Tablespoonful of Butter.
1 Tablespoonful of Flour.
½ Pint of Milk.  ½ Can of Mushrooms.
A Pinch of Grated Nutmeg.
Salt and Pepper to Taste.

Roast or broil the chicken nicely. Make a Puff Paste. (See recipe.) Cut a dozen rounds with a biscuit cutter; mark a smaller round or top for a cover. Brush with a beaten egg, and mark on the surface of each with the cutter, dipping it each time in hot water, so that the marked outline may remain perfect. Set in a brisk oven and let them brown nicely for twelve minutes. Then remove the covers gently with a knife and fill with the following garnishing. Remove all the chicken meat from the bone and chop very fine. Put a tablespoonful of butter in a sautoire or stewpan and add a tablespoonful of sifted flour. Stir till smooth. Pour in gradually a half pint of hot milk till the same reaches the consistency of a thick cream. Season to taste with salt and pepper and a little nutmeg, and add one-half can of mushrooms finely chopped and the chicken. Stir constantly and let it come to a boil. Then remove from the fire and fill the patties. Set the covers on, serve on a hot dish. Pork tongues, blanched sweetbreads and all other "Bouchées" are prepared in the same manner.

### Boned Chicken.
Galatine Truffée à la Gelée.

Proceed in exactly the same manner as for boned turkey and serve. (See recipe Boned Turkey.)

### Chicken Croquettes.
Croquettes de Volaille.

1 Young Chicken.
2 Small Onions.  1 Bay Leaf.
4 Sprigs of Parsley.
1 Large Tablespoonful of Butter.
1 Cup of Milk.
1 Teaspoonful of Salt.
Cayenne and Pepper to Taste.

Boil the chicken as directed in the recipe for boiling. Then, when cold, remove all the tough fibers and nerves. Hash the chicken well and season with the minced vegetables and sweet herbs, mixing all thoroughly. Then take a cup of the soft of the bread, wet it and squeeze, and soak in milk, in which you have beaten two eggs. Mix all this with the chicken very thoroughly and season to taste. When well mixed form the meat into cylindrical shapes and brush with a little butter. Then roll in a beaten egg and roll again in powdered bread crumbs. Fry in boiling lard and serve hot on a plate garnished with fried parsley.

Remains of cold turkey or cold chicken may be utilized in this way.

### Chicken Balls, Queen Style.
Boudins à la Reine.

1 Young Chicken.
2 Small Onions.  1 Bay Leaf.
4 Sprigs of Parsley.  1 Cup of Milk.
2 Eggs.  ¼ Grated Nutmeg.
1 Tablespoonful of Butter.
Salt and Pepper to Taste.

Boudins à la Reine are made in exactly the same manner as croquettes, only the mixture is placed in a frying pan and fried in butter, using about a tablespoonful. To this is added about one pint of milk. Beat the chicken thoroughly in this, add a grated nutmeg, then take off the fire and add two eggs, well beaten. Fill custard cups with the mixture, place in the oven setting in a pan of boiling water and covering with paper. Let them bake thus as you would a cup custard for twenty minutes, and take off the paper and let them brown. Serve hot. All cold roasts, whether of turkey or chicken, may be thus utilized.

### Boulettes.
Boulettes are prepared in exactly the same manner as boudins, only the meat is formed into boulettes, or

small balls, and patted on either side to flatten slightly.

### Chicken Salad, Mayonnaise Sauce.
#### Mayonnaise de Volaille.
Remains of Cold Chicken,
or Freshly Boiled.
3 Hard-Boiled Eggs.
Celery.   1 Onion.
Celery, Asparagus Tips and Boiled Beets to Garnish.
A Sauce a la Mayonnaise.

The remains of cold chicken are used for this. But it is always preferable for dinners to boil the chickens nicely and use only the white meat, if you wish the dish to be recherché. The dark meat, however, is equally good, though it may not look so pretty. After cooking the chickens very tender, pick out all the white meat into small pieces of about an inch or less, and add chopped celery of the whitest fiber and very tender. Mix thoroughly, using good judgment in having parts of the celery and chicken in the proportion of one-third celery. Chop an onion very fine, and add. Season all with salt and pepper to taste. Place on a dish and spread over a nice Mayonnaise dressing (see Sauce à la Mayonnaise), and garnish prettily with celery tips, asparagus tips, olives, and very delicately sliced red beets, and sliced lemon.

### Chicken Livers.
#### Foies de Volaille.

Chicken livers may be prepared as "Foie de Volaille Sauté," or "Foie de Volaille en Brochette." They are prepared in exactly the same manner as in the recipes for cooking beef's liver. (See recipe.)

### CAPONS.
#### Chapons.

Capons of either turkey or chicken are cooked in exactly the same manner, generally being best when boiled or roasted.

Chapon Farcie à la Crême corresponds to Creamed Chicken, and Chapon à la Poêle corresponds to Poularde à la Poêle, and are particularly recommended. (See recipes.)

### GUINEA FOWL.
#### Pintade.

The Guinea Fowl is only eaten when very young, and then it makes a nice, palatable dish. All the preparations given for cooking turkey may be followed in preparing this fowl, and it is unnecessary to repeat them here. (See recipes for Cooking Turkey.)

### GOOSE.
#### Oie.

The goose is a much tougher fowl than either the chicken or turkey and requires longer to cook. It is also dryer meat, and in roasting requires to have a little water poured over it. Never roast a goose that is more than eight months or a year old, and never eat a goose over three years old. The happy age for general cooking is when the goose has reached one year or one year and a half. Young wild geese of not more than one year, and yard ducklings of similar age, are broiled in the same manner as spring chicken. The fatter the goose, the more tender and juicy the meat.

### Roast Goose.
#### Oie Rotie.
1 Young Goose.   4 Onions.
1 Cup of Mashed Potatoes.
½ Teaspoonful of Thyme.
2 Sprigs of Parsley.
4 Apples.   1½ Tablespoonful of Lard.
Salt and Pepper to Taste.

A roast goose, properly preparerd, is a very savory dish, whether the fowl is wild or tame. But, as mentioned above, the goose must be tender. If the breastbone yields easily to pressure and the pinions are very tender, the legs smooth and yellow and free from feathers, the goose is young. In picking a goose never scald it, as this utterly ruins the flesh. The goose must be hand picked. Then singe and clean, and season well and roast as you would a turkey, allowing, however, twenty-five minutes to every pound. It may be served with a Giblet Sauce as roast chicken. Apple Sauce or Currant Jelly is always served with Roast Goose, preferably the Apple Sauce. Any stuffing used in baking a turkey may be used for roast goose, such as oyster or egg, etc. But the following is an excellent special dressing and seems to bring out more than any other the flavor of the goose.

Take one cup of mashed potatoes, four apples, peeled nicely and cored, and four onions, one-half teaspoonful of sage, powdered well; one-half teaspoonful of thyme, and pepper and salt to taste. Place the apples and onions and herbs in a saucepan and add water sufficiently to cover nicely. Let all cook together till soft. Then mash well and rub through a sieve. Add the cup of mashed potatoes and mix well, seasoning with salt and pepper. Stuff the body and craw, sew up and truss the goose. Put into the roasting pan, rubbing a half tablespoonful of lard over it and pouring over a half cup of water, boiling. Baste the goose very frequently, say every ten minutes, so that it will be fine and juicy. It generally requires at least an hour and a half to roast well, but the rule of twenty-five minutes to the pound is a good one to follow. A "Green

Goose" is always best for roasting, but this must be covered from the beginning with a piece of buttered paper, else it will brown before cooking. Serve with Apple Sauce.

### Goose Daube.
### Oie en Daube.

Prepare in exactly the same manner as Turkey Daube (see recipe). A goose that is not so young may be cooked à la Daube.

### Goose à la Chipolata.
### Oie à la Chipolata.

1 Fine Young Goose.
½ Pound of Chaurice. 1 Can of Mushrooms.
1 Dozen Large Chestnuts, nicely roasted and skinned.
1 Sprig Each of Thyme and Bay Leaf.
3 Sprigs of Parsley.
The Juice of 2 Lemons.
4 or 5 Bits of Lemon Peel.
2 Onions. 1 Pint of BoilingWater.
½ Tablespoonful of Lard or Butter.
1 Spoon of Flour.

Place the lard or butter in the stewpot and when it melts add the onions, which have been nicely sliced. As they brown add the goose, which has been cleaned, singed and nicely cut at the joints into pieces, and well rubbed with salt and pepper, and the sausage, which must be cut in halves. Let simmer for about ten minutes, until every portion is slightly browned, and then add the minced herbs and garlic. After three minutes add the spoonful of flour, mixing well, and let it all simmer for ten minutes longer, then pour in the can of mushrooms and their water, and add immediately the chestnuts. Let the goose cook till tender and serve hot.

### Fat Livers.
### Des Foies Gras.

The livers of geese that have been caged tightly, so that they can make no movement, and which have been kept in a very high temperature, much higher than that of the atmosphere—geese which have been deprived of every ray of light—are used for the famous dish, "Foies Gras." The French first discovered this manner of caging geese, doing it at their ancient stronghold of Strasbourg. At Toulouse the livers of tame ducks were treated in the same manner. The Creoles, descendants of the French, brought over the custom to the old French colony of Louisiana, whence it has spread to all portions of the United States. Before the war, on the spot now known as the New Orleans Fair Grounds, there was a famous "Foie Gras" farm. It was kept by an old Creole woman, and she made a fortune from the profits. She followed the old French method of caging the geese so tightly that often, as in Strasbourg, the feet were nailed down, to prevent the least movement. The farm closed in 1861. While the livers of the geese or ducks become soft and fat under this treatment, the rest of the body suffers, and becomes so very fat that the goose flesh is good for nothing, or, as the Creoles say, "Plus bonne à rien." Foies Gras are now sold in cans in every large grocery establishment in the United States. They come already cooked, in such shape that they can easily be made into any of the delectable dishes that so delight the old Creole or French "bon vivants." The most famous of these dishes is the

### Patties of Foies Gras.

Paté de Foie Gras.
1 Terrine of Foies Gras.
1 Pound of Fat Pork.
1 Pound of Goose Fat.
½ Can of Truffles.
Salt and Pepper to Taste.
A Glass of Sherry Wine.
A Puff Paste.

Procure the fat livers of geese. (They are no longer to be bought except already prepared in cans, Terrine de Foie Gras aux Truffles du Perigord, Strasbourg.) To this allow one pound of fat pork and one pound of the fat of geese. Chop these and the livers very fine, allowing pound for pound of the fat meat and goose fat to the same quantity of livers. Season well with salt and pepper, and moisten it well with Sherry wine. Chop a half can of truffles and mix, and put all in a quart or pint measure baking pan, which you will have lined with Puff Paste. (See recipe.) The pan must be about two and a half or three inches deep. Bake this paste, and then fill in with the foies gras. Cover with a light cover of the dough, and decorate around the edges with the clippings of dough that remain. Place the pie in the oven, and let it bake for about an hour to a nice brown, covering for the first three-quarters of an hour with a piece of paper, to prevent burning. When done, serve in the dish in which it was baked. This is the real Creole Paté de Foie Gras.

### Stewed Foies Gras.

Foies Gras en Matelote.
1 Terrine of Foies Gras.
Thin Strips of Bacon.
1 Carrot. 1 Onion.
1 Tablespoonful of Chopped Parsley.
1 Wineglassful of White Wine.
2 Spoonfuls of French Brandy.
Salt and Pepper to Taste.

Get the prepared Foies Gras. Cut them into slices or filets. Lard them with a larding needle and then place at the bottom of the saucepan small strips of bacon, cut very thin and fine. Add one carrot, nicely sliced; one onion, nicely sliced, and a tablespoonful of chopped parsley. Cover this with narrow strips of bacon, and moisten with sufficient white wine to cover well, and two spoonfuls of brandy. Add the juice of a lemon and let it simmer well for a few minutes. Then add the livers, and let them simmer for ten minutes longer. Season to taste, cook five minutes more and serve hot. In seasoning the lvers prepared in this manner must always have a stimulating taste.

### Loaf of Foies Gras.

#### Pain de Foie Gras.

Foies. Gras. ½ Can of Mushrooms.
¼ Can of Truffles. 2 Shallots.
1 Sprig Each of Thyme, Parsley and Bay Leaf.
1 Leaf of Rose Geranium.
¼ Teaspoonful Each of Ground Cinnamon, Allspice, Cloves and Mace.
1 Young Sweetbread.
½ Cup of the Soft of Bread.
The Yolk of an Egg.
Grated Bread Crumbs.

Choose sufficient livers for the number of guests, for this is never an every-day dish, and place them in a saucepan with a tablespoonful of butter. Let them simmer gently and add a half can of mushrooms and a quarter of a can of truffles, two shallots, nicely minced; a sprig each of thyme, bay leaf and parsley, minced fine; salt and pepper to taste, and a half teaspoonful of prepared mustard; the leaf of one geranium, minced fine, and a quarter teaspoonful each of ground cinnamon, allspice, cloves and mace. Mix this thoroughly and let it simmer in the juice of the mushrooms for about twenty minutes. Then take a young sweetbread and cook according to recipe for Plain Fried Sweetbreads, and add a half cup of the soft of the bread, well moistened with milk. Mix this with the hashed sweetbreads, and add the yolk of an egg. Place this in a mortar with the foies gras and mix well. Then turn into a pan and brush lightly with the beaten yolk of an egg, and sprinkle grated bread crumbs over. Set in a pan of boiling water (Bain-marie), and bake in the oven for about a half hour.

### Foies Gras Loaf Jellied.

#### Pain de Foies à la Gelée.

Foies Gras. 1 Slice of Fat Fresh Pork.
1 Slice of Lean Pork (Grated.)
½ Can of Mushrooms.
¼ Can of Truffles.
1 Calf's Foot. 1 Bay Leaf.
Grated Bread Crumbs.
1 Sprig Each of Thyme and Parsley.
¼ Teaspoonful of Ground Allspice, Cinnamon Cloves and Mace.
½ Cup of the Soft of Bread.
The Juice of 1 Lemon.
Bits of Lemon Peel.
1 Tablespoonful of French Brandy.

This is prepared in exactly the same manner as the above, only the sweetbreads are omitted, and in their place is added an egg, well beaten, and a piece of grated lean and fat fresh pork meat. Add a half can of mushrooms again and a quarter of a can of truffles, and a piece of calf's foot. Cook into a mixture of the consistency of gravy, mash well and strain in a sieve after seasoning very highly; add the juice. Let this simmer for about five minutes and add the pint of boiling water. Set upon the back of the stove, and let it cook for about two hours, or an hour and a half, according to the age of the goose, throwing in the bits of lemon peel. When done, skim carefully of all grease, and at the moment of serving add the juice of one lemon to the mixture and serve. This is a very rich dish, and is served as an entrée.

## CHAPTER XVII.

### PIGEONS.

Pigeons.

Pigeons are of two kinds, those of the dovecot and those that are shot on the wing, commonly called doves. The latter are always broiled, just as one would broil any other bird or a tenderloin beefsteak; else they are roasted in little bands of bacon. The former are prepared in various ways, as, indeed, the latter may be also, only the wild taste is more apparent when broiled or roasted.

#### Broiled Pigeons.

Pigeons Grillées.

6 or 8 Young Squab.
3 Tablespoonfuls of Melted Butter.
6 or 8 Pieces of Buttered Toast.
The Juice of 1 Lemon.
Chopped Parsley to Garnish.

Squab are always best for broiling. Pluck and clean nicely inside and out. Wipe with a damp towel. Split down the back and spread open as you would a broiled chicken. Have the gridiron very hot. Rub the pigeon inside and out with salt and pepper, and brush lightly with butter. Place the broiler over a moderate furnace fire, from which all the gas has been exhausted, and let it broil slowly ten minutes on the inner side and five minutes on the outer. In the meantime toast a piece of bread for every pigeon that you broil. Moisten well with butter. Place the squab upon the toast, allowing one squab for each piece of toast, sprinkle with chopped parsley and butter, and serve hot. It is always well to rub the pigeon with a little lemon juice, as that renders the flesh nice and white.

#### Broiled Pigeons à la Crapaudine.

Pigeons à la Crapaudine.

4 Pigeons. The Yolk of an Egg.
1 Cup of Milk. 1 Tablespoonful of Butter.
Salt and Pepper to Taste.
A Tomato Sauce.

This is a famous Creole dish, and the object is to so dress the pigeons that they will resemble little frogs, hence the name, "Pigeons à la Crapaudine."

Clean the pigeons nicely, inside and out, and then carefully cut the breast from the loin joints, without separating entirely. Raise the breast up from the shoulder joints, and pass it over the head of the pigeon, without separating it from the shoulders. Then press it down very firmly with your hands or a masher. Have ready the yolk of one egg, well beaten in a cup of milk. Season well with salt and pepper. Soak the pigeons in it well, so that they will absorb the milk and be thoroughly impregnated Roll over and over, so that they will gather up the seasoning. Then pass them through bread crumbs, rolling and then patting each pigeon with your hands, so that the crumbs will hold. Brush each with a little melted butter. Have ready a double broiler, well heated, but on a slow fire. Place the pigeons on it, broiling very slowly. Broil for fifteen or twenty minutes, allowing from seven to ten minutes to each side, and serve with Tomato Sauce. (See recipe.)

#### Roasted Squab.

Pigeons Rotis sur Canapés.

6 or 8 Young Squab.
6 or 8 Thin Slices of Fat Bacon.
4 Tablespoonfuls of Butter.
Truffles (if desired.)
2 Tablespoonfuls of Water.
6 or 8 Slices of Buttered Toast.

Use squab only for roasting. Clean nicely, and then truss the pigeon as you would a turkey, only use wooden skewers to hold the wings and legs in place. Take a slice of nice fat pork and fasten it around the body of each pigeon, passing over the breast. Put a bit of butter about the size of a pecan in each bird, and, if you can afford to do so, you may stuff with truffles. But this is a matter of taste. Put the pigeons in the roasting pan, and add a tablespoonful of butter and about two tablespoonfuls of water. The oven should be hot, but must not be scorching. Baste the birds frequently, and let them roast from fifteen to twenty minutes, according to their size. Prepare toasted bread, one slice for each pigeon. Butter well, and then remove the fat pork and place the pigeons on the toast. Pour over each a little of the gravy which has been made in the roasting pan, allowing it to soak into the bread. Serve hot, with a jelly, preferably Cranberry Sauce. (See recipe.)

### Compote of Pigeons.
Pigeons en Compote.

6 Fine Fat Squab. A Half Can of Mushrooms.
1 Clove of Garlic.
2 Sprigs Each of Thyme and Parsley.
1 Bay Leaf.  1 Onion.
2 Tablespoonfuls of White Wine.
1 Tablespoonful of Butter.
½ Cup of Consomme.

Clean the squabs nicely; singe, draw and truss, with their legs inside. Rub well with salt and pepper and three cloves, ground very fine, and three allspice, also ground very fine. Take a tablespoonful of butter and melt in a saucepan. Add the sliced onion, and as it browns add the sliced carrot. Let this simmer gently for three or four minutes, and then add a minced sprig of thyme, and parsley, and one bay leaf, and the clove of a garlic, minced very fine. Let all this brown, and then place on top the pigeons, which you will have bound in thin strips of bacon tied around the body. Add two tablespoonfuls of white wine and cover well. Let this simmer for about fifteen minutes, till the pigeons are nicely browned, and then add a half cup of consommé if you have it, if not, a half cup of boiling water. After ten minutes add a half can of mushrooms. Let all simmer gently for an hour longer, being careful not to let the pigeons go to pieces. Watch, therefore, very carefully. Place each pigeon on a slice of toasted Croûton, and garnish with the mushrooms. Pour over the gravy, and serve hot. This is a most excellent compote.

### Squab With Green Peas.

Pigeons Étouffés aux Petit Pois.

3 Pigeons.  1 Pint of Green Peas.
¼ Inch of Ham.  2 Onions.
1 Tablespoonful of Butter.
1 Bay Leaf.
1 Sprig Each of Thyme and Parsley.
1 Clove of Garlic.
Salt and Pepper to Taste.

Clean the pigeons nicely, leaving them whole, as you would a fowl that is to be roasted, and truss nicely. Take two onions and slice well, and place in a saucepan with a tablespoonful of melted butter. Let them brown slightly, and lay the pigeons that have been rubbed well with salt and pepper, inside and out, on top of the onions. Cover closely and let them smother. Then add for one pigeon one-half or one-quarter of an inch of nice ham, minced very fine, to give a good seasoning. Then add one sprig of thyme and one bay leaf, and the clove of a garlic, minced very fine. Let this smother very slowly for ten or fifteen minutes. When well browned, moisten with a cup of consommé or broth, and add one pint of fresh green peas, or one can. Cover tight, and let all simmer over a slow fire for one hour, or more if the pigeons are not very tender. Serve on a platter, placing the pigeons in the center and heaping the green peas around. This is delicious, and the real Creole method of cooking pigeons with green peas.

### Pigeons and Crawfish.

Pigeons à la Cardinale.

3 Pigeons.  2 Dozen Crawfish.
1 Slice of Fat Bacon. 1 Square Inch of Ham.
1 Onion.  1 Carrot.  1 Herb Bouquet.
1 Tablespoonful of Butter.
Salt and Pepper to Taste.

Clean the pigeons nicely, and rub inside and out with the juice of a lemon. Then rub with salt and pepper, and brush with melted butter. Place thin strips of fat bacon in the bottom of a saucepan, lay the pigeons on this, and cover with another thin layer of strips of bacon. Cover with butter and set in a slow oven, and let them simmer gently. In the meantime prepare a "Poêle" as follows: Take a small square inch of ham, chop or mince very fine, and fry in a tablespoonful of butter. Add an onion and a carrot, chopped fine. Let these brown, and then add an herb bouquet, minced very fine. When brown, add a cup of bouillon, and let it boil for ten minutes. Pour this sauce over the baking pigeons, and let them cook slowly for about an hour, or until done. In the meantime boil about two dozen nice crawfish, according to recipe (see Crawfish), and, when the pigeons are done, place them on buttered Croûtons and place between each a garnish of crawfish. Add about a half cup of the broth in which the crawfish have been boiled to the gravy in the baking dish. Let it simmer for five minutes till reduced slightly, and pour over the pigeons. This is Creole to the letter.

### Pigeon Pie.

Vol-au-Vent de Pigeons.

6 Young Wild Pigeons.
1 Onion. 1 Tablespoonful of Lard.
1 Tablespoonful of Flour.
1 Sprig Each Thyme, Bay Leaf and Parsley.
Pie Paste.

Clean and cut the young pigeons into small pieces of about two inches in length and make a plain fricassée. (See Fricassée Brown Gravy.) Prepare a Vol-au-Vent Paste (see recipe) and fill a tin pan of about two quarts with the paste. Pour in pigeons and gravy, and let bake in the oven till the top crust is nicely browned. Always bake the under crust first. This is a delightful entrée at any feast.

Again, the pie may be prepared as follows: After cleaning the pigeons, stuff each daintily with oyster or egg dressing and then loosen the joints with a knife without separating them. Put into a stewpan and make a plain fricassée as above indicated. Let them cook until tender, and season with salt and pepper. Fill the pie dish with the pie paste; put in the birds, pour over the gravy, cover with a crust and bake.

## CHAPTER XVIII.

## GAME.

### Gibier.

The number and variety of the game of the Louisiana forests have been the subject of many a magazine and newspaper article, and the admiration and joy of the chasseurs, or hunters, from earliest days. Our birds alone are so distinct and remarkable that the great Audubon devoted his life to their study, and his volume on the birds of Louisiana stands out as the greatest work extant upon birds. The fact is, that all through the year, from January to December, fancy game may be found in the New Orleans markets, though the game laws are very strict, and no bird is allowed to be shot out of season.

The venison brought to New Orleans from the woods of St. Tammany's forest and the Teche rivals in flavor that of any section, and to leave New Orleans without having eaten "Filet de Chevreuil à la Poivrade," or "Salmi de Chevreuil à la Créole," is to have lost, in the opinion of old Creole gourmets, half the pleasure of your visit. In the same manner your visit would be considered a failure if you failed to eat our famous Louisiana bird, "Pababotte à la Créole," or our noted "Cailles de Laurier Roties," or Snipe, in that wonderful dish. "Bécassine Sautée à la Créole"; or our distinctive Mallard and Canvasback Ducks, in "Salmi de Canards Français," or "Salmi de Canards Chevals."

The following are the most accepted methods of preparing our "Fancy Game." The Picayune uses the words "Fancy Game" because, while blackbirds and all such game as are commonly found in forests abound in Louisiana, there is always such an abundance of our famous wild ducks, Poule d'Eau, Quail, Pababotte, Snipe, Woodcock, Grassets, Larks, Robins, Reed Birds and other delicious game in their season, that even the humblest seldom think of placing any other upon their tables. Our hunting clubs are many, and the Creole chasseurs, from the highest to the lowest rank, are famous shots, bagging great quantities of game while on the hunt, and often as not courteously supplying the tables of their neighbors for squares around when they return from their weekly sport. It is quite the proper thing among ancient families, when the gentlemen go on a hunt, for them to send, upon their return, a pair of Teal, Mallard or Canvasback Ducks, or a dozen Quail or Pababottes, Bécassines or Bécasses, to Madame or Mademoiselle So-and-So, "Avec les Compliments de Monsieur ————, le Chasseur." These pretty little neighborly courtesies are among the most delightful forms of life in the Old French Quarter.

### Something to Remember When Cooking Game.

Game should never be fried. This is horrible. The larger game is roasted or broiled, or, as with ducks and venison, squirrels and rabbits, made into stews or "salmis." The smaller game is roasted or broiled.

### VENISON.

### Du Chevreuil.

The meat of Venison may be kept in cold weather at least ten or twelve days, if hung in a cold place; in warm weather for much less time, unless dried. The meat of fresh Venison is of a fine grain, and is always nicely covered with fat. The age of the deer can always be told by examining the hoofs; if it is young, the hoofs will be very slightly opened; if old, they will stand apart. Of all meats, Venison cooks the most rapidly. Venison is always best when the deer has been killed in the autumn. Wild berries are then plentiful and the animal has then abundant opportunity to fatten upon this and other fresh, wild food.

### Roast Haunch of Venison.
Cuissot de Chevreuil Roti.

A Haunch or Saddle of Venison.
Melted Butter.
Salt and Pepper to Taste.
Watercress to Garnish. Currant Jelly.

Prepare the haunch or saddle of Venison in the same manner as you would the roast beef. (See recipe Roast Beef.) Only pour a cup of water over the venison when putting in the oven, for it is a dry meat, and requires a little moistening if roasted. Bake in a quick oven, allowing ten minutes to the pound. A haunch of Doe Venison will require in the aggregate half an hour less time to roast than Buck Venison. To prevent the hoof and hair just above changing color in cooking always bind this with a coarse piece of muslin, in four or five pieces of thickness, covering the hoof and hair. Wet with cold water, and bind a buttered paper tightly around and over it. Baste every ten minutes, with melted butter first, and then with the drippings of the Venison. When half cooked, turn the venison over, so that the other side may cook. Unbind the hoofs and garnish them with quilled paper. Place the venison on a dish garnished with Watercress. Serve with Currant Jelly. (See recipe.)

### Saddle of Venison, Currant Jelly Sauce.
Selle de Chevreuil, Sauce Groseille.

A Saddle of Venison Weighing About 5 Pounds.
1 Onion.   1 Carrot.
½ Tablespoonful of Butter.
½ Glass of Madeira Wine.
1 Gill of Consomme.
Currant Jelly Sauce.

Skin the Venison neatly and remove all the sinews from the surface. Take fine larding needles and lard closely. Tie the saddle around four times. Slice the carrot and onion and put in the rosting pan. Place the Saddle of Venison on top of these sprinkle lightly with a pinch of salt, and spread a half tablespoonful of butter over. Set in a brisk oven and roast for forty minutes, frequently basting the venison with its own gravy. Before taking it from the pan, remove the cord which binds it and place the saddle in a hot dish. Then pour the Madeira wine and a gill of veal consommé into the pan, set on the stove and let it come to a boil. Then skim the gravy of all fat and strain over the veinson. Serve with a hot Currant Jelly Sauce as follows: Take a half pint of Currant Jelly and stir till it is thoroughly dissolved. Then put in a saucepan a wineglassful of good old Port wine, and set on the stove and let it come gradually to a boil. Add the currant jelly and mix till thoroughly dissolved; then add a tablespoonful of Sauce Espagnole (see recipe) and let it again come to a boil. Serve with the venison, sending each to the table separately.

Venison steaks broiled may also be served with this sauce. The steaks are placed in a dish, one overlapping the other; the hot sauce is poured over and thus sent to the table.

### Venison Steaks à la Poivrade.
Filet de Chevreuil à la Poivrade.

6 Filets or as Many Filets as Desired.
Salt and Pepper to Taste. A Sauce Poivrade.

The filets or Venison steaks are taken from any part of the Venison. The best are from the haunch or leg, and cut three-quarters of an inch in thickness. Rub them well with salt and pepper, and then fry in butter, allowing about five minutes to the steak. Venison must be served on a very hot dish and eaten hot. Place in a heated dish, and garnish with melted butter and chopped parsley, and serve with a Sauce Poivrade for Venison (see recipe), pouring the sauce over the steaks. This is a delicious dish.

### Venison Cutlets Broiled.
Cotelettes de Chevreuil Grillées.

6 Venison Cutlets.
2 Tablespoonfuls of Melted Butter.
Chopped Parsley.
Salt and Pepper to Taste.
Watercress to Garnish.

Trim the cutlets nicely, rub well with salt and pepper, brush with a little butter, and broil over a quick clear fire, allowing about eight minutes, or less, according to size, to each cutlet. They must always, like all Venison, be underdone. When cooked, place in a very hot dish, pour over a little melted butter and chopped parsley, garnish with water cress, and serve with Currant Jelly.

### Stewed Venison à la Créole.
Salmi de Chevreuil à la Créole.

Venison Steaks, or Rougher Part of the Deer.
2 Onions. 1 Square Inch of Ham.
1 Tablespoonful of Butter.
1 Clove of Garlic, Chopped Very Fine.
1 Herb Bouquet, Chopped Fine.
1 Glass of Claret. 1 Cup of Water.
1 Can of Mushrooms.

The rougher parts of Venison are usually used for stewing, but the dish is most delicious when made of the Venison steaks. Cut the Venison into two-inch square pieces, and rub well with salt and pepper. Chop two onions very fine, and put them in a stewpan with a tablespoonful of melted butter. Let them brown slightly; then add the Venison meat. Let it brown slightly, and then add one tablespoonful of flour, and let this brown a little. Chop the square inch of ham very fine, mincing it, and add. Then add the clove of garlic, and two sprigs each of thyme and parsley and a bay leaf, minced fine. Let this brown nicely, and pour over one glass of good Claret. Let this cook for ten minutes, stirring it constantly, so that it will not burn, and then add one cup of boiling water. Stir well, season again to taste, and let it boil for thirty minutes, and serve hot. This dish will be improved beyond estimation if a can of mushrooms is added immediately after adding the water. But it may be made without the mushrooms. Serve very hot.

### Venison, Hunters' Style.

Chevreuil à la Chasseur.

3 Pounds of Venison Meat.
2 Tablespoonfuls of Butter.
1 Onion.   1 Square Inch of Ham.
1 Tablespoonful of Flour.
1 Clove of Garlic. 2 Sprigs of Thyme.
2 Bay Leaves.
½ Box of Mushrooms. The Zest of a Lemon.
1 Glass of White Wine.
Salt and Pepper to Taste.
Croutons to Garnish.

Cut the venison into pieces of about two inches square. Salt and pepper well. Put two tablespoonfuls of butter into a saucepan with the venison and let it brown slowly. When nearly brown, add an onion, chopped fine, and let this brown slightly; then add the ham, minced very fine, and the clove of garlic and bay leaves and thyme, minced very fine. Stir in with the rabbit and let these brown for about two minutes. Then add a tablespoonful of flour and brown for a few minutes more. Add a half bottle of White Wine and let all simmer for five minutes. Then add a quart of consommé or water and let all cook for about one hour. Season again according to taste and add a half can of mushrooms chopped fine and the zest of a lemon and season again to taste. Let all cook a half hour longer and serve on a hot dish with Croûtons fried in butter.

### Stewed Venison, French Style.

Civet de Chevreuil à la Française.

2½ Pounds of Venison (the lower and lean part preferable.)
A Handful of Parsley.   1 Onion.
1 Sprig of Thyme.   2 Bay Leaves.
12 Whole Peppers. A Half Glass of Vinegar.
1½ Glass of Claret.
1 Pint of Veal Consomme.
1 Ounce of Salt Pork. 12 Small Onions.
1 Dozen and a Half Mushrooms.
1 Herb Bouquet.
Salt and Pepper to Taste. Croutons.

Cut the venison into small pieces of about two inches square. Make a "Marinade" by placing the venison in an earthen jar with one large onion sliced, a handful of parsley, the chopped thyme and bay leaf, the whole peppers, a light seasoning of salt and black pepper, and the vinegar. Let the venison marinate for twelve hours. Then drain it from the juice and place it in a saucepan with one tablespoonful of the best butter, and let it brown over a moderate fire. After ten minutes add three tablespoonfuls of flour and stir constantly. Then moisten with the consommé and the claret. Season again to taste with salt and pepper, and stir until it comes to a boil. Then add the small onions which have been nicely peeled, and one ounce of salt pork and the herb bouquet. Let all cook about forty minutes, and about five minutes before serving add the mushrooms. Take the herb bouquet from the preparation; place the latter on a hot dish and decorate nicely with toasted Croûtons, and serve hot.

### Venison in a Chafing Dish.

Chevreuil au Réchaud.

8 or 10 Slices of Venison.
2 Tablespoonfuls of Butter.
1 Tablespoonful of Currant Jelly.
1 Tablespoonful of Water.
Salt and Pepper to Taste.

This is a most delicious way of preparing Venison. The old Creoles use, if a chafing dish is not available, a little alcohol lamp and a frying pan. Even the humblest families can thus enjoy this delightful dish. Slice the venison very thin in pieces about two inches long and one inch wide, and about the thickness of a silver dollar. Have the chafing dish or alcohol lamp on the dining table, as you sit to eat. The pan must be very hot. The meat must be well-seasoned with salt and pepper, and ready to put into the pan. Put a tablespoonful of butter into the dish. Let it get very hot, without burning. Put the slices of Venison in the dish. In one minute turn them over. Take a tablespoonful of melted butter, and blend well with a tablespoonful of Currant Jelly and a tablespoonful of water. Spread this over the cooking Venison. Turn again. Let it cook for five minutes only, and serve very hot. This is one of the finest old-fashioned Creole dishes, and is good for breakfast, luncheon or supper. Bear in mind that to be effective it must be made at the table, as it will lose half its flavor if brought from the kitchen to the table.

### Venison Hash.

Hachis de Chevreuil.

3 Cups of Left Over Venison.
6 Potatoes.   1 Herb Bouquet.
Salt and Pepper to Taste.
1 Tablespoonful of Lard or Butter.

This is a splendid way of utilizing

the left-over venison. After having taken off all the rough edges of the roast and cut out the gristle and hard membrane, hash the Venison into pieces of about one-inch in size. Take six left-over tomatoes, or freshly boiled, and cut into quarters. Chop fine one herb bouquet. Place a tablespoonful of butter or a half tablespoonful of lard into the stewpot, and as it melts add the venison, seasoned well, and a few minutes later the fine herbs. Mince the clove of a garlic if the flavor is liked and add. Stir constantly without browning much, and add a tablespoonful of flour. Let this brown very slightly, and then add the tomatoes. Cover and let all simmer for about twenty minutes, and then pour over a pint of boiling water. Season again to taste and set back on the stove and let it simmer gently for about three-quarters of an hour. Cut some Croûtons and fry them in butter; place on a dish and serve with the hash.

### WILD TURKEY.

#### Dinde Sauvage.

The wild turkey abounds in Louisiana. It is roasted in the same manner as the domestic fowl (see recipe) and always served with Cranberry Sauce. (See recipe.)

### WILD DUCKS.

#### Canards Sauvages.

The wild ducks so much enjoyed in Louisiana are many, but the most famous are the Canvasback Ducks, or "Canards Cheval," the more delicate "Teal Ducks," or "Sarcelles," and the noted Mallard Ducks, or "Canards Français." Then we have a species of water fowl called the "Poule d'Eau," or water chicken, which lives exclusively in the waters of the Louisiana bayous and marshes; as it never comes on dry land, it has been classed by the ancient Creoles among the fish, and is eaten on Fridays and fast days, when flesh meat is prohibited to Catholics.

In following the recipes given below, it must be borne in mind that all tame or domestic ducks may be cooked in the same manner as the wild ducks. For this reason it would be superfluous to give a special section to the former. But the flavor of the wild duck is such that it is always preferred on Creole tables as the superior bird. Ducks are stewed or roasted. The wild goose, or "Oie Sauvage," is cooked in the same manner as the wild duck and the domestic goose. The "Duckling," or "Canneton," in the same manner as the delicate "Teal Duck" or "Sarcelle."

In cleaning all game, remember that they must be hand picked, and never scalded, as scalding utterly ruins their flavor. Wild Duck should not be dressed too soon after being killed.

### Canvasback Duck.

#### Canard Cheval.

Epicureans declare that the Canvasback Duck is the King of Birds. And as it feeds mostly on wild celery, it requires no flavors or spices to make it perfect. The bird partakes of the flavor of the celery on which it feeds. This delicious flavor is best preserved when the duck is roasted quickly with a hot fire. And so also with the dainty Mallard or French Ducks.

### Mallard Ducks or Canvasback Ducks Roasted.

#### Canards Français ou Canard Cheval Rotis.

1 Pair of Wild Ducks.
1 Tablespoonful of Butter. Salt and Pepper to Taste.

Clean the ducks as you would a chicken, without scalding, however. Rinse out the inside and wipe well inside and out with a wet towel. But do not wash the duck unless you have broken the gall bladder, as the washing destroys their flavor. Rub the inside well with salt and pepper, and rub outside as thoroughly. Place a three-inch lump of butter on the inside. Truss nicely and place the ducks in a baking pan, and brush the tops with melted butter. Pour over two tablespoonfuls of water, and set in a very hot oven, and allow them to bake twenty minutes, if they are not very large, and thirty minutes, if larger than the ordinary size of Canvasback ducks. A wild duck is never cooked dry. It must reach the point where the blood will not run if the flesh is pierced with the fork in carving. When done, place the ducks in a very hot dish, and serve with their own gravy poured over them. Garnish nicely with parsley or water cress. Serve with Currant Jelly. Always have the plates very hot in which you serve the ducks at table.

### Broiled Canvasback Ducks.

#### Canards Cheval Grillées.

1 Pair of Ducks.
1 Tablespoonful of Olive Oil.
Salt and Pepper.
Drawn Butter Sauce.
The Juice of 1 Lemon.
Minced Parsley to Garnish.

The Canvasback Duck is very excellent when broiled. Hunters often serve it thus when on long hunts, and it is said the taste of the game just bagged is beyond estimate. Broiled Canvasbacks are served as follows on the Creole table: Clean the duck nicely, as for broiling a chicken, wipe well and split down the middle of the back in the same manner as for a chicken. Season well with salt and pepper. Rub the duck well with olive oil of the best quality, and place on the broiler. Turn it over at least twice, so that it will cook thoroughly through and through without burning. Let it cook from seven to ten minutes on either side. Place on a dish that is very hot, pour over a Drawn Butter Sauce, in which you will have squeezed the juice of a lemon, and mixed some minced parsley. Decorate with water cress or parsley sprigs. Bring to the table covered and very hot, and serve on heated plates. This dish is very elegant.

### Stewed Wild Ducks.
Salmi de Canards Sauvages à la Créole.

1 Pair of Ducks.
1 Square Inch of Ham. 2 Onions.
1 Tablespoonful of Butter. 1 Clove of Garlic.
1 Herb Bouquet Chopped Very Fine.
1 Glass of Claret. 1 Cup of Water.

Clean and pick the ducks nicely. Cut into joints, or stew whole, as desired. The Creoles generally cut them into joints. Rub well with salt and pepper. Chop two onions very fine. Put them into the stewpan with a tablespoonful of melted butter, and let them brown slightly. Then add the well-seasoned ducks. Let these brown well and add the one square inch of finely minced ham. Add the clove of garlic and two sprigs each of thyme, parsley and one bay leaf, minced very fine. Let this brown with the ducks, stirring frequently, and then pour over one good glass of claret. Let this simmer for ten minutes, stirring constantly, so that it will not burn, and add one cup of boiling water. Season well to taste, and let the ducks simmer well for about an hour.

### Ducks Stewed With Mushrooms.
Salmi de Canards aux Champignons.

1 Pair of Ducks. 1 Square Inch of Ham.
2 Onions. 1 Tablespoonful of Butter.
1 Clove of Garlic.
1 Herb Bouquet, Chopped Very Fine.
1 Glass of Claret. 1 Cup of Water.
1 Can of Mushrooms.

Prepare the Ducks for cooking exactly as in the above recipe and proceed to cook accordingly. Immediately after adding the boiling water add a can of mushrooms, and continue cooking according to recipe. The mushrooms add a delicous flavor to the dish. Serve hot, using the mushrooms as a garnish.

### Wild Ducks, Hunters' Style.
Salmi de Canards Sauvages à la Chasseur.

2 Fine Canvas-Back Ducks.
½ Pint of Veal Broth or Water.
1 Tablespoonful of Butter.
1 Dozen Mushrooms. Sliced.
3 Fresh or Canned Tomatoes.
1 Onion.
¼ Glass of Madeira Wine or Lemon Juice.
½ Pint of Sauce Espagnole.
The Zest of 1 Lemon.
Croutons.

Pick the ducks; singe, draw, and, after rinsing clean within, wipe neatly within and without; cut off the wings, legs and breasts; then take the two carcasses and sprinkle rightly with salt and place in the oven to bake about six minutes. Then remove the carcasses and hash them up. Put them into the saucepan; add a pint of veal broth, consommé or water in lieu of either of these. Add a herb bouquet tied together, and let the preparation simmer for about a quarter of an hour over a moderate fire. Put a tablespoonful of butter into a saucepan, and lay in the wings, breasts and legs of the Ducks; season lightly with salt and pepper, and set on a very brisk fire and let cook for a few minutes, on either side. Now add a half glassful of Madeira wine and a half pint of Sauce Espagnole and the grated zest of a lemon. Take the gravy from the carcasses and strain over the Ducks, and allow all to cook about a quarter of an hour. Then place on a hot dish and decorate nicely with Croûtons fried in butter and cut in dice shape.

### Ducks à la Bourgeoise.
Salmi de Canards à la Bourgeoise.

2 Fine Canvas-Back Ducks.
1 Tablespoonful of Butter.
3 Tomatoes (fresh or canned).
12 Onions. 2 Carrots.
½ Glass of Madeira Wine.
The Zest of 1 Lemon.
½ Pint of Sauce Espagnole.
½ Pint of Consomme or Water.
Salt and Pepper to Taste.

Prepare the Ducks, and cook according to above recipe. After placing finally in the saucepan, add twelve small onions which have been nicely glazed (see recipe "Glaze"); add the two carrots cut into small dice and which have been cooked in salted water for two minutes, before adding to the ducks; also add a half ounce of salt pork cut into half-inch pieces. Let these cook for fifteen minutes with the ducks and serve on a hot dish with Croûtons.

### Stewed Ducks With Turnips.
Salmi de Canards aux Navets.

1 Pair of Ducks. 6 Turnips.
1 Tablespoonful of Butter.
2 Onions, Chopped Fine.
1 Square Inch of Ham, Minced Very Fine.
1 Bay Leaf. 1 Tablespoonful of Flour.
Salt and Pepper to Taste. 1 Clove of Garlic.
3 Sprigs Each of Thyme and Parsley.

This is one of the most delightful ways of cooking wild ducks. The turnip blends well with the flavor of the wild ducks, and a nicer way of serving this vegetable in combination does not exist. Clean the Ducks, and cut into pieces at the joints. Put a tablespoonful of butter into the pot, and as it melts, add the onions, chopped fine. Let this brown, and then add the pieces of Ducks. Let them brown, and add the minced ham. Immediately after add the turnips, sliced or cut in quarters, a tablespoonful of sifted flour. Stir well, let the flour brown slightly, and add the minced thyme, parsley and bay leaf, and one clove of garlic, minced very fine. Stir well again, and let it smother for about fifteen minutes, stirring frequently, so that it will not burn. Then add water, almost sufficient to cover the Ducks, and stir well. Cover tight, and let the mixture smother for a half hour longer. You will have one of the nicest dishes that ever graced a table.

### Wild Ducks With Olives.
Salmi de Canards aux Olives.
3 Cups of Left-Over Duck.
1 Tablespoonful of Butter.
1 Tablespoonful of Flour.
1 Onion.
2 Sprigs Each of Thyme and Parsley.
1 Bay Leaf.
1 Cup of Broth or Water.
1 Glass of Claret.
2 Dozen Spanish Olives.
Toasted Croutons.

This is a nice way to utilize the left-over Duck; take all the remains of the Duck and select the good parts, and cut them into pieces of about an inch and a half square. Put a tablespoonful of butter into the stewpan, and, as it browns, add one onion, chopped fine. Let this brown and then add the Duck. Stir well; add the tablespoonful of sifted flour, stir again, and in four or five minutes add two sprigs each of thyme and parsley and one bay leaf, minced very fine. Let this brown well, and smother nicely for about ten minutes. Add a pint of good broth if you have it; if not, a cup of boiling water. Stir well, and season again according to taste. Pour in a half glass of good Claret, and add about two dozen fine olives, stoned. Let all boil for thirty minutes longer, and serve hot, with garnish of diamond-shaped toasted Croûtons.

### Stewed Ducks, Peasant Style.
Salmi de Canards à la Paysanne.
1 Pair of Fine Ducks, French or Canvas-Back.
1 Dozen Glazed Onions. 2 Carrots.
1 Square Inch of Ham.
1 Cup of Green Peas.
1 Bay Leaf.
2 Sprigs Each of Thyme and Parsley.
1 Clove of Garlic. 1 Tablespoonful of Flour.
1 Tablespoonful of Butter.
Salt and Pepper to Taste.
1 Glass of Madeira or Sherry Wine.
The Zest of 1 Lemon.

Prepare the Ducks exactly as in the recipe for "Stewed Ducks With Turnips (see recipe), only the turnips are omitted. Add two carrots cut into dice pieces, and twelve glazed onions and the green peas. A quarter of an hour before serving add a glass of Madeira wine. Serve on a hot dish, with Croûtons fried in butter, using the onions as a garnish with the Croûtons.

### Stewed Ducks, French Marshal Style.
Salmi de Canards à la Marechale Française.
1 Pair of Fine Ducks, French or Canvas-Back.
12 Godiveau Quenelles. 12 Mushrooms.
2 Onions Chopped Fine. 1 Bay Leaf.
3 Sprigs Each of Thyme and Parsley.
1 Clove of Garlic. 1 Square Inch of Ham.
1 Tablespoonful of Butter.
1 Tablespoonful of Flour.
Salt and Pepper to Taste.
1 Glass of Madeira or Sherry Wine.
Croutons to Garnish.

Prepare the Ducks exactly as in the recipe for "Stewed Ducks With Turnips," omitting the turnips. Add ten minutes before serving, twelve small Godiveau Quenelles (see recipe) and the wine. Garnish the dish with Croutons (see recipe) and twelve nicely cooked mushrooms, cut in two. Send to the table hot.

### Cold Wild Duck.
Canards Sauvages Froid.
Remains of Cold Duck.
1 Tablespoonful of Butter.
½ Tumbler of Currant Jelly.
2 Tablespoonfuls of Port Wine.

Cut the cold Wild Duck nicely in thick slices, and serve with a sauce made as follows: Take one tablespoonful of butter, one-half tumbler of Currant Jelly, and two tablespoonfuls of good Port wine. Warm the butter in the saucepan, add the wine and jelly, thoroughly blended; mix well, and serve with the slices of cold duck. The duck may also be served very deliciously with Currant Jelly alone, and buttered toast.

### Teal Duck.
Sarcelle.

The Teal Duck is the smallest and most delicate of the wild ducks. It is prepared in the same manner as the Mallard, preference, however, being always given to roasting and broiling, on account of its size. The Teal Duck is always broiled whole, without splitting on the back.

### Teal Ducks Roasted.
Sarcelles Roties.
3 Pairs of Teal Ducks.
6 Thin Strips of Bacon.
6 Truffles. 1 Tablespoonful of Butter.
2 Tablespoonfuls of Water.
6 Slices of Toast.
Currant Jelly.

Clean the duck nicely and put one

truffle and a lump of butter about the size of a peanut, with salt and pepper, on the inside. Rub well with salt and pepper and a little butter melted. Take a thin strip of bacon and bind it around the body of the duck, fastening with a skewer. Place a tablespoonful of butter in the roasting pan, and pour about two tablespoonfuls of water in it, dropping slightly over each bird. Set in a quick oven and bake for thirty minutes, or until done. The bird should always be served underdone. Have ready a hot dish, garnished with parsley, and a slice of toast buttered for each bird. Place the birds on them, sprinkle over chopped parsley, and take the juice in which the birds have been roasted, pour a little over each bird, so that it sinks down into the toast, and squeeze a little lemon juice over each, and serve hot.

The truffle may be omitted, but it is considered very elegant. The bird is just as good without, however, and it is within the reach of the poorest, simply for the hunting. Serve with Currant Jelly.

### Teal Duck Broiled.
Sarcelle Grillée.

3 Pairs of Teal Ducks.
6 Strips of Bacon.
Melted Butter.   Chopped Parsley.
Olives and Silces of Lemon to Garnish.
6 Slices of Toast.

Clean and prepare the duck in exactly the same manner as for roasting, binding with the strip of bacon. Place on a broiler, turning frequently, and let it broil for about thirty minutes, very slowly. Serve with melted butter and chopped parsley spread over, and the juice of a lemon squeezed in. Garnish the dish nicely with sprigs of parsley, slices of lemon and olives. Serve with Currant Jelly.

### Teal Duck à la Bigarade.
Sarcelle à la Bigarade.

3 Pairs of Teal Ducks.
1 Brigarade or Sour Orange.
Salt and Pepper to Taste.
A Sauce a l'Espagnole.

Clean the ducks and take the livers and fry them in a little melted butter. Season well with salt and pepper and a slight pinch of ground allspice and cloves and the zest of a "bigarade," or sour orange. If the orange is not available, take the zest of a lemon. The zest is the skin of the orange or lemon, scraped off without touching the inner pulp, or white skin. Place this in the interior of the ducks (you must have the boiled livers of five or six for the garnishment of two ducks), and then rub the outside well with salt and pepper. Bind with a strip of bacon and place on the broiler. In about thirty minutes it will be done. Cook over a slow fire, turning frequently. In the meantime prepare a "Sauce à l'Espagnole," and as soon as the birds are done pour off from the broiler all the juice that has fallen, and put this into the sauce, with the juice of two sour oranges or citrons. Let it warm without boiling, pour over the birds, which you have placed on buttered toast, and serve hot. This is an ancient Creole dish, almost lost in our day, but which deserves to be resurrected.

### Stewed Rabbit.
Salmi de Lapins.

A Pair of Rabbits.
2 Onions.   1 Square Inch of Ham.
1 Tablespoonful of Butter.
1 Clove of Garlic, Chopped Very Fine.
1 Herb Bouquet, Chopped Fine.
1 Glass of Claret.   1 Cup of Water.
1 Can of Mushrooms.

Stewed rabbit is a great dish among the Creoles. They say that this is the only way to cook a rabbit. Proceed as follows:

Skin and clean the rabbit. Wash well and cut into pieces at the joints, and rub well with salt and pepper. Chop two onions very fine, and put them in the stewpan with a tablespoonful of melted butter. Let them brown slightly; then add the rabbit. Let it brown slightly, and then add one tablespoonful of flour, and let this brown a little. Chop the square inch of ham very fine, mincing it, and add. Then add the clove of garlic, and two sprigs each of thyme and parsley and a bay leaf, minced fine. Let this brown nicely, and pour over one glass of good Claret. Let this cook for ten minutes, stirring it constantly, so that it will not burn, and then add one cup of boiling water. Stir well, season again to taste, and let it boil for thirty minutes, and serve hot. Green peas or potatoes, boiled or mashed, make a nice entrée for this dish.

### Rabbit, Hunters' Style.
Lapin à la Chasseur.

A Pair of Rabbits.
1 Tablespoonful of Butter.
1 Onion.   1 Slice of Ham.
1 Tablespoonful of Flour.
1 Clove of Garlic.   2 Sprigs of Thyme.
2 Bay Leaves.
½ Box of Mushrooms. The Zest of a Lemon.
½ Bottle of Claret Wine.
Salt and Pepper to Taste.
Croutons to Garnish.

Prepare the rabbit; clean and draw, and cut into pieces at the joints. Rub well with salt and pepper; put a tablespoonful of butter into the saucepan with the rabbit and let it brown slowly. When nearly brown, add the onion, chopped fine, and let this brown slightly. Then add the ham, minced very fine, and the clove and garlic and bay leaves and thyme, minced very fine. Stir with the rabbit, and let these brown for about two minutes; then add a tablespoonful of flour and brown for a few minutes; add a half bottle of Claret wine and let all simmer for five minutes; then add a quart of consommé or water, and let all cook for about one hour. Season according to taste. Add a half can of mushrooms, chopped fine, and the zest of a lemon and again season to taste. Let all cook for a half hour longer and serve on a hot dish, with Croûtons fried in butter.

### Rabbit en Matelote.

Lapin en Matelote.

A Pair of Rabbits.
2 Tablespoonfuls of Lard or Butter.
2 Tablespoonfuls of Flour.
6 Fresh, Large Tomatoes, or a Half Can.
1 Large Onion, Chopped Fine.
3 Sprigs Each of Thyme, Sweet Marjoram, Parsley and Bay Leaf.
1 Glass of Good Claret, or the Juice of 1 Lemon.
1 Quart of Water or Consomme.
Salt and Pepper to Taste.
A Dash of Cayenne.

Skin, clean, wash and cut the rabbit into pieces at the joints. Put the lard or butter into a deep stewpan or kettle. When hot, add gradually two tablespoonfuls of flour, stirring constantly to prevent burning. Throw in about ten or twelve well-mashed allspice, and three sprigs each of chopped thyme, parsley, bay leaf and sweet marjoram, one clove of garlic, and one large onion, chopped very fine. Add six fresh large tomatoes, chopped fine, or one-half can of tomatoes. Pour in one glass of good claret, add about one quart of water, and let it boil well. Then add salt and Cayenne to taste, and, when this has boiled about five minutes, add the rabbit, putting in piece by piece. Add the juice of a lemon, and let all boil about ten minutes. Serve with French Fried Potatoes, Mashed Potatoes, or Potato Croquettes.

### HARE.

Lièvre.

The hare and the rabbit are very much alike, the closest relationship existing between the two. The principal difference is that the rabbit is smaller in size than the hare, and its ears and legs are shorter.

The hare may be cooked in almost any manner in which rabbits are served. There are, however, some special methods in vogue among the Creoles which are here appended. In preparing the hare for roasting, it should be first skinned, and then washed well in cold water and rinsed thoroughly in tepid water. If the hare seems a little musty from being emptied before being hung up, rub the insides well with vinegar and again wash thoroughly in warm water. Prepare for cooking as you would a rabbit, wipe well with a soft towel, dress nicely, sew the animal up and truss it, and allow it to roast from three-quarters of an hour to one hour, according to size. Baste occasionally with butter, just before serving. Of late, the hare is much affected by epicures. Many consider the meat far more tender and of more delicate flavor than the rabbit. It is generally served with Currant Jelly.

### Hare, Roasted and Stuffed.

Lièvre Roti.

2 Fine Hares. 3 Onions.
1 Carrot. 3 Apples.
2 Ounces of Sausage Meat.
6 Mushrooms. 1 Lemon.
1 Sprig of Thyme. 1 Bay Leaf.
2 Cloves. 3 Sprigs of Parsley.
1 Glass of White Wine or Cider.
1 Pint of Consome.
1 Tablespoonful of Butter.
2 Slices of Bacon.
½ Tablespoonful of Pepper.
½ Tablespoonful of Salt.
Croutons.

Select two fine Hares, and cut them in half. Separate the hindquarters from the fore and then bone them down to the legs. Do not bone the legs. Place the Hares in an earthern dish that is quite deep, then make a marinade as follows: Pour in a glassful of white wine; add a small lemon nicely sliced, and a small onion minced fine, one sprig of thyme and one bay leaf, all minced very fine. Season this preparation with a tablespoonful of salt and a tablespoonful of pepper and two mashed cloves. Take the saddles of the Hares and roll them well in this, and let the entire Hares steep well in the marinade for twelve hours.

Chop an onion very fine and put it in a saucepan on the stove, and, when well heated, put in a tablespoonful of butter, cook for one minute, and then add two ounces of fine chaurice (sausage) (see recipe), chopped very fine; six mushrooms, chopped very fine; a teaspoonful of minced parsley, a teaspoonful of salt and a half teaspoonful of pepper; mix well and let all cook for about five minutes. Take three fine apples and cut them fine, carefully removing the cores; place them in a clean saucepan on the fire, with a half glassful of good White Wine or the best Cider. Let this boil about five minutes, and then add the stuffing and mix well together. Then set the mixture to cool. Take the Hares from the marinade and stuff the boned saddles very carefully and evenly, and give a nice round, even shape; tie them to keep them firm; then place a fine slice of bacon over each saddle, tying firmly. Cut up a carrot and onion into fine slices and place in the bottom of the roasting pan; lay the Hares over these and pour one pint of consommé over the Hares. Place them in a hot oven and roast for three-quarters of an hour, basting frequently with their own gravy. Then remove from the oven and untie. Place the Hares on a hot dish nicely decorated with dice-shaped Croûtons, and pour the gravy over the Hares and serve very hot.

### Hare, Creole Style.

Civet de Lièvre à la Créole.

1 Fine, Tender Hare
1 Tablespoonful of Butter.
2 Tablespoonfuls of Flour.
1 Large Onion.     1 Dozen Small Onions.
3 Tomatoes.
1 Ounce of Minced Ham.
2 Sprigs of Thyme.     2 Bay Leaves.
½ Glass of White Wine.
½ Glass of Red Wine.
1½ Tablespoonfuls of Salt.
1½ Tablespoonfuls of Pepper.
1 Pint of Consomme or Water.

Skin, clean, draw and thoroughly wash a fine tender Hare. Preserve the liver and heart. Cut the Hare into pieces at the joints. Make a marinade by taking a half glass of White Wine, one large finely-sliced onion, the thyme and bay leaves (finely minced), and place in a stone jar. Add a half teaspoonful of grated nutmeg and a tablespoonful of salt, and place in this mixture the cut-up Hare, and let all steep for six hours. Then lift the pieces out carefully; have ready a saucepan into which you will have placed a teaspoonful of butter, and add twelve small onions, glazed (see recipe); one ounce of ham, minced fine; put the Hare into the pan and let all brown nicely for about ten minutes. Then add the flour, finely rubbed, stir well and let brown. Add the tomatoes, peeled and sliced fine; let all brown ten minutes longer, and add the red wine and the consommé or water. Stir till it begins to boil; then season according to taste, with salt and pepper. Let all cook for three quarters of an hour, and add the heart and liver, which you will have finely chopped and thoroughly mixed together. Let all cook for a quarter of an hour longer and serve with toasted Croûtons.

### Stewed Hare With Onions.

Gibelotte de Lièvre.

1 Fine Hare.
1 Tablespoonful of Butter.
1 Tablespoonful of Flour.
1 Large Onion.     1 Dozen Small Onions.
1 Ounce of Ham.
2 Sprigs of Thyme.     2 Bay Leaves.
1 Glass of White Wine.
½ Can of Mushrooms.
1 Pint of Consomme or Water.
Salt and Pepper to Taste.

Prepare in exactly the same manner as above indicated, only do not use the tomatoes or red wine; use instead of the claret, one pint of broth or consommé, and add a half can of mushrooms about ten minutes before serving.

### Filet of Hare, Sauce Poivrade.

Filet de Lièvre, Sauce Poivrade.

2 Fine Hares.     2 Onions.
2 Carrots.     A Half Glass of White Wine.
1 Tablespoonful of Lard or Butter.
1 Cup of Broth or Water.
Sauce a la Poivrade.

Take two fine Hares, clean neatly and cut the filets neatly from the rack. Lard the surface carefully with fine needles. Season well with salt and pepper. Make a marinade with half a glass of White wine, one onion and one carrot, minced very fine. Let all steep together for two hours; then place the butter or lard in a baking dish, with an onion and carrot, sliced fine. Put the filets of Hare over this and set in the oven and let it cook for a half hour. Baste frequently with the Hare's own juices. Place the filets on a hot dish, add a tablespoonful of broth to the gravy in which the Hares were cooked; let all come to a boil on the stove; strain the gravy and pour over the filets. Bring to the table hot and serve with a Sauce à la Poivrade.

### Stewed Squirrel.

Salmi d'Écureuil.

A Pair of Squirrels.
2 Onions.     1 Square Inch of Ham.
1 Tablespoonful of Butter.
1 Clove of Garlic, Chopped Very Fine.
1 Herb Bouquet, Chopped Fine.
1 Glass of Claret.     1 Cup of Water.
1 Can of Mushrooms.

Skin and clean the Squirrels; wash well and cut into pieces at the joints. Chop two onions very fine and put them in a stewpan with a tablespoonful of melted butter. Let them brown slightly; then add the Squirrel. Let it brown slightly, and then add one tablespoonful of flour, and let this brown a little. Chop the square inch of ham very fine, mincing it, and add. Then add the clove of garlic, and two sprigs each of thyme and parsley and a bay leaf, minced fine. Let this brown nicely, and pour over one glass of good Claret. Let this cook for ten minutes, stirring it constantly, so that it will not burn, and then add one cup of boiling water. Stir well, season again to taste and let it boil for thirty minutes and serve hot. This dish will be improved beyond estimation if a can of mushrooms is added immediately after adding the water. But it is very nice without the mushrooms. Serve very hot.

**Squirrel, Hunters' Style.**
Écureuil à la Chasseur.

Procure two fine Squirrels, and prepare in exactly the same manner as in the recipe, "Rabbit, Hunters' Style." (See recipe.)

**Squirrel en Matelote.**
Écureuil en Matelote.

Procure two fine Squirrels, and prepare in exactly the same manner as in the recipe for "Rabbit en Matelote." (See recipe.)

## CHAPTER XIX.

### BIRDS.

Des Oiseaux.

As already mentioned, Louisiana points with pride to the quality and variety of the Birds found in her forests. Fine game birds are always heavy for their size; the flesh of the breast is plump and firm, and the skin clear. To be sure that the bird is fresh if purchased from dealers, pluck off a few feathers from the inside of the legs and around the vent; in a freshly-killed bird the flesh will be fat and fresh-colored; if the game has been hung a long time, the flesh will be dark and discolored. These are infallible guides in selecting game birds. In serving birds, remember that young Green Peas, or "Petits Pois Français," as they are generally called, are a nice entrée for all birds. The following are the recognized Creole rules and methods of preparing our delightful "Fancy Game."

**Invariable Rule for Broiling Birds.**
Oiseaux Grillées.

Prepare the birds by hand picking. If of the very small variety, such as grassets, reed birds, robins, etc., do not pick out the entrails, for there will be little left of the bird but a charred mass. Rub the bird well with salt and pepper, and then with melted butter. Tie a strip of very finely-sliced bacon around the body of the bird, joining with a skewer, and place on a broiler over a slow fire, and let it cook for ten, fifteen or twenty or even thirty minutes, according to the size of the bird. Turn frequently, so that it may cook well without burning. When done, take off the broiler. Have ready always buttered French toasts, and place the birds upon them, allowing a slice of toast for each bird. Trim away the rough edges of the toast. It is a matter of taste whether the strip of bacon be removed or not. But in the most exclusive homes of Creole New Orleans it is retained, being removed at the table by the person to whom it is served, the hot bacon keeping the bird hot, juicy and tender. Always pour over the bird a little of the juice that has run from it in broiling, and let it soak down into the toast. Pour over a little melted butter and chopped parsley, and lemon juice if you like. Garnish with sliced lemon and parsley sprigs, and bring to the table hot.

**Invariable Rule for Roasting Birds.**
Oiseaux Rotis.

Prepare the birds in exactly the same manner as for broiling, cleaning out the entrails of the larger birds, and leaving the small ones untouched, with the exception of the Pababotte, the gizzards of which must never be eaten, for the Pababotte is a very rich bird. Rub with salt and pepper and melted butter. In the larger birds, if you can afford it, put a truffle or two, for stuffing, and in all put a little lump of butter and a little salt and pepper, a pinch of chopped thyme, parsley and bay leaf, and a small pinch of the four spices, but very, very small indeed. Bind with strips of bacon, and place in a baking pan with a tablespoonful of butter. Let them bake or roast thirty minutes or less, according to size, and serve always on buttered French toast, over which you will pour, when you have placed the bird upon it, a bit of the gravy made when cooking. Prepare this gravy by simply adding a tablespoonful of water, letting it cook for two minutes; then strain; let it cook for two minutes more, and pour upon the breast of the bird, so that it will soak down into the toast. Garnish nicely with sprigs of parsley and lemon, and serve hot.

Bear in mind that all large game should be roasted; the small may be roasted or broiled, according to taste.

### Pababotte.

The Pababotte is one of our most récherché and distinctive birds. The Pababotte is a summer bird, and is with us from the latter part of the month of June to September. The game laws are very strict, and it is not allowed to be killed out of season. The first Pababottes in the market, like the first Pompano, are much sought after. It is a rich bird and is the joy of the ancient Creole gourmets. "Pababotte à la Créole!"—"Ah!" they will tell you, "you have a dish that is enough to make a dead man turn alive!" Thus prepared, the dish is sometimes called "à la Français-Créole," not because the bird has been ever cooked by the French in their own domains, for it is unknown in French forests, but because the Creoles, in cooking it to the best advantage, adopt the French dressing which will be explained in stuffing the bird, according to the subjoined distinctive Creole recipe:

### Pababotte à la Créole.
Pababotte à la Créole.

6 Pababottes.  6 Truffles.
6 Thin Slices of Bacon.  6 Slices of Toast.
3 Tablespoonfuls of Butter.
3 Tablespoonfuls of Water.
The Zest of a Lemon. The Juice of 1 Lemon.
Olives and Sprigs of Parsley to Garnish.

Clean the Pababotte as you would a chicken, and take out the entrails. Separate the gizzards, and be sure to throw them away, retaining all the rest of the entrails for stuffing. Chop the remaining entrails very fine, and season well with salt and pepper. Fry them in about a quarter of a spoon of butter. In the meantime take the Pababotte and rub well with salt and pepper, and put a small piece of butter, about the size of a peanut, with a little salt and pepper, in the Pababotte. Place in the interior one truffle. Bind a strip of thin bacon around the body. Place a tablespoonful of butter in a baking dish, and set the Pababotte in it, and add about two tablespoonfuls of water. Set the dish in a quick oven, and let the birds roast thirty minutes, turning over once, so that they may be perfectly done. When the entrails are done, add two inches of the zest of the lemon and a little juice. Take slices of toast, allowing one slice for each bird, and spread over each a coating of the entrails, or farcie. Place a bird on each slice of toast, after taking off the binding of bacon, or leaving it on, according to taste. Add one spoon of water to the gravy in which the Pababottes have been cooking, strain it, then warm for two minutes, and pour hot on top of the breast of the bird, allowing it to melt down into the French toasts. Garnish the dish nicely with sprigs of parsley and olives, and serve hot.

### Broiled Pababotte.
Pababotte Grillé.

6 Pababottes.  6 Fine Strips of Bacon.
6 Slices of Buttered French Toast.
3 Tablespoonfuls of Melted Butter.
Juice of 1 Lemon.
1 Tablespoonful of Chopped Parsley.
Sliced Lemon and Parsley Sprigs to Garnish.
Salt and Pepper to Taste.

Clean the Pababotte well, removing the entrails, and be particularly careful to throw away the gizzard. Rub the birds with salt and pepper and then with melted butter. Tie a strip of very finely-sliced bacon around the body of each bird, joining the bacon with a skewer, and place the birds on a broiler over a slow fire and let them cook fifteen, twenty or even thirty minutes, according to the size of the birds. Turn frequently, so that they may broil without burning. When done, take off the broiler; have ready the slices of buttered French toast, and place a bird upon each slice. Trim away the rough edges of the toast. Pour over the birds a little of the juice that has run from them in broiling, and let this soak down into the toast. Pour over a little melted butter and chopped parsley, and add a little lemon juice, if desired. Garnish with slices of lemon and parsley sprigs and bring to the table hot.

### Roast Pababotte.
Pababotte Roti.

6 Pababottes.  6 Truffles (if desired).
3 Sprigs of Chopped Thyme and Parsley.
1 Bay Leaf, Minced.
6 Thin Strips of Bacon.
3 Tablespoonfuls of Butter.
1 Tablespoonful of Water.
6 Slices of French Toast.
Salt and Pepper to Taste.
Sprigs of Parsley and Thin Slices of Lemon to Garnish.

Prepare the Pababottes as indicated in above recipe. Rub with salt and pepper and melted butter; put a truffle or two into each Pababotte, if you can afford it, and put in each bird a little lump of butter about the size of a peanut, a pinch of salt and pepper, and a pinch of chopped thyme and parsley and bay leaf. Bind the birds with the strips of bacon and place in a baking pan with a tablespoonful of butter. Let them bake or roast for thirty minutes or less, according to size. When done, place each bird on a slice of buttered French toast, and, when you have placed the bird thus, pour over a bit of the gravy which you will have made by adding to the birds while cooking, and just four minutes before serving, add a tablespoonful of water, letting it cook for two minutes; then strain this gravy, and let it cook two minutes more. Pour a little over the breast of each bird, so that it will soak down into the toast. Garnish nicely with sprigs of parsley and sliced lemon and serve hot.

### PARTRIDGES.
### Perdreaux.

The Partridge may be roasted or broiled; being a large bird, if roasted it may be stuffed with truffles or any stuffing, such as oysters or egg, and served on toast, as indicated in the recipes for broiling and roasting birds.

The term "Perdreaux" is applied by the French to young Partridges, and "Perdrix" to the older birds. In the young birds the tips of the long wing feathers are pointed; in the old birds the tips of the wing feathers are round.

### Roast Partridge.
Perdreaux Rotis, ou Perdreaux Piqués Sur Canapés.

6 Fine Young Partridges.
6 Thin Slices of Bacon.
3 Tablespoonfuls of Butter.
2 Sprigs of Thyme.
2 Sprigs of Parsley.   1 Bay Leaf.
Salt and Pepper to Taste.
Toasted Bread.

Parsley or Watercress to Garnish.

Clean, singe and draw and wipe the birds neatly; rub each bird well with salt and pepper, and then with melted butter. If it can be afforded, stuff the bird with truffles, placing one or two in each bird, and place within the bird a pinch of salt and pepper, a lump of butter about the size of a peanut, and a pinch of chopped thyme, parsley and bay leaf, all minced very fine. Bind the birds with thin strips of bacon, and fasten each strip with a skewer. Put the Partridges in a baking pan in a brisk oven, and add two tablespoonfuls of butter and one of water. Let them bake from twenty-five to thirty minutes, according to size, basting occasionally with their own juice. When done, have ready the buttered French toast; place the birds upon the toast and pour over a bit of the gravy made when cooking. Prepare this gravy by adding two tablespoonfuls of water to the Partridge juice after removing the birds; let it cook for two minutes, and then strain and let it cook two minutes more. Pour upon the breast of the birds, so that it will soak into the toast. Garnish the dish nicely with sprigs of parsley or watercress and serve hot.

### Roast Partridge, Bread Sauce.
Perdreaux Rotis, Sauce au Pain.
3 Fine Young Partridges.
Slice of Toast Bread.
1½ Ounces of Fresh Bread Crumbs.
1 Tablespoonful of Butter.
½ Cup of Cold Water.
½ Cup of Cream or Milk.
½ Teaspoonful of Salt. 6 White Peppers.

Prepare the Partridges and roast according to recipe for "Roast Partridge." (See recipe.) Make a bread sauce as follows: Crumble one and a half ounces of fresh bread crumbs and place in a saucepan with a half cup of cold water; add, when the water heats, a tablespoonful of butter, six whole white peppers and a half teaspoonful of salt. Cook for five minutes; then add a half cup of rich milk or cream. Let the whole cook five minutes more. Remove the white peppers. Place the Partridges on the toasted bread, and garnish the dish nicely with parsley sprigs or watercress. Send to the table hot, with the sauce in a separate dish. Pour the sauce over the Partridges when serving.

### Broiled Partridges
Perdreaux Grillés.

3 Fine Young Partridges.
6 Slices of French Toast.
2 Tablespoonfuls of Butter.
Salt and Pepper to Taste.
The Juice of a Lemon.
Parsley Sprigs and Sliced Lemon to Garnish.

Prepare the birds as in the above recipe. Cut them in two by splitting down the back, as in broiling a chicken. Rub with salt and pepper and melted butter. Place on a broiler and let them broil from fifteen to twenty minutes, allowing from seven to ten minutes, according to the size of the bird, to either side during the broiling process. Turn frequently to avoid burning. Have ready the buttered French toast; place the birds upon it and pour over a little of the juice that ran from the bird while broiling. Let it soak down in the bread; pour over melted butter and chopped parsley, and add a little lemon juice, if desired. Garnish the dish nicely with sprigs of parsley or watercress and send to the table hot.

### Partridge With Sour Orange Sauce.
Perdreaux aux Bigarades.
3 Fine Partridges.
2 Tablespoonfuls of Butter.
The Juice of a Sour Orange.
Toasted Croutons.
Watercress or Parsley to Garnish.

Broil the Partridges according to recipe for "Broiled Partridge." (See recipe.) Prepare a "Drawn Butter

### Partridges, Hunters' Style.

Perdrix Sautées à la Chasseur.

3 Fine Partridges.
2 Tablespoonfuls of Butter.
2 Tablespoonfuls of Flour.
1 Finely Chopped Onion. 12 Whole Mushrooms.
2 Sprigs Each of Thyme and Parsley.
1 Bay Leaf. Salt and Pepper to Taste.
½ Glass of Sherry or Madeira Wine.
1 Cup of Water or Consomme.
Croutons.

The older birds are used for stewing purposes. Clean the Partridges; singe, draw and wipe well. Cut up the birds as you would a young chicken. Rub well with salt and pepper, and place in a stewpan with two tablespoonfuls of butter. After letting them brown well on either side, about three minutes, add the finely-chopped onion and carrot, and the minced herbs. Let these brown for two minutes, and add the flour and let all brown nicely. Then add a cup of water or consommé and the wine and the chopped mushrooms. Cover closely and cook for fifteen minutes and then serve, using toasted Croûtons as garnish.

### Partridge, Creole Style.

Perdrix Sautées à la Créole.

3 Fine Partridges.
2 Tablespoonfuls of Butter.
1 Tablespoonful of Flour.
3 Large Tomatoes.
2 Sprigs Each of Thyme and Parsley.
1 Bay Leaf.
½ Glass of Sherry or Madeira Wine.
1 Cup of Water or Consomme.
Salt and Pepper to Taste.
Croutons to Garnish.

Clean the Partridges; singe, draw and wipe well. Cut up the birds as for Fricasseed Chicken. Rub well with salt and pepper and place in a stewpan, and let them brown well on either side. Then add the finely-chopped onion and the herbs, minced very fine. Let these brown, and add the tablespoonful of flour. Let brown nicely, and add the chopped tomatoes and their juice; cover and let simmer about five minutes, and then add the wine and a cup of water or consommé. Cover closely and let all cook for fifteen minutes and serve hot, using toasted Croûtons for a garnish.

### Partridge à la Financiére.

Perdreaux à la Financiére.

3 Fine Young Partridges.
1 Carrot. 1 Onion. 1 Bay Leaf.
2 Sprigs of Thyme. 1 Tablespoonful of Salt.
1 Tablespoonful of Pepper.
A Dash of Cayenne. 2 Sprigs of Parsley.
½ Pint of Consomme or Water.
3 Tablespoonfuls of Butter.
1 Tablespoonful of Flour. 3 Truffles.
2 Dozen Stoned Olives.
3 Blanched Chicken Livers.
1 Dozen Mushrooms.
1 Dozen Quenelles of Veal or Chicken.
1 Pint of Madeira or Sherry Wine.

Clean the partridges according to the recipe given. Singe, draw, wipe well and then truss neatly. Rub well with salt and pepper. Take a piece of fat salt pork and cut into strips and lard the partridges with these thin strips, using a larding needle. Then put two tablespoonfuls of butter into a shallow saucepan, let the butter melt, add the onion and carrot sliced fine and the minced parsley and bay leaf; lay the partridges over these, cover the saucepan and let the partridges brown till they reach a nice golden color. Then add a half pint of chicken or veal consommé, or if these are not convenient add a half pint of water. Cover the saucepan and let them simmer down for twenty minutes, turning occasionally so that they may be thoroughly cooked. Then remove the birds, placing them on a hot dish in the oven. Make a Sauce à la Financiére by adding to the gravy in which the partridges were cooked; one tablespoonful of flour; let it brown and add one pint of rich chicken broth, one tablespoonful of butter, three sliced truffles, two dozen stoned olives, three blanched chicken livers cut in pieces, one dozen mushrooms, one dozen small balls or quenelles (see recipe) of minced veal or chicken (may be omitted), and a pint of Sherry or Madeira wine. Season well with salt and pepper, and add a dash of Cayenne. Let all cook for twenty minutes, using a wooden spoon to stir. The sauce should be of the consistency of rich cream. After twenty minutes place the partridges back in the sauce and let them warm for about three or four minutes. Place in the dish, pour the sauce over them and serve hot with garnish of toasted Croûtons.

### Partridge and Cabbage.

Perdrix aux Choux.

3 Fine Partridges.
A Fine Tender Head of Cabbage.
12 Chaurice (Sausage). ½ of a Pound of Salt Pork.
1 Onion. 1 Carrot. 4 Cloves.
½ Tablespoonful of Butter. 1 Herb Bouquet.

1 Pint of Veal or Chicken Broth (White).
1 Pint of Beef Broth or Water.
Salt and Pepper to Taste.

Clean the partridges, selecting large and older partridges in preference to the young. Clean, singe, draw and wipe well. Then truss them neatly, rub with salt and pepper and butter and place in a roasting pan. In the meantime take a fine, tender head of cabbage, clean thoroughly and cut into four parts. Wash the cabbage well in cold water and put into boiling salted water for five minutes. Then take the cabbage out of the water and drain well; make a hollow in the center of each piece of cabbage; place within the partridges, cover with the other pieces and tie together. Put in a saucepan the quarter of a pound of salt pork which has been well scalded and washed of all salt and cut into six slices. Add one carrot cut into four pieces, one whole onion into which you will have stuck four cloves, the herb bouquet, the sausage and one pint each of white veal broth or chicken broth, and one pint of water or beef broth. Season with a small pinch of salt, and a good pinch of pepper, and place the cabbage in this preparation. Put the partridges in the oven and let them roast for ten minutes. Then remove and take the cabbage from the mixture, make a hollow in the center of the cabbage, place within the partridges and cover with the remaining portion of cabbage; tie each half separately together; then return to the saucepan, placing a piece of buttered paper over to keep all air from escaping. Put the lid on the saucepan, set in the oven and let the partridges cook thus for an hour. Remove the lid and paper, skim off all that may adhere to the surface, drain the cabbage and slice; dress neatly on a hot dish. Untruss the partridges and lay them on the cabbage, placing on each dressed section a piece of sliced boiled pork, a sausage cut in half; slice the carrots nicely in round pieces, and use these as a decoration, placing them artistically around the dish. Strain the sauce in which the partridges were cooked and let it reduce slightly. Serve with the cabbage and partridge, bringing it to the table in a separate bowl and pouring over the cabbage when serving.

### Chartreuse of Partridge.

Chartreuse de Perdrix.

3 Fine Partridges.
A Fine Tender Head of Cabbage.
12 Chaurice (Sausage). ¼ Pound of Salt Pork.
3 Small Onions.
2 Turnips. 2 Carrots. 4 Cloves.
1½ Tablespoonfuls of Butter.
½ Cup of Green Peas.
1 Herb Bouquet.
1 Pint of Veal or Chicken Broth.
1 Pint of Consomme.
½ Pint of Demi Glace, or Madeira Sauce.

Prepare the partridges and cabbage exactly as for the recipe „Partridges and Cabbage."

Butter a three-pint mold lightly; cut the turnips, carrots and onion into small even pieces, using a vegetable tube; put a layer of the cut vegetables in the bottom of the mold; lay on top a layer of the cooked cabbage, cut the partridges into pieces and place a layer of them on the cabbage, filling in the hollow spaces with cabbage chopped fine and the chopped vegetables; fill in further with the sliced sausage and lay on top six slices of the salt pork; then place another layer of the partridges, fill in the hollow places with the sliced turnips and carrots and onions and the sausage; place on top another layer of cabbage, covering the top well with the cabbage and pressing down very carefully; decorate the mold prettily around the edges with the sliced carrots and turnips and place in a tin baking pan and set in a moderate oven for fifteen minutes. Have at hand a hot dish turn the mold upside down and carefully draw it off the preparation. Send to the table hot and serve with Demi Glace, or Madeira Sauce. (See recipe.)

### Breasts of Partridge, Truffle Sauce.

Suprême de Perdreaux, Sauce Périgueux.

3 Fine Young Partridges. 3 Truffles.
12 Mushrooms.
½ Glass of Madeira Wine.
2 Ounces of Chicken Forcemeat.
A Pint of Sauce a la Hollandaise.
2 Gills of White Wine.

Clean, singe, draw and wipe the partridges carefully. Then remove the skin from the breasts. By a delicate manipulation with a very sharp small knife make an incision on the top of each breastbone from end to end and cut off the entire breast, including the wing bone, from the carcass. Carefully remove the small filet which lies under each breast and place on a dish aside for further use. Then cut an incision two inches square and 1 inch in depth into each breast, on the inner side. Rub well with salt and pepper, and stuff the incision with two tablespoonfuls of chicken forcemeat, to which has been added six finely-chopped mushrooms and two thinly-sliced truffles. Butter the inside of a tin saucepan and lay the six breasts very carefully within. Then take each of the six small filets that have been laid aside; rub them well with salt and pepper and make a small incision on the top of each and place within a thin slice of truffle and brush lightly with melted butter. Lay these filets lightly on top of each of the breasts, and again brush lightly with melted butter. These filets and breasts thus arranged constitute supremes. Pour into the pan a half glass of Madeira wine and two tablespoonfuls of the chicken liquor, cover the pan tightly and place in a hot oven for fifteen minutes.

Take one pint of Hollandaise Sauce, add one finely-minced truffle and a half dozen minced mushrooms and two gills of White Wine. Place the sauce in a saucepan of hot boiling water and let the sauce heat well without boiling. Pour this sauce into a hot dish and then take the pan with the partridges out of the oven, remove the breasts and filets, or "Suprêmes," place them on the dish with the sauce, garnish nicely with Croûtons and send to the table hot.

## QUAIL.
### Cailles.

The quail is a most delicious and tempting bird. It delights the most fastidious, and that famous preparation, "Quail on Toast," or "Cailles sur Canapés," is a dish that no great dining is considered complete without, when quail are in season.

We have two kinds of quail, the blue and the yellow spotted, or pivéle. Both are excellent. If purchased in the market or city stores, see that the skin is clear and the breasts full and tender. The quail is either broiled or roasted, following exactly the same directions given in the recipes for broiling and roasting. In broiling, allow from twelve to fifteen minutes. In roasting, from twenty to twenty-five. Always cook slowly on a slow fire.

### Roasted Quail.
#### Cailles Roties.

6 Quails.
1 Tablespoonful of Butter.
1 Tablespoonful of Water.
The Juice of 1 Lemon. 6 Slices of Toast.
Salt and Pepper to Taste.
Sliced Lemon and Parsley Sprigs, or Watercress to Garnish.

Select six fine, fat, tender quail. Pick, singe, clean and wipe them well. Butter the inside of each quail nicely and sprinkle lightly within with salt and pepper. Rub lightly on the outside with butter, then truss the bird and bind the body round with a thin strip of bacon. Put a tablespoonful of butter in a roasting pan and set the birds in the pan and cook in the oven from twenty to thirty minutes, according to size. Have ready the buttered toast. Place on a hot dish, lay a bird on each slice of toast. Add a little butter to the gravy in which the quails have been roasted, a tablespoonful of water and the juice of one lemon. Let this cook for three or four minutes, strain and set on the stove for two minutes longer and pour over the breast of the birds so that it will soak into the bread. Garnish the dish nicely with parsley and sliced lemon or sliced lemon and watercress, and send to the table hot. When served with a garnish of watercress the dish is called "Cailles aux Cressons."

### Quail Roasted in Grape Leaves.
#### Cailles de Laurier aux Feuilles de Vignes.

6 Fine Quails.
2 Tablespoonfuls of Butter.
1 Tablespoonful of Water. The Juice of 1 Lemon.
6 Slices of Buttered Toast. 12 Grape Leaves.
Green Grape Jelly.

Follow the directions given in the above recipe for roasting quails, only do not wrap the quails in strips of bacon. Instead rub the bodies well with butter and then envelop the birds in fresh grape leaves; set in a baking pan and proceed to roast according to the directions given above. Garnish a dish nicely with fresh young grape leaves, place the quails on slices of toast and lay upon the leaves and send the dish to the table hot. Serve the quails with Green Grape Jelly. This is, of course, a rare dish, and can only be served at the season when the grape vine is in leaf. It is much affected at such times by epicures, but it is a dish within the reach of any who may have a grape vine near. The grape leaves impart a very peculiar and grateful flavor to the quail.

### Roasted Quail.
#### Cailles de Laurier Roties.

6 Fine Tender Quails.
2 Tablespoonfuls of Butter.
1 Tablespoonful of Water. 6 Truffles.
6 Thin Strips of Bacon. The Juice of 1 Lemon.
Parsley Sprigs and Sliced Lemon to Garnish.

To make this delicious dish, clean the quail and butter inside and throw in a little salt and pepper. Stuff with truffles, and bind the body, after rubbing, with a strip of bacon. Set in the oven in a baking pan in which you have placed a tablespoonful of butter, and let it roast twenty or thirty minutes, according to size. Have ready buttered toast. Put the birds on the toast. Add a little butter to the gravy in which they have been roasted, and a tablespoonful of water, and the juice of a lemon. Let this cook for three or four minutes, strain, set on the stove for two minutes longer, and pour over the breast of the bird, so that it will soak into the bread, and serve with a nice garnish of parsley and sliced lemon, and with green peas as an entrée.

### Broiled Quail on Toast.
#### Cailles Grillées sur Canapés.

6 Fine Fat Quails. 6 Strips of Bacon.
2 Tablespoonfuls of Butter. 6 Slices of Buttered Toast.
The Juice of 1 Lemon.
Parsley Sprigs to Garnish.

Rub the bird well with salt and pepper, and then with melted butter. Tie a strip of very finely-sliced bacon around the body of the bird, joining with a skewer, and place on a broiler over a slow fire, and let it cook for ten, fifteen or twenty, or even thirty minutes, according to the size of the bird. Turn frequently, so that it may cook well without burning. When done take off the broiler. Have ready always buttered French toasts, and place the birds upon them, allowing a slice of toast for each bird. Trim away the rough edges of the toast. It is a matter of taste whether the strip of bacon be removed or not. But at the most elegant dinings in Creole New Orleans it is retained, being removed at the table by the person to whom it is served, the hot bacon keeping the bird hot, juicy and tender. Always pour over the bird a little of the juice that has run from it in broiling, and let it soak down into the toast. Pour over a little melted butter and chopped parsley, and lemon juice, if you like. Garnish with sliced lemon and parsley sprigs, and bring to the table hot.

### Quails Broiled With Bacon.
#### Cailles Grillées et Bardées.

6 Fine Fat Quails.
1 Tablespoonful of Butter.
1 Tablespoonful of Salt. ½ Tablespoonful of Pepper.
6 Slices of Bacon. 6 Slices of Toast.
2 Tableapoonfuls of Sauce a la Maitre d'Hotel.
Watercress and Sliced Lemon to Garnish.

Clean the quails, singe and wipe well. Split them through the back without separating the breast and break the leg bones. Rub well with salt and pepper and a little melted butter, mixed together, and put the quails on a broiler and let them broil on a moderate fire for fifteen minutes, allowing seven and a half minutes to either side, and turning frequently, to prevent burning. Have ready a hot dish with six slices of buttered toast, lay the quail on top and pour over a little melted butter (Sauce à la Maitre d'Hotel), and then decorate the dish with parsley sprigs, on which lay six nicely broiled slices of breakfast bacon.

### Smothered Quail.
#### Cailles Braissées.

6 Fine Fat Quails. ½ Carrot.
½ of an Onion. ⅓ Cupful of Water.
2 Tablespoonfuls of Butter.
Salt and Pepper to Taste.
6 Thin Strips of Bacon.

Select fine fat quails, clean, singe and wipe well. Truss neatly and cover with a thin layer of bacon. Then place two tablespoonfuls of butter in a saucepan; place the quails in the pan; add half of an onion and carrot minced very fine, cover and let the quails brown to a nice golden color. Then moisten with a half cup of water and set the pan in the oven. Cover with buttered paper and let the quails cook for twenty minutes. Serve on a hot dish nicely garnished with parsley sprigs or lettuce leaves.

### Braised Quails, Celery Sauce.
#### Cailles Braissées à la Sauce Céleri.

Proceed to clean and cook the quails as in the recipe given above and serve with a pint of hot Celery Sauce (see recipe) poured over.

### Quails Braised à la Financière.
#### Cailles Braissées à la Financière.

Braise the quails as in the recipe for "Braised Quails," and serve with a pint of hot Sauce à la Financière poured over.

### WOODCOCK.
#### Bécasse.

The "Bécasse" is a rare bird. It is in season from December till April. In purchasing see that the skin is clear, the breasts firm and plump and the wings tender to the touch. Pluck and clean, but never draw these birds. The olden epicurean ideas of Creole cookery forbid this. If you were to serve the Bécasse to an old Creole bon vivant without the entrails he would consider it quite shocking, and his indignation would vent itself immediately in unmistakable terms. The "Bécasse" is always broiled or roasted and served on buttered French toast. If roasted, always put, if you can, one truffle in the body as a stuffing, and when serving a little melted butter on top of the breast.

### Roast Woodcock on Toast.
#### Bécasses Roties sur Canapés.

6 Fine Woodcock.
6 Slices of Buttered Toast.
6 Strips of Bacon.
2 Tablespoonfuls of Butter.
1 Sprig Each of Thyme and Parsley. 1 Bay Leaf.
Sliced Lemon and Sprigs of Parsley or Watercress to Garnish.

Prepare the birds as in the "Invariable Rule for Roasting Birds." (See recipe.)

Rub with salt and pepper and melted butter. If you can afford it, put a truffle in each bird for stuffing, and in all put a little lump of butter and a little salt and pepper, a pinch of chopped thyme, parsley and bay leaf, and a small pinch of the four spices, but very, very small, indeed. Truss neatly. Bind with strips of bacon, and place in a baking pan with a tablespoonful of butter. Let them bake or roast thirty minutes or less, according to size; remove from the oven and place on buttered French toast on a hot dish, cover and set over a pot of boiling water to keep warm. Prepare gravy by simply adding a tablespoonful of water to the gravy made when cooking the birds, let it cook for two minutes; then strain; let it cook for two minutes more, and pour upon the breast of the bird so that it will soak down into the toast. Garnish nicely with sprigs of parsley and lemon, and serve hot.

### Broiled Woodcock on Toast.

Bécasses Grillés sur Canapés.

6 Fine Fat Woodcock. 6 Slices of Buttered French Toast.
6 Fine Strips of Breakfast Bacon.
2 Tablespoonfuls of Butter. Parsley Sprigs and Sliced Lemon to Garnish.

Prepare the birds by hand picking. Singe and wipe well. Rub the bird well with salt and pepper, and then with melted butter. Tie a strip of very finely-sliced bacon around the body of the bird, joining with a skewer, and place on a broiler over a slow fire, and let it cook for ten, fifteen or twenty, or even thirty minutes, according to the size of the bird. Turn frequently so that it may cook well without burning. When done take off the broiler. Have ready always buttered French toasts, and place the birds upon them, allowing a slice of toast for each bird. Trim away the rough edges of the toast. Always pour over the bird a little of the juice that has run from it in broiling, and let it soak down into the toast. Pour over a little melted butter and chopped parsley, and lemon juice, if you like. Garnish with sliced lemon and parsley sprigs, and bring to the table hot. In cooking, and in serving, follow the "Invariable Rule for Broiling Birds." (See recipe.

### SNIPE.

Bécassine.

The snipe is one of our finest birds, and is much sought after by epicures. But the glory of our Louisiana forests is that the rich gifts of nature may be had by the poor as well as the millionaire.

The Bécassine is a welcome dish at the most exclusive tables. It is a winter bird, and is with us from December till April, as also the "Bécasse," or "Woodcock." If you tell an old Creole that you are going to treat him to "Bécassines" or "Bécasses," he will smack his lips and say: "Ah! you are a connoisseur."

"Bécassines" are either roasted or broiled; follow implicitly the directions given in the rules for broiling and roasting birds. Serve in the same manner, with a garnish of cresses or parsley, and always on buttered French toasts. In selecting snipe, see that the flesh is clear and firm and the breasts full and tender.

### Roast Snipe on Toast.

Bécassines Roties sur Canapés.

6 Fine Snipe. 6 Slices of Buttered French Toast.
6 Strips of Bacon.
2 Tablespoonfuls of Butter.
1 Sprig Each of Thyme and Parsley. 1 Bay Leaf.
Sliced Lemon and Sprigs of Parsley or Watercress to Garnish.

Prepare the birds as in the "Invariable Rule for Roasting Birds." Rub with salt and pepper and melted butter. If you can afford it, put a truffle into each bird for stuffing, and in all put a little lump of butter and a little salt and pepper, a pinch of chopped thyme, parsley and bay leaf, and a small pinch of the four spices, but very, very small, indeed. Bind with strips of bacon, and place in a baking pan with a tablespoonful of butter. Let them roast thirty minutes or less, according to size, then remove and place always on buttered French toast on a hot dish, and cover and set over a pot of boiling water to keep warm and juicy. Meanwhile prepare a gravy by simply adding a tablespoonful of water to the gravy made in cooking the birds; let it cook for two minutes; then strain; let it cook for two minutes more and pour a little upon the breast of each bird so that it will soak down into the toast. Garnish nicely with sprigs of parsley or watercress and slices of lemon, and serve hot.

### Broiled Snipe on Toast.

Bécassines Grillées sur Canapés.

6 Fine Fat Snipe.
6 Slices of Buttered French Toast.
6 Strips of Bacon.
2 Tablespoonfuls of Butter. Parsley Sprigs and Sliced Lemon to Garnish.

Prepare the bird by hand picking, singing and trussing neatly, following the "Invariable Rule for Broiling Birds." (See recipe.)

Rub the bird well with salt and pepper, and then with melted butter. Tie a strip of very finely-sliced bacon around the body of the bird, joining with a skewer, and place on a broiler over a slow fire, and let it cook for ten, fifteen or twenty, or even thirty minutes, according to the size of the bird. Turn frequently, so that it may cook well without burning. When done take off the broiler. Have ready always buttered French toasts, and place the birds upon them allowing a slice of toast for each bird. Trim away the rough edges of the toast. It is a matter of taste whether the strip of bacon be removed or not. Always pour over the bird a little of the juice that has run from it in broiling, and let it soak down into the toast. Pour over a little melted butter and chopped parsley, and lemon juice if you like. Garnish with sliced lemon and parsley sprigs, and bring to the table hot.

**Grassets, Reed Birds, Robins, Larks, Broiled or Roasted.**

Grassets, Ortolans, Grives, Alouettes, Grillées ou Rotis.

6 or 8 Birds. 6 or 8 Slices of Toast.
2 Tablespoonfuls of Butter.
6 or 8 Strips of Bacon. Salt and Pepper to Taste.
Sliced Lemon and Sprigs of Parsley or Water creas to Garnish.

Grassets, Reed Birds, Robins and Larks are delightful small game that come in the summer. They are with us from July, through October. The Reed Birds, or Ortolans, are the terror of the rice planters of Louisiana. They peck at the rice and spoil the growth, and are, consequently, shot in this season, when the rice is maturing, in order to rid the rice fields of their presence. They are delicate eating, as are also the Louisiana Robins, Larks, and the Grassets, which latter are fat, plumpy birds of the Robin order. The name Grasset is given to indicate fatness and plumpness. These birds are always broiled or roasted, following the invariable rules laid down above. They should be broiled over a clear fire, and do not require much more than five minutes to broil; ten minutes to roast in a quick oven. Serve whether broiled or roasted, on buttered French toast, and garnish with cresses of parsley sprigs. All these little birds should be broiled "en brochette," that is, a skewer should be run through the body. Salt and pepper after, and pour melted butter and chopped parsley over them. If roasted, they may be served with a brown gravy.

**POULES D'EAU.**

Poules d'Eau.

2 Pair of Poules d'Eau.
6 Turnips.   1 Tablespoonful of Butter.
1 Tablespoonful of Flour.
2 Onions, Chopped Fine.
1 Square Inch of Ham, Minced Fine.
1 Bay Leaf.   1 Clove of Garlic.
3 Sprigs Each of Thyme and Parsley.
Salt and Pepper to Taste.

The Poule d'Eau is a species of water duck resembling both a chicken and a duck. The Creoles gave it the name of "Poule d'Eaux," or "Water Chicken." As it lives entirely in the water and marshes, never coming on dry land, it is classed by the Creoles among the fish and served as a Friday or fast-day dish. It makes a very delightful entrée, either stewed plain or with turnips. It is never cooked in any other way. As it feeds much on fish, it often has the flavor of fish. In the hands of an inexperienced cook it is sometimes unpalatable on that account. Before cooking parboil a few minutes if there is the slightest odor of fish; add a small peeled carrot or onion to the water, and this will absorb the flavor of fish.

**Stewed Poules d'Eau.**

Poules d'Eau à la Créole.

1 Pair of Poules d'Eau.
1 Square Inch of Ham.   2 Onions.
1 Tablespoonful of Butter. 1 Clove of Garlic.
1 Herb Bouquet, Chopped Very Fine.
1 Glass of Claret.   1 Cup of Water.
1 Can of Mushrooms.

Clean and pick the Poules d'Eau nicely. Cut into joints or stew whole, as desired. The Creoles generally cut them into joints. Rub well with salt and pepper. Chop two onions very fine. Put them into the stewpan with a tablespoonful of melted butter, and let them brown slightly. Then add the well-seasoned ducks. Let these brown well, and add the one square inch of finely minced ham. (Omit the ham on fast days.) Add the clove of garlic and two sprigs each of thyme, parsley and one bay leaf, minced very fine. Let this brown with the Poules d'Eau, stirring frequently, and then pour over one good glass of claret. Let this simmer for ten minutes, stirring constantly so that it will not burn, and add one cup of boiling water. Season well to taste, and let them simmer well for about an hour. Serve hot with Croûtons for a garnish.

**Stewed Poules d'Eau With Turnips.**

Salmi de Poules d'Eau aux Navets.

1 Pair of Poules d'Eau.
6 Turnips.
1 Tablespoonful of Butter.
2 Onions Chopped Fine.
1 Square Inch of Ham, Minced Very Fine.
1 Bay Leaf.   1 Tablespoonful of Flour.
Salt and Pepper to Taste. 1 Clove of Garlic.
3 Sprigs Each of Thyme and Parsley.

This is the most delightful way of cooking Poules d'Eau. The turnip blends well with the flavor, and a nicer way of serving this vegetable in combination does not exist. Clean the Poules d'Eau and cut into pieces at the joints. Put a tablespoonful of butter into the pot, and as it melts add the onions, chopped fine. Let this brown and then add the pieces of Poules d'Eau. Let them brown, and add the minced ham. (Omit the ham on fast days.) Immediately after add the turnips, sliced or cut in quarters, and a tablespoonful or sifted flour. Stir well, let it brown slightly, and add the minced thyme, parsley and bay leaf, and one clove of garlic, minced very fine. Stir well again, and let it smother for about fifteen minutes, stirring frequently, so that it will not burn. Then add water almost ufficient to cover the Poules d'Eau, and stir well. Cover tight and let the mixture smother for a half hour longer. You will have one of the nicest dishes that ever graced a table.

### Game Pie.
Pâté de Gibier.

1 Dozen Small Birds. 1 Dozen Eggs.
A Rich Pie Crust. 1 Dozen Hard-Boiled Eggs.
2 Cups of Egg Dressing.
Salt and Pepper to Taste.

Take one dozen small birds, Snipe, Quail, Woodcock, etc., and clean well, inside and out. Stuff each one with a dressing the same as for turkey, using either egg or oysters as desired. Loosen the joints with a knife but do not separate them. Put them in a stewpan, with water enough to cover them, and let them cook till nearly tender. Then season with salt and pepper again and two tablespoonfuls of butter. Thicken the gravy with one tablespoonful of flour, let cook for ten minutes more and then remove and set to cool. Butter a pudding dish and line the sides with a rich pie crust (see recipe). Have ready the hard-boiled eggs, cut in slices. Put in a layer of the eggs and a layer of the birds until the dish is full. Pour over the gravy and then cover the pie with a crust and bake to a light brown.

The pie may also be made very nicely by stewing the birds as one would a chicken (see recipe), and then line a pie pan with a rich pie crust; bake lightly, fill in with the stewed birds, pour over the gravy, place a cover of the pie crust on top, set in the oven and bake to a light brown.

### Chaud-Froid of Game.
Chaud-Froid de Gibier.

The Breasts of 3 Ducks, or 1 Dozen Breasts of Small Game.
1 Cup of Chicken Forcemeat.
2 Tablespoonfuls of Butter.
1 Pint of Aspic Jelly.
1 Pint of Poulette Sauce.
3 Truffles. Watercress to Garnish.

This is a most recherché dish, seldom made in these days on account of the cost, but in old Creole days it was a standing dish at every great feast. It may be made with Canvasback or French or Teal Duck, or with Woodcock, Snipe and other small game. The dish demands such beautiful decoration that it requires an artist to make a real Creole Chaud-Froid.

Clean the ducks or game or spring chicken, if the latter is used; wash and truss neatly. Then wrap in buttered paper and smother according to recipe for Smothered Chicken (see recipe.) When done take out of the paper and separate the breasts of the game or chicken from the legs. Trim them neatly and stuff the portion between the breasts proper and the filets with a chicken forcemeat. (See recipe.) Mix together equal parts of Aspic Jelly and Poulette Sauce. (See recipes.) Stir till thick and surround with crushed ice. Then dip the breasts of the game or chicken into this mixture. Take a fine baking sheet or dish and arrange the breasts in fanciful or pyramidal figures on this dish, and when set decorate them nicely with sliced truffles and the remaining sauce that has been poured into timbale molds that have been previously lined with Aspic Jelly, and which have become set. Decorate nicely with these timbales of Aspic and Poulette Sauce, and garnish the dish with Croûtons, on which you will have placed portions of Aspic Jelly. Decorate the edges of the dish with Watercress, and place on the table cold. When ready to serve, serve a portion of the breast of the duck or the entire breast of the small game on a croûton of Aspic Jelly, with the timbale turned out on the end of the chicken or game and the other end garnished with Watercress. If chickens are used be careful to have spring chickens of one and a half pounds in weight. This is the real Creole Chaud-Froid that was served at the great feasts and banquets in the days gone by, when parties paid from $10 to $20 a plate. It is always an expensive dish, both from the cost of the ingredients and the care required in making it.

## CHAPTER XX.

### STUFFINGS AND DRESSINGS FOR POULTRY, GAME, FISH, ETC.

#### FORCEMEAT.

Des Farcies—Des Quenelles.

The Creoles claim that oysters, eggs, chestnuts or truffles are the only elegant dressings for poultry or game, and oysters or egg stuffing for fish. The following are the methods of preparing these dressings:

#### Oyster Dressing.

Farci aux Huîtres.

2 Dozen Oysters.
1 Cup of Bread, Wet and Squeezed.
1 Onion, Chopped Very Fine.
½ Square Inch Ham. 1 Tablespoonful Butter.
½ Teaspoonful of Sage.
1 Sprig Each of Thyme, Parsley and Bay Leaf, Minced Very Fine.
Salt and Pepper to Taste.

Wet the soft of the bread and squeeze thoroughly till you have one cup, judging the quantity of stuffing always by the size of the fowl to be stuffed, and adding more in proportion, if needed. Season the bread well with salt and pepper, and add the minced herbs, mixing well. Take a tablespoonful of butter and put in the frying pan. As it melts, add the onion, which must be chopped very fine. Let this brown for about five minutes, and while frying add the bread and stir well. Then add the square inch of ham, minced very fine. Mix well and let all fry well. Season again to taste. Then add the two dozen oysters, cut in two, with all the hard portions taken off. Mix all well, and fry for a few minutes longer. Then, if you prefer a dry dressing, place the pan in the oven and let the dressing bake for ten minutes. If you prefer, as many do, the moister and richer dressing, stuff the fowl or fish immediately, and proceed to bake. Arrange and bake the fowl as in the directions on these special subjects. Twice the above qauntity of bread will be needed, and perhaps a little more, in stuffing turkey. Nothing is more elegant or recherché than an oyster dressing. The flavor of sage is very much liked by some and disliked by others. If used—and the Creoles always use it—add a teaspoonful sifted, and mix thoroughly with the bread before putting it in the frying pan, if two cups of dressing are used, and less for one cup, in proportion.

#### Oyster Stuffing for Poultry.

Farci d'Huîtres.

All depends upon the size of the fowl. For the ordinary-sized fifteen or sixteen pound turkey, take
3 Dozen Oysters.
1 Quart of Stale Bread, Wet and Squeezed.
1 Tablespoonful of Butter.
1 Tablespoonful of Parsley.
1 Sprig of Thyme.
1 Bay Leaf. 3 Tablespoonfuls of Sage.
Salt and Pepper to Taste.

Drain the oysters; wet the stale bread with hot water, squeezing thoroughly. Chop fine the liver and gizzard of the fowl, and put a tablespoonful of lard into the frying pan. Mix in the chopped onions and add the chopped liver and gizzard. As it begins to brown, throw in the chopped herbs, and then add the bread which has been mixed well and seasoned with the chopped sage. Mix well. Add to this one tablespoonful of butter and stir, blending all thoroughly. Now add the pint or so of oyster water, and as it is reduced mix in the oysters. Stir for three or four minutes and take off and dress the fowl. This dressing is highly recommended.

#### Stuffing of Truffles.

Farci aux Truffes.

¼ Can of Truffles.
1 Cup of Bread, Wet and Squeezed.
1 Onion, Chopped Very Fine.
½ Square Inch of Ham.
1 Tablespoonful of Butter.
2½ Teaspoonfuls of Sage.
1 Sprig Each of Thyme, Parsley and Bay Leaf, Minced Very Fine.
Salt and Pepper to Taste.

Proceed in exactly the same manner as for egg or oyster stuffing, using a quarter of a can of truffles chopped, instead of the oysters or egg. But bear in mind that this is an expensive stuffing. Some fastidious epicures stuff the fowl entirely with truffles, but this will make the dish of turkey dressed in such manner cost at least $10.

#### Egg Dressing.

Farcis aux Oeufs.

4 Hard-Boiled Eggs.
1 Cup of Bread, Wet and Squeezed Thoroughly.
1 Chopped Onion. ½ Square Inch of Ham.

1 Teaspoonful of Butter.
½ Teaspoonful of Sage.
1 Sprig Each of Thyme, Parsley and Bay Leaf.
Salt and Pepper to Taste.

Wet the bread and squeeze thoroughly. Chop the eggs fine and mix with the bread. Mince the herbs and add. Season well with salt and pepper. Chop the onion and fry it in one tablespoonful of butter. As it browns add the bread, into which you have mixed the sifted sage, if desired. Add, as it fries, the half square inch of ham, minced very fine. Season again to taste, and let all fry about ten minutes. Take off the stove and stuff the fowl or fish and proceed with the arrangement for baking. Egg dressing is a very nice stuffing for fish, if oysters cannot be had.

### Stuffing for Ducks.
Farci Pour les Canards.

2 Dozen Oysters.
1 Cup of Bread, Wet and Squeezed.
1 Onion Chopped Very Fine.
½ Square Inch of Ham.
1 Tablespoonful of Butter.
½ Teaspoonful of Sage.
1 Sprig Each of Thyme, Parsley and Bay Leaf, Minced Very Fine.
Salt and Pepper to Taste.

The Creoles generally stuff the domestic duck when roasted, using an oyster stuffing. (See recipe.) But many hold that the flavor of the wild duck is finer when not stuffed. This is a matter of taste. The wild duck stuffed with oysters is a most delectable dish.

Ducks may be stuffed with truffles. This is much affected by epicures when serving the famous Mallard or Canvasback Ducks at great dinings. But a duck stuffed with truffles is a very expensive dish.

The domestic duck is always roasted and stuffed. Serve with Currant Jelly.

### Stuffing for Goose.
Farci Pour l'Oie.

1 Cup of Mashed Potatoes. 4 Apples.
4 Onions. ½ Teaspoonful Powdered Sage.
½ Teaspoonful of Thyme.
Salt and Pepper to Taste.

Any stuffing used in baking a turkey may be used for roast goose, such as oyster or egg, etc. But the following is an excellent special dressing and seems to bring out more than any other the flavor of the goose:

Take one cup of mashed potatoes, four apples (peeled ncely and cored) and four onions; one-half teaspoonful of sage, powdered well; one-half teaspoonful of thyme and pepper and salt to taste. Place the apples and onions and herbs in a saucepan and add water sufficient to cover nicely. Let all cook together till soft. Then mash well and rub through a sieve. Add the cup of mashed potatoes and mix well, seasoning with salt and pepper. Stuff the body and craw, sew up and truss the goose, and bake according to recipe. (See recipe for "Roast Goose.")

### A Simple Bread Stuffing.
Farci de Pain.

1 Pint of Stale Bread, Wet and Squeezed Thoroughly.
1 Tablespoonful of Butter.
1 Tablespoonful Each of Chopped Parsley and Thyme.
1 Bay Leaf. Salt and Pepper to Taste.

Wet the bread and squeeze. Add the minced herbs and season well with salt and pepper. Mix all thoroughly and fry in butter.

### Onion Stuffing.
Farci aux Ognons.

1 Pint of Stale Bread, Wet and Squeezed Thoroughly.
1 Tablespoonful of Butter.
1 Tablespoonful Each of Chopped Parsley and Thyme.
1 Bay Leaf. Salt and Pepper to Taste.

Proceed in exactly the same manner as for bread stuffing, using also one large onion, chopped very fine, and mixed thoroughly. This is a very nice dressing and cheap.

### FORCEMEATS.
Quenelles.

Quenelles are small balls of fowl, fish meat or other chopped and hashed ingredients rolled nicely, and used as a garnish for poultry and fish, and fish or meat sauces, often adding both to the taste and beauty of a dish.

### Creole Forcemeat.
Quenelles à la Créole.

Calf's Liver. A Slice of Pork Fat.
1 Onion. 2 Sprigs of Thyme.
2 Sprigs of Parsley. 1 Bay Leaf.
½ Teaspoonful of Grated Nutmeg. 1 Tablespoonful of Butter.
Salt and Pepper to Taste.

Take calf's liver and pork fat, in the proportions of two-thirds liver and one-third fat. Grind both together very, very fine. Then mince an onion, and two sprigs each of thyme and parsley, and one bay leaf, and mix with the ground meat; add a half teaspoonful of grated nutmeg and salt and pepper to taste. Mix well. Put one tablespoonful of hot butter in a frying pan and throw in the chopped meat. Let all blend well together without cooking for about two minutes, stirring all the time. Take the mixture off, and, when it cools, form into little balls about the size and shape of a pecan. Roll these in flour, and then parboil in boiling water that has been well seasoned with pepper and salt. The balls then become Quenelles, and are used as a garnish for meats, etc. Place around the meat and pour the sauce over and serve hot. These are the genuine Quenelles.

### Sausage Forcemeat.

Quenelles de Saucisses.
¼ Pound of Fresh Pork.
2 Square Inches of Lean Raw Ham.
1 Sprig of Thyme. 1 Bay Leaf. 1 Sprig of Parsley.
A Pinch of Grated Nutmeg.
Salt and Pepper to Taste.

Hash the pork; season well with salt and pepper, according to taste, adding a pinch of grated nutmeg and the chopped herbs and minced ham. Hash all very fine and make into small balls and use as desired. This is a nice garnishing for meat when served with sauces.

### Godiveaux Forcemeat.

Quenelles Godiveaux.
¼ Pound of Suet. ¼ Pound of Lean Veal.
1 Tablespoonful of Flour.
1 Tablespoonful of Butter. ½ Gill of Cold Milk.
1 Teaspoonful Each of Minced Thyme and Parsley. 1 Bay Leaf.
2 Raw Eggs. A Pinch of Grated Nutmeg.
Salt and Pepper to Taste.

Remove all the stringy tissue from the suet and pound in a mortar; hash the veal well and mix with the meat. Take a tablespoonful of flour and blend well with half a gill of cold milk and a tablespoonful of melted butter and add to the suet and veal and blend well. Season highly with salt and pepper, and add a pinch of grated nutmeg. Then add the yolks of two raw eggs and the white of one egg, and, when well blended, strain all through a sieve, roll into balls and use as needed. In making this forcemeat, poultry or game may be used instead of veal.

### Chicken Forcemeat.

Quenelles de Volaille.
2 Raw Chicken Breasts.
The Yolks of 4 Eggs. Bread Soaked in Water.
1 Teaspoonful of Butter.
1 Bay Leaf. 1 Teaspoonful Each of Thyme and Parsley.
Salt and Pepper to Taste.
A Pinch of Grated Nutmeg.

Cut up the chicken and pound in a mortar; add an equal quantity of bread soaked in milk or water and well squeezed; add the butter and the yolks of the eggs; blend well and season highly with salt and pepper and the minced herbs, and add a pinch of grated nutmeg. Mix all together and roll into balls, and use as desired.

### Game Forcemeat.

Quenelles de Gibier.
The Breasts of Any Birds. 4 Eggs.
1 Teaspoonful of Butter.
1 Bay Leaf. 1 Sprig of Thyme. 1 Sprig of Parsley.
Salt and Pepper to Taste.

In making a forcemeat of game, use judgment in regard to quantity. The partridge is the best bird for a game forcemeat. Take two breasts of partridges, cut into pieces and pound in a mortar. Add the same quantity of bread that has been wet with milk or water and squeezed well. Add the butter and the yolks of four eggs, and season highly with salt and pepper and a pinch of grated nutmeg. Mix thoroughly and press all through a sieve. Two well-pounded truffles may be added. Use as desired.

### Fish Forcemeat.

Quenelles de Poisson.
½ Pound of Firm Fish.
The Whites of 3 Eggs.
¼ Pint of Cream or Milk. 1 Bay Leaf.
1 Teaspoonful Each of Minced Thyme and Parsley.
Salt and White Pepper to Taste.
A Pinch of Grated Nutmeg.

The left-over fish may be utilized for these Quenelles, or take a half pound of any firm fish—Sheepshead, Redfish or Red Snapper. Take out all the bones and remove the skin. Pound the fish well in a mortar, and add gradually the well-whipped whites of three eggs. Add gradually the cream or milk, and season to taste with salt and pepper, using white pepper. Add the grated nutmeg and minced herbs. Mix thoroughly, drain through a sieve, form into little balls, and use when needed.

### Crab Forcemeat.

Quenelles des Crabes.
The Meat of 12 Crabs. 1 Onion.
1 Tablespoonful of Butter.
1 Tablespoonful of Flour. ½ Teaspoonful of Salt.
1 Teaspoonful of White Pepper.
A Dash of Cayenne. 1 Clove of Garlic.
12 Mushrooms, if desired.
The Yolks of 3 Eggs.

Chop the onion very fine and fry in one tablespoonful of butter until a golden brown; then add a tablespoonful of flour and moisten with a quarter of a pint of water, or oyster juice, till the sauce begins to thicken well; season with the salt and pepper and a dash of Cayenne. Add the clove of garlic, finely minced, and the herbs. Then add the crab meat, finely minced, and the mushrooms, if desired. Cook for a half hour in the saucepan, and then take off the fire and add the yolks of the eggs. Stir again for a moment, cool, and roll into balls and use as desired.

## CHAPTER XXI.

### SAUCES FOR FISH, MEATS, POULTRY, GAME, ETC.

Des Sauces Pour les Poissons, des Viandes, la Volaille, le Gibier, etc.

The Creoles, like their French ancestors, hold that the three mother sauces, or "Sauces Méres," are Brown Sauce, or "Sauce Espagnole"; the White Sauce, or "Sauce Allemande," and the "Glace," or "Glaze." These are the foundation of all sauces, and upon their successful making depends the taste and piquancy of the numberless variety of fancy sauces that give to even the most commonplace dish an elegance all its own. The Creoles are famous for their splendid sauces, and the perfect making of a good sauce is considered an indispensible part of culinary art and domestic economy. The first thing to learn in making sauces of every kind is how to make a good "Roux," or the foundation mixture of flour and butter, or flour and lard. We have the Brown Roux and the White Roux. In making a Brown Roux, this unfailing rule must be the guide: Never, under any consideration use burnt or over-browned flour.

### Brown Roux.

Roux Brun.

1 Tablespoonful Butter. 1 Tablespoonful Flour.

In making the roux, which is the foundation of a fancy sauce, melt the tablespoonful of butter slowly, and add gradually the flour, sprinkling it in and stirring constantly, till every portion is a nice, delicate brown. Never make it too brown, because it must continue browning as the other ingredients are added in the order given in every recipe in this book. It is a great mistake to pile all ingredients, one after another, pell-mell, into a dish, in the course of preparation. The secret of good cooking lies in following implicitly the gradual introduction of the component parts in the order specified.

In making a roux for cooking gravies or smothering meats, the proportions are one tablespoonful of lard and two of flour. butter always making a richer gravy than lard, and sometimes being too rich for delicate stomachs. It is a great fad among many in our day to use nothing but butter in cooking. The Creoles hold that butter should be used in its proper place, and lard in its own. The lard is not only less expensive, but is far preferable to an inferior quality of butter, and in many cases preferable to the best butter, according to the dish in course of preparation. Properly made, the taste of lard can never be detected, and it is feared that butter is used by many to cover up, by its taste, the deficiencies of having made the roux improperly. If there is the slightest indication of burnt odor or over-browning, throw the roux away and wash the utensil before proceeding to make another. Remember that even a slightly burnt sauce will spoil the most savory dish.

### White Roux.

Roux Blanc.

1 Tablespoonful Butter. 1 Tablespoonful Flour.

The White Roux is made exactly like the Brown Roux, only that the butter and flour are put simultaneously into the saucepan, and not allowed to brown. It is then moistened with a little broth or boiling water, and allowed to boil a few minutes till thick. The White Roux is the foundation of all white sauces, or those containing milk and cream. It is also used in nearly all purées. In the Sauce Velouté it should be colored.

### GLAZE.

Glace.

5 Pounds Rump of Beef. 5 Pounds of Bones.
2 Calf's Feet.
1 Large Herb Bouquet. 1 Stalk of Celery.
3 Large Carrots.
Salt and Pepper to Taste.

Glace is the foundation of all sauces for roasts, filets, etc. In other words, it is Liebig's Beef Extract, which every housekeeper may make and keep on hand for gravies for meats. It is made as follows: Roast five pounds of the rump of the beef. Take five or six pounds of bones of beef and two calf's feet. After roasting the beef well and brown, but rare, chop it in small pieces, and put in a pot with two gallons of water. Add to this the bones and calf's feet, all raw. Then add a large herb bouquet, and one stalk of celery and three large carrots. Let the whole come to a boil. As the scum rises skim, and then season with salt and pepper to taste. Let all boil till reduced to one quart. Strain this, and it will make a jelly or glace when cold. Do not add any flour or grease. The good Creole cook considers it little short of a crime to add flour to the gravies of roast or broiled beef. This glace is then used as a "demi-glace" for sauces for sweetbreads, when they are prepared in sautés, filets of beef, etc. In making this "demi glace," take one tablespoonful of the glace, and add a spoonful of Madeira or Sherry wine. It should always be a light sauce. Use this for thickening Sauce Espagnole.

### Anchovy Sauce.
Sauce aux Beurre d'Anchois.

1 Tablespoonful of Anchovy Butter.
1½ Tablespoonfuls Flour.
1½ Tablespoonfuls Butter.

Make a White Sauce (see recipe), and add to this a tablespoonful of Anchovy butter, which comes prepared. Let it melt, season to taste in the sauce, and serve. An Anchovy Sauce may be either brown or white. Serve with boiled fish.

### Apple Sauce.
Sauce Marmalade de Pommes.

6 Large Apples.
2 Tablespoonfuls of Butter. 4 Cloves.
1 Stick Cinnamon. 1 Cup Water.

Cut the apples into pieces, peel, and let them boil till mashed into a jelly, stirring frequently, to prevent burning. Add the ground cloves and the stick of cinnamon, ground fine. Let them boil at least three-quarters of an hour, mashing as they become tender. Then take off the fire and press them through a coarse sieve. Add sugar to taste, add the butter, and set all back on the fire, and let it simmer gently for five minutes longer. Set to cool in a dish, and serve with Roast Pork or Roast Goose. The sauce must not scorch, or the taste will be spoiled.

### Béarnaise Sauce.
Sauce Béarnaise.

6 Shallots. ½ Clove of Garlic.
½ Gill of French Vinegar.
1 Tablespoonful Each of Flour and Butter.
Yolks of Four Eggs.
A Grated Nutmeg. ½ Lemon's Juice. Glace.

Chop the shallots and mince the garlic very fine. Blend the butter and flour, or take a good tablespoonful of Glace (see recipe), and moisten with a tablespoonful of White Wine and good white consommé, till you have about a pint. Set on the stove, in a porcelain-lined saucepan. Add the pepper and salt and butter, and a quarter of a teaspoonful of grated nutmeg. Add half a gill of vinegar and the juice of a lemon, according to taste and acidity. When of the consistency approaching starch, take from the fire and add the yolks of four eggs, beaten well, and stirring all the time, till you have the consistency of a thick starch. Serve immediately, with broiled steak, broiled chops, broiled fish, etc.

### Béchamel Sauce.
Sauce Béchamel.

2 Ounces of Raw Ham. 2 Fresh Mushrooms.
1 Tablespoonful of Butter.
1 Pint of Veloute Sauce. 2 Gills Rich Cream.
1 Stick of Celery, Cut Very Fine.
½ Carrot, Cut Very Fine.
½ Onion, Chopped Very Fine.
1 Bunch Sweet Herbs. 2 Cloves. 4 Allspice.
Blade of Mace.

Put the butter in a saucepan, and as it melts add the chopped onion, and let it stew until very tender, but do not let it brown. Mince the ham and cut the vegetables very fine, and add first the ham, letting it brown a minute, and then the vegetables, herbs and spices. Let all simmer gently for ten minutes, without browning. Add the Veloutée Sauce (see recipe,) stir in well, and bring all to a boil. Let it boil ten minutes, and be sure to stir constantly. Then add, by gentle degrees, the cream, which should not be heated, but which must be very rich and sweet (if not perfectly sweet it will spoil the sauce). When all this is blended, the sauce is of a velvet smoothness, and very delicious. Strain and set on the fire a minute longer to heat, and serve hot. It is served with fish, chicken and sweetbreads.

### Bordelaise Sauce.
Sauce à la Bordelaise.

2 Shallots. ½ Glass Claret.
3-4 Pint of Sauce Espagnole.
A Dash of Red Pepper.

Cut two shallots very fine; put in a saucepan with a half glassful of Claret; reduce one-half; add three-quarters of a pint of good Sauce Espagnole (see recipe) and a dash of red pepper. Cook for twenty minutes and serve hot. In serving this sauce, the flavor may be increased by adding a dozen round slices of blanched Marrons.

### Bordelaise Sauce, Creole Style.
Bordelaise Sauce à la Créole.

1 Onion or 2 Shallots.
1 Tablespoonful of Olive Oil.
Salt and Pepper to Taste.

Peel the onion or shallots and chop fine. Put in a saucepan with one tablespoonful of olive oil; let the onion sauté well, and pour the sauce over tenderloin filets or sirloin steaks when it is desired to serve these à la Bordelaise. A tablespoonful of Red Wine may be added to the sauce.

### Brown Sauce.
Sauce Espagnole.

1 Pound of Neck or Brisket of Veal.
Bones of Beef.
1 Gallon of Water. 2 Tablespoonfuls of Lard.

½ Can Mushrooms or ¼ Can Truffles.
2 Carrots. 2 Tablespoonfuls of Flour.
2 Cloves Garlic. 1 Herb Bouquet.
1 Wineglass of Sherry.

Take a good quantity of bones, place in a gallon of boiling water, and make a strong consommé, seasoning well with salt and pepper. Take a piece of the brisket or neck of the beef, and roast rare, so that the blood spurts out when pricked with a needle. After roasting cut it in pieces of about one inch square. Take two tablespoonfuls of lard and three of flour, and brown slightly, stirring all the time. After browning, add the water of the consommé, which has been reduced to about half a gallon, pouring it in slowly and stirring constantly. Then add all the pieces of the roast beef which you have cut. Add three carrots, two cloves of garlic, one onion, an herb bouquet (tied together of thyme, parsley and bay leaf), and let the whole boil well two hours, stirring every five minutes until reduced to the consistency of starch. Then strain well through a strainer or sieve, season to taste, and set back on the stove to cook a few minutes longer. Taste, and if sufficiently seasoned take it off and allow it to get cool. This sauce is then used as a foundation sauce, and will keep for at least one month in our climate of New Orleans, if put in a cool place in winter or the ice box in summer.

The Brown Sauce, or Sauce Espagnole, is made by taking out of this foundation sauce one tablespoonful at a time, and then adding one wineglass or two tablespoonfuls of Sherry, to dissolve, and a half pint of broth. Set it to boil again, and add a half can of mushrooms or truffles, as desired. It is used for all meats, fish or fowl, served hot.

If one does not desire to keep it, and it is a matter of economy to do so, it can be made by reducing the proportions for the dish to be prepared, simply browning one tablespoonful of butter and two of flour, adding at the right time a pint of boiling broth, and Sherry to taste.

### Brown Butter Sauce.
Sauce aux Beurre Noir.
¼ Pound of Butter.
2 Tablespoonfuls of Cut Parsley (not chopped).
3 Tablespoonfuls Juice of Lemon or Vinegar.
Salt and Pepper to Taste.

Melt the butter in a saucepan, and when it begins to smoke it is browning. Then add two tablespoonfuls of cut parsley, and let it brown half a minute longer. Then add three tablespoonfuls of the juice of a lemon or Tarragon Vinegar, and let it simmer two minutes longer, and serve with Stingaree or Rai aux Beurre Noir (see recipe), calves' brains or crawfish boiled.

### Bread Sauce.
Sauce de Pain.
1½ Ounces of Fresh Bread Crumbs.
½ Cup of Cold Water.
½ Ounce of Butter.
1 Cup of Cream or Milk.
6 Whole Peppers.
Salt and Pepper to Taste.

Crumble the bread and place in a saucepan with the water; add the butter, salt and peppers. Cook for five minutes and add the milk. Cook five minutes longer, remove the peppers and serve hot.

### Caper Sauce.
Sauce aux Câpres.

Make a White Sauce, as above, and add a half cup of finely-cut French capers before serving. This sauce is served with boiled mutton.

### Cauliflower Sauce.
Sauce aux Chouxfleurs.

For this sauce, as a foundation, first make the Cream Sauce (see recipe), and add to it the flowerets of the cauliflower, which you will have previously boiled till tender, and cut very fine. Serve with boiled fish, veal sauté, boiled cauliflower, etc.

### Chambord Sauce.
Sauce à la Chambord.
1 Tablespoonful of Butter.
1 Large Onion Minced. 1 Sprig of Thyme.
1 Bay Leaf. 3 Large Tomatoes.
1 Truffle, If Desired.
6 Thinly Sliced Mushrooms.
1 Pint Oyster Water.
Salt and Pepper to Taste.
2 Sprigs of Parsley. 2 Cloves, Mashed.
4 Allspice, Ground.

Brown the onion in the butter, but do not let it burn. Add three large tomatoes, chopped fine, with their juice and the finely-minced herbs, the thinly-sliced truffles and mushrooms. Let these brown well for about ten minutes. Then add the pint of oyster water, and season to taste. Add, if you have them, three or four crawfish, chopped fine, and one dozen oysters. Let all boil twenty minutes longer, and season to taste. Serve with Baked Red Snapper and other baked fish.

### Champagne Sauce.
Sauce au Champagne.
1 Glass of Champagne. 2 Cloves.
6 Whole Peppers. 1 Bay Leaf.
3-4 of a Pint of Sauce Espagnole.
½ Teaspoonful of Powdered Sugar.

Put the Champagne, cloves, peppers, bay leaf and sugar in a saucepan; set on the fire and reduce for five minutes. Then moisten the mixture with three quarters of a pint of Sauce

Espagnole and let it cook for fifteen minutes longer. Strain well and serve.

### Chili Sauce.
### Sauce au Chili.

6 Tomatoes. 4 Green Peppers. 1 Onion.
1 Tablespoonful of Salt.
1 ½ Cups of Vinegar.
Cayenne and Chili Pepper to Taste.

Boil the vinegar and add the chopped tomatoes and green peppers and the minced onion, adding a tablespoonful of sugar. Let all boil one hour. Season to taste, strain, and serve with any fish or meats.

### Chestnut Sauce.
### Sauce aux Marrons.

1 Pint of Large Roasted Chestnuts.
1 Pint of Boiling Stock.
1 Tablespoonful Flour. 1 Tablespoonful Butter.
Salt and Pepper to Taste.

Roast the chestnuts, and peel and mash them very fine. Make a Brown Roux with the flour and butter, and add the boiling stock. Let it boil for about five minutes, and add the mashed chestnuts, stirring constantly, and seasoning to taste. Let it boil for two minutes, take off and serve hot, with Broiled Dindonneau (turkey chicks). This is a great Creole dish and is considered a most recherché and delicate one. The sauce may also be served with Roast Turkey.

### Celery Sauce.
### Sauce au Céleri.

Mince the celery well; put it in a saucepan and cover with boiling water. Let it boil about thirty minutes, until tender. Then make a Cream Sauce.

### Colbert Sauce.
### Sauce Colbert.

½ Pint of Madeira Sauce.
1 Tablespoonful of Butter.
2 Tablespoonfuls of Consomme.
1 Teaspoonful of Chopped Parsley.
The Juice of Half a Lemon.

Put a pint of very thick Madeira Sauce (see recipe) in a saucepan, add gradually the butter and consommé and mix well without allowing the mixture to boil. When ready to serve add the juice of half a lemon and a teaspoonful of chopped parsley.

### Cream Sauce.
### Sauce à la Crême.

1 Tablespoonful Butter. 1 Tablespoonful Flour.
2 Gills of Fresh Milk or Cream.
Salt and Pepper to Taste.

Melt the butter in the saucepan, and add the flour gradually, letting it blend without browning in the least. Add the boiling milk or cream and stir without ceasing. Add salt and white pepper to taste, and serve immediately with boiled fish, etc.

### Cranberry Sauce.
### Sauce aux Airelles.

Wash the cranberries in cold water, and pick well, rejecting all those that float on top or are in any manner over-ripe and spoiled. Put them in a porcelain-lined saucepan, with one pint of water, and let them boil over a moderate fire, stirring occasionally with a wooden spoon, and mashing the fruit as much as possible. When the berries have cooked about twenty minutes, remove the saucepan from the fire, and add the sugar stirring in sufficient to sweeten nicely. Let them cook at least ten or fifteen minutes longer, after adding the sugar, and put into an earthern bowl, and let the sauce cool. Never strain the sauce. Many do, but the Creoles have found out that cranberry jelly is a very poor and insipid sauce, compared with that of the whole fruit, when formed into a sauce in an earthern mold. Liquid cranberry is a very poor apology for the dainty crimson mold of the native fruit. The following directions for cooking this fruit are given in detail, because so few know how to purchase and prepare it properly:

Never, when buying cranberries, select the pale, whitish fruit. They are unripe and unfit for use. Select fine, large, crimson-colored fruit.

Never cook cranberries in a metal saucepan; nor even in one of agate or the brightest tin. The berries absorb the taste, as they are an acid fruit, and your best efforts will fail in making a fine sauce. Use always a porcelain-lined saucepan.

Do not put much water in the cranberries. The proportion of a half a pint cupful to every quart should be rigidly observed.

Never add the sugar to the cranberries until they have first boiled steadily at least twenty minutes, or else the cranberries are liable to burn. After twenty minutes, add sugar to taste. Do not be sparing of the sugar. Be careful to measure out a good, full pint for every quart of berries you are cooking. Take the cranberries off the stove, and stir in the sugar thoroughly, and let them boil again at least ten or fifteen minutes after you have added the sugar. Stir them often to keep from burning.

Never put the cooked cranberries into tin or metal molds. Use always an earthenware bowl or mold.

Never dip the molds into water before putting in the cranberries. Let them be well washed and dried some time, as dipping them into water renders the cranberries bitter. When you wish to remove the cranberries from the bowl or mold press them on the top, and gently loosen them at the bottom by setting the mold into hot water long enough to warm it through, and thus loosen the cranberries, without warming them.

And, finally, remember never to strain the cranberries, and not to use them on the same day on which they were cooked. Let them stand at least overnight, or twenty-four hours, in a cool place, before serving. Serve Cranberry Sauce with Roast Turkey.

### Crapaudine Sauce.

Sauce à la Crapaudine.

1 Pint of Sauce Piquante.
8 Chopped Mushrooms.
1 Teaspoonful of Dry Mustard.
2 Teaspoonfuls of Tarragon Vinegar.

Put a half pint of very light Piquante Sauce on the fire, add the mushrooms finely chopped and a teaspoonful of dry mustard, which has been well diluted in two tablespoonfuls of Tarragon vinegar. Let the sauce boil for five minuetes and serve hot.

### Creole Sauce.

Sauce à la Créole.

2 Tomatoes. 6 Shallots.
1 Chopped Sweet Pepper.
1 Glass Sherry. Salt and Cayenne to Taste.

Make a Tomato Sauce quite brown. (See recipe.) Add the chopped shallots and sweet pepper, and, when these are browned, add one wine glass full of Sherry wine, seasoning highly. Serve with meats.

### Cucumber Sauce.

Sauce aux Concombres.

1 Nice. Tender Cucumber.
2 Tablespoonfuls of Prepared Mustard.
The Yolk of One Egg. Seasoning to Taste.

Peel and grate the cucumber, and add the mustard, mixing thoroughly. Add the juice of one lemon and the yolk of one egg, beaten thoroughly. This is a delicious salad dressing.

### Currant Jelly Sauce.

Sauce à la Gelée de Groseilles.

½ Tumbler of Currant Jelly.
4 Tablespoonfuls of Butter. 1 Gill Water.
1 Gill of Port or Madeira Wine.

Melt the butter, and add the jelly, blending well, and then add the gill of wine and water. Add a little salt and sugar to taste. The sauce is much finer when made of wine without water, but this is a question of taste. If the wine only is used, double the proportions, or according to taste. This sauce is served with Venison and other game.

### Drawn Butter Sauce.

Sauce aux Beurre.

2 Tablespoonfuls of Butter.
1 Tablespoonful Chopped Parsley.
Juice of 1 Lemon.

This sauce is made simply by melting butter and adding a little chopped parsley. Add the juice of a lemon, if desired. It is used as a garnish for broiled meat, fish, chicken, etc.

### Demi-Glace.

Demi-Glace.

1 Pint of Sauce Espagnole.
1 Glass of Madeira Wine.
1 Glass of Mushroom Liquor.
1 Herb Bouquet. 1 Teaspoonful of Pepper.
Salt to Taste.

To one pint of Sauce Espagnole (see recipe) add a glass of Madeira wine and a glass of mushroom liquor, a herb bouquet and a teaspoonful of pepper. Carefully remove all fat and set on the fire and cook for thirty minutes, Strain and use when needed. This sauce is used in all recipes where Madeira Sauce is indicated as a foundation sauce.

### Devil's Sauce.

Sauce à la Diable.

1 Onion. 2 Cloves of Garlic.
3 Tablespoonfuls of Butter.
1 Pickle a Finger Long. 1 Teaspoonful of Mustard.
2 Gills of Consomme. Salt and Cayenne.
1 Glass of White Wine. Juice of a Lemon.

Brown the onion in butter, and add the two cloves of garlic, minced very fine. When brown, add one pickle, minced very fine, and add a teaspoonful of mustard prepared. Then add two gills of consommé and one glass of White Wine, and the juice of a lemon, and allow it to cook slowly. Season with salt and hot pepper (piment fort), and serve with shell fish, chicken, sweetbreads, etc. This is a hot sauce.

### Duxelle Sauce.

Sauce Duxelle.

1 Pint of Madeira Sauce.
½ Glass of White Wine.
12 Mushrooms. 2 Shallots.
½ Ounce of Beef Tongue.
½ Tablespoonful of Butter.
Salt and Pepper to Taste.

Put half a pint of Madeira Sauce and a half glass of White wine in a saucepan. Add the mushrooms, which must be chopped very fine. Then add the shallots, which will have also been chopped fine and browned in butter. Let this reduce slightly and add half an ounce of finely chopped cooked beef tongue. Let all boi for five minutes and serve hot.

### Egg Sauce.
#### Sauce aux Oeufs.

The Yolks of 3 Eggs.
2 Chopped Hard-Boiled Eggs.
1 Bay Leaf, Minced Fine.   1 Onion.
6 Peppers.
2 Tablespoonfuls of Flour.   2 Tablespoonfuls of Butter.
½ Teaspoonful of Grated Nutmeg.
1 Pint of Veal or Chicken Broth.

Chop the onions and put in the saucepan with the butter and bay leaf. Stir in the flour to thicken and moisten with the broth. Mix well, and add the nutmeg, and salt and pepper to taste. Beat the yolks of the eggs separately with the juice of half a lemon. Pour gradually into the sauce, but do not let it boil after they are added. Press through a sieve, and, when ready to serve, sprinkle with two chopped hard-boiled eggs and a teaspoonful of minced parsley.

### Hard-Egg Sauce.
#### Sauce aux Oeufs Durs.

Make a White Sauce, as above, and add three or two hard-boiled eggs, chopped, but not too fine, and a little finely-minced parsley as a garnish. This sauce is served with boiled fish or boiled chicken or other fowl.

### Genoese Sauce.
#### Sauce à la Genoise.

1 Tablespoonful of Butter.
2 Tablespoonfuls of Flour.
1 Glassfull of Claret.
1 Tablespoonful of Chopped Parsley.
½ Pint of Water.
Salt, Pepper, Nutmeg, and Allspice to Taste.

Melt a tablespoonful of butter, stir in two tablesponfuls of flour, and mix well till smooth. Then add a wineglassful of Claret, stirring all well. To this add about half a pint of water, and season with pepper and salt and a little nutmeg and allspice. Let the sauce simmer and reduce to about one-half. Add parsley as a garnish and serve with boiled fish or boiled meat.

### Giblet Sauce.
#### Sauce d'Abbattis.

The Turkey Giblets.   1 Cup of Water.
Salt and Pepper to Taste.

Put the giblets or simply the gizzard into a saucepan and cover well with water. Let them simmer as long as the turkey roasts, then cut them fine and take the turkey out of the pan on which it has been roasted. Add the giblets and stir well, and then add a cup of the water in which the giblets have been boiled. Season to the taste and serve in a sauce dish, pouring over the dressing when serving the turkey.

### Hollandaise Sauce.
#### Sauce à la Hollandaise.

1 Tablespoonful of Melted Butter.
The Juice of Half a Lemon.   Yolk of 1 Egg.
Salt and Pepper to Taste.
1 Teaspoonful of Chopped Parsley.

Sauce à la Hollandaise is nothing more than a Drawn Butter Sauce, to which the juice of a lemon and the yolk of an egg have been added. Melt the butter; add the juice of half a lemon; mix well and take off the stove and add the yolk of one egg, well beaten. Add a teaspoonful of chopped parsley, beating steadily. This sauce is very light, and as soon as removed from the fire is served hot with the fish.

### Horseradish Sauce.
#### Sauce au Raifort.

3 Eggs.   1 Cup Cream.   Grated Horseradish.
Salt and Pepper to Taste.
½ Pint of Consomme or Broth.

Grate the horseradish in sufficient quantity for use, and place it in a saucepan with the boiling stock. Let it boil about ten minutes, or less, until tender. Season to taste. In the meantime rub the eggs in a bowl with the cream, beating and mixing thoroughly. Add these to the horseradish, stirring constantly, but do not let the sauce boil, or the horseradish will curdle. Serve with roast meats or with baked fish.

### Hunters' Sauce.
#### Sauce à la Chasseur.

2 Tablespoonfuls of Butter.
2 Tablespoonfuls of Flour.
3 Tomatoes.   2 Onions.   6 Mushrooms.
1 Pint of Consomme.

Put the flour and butter into a saucepan and blend well; then moisten with one pint of consommé or water; add the chopped tomatoes, onions and mushrooms and season with a pinch of salt and pepper; add an herb bouquet and let it boil for an hour; before serving add the juice of a lemon or six drops of vinegar. If you have fresh game two tablespoonfuls of blood may be added but do not let it boil after this.

### Italian Sauce.
#### Sauce à l'Italienne.

1 Tablespoonful Butter.   1 Tablespoonful Flour.
8 Shallots, Greens and White.
1 Tablespoonful of Chopped Parsley.
½ of a Lemon's Juice.   ½ Can Mushrooms.
Consomme.   Salt and Pepper to Taste.
Cayenne to Taste.

A Sauce à l'Italienne may be either brown or white. If mushrooms are used, make a white sauce, that is, let the butter and flour blend without browning. Add a half cup of consommé and a half can of chopped mushrooms, the white of the shallot (chopped very fine) and the juice of half a lemon. If a brown sauce, add the shallots to the butter and flour, which you will have browned, using the chopped white and green of the shallots. Then add a half pint of consommé, and let it simmer for about an hour, and add the juice of a lemon and serve.

The white sauce is used for fish, the brown for meats. Always season to taste.

### Financier Sauce.

Sauce à la Financiére.

2 Tablespoonfuls of Butter.
1 Tablespoonful of Flour.
6 Stoned Olives.   12 Mushrooms.
1 Glass of Sherry Wine.
Salt and Pepper to Taste.
A Dash of Cayenne.

Melt the butter, then remove from the fire and add the flour. Blend with a wooden spoon till smooth. Moisten with one pint of consommé till it reaches the consistency of cream. Then add the chopped mushrooms, stoned olives, pepper, salt and Cayenne. Before serving add the wine. Serve hot.

### Jolie Fille Sauce.

Sauce à la Belle Créole.

The Yolks of 2 Hard-Boiled Eggs.
½ Cup Bread Crumbs.
1 Tablespoonful of Chopped Parsley.
1 Tablespoonful Butter.   ½ Cup of Cream.
Salt and Pepper to Taste.

Put the butter into the saucepan, and add the flour, letting it blend well, without burning or browning, for this is a white sauce. When it becomes a delicate yellow, add the bread crumbs, stir for one minute, and add the half cup of consommé or broth. Stir well, and add a half cup of cream, and salt and pepper to taste. Add the chopped parsley as a garnish, and a little onion juice. Take off the fire and add the well-chopped yolks of two eggs, and a tablespoonful of lemon juice. Serve with boiled fish or boiled meats of any kind.

### Lyonnaise Sauce.

Sauce à la Lyonnaise.

1 Dozen Tomatoes.   Equal Parts of Onions.
⅓ Spoon of Butter.  2 Cloves of Garlic.
1 Sprig Each of Thyme and Bay Leaf, Minced Fine.
Sherry to Taste.   1 Tablespoonful of Flour.
Salt and Pepper and Cayenne to Taste.

Make a good Tomato Sauce (see recipe), and add to this the equal parts of onion browned in butter. Stir well, add a little lemon juice, and serve with any meats.

### Madeira Sauce.

Sauce Madère.

2 Gills of Espagnole Sauce or Brown Sauce.
1 Gill of Truffles, Cut in Two.
1 Gill of Mushrooms, Cut in Two.
1 Glass of Madeira Wine.

Make a Sauce Espagnole (see recipe), and let it boil for about five minutes. Add salt and pepper to taste, and the mushrooms and truffles, cut in pieces. Let them boil for ten minutes, and then stir in the wine. If you have not the Madeira, use Sherry wine. Serve with Filet of Beef Roasted, etc.

### Maître d'Hotel Sauce.

Sauce à la Maitre d'Hotel.

1 Tablespoonful Butter. 1 Tablespoonful Flour.
The Juice of ½ a Lemon.
1 Tablespoonful of Chopped Parsley.
1 Pint of Clear Water.

Put the butter and the flour in the saucepan and let them blend without burning. Mix well over a slow fire, and add one pint of consommé. Add the juice of half a lemon and the chopped parsley, and let all boil about fifteen minutes. When it reaches this point take off the stove and add the yolk of one egg, well beaten; mix well, stirring round, and serve with boiled fish, etc.

Never add egg while the sauce is on the fire, as it will curdle immediately.

### Mayonnaise Sauce.

Sauce Mayonnaise.

Yolk of 1 Egg.
Sweet Oil.    Lemon.    Vinegar.
Pepper and Salt.

Take the yolk of one fresh egg, raw, and put in a bowl. The egg and the oil must be cold, and in summer it is well to keep the soup plate in which you make the dressing on cracked ice in a pan, so that the oil will not run. Put the yolk in a plate; add, drop by drop, a little sweet oil from the bottle. When you have dropped about a spoonful, being careful to work it into the yolk of the egg drop by drop and blend all the time, take a lemon and drop a few drops into the mixture. It will at once begin to harden as you stir it in. Continue stirring till the egg grows hard, and then steadily, drop by drop, let the oil fall, working it all the time with your fork into the egg. Have another spoon, begin to drop in the lemon juice, working it the same way again till it hardens the egg. Then begin again with the oil and work again, and again drop the lemon till you have the juice of half a lemon and about two gills of oil, finishing with the oil. When the egg begins to curdle, add a little salt, but do not add this salt till the mayonnaise is complete. Serve very cold, with salads, etc.

Mayonnaise is the standing sauce for chicken salad, shrimp salad, crab salad, etc. When making for these large salads, as a garnish use three yolks of eggs and other ingredients in proportion.

### Mushroom Sauce.
### Sauce aux Champignons.

½ Pint of Broth (white) or Boiling Water. Lemon Juice. 1 Can of Mushrooms.
1 Tablespoonful Butter. 1 Tablespoonful Flour.
Salt and Pepper to Taste.

Make a Brown Roux, melting the butter in the saucepan, and adding the flour, and stirring till well browned. Then stir in the boiling stock, or water, if you have not the stock; add the mushrooms, and salt and pepper to taste. Add the juice of half a lemon and let it cook for about fifteen minutes longer. This is a fine sauce for Roast Filet of Beef. Pour the sauce over the filet, and serve hot.

### Mint Sauce.
### Sauce Menthe.

1 Good Handful of Mint, Chopped Very Fine.
1 Tablespoonful of Tarragon Vinegar.
1 Teaspoonful of Sugar.
A Pint of White Beef Stock.
Salt and Pepper to Taste.

Chop one good handful of fresh mint and put it in a bowl; add a teaspoonful of Tarragon Vinegar and one teaspoonful of sugar. To this add one pint of good white beef stock. Mix all together and place in a bain marie or hot-water bath —that is, stand in a saucepan of hot water on the fire and let it warm without boiling. If the mint boils, it will be very bitter. Serve with roast lamb.

### Normandy Sauce.
### Sauce à la Normande.

1 Pint of Sauce Velouté.
2 Tablespoonfuls of Mushroom Liquor.
2 Tablespoonfuls of Fish Stock. The Yolks of 2 Eggs.
The Juice of Half a Lemon.

Make a pint of Sauce Velouté (see recipe) and add the mushroom liquor. Reduce for about ten minutes and add two tablespoonfuls of Fish Stock or Oyster Juice; if not at hand add hot water. Let it all boil again, and then add the yolks of two eggs and the juice of a lemon. Strain through a fine sieve, and add a teaspoonful of fresh butter and serve with fish. The sauce should be of the consistency of cream.

### Onion Sauce.
### Sauce Soubise.

8 Onions. 1 Tablespoonful of Butter.
1 Tablespoonful of Flour. Lemon Juice.

Boil the onions until quite tender, adding salt and pepper. When soft, mash well and pass through a sieve. Take one spoon of butter and one of flour and melt, blending together without burning, or allowing to brown. In this cream dissolve the purée of onions, boiling gently for ten minutes and stirring well. Add the juice of a lemon, a teaspoon of vinegar, and serve with cutlets of lamb, fried sweetbreads, etc.

### Oyster Sauce.
### Sauce aux Huitres.

2 Dozen Oysters. The Oyster Water.
1 Tablespoonful Butter. 1 Tablespoonful Flour.
Salt and Pepper to Taste.

Boil the oysters in their own water. Add a nice herb bouquet while boiling. Take a tablespoonful of butter and one of flour and put into a saucepan, and mix well without browning; water this with the juice of the oysters, sufficient to make one pint; season to taste. Let it boil for ten or fifteen minutes, and, when it reaches a thick consistency, serve with freshly added oysters, taking the old ones out, because oysters that have boiled more than three minutes are unfit for eating, being hard and indigestible; or the sauce may be served without the oysters. This is a sauce for boiled fish, etc.

### Parsley Cream Sauce.
### Sauce à la Crème de Persil.

A Tablespoonful and a Half of Butter.
A Tablespoonful and a Half of Flour.
Half a Cup of Water or White Broth.
Salt and Pepper to Taste.

To the recipe for White Sauce add one tablespoonful and a half of finely minced parsley. You may also add a tablespoonful of cream. This is nice with boiled fish or boiled chicken.

### Pepper Sauce.
### Sauce Poivrade.

1 Carrot, Minced Fine.
2 Sprigs Each of Thyme and Parsley.
1 Onion, Minced Fine.
½ Pint of Consomme. 1 Bay Leaf.
1 Wineglass of Sherry or Madeira.
½ Grated Lemon. 1 Small Piece of Celery.
Salt and Black Pepper to Taste.
1 Tablespoonful Butter. 1 Tablespoonful Flour.
A Dash of Cayenne.

Put the butter in the saucepan, and, as it melts, add the flour. Let it brown slowly, and then add one pint of Consommé. Let it boil, and add the minced herbs and vegetables and the zest or outer skin of half a grated lemon. (The zest is the skin of a lemon, grated off without touching the inner white skin or pulp.) Let all boil slowly for an hour and a half. Add a wineglassful of Sherry or Madeira and season with salt and black pepper (hot) and a dash of Cayenne. Let it boil for ten minutes longer, take off the stove and strain, and serve with any game.

### Pepper Sauce for Venison.
Sauce Poivrade pour le Chevreuil.

1 Carrot, Minced Fine.
2 Sprigs Each of Thyme and Parsley.
1 Onion, Minced Fine.
½ Pint of Consomme. 1 Bay Leaf.
1 Wineglass of Sherry or Madeira.
½ Grated Lemon. 1 Small Piece of Celery.
Salt and Black Pepper to Taste.
1 Tablespoonful Butter. 1 Tablespoonful Flour.
A Dash of Cayenne.

This sauce is made in exactly the same manner as Sauce Poivrade (see recipe), with this difference, that when it is to be served with venison a half glass of Currant Jelly is added, and the sauce allowed to boil ten minutes longer.

### Pickle Sauce.
Sauce aux Cornichons.

A Tablespoonful and a Half of Butter.
A Tablespoonful and a Half of Flour.
Half a Cup of Water or White Broth.
Salt and Pepper to Taste.

To the recipe for White Sauce (see recipe) add chopped gherkins, or any other vinegar pickles, using about two or three. Add, just before serving. Serve with fish.

### Piquant Sauce.
Sauce Piquante.

2 Onions. 1 Tablespoonful of Butter.
2 Cloves of Garlic.
1 Sprig Each of Thyme, Parsley and Bay Leaf.
2 Pickles, 2 Inches in Length.
1 Teaspoonful of Strong French Vinegar.
Salt and Pepper to Taste.
Cayenne or Hot Pepper.

Chop two onions very fine. Smother in a tablespoonful of butter. When well cooked, without burning, add one tablespoonful of consommé or water. Add two cloves of garlic, minced very fine, and the herbs minced very fine. Season to taste with hot pepper. Take two pickles about two inches in length, and cut into thin slices of about a quarter of an inch in thickness. Put this into the sauce, with a teaspoonful of strong vinegar, and let the whole boil about five minutes. Serve with boiled beef, boiled beef tongue, boiled pork tongue, or any boiled meats.

### Poulette Sauce.
Sauce à la Poulette.

1 Tablespoonful Butter. 1 Tablespoonful Flour.
The Yolks of 2 Eggs.
1 Tablespoonful of Chopped Parsley.
½ Pint of Consomme or Water.
Juice of an Onion. Salt and Pepper to Taste.
The Juice of Half a Lemon.

Melt the butter and flour, blending well without browning. Add a half pint of water, or consommé, the juice of one lemon, and let it simmer twenty minutes. Season to taste. Take from the fire, add the yolks of two well-beaten eggs and the juice of a lemon and serve immediately. No sauce into which the yolks of eggs are beaten must be set on the fire after adding these. If necessary to keep warm, set in a bowl of boiling water (a "bain-marie") till ready to serve. It is best served immediately.

### Ravigote Sauce (Cold.)
Sauce Ravigote.

12 Shallots. 2 Cloves of Garlic. 1 Pickle.
1 Tablespoonful of Mustard.
1 Tablespoonful of Vinegar.
The Yolk of an Egg.
4 Sprigs of Chopped Parsley.
1 Sprig Each of Thyme and Bay Leaf.

Chop the shallots, greens and white all very fine, and mince the cloves of two garlics very fine. Put these in a bowl, and add one pickle of about three inches long, chopped very fine; drain the pickle first of all water; add a good bunch of parsley, chopped very fine. Mix all this together in a bowl, and add one tablespoonful of mustard. Mix well. Add a good tablespoonful of vinegar and salt and pepper to taste. Beat the yolk of an egg and mix well in the sauce. This sauce is to be served cold, with cold meats, turkey or fowl.

### Ravigote Sauce (Hot).
Sauce Ravigote.

12 Shallots. 1 Tablespoonful of Vinegar.
2 Tablespoonfuls of Chopped Parsley.
Salt and Pepper to Taste.

Chop the parsley very fine. Have ready a "Sauce Veloutée." (See recipe.) Add the other ingredients. Mix well. Place in a saucepan and set in boiling water and let it heat, and serve hot with fish, white meats of chicken, etc.

### Sauce Rémoulade.
Rémoulade (Cold).

3 Hard-Boiled Eggs. 1 Raw Yolk of Egg.
1 Tablespoonful of Tarragon Vinegar.
3 Tablespoonfuls of Olive Oil.
½ Clove of Garlic, Minced Very Fine.
½ Teaspoonful of Prepared Mustard.
Salt and Cayenne to Taste.

A Rémoulade is a cold sauce, and is always served with cold meats. Boil the eggs till hard. Remove the shells and set aside the whites, which you will have crumbled fine for a garnish. Put the yolks into a bowl mash very fine, till perfectly smooth, add the mustard and mix well, and the seasonings of vinegar and salt and Cayenne to taste. Then add the olive oil, drop by drop, working in the egg all the time, and then add the yolk of the raw egg, and work in thoroughly, till light. Then add the juice of half a lemon. Mix well, increasing the quantities of oil or vinegar, according to taste, very slightly. If the sauce is not thoroughly mixed, it will curdle. It is now ready to be served with cold meats, fish or salads.

### Green Rémoulade.
#### Rémoulade Verte.

3 Hard-Boiled Eggs. 1 Raw Yolk of Egg.
1 Tablespoonful of Tarragon Vinegar.
3 Tablespoonfuls of Olive Oil.
½ Clove of Garlic, Minced Very Fine.
½ Teaspoonful of Prepared Mustard.
Salt and Cayenne to Taste.

A Green Rémoulade is made in exactly the same manner as the above, only it is colored with the juice of spinach or parsley, using about two tablespoonfuls of either.

### Robert Sauce.
#### Sauce Robert.

2 Onions. 1 Tablespoonful of Butter.
2 Cloves of Garlic.
1 Sprig Each of Thyme, Parsley and Bay Leaf.
2 Pickles, 2 Inches in Length.
1 Teaspoonful of Strong French Vinegar.
Salt and Pepper to Taste.
Cayenne or Hot Pepper.

Make a Sauce Piquante (see recipe) and add a teaspoonful more of prepared mustard, and two more of minced parsley, the juice of a lemon, and let it boil up once, and serve with steak, pork chops, liver sauté, turkey or goose.

### Spanish Sauce.
#### Sauce Espagnole.

¼ Pound of Brisket or Veal.
Bones of Beef.
1 Quart of Water. 1 Tablespoonful of Lard.
½ Can Mushrooms or ¼ Can Truffles.
1 Carrot. 1 Tablespoonful of Flour.
1 Clove of Garlic.
2 Sprigs Each of Thyme and Parsley.
1 Bay Leaf.
1 Wineglass of Sherry.

Take a good quantity of bones, place in a quart of boiling water, and make a strong consommé, seasoning well with salt and pepper. Take a piece of the brisket or neck of the beef, and roast rare, so that the blood spurts out when pricked with a needle. After roasting cut it in pieces of about one inch square. Take two tablespoonfuls of lard and three of flour, and brown slightly, stirring all the time. After browning add the water of the consommé, which has been reduced to about half a pint, pouring it in slowly and stirring constantly. Then add all the pieces of the roast beef which you have cut. Add three carrots, two cloves of garlic, one onion, a herb bouquet, tied together, of thyme, parsley and bay leaf, and let the whole boil well two hours, stirring every five minutes, until reduced to the consistency of starch. Then strain well through a strainer or sieve, season to taste, and set back on the stove to cook a few minutes longer. Add one wineglass or two tablespoonfuls of Sherry to dissolve, and a half pint of broth. Set it to boil again, and add a half can of mushrooms or truffles, as desired. It is used for all meats, fish and fowl, served hot.

### Sauce Tartare.
#### Sauce à la Tartare.

A Mayonnaise Sauce. 6 Shallots.
½ Clove of Garlic. 1 Pickle.
A Handful of Parsley. Minced Fine.
1 Teaspoonful Mustard.

Prepare the Mayonnaise as directed above. Put in a bowl a half dozen shallots, greens and all, and chop fine; add a handful of parsley, chopped fine; and the half-minced clove, and one whole pickle, well chopped. Mix all this together and put in a cloth and strain out the juice by pressing. Add this juice to the Mayonnaise, and add one teaspoonful of mustard, salt, Cayenne and black pepper to taste. This is served with filet of trout, etc.

### Tomato Sauce.
#### Sauce aux Tomates.

1 Dozen Tomatoes.
½ Spoonful of Butter. 2 Cloves of Garlic.
1 Sprig Each of Thyme and Bay Leaf.
Minced Fine.
Sherry to Taste.
1 Tablespoonful of Flour.
Salt and Pepper and Cayenne to Taste.

Take one dozen large tomatoes, or one can, and put in a pot to boil, with one-half tablespoonful of butter. Add salt and pepper to taste, and one pint of water. Let it cook for about ten minutes and add minced thyme, parsley and bay leaf, very fine, and two cloves of garlic, minced fine. Let it boil, and, when well boiled, take from the fire and mash through a sieve, reducing to a pulp. Take a tablespoonful of flour and put in a saucepan, and add a half spoon of flour. When it blends and browns nicely, add the tomato juice, season nicely to taste, and, when ready to serve, add chopped parsley as a garnish. Serve with meat, fish or game.

### Velouté Sauce.
#### Sauce Veloutée.

3 Ounces Butter, or 1 Tablespoonful and a Half.
1 Tablespoonful and a Half of Flour.
2 Gills of Water.
The Well-Beaten Yolks of 2 Eggs.
Salt and Pepper to Taste.
Juice of a Lemon.
1 Tablespoonful of Chopped Parsley.

Blend the flour and butter as in White Sauce, only letting it become slightly yellow. Add by degrees the boiling water, and season to taste. A tablespoonful of white wine is a fine addition. Add the juice of half a lemon, and a tablespoonful of chopped parsley. Let it simmer for about ten minutes, and take from the fire, and add the well-beaten yolks of two eggs. Serve immediately with any boiled fish or meats.

### Vinaigrette Sauce.
### Sauce Vinaigrette.

12 Shallots. 2 Tablespoonfuls of Vinegar.
5 Tablespoonfuls of Oil.
2 Tablespoonfuls of Chopped Parsley.
Salt and Pepper to Taste.

Mix all together as in a Sauce Ravigote, cold (see recipe), and add the oil and vinegar; serve cold, with cold boiled meat, cold boiled fish, etc.

### White Sauce.
### Sauce Blanche.

A Tablespoonful and a Half of Butter.
A Tablespoonful and a Half of Flour.
Half a Cup of Water or White Broth.
Salt and Pepper to Taste.

Blend the flour and butter in the saucepan without browning in the least. Add by degrees the boiling water or White Consommé of veal or chicken, stirring until smooth, and boiling three minutes. Salt and pepper to taste. Add the juice of half a lemon. If the sauce is to have other ingredients, this is the foundation for them. It must be of the consistency of thick starch to begin with, in the latter case.

### White Sauce.
### Sauce Allemande.

4 Pounds of Raw Veal.
The Bones of a Chicken.
1 Gallon of Water. 1 Carrot. 1 Turnip.
Celery Tops.
2 Tablespoonfuls of Butter.
2 Spoonfuls of Lard.
1 Herb Bouquet of Thyme, Parsley, Bay Leaf.
1 Stalk of Celery. 2 Long Carrots.
1 Wineglassful of Madeira or Sherry Wine.

Take the veal and the bones of the chicken and put into a pot with a gallon of water. Add the herb bouquet, tied together, and one chopped carrot, one turnip chopped, celery tops, and other ingredients of a good "pot-au-feu." Let all boil slowly for three hours until it is reduced one-half. Then salt and pepper to taste. This will give a white broth or consommé blanc. When boiled to this point, take off the fire and strain the broth into a jar. Now take two tablespoonfuls of butter and three of flour, and put into a saucepan together, letting the butter and flour blend, without browning. Add all the broth to this, stirring slowly while on the fire. Add a good, strong bouquet of herbs, thyme, parsley and bay leaf, all tied whole together. Add two large carrots, and let it boil till reduced to one-half again. After it has reduced, season to taste, and when it has reached the consistency of starch take off the fire and strain and let it get cool. This sauce is used for all white meats and fish. When used for fish take one tablespoonful and moisten with a little fish broth. Add a wineglass of Sherry or Madeira, and set on the fire to heat, and add a pint of consommé or broth. This sauce Allemande will keep at least one month in our climate, in the ice box. If one prefers to make it as needed, follow the proportions of one tablespoonful of butter, two of flour, and one pint of boiling broth.

---

## CHAPTER XXII.

### SALADS.

#### Des Salades.

The Creoles have always been famous for the excellent salads which grace their tables. Salad, like soup, or gumbo, is the daily accompaniment of dinner in even the most humble Creole home. They hold, one and all, that a good salad is a most delightful dish, but a poor one is worse than none at all.

The old Spanish proverb that "to make a perfect salad there should be a miser for vinegar, a spendthrift for oil, a wise man for salt, and a madcap to stir all these ingredients, and mix them well together," still holds as the unfailing Creole rule in making a good salad. The reason is clear. For the dressing of the salad should be saturated with the oil, before the salt, pepper and vinegar are added. Results have proven however, where the salad is dressed in the bowl, that there can never really be too much vinegar, for, from the specific gravity of vinegar, compared to the oil, what is useless will fall to the bottom of the bowl. By dissolving the salt in the vinegar, instead of the oil, too it becomes more thoroughly distributed throughout the salad. But this will not hold where each makes his own salad dressing at table, as is common in Creole families.

The simple French Dressing for salads is always the best for daily use, and also for formal dinners. It is not only lighter, as compared to the Mayonnaise Dressing, and, therefore, far more acceptable at dinners where the courses are many, but the Creoles hold, like the French, that it is the only dressing for salads that are not intended for luncheons or teas, such as chicken, shrimp or crab salads. A Mayonnaise Dressing for salad should never be used at the family dinner or formal dinings.

A meat salad is never an economical article of food, if one counts all the items of cost. The wretched combinations, too, which pass for Mayonnaise, and which are nothing more than a paste spread over the top of the salad, or stirred through with a mixture of pepper, vinegar and salt, cannot be too greatly condemned. The making of a good Mayonnaise is a matter of art, and requires the skill that comes from experience. Practice will teach that there is no need for useless expenditure of time in making this dressing, and that once you have learned the simple trick of securing the good start in the way of blending, or rather "working," the oil into the egg, drop by drop, the task of making a fine Sauce à la Mayonnaise, becomes a very simple and easy one. The Mayonnaise, which is intended, as stated above, only for meat dressings, and the French Salad Dressing are the only two in general use in Creole households.

The Creoles serve salads for breakfast, luncheon and dinners, while no elegant supper is considered complete without a salad. The ancient Creole dames have always declared that for health the green salad, with the simple French Dressing, is the proper one. Such a salad is to be found daily on their tables. Make the French Dressing according to the directions given in the subjoined recipes, and pour this over the lettuce, with a tablespoonful of parsley, cut very fine, sprinkled over again. Salads of this order, are, indeed, the most healthful in the world. The old Creoles say that the family that eats much oil will never know a headache, and the medicinal virtues of lettuce and celery are such as are acknowledged by physicians, and all nervous and energetic people require them as sedatives. The French say that the Americans eat too much meat, and too little vegetables. Happily, the Creoles know how to blend both, and they declare that this accounts for the longevity and good health of the ancient members of the race.

### Plain French Dressings for Salads.

Assaisonment Français.

3 Tablespoonfuls of the Best Olive Oil.
1 Tablespoonful of Vinegar, According to Taste.
¼ Teaspoonful of Salt.
¼ Teaspoonful of Black Pepper.

First put the oil into a small bowl. Then add gradually the salt and pepper until all are thoroughly mixed. Then add gradually the vinegar, stirring continually for about a minute. It is now ready to pour over the salad, and remember that it must be mixed thoroughly. The proportion of vinegar varies according to the salad to be dressed. Lettuce salad requires but little; tomato salad, corn salad or Doucette require more. Serve this dressing with lettuce, tomato, onion, cucumber and other vegetables and green salads.

### French Dressing No. 2.

Assaisonment Français.

3 Tablespoonfuls of Oil.
1 Tablespoonful of Tarragon Vinegar.
A Saltspoon Each of Black Pepper and Salt.
Chopped Onion and Parsley.
The Juice of Half an Onion.

Mix these in the order given above, adding the onion juice and parsley, well chopped, last. This is a more elaborate French dressing. Serve with the same salads as above. The oil may be omitted for those who do not like it, but it will be no longer in either of these recipes a French Dressing. The Creoles hold that the oil is a very healthy, digestible and essential ingredient.

### Mustard Dressing.

Assaisonment à la Moutarde.

1 Tablespoonful of Vinegar.
1 Teaspoonful of Prepared Mustard.
2 Tablespoonfuls of Olive Oil.
The Yolk of 1 Egg, If Desired.
Salt and Pepper to Taste.

Blend the mustard and the oil, adding the latter, drop by drop at first, and then proceeding more confidently. Whenever the dressing appears to be curdling, add a few drops of vinegar, and work rapidly till it becomes smooth again. Add the salt and pepper, and when the dressing is finished, use it for celery salad, fish, tomatoes, potatoes, etc. If the oil appears to separate from the other ingredients, it can always be rubbed into them smoothly again by adding a few drops of vinegar. In all these salads the question of oil and its measurements can only be approximated. Good judgment must always be the final test.

## Creole French Dressing.
### Assaisonment à la Créole.

3 Tablespoonfuls of the Best Olive Oil.
1 Tablespoonful of Vinegar.
1 Teaspoonful Mustard.
The Yolk of a Hard-Boiled Egg.
Salt and Pepper to Taste.

Blend the oil and salt and pepper in the manner above indicated, and then add these to the mustard drop by drop, alternating with the vinegar. When well blended add the well-mashed yolk of a hard-boiled egg. Stir well, and serve with lettuce, celery or potato salad.

## Mayonnaise Dressing.
### Sauce Mayonnaise.

Yolk of 1 Egg.
Sweet Oil. Lemon. Vinegar.
Pepper and Salt.

Take the yolk of one fresh egg, raw, and put it in a bowl. The egg and the oil must be cold, and in summer it is well to keep the soup plate in which you make the dressing on cracked ice in a pan, so that the oil will not run. Put the yolk in a plate; add, drop by drop, a little sweet oil from the bottle. When you have dropped about a spoonful being careful to work it into the yolk of the egg drop by drop and blend all the time, take a lemon and drop a few drops into the mixture. It will at once begin to harden as you stir it in. Continue stirring till the egg grows hard, and then steadily, drop by drop, let the oil fall, working it all the time with your fork into the egg. Have another spoon, begin to drop in the lemon juice, working it the same way again till it hardens the egg. Then begin again with the oil and work again, and again drop the lemon till you have the juice of half a lemon and about two gills of oil, finishing with the oil. When the egg begins to curdle, add a little salt, but do not add this salt till the Mayonnaise is complete. Serve very cold, with salads, etc.

Mayonnaise is the standing sauce for chicken salad, shrimp salad, crab salad, etc. When making for these large salads, as a garnish use three yolks of eggs and other ingredients in proportion.

## Rémoulade Dressing.
### Sauce Rémoulade.

3 Hard-Boiled Eggs. 1 Raw Yolk of Egg.
1 Tablespoonful of Tarragon Vinegar.
3 Tablespoonfuls of Olive Oil.
½ Clove of Garlic, Minced Very Fine.
½ Teaspoonful of Prepared Mustard.
Salt and Cayenne to Taste.

A Rémoulade is a cold sauce, and is always served with cold meats. Boil the eggs till hard. Remove the shells and set aside the whites, which you will have crumbled fine for a garnish. Put the yolks into a bowl, and mash very fine, till perfectly smooth. Add the mustard, and mix well, and the seasonings of vinegar and salt and Cayenne to taste. Then add the olive oil, drop by drop, working in the egg all the time, and then add the yolk of the raw egg, and work in thoroughly, till light. Then add the juice of half a lemon. Mix well, increasing the quantity of oil or vinegar, according to taste, very slightly. If the sauce is not thoroughly mixed, it will curdle. It is now ready to be served with cold meats, fish or salads.

## Vinaigrette Dressing.
### Sauce Vinaigrette.

12 Shallots. 2 Tablespoonfuls of Vinegar.
5 Tablespoonfuls of Oil.
2 Tablespoonfuls of Chopped Parsley.
Salt and Pepper to Taste.

Mix all together, as in a Sauce Ravigote, cold (see recipe), and add the oil and vinegar; serve cold, with cold boiled meat, cold boiled fish, etc.

## Anchovy Salad.
### Salade d'Anchois.

1 Box of Anchovies.
A Plain French Dressing.

Cut the sardines into pieces of about an inch in length. Season nicely with a French Dressing and serve. This is a delicious luncheon dish.

## Artichoke Salad.
### Artichauts en Salade.

1 Pint of Cold Boiled Artichokes.
1 Teaspoonful of Vinegar.
1 Teaspoonful of Chopped Parsley.
French Dressing.

Boil the Artichokes. (See recipe). When cold, peel them and cut into quarters. Add chopped parsley and the French dressing; mix, and serve very cold.

## Tips of Asparagus Salad.
### Pointes d'Asperges en Salade.

1 Pint of Asparagus Tips.
A Plain French Dressing.

Boil the Asparagus tips. (See recipe.) When cold, place on a dish and garnish nicely. Serve very cold, with French Dressing.

## Bean Salad.
### Salade d'Haricots.

1 Pint of Cold Beans.
Vinaigrette Sauce.

This is a nice way of utilizing cold left-over red or white beans. Serve with a Vinaigrette Sauce. (See recipe.)

### Beet Salad.
Salade de Betteraves.

4 Large Red Beets.   French Dressing.

Boil the beets till done, and then peel and slice nicely. Set them to cool and pour over them a French dressing or a plain dressing of vinegar, salt and pepper. This is a nice spring or winter salad in New Orleans.

### Cauliflower Salad.
Chou-fleur à la Vinaigrette.

1 Pint of Boiled Cauliflower.
1 Teaspoonful of Chopped Parsley.
1 Teaspoonful of Tarragon Vinegar.
A French Dressing (plain).

Boil the cauliflower as directed. (See recipe.) Then separate the flowerets; mix them with parsley, and cut the remainder very fine and mix also. Let it cool. Serve with a French dressing, after adding first an extra teaspoonful of Tarragon vinegar. This is a famous and very popular Creole way of serving cauliflower.

### Celery Salad.
Salade de Celeri.

1 Pint of Crisp French Celery.
2 Hard-Boiled Eggs.   French Dressing.

Cut the celery into pieces of about a quarter of an inch. Chop two hard-boiled eggs, not too fine, and mix well with the chopped celery. Blend all with French dressing and serve. This is a delicious salad.

### Celery Mayonnaise.
Mayonnaise de Celeri.

1 Pint of Crisp White Celery.
A Mayonnaise Sauce.

Chop the celery, or rather cut fine, as indicated in the above recipe. Mix the Mayonnaise with it. Garnish nicely with celery tips and serve. The mustard dressing is even nicer than the Mayonnaise for this salad.

### Chervil Salad.
Salade de Cerfeuil.

1 Pint of Chervil.
A Plain French Dressing.

Chervil is a delicious salad herb, much affected by French and Creole gourmets. It is served cut fine between bits, in the same manner as Lettuce Salad, with a French Dressing.

### Chicken Salad.
Mayonnaise de Volaille.

1 Pint of Cold Boiled Chicken.
½ Pint of Mayonnaise Sauce.
1 Head of Crisp Fresh Lettuce.

Cut the chicken into small dice. Chop half of the lettuce very fine, and season well with salt and pepper. Make a bed of the remainder of the lettuce leaves, and place first a layer of the chicken and then of the lettuce, until you have used all. Spread the Mayonnaise Sauce over the top nicely, and garnish prettily with slices of cold hard-boiled eggs, sliced beets, celery tips, etc. For chicken and celery salad follow the recipe for Volaille en Salade, given under the heading of "Poultry." (See recipe.) Left-over chicken may be utilized in either of these salads.

### Crab Salad à la Mayonnaise.
Mayonnaise de Crabes.

1 Pint of the Meat of Crab (hard shell).
Mayonnaise.
Hard-Boiled Eggs.   Garnishes.

Boil and pick crabs sufficient to give a pint of meat. (See recipe for Boiling Crabs.) Season well with salt and pepper. Place in a dish, on a bed of crisp lettuce leaves, spreading over them the Mayonnaise Sauce, and garnish nicely with hard-boiled eggs, sliced beets and tips of celery.

### Crawfish Salad.
Mayonnaise d'Écrevisses.

3 Dozen Crawfish.
A Sauce a la Mayonnaise.

Boil the crawfish, pick the meat out of the shells, heads and tails, break them into pieces, and prepare in exactly the same manner as Shrimp Salad.

### Cress Salad.
Salade de Cresson.

Cress.   Vinegar.   Salt and Pepper.

Prepare in exactly the same manner as lettuce, washing and bringing to the table firm and crisp. In this salad use for dressing only Tarragon vinegar, salt and pepper to taste.

### Cucumber Salad.
Salade de Concombres.

2 Fine Cucumbers.
A Plain French Dressing.

Wash and slice two nice young cucumbers, and use a plain dressing of vinegar, salt and pepper. This is a very delicious salad. There are many so-called elegant novelties introduced lately in the way of serving cucumbers, such as stuffed cucumbers, fried cucumbers, etc. The Creoles look with disdain, and justly, on these silly innovations in the serving of a vegetable which nature intended to be used for salad purposes, and nothing else.

### Corn Salad.
Salade de Maches, ou Doucette.

1 Pint of Corn Salad.
A Plain French Dressing.

This is an excellent salad, and is prepared and served with a French dressing. Take one pint of fresh Doucette and pare off the outer stale leaves, if there are any; cut off the roots. Wash the Doucette well in two waters, drain in a napkin and place in the salad bowl. When ready to serve add a plain French dressing but not before. Mix well, so that every portion will be impregnated with the dressing. Serve very cold. A garnish of two hard-boiled eggs, sliced or cut in quarters, or of two medium-sized beets, which may be added both for taste and effect.

### Dandelion Salad.

Salade de Dent-de-Lion

1 Pint of Fresh White Dandelion.
A Plain French Dressing.

Cut off the roots and green portion of the leaves; wash and steep in salt and water. When they become crisp, drain and press dry; rub the salad bowl with a clove of garlic and season the dandelions with French dressing. This salad may also be served with two hard-boiled eggs cut in quarters or sliced and laid over; or with two medium-sized beets, sliced, and seasoned with a plain French dressing.

### Endive Salad.

Salade de Chicorée.

1 Pint of Endives. French Dressing.
1 Teaspoonful of Chervil, Chopped Very Fine.

Prepare the endives in the same manner as the lettuce. When ready to serve, add the chervil and the French dressing. If endives stand, like lettuce, they will wilt after being dressed. Serve immediately.

### Fish Salad.

Salade de Poisson à la Mayonnaise.

1 Piot of Cold Boiled Fish.
1 Head of Lettuce. Mayonnaise Sauce.

Use cold boiled left-over fish, picking nicely into bits of about an inch and a half square. Follow the same directions as in the above recipes, only do not mix lettuce and fish in layers. There is nothing nicer than a fine fish salad.

### Green Pepper Salad.

Salade de Piments Doux à la Créole.

4 Tomatoes. 2 Green Peppers. 1 Large Onion.
French Dressing, Plain.

Slice the tomatoes, onions and green peppers nicely and thin, arrange on a dish, placing a layer of tomatoes, an alternate layer of onion and green pepper, and tomatoes mixed. Dress either before bringing to the table, or at the table, with French dressing. This is a great Creole family salad, and a very healthy one.

### Green Peppers à l'Espgaole.

Piments Verts en Salade à l'Espagnole.

6 Green Peppers. 3 Tomatoes.
A Plain French Dressing.

Parboil the peppers so that they will peel easily, and scald the tomatoes. Peel them, removing the seeds of the peppers. Cut the peppers into one-inch pieces, slice the tomatoes, and serve with plain French dressing as a salad.

### Lentil Salad.

Salade de Lentilles.

1 Pint of Lentils.
A Vinaigrette Sauce (See Recipe).

Lentils are prepared in the same manner as Bean Salad (see recipe), and served with Vinaigrette Sauce. They make a cheap, excellent and healthy salad.

### Lettuce Salad.

Salade de Laitue.

3 Heads of Lettuce.
French Dressing. 2 Eggs.

Take fresh, crisp lettuce of sufficient quantity for the number to be served, three young heads being enough for six. Dip in cold water examining each leaf, and pick over carefully, and select the fresh crisp leaves. Place all these in a salad bowl, and garnish nicely with sliced hard-boiled egg. Never dress the lettuce before bringing to the table. The vinegar causes the leaves to wilt utterly, and takes away all the relish which one experiences from looking at a fresh, crisp dish, and also spoils a fine table garnish. Bring to the table, and let the sauce, always a plain French dressing or Creole dressing preferred, be made at the table. Generally each makes the dressing to suit himself or herself, using proportions of greater or lesser quantity than those mentioned in the recipe. If one person dresses the salad for the table, use the proportions given above in any of the French salad dressings for this amount of lettuce. This is one of the nicest and most refreshing as well as one of the healthiest of all salads.

### Louisiana Salad.

Salade Louisianaise.

2 Lettuce Heads. 6 Pickled Cucumbers.
2 Dozen Pickled Onions. A Plain French Dressing.

Use, in this fancy salad, lettuce, pickled cucumbers, pickled onions, cut in dice, and serve with a French dressing.

### Okra Salad.

Salade de Fevi.

4 Dozen Boiled Young Okras.
French Dressing.

Boil the okra as directed. (See recipe.) When cold, dress nicely with vinegar, salt and pepper, or, if preferred, the plain French dressing, and serve very cold. This is a most delightful summer salad, the okra being very cooling in our tropical climate.

### Spanish Salad.
Salade à l'Espagnole.

4 Sliced Tomatoes. 2 Dozen Pickled Onions.
½ Pint of Mayonnaise Dressing.

This is a very much affected salad, made of sliced tomatoes and pickled onions, prettily arranged around a small bed of Mayonnaise heaped in the center.

### String Bean Salad.
Haricots Verts en Salade.

1 Pint of Cold Boiled String Beans.
French Dressing (plain).

Only very young and tender beans should be used for this salad. Boil as directed under the heading "Vegetables," and put the beans in a salad bowl and allow to cool well. Serve with a plain French dressing, or, better still, a simple dressing of vinegar and a dash of Cayenne.

### Tomato Salad.
Salade de Tomates.

4 Fresh Fine Tomatoes.
French Dressing.

Slice the tomatoes nicely and place on a salad dish. Never peel or scald tomatoes intended for salad. Serve nicely with a plain French dressing or any of the above dressings. Tomatoes may also be served with Mayonnaise dressing. In this case place them on a bed of crisp, fresh lettuce, whole, and serve one to each person, or cut them in halves. Tomatoes with Mayonnaise is a luncheon dish, or a supper dish.

### Iced Tomatoes.
Tomates Frappé.

6 Whole Tomatoes. 1 Pint Mayonnaise Sauce.
A Garnish of Chopped Ice.

Take the tomatoes whole. Lay on a bed of lettuce or cress, as indicated above. Garnish with chopped ice, and serve very cold with Mayonnaise Sauce. This is delicious and very elegant.

### Tomato, Green Pepper and Onion Salad.
Salade à la Créole.

4 Tomatoes. 2 Green Peppers. 1 Large Onion.
French Dressing, Plain.

Slice the tomatoes, onions and green peppers nicely and thin; arrange on a dish, placing a layer of tomatoes, an alternate layer of onion and green pepper, and tomatoes mixed. Dress either before bringing to the table, or at the table, with French dressing. This is a great family salad among the Creoles, and a very healthy one. The Creoles follow the old adage, that the taste of the onion must only lurk within the bowl when using it for salad. More than this renders the salad disagreeable and coarse.

### Watercress Salad.
Salade de Cresson.

1 Pint of Watercress.
Minced Potato, if desired.
A Plain French Dressing.

This salad is made of watercress simply, or watercress and minced potatoes, mixed in equal quantities, and served with a French dressing. It is a most healthy, light and excellent salad, especially in summer. The salad is delightful without the potatoes. They may be added if desired.

### The Gardener's Wife Salad.
Salade à la Jardinière.

1 Carrot   3 Beets.
½ Cup of Green Peas.   1 Cup String Beans.
A Plain French Dressing.

Take fine strips of vegetables of different colors, cooked and cold, with green peas and string beans, and dress nicely with oil and vinegar and serve.

### Sardine Salad.
Salade de Sardines.

1 Box Sardines.
A Plain French Dressing.

Cut the sardines into pieces of about half an inch in length. Season nicely with a French dressing and serve. This is a delicious luncheon dish.

### Potato Salad.
Salade de Pommes de Terre.

3 Large Cold Boiled Potatoes.
2 Hard-Boiled Eggs.
9 Tablespoonfuls of Olive Oil.
3 Tablespoonfuls of Vinegar. 1 Large Onion.
1 Teaspoonful of Salt.
4 Sprigs of Parsley.

This is a nice way of utilizing cold left-over potatoes. But the freshly boiled potatoes always make the nicest salad. Pare and peel the potatoes, if freshly boiled, and let them cool. Prepare the salad dressing, following implicitly the directions given for plain French dressing, only here the quantities are larger in proportion. Add the vinegar, stirring constantly. A dash of mustard may be added, if desired. Mince the onion very fine, and cut the potatoes into dice or slices, and mix them carefully with the onion. Then add the dressing, turning the potatoes into it without breaking. Sprinkle all with parsley, nicely chopped, and serve cold.

### Russian Salad.
### Salade à la Russe.

| | |
|---|---|
| 2 Carrots. | 2 Parsnips. |
| 1 Cup of Cold Minced Fowl. | 3 Anchovies. |
| 1 Dozen Olives. | 3 Caviares. |
| 1 Tablespoonful of Sauce a la Tartare. | |
| 1 Teaspoonful of Mustard. | |

This salad is made of cooked carrots, parsnips, beets, cold roast beef, cold ham, a truffle (if it can be afforded), all cut into fancy or dice-shaped pieces. Use one ounce of each of the meats, or simply one cup of cold minced fowl, as it may not be convenient to have all these meats at hand in households. Add six boned anchovies, and one dozen olives and two caviares, and serve with Tartare Sauce, or with a French salad dressing, to which mustard has been added. It is a heavy salad.

### Shrimp Salad.
### Salade de Chevrette à la Mayonnaise.

2 Pints of Cold Boiled Shrimp.
1 Head of Crisp Lettuce.  Mayonnaise Sauce.

Take Lake Shrimp and River Shrimp combined, if you have them. Cut the larger Lake Shrimp into two. Season well with salt and pepper. Chop some lettuce. Season well. Place first a layer of shrimp and then of lettuce, and spread over all a Mayonnaise Sauce. Garnish nicely with sliced hard-boiled eggs, sliced beets and celery and lettuce tips, and serve very cold.

## CHAPTER XXIII.

## EGGS.

### Des Oeufs.

A chapter on eggs would be superfluous in any cook book, were it not for the fact that there are many, many women who cannot tell for a certainty just how long to boil an egg soft or hard, just when the exact point is reached when the omelette is cooked to a nicety, and how to send to the table in all the perfection of good cooking that most delicate and palatable dish, the "Scrambled Egg."

This book will not deal with the many new and more or less unpalatable and undigestible methods of cooking eggs, methods which, under high-sounding names, nevertheless rob the egg of all possible beneficial effects by "cooking it to death," for an egg that has been cooked or boiled for twenty or twenty-five minutes is about as indigestible an article of food as can be conceived. And as for the flavor of the egg, it has disappeared.

The Creoles have very wisely eschewed all innovations in cooking eggs that require more than five to eight minutes to cook to perfection. They cling to the old-fashioned soft-boiled egg, the hard-boiled egg, fried egg, scrambled and poached eggs. They have retained many ancient French and Spanish methods of cooking eggs, but none of these, followed properly, according to the time-honored customs, calls for more than five or eight minutes at the most in cooking.

The first and most important point to be considered in preparing eggs for the table is to ascertain whether they are perfectly fresh. The fresher the egg the better. The egg which appears moldy or in the least bit ancient should be rejected. Never, under any circumstances, put a tainted egg in any dish, under the impression that other ingredients will hide the flavor. Never put such an egg in a cake. The presence of one egg that is not fresh will ruin an entire dish. As a matter of health, above all other considerations, such eggs should be rejected.

The old Creole darkies, in common with many other people, have a way of finding out whether an egg is fresh by inclosing it in the hollow of the hand and looking through it with one eye, while shutting the other. They aver that if you can distinctly trace the yolk in one solid mass, and if the white around it looks clear, the egg is good. A more simple and scientific way, and by far a surer one, is to drop the eggs into cold water. The fresh ones will sink immediately to the bottom, the doubtful ones will swim around a little before reaching the bottom, and the bad ones will float.

Eggs are among the most nutritious articles of food substances. They are rich in albumen, and their free use cannot be too highly recommended to the delicate, to hard brain workers, and to families generally.

### Boiled Eggs.

### Oeufs à la Coque.

Have ready a saucepan of boiling water. Use only fresh eggs. Put them in the boiling water without cracking the shells. If you desire soft-boiled eggs, or "Oeufs Mollets," let the eggs boil from two minutes to two minutes and a half by the clock, keeping the exact time, minute by minute. The whites will then be set. If you desire the yolk to be set also in the soft-boiled egg, let the eggs boil three minutes, but not a second longer. For hard-boiled eggs, five minutes is sufficient. Bear in mind always that the water must be boiling hard before you put the egg into it, and that the exact time for boiling must be followed by the clock or with the watch in hand.

### Poached Eggs.
### Oeufs Pochés.

Have the frying pan filled with boiling water. Add salt. Some add also a tablespoonful of vinegar, but this is a matter of taste. The eggs must be absolutely fresh. Break the eggs into a saucer, one by one, and gently slip off into the water, without breaking the yolk. Break another and another, until you have four in the pan, and allow the eggs to stand apart. Let them boil thus on the water, till the white forms a thin veil over the yolks. Then the eggs are done. Take them up gently, neatly round off the ragged edges, sprinkle the top with a little black pepper, place on buttered toast, and serve immediately.

### Fried Eggs.
### Oeufs Frits.

6 Eggs.    2 Tablespoonfuls of Lard.

The lard must be very hot. Break the eggs gently into a saucer, one by one, and drop gently into the lard, without breaking the yolks. With the spoon take up a little of the hot lard and drop gently over the top of the egg, if you wish it to be quite done. Otherwise simply fry till the yolk is set. Slide out on a batter cake turner, and place in a dish. Sprinkle with salt and black pepper, and add, if you wish, a little parsley garnish, and serve very hot.

### Ham and Eggs.
### Oeufs au Jambon.

6 Slices of Ham.    6 Eggs.
1 Tablespoonful of Lard.

The ham should always be soaked in hot water before frying. Cut slices of about half an inch in thickness, of sufficient size to lay an egg upon them. Lay the ham in the hot frying pan, and let it fry until the fat becomes transparent. Then take the slices out and put them on a hot dish. Break the eggs, one by one, into a saucer, and slip them into the frying pan, and fry in the same lard in which you have fried the ham. When the yolks are quite set, take them out, and lay one egg on each slice of ham. Garnish nicely with parsley, and serve hot. This is a great Creole breakfast dish.

### Scrambled Eggs.
### Oeufs Brouillés.

6 Fresh Eggs.    A Tablespoonful of Butter.
Salt and Pepper to Taste.

Break the eggs into a saucer, one by one, and then transfer to a bowl. Season well with salt and pepper. Have the frying pan very hot. Put into it the butter, and add immediately the eggs, and keep stirring around and around and across for about three or four minutes, judging by the consistency of the egg, which must be like a thick mush as you take it from the fire. Keep stirring a few seconds longer after you have taken the pan off the fire, and put the eggs into a hot dish, and garnish with parsley and serve immediately with buttered toast or broiled ham. The beauty of the scrambled egg is that the whites and yolks are delicately blended. The practice of beating the yolks and whites thoroughly together, as for an omelette, before scrambling the eggs is to be condemned as against the best ethics of Creole cookery. There is no comparison in the taste of the scrambled egg cooked according to the above method, and the eggs in which the yolks and whites have been previously beaten together.

### Eggs Scrambled in Ham.
### Oeufs Brouillés au Jambon.

6 Eggs.
3 Tablespoonfuls of Finely Minced Boiled Ham.
A Tablespoonful of Butter.

Mince the ham very fine, and break the eggs, one by one, into a saucer, and add to the bowl in which you have minced the ham. Mix all together. Place a tablespoonful of butter in the frying pan, add the eggs and ham, stir briskly, and when it comes to the consistency of starch take off the fire, and serve hot on buttered toast.

In the same manner eggs may be scrambled with minced truffles, mushrooms, onions, celery or tomatoes.

### Eggs Scrambled With Preserves.
### Oeufs Brouillés aux Confitures.

6 Eggs.    1 Tablespoonful of Butter.
2 Tablespoonfuls of Fruit Marmalade.

Eggs may also be scrambled with marmalade of apricots or prunes, in which case they are called "Oeufs Brouillés aux Confitures." Follow above recipe, using the marmalade instead of the ham.

### Eggs Fondus.
### Oeufs Fondus au Fromage.

6 Eggs.
4 Hesping Teaspoonfuls of Gruyere Cheese, Grated.
1 Tablespoonful of Butter.

Break the eggs into a saucepan,

add the butter, the grated cheese, a little salt and pepper. Place the saucepan on a hot fire, stir the mixture around and around till the edges begin to thicken, and when of the consistency of a thick starch take off the fire and serve immediately on buttered toast.

### Eggs With Asparagus Tips.
Oeufs aux Pointes d'Asperges.

6 Eggs.
2 Tablespoonfuls of Asparagus Tips.
1 Tablespoonful of Butter.
1 Tablespoonful of Milk. Salt and Pepper.
Buttered Toast.

Boil the asparagus tips (see recipe), and put the eggs into a saucepan, with the butter, after seasoning well with salt and pepper, and mixing the milk. Stir a second, and throw in the asparagus, and proceed to scramble as in preceding recipe. Serve on buttered toast.
Cauliflower may be prepared with eggs in the same way.

### Shirred Eggs.
Oeufs sur le Plat.

6 Eggs. 1 Tablespoonful of Butter.
Salt and Pepper to Taste.

Break the eggs into a thin dish, in which they are to be served, having first buttered the bottom of the dish or pan. Sprinkle them with salt and pepper, pour over a little melted butter, place in a quick oven, and let them bake until the yolks are set. Serve in the dish in which they have been cooked.

### Eggs à la Poulette.
Oeufs à la Poulette.

6 Eggs.  ½ Pint of Sauce a la Poulette.
Boil the eggs hard and slice. Pour over a Sauce à la Poulette (see recipe), and serve hot.

### Beauregard Eggs.
Oeufs à la Beauregard.

6 Eggs.  ½ Pint of Fresh Milk.
1 Tablespoonful of Butter.
1 Tablespoonful of Cornstarch.
Salt and Pepper to Taste.

Boil the eggs for five minutes, till hard. Then take out of the water and cool, take off the shells, and separate the whites from the yolks, rubbing the latter through a sieve, and chopping the former very fine. But do not mix them. Have the milk ready to boil, and rub the butter and cornstarch together, and add to the boiling milk. Then add the whites of the eggs, and salt and pepper to taste. Prepare previous to this some buttered toast, and cover it now with a layer of this white sauce, and then add a layer of the yolks of the eggs. Add another layer of the sauce, and another layer of the yolks, and then the remainder of the sauce. Sprinkle the top with a little salt and pepper, and set in the oven and let it stand two minutes, and serve hot.

### Plain Omelet.
Omelette.

4 Fresh Eggs.  1 Tablespoonful of Butter.
Salt and Pepper to Taste.

If you wish to have the omelet very nice, break the whites and yolks separately, and beat the former till they come to a light froth, and the latter till they are quite light. Then beat the whites and yolks together. Season well. Melt the butter in a frying pan, letting it grow hot, but not by any means brown. Pour in the mixture of egg. Let it stand about two minutes, shaking occasionally to prevent it from sticking to the pan. Continue shaking over a quick fire until the eggs are set. Then roll the omelet, folding it in two or three rolls and making it long and narrow. Take a hot dish, turn the omelet into it, garnish with parsley, and serve hot immediately, or it will fall. It is always easier to make several small omelets and have them pretty and sightly, than to succeed perfectly in making a large one.

### Creole Omelet.
Omelette à la Créole.

6 Fine, Ripe Tomatoes. 2 Onions. 6 Eggs.
1 Tablespoonful of Butter.
2 Tablespoonfuls of Minced Ham.
½ Clove of Garlic.
Salt and Pepper to Taste.

Scald and skin six fine, ripe tomatoes, and chop them fine. Chop two onions, and mince the garlic very fine, and add a large spoonful of bread crumbs. Fry them with a tablespoonful of butter in a saucepan till quite brown. Then add the tomatoes, and salt, pepper and Cayenne to taste, and let all stew for an hour, at least. Prepare the eggs as for Ham Omelet (see recipe), and when the tomatoes are quite done have ready a heated frying pan and a half tablespoonful of butter. Pour this into the pan. As they become set pour in the center the tomatoes, and fold the omelet over, and cook for two minutes longer. Roll gently into a dish and serve hot.

### Ham Omelet.
Omelette au Jambon.

4 Eggs.  ½ Teaspoonful of Flour.
2 Tablespoonfuls of Milk.
2 Tablespoonfuls of Chopped Ham.
½ Grated Onion.
1 Tablespoonful of Chopped Parsley.
Salt and Pepper to Taste.

Beat the yolks to a cream, and add the other ingredients. Rub all these smoothly together, and then add the whites of eggs, beaten to a froth. Beat all thoroughly together. Put a tablespoonful of butter in the frying pan. When it melts add the omelet. Let it sand, shaking occasionally to prevent from sticking to the pan, till the eggs are quite set. Then fold as in a plain omelet, turn into a hot dish, and serve.

### Kidney Omelet.

Omeletts aux Rognons.

3 Kidneys.  6 Eggs.
1½ Tablespoonfuls of Butter.

Cut the fat from the kidneys, wash well, and cut into small pieces. Mix these with the eggs, which you will have prepared as for a plain omelet, and proceed as in Ham Omelet. This is very nice served with Tomato Sauce.

### Mushroom Omelet.

Omelette aux Champignons.

6 Eggs.  ¼ Can of Mushrooms.
1½ Tablespoonfuls of Butter.

Stew the mushrooms a few minutes. Then chop them fine. Make a plain omelet. When it is ready to fold, place the mushrooms across the center, fold twice over, let it cook two minutes longer, and serve hot.

### Onion Omelet.

Omelette à l'Ognon.

4 Eggs. 1 Tablespoonful of Butter.
1 Large Onion Minced Very Fine.

Beat the eggs as for a plain omelet. Then stew the onions in the butter till quite tender. Stir in the omelet once, and then let it cook as in a plain omelet. Roll in folds, and serve hot.

### Omelet Soufflé.

Omelette Soufflée.

The Whites of 6 Eggs. The Yolks of 4 Eggs.
The Juice of Half a Lemon, or a Spoon.
of Orange Flower Water or Kirsch.
4 Tablespoonfuls of Powdered White Sugar.

Have a baking dish ready, greased with butter, and be sure that the oven is very hot. Beat the whites of the eggs to a stiff froth. Beat the yolks and the sugar to a cream, and add the juice of half a lemon or a tablespoonful of orange flower water or Kirsch. Add the whites of the eggs. Stir carefully and heap all quickly into the baking dish and bake about fifteen minutes, till the top is a delicate brown. Serve immediately, as it will fall if allowed to stand. This may be served as a sweet entremet or as a dessert.

### Parsley Omelet.

Omelette au Persil.

6 Eggs.  1½ Tablespoonfuls of Butter.
1 Tablespoonful of Cut Parsley.

Proceed in exactly the same manner as for Plain Omelet, only mix a tablespoonful of cut parsley in the omelet before putting in the frying pan.

### Truffle Omelet.

Omelette aux Truffes.

6 Eggs.  2 Truffles.
1½ Tablespoonfuls of Butter.

An omelet with truffles is made in the same manner as a Mushroom Omelet.

### Rum Omelet.

Omelette au Rhum.

3 Eggs.  1 Glass of Jamaica Rum.
1 Teaspoonful of Milk.
1 Tablespoonful of Butter.

Beat the yolks well; add the milk, and then add the whites of the eggs, beaten to a stiff froth. Beat all together. The longer the eggs are beaten, the lighter will be the omelet. Make a plain omelet. (See recipe.) Fold and turn quickly into a hot dish; place three lumps of loaf sugar on top of the omelet, and bring to the table hot. As you place it on the table, pour the rum over the omelet and around. Set the rum on fire with a match, and with a tablespoon dash the burning rum over the omelet till all the sugar has melted over it and all the rum has evaporated. When it ceases burning serve immediately. This is served as a sweet entremet.

## CHAPTER XXIV.

### LOUISIANA RICE.

Le Riz de la Louisiane.

The cultivation of rice began in Louisiana nearly a hundred years after it commenced in Georgia and South Carolina, but Louisiana now produces more of this beautiful grain than both these States combined. It is one of the great Louisiana staples, and New Orleans is the distributing point of the immense crop that yearly make our immense rice fields of southwestern Louisiana the wonder and admiration of tourists.

In no section of the world can rice be grown at so small a cost as in Louisiana. The cost of growing the grain in our matchless clime is small, and it requires but little capital to begin.

As remarked in the beginning of this book, the consumption of rice has increased enormously of late, and it will continue to become more and more a popular article of food when the people of the great North and West learn how to cook it as well as the Creoles of Louisiana.

The folloing recipes, carefully selected from among many that are used in this old Creole city of New Orleans, will give an idea of how rice is prepared and made such a delightful article of food in our Creole households:

#### How to Prepare Rice for Cooking.

The whiteness of the rice depends in a great degree, upon its being washed thoroughly. Pick the rice clean, and wash it well in cold water before attempting to cook, rubbing the rice well with the hands, to get all the dust off. Pour off the first water, and add fresh; then pour off this, and add fresh again. The rice will then be ready to cook.

#### How to Boil Rice.

When properly boiled, rice should be snowy white, perfectly dry and smooth; and every grain separate and distinct. To attain this end, put a quart of water on the fire, and let it boil well, with a teaspoonful of salt. Wash a cup of rice well in cold water. When the water commences to boil well add the rice. Stir occasionally, and gently with a wooden spoon. The boiling water will toss the grains of rice, and prevent them from clinging together. As soon as the grains commence to soften, do not, under any circumstances, stir or touch the rice again. Let it continue to boil rapidly for about twenty minutes, or until the grains begin to swell out, and it appears to thicken. This is easily ascertained by touching one of the grains with your finger. When it has reached this stage, take the cover off and pour off the water, and set the pot in the oven, so that the rice may swell up. Let it stand in the oven about ten minutes. Do not let it brown, but simply dry—that is, let the water which rises dry out of the rice. Take it off, and let it stand a few minutes. Then pour out into a dish. Every grain will be white and beautiful, and stand apart because the drying in the oven will have evaporated the moisture, leaving the rice soft, snowy white and perfectly dry.

Boiled rice is delicious served with chicken, turkey, crab or shrimp or okra gumbo, as also with many vegetables, all daubes, and with gravies of all kinds. It is the standing dish on every Creole table.

#### Things to Remember in Boiling Rice.

Never set the rice to cook in cold water, or you will have a thick, mushy dish that is most unpleasant to the sight, and equally so to the taste.

Always use boiling water. Boil rapidly from the time that you cover the pot until you take it off, for this allows each grain to be tossed away from the other constantly, and also allows it to swell to three times its normal size. The constant motion of the water prevents the grains from sticking together.

Do not stir from the moment it begins to boil, for it will be noticed that when first the rice is put into the water it will cease boiling till the rice is heated. Stir occasionally during this period, to keep it from sinking to the bottom and burning, but do not touch it with a spoon or fork or anything, once it has commenced boiling. Follow implicitly the directions about setting in the oven and allowing the rice to "sweat," as the old Creoles say. You will then have a dish that is not only very beautiful and tempting to the sight, but most delectable to the taste.

#### Creole Jambalaya.

Jambalaya à la Créole.

Jambalaya is a Spanish-Creole dish, which is a great favorite in

New Orleans, and is made according to the following recipe:

One and a Half Cups of Rice.
1 Pound of Fresh Pork.  1 Slice of Ham.
1 Dozen Fine Chaurice (Pork Sausage.)
2 Onions.  1 Tablespoonful of Butter.
2 Cloves of Garlic.
2 Sprigs Each of Thyme and Parsley.
2 Bay Leaves. 2 Cloves Ground Very Fine.
3 Quarts of Beef Broth or Hot Water (Broth Preferred.)
½ Spoonful of Chili Pepper.
Salt, Pepper and Cayenne to Taste.

Cut the pork very fine, lean and fat, into pieces of about half an inch square. Chop the onions very fine, and mince the garlic and fine herbs. Grind the cloves. Put a tablespoonful of butter into the saucepan, and add the onions and pork, and let them brown slowly. Stir frequently, and let them continue browning slightly. When slightly brown, add the ham, chopped very fine, and the cloves of garlic. Then add the minced herbs, thyme, bay leaf and parsley and cloves. Let all this brown for five minutes longer, and add a dozen fine Chaurice, cut apart, and let all cook five minutes longer. Then add the three quarts of water or broth, always using in preference the broth. Let it all cook for ten minutes, and when it comes to a boil add the rice, which has been carefully washed. Then add to this a half teaspoonful of Chili pepper, and salt and Cayenne to taste. The Creoles season highly with Cayenne. Let all boil for a half hour longer, or until the rice is firm, and serve hot. Stir often, to mix all well. You will then have a real Creole Jambalaya. Some use the brisket of veal instead of the pork, but there is no comparison in the flavor, the pork being so superior. But, again, this is a matter of taste.

### Crab Jambalaya.
Jambalaya aux Crabes.

1 Dozen Fine, Large Crabs.
1½ Cups of Rice.  3 Quarts of Broth.
3 Tomatoes.  2 Onions.
1 Tablespoonful of Butter.
1 Tablespoonful of Flour. 2 Cloves of Garlic.
2 Sprigs of Thyme.  2 Bay Leaves.
½ Teaspoonful of Chili Pepper.
Salt and Black Pepper to Taste.

Boil the crabs according to recipe. (See Boiled Crabs.) Then cut in pieces, cutting the bodies into quarters. Proceed in exactly the same manner as in making Shrimp Jambalaya.

### Jambalaya au Congri.
Jambalaya au Congri.

1 Cup of Rice.
1 Pint of Cowpeas.
1 Large Onion.
¼ Pound of Salt Meat. 1 Square Inch of Ham.

Chop the small meat, after washing, into dice, and mince the ham. Boil the cowpeas and the salt meat and ham together. Add the onion, minced very fine. Boil the rice according to recipe for boiled rice. (see recipe.) Chop the meat well. After the peas and the rice are cooked, pour the rice into the pot of peas, which must not be dry, but very moist. Mix well. Let all simmer for five minutes, and then serve hot. On Fridays and fast days the Creoles boil the peas in water adding a tablespoonful of butter, but no meat. It is again buttered according to individual taste at table. The jambalaya, however, is much nicer when made with the meat.

### Shrimp Jambalaya.
Jambalaya aux Chevrettes.

1½ Cups of Rice.  3 Tomatoes.
80 Lake Shrimp.
2 Onions.  Cayenne to Taste.
1 Tablespoonful Butter. 1 Tablespoonful Flour.
½ Teaspoonful of Chili Pepper.
Salt.  Pepper.  2 Cloves of Garlic.
2 Sprigs Each of Thyme and Bay Leaf.

Chop two onions very fine, and put them in a saucepan to brown with a tablespoonful of butter. After a few minutes add a tablespoonful of flour and stir well. Then add chopped thyme, bay leaf and parsley, and two cloves of garlic, minced very fine. Let all of this fry five minutes longer, and be careful not to let it burn or brown too much. Add a half teaspoonful of Chili pepper, and three large tomatoes, chopped fine, and also add the juice. Let all brown or simmer for ten minutes longer. When cooked, add three quarts of broth or water, or, if on Friday, and you do not eat meat, add oyster water or plain water (the former preferred) which has been heated to the boiling point. Let all boil well, and then add the lake shrimp, which you will alreay have boiled according to recipe. (See recipe for Boiled shrimp.) Let the mixture boil again for five minutes, and add one cup and a half of rice, or half a pound, which has been well washed. Mix all well, and let boil for a half or three-quarters of an hour longer, stirring every once in a while, so as to mix all together. Serve hot.

### A French Pilou.
Pilou Français.

2 Chickens.  ½ Cup of Rice.
2 Tableapoonfuls of Butter.
The Yolks of 2 Eggs.  Bread Crumbs.

Boil the fowls according to recipe. (See recipe Boiled Chicken.) When done, take out about a pint of the liquor in which it was boiled, and put the rice, which you will have washed well, into the remaining boiling broth. Let it cook well for twenty minutes, and then add two tablespoonfuls of butter to the rice. Butter the bottom of a dish, and put upon it one-half of the rice, spreading out nicely. Lay upon it the chickens, which have been disjointed and buttered. Add the remaining chicken broth, pouring over the chicken. Then cover the fowls with the other half of the rice. Make the top perfectly smooth. Spread over it the yolks of two eggs, which have been well beaten. Sprinkle with bread crumbs, and dot with little bits of butter here and there. Set in the oven, let it brown, and serve hot.

### Chicken With Rice.
### Poulet au Riz.

1 Young Chicken.   ½ Cup of Rice.

This is a most delightful Creole way of preparing chicken and rice. It is highly recommended. Prepare and cook the chicken as in Poulet au Riz, only do not cut up the chicken, but stew whole. When three-fourths done, add the rice, and in serving place the chicken in the center of the dish and heap the rice around. Young chickens are best for this dish. An old chicken may be cut up and cooked till tender, as in Poulet au Riz. (See recipe Poulet au Riz, under chapter on Meat Soups.)

### Pilaff of Chicken.
### Pilaff de Volaille.

1 Chicken About Four Pounds.
½ Cup of Rice.   1 Tablespoonful of Butter.
Salt and Pepper to Taste.

Clean and cut the chicken as you would for a fricassé. Put in a stewpan and cover well with water. Add salt and pepper again to taste, having, of course, previously rubbed the fowl with salt and pepper. Let the chicken simmer gently for about an hour. Then take a half cup of rice and wash it thoroughly. Add it to the chicken. Salt again to taste. Cover and let all simmer for about twenty minutes longer. Then make a Tomato Sauce (see recipe). Dish the chicken and rice together, setting the chicken in the center of the dish and the rice around for a border. Serve hot. This dish can be nicely made from the remains of cold chicken or mutton.

### How to Make a Rice Border.
### Bordure de Riz.

1 Cup of Rice.   1 Quart of Boiling Water.
1 Tablespoonful of Butter.   Salt to Taste.

Boil the rice according to recipe given above, using one cup to one quart of boiling water. Boil rapidly for fifteen minutes. Pour off any water that remains on top. Set in the oven to dry for about ten minutes, then drain. Season with salt and pepper, and press into a well-buttered border mold. Put it in the oven and let it bake ten minutes. Take out. Place a dish on the mold. Turn it upside down, and remove the mold. The hollow space in the center can be filled with a White or Brown Fricassée of Chicken or Curry of Crawfish.

### Curry of Crawfish.
### Écrevisses au Kari.

1 Cup of Rice.   3 Dozen Crawfish.
2 Ounces of Butter.   1 Clove of Garlic.
2 Sprigs of Thyme.   2 Sprigs of Parsley.
1 Bay Leaf.   Juice of Half a Lemon.
1 Tablespoonful of Curry Powder.
1 Tablespoonful of Flour.   1 Quart of Water.
Salt and Pepper to Taste. A Dash of Cayenne.

Boil the crawfish according to the recipe given. (See Boiled Crawfish.) Clean and pick the crawfish the same as for a fricassée. Put two ounces of butter in the frying pan. Cut one onion in slices, add it to the butter, letting it brown nicely. Then add the well-seasoned crawfish, and fry them to a golden brown. Add one clove of garlic, finely minced, and minced thyme, parsley and bay leaf. Let this brown. After five minutes, add a quart of boiling water. Stir well. Season to taste with salt, pepper and a dash of Cayenne. Simmer gently until the crawfish are very tender. When done, add the juice of half a lemon, and mix one even tablespoonful of Curry Powder and one of flour with a little water. Bring it to a smooth paste by rubbing well, and add it to the crawfish. Stir constantly, and let it boil five minutes longer. Serve with a border of boiled rice heaped around it. Curry of Chicken is made in the same manner, by adding the Curry Powder.

### Boiled Rice, Italian Style.
### Riz Bouilli à l'Italienne.

1 Cup of Rice.   A Slice of Breakfast Bacon.
1 Tablespoonful of Grated Parmesan.
1 Pinch Saffron.   Salt and Pepper to Taste.
1 Tablespoonful of Butter.

Wash one cup of rice. Take boiling water, using about a quart. Add a slice of bacon and a tablespoonful of grated Parmesan cheese, and a pinch of saffron. Let it boil well for five minutes. Then add the rice gradually, continuing to cook according to the recipe for boiled rice. When done, remove the bacon, dot the top with bits of butter, set in the stove to dry for ten minutes, and serve hot.

### CALAS.
### "Belle Cala!. Tout Chaud!"

Under this cry was sold by the ancient Creole negro women in the French Quarter of New Orleans a delicious rice cake, which was eaten with the morning cup of Café au Lait. The Cala woman was a daily figure in the streets till within the last two or three years. She went her rounds in quaint bandana tignon, guinea blue dress, and white apron, and carried on her head a covered bowl, in which were the dainty and hot Calas. Her cry, "Belle Cala! Tout Chaud!" would penetrate the morning air, and the olden Creole cooks would rush to the doors to get the first fresh, hot Calas to carry to their masters and mistresses with the early morning cup of coffee. The Cala women have almost all passed away, for, as remarked at the beginning of this book, there is a "new colored woman" in New Orleans, as elsewhere in the south, and she disdains all the pretty olden industries and occupations which were a constant and genteel source of revenue to the old negro mothers and grandmothers. Only two or three of the ancient Cala women remain. The cries of "Belle Cala! Tout Chaud!" are now few and far between. Once in a while, like some ghostly voice of the past, one starts up in bed of an early morning as the weak old voice faintly penetrates your chamber. In a second more it is lost in the distance, and you turn over with a sigh for the good old times and the quaint customs of old Creole days, which gave such a beautiful and unique tinge to the life of the ancient quarter.

But the custom of making Calas still remains. In many an ancient home the good housewife tells her daughters just how "Tante Zizi" made the Calas in her day, and so are preserved these ancient traditional recipes.

From one of the last of the olden Cala women, one who has walked the streets of the French quarter for fifty years and more, the Picayune has gotten the following established Creole recipe:

½ Cup of Rice.  3 Cups Water (boiling).
3 Eggs.  ½ Cup of Sugar.
½ Cake of Compressed Yeast.
¼ Teaspoonful of Grated Nutmeg.
Powdered White Sugar.  Boiling Lard.

Put three cups of water in a saucepan and let it boil hard. Wash half a cup of rice thoroughly, and drain and put in the boiling water. Let it boil till very soft and mushy. Take it out and set it to cool. When cold, mash well and mix with the yeast, which you will have dissolved in a half cup of hot water. Set the rice to rise overnight. In the morning beat three eggs thoroughly, and add to the rice, mixing and beating well. Add a half cup of sugar and three tablespoonfuls of flour, to make the rice adhere. Mix well and beat thoroughly, bringing it to a thick batter. Set to rise for fifteen minutes longer. Then add about a half teaspoonful of grated nutmeg, and mix well. Have ready a frying pan, in which there is sufficient quantity of lard boiling for the rice cakes to swim in it. Test by dropping in a small piece of bread. If it becomes a golden brown, the lard is ready, but if it burns or browns instantly it is too hot. The golden brown color is the true test. Take a large deep spoon, and drop a spoonful at a time of the preparation into the boiling lard, remembering always that the cake must not touch the bottom of the pan. Let fry to a nice brown. The old Cala women used to take the Calas piping hot, wrap them in a clean towel, basket or bowl, and rush through the streets with the welcome cry, "Belle Cala Tout Chaud!" ringing on the morning air. But in families the cook simply takes the Calas out of the frying pan and drains off the lard by laying in a colander or on heated pieces of brown paper. They are then placed in a hot dish, and sprinkled over with powdered white sugar, and eaten hot with Café au Lait.

The above quantity will make six cakes. Increase in proportion.

Calas may also be made of rice flour. In olden days the Cala women used to pound the rice themselves in a mortar till they reduced it to a fine powder or flour. Then it was mixed and set to rise overnight. If the rice flour is used, one tablespoonful of wheat flour is sufficient to bind.

Often in large Creole families, where rice is left over from the day before, the quantity is increased by adding a cup of well-sifted self-raising flour. But these cakes, though very nice and palatable, are not the true "Calas," which are made entirely of rice, with only a little flour to bind, as directed above.

### Rice Waffles.
#### Galettes de Riz.

1½ Cups of Softly Boiled Rice.
2 Ounces of Butter. 1 Pint of Scalded Milk.
3 Eggs. 1 Teaspoonful of Baking Powder.
½ Teaspoonful of Salt.
1 Tablespoonful of Wheat Flour.

The rice must be cold and well mashed. Melt the two tablespoonfuls of butter into the milk, which has been allowed to cool. Beat the yolks of the eggs and the whites seperately, making the latter come to a stiff froth. Mix the rice and milk. Beat thoroughly, and then add a half teaspoonful of salt and one of baking powder, and the flour. Put the yolks into the batter, first blending well, and lastly add the whites, and beat well again. The waffle iron should be very hot, and well greased in every part. Always have a little brush with which to grease the waffle irons. Pour the batter into a pitcher, so that you may more easily fill the irons. Open the irons, pour the batter from the pitcher and fill the iron quickly. Then close quickly and set on the fire. As soon as the edges are set, turn the iron and bake on the other side. Two minutes should be all the time required to bake a waffle nicely. The waffle must be baked evenly. Always select the simple waffle baker with four compartments in preference to the more elaborate designs. Better results will be achieved. When the waffles are baked, remove them carefully, place on a hot dish, piling them in double rows, and butter them generously. Rice waffles are generally served with ground cinnamon and sugar mixed and sprinkled over. But this is a matter of taste. They are very delicious when served with butter and Louisiana Syrup or Molasses.

### Rice Griddle Cakes.

### Gateaux de Riz.

1 Pint of Milk. 1½ Cups of Cold Boiled Rice.
1½ Cups of Flour. 2 Eggs.
2 Heaping Teaspoonfuls of Baking Powder.
1 Large Teaspoonful of Salt.

Scald the milk and set it to cool. Press the rice through a sieve, and then add the well-beaten yolks of two eggs, then the salt, yeast powder and flour, blended, and beat well. Then add the milk, blending thoroughly, and finally the whites of the eggs, beaten to a stiff froth. Mix thoroughly and bake on a hot griddle.

### Rice Bread.

### Pain de Riz.

1 Cup of Cold Boiled Rice.
2 Cups of White Indian Meal. 3 Eggs.
1 Tablespoonful of Melted Butter.
2 Heaping Teaspoonfuls of Baking Powder.
1¼ Pints Milk. 1 Teaspoonful Salt.

Beat the yolks and whites of the eggs together until very light, and then pour in the milk, mixing gradually. Add the well-prepared meal, into which you will have mixed the salt and baking powder. Beat well. Then add the melted butter and the rice, which you will have pressed through a sieve. Mix all thoroughly and beat till very light. Then grease the bottom of a shallow pan and turn the mixture in and bake half an hour in a hot oven. Serve hot, buttering the slices freely. This is a delicious breakfast bread, and, as in any of the above recipes, cold rice left over may be utilized in its making.

### Rice Croquettes With Parsley.

### Croquettes de Riz au Persil.

1 Cup of Rice. 1 Quart of Milk.
1 Tablespoonful of Chopped Parsley.
The Yolks of 4 Eggs.
Salt and Pepper to Taste.

Wash the rice well, and put it on to boil in a farina boiler with the milk, or use cold boiled rice, and set it to boil with the milk, after pressing through a sieve. If the rice has not been cooked, let it boil about an hour. If it has already been cooked, twenty minutes will suffice. When very thick take from the fire and beat until very smooth, mashing all the grains. Then add the well-beaten yolks of the eggs, and cook for about eight or ten minutes longer. Add the parsley and seasoning, using the white pepper. Take from the fire and mix well, and turn out on a plate, and let it cool. When cool, form it into pretty cylinders of about three inches in length and one and a half in thickness. Roll these in a beaten egg, to bind, and then in bread crumbs, and fry in boiling lard. Drain and serve with any daube, or with any meat cooked with gravy.

### Rice Croquettes With Fruits.

### Croquettes de Riz aux Fruits.

½ Cup of Rice. 1 Pint of Milk.
2 Large Tablespoonfuls of Sugar.
¼ Cup of Currants. ¼ Cup of Raisins.
¼ Cup of Citron.
½ Teaspoonful of Vanilla Essence.
The Yolks of Two Eggs.

Put the milk into a farina boiler, and add the rice which you will have washed well. Boil until very thick. Seed the raisins and prepare the other fruits. Beat the eggs well and add them to the rice, and then stir in the sugar. Beat until very smooth. Then take from the fire, and add the essence of vanilla, the raisins and currants, and the citron. Turn out all into a dish to cool. Then form into pretty pyramids, and dip first in a well-beaten egg, and then in bread crumbs. Fry in boiling lard. Drain well. When about to serve, put a small piece of Currant Jelly on the top of each croquette. Then dust the whole with powdered sugar, and serve with Sauce à la Vanille. (Vanilla Sauce, see recipe.)

### Rice Flour Croquettes.

### Croquettes de Farine de Riz.

1 Quart Milk. ½ Split Vanilla Stick.
6 Ounces of Ground Rice. ¼ Pound of Sugar.
2 Ounces Butter. Yolks of 8 Eggs.
1 Ounce of Pineapple. 2 Ounces of Apricots.
3 Ounces of Cherries.
1 Ounce of Orange Peel. A Cream Sauce.

Boil a quart of milk, and add to it while boiling the split vanilla stick.

Take out the vanilla after you have cut all the fruit and orange peel into small dice, throwing away the seeds. Drop the ground rice like a shower of rain into the boiling milk, stirring it continuously with a whisk of the hand. When it begins to soften, set it back, and let it cook for fifteen minutes longer. Then mix in the cut fruits, and add the butter, which you will have melted. Add the eggs, which have been beaten very light in the sugar. Mix thoroughly, and add the orange peel; cut into quarter dice. When the mixture is very light, set it to cool, by spreading it out on a baking sheet, covered with white paper. When cold, divide it into small balls, roll these in powdered Macaroons (see recipe Macaroons), dip in beaten egg, and then roll in white bread crumbs. Fry in boiling lard. Drain in a heated colander or on a piece of brown paper. Then dress the croquettes nicely on a dish, sprinkle with vanilla sugar, and serve each separately, with a Cream Sauce. (See recipe.) This is a delicious dish.

### Rice Custard.
### Riz au Lait.

1 Cup Rice. 3-4 Cup Sugar. ½ Grated Nutmeg.
1 Teaspoonful of Vanilla.
The Peel of a Quarter of an Orange, Cut in Dice.

Boil the rice very soft, and then add the milk, and let it come to a good boil. Add the orange peel, cut in quarter dice. Beat the eggs and sugar well together till very light, and add to the boiling custard. Cook for one minute longer. Then take from the fire, and add the vanilla and one-quarter of the grated nutmeg. Place all in a dish to cool. Sprinkle the top with grated nutmeg, and serve cold. This is a famous Creole dish.

If you wish to have a baked custard, Place the custard in a pan or in cups. Set in the oven to brown, and serve hot, with a Cream Sauce. The above amount will fill about eight cups.

### Rice Dumplings.
### Echaudés de Riz.

It was the old Creole negro cooks who first evolved that famous Creole dessert, Rice Dumplings. They are made as follows:

½ Cup of Flour. 3 Cups of Ground Rice.
8 Apples, Tart and Not Overripe.
2 Quarts of Milk. Sugar and Cinnamon.
¼ of the Peel of an Orange.
½ of a Grated Nutmeg.

Pare the apples and take out the cores, leaving the apples whole. Take the ground cinnamon and sugar, and mix well, and fill the cores with this mixture. In the meantime boil the rice in milk till it comes to the consistency of flour, having added the grated peel of an orange and a half teaspoonful of grated nutmeg and a half cup of flour. Take off the fire, and let it cool. Then cover each apple all over with a very thick coating of the rice, and tie each dumpling in a cloth very tightly, and put them in a pot of cold water. Bring the water to a quick boil, and boil the apples for three-quarters of an hour. When done, untie the cloth and place the dumplings carefully on a large dish. Sprinkle each with a little grated nutmeg, put on top of each a dot of butter, set in the oven for five or ten minutes to brown, and serve with a Hard or Cream Sauce. They are most delicious with a Hard Sauce. They may be served without setting in the oven, immediately after they have been taken from the water, or they may be served cold.

Again, in large families, the apples may be cut in halves or quarters, and boiled in the same manner, covering with the coating of rice, as in the following recipe:

### Apples and Rice.
### Riz à la Condé.

Take three large, fine apples, and cut in halves. Pare and core. Then bake in the oven until quite done and juicy. Make a Rice Pudding (see recipe), using only one cup of rice and other ingredients in proportion. When the apples are cold, set in a dish, placing each apple over a small bed of Rice Pudding. Place the same quantity on top of the apple, so that it will be inclosed between the rice as in a ball. Serve in saucers, and pour over each riced apple two tablespoonfuls of Brandy or Cream Sauce. (See Sauces for Puddings, etc.)

### Rice Meringue.
### Meringue de Riz.

1 Cup Rice. 6 Creole Eggs. 2 Cups Sugar.
1 Pint Milk. 2 Tablespoonfuls Butter.
The Grated Rind of a Lemon.

Wash the rice thoroughly, and boil it in a quart of boiling water. When very soft, drain the rice of all water by pressing through a colander, and add it to the milk. Beat the yolks of the eggs and the sugar together till very light, and add the butter. Then add the juice and the grated rind of a lemon, and mix thoroughly. Place the whole mixture into a baking dish, and bake for half an hour in a quick oven. Beat the whites to a stiff froth, and add gradually six tablespoonfuls of powdered sugar (white), beating them well all the time. Continue beating till the whites are stiff enough to stand alone. Pour this over the top of the rice, and set it back in the oven a few minutes to brown. It may be served either hot or cold.

### Rice Soufflé.
### Soufflé de Riz.

¼ Pound of Rice Flour. ½ Pound of Sugar. ½ Pint Cream. 6 Fresh Creole Eggs. 1 Teaspoonful Vanilla. ¼ Teaspoonful Salt. The Grated Peel of Half an Orange.

Boil the rice well, according to recipe, and when very soft add the half pint of cream, and let it come to a boil. Beat the butter and sugar and the yolks of the eggs together until very light. Then add the rice, which has been boiled in the milk. Set on the fire, and add the grated peel of a half orange, and stir continually till it thickens. Add the salt. Stir well. Then take from the fire, and add the vanilla. Have the whites of the eggs beaten to a stiff thick froth. Pour this over the rice. Set in the oven a few minutes to brown, and serve immediately while very hot, or it will fall.

### Snowballs.
### Riz à la Neige.

1 Cup Rice. 1 Pint Milk. ¼ Cup White Sugar. The Whites of Six Eggs. A Cream Sauce.

Boil the rice with the milk, and add the whites of three eggs, well beaten with the sugar. Stir well. and flavor with the juice of one lemon. The mixture should be white as snow. Take from the fire as it thickens well, and set in a dish to cool. Form the rice into small balls of about two and a half inches square (little "boulettes," as the Creoles call them.) Have the rest of the eggs beaten to a stiff froth, with two tablespoonfuls of powdered sugar. Cover the tops of the balls with the mixture and place in the stove to heat. Let the balls remain about four minutes, without browning. Take out, and serve with a Cream Sauce (see recipe Sauces for Puddings,) or just as they are.

### Rice Cream Pudding.
### Pouding de Riz à la Crème.

1 Cup of Boiled Rice. 3-4 Cup of Sugar. 1 Ounce of Pineapple. 2 Ounces of Raisins. 2 Ounces of Currants. 1 Ounce of Grated Orange Peel. 1 Quart of Milk. The Yolks of 6 Eggs. ¼ of a Grated Nutmeg.

Boil the rice well, and then drain through a colander and set to boil with the milk. When it has cooked for twenty minutes, add all the fruits, being careful to have the pineapple cut into dice, and the raisins seeded, and the currants picked, washed and dried. Then add the orange peel and grated nutmeg, and finally the eggs, which have been well beaten in the sugar till very light. Let all simmer for just one minute. Then take off the stove, place in a baking pan, and set to brown nicely in a quick oven for about twenty-five minutes. When well browned, have ready a meringue, which you will have made by beating the whites of two eggs to a froth (reserve the whites of two eggs), and add to this two tablespoonfuls of powdered white sugar. Spread all this over the pudding. Let it brown slightly in a hot oven, or the meringue will fall. Serve either hot or very cold. The pudding may be made without the addition of the pineapple.

### Frozen Rice Custard.
### Crème de Riz Glacée.

1 Cupful of Rice. 1 Quart of Milk. A Pint of Cream. 1 Cup of Sugar. 1 Teaspoonful of Salt. 6 Oranges.

Prepare exactly as above, as far as boiled, but omit the fruits and use only the grated rind of an orange in making the pudding. When cold, add the juice of an orange and the cream, beaten or whipped to a froth. Four tablespoonfuls of wine or lemon juice may be substituted for the orange juice, according to taste. Then freeze, the same as you would ice cream, and serve with an Orange Sauce, prepared as follows:

Boil together for ten minutes one cupful of water, one-half cup of sugar, the grated yellow rind or zest of two oranges. Add to this the strained juice of four oranges. Cool and set to freeze. Boil three tablespoonfuls of sugar with three of water for two minutes. Beat this into the white of one egg, which has already been brought to a stiff froth. Stir this meringue into the frozen mixture, and the sauce will be ready to serve with the pudding or custard.

### Rice With Compote of Oranges.
### Riz à la Compote d'Oranges.

3-4 Cup Rice. 1½ Pints Milk. 1 Quart Cream. 1½ Cups Sugar. Yolks of 8 Eggs. 1 Tablespoonful of Vanilla. The Grated Peel of an Orange. 12 Sweet Louisiana Oranges. 1 Pound Sugar. 1 Gill Water. ¼ of a Grated Nutmeg.

Wash the rice clean, and boil according to recipe in about a pint and a quarter of water. In half an hour take off and drain of all water, and press through a sieve. Then add it to the milk, and let it boil slowly a half hour longer without burning. Whip the cream to a stiff froth, and add the drain to the rice or milk, and set the whipped cream to cool until it is needed. Beat the yolks of the eggs and the sugar until they are very light. Add them to the boiling rice, stirring constantly and well, and let it cook for two minutes, adding in the meantime the grated peel of the orange. Take the mixture from the fire. Then add the tablespoonful of vanilla, and the grated nutmeg. Mix well and set out to cool. Remove the dasher from the ice cream freezer, and when the mixture has become very cool, turn it into the freezer and let it set packed in rock salt and ice for three hours.

In the meantime take a dozen sweet Louisiana oranges, and peel and cut them crosswise into halves. Take out the cores with the sharp point of a' penknife, and set them in a dish ready for use. Put a round of sugar to boil with one gill of water, and after ten minutes add the juice of half a lemon. Put a few pieces at a time of the oranges into this boiling liquid, and lay them out side by side in a flat dish. Pour over them the syrup that remains from the boiling, and set the dish in the ice box to cool. When ready to serve, wipe thoroughly the outside of the can that contains the pudding, and all around the edges, so as to remove any traces of salt. Wet a towel in boiling water and stand the can upon it. Open the can. Put a round dish on top, and then turn quickly upside down, and remove the can. If the pudding adheres, repeat the applications of the hot towel at the bottom and around. Place the oranges on top and all around the pudding, and pour over them the syrup, which has become cool, but not frozen. Serve immediately. This is one of the most delicious, as well as one of the most typical of our Louisiana methods of serving rice as a dessert.

### Left-Over Rice.

Enough has been said and written in these recipes to give an idea of the possibilities of Louisiana rice under proper methods of culinary preparation. It enters into many different combinations in cooking, and among the poorer Creoles of large families it takes, in a great measure, the place of bread. A meal of boiled rice, with Grillades à la Sauce, and Red Beans or White Beans, is very popular among the Creoles, especially those of limited means, all of these being good, nourishing, as well as economical, dishes, the rice not only saving the expenditure of money for bread, but making a most welcome and palatable substitute. The family that uses rice daily will note the economy that follows in the purchase of bread.

Left-over rice may be utilized in almost any of the above dishes, but it is more generally used in the making of rice waffles or rice cakes for breakfast, Calas, etc. It is also fried or made into rice fritters, as follows:

### Fried Rice.
### Riz Frit.

Take the left-over rice from the day before, and cut it into slices of proper thickness, and fry to a nice brown, turning it carefully, to avoid breaking the slices. This makes an excellent breakfast dish, with Grillades à la Sauce. (See recipe.)

### Rice Fritters.
### Beignets de Riz.

Take the left-over rice and mash very fine. If you have only a cupful, take three eggs, a half cup of flour, one teaspoonful of yeast powder, and sugar to taste, and beat all into a light, thick batter. Cook by dropping a spoonful at a time into boiling lard. This is a sweet entremet, as also an excellent breakfast dish.

### Parched Rice.
### Riz Grillé.

Rice may be parched in the same manner as popcorn. It is a method of cooking rice that came to New Orleans from the West Indies, and was brought into general use by the San Domingo refugees, who came to New Orleans in numbers after the great insurrection. When the culture of rice became general in the southwestern parishes of our State, these old settlers began to give rice-parching parties, and they became very fashionable. The Creole children and the belles and beaux of eighty years ago enjoyed parching rice just as much as northern children, youths and maidens enjoy roasting chestnuts or parching corn. Rice is parched in the same manner as the Creoles parch popcorn. The parched grain of rice becomes a beautiful open ball, which is eaten with salt or sugar, and is very delicious.

## CHAPTER XXV.
### CEREALS.

Under the heading of Céreals are classed Wheat, Rye, Barley, Oats, Corn, Maize or Indian Corn, Buckwheat and Rice. Rice being one of our great Louisiana staples, and the proper methods of preparing it so little known, has been separately treated in the preceding chapter. The other Cereals are in general use in every section of our country, and will require less amplification.

### WHEAT.
#### Du Froment.

On account of its universal consumption and great nutritive qualities, Wheat is considered the principal cereal. In the form of bread, it has long been distinguished as the "Staff of Life."

The structure of the grain, like that of other cereals, consists of a gritty, woody center covering, which is indigestible, and which is gotten rid of, after the grain has been ground, by "sifting." In the whole wheat grain is found a perfect food, for it contains all that is necessary to support life—starch, gluten, sugar, nitrogenous and carbonaceous matter, water, salts, potash, soda, lime, phosphoric acid, magnesia, etc.

In what is called "whole meal," the bran and pollards derived from the outer covering are retained. From this wheat is made "Brown Bread," and though this kind of bread contains far more nitrogenous matter than white bread, it is not in general use, on account of its indigestibility. It should never be eaten by persons of weak digestion.

From wheat are derived not only flour in all its various degrees of refinement, but several delightful and nutritious breakfast cereals, such as "Cracked Wheat," which is generally and very wisely used among the Creoles as an article of food. "Farina," an excellent preparation, which is delicate and acceptable to the most fastidious stomach, and, being rich in nitrogenous matter, is not only a most excellent food for adults, but is considered far superior in nutritive value to arrowroot or cornstarch for children. Again, we have "Wheatena," and "Cerealine," both muscle and brain feeding preparations of Wheat.

Wheat contains a gluten, which is a gray, elastic, tough substance. This gluten is especially abundant in wheat grown in warm climates. From this gluten paste Macaroni and Vermicelli are made.

#### Cracked Wheat.
#### Froment Crevé.

1 Cup of Cracked Wheat.
1 Quart of Water.
1 Teaspoonful of Salt.

Under the name of "Cracked Wheat" there is sold in the markets whole wheat grains which are cooked by boiling in a double boiler until the entire envelope of the grain bursts open. It will require four hours of good boiling, therefore, it is best to soak the grain over night in a quart of cold water. In the morning set the kettle containing the grain in another kettle of cold water, add the salt, and let it gradually heat and boil for at least an hour and a half. It should be thoroughly cooked. Serve with sugar and cream for breakfast.

Wheatena may be cooked without soaking, as also Cerealine. If a single boiler is used, be very careful to stir often, to prevent burning.

#### FARINA.
#### Fécule.

½ Cup of Farina.
1 Quart of Water or Milk.
1 Teaspoonful of Salt.

Add the salt to the milk or water, and then sift in slowly sufficient Farina to make a thick gruel. Set in a double boiler, and let it cook for about a half hour, stirring frequently while it boils.

#### Farina Gruel.
#### Gruau de Fécule.

1 Cup of Boiling Water.
1 Cup of Fresh Milk.
1 Large tablespoonful of Farina.
2 Tablespoonfuls of White Sugar.

In preparing this splendid food for infants, take a cup of boiling water, one cup of milk, and a pinch of salt. Slightly salt the water. Set one boiler within another, the latter boiler being filled with boiling water. Stir the Farina into the cup of boiling water, and let it boil, stirring constantly, till it thickens. Then add the milk, stirring it gradually, and let it boil about fifteen minutes longer. Sweeten, and when it is cool give to the child. Enough may be made to last all day. Warm, when it is needed, with a little boil-in milk.

## RYE.
### Seigle.

Rye Meal, once such a common article of food in New Orleans, is still extensively used by the German population, both in making Rye Bread and in making Rye Mush. As regards nutritive quality, Rye ranks slightly less than flour.

### Rye Mush.
### Bouillie de Seigle.

3-4 Cup of Rye Meal.
1 Quart of Boiling Water.

Sift the meal into the boiling water, and stir constantly while doing so. Add the salt, and continue stirring till the mixture begins to boil. Then cover and let it cook slowly for at least an hour and a quarter. Serve hot for breakfast, with sugar and cream.

## OATS.
### Avoine.

From Oats, which are used so extensively as food for beasts, is produced Oatmeal, which heads the list of flesh-producing and strengthening grains, being far richer than flour in nitrogen and fat, and therefore more nutritious. With oatmeal porridge for breakfast, oatmeal cakes for dinner, milk, potatoes and a few vegetables, the hard-working laborer or brain worker need require little else for sustenance from year's end to year's end. The coarsely ground Scotch oatmeal is the most nutritious, though we have many refined preparations, such as "Nudavene," "Rolled Oats," etc., which are very palatable to delicate stomachs. With good milk, oatmeal makes a most nutritious breakfast or supper for children or adults. It is in far more general use in New Orleans than in former years. A gruel of oatmeal is about the healthiest article of food that any mother, whether rich or poor, can give to her growing babies. Oatmeal is a heat-producing food. It is used extensively in spring, autumn and winter in our climate; in summer we have our own splendid Creole substitutes, Hominy and Grits.

### OATMEAL.
### Gruau d'Avoine.

1 Cup of Oatmeal.
1 Quart of Boiling Water.
1 Teaspoonful of Salt.

It is best to soak the oatmeal, when the coarse Scotch Oats are used, over night. Then cook for a half hour in the morning, boiling constantly, and salt to taste. If the oatmeal is not soaked, it will require at least an hour to cook. It burns very easily, and, therefore, it is always best to set in a double boiler. Serve with cream.

The more delicate preparations of oatmeal, such as "Nudavene," "Rolled Oats," etc., require only fifteen or twenty minutes to cook, and need no soaking. Always put the preparations in boiling water.

### Steamed Oatmeal.
### Gruau d'Avoine à la Vapeur.

1 Teacupful of Oatmeal.
1 Quart of Boiling Water.
1 Teaspoonful of Salt.

Add the oatmeal to the water, and then add the salt, and set the steaming vessel over a pot of cold water, and let it gradually heat, and then steam for an hour and a half. Keep closely covered. When done, serve with cream.

### Oat Flakes.
### Flocons d'Avoine.

1 Teacupful of Oat Flakes.
1 Quart of Boiling Water.
½ Teaspoonful of Salt.

This delicate preparation from oatmeal is prepared by putting the quart of water into a porcelain-lined saucepan, and letting it come to a boil. Add the salt, and when it is boiling stir in gradually the oat flakes. Keep stirring to prevent burning. Let the preparation boil for about fifteen or twenty minutes, and serve with sugar and cream, or simply cream or milk.

It might be emphasized here that ordinary coarse oatmeal that has not been soaked requires from two to two and a half hours of steady cooking to render it palatable and digestible. Never be afraid of cooking any cereal or preparations from cereals, except rice, too long, no matter how the directions read. A half hour or so longer cooking does not injure them, but, on the contrary, renders them easier of digestion.

## CORN.
### Du Maïs.

Under this heading are included Corn proper and our own Indian Corn, or Maize. From these come such staple dishes as "Grits," "Big Hominy," "Little Hominy," "Lye Hominy," or "Samp."

Corn contains far greater force-producing and fattening matter than Wheat. Scientists declare that cornmeal contains six times as much oil as wheat. Corn Bread is, therefore, an excellent winter diet, as also the delicate "Grits" and "Big and Small Hominy." "Samp," or "Lye Hominy," is used throughout the summer, as less heatening. Preparations of Corn are among the cheapest, if not the very cheapest articles of food and considering their high nutritive value, are especially recommended to the families of the poor. But, whether rich or poor, there are few Creole families in New Orleans who sit to breakfast without a good dish of Grits or Hominy.

### GRITS.
#### Du Gru.

Under the heading of corn might properly be classed the white corn grits, without which no breakfast in Louisiana is considered complete. Grits are not only used for breakfast, but may appear on the table several times a day, the left-over grits from breakfast being utilized either in dainty cakes or entremets, or else warmed over and served with gravies. Grits is the ground dried corn. We have yellow grits, or grits from which the outer yellow covering of the corn has not been removed, and white grits, the latter considered the daintier preparation. From these comes the "Small Hominy," or corn ground to superfineness. Grits are always boiled. Left-over may be fried or warmed up again, or beaten with eggs and milk and baked. This is a most delicious dish.

In ante bellum days, and up to about fifteen years ago, the "grits man" was as common a figure in the streets of the old French quarter as the "ring man," the "bottle man," or the "Cala woman." The "toot-toot," long drawn out of his great tin horn, nearly three feet in length, was as usual a cry as that of "Belle calas! Belle chaurice! Belle fromage!" for everything that was worth selling was considered "belle," or "beautiful," in New Orleans. The "grits man" went his rounds in a covered wagonette, labeled "Grits," and when his great horn was heard the housekeepers rushed to the doors to make bargains in the dainty breakfast cereal. But, like the "Cala woman," the "Grits man" is fast becoming a memory of other days.

#### Boiled Grits.
#### Du Gru Bouilli.
##### 2 Cups of Grits.
2 Quarts of Water. 2 Teaspoonfuls of Salt.

Wash the grits in fresh cold water, and throw off the refuse. Wash again and drain. Into two quarts of cold water put the grits. Add the salt, and stir frequently while they are coming to the boiling point. Then set back on the stove and let them cook slowly for about an hour. It must be of the consistency of a very thick starch, or drier, if preferred. For invalids it may be cooked like a cornmeal mush. Serve hot. with any meat, with gravy, or serve with milk, as oatmeal, as a preliminary to breakfast, or, again, simply eat with butter. In any manner in which they are served they are always relishable and palatable. If half milk, instead of water, is added in cooking, the dish is all the more delicious.

#### Baked Grits.
#### Du Gru aux Oeufs.
##### 1 Cup of Grits.
½ Quart of Water. ½ Quart of Milk. 2 Eggs. Salt to Taste.

Boil the grits in the water and milk, mixed. Season, and when quite dry, take off the stove and let it cool a little. Beat the whites and yolks separately, and when the grits is cool beat in the yolks, and blend thoroughly. Then add the whites, and beat till very light. Add a gill of cream. Set in an oven and bake to a beautiful browin, and serve hot. This is an ideal Creole breakfast dish. Cold grits may be thus utilized.

### HOMINY.
#### Saccamité.

Hominy is called by the Creoles the older sister of Grits. It was the Indians around Louisiana who first taught the use of hominy. They used to take all the dried Indian corn and thresh it till all the yellow, hardened outer germ or hull came off, the grain being left white. Then they would bring the large whitened grains into the city to sell. Hominy became a great industry, and was extensively manufactured and sold all over the south. It was the chief food of the southern negroes. But it was also a standing dish on the most elegant tables. The little Creole children were reared on "La Saccamité." The hominy was boiled in water in the same proportions as grits, but, of course, allowed to cook much longer, till the great white grains of corn were very soft, and yielded easily to pressure. It is still cooked in the same way, and eaten with milk or with sugar, the latter being a favorite dish with the Creole children. It is also eaten with meat and gravy, or simply with salt and butter. Left-over hominy is utilized in making hominy griddle cakes. So general is the use of hominy in Creole homes, that the ancient dames have a saying when any one is dissatisfied with home, and longs to pass beyond its environments, "Tempi, pour toi! La Saccamité te raménera!" "Never mind! Hominy will bring you back!"

We have also "Lye Hominy," or Hominy soaked in Lye till the coarse outer germ comes off. This is the great summer breakfast dish of the city and parishes. The hominy is made in the parishes, and shipped to New Orleans. It is also pounded and used for making "Lye Hominy Bread."

In our day, oatmeal, cracked wheat,

en favorites, grits and hominy, in popular favor in New Orleans. These, as shown in this chapter, are also cooked like grits, in the proportion of one cup of the grain to one quart of water. Simple breakfast hominy is the hulled grain broken up into a number of small pieces.

### Boiled Hominy.
### La Saccamité Bouillie.

1 Pint of Hominy.
2 Quarts of Water. Salt to Taste.

Hominy should always be soaked over night in cold water. Wash the hominy, and put into two quarts of water to soak. In the morning turn both hominy and water into a saucepan, and let it boil slowly for three or four hours. Serve with sugar and cream. It may also be eaten with butter and salt and pepper.

### Hominy Croquettes.
### La Saccamité en Croquettes.

These are made from the left-over hominy. They are prepared in exactly the same manner as rice croquettes. (See recipe.) Grits may be made into croquettes in the same manner.

### Fried Grits or Hominy.
### Gru ou Saccamité Frite.

To fry grits or hominy, after the grain is boiled, let it cool. Then season with salt and pepper, and spread on a biscuit board. When perfectly cold, cut into slices and dust each slice with a little flour. Brush again with a beaten egg, and fry in lard till a light brown.

### Lye Hominy or Samp.
### Saccamité à la Lessive.

This is an old-fashioned Creole way of preparing hulled corn. It is and has been much in vogue for many generations throughout rural Louisiana. The corn is allowed to get very ripe, put to dry, and then hulled. It is then allowed to lie for many days, spread out upon a cloth, till thoroughly dried. An immense pot is then filled with water, and a bag containing at least a quart or more of hard wood ashes is put into it. A good peck of the old, ripe, dry, hulled corn is thrown in, and it is allowed to soak for at least twenty-four hours. The corn is then put to boil in these ashes till the husks or outer germs come off easily. Then the corn is thrown into the cold water and divested of the hulls by thorough rubbing with the hands. It is then washed in four or five waters, till every taste of potash disappears.

Another way the Creoles of rural Louisiana have of preparing Lye Hominy is to dilute the strong lye in water, and then boil the corn in this till the hull comes off. After thoroughly washing, the corn prepared after either way is sent in large quantities to New Orleans, as well as used for home consumption. In cooking Lye Hominy, it is either boiled in water until the kernels are soft, as in other recipes for Hominy, making a delicious dish when served with milk, or cream, or it is ground or pounded into a flour, from which is made that famous Louisiana breakfast offering, "Lye Hominy Bread." (See recipe under chapter on Breads.) This flour also finds a ready sale among the Creoles during summer.

In preparing Hominy after the fashion, the Creoles again demonstrate how perfectly they understand conditions of life in Louisiana and the peculiarities of our climate. Lye is an alkali, and when the corn is soaked in it, much of the oil, which gives it such heat-producing power, is lost. The Hominy thus prepared and distinguished as "Samp," becomes a splendid summer food, while "Big Hominy" and "Little Hominy" and "Grits" supply heat for winter. Any family may make its own Lye Hominy at home in small quantities by following the above recipes, first making the lye by boiling two handfuls of clean, hardwood ashes in cold water for twenty-five minutes, and when the lye is strong and slippery add the corn. As the hulls begin to start, skim out the corn and throw it into a pan of cold water and proceed as above.

### Cornmeal Mush.
### Bouillie de Farine de Maïs.

1½ Cups of Cornmeal.
2 Quarts of Boiling Water.
1½ Teaspoonfuls of Salt.

Set the water to boil in a porcelain-lined or agate stewpot; add the salt, and when the light scum comes on top, skim it off. Then add the fresh, sweet white cornmeal, putting a handful at a time into the water, and stirring with a spoon, or a pudding stick, round and round, as the meal falls lightly from the hand. When one handful is exhausted, refill it, and continue stirring and letting the meal fall by degrees, until the pudding stick will stand in it. This is the test. Continue stirring, and when sufficiently cooked, which will be in a half hour, as the bubbles begin to puff up, turn into a bowl, bring to the table (either hot or cold) and eat with milk, butter, sugar, syrup or with meat and gravy.

In preparing this as a gruel for infants, take one-half cup of cornmeal, a quart of water, and let it boil for at least one hour, stirring often. When done, soften with boiled new milk, sweeten to taste and feed the infant with a spoon.

Graham Meal Mush is prepared in the same manner as either of the above recipes.

### Milk Porridge.
### Bouillie de Lait.

2 Tablespoonfuls of Indian Meal.
1 Spoon of White Flour.
3 Cups of Milk.
1½ Cups of Boiling Water.
A Pinch of Salt.

Bring the flour to a paste with a little cold water, and also scald the meal with a little hot water. Have the water boiling in the proportion given above; add the meal, and then add the flour, stirring constantly. Then let it boil for about twenty minutes, and add the pinch of salt and the milk, stirring almost constantly; then let all cook for ten minutes more, stirring often. Serve while hot, with sugar and milk. This is excellent for little children and invalids.

### BARLEY.
### Orge.

Barley is extensively used by the Creoles, especially in summer, for making soups. A good barley soup is considered not only a most nutritious dish, but a very cooling one, and especially suited to a summer diet. A half cupful is thrown into the soup. (See recipe for Barley Soup.) Barley water is also extensively used to cool the system, and also for delicate infants, with whom very often even sterilized milk does not agree, and it is found absolutely necessary to substitute some other article of diet. The Creole mothers first soak two tablespoonfuls of barley in a little cold water for about an hour, and then, without draining pour this into the boiling water, which has been very slightly salted. This water is stirred very frequently and allowed to simmer for at least an hour. It is then strained and sweetened before it is used. Barley thus prepared is used extensively for invalids. Barley must always be picked over and washed thoroughly in several waters before using and soaked in a little cold water.

### BUCKWHEAT.

Froment de Sarrasin.

Buckwheat is not by any means a nutritive food, being far inferior to wheat and corn. It is never eaten alone, but in combination with flour, is used in making those delightful breakfast accompaniments, "Buckwheat Cakes." (See recipe, under Chapter on Breads.)

---

## CHAPTER XXVI.

### MACARONI.

#### Macaroni.

Macaroni is a general article of food in New Orleans among the rich and the poor. It is very cheap, and is a most excellent dish. We have in New Orleans large Macaroni factories, where not only Macaroni is made by the Italians themselves, but the twin sisters of Macaroni, Spaghetti and Vermicelli, are also manufactured fresh daily. While there is no city in the United States in which Macaroni is cooked in real Italian style but New Orleans, which has long been a favorde point of migration for the sons of sunny Italy, the Creole cooks have modified and improved upon the Italian methods, so that Macaroni à la Créole is just as famous a dish as Macaroni à l'Italienne, and by many considered far superior.

Macaroni is used extensively in New Orleans in making soups. In this particular it was treated under the special chapter allotted to soups. (See Macaroni Soup.)

#### How to Boil Macaroni.

Always purchase the best quality of Macaroni. The cost is small and more satisfactory results are obtained in cooking. Avoid breaking the macaroni as much as possible. Immerse it whole in a large saucepan of boiling water; add a tablespoonful of salt and one of butter. Let the macaroni cook from twenty to twenty-five minutes; remove from the fire and drain in a colander. If not intended for immediate use, cover at once with cold water. When cool, drain and use as needed.

### Boiled Macaroni, Italian Style.
Macaroni à l'Italienne.

½ Pound of Macaroni.
1 Pound of Grated Parmesan Cheese.
1 Tablespoonful Flour.
1 Tablespoonful Butter.
Salt and Pepper to Taste.

Break the macaroni into convenient lengths, and set to boil in a kettle filled with boiling water and in which you have thrown a spoonful of salt and black pepper. Be careful to keep the lengths of macaroni firm. When cooked till tender, take off and strain the water. Take one tablespoonful of butter and one of flour and put them on the fire, blending well. Have one pound of Parmesan cheese grated; add one-half of it to the flour and butter, and one pint of the water in which the macaroni was boiled; the mixture must not be allowed to brown; stir briskly Place the macaroni by lengths into a dish, season well with salt and pepper, and warm a few minutes in the oven. When warm, take out the dish and sprinkle over it one-quarter of the pound of cheese that still remains; pour the hot sauce over this, and sprinkle the rest of the cheese on top; serve hot.

### Boiled Spaghetti, Italian Style.
Spaghetti à l'Italienne.

½ Pound of Spaghetti.
1 Pound of Grated Parmesan Cheese.
1 Tablespoonful of Butter.
1 Tablespoonful of Flour.
Salt and Pepper to Taste.

Spaghetti à l'Italienne is prepared in the same manner as in the above recipe. Spaghetti is a more delicate form of macaroni.

The Italians in New Orleans also simply boil the macaroni or spaghetti as mentioned above, sprinkle it with grated cheese and salt and pepper, and serve with a rich tomato sauce (see recipe), and grated cheese, the latter served in separate plates. This latter is a very rich dish.

Macaroni or Spaghetti thus cooked is served with daube and is a very palatable dish.

### Macaroni with Tomato Sauce.
Macaroni à la Sauce Tomate.

½ Pound of Macaroni.
1 Gill of Tomato Sauce.
1 Gill of Madeira Sauce, or Wine.
¼ Pound of Grated Parmesan Cheese.
1 Onion.    1 Tablespoonful of Butter.
Salt and Pepper to Taste.
A Dash of Cayenne.

Boil the macaroni in salted water for twenty minutes, adding a tablespoonful of butter and an onion, with two cloves stuck in it. Then drain the macaroni of all water; place it in a saucepan with a gill of Tomato Sauce and one of Madeira Sauce or Madeira Wine. Add a quarter of a pound of grated Parmesan cheese;season well with salt and pepper; add a dash of Cayenne, and let the mixture cook slowly for ten or fifteen minutes, tossing frequently to prevent burning. Place the Macaroni on a hot dish, pour the sauce over it, and serve with grated Parmesan cheese passed in a separate dish. Spaghetti may be prepared and served in the same manner.

### Macaroni, Creole Style.
Macaroni à la Créole.

½ Pound of Macaroni.
½ Can of Tomatoes, or 6 Fresh Ones.
1 Tablespoonful Butter.
1 Tablespoonful Flour.
Salt and Pepper to Taste.

Boil the macaroni according to the recipe given above. When done, drain through a colander without breaking the lengths. Season well with salt and pepper. Put one tablespoonful of butter in a frying pan and add one tablespoonful of flour; blend well and as it browns add the tomatoes, which have been chopped fine in their own juice. Let this stew, after stirring well for about ten minutes, and when it begins to boil add the macaroni or spaghetti, mixing well without breaking the lengths. Let it boil up once, and then serve hot. The dish may be served with any meats.

### Macaroni or Spaghetti Milanaise Style.
Macaroni ou Spaghetti à la Milanaise.

½ Pound of Macaroni.
¼ Pound of Cold Boiled Ham.
1 Pound of Grated Parmesan Cheese.
1 Onion.    2 Cloves of Garlic.
1 Can Tomatoes.
2 Sprigs Each of Thyme and Parsley.
1 Bay Leaf.
Salt, Pepper and Cayenne to Taste.

Boil the macaroni in water and salt as in the recipe given for Boiling Macaroni. When tender, drain well through a colander. In the meantime, while it is boiling, put a tablespoonful of butter in a saucepan, and as it melts, add the grated onion. Let this brown, and then add the ham which you will have minced very fine. Let this brown; add the cloves of garlic, minced very fine, and the herbs, minced very fine. Then add almost immediately, as these begin to brown, for bay leaf burns quickly, a half can of tomatoes, or six fresh large tomatoes. To this, as it stews, add a half pound of grated Parmesan cheese, and let all stew for about ten minutes; then add the macaroni or spaghetti, and let all simmer gently for about twenty minutes longer. Serve hot, and pass at the same time a small plate of grated Parmesan cheese to each person.

### Macaroni, Neapolitan Style.
Macaroni à la Napolitaine.

½ Pound of Macaroni.
¼ Pint of Sauce Espagnole.
¼ Pint of Tomato Sauce.
¼ Pound of Grated Parmesan Cheese.
6 Mushrooms.   2 Truffles.
1 Ounce of Smoked Beef Tongue.
Salt and Pepper to Taste.
¼ Bottle of Claret.
1 Carrot.   1 Herb Bouqute.
2 Sprigs of Celery.

Boil the macaroni, and cut into pieces of about two inches long, after draining thoroughly. Place it in a saucepan with a half pint of Tomato Sauce and Sauce Espagnole (see recipe), and add the cheese. Add the herb bouquet, tied together; cut the truffles and mushrooms and carrot into dice-shaped pieces; mince the celery and add; then add the beef tongue cut into small dice-shaped pieces. To this add the Claret. Let all cook for about fifteen minutes, tossing frequently in the meantime. When ready to serve, remove the herb bouquet and send to the table hot.

### Macaroni au Gratin.
Macaroni au Gratin.

½ Pound of Macaroni or Spaghetti.
1 Pound of Parmesan Cheese (Grated).
1 Tablespoonful of Flour.
1 Tablespoonful of Butter.
Salt and Pepper to Taste.

Boil the macaroni by its length in water until soft. Do not let it cook too much, but just enough to be soft, and lift out of the water without breaking. This will require about a half hour of rapid boiling. When done, take out of the water in which it was boiled, and season well with salt and black pepper. Put a tablespoonful of butter, blended well with flour, into a pint of milk. Let it boil two minutes. Place a layer of the spaghetti or macaroni in the pan in which it is to be baked, seasoning again to taste, and mix in a layer of the grated cheese; sprinkle with pepper and salt; then put in alternately a layer of the macaroni and a layer of cheese, and so on until three-fourths of the cheese is used. Do not break the macaroni or spaghetti. Pour over this the boiling milk. Take the remaining quarter pound of cheese and sprinkle thickly on top, dot here and there with bits of butter, and put in a quick oven and let it bake to a nice brown. Serve in the dish in which it was baked. In cooking macaroni or spaghetti, cream or milk may be used always instead of water, using a pint of either in the above proportions. If you have not the milk, a pint of the water in which the macaroni was boiled will answer equally well. This recipe is highly recommended as the nicest way of preparing macaroni.

### Macaroni or Spaghetti With Daube.
Daube au Macaroni ou au Spaghetti.

½ Pound of Macaroni.
A Veal or Beef Daube.
1 Pint of Hot Water or Broth.

This is a popular Creole dish, and a very good one, too. Prepare a daube. (See recipe, "Boeuf à la Mode ou Daube.) After it has cooked about an hour and a half, and is about two-thirds done, add the macaroni according to the number to be served, using between a quarter and a half pound for six, and cutting the macaroni into lengths of about five inches, to facilitate serving. Let it boil for about three-quarters of an hour in the daube, and if you see, on adding it, that there is not sufficient gravy for it to cook well, add a half pint or a pint more of hot water or hot broth, according as the macaroni appears to absorb after it has been in the pot four or five minutes. Cook until very tender, and on serving place the daube in the center of the dish and heap the macaroni around. Chicken and macaroni may be prepared in the same way. Both are excellent and favorite New Orleans ways of serving macaroni. They are also very healthy and nutritious family dishes.

Spaghetti may also be cooked in either of these ways, and makes a more delicate dish.

### Timbale of Macaroni.
Macaroni en Timbale.

¼ Pound of Macaroni or Spaghetti.
1 Head of Edam's Cheese.
½ Pound of Grated Parmesan Cheese.
1 Tablespoonful of Flour.
1 Tablespoonful of Butter.
Salt and Pepper to Taste.

Nearly every family keeps a head of Edam's cheese for general use. When you have finished scooping out the cheese, do not throw away the head, but keep it to make a Timbale of Macaroni. Boil a little over one-quarter of a pound of macaroni, or sufficient to fill the head, according to the above directions (Boiled Macaroni.) When boiled, take out of the water and set in a dish. Take about half a pint of the liquor in which the macaroni was boiled, strain it and set it back on the stove; add the flour and butter blended, and three-quarters of the grated cheese, and let it boil five minutes. Then pour this sauce over the macaroni in the dish and mix well, seasoning with salt and pepper to taste. Fill the head with this mixture, and sprinkle on top the rest of the grated cheese. Set in the stove to bake, and, when nicely browned, serve hot from the shell of the cheese. The macaroni may also be baked in molds, but there is no comparison to the Timbale when made in the empty cheese head. This is a genuine Timbale of Macaroni, and the only way to really make the dish.

### Macaroni Balls.

Boulettes de Macaroni.

1 Cup of Cold Boiled Macaroni.
1 Cup Boiling Milk. 1 Tablespoonful Butter.
2 Tablespoonfuls Flour.
2 Tablespoonfuls of Grated Cheese.
The Yolks of 4 Eggs.
Salt and Pepper to Taste.

Put the butter into a saucepan, and as it melts add the flour, but do not let it brown. Add the cup of boiling milk and stir well. When it begins to thicken add the grated cheese, and let it simmer for a few minutes longer; then take from the fire and add the beaten yolks of four eggs. Have the macaroni cut into tiny bits and work it well into this mixture. Then set it aside to cool. When cold, take a little flour, rub it on your hands, and form the macaroni into small balls about two inches in length and one in thickness. Dip the balls into a well-beaten egg, roll well and then roll in grated cracker crumbs. Fry in boiling lard, and serve hot.

## CHAPTER XXVII.

### CHEESE.

Du Fromage.

Cheese is one of the most nutritious of all food substances, being not only substantial, but especially rich in nitrogenous matter. Among scientists it ranks very high as an article of food. Being somewhat expensive, it is not as economical as other kinds of food, but the Creole family must be very poor indeed in which cheese of some kind is not served after each meal, especially after dinner. They hold that cheese is a good aid to digestion, and if it is simply the Gruyére cheese or the plain "Fromage à l'Americain," you will always see it passed around as a proper finish to a meal just before the coffee is brought in.

So much for the cheese in its natural state. In cooking, the Creoles use some very delightful forms, chief among which is that old French preparation known as

### Cheese Ramakins.

Ramequins de Fromage.

6 Tablespoonfuls of Grated Cheese.
1½ Gills of Milk.
The Yolks of Three Eggs.
2 Tablespoonfuls of Butter.
2 Ounces of Bread.
½ Tablespoonful of Prepared Mustard.
The Whites of Three Eggs.
Cayenne and Salt to Taste.

Put the milk on to boil, and add the bread, which you will have minced fine. Stir the milk and bread until very smooth, and then add the butter, stirring well, and finally the grated cheese. Stir this for five minutes, letting it boil, and then take off the fire and add the beaten yolks of three eggs. Have the whites ready, beaten to a stiff froth, and stir them in very gently. Season to taste. Grease a baking dish with butter and pour the mixture into the dish, set in a quick oven, and let it bake for a quarter of an hour. Serve hot.

### Cheese Soufflé.

Soufflé de Fromage.

¼ Pound of Grated Cheese.
1 Gill of Fresh Cream or Milk.
3 Creole Eggs.   1 Teaspoonful of Flour.
2 Tablespoonfuls of Butter.
1 Pinch of Grated Nutmeg.
1 Pinch Cayenne.   Salt to Taste.

Grate the cheese very fine and then add to it the boiling milk; add gradually the pepper, Cayenne and salt. Then add the butter and flour, rubbed well together. When the cheese is well dissolved, take the mixture off; then add nutmeg and the beaten yolks of three eggs and the whites of two eggs beaten to a froth; stir the whole well. Place all in a shallow earthern dish, add a little butter that has been well melted and put in the stove for a few minutes till it begins to solidify well; then take out and spread on top the white of one egg, beaten to a stiff froth. Set one minute in the stove, let it brown slightly and serve immediately. If you cannot attain the acme of browning the whites of eggs without letting them fall, stir the whites into the mixture with the eggs and serve hot, after letting it brown slightly. Some add a little mustard to the mixture, but it is better without it.

### Toasted Cheese.

Fromage sur Canapés.

½ Pound of Cheese.  6 Slices of Bread.
Salt and Cayenne to Taste.

Toast the bread nicely and butter it. Cut the cheese into very thin slices and hold to the fire, letting it toast nicely, first on one side and then on the other. Lay this upon the buttered toast and serve hot. This is a very nice delicacy for breakfast, or for an evening in winter when seated around the home fire.

### Cheese Straws.

Pailles de Fromage.

1 Cup of Grated Parmesan or Gruyere Cheese.
1 Cup Flour.  1 Tablespoonful Butter.
Yolk of an Egg.
Salt and Cayenne to Taste.

Blend the flour and cheese together and add at the same time the salt and Cayenne; then moisten with a well-beaten egg and one tablespoonful of melted butter, and work all gently into a paste. Roll out on a biscuit board into thin strips of not more than an eighth of an inch in thickness, and cut into strips of four inches in length and one-eighth of an inch in width. Place on buttered sheets of paper and bake in a very hot oven until a light brown. It is very pretty to make little rings of some of the strips and pass the others through them in little bundles like gathered bound bits of straw. This is a very dainty dish.

### Welsh Rarebit.

Fromage Fondu à la Bière.

2 Cups of Grated Cheese (Very Rich).
½ Cup of Milk.  The Yolks of Two Eggs.
Salt and Cayenne to Taste.

The old English dish, "Welsh Rarebit," under this name crossed the channel to France, and thence to New Orleans. Toast the bread nicely in square slices and cut off the crusts. Butter nicely while very hot and then plunge them into a bowl of boiling milk. Place them on a heated dish and stand in the oven to keep hot while you proceed to make the "Rarebit." Have a porcelain-lined saucepan; and set a half cup of milk in it over a moderate fire; when it is boiling hot, add the cheese which has been finely grated; stir unceasingly till the cheese melts, and then add the salt, Cayenne and the yolks of the eggs and pour over the toasted bread. Serve hot. In making this "Délicatésse," the cheese must be very rich or it will be tough and stringy, because poor cheese will not melt.

### Cheese Biscuits.

Biscuits de Fromage.

¼ Pound of Butter.  ¼ Pound of Flour.
5 Ounces of Grated Swiss Cheese.
½ Tablespoonful of Mustard.
Yolks of 2 Eggs.  A Dash of Cayenne.

Beat the butter to a cream; add the yolks of the eggs, well beaten, and mix well. Then add gradually the grated cheese, mustard and Cayenne. Add the flour gradually, beating in thoroughly and make a stiff dough. Roll it out and cut into square or round biscuits. Bake in a rather slow oven for twenty minutes and serve.

### Cheese Fondu.

Fromage Fondu.

1 Cup of Grated Parmesan or Gruyere Cheese.
2 Tablespoonfuls of Sifted Flour.
2 Tablespoonfuls of Butter.  3 Creole Eggs.
½ Cup of Fresh Milk or Cream.
A Pinch of Grated Nutmeg.
Salt and Pepper to Taste.

Put the butter into a saucepan and melt, and add the flour, blending without allowing it to brown. Add immediately the boiling milk, and let it boil for two minutes. Then remove from the fire and stir in the yolks of three eggs, well beaten; then salt, pepper, nutmeg and the grated cheese. Mix all thoroughly. Have ready a small pudding dish, or, better still several small souffle dishes. Butter these well. Have the whites of the eggs beaten to a stiff froth, beat them into the mixture and fill the dishes about two-thirds full. Then bake in a moderate oven for about twenty-five minutes. Serve immediately, or the mixture which has risen to the top of the dishes will fall.

### Cream Cheese.

Fromage à la Crème.

Cream Cheese is always made from clabbered milk. The "Cream Cheese Woman" is still as common a sight on our New Orleans streets as the Cala woman was in the days gone by. She carries a covered basket in which are a number of small perforated tins in which the cheese are. In her other hand she carries a can of fresh cream. She sells her wares to her regular customers, for the old Creoles who do not make their own cream cheese are very particular as to whom they buy from, and when once a good, clean, careful woman gets a "customer" she keeps her during her period of business, coming early every fast day and Friday with her cheese and cream, for this is a fast-day breakfast and luncheon dish.

Many of the Creoles, however, make their own cream cheese, as follows: The clabber is placed in a long bag of muslin and put to drain, the bag being tied tightly and hung out over night in a cool place. When ready for use, the bag is opened and the cheese is taken out and beaten till light. It is then placed in these perforated molds, and when the time comes for serving it is taken out placed in a dish, and sweet cream is poured over it. It is eaten with sugar or salt, more generally sugar.

Frozen cream cheese is a very delicious summer dish with the Creoles. Some persons, after skimming the cream from the sour milk, stand the pan on the back of the stove, and scald the clabber with about three quarts of boiling water before putting in the bag to drain. Again, some use only the perforated tins, instead of the muslin bag, but the best results are obtained by the former ancient Creole method. Cream cheese corresponds to the German "Schmier Kase."

## CHAPTER XXVIII.

### CANAPÉS.

#### Canapés.

No book on Creole cookery would be complete without reference to the delightful "Canapés" that are so extensively used at breakfasts, luncheons, dinners or suppers, and whose methods of preparation, distinctively Creole, have added to the reputation of the Creole cuisine. "Canapé" is a French term, literally meaning a "couch" or "bed." In the culinary sense it is used as a bed on which to rest savory foods. Usually the Canapé is the form of sliced bread, or toast, or crackers, covered with finely minced meats, pastes, etc., and handsomely decorated. It is a term that is also applied to the ordinary "Sandwich."

#### Anchovy Canapés.
Canapés d'Anchois.

6 Slices of Dry Toast.
1 Ounce of Anchovy Butter.
2 Dozen Anchovies.

First prepare the Anchovy Butter, by adding to one ounce of good regular butter one teaspoonful of Anchovy Essence. Mix well and set on ice till ready to use.

Prepare six slices of bread, slicing them about one-half an inch thick and toasting to a golden brown. Trim the edges nicely and spread over each a little Anchovy Butter and then cover each with four Anchovies cut in halves, or pounded to a paste, according to taste. Place the toasts on a tin baking sheet in an oven for one minute, and then arrange neatly on a folded napkin on a dish and serve.

#### Anchovy Canapés With Hard-Boiled Eggs.
Canapés d'Anchois aux Oeufs Durs.

6 Slices of French Toast.
1 Dozen Anchovies.   2 Hard-Boiled Eggs.
1 Ounce of Anchovy Butter.

Prepare six slices of French toast (see recipe), spread over each a little Anchovy Butter, and then spread over this buttered toast the Anchovies and hard-boiled eggs, which have been finely minced and mixed together. Place on a folded napkin in a dish and serve.

#### Anchovy Canapés, Creole Style.
Canapés d'Anchois à la Créole.

6 Slices of French Toast.
1 Dozen Anchovies.   1 Ounce of Grated Ham.
6 Gherkins.   ½ a Truffle.
1 Tablespoonful of Salad Oil.
1 Teaspoonful of Caper Vinegar.
1 Ounce of Aspic Jelly.

Prepare the French toasts (see recipe); trim the edges neatly. Chop the Anchovies very fine and mix with the ounce of grated boiled ham, and the truffle and gherkins, all minced very fine; moisten this with the salad oil and vinegar, which have been well mixed. Spread over the toast and garnish nicely with the aspic jelly, and place on a folded napkin and serve. The Anchovy preparation may also be used to fill very small patty cases; in this case, serve with a garnish of delicate pieces of toast and Aspic Jelly.

#### Anchovy Canapés With Gruyère Cheese.
Canapés d'Anchois au Fromage de Gruyère.

6 Slices of French Toast.
2 Ounces of Gruyere Cheese.
16 Anchovies.
6 Minced Gherkins. 1 Ounce of Anchovy Butter.

Prepare the French toast (see recipe); pound the Anchovies to a paste with the Gruyère cheese; line very shallow gem pans with a pie paste. (See recipe.) When baked, set to cool, and then fill in with the Anchovy preparation. Then invert this on a circle of nicely buttered Anchovy toast; garnish with the minced gherkins and serve.

### Cracker Anchovy Canapés.
#### Canapés d'Anchois aux Biscuit.
1 Dozen Soda Crackers or Butter Crackers.
2 Dozen Anchovies.
1 Ounce of Anchovy Butter.

Cut the Anchovies into halves. Butter one side of six crackers with the Anchovy butter; lay on this four Anchovies sliced in half; cover each with a cracker; place on a folded napkin on a dish and serve. A very pretty conceit at luncheons is to tie the crackers across and around with narrow green ribbon, making a delicate knot in the center.

### Swiss Canapés.
#### Canapés à la Suisse.
1 Ounce of Anchovy Butter.
3 Hard-Boiled Eggs. 6 Stuffed Olives.
3 Minced Green Gherkins.
6 Slices of Toast.

Prepare the French toast, and cut six delicate pieces into the shape of a triangle. Spread these with Anchovy butter; decorate along one side with the whites of the eggs, finely minced; along the second triangular edge with the minced yolks of the eggs and on the third with the minced green gherkins. Place a stuffed olive (see recipe) in the center, and arrange nicely on a folded napkin on a dish and serve.

### Caviar Canapés.
#### Canapés de Caviar.
6 Slices of French Toast.
½ of a Box of Russian Caviar.
2 Tablespoonfuls of Cream.

Prepare the toast and cut in delicate circles. In the meantime put half the contents of a small box of Russian Caviars into a sautoire or saucepan; add two tablespoonfuls of cream and heat one and a half minutes on the stove. Be careful to stir constantly. Pour this over the toast; place on a dish on a folded napkin and serve. Again, the circles of toast may be used as a foundation, the edges being spread with Anchovy butter, with an onion ring at its base. Fill this decorated ring with the Caviars, place on a folded napkin on a dish and serve.

### Canapés, Hunters' Style.
#### Canapés à la Chasseur.
6 Slices of Toast.
1 Cup of Forcemeat of Game (White Meat).
½ Cup of Forcemeat of Game (Dark Meat).

Prepare triangular-shaped pieces of toast, butter nicely and spread over with a game forcemeat (Woodcock, Snipe, Reed Birds, etc.) Decorate the edges with a forcemeat of game of different color, for effect, and serve.

The wild duck, the meat of which is dark, may be utilized in this garnish. Left-over game also may be thus nicely utilized at luncheon or supper.

### Crab Canapés.
#### Canapés de Crabes au Canapés
#### Lorenzo.
6 Slices of Toast.
8 Hard-Shelled Crabs. 1 Ounce of Butter.
1 Small Onion.
2 Tablespoonfuls of Butter. 2 Tablespoonfuls of Flour.
1 Gill of Broth or Water.
2 Ounces of Grated Parmesan Cheese.
2 Ounces of Grated Swiss Cheese.

For this recipe first prepare the "Deviled Crabs" as follows: Boil the crabs. (See recipe Boiled Crabs.) Then pick out all the meat from the claws and bodies, and season nicely with salt and pepper. Put one ounce of butter into the saucepan, and add a finely minced onion; let this cook on a slow fire for two minutes, but by no means allow either butter or onion to brown. Add a tablespoonful of flour, and stir constantly for a minute and a half, and then add a gill of broth or water, if the broth is not convenient. Stir well and let this mixture cook for five minutes, stirring constantly. Now add the crab meat and let it cook for fifteen minutes longer, stirring occasionally with a wooden spoon. Turn the mixture into a dish and let it cool for about a quarter of an hour. Put a tablespoonful of butter into a saucepan, and add immediately a tablespoonful of flour and blend well; let this cook for three minutes, stirring all the time, and then add two ounces of grated Parmesan and two ounces of grated Swiss cheese. Stir all well together, blending thoroughly, and then turn into a vessel to cool. Cut six slices of bread the full length and width of the loaf, using preferably the "Pan Bread," or delicate French loaf. Let the thickness of each slice be about a quarter of an inch; neatly trim off the crust, and fry the bread in a saucepan with a tablespoonful of butter till they have reached a golden brown. Then let them cool, draining off all butter. Divide the crab forcemeat and the cheese separately into six equal parts; place a layer of the crab forcemeat one-quarter of an inch thick on each slice of toast. Take the six portions of cheese and roll each into a ball-shaped form about two inches in diameter, and arrange them on each portion of toast nicely and equally; place in a dish and brown in the oven for five minutes, and send the Canapés to the table hot in the same dish in which they were baked.

### Chicken Canapés.
#### Canapés de Volaille.
6 Slices of Toast.
1 Cup of Chicken Forcemeat. Ounce of Butter.
1 Gill of Cream.
The Whites of 2 Hard-Boiled Eggs.
2 Ounces of Parmesan Cheese.

Prepare a Chicken Forcemeat (see recipe), and then prepare six slices of toast, cut square or in circles. Add an ounce of butter and one gill of cream to the chicken forcemeat; work well together, and then set to cool. Spread the toast lightly with butter, and spread over each slice a portion of the chicken forcemeat to the thickeness of one-quarter of an inch; sprinkle with grated Parmesan cheese, set in the oven and bake for five minutes, and then decorate in the center with delicately cut pieces of the white of hard-boiled eggs and serve.

### Canapés of Chicken Livers.
#### Canapés de Foies de Volaille.
1 Dozen Chicken Livers.   1 Onion.
6 Slices of Toast.
Dash of Anchovy Essence. 1 Ounce of Butter.
Salt and Red Pepper to Taste.
Pimentos and Red Chili to Garnish.

Sauté the Chicken Livers (see recipe) with a finely minced onion till tender; then pound them to a paste, adding first a dash of Anchovy Essence, one tablespoonful of butter, salt and red pepper to taste. Cut the bread the full width of the loaf and trim the edges nicely; then fry in butter to a golden brown; take out and drain, and place in a silver dish, or in the dish in which they are to be served, and pile up the chicken liver preparation in pyramidal shape on top of the toast; smooth nicely all around with a knife and set in the oven for two or three minutes; then decorate the edges of the bread with slices of Pimentos and rings of Red Chilis and serve hot.

### Creole Canapés.
#### Canapés à la Créole.
Cup of Grated or Minced Boiled Ham.
1 Onion. 1 Clove of Garlic.
1 Peeled Tomato.   1 Minced Green Pepper.
6 Slices of Buttered Toast.
1 Tablespoonful of Butter. 2 Ounces of Parmesan Cheese.
Salt and Pepper to Taste.

Grate and mince only the lean portion of ham till you have a cupful. Put this in a saucepan with a tablespoonful of butter, and add the finely minced onion and garlic. Let this cook for three minutes, and then add the finely-cut tomato and minced green pepper. Season to taste with salt and pepper; add a dash of Cayenne, and let the preparation stew down dry; then spread on strips of buttered toast and dredge with grated Parmesan cheese. Set in the oven in the dish in which it is to be served and bake for five minutes and send to the table hot.

### Cheese Canapés.
#### Canapés de Fromage.
6 Slices of Swiss Cheese.
6 Slices of Toast.
1 Gill of Sauce Piquante.

Take six slices of bread cut the whole width of the loaf, one-half inch in thickness, and hollow out one-half of the inner portion. Toast this nicely and spray the inner part with Piquante Sauce. (See recipe.) Have ready six slices of toasted or baked Swiss cheese; fit a slice into each cavity in the sliced toast; set in the oven for a few minutes and serve very hot.

### Codfish Canapés.
#### Canapés de Cabillaud ou de Morue.
1 Cup of Boiled Salt Codfish.
1 Green Pepper.   3 Young Onions.
1 Teaspoonful of Tarragon Vinegar.
Capers to Garnish.

Boil the codfish (see recipe), or utilize left-over fish; mince finely and mix thoroughly with the minced green peppers and young onions, and season with one teaspoonful of Tarragon vinegar. Spread on triangular-shaped pieces of toast placed on a dish on a folded napkin. Decorate nicely with capers and serve.

### Ham Canapés.
#### Canapés de Jambon.
6 Slices of Lean Ham.
6 Slices of Toast.
1 Tablespoonful of French Mustard.
1 Gill of Cold White Sauce.
1 Boiled Onion.   1 Cooked Garlic.
2 Ounces of Grated Parmesan Cheese.

Prepare the toast nicely, cutting the slices the full width of the bread, paring the edges nicely and toasting and buttering well. Lay on each piece of toast a thin slice of very lean ham, which has been lightly spread with French mustard. Spread lightly over this a cold White Sauce (see recipe White Sauce, Sauce Blanche) to which has been added while cooking a finely-minced onion and clove of garlic, and a dash of Parmesan cheese. Dredge the top of the Canapé with Parmesan cheese, then sprinkle lightly with finely-grated bread crumbs. Set in the oven for five minutes and bake and send to the table hot.

### Fish Canapés.
#### Canapés de Poisson.
1 Cup of Minced Left-Over Fish.
1 Tablespoonful of French Mustard Dressing.
1 Gill of Sauce Piquante.
2 Ounces of Parmesan Cheese.
6 Slices of Toast.

Utilize in this form of Canapé any kind of white-fleshed Fish, Red Fish,

Red Snapper, Sheephead or Trout, etc. Prepare a forcemeat (see recipe) and season with the French Mustard and the Piquant Sauce. Spread a layer one-quarter of an inch thick over delicate strips of toast, dredge with grated Parmesan Cheese, set in the oven, and bake for five minutes and serve hot.

### Canapés of Potted Ham.
Canapés de Jambon en Conserve.

1 Box of Potted Ham.
2 Ounces of Grated Boiled Ham.
Thin Slices of Green Gherkins.
6 Slices of Toast.

Prepare delicate strips of Toast, spread with Potted Ham to a quarter of an inch in thickness, then sprinkle lightly with grated ham and decorate the edges, and cover fidesired, with thinly-sliced Green Gherkins. The grated Boiled Ham may be omitted.

### Indian Canapés.
Canapés à l'Indienne.

1 Box of Potted Ham. 1 Ounce of Chutney.
6 Slices of Toast.
2 Ounces of Grated Parmesan Cheese.

Cut six slices of bread into delicate circles, and fry in butter. Spread first with Potted Ham and then with Chutney. Sprinkle with grated Parmesan Cheese. Set in the oven to brown for five minutes, and serve hot.

### Oyster Canapés.
Canapés d'Huîtres.

3 Dozen Oysters. 6 Slices of Toast.
2 Tablespoonfuls of Hollandaise Sauce.
Parsley Sprigs.

Blanch the oysters (see recipe) and then mince very fine. Mix with two tablespoonfuls of Hollandaise Sauce, and then spread over thin strips of Buttered toast. Sprinkle lightly with Parsley, which has been grated so fine as to be almost a dust. Put a bit of butter on top of each Canapé set in the oven for a few minutes, and send to the table hot.

### Olive Canapés.
Canapés d'Olives.

6 Stuffed Olives. 6 Slices of Buttered Toast.
6 Anchovies.
Capers and Minced Olive to Garnish.

Prepare the toast and cut into delicate circles. Place on each circle a coiled Anchovy, and set a Stuffed Olive in the center of the coil. Decorate lightly with Olives and Capers minced very fine, and serve. Again, this Canapé may be prepared by frying the circles of toast in butter, and spreading them with Anchovies pounded to a paste, and decorating on top with minced Capers and Olives.

### Canapés of Potted Tongue.
Canapés de Langue de Boeuf en Conserve.

1 Box of Potted Tongue.
Strips of Cooked Pork Tongue.
6 Slices of Toast.

Prepare the toast and cut into delicate circles. Spread with a layer of Potted Tongue one-quarter of an inch in thickness, and decorate with strips of cooked Red Tongue in lattice forms, that is with strips laid one over the other, like a lattice work.

### Louisiana Canapés.
Canapés à la Louisiane.

Two Breasts of Chicken. ¼ of a Red Tongue.
2 Ounces of Grated Lean Boiled Ham.
A Dash of Curry Powder.
2 Tablespoonfuls of Thick Veloute Sauce.
2 Tablespoonfuls of Grated Parmesan Cheese.

Mince very fine the cooked breasts of the chicken, and cut the ham and tongue into small dice shapes; mix well with the chicken, and season with salt and a dash of Cayenne. Add a dash of Curry Powder, and then work the entire forcemeat well with two tablespoonfuls of thick Velouté Sauce. (See recipe.) Spread the mixture in layers one-quarter of an inch thick on each slice of delicate circles of toast, dredge lightly with Parmesan Cheese, set in the oven for five minutes and bake. Send to the table hot.

### Sardine Canapés.
Canapés de Sardines.

6 Triangular Slices of Toast.
1 Box of Sardines. 3 Hard-Boiled Eggs.
The Juice of 1 Lemon. 6 Anchovies.
A Dash of Red Pepper.

Pound the sardines and the hard-boiled eggs to a paste, season with a dash of Red Pepper and the juice of a lemon and spread the buttered toast with the mixture. Decorate in the center with a coiled Anchovy. Or, simply pound the sardines to a paste, season with a dash of red pepper and the juice of a lemon, and spread on the slices of buttered toast.

### Spanish Canapés.
Canapés à l'Espagnole.

6 Circular Pieces of Buttered Toast.
1 Cup of Finely Minced White Fleshed Fish.
3 Sweet Pickles.
1 Tablespoonful of Madras Chutney.
2 Tablespoonfuls of Hollandaise Sauce.
2 Tablespoonfuls of Parmesan Cheese.

Prepare circular pieces of buttered toast, make a mixture of a cup of any white-fleshed fish, the Madras Chutney moistened with the Hollandaise Sauce and minced pickles, all pounded together. Spread this over the toast and dredge with grated Parmesan Cheese. Set in the oven and bake for five minutes.

## CANNELONS.

Cannelon is a term applied to peculiar hollow lengths of puff paste or noodle paste, made by taking a piece of piping or tubing and cutting the paste into strips and twining around the tubing or piping. Bake or fry this preparation, remove the tubing and fill in the cannelons with a forcemeat of sausage, chicken croquette mixture, preserves, jellies or creams.

# CHAPTER XXIX.

## VEGETABLES.

### Des Légumes.

Louisiana is peculiarly favored in respect to the variety of vegetables that can be grown on her soil. Almost all the sturdier varieties of vegetables and all the more delicate and recherché are grown here in abundance. The soil is so rich and fruitful that it has been said that if you simply scatter the seed over the ground, without any effort at cultivation, it would still take root and a good crop would follow. Our climate also admits of two seasons of planting, so that we have both an early spring and autumn crop; the one extends far into the summer and verging upon the autumn, and the other till late in the winter and verging upon the early spring. Consequently, vegetables are always to be found in abundance in our markets.

The nutritive value of vegetable food is high, especially of peas, beans and lentils. Among the succulent vegetables, the potato ranks as the most nutritious, and there is scarcely a table in New Orleans on which the potato in some form is not served every day. Turnips, carrots, cabbage, parsnips, beets, onions, asparagus, spinach, cauliflower, artichokes and egg plants are all highly nutritious, and most of them possess medicinal qualities that make them of great value as blood purifiers. The old Creoles hold that the family that makes it a daily practice to eat vegetables and fruits, when in season, will never have need of a physician. All green vegetables should be freshly gathered when bought, and should be well washed in cold water before cooking. Some vegetables, such as dried beans, split peas and lentils, do not boil to softness in hard water, that is, when put into boiling water. The seeds contain salts of lime, or sulphates, and these at once coagulate if the vegetable is put into hot water to boil, and no after amount of boiling can ever bring them quite to softness. Always put such vegetables to cook in cold water, allowing it to heat gradually with the vegetables.

On the other hand, young green vegetables, such as green peas and string beans, are best cooked in hard or boiling water, for the cold water has such solvent powers that it immediately destroys the firmness of the outer coating of the vegetable, and the color also, the juices passing out into the water. Onions should be set to boil in hot water.

Some vegetables such as green peas, spinach, string beans, Brussels sprouts, should be boiled uncovered, if you wish them to retain freshness of color.

A most important rule is to allow the vegetable to cook until done or tender, and not a moment longer, or it will be wet and soggy. Remove the vegetable from the fire the moment it is done, and do not allow it to stand in the water, but be careful to drain at once thoroughly. It is a wise rule to calculate the time that will be required in cooking the vegetable and the hour at which you intend to serve it, and so arrange that it will be put on at the proper time, and be "just done" at the proper hour for serving. Above all, don't let the vegetable stand in a hot oven and dry up while waiting for the meal to be served. Place in a dish over a pot of boiling water, and this will keep it hot and moist.

In the following recipes the vegetables found in our New Orleans markets are treated systematically. It will be noticed that new-fangled recipes, with high-sounding titles that mean nothing but some old-time method of cooking in a new dress, have been carefully eschewed. Dishes have been called by their proper names, and care taken not to confuse by a vast number of recipes, whose value is worthless. The Creoles believe that the flavor of a vegetable should be dominant in every way in which it is served. They, therefore, cling with singular tenacity to the old-fashioned methods, rather than the so-called elegant novelties, whose chief aim seems to be, judging from the combinations that enter into the recipes, to utterly destroy the original taste of the vegetable itself.

## ARTICHOKES.
### Des Artichauts.

Artichokes are of two kinds: The French or Green Globe Artichokes, which have large scaly heads, like the cones of a pine, and the Jerusalem Artichokes. The latter are little esteemed by the fastidious, the preference being always given to the former, which is a more delicate and tender variety, and a popular favorite. In Louisiana the Jerusalem Artichoke is cultivated principally for its tubers, which are very valuable for stock and hog feeding, owing to their fattening properties. But, if boiled or made into a purée, these artichokes will be found not only a pleasant, but most nutritious food. French artichokes may be boiled or stuffed or fried.

To tell if a French Artichoke is tender, lift up one of the scales that lie near the body of the vegetable. If it breaks without effort, the vegetable is young; otherwise, the artichoke will be tough and disagreeable to eat.

### French Artichokes Boiled.
Artichauts Français Bouillis.

6 Tender Fresh Artichokes. 1 Tablespoonful of Vinegar.
1 Teaspoonful of Salt. Sauce, according to Taste.

Strip off the coarse outer leaves, or, better still, cut the stalks close with a pair of scissors, and trim the sharp points from the leaves, removing about a quarter of an inch of each. Cut the stalks about an inch from the bottom. Throw in cold water and wash well, adding a little vinegar to draw out any lurking insects. Have on the stove a pot of boiling water, and add a teaspoonful of salt. Throw in the artichokes and boil gently until it is possible to draw out a leaf easily, or until the outer leaves are tender. Take from the fire and drain upon a dish, placing them upside down, so that the water may all run off. Stand on their stalks in another dish when thoroughly drained, and serve hot with a Drawn Butter Sauce, Sauce à la Maitre d'Hotel or a Sauce à la Hollandaise.

The time for boiling an artichoke depends entirely on the age and size of the vegetable and requires all the way from twenty-five minutes to an hour.

### Jerusalem Artichokes Boiled.
Topinambours Bouillis.

6 Jerusalem Artichokes. Sauce a la Maitre d'Hotel or a la Creme.

Wash the artichokes in cold water, and scrape them. Then throw them into cold water, and let them soak for an hour or so. Take out and drain. Put them in a saucepan; cover with boiling water, and let them boil slowly until tender; watch carefully, as they will easily harden again Serve with a Sauce à la Maitre d'Hotel or a Cream Sauce. (See recipes.)

### Purée of Jerusalem Artichokes.
Purée de Topinambours à la Crème.

6 Artichokes. 1 Tablespoonful of Butter.
Salt and Pepper to Taste.

Wash and skin the artichokes, and boil until tender in a pint of water. Press them through a colander, and return to the fire in a saucepan in which you have placed a tablespoonful of butter, salt and pepper. Stir well, and let them simmer for five minutes longer, and serve with a Cream Sauce. (See recipe.)

### Fried Artichokes.
Artichauts Frits.

6 Artichokes. 2 Tablespoonfuls of Butter.

Pluck off the coarse scales of the artichoke, and then throw the vegetable into cold water. Let it stand for an hour. Then drain. Cut the meat into delicate slices, and fry in butter, just as you would potato chips. Serve with Filet of Beef, Veal Sauté, Smothered Chicken, etc.

### Artichokes Sautés.
Artichauts Sautés.

6 Fine Tender Artichokes. 2 Tablespoonfuls of Butter.
1 Tablespoonful of Vinegar. Any Sauce Desired.

Take six fine artichokes and cut into quarters. Remove the choke entirely. Trim the leaves neatly and parboil in hot water for five minutes, being careful to add a teaspoonful of salt and a tablespoonful of vinegar to the water. After five minutes remove the artichokes and drain thoroughly. Place in a saucepan or sautoire, with two good tablespoonfuls of butter. Cover the pan tight and set to cook in a moderate oven for twenty-five minutes. Then take the artichokes from the pan and place in a deep serving dish and serve with a Sauce à la Maitre d'Hotel, a Drawn Butter Sauce, a Hollandaise Sauce, or any sauce desired.

### Artichokes à la Vinaigrette.
Artichauts à la Vinaigrette.

6 Fine, Tender Young Artichokes. 3 Tablespoonfuls of Butter.
2 Tablespoonfuls of Vinegar. 1 Shallot.
The Yolk of a Hard-Boiled Egg.
Salt and Pepper to Taste.

Prepare and boil the artichokes as in recipe for French Artichokes Boiled (see recipe.) Serve with the following sauce: Take the yolk of a hard-boiled egg, dilute it with two teaspoonfuls of vinegar, blend well, season to taste with salt and pepper;

chop the shallot very, very fine, add to the mixture, and then add gradually three tablespoonfuls of Olive Oil. Mix all together well. Place the artichokes on a folded napkin on a dish, and send to the table with the sauce in a separate dish.

### Stuffed Artichokes.
Artichauts Farcis à la Barigoule.

3 Quarts of Boiled Artichokes.
1 Onion, Minced. 2 Cloves of Garlic.
½ Square Inch of Ham.
1 Tablespoonful Butter. ¼ Can of Mushrooms.
Salt and Pepper to Taste.

Clean and boil the artichokes according to recipe. (Boiled Artichokes.) When the leaves begin to be tender and it is possible to pull out a leaf without difficulty, take the artichokes off the fire. Pull off a few of the coarse leaves, and then scoop out the artichoke, without touching the "fond," or bottom meat, and without breaking the outer scales or leaves from the sides and around. The artichoke must be apparently whole and undisturbed. Then chop an onion, or, rather, mince it very fine, and mince two cloves of garlic and half a square inch of ham very, very fine. Take a quarter of a can of mushrooms and mince them fine. Mix all this together as a stuffing, and season well with salt, pepper and Cayenne. Put a tablespoonful of butter in a frying pan, and fry the dressing in it for about five or ten minutes. Take off the fire, and stuff each artichoke from the center, which you will have scooped, beginning just above the heart or "fond" of the artichoke. Pour over each a spoonful of broth or consommé, or water; sprinkle lightly with bread crumbs; put a dot of butter on each, and set in the oven and bake for five minutes, till the crumbs are nicely browned. Serve immediately, using, if you wish, a Drawn Butter Sauce, but it is unnecessary. (See Beurre à la Maître d'Hotel.)

### ASPARAGUS.
Des Asperges.

Asparagus is a vegetable of very delicate flavor, and is much sought after and highly esteemed by epicures. It is a dainty accompaniment to the most elegant feast.

### Boiled Asparagus.
Asperges en Branches.

1 Can of Asparagus or 2 Bunches of Fresh Asparagus.
½ Pint of Hollandaise or 1 Gill of Drawn Butter Sauce.

When it is possible to get fresh asparagus, carefully wash it in cold water, and cut off the tough white ends. Scrape the white part well, and throw it into cold water, to soak for half an hour. Then tie it in small bundles, and put it in a saucepan lined with porcelain. Pour over boiling water, and let it cook for twenty minutes. Add a teaspoonful of salt and cook ten minutes longer. Take the asparagus up nicely. Drain off all water. Lay on a folded napkin, and serve with a Drawn Butter Sauce. (See recipe.) Asparagus is generally bought in New Orleans in cans, being very nicely prepared. It requires simply to be set on the stove and allowed to heat, as it is already cooked. Take out of the can by turning it downward in a dish, letting the asparagus slide gently out. Drain off all water, and place on a folded napkin, and serve with a Drawn Butter Sauce. (See recipe.)

### Asparagus Vinnigrette Sauce.
Pointe d'Asperges à la Sauce Vinaigrette.

1 Can of Asparagus. ½ Pint of Vinaigrette Sauce.

Prepare the asparagus as in the above recipe. Drain and set to cool. Serve with a half pint of Vinaigrette Sauce. (See recipe.)

### Asparagus Tips With Green Peas.
Pointes d'Asperges aux Petit Pois.

1 Can of Asparagus or 2 Bunches of Fresh Asparagus.
1 Can of Green Peas or 1 Pint of Fresh Green Peas.
1 Tablespoonful of Butter. 6 Tablespoonfuls of Cream Sauce.
6 or 8 Buttered Croutons.

Cut the tender parts of the asparagus into pieces of about one inch in length. Take the asparagus water, in which they were put up, and set on the stove to heat, and add the canned green peas to the fresh peas that have already been boiled. Throw in the asparagus tips, and add water sufficient to cover. Boil rapidly for ten minutes; then drain very thoroughly and return to the fire, having added one tablespoonful of butter, salt, pepper and six tablespoonfuls of Cream Sauce. (See recipe.) Stir carefully, so that you may not break the tips and serve on neat Croûtons of buttered toast, or place in a dish and bring piping hot to the table as an entré. The coarse ends of the asparagus must not be thrown away, but may be utilized in a very nice Cream of Asparagus Soup. (See recipe.)

### BEANS.
Des Haricots.

Beans, whether white or red, are among the most nutritious of food substances. In all the ancient homes of New Orleans, and in the colleges and convents, where large numbers of children are sent to be reared to be strong and useful men and women, several times a week there appear on the table either the nicely cooked dish of Red Beans, which are eaten with rice, or the equally wholesome White Beans à la Crême, or Red or White Beans boiled with a piece of salt pork or ham. String Beans à la Sauce de Maître d'Hotel, or boiled with a piece of salt pork or or ham, are also classed among the especially nutritious beans. The Creoles hold that the boys and girls who are raised on beans and rice and beef will be among the strongest and sturdiest of people.

### String Beans With Butter Sauce.

Haricots Verts à la Maitre d'Hotel.

2 Quarts of Fresh, Tender String Beans.
2 Tablespoonfuls of Butter. Salt and Pepper to Taste.

Always select tender beans. Break the blossom end, and pull it backward, removing the string. Then be careful to pare the thin strip from the other end of the bean pod. It is only in this way that you will be sure that every inch of string is removed. Split the larger beans down the pod, and let the younger and more tender remain whole. Wash them in clear, cold water, letting them stand about ten minutes. Then drain off the water, put the beans into a saucepan, cover well with boiling water, and let them boil for forty minutes or an hour, according to the tenderness of the beans. Just before serving drain off water, put a large tablespoonful of butter into the beans, mix well, sat and pepper to taste, and serve hot.

### String Beans with Cream Sauce.

Haricots Verts à la Crême.

2 Quarts of Fresh String Beans. 1 Tablespoonful of Butter.
1 Tablespoonful of Flour. ½ Cup of Fresh Milk or Cream.
Salt and Pepper to Taste.

String and wash the beans according to the first recipe. Place in a saucepan and cover with boiling water. Let them boil for an hour. Then drain off the water. Take a tablespoonful of butter and one of flour, and blend well. Add a half cup of fresh milk or cream, or one-half pint of the water in which the beans have been boiled. Season nicely with salt and pepper. Stir in the beans; set them back on the stove for several minutes; let them simmer gently. Season again with salt and pepper to taste, and serve hot. The flour may be omitted, and, instead, dilute the milk with the yolk of two eggs, but do not boil after adding the eggs.

### String Beans, Brittany Style.

Haricots Verts à la Bretonne.

2 Quarts of Fresh String Beans.
2 Tablespoonfuls of Butter. 1 Tablespoonful of Flour.
1 Pint of Chicken Consomme or Water.
1 Medium-Sized Onion.
Chopped Parsley to Garnish. Salt and Pepper to Taste.

Take a medium-sized onion, peel and cut into small dice-shaped pieces. Put the onion in a saucepan with the butter and let it sauté to a golden brown. Add the flour gradually, blending well, and moisten with the consommé or water. Let the mixture come to a boil and skim the broth; then add the string beans, which have already been boiled and drained. Let them simmer for ten minutes, adding in the meantime one finely-minced clove of garlic. After ten minutes, place the beans in a hot dish, sprinkle with chopped parsley and serve hot.

### String Beans à la Vinaigrette.

Haricots Verts à la Vinaigrette.

2 Quarts of String Beans.
A Sauce a la Vinaigrette.

Boil the string beans according to recipe. (See recipe String Beans with Butter Sauce.) When done, drain and serve with a Vinaigrette Sauce. Garnish the dish with sliced lemon dipped in parsley, which has been chopped very fine, and small gherkins cut in fan shapes.

### String Beans à la Poulette.

Haricots Verts à la Poulette.

2 Quarts of String Beans.
A Sauce a la Poulette.

Boil the beans as in the recipe for String Beans with Drawn Butter Sauce. Drain and serve with a Sauce à la Poulette poured over.

### String Beans Boiled With Ham.

Haricots Verts au Jambon.

2 Quarts of String Beans.
1 Pound of Lean Ham or Salt Pork.
Salt and Pepper to Taste.

Proceed to prepare the beans in exactly the same manner as mentioned above. Throw them into cold water, and let them stand for about ten minutes. Have ready a large saucepan of boiling water in which you will have placed a pound of salt pork or ham, and allowed to boil for almost an hour. Drain the beans and put them into this, and let them boil forty minutes or an hour longer. Season with pepper only, and serve, placing the salt pork or ham in the center of the dish, and heaping the beans around. This is an excellent way of utilizing the ham bone which is left over from the boiled ham. The Creoles like the flavoring of ham or salt pork in vegetables. A bit of fine herbs, nicely minced, and one onion, minced fine, greatly add to the flavor of this dish.

### String Beans Panachés.
#### Haricots Verts Panachés.

1 Pint of String Beans.
1 Pint of Lima Beans. 2 Tablespoonfuls of Butter.
Salt and Pepper to Taste.

Boil the string beans and cut them into pieces of about three-fourths of an inch in length; mix them with an equal quantity of boiled Lima beans (see recipe); put them in a saucepan with two tablespoonfuls of butter; let them saute for five minutes, and toss continually while cooking. Season with salt and pepper to taste, place on a hot dish, sprinkle with finely-chopped parsley and serve hot.

### RED BEANS.
#### Haricots Rouges.

Red Beans are the favorite dish among Creole families, the great amount of sustenance to be found in this and the White Bean commending it especially as a food for growing children and adults who labor hard. The beautiful color and excellent flavor of the Red Bean has won for it a place among the most highly esteemed legumes.

### Red Beans, Plain Boiled.
#### Haricots Verts au Naturel.

1 Pint of Dried Red Beans.
½ spoonful of Lard or Butter.
Salt and Pepper to Taste.

This is an excellent way of preparing red beans for Fridays and fast days. Soak the beans in cold water over night, or at least five or six hours, and drain off the water, and place them in a pot of cold water, using at least a quart of water to a pint of beans. Let them boil for at least an hour and a half or two hours, and then season nicely with salt and pepper. Add a half tablespoonful of lard or butter, let them cook for fifteen minutes more, and serve in their own juice. This dish is excellent with boiled rice.

### Red Beans, Burgundy Style.
#### Haricots Rouges à la Bourguigonne.

1 Quart of Red Beans.
1 Ounce of Butter. 1 Onion. 2 Cloves.
1 Herb Bouquet.
Salt and Pepper to Taste.
1 Glass of Claret Wine. 6 Small Glazed Onions.

Pick and wash the beans and let them soak in cold water for six hours Drain thoroughly, and put in a sucepan, with sufficient fresh cold water to cover. Add a tablespoonful of butter, and a medium-sized onion, with two cloves stuck in it. Boil for about twenty minutes, and then add a glass of Claret. Stir well, and let the beans cook for three-quarters of an hour longer, stirring frequently to keep from scorching. Then remove from the fire, take out the herb bouquet and onion, pour the beans into a hot dish, and decorate the edges with a half dozen small glazed onions. (See recipe.) Serve hot.

### Red Beans à la Condé
#### Purée à la Condé

See recipe under heading "Soups." This is a most nutritious dish.

### Red Beans and Rice.
#### Haricots Rouges au Riz.

1 Quart of Dried Red Beans.
1 Carrot. 1 Onion. 1 Bay Leaf.
1 Tablespoonful of Butter.
1 Pound of Ham or Salt Meat.
Salt and Pepper to Taste.

Wash the beans and soak them over night, or at least five or six hours, in fresh, cold water. When ready to cook, drain off this water and put the beans in a pot of cold water, covering with at least two quarts, for beans must cook thoroughly. Let the water heat slowly. Then add the ham or salt pork, and the herbs and onion and carrot, minced fine. Boil the beans at least two hours, or until tender enough to mash easily under pressure. When tender, remove from the pot, put the salt meat or ham on top of the dish, and serve hot as a vegetable, with boiled rice as an entrée, with Veal Sauté, Daube à la Mode, Grillades à la Sauce, etc.

### Purée of Red Beans.
#### Purée d'Haricots Rouges.

1 Quart of Dried Red Beans.
1 Carrot. 1 Onion. 1 Bay Leaf.
1 Tablespoonful of Butter.
½ Pound of Ham or Lean Salt Pork.
½ Pint of Cream or Milk.
Salt and Pepper to Taste.

Prepare the beans as in the preceding recipe if it is desired to make a purée (not a soup). Remove the beans from the fire as soon as they will mash very easily under pressure. Take out the bits of ham. Press the beans through a colander. Add a tablespoonful of butter as you return them to the pot in which they have been boiled, and a half pint of cream or milk, or sufficient according to quantity to make the purée of the consistency of thick starch or mashed potatoes. Season with salt and pepper, and serve. Thus prepared, red beans may be eaten by the most delicate invalid with excellent results as to recuperation.

### Bacon and Beans à la Créole.
Haricots au Petit Salé à la Créole.

1 Quart of Dried Red Beans. 1 Pound Bacon.
Salt and Pepper to Taste.

Soak the beans over night. Drain off all water. Place in a pot and cover well with cold water, in the proportions already mentioned. Add the bacon, leaving it in a single square piece. When both have boiled about two hours, season well with pepper and a little salt, if necessary, and place the bacon in the center of a baking dish. Drain the beans and put them around the bacon. Fill the pan to the top with liquor in which the beans have been boiled, and bake one hour and a half, or until the liquor is nearly all absorbed. Then serve hot. This is a favorite dish with the little Creole children, and is most wholesome and palatabe. White or red beans may be cooked in this fashion.

### Bean Polenta.
Polente d'Haricots.

2 Cups of Dried Beans.
1 Tablespoonful of Molasses. ½ Tablespoonful of Mustard.
1 Tablespoonful of Butter. 1 Tablespoonful of Vinegar.
Juice of 1 Lemon. Salt and Pepper to Taste.

Use either white or red beans. Wash two cupfuls of dried beans, having previously soaked them over night. Pour off the water. Put the beans in the stewpan and cover with fresh cold water, and cook the beans until tender. Pour into a colander, and press the beans through. Put this pulp into the stewpan, and add one tablespoonful of ready-made mustard, one tablespoonful of molasses, one of butter, one of vinegar, the juice of an onion, and salt and pepper to taste. Serve very hot, as a vegetable.

### WHITE BEANS.
Des Haricots Blancs.

White Beans may be prepared in exactly the same manner as red beans, using any of the above recipes. By many the white bean is preferred as the more delicate bean.

### White Beans à la Maître d'Hôtel.
Haricots Blancs à la Maître d'Hôtel.

1 Quart of White Beans.
2 Sprigs of Minced Thyme and Parsley.
1 Bay Leaf.
Sauce a la Maître d'Hôtel.

Prepare the white beans and cook in exactly the same manner as red beans à la Maître d'Hôtel. Before adding the butter, however, add a minced sprig of thyme, bay leaf and parsley, and salt and pepper to taste. Let them simmer for a few minutes on the fire, and then take off and add the juice of a lemon.

### DRIED PEAS.
Des Pois Secs.

All dried peas, whether the Blackeyed Peas, Lady Peas, etc., may be cooked according to any of the above recipes. Be careful to soak them over night in cold water, or at least six hours from the early morning, before beginning to cook.

### COWPEAS.
Pois Congris.

These peas are utilized by the Creoles in making that famous dish, "Jambalaya au Congri." (See recipe under heading "Louisiana Rice.') On Fridays the rice and peas, which are always boiled separately, must not be cooked with meat, if this day is kept as a fast day. The peas and rice are mixed well together and are eaten with butter.

### BUTTERBEANS.
Féves Plates.

1 Pint of Butterbeans. 2 Pints of Water.
1 Tablespoonful (heaping) of Butter.
Salt and Pepper to Taste.

The butterbean is one of the most recherché and delicate of our Louisiana vegetables. Soak the butterbeans for about a half hour in water. Pour off this cold fresh water, and then put them in a porcelain lined saucepan, or one of agate, and cover with two pints of water. Let them boil well for about an hour, or less, if they are very tender. As soon as they crush easily under pressure, take off the fire, drain off water, season well with salt and pepper. Butter well with a heaping tablespoonful of butter, add a teaspoonful of parsley, minced very fine, and serve hot. This is a delicious and welcome dish at the most elegant tables. Butterbeans are raised so extensively in Louisiana that they are very cheap and may always grace the poor mans table as well as the rich.

### LIMA BEANS.
Haricots à Rames.

1 Pint of Lima Beans. 3 Pints of Water.
1 Tablespoonful of Flour.
1 Tablespoonful of Butter. ½ Pint of Cream.
Salt and Pepper to Taste.

The younger the Lima beans the better . It is a great mistake to allow the beans to grow large and hard. Sort the beans as you shell them, and save the very large ones for a purée. Soak the small ones over night. Drain the water when about to cook, and put in a porcelain or agate saucepan, and cover with three pints of boiling water. Boil them until very tender, which will require at least two hours. After they have boiled one hour, add a teaspoonful of salt, or salt to taste. When done, drain the beans and return to the saucepan. Add a half pint of cream or milk, a tablespoonful of flour, blended well with butter, salt and pepper to taste, a sprig each of thyme and parsley and bay leaf minced very fine. Let all simmer for ten minutes, and then serve hot. Or the beans may be served without the cream, simply buttering well and adding salt and pepper to taste. All shelled beans, such as the Kidney and the small French bean, may be cooked in the same way. The larger Lima Beans may be saved, and will serve some day during the week for a purée.

### Bean Croquettes.
Haricots en Croquettes.

1 Pint of Beans. 1 Tablespoonful of Butter.
Salt and Cayenne to Taste.

Any remains of left-over beans may be nicely utilized in this way. Mash the beans well by pressing through a colander. Then add salt and pepper to taste, a teaspoonful of vinegar, and a tablespoonful of melted butter. Form into small boulettes, or balls, and dip in a raw egg, well beaten, and then roll in the bread crumbs. Fry in boiling fat, and serve hot.

### BEETS.
Des Betteraves.

We have in New Orleans two crops of beets, the winter beet and the summer beet. Summer beets require less time to boil than the winter. Good judgment must always be the guide.

Beets may be kept several days when boiled, and make a beautiful garnish.

The small winter beets may be served aux Beurre Maitre dHotel, or they may be sautéd in butter or served Sautées à la Crème or à la Bechamel. Beet roots are generally served as a salad or garnish. Always cut off and save the green tops of the beets. These may be boiled with salt meat, or made into a purée, or used in the famous Creole Gumbo aux Herbes.

### Boiled Beets.
Betteraves Bouillies.

6 Beet Roots. 2 Quarts of Water.
A Plain French Dressing (if served as a salad).

Cut off the beet tops and save for boiling or purée or gumbo. Soak the beets in cold fresh water, and wash well, taking off every particle of earth that may adhere. Wash them carefully, without scraping them. If the beet is very tender, it will cook in an hour. Older beets require all the way from three to four hours, according to size. If the beet is wilted or tough, no amount of boiling will ever make it perfectly tender. If you break the skins of the beets before cooking, the flavor will be lost, as well as the color, when boiled. Put the beets into a pot of cold water, covering well, and boil until tender. Then set them to cool. When cold, slice nicely and sprinkle with salt and pepper to taste, and add vinegar, and set aside for an hour, for the vinegar to penetrate thoroughly. Serve as a salad.

### Buttered Beets.
Betteraves au Beurre.

6 Beet Roots. 1 Tablespoonful of Butter.
Salt and Pepper to Taste.

The small winter beets may be served aux Beurre Maître d'Hotel, by cooking very tender and then slicing nicely, and pouring over them a tablespoonful of melted butter, and sprinkling nicely with salt and pepper. Vinegar may also be added at the table, according to the taste.

### Beet Roots Sautéd in Butter.
Betteraves Sautées au Beurre.

6 Beets. 1 Tablespoonful of Butter.
A Pinch of Black Pepper.
2 Tablespoonfuls of Powdered Sugar.

Boil the beet roots as in recipe for Boiled Beets. (See recipe.) When cooked, peel neatly and cut up into dice-shaped pieces. Put them in a saucepan with a tablespoonful of butter, season with a little pinch of black pepper and salt to taste, and sprinkle the powdered sugar over them. Let them cook for five minutes, tossing them lightly and almost constantly. Send to the table hot as a vegetable.

### Beet Roots Sauté à la Bechamel ou à la Crème.
Betteraves Sautées à la Bechamel ou à la Crème.

6 Beet Roots. 1 Ounce of Butter.
Salt and Pepper to Taste.
½ Pint of Bechamel or Cream Sauce.

Prepare the beets exactly as in the preceding recipe, and about five minutes before serving add half a pint of hot Bechamel or Cream Sauce. Serve as a vegetable.

### Borecole or Curled Kale.
Chou Vert.

This is a vegetable cultivated by Louisiana truck farmers principally for family use. It requires frost to make it good for the table. It is treated and served in the same manner as cabbage; all recipes for cooking cabbage may, therefore, be used in preparing Chou Vert.

### BROCCOLI.
Chou Broccoli.

Broccoli is a vegetable of the same order as the Cauliflower, and resembles it very much, only the plant does not form such compact heads, and is not quite so white, being of a greenish cast. Such fine Cauliflower is raised in and around New Orleans that very little Broccoli is planted. Further north than New Orleans, however, where Cauliflower does not succeed, it is substituted for it, as the hardier plant. It thrives easily, and in season is always to be found in the New Orleans market, selling much cheaper than Cauliflower, and is used very frequently as a substitute. It is prepared and served in all ways in which Cauliflower is served. (See recipes for Cauliflower.)

### BRUSSELS SPROUTS.
Choux de Bruxelles.

1 Quart of Brussels Sprouts.
½ Gallon of Water. 1 Tablespoonful of Salt.

Pick the sprouts carefully, rejecting all loose, dead leaves, and then throw the sprouts into cold fresh water, so that any lurking insects may be drawn out. Wash and pick carefully after the sprouts have remained about twenty minutes in the water. Then put them into half a galon of boiling water, and add immediately a tablespoonful of salt and a quarter of a spoon of bicarbonate of soda (cooking soda). Let the sprouts boil (uncovered) for twenty minutes, or just long enough to make them tender all through. By no means must they be soft, or go to pieces. Boil rapidly. Then drain in a colander, season well with pepper and salt, and serve in a heated dish with a Drawn Butter Sauce poured over. (See sauces.)

### Brussels Sprouts Sautéd in Butter.
Choux de Bruxelles Sautés au Beurre.

1 Quart of Brussels Sprouts.
2 Tablespoonfuls of Butter.
1 Teaspoonful of Chopped Parsley.
Salt and Pepper to Taste.

Prepare the Brussels Sprouts carefully as in the preceding recipe. After washing, drain thoroughly and boil them in salted water for ten minutes. Take out of the hot water, drain and put into cold water. Drain again and put them in a saucepan, with two tablespoonfuls of butter. Season according to taste with salt and pepper, and add a teaspoonful of chopped parsley. Let them cook slightly for ten minutes more, or less if very tender, and serve hot.

### Brussels Sprouts à la Crème.
Choux de Brussels à la Crème.

1 Quart of Brussels Sprouts.
2 Tablespoonfuls of Butter.
1 Teaspoonful of Chopped Parsley.
½ Cupful of Cream or Milk.
A Pinch of Nutmeg.
Salt and Pepper to Taste.

Prepare and boil the Brussels Sprouts as in the preceding recipe. Drain thoroughly, and put in a saucepan, with two tablespoonfuls of butter, and season with salt and pepper to taste, and a pinch of nutmeg. Add a half cup of cream or milk, and toss lightly for five or ten minutes, but do not let them boil. Place on a hot dish, garnish nicely and serve hot.

### CABBAGE.
Du Chou.

Cabbage is said to be the most nutritious of all vegetables. It enters largely into the daily life of the Creoles, not only in the boiled and creamed and stuffed states, but also in that most delightful Creole dish, Gumbo Choux. In many a Creole family of limited means the good dish of Gumbo Choux and rice, and a dish of Grillades, make not only a most appetizing and nutritious, but a most hearty meal. We have two crops of cabbage in New Orleans, the summer and winter. It is said that when cabbage is cooking the odor fills the house. But the Creoles overcome this by using a very large pot when boiling cabbage, dropping in a bit of charcoal, and not filling it too near the brim, as the old darkies say it is the boiling water that forms into steam and causes the odor. Again, they tie a piece of bread in a very fine and thin white piece of cloth. After it has been in the pot about twenty minutes remove it and burn, for the odor of the cabbage has clung to it. Repeat the process with a fresh piece of cloth and bread for about three-quarters of an hour.

### Boiled Cabbage.
Chou Bouilli.

A Fine Head of Green and White Cabbage.
1 Teaspoonful of Salt. 1 Red Pepper Pod.
1 Teaspoonful of Chili Pepper.

For boiling, select a fine white head in which the green and white are prettily mingled. The white makes the prettiest dish. Remove all the outside leaves and reject them. Then cut the cabbage head into quarters, and let it soak in cold water for about an hour. Then drain well, and pull off each leaf separately to discover any lurking insects, and throw each leaf into a pan of fresh water. Drain thoroughly, and put into a large pot of boiling water with a pound of ham or salt pork, and let it cook for an hour or more, until tender. After it has been in the water ten minutes, add a teaspoonful of salt and a red pepper pod, cut in two. Add a teaspoonful of Chili pepper. Cover the cabbage and boil for one hour, if the cabbage is very young and tender; boil for two hours or more if not. When done, drain well of all water, and place in a dish with the salt meat or ham on top.

and serve hot. Cabbage is always eaten with a little vinegar. The Creoles serve boiled cabbage with the pepper vinegar which they put up themselves.

### Cabbage and Corned Beef.
### Chou et Boeuf au Mi-sel.
1 Fine Head of Cabbage. 1 Pound of Corn Beef.
1 Red Pepper Pod.
1 Teaspoonful of Chili Pepper.

To boil corned beef and cabbage, wash the meat in cold water and put it in a large kettle; cover with cold water. Let it simmer gently for two hours. Then add the cabbage, which you will have prepared according to directions in the above recipe, and let all boil for two hours longer. When done, put the cabbage in a dish, with the meat in the center, and serve with tomato catsup or horseradish or mustard sauce. The cabbage may be put in the pot after having been cut in four quarters and soaked, but it is always safer to pick over each leaf, for fear of insects.

### Stewed Cabbage.
### Chou Etouffé.
1 Head of Cabbage. 1 Pound Ham or Salt Pork.
Salt to Taste. Pinch of Red Pepper Pod.
1 Tablespoonful of Lard.

Parboil the cabbage after cutting into quarters. Let it boil well about half an hour. Then take it out of the water and drain nicely, separating the leaves down to the heart as it cools. Cut the ham into pieces of about two inches long. Take a tablespoonful of lard, and put in a stewing pan, which must be very deep, or a pot. Put into this the ham or salt meat, and let it fry well. Add two chaurice, or sausage. As these brown well, moisten with half a cup of boiling water, and let simmer gently for fifteen minutes. When well browned, add, little by little, the cabbage, stirring it well, and let it simmer gently for an hour and a half or longer, covering well, and stirring frequently to prevent burning. Add an inch of red pepper pod, cut fine, and salt to taste if you use ham, and none at all if you use salt meat. Serve hot.

### Cabbage Stewed With Sausage.
### Saucissons aux Choux.
2 Dozen Fine Sausage. (Chaurice Preferred.)
1 Head of Cabbage.
1 Tablespoonful of Lard. Salt to Taste.
1 Inch of Red Pepper Pod.
1 Pound Fresh Pork.

This is a famous Creole dish, for many generations in vogue in New Orleans, and dearly loved by the little Creole children. Wash the cabbage well, after having cut it into quarters and allowed it to soak half an hour. Cut the cabbage into shreds of about one inch in width and five in length, according to the leaf. Then scald the cabbage with boiling water for about fifteen minutes. Throw off this water, and cover it again with boiling water, and let it boil for twenty minutes. In the meanwhile prick each sausage in several places, and cut the meat into pieces of about two inches in length and one in thickness; put the lard in the frying pan and fry the sausage and meat until they are about half done; then drain the cabbage and turn into the sausage and meat and the fat drippings. Cover and stew gently where it will not scorch, for at least forty minutes; season with salt, and add, immediately after turning in the cabbage, an inch of red pepper pod. Let all simmer till the cabbage is quite done, and then put in a dish with the sausage and meat piled in the center, and the cabbage heaped around as a border.

### Creamed Cabbage.
### Chou à la Crème.
1 Head of Tender White Cabbage.
A Cream Sauce.

Take a fine delicate head of white cabbage; cut it in quarters and soak in cold water for an hour. Then remove all the hard parts, and cut the remainder into fine shreds. Put it into the stewing pan and pour over boiling water enough to cover; season with salt and pepper; let it boil at least thirty minutes, and then drain in a colander. Have ready a heated dish; turn the cabbage into this and pour over a Cream Sauce. (See recipe.)

### Cabbage Sautéd With Cream.
### Chou Sauté à la Crème.
A Fine Head of White Cabbage.
1 Cupful of Cream or Milk.
2 Tablespoonfuls of Butter. 1 Tablespoonful of Flour.
A Pinch of Black Pepper. Salt to Taste.

Prepare the cabbage according to recipe. Blanch in hot water for ten minutes, then drain and throw into cold water. Drain again, and chop up the cabbage and put into a saucepan with two tablespoonfuls of butter; add the salt to taste, and the black pepper. Take a tablespoonful of flour and blend well with a little milk, and then mix well with a cup of cream or milk. Add this to the cabbage and mix well, and let all cook for three-quarters of an hour or an hour, till done; arrange neatly on a hot dish and serve.

### Stuffed Cabbage
### Chou Farci.
1 Head of Fine White Cabbage.
1 Dozen Fine Chaurice. 2 Onions. 1 Tomato.
1 Clove of Garlic.
1 Square Inch of Ham. 1 Spoonful of Butter.
Thyme, Parsley and Bay Leaf.
Salt and Pepper to Taste.

Select a fine head of cabbage. Take away the big, green leaves, and select about twelve of the finest and nicest of the large white leaves. Put them in cold water for about an hour; then parboil for about twenty minutes in boiling water. In the meantime, prepare a stuffing with a dozen fine chaurice, one onion (chopped fine), a tablespoonful of butter and a tomato. Mince the sausage meat very fine after taking out of the cases, and also the onion and tomato. Mince fine one sprig each of thyme, parsley and bay leaf; add one square inch of finely-minced ham. Put the butter in the frying pan, and as it browns add the onions; let these brown, and add the sausage meat and the ham. Mince four or five of the tender white leaves of the cabbage very fine and add; then add the minced clove of garlic and onion; let these brown for five minutes, and then let all simmer for about ten minutes. Take out, and take each leaf by leaf of the cabbage and drain dry; lay open on the table and put in each leaf equal quantities of the stuffing; fold over and close nicely. Then take slender strips of bacon and lay at the bottom of a wide and deep frying pan; place the stuffed leaves on top of these, and place other strips of bacon on top; cover and let them cook for a half hour, or until the cabbage leaves are very tender. Take out of the pan and lay in a heated dish and serve very hot. The Creoles also have a way of making a nice sauce to serve with these. After laying the stuffed cabbage leaves in the frying pan, add one square inch of ham, minced very fine; two carrots, sliced fine; one onion, chopped very fine, and sprigs of thyme, parsley and bay leaf. Moisten this with a cup of good bouillon or water, a gill of White Wine, and cover the pan and allow all to simmer well with the cabbage. At the moment of serving, place the cabbage in a heated dish and allow the sauce to reduce for five minutes longer; then strain it through a fine sieve and pour over each stuffed leaf of cabbage as it is served. The stuffed cabbage leaves may also be thrown into boiling water for thirty minutes, after being tied together well, and served with a Cream Sauce. (See recipe.)

**Stuffed Cabbage With Cream Sauce.**

Chou Farci à la Crème.

1 Fine Head Cabbage. 1 Dozen Fine Chaurice.
1 Onion.
3 Sprigs each of Thyme, Parsley and Bay Leaf.
1 Square inch of Ham.
1 Inch of a Red Pepper Pod.
Salt and Pepper to Taste.

Select a fine tender head of cabbage. Pick off the outer leaves, and let it soak in cold fresh water for an hour. Then throw the whole head into a pot of boiling water for about three-quarters of an hour. In the meantime make a stuffing by taking one dozen fine Chaurice, or sausage-meat, one onion, and three sprigs each of thyme and parsley, and one bay leaf. Mince the herbs and onion very fine, and add to them one square inch of finely minced ham. Chop the sausage meat over, and mingle this with the ham and herbs, and then add the finely minced onion and one clove of finely minced garlic. Mix these well together. Season to taste. Take the cabbage out of the water, and open carefully to the very heart, and put in a teaspoonful of the dressing. Fold over this two or three leaves, and then insert the mixture in between another layer of leaves, and so continue until each layer of leaves has been nicely stuffed. Press all firmly together, and then tie in the large leaves, which you will have boiled with the cabbage head. Put it into the kettle of boiling water, and add a little salt and two inches of a red pepper pod, thyme, parsley and bay leaf. Let it boil for two hours. When done carefully untie the larger leaves in which you have cooked the cabbage, and lay the head in a well-heated dish. Pour over all a Cream Sauce, and serve hot. (See Cream Sauce.)

**SAUERKRAUT.**

Chou Croûte.

1 Fine Head of Cabbage. 1 Pint of Vinegar.
1 Bottle of White Wine.
1 Glass of Brandy or Whisky.
Salt in Sufficient Quantity to Allow 3 Ounces for each Layer of Cabbage.

The French learned how to eat Sauerkraut from the Germans, but the ancient French cuisinières held that the French adaptation, Chou-Croûte, was a very poor way indeed of expressing what the German term Sauerkraut intends to convey. The Creoles, while not overfond of Sauerkraut, nevertheless know how to make it, and occasionally cook it after ol French methods.

To prepare Chou-Croûte, take a large head of cabbage, and take off the green leaves. Shred the cabbage into fine pieces, of about five inches long and one wide. Then get an earthern vessel or a keg, and line the bottom and sides with the green leaves of the cabbage Put in a layer of salt, of about three ounces, and lay over this a layer of cabbage leaves of about three inches in thickness. Cover again with a layer of salt, and pound down well, and so continue until you have used up the cabbage. Pour over this sufficient vinegar to cover, and also, if possible, a bottle of White Wine and a glass of brandy or whisky. Take some boards or the cover of the keg and line them with cabbage leaves, and cover the keg closely. Put the cover on the keg, or the board over the bowl, with a fifteen-pound weight on top. Set it in a place of even moderate temperature. Bore a hole in the bottom of the keg, and insert a piece of wood. When the cabbage begins to ferment, take the piece of wood out, and let the liquor from the fermentation flow through this canal. This will be in about four or five days. After this first operation open the keg and renew the vinegar and wine, skimming the fermentation from the top, and so continue until the cabbage is clear and without odor. The Chou-Croûte, should be placed in a cool place. When ready to use, take it out and let it soak for two or three hours in cool fresh water, and when quite fresh-looking put it into a saucepan and cook as you would cabbage, with salt meat, pork, sausage or corned beef.

### CAULIFLOWER.
#### Choux-Fleurs.

Cauliflower may be either boiled and served with various sauces or made into that delightful dish, "Cauliflower au Gratin."

#### Boiled Cauliflower, Cream Sauce.
Choux-Fleurs à la Crème.

2 Medium-Sized Cauliflowers.
1 Teaspoonful of Salt.
A Cream Sauce. 2 Lemons Cut in Quarters.

To boil the cauliflower, pick off the outer leaves, leaving only the one delicate row near the bottom of the flowerets. Cut the stem close to the flowerets. Wash the cauliflower well in cold fresh water, and then soak, with the head downwards, about twenty minutes, to drain off all possible insects. Have ready a pot of boiling water. Take a nice, clean piece of cheesecloth, and tie the cauliflower in it, to prevent breaking while boiling. Put the cauliflower in the kettle of boiling water, with the stem downwards. Add a teaspoonful of salt, and cover the kettle. Let the cauliflower boil from thirty to forty minutes, according to size, or until the vegetable is tender. When cooked, lift it gently out by the cheesecloth, untie and set it in a dish, stem downward. Pour over it a Cream Sauce and serve hot. Place on each plate, when serving, a quarter of a lemon, nicely cut.

#### Cauliflower Boiled With Butter.
Chou-Fleur Bouilli au Beurre.

2 Medium-Sized Cauliflowers.
2 Tablespoonfuls of Butter.
A Tablespoonful of Salt. A Pinch of Pepper.
1 Tablespoonful of Vinegar.

Prepare the cauliflower as in recipe Boiled Cauliflower, Cream Sauce. After picking and washing thoroughly put in a saucepan and cover with cold water. Add the salt and pepper and a tablespoonful of butter. Let it cook for a half hour and then take the cauliflower from the pan and drain through a colander. Place them on a dish and add a sauce made of one tablespoonful of butter, one of vinegar and a dash of salt and pepper, all mixed thoroughly, and serve hot.

#### Cauliflower With White Sauce.
Choux-Fleurs à la Sauce Blanche ou au Jus.

1 Large or 2 Small Cauliflowers.
A Teaspoonful of Salt.
A White Sauce or Sauce Allemande.

Separate the cauliflower, piece by piece, having taken off the outer leaves and cut off the rough stalk. Place them in a pot of boiling water, with a teaspoonful of salt, and let them boil rapidly for about half an hour, till the stalks are tender. When done, take them out gently with a skimmer, that you may not break them. Place in a bowl and pour over a Sauce Blanche or Sauce Allemande.
Cauliflower prepared in this manner may be served with a Hollandaise Sauce.

#### Cauliflower à la Vinaigrette.
Choux-Fleurs à la Vinaigrette.

1 Large or 2 Medium-Sized Cauliflowers.
1 Tablespoonful of Vinegar.
Salt and Pepper to Taste.

Boil the cauliflower as above, and serve "à la Vinaigrette," that is, with vinegar, pepper and salt. This is a common and pleasant way that the Creoles have of serving the vegetable.

#### Cauliflower à la Maître d'Hotel.
Choux-Fleurs à la Maître d'Hotel.

1 Large or 2 Medium-Sized Cauliflowers.
1 Teaspoonful of Salt.
A Sauce a la Maître d'Hotel.

Boil the cauliflower whole, as in the first recipe. Bring them to the table whole, like blooming flowerets, in a dish nicely garnished, and serve with a Sauce à la Maître d'Hotel and lemon cut in quarters.

#### Culiflower au Gratin.
Choux-Fleurs au Gratin.

1 Ord'nary-Sized Head of Cauliflower.
1 Pint of Cream.
½ Pint of Grated Parmesan and Gruyere Cheese, Mixed.
Salt and Pepper to Taste.
1 Tablespoonful of Butter. 1 Tablespoonful of Flour.

Boil the cauliflower as in the first recipe. When boiled, take it off the fire and take out of the cheesecloth in which it was enveloped. Let it cool. Put a tablespoonful of butter into the frying pan, and as it melts add a tablespoonful of flour. Let these blend nicely, without browning, and add immediately half a pint of milk and half a pint of grated Parmesan or Gruyére cheese. Mix this thoroughly in the sauce, and let it cook well for about ten minutes. Put the cauliflower in a pan, or the dish in which it is to be served, having greased the dish with butter. Take some grated cheese, sprinkle well over the cauliflower, and then cover the cauliflower with the sauce, forcing it down into every nook and crevice. When these crevices are full, and the cauliflower seems to have absorbed all, wipe the edges and all around the dish with a napkin. Then add grated bread crumbs, sprinkling them over the cauliflower; dot it in about a dozen places with little bits of butter. Set it in the oven, let it brown, and serve hot. Let it bake about twenty minutes, or until brown.

## CARROTS.

### Des Carottes.

Carrots are among the most important of the vegetables used in seasoning. They enter largely into the making of soups, daubes, stews, etc., giving to all a delightful flavor, which no other vegetable can. Eaten "au jus" or in their natural state, they may be stewed, fried or smothered. Any one of these dishes makes a delightful and appetizing entrée.

### Stewed Carrots.

Carottes à la Crème.

4 Carrots of Good Size.
1 Tablespoonful Butter. 1 Tablespoonful Flour.
½ Pint of Milk.
Salt and Pepper to Taste.

Scrape the carrots and throw them into cold water for about a quarter of an hour. Then put them in a saucepan, and cover with boiling water. Add the salt, and let them cook for an hour and a half, boiling steadily. After this time expires, take them out and drain off all water. Then cut neatly into one-half inch dice pieces, or slice thin. Put a tablespoonful of butter in the frying pan, and add the flour, blending well, but without browning. Then add the milk, and let it simmer to a rich cream sauce. Add the carrots to this, and let them simmer gently for about twenty minutes. Then add a little chopped parsley and sugar, and serve hot.

### Carrots à la Maitre d'Hotel.

Carottes à la Maitre d'Hotel.

4 Good-Sized Carrots.
1 Tablespoonful of Butter.
3 Sprigs Each of Thyme and Parsley.
1 Bay Leaf.
Salt and Pepper.

Scrape the carrots and boil them at the same time that you are making your soup, or bouillon, leaving them whole. When done and ready to serve, skim out of the soup, and place in a dish. Cut them into pieces, more or less large, and then place them in a frying pan with a tablespoonful of butter, minced parsley, thyme, bay leaf. Add salt and pepper to taste, and when they have cooked for about ten or fifteen minutes pour over a Sauce à la Maitre d'Hotel, and serve hot. The carrots may also be simply boiled, seasoned, and served with a Drawn Butter Sauce.

### Carrots à la Lyonnaise.

Carottes à la Lyonnaise.

3 Carrots. 1 Tablespoonful of Butter.
1 Onion, Minced Very Fine.
Salt, Pepper, Thyme and Bay Leaf.

Boil the carrots according to recipe given above, and then cut into thin slices. Fry an onion in butter, add the carrots. Sprinkle well with salt and pepper, and add minced thyme, parsley and bay leaf. Fry ten minutes, and serve hot.

### Carrots Sautés à la Créole.

Carottes Sautées à la Créole.

9 Nice Tender Carrots. 1 Tomato.
1 Square Inch Ham. 1 Tablespoonful Butter.
6 Fine Chaurice or Sausages.
3 Shallots. 1 Onion. ½ Pint of Bouillon.
Salt and Pepper to Taste.
1 Gill White Wine.
Thyme, Parsley, Bay Leaf. ½ Clove Garlic.

Boil the carrots for one hour and a half. Then cut into dice or nice slices. Put the butter in the saucepan, and add the onions, minced very fine, and the shallots, greens and whites. Let these brown for a few minutes, and then add the half square inch of ham and three Chaurice whole. Let these simmer for three minutes, and add the minced herbs. Then add the tomato and its juice, mincing it well. Let all simmer for three minutes more, till the tomato has browned, and add a half pint of bouillon and one gill of White Wine. if you can afford it. Let all this simmer for ten minutes, and then add the carrots, nicely seasoned. Stir well. Cover and let them simmer for about half an hour. Serve hot. This is a true dish of Carrots à la Créole. Eat with Daube, Roast, etc.

## CELERY.
### Du Céleri.

Celery may be eaten "au naturel," that is in its natural state; or in salad, or it may be cooked. When cooked, it is best à la Crème, or in a Purée of Celery. (See recipe.)

### Celery au Naturel.
#### Céleri au Naturel.

Scrape and wash the celery nicely. Then cut off the long outer leaves, leaving the tips nice and crisp. Set in a celery glass or bowl, with about one inch of salt and water, and serve as an appetizer, or hors d'oeuvre, at the beginning of the meal.

Celery makes a pretty decoration for any table. The leaves that have been cut off should be saved and used as garnishes, and also for seasoning.

### Creamed Celery.
#### Céleri à la Crème.
1 Pint of Cut Celery.
1 Cupful of Milk or Cream.
1 Tablespoonful Butter. 1 Tablespoonful Flour.
Salt and Pepper to Taste.

Cut fresh, crisp celery into pieces of an inch, until you have a pint. Wash thoroughly, and put in boiling water and cook until tender, which will be in about twenty-five minutes or a half hour. Then put a tablespoonful of butter in a saucepan, and add the flour, blending without allowing to brown. When perfectly smooth, add the cream or milk, and let it come to a boil. Then add salt and pepper to taste. Drain out the celery, and add it to the sauce, and stir gently, letting it cook twenty minutes longer. Serve hot. The dish should be kept covered while cooking.

Celery root and the green stalks of the celery, which you do not serve at table, may also be utilized in this way, making a most acceptable and palatable dish.

### Celery à l'Espagnole.
#### Céleri à l'Espagnole.
4 Stalks of Celery. 2 Hard-Boiled Eggs.
1 Onion.
Salt and Pepper and 1 Tablespoonful Vinegar.

This is a form of celery salad. Wash and scrape the celery well, and then chop it fine. Chop an onion very fine, and also several sprigs of parsley. Take a hard-boiled egg and cut fine. Mix all these together, pour over a little Tarragon vinegar and oil, if desired, and serve as a salad.

### Celery Salad.
#### Céleri en Salade
See recipe for Celery Salad.

### Celery aux Petit Pois.
#### Céleri aux Petit Pois.
6 Stalks of Celery. 1 Egg.
1 Tablespoonful Butter. 1 Tablespoonful Flour.
1 Cup of Milk or Bouillon.

Cut the celery into pieces and blanch and boil for about thirty minutes. Then drain. Put a tablespoonful of butter into a saucepan, and add the flour, blending without browning. Add the milk and salt and pepper to taste. When it begins to boil add the chopped celery. Let all simmer for twenty minutes longer, and then take off the fire and add the well-beaten yolk of an egg. Season again to taste, and serve. Bouillon or water may be substituted for the milk.

### Celery With Beef's Marrow
#### Céleri à la Moelle de Boeuf.
3 Fine Heads of Celery. 2 Dozen Slices of Beef's Marrow.
1 Pint of Madeira Sauce.

Cut off the green leaves of the celery and pare nicely. Wash well and drain. Then tie each head near the end where the green portion has been taken away. Put them into boiling salted water and let them blanch for ten minutes. Take out of the water and drain through a colander. Make one pint of Madeira Sauce (see recipe), add the celery to this and let it cook for a quarter of an hour. Then take the celery, place on a dish and untie. Add to the sauce in the saucepan about two dozen slices of beef marrow cut half an inch thick; cook for two minutes; do not allow the marrow to break, put in the dish with the celery, pour the sauce over and serve hot.

### Celery Patties.
#### Pátés de Céleri.
The Hearts of 3 Heads of Celery. ½ Cupful of Grated Ham.
½ Cupful of Cream. ½ Cup of Fine Bread Crumbs.
1 Tablespoonful of Butter.
Salt and Pepper to Taste.

Boil the celery hearts till tender, then drain and pound to a paste, with a cupful each of grated ham, cream and fine bread crumbs; season to taste with salt and pepper and add a tablespoonful of butter. Steam the mixture till it thickens, then fill small patty cases with it and serve hot.

### Celery Fritters.
#### Beignets de Céleri.
3 Heads of Celery. 1 Tablespoonful of Butter.
2 Ounces of Parmesan Cheese.
Salt and Pepper to Taste.

Cut the celery into stalks three inches long, tie the stalks in bundles, allowing three to a bundle; boil till tender in salted water, then take out; remove the strings and drain; season with salt and pepper, and the grated Parmesan cheese. Dip in batter and fry and serve as a vegetable.

## CEPS.
### Ceps.

Ceps the strongly flavored, flat-headed mushrooms preserved in cans and imported to this country. They are much affected by Creole epicures. They are quite expensive, and are, therefore, not as generally used in household cookery as the less expensive mushroom.

### Ceps on Toast.
#### Ceps sur Canapés.

3 Ceps. The Juice of 1 Lemon.
1 Tablespoonful of Chopped Parsley.
6 Slices of Toast.

Drain the Ceps from their oil, slice nicely and fry lightly in a frying pan. When thoroughly heated take from the pan, sprinkle lightly with chopped parsley and lemon juice, arrange daintily on slices of toast and send to the table hot.

### Stewed Ceps.
#### Ceps Sautés.

3 Ceps. 1 Onion, Minced Fine. 1 Clove of Garlic.
1 Tablespoonful of Butter. 1 Tablespoonful of Flour.
1 Tablespoonful of Chopped Parsley.
½ Cup of Milk.

Drain the Ceps from their oil; slice nicely; put a tablespoonful of butter in a saucepan, add the minced onion and the clove of garlic minced very fine; moisten with a half cup of milk, let the mixture simmer gently for twenty minutes, then serve the Ceps on slices of toast with the sauce poured around.

### Broiled Ceps on Toast.
#### Ceps Grillés sur Canapés.

3 Ceps. ½ Pint of Sauce a la Maitre d'Hotel.
Grated Bread Crumbs. Sliced Lemon and Chopped Parsley to Garnish.

Drain the Ceps from their oil; season well with salt and pepper; roll in fresh bread crumbs finely grated, broil nicely on double broiler, arrange nicely on toast. Pour over each slice some of the Sauce à la Maitre d'Hotel, garnish nicely with sliced lemon and serve hot.

## CHERVIL.
### Cerfeuil.

Chervil is an aromatic plant, resembling parsley, and much used for seasonings, especially in oyster soups. It is also considered a delightful salad herb, and is often cut and mixed between lettuce, and served as a salad. It is found in small quantities, chopped, in nearly all salads prepared to suit the taste of epicures. It is a plant little known in the North, but in this section there is scarcely a garden where it is not found. It is especially used by the Creoles as a flavoring for breakfast salads, a few leaves imparting a delightful flavor.

## CHESTNUTS.
### Marrons.

Chestnuts are much used by the Creoles in stuffing for poultry and game. They are also stewed, boiled or made into purées. (See recipe Purée de Marrons.)

### Stewed Chestnuts.
#### Marrons Sautées.

1 Pint of Chestnuts. 1 Pint of Milk.
1 Tablespoonful Flour. 1 Tablespoonful Butter.
Salt and Pepper to Taste.

Shell the chestnuts, and then throw them into a saucepan of boiling water for twenty minutes. Take them out, and remove the dark outer skin. Remove the boiling water in the saucepan, and add the chestnuts and let them cook for twenty minutes more, or until they may be easily pierced with a fork. Then take them out and drain, and put a tablespoonful of butter in a saucepan. Add the flour. Blend gradually, without browning. Add the pint of milk and then add the chestnuts, and let all cook for fifteen minutes longer. Season to taste.

### Chestnuts With Brown Sauce.
#### Marrons Sautés à la Sauce Espagnole.

1 Pint of Chestnuts. 1 Pint of Brown Sauce.

The chestnuts may be cooked in the same manner as Stewed Chestnuts, as far as boiling. Then make a Brown Sauce (see Sauce Espagnole) add the chestnuts to it, sauté for fifteen minutes longer, letting all simmer gently, and serve hot.

### Boiled Chestnuts.
#### Marrons Bouillis à la Sauce Maitre d'Hotel.

1 Pint of Chestnuts. 1 Pint of Sauce a la Maitre d'Hotel.

Prepare and boil the chestnuts according to above directions. When done, drain and press through a colander. The chestnuts must be cooked very soft for this dish. Add a Drawn Butter Sauce, and sprinkle with salt and pepper or a Sauce à la Maitre d'Hotel, and serve as an entrée, like mashed potatoes.

## CHIVES.
### Cives.

Chives are small bulbous plants of the onion tribe. The leaves are long and slender and impart a very pleasant flavor to soups, salads, etc. Chives are especially used in seasoning stews of rabbits and hare, hence, the name "Civet," applied to these stews in particular, on account of the high seasoning.

## COLLARDS.

This is a variety of cabbage which does not head, but the leaves are cooked and served in the same manner as other cabbage. But they are served, principally as "greens," boiled with a piece of salt meat. This vegetable is not as popular now in New Orleans as it was in former years.

## CORN.

### Du Maïs.

Corn in various ways is served on the Creole tables. The first young corn in the market is highly prized, but in a few days there is such an over-abundance that it can be had all summer and late in the fall at prices within the reach of all. There is not a healthier or more nutritious vegetable. The following are some of the dainty ways of preparing this delightful dish:

### Corn on the Cob.

#### Épis de Maïs Bouillis.

6 Ears of Corn.  2 Quarts of Boiling Water.
1 Tablespoonful of Salt.

Only young and tender corn should be boiled. Have ready a pot of boiling water. Remove the green outside husks and the silk, as far as possible. Put the corn into the kettle of boiling water, and let it boil rapidly twenty or thirty minutes, if the ears are large. More than this will cause the corn to lose its sweetness. Serve immediately after removing again all the silk, which easily comes to the surface in boiling. Heap the corn on a platter, and serve to each person an ear, with a small butter plate of butter, pepper and salt.

### Green Corn, Planter's Style.

#### Maïs Tendre à l'Habitant.

6 Ears of Corn.
2 Quarts of Boiling Water.
1 Tablespoonful of Salt.

Husk the corn and pull off the silk, leaving one layer of leaves close to the kernels; put to cook in cold water. When the water begins to boil, after ten minutes, add the salt, but do not let the corn boil longer than five minutes after adding the salt, as boiling longer will harden it. Corn cooked in this manner preserves its sweetness and is most palatable and tender.

### Roasted Corn.

#### Maïs Rotis.

Place the ears of corn which have not been removed from the husks in a hot oven, or, better still, if you can, in hot ashes, and let them roast for a half hour or more, until tender. Then take out of the oven or hot ashes and remove the husks and silk and serve in the same manner as boiled corn.

### Creamed Corn.

#### Maïs à la Crème.

8 Fine Ears of Corn.  1 Pint of Milk Cream.
1 Teaspoonful of Salt.
¼ Spoonful of Black Pepper.
1 Dessertspoonful Butter.

Score the corn down the center of each row of grains, and then cut from the cob. With the knife press out all the pulp from the cob, leaving the hull on the cob. Set a porcelain or agate saucepan on the fire, and put into this the corn cobs, which you will have cut into pieces. Cover with water, and let them boil until you have extracted all the juices. When the liquid is reduced to about one pint, add the corn, and let it boil for about twenty minutes. Then stir in a quarter of a pint of milk, season with salt and pepper to taste, add a teaspoonful of butter, and serve hot. Or, if you can afford it, boil the corn in the milk, using at least one pint, having first added a half cup of the water in which the corn cobs were boiled. Let all simmer gently for about a half hour, and then add salt and pepper to taste, and a spoonful of butter, and serve. Some like the addition of a teaspoonful of sugar, but this is a matter of taste.

### Corn Sautéd With Butter.

#### Maïs Tendre Sauté au Beurre.

8 Fine Ears of Corn.
1 Teaspoonful of Salt.
1 Cup of Milk or Water.

Boil the corn, and then cut the grains from the cob with a sharp knife. Put in a saucepan and add one tablespoonful of butter; add the milk, and season nicely to taste. Let the corn boil for about ten minutes and serve hot.

### Corn Pudding.

#### Pouding de Maïs.

1 Dozen Ears of Tender Corn.  1 Quart Milk.
4 Eggs.  2 Tablespoonfuls of Butter.
1 Tablespoonful of White Sugar.

Score the corn down each row of grains, and grate it from the cob. Beat the whites of the egg and the yolks separately. After beating the yolks, add them to the sugar and butter, which you will have rubbed well together. Beat all this very light, and then add the milk and a half teaspoonful of salt. Blend well, and add the grated corn. Beat again, and blend thoroughly, and add the whites of the eggs beaten to a stiff froth. Stir it well, and set the mixture in the oven with a piece of brown paper on top. Bake slowly for about an hour, and serve hot. Corn thus prepared is delicious; it is served with daube or roast filet of beef, etc.

### Baked Corn à la Crème.
#### Maïs Roti à la Crème.

1 Dozen Large Ears of Young Corn.
1 Pint of Milk. 4 Eggs.
1 Teaspoonful of Salt.
¼ Teaspoonful of Black Pepper.
1 Dessertspoonful of Butter.

Score the ears of corn down each row with a knife, and then cut from the cob. With the knife press out all the pulp and corn juice, leaving the hulls in the cob. Beat the yolks of the eggs well, and then add the corn. Season to taste with salt and pepper. Add melted butter, and then add the whites of the eggs beaten to a stiff froth. Stir in carefully, and place the whole in a dish, which you will have buttered. Set in the oven and bake for an hour, slowly at first, more rapidly towards the end of the last fifteen minutes. Serve with roast beef, veal or lamb.

### Fried Corn.
#### Maïs Frit.

1 Dozen Ears Young, Tender Green Corn.
1 Tablespoonful of Lard.
Salt and Pepper to Taste. 1 Minced Onion.

Score the corn along each row, and then cut from the cob with a knife. Press out all the pulp and corn juice from the cob. Mix all and season well with salt and pepper. Mince the onion fine, and blend with the lard, which you will have put into the frying pan. Add the corn when the onions begin to brown slightly, and keep stirring and stirring till the grain is cooked, which will be in about fifteen or twenty minutes. This is a very nice breakfast dish or dinner entrée.

### Corn Soup.
#### Purée de Maïs.

This is a delightful summer soup in New Orleans. (See recipe Creole Summer Soup.)

### Corn Fritters.
#### Beignets de Maïs.

6 Ears of Corn. ¼ Pint of Milk. 1 Egg.
½ Cup of Flour. 1 Tablespoonful Butter.
Salt and Pepper to Taste.

Grate the corn. Then beat the egg well, whites and yolks together, and by degrees add the corn, beating in thoroughly and very hard. Add a tablespoonful of melted butter, and then stir in the milk. Add a tablespoonful of flour, or just sufficient to thicken and bind, and then fry like fritters, in boiling lard, dropping in a deep spoonful at a time. Serve hot.

### Corn Cakes.
#### Gateaux de Maïs.

6 Ears of Corn. ½ Pint of Milk.
1 Egg. ½ Cup of Flour. 1 Tableapoonful of Butter.
Salt and Pepper to Taste.

Prepare the batter in exactly the same manner as above, and bake on a griddle like batter cakes, and serve hot, with generous layers of butter between. These cakes are delicious.

### Corn and Tomatoes.
#### Maïs Sautés aux Tomates.

1 Pint of Corn, Cut from the Cob.
1 Pint of Fresh Tomatoes, Peeled and Chopped.
2 Tablespoonfuls of Butter.
Salt and Pepper to Taste.
Sprigs Each of Thyme, Parsley and Bay Leaf.

Place the butter in a frying pan, and when it heats well without browning, add the tomatoes. Let them simmer for about five minutes, stirring well, and then add the minced herbs. Let these stew for three minutes, and add the corn, which has been scored and cut from the cob. Mix all thoroughly. Add salt and pepper to taste, and a teaspoonful of sugar, or less, according to taste. Let all stew or sauté for about twenty minutes, and then stir in a teaspoonful more of butter. Serve hot, after cooking ten minutes longer. Serve with roast meats or grillades or daube.

### Corn Salad.
#### Mache ou Doucette.

This is a delicious variety of corn, and is much used for salads during the winter and early spring months in New Orleans. The Corn Salad, for that is the name given to the vegetable, is boiled and then served "à la Vinaigrette," that is, with vinegar salt and pepper, or with a plain French Dressing; or with beets, sliced. Still again, it is served with hard-boiled eggs. (See recipe.)

### CRESS.
#### Cresson.

This is one of the most popular Creole winter and spring salad plants and is also considered a great appetizer, being served as an hors d'oeuvre, and eaten simply with salt. As a salad it is most cooling, refreshing and healthy. We have two varieties, the broad-leaved winter "Curled or Pepper Grass," and the "Water Cress." The latter can only be planted by the side of running water, or near springs. It is delicious. It is found all through the Louisiana forests, along the streams especially in the vicinity of Abita Springs and Covington.

## CUCUMBER.
### Concombre.

The Creoles hold, and justly, that the only proper way to eat a cucumber is "en salade." No fashionable method of cooking this vegetable can ever make up for the delicate flavor that has been destroyed by submitting it to heat.

Cucumbers are best when freshly picked from the vine. When they are thrown around the market for a number of days and become whited they are not fit for table use. Cucumbers are extensively used by the Creoles for salad and pickling purposes. For salad preparations, see special recipes under Chapter on Salads. The word "Gherkin" is applied to all kinds of pickled cucumbers; properly, however, the terms should be applied to the small prickly variety. Cucumbers, besides being served as salads and pickles, are used as relishes and as a garnish.

### Cucumbers as a Relish.
### Concombres Comme Hors d'Oeuvres.

4 Fine Cucumbers. A French Salad Dressing.

Wash the cucumbers, cut off the bitter end, and pare the skin to a sufficient depth to remove the green portion. Then score them lengthwise with a table fork. Put them into a salad earthen bowl and sprinkle with salt. Set in an ice box for three hours; then cut into delicate slices and serve with a French Salad Dressing, the dressing being served in a separate dish. In preparing cucumbers to serve as a relish with fish, this is the proper mode of preparation.

### Cucumbers as a Garnish.
### Concombres Comme Garniture.

3 Fine Cucumbers.
1 Tablespoonful of Vinegar. 1 Large Onion.

Peel and slice three fine cucumbers, and then make a marinade of one teaspoonful of salt, one of black pepper and a tablespoonful of vinegar. Add one finely-sliced onion. Let the cucumbers marinate in this for an hour, and then drain and use as a garnish for cold meats, especially cold Bouilli.

## CURRY.
### Kari.

Curry is a condiment composed of pulverized Cayenne pepper, coriander seed, timeric, onions, garlic, ginger root, cloves cinnamon cardamon and salt, all pulverized together and thoroughly mixed. It is extensively used in the making of stews of fish meats and some vegetables.

## DANDELION.
### Dent-de-Lion.

The Creoles long ago discovered the possibilities of the dandelion under cultivation. The wild dandelion, as all know, is a common and hardy perennial plant. It is found in luxuriance in the Louisiana meadows and pastures. The deeply-notched leaves closely resembling chicoree, so extensively used as a salad and as a green. Through cultivation, the dandelion is now numbered among the best of the early spring salads. (For recipe for Dandelion Salad, see Chapter on Salads.)

### Dandelion Greens.
### Dent-de-Lion Bouilli.

1 Quart of Dandelion Greens.
A Ham Shank.
1 Tablespoonful of Butter, Salt and Pepper to Taste.

Cut off the coarse roots; wash the leaves thoroughly; steep in salt and water for five hours to remove the bitterness. Boil a ham shank for two hours, throw in the dandelions, and cook gently for forty-five minutes; then drain, chop fine; season with butter, pepper and salt. Mince the ham very fine and sprinkle over the greens; spread over sliced hard-boiled eggs and serve hot.

## EGGPLANTS.
### Des Auberfines.

This is one of our most esteemed and useful vegetables, and is served in the following delightful ways:

### Stuffed Eggplant.
### Aubergines Farcies.

6 Eggplants of Good Size.
1½ Cups of Bread, Wet and Squeezed.
1 Tomato. 1 Onion. 1 Clove of Garlic.
Thyme, Parsley, Bay Leaf.
2 Tablespoonfuls of Butter.

Cut the eggplant in the middle, and put to boil in cold water for about half an hour, or until tender. Then take out of the water and set to cool. When quite cool, take out the seeds and throw away. Then scoop out carefully the soft meat of the eggplant, and leave the skins unbroken. Set these skins carefully aside. Chop the soft eggplant fine, and then wet and squeeze one and a half cups of bread. Chop the onion and tomato fine, and mince the herbs and garlic very fine. Season the eggplant well with salt and pepper. Put the butter in the frying pan (use a tablespoonful of lard, if you have not the butter), and brown the onion in it slightly. Then add the chopped tomato and its juice, and let this fry for four or five minutes. Then add the minced herbs and the clove of garlic, and almost immediately the chopped eggplant. Then add the bread at once, and mix all well. Season again to taste, and let all fry for about five minutes. Take off and fill the shells with the stuffing, sprinkle the top lightly with bread crumbs, dot with butter, and set in the oven to bake to a nice brown.

### Fried Eggplant

Aubergines Frites.

2 Young Eggplants. 2 Eggs.
Flour to Make a Light Batter.
2 Tablespoonfuls of Lard.

Slice the eggplants very thin, paring them if large, and leaving the skin on if very young and tender. Make a light batter with the eggs and flour. Season the eggplant well with salt and pepper. Soak the slices in the batter. Lift out and fry in the boiling lard. When done on one side, turn on the other with a cake turner. Remove the eggplants. Drain them on brown paper in the mouth of the oven, and serve hot on a flat and open dish or platter.

### Eggplant Fritters.

Aubergines en Beignets ou au Naturel.

2 Young Eggplants. ½ Pint of Milk.
Salt and Pepper. Flour.

Slice the eggplants nicely and thin. Roll them in milk in which you have put salt and pepper to taste. Pass the eggplant in flour, dusting lightly, and fry in boiling lard. The eggplant must float in the lard. Drain on brown paper in the mouth of the oven, and serve hot.

### Stewed Eggplant.

Aubergines à la Créole.

3 Eggplants. ½ Can of Tomatoes.
1 Square Inch of Ham.
2 Cloves of Garlic. 2 Onions.
1 Tablespoonful of Butter. Salt and Pepper to Taste.

Parboil the eggplant for about thirty minutes. Take out of the boiling water and let cool slightly. Then skin and cut into pieces half an inch square. Chop two onions very fine. Take one tablespoonful of butter, and brown the onion in it. As it browns, add half a can of tomatoes, or six fresh, chopped fine. Add the square inch of ham, chopped very fine. Add then two cloves of garlic, minced very fine, and season with salt and pepper to taste. Let this simmer for three or four minutes, and then add the eggplant sufficient to make a pound. Let all cook, smothering slowly and well, keeping tightly covered, and stirring often to prevent burning. Season again to taste. After it has cooked for half an hour serve very hot. This is a splendid dish, and was first the production of a Creole cuisinière.

### ENDIVES.

De la Chicorée.

Endive, or Chicorée, is served both as a salad plant and as a vegetable. It is very popular among the Creoles, and is much cultivated for the market, especially for summer use. Chicorée as a salad is served in exactly the same manner as Lettuce Salad. (See recipe under chapter on Salads.)

### Endive With Cream Sauce.

Chicorée, Sauce à la Crème.

3 Heads of Chicory. 4 Tablespoonfuls Butter.
2 Glasses of Cream or Milk.
A Pinch of Nutmeg. Salt and Pepper to Taste.

Pick nicely three heads of Chicorée, casting away all the outer green leaves. Then wash the heads carefully in fresh cold water; drain and wash again, and blanch for ten minutes in boiling salted water; remove and throw into cold water to cool. Then drain of all the water, and chop the Chicorée very fine. Put in a saucepan with four tablespoonfuls of butter and let cook for a quarter of an hour. Pour two glassfuls of milk or rich cream over it; add a pinch of grated nutmeg, and salt and pepper to taste. Mix all thoroughly together for five minutes on the stove; then remove, put in a dish, garnish nicely with Croutons fried in butter, and serve hot.

### Endives With Gravy.

Chicorée au Jus.

4 Heads of Chicory. 1 Onion. 1 Carrot.
1 Herb Bouquet.
¼ Pound of Bacon. Salt and Pepper to Taste.
1 Pint of Veal or Chicken Consomme.

Clean and pick the Chicorée well, pare off all the outer leaves, and wash the heads well in several waters. Then drain and put to blanch in salted water for ten minutes. At the end of this time, throw them in the cold water to cool; drain and cut into quarters. Put the piece of bacon in the bottom of a sautoire or stewpan, and add an onion and carrot and herb bouquet, minced very fine. Lay the Chicorée on top of this, season with a teaspoonful of salt and a half teaspoonful of black pepper, and cover with a buttered paper. Then set the sautoire in the oven, and let the Chicorée cook for ten minutes, when it will be a golden brown. Moisten with half a pint of veal or chicken consommé, cover and again set in the oven for thirty minutes. At this point it will be ready to serve. Arrange the Chicorée on a hot dish; strain the sauce, pour over and serve.

### GARLIC.

De l'Ail.

Garlic is a great Creole vegetable, a bulbous-rooted plant, with a strong penetrating odor, and highly esteemed as a flavoring for soups, stews, roasts and various other dishes. Garlic is a staple product of the lower Louisiana parishes, and is raised for home consumption and for shipping. More garlic is grown and used in Louisiana than in all the other states together. It is cultivated like the onion. In the spring the bulbs are taken up and plaited together in long strings. One of these strings contains from fifty to sixty heads in double rows. They are then hung up in a dry, airy place, or stored away. They will keep from six to eight months. Great strings of garlic adorn the stalls of the French Market daily.

### HORSERADISH.
### Raifort.

The roots of the horseradish are extensively used as an appetizer on Creole tables. They are an agreeable relish, with a fine, sharp, pungent taste. Scraped and grated very fine, and set on the table in small cups, they are used as a condiment. In cookery the horseradish is used in the preparation of sauces and salads.

### KOHLRABI, OR TURNIP-ROOTED CABBAGE.
### Chou-Navet.

This vegetable is used in making soup purées or vegetable purées, and is also prepared in the same manner as cauliflower. (See recipes Purées and also Cauliflower.) The finest variety, the "Early White Vienna," is the only variety planted and sold in New Orleans. It is an excellent table vegetable, very popular among the Italian and other European population of the city especially, and very largely cultivated.

### LEEKS.
### Poireau.

This popular vegetable is a species of onion, highly esteemed for flavoring soups, etc. It is used altogether as a seasoning.

### LENTILS.
### Des Lentilles.

Lentils are among the most nutritious of all vegetables. They may be made into a purée (see recipe under chapter on Soups), or may be cooked in every manner in which red and white beans are cooked. On Fridays and fast days they are simply boiled over a slow fire, with a little butter, salt and pepper, and a bouquet of parsley, and an onion cut in quarters. Again, the Creoles boil Lentils with sausage, or chaurice. Still again, they are simply boiled in salt and water, and served with a Sauce à la Vinaigrette, Sauce Soubise, or a Sauce à la Maître d'Hotel. (See recipes.)

### MUSHROOMS.
### Des Champignons.

Mushrooms constitute one of the greatest flavoring vegetables known to the scientific cuisinier. They are used in all manner of sauces, and when veal, game or fish are cooked "en braisé," or "en sauté." They are used in "matelotes," and in nearly all forms of farcies. The Creoles, like the French, think it a crime to cook this vegetable in any form that would destroy its own peculiar flavor, or that which it is capable of imparting to the most ordinary dish.

#### Stewed Mushrooms on Toast.
Champignons Sautés sur Canapés.

1 Pint of Mushrooms.
1 Tablespoonful of Butter. The Juice of 1 Lemon.
1 Teaspoonful of Chopped Parsley.
6 Slices of Toast.

Drain the mushrooms of their liquor, and place in a stewpan with the butter; season to taste with salt and pepper; cover and let them cook for ten minutes, tossing almost constantly. Add the juice of a lemon and the chopped parsley. Place six slices of toast on a dish, garnish these nicely with the mushrooms and serve. The toast may be omitted if it is desired simply to stew the mushrooms and serve as a vegetable.

#### Mushrooms With Cream.
Champignons Sautés à la Crème.

1 Pint Mushrooms. 1 Tablespoonful Butter.
½ Cup of Cream.
The Yolk of 1 Egg. 1 Tablespoonful Flour.
Salt and Pepper to Taste.

Put the mushrooms with their juice, into a saucepan, porcelain-lined or agate. Let them simmer for fifteen minutes. Then add one tablespoonful of butter, blended well with the same amount of flour, and mixed thoroughly with the cream. Season with salt and pepper. Stir well. Bring it to a good boil, and remove from the fire, and stir in the yolk of an egg, which has been beaten with Sherry Wine. Serve immediately in a very hot dish or bowl.

To stew canned mushrooms, drain them of their liquor. Melt the butter in a porcelain-lined saucepan, and gradually add the flour, without letting it burn. Blend smoothly. Add the boiling milk, and let it boil for about two minutes. Then add the mushrooms, salt and pepper to taste. Remove from the fire after five minutes. Serve on buttered toast or Croutons fried in butter. Again, the milk may be omitted, and the mushrooms stewed in their own liquor.

### Mushrooms With Cream.

Champignons Sautés à la Crême.

1 Pint Mushrooms. 1 Tablespoonful Butter.
½ Cup of Cream.
The Yolk of 1 Egg. 1 Tablespoonful Flour.
Salt and Pepper to Taste.

Put the mushrooms with their juice into a saucepan, porcelain-lined or agate. Let them simmer for fifteen minutes. Then add one tablespoonful of butter, blended with the same amount of flour, and mixed thoroughly with the cream. Season with salt and pepper. Stir well. Bring it to a good boil, and remove from the fire and stir in the yolk of an egg, which has been beaten with Sherry Wine. Serve immediately in a very hot dish or bowl.

To stew canned mushrooms, drain them of their liquor. Melt the butter in a porcelain-lined saucepan, and gradually add the flour, without letting it burn. Blend smoothly. Add the boiling milk, and let it boil for about two minutes. Then add the mushrooms, salt and pepper to taste. Remove from the fire after five minutes. Serve on buttered toast or Croûtons fried in butter. Again, the milk may be omitted, and the mushrooms stewed in their own liquor.

### Stewed Mushrooms, Spanish Style.

Champignons Sautés à l'Espagnole.

1 Pint or 1 Can of Mushrooms.
1 Tablespoonful of Olive Oil.
1 Tablespoonful of Chopped Parsley. 1 Clove of Garlic.
1 Teaspoonful of Chives. 1 Dozen Whole Peppers.
Salt and Black Pepper to Taste.

Drain the mushrooms of their liquor; cut them in lozenge-shaped pieces, and put them in a dish and sprinkle with a tablespoonful of olive oil, and salt and pepper to taste. Let the mushrooms soak in this marinade for two hours. At the end of this time, take them out and put in a saucepan and let them stew for ten minutes. Make a sauce of three tablespoonfuls of olive oil, the clove of garlic, minced very fine, a tablespoonful of minced chives, and blend well. Add this to the mushrooms and let them sauté for five minutes longer on a very slow fire, without boiling, and serve hot.

### Fried Mushrooms.

Champignons à la Bordelaise.

1 Pint Mushrooms. 1 Tablespoonful Olive Oil.
6 Shallots, Minced Very Fine.
Thyme, Parsley and Bay Leaf, Minced Fine.
1 Clove of Garlic, Minced Fine.
Salt and Pepper to Taste.

Put the oil into a frying pan, and, when heated, add the shallots, minced very fine. Let these brown slightly, and add the minced garlic and fine herbs. Let these brown for three minutes or so, and then add the mushrooms. Stir well and fry for about five minutes. Add one tablespoonful of White Wine or Sherry, and serve the mushrooms on slices of French toast.

### MUSTARD.

De la Moutarde.

Mustard is grown extensively in Louisiana, especially the large-leaved or curled, which has grown to be a distinct Louisiana variety, quite different from the European. The seed is black, and is raised in Louisiana, and the plant is being more extensively cultivated every year. The large leaves are cooked the same as Spinach (see recipe), or they may be boiled with salt meat and served as greens.

Our Creole mustard seeds are famous not only in making sauces, but for medicinal purposes.

### OKRA.

Du Févi.

Okra is a great summer dish with the Creoles. It may be made into Gumbo (see recipe Okra Gumbos) or boiled and served en salade.

### Boiled Okra.

Févi Bouilli.

1 Quart Young Okra. 1 Tablespoonful Vinegar.
Salt and Pepper to Taste.

Wash the okra well in cold water, and put in a porcelain-lined or agate saucepan. Add a pint of water and a teaspoonful of salt. Cover the pot, and let the okra simmer for about half an hour. Take from the pot, season with salt and pepper to taste, pour over a tablespoonful of Tarragon vinegar and set to cool. Serve as a salad, and with all meats, such as daube, roast, etc.

### Stewed Okra, Creole Style.

Févi Sauté à la Créole.

4 Dozen Okras. 1 Tablespoonful Butter.
3 Nice Potatoes.
1 Onion. 1 Green Pepper. 1 Clove of Garlic.
1 Teaspoonful of Chopped Parsley.

Wash the okras and pare the ends. Place in a saucepan with one tablespoonful of butter; add a finely-minced onion and clove of garlic and green pepper. Let all cook for six or eight minutes, and then add the three tomatoes, chopped fine; also add the juice of the tomatoes. Season to taste with salt and pepper; add a dash of Cayenne and a teaspoonful of chopped parsley. Now add the okras, and let all simmer slowly for twenty minutes. Place in a hot, deep serving dish, and cover and send to the table.

## ONIONS.

### De l'Ognon.

Onions have always been conceded by the Creoles, as also by all scientists, among the healthiest of food substances. The onion is indispensable in the kitchen. It is used in almost every kind of meat and fish or vegetable seasoning, and imparts a flavor that cannot be claimed by any other vegetable. Onions are also acknowledged as a great sedative. The onion juice, mixed with sugar, is largely used by the old Creoles in coughs and colds, and is almost an infallible remedy. The onion is used as a salad, or it may be cooked in some very delightful ways. There are those, who, being over-fastidious, object to eating onions on account of the perceptible odor that clings to the breath, especially in eating the raw onion in salad. This should never interfere in the consumption of a vegetable that carries within it such important chemical juices that operate so largely in the upbuilding of the general system. A glass of milk, taken after eating a raw onion, will destroy every particle of odor or taste that remains in the mouth.

The Louisiana Creole onion is famous. The origin of the Creole onion is lost in the mist of years. It has been planted in Louisiana for generations, and is to-day the most valuable of all existing varieties of onions in the Southern States. The bulb is supposed to have been brought to Louisiana from the south of Europe over a century and a half ago and has been cultivated here so long that it has become a distinct kind. It is a singular fact that no northern seed has ever yet produced an onion in Louisiana soil. The Red Bermuda Onion is also cultivated in this State. It is flat, like the Creole, but a little lighter in color. Both are prepared after the following methods:

### Boiled Onions.
#### Ognons Bouillis.

1 Dozen Nice, Small White Onions.
1 Tablespoonful Butter.
Salt and Pepper to Taste.

Throw the onions in their skins into cold water, and peel them. Then put them into a saucepan of boiling water. Add a teaspoonful of salt, and let them boil about forty minutes, or until you can pierce them easily with a fork. Then put into a dish, and drain off all water. Sprinkle with salt and pepper to taste, and pour over a Drawn Butter Sauce (see Beurre à la Maître d'Hotel), and serve hot. The large Spanish onions will require about an hour longer to boil tender.

### Creamed Onions.
#### Ognons à la Crème.

1 Dozen Small, White Onions.
1 Tablespoonful Butter. 1 Tablespoonful Flour.
½ Pint of Milk or Cream.
Salt and Pepper to Taste.

Boil the onions as directed in the above recipe. When very tender, take off the fire and drain. Pour over them the following cream sauce, which you will have prepared when almost ready to serve: Put one tablespoonful of flour into a saucepan, and add a tablespoonful of butter. Set on the fire, and let all blend well together, rubbing very smooth, without browning. Then add half a pint of milk. Stir continually till it boils. Season with salt and pepper to taste, and pour over the onions, and serve hot. The young Creole onions are most delicious when prepared in this manner.

### Fried Onions.
#### Ognons Frits.

½ Dozen Nice, Tender Onions.
1 Tablespoonful Butter. 1 Tablespoonful Salt.
Pepper to Taste.

Throw the onions into cold water. Peel them, and then cut them into thin slices. Cover them with boiling water, and let them boil about twenty minutes. Drain off the water thoroughly, and put them into a frying pan with a large tablespoonful of butter, and season to taste, and let them fry slowly for about ten minutes. Turn frequently, to prevent them from burning. Again, the onions may be fried without previous boiling, some preferring this latter method, as it admits of the onion retaining its flavor. Simply peel and pare and slice into round-shaped pieces. Lay the pieces in milk, and then in grated bread crumbs or flour, and fry them in boiling fat for about ten minutes. Lift them out of the fat, drain well, and serve on a hot dish with fried parsley as a garnish. Young shallots may be fried by washing well in cold water, cutting off the rough roots of the shallots, and then cutting the green and white together into half-inch dice. Season well with salt and pepper, and fry in butter for about five minutes. Garnish a dish with parsley sprigs. Lay the shallots on these and serve hot.

### Smothered Onions.
#### Ognons Sautés.

1 Dozen Small Onions.
1 Tablespoonful of Butter. 1 Quart of Broth.
Salt and Pepper to Taste.

Put the onions into cold water, and remove their skins. Then put them into a saucepan, and cover with a soup stock (pot-au-feu or bouillon), if you have it, otherwise use water, and let them stew slowly for an hour and a half, till they are almost falling to pieces. Then drain the onions through a colander, and save the stock. Put a tablespoonful of butter into a frying pan, and add a tablespoonful of flour, and make a Brown Roux. (See recipe.) When brown, add a half pint of the broth in which the onions were boiled. Season well with salt and pepper and a dash of Cayenne. Put the onions into this and let them simmer gently for about twenty minutes longer. Serve hot.

### Stuffed Onions.
### Ognons Farcis.

½ Dozen Large Spanish Onions.
A Stuffing of Chaurice.
Salt and Pepper to Taste.

Take a half dozen fine, large Spanish onions, and put them in hot ashes to roast. When they are sufficiently cooked, which will be in about half an hour, take them out of the ashes, dust off, and peel well. Then open the interiors and fill with a stuffing made as follows: Take a tablespoonful of butter and put in a frying pan, and add three chaurice, which you will have taken out of the casings and chopped finely again. Add a cup of bread, which has been wet and squeezed, and mix well. Then add an inch of ham, finely chopped, and a sprig each of thyme and parsley and sweet marjoram, and one bay leaf, all finely minced. Season with salt and pepper to taste. Fry about fifteen minutes, and then stuff the onions as far down in the center as possible, and between the folds. Sprinkle the top with powdered bread crumbs and put a little dot of butter on top of each. Set in the oven and let them bake for about thirty or forty minutes. Serve with roast beef.

Another nice way of stuffing onions is to peel the onion, scoop out the centers with a vegetable scoop, parboil them for ten minutes, and then fill the insides with the sausage forcemeat, as directed above. Line the bottom of a stew pan with fine strips of bacon. Lay over these an onion and a carrot both minced very fine. Place the onions on top of this and moisten with a pint of Chicken or Veal Consommé. Set in the oven to bake for about three-quarters of an hour and baste frequently. Serve in a hot dish, with the sauce poured over.

### Baked Onions.
### Ognons Rotis.

1 Dozen Large Spanish Onions.
Salt and Pepper to Taste.

Trim the onions nicely, but do not peel them. Then put them into a kettle of boiling water, and let them boil rapidly for about an hour. Drain in a colander. Then put them in a baking pan, and let them bake slowly for about an hour. Take out and remove the skins, and place in a vegetable dish, and sprinkle with salt and pepper, and serve with Drawn Butter Sauce. (See Beurre à la Maître d'Hotel.

After taking the onions out of the boiling water, if you wish to serve with "Roast Beef aux Ognons," peel the onions and place around the beef roast in the oven. Baste them as often as you baste the roast, with the juices that come from it. Serve with the roast, using them as a garnish around the dish.

### Glazed Onions.
### Ognons Glacés.

1½ Dozen Small Onions of Uniform Size.
1 Tablespoonful Sugar. 1 Cup Water.
1 Large Teaspoonful Butter. Salt to Taste.

Select small Creole onions of uniform size, top the heads and the stems, and remove the skins, but not too closely, lest they should break up when boiling. Then take a frying pan, large enough for the onions to lie in it, side by side. Put the butter in it first, and when melted add the onions. Then sprinkle with the sugar and water, and season with salt to taste. Set on the back of the stove, where they can simmer gently for an hour. When nearly done, and tender all through, add a tablespoonful of flour, mixed in water, blended well. Then set in the oven, with a paper on top. Let them stand for about half an hour, and use as a garnish for beef, veal, etc. The onions will be nicely glazed, and will make the dish appear very beautiful.

### SHALLOTS.
### Échallottes.

Shallots are small-sized onions, grown in clumps. They are very delicate and mild in flavor, and much used in soups, stews, salads, etc. In the green state they are also chopped and fried in butter. (See recipe Fried Onions.)

### PARSLEY.
### Persil.

Parsley is one of the most important of all vegetable herbs, entering, as it does, into the seasoning of all soups, meats, fish and even vegetables. It is one of the most beautiful of all garnishes, and gives a pretty touch to the homeliest dish. The "Plain-Leaved," the "Double Curled," or the "Beautiful Garnish" varieties are always to be found in the New Orleans market. A handful of parsley is always thrown into the market basket for "Lagniappe."

### Fried Parsley.
Persil Frit.
6 or 8 Sprigs of Parsley.
1 Tablespoonful of Lard.

Pick off the delicate leaves and branches of very young parsley, wash well, drain and put in a frying pan, in which you will have placed a tablespoonful of lard and allowed to reach a medium hot state. Fry slowly and drain and use as a garnish or as needed.

### Chopped Parsley.
Persil Haché.

Wash the parsley in cold water, trim off the coarse stems and branches and leaves, immerse in very cold water again, drain, press dry and chop very fine. Use as needed.

### Parsley Green.
Persil au Jus.

Take young parsley, wash well, strip of all coarse stems, and branches, plunge into very cold water, chop very fine, squeeze in a strong kitchen towel and save the juice for coloring purposes.

### Parsley for Garnishing Purposes.
Garniture de Persil.

Take several bunches of fresh parsley, trim off all the coarse stems, wash in slightly salted water, drain and place in a colander. Set over a watertight vessel. Shave some ice, cover the parsley with it and let it keep fresh and cool for table garnishes. Never lay parsley that is intended for garnishing purposes in water, as the freshness will be quickly destroyed, and it will become dark, discolored, limp and slimy and devoid of all beauty or crispness.

### PARSNIPS.
Des Panais.
6 or 8 Parsnips.
½ Pint of Sauce a la Maitre d'Hotel.

To boil parsnips, if they are young, simply scrape them and lay them in cold water. If the parsnips are old, pare them and cut them in quarters, or, better still, split lengthwise. Let the young parsnips cook in salted boiling water in a porcelain-lined saucepan for forty-five minutes; let the older ones cook for an hour and a quarter. When done, take them out of the saucepan, and drain and serve on a heated dish with a Drawn Butter Sauce. (See Beurre à la Maitre d'Hotel.)

### Boiled Parsnips With Cream Sauce.
Panais Bouillis à la Crème.
6 or 8 Parsnips. A Cream Sauce.

Proceed exactly as above in peeling and boiling the parsnips. When done, drain and put into a heated dish, and serve with a Cream Sauce poured over them. (See recipe Cream Sauce.) Serve the parsnips with boiled salt or fresh fish or boiled corn beef.

### Fried Parsnips.
Panais Frits.
5 Parsnips. 1 Tablespoonful Butter.
2 Tablespoonfuls of Drippings of Roast Beef.
Salt and Pepper to Taste.
Chopped Parsley to Garnish.

Brush and scrape or peel the parsnips as directed above. Then boil as directed in salted water till tender. When done, drain off the water and cut the parsnips into slices lengthwise of about half an inch in thickness. Put two tablespoonfuls of the drippings of the roast beef in the saucepan, and add a teaspoonful of butter. When hot add the sliced parsnips. When they are brown on one side, turn on the other and let this brown also. Place on a hot platter, sprinkle with chopped parsley and salt and pepper, and serve with roast meats.

### Smothered Parsnips.
Panais Sautés.
6 or 8 Parsnips. 2 Tablespoonfuls of Butter.
Salt and Pepper to Taste.
Chopped Parsley to Garnish.

Boil the parsnips as directed, and then cut into strips of the length of the parsnip, and half an inch in width. Put a big cookingspoonful of butter into the saucepan, and add the parsnips. Sprinkle well with salt and pepper. Cover and let them fry, but only slightly brown, on either side. Serve with chopped parsley as a garnish.

### Mashed Parsnips.
Purée de Panais.
6 or 8 Parsnips. 1 Tablespoonful of Butter.
1 Tablespoonful of Flour. 1 Pint of Milk.
Salt and Pepper to Taste.

Boil the parsnips until so tender that they break easily under pressure. Then mash them well, after draining off all water. Put a tablespoonful of butter in a saucepan, and add a tablespoonful of flour. Blend, without browning, and add a half pint of milk or cream. Stir well, and as the mixture begins to boil, add the parsnips. Mix thoroughly, season with salt and pepper, and serve in a dish, heaping up the parsnips in pyramidal shape. Serve with veal cutlets.

### Parsnip Balls.
Boulettes de Panais.
3 Large Parsnips. 2 Eggs.
Salt and Pepper to Taste.

Boil the parsnips as directed above, until very, very tender. Then drain and mash through a colander. Beat two eggs very light, and add the parsnips, using proportions of three large parsnips to the eggs. Then form the parsnips into little balls or boulettes, and fry in boiling lard, or make into little cakes and fry on a griddle.

### Parsnip Fritters.
### Beignets de Panais.

5 Parsnips.  1 Tablespoonful of Butter.
1 Cup of Water.   2 Eggs.
¼ Pound of Flour. 1 Teaspoonful of Salt.
1 Teaspoonful of Pepper.

Boil the parsnips as directed above till very tender. Then cut into long, narrow strips. Make a batter by mixing the flour with the yolks of the eggs, beaten well. Then add the salt and pepper, and gradually one cup of water, till it is absorbed. Then add the whites of the eggs, beaten to a stiff froth. Mix thoroughly. Add the parsnips to the batter. Dip out one at a time, in a spoon of butter, and fry in boiling lard. Serve as an entrée at dinner.

### PEAS.
### Des Pois Secs.

All dried, split, kidney or black-eyed peas may be cooked in the same manner as beans. (See recipe.)

### GREEN PEAS.
### Des Pois Verts.

Green peas are abundant in our New Orleans market, with but a short respite, almost all the year. We have two crops, the spring and fall. The large peas, or older ones, are called "Des Pois Verts," and the smaller, or French peas, "Des Petits Pois." The latter are great delicacies when boiled and served with butter; the former may be utilized in making that most delectable dish, "Purée des Pois Verts." (See recipe in Chapter on Soups.)

### To Cook Canned Green Peas.
### Petits Pois en Conserve.

The delightful preparations of French peas that come put up in cans do not require much cooking, being, like all canned vegetables, already cooked. To cook these drain the peas from all liquor after opening the can, and put them in a saucepan; add a tablespoonful of butter and pepper and salt to taste. Set on the fire, and, when thorouhgly heated, serve immediately. Green peas are served with all roast, and broiled and sautéd meats, fowls or game. There is scarcely a vegetable that admits of such various uses with entrées.

### Boiled Green Peas.
### Petit Pois au Naturel.

1 Pint of Fresh Young Green Peas.
1 Tablespoonful of Butter.
Salt and Pepper to Taste.

Shell the peas, and when you have a pint (sufficient for six), put the peas into cold water, drain and put into a saucepan of boiling water; add a teaspoonful of salt to prevent the peas from cracking, and let them boil rapidly for at least twenty minutes. To ascertain if they are done, take one out and press with a fork. The great art in cooking green peas properly is to have plenty of water, to cook the peas very rapidly, and not to let them boil a moment longer than necessary, if you would keep them from being soggy and preserve their fresh color and sweetness. Fresh peas should never be shelled until the moment when you wish to cook them. When cooked, they must be eaten immediately. As soon as done, drain off all water; put a large tablespoonful of butter into the saucepan with the peas, season with pepper to taste, pour into a vegetable dish and serve hot. This is the very nicest way of cooking this dainty vegetable.

As the peas grow older and larger, they may be made into purées, or cooked as follows:

### Green Peas à la Bourgeoise.
### Pois Verts Sautés à la Bourgeoise.

1 Pint of Peas.
1½ Tablespoonfuls of Butter.
1 Ounce of Chopped Onion.
1 Herb Bouquet, Minced Fine.
1 Tablespoonful of Flour.
½ Pint of Cream or Milk or Water.

Shell and boil the peas according to the above recipe. Add sprigs of parsley, thyme and bay leaf, finely minced. When done, which will be in about forty minutes, if the peas are large, or perhaps, a few minutes longer (easily ascertained by taking out a pea and pressing it with a fork), drain off all water and add one tablespoonful and a half of butter. Then blend the flour, and add the milk, preferably, mixing together and stirring well, to prevent browning or burning. Serve hot. Some add the yolk of an egg, well beaten, after taking the peas off the fire, but this is a matter of taste; the flavor of the peas is more perceptible without it.

### Green Peas, Country Style.
### Petits Pois Verts à la Paysanne.

1 Pint of Green Peas. 3 Small Carrots.
1-8 of a Head of Green and White Cabbage.
A Tablespoonful of Butter.
½ Pint of Consomme of Veal or Chicken.
Salt and Pepper to Taste.

Shell the peas; take three small carrots, and one-eighth of a head of cabbage, and one-quarter head of lettuce, and cut into small dice-shaped pieces. Put a tablespoonful of butter in a saucepan and let the dice-shaped vegetables smother for about fifteen minutes over a slow fire without browning. Add the green peas and the consommé, and let all cook for a half hour, stirring frequently to prevent burning. Season to taste with salt and pepper, and use a sprinkling of chopped parsley as a garnish.

### Green Peas, French Style.
Petit Pois Verts à la Française.

1 Pint of Fresh Green Peas, or 1 Can.
2 Tablespoonfuls of Butter. ½ Cup of Water.
1 Herb Bouquet. 1 Lettuce Heart. 1 Onion.
1 Teaspoonful of Powdered Sugar.
Salt and Pepper to Taste.

Shell the peas and wash and drain them. Put them into a saucepan, with one tablespoonful of butter; add the herb bouquet, the onion whole, and the lettuce heart, and cover with cold water, and let them simmer slowly for about twenty minutes, or until tender. Then drain off the water, remove the onion and herb bouquet, lay the lettuce heart on a dish, and add another tablespoonful of butter to the peas. Let them cook for five minutes longer. Pour the peas over the lettuce heart and send to the table hot, and serve with chops or cutlets as a vegetable.

### Green Peas, Old Creole Style.
Petits Pois Verts à l'Ancienne Mode Créole.

1 Pint of Young Green Peas.
3 Tablespoonfuls of Butter. ¼ Cup of Cream.
The Yolk of 1 Egg.
1 Teaspoonful of Powdered Sugar.
Salt and Pepper to Taste.

Shell and clean the peas carefully. Put them in a saucepan with three tablespoonfuls of butter, and cover with a cup of water; season wtih a pinch of salt, and let them cook for twenty minutes, or until tender. Take three tablespoonfuls of cream and beat with the yolk of one egg; add a half pinch of white pepper, and mix thoroughly with the peas. Add a teaspoonful of powdered sugar, stir well, and let all cook together for five minutes and serve hot.

### Purée of Green Peas à la Créole.
Purée de Pois Verts à la Créole.

1 Pint of Green Peas. 1 Cup of Milk or Cream
A Pinch of Salt and White Pepper.
1 Teaspoonful of Powdered Sugar.

Shell and clean the peas well; then put them in a saucepan with the cream and a half cup of water, and let them simmer till they become quite soft. Then remove the pan from the fire; rub the peas through a fine sieve; season well with the salt and pepper and sugar; add a tablespoonful of butter; beat the butter in well with the peas; set on the stove for five minutes and serve hot. Peas thus prepared are served as a vegetable with entrées and other meats.

### Purée of Green Peas à la St. Germain.
Purée de Pois Verts à la St. Germain.

1 Pint of Green Peas. 1 Pint of Chicken Broth.
1 Pint of Sweet Cream. 1 Herb Bouquet.
2 Sprigs of Mint.
A Pinch Each of Salt and White Pepper.
1 Teaspoonful of Powdered Sugar.
8 Chicken Quenelles to Garnish.

Shell and clean the peas and put them in a saucepan or sautoire, with one pint of chicken broth and one pint of sweet cream. Add an herb bouquet, in which you will have tied two sprigs of mint. Let the peas cook for twenty minutes, or until very tender, and then remove the herb bouquet and mint; take from the fire, and run the peas through a sieve. Season with salt and pepper and a little powdered sugar; add a tablespoonful of butter; set on the fire five minutes longer, and then serve on a hot dish with Chicken Quenelles (see recipe) to garnish. Make the quenelles from the chicken left over from the broth. This is a very recherché dish. Serve as an entrée.

### POTATOES.
De la Pomme de Terre.

Potatoes may be cooked in a greater variety of ways than any other vegetable. They are most nutritious and are always economical as well as palatable dish on the table.

### Steamed Potatoes.
Pommes de Terre à la Vapeur.

8 Nice Potatoes.
A Pot of Boiling Water. Salt.

Wash the potatoes well, scrubbing thoroughly, to take off every particle of earth that adheres. Then put them in a potato steamer, and set over a pot of boiling water. Cover tight and steam till you can pierce with a fork. Potatoes should never be boiled if you can steam them conveniently, as they are naturally watery. When done, remove the jackets, or skin, and sprinkle with salt and pepper; add a tablespoonful of butter in which you have mingled chopped parsley; and serve immediately. Or they may be served just as they are, in a covered dish. A potato should always be mealy, and not sogged with water, if cooked properly. In cooking potatoes the time depends on the size of the potato. An unfailing test is to cook till the potato can be easily pierced with a fork.

### Boiled Potatoes.
Pommes de Terre au Naturel.

6 Potatoes, of Uniform Size, if Possible.
Boiling Water.

Potatoes should always be boiled in their skins, or jackets, if possible.

Never be guilty of paring a new potato before boiling. Towards the close of winter, just before the new crop comes in, the potatoes may be pared, so that blemishes may be removed. But this is scarcely necessary in our State, unless the old potatoes have sprouted and shriveled.

Wash and scrub the potatoes well, and put them on in their jackets in a pot of boiling water, which has been well salted. Let them cook until they are soft enough to be pierced with a fork. Do not let them remain a moment longer, or they will become waxy and watery. Nothing is more disagreeable than a watery potato. When done, take them out and drain dry. Put into steamer, sprinkle with salt, and cover and let them stand over the kettle (lid open) on the fire for a few minutes for the water to evaporate. After five minutes take off and peel quickly, and serve in a covered vegetable dish. Nothing is more unpleasant than to be given a cold potato at the table. Properly cooked, the potato should be dry and flaky and most acceptable.

If the potatoes are old and beginning to sprout, it will be found better to put them on in cold water after paring or peeling, and let them cook gradually.

The Creoles use the water in which the potatoes have been boiled for destroying the green flies and insects that infest rose bushes.

### Potatoes With Drawn Butter.
Pommes de Terre aux Beurre Maître d'Hotel.
6 Potatoes.
1 Tablespoonful of Butter. Salt and Pepper.

Boil the potatoes according to the above recipe. Peel and pour over them a tablespoonful of melted butter, in which you have mingled chopped parsley. Salt and pepper to taste. Potatoes prepared in this way are delicious.

Or, if you wish to have mashed potatoes, or a "Puree of Potatoes," as a vegetable, mash the potatoes well, and add two tablespoonfuls of butter. Salt and pepper to taste. Place in a dish, mold prettily, and serve hot with meats, fish, poultry, etc. A half cup of milk or cream may be added to the purée with very delicious results. (For Purée of Potatoes as soup, see recipe under heading Soups.)

### Creamed Potatoes.
Pommes de Terre à la Créme.
6 Potatoes. A Cream Sauce.

Boil the potatoes as above, and pour over them (remembering always to keep them whole) a Cream Sauce. (See recipe.) Serve hot with fried chicken. Add the juice of a lemon.

### Potatoes à la Maître d'Hotel.
Pommes de Terre à la Maitre d'Hotel.
6 Potatoes. Sauce a la Maitre d'Hotel.

Boil the potatoes whole, according to recipe, and serve hot, with a Sauce à la Maître d'Hotel poured over them.

### Potato Puffs.
Pommes de Terre Soufflé à la Créole.
2 Cups of Cold Mashed Potatoes.
2 Eggs. 3 Tablespoonfuls of Cream or Milk.
1 Tablespoonful Butter.
Salt and Pepper to Taste.

This is a nice way to utilize left-over potatoes. Mash the potatoes well, and put them into a frying pan with the butter. Add the yolks of 2 eggs well beaten, and stir well, and almost add immediately the cream. Let it get very hot, stirring all the time. Then take the potatoes from the fire, and add the whites of the eggs, beaten to a stiff froth. Butter a baking dish or biscuit pan, and fill with the mixture. Let it bake in a quick oven till brown. This is an old Creole way of preparing potatoes, and highly recommended.

### Potato Snow.
Pommes de Terre à la Neige.
6 Potatoes. Salt to Taste.

Boil the potatoes with their jackets on. Then peel them and set them before the fire, to allow all the water to evaporate. Sprinkle lightly with salt. Then rub them through a sieve or colander. Let the potato fall in light, flaky drops, like snow flakes. Do not touch the flakes as they fall. Serve on the dish in which the flakes have fallen. This dish is very delicious.

### Potato Croquettes.
Pommes de Terre en Croquettes.

2 Cups of Mashed Potatoes.
1 Tablespoonful of Chopped Parsley.
2 Tablespoonfuls of Cream.
1 Teaspoonful of Onion Juice.
1 Teaspoonful of Salt. 1 Ounce of Butter.
The Yolks of 2 Eggs. A Dash of Cayenne.

Beat the yolks to a cream and add them to the potatoes. Mix well and then add the cream and all the other ingredients. Mix well, and put into a saucepan over the fire, and stir until the mixture leaves the side of the vessel. Take off the fire, and set to cool. When cold, form into cylinders of about two and a half inches in length and one in width. Roll first in a beaten egg, to bind, and then in bread crumbs, and fry to a golden brown in boiling lard. (See general directions for frying.) When done, lift out of the lard with a skimmer, and drain on brown paper in the mouth of the oven. Serve for breakfast, or as a garnish for meats. Utilize left-over potatoes in this way. Serve with fish, fried, broiled or baked.

Boulettes are prepared in exactly the same manner, only thyme and bay leaf, minced very fine, are added, and the potatoes are formed into balls or boulettes. Boulettes are eaten more generally at breakfast, and croquettes at dinner, especially with fish.

### Potatoes au Gratin.
Pommes de Terre au Gratin.

5 Cold Boiled Potatoes.
½ Pint of Cream. 2 Tablespoonfuls of Butter.
1 Tablespoonful of Flour.
3½ Heaping Tablespoonfuls of Gruyere or Parmesan Cheese.
The Yolks of 4 Eggs.
½ Pint of Consomme or Water.
Salt and Cayenne to Taste.

Put the butter in the frying pan, and as it melts, add the flour, and let it blend, rubbing smooth, without browning. Then add the consommé or water and the cream, and stir constantly till the mixture boils. Then take the saucepan from the fire, and add the cheese, well grated, and the well-beaten yolks of the eggs. Salt and pepper to taste. Beat all thoroughly till light. Mash the potatoes well, and place, first, a layer of the sauce in the saucepan, and then of the potatoes, and so on till the sauce forms the top layer. Sprinkle this lightly with bread crumbs, and set in the oven and let bake ten minutes. When it comes to a nice brown, serve in the dish in which it was baked.

### Potato Soufflé.
Pommes de Terre en Soufflé.

2 Cups of Mashed Potatoes.
2 Tablespoonfuls of Melted Butter. 2 Eggs.
¼ Cup of Cream.
Salt and Pepper to Taste.

Mash the potatoes well, pressing them through a colander. Then add the butter, and beat till smooth and light. Add the cream and the well-beaten yolks of the eggs, and salt and pepper to taste. Then add the whites, which must be beaten to a stiff froth. Then heap this into a dish, leaving the mound rough and uneven, so that the dish will look pretty with the tips nicely browned. Set in the oven and bake to a beautiful brown, and serve in the dish in which it was baked.

Scalloped potatoes are cooked in the same manner, only the potatoes are cut into dice, a Cream Sauce is made, and a layer of potatoes and a layer of the sauce is put into a pan or shells, and then alternate layers, with a layer of sauce on top. Sprinkle lightly with bread crumbs, and serve in the shells or in the dish in which it was baked.

### French Fried Potatoes.
Pommes de Terre à la Française.

6 Potatoes. Boiling Lard.
Chopped Parsley to Garnish.

Peel the potatoes and then cut into three-inch dice, or sections like an orange. Have ready a frying pan of very hot, boiling lard, and let them fry to a golden yellow or brown. Do not burn. Take them out with a skimmer, and drain in a heated colander. Stand the colander in the mouth of the oven while you fry the remainder of the potato. When done, sprinkle with salt, garnish with chopped parsley, and serve hot.

### Julienne Potatoes.
Pommes de Terre à la Julienne.

4 Potatoes. Boiling Lard.

Peel and cut the potatoes into long, thin strips. Then fry in boiling lard, and serve with beefsteak, grillades, etc.

### Potato Chips.
Pommes de Terres Frites.

2 Potatoes   Boiling Lard.
Parsley Sprigs to Garnish.

Have two medium-sized potatoes, and slice them just as thin as possible, and fry in boiling lard. (See directions for frying.) Use a vegetable cutter, if you have one, for slicing the potato. Drop a few pieces at a time into the lard, and be sure to have the lard about three inches deep. Stir the slices occasionally, to keep them from overlapping the others. When a light brown, take out of the pan and drain on a piece of brown paper, which you have put in a colander. Stand in the open oven, and continue frying. As you finish the second frying turn the first from the colander into a heated dish, and so continue till all the potatoes are fried. Serve hot. Garnish, if you wish, with parsley sprigs.

Pommes de Terre Frites correspond to the American dish of Saratoga chips.

### Lyonnaise Potatoes.
Pommes de Terre à la Lyonnaise.

2 Pints of Cold Boiled Potatoes, Cut in Dice.
2 Onions. 2 Large Tablespoonfuls Butter.
Salt and Pepper to Taste.

Take cold boiled potatoes, and cut them into slices. Slice the onions fine. Put the lard into the frying pan and as it melts add the onions. Let them fry until half done, and then add the potatoes. Fry and stir gently until the potatoes are a light yellow. They must not be fried brown or crisp, but merely sautéd, or smothered, in the onions. The dish is really Pommes de Terres Sautées à la Lyonnaise. When done, turn into a hot dish, garnish with chopped parsley, and serve very hot, with beefsteak, etc.

### Brabant Potatoes.
Pommes de Terre Brabant.

3 Boiled Potatoes.
1 Tablespoonful of Butter.
1 Tablespoonful of Chopped Parsley.
2 Tablespoonfuls of Lard.
1 Teaspoonful of Vinegar.

Cut the potatoes into small dice-shaped pieces and fry them for a few minutes in the lard. When half brown, take out of the lard and finish frying in the butter to a light brown. When ready to serve, add three sprigs of chopped parsley, and salt and pepper, and the juice of a lemon, and serve hot.

### Potatoes à la Bourgeoise.
Pommes de Terre à la Bourgeoise.

6 Potatoes. 1 Pint Gravy or Broth.
1 Onion. 1 Leak.
Salt and Pepper to Taste.

Take cold boiled potatoes and cut into quarters, and then drain and put into a saucepan, and cover with any meat gravy or soup stock that may have remained, and chopped onion, chopped leak, pepper and salt. Set on the stove and let stew or simmer for half an hour. This is an excellent family dish, that can be made with left-over potatoes, and may be used for breakfast or luncheon.

### Potatoes With Butter.
Pommes de Terre au Beurre.

16 Small New Potatoes.
1 Tablespoonful of Butter.
1 Tablespoonful Parsley.

Select for this dainty dish small, round new potatoes, about the size of a marble. Boil them for about half an hour or twenty minutes, according to the touch when pierced with a fork. Then drain off water, peel quickly, and put into a saucepan, with a tablespoonful of butter. Let them brown lightly, and serve with Drawn Butter Sauce, in which you have put a tablespoonful of chopped parsley.

### Potatoes à la Créole.
Pommes de Terre à la Créole.

8 Potatoes. 1 Spoonful of Flour.
Yolks of 2 Eggs. 2 Teaspoonfuls of Vinegar.
2 Tablespoonfuls of Butter.
Salt and Pepper.

Boil the potatoes according to recipe. Then take out of the water, drain and set to the side of the stove for five minutes, to evaporate. Then take off and pour over the following sauce: Blend one tablespoonful of flour with two of butter, and, as it melts, add about three large tablespoonfuls of water. Let it come to a boil, and take off the stove and add the yolk of an egg, which has been beaten very light. Add two teaspoonfuls of vinegar. Beat well, and pour over the potatoes, and serve either hot or cold à la salade.

### Potatoes à la Diable.
Pommes de Terre à la Diable.

2 Dozen New Potatoes, About the Size of Marbles.
1 Teaspoonful of Mustard.
2 Large Tablespoonfuls of Butter.
A Dash of Cayenne. Salt to Taste.

To appreciate this dish, one must first hear the funny old Creole story connected with its origin. Tradition relates that Jean Marie, who was one of "dose no-count Creole, what love one good game of card, one good story, and one good glass wine wid Jacques and Jules more better than work for make money for his famille," was one day told by his wife, Madame Jean Marie, to "take dat basket and go for dat French market, and buy some of dose new pommes de terre." It was a familiar saying in the old quarter that Madame Jean Marie, who was the support of her large family, also wore the "culottes" or trousers. There were constant squabbles between her and her good-for?nothing spouse, but she frequently managed to make him help her a little in the "ménage." On this particular day, Monsieur Jean Marie resented her interference with his pleasure. Then, too, floating visions of his companions at his dear familiar haunts, jeering him as he passed with the market basket on his arm, and telling him, "Parbleu, but Jean Marie, you would make one good woman, ya-as!" rose before his mental vision. He rebelled against his wife's authority, and told her point blank that he would not go. Approaching him, with the market basket in her hand, the enraged wife shook her fist in his face, and told him if he "didn't make quick for go to dat market and get pommes de terres, dat she would show him de next world before it bin come." And she thrust the market basket in his hands. "Pommes de terre aux diable!" cried out Monsieur Jean Marie, groundflinging the basket on the ground. Madame Jean Marie eyed him for one moment. Then going up to him, with a most determined air, she coolly picked up the basket and said in a tone of voice that he had learned to know too well: "Now, I is one patient woman, yas, mais I don't let no man 'aux diable' at me. You hear dat hein. Now, if you don't go for dat market, as I bin tell you, I gone make you eat one dish à la diable dat bin make you wish all your life long you bin walk more quick." Jean Marie sullenly picked up the basket and went to market. But tradition also relates that he lingered so long that when he returned Madame Jean Marie swore that she would keep her promise. While cooking the potatoes she poured a quantity of mustard into them, and, to still further "burn his tongue, and keep him from talk so long wid dose vieux camarades, Jacques and Jules," she added a good dash of Cayenne. "Now," she said, as she brought the dish to the table in her anger, "I go'ne make you eat pommes de terre à la diable, for sure!" But her revenge was neither long nor sweet. The improvised dish that was intended for a punishment proved such a success that Jean Marie laughed heartily as he lolled back in his chair, and declared that he was going to "make three, four dollar quick for ax Jacques and Jules come to one grand déjeuner à la fourchette, and eat some pommes de terre à la diable with him." And so the dish was christened, and the quaint name has remained to this very day. It is made as follows:

Take nice, fresh new potatoes and boil them. (See recipe for boiling potatoes.) When done, take off and let evaporate, being careful not to have cooked them too much. Take a deep frying pan, and heat the lard to the boiling point. When it begins to boil, drop in the potatoes, and let them fry for about five minutes. Lift out with a skimmer, drain quickly, and put them into a saucepan with two tablespoonfuls of melted butter into which you have rubbed well a teaspoonful of prepared mustard. Add a dash of Cayenne and two teaspoonfuls of vinegar. Let it cook for three or four minutes, shaking constantly, and then take off. Add the yolks of two eggs, well beaten, and serve immediately with Grillades à la Sauce or Grillades Panées. (See recipes.)

### Duchess Potatoes.

Pommes de Terre à la Duchesse.

1 Dozen Boiled Potatoes.
The Yolk of 1 Egg.

Take one dozen boiled potatoes, mash them, and form into small square cakes. Criss-cross them gracefully with a knife, brush with the yolk of an egg beaten in water or milk, and set in the oven to bake to a delicate brown.

### Potatoes à la Parisienne.

Pommes de Terre à la Parisienne.

8 Potaoes.
1 Kitchenspoonful of Butter.
½ Pint of Milk or Water. 2 Eggs.

Peel the potatoes and let them boil till tender in salt and water. Take them out of the water, and grate and mash them into a paste. Put this potato paste in a saucepan with a kitchenspoonful of butter and a half pint of milk or water, more or less, according to the dryness of the potatoes. Season lightly with salt, and add a teaspoonful of orange flower water, to give a pleasant taste.

Let all boil together, stirring constantly until a smooth and thick paste is formed. Then turn the mixture into another pan, in which you have already beaten two eggs until very, very light. Mix thoroughly, and make small boulettes or balls of this paste. Have ready a pan of boiling lard, place the boulettes in it, and when they are a beautiful golden brown take them out, drain and serve hot. The orange flower water may be omitted. The boulettes may also be sprinkled with fine white sugar, according to the true Parisian style. The Creoles serve them with or without the sugar, according to taste.

Sweet potatoes may also be prepared after this manner, and are delicious. The sweet potatoes are always sprinkled with white sugar.

### Potato Balls.

Pommes de Terre en Boulettes.

8 Potatoes.
1 Kitchenspoonful of Butter.
½ Pint of Milk. 2 Eggs.
Parsley to Garnish.

Cook the potatoes as above, or use cold left-over potatoes for this dish. Mash the potatoes well, and add an equal quantity of cold left-over meat or pork, minced very fine. Sausage may also be used, with or without the meat. Season well with salt and pepper, minced parsley and shallots or onions. Mix well with the yolks of two eggs, and form into balls of medium size. Brush with the whites of the eggs, beaten to a stiff froth, and fry in boiling lard. Serve with garnish of chopped parsley or with meat gravy.

### Potato Quenelles.

Quenelles de Pommes de Terre

6 Potatoes
1 Tablespoonful of Butter. 2 Eggs.

Boil the potatoes, peel and mash very fine. Add the butter and minced parsley, and a half onion minced very fine. Add the yolks of the eggs, beaten very light, and then form the potatoes into balls and throw them for two minutes into boiling water. Take out, brush with the whites of the eggs, roll lightly in powdered bread crumbs, and fry in boiling lard. Drain and serve with fish, meat or any sauce.

### Baked Potatoes.

Pommes de Terre Roties.

6 or 8 Potatoes.
A Drawn Butter Sauce, or Sauce a la Hollandaise.

To bake potatoes without meat, wash the potatoes well, set them in the oven in their skins, and in about an hour open the oven slightly and take the potatoes ont, one by one, in a cloth, and press lightly to see if they are quite soft to the touch. Then either bring to the table in their jackets, as many prefer, or pare and serve with a Drawn Butter Sauce, or with daubes, meats, sautés, etc., or with any fish or meats with gravies.

### Stuffed Potatoes à la Créole.
Pommes de Terre Farcies à la Créole.

6 or 8 Potatoes. Chaurice (Sausage) Forcemeat.
1 Tablespoonful of Butter.

This is a delightful Creole variation for preparing potatoes. Select fine large potatoes, and have ready several nice Chaurice. Wash and peel the potatoes.

Potatoes may also be stuffed after washing, by peeling carefully and scooping out the insides nicely with a spoon or sharp-pointed knife. Then make a sausage forcemeat (see recipe), and heap up lightly on top. Butter a baking dish nicely, place the potatoes upon it, and let them bake in a slow oven for a half hour or forty-five minutes, till nicely browned, and send to the table hot.

### Stuffed Potatoes, Lenten Style.
Pommes de Terre à la Crème.

6 Large Potatoes. The Yolk of 1 Egg.
1 Tablespoonful of Butter.
1 Tablespoonful of Chopped Parsley.
½ Cup of Milk or Cream.
½ Teaspoonful of Grated Nutmeg.

Bake the potatoes in the oven, and, when done, cut one end and scoop out the meat without breaking the skin. Add the yolk of one egg, the butter, chopped parsley, salt and pepper to taste, and the grated nutmeg, and moisten all with the cream or milk. Mix well and beat very light. Then refill the skins and return to the oven for a few minutes, till very hot and slightly browned, and serve.

### Stuffed Potatoes, Swiss Style.
Pommes de Terre Farcies à la Suisse.

6 or 8 Potatoes. 1 Tablespoonful of Butter.
½ Cup of Hot Milk.
1 Teaspoonful of Salt. Pepper to Taste.
The Whites of 2 Eggs.

Bake the potatoes, and, when they are done, cut off the tops, and scoop out the meat into a hot bowl; mash very fine, and add the butter, the milk and salt and pepper. Some add a little grated Gruyere cheese; this is a matter of taste. Beat all till very light, and add the beaten whites of two eggs, and stir lightly, Fill the potato skins with this preparation, heaping the flaky potatoes nicely on top. Brush over lightly with the yolks of the eggs, set in the oven to brown and serve hot.

### Potatoes as a Garnish.
Pommes de Terre pour Garniture.

6 Potatoes.
Beef, Veal or Mutton Drippings.

Select nice, round potatoes, if you wish to roast them with beef. Wash them, clean, boil, or, better, steam them; peel and lay them in the pan with the beef or mutton or veal, and let them brown awhile before the meat is done, basting them when you baste the meat with the drippings from the roast. Place as a garnish around the roast, and bring to the table hot.

## SWEET POTATOES.
Des Patates Douces.

Sweet potatoes may be boiled, baked, fried or made into purées, and used in puddings and pies. The sweet potato is one of our most common vegetables. Possessing saccharine properties, it is especially nourishing and palatable.

Cooking the sweet potato is an art, for the delicate flavor of the potato is lost if it is not properly cooked. As mentioned above, sweet potatoes may be boiled, steamed or baked. Baking is the best method of preserving the flavor, and steaming is better than boiling. Sweet potatoes cannot be properly cooked, if they are cooked too quickly. Time is an essential element. To properly bring out the flavor of the sweet potato in baking, it should be kept at least an hour in the oven. The old Creole negroes often bake the sweet potatoes in ashes, covered with coals. The old corn field slaves used to put the potatoes in the ashes after one meal, go back into the field, and leave it there till the next meal. The delicate flavor was most grateful.

### Boiled Sweet Potatoes.
Patates Douces Bouillies.

6 Potatoes. A Drawn Butter Sauce.

Wash the potatoes well, using a cloth or brush, and removing every particle of earth. Clip the edges of the roots that adhere. Put them to boil in a kettle of boiling water, and let them cook till they may be easily pierced with a fork. Then drain off the water, and set the kettle on the back of the stove. Cover and let the potatoes steam a few minutes. Take them out after five minutes or so, and peel and serve them with Drawn Butter Sauce, or cut in slices and spread butter over them, and set in the oven for a few seconds, and serve hot with daubes, fish, grillades, etc. Sweet potatoes are in particular the vegetable that is served with roast pork.

### Fried Sweet Potatoes.
Patates Douces Frites.

4 Potatoes. 3 Tablespoonfuls of Butter.

Cut the boiled potatoes lengthwise in slices. Fry in very hot butter until brown, and serve hot. This is a very nice way to utilize left-over potatoes.

To fry uncooked potatoes, the great breakfast dish for fast days among the Creoles, slice the potatoes not lengthwise, but by rounds, and fry in boiling lard. Bring to the table when a beautiful brown, and eat with butter, spread generously over.

### Sweet Potatoes au Caramel.
Patates Douces au Caramel.

4 Potatoes.   Boiling Lard or Butter.
4 Tablespoonfuls of Sugar.

Boil the potatoes, and then cut them lengthwise in halves. Fry in boiling lard or butter, and, while frying, sprinkle generously with sugar. This is a delicious sweet entrée.

### Baked Sweet Potatoes.
Patates Douces Roties,

6 or 8 Potatoes. 1 Tablespoonful of Butter.
Wash the potatoes, and scrub the skins, but do not peel them. By rubbing the skins of the potatoes lightly all over with a little lard, butter, or fat bacon, it will render the skins soft and pliable to the touch when baked; they will peel readily, without crumbling from dryness, as baked potatoes often do, the peeling coming off in thin strips, leaving the potato intact. Put the potatoes in a baking pan in the oven, and let them cook until their centers are mellow to the touch. Serve in their jackets immediately. Serve with roast meats, daubes, grillades, etc., or as a Friday dish, to be eaten with butter.

To roast potatoes with meat or pork, wash and boil the potatoes well, and a half hour before the roast pork or beef is done pare the potatoes, drain well, and place in the baking pan, around the pork or beef, and baste frequently with the drippings from the roasting meat. Or put in the pan without boiling, and bake a half hour longer. The former is the best method.

### Sweet Potato Fritters.
Patates Douces en Beignets.

4 Boiled Sween Potatoes.
1 Glass of Milk, White Wine or Brandy.
1 Teaspoonful of Sugar.
Juice of Lemon.   Powdered Sugar.

Cut the boiled sweet potatoes into slender round slices, and steep them for a half hour in a little White Wine or brandy or milk. Then make a light batter, to which you will have added a tablespoonful of sugar. Add the juice of a lemon to the soaking potatoes. Take each slice at a time, dip it in the batter, and let it drop from the spoon into the boiling lard. When fried to a nice golden brown place on a piece of brown paper, and drain in the oven. Then place in the dish in which they are to be served. Sprinkle with powdered white sugar, and serve hot as a sweet entremet.

### Sweet Potato Padding.
Pouding de Patates Douces.

6 Sweet Potatoes.   3-4 Pound of Fine Sugar.
3-4 Pound of Butter.
The Zest of a Lemon, Grated Fine.
1 Wineglass of Good Brandy.
½ Grated Nutmeg.   4 Ground Allspice.
1 Piece of Ground Cinnamon.
1 Pint of Milk or Cream.

Boil or bake the potatoes, peel and press them through a very fine sieve, the finer the better. Add to them the yolks of six eggs, and beat well. Then add the butter, beating well and thoroughly, and add the sugar and milk. Beat all very light, and add the whites of the eggs, beaten to a stiff froth. Mix thoroughly, and add the grated nutmeg, ground spices, and blend well with the potatoes. Add finally, if desired, a wineglassful of good old brandy or whisky, and set the pan with the potatoes in an oven, and let it bake for an hour. Place a brown paper on top for the first three-quarters of an hour, and take it off at the last quarter for the frangipane to brown nicely. Sprinkle with powdered sugar, and serve hot or cold.

### Sweet Potato Waffles.
Gaufres de Patates Douces.

4 Left-Over Potatoes.
Other Ingredients in Proportion Given.

This is a good way to utilize left-over potatoes. To every two tablespoonfuls of mashed potatoes add one of butter, one of sugar, one pint of milk, and four tablespoonfuls of flour. Beat all well together, and add one egg, well beaten. Bake in waffle iron, and serve with butter spread over.

### Sweet Potato Pone.
Pain de Patates Douces.

4 Large Sweet Potatoes.
1 Teacupful of Brown Sugar.
1 Teacupful of New Orleans Molasses.
1 Teacupful of Milk.
1 Teacupful of Butter.   4 Eggs.
The Zest of One Lemon, Grated.
A Small Bit of Orange Peel Grated Very Fine.
½ Teaspoonful of Nutmeg.
½ Teaspoonful of Ground Cloves.
½ Teaspoonful of Ground Cinnamon.

Grate the potatoes and the zest of the lemon and orange. Beat the eggs well; beat the butter and sugar till creamy, add the eggs, beat well, then add the grated potato and spices and milk; beat all well together; add the grated zest of the orange and lemon, put the mixture in a well-buttered pan and bake slowly for

## PEPPERS.
### Du Piments.

More peppers are raised in Louisiana than in any other section of the country. The hot varieties, or "Pimentos," as the Creoles call them. "Chili," "Red Pepper," "Cayenne," "Tabasco," etc., are used extensively for seasoning and for making our famous Creole pepper sauces. The mild varieties, "Sweet Peppers," or "Green Peppers," "Mangoes," etc., are highly esteemed, and are used not only in making salads, but in other delightful dishes. The Creoles are famous for the uses to which they have adapted all peppers.

### GREEN PEPPERS.
### Des Piments Verts.

Green Peppers may be used in salads, as seasonings for various dishes, or they may be stuffed or sautéd. For Green Pepper Salads see recipe under chapter on "Salads."

### Stuffed Green Peppers.
### Piments Verts Farcis.

2 Dozen Fresh Green Peppers.
1 Tablespoonful of Butter.
½ Onion, Chopped Very Fine.
½ Inch of Boiled Ham. 1 Clove of Garlic.
½ Cup of Bread, Wet and Squeezed Thoroughly.

Parboil one dozen of the peppers, Then take off the skins and cut the topmost tip, and clean the inside of the peppers, throwing these seeds away. Then take a dozen or more raw peppers, cut off the stalk or stem, and clean the insides of all seeds, throwing the seeds away. Chop the peppers very fine, and then put a tablespoonful of butter on the fire. Add one-half of an onion, minced fine, and let it brown slightly in the butter. Then add the peppers, minced very fine, almost mashed into a jelly, and the half inch of ham, minced very fine. As these brown, add the clove of garlic, minced fine, and when the peppers are well-cooked add one-half a cup of bread that has been wet in water and squeezed thoroughly. Season with salt and pepper to taste, and let it brown. Add a dash of Cayenne pepper. When the stuffing is well browned and well seasoned, take from the stove and stuff the peppers. Sprinkle a little grated bread crumbs on top, and a dot of butter on each pepper top. Put it in the stove, let it brown, and serve hot with meats, broiled or roasted, chicken, etc.

about an hour. It may be served hot or cold cut in slices. It is delicious when served at luncheon cold with a glass of fresh milk.

### Green Peppers Sautéd.
### Piments Verts Sautés.

1 Dozen Large Green Peppers.
1 Tablespoonful of Butter.
2 Chopped Shallots.   2 Sprigs of Parsley.
A Dash of Sweet Tapioca.
Salt to Taste.

Plunge the peppers into hot boiling fat and rub off the skin. Then cut them into halves and cut off the stem and take out the seeds. Carefully cut away the ribs and let the peppers sauté for ten minutes in a tablespoonful of butter. Then moisten with a pint of consommé; season with the chopped shallots, parsley and sweet paprika, and let all cook slowly for a half hour, or until done. Prepare fancy slices of toast, and serve the peppers on these with a delicate garnish of chopped yolks of hard-boiled eggs.

### MANGOES.
### Mangos.

This is a bright, waxy, golden-yellow sweet pepper, very brilliant and handsome, and exempt from fiery flavor, and may be eaten as readily as an apple. Mangoes are generally served as an appetizer (hors d'oeuvres.)

### PUMPKIN.
### Des Citrouilles—Des Giraumonts ou Potiron.

We have two varieties of pumpkin in Louisiana, one a large immense globe pumpkin, and the other a more delicate and much more highly appreciated variety, called the Cashaw. The former is called by the Creoles "Citrouille," and the latter "Giraumont," or "Potiron." Both are cooked according to the following methods:

### Stewed Pumpkin.
### Citrouille à la Créole.

2 Pints of Pumpkin or Cashaw.
4 Tablespoonfuls of Butter.
1 Teaspoonful of Salt.
1 Teaspoonful of Ground Mace.
1 Teaspoonful of Ground Cinnamon.
1 Teaspoonful of Ground Cloves.
2 Gills of Good Whisky or Brandy.

Cut the pumpkin into halves and then into quarters, and pare. Then cut it into pieces of about one inch square. Place them all in a deep pot, and add sufficient water to cover. Let the pumpkin stew slowly for about an hour, stirring frequently to prevent burning. Then take out of the pot, press through a colander, and set back on the stove. Add, for every pint of pumpkin, two large tablespoonfuls of butter, and a half teaspoonful of salt, one of ground mace, one of ground cinnamon and one of ground allspice. A gill of good whiskey or brandy may be added, and improves the flavor. Mix all thoroughly, and add sugar to taste. Let it simmer slowly for half an hour longer, and serve hot with daubes, Grillades à la Sauce, etc. If the pumpkin cooks till very tender, so that it mashes easily, it need not be pressed through a colander.

If the Citrouille, or large pumpkin is used, never cook all in one day. Cut it in half, and save the other half for some other day in the week. The Cashaw will depend on the size. Generally one is cooked at a time. Left-over pumpkin can be utilized in making pumpkin pie. (See recipe.)

### Baked Pumpkin.
### Giraumont Roti.

2 Pints of Pumpkin or Cashaw.
A Dressing of Butter or Gravy.

Cut the pumpkin in halves and then into quarters. Two quarters are enough for a family of six, if the pumpkin is large. Remove the seeds, but do not peel the rind. Place in a baking pan with the rind downwards, and bake until so tender that it may be pierced easily with a fork. Serve in the rind at the table, helping it by spoonfuls. It is eaten with butter or gravy.

Baked pumpkin is liked by some, but the majority of the Creoles prefer the stewed pumpkin. The above is the recipe that has been in use for generations. Once eaten in this way, you will never look again upon a baked pumpkin or Cashaw.

### RADISHES.
### Des Radis.

Radishes are eaten as a relish, or hors d'oeuvres. They are great appetizers, and help the digestion. The "Half Long Scarlet French Radish" is the only red Radish raised for the New Orleans market, and it is said that all the other cities of the Union put together do not consume as much of that one variety as New Orleans does.

There is an art in preparing the radish properly for the table. Cut the tops, and save them for Gumbo aux Herbes. Throw the radishes into a bucket of cold water and wash well. Have at hand another bucket of water. Cut the remaining tops about an inch from the body of the radish, so that only the dainty green will appear. Hold the radish by the top root, upwards, and cut the skin downwards in four or six parts, without detaching the radish from the stalk. In other words, open as you would an orange, without breaking to pieces. Throw the radishes into the fresh bucket of cold water, and in about fifteen minutes they will have opened like a rose, and the effect of the white against the red is very pretty. Fill glass bowls with these, using taste in arranging, and you will not only have a very dainty dish, as far as a relish is concerned, but a pretty table decoration.

Another way is to scrape the radish in spots or lengths, alternating so that there will be a streak of red and one of white. The radish is not cut open in this case. Either way is pretty and inviting, if properly done. One or two dainty leaves may be left near the stalk to improve the appearance of the dish.

Radishes may be served at breakfast, dinner or luncheon. The horseradish is used as an appetizer, and also in sauces.

### ROQUETTE.
### Roquette.

This is a salad vegetable, resembling Cress in taste. It is served as a salad in the same manner, and is very popular with the Creoles.

### SALSIFY, OR OYSTER PLANT.
### Salsifis.

All recipes given for cooking parsnips may be applied to Salsify, which, by the way, is considered the most delicate of the two, both belonging to the same order. Salsify partakes somewhat of the flavor of oysters, hence the name "Oyster Plant." (See Parsnips.)

### Oyster Plant à la Crème.
### Salsifis à la Crème.

A Bunch of Fresh Oyster Plant.
½ Pint of Cream Sauce.

Wash and scrape the roots of the plant thoroughly. Then throw them into cold water immediately as you scrape them, or they will turn black and appear unpalatable. Have ready a kettle of boiling water, and cook for an hour, or longer, till tender. Drain and serve with a Cream Sauce poured over. (See recipe Cream Sauce.)

### Oyster Plant à la Poulette.
### Salsifis à la Poulette.

A Bunch of Salsify or Oyster Plant.
½ Pint of Sauce à la Poulette.

Prepare exactly as in the manner indicated above, using instead of the Cream Sauce a Sauce à la Poulette.

### Oyster Plant Sautéd in Butter.
### Salsifis Sautés au Beurre.

A Good Bunch of Oyster Plant.
4 Tablespoonfuls of Vinegar.
4 Tablespoonfuls of Flour.
A Tablespoonful of Salt.
The Juice of 1 Lemon.
A Teaspoonful of Chopped Parsley.
A Pinch of Black Pepper.

Scrape the oyster plant well and throw into cold water into which put two tablespoonfuls of vinegar to prevent the salsify from turning black. Take from the water, drain and cut into pieces one and a half inches in length. Put into a saucepan with two tablespoonfuls of vinegar and flour well mixed and cover with a quart of cold water. Add a tablespoonful of salt, cover well and let boil slowly for three quarters of an hour. Drain and return to the saucepan and add two tablespoonfuls of the best butter, the pepper, chopped parsley, juice of a lemon, and a pinch of black pepper. Mix well and let it heat for five minutes, tossing almost constantly. Put into a deep dish and serve hot.

### Salsify Fritter.

Salsifis en Beignets.

A Bunch of Salsify.
1 Tablespoonful of Butter.
1 Cup of Water. 2 Eggs.
¼ Pound of Flour. 1 Teaspoonful of Salt.
1 Teaspoonful of Pepper.

Clean and scrape the salsify and boil as directed in recipe Boiled Parsnips (see recipe) till very tender. Then cut into long, narrow strips. Make a batter by mixing the flour with the yolks of the eggs, beaten well. Then add the salt and pepper, and gradually one cup of water, till it is absorbed. Then add the whites of the eggs, beaten to a stiff froth. Mix thoroughly. Add the salsify to the batter. Dip out one spoon at a time of the batter, and fry in boiling lard. Serve as an entrée at dinner.

### SPINACH.

Des Épinards.

Spinach is one of the healthiest of vegetables, but, unfortunately, it is generally so badly prepared by the majority of cooks as to be not only most unrelishable, but unsavory as well. The great art in cooking Spinach is to cook it just long enough and no longer; to drain thoroughly and to have it of just such consistency as will enable it to retain a neat shape when arranged on a dish in mound shape. The most important point in cooking Spinach is to drain it perfectly dry the moment it is taken from the fire. If allowed to cook too long, it loses its color. If it stands in the water it becomes tasteless. The following are the Creole methods of serving Spinach. It is one of the cheapest of all dishes served among the Creoles, and a very good dish, too.

### Spinach, Plain Boiled.

Épinards au Naturel.

½ Peck of Fresh Young Spinach.
1 Cupful of Water. 1 Tablespoonful of Butter.

Always select young and tender spinach. Carefully pick it over, and reject all wilted leaves and coarse fibers and nerves. Cut off the roots. Wash and drain it well in cold water, and press out all the water. It will take about half a peck or four pints, to make a good dish, as it boils down. Put the spinach in a kettle, and add one cupful of water. Place on a moderate fire and let it simmer for ten minutes. As soon as it appears to wilt, take off the fire, for that is all the cooking that is needed. Then drain the spinach of all water through a colander, and then press through a very fine sieve, to drain off the remaining water from the vegetable. Chop the spinach very fine. Then put a tablespoonful of butter in a saucepan, and add the spinach to it. Stir well. Add a few spoonfuls of water, just sufficient to thin, if a little thick, and let it heat thoroughly. Otherwise, if of the right consistency, no water need be added. Good judgment must here prevail. Season with salt and pepper to taste.

At this point the spinach may be served in various ways, as Spinach à la Crème, Spinach au Jus, Spinach with Hard-Boiled Eggs, Spinach à la Maître d'Hôtel, etc. The plain boiled spinach may be served with vinegar as a salad. (See recipe under Chapter on Salads.)

### Spinach à la Crème.

Épinards à la Crème.

½ Peck of Spinach. 1 Cupful of Water.
1 Tablespoonful of Butter. 1 Tablespoonful of Powdered Sugar.
6 Croutons.
A Cream Sauce.

Prepare the spinach as above. When ready to take from the saucepan, have ready slices of buttered toast, or Croûtons fried in butter. Roll the Croutons in sugar before frying. Heap the spinach in little mounds upon them, sprinkle lightly with sugar, and pour over a Cream Sauce (see Cream Sauce), and serve hot.

### Spinach au Jus à la Bourgeoise.

Épinards au Jus à la Bourgeoise.

½ Peck of Spinach.
2 Hard-Boiled or Poached Eggs.
1 Cup of Gravy or Consomme.

Boil the spinach according to the above recipe. When ready to take from the saucepan, after adding the butter and seasonings, put it in a saucepan and pour over a cup of roast beef gravy or consommé, let it cook for twenty minutes, and serve hot.

### Spinach with Hard-Boiled Eggs.
#### Épinards aux Oeufs Durs.

½ Peck of Spinach.
1 Cupful of Water. 1 Tablespoonful of Butter.
3 Hard-Boiled Eggs.

Boil the spinach and prepare to the point indicated in recipe for Spinach (Plain Boiled). Then take the spinach from the saucepan, and arrange in a mound on a dish, and garnish with slices of hard-boiled eggs.

### Spinach à la Maître d'Hotel.
#### Épinards à la Maître d'Hotel.

½ Peck of Spinach. 1 Cupful of Water.
1 Tablespoonful of Butter. A Sauce a la Maître d'Hotel.

Prepare the spinach as directed in recipe Plain Boiled Spinach. Pour over a Sauce à la Maître d'Hotel, cook a few minutes, and serve hot.

### Spinach à la Cuisinière.
#### Épinards à la Cuisinière.

½ Peck of Spinach. ½ Tablespoonful of Butter.
1 Tablespoonful of Flour. 1 Cup of Milk.
6 Toasted Croutons.

Prepare the spinach as above, hash fine, and put in a saucepan with a tablespoonful of butter. Season with salt and pepper, add a tablespoonful of flour, mixed with a cup of milk and a spoon of melted butter, and serve with toasted dice Croûtons on the spinach.

### BEET TOPS, RADISH TOPS, TURNIP TOPS, ETC.

Never throw away any beet, turnip, or radish tops. They may all be cooked in the same manner as spinach au jus, or they may be cooked with salt meat, and make very good and healthy dishes. The humble Creole families in New Orleans prepare turnip tops and beet tops in such a way that a king might not disdain what is commonly held as kitchen refuse.

All these may be made into nice purées. (See recipe for making purées.)

### SORREL.
#### De l'Oseille.

Sorrel is used for various purposes in the kitchen. It is made into soups and purées, served as a salad, or cooked in exactly the same manner as in the recipe for cooking spinach. (See recipes Spinach.)

### Purée of Sorrel.
#### Purée d'Oseille.

In preparing Sorrel after this recipe, make a purée, to be served as a vegetable or as a soup. (See recipe.) A vegetable purée is of course of far denser consistency than a purée intended for soup.

### Sorrell au Gras.
#### Oseille au Gras.

Prepare the sorrel in exactly the same manner as spinach, or "Épinirds au Jus." (See recipe.) Reject all fibrous portions. After you have scalded it, it is important to drain thoroughly. Then chop and press through a colander. Garnish nicely with Croûtons fried in butter.

Sorrel is very acid, and to those who do not like much acidity this may be modified by mingling with equal parts of spinach or lettuce.

### Sorrell au Maigre.
#### Oseille au Maigre.

Prepare exactly as above, only, instead of using broth or gravy, add milk and the well-beaten yolks of two eggs.

### SQUASH.
#### Courge.

3 Young Squash. 2 Tablespoonfuls of Butter.
Salt and Pepper to Taste.

Cut the squash into quarters and pare and remove the seeds. Then cut into small squares of about an inch. Wash in cold water, and then put into a porcelain-lined or agate saucepan, and half cover with water, for squash is a watery vegetable. Let it simmer gently for about twenty minutes or half an hour. Then drain through a colander, pressing gently. Mash the squash very fine after draining, and return to the saucepan. Add two tablespoonfuls of butter, and salt and pepper to taste, and stir until thoroughly heated, and it begins to simmer gently. Do not cease stirring, or it will burn. Serve hot. This is the most delicate way of serving squash, and the only one that the good taste of the Creoles will tolerate. Baked squash are often served, but stuffed squash and the like offend the good ethics of the Creole kitchen.

### TOMATOES.
#### Des Tomates.

Like the onion, tomatoes are among the indispensible adjuncts of good cooking, entering, as they do, so much into the good seasoning and delicate flavoring of various dishes. They are also excellent in salads. (See Salads.) Tomatoes, however, form very dainty dishes, when cooked, and among these are the following:

### Stewed Tomatoes.
#### Tomates Sautées.

12 Tomatoes. 1 Tablespoonful of Butter.
1 Teaspoonful of Sugar. 1 Onion.
Salt and Pepper to Taste.
½ Cup of Bread Crumbs. 1 Inch of Ham.
Salt and Pepper and Cayenne to Taste.
1 Sprig Each of Thyme, Parsley and Bay Leaf.

Scald the tomatoes, and let the water remain over them about five minutes. Then peel the tomatoes, slipping the skins off easily, and cut them into small pieces. Put a tablespoonful of butter into a saucepan, and as it melts add the onion, which you will have chopped very fine. Let it brown, and add one inch of ham, chopped very fine. Then add the tomatoes, and let them brown, slowly adding in the meantime a half cup of dry bread crumbs. Let all simmer gently, and add one sprig each of thyme, parsley and bay leaf. Stew gently for an hour longer, and serve hot.

### Broiled Tomatoes.

Tomates Grillées.

6 Tomatoes. 2 Tablespoonfuls of Butter.
1 Tablespoonful of Chopped Parsley.
The Juice of 1 Lemon.

Take six tomatoes and cut them in halves on the cross. Do not peel. Put them on the broiler and broil on a slow fire till tender. Turn the broiler from one side to the other often, to prevent burning. In about ten minutes they will be done. Put on a hot dish; put a little melted butter, a little chopped parsley and the juice of a lemon on each, and serve hot.

### Fried Tomatoes.

Tomates Frites.

6 Nice, Large, Firm Tomatoes.
1 Egg.   ½ Cup of Bread Crumbs.
2 Tablespoonfuls of Lard.

Slice the tomatoes very thin, and then dust with salt and pepper. Beat the egg very light. Dip the tomatoes first in this and then in the bread crumbs, and drop into the lard, covering the bottom of the pan. When brown on one side, turn on the other. Turn carefully with the cake turner into a heated dish. Keep warm while you are frying the rest, and serve very hot.

### Tomatoes au Gratin.

Tomates au Gratin.

6 Tomatoes.   2 Tablespoonfuls of Butter.
1 Cup of Grated Bread Crumbs.
Salt and Pepper to Taste.

Scald and skin the tomatoes. Then place a layer of them at the bottom of a baking dish, cover with a layer of bread crumbs, spread very thick, and season with salt and pepper and dots of butter at intervals. Continue in this way till the last layer is reached, finishing with a layer of bread crumbs, sprinkle with salt and pepper, dot with butter, and put in an oven to bake for an hour and a quarter. Canned tomatoes will require about half this time.

### Scalloped Tomatoes.

Tomates en Coquilles.

6 Tomatoes. 1 Cup of Grated Bread Crumbs.
2 Tablespoonfuls of Butter.
Salt and Pepper to Taste.

Proceed exactly as above, only bake the tomatoes in layers in small cups or silver shells.

### Stuffed Tomatoes.

Tomates Farcies.

6 Tomatoes. 1 Tablespoonful of Butter.
1 Cup of Wet Bread, Squeezed Thoroughly.
Salt, Pepper and Cayenne to Taste.
1 Clove of Garlic (If desired.)   1 Onion.
¼ Inch of Ham.

Wash the tomatoes, selecting fine, large, smooth ones for this purpose. Either cut the tomato in two, or else cut one slice from the stem end. Scoop out the inside of the tomato, and put it in a dish and save the skins. Take one onion and one quarter of an inch of ham and chop very fine. Put a tablespoonful of butter into a saucepan, and add the onion, letting it brown nicely. Then add the ham. Let it brown. Add the insides of the tomatoes, and then add, almost instantly, a cup of bread that has been wet and squeezed. Beat all well together as it fries, and add salt and pepper to taste. Let it cook well, and then take off, and stuff the tomatoes, cut in halves or whole. The former is the daintier way. Sprinkle the tops with bread crumbs, and dot with butter. Place in the oven for fifteen or twenty minutes, till brown, and serve hot with filet of beef or chicken, etc.

### Stuffed Tomatoes à la Créole.

Tomates Farcies à la Créole.

¼ Pound of the White Meat of a Chicken.
2 Inches of Ham.
1 Egg.  1 Tablespoonful of Parsley.
1 Onion, Minced Fine.  ½ Cup Bread Crumbs.
Thyme and Bay Leaf.
Salt, Pepper and Cayenne to Taste.

Chop the chicken meat very fine. Cut the tomatoes into halves, and scoop out the insides without breaking the outer skins. Take the inside meat and chop fine. Put a tablespoonful of butter into the saucepan, and as it melts add the chopped onion, and let it brown. After a few minutes, add the ham and chicken, and let these brown. Then add the tomatoes, and, as they brown the bread crumbs. Add the minced herbs and a clove of garlic, if desired. (The garlic must be added before the tomatoes, if it is used.) Let all simmer gently. Season to taste with salt and pepper and a dash of Cayenne. When well cooked, remove from the fire, when about the consistency of thick starch. Let it cool slightly, and then stuff each tomato shall. Sprinkle bread crumbs grated on top, and dot with butter. Place in the oven for about half an hour, and serve as an entremet with chicken or veal.

### Tomato Salad.
Tomates en Salade.

See recipe under chapter on Salads.

### Purée of Tomatoes.
Purée de Tomates.

See recipe under chapter on Soups.

### TURNIPS.
Des Navets.

Turnips are cheap in New Orleans, and many delightful dishes may be made with them, if properly prepared. The turnip tops also make good, substantial home dishes, that none should disdain. The Creoles, who have applied the art of cooking to the most humble even of the vegetable kingdom, have learned to so prepare turnip tops as to make them a welcome dish on the most exclusive tables.

Turnips are largely used, like the tomato and onion, though not to such an extent, in seasoning food substances. They are indispensible with the pot-au-feu, the bouillon, or the well-made consommé.

### Mashed Turnips.
Purée de Navets.

6 Turnips. 2 Tablespoonfuls of Butter.
Salt and Pepper to Taste.

Wash and pare the turnips, and cut them into quarters, and cover with boiling water and boil until very tender, which will be in about thirty to forty-five minutes, according to the tenderness of the turnips. If you boil them whole it will take an hour and a quarter. If you cut the turnips as soon as tender take out of the water and drain through a colander of all water. Then press them lightly, to squeeze all remaining water out, and hash well. Add a tablespoonful of butter, salt and pepper to taste, and serve hot. Serve with roast meats or roast ducks.

Turnips may be mixed with equal quantities of potatoes, mashed and buttered.

### Plain Boiled Turnips.
Navets Bouillis au Naturel.

6 Turnips. A Drawn Butter Sauce.

Boil the turnips whole, selecting very tender ones. They will require about an hour of boiling. Always use hot water in putting on the turnips. Drain off water, when tender, and serve with a Drawn Butter Sauce, pepper and salt. Serve with roast beef, mutton or roast duck.

### Creamed Turnips.
Navets à la Crème.

6 Turnips. A Cream Sauce.

Cut large turnips in quarters for this dish. Small ones may be boiled whole. When tender, drain and put into a colander and press out all water. Then make a rich Cream Sauce (see recipe) and pour over the turnips. Serve with boiled leg of mutton, either by placing the turnips around the leg of mutton on the dish and pouring the sauce over, or separate, as a vegetable.

### Turnips Baked With Mutton.
Mouton Roti aux Navets.

6 Turnips. Salt and Pepper to Taste.
Roast Mutton Drippings.

Boil the turnips until nearly tender. Then drain in a colander. If very large, cut in quarters; if small, let them remain uncut. Lay them on the pan, around the roasting leg of mutton, and let them bake about an hour, basting frequently with the drippings from the mutton. When done, place around the leg of mutton as a garnish, and serve.

### Glazed Turnips.
Navets Glacés.

6 Turnips of Uniform Size.
1 Tablespoonful of Sugar. 1 Cup of Water.
1 Large Tablespoonful of Butter.
Salt to Taste.

Select fine, small and tender turnips of uniform size (top the heads and the stems, and remove the skins, but not too closely, lest they should break up when boiling. Then take a frying pan large enough for the turnips to lie in it, side by side. Put the butter in first, and when melted add the turnips. Then sprinkle with the sugar and water, and season with salt to taste. Set on the back of the stove, where they can simmer gently for an hour. When nearly done, and tender all through, add a tablespoonful of flour, mixed in water, blended well. Then set in the oven, with a paper on top. Let them stand for about half an hour and use as a garnish for beef, veal, etc. The turnips will be nicely glazed, and will make the dish appear very beautiful.

### Turnips Fried in Butter.
Navets Sautés au Beurre.

6 Turnips. 2 Tablespoonfuls of Butter.
Salt and Pepper to Taste.

Boil the turnips according to directions, and, when very tender, drain in a colander. Put two tablespoonfuls of butter into a frying pan, and when it is hot, add the turnips. Season well with salt and pepper, and, when nicely browned, dish on a hot platter and serve with roast ducks.

### Boiled Turnip Tops à la Créole.
#### Navèts à la Créole.

¼ Peck of Turnip Greens.
1 Tablespoonful of Salt and a Pound of Fresh Pork or 1 Pound of Salt Pork.
Pepper to Taste.

Wash the turnip tops, and put into a kettle of boiling water with a piece of fresh or salt pork. Let them boil slowly till tender, and then season well with salt and pepper. When tender, take out and chop, but not too fine, or leave them just as they are. Drain of all water, and serve as you would boiled cabbage, piling the turnip tops around the dish, and the salt meat or pork in the center.

Again, the Creoles boil the white turnips with the greens, cutting the former portions into quarters or semi-quarters, according to their size, and chopping the greens after cooking. Eat with pepper vinegar, as you would boiled cabbage.

### TRUFFLES.
#### Des Truffes.

The Truffle is a most expensive vegetable. It belongs to the family of Mushrooms, and is a subterranean production, of a fishy, fungous structure and roundish figure. Its aroma is particularly marked, and it is much esteemed by epicures, for, when mixed in proper proportions it adds a zest and flavor to all sauces for Fish, Filets of Beef, Turkey, Chicken, Game and Omelets that cannot be found in any other plant in the entire vegetable kingdom. The name "Truffle" is supposed to be derived from the French "Truffe," or the Spanish "Trufa," signifying deceit or imposition, the growth of the plant under ground seeming to accord with the name.

Truffles come prepared in cans, being put up in France, those of "Perigord" being the brand most in use. The Creoles use Truffles mostly as a condiment for fish, meats, stuffings for poultry, game, etc. They are very expensive, costing as much as $3 a can, and a small can at that. In cooking filets, they are prepared simply "Truffée," or whole or cut in halves, or "à la Perigueux," that is, the Truffles are cut or minced very fine. They are also served after the following manner as entremets or hors d'oeuvres.

### Truffles in Spanish Style.
#### Truffes à l'Espagnole.

10 Truffles.
2 Tablespoonfuls of Salad Oil or Butter.
1 Tablespoonful of Minced Parsley.
3 Finely Minced Shallots.
3 Sprigs of Minced Parsley.
½ Glass of White Wine. Sauce Espagnole.

Slice the Truffles very fine, and place in a saucepan on a slow fire, with a tablespoonful of butter or two of oil, salt and pepper to taste and the minced parsley and shallots. After letting them smother for a few minutes, moisten well with the White Wine or Champagne and a Sauce Espagnole, using equal proportions of the wine and sauce. Quicken the fire slightly, and let them cook slowly till done. Skim off all grease, and serve hot with ragouts, etc.

### Truffles With Champagne.
#### Truffes au Vin de Champagne.

6 Truffles. 1 Glass of Champagne.

Make a "Marinade," that is, a liquor with spices and vinegar; set to cook, and add a glass of champagne. Add the Truffles, and season again to taste. Let all cook for upwards of half an hour. Then take the Truffles from the sauce. Let them cool, and serve on a folded napkin as an hors d'oeuvre.

### Truffles on Minced Toast.
#### Truffes en Croustades.

4 Truffles. 2 Tablespoonfuls of Butter.
1 Clove of Garlic.
Salt and Pepper to Taste.
8 Croutons Fried in Butter.

Prepare the Truffles as in the recipe "à l'Espagnole," or simply "à la Provençale," that is, slice them very fine, let them stew or sauter them in butter, and season well with salt and pepper and the clove of a garlic minced very fine. When done, add the juice of a lemon. Take some slices of bread, cut in fancy shapes, and fry in butter, or toast. Cover each piece with some of the Ragout of Truffles, and serve hot.

### VEGETABLE PEAR.
#### Mirliton.

The Vegetable Pear, or "Mirliton," as the Creoles have named this vegetable, belongs to the gourd family. It is known to botanists by the name of the "One-Seeded Cucumber." Like almost all the gourds, the plant is a vine, and is trained by the Creoles upon trellis, fences or arbors around their homes. It is not only a very ornamental vine, but an abundant bearer. The fruit, if properly prepared, as the Creoles know so well how to prepare it, is a delightful dish, and is of a very much finer flavor than eggplants, squashes or pumpkins. It may be cooked in a half dozen ways, stuffed and stewed and fried, as the eggplant (see recipes), or stewed or baked, like the pumpkin, squash or cashaw. It is particularly fine when prepared like stewed cashaw. (See recipes.) It may also be made into fritters, like eggplants, or baked cakes. In any way that it is served it is delicious, and is a great favorite with the Creoles, especially the little children.

## MELONS.
### Des Melons.

The New Orleans market cannot be excelled by any market in the world in the splendor and variety of the Melons found in the beginning of the summer, and till late in the fall, in its great market stalls and fruit stalls, which intersect every portion of the city. Especially is this the case with the Muskmelon, or Canteloupe. No northern variety of melons can compare with our special varieties, and it is familiarly said that it requires Louisiana sun to bring the seed to perfection. Muskmelons and Watermelons are among our most common articles of food, and are within the reach of all classes, rich and poor, white and black, in season. The Creoles serve Melons both as a fruit and a dessert.

### MUSKMELON.
### Cantaloup.

Muskmelons, or Canteloupes, are cultivated extensively in the vicinity of New Orleans. The quality is fine, and the flavor delicious. They are served by the Creoles both as a fruit and as a dessert—as a fruit at the beginning of breakfast, and as a dessert at the close of luncheon or dinner. The melon is always served very cold, being kept on ice several hours before serving, and when cut in halves and cleansed of seed, crushed ice is placed within each half, and it is brought to the table and served. It is a most refreshing accompaniment to breakfast, at which meal it is more generally served.

### WATERMELON.
### Melon d'Eau.

The Watermelon is as great a favorite among the Creoles for luncheon and dinner and supper desserts as the Muskmelon is a general breakfast and luncheon favorite. Indeed, at all hours during the summer, except in the early forenoon, a watermelon is considered in place as a most refreshing and welcome summer offering. Watermelons are kept on ice continually by fruit dealers, and whenever a family chooses to have a "Melon on Ice," they have simply to send to the fruit stand within the radius of a square, and a splendid rosy-fruited melon is to be had, cold and delicious, and just ready to be cut. The Creoles as a rule, cut the melon in great round slices, so that each person may have a piece of "the heart" of the fruit; or it may be cut in lengthwise slices, according to taste. The new-fangled practice of "scooping the melon out with a spoon," and thus serving it, is disregarded by the Creoles. The only proper way to eat a melon and enjoy it is in the good old Creole style: Give every guest a fine round slice, glowing with "a heart of red," and thus will the fruit be enjoyed as it deserves.

## GARDEN HERBS.

The old-time garden herbs are part of every well-regulated Creole kitchen garden. Thyme, Sage, Rosemary, Mint, Sweet Marjoram, Basil, Lavender, Anise, Carraway, Bene, Borage, Catnip, Coriander, Dill, Fennel, Horehound, Pot Marigold, Pennyroyal, Rue, Summer Savory, Tansy, Tarragon, Wormwood—all these thrive in our gardens, and are used by the Creole housewives, some for culinary, others for medicinal purposes. "The Bouquet Garni," or herb bouquet, has already been spoken of in the beginning of this book. To prepare such herbs as Sage, Thyme, Summer Savory, Mint, Basil, or any of the sweet or medicinal herbs, for winter use, the Creole housewife gathers them from her own little garden patch when they are fresh in their season, or she procures them from the markets. After examining them well, and discarding all poor or sickly looking sprigs, she washes and shakes the herbs. Then she ties them into small bundles, and ties an old piece of mosquito netting about them, to keep them from picking up any dust. The herbs are then hung, leaves downwards, in a warm, dry place. In a few days they will be thoroughly dry and brittle. She then picks all the leaves off, and puts them in clean large-mouthed bottles, and corks and labels them. When needed for use, they are rubbed very fine between the fingers and passed through a sieve. The bottle is always kept corked, as exposure to the air will cause the herbs to lose strength and flavor.

Herbs, such as Sweet Marjoram, Thyme, etc., are in daily use in our kitchens. In like manner the Creole housewife gathers the leaves of the Laurel, or Bay Leaf, and, after washing and drying thoroughly, the leaves are bottled for use. But fresh herbs are nearly always to be found in our gardens.

# CHAPTER XXX.

## RELISHES.

### Hors d'Oeuvres.

Hors d'Oeuvres are relishes and may be served either hot or cold. Ordinarily, in daily household life, only the cold hors d'oeuvres, such as cress, celery, olives, radishes, etc., are served; they are set upon the tables as a decoration and passed as appetizers or relishes between the courses. At more formal affairs, hot hors d'oeuvres are served, some of them being most elegant and recherché dishes. The hot hors d'oeuvre does not preclude the cold at the same dining.

The following form the list of the greater number of

### Cold Relishes.

### Hors d'Oeuvres Froids.

Radishes, Celery, Olives, Cress, Lettuce, Roquette, Pickled Onions, Sliced Cucumbers, Sliced Tomatoes, Pickles, Mangoes, Melons, Anchovies, Sardines, Lyonnaise Sausage (Saucissons Lyonnaise), Bread and Butter, Crackers, Anchovy Sandwiches, Ham Sandwiches, Cheese Sandwiches, Bologna Sausage cut and sliced, Cold Ham, Pigs' Feet, a Crawfish Bush (Buisson d'Écrevisses), a Shrimp Bush (Buisson de Chevrettes), Boiled Crawfish, River Shrimp on Ice, Oysters on Half Shell, Raw Oysters, Sliced or Quartered Lemon, Salted Almonds, Salted Peanuts, Canapés of Caviare, Ham, Crab, etc.

Among the more elegant

### Hot Relishes

### (Hors d'Oeuvres Chauds)

may be mentioned the following:

Petits Pâtes au Jus (or small hot patties of meats, etc.), Boudins Noirs et Blancs (Boudin Sausages, white and black), Rissoles, Sausages with or without Truffles, Rognons à la Brochette or Broiled Kidneys, Pigs' Feet, Bouchées d'Huîtres or Oyster Patties, Fried Brains (whether of mutton or veal), Calves' Feet, Oxtail with Vinegar or Mustard Sauce.

Almost all the above named Hors d'Oeuvres, whether hot or cold, have been already treated in the special departments, whether of vegetables or meats, to which they pertain. The subjoined recipes, however, have been especially prepared, the number and variety of our Creole Hors d'Oeuvres being such as to warrant a special chapter on the subject.

### Anchovies in Oil.

Anchoix à l'Huile.

1 Pint Bottle of Boned Anchovies.
1 Hard-Boiled Egg.
Chopped Parsley to Garnish.

Take the contents of one pint bottle of boned Anchovies; drain them of all oil on a cloth and then arrange nicely in a flat glass or china celery or radish dish. Take a hard-boiled egg, hash or slice daintily and decorate the dish with this. Sprinkle over some chopped parsley and serve.

### Sardines in Oil.

Sardines à l'Huile.

1 Box of Sardines.
Parsley to Garnish.

Take the sardines carefully from the box and avoid breaking them. Decorate a dish nicely with sprigs of parsley or watercress and lay the sardines upon it and serve.

### Coquilles of Chicken, Creole Style.

Coquilles de Volaille à la Créole.

The Breast of a Roasted Chicken.
1 Ounce of Butter.  1 Truffle.
4 Mushrooms.  1 Dozen Godiveau Quenelles.
1½ Pint of Madeira Sauce.
Grated Bread Crumbs.

Cut the chicken into dice-shaped pieces; take an ounce of butter and place in a saucepan; add the chicken; chop four mushrooms and one truffle and add. Make a dozen small Godiveau Quenelles (see recipe), and add to the mixture in the saucepan; pour over a half pint of Madeira Sauce (see recipe), stir well and let all cook for five minutes. Take a half dozen table shells and fill with this mixture. Sprinkle grated fresh bread crumbs over the tops, spread a little melted butter over each and place the shells on a baking dish. Place in a very hot oven and let them brown to a beautiful golden color. This will require about six minutes. Place a folded napkin on a dish, set the shells upon it and send to the table hot.

### Cromesquies with Truffles.

Cromesquies aux Truffes.

1 Roasted Chicken.  2 Truffles.
1 Pint of Velouté Sauce.
6 Pieces of Crepinette.
Salt and Pepper to Taste. A Dash of Nutmeg.

Roast the chicken, then bone and hash the meat. Make a pint of Velouté Sauce; chop the truffles very fine and place the chicken and the truffles and sauce in a saucepan together. Season to taste with salt and pepper, and add a dash of nutmeg. Cover and let all cook for ten minutes, occasionally, however, stirring to prevent burning. Then take from the fire and let cool by pouring into a flat dish. Spread out to about an inch in thickness and divide into six parts. Prepare six pieces of Crepinette and roll each one of the six parts of chicken into the skin. Have ready a flour batter and dip each Crepinette into the batter and fry in boiling lard for five minutes, or until slightly brown. Drain thoroughly on a cloth, place a nice folded napkin on a dish; set the cromesquies upon it; decorate with fried parsley and serve hot.

Cromesquies of game, veal or any meats may be made in the same manner.

### Creole Timbales.
### Timbales Créoles.

2 Raw Chicken Breasts.
1 Cup of Bread, Soaked in Milk.
½ Tablespoonful of Butter.
The Yolks of Four Eggs.
3 Tablespoonfuls of Velouté Sauce.
Salt and Pepper to Taste.
6 Plain Pancakes.  1 Gill Madeira Sauce.

Cut up into medium-sized pieces two raw chicken breasts; pound them in a mortar with the same quantity of bread soaked in milk, a half tablespoonful of fresh butter and the yolks of four eggs; season with salt and pepper and a dash of Cayenne; mix all well together, and then mix in a bowl with three tablespoonfuls of Velouté Sauce. (See recipe.) Butter the half dozen small timbale molds and line them with plain pancake. (See recipe). Fill the molds with the chicken mixture and cover with small round pieces of pancake. Steam them in a moderate oven for about ten minutes. Then take out of the oven and remove the timbales from the mold; garnish a hot dish nicely with sprigs of parsley, place the timbales upon it, pour over a gill of hot Madeira Sauce and send to the table hot.

### Queen of the Carnival Croustades.
### Croustades à la Reine du Carnaval.

6 Quenelles (Chicken or Godiveau). 2 Truffles.
1 Sweetbread.  6 Kidneys.
1 Pint of Allemande Sauce.
½ Glass of White Wine.
¼ Pound of Foundation Paste.
Cracker Dust for Filling.

Prepare six Quenelles, either chicken or Godiveau (see recipe) and place in a saucepan with a half glass of white wine. Season the wine first with a little salt and pepper. Add the mushrooms and the truffles all cut into dice-shaped pieces. Poach for six or eight minutes, and then take one pint of hot Allemande Sauce and put all this mixture into it. Let all stand on the hot stove for five minutes and in the meanwhile spread out a quarter of a pound of Foundation Paste (Pâte-à-Foncer, see recipe) to the thickness of an eighth of an inch; line six tartlet molds with this and fill with cracker crumbs that have been pounded into a dust. Cover with a buttered paper and set in the oven and bake for ten minutes. Then take out, remove all the cracker dust and fill the molds with the hot mixture of chicken, etc. Set in the oven for three minutes, dress nicely on a hot dish and serve hot.

### Lamb Sweetbreads in Cases.
### Riz de Veau d'Agneau en Petites Caisses.

6 Lamb Sweetbreads.
2 Tablespoonfuls of Butter.
1 Glass of Madeira Wine.
1 Small Onion.  1 Shallot.  6 Mushrooms.
½ Clove of Garlic.
1 Tablespoonful of Chopped Parsley.
1 Gill of Sauce Espagnole.

Clean and pare and blanch the sweetbreads. (See recipe.) Then set aside to cool. Lard nicely with very fine larding needles. Put two tablespoonfuls of butter in a saucepan and add the sweetbreads. Pour over one glass of Madeira Wine, cover well with the onion, shallot, mushrooms, clove of garlic and parsley, all minced very fine. Cover with a piece of buttered paper and set in the oven for ten minutes or until they are a nice golden brown color. Then take out of the oven and lay the sweetbreads on a dish. Set the saucepan back on the stove and add a gill of Sauce Espagnole (see recipe.) Let all cook for five minutes. Have ready six small boxes of buttered paper; pour a little of the gravy in the bottom of each case, then place a sweetbread in each and set in a baking dish; set the dish in the open oven for five minutes; then arrange a napkin nicely in a dish, set the cases of sweetbreads upon it and send to the table hot.

### Macaroni Croquettes.
### Croquettes de Macaroni.

¼ Pound of Macaroni.
1 Tablespoonful of Butter.
½ Tablespoonful of Grated Parmesan Cheese.
1 Tablespoonful of Cooked Smoked Tongue, Cut Very Fine.
1 Minced Truffle.  1 Egg.
3 Tablespoonfuls of Grated Fresh Bread Crumbs.

Boil the Macaroni. (See recipe.) Then drain well. Put a tablespoonful of butter into a saucepan, add the

Macaroni, and sprinkle over the grated cheese and the minced smoked tongue and truffle. Toss all together nicely and then spread out evenly. Then set aside to cool. When cool, cut the preparation into six equal parts and roll each in grated Parmesan cheese, then in a well-beaten egg, and afterwards in freshly-grated bread crumbs. Have ready a pan of boiling lard, fry the Croquettes in the lard for five minutes, then drain well, place on a dish on a folded napkin and serve hot.

### Royal Salpicon.
#### Salpicon Royale.

Sweetbreads.  1 Tablespoonful of Butter.
12 Mushrooms.   2 Truffles.
1 Pint of Sauce Allemande.

Clean, pare and blanch the sweetbreads. Then cut into very small pieces and put them into a saucepan with two tablespoonfuls of butter; let them sauté a moment and then add the mushrooms and truffles all cut very fine. Add a pint of Sauce Allemande (see recipe), and let the mixture cook on a slow fire for six or eight minutes, tossing gently all the while. Add a teaspoonful of butter, stir well and use for any garnishing desired.

### Salpicon, Hunters' Style.
#### Salpicon à la Chasseur.

The Breasts of 2 Fine Partridges.
1 Tablespoonful of Butter.  12 Whole Peppers.
1 Glass of Madeira Wine.
1 Glass of Good Sherry Wine.
6 Blanched Chicken Livers.
1 Carrot.    ½ Onion.
1 Ounce of Cooked Beef Tongue.
2 Truffles.   6 Mushrooms.   1 Bay Leaf.
1 Sprig of Thyme.  Square Inch of Lean Ham.
1 Quart of Consomme or Broth.

Cut the breasts of the Partridges into dice-shaped pieces, and then put them into a saucepan with a tablespoonful of butter. Pour over a glass of good Sherry wine and set on a hot fire. Add the blanched chicken livers, the truffle cut into dice-shaped pieces and the mushrooms cut very fine. Have already prepared a "Fumet of Game," made by placing one carrot, one-half of a small onion, one bay leaf, one square inch of ham, one sprig of thyme, and the carcass of the partridge into a covered saucepan with a tablespoonful of butter. Let these brown well and add a glass of Madeira Wine. Let it come to a boil, then moisten with one quart of broth or consommé, and salt and pepper to taste; add twelve whole black peppers. Let all cook for three-quarters of an hour, until it is reduced to a pint, and strain through a napkin. Add this to the salpicon and let all cook for five minutes longer. Use as a garnish for any dish desired.

### Creole Salpicon.
#### Salpicon à la Créole.

2 Dozen Crawfish.   3 Tomatoes.
1 Dozen Mushrooms.
2 Tablespoonfuls of Butter.
2 Tablespoonfuls of Flour.
1 Pint of Boiling Milk.
1 Teaspoonful of Grated Nutmeg.
1 Herb Bouquet.  12 Whole Black Peppers.

Put two tablespoonfuls of butter into a saucepan and add the flour; stir constantly for about five minutes; then moisten well with the milk, pouring it in gradually and then whisking. Add the grated nutmeg, salt to taste, and the twelve whole peppers. Add a herb bouquet, minced fine, and let all cook for a quarter of an hour. Then rub well through a sieve; and put into a saucepan with the tomatoes, skinned and chopped fine, and the meat of the crawfish cut into dice-shaped pieces, and the minced mushrooms. Let all cook for five minutes and serve.

### Louisiana Salpicon.
#### Salpicon Louisianaise.

50 Lake Shrimp.  1 Dozen Mushrooms.
1 Truffle.   2 Tablespoonfuls of Butter.
2 Tablespoonfuls of Flour.
1 Grated Nutmeg.  1 Herb Bouquet.
1 Glass of White Wine.
3 Tomatoes.

Clean and scale the Shrimp and boil according to recipe. Then follow in all particulars the recipe given above for Salpicon Creole, with the exception that White Wine is used instead of milk, and a truffle is added to the minced vegetables. Send to the table hot.

### Salpicon à la Montglas.
#### Salpicon à la Montglas.

The Breasts of 2 Small Chickens, or Any Game.
1 Ounce of Lean Ham.
1 Gill of Madeira Sauce.
1 Gill of Tomato Sauce.
6 Mushrooms.   1 Truffle.

Mince the breasts of the chicken or game very fine, mince the ham, truffles and mushrooms, and put all into a saucepan with a gill of Madeira Sauce and one gill of Tomato Sauce. Let all cook for five minutes, and then use as a garnish.

### Salpicon, Financier Style.
#### Salpicon à la Financiére.

The Legs and Breasts of a Chicken.
1 Tablespoonful of Butter.
1 Dozen Small Godiveau Quenelles.
1 Square Inch of Ham.   1 Truffle.
8 Mushrooms.   1 Pint of Madeira Sauce.

Cut the chicken into dice-shaped pieces, and put into a saucepan with the butter; add the square inch of ham, the truffles and mushrooms, all minced fine; and then add twelve small Godiveau Quenelles. (See recipe.) Add a pint of Madeira Sauce (see recipe); set on the stove, and let all cook for five or eight minutes, and the Salpicon is ready to be served as a garnish for any dish desired.

### Reed Bird Patties.
### Pâtés d'Ortolans.

1 Dozen Reed Birds.    1 Salpicon Royal.
¼ Pound of Foundation Paste.

Pick and clean the birds and season well; then bind each with a thin strip of bacon. Make a Foundation Paste (Pâté-à-Foncer) and line six patty molds with this. Put in a moderate oven and bake for fifteen minutes; then empty them and let them dry well in the open oven for five minutes. Let them cool. Then fill the bottom of each mold with a tablespoonful of Salpicon Royal (see recipe), and place in each mold two of the nicely prepared birds. Lay the patties on a baking dish or roasting pan and set in the oven, whose heat must be moderate, and let them roast for fifteen or twenty minutes. Then remove from the oven, moisten each patty with a tablespoonful of hot Madeira Sauce, and send to the table hot.

### Tamales.
### Des Tamales.

1 Tender Young Chicken.
1 Cup of Boiled Irish Potatoes.
1 Large Onion.    1 Clove of Garlic.
2 Sprigs of Parsley.    1 Bay Leaf.
1 Sprig of Thyme.    1 Spoon of Butter.
1 Cup of Cracker Crumbs.
Salt and Pepper to Taste.
A Good Dash of Cayenne.

Boil a young chicken until the meat can be picked off the bones. Then chop up very fine. Mince the onion, clove of garlic, thyme, bay leaf, and parsley, very fine. Put the onion and butter into a saucepan and let brown slightly; and add the minced garlic, thyme, parsley and bay leaf. Add the chicken immediately and one cup of mashed potatoes and grated cracker crumbs. Stir well, and season to taste with salt and Chili pepper. Add a good dash of Cayenne, for this is a very hot dish. Mix all well by stirring and let cook for five minutes. Have ready a pot of boiling water and about a dozen nice, clean corn-shuck leaves. Cut the leaves into nice oblong shapes, and divide the chicken mixture into equal parts. Roll each of these parts into a corn leaf and tie, and immerse in boiling water for five minutes. Then drain off the water, arrange the husks on a dish and send to the table hot, serving just before the meal begins as an appetizer. This is a famous Mexican-Creole Hors-d'Oeuvre. Tamales are also eaten hot for supper or luncheon.

### Pickled Tunny.
### Thon Mariné.

In New Orleans we only get the tunny in its pickled or other prepared states. Take a radish or flat celery dish; decorate nicely with fresh parsley sprigs, or cress, or asparagus tips; lay the tunny upon it, and serve as a cold Hors d'Oeuvre.

### Lyonnaise Sausage.
### Saucissons de Lyonnaise.

12 Thin Slices of Lyonnaise Sausage.
Parsley Sprigs to Garnish.

Cut from a medium-sized Lyonnaise sausage twelve nice and very thin slices; decorate a dish nicely with parsley leaves on the outer edges. Lay the saucisson de Lyons in the center and serve as a cold hors d'oeuvre.

---

## CHAPTER XXXI.

### SWEET ENTREMETS.

### Des Entremets Sucrés.

Sweet entrées and entremets are not the least part of the real Creole cuisine. The ancient French colonists brought the custom of serving sweet entremets and entrés, such as Beignets, Compotes, Soufflés, Gelées, etc., from the old mother country to Louisiana. The Creoles applied these to the various delightful and refreshing fruits which abound in Louisiana. When the little Creole children, taking a peep into the kitchen, as children will do in every clime, saw that the fat and cheery old negro cook was going to make Apple Fritters, Orange Fritters, or cook fried bananas for dinner, there was always some very endearing term applied to the old Creole cuisinière, and she never failed to respond in the wholesome and practical way that the Creole cooks of those days did, by handing a beautiful golden beignet, piled with snowy sugar, to the expectant little ones. The custom of serving these sweet entremets spread from New Orleans to other portions of the United States, till now no fastidious chef would think of keeping a fashionable hotel or restaurant without including some of these in the daily bill of fare. The following are the ancient and most accepted forms of preparing sweet entrées and entremets à la Créole. All compotes of fruits may be served either as entremets or desserts.

### FRITTERS.

### Des Beignets.

The most important rule to be observed in making fritters, whether of fruit or plain, is to have the batter of the proper consistency. This is particularly important in making fruit fritters. "La Pâtes à Beignets," as the Creoles call the batter, must be of sufficient consistency to envelop in one single immersion the fruit or other substance with which it is intended to make the fritters.

#### Fritter Batter à la Créole.

Pâte à Beignets à la Créole.

1 Cup Flour. 2 Eggs. 2 Tablespoonfuls Brandy.
¼ Teaspoonful of Salt.
Cold Water. 1 Tablespoonful Butter, Melted.

Beat the yolks of the eggs well, and add the flour, beating very light. Now add the melted butter and the brandy, and thin with water to the consistency of a very thick starch. Add the whites of eggs, beaten to a stiff froth, and then dip the fruit into this, immersing well at one dipping. Lift out with a large cooking spoon, drop into the boiling lard, and fry to a golden brown. The batter must be thick enough to coat the fruit all around in one immersion, yet it must not be so thick as to be over-heavily coated or tough.

Many of the Creoles substitute, according to the fruit which they intend to make into fritters, White Wine or Sherry or lemon juice for the brandy. A fruit fritter must always be sprinkled nicely and lightly with powdered sugar, and, if served as an entremet, it must be hot. Fruit fritters often take the place of desserts among the poorer Creole families.

#### French Fritter Batter.

Pâte à Beignets à la Française.

1 Cup of Sifted Flour. ½ Cup of Cold Water.
2 Eggs. ½ Cup of Sugar.
1 Tablespoonful of Best Olive Oil.
2 Tablespoonfuls of Brandy or Orange Flower Water.
¼ Teaspoonful of Salt.

Beat the whites well into a stiff froth. Beat the yolks of the eggs into the flour until very light, and add the sugar, blending well. Add brandy or orange flower water, and beat light, and then add the water and oil, making the batter of the consistency of a very thick starch. Now add the whites of the egg, beat well, and proceed to drop in the fruit, as in above recipe.

#### Plain Fritters.

Beignets de Pâte.

1 Pint of Flour. 1 Pint of Milk.
1 Teaspoonful of Baking Powder. 4 Eggs.
The Zest of Half a Lemon.
¼ Cup of Sugar. Flavoring to Taste.
½ Teaspoonful of Salt.

Beat the yolks of the eggs and the whites separate. Sift the baking powder into the flour, and add the yolks of the eggs, well beaten. Beat well, and add the milk, and flavoring of orange, vanilla or brandy to taste. (The flavoring may be omitted altogether.) Add the zest of a lemon, grated very fine, and salt in quantity given above. Lastly, add the whites, beaten to a stiff froth, and have the batter of such consistency that it will pour from the spoon. Drop it in the boiling lard by large kitchen spoonfuls, and let it fry to a golden yellow. (See General Directions for Frying.) Lift out with a skimmer, and drain and place on a heated dish, and sprinkle freely with powdered white sugar, and serve hot. In arranging them in the dish, make the fritters rise into a pretty pyramid and sprinkle with the sugar. Never pierce fritters with a fork, as it will cause the steam to evaporate and make the fritters heavy. A fritter that is well made should be light and puffy.

#### Plain Fritter Batter for Meats, Poultry, etc.

Pâte à Beignets pour les Viandes, les Volailles, etc.

1 Cup Flour. 1 Cup of Water. 2 Eggs.
½ Teaspoonful of Salt.
1 Tablespoonful of Melted Butter.

Beat the yolks of the eggs and the flour together, and add the melted butter and the salt. Then add the water, and beat well, and finally add the whites of the eggs, beaten to a stiff froth. Some add a half teaspoonful of baking powder. This is according to taste. If the eggs are well beaten, there will be no need for the baking powder.

This batter is used in making pork, kidney or chicken fritters, or fritters of left-over meats, and also for all meats or fish which must be rolled in batter.

### Apple Fritters.
Beignets de Pommes.

3 Fresh Apples.
1 Gill of Brandy or Rum (if desired).
Grated Peel of ½ Lemon.
Powdered Sugar.

Peel and core the apples, which will be all the nicer if they are a little tart. Take out the seeds and core. Cut them into slices, more or less thick or thin, according to taste. The thin slices are recommended. Soak them in brandy or good whisky, or rum, for the space of two hours, sprinkling with the grated zest of a lemon and sugar, according to judgment. Two tablespoonfuls of sugar should be sufficient for the zest or rind of half a lemon. Make a batter à la Créole and have ready a deep saucepan of boiling lard. Drain the apples. Dip the slices, one at a time, into the batter, lift out with a large kitchen spoon, drop into the boiling lard, and fry to a golden brown. Then lift out with a skimmer, and set on brown paper, in the mouth of the oven, and drain. Sift powdered white sugar over them, and serve hot, piling high in pyramidal shape, and sprinkling again with powdered white sugar. Serve as an entremet or as a dessert. The liquor may be omitted, and the apples simply cut into very thin slices; then proceed with the dropping in batter and frying.

### Apricot Fritters.
Beignets d'Abricots.

6 Fresh or a Half Can of Apricots.
1 Glass of Madeira Wine.
3 Tablespoonfuls of Sugar.
Grated Lemon Peel.

If the apricots are fresh, peel and stone them, and cut into halves. Then sprinkle them with the grated zest of a lemon and sugar, and pour over them sufficient Madeira Wine to thoroughly saturate. Cover and set aside for two hours. Then drain off the liquor. Make a Fruit Fritter Batter à la Créole, and have ready a saucepan filled deep with boiling lard. Dip the apricots, one by one, into the batter, and drop from the spoon into the lard, and let them fry to a golden brown. In serving, proceed in exactly the same manner as in the directions given for Apple Fritters. (See recipe.)

### Banana Fritters.
Beignets de Bananes.

3 Bananas. Fritter Batter a la Creole.

Make a Fritter Batter à la Créole. Peel the bananas and then cut them in halves. Slice them incely, according to length. Dip in the fritter batter, and proceed to cook and serve as in the recipe for Apple Fritters. The bananas may also be cut into round slices. In this case, two or three slices at a time must be put in each fritter. The method of cutting by lengths is recommended.

### Banana Fritters with Cognac or Rum.
Beignets de Bananes au Cognac ou au Rhum.

3 Bananas. Fritter Batter a la Creole.
Fritter Batter a la Creole.

If "Beignets de Bananes au Cognac" or "au Rhum" are desired, slice the banana and sprinkle with sugar, and cover with sufficient Cognac or Rum to saturate well. Set them aside for half an hour, then drain, and proceed as in Apple Fritters.

### Brioche Fritters.
Beignets de Brioches.

3 Small Brioches.
1 Tablespoonful of Essence of Vanilla.
Lemon or Orange Flower Water.
Creole Fritter Batter. Powdered White Sugar.

Cut the Brioche (see recipe under chapter on Breads) into slices, more or less thin, and soak them in sweetened milk, to which you have added the essence of orange flower water, vanilla or lemon. Drop them into a light fritter batter, or simply drop them into boiling lard, fry to a golden yellow, sprinkle with white sugar, and serve.

### Cherry Fritters.
Beignets de Cerises.

1 Pint of Fine Cherries. 1 Egg.
1 Pint of Milk.
1 Tablespoonful of Madeira or Malaga Wine.
1 Tablespoonful of Sugar.
The Zest of a Lemon.

Prepare the cherries by taking out the stones. Make them into a thick marmalade, adding a tablespoonful of Madeira or Malaga Wine. Soak nice slices of bread in milk and egg, seasoned well with a tablespoonful of sugar and the grated zest of a lemon. Take the slices, when well-soaked, and spread the marmalade well over them, making it adhere very thickly and closely into the meshes of the bread. Then fry in boiling lard, sprinkle nicely with powdered sugar, and serve hot. Or mix the cherries in Creole Fritter Batter, drop by spoonfuls into the boiling lard, fry to a golden brown, drain in the oven, and sprinkle with powdered white sugar and serve hot.

### Corn Fritters.
Beignets de Farine de Maïs.

1 Pint of Corn Meal. 1 Pint of Boiling Milk.
1 Tablespoonful of Butter.
3 Eggs. ¼ Cup of Sugar. Flavoring to Taste.
¼ Spoonful of Salt.

Beat the yolks of the eggs and the cornmeal together, and add the melted butter and the milk, stirring and beating well. Add the salt and any flavoring extract preferred, and, lastly, the whites of the eggs, beaten to a stiff froth. Fry in boiling lard, dropping in the lard by spoonfuls. By omitting the sugar you will have nice corn cakes to eat with butter. In this case do not use the same quantity of lard, but bake on a griddle.

### Elderflower Fritters.

Beignets à la Fleur de Sureau.

1 Cup of Tender White Elder Flowers.
1 Cup of Sugar.
White of 2 Eggs.   Creole Fritter Batter.

Select a sufficient quantity of beautiful, tender white flowers, and soak them in the whites of two eggs, beaten to a snowy froth, and well blended with white sugar. Dip them by spoonfuls into the fritter batter, and fry according to directions. This is an old time Creole recipe, almost lost in our day.

### Fig Fritters.

Beignets de Figues.

1 Pint of Fresh Figs.
½ Cup of Sugar.
Creole Fritter Batter.

Pare the figs, taking off every particle of the skin. Then cut up nicely, sprinkle with sugar and let them stand for half an hour. Then add the juice to fritter batter and proceed as in Apple Fritters. (See recipe.)

### Fritters Soufflé à la Vanille.

Beignets Soufflé à la Vanille.

3 Ounces of Flour.   1 Tablespoonful Butter.
½ Pint of Milk.
1 Tablespoonful of Sugar.
The Yolks of 2 Eggs.   The White of 1 Egg.
1 Spoonful of Whipped Cream.
1 Vanilla Bean.   Powdered White Sugar.

Put the milk into a a saucepan and infuse the vanilla bean, and let the milk reduce to one-half. Then remove the bean, and add a tablespoonful of butter, and, when it comes to a good boil, add the flour, well sifted; stir briskly till a stiff paste is formed that will not adhere to the saucepan. Then take off the fire and add an ounce of powdered white sugar that has been beaten well with the yolks of two eggs. Have ready the white of one egg beaten to a stiff froth, and mix a spoonful of whipped cream with this, and add to the paste. Mix well, and then roll the paste out on a flour board that has been slightly sprinkled with flour, and sprinkle lightly on top with the flour. Cut into small cakes, drop into very hot lard, and let them cook to a golden brown. Then arrange nicely on a dish, sift powdered sugar over them, and send to the table hot.

### Lemon Fritters.

Beignets de Citron.

1 Pint of Creole Fritter Batter.
The Juice of 1 Lemon.
2-3 Cup of Sugar.

Make a plain Creole batter for fruit fritters, and add the juice of a lemon, and sugar to taste, and proceed as directed in cooking and serving Apple Fritters.

### Orange Fritters.

Beignets d'Oranges.

2 Large Louisiana Oranges.
Creole Fritter Batter.

Pare the oranges, taking off every particle of the white inner skin. Then slice nicely, and take out the seeds. Sprinkle with sugar, and let them stand for an hour. Then add the juice to the fritter batter, and proceed as in Apple Fritters. Or, better still, place the oranges thus sliced over a slow fire, add a little water and several tablespoonfuls of sugar, and let them cook till you have a light marmalade. Take it off, let it cool, cover the slices of orange well with the jellied juice, dip in the batter, and proceed as directed in recipe for Apple Fritters. (See recipe.)

### Peach Fritters.

Beignets de Pêches.

6 Fresh or Canned Peaches (½ Can.)
Madeira Wine.   3 Tablespoonfuls of Sugar.
Grated Lemon Peel.

If the peaches are fresh, peel and stone them, and cut in halves. Then sprinkle them with the grated zest of a lemon and sugar, and pour over them sufficient Madeira Wine for them to be saturated. Cover and set aside for two hours. Then drain off the liquor. Make a Fruit Fritter Batter à la Créole, and have ready a saucepan filled deep with boiling lard. Dip the peaches, one by one, into the batter, and drop from the spoon into the lard, and let them fry to a golden brown. Then proceed in exactly the same manner of serving as in the directions given for Apple Fritters. (See recipe.)

### Pear Fritters.

Beignets de Poires.

3 Fresh Pears or 4 Canned Pears.
Brandy or Rum (if desired).
Grated Lemon Peel.   Powdered Sugar.

Peel and core the pears, which will be all the nicer if they are a little tart. Take out the seeds and core. Cut them into slices, more or less thick or thin, according to taste. The thin slices are recommended.

Soak them in brandy or good whisky or rum for the space of two hours, sprinkling with the zest of a lemon and sugar, according to judgment. Two tablespoonfuls of sugar should be sufficient. Make a batter a la Creole, and have ready a deep saucepan of boiling lard. Drain the pears. Dip the slices, one at a time, into the batter; lift out with a large kitchen spoon, drop into the boiling lard, and fry to a golden brown. Then lift out with a skimmer, and set on brown paper, in the mouth of the oven, and drain. Sift powdered white sugar over them, and serve hot, piling high in pyramidal shape, and sprinkling again with powdered white sugar. Serve as an entremet or as a dessert. The liquor may be omitted, and the pears simply cut into very thin slices; then proceed, dropping in batter and frying. Serve as directed above.

### Pineapple Fritters.
Beignets d'Ananas.
½ a Pineapple. Fritter Batter.
½ Cup of Sugar. 1 Gill White Wine.

Slice the pineapple, and cut the slices in halves. Sprinkle with sugar and White Wine, and let them soak for an hour. Then proceed as in Apple Fritters. Or, simply sprinkle with sugar, let them stand one hour, add the juice to the fritter batter, and proceed as above.

### Pineapple Cream Fritters.
Beignets d'Ananas à la Crème.
½ a Pineapple. ½ Cup of Sugar.
1 Gill of White Wine.
Cream Puff Paste.

For these fritters it is necessary to make a Cream Paste. (See recipe.) Prepare the pineapple as in the above recipe; then dip in the Cream Puff Paste and proceed as in Apple Fritters. (See recipe.)

### Queen Fritters.
Beignets à la Reine.
1 Cup of Cream Puff Filling.
A Cream Puff Batter.
¼ Cup of Grated Almonds.
1 Glass of Sherry Wine.
Cold Sherry Wine Sauce or French Sauce.

Prepare a Cream Puff Batter and a Cream Puff Filling. (See recipe.) If the flavor of almonds is desired, add a few finely-grated almonds that have been steeped in Sherry Wine. Have ready the frying pan, with boiling lard. Roll the cream batter into small balls, and fry till they swell to the size of an egg. Skim out with a skimmer, and drain, and, when cold, split one side with a very sharp knife, and fill with the filling; close, and continue till all are filled. Serve cold with Sherry Wine Sauce or Peach Sauce.

### Rice Fritters.
Beignets de Riz.
1 Cup of Cold Rice.
1 Tablespoonful of Butter. Yolks of 2 Eggs.
1 Tablespoonful of Orange or Lemon Essence.
A Pinch of Cinnamon.

Take one cup of cold rice, mash it well, and then pass through a sieve. Season with the orange essence or lemon, a pinch of cinnamon, and a tablespoonful of butter. Add the beaten yolks of two eggs. Then make the rice into small boulettes or balls, roll in a beaten egg, fry to a golden brown, sprinkle with white sugar and serve.

### Sago Croquettes.
Croquettes de Sagou.
Equal Parts of Sago Marmalade and Rice Croquettes.
Creole Fritter Batter.
Port Wine Sauce.

Prepare Croquettes of Rice (see recipe), adding equal parts of Sago Marmalade. Dip in fritter batter, and fry to a golden brown, and serve with Port Wine Sauce.

### Strawberry Fritters.
Beignets de Fraises.
1 Pint of Fine Large Strawberries.
2 Tablespoonfuls of White Wine.
Grated Zest of ½ Lemon.

For this purpose have fine, large strawberries. Make a Fritter Batter à la Créole, only just before adding the whites of the eggs add the grated zest of half a lemon and two tablespoonfuls of White Wine. The batter must be of the consistency of thick cream. Stem the strawberries, and drop them into the batter. Proceed to fry as in recipe given for Apple Fritters (see recipe), allowing two or three strawberries to each fritter. Or make a marmalade of the strawberries, keeping them whole and proceed as in Orange Fritters. (See recipe.)

### Surprise Fritters.
Beignets en Surprise.
6 Nice, Small Ripe Apples.
1 Glass of Brandy.
The Zest of 1 Lemon. The White of 1 Egg.
¼ Teaspoonful of Ground Cinnamon.
½ Teaspoon of Ground Allspice.

Take nice, small, ripe apples, and peel them. Cut off about an inch at the top end, and then scoop out the interior, leaving the apple frame whole. Take out all the seeds and cores from these cuttings, and mince them very fine. Then put them into a dish and put also the apple frames, and cover them with brandy. Sprinkle well with the grated zest of a lemon and ground cinnamon and allspice, and add to the minced portion of the apples a few apricots, well minced. After an hour, take the frames out of the marinade. Then drain the apple stuffing of the brandy and add to it the white of an egg, well beaten to a stiff froth. Mix this well, and then fill the interiors of the apple frames with it. Cover with the pieces of apple that were taken from the tops, and which must be immersed in the marinade, like the frames, covering this opening well. Take the fritter batter, and immerse each piece gently, just enough for the batter to cover, and place in a frying pan of boiling lard, and fry to a golden brown. Place on a dish, sprinkle well with powdered sugar, and serve hot. Or the apples may be simply placed in the oven, sprinkled with sugar, a little water added, and let them bake till a beautiful golden brown. This is an excellent old-fashioned Creole recipe.

### Sweet Omelet Fritters.

Beignets d'Omelette au Sucre.

A Plain Omelet.
2 Tablespoonfuls of Sugar.
1 Tablespoonful of Brandy.
Creole Fritter Batter. Powdered White Sugar.

Make an omelet (see recipe), and add two tablespoonfuls of sugar and a tablespoonful of good brandy. Cook it nicely and very soft, and then cut it into small slices. Plunge these into the fritter batter, let them fry to a golden brown, and then drain in the mouth of the oven on brown pepper. Place in a heated dish, sprinkle well with fine white sugar, and serve hot.

### Stewed Apples.

Compote de Pommes.

6 Apples, Large and Firm.
Sugar to Taste. The Zest of Half an Orange.
1 Blade Mace.
1 Stick Ground Cinnamon. 4 Ground Allspice.

Pare the apples and cut into quarters or semi-quarters, removing the cores and seeds. Add half a cup of water. Put them into an agate or a porcelain-lined saucepan; and strew generously with sugar. Let them simmer gently for half an hour. Then add the zest of half an orange, grated, and the ground spices. Let all simmer gently till they form a rich tender compote, that is, until not the least semblance remains of being uncooked. This compote may be served hot during the meal, or it may be used as a dessert, with cream or milk.

Apples may be stewed whole in the same manner, only remember to extract the core with a fine knife.

### Baked Apples.

Pommes Roties.

6 Fine Apples.
6 Spoonfuls of Sugar.  1 Cupful of Water.

Cut the blossom end of the apple, and wash, but do not peel. Set them in a baking pan, heap a spoonful of sugar over each in the little place scooped out at the blossom end, and pour a cupful of water in the bottom of the pan. Set in the oven, and bake till very tender. Place in a dish, pour over the syrup, and serve either hot or cold. They are much nicer served cold, with a glass of milk. They are then used as a dessert.

### Fried Apples.

Pommes Frites.

3 Fine Apples.  Boiling Lard.
½ Cup of White Powdered Sugar.

Pare the apples and cut into round slices. Have ready a pan of boiling lard, and fry to a delicate golden brown. Place in a colander, heated, and in which you have placed a piece of brown paper. Drain in the mouth of the oven. Place in a dish, and sprinkle with sugar, and serve hot with roast meat, roast pork, etc.

### Apple Charlotte.

Charlotte de Pommes.

6 Large Apples.  6 Apricots.
3 Tablespoonfuls of Butter.
1 Cup of Sugar, or Sugar to Taste.

Pare the apples and then cut them into slices, taking out the seeds and core. Then put them in a saucepan with three large tablespoonfuls of butter. Add a little water to stew gently, and add the apricots, if you have them. In this case use four tablespoonfuls of butter and ground cinnamon, and allspice to taste. Let all cook to a nice marmalade. Then take off and add a quarter of a grated nutmeg. Then cut six slices of bread, and butter well. Butter a pan and garnish it around the bottom and around with the slices of bread, which must be very thin. Then fill with the apples, and cover on top with the bread. Dot with butter and sprinkle with sugar, and put in an oven and bake to a golden brown. When done, carefully loosen the edges and turn into a dish. Serve it hot, with sugar and cream, or with a Custard Sauce, flavored with good brandy. (See recipe.)

### Cherry Charlotte.

Charlotte de Cerises.

1 Pound Cherries.  1 Pound White Sugar.
2 Tablespoonfuls of Butter.
The Soft of Bread.

Seed the cherries, and butter the bottom of a pudding dish. Cover the bottom with a layer of the bread crumbs which must be soft. Then add a layer of the cherries, which have been cooked like the apples, into a marmalade. Sprinkle with sugar, and add another layer of cherries, and then a layer of bread crumbs, alternating till the dish is filled, letting the last layer be of crumbs, which you will dot with bits of butter. Put in an oven and bake for an hour. Serve cold with cream.

### Currant Charlotte.
Charlotte de Groseilles.

1 Pound of Currants.
1 Pound of White Sugar.
2 Tablespoonfuls of Butter.
The Soft of Bread.

Proceed exactly as for Cherry Charlotte, making a marmalade of the currants, and using the same proportion as above.

### Raspberry or Blackberry Charlotte.
Charlotte de Bramboises ou de Mûres.

1 Pound of Raspberries or Blackberries.
1 Pound of White Sugar.
2 Tablespoonfuls of Butter.
The Soft of Bread.

Stew the berries, making a marmalade, and proceed exactly as in the recipe for Cherry Charlotte.

### Fruit Toasts With Cherries, Apricots or Raspberries.

Croûtes de Fruites aux Cerises aux Abricots ou aux Framboises.
6 Slices of French Toast.
1 Cup of Fruit Marmalade.
Cream to Serve.

Prepare thin slices of very dry French toast, and butter generously. Take a dish, and lay on each slice of toast generous allotments of the fruits you wish to serve. The fruit must be made into a marmalade. Pour all remains of syrup over the toast, and serve with cream.

### Fried Bananas.
Bananas Frites.

4 Bananas.       Boiling Lard.
White Powdered Sugar.

Peel the bananas, and cut them in two, lengthwise. Then slice lengthwise about a quarter of an inch in thickness. Have ready a pan of boiling lard. Lay the bananas in it, and fry brown, first on one side and then on the other, sifting with a little powdered sugar. When done, skim out of the pan, place neatly in a dish, sprinkle with powdered sugar again, and serve hot, as an entrée. This is a celebrated and cheap Creole dish, and is seen on the tables of all classes. The banana stalls in the French market are famous, and at every corner or so, here and there throughout the city, there are fruit stalls, where the banana is always to be found in a perfect state, and very fresh and inviting. Bananas are also served in their natural state, as a fruit dessert

### Stewed Peaches.
Compote de Peches.

10 Medium-Sized Peaches.
1 Pint of Cold Water.
½ Pound of Granulated Sugar.
1 Gill of Kirsch or Brandy, if desired.

Peel the peaches and cut them into quarters, carefully removing the stones. Put them into a saucepan, with a pint of cold water and a half pound of granulated sugar; set on the stove, and, when they begin to boil, skim well. Then let them cook for six minutes longer, stirring slowly; avoid mashing the peaches. Remove from the fire and add, if desired, a gill of Kirsch or Brandy; mix well and pour the peaches into a dessert dish to cool. Serve cold, either plain or with cream. The peaches may be boiled whole.

### Orange Salad.
Salade d'Oranges.

6 Fine Louisiana Oranges.
3-4 Pound of Powdered Sugar.
1 Glass of Rum or Brandy.

Peel the oranges whole, removing the peel entirely down to the tips of the stem end. Cut in slices, and cut out the seeds. Pile the oranges in a neat heap in a dish. Sprinkle with powdered sugar. Boil some sugar to a syrup, using about half a pound to half a pound of oranges. Add a glass of rum or brandy, and, when cold, pour over the oranges and serve.

### Sweet Omelet Entremets.
Entremets d'Omelettes au Sucre.

Rum Omelet, Omelette Soufflé, Omelet aux Confitures, etc., are also served as Sweet Entremets These were specially treated under the chapter on "Eggs." (See recipes.)

### Wine and Liquor Entremets.
Entremets au Vin et aux Liqueurs.

Roman Punch, Punch à la Cardinale, Sorbet à la Royale, and other fancy concoctions of ices or sherbets and liqueurs, are also served as entremets. Indeed, no elegant feast is considered complete without a Punch à la Romaine, Ponche à la Cardinale, or a Sorbet à la Royale, etc. (See recipe.)

### DOUGHNUTS.
Croxignolles.

½ Cup Sugar.   1 Pint of Milk.   3 Eggs.
2 Tablespoonfuls of Butter.
½ Cake of Compressed Yeast.
1 Teaspoonful of Salt.
Flour in Sufficient Quantity to Make a Dough.

Scald the milk, and then add the butter, and let it stand and cool.

When it has cooled, add the yeast and the sugar, and beat in the flour gradually. Beat well, and then cover, and set the mixture in a warm place over night. But be careful to have the warmth only moderate. In the morning beat the eggs till very light, and stir them into the butter. Then add more flour, sufficient to make a dough, which must be soft. Knead this dough lightly, and stand it away to rise. When it has risen well, take one-half of the dough and roll it on the biscuit board, and then cut into doughnuts, using a large cake or biscuit cutter. Then take a small cutter and make a small hole in the center of each doughnut. They may also be cut into square shape, and slashed gently with the cutter or knife. Spread a clean towel over the table, and dust it lightly with flour, and let the doughnuts stand upon it for half an hour, being well covered, either with a towel or some other cover. Let the frying kettle then be ready, with boiling fat or lard. It must be so deep that the doughnuts can swim in it. Put the doughnuts into the boiling lard, and let them fry to a golden brown. Do not stick the doughnut through with a fork, or it will fall immediately. When a beautiful dark golden brown, drain out of the pan with a skimmer, place on a hot dish, sprinkle with powdered sugar, and serve hot. You will have the true Creole "Croxignolle."

## PANCAKES.

### Crépes.

8 Eggs. 3-4 Pound of Sugar.
1 Cup of Milk.
¼ Teaspoonful of Salt.

Many there are in New Orleans today who remember the delightful old-time crepe parties that the belles and beaux used to give. The word would go from mouth to mouth that some great, cheery kitchen in the rue Esplanade, the rue Royale or the rue Rampart would be at the disposal of the young folks for the evening for a "crépe" party, and thither the young gallants and numbers of "Ma Belle Créole" would gather, and the dexterity with which a young lady could toss a "crepe," was often the open sesame to some young man's heart. The great secret in tossing a "crépe" was to do it with accuracy and celerity, and so neatly that it would settle down in its place in the frying pan just as though it had not been touched, with no rough edges around, and as smooth and round as a young globe. The old Creole darky cooks prided themselves on the way that they could toss a "crépe," and the great secret that they had mastered in making them as thin as possible, and exceedingly tender.

As the "crepes" were tossed by the girls, they were caught by the young men and piled in a hot plate. Then they were served hot, with butter, and molasses, and were each spread with sugar and cinnamon and butter mixed and rolled. There was as much art in rolling the "crepes" as in serving them. But more generally they were simply buttered and rolled in our unexcelled Louisiana molasses, or "La Cuite," a deposit of sugar which comes from the molasses.

These innocent diversions of long ago, like the old-time molasses candy pullings, or "soirees de candi tire," and the quaint old-time "eau sucré" parties have passed out of the life of the old French quarter. They are among the most gentle memories of those ancient days.

"Crepes" are made as follows, the quantity of ingredients given above being sufficient for six persons:

Beat the yolks and whites of the eggs together. Then add the flour, and beat very light. Add the milk, pouring gradually, and having the batter no thicker than cream. Add the salt, and mix well. Now comes the most important part, the baking. Unless this is properly done, your labor has fallen to naught. Have a wide pancake pan, and let it be very hot. Grease it with butter, or, better still, with a piece of fat bacon. This is the safest way, as you will not have a pancake swimming in grease, a most undesirable offering at any table. Pour in batter sufficient to just cover the bottom of the pan. In a minute, or perhaps less time, the cake must be ready to turn. This is the critical moment that the old Creole cooks used to understand so well. By a peculiar sleight of hand that comes only by experience, the cake was tossed and caught in the pan, and the brown side was brought up without failure, and the cake lay just as smooth as though untouched. Those who wish to learn the art must begin slowly at first. If you have never tossed a pancake, and attempt to do it before you have caught the trick, as the old Creoles used to call it, you will make a miserable failure, and have only a mingled heap of batter. Go slowly, and learn. The old darkies used to say, when one of their number could toss a "crépe" to the top of the chimney and bring it down again slick and smooth, with the brown side up, tossing minute after minute, "like lightning," that the woman was "for sure one hoodoo, and the old devil himself had taught her to toss and fry." But the pancakes thus tossed savored neither of fire nor brimstone, and, when rolled up with infinite art and ready to serve hot on a dainty china dish, many were the encomiums that masters and mistresses bestowed upon their faithful old slaves. "Crêpes" may be served as an entrée at breakfast, dinner or supper. They make an excellent luncheon dish.

### French Pancakes.

Crêpes à la Française.

¾ Pound of Flour. 4 Eggs.
½ Pint of Cold Milk.
4 Ounces of Powdered Sugar.

Sift the flour into a bowl. Break in the eggs; beat well, and add one ounce of powdered sugar. Mix thoroughly with a spatula, and then add the cold milk, pouring it in gradually. Mix well for six minutes. Have ready a clean griddle; butter lightly, and, when hot, drop on it about two large spoonfuls of the batter at a time. Let the cakes bake two minutes on each side, and then turn and bake two minutes on the other. Turn the pancake on a dish; sprinkle generously with powdered sugar. Continue baking the cakes and turning on the dish, sprinkling each in turn with the powdered sugar, till all is used. The above quantity of batter will make one dozen pancakes.

### French Pancakes With Jelly.

Crêpes Français à la Gelé.

¾ Pound of Flour. 4 Eggs.
½ Pint of Cold Milk.
4 Ounces of Powdered Sugar.
1 Glass of Jelly.

Prepare the batter exactly as in the above recipe. When the pancakes are nicely cooked, arrange them neatly on a dish, and spread over each a half tablespoonful of apple, strawberry, raspberry, currant, peach or any kind of jelly desired; then roll them up nicely and dress on a dessert dish and sprinkle powdered white sugar over them. Send to the table hot. Some glaze the surface of each pancake with a red hot iron. But this is a matter of taste and decoration.

## CHAPTER XXXII.

### DESSERTS.

Des Desserts.

Desserts are many and varied. They comprise Compotes, Puddings, Pies and Pastry, Cakes, Ices, Creams, etc., all of which are specially treated in order. The Creoles are famous for their dainty and delightful desserts.

### COMPOTES.

Des Compotes.

Compotes are fruits preserved in very little sugar, and made as needed in the household. The fruits are always blanched, and a little sugar is added for them to absorb, and then they are put into dishes, and the syrup is poured over them. The Creoles often cut the fruits into many pretty shapes, especially apples and peaches. It is always better to blanch the fruits in thinned syrup than in water. To preserve the whiteness of the peeled fruits, they should be peeled as rapidly as possible, and put into the saucepan with the water or syrups and blanched only long enough to soften, and then arranged in the dish and covered with the syrup. If the fruits are not ripe, they ought to be put into syrup over the fire to cook a little.

All compotes may be served as desserts or entremets.

### Compote of Apples.

Compote de Pommes.

1 Dozen Apples. 1 Pound of Sugar.
½ Cup of Water.

Pare the apples, cut them in quarters, cut out the cores, and pierce them several times, to drain the juice. Boil six apples in one pound of sugar and half a cup of water, and add the finely cut peel of a lemon, together with the lemon juice. When they are well blanched, take them out, without letting them cook too much, and place in a dish. They must be soft, but not pithy. Put the apples that you have cut into quarters into the syrup, and let hem boil o a jelly in the juice. Then drain well, and pour over the apples. Sprinkle with a little grated nutmeg and powdered sugar. This is excellent.

To make a compote of whole apples, first remove the core its whole length, by inserting a long tin cutter at one end, and then at the other end, and with the finger force the core out. In this way you will not split the apple. Finish as in the above recipe.

### Stuffed Apple Compote.
#### Compote de Pommes Farcies.
1 Dozen Apples. 1 Pound of Sugar.
1 Cup of Orange or Apricot Marmalade.
* Cup of Water.
¼ Teaspoon of Ground Cinnamon.
¼ of a Grated Nutmeg.

Pare fine, large apples, take out the core, and be careful to leave the apple entire. Then fill the opening with orange or apricot marmalade, and put them together in a pan with a pound of clarified sugar. Add a half cup of water. Let them cook soft in the oven, sprinkling first with grated cinnamon. Add grated nutmeg when done, and serve either hot or cold.

### Apricot Compote.
#### Compote d'Abricots.
1 Dozen Apricots. 1 Pound of Sugar.
¼ Pound of Apple Jelly.

Cut the apricots in two, and peel. Rinse them in cold water, and then proceed to cook them in syrup made of sugar and a little water. Add a little Apple Jelly to the sugar after you have taken out the apricots. Mix the jelly well with the syrup, pour over the apricots and serve.

### Banana Compote.
#### Compote de Bananes.
1 Dozen Bananas. ½ Pound of Sugar.
The Juice of Half a Lemon.
½ Cup of Water.

Peel the Bananas and cut them into halves. Put the sugar and the water on to boil, and after ten minutes add the lemon juice. Then put the bananas, a few at a time, into the hot syrup and let them stew gently. After a half hour take them out lay in a dish, pour over the hot liquid syrup, and serve either hot or cold.

### Compote of Banana Cassa.
#### Compote de Banane Cassa.
1 Banana Cassa.
1¼ Pounds of Granulated Sugar.
1 Quart of Water.
¼ Teaspoonful Each of Ground Allspice, Cinnamon and Mace.
¼ Grated Nutmeg.
1 Teaspoonful of Vanilla or Lemon Extract.

The "Banana Cassa" is a form of vegetable fruit that is very much used among the Creoles in making compotes, etc. It grows on a vine similar to the gourd or "Mirliton," only, unlike the latter, it is considered a fruit, and is served as a dessert. It is a long, pear-shaped fruit, resembling the banana in color and odor and shape, only it is longer and and broder. Hence the name, "Banana Cassa." It is prepared as follows:

Take the ripe fruit, peel it, and cut into slices of about an inch in thickness. Remove the seeds and place the fruit in a bowl of water, to which you will add a small piece of lime; or simply immerse in lime-water. Let it soak for three hours. Then remove it and rinse in cold water. Prepare a syrup, allowing one and a quarter pounds of granulated sugar to one quart of water, and when it begins to boil well add the fruit, ground spices and nutmeg, and let all boil till the fruit becomes transparent. If flavoring is preferred to the natural taste, add, according to taste, a tablespoonful of Extract of Lemon or Vanilla. Let it cool and serve as a dessert. It is delicious with Whipped Cream.

### Compote of Blackberries.
#### Compote de Mûres.
1 Quart Blackberries.
¼ Pound of Sugar.

Select fine berries, but not too ripe. Wash them in cold water, and drain through a sieve. Boil the sugar, and add the berries, and let them boil up once very gently. Put them into a dish, pour the jelly over and serve.

### Cherry Compote.
#### Compote de Cerises.
1 Quart of Cherries. ¾ Pound of Sugar.
¼ Cup of Water.

To one pound of stoned cherries allow the above amount of sugar. Put the sugar and water into a saucepan, and when it makes a syrup add the cherries. Let them boil up several times. Then drain them with the skimming spoon, and put them in a dish, and add to the juice a glassful of Currant Jelly. Let it boil to a thin jelly, and pour it, when half cold, over the cherries. The Currant Jelly may be omitted and the reduced cherry syrup used alone.

### Compote of Cocoanut.
#### Compote de Coco.
1 Cocoanut. The Juice of 1 Lemon.
½ Teaspoonful of Salt.
1 Pound of Fine White Loaf Sugar.
1 Tablespoonful of Vanilla Exeract.

Divide the cocoanut into quarters Peel off all the brown skin, and then soak the clean, white pieces in cold water, with a little lemon juice and a little salt. Cut them in thin slices first, and then in thick threadlike shreds, just as you would vegetables for Julienne soup. This must be done, however, before soaking in the lemon juice and salt. Then drain the shreds in a clean sieve, and wash them in another water, to free them entirely from oil. Drain well. Boil one pound of the finest white loaf sugar. Then remove it from the fire, and throw in the prepared cocoanut, and set back on the fire. Let it come to a good boil, stirring lightly with a silver fork. Then lift them out with the fork, after they have boiled up once, and place the cocoanut shreds in a sieve. Let the sugar boil up well again. Add the juice of a lemon to the syrup, boil it very thin, and then throw in the cocoanut shreds, mixing them very lightly in the syrup. Separate the shreds carefully with two silver forks, holding one fork in each hand; dish up in a raised pile in a dish; when cold, pour over the clear syrup, flavoring with any extract you wish, preferably vanilla, and serve.

### Compote of Cranberries.
Compote d'Airelles.

1 Quart of Cranberries. 1½ Pounds of Sugar.
The Juice of 1 Lemon.

Wash and drain the cranberries. Then boil as in Cranberry Jelly, only do not let the cranberries get mashed. Take them out with a skimmer, and add a half pound of sugar to the syrup, and the juice of a lemon. Boil to a syrup and pour over the berries and serve cold.

### Compote of Currants.
Compote de Groseilles.

1 Quart of Currants. ¾ Pound of Sugar.
½ Cup of Water.

Select nice berries and pick clean and wash well in cold water, and drain them through a sieve. Boil the sugar and add the berries. Let them boil up once very gently. Put them in a dish, pour the syrup over and serve.

### Compote of Damsons.
Compote de Prunes.

1 Quart of Damsons.
¾ Pound of Sugar. ¼ Cup of Water.

Pick off the stems of the damsons and prick them all over with a pin. Let them simmer in sugar, which you will have boiled to a syrup for about fifteen minutes. Then proceed as in a Compote of Cherries. (See recipe.)

### Compote of Dried Fruits.
Compote de Fruits Secs.

½ Pound of Dried Fruit.
½ Pound of Sugar. ½ Cup of Water.
The Juice of 1 Lemon.

All dried fruits, such as apples, peaches, apricots, crab apples, etc., are prepared in the same manner as compote of apples and peaches. Only allow the dried fruit to soak in cold water a long while, say about two hours, to swell up. Then boil, and afterwards pour into a syrup of boiling sugar, and proceed as in other compotes.

### Compote of Figs.
Compote de Figues.

1 Quart of Figs. ½ Cup of Water.
1 Pound of Sugar.
The Juice of 1 Lemon.

Use figs that are not quite ripe. Break off the stalks, and prick them all over, and let them simmer in a syrup, as above. Then proceed in exactly the same manner as for Compote of Cherries. (See recipe.)

### Figs à la Créole.
Figues à la Créole.

1 Quart of Ripe Figs.
½ Pound of Sugar.

Stem and peel and cut the figs in quarters. Figs are always abundant with us in August and September. Place in a dish, sprinkle well with sugar, and serve with their own syrup, ice cold.

### Compote of Lemons.
Compote de Citrons.

½ Dozen Lemons.
1 Pound of Sugar. 1 Cup of Water.

A Compote of whole lemons is prepared in exactly the same manner as the above, using twice the amount of sugar, or sugar to taste. When squeezed thoroughly and boiled they make an excellent Creole remedy for colds and coughs.

### Compote of Malaga Grapes.
Compote de Raisins Blancs.

1 Pound of Malaga Grapes.
¾ Pound of Sugar. ½ Cup of Water.

Wash the grapes, then cut a slit in the grape on one side, and take out the seeds. Put the fruit in cold water, and let it boil. Take off the fire, and let it stand uncovered for a time, and then put in cold water. When cold lift them out with a skimming spoon. Put the grapes in clarified sugar, which you will have boiled almost to a thread, and let them boil up once. Skim them out, and put in a dish. Boil the sugar to half the quantity in syrup, and pour over, and serve.

### Compote of Mespilus or Japan Plums.
Compote de Mespilus.

1 Quart of Mespilus. 1½ Cups of Water.
¾ Pound of Sugar.
Juice of 1 Lemon.

This is a species of delicious Japan plum very common in our State. Peel, stone and proceed in exactly the same manner as for Compote of Cherries. (See recipe.)

### Compote of Oranges.
Compote d'Oranges.

1 Dozen Louisiana Oranges.
1 Pound of Sugar. The Juice of Half a Lemon.
½ Cup of Water.

Peel the oranges, and cut them into halves crosswise, and take out the seeds and the inner pulp. Put the sugar and the water on to boil, and after ten minutes add the lemon juice. Then put a few of the oranges at a time into the hot syrup, and let them stew gently. After a half hour take them out, lay in a dish, pour over the hot liquid syrup and serve either hot or cold.

### Compote of Whole Oranges.
Compote d'Oranges Entiéres.

1 Dozen Louisiana Oranges.
1 Pound of Sugar.

Boil the oranges, with their peel, gently in water for twenty minutes. Turn the oranges very thinly and spirally, scoring out, if possible, all the inner pulp and peeling. Make a syrup by boiling the sugar, and add the oranges. Let them simmer for twenty minutes longer. Take off, and allow the oranges to remain in their juice for several hours. Dish them up in a compote dish, and pour over their syrup on the instant of sending to the table.

### Oranges, Creole Style.
Oranges à la Créole.

1 Dozen Fine Louisiana Oranges.
¼ Pound of Sugar.

Peel the oranges and cut in slices, and sprinkle with sugar, to form a syrup. Let them stand for several hours in a cool place, and serve either as a preliminary to breakfast or as a dessert. This is a delightful Creole way of serving oranges.

### Compote of Peaches.
Compote de Pêches.

1 Dozen Peaches. 1 Pound of Sugar.
½ Cup of Water.

Take well-grown, somewhat unripe peaches. Then cut them in two, and take out the stones. Put the peaches into boiling water, and let them stand till they are soft, and then throw in cold water till cold. Peel them and put them into the sugar, adding a little water, and let them boil up several times. Then drain with the skimmer, lifting them into the dish gently. Pour over the reduced syrup, and serve with milk or whipped cream.

### Compote of Pears.
Compote de Poires.

7 Large, Fine Pears.
1 Pound of Sugar. The Juice of a Lemon.
½ Cup of Water.

Scrape the pears spirally from head to stalk with a tapering tin cutter, to take out the cores. Then put the sugar and one-half cup of water on the fire, and add to it four or five pears, which you will have cut into pieces. As this forms a syrup place the whole pears in it, and let them simmer, adding the lemon juice to keep them white. When done, place the pears in order in a dish. Let the syrup stew down to a nice jelly, and then pour over and serve. Apple jelly may be spread over the pears first, and the syrup poured afterwards. This increases the flavor of this delightful compote.

### Compote of Plums.
Compote de Prunes.

1 Quart of Plums.
¾ Pound of Sugar. ½ Cup of Water.

Pick off the stems of the plums and prick them all over with a pin. Let them simmer in sugar, which you will have boiled to a syrup for about fifteen minutes. Then proceed as in a Compote of Cherries. (See recipe.)

### Compote of Pineapple.
Compote d'Ananas.

1 Pineapple. ½ Pound of Sugar.
½ Cup of Water.

Peel the pineapple, and cut in slices, very thin. Put it into a syrup made of half a pound of sugar, and let it boil up once. Take out, and let the syrup simmer a few minutes longer, pour over the pineapple, and serve.

Another method very common among the Creoles, and often preferred to the former by many, is to slice the pineapple nicely, place in a dish, sprinkle with powdered white sugar, let the pineapple form a natural syrup and serve. This is delicious. Some add Claret or White Wine to this compote.

### Compote of Plantain, Creole Style.
Compote de Plantain à la Créole.

6 Plantains.
½ Pound of Sugar.
The Juice of Half a Lemon.
1 Cup of Water.

Peel the plantains and cut into halves or quarters. Put the sugar and water on to boil, and, after ten minutes, add the lemon juice. Then put the pieces of plantain, a few at a time, into the hot syrup and let them stew gently. After half an hour, or forty-five minutes if not tender, take them out, lay in a dish, pour over the hot syrup, and serve either hot or cold.

The plantain is a variety of banana, and may be prepared in every manner in which bananas are cooked, such as fried bananas, stewed bananas, banana fritters, pudding, cake and pie. (See recipes.) Unlike the banana, however, the plantain is never eaten raw, as it is a fruit of much coarser fiber; but, when cooked, equals the banana in delicacy of taste. It is a favorite dish on Creole tables.

### Compote of Plantain, Old Style.

Compote de Plantain à l'Ancienne Mode.

6 Plantains.
½ Pound of Sugar.
1 Pint of Rum.
Kirsch or Maraschino Sauce.

The following is a famous Creole way of cooking plantains that has fallen in desuetude, but which deserves to be resurrected as one of the most delightful methods of preparing plantains: Have ready a pile of hot ashes in the oven. Put the plantains (unpeeled) into the ashes and cover well with ashes. Let them roast thus for half an hour; then take out, peel, cut into quarters and sprinkle with sugar. Set in the oven a few minutes and serve hot, with a Rum, Kirsch or Maraschino Sauce.

### Compote of Pomegranates.

Compote de Grenades.

1 Dozen Pomegranates.
¾ Pound of Sugar.
½ Cup of Water.
1 Tablespoonful of Orange Juice or Maraschino.

Cut a circle about the size of a five-cent piece out of the peel of the pomegranate, using a sharp-pointed knife. Then split down the sides of their skins, and carefully remove all the bright ruby pips, without bruising them. Throw these into a dish. Make a syrup, flavored with orange juice or Maraschino, and pour over and serve.

### Compote of Prunes.

Compote de Pruneaux.

1 Pound of Prunes    ¼ Pound of Sugar.
1 Glass of Claret.

Soak the prunes over night in cold water, and drain. Put them into a saucepan with water, cover the saucepan, and let them boil over a moderate fire. When they begin to soften, add a glass of red wine and a quarter of a pound of sugar. Let it boil, stirring frequently, till the prunes are cooked well. Then take them from the fire, rub a piece of sugar over an orange or a lemon, and when it is completely saturated with the zest, put into a dish, pour the prunes in with their juice, and serve cold.

It is not absolutely necessary to soak the prunes over night, but they cook much more easily if you do. Prunes are very healthy and are served twice a week in every convent in New Orleans.

Stewed prunes are prepared in exactly the same manner as above, only the sugar is put on with the prunes and the wine is omitted.

### Compote of Raspberries.

Compote de Framboises.

1 Quart of Raspberries.   ¾ Pound of Sugar.
Select fine Raspberries, but not too ripe. Wash them in cold water, and drain through a sieve. Boil the sugar, and add the berries and let them boil up once very gently. Put them into a dish, pour the jelly over and serve.

### Strawberry Compote.

Compote de Fraises.

1 Quart of Strawberries.   ¾ Pound of Sugar.
Select fine strawberries, but not too ripe. Wash them in cold water, and drain through a sieve. Boil the sugar, and add the berries, and let them boil up once very gently. Put them into a dish, pour the jelly over, and serve.

### HOW TO SERVE FRESH FRUITS AND DESSERTS.

Fruits are served in New Orleans tables every day. There is always a variety of fruit in our markets. We have out own magnificent Louisiana oranges, peaches, pears and plums, grapes of all varieties, mangoes, mespilus, in their season, pomegranates, strawberries, raspberries, blackberries, which are to be had for the picking, bananas and plantains galore, lemons, citrons—in a word, all the fruits of the tropical and temperate zones.

In arranging fruits on the table, the higher they are elevated the prettier the effect, and the more tempting the sight.

It is out of taste to mix fruits, cakes and bonbons on the same dish. Serve each in its own dish, and these alternating when the dessert is brought on, tend much to tempt the appetite of the guest. Fruits are most wholesome when ripe, and form a part of the well regulated family meal for breakfast, as a preliminary, and for dinner as an after dessert. In serving the desserts that are cooked, always be careful to dish them nicely and neatly.

Always serve raw fruits ice cold. This end is easily attained by placing the fruit in an ice box or refrigerator.

## CHAPTER XXXIII.

### PASTRY AND PIES.

#### Patisserie.

The most important point in making pastries of all kinds is to make the pastry crust of the proper consistency. The crust of pies should always be light, flaky and delicately crisp. To attain this end, only the best flour should be used. In making Puff Paste, always use ice water. In making pie crust, use tepid water if you wish for the best results. The great secret of all pastry depends upon the proper manipulation with the fingers.

#### PUFF PASTE.
#### Pâté Feuilletée.

1 Pint of Flour.
1 Pound of Good Butter, or Half Lard and Half Butter.
1 Teaspoonful of Salt.
1 Cup of Ice Water.   1 Egg.

Have the flour dry and fresh and the butter of the freshest. Wash the butter well, till it becomes clear and elastic to the touch, and cut it into four equal parts, and place it in a bowl, which you will have cooled with ice water. Set it away to cool and harden. Have your flour sifted and ready, and the egg beaten and at hand. Put the flour into a bowl and add to it a lump of butter; work it with your hand, handling always as lightly as possible; add the egg, then salt, and, if the paste is intended for cakes, a teaspoonful of sugar. Work all well, but very lightly, with the fingers and thumb, and then gradually add the ice water, working it well and lightly into the flour. When all is worked in, knead lightly for about five minutes, just as though you were making bread. Then cut the dough into halves; sprinkle the board lightly with flour; take the rollingpin and roll the paste out very thin, rolling each half into a half sheet. Break the butter into bits; take about one-quarter of the remainder, quickly spread this over the paste; then dredge it very lightly with flour and lay over it the other sheet. Dredge this with flour lightly and pound with the rollingpin lightly; then roll this from you into a long thin sheet. Spread a thin coating of butter over this, and then fold the paste over from the sides to the center, and then back again, till you have three folds. Then turn and roll this again till quite thin; add a second quarter of butter broken into bits; dredge lightly with flour and fold and roll as before, always in the same direction—from you. Repeat this process, folding and rolling, till all the butter is used. Then cut the paste into three or four parts, according to quantity, and set in the ice box in tin plates for twenty minutes, or until you are ready to use. It may be kept for several days, if rolled in a napkin and set in a cool place. This is the paste used in making Vol-au-vents, small patés, etc. The most important point is the baking. The oven should be very hot. If you have used all the best materials that wealth can procure, and yet do not have the oven properly heated, all your efforts will have been in vain. Do not set the crust too near the inner fire part of the oven, as it will bake unevenly, and one side will be higher than the other. It is always well to bake small patés with a strong underheat, thus allowing them to rise to their full height before browning. If the oven be too hot, and the paste begins to brown as soon as put in, quickly open the drafts of the stove and reduce the temperature.

It is well to bake the under crust first before putting in the filling in meat pies.

In baking small patties, cut the dough out with a biscuit cutter, leaving the outer rounds distinct from the center. Remove the center and cut out other little rings, and place these one on top of the other, above the bottom crust, which should be solid. In this way is produced the effect of each section being crisp and apparently separate from the other. Some use the white of an egg only; others omit it entirely. It is optional.

#### PIE CRUST.
#### Pâte Brisée.

3 Cups of Sifted Flour.
1½ Cups of Butter.
1 Tablespoonful of Salt.
Nearly a Cup of Tepid Water.

This quantity will make crusts and coverings for three ordinary pies. Rub the flour and butter very lightly together, being careful not to allow it to harden under touch; keep on kneading a little butter at a time into the flour till you have used up all and the dough feels greasy to the touch. Always remember to add the salt before putting in the butter. Some add a tablespoonful of sugar, but the sweetned filling will be generally found sufficient. Then add, little by little, the water, kneading gently, till you have a nice, soft dough, lifting out the portion that is wet and continuing to knead as you mix the flour and water. Always be very careful in adding the water, and never wet the flour twice in the same place. Mix all together lightly with your hands when all is moisened, using always your own good judgment in adding water. Do not work the dough; simply mix lightly and thoroughly, and then dredge the board lightly with the flour. If you intend to make two pies, cut the dough into four parts. Turn the paste out upon the board and roll lightly and quickly into long, thin sheets. Use as little flour as possible in rolling, as your dough will grow tough the more you work it, and the more you add flour and roll it. Remember always that the less flour used in rolling, the tenderer will be the paste. Therefore always cut the dough in as many sections as you intend to make pies, allowing for an upper and an under crust; this will obviate the necessity of rolling it again. Take the pie pans immediately, and place a sheet of dough over each, and trim the edges nicely. Set in the stove, let them bake lightly, and then add the filling of fruits. Place a light thin cover of crust over them, and trim the edges; decorate the edges prettily, using the end of a fork or spoon, and set in the hot oven to bake quickly. When done, set to cool. Sprinkle, when cool, with powdered white sugar, rolling the loaf sugar into a powder, rather than using the pulverized, if you wish an elegant taste. Thus made, the pies ought to have a rich, light, flaky crust, that will, as the old Creole darkies used to say, "melt in your mouth." You cannot attain this end if you use ice-cold water in making this kind of paste.

Paste made with lard may be used for meat pies and dumplinge, and for stews and chicken, when cooked with dumplings. Only roll very thin. Some persons use lard for pie crust. This is to be deprecated. The crust will never have the same flavor as when made with butteer. Others, again, mix the butter and lard. This, too, is to be condemned if you wish for the best results.

If any pie crust is left, do not think of throwing it away. Take all the bits left from cutting around the edges of the pie pans; roll very thin into small squares; bake lightly, and save for tea or luncheon. Put a spoonful of orange, pineapple, lemon or raspberry jelly on each square, and they will be found delicious.

## FOUNDATION PASTE.
### Pâte à Foncer.

½ Pound of Flour.  ¼ Pint of Water.
1 Ounce of Butter.  ½ Teaspoonful of Salt.

Sift the flour well; mix with the salt; then rub the flour and butter lightly together, being careful not to let it harden under the touch. When the butter and flour are well kneaded, add the water gradually, kneading little by little, till well kneaded. Do not work the dough; simply mix lightly and thoroughly. Flour the table lightly, turn the paste out upon it, and press in the center and around the edges, repeating this operation three or four times. Then flatten the paste, lay on a dish and cover with a towel and set in a cool place till ready to use, which should be in about twenty-five minutes, at least.

## PLAIN PASTE FOR DUMPLINGS.
### Pâte à Dresser.

2 Cups of Sifted Flour.
1 Large Heaping Kitchenspoonful of Butter, or Lard.
¾ Cup of Tepid Water.
¼ Teaspoonful of Salt.

Blend the salt and the flour, and then gradually mix in the butter, if for apple dumplings or rolls. Use lard if intended for dumplings for chicken stews, veal stews, etc. Follow the same directions given for making pie paste. Add the water by degrees, using good judgment always, and lifting the dough out as you wet it, never wetting twice in the same place. Mix and knead lightly, and then sift a light coating of flour on the board, and roll out with the rolling pin, and use for all purposes in this book where Plain Paste is indicated. If necessary to keep the paste awhile, place in a napkin in the ice box. But do not use ice water in mixing it, or you will have a tough dough. To attain perfect success in making all pastes, mix quickly, knead slightly, roll quickly and bake rapidly, using always as little flour as possible in rolling. Never beat pie crust or plain paste. You will harden it and make it just the reverse of the light, palatable paste you desire. Use above paste for chicken dumplings, meat dumplings and apple dumplings, rolling out the dough exceedingly thin in small pieces of about two and a half inches in length one in width, and at least one-eighth of an inch in thickness.

With these preliminary instructions, the Picayune will proceed to give the recipes for the various pies made in Creole households.

## Apple Pie.

### Tarte aux Pommes.

4 Large Apples (tart).  1 Cup Sugar.
1 Teaspoonful Sweet Spices, Blended Equally.
2 Tablespoonfuls of Water.
1 Tablespoonful Butter.

Pare and slice the apples nicely. Then put them in a porcelain-lined saucepan, and let them stew gently, adding the water and the butter. Season well with a little ground cinnamon, mace and allspice. When done, take off and allow to cool a little. Make a flaky pie crust (see recipe), and line the tin plates, after greasing slightly with butter, and bake the bottom crust slightly brown. Take out and fill in with the apples, and then cover the top with a thin layer of crust. Decorate the edges, and set in the oven to bake. When a nice, delicate brown, take out and let them cool. Remove from the tin plate by slightly loosening the outer edge with a knife. Turn over into a china plate, sprinkle with white powdered sugar, and serve cold or hot. A pie is always better served cold when made of fruit.

The above is the general rule to be observed in making pies. Sometimes the pies are left open, being covered with tiny strips of paste. This is a matter of taste. Utilize odd bits of paste and fruits thus.

### Apple Tarts.

### Tartelettes aux Pommes.

4 Ounces of Pie Paste.  8 Ounces of Apple Marmalade.  3 Apples.
2 Ounces of Powdered Sugar.
1 Pint of Water.

Prepare the Pie Paste (see recipe), and line six tart molds with it. Peel and core the apples and cut into quarters, and put into a saucepan with a pint of cold water. Let them cook on a hot stove for ten minutes. Then remove and drain, and let cool for half an hour. Then cut the quarters into three slices each; line the bottom of the molds with the marmalade divided evenly; arrange the sliced apples nicely over the marmalade, and dredge nicely with two ounces of powdered sugar. Set in a baking dish and bake for twenty minutes, or a half hour if necessary, in a moderate oven. Take out and spread nicely with apple marmalade and serve.

A simpler way is as follows: Pare and quarter the apples. Sprinkle lightly with sugar. Make a pie crust; roll into small bits; place the apples in the open crust, fold over, fasten by pressing in an ornamental way with a fork, and bake in a quick oven until the apples are very tender.

## Apple Meringué Pie.

### Tartes de Pommes Meringuées.

4 Large Apples.  ¾ Cup of Sugar.
1 Tablespoonful of Butter.
1 Teaspoonful of Sweet Spices, Blended Equally.
2 Tablespoonfuls of Water.
Whites of 3 Eggs.
1 Tablespoonful of Vanilla or Lemon Essence.

Peel, slice and stew ripe, juicy apples, and mash them through a sieve. Season with a little grated nutmeg, using the proportion all through this recipe given in Apple Pie. (See recipe.) Fill the pie plates with the crust, bake and fill with the stewed apples. Let them bake for about twenty minutes, and then spread over the top a thick meringue, made by beating the whites of three eggs for each pie, with three tablespoonfuls of powdered sugar, if you desire a deep, rich meringue; otherwise, allow the white of one egg and one tablespoonful of sugar. Flavor with vanilla or lemon, and continue beating till it will stand alone. Cover the pies with this meringue three-quarters of an inch or one-quarter of an inch thick, according to quantity used; set in the stove and let brown, and eat cold.

### Banana Pie.

### Tarte de Bananes.

4 Large Bananas.
½ Cup of Sugar.
1 Teaspoonful of Sweet Spices, Blended Equally.
1 Tablespoonful of Butter.
2 Tablespoonfuls of Water.

Peel, slice and stew the bananas and mash through a sieve. Prepare a Pie Paste and proceed as in Apple Pie. (See recipe.)

### Banana Meringué Pie.

### Tarte de Bananes Meringués.

4 Large Bananas.
½ Cup of Sugar.
1 Tablespoonful of Butter.
1 Teaspoonful of Sweet Spices.
Whites of 3 Eggs.
1 Tablespoonful of Vanilla Essence.
1 Teaspoonful Grated Nutmeg.

Peel, slice and stew the bananas and mash through a sieve; then proceed as in directions for Apple Meringue Pie. (See recipe.)

### Blackberry Pie.

### Tarte de Mures.

1 Quart of Blackberries.  1 Cup of Sugar.
1 Teaspoonful of Sweet Spices.  2 Tablespoonfuls of Water.

Stew the blackberries and proceed in exactly the same manner as for Apple Pie, using the same proportions for two pies. (See recipe.)

### Cherry Pie.
Tarte de Cerises.

1 Quart of Cherries.   1 Cup of Sugar.
1 Tablespoonful of Water.

All fruit pies arer best when the fruit is previously cooked. Stew the cherries gently, as for a marmalade, and prepare the pie crust according to directions, and proceed as in directions for making pies.

### Chocolate Cream Pie.
Tarte à la Crème de Chocolat.

2 Quarts of Milk.
¼ of a Cake of Vanilla or French Chocolate.
¾ Cup of White Sugar.
6 Eggs.   2 Teaspoonfuls of Vanilla.

First dissolve the chocolate in a little milk, and then stir into the boiling milk. Let it boil about four minutes. Then set to cool. When almost cool, add the yolks of all the eggs and the whites of three, saving the remainder for the meringue. Stir these eggs well into the chocolate, and add the essence of vanilla. Then put into pie pans, in which you will already have baked the under crust. Set in the oven and let the custard grow to a "set" state. When half done, spread over the whites of the eggs, which have been whipped to a stiff froth, with two tablespoonfuls of powdered sugar. Let the pies brown lightly, and serve cold. By baking the above preparation, without the paste, in cups set in boiling water, you will have a Chocolate Cup Custard.

### Cocoanut Pie.
Tarte de Coco.

1 Pint of Milk.   ½ Cup of Sugar.
1 Cup of Grated Cocoanut.   2 Eggs.
½ of a Grated Nutmeg.

Beat the eggs very light. Add the sugar and beat with the eggs until very light. Add the grated nutmeg, and finally the cocoanut. Make a pie crust (see recipe), using half the quantity, as a cocoanut pie is always an uncovered pie. Fill with the mixture, and bake in the oven for about half an hour.

### Creole Cocoanut Pie.
Tarte de Coco à la Créole.

½ Pound of Grated Cocoanut.
2 Tablespoonfuls of Melted Butter.
¼ Pound of White Powdered Sugar.
The Whites of 6 Eggs.
1 Glass of White Wine.
1 Pint of Milk.
2 Teaspoonfuls of Vanilla.
1 Tablespoonful of Nutmeg.

Beat the sugar and butter to a light cream, and then add the wine and the essence of vanilla. Gradually add the cocoanut, beating in as lightly as possible. Add the scalded milk, which has been allowed to cool, and finally beat in lightly the whites of the eggs, which have been whipped to a very stiff froth. Do this latter with a few swift strokes, so that the cocoanut may stand out fresh and flaky, like snow. Bake in pie crusts which have already been set in the oven. Serve cold, sprinkling over white powdered sugar. This is a famous Creole pie.

### Cream Pie.
Darriole.

1 Pint of Milk.   The Whites of Four Eggs.
1 Tablespoonful Flour.   ½ Cup Sugar.
1 Tablespoonful of Butter.
1 Teaspoonful of Vanilla Essence or Lemon Juice.

Blend the flour and butter well together, and when light add the milk gradually. Cornstarch may be substituted for the flour. Add the essence of vanilla or the juice of a lemon, and then add the whites of the eggs, beaten to a stiff froth. Stir them well into the boiling mixture, and then fill the pie pans, which you have filled with crust, baked according to directions. Place in the oven and bake until a nice brown. A cream pie should be served very cold.

### Cranberry Pie.
Tarte d'Airelles.

1½ Pints of Cranberries.   1 Cup of Sugar.
Plain Pie Crust.

Cook the cranberries as for Cranberry Sauce. (See recipe.) Do not strain the berries. Prepare the pie crust. Bake the lower crust, and fill with the fruit, and proceed as in general directions for making pies given under the heading "Apple Pie." A cranberry pie, properly made, is one of the most delicious of all pies.

### Custard Pie.
Flan.

1 Pint of Milk. 3 Eggs. ¼ Cup of Sugar.
Vanilla or Lemon Extract.
A Pinch of Salt.

Line the pie pans with the pie crust. (See recipe.) Beat the eggs lightly in a bowl. Add the sugar and the flavoring extract. Set the milk to boil in a farina boiler. When it boils, pour it gently upon the eggs, and stir till all is thoroughly blended. Then fill the pie pans with this filling. Place in a moderate oven, and bake for twenty or twenty-five minutes.

### Currant Pie.
Tarrte de Groseilles Rouges.

½ Pint of Currants.   ½ Cup of Sugar.
Plain Pie Paste.

Clean and pick and wash the currants well; drain nicely, and then put into a saucepan with one-half cup of sugar. Stew nicely, and then proceed as in the directions given for making Apple Pie. (See recipe.)

### Frangipani.
### Frangipane.

8 Ounces of Shelled Almonds. 3 Tablespoonfuls of Powdered Sugar.
2 Tablespoonfuls of Melted Butter. 2 Eggs.
½ Spoonful of Ground Cinnamon. ½ Teaspoonful of Orange Flower Water.
½ Gill of Rum.

Prepare a pie paste, and peel three ounces of shelled almonds. Then put them into a mortar and pound to a paste, with the powdered sugar and a raw egg. When reduced to a very fine paste, add the melted butter, ground cinnamon and the orange flower water. Beat the yolk of an egg well, and then beat the white to a stiff froth and mix thoroughly. Now add the rum and mix again. Line the pie pans with the pie paste, and fill with the preparation of almonds. Set in a moderate oven for thirty-five or forty minutes; then set to cool for a half hour. In the meantime prepare a "Glace a l'Eau" as follows: Put one ounce of white granulated sugar into a saucepan, with one tablespoonful of cold water, and let it come to a boil. Take off the fire and add immediately a tablespoonful of curacoa; mix thoroughly, and then glaze theh surface of the cake with this. Let it cool an send to the table.

### Gooseberry Pie.

Tarte de Groseilles Blanches.

1 Quart of Gooseberries. 1¾ Cups of Sugar. A Plain Pie Paste.

Top and tail the gooseberries. Line two deep pie dishes with a plain Pie Paste (see recipe); fill with berries; add nearly one cup of sugar to each pie, and proceed as in recipe for Apple Pie. Set in the oven and let the pies bake for three-quarters of an hour. If the gooseberries are stewed as blackberries, it will require less time to bake.

### Green Gage Pie.

Tartre de Reine-Claude.

8 Ripe Greengages. 3 Ounces of Apple Marmalade.
½ Pound of Feuilletage Paste.

Prepare a half pound of Feuilletage Paste (see recipe) and line six tart molds with it. Then spread nicely on the bottom of each three ounces of Apple Marmalade. (See recipe.) Take the greengages, wipe well and remove the stones; cut into quartered pieces and lay nicely over the marmalade. Sprinkle two ounces of powdered sugar evenly over them in a moderate oven and bake for twenty-five minutes. Remove; let cool; spread apple marmalade nicely over the top and send to the table.

### Huckleberry Pie.

Tarte de Mûres de Ronce.

1 Quart of Huckleberries. ½ Cup of Sugar. A Plain Pie Paste.

In making this delicious pie, proceed in the same manner as in the recipe given for Cherry Pie. (See recipe.)

### Lemon Pie.

Tarte de Citron.

1½ Cups of Sugar. 1 Cup of Water.
1 Tablespoonful of Corn Starch or 2 of Flour.
2 Eggs. 1 Tablespoonful of Butter.
The Juice and Inner Fruit and Zest of Two Grated Lemons.

Beat the sugar and butter to a cream; add the eggs, the yolks and the white beaten separately, and then add the hot water and the juice and meat of the lemon and the grated zest. Moisten the flour or cornstarch with a little cold water, and stir into the mixture. Line the pie pans with plain paste or pie crust. (See recipe.) Bake the under crust a few minutes. Then fill the pans with the mixture, cover with an upper crust, and bake in a quick oven for half an hour.

Or cook the custard first, as many of the Creoles do, declaring that thus they reach better results. Boil the water, and then wet the flour, or cornstarch with a little cold water, blending thoroughly. Stir this into the water, and let all come to the boiling point. Then add the sugar, and, if you wish, the butter. Let it boil up once. Take off, and add immediately the beaten eggs, and set to cool. Then add the lemon juice and grated lemon zest, stirring well. Bake the under crust of the pie, fill with this mixture, and set in the oven to brown nicely. This should be an open pie. Indeed, all lemon pies should be open, as custard pies always are. The above measurements will make two pies.

### Lemon Meringue Pie.

Tarte de Citron Méringuée.

1½ Cups of Milk or Water.
1½ Cups of White Sugar. 3 Eggs.
1 Tablespoonful of Flour or Cornstarch.
2 Tablespoonfuls of Powdered White Sugar.
The Juice and Grated Zest of 2 Lemons.

Have ready the pie pans, with the baked crust. Beat the sugar and the yolks well together, and add the juice and grated zest of the lemons. Blend the flour and milk gradually, and pour it through a sieve into the eggs. Mix thoroughly. Fill the lined pans with this, and set in the oven to bake for twenty or thirty minutes. Add gradually three tablespoonfuls of powdered sugar to the whites of the eggs, beating steadily all the time, and when it is all absorbed beat it to a stiff froth. Place this over the top of the pie by spoonfuls, and then smooth lightly with the spoon, place in the oven, and let it brown. This is a delicious pie.

### Mince Pie.

#### Pâté de Noel.

3 Pounds of Beef, Chopped Very Fine.
1 Pound of Beef or Mutton Suet.
4 Pounds of Apples, Pared and Chopped.
2 Pounds of Raisins, Seeded and Chopped.
1 Pound of Sultana Raisins, Picked and Washed.
2 Pounds of Currants, Picked and Washed.
1 Pound of Citron, Cut Very Fine.
½ Pound of Lemon Peel, Grated Very Fine.
2 Pounds of Brown Sugar.
Pound of Candied Lemon Peel, if desired.
2 Grated Nutmegs.
1 Tablespoonful Each of Ground Cloves and Allspice.
2 Tablespoonfuls of Ground Mace.
1 Tablespoonful of Fine Salt.
2 Tablespoonfuls of Ground Cinnamon.
1 Quart of Good Sherry or Madeira.
1 Quart of the Best Brandy.
The Juice of Two Lemons.
The Juice of 2 Oranges, and the Rind, Grated Fine.

The meat should be good and lean, and should be boiled the day before needed, or early in the morning, and allowed to cool. In boiling the meat, plunge it into boiling (not cold) water, for the boiling water enables it to retain its juices. Boil steadily till tender. Then stand away to cool. Chop the meat very fine, and clear away all gristle and skin. Shred the suet, and chop, or, rather mince it very, very fine. Then pare and core the apples, and chop very fine. Stone the raisins, and cut the citron fine. Many prefer to leave out the candied lemon. That is according to taste. The mince meat is heavier with it. The taste is much more delicate and the pie much more digestible without. Grate the orange and lemon peel very fine. Then mix the meat and suet together, chopping again, and add all the ingredients, mixing well together. Add the juices of the lemon and orange, and the grated rinds, and then mix all well again, and pack in a stone jar. Pour over this the quart of brandy, and the wine, and cover very tightly, and set in a very cool place. Mince meat made in this manner should keep all winter. The Creoles generally begin to make it, like their fruit cakes, just before Thanksgiving time, and set it away, having recourse to it for Christmas and New Year's pies, or whenever needed. When ready to use the meat, dish out the quantity you desire, and thin to the desired consistency with good Sherry or Madeira wine. Be very careful in picking the currants carefully, seeding out all grains of sand or dirt and pieces of twigs of trees. Wash them very, very carefully, in cold water, separating the good from the bad, and the great quantity of refuse that always lurks in bought currants.

The Creoles often use the fresh beef tongue or the heart of the beef, well chopped and boiled, in making this mince meat. The filet of beef is best. Mince meat made in this manner never need cause dyspepsia. If the housekeeper is careful in using it, and in properly keeping it, it need not be made more than once or twice during the winter. It should be made at least twenty-four hours before using.

To make the pies, line the bottom of the pie pans with the pie crust, bake the bottom layer, and then fill with the mince meat. Cover the pies with a thin crust, or leave open, if preferred, bake till a nice, delicate brown, sprinkle lightly with white sugar, and serve hot. Mince pies kept from day to day should be warmed over before serving.

### Plain Mince Meat.

#### Pâté de Noel Simple.

A plain mince meat for every day use may be made as follows:
2 Pounds of Meat. 2½ Pounds of Apples.
2 Pounds of Seeded Raisins.
2 Pounds of Currants. 1 Pint of Brandy.
½ Pint of Good Sherry.
1 Teaspoonful Each of Cinnamon, Cloves, Nutmeg and Mace, Grated.
2 Pounds of Brown Sugar.
The Juice and Rind of 1 Lemon. The Juice and Rind of 1 Orange.
¾ Pound of Mutton or Beef Suet.
½ Pound of Chopped Citron.

Proceed to prepare the meat and the pies as in above recipe.

### Lenten Mince Pies.

#### Pâté de Noel au Carême.

4 Pounds of the Best Apples, Cored and Minced.
2 Pounds of Raisins, Stoned and Minced.
8 Hard-Boiled Eggs, Chopped Fine.
1 Teaspoonful Each of Ground Spices, as Above.
Juice and Rind of 2 Lemons, Grated.
The Juice of an Orange, and Rind, Grated.
2 Pounds of Currants.
2 Pounds of Sugar, or Sugar to Taste.
½ Pint Each of Brandy and Sherry.

Mix all well together in lesser proportions, according to the number of pies you wish to make, and proceed as above. (See recipe Mince Pie.)

### Molasses Pie.
#### Tarte de Melasse.
2 Cups of New Orleans Molasses.
½ Cup of Sugar.
The Juice of 2 Lemons.   3 Eggs.
2 Tablespoonfuls of Flour.
½ Teaspoonful Each of Nutmeg and Cinnamon.
2 Tablespoonfuls of Butter.

Blend the lemon juice and molasses well, and gradually beat in the flour, which you will have moistened with a little water. Then add the spices and the butter, melted, and the yolks of the eggs, beaten very light with the sugar. Finally, add the whites, beaten to a stiff froth. Mix well. Line the pie pans with a pie crust (see recipe), bake, fill with the mixture, and bake again for half an hour. One-quarter of a cup of vinegar may be substituted for the lemon juice, but always use the latter if you have it.

### Orange Pie.
#### Tarte d'Oranges.
2 Fine Louisiana Oranges and Their Juice.
The Rind of 1 Orange, Grated.
2 Tablespoonfuls of Butter.
1 Tablespoonful of Cornstarch.   3 Eggs.
1 Cup of Powdered Sugar.
½ Teacupful of Boiling Water.

Beat the butter and sugar to a cream. Then blend the cornstarch with sufficient cold water to moisten and mix well, and stir into the teacup of water, which should be boiling in a saucepan. Let it cook, stirring constantly, for two minutes only. Then add the butter and sugar, and stir well. Remove from the fire, and add the well-beaten yolks of two eggs. Line the pie plates with pie crust (see recipe), and bake the under crust. Add the custard, and let it get slightly brown in the oven. Then take out, and spread over the whites of two eggs, beaten to a stiff froth, with two tablespoonfuls of fine white powdered sugar. Let it bake for about three minutes longer in a quick oven, and serve cold. The meringue on top must be slightly browned.

### Peach Pie.
#### Tarte de Pêches.
1 Dozen Large Peaches.   1 Cup of Sugar.
A Plain Paste.

Pare and cut the peaches into slices. Stew the peaches and proceed in exactly the same manner as for Apple Pie. (See recipe.) Sprinkle the tops of the covers with fine white powdered sugar when ready to serve.

### Peach Meringue Pie.
#### Tarte de Pêches Méringuées.
1 Dozen Peaches.   Sugar to Taste.
Whites of 6 Eggs.   6 Tablespoonfuls of Sugar.
1 Teaspoonful of Vanilla.

Pare and stone the peaches, and stew according to recipe. (See recipe Stewed Apples or Peaches.) Line the bottoms of two pie pans with a rich pie crust, and then fill in with the peaches, which you will have sweetened to taste. Bake in a quick oven twenty or twenty-five minutes. Beat the whites of six eggs to a stiff froth with the sugar, which should be fine white powdered. Add a teaspoonful of vanilla. When the meringue can stand alone, cover the tops of the pies three-quarters of an inch thick, after baking, and set back in the oven and bake for two or three minutes, to a nice, delicate brown.

All fruit meringue pies are made in the same way.

### Pear Pie.
#### Tarte de Poires.
6 Fine Pears.
½ Cup of Sugar.   2 Tablespoonfuls of Water.
A Plain Paste.

Peel and core and slice six fine pears. Put them in a vessel with the sugar and water, and stew. Prepare a plain paste, and proceed in exactly the same manner as for Apple Pie. (See recipe.)

### Pineapple Pie.
#### Tarte d'Ananas.
1 Fine Pineapple.   ½ Cup of Sugar.
A Plain Pie Paste.

Peel and slice into very fine, thin slices one pineapple. Place with the juice in a saucepan with the sugar, and stew slightly. Prepare a plain pie paste, and proceed in the same manner as for Apple Pie. (See recipe.)

### Plantain Pie.
#### Pâté de Plantain.
2 Plantains.
½ Cup of Sugar.
A Plain Paste.

Peel, slice and stew the plantains, and proceed in the same manner as for Apple Pie. (See recipe.)

### Plantain Meringue Pie.
#### Pâté de Plantain Méringue.
2 Plantains.
½ Cup of Sugar.
1 Tablespoonful of Butter.
1 Teaspoonful of Sweet Spices.
Whites of 3 Eggs.
1 Tablespoonful of Vanilla Essence.

Peel, slice and stew the plantains, mash through a sieve, and proceed as in recipe for Apple Meringue Pie. (See recipe.)

### Pumpkin Pie.
#### Tarte de Citrouille.
Use the delicate Cashaw for this pie. Take
1 Pint of Mashed, Stewed Pumpkin.
1 Pint of Milk. 3 Tablespoonfuls of Butter.
4 Eggs.   1 Cup of Sugar.
½ Teaspoonful Each of Ground Mace, Cinnamon and Allspice.

Boil a quart of pumpkin, cut into

dice-shaped pieces, putting it on with just enough water to keep from burning, say about a quarter of a cupful. Let it stew slowly for an hour, at least, or until tender. Then drain and press through a colander. Add a good tablespoonful of butter and a quarter of a teaspoonful of salt. Mix well; and let it cool. When cool, put the pumpkin, using one pint, into a large bowl, and add the pint of milk, the ground spices, and mix all well together, and add the above amount of sugar, or sugar to taste. Then beat four eggs well and add to the mixture. Add a tablespoonful of brandy, if desired. Line the pie pans, and bake the under crust. Fill with the mixture, and bake in a quick oven for half an hour. When cold, sprinkle lightly with white powdered sugar, and serve. This quantity will make three pies.

### Raspberry Pie.

Tarte de Framboises.

1 Quart of Berries.
1 Cup of Sugar.
1 Teaspoonful Sweet Spices, Blended Equally.
½ Cup of Water.
1 Tablespoonful of Butter.

Pick, wash and stem the berries; then put them in a porcelain-lined saucepan, and let them stew gently, adding the water and the butter. Season well with a little ground cinnamon, mace and allspice. When done, take off and allow to cool a little. Make a flaky pie crust (see recipe), and line the tin plates, after greasing slightly with butter, and bake the bottom crust slightly brown. Take out and fill in with the berries, and then cover the top with a thin layer of crust. Decorate the edges, and set in the oven to bake. When a nice, delicate brown, take out and let them cool. Remove from the tin plate by slightly loosening the outer edge with a knife. Turn over into a china plate, sprinkle with white sugar, and serve cold or hot.

### Strawberry Pie.

Tarte de Fraises.

1 Quart of Berries.
1 Cup of Sugar.
½ Cup of Water.
1 Tablespoonful of Butter.
1 Teaspoonful Sweet Spices, Blended Equally.

Proceed in exactly the same manner as for Raspberry Pie. (See recipe.)

It might be remarked that all the above fruit pies may be made into meringue pies, the same as the Peach Meringue and Apple Meringue pies.

All fruit pies are delightful eaten with a glass of fresh milk or cream.

### Sweet Potato Custard Pie.

Flan de Patates Douces.

3 Boiled Sweet Potatoes.
3 Eggs. 1 Cup of Milk. 1 Cup of Sugar.
2 Tablespoonfuls of Butter.
½ Teaspoonful of Cinnamon.
The Grated Zest and Juice of an Orange.
2 Tablespoonfuls of Brandy, if Liquor is Desired.

Wash the potatoes well, and boil them until tender, but not overdone. Thirty minutes will suffice. When cold, peel and grate them, and then beat together the butter and sugar till light. Add the yolks of the eggs, beaten till light, and then beat in the potatoes, stirring first gradually, and then beating lightly and steadily. Add the spices and the orange, and brandy, if desired, and then line one deep pan or two small pie pans if preferred, with the pie crust. (See recipe.) Bake lightly, fill in lightly with the potatoes, and bake in a quick oven for a half hour. Beat the whites of the eggs to a stiff froth, and while beating add two tablespoonfuls of white powdered sugar. When the pies are baked, heap the meringue on the top, set back in the oven, and let them bake for two or three minutes only, to a light brown.

### Vol-au-Vent.

1 Pound of Flour.
1 Pound of Butter, or Half Butter and Half Lard.
1 Teaspoonful of Salt. 1 Cup of Ice Water.
1 Egg.

Vol-au-vent Paste is always difficult to make, and should never be attempted by inexperienced housekeepers, if they are expecting company. Practice first before essaying to make others eat your efforts. Make the Puff Paste as directed (see Puff Paste), and let it stand in a cool place at least six hours. Roll the paste out very thin, and then line the deep pan in which you intend to cook the chicken or meat. Cut around the edge nicely with a knife. Then take another small pan and cover it only half way with the paste. Cut around the edges, trimming off all strings of dough. Then brush the paste all around the top with a beaten egg. Put it on a sheet iron or square tin, and set it on the ice till very cold. Then set it in a very hot oven to bake for about half an hour. Do not let it burn or scorch. When done, fill the inside with chicken, pigeon or other meat (already fricasseed.) with which you intend to make the Vol-au-Vent and then cover with the top crust. Fill around the edges with strips of paste left over, and piled one over another for about three thicknesses, set in the oven to bake, and serve hot.

This is the true Vol-au-vent paste,

and chicken, pigeons, small birds, veal or meats may be used for filling. But the best chicken pie is the old-fashioned one, made by filling the pan with pie crust (see recipe), baking it, and the edges which you have cut around lightly, and then filling in with the chicken and strips of dough between, and covering with a thin cover of the paste, baking brown and serving hot.

### Oyster Patties.
Bouchées d'Huîtres.

Prepare a puff paste, and proceed in exactly the manner outlined under the chapter on "Oysters." (See Oyster Patties.)

## CHAPTER XXXIV.

## PUDDINGS.
Des Poudings.

We have no real French word for pudding. Puddings are essentially English in origin. French chefs introduced them into France, retaining, with a slight modification of spelling, the expressive name for the dish. The Creoles adapted the dish to many of the delightful fruits of Louisiana.

Puddings may be either boiled or baked. One rule may be given for the baked pudding, and one for the boiled, or more properly, the "roll," and these will be the guides of the intelligent cook. In the boiled puddings it is generally necessary to make a dough, using the Plain Paste (see recipe), and then the dough is rolled out, and the raw fruit placed within. The dough is then rolled over and over, so as to form layers first of dough, and then of fruit. Sew up in a clean cloth, and boil till done.

### Blackberry Roll.
Bourrelet aux Mûres.
1 Quart of Blackberries.
A Plain Paste, Not Too Flaky.

Make a Plain Paste, which should be rather firm, to prevent the berries from escaping. Roll this out to about one and a half feet in length, or one foot, according to the size of the family, and the number of guests, one foot being ample for a family of six. Spread the blackberries, which you will have carefully picked, over this paste, and then carefully roll over and over until the entire paste is taken up. Then sew in a clean piece of white muslin, and put into a kettle of boiling water. Let it boil continuously for at least two hours and a half. Then take out, let it cool slightly, rip the cloth which binds it, and serve immediately with a Hard Sauce or Cream or Brandy Sauce. (See recipes Sauces for Puddings, etc.)

Peach Rolls, Apple Rolls, Banana, Strawberry, Raspberry, Cherry and Currant Rolls, and Plantain Rolls, are made in the same manner. Always slice and peel the peaches and stone them; also stone the cherries, and peel and seed the apples. Peel the plantains and bananas and slice very thin before rolling in the dough. Some serve the roll cold, but then it is always a little tough, for the boiled dough hardens easily. A boiled pudding should always be eaten hot. The pudding may be boiled in a mold, in which case it should be well-covered, and the mold first buttered.

The fruits may be mixed, in which case excellent results are produced.

### Boiled Dumplings.
Échaudés à l'Anglaise.
8 Large, Fine, Rosy Apples.   Sauce.

Prepare a Plain Paste (see recipe), and cut into squares, and put in the center of each a fine, juicy apple, pared and cored, or a half apple, pared and cored. Wrap the fruit up in the dough, and place these in small dumpling cloths (the Creoles sometimes do not use cloths), and put them into boiling water, and let them boil for at least an hour. On taking out the apple, if so desired, the inner core may be filled with some delicate jelly or marmalade. Serve with Hard, Cream or Brandy Sauce. (See recipes Sauces for Puddings, etc.)

Dumplings of other fruits are made in the same way. In making a peach dumpling, cut the peach in half, stone it, put together again, or place the halves each in separate pieces of dough in dumpling cloths. Cut bananas and plantains into quarters. Always dip the pudding and dumpling cloths first in hot water before sewing up the pudding or dumplings in them. Dumplings must be served as soon as done.

### Old-Fashioned Creole Apple Dumplings.

Échaudés de Pommes à l'Ancienne Mode Créole.

8 Large, Fine, Rosy Apples.
1 Large Kitchen Spoonful of Butter.
2 Large Kitchen Spoonfuls of Sugar.
1 Cup of Seeded Raisins. The Grated Zest of 1 Orange.

An old-fashioned Creole apple dumpling, much to the taste of little children, is made by dropping the dumpling into the boiling water without wrapping them in cloths. After they have boiled an hour, beat one large kitchen spoonful of butter and two of sugar to a thick cream, and stir into the water with the dumplings. Add one cup of seeded raisins, and the grated zest of one orange. Let all boil twenty minutes longer. Put the dumplings into a dish, pour the sauce over, and serve hot or cold.

### Baked Dumplings.

Échaudés Rotis.

8 Large, Fine, Rosy Apples.
Sauce.

Prepare a Plain Paste. (See recipe.) Cut into squares and proceed to prepare the dumplings in exactly the same manner as in the recipe for Boiled Dumplings (see above recipe), only, instead of boiling the dumplings set in the oven in a baking dish, and bake to a delicate brown. Serve with a Hard, Cream or Brandy Sauce. (See recipes Sauces for Puddings.) Dumplings of other fruits are made and baked in the same way.

### Rice Dumplings.

Échaudés de Riz.

¼ Pound of Mashed, Cold, Boiled Rice.
½ Dozen Apples.
3 Tablespoonfuls of Flour.
1 Egg.

Pare the apples and take out the cores. Fill the interiors with sugar and cinnamon. Beat the egg and the rice together, add the flour, and knead to a dough. Cover the apples with a thick coating of rice, and then tie each in a dumpling cloth, and put them in a pot of boiling water. Let them boil for three-quarters of an hour. When done, turn out carefully on a dish, and serve with a Hard or Cream Sauce. Or the dumplings may be baked in the oven.

### Roly Poly.

Bourrelet.

½ Pound of Flour.   5 Ounces of Suet.
1 Pint of Fresh Fruit, Jam or Jelly.
¼ Teaspoonful of Salt.

Cut away all the fibers from the suet, and then mince very fine. Add the flour and salt to it, and mix well together, and gradually add sufficient water to make a dough. Roll it out about half an inch in thickness on a baking board, and then spread over thinly with minced fresh fruits, mingled, or with fruit jam or preserves, singly or mingled. Roll it up, and put in a cloth, leaving room for it to swell. Then plunge into boiling water, and let it boil for two hours. Serve with Hard, Cream or Brandy Sauce.

An Orange Roly Poly is made by seeding the oranges and laying them thinly sliced all over the sheet of dough. Sprinkle lightly with white sugar, and roll up and fasten closely in the pudding cloth. Boil for one hour, and eat with Lemon or Orange Sauce.

Peaches and apples and other fruits may be used in making these delightful roly polys.

### Plum Pudding.

Pouding aux Raisins.

1 Pound of Raisins.   1 Pound of Currants.
¼ Pound of Citron.
½ Pound of Butter.   ½ Pound of Suet.
½ Pound of Sugar.   ¼ Pound of Flour.
6 Eggs.   ½ Pint of Milk.
½ Cup of Brandy.   1 Grated Nutmeg.
¼ Ounce Each of Ground Cloves, Mace, Cinnamon and Allspice.
The Grated Zest of 1 Lemon.
The Grated Zest of Half an Orange.

Seed the raisins and chop them fine. Seed the currants, after washing and picking over very carefully. Mince the citron, and grate the zest of the orange and lemon. Then proceed as follows: Beat the butter and sugar to a cream, and then beat in the yolks of the eggs, which have been previously beaten to a perfect degree of lightness. Then add the flour, beating in by degrees till very light, and the whites of the eggs, which have been beaten to a stiff froth. Add the spices and beat in well. Mince the suet and the fruits very fine and add, and lastly add the brandy, which you will beat thoroughly into the pudding. When all is well-mixed, have ready the pudding cloth; wet with hot water, and wrung perfectly dry. Dredge it slightly with flour, and wrap the pudding in it. Sew it up, and put into a kettle of boiling water, and let it boil for six hours. Serve with a Hard or Brandy Sauce.

### Old-Fashioned Creole Plum Pudding.

Pouding aux Raisins à l'Ancienne Mode Créole.

2 Pounds of Beef Suet.   1½ Pounds of Flour.
1 Pound of Sugar. The Yolks of 8 Eggs.
1 Pound of Raisins. 1 Pound of Currants.
¼ Pound of Citron.
1 Glass of Madeira Wine. 2 Glasses of Brandy
1 Nutmeg.
A Pinch of Cinnamon. A Hard or Brandy Sauce.

Chop finely two pounds of beef suet. Take one and a half pounds of flour, mix with suet; add to this one pound of sugar, the yolks of eight eggs, one pound of raisins, stoned and floured; one pound of currants, one-quarter pound citron, chopped fine; one glass Madeira wine, two glasses brandy, one nutmeg, grated, and a little cinnamon. Beat the whole well together, adding milk till of proper consistency. Wrap in a cloth, previously scalded and floured, leaving room for the pudding to swell; boil six hours, and serve with Brandy or Hard Sauce.

### Baked Puddings and Dumplings.

Des Poudings et des Échaudés au Flour.

In baked puddings this invariable rule must be observed—the whites and the yolks of the eggs must be beaten separately, if you would achieve the best results. Custards come under the same class as puddings, in a way, and when baked both should be put into the oven the moment they are made, and baked instantly. Once done, they should be taken out, and if to be eaten hot, should be served at once; if cold, they should be set in a cool, sweet, fresh place. Nothing so absorbs as milk, and when this ingredient enters into the composition of any dish if it is to be eaten cold, care should be taken to keep it in a cool, fresh place.

### Apple Pudding.

Pouding de Pommes.

1 Pint of Apples.
3 Tablespoonfuls of White Sugar.
1 Tablespoonful of Butter.
¼ Teaspoonful Each of Nutmeg, Mace, Allspice and Cinnamon, Grated.
1 Spoonful of Vanilla Essence.

Stew the apples according to recipe (see recipe), and while the apples are boiling stir in the butter and the spices. Then take from the fire, and add the well-beaten yolks of the eggs. Beat all very light. Beat the whites of the eggs to a stiff froth, and beat well into the pudding. Put into a buttered dish, and bake for fifteen minutes in the oven. When nicely browned, grate nutmeg on top, and serve cold, with cream or milk.

### Apple Meringue Pudding.

Pouding Méringué au Pommes.

1 Pint of Apples.
3 Tablespoonfuls of White Sugar.
1 Tablespoonful of Butter.
¼ Teaspoonful Each of Nutmeg, Mace, Allspice and Cinnamon, Grated.
1 Spoonful of Vanilla Essence.

Stew the apples according to recipe (see recipe), and while the apples are boiling stir in the butter and the spices. Then take from the fire, and add the well-beaten yolks of the eggs. Beat all very light, and put into a buttered dish, and bake for fifteen minutes in the oven. Then cover with a meringue made with the whites of the eggs, the essence, and the white powdered sugar, beaten to a stiff froth. Bake to a light brown, and serve cold with fresh milk or cream.

Peach Meringue Pudding, Cherry Meringue Pudding, Pear Meringue Pudding, Orange Meringue Pudding, Blackberry Meringue Pudding and Fig Meringue Pudding are all made in the same way, only the figs must not be overripe when cooked.

The same fruits may be made into the plain pudding by following the first recipe. All are most excellent, and in their season these fruits are so cheap in our clime that there is no reason why the poorest may not enjoy these delightful desserts.

### Banana Pudding.

Pouding de Bananes.

6 Bananas. Stale Cake.
1 Pint of Milk. 3 Eggs. ½ Cup of Sugar.

Cut the stale cake very thin. Peel and slice the bananas. Put a layer of cake at the bottom of a buttered baking dish. Place over this a layer of the sliced bananas. Pour over this a layer of milk custard, made from the above ingredients, and boiled very thin. (See Custard.) Add another layer of cake, then one of banana and custard, and so continue till you have used up all. Make the top layer of the custard. Put in an oven, cover with a piece of paper, bake for half an hour, and let the top brown slightly, and serve cold.

### Bird's Nest Pudding.

Pouding au Nid d'Oiseau.

6 Apples. 1 Pint of Rich Cream.
2 Cups of Flour. 1 Teaspoonful of Soda.

Pare and core the apples, and then put them in the bottom of a buttered dish. Mix the cream with the flour until smooth, and add a teaspoonful of baking powder, which you will have dissolved well in a tablespoonful of boiling water. Mix again thoroughly, and pour over the apples. Set in a moderate oven, and bake for one hour. Serve with Hard, Cream or Brandy Sauce. (See recipe.)

### Bread Pudding.

Pouding de Pain.

Utilize left-over stale bread in this pudding.

1 Quart of Stale Bread.
3 Eggs. 1 Cup Raisins. 1½ Pints of Milk.
1 Teaspoonful of Vanilla.

Beat the eggs well, and mix, and then, when very light, add the milk. If you use stale cake, add two tablespoonfuls of sugar; if you use stale bread, add half a cup of sugar. Mix thoroughly. Wet the bread and squeeze it. Then mix in it a cup of seeded raisins. Beat the egg mixture thoroughly into this, and place in the oven and bake for an hour. Serve with Hard, Cream, Brandy or Lemon Sauce. (See recipes.)

### Brown Betty Pudding.
#### Pouding à la Mulâtresse.

1 Cup of Bread Crumbs.
2 Cups of Chopped Apples. 1 Cup of Sugar.
2 Tablespoonfuls of Butter.
¼ Spoonful Each of Ground Spices.

Utilize stale bread crumbs for this pudding. Butter the bottom of a baking pan, and put in a layer of the apples, which you will have stewed nicely. Put over this a layer of bread crumbs, and sprinkle with sugar and dot with butter. Sprinkle lightly with the spices. Continue this till you have used up all the apples. Put a layer of bread crumbs on top. Place in a moderate oven, and bake to a nice brown. Serve hot, with Cream Sauce or Hard Sauce.

### Cake or Bread Pudding.
#### Pouding de Gateau ou de Pain.

1 Quart of Stale Cake.
3 Eggs. 1 Cup Raisins. 1½ Pints Milk.
1 Teaspoonful of Vanilla.

Utilize left-over cake in this pudding. Beat the eggs well, and mix and then, when very light, add the milk. If you use stale cake, add two tablespoonfuls of sugar; if you use stale bread, add half a cup of sugar. Mix thoroughly. Spread the bottom of the pan with the raisins, and then put a layer of cake over them, sliced very thin. Sprinkle this with raisins, and continue adding the cake and raisins alternately till all are used. Add a little essence of lemon or vanilla to the egg mixture, and pour all this over the cake. Set in the oven and bake for an hour. Serve with Hard or Lemon Sauce. Some add a little Sherry Wine. That is according to taste and the methods of the family.

### Chocolate Pudding.
#### Pouding au Chocolat.

3 Ounces of Grated Chocolate.
3 Eggs.
1 Quart of Milk. ¾ Cup of Powdered Sugar.
¾ Cup of Powdered Crackers.
¾ Cup of Butter. 1 Pinch of Salt.

Soak the cracker crumbs in water for a few minutes, to dissolve them, and then squeeze out thoroughly. Dissolve the chocolate in a little milk, and add the other ingredients. Pour all into a buttered dish, and let bake for twenty minutes. Then take out, and let it cool slightly. Spread over the top a meringue made of one cup of powdered sugar and the whites of three eggs. Set back in the oven to brown slightly for two minutes, and serve cold.

### Cottage Pudding.
#### Pouding de Ménage.

1 Cup of Milk. 1 Cup of Sugar. 3 Eggs.
1 Tablespoonful of Butter. 1½ Cups of Flour.
1 Teaspoonful of Baking Powder.

Beat the sugar and the yolks of the eggs, and then add the milk and the flour. Add the whites, beaten to a stiff froth. Beat carefully into the pudding. Add the baking powder, and pour into a buttered pan, and cook in a moderate oven for three-quarters of an hour. Serve this pudding hot, with Vanilla, Cream or Lemon Sauce.

### Cocoanut Pudding.
#### Pouding de Coco.

1 Grated Cocoanut. 1 Quart of Milk.
1 Cup of Sugar. 1 Tablespoonful of Vanilla.
4 Tablespoonfuls of Cornstarch.

Put the milk in a boiler and add the cornstarch as it commences to boil, first moistening the cornstarch with a little water. Stir until very smooth. Then add the yolks of the eggs, well beaten, and then the sugar. Lastly, add the whites, beaten to a stiff froth. Then add the grated cocoanut, turn into the baking pan, and bake for half an hour. Serve cold, with Vanilla Sauce. (See recipe.)

### Cream Pudding.
#### Pouding à la Crème.

6 Eggs. ½ Cup of Sugar.
1 Pint Flour. 1 Pint Milk. 1 Grated Lemon.
1 Pint of Rich Cream. A Pinch of Salt.

Mix the sugar and the grated lemon. Beat the yolks of the eggs well, and add to the mixture. Then add the flour, well-sifted; beat light, and add one pint of milk and one pint of rich cream. Beat the whites to a stiff froth and add. Bake a half hour in a buttered dish. Serve with Lemon Sauce. (See recipe.)

### Creole Fig Pudding.
#### Pouding de Figues à la Créole.

½ Pound of Figs.
¼ Pound of Grated Bread Crumbs.
1 Teacupful of Milk. 2½ Ounces of Sugar.
3 Ounces of Butter. 2 Eggs.

Chop the figs fine, and beat the sugar and the yolks of the eggs to a thick cream. Add the melted butter and the bread crumbs, which have been wet and squeezed thoroughly. Add the milk and the whites of the eggs, beaten to a thick froth. Butter a mold and sprinkle with flour. Steam lightly for three hours. Serve with a Hard, Cream or Brandy Sauce.

### Fig Pudding.
#### Pouding de Figues.
1 Pint of Fresh Figs. 1 Cup of Sugar.
1 Cup of Milk. 1 Cup of Flour.
1 Teaspoonful of Baking Powder.
¼ Teaspoonful of Grated Nutmeg.
½ Cup of Butter.

Peel the figs and cut fine. Then make a batter of the eggs, flour and milk, according to recipe (Apple Batter Pudding). When smooth, add the fruit. Turn into a baking pan, and bake for an hour. Serve with Wine Sauce. (See recipe.)

This pudding may be boiled by adding two cups of flour to the batter, and rolling and sewing in a well-floured dumpling cloth and boiling for three hours. (See recipe.)

### Indian Pudding.
#### Pouding à l'Indienne.
2 Cups of Indian Meal.
½ Cup Butter. 1 Cup Sugar. 2 Cups Milk.
½ Cup of Molasses.
1 Cup of Seeded Raisins.

Pour sufficient boiling water on the meal to wet it thoroughly, and then beat in the butter. Add the sugar, beating thoroughly, and the salt. Then add the milk, stirring well, also the molasses and the raisins. Add one teaspoonful of extract of cinnamon, and one-quarter of a grated nutmeg. Mix thoroughly. Bake for two and a half or three hours, and serve cold with cream.

### Baked Lemon Pudding.
#### Pouding de Citron au Four.
¾ Pound of Butter.
¾ Pound of Powdered Sugar.
1 Gill of Sherry and Brandy, Mixed.
1 Small Stale Sponge Cake. 6 Eggs.

Grate the rind of the oranges, and squeeze out the juice after removing the seeds. Grate the inner meat. Beat the butter and sugar to a thick cream, and then add the wine. Add these to the oranges, grated with the rind. Beat the whites of the eggs to a stiff froth, and the yolks separately. Add them in order to the mixture. Place in a moderately quick oven, and let it bake for about a half hour. When done, let it cool slightly. Place a meringue on top, as in Apple Meringue Pudding (see recipe), and set back to bake two minutes more. Serve cold.

The pudding may be baked in a rich pie crust, set in a deep pan.

### Molasses Pudding.
#### Pouding de Melasse.
1 Cup of New Orleans Molasses.
1 Cup of Milk. ½ Cup of Melted Butter.
½ Cup of Sherry Wine.
3 Cups Flour. ½ Teaspoonful Baking Powder.
½ Teaspoonful Each of the Four Spices.

Dissolve the baking powder in the flour, mixing thoroughly. Melt the butter and add it to the molasses, and then add the milk, mixing thoroughly. Add the flour, gradually mixing well, and then add the wine, and lastly the spices. Blend all well together. Pour into a well-buttered pan, and let it bake for about two hours. Serve with Foamy Sauce.

This pudding may also be boiled by sewing in a well-floured dumpling cloth and boiling for three hours.

### Nesselrode Pudding.
#### Pouding Nesselrode.
½ Pint of Chestnuts.
½ Pint of Almonds. 1 Pint of Cream.
1 Pint of Boiling Water.
½ Pound of Mixed French Candies of the Finest Kind.
½ of a Grated Pineapples, or ½ of a Can.
The Yolks of Six Eggs.
1 Tablespoonful of Vanilla Essence.

Shell the chestnuts and throw them into boiling water to blanch. Then take off the brown skin, and set them in a saucepan and cover with boiling water, and let them boil for twenty minutes. Then drain and press them through a colander. Shell the almonds and blanch them for twelve minutes in boiling water. Then take them out and pound them, and cut the fruit into very small pieces. Put the sugar and the water on to boil together, and let the mixture boil for ten minutes. Then beat the yolks of the eggs very, very light, and add them to the boiling syrup. Let it boil up once, and take off, and then beat very lightly with an egg beater till cool. (Use a wire beater.) Add all the fruits, the almonds and chestnuts, and the pint of cream, and a tablespoonful of Vanilla Essence. Beat well, and add four tablespoonfuls of Sherry. Put the pudding into a freezer to freeze and ripen, and let it stand covered with a carpet for four or five hours, or till frozen, renewing the ice and salt and draining off water as necessary. This will serve eight persons nicely. Some of the cream may be worked in with Spinach greenery, as in Pistachio Ice Cream (see recipe), and a delicate coating of green given to the pudding, which adds to the effect. The pudding may be served with cream whipped to a stiff froth.

### Orange Pudding.
#### Pouding d'Orange.
2 Large Louisiana Oranges.
¾ Pound of Butter.
¾ Pound of Powdered Sugar.
1 Gill of Sherry and Brandy, Mixed.
1 Stale, Small Sponge Cake. 6 Eggs.

Grate the rind of the oranges, and squeeze out the juice after removing the seeds. Grate the inner meat. Beat the butter and sugar to a thick cream, and then add the wine. Add these to the oranges, grated with the rind. Beat the whites of the eggs to a stiff froth, and the yolks separately. Add them in order to the mixture. Place in a moderately quick oven, and let it bake for about a half hour. When done, let it cool slightly. Place a meringue on top, as in above recipe, and set back to bake two minutes more. Serve cold.

### Peach Batter Pudding.
Pouding de Pêches.

1 Pint of Milk.    2 Cups of Flour.
3 Eggs.    8 Peaches.
2 Teaspoonfuls of Baking Powder.
½ Teaspoonful of Salt.
2 Tablespoonfuls of Melted Butter.

Beat the yolks and whites of the eggs till very light, and mix, and add the milk. Beat steadily until smooth. Then add the melted butter, the salt and the baking powder. Have the peaches stewed till almost cooked, and stir them into the pudding, after cutting fine. Then turn the pudding into the mold or pan in which it is to be baked. Bake for an hour, and serve hot, with Cream, Brandy or Hard Sauce. (See recipes Sauces for Puddings, etc.)

### Fruit Batter Puddings.
Poudings de Fruits.

Cherry Batter Pudding, Apple Batter Pudding and all fruit batter puddings are made in the same way as Peach Batter Pudding. (See recipe.)

### Pineapple Pudding.
Pouding d'Ananas.

1 Fine Pineapple.    1 Pint of Milk.
½ Pound of Flour.
3 Eggs.    3 Tablespoonfuls of Butter.
½ Cup of Sugar.
A Sauce au Kirsch.

Boil the milk in a saucepan and add the butter. Sift the flour and add gradually to the mixture, stirring briskly for three minutes. Take off the fire, and add the yolks of the eggs, beaten very light. Stir well, and add the powdered sugar. Beat the whites of the eggs to a stiff froth, and add gradually to the milk. Then take a pudding mold and butter well; sprinkle with sugar and put a layer of the milk-and-egg preparation about half an inch thick at the bottom. Put over this a layer of finely-sliced pineapple, then add another layer of the milk and eggs and a layer of the pineapple, and continue till all the pineapple and the mixture are used up. Set the mold in a tin pan of warm water, and place in the oven and cover with buttered paper. Let the pudding steam for one hour; then remove from the oven, turn into a pudding dish, and serve with a Sauce au Kirsch. (See recipe Sauces for Puddings, etc.)

### Raspberry Pudding.
Pouding de Framboises.

1 Quart of Raspberries.
¾ Pound of Powdered Sugar.
¾ Pound of Butter.
1 Gill of Sherry Wine and Brandy Mixed.
1 Stale Small Sponge Cake.    6 Eggs.

Stew the berries and proceed in the same manner as for Orange Pudding. Bake for about twenty minutes or half an hour after adding the fruit, and serve cold, with a Cream or Hard Sauce.

These fruit puddings are the most delicious of Louisiana puddings.

### Sago Pudding.
Pouding au Sagou.

1 Quart of Milk.    ¼ Pound of Sago.
½ Cup of Powdered Sugar.    4 Eggs.
1 Teaspoonful of Vanilla Essence.

Boil the milk and add the sago, and stir briskly for ten or fifteen minutes. Then take off the stove and set to cool. Add the sugar and mix thoroughly. Then add the eggs and a tablespoonful of Vanilla Essence. Mix thoroughly. Butter a pudding mold or pan and fill with the mixture. Set in a tin pan and fill the latter with hot water. Place in the oven and let it steam for half an hour. Remove from the fire, turn into a dessert dish and send to the table hot. Serve with a Cream Sauce.

### Snow Pudding.
Pouding à la Niege.

½ Box of Gelatine. 1 Pint of Boiling Water.
2 Cups of Sugar.
The Whites of 3 Eggs. The Juice of 3 Lemons.

Dissolve the gelatine in the boiling water, and, when nearly cool, add one cup of powdered sugar and the juice of one lemon. Beat well and lightly, and strain. When cold, beat as white as snow, and add the whites of the eggs, beaten to a stiff froth. Beat all thoroughly, and pour into a mold. Stand in a cold place for four hours to harden. Then make a Custard Sauce by beating the yolks of the eggs together with a half cup of sugar till very light. Stir them into the milk, which should be boiling. Let them cook, stirring constantly, for two or three minutes. Then add a teaspoonful of Vanilla, and set to cool. Serve with the pudding, pouring the sauce upon it.

### Strawberry Pudding.
Pouding de Fraises.

1 Quart of Strawberries. ½ Pound of Sugar.
1 Gill of Sherry and Brandy, Mixed.
1 Stale Small Sponge Cake. 6 Eggs.

Stew the berries and proceed in the same manner as for Raspberry Pudding.

Quince pudding is prepared in the same manner.

### Sweet Potato Pudding.
Pouding de Patates Douces.

1 Pint of Mashed Sweet Potatoes.
½ Pound of Sugar. ½ Pound of Butter.
8 Eggs.
The Juice and Rind of an Orange and Lemon.
¼ Spoon of Ground Mace.
The Same of Cinnomon and Allspice.
¼ Grated Nutmeg.
2 Tablespoonfuls of Brandy. ½ Cup of Sherry.

Grate the potatoes and mash them through a sieve, if you use them raw. If you use the cold boiled potatoes, simply mash them. Beat the butter and the sugar to a rich cream, and add the well-beaten yolks of the eggs, and then add the grated potatoes, and the spices, and finally the whites of the eggs, beaten to a stiff froth. Mix all well. Add the liquors. Turn into a buttered baking pan, and let the pudding bake in a moderate oven for three-quarters of an hour. The addition of the liquors is optional. Serve hot or cold, with Cream Sauce. (See recipe.)

### Tapioca Pudding.
Pouding au Tapioca.

1 Quart of Milk. 1 Cup of Tapioca.
½ Cup of Sugar. 1 Teaspoonful of Vanilla.
1 Teaspoonful of Salt.

Wash the tapioca well, and then add it to the milk and let it soak for at least two hours and a half. Then beat the eggs separately until light. Add them in order to the sugar, beat very light, add the salt and the tapioca, and bake for forty-five minutes in a moderate oven. The pudding may be served either hot or cold.

To make Tapioca Fruit Pudding, add one pint of preserved raspberries to the above.

### The Queen of All Puddings.
La Reine des Poudings.

1 Pint of Bread Crum's.
1 Quart of Milk. 1 Cup of Sugar. 4 Eggs.
2 Tablespoonfuls of Butter.
The Juice of a Lemon.
½ Pint of Seeded Currants.
½ Pint of Raisins.

Soak the bread crumbs in water for about an hour. Then squeeze thoroughly. Beat the yolks of the eggs and the sugar very light, and then add the milk and the bread crumbs, beating all light. Add the melted butter and the seeded raisins and the currants, and the juice of one lemon and the grated zest of half a lemon. Beat all thoroughly together, and set in a moderate oven for a half hour. In the meantime, beat the whites to a very stiff froth. Add four tablespoonfuls of powdered sugar, and beat thoroughly till very stiff. After half an hour take the pudding out of the oven, if it is nicely browned, and put over the top a layer of some fruit jelly, and then a layer of the whites, and then another layer of the jelly, and a last layer of the whites of the eggs. Set it back in the oven to brown for several minutes, and serve cold with Cream or Wine Sauce. This pudding, however, is so delicious that it may be served without any sauce. The above proportions will serve a family of six and two guests.

### Tipsy Squire.
Pouding au Bon Camarade.

Left Over Sponge Cake.
1 Glass Sherry Wine.
A Boiled Custard.

Saturate left-over sponge cake with Brandy or Sherry Wine. Then take a rich Boiled Custard (see recipe); place the cake in a deep glass dish, and pour the custard over it. Decorate with blanched lemons, and serve cold.

## CHAPTER XXXV.

## CUSTARDS, CREAMS, AND OTHER DESSERTS.

Des Flans, Des Crèmes, et Autre Desserts.

### Blanc Manger.

1 Quart of Cream.
½ Cup of Sugar.  ½ Ounce of Gelatine.
1 Teaspoonful of Vanilla.

Dissolve the gelatine in water, and then mix with the milk and cream, Let it come to a boil, add the Vanilla, pour into a mold, let it harden and serve cold.

### Cornstarch Blanc Manger.

Blanc Manger à la Fécule de Maïs.
1 Quart of Milk.
3 Tablespoonfuls of Cornstarch.
3 Tablespoonfuls of Sugar.
The Whites of 3 Eggs.
1 Teaspoonful of Lemon Extract.

Dissolve the cornstarch lightly in one pint of milk, and then add the sugar and the whites of the eggs, beaten to a stiff froth. Put this mixture into a pint of boiling milk. Let it come to a boil. Flavor with the lemon; pour into cups to cool. Then, when very cold, turn out, and serve with jelly and cream. This will serve six persons. Serve, if you wish, with a Cream Sauce.

### Neapolitan Blanc Manger.

Blanc Manger à la Neopolitaine.
1 Quart of Milk.
3 Tablespoonfuls of Cornstarch.
3 Tablespoonfuls of Sugar.
The Yolk of 1 Egg.   The Whites of 3 Eggs.
1 Teaspoonful of Lemon Extract.
1 Tablespoonful of Grated Vanilla Chocolate.
Whipped Cream.

To make a Neopolitan Blanc Manger, first make the above preparation, and then separate it into four parts. Put the first into a mold, and then stir into it, while warm, one heaping tablespoonful of grated Vanilla chocolate. Pour the white preparation into the same mold, on top of this. Then a layer of the chocolate, and then the white. Cover the last layer with the yolk of an egg, and set to cool and harden. Serve cut into thin slices, with whipped cream.

### Velvet Blanc Manger.

Blanc Manger Velouté.
2 Cups of Cream.
½ Cup of Powdered Sugar.
½ Cup of Gelatine, Dissolved in Water (hot).
1 Glass of White Wine.

Boil the cream, sugar and gelatine together, stirring until smooth. Take a teaspoonful of Almond Extract. Mix well, and pour into a mold, and set to cool and harden.

### Boiled Custard.

Oeufs au Lait.
1 Quart of Milk.   4 Eggs.
2 Tablespoonfuls of Cornstarch.
½ Cup of Sugar.
1 Teaspoonful of Vanilla.

Set the milk to boil. Beat the yolks of the eggs and the sugar very light. Beat the whites to a stiff froth, and stir carefully into the yolks and the sugar. Moisten the cornstarch with a little cold milk, and stir into the boiling milk. Continue to stir until it commences to thicken. Then add the sugar and the eggs. Stir and let it cook for one moment longer, and take from the fire, add the vanilla, and turn into a dish to cool. Serve very cold.

The cornstarch is added to thicken the custard. If the milk is rich, it may be omitted. The custard is far more delicate without it.

Baked custard without corstarch is made in he same manner; the custard is put in a baking dish, setting in the oven, and allowed to bake till quite firm. By adding two tablespoonfuls more of cornstarch the custard may be thickened, if desired.

### Cup Cnstard.

Oeufs au Lait.
4 Eggs.   1 Quart of Milk.
2 Tablespoonfuls of Cornstarch (if desired).
½ Cup of Sugar.
1 Teaspoonful of Vanilla Extract.

Beat the eggs together until light, and then add the sugar, and beat till very light. Now add the milk and the nutmeg, and put a pan into the oven. Fill the pan with boiling water. Pour the custard into cups or into ｎaller pan, and set in the boiling    er, and let it bake till firm in   ｅ center. Set to cool, and serve in the cups if they have been used.    Otherwise serve in dessert plates.

### Custard Soufflé.

Flan Soufflé.
1 Cup Milk. 4 Eggs. 2 Tablespoonfuls Butter.
2 Tablespoonfuls of Sugar.
2 Tablespoonfuls of Flour.
1 Tablespoonful Vanilla.

Boil the milk. Blend the butter and the flour nicely, and add to the boiling milk. Stir constantly over the fire for ten minutes. Beat the yolks of the eggs and the sugar together, and add these to the milk. Then set the mixture to cool. When cool, beat the whites of the eggs to a stiff froth, and add to the mixture. Turn into a buttered baking dish, and bake in a quick oven for twenty minutes. Serve with Cream Sauce, while hot, otherwise it will fall.

### Tapioca Custard.
Flan au Tapioca.

½ Cup of Tapioca. ½ Cup of Sugar.
4 Eggs. 1 Pint of Water.
1 Tumbler of Currant or Strawberry Jelly.

Wash the tapioca well several times, and then soak it well in the pint of water for two hours. Add it to the jelly, mixing thoroughly, and then add the sugar, and mix again until the tapioca is very clear. Beat the whites of the eggs to a very stiff froth, and add them to the tapioca, and turn it into a mold and set away to harden. Make a Vanilla Cream Sauce with the yolks of the eggs, and serve cold with the custard. (See Vanilla Cream Sauce.)

### Almond Custard.
Flan d'Amandes.

1 Pint of New Milk. 1 Cup of Sugar.
¼ Pound of Blanched Almonds (scalded).
The Yolks of 4 Eggs.

Blanch the almonds after shelling, and chop very fine. Blend the eggs and sugar, beating thoroughly, and add to the boiling milk. Then add the almonds. Stir well, set into cups to cool. Place on top a meringue made of two tablespoonfuls of white powdered sugar and the whites of the eggs, beaten to a stiff froth. Set in the oven for a few seconds to brown, and serve cold.

### Macaroon Custard.
Flan de Macarons.

1 Quart of Milk.
The Yolks of 6 Eggs. ½ Tablespoonful Butter.
3 Tablespoonfuls of Flour.
½ Cup of Sugar. 1 Dozen Macaroons.

Set the milk to boil. Blend the butter and the flour, and stir into the boiling milk. Beat the yolks of the eggs with half a cup of sugar, very light, and add this to the milk, stirring constantly for one minutes, and take from the fire to cool. Add a tablespoonful of orange juice or extract of orange. When cool, crumble one dozen macaroons over the top of the dish. Make a meringue with the whites of the eggs and two tablespoonfuls of powdered white sugar. Beat to a stiff froth, pile on the custard, and set in the oven for a few minutes to brown. Serve very cold.

### Rice Custard.
Riz au Lait.

See Rice Custard under chapter on Louisiana Rice.

### Charlotte Russe.

1 Quart of Good Cream.
¾ Cup of Powdered White Sugar.
½ Box of Gelatine. 1 Teaspoonful of Vanilla.
2 Tablespoonfuls of Sherry Wine.
½ Pound of Lady Fingers.

Line a glass dish with the lady fingers, or with small slices of cake. Soak the gelatine in cold water, just covered, for half an hour. Whip the cream, and then dissolve the soaked gelatine with the Sherry Wine. Add the Vanilla Extract. Add the sugar to the cream carefully, and then strain in the gelatine very carefully. Stir immediately, and then pour the cream over the lady fingers, and set away to harden.

### Parisian Charlotte Russe.
Charlotte Russe à la Parisienne.

¼ Pound of Stale Lady Fingers.
¼ Box of Gelatine. 1 Cup Grated Cocoanut.
¼ Pound of Macaroons.
4 Eggs. 2 Tablespoonfuls of Sugar.

Soak the gelatine in cold water for about half an hour. Put one-half of the cream to one side, and whip the rest. Put the remaining pint to boil, and stir into it the sugar and eggs, beaten together till very light. Stir about one minute, and as it thickens add the gelatine, which you will have dissolved either in a little warm water or Sherry Wine. Then add the lady fingers and a teaspoonful of the vanilla; add the macaroons and the grated cocoanut. Turn all this into a bowl or tin basin, place it on ice, and stir continually until it begins to harden. Add the whipped cream, and stir all very carefully. When well-mixed, wet a fancy dish of glass or a mold, turn the Charlotte Russe into it, and stand on the ice to harden.

Some utilize a stale sponge cake in making Charlotte Russe, cutting out the inside and leaving the sides and bottom about an inch in thickness. The mixture is poured into this cake, and served cold, with sauce.

### Floating Island.
Oeufs à la Neige.

1 Quart of Milk.
4 Eggs. 4 Tablespoonfuls of Sugar.
1 Tablespoonful of Vanilla.
½ Cup of Currant Jelly.

Put the milk to boil in a farina boiler. Beat the yolks of the eggs with the sugar till very light, and stir them into the milk as it begins to boil. Let it thicken one minute Then take from the fire, and add the vanilla and set aside to cool. Beat the whites of the eggs to a stiff froth, and when the mixture is cold pour it into a glass dish, heap on the whites of the eggs, and dot here and there with bits of Currant Jelly. Dust these with powdered sugar, and serve very cold. Some add a tablespoonful of cornstarch to the boiling milk, if it is desired to thicken the preparation. But the taste of cornstarch is never as delightful as that of the mixture pure and simple.

### Apple Snow.
#### Neige aux Pommes.

6 Fine Apples. 1 Cup Fine White Sugar.
The Whites of Six Fresh Creole Eggs.
The Juice of One Lemon.

Pare and core and cut up the apples, and steam them in two tablespoonfuls of water, with a little grated lemon peel, till quite soft. Then press them through a sieve, and add the sugar and the lemon juice. Beat the whites of the eggs to a very stiff froth, and add two-thirds to the apples, stirring all the whites, and when the eggs and apples are very light beat this with a little powdered white sugar to form a meringue. Place the apples in custard glasses, heap on the meringue, and serve immediately.

This preparation may be improved by putting the apples into a dish, heaping on the meringue, and baking for one minute in the oven, and serving very cold.

### Pineapple Snow.
#### Neige à l'Ananas.

1 Pineapple. The Whites of Four Eggs.
1 Pint of Whipped Cream.
½ Cup of Powdered Sugar.

Pare the pineapple, and grate it. Beat the whites of the eggs until foamy, and then add by degrees the sifted sugar. Add one tablespoonful of Sherry. Stir the whipped cream, which must be very cold from standing on ice, and when all is very stiff beat in the pineapple, pulp and juice, adding as much as the cream and the meringue will hold without becoming too soft. Place in glasses, and serve very cold. This is a delightful summer dessert.

### Orange Snow.
#### Neige d'Oranges.

6 Fine Louisiana Oranges.
A Snow Cream, as Above.

Prepare this dish in exactly the same manner as above.
First slice the oranges, and removing the seeds, sprinkle sugar over them before adding the snow cream.
Lemon Snow may be made in the same manner.

### Snow Cream.
#### Neige à la Crème.

The Whites of Four Eggs.
1 Pint of Cream. 1 Teaspoonful of Vanilla.
½ Cup of Powdered Sugar.
1 Tablespoonful of Sherry.

Whip the cream and set on ice. Beat the whites of the eggs to a foam, and then add the sifted white sugar, and beat steadily till the mixture becomes very stiff and glossy. Add the Sherry and Vanilla. Stir the whipped cream carefully into the meringue, and set it in small custard glasses to get cold. The Creoles often add a few blanched almonds. Serve very cold, as a summer dessert.

Strawberries, blackberries, peaches, pears, figs, etc., in their natural state, may all be made into "snows" by following the directions given in Pineapple Snow; only the peaches and pears and figs and bananas must be chopped, and strawberries and other berries must be served whole in the snow. Grated cocoanut may also be served in the same manner.

### A Creole Summer Pudding.
#### Pouding d'Été.

1 Pint of Lemon Jelly.
1 Cup of Stoned Cherries.
1 Cup of Malaga Grapes. 2 Oranges.
2 Bananas. ½ a Pineapple.
1 Pint of Snow Cream.

Make a Lemon Jelly (see recipe); add stoned cherries, a few Malaga grapes, and the meat of two oranges, two bananas and half a pineapple, sliced. Pour a little jelly into each custard glass. Put a layer first of one fruit, then of another, then a layer of snow cream, and continue alternating till the glass is filled with the snow on top. Serve ice cold.

Or the layers may be made in a dish, and when ready to serve pour over a thin custard, made of the yolks of four eggs and a quart of milk and a half cup of sugar. Serve very cold.

### Apple Sponge.
#### Soufflé de Pommes.

1 Pound of Apples.
1 Pound Sugar. 3 Eggs. ½ Box of Gelatine.
The Grated Zest of a Lemon.
½ Pint of Boiling Water.

Boil the sugar and water, and when very clear skim the surface. Have the apples pared and cored and sliced nicely, and place them in the syrup. Let them stew until very tender. Then add the gelatine, which has been soaked in cold water, to the mixture, and when well done press all through a sieve. Then add the rind and juice of the lemons, using only the zest of the rind in grating the lemon. Stir until it begins to cool and thicken. Then add the whites of the eggs, beaten to a stiff froth, stirring and beating until cool and thick. Use the yolks for a Vanilla Sauce (see recipe), and turn the Apple Sponge in a dish and serve with the sauce poured over it.

Peach Sponge is made in the same way.

### Strawberry Sponge.
Soufflé de Fraises.

½ Pint of Strawberries.
½ Cup of Sugar.   4 Eggs.
1 Pint of Boiling Water.

Stew the strawberries gently, and press them through a sieve. Soak the gelatine in a cup of cold water for an hour, and then dissolve with a tablespoonful of sherry wine. Pour it into the boiling water, and let it dissolve well. Add the sugar, and let it thicken gently. Then strain, and add the strawberries, an set it upon ice to cool. Occasionally stir to prevent the fruit from settling at the bottom. Beat the whites of the eggs to a stiff froth, and add them to the sponge, beating steadily till very smooth. Set in a fancy bowl to harden, and serve with Vanilla Sauce poured over it. (See Vanilla Sauce.)

Blackberry Sponge, Lemon Sponge, Orange, Raspberry, Currant and Fig and Pineapple Sponge are made in the same way.

### Apple Sago.
Pommes au Sagou.

1 Cup of Sago.   8 Large Apples.
1 Quart of Boiling Water. Sweetened Cream.

Soak the Sago for half an hour in cold water, and then put it in a farina boiler and add one quart of boiling water. Pare the apples, and add to the Sago, and let all boil together till very tender. Sweeten to taste. Then bake in a moderate oven for twenty minutes, and serve with cream.

Tapioca may be used instead of the Sago, and you will then have Apple Tapioca. Cherry, Orange, Peach and other fruit tapiocas and sagoes are made in the same way.

### AMBROSIA.
Ambroisie.

1 Dozen Sweet Louisiana Oranges.
1 Cup of White Sugar.   1 Cocoanut.

Grate the cocoanut after paring. Then peel and slice the oranges, taking out the seeds. Have a nice large glass dish. Put first a layer of oranges in the dish, sprinkle with sugar, and then a layer of cocoanut, till all the oranges and cocoanut are used, the layer of cocoanut being the last. Sprinkle with powdered white sugar, and let it stand about two hours before serving. This is a famous Creole dessert.

### Pineapple and Orange Ambrosia.
Ambroisie d'Ananas et d'Oranges.

1 Large, Ripe Pineapple.
6 Oranges.   1 Cup of Sugar.
1 Glass of Sherry or White Wine.

Slice one large, ripe pineapple and six oranges. Put in a glass bowl one layer of oranges, sprinkle pulverized sugar over them; then one layer of pineapples, also sprinkled with sugar and continue till all the fruit is used. Pour a wineglassful of Sherry or White Wine over the top. Let it stand about two hours before serving. This is a typical Creole dessert.

### Minute Cake.
Tot Fait.

6 Eggs.   5 Tablespoonfuls of Sugar.
3 Tablespoonfuls Flour. 2 Tablespoonfuls Milk.
The Juice and Rind of a Lemon.

Beat the yolks of the eggs to a cream, and then add the sugar, beating thoroughly till very, very light. Then blend the flour and milk until smooth, and add. Add the juice of the lemon and the grated zest, and beat well again. Then add the whites of the eggs, beaten to a thick froth, turn into a buttered dish and bake fifteen minutes in a quick oven.

### Strawberry Short Cake.
Pâte Brisée aux Fraises.

½ Pound of Sifted Flour.   ¾ Pound of Sugar.
2 Quarts of Strawberries.
2 Teaspoonfuls of Baking Powder.   6 Eggs.
1 Quart of Cream.
½ Pound of Powdered Sugar.

Stem the strawberries. Sweeten to taste, and slightly mash. Then set them aside. Blend the sugar and butter together until very smooth, and add the baking powder, and blend well. Add the salt. Then add the eggs, breaking them in whole, one at a time, and beat all well for ten minutes. Add the grated zest of half a lemon; by degrees add the flour, and mix all together very gently. Divide into two parts; put one into well-buttered baking tins and bake in a moderate oven thirty minutes. When done, remove the cakes and allow them to cool. Detach the cakes from the tins by passing a knife gently around. Have a dessert dish ready and lay one of the cakes upon it. Spread two tablespoonfuls of whipped cream over, and then cover liberally with strawberries. Cover with another cake and spread as before with cream and then with strawberries. Lay the other cake on top and sprinkle with powdered sugar. Serve with "Whipped Cream à la Vanille" (see recipe), or with rich cream or milk.

Peach Short Cake, Raspberry Short Cake and Blackberry Short Cake are made in the same way.

## CREAMS.
### Des Crèmes.
### General Directions for Making Cream Desserts.

In making creams for desserts, one unfailing rule must be observed. In making a cream to serve six or eight persons, use either a half box of prepared gelatine, or half a pint of home-made gelatine. The latter if properly made, is always the best, as well as the most economical. The gelatine must be soaked for about half an hour before using in water just sufficient to cover. This is for the purpose of softening it. Or it may be moistened with a little Sherry or Madeira wine. This is according to the taste and the usages of the family. The cream must always be whipped, the yolks of the eggs must be beaten separately from the whites; and the whites of the eggs must be beaten to a stiff froth. In using flavoring extracts, select, according to taste, Essence of Vanilla, Lemon, Pineapple, Almonds, Aromatic Roses, Orange Flower Water, etc.

### Calf's Foot Jelly or Gelatine.
### Gelée de Pieds de Veau.

4 Calf's Feet. 5 Quarts of Cold Water.
1 Pint of White Wine or Sherry.
Juice of 2 Lemons. Juice of 2 Oranges.
½ of the Zest of a Lemon, Grated.
The Whites and the Crushed Shells of Two Eggs.
1 Pound of White Sugar.
2 Teaspoonfuls of Grated Nutmeg.
1 Stick of Grated Cinnamon.

Wash the feet well, scrubbing them thoroughly, in cold water. Then put them into a kettle to boil with the five quarts of cold water given above. Let them simmer slowly for at least seven or eight hours, till the liquor is reduced one-half. Then strain the liquid into an earthen bowl, and set it away for at least twelve hours, or over night. Then skim carefully every particle of fat from the surface, and remove all sediment or dregs from the jelly. Put it into a porcelain-lined kettle, and set over the fire, and let it melt slowly. Add the whites of the eggs, well beaten to a froth, and the crushed shells, the ground cinnamon, the nutmeg, the sugar and lemon and orange juice, and the zest of the lemon. Mix all these ingredients thoroughly, and let the jelly boil hard, without stirring again, for twenty minutes. Then add half a cup of water, and let it come again to a boil. Set it back on the stove, where it cannot boil, and keep it closely covered for half an hour. Have ready a flannel bag, and dip it into boiling water. Hang it up with a bowl underneath, and pour the jelly into the bag, suspending the bag from the end of a thick, short pole, where it can drip easily. Tie the end of the bag, and let the jelly drip freely. On no account squeeze or touch it, if you wish to have an unclouded jelly. Then the drippings into a bowl or mold, add the wine, and set to cool in a cool place. You will then have the genuine Calf's Foot Jelly, and will know that it has not been made of the horns and hoofs of animals, etc.

### Whipped Cream.
### Crème Fouettée.

1 Pint of Sweet Cream.
2 Tablespoonfuls of Powdered Sugar.
6 Drops of Jamaica Rum.

In whipping cream remember that the first great essential is to have good cream, and that the great secret of whipping depends upon the right, steady stroke. Always set the cream on ice for several hours before using. Then sweeten it to taste, and add a few drops of Jamaica rum. Have ready a second bowl, beat the cream, or, rather, whip it, as you would in beating eggs to a froth, with clear, steady strokes, using an egg beater, or, if you have a small crank churn, which is better, use it, pressing the dasher up and down very hard, and removing the cream as it rises around the dashboard. In the same way remove the cream as it rises, while beating with the egg beater, putting the whipped portion into the second bowl, and continuing the process of whipping until all the cream is drained. Set on ice, and it will keep cool, fresh and sweet and firm.

The above process is intended when the cream is to be used as a garnish for desserts. Any essence may be used, instead of the rum. When whipping cream for coffee, or when you desire the plain whipped cream, do not use sugar or essence, but simply proceed to whip the cream as directed above. Good, rich milk may be whipped into the cream.

Having given the above explicit directions, it will be easy for even the veriest amateur to make any of the following delightful Creole cream desserts:

### Whipped Cream and Strawberries, Raspberries, Blackberries, etc.

Crème Fouettée aux Fraises ou aux Framboises ou aux Mûres, etc.

1 Pint of Berries.
1 Pint of Whipped Cream.
1 Cup of Sugar.

Stem the berries, sprinkle nicely with white sugar, and set aside for several hours in a cool place. Serve with the whipped cream, dishing the berries first in serving, and heaping the cream prettily on top.

### Whipped Cream With Peaches, Cherries, etc.

Crème Fouettée aux Pêches, aux Cerises, etc.

1 Pint of Fruit, Peaches, or Cherries, or Bananas, or Pears, etc.
1 Pint of Whipped Cream.
1 Cup of Sugar.

Stone the peaches, and slice or cut them nicely, adding sugar to taste. In like manner stone, but do not cut, the cherries if this fruit is used. If bananas or pears are preferred peel and slice nicely. Seed the pears. Sprinkle the fruit with sugar, an set it aside in a cool place for two hours; and serve with the whipped cream, heaping it in generous measure at the moment of serving. All fruits that may be eaten with cream are prepared in the same manner.

### Whipped Cream With Liquors.

Crème Fouettée aux Liqueurs.

½ Gill of Liqueur.
1 Pint of Whipped Cream.

It is simply necessary just before whipping the cream, to add a few drops of the liqueur with which you wish to flavor the cream.

### Whipped Cream With Vanilla, etc.

Crème Fouettée à la Vanille, etc.

1 Pint of Cream.
2 Ounces of Powdered Sugar.
1 Teaspoonful of Vanilla Extract.

Put a pint of sweet cream into a basin, add the sugar and the essence and proceed to whip according to the directions given in "Whipped Cream" (see recipe.) Always remember to add the essence before whipping the cream. This is the unvarying rule to be observed whenever you wish to flavor with any extract.

### Foamy Cream.

Crème en Mousse.

1 Pint of Whipped Cream.
1 Gill of any Liqueur Desired.

Proceed exactly as in the above recipe, using a gill of any liquor desired.

### Foamy Cream With Rum.

Crème en Mousse au Rhum.

1 Pint of Whipped Cream.   1 Gill of Rum.
2 Ounces of Powdered Sugar.

Whip a pint of fresh sweet cream, adding a gill of rum and whipping till it reaches a stiff froth. Then transfer to a china bowl and set on ice till ready to use. Have a dessert dish ice cold when ready to serve and drop the cream into this spoon by spoon, with greatest care so that it will not fall, and pile up high in a pretty pyramid shape and serve immediately.

### Whipped Cream With Kirsch.

Crème Fouettée au Kirsch.

1 Pint of Whipped Cream.  1 Gill of Kirsch

Prepare the cream exactly as in above recipe, only, instead of the rum, substitute a gill of Kirsch.

### Whipped Cream With Maraschino.

Crème Fouettée au Maraschino.

1 Pint of Whipped Cream.   1 Gill of Maraschino.

Prepare exactly as in the direction for Crème en Mousse with Rum, substituting a gill of Maraschino instead of the Rum.

### Whipped Cream With Cognac.

Crème Fouettée au Cognac.

1 Pint of Cream.   2 Tablespoonfuls of Powdered Sugar.

Proceed in exactly the same manner as in the directions for Whipped Cream with Rum, substituting instead a gill of good old Cognac. Serve in the same manner directed.

### Whipped Cream With Curacoa.

Crème Fouettée au Curaçoa.

1 Pint of Cream. 2 Ounces of Powdered Sugar.
1 Gill of Curaçoa.

Proceed in exactly the same manner as in the directions for Whipped Cream with Rum, adding, instead of the Rum, one gill of Curaçoa.

### Whipped Cream With Coffee.

Crème Fouettée au Café.

1 Pint of Whipped Cream.
2 Ounces of Powdered Sugar.
3 Ounces of Extract of Coffee.

Make three ounces of Créole Café Noir. (See recipe.) Take three tablespoonfuls and add to the cream and sugar. Then proceed in exactly the same manner as in Whipped Cream with Vanilla. When ready to serve, heap the cream in the center of a very cold dish, using artistic taste, and serve immediately.

### Light Cream.
### Crème Légère.

1 Pint of Milk.   1 Pint of Cream.
4 or 5 Tablespoonfuls of Powdered White White Sugar.
2 Fresh Eggs.
1 Tablespoonful of Orange Flower Water.

To one pint of milk add the same quantity of cream, and four or five tablespoonfuls of powdered white sugar. Let it boil till reduced to one-half the quantity. Take off the stove, and whip in the whites of two fresh Creole eggs, and, when it is as white as snow, add a half pint of whipped cream. Place upon the fire, and let it simmer gently, stirring continually. Add a tablespoonful of orange flower water, or other essence, take off, let it cool, and serve when cold.

### Sweet Almond Cream.
### Crème d'Amandes Douces.

6 Nice Almonds.
1 Quart of Milk. The Whites of 2 Eggs.
4 Ounces of Powdered White Sugar.

Take six nice almonds and shell them. Then blanch them by throwing into boiling water, and letting them stand on the back of the stove for five minutes. Then throw into cold water, and take out the inner skins by rubbing them together with the hands. Whip in one quart of milk, the whites of two eggs, and four ounces of powdered sugar. Let the milk boil slowly on the fire till it is reduced one-half, and then add the almonds, which you will have chopped fine, and add a tablespoonful of Orange Flower Water, and let the mixture boil for three minutes longer. Set it to cool. Then garnish with almonds that have been passed in Caramel or melted sugar and allowed to cool.

### Burnt Cream.
### Crème au Caramel.

1 Pint of Milk.   1 Pint of Cream.
4 Ounces of Powdered Sugar. The Yolks of 3 Eggs.
1 Teaspoonful of Caramel.

Boil one pint of milk and one pint of cream together. Add four ounces of powdered white sugar and the yolks of three eggs, nicely beaten together till very light. Add one teaspoonful of Caramel (see recipe), let it reduce one-half, strain, garnish nicely with any fruits, and serve cold.

### Creamed Coffee.
### Crème au Café.

2 Ounces of Finely Ground Coffee.
1 Pint of Milk. ½ Pint of Cream.
4 Ounces of Powdered Sugar.
The Yolks of 3 Eggs.

Boil two ounces of finely ground and powdered coffee in one pint of milk. Add one-half pint of cream as it begins to boil. Then add the yolks of three eggs, which have been well beaten with four ounces of powered sugar. Let it reduce one-half, take off and strain till clear, let it cool and serve.

### White Coffee Cream.
### Crème Blanche au Café.

2 Ounces of Coffee.   1 Pint of Milk.
½ Pint of Cream. 4 Ounces of Powdered Sugar.
The Yolks of 3 Eggs.

To make a "Crème Blanche au Café," parch two ounces of coffee, and throw the grains, while hot, into the boiling milk. Then proceed exactly as above.

These are famous old-time Creole recipes.

### Chocolate Cream.
### Crème au Chocolat.

1 Pint of Milk.   1 Pint of Cream.
Yolks of 3 Eggs.   4 Ounces of Sugar.
2 Ounces of Grated Chocolate.

Boil one pint of milk and one pint of cream. Add, while boiling, three yolks of eggs, beaten well with four ounces of sugar. Stir constantly, and let it reduce one-half. Add two ounces of grated chocolate. Let it boil three or four minutes, take off, and serve when very cold.

### Macaroon Cream.
### Crème au Macarons.

6 Macaroons.   1 Pint of Milk.
1 Tablespoonful of Orange Flower Water.
½ a White Praline.
2 Ounces of Powdered White Sugar.
The Yolks of 4 Fresh Eggs.

Crumble six macaroons (a macaroon is a small cake, made of almonds and sugar—see recipe), soak them in a pint of milk; add one tablespoonful of Orange Flower Water, in which you have put one-half of a mashed Praline (see recipe Pralines), and add two ounces of sugar, and the yolks of four fresh Creole eggs, well beaten till light. Set on the stove and let it simmer constantly till reduced almost one-half. Let it cool, and serve in the glass in which it was cooled.

### Chestnut Cream.
### Crème de Marrons.

2 Dozen Chestnuts.
Yolks of 2 Eggs.
1 Tablespoonful of Butter. 1 Pint of Cream.
1 Pint of Milk.
4 Ounces of Powdered Sugar.

Shell the chestnuts and blanch them, and pound sufficient quantity to make two ounces reduced to flour. Or roast two dozen chestnuts and peel them (which is far better), and pound them till very fine, and blend with a little milk till you have a thick paste. Add the yolks of two eggs, well beaten, and two tablespoonfuls of the best butter. Beat well, and add four ounces of powdered white sugar. Beat all this very light, and put into one pint of boiling milk, or half milk and half cream. Let it boil for about ten minutes, and then take off, strain, decorate in a glass dish, and serve cold. This is the true Créole Crème de Marrons.

### Peanut Cream.
#### Crème aux Pistaches.

4 Ounces of Fresh Peanuts.
The Zest of 1 Lemon. 1 Gill of Water.
½ Pint each of Milk and Cream.
1½ Ounces of Powdered White Sugar.
1 Ounce of Gelatine.

Peel four ounces of fresh peanuts, and pound them into a flour. The quantity must equal four ounces shelled. Add the grated zest of a lemon, and a little water, sufficient to make all into a thick paste. Boil equal quantities of milk and cream to equal a pint and a half, and add an ounce and a half of white powdered sugar. Let it cool, and add a piece of gelatine, blended with one spoon of water. Mix well and then strain through a sieve. Put the cream back on the fire to heat, and add the peanuts. Let all come to a good boil, take off and set it to cool in a cool place, and serve cold.

### Snow Cream.
#### Crème à la Neige.

1 Pint of Fresh, Sweet Cream.
8 Tablespoonfuls of White Powdered Sugar.
The Whites of 2 Eggs.
1 Coffeespoon of Orange Flower Water.

Add to one pint of fine, fresh, sweet cream, eight tablespoonfuls of white powdered sugar, the whites of two eggs, well beaten to a froth, one coffeespoonful of Orange Flower Water, and whip all together steadily till the cream rises, taking it out as it does, and putting in another bowl, as in "Crème Fouettée" (see recipe), till all is drained. Place it in a little basket, lined with a fine linen napkin, and serve as quickly as possible.

The cream may be varied by coloring it with a little Saffron Powder make it yellow, with carmine or cochineal to make it pink and rosy, only, when doing this, add a little aromatic essence, such as vanilla, lemon or pineapple.

All the above creams may be served with plain or whipped cream.

### Bavarian Creams.
#### Bavaroise.

1 Quart of Cream.
½ Pint of Gelatine, or ½ Box.
1 Gill of Cold Water. ½ Cup of Sugar.
The Yolks of 4 Eggs.
1 Tablespoonful of Vanilla or Rum.

First of all, in making all Bavarian creams, follow implicitly the general directions given for making Cream Desserts, viz: Soaking the gelatine, and, before whipping the cream, cool it for at least an hour on the ice. Then put one pint of fresh cream or milk in a farina boiler, and add the sugar, and bring it to a boil. As it boils, pour in the gelatine. Stir constantly till the latter is well dissolved and blended, and set aside to cool. Beat the yolks of the eggs to a cream, an stir them in the cold cream, blending and beating vigorously. Then add the Vanilla or Rum, and set it away on the ice. When the boiled cream is quite cold, and has begun to thicken, stir it till perfectly smooth, and then stir in the whipped cream with a few light strokes. Have ready the mold or freezer, well rinsed, and fill with the cream. Set it away to cool and when quite firm turn it out, and serve with plain cream or whipped cream.

### Apricot Bavarian Cream.
#### Crème Bavaroise aux Abricots.

1 Pint of Fresh Apricots or 1 Pint Can.
½ Box of Gelatine, or ½ Pint.
1 Pint of Cold Water. 1 Pint of Cream.

Soak the gelatine and whip the cream. If the apricots are fresh, stew them and sweeten to taste. If canned, press them through a colander or sieve. Proceed to add the gelatine, which has been dissolved in a little boiling water, and then turn into a bowl. Stand upon cracked ice, and stir constantly till it begins to thicken, and then add the whipped cream stirring constantly till mixed well. Turn into a mold to harden and serve with whipped cream.

Peach or Plum Bavarian Cream may be made in exactly the same manner as the above, using eight or nine fresh peaches, stoned, or a one-pint can of fresh ones. Use one pint of plums.

### Strawberry Bavarian Cream.
#### Crème Bavaroise aux Fraises.

1 Quart of Fresh, Stemmed Strawberries.
½ Box of Gelatine, or ½ Pint.
1 Pint of Cream. 1 Cup of Sugar.
3 Tablespoonfuls of Water.

Soak the gelatine, and prepare the whipped cream. Then mash the strawberries and press them through a sieve. Add the white powdered sugar. Melt the gelatine by standing over boiling water, and then add it to the strawberry juice. Mix thoroughly. Then turn it into a tin pan or mold, set the basin on a pan of cracked ice, stir constantly till it begins to thicken, and then add the whipped cream, stiring it gradually till all is thoroughly mixed. Then pour into a mold and stand in an ice-cold place to harden.

### Raspberry Bavarian Cream.

Crème Bavaroise aux Framboises.

1 Pint of Raspberry Juice.
1 Pint of Cream. ½ Cup of Sugar
½ Pint of Gelatine.

Proceed in exactly the same manner as for Strawberry Bavarian Cream.

### Pineapple Bavarian Cream.

Crème Bavaroise à l'Ananas.

1 Pint of Grated Pineapple. 1 Pint of Cream.
1 Cup of Sugar. ½ Pint of Gelatine.
½ Cup of Cold Water.

Cover the gelatine with the water, and let it soak for half an hour. Then stand it over boiling water, and let it melt. Grate the pineapple, and add the sugar, and let it simmer gently till reduced to a liquid. Then stir the gelatine into the pineapple, and dissolve thoroughly. Place it in a tin vessel, and stand over cracked ice, stiring constantly. When it begins to thicken, add the whipped cream, and set away to harden, after turning into a mold. Serve with whipped cream.

Lemon Bavarian Cream is made in the same maner.

### Coffee Bavarian Cream.

Crème Bavaroise au Café.

1 Strong Cup of Cafe Noir. (See Recipe).
1 Teaspoonful of Vanilla.
½ Pint of Gelatine. 1 Cup of Sugar.
½ Cup of Water. 1 Pint of Whipped Cream.
The Yolks of 4 Eggs.

Soak the gelatine and whip the cream. After half an hour, pour it into the boiling coffee, and dissolve thoroughly. Then add the sugar, and stir thoroughly. Then add the milk. Let it boil up once, and remove from the fire, and stir in the well-beaten yolks of the eggs. Stir steadily and carefully until all the ingredients have thoroughly blended. Then set it on the fire to thicken slightly, stirring all the time, but be careful not to let it boil, or the eggs will curdle. Then set aside to cool slightly; pour it into a basin, and set over cracked ice, and add the whipped cream as it thickens. Then turn into a mold, and set in a cool place to harden. Serve with whipped cream.

### Caramel Bavarian Cream.

Crème Bavaroise au Caramel.

½ Pint of Gelatine.
1 Cup of Sugar. ½ Cup of Water.
1 Pint of Whipped Cream. 1 Gill of Sherry Wine.
2 Tablespoonfuls of Caramel.

Proceed exactly as above, using the same ingredients, except the eggs and coffee, substituting instead of the coffee, a gill of the best Sherry Wine and two tablespoonfuls of Caramel. (See recipe.)

### Chocolate Bavarian Cream.

Crème Bavaroise au Chocolat.

2 Large Tablespoonfuls of Chocolate.
1 Pint Milk. 1 Pint Cream. ½ Cup Sugar.
½ Pint of Gelatine.
Yolks of 4 Eggs.
1 Tablespoonful of Vanilla or Rum.
2 Ounces of Best French Chocolate.

Prepare the gelatine and cream according to general directions. (See recipe.) Grate the chocolate and set the milk to boil. Then add the grated chocolate, stirring slowly until all is dissolved. Take the saucepan from the fire, and add the sugar, mixing well, and the vanilla and rum. Turn it into a tin vessel to cool; set the vessel over cracked ice, and stir constantly till it begins to thicken. Then stir the whipped cream in carefully, and pour the mixture into a mold, and set in a cool place to harden. Serve with whipped cream.

### Orange Bavarian Cream.

Crème Bavaroise à l'Orange.

6 Louisiana Oranges. The Yolks of 5 Eggs.
1 Pint of Cream. 1 Pint of Milk.
1 Cup of Sugar. ½ Box Gelatine, or ½ Pint.

Whip the cream and prepare the gelatine according to general directions. (See recipe Bavarian Cream.) Set the milk to boil, and when it begins to boil, add the gelatine. Beat the yolks of the eggs very light, and add the sugar, beating very light; strain the milk and gelatine, and add the sugar and yolks stirring constantly till well mixed. Set over the fire for two minutes, and then set it away to cool. When cold, stir in the orange juice, which you will strain through a sieve. Set the basin in a pan of cracked ice, and stir until it begins to thicken, and then stir in the whipped cream very carefully, and proceed to turn into a mold to harden. Always wet the mold first with cold water before turning in the cream. When cold, serve with whipped cream.

### Velvet Cream.
#### Crème Velouté.
1 Pint of Cream.  1 Pint of Milk.
5 Ounces of Sugar.
Juice of 1 Lemon.  3 Tablespoonfuls Milk.
½ Pint of Gelatine.

Soak the gelatine in the water, and let it dissolve well. Set the milk to boil, and add the powdered sugar. Then dissolve the gelatine in it. Take off the fire, and add, as it cools, esence of vanilla or orange, using about two tablespoonfuls. Mix well. Then add the whipped cream, set over the fire one minute, pour into a mold to harden, and serve cold.

### Wine Cream.
#### Crème au Vin.
The Yolks of 8 Eggs.
1 Cup Sugar.
1 Quart of Madeira or Sherry Wine.

Beat the sugar and eggs well together, and add gradually one quart of Madeira or Sherry Wine, flavored with lemon or vanilla. Set the vessel in which they were mixed in another containing boiling water. Let the mixture simmer until the cream is perfectly formed, and then set to cool. Serve with whipped cream.

### Spanish Cream.
#### Crème à l'Espagnole.
1 Quart of Milk.  The Yolks of 5 Eggs.
1 Cup of Sugar.  ½ Pint of Gelatine.
1 Teaspoonful of Vanilla.

Soak the gelatine and whip one pint of cream. Set the milk to boil, and add the gelatine, which you will have dissolved in two tablespoonfuls of milk. Have the eggs and sugar beaten very light, and, as the milk boils up, add the sugar and eggs, but do not let them boil, or the eggs will curdle. Stir well, and turn the gelatine, which you will have dissolved well, into the milk. Then remove from the fire and strain, and add the essence of vanilla. Have the mold ready, clean and well rinsed and turn the cream into it. Set it on ice to harden, and, when ready, to serve, make a cream by whipping the whites of the eggs into the cream which has been whipped with powdered sugar. Turn the cream into a dish, heap this delicious meringue cream over it, and serve very cold.

Italian cream is made in exactly the same manner as above, only a wineglassful of Brandy is added.

## CHAPTER XXXVI.

### PUDDING SAUCES.

Sauces de Poudings.

### Apple Sauce.
#### Sauce aux Pommes.
6 Apples.  1 Pint of Cold Water.
¼ of a Lemon.
½ Pound of Powdered White Sugar.
A Teaspoonful of Ground Cinnamon.
1 Gill of Brandy.

Peel and quarter and seed the apples, and put them into a saucepan, with a pint of cold water and a quarter of a lemon. Let them boil for half an hour. Then press the cooked apples through a sieve into a bowl, and add the powdered sugar and the cinnamon and brandy. Set back on the stove and let the juice boil for five minutes, and serve with apple puddings, baked apples, dumplings, etc.

### Apricot Sauce.
#### Sauce d'Abricots.
4 Ounces of Apricot Marmalade.
1 Tablespoonful of Butter.
1 Gill of Water.  1 Gill of Brandy.

Take four ounces of Apricot Marmalade (see recipe) and put into a saucepan; add the butter and water, and set on a brisk fire; stir constantly until it comes to a boil, and then add a gill of good brandy. Let the mixture cook for two minutes more, and serve with baked apple dumplings, boiled dumplings, or apple pudding, as desired.

### Brandy Sauce.
#### Sauce au Cognac.
4 Tablespoonfuls of Butter.
1 Cup of Powdered Sugar.  Whites of 2 Eggs.
1 Gill of Brandy.
1 Gill of Boiling Water.

Beat the butter and sugar together to a cream, and add the sugar, beating until light and very white; add the whites of the eggs, beaten to a stiff froth, putting in one at a time; whip these well together, and add the boiling water and the brandy. Set over the fire in a bain-marie (boiling water) and stir till creamy and no longer. Serve either hot or cold. Do not let it boil. This sauce is excellent with Blackberry Roll, Bread Puddings, etc.

When a loaf of stale bread is left over, it may be wet and squeezed; add the yolks of three eggs, well beaten, and a pint of seeded raisins; mix well, and set to bake in the oven. Serve with the sauce above. This makes a very excellent and economical pudding.

### Hard Brandy Sauce.
#### Sauce Dure au Cognac.
1 Cup of Powdered Sugar. ½ Cup of Butter.
1 Wineglassful of Brandy.
¼ Teaspoonful of Ground Cinnamon.

Beat the butter and sugar to a cream; add the brandy and the powdered cinnamon and serve cold.

### Caramel Sauce.
#### Sauce au Caramel.
1 Cup of Sugar. 1 Cup of Water.
1 Tablespoonful of Sherry.
2 Ground Cloves. 1 Stick of Cinnamon.
Grated Zest of ¼ Lemon.

Put the sugar in a saucepan and let it melt and brown to a golden yellow; add the water and the wine, or essence and spices, etc., and set to cool after it has boiled three minutes.

### Chaufausen Sauce.
#### Sauce Chaufausen.
1 Pint of Chaufausen Wine.
1 Pint of Cold Water.
3 Tablespoonfuls of Powdered White Sugar.
6 Cloves. The Zest of 1 Lemon.
1 Inch of Cinnamon. 1 Ounce of Cornstarch.

Put the sugar, cinnamon, zest of lemon, cloves and water into a saucepan and set on a good fire and let them come to a boil, which will be in about five minutes. Then add the cornstarch diluted in a tablespoonful of cold water and stir it briskly into the water. After three minutes of stirring add one pint of Chaufausen wine, let it cook for two minutes longer and then take off the fire, drain through a sieve and serve with puddings, especially Apple Pudding.

### Cream Sauce.
#### Sauce à la Crème.
1 Pint of Sweet, Fresh Cream.
2 Tablespoonfuls of Powdered Sugar.
1 Nutmeg, Grated.
1 Teaspoonful of Vanilla, or Sherry or Madeira.

Add the sugar essence or wine to the cream; then stir constantly till thoroughly dissolved. Beat vigorously, and then add the nutmeg and set to cool. Serve with stewed apples and other stewed fruits, or fruit puddings.

### Cream of Butter Sauce.
#### Sauce à la Crème de Beurre.
½ Cup of Butter.
½ Cup of Powdered White Sugar.
4 Tablespoonfuls of Milk or Cream.
The Juice and Rind of a Lemon.

Beat the butter and sugar to a thick cream, and add the milk or cream gradually. Then place the mixture in a bowl and stand in a small tin of boiling water (bain-marie) and stir slowly till the sauce is very creamy, but do not allow it to simmer or boil. It will take just three or four minutes. As the thick cream forms, take from the fire, add the lemon and serve with any pudding.

### Cream of Vanilla Sauce.
#### Sauce à la Crème de Vanille.
1 Pint of Milk.
2 Tablespoonfuls of Powdered White Sugar.
The Yolks of 3 Eggs.
1 Tablespoonful of Vanilla Essence.
½ Gill of Maraschino or Good Cognac.

Beat the yolks of the eggs and the sugar well together, and add the vanilla essence. Beat thoroughly. Boil the milk and add the beaten egg to the milk as it comes to a boil. Stir briskly till it comes to a boil once more. Then take from the fire and add the maraschino or brandy according to taste.

### Custard Sauce.
#### Sauce Duchesse.
1 Pint of Milk.
½ Cup of Powdered Sugar. 3 Eggs.
1 Teaspoonful of Vanilla.

Set the milk to boil. Beat the eggs and sugar to a thick cream and very light, and then stir them into the boiling milk. Stir over the fire till the sauce begins to thicken, and no longer. If you stir too long the sauce will curdle. Take it from the fire and add the Vanilla and serve cold.

### Foaming Sauce.
#### Sauce à la Neige.
The Whites of 3 Eggs. 1 Cup of Sugar.
1 Gill of Boiling Water.
1 Glass of Sherry Wine or a Tablespoonful of Vanilla.

Beat the whites of the eggs to a stiff froth; melt the sugar in the boiling water, and then add a wineglass of Sherry. Stir in the frothy whites, and set to cool.

### Fruit Sauce.
#### Sauce aux Fruits.
4 Peaches, Apples, Apricots or Pears.
1 Cup Sugar. ½ Cup Water. 1 Pint of Cream.
Whites of 2 Eggs.
2 Tablespoonfuls of Brandy.

Pare the fruit; take out the stones or core; slice and put into a saucepan with the water and sugar, and let it stew gently until very tender. Then press through a colander or sieve. Set the cream to boil, and then beat it into the fruit thoroughly. Take off the fire, add the whites of the eggs beaten to a stiff froth, set to cool, and serve with fruit puddings made of the same fruits.

### Golden Sauce.
#### Sauce d'Or.

The Yolks of 2 Eggs. Juice of 1 Lemon.
1 Cup of Sugar.
1 Gill of Brandy or Sherry.

Beat the eggs and sugar until creamy. Set the saucepan in a kettle of boiling water over the fire; add the eggs that have been beaten well with the brandy or sherry; stir until the sauce becomes a thick cream; then take from the fire, add the juice of a lemon and serve very hot.

### Hard Sauce.
#### Sauce à la Crème Dure.

¼ Cup of Butter.
1 Cup of Powdered White Sugar.
The Whites of 2 Eggs.
1 Teaspoonful of Vanilla.

Beat the butter and sugar to a cream and gradually add the whites of the eggs beaten to a stiff froth; add the flavoring and heap on a small butter dish, sprinkle with grated nutmeg and serve cold.

### Hard Sauce à la Créole.
#### Sauce Créole.

¼ Cup of Butter. 1 Cup of Powdered Sugar.

Beat the sugar and butter to a rich cream, add a teaspoonful of vanilla, or a tablespoonful of good brandy, and serve cold. This is a very excellent sauce for baked dumplings, etc.

### Kirsch Sauce.
#### Sauce au Kirsch.

½ Gill of Kirsch.
1 Pint of Cold Water. ½ Pound of Sugar.
1 Tablespoonful of Cornstarch.

Mix the sugar and water in a saucepan and set on the stove on a brisk fire; let it come to a boil; then add a tablespoonful of cornstarch which has been diluted in a tablespoonful of water. Stir well for three minutes, and then take from the fire and add immediately a half gill of Kirsch. Mix well, strain through a sieve and serve with puddings.

### Lemon Sauce.
#### Sauce au Citron.

1 Tablespoonful of Cornstarch.
1 Tablespoonful of Butter.
1 Pint of Boiling Water. ½ Cup of Sugar.
1 Egg.
The Juice and Grated Zest of a Lemon.

Beat the butter and sugar to a cream; add the well-beaten egg, and then add the cornstarch, which you will have dissolved in a teaspoonful of water. When well-blended pour in slowly the boiling water, stirring all the time, and set over the fire till it thickens; stir about three minutes. Take from the fire and add the juice and rind of a grated lemon. This sauce is much improved by adding the white of an egg beaten to a stiff froth, after you have taken it from the fire.

### Madeira Sauce.
#### Sauce au Vin de Madère.

2 Cups of Sugar. ¼ Grated Nutmeg.
½ Cup of Butter. ½ Cup of Boiling Water.
2 Wineglasses of Madeira.

Beat the butter and the sugar to a cream, using powdered sugar, and then add one cup of boiling water. Stir in gradually two wineglasses of good Madeira wine or Sherry, and add one teaspoonful of grated nutmeg. Put into a double boiler and stir until the sauce is hot, but do not let it boil. Serve, either hot or cold, with any pudding.

### Madeira Sabayon Sauce.
#### Sauce Sabayon au Madère.

The Yolks of 4 Eggs.
2 Tablespoonfuls of Powdered White Sugar.
2 Gills of Madeira Wine.
The Zest of Half a Lemon.

Beat the yolks of the eggs and the sugar well together, and when they come to a rich cream set on the stove and whip well for two minutes. Then add the zest of a lemon or one tablespoonful of a lemon, or one tablespoonful of lemon essence, and drop in gradually the Madeira wine. Stir without ceasing for two minutes more, and then serve very hot with Fruit, Bread Puddings, etc.

### Orange Sauce.
#### Sauce d'Orange.

1 Cup of Sugar. 2 Tablespoonfuls of Butter.
½ Cup of Water.
The Juice and Grated Zest of 2 Oranges.
2 Eggs. 1 Teaspoonful Grated Nutmeg.

Beat the sugar, butter and yolks of the eggs to a cream. Then add the water and the juice and grated zest of two oranges. Set to boil in a double boiler; add, if desired, when it begins to simmer well, one tablespoonful of wine; take off the fire and add the whites of the eggs, beaten to a froth. Serve either hot or cold. If served cold, add the whites of the eggs at the moment of serving, as also the grated nutmeg. Serve with Orange Pudding, Orange Roly-Poly, etc.

### Punch Sauce.
#### Sauce au Ponche.
1 Gill of Good Cognac or Rum.
5 Ounces of Powdered Sugar.
The Juice of 3 Oranges.
The Zest of Half a Lemon.
The Grated Rind of Half an Orange.
1 Teaspoonful of Vanilla Essence.

Put the rum or brandy, the sugar, orange rind, lemon zest and vanilla essence into a saucepan and set on the stove. As soon as the ingredients light into a flame, cover tightly with a lid and let all infuse together for two minutes. Then take from the fire and add the juice of three Louisiana oranges. Serve very hot as a pudding sauce.

### Rum Sauce.
#### Sauce au Rhum.
1 Gill of Jamaica Rum.
6 Ounces of Granulated Sugar.
1 Tablespoonful of Caramel.
1 Tableapoonful of Cornstarch.
1 Pint of Water. The Zest of 1 Lemon.

Put the sugar and caramel (see recipe) and lemon zest in a saucepan, and when it begins to boil add a tablespoonful of cornstarch diluted in four tablespoonfuls of cold water. Let all cook for three minutes, and then remove from the fire, and add the rum. Mix well, then strain through a sieve into a sauce bowl and serve hot with fruit puddings especially.

### Silvery Sauce.
#### Sauce Argentée.
1 Cup of Sugar. 1 Tablespoonful of Butter.
The Whites of 2 Eggs.
1 Tablespoonful of Vanilla or Lemon.
2 Cups of Milk. 1 Tablespoonful of Brandy.

Beat the sugar and the butter to a cream. Set the milk to boil, and as it begins to simmer, add the sugar and butter. Let it simmer gently for a few minutes, and then take from the fire and add the whites of the eggs, beaten to a stiff froth. Add the essence, stirring till thoroughly mixed. Add the brandy and serve, either hot or cold, with any berry pudding.

### Strawberry Sauce.
#### Sauce aux Fraises.
1 Cup of Cream. The Whites of 2 Eggs.
1 Cup of Sugar. ½ Cup of Butter.
1 Cup of Fresh Mashed Strawberries.

Mash the strawberries, and press them through a sieve. Beat the butter and sugar to a cream; whip the cream and beat in the strawberries; then add the berry juice and mix thoroughly. Add two tablespoonfuls of sherry, if desired, or brandy, and serve with strawberry pudding, strawberry shortcake, or strawberry pie. It may also be served cold with a plain bread pudding. Blackberry Sauce may be made and served in the same way. Add a gill of Brandy to the Blackberry Sauce.

### Vanilla Sauce.
#### Sauce à l'Essence de Vanille.
1 Tablespoonful of Vanilla. 4 Eggs.
1 Pint of Milk. 2 Tablespoonfuls of Sugar.
1 Teaspoonful of Grated Nutmeg.

Set the milk to boil, and beat the yolks of the eggs and sugar very light; add them to the boiling milk; stir for two minutes over the fire. Take off and add the Vanilla and the whites of the eggs beaten to a froth; mix thoroughly, and serve either hot or cold.

### Velvet Sauce.
#### Sauce Veloutée.
1½ Cups of Powdered Sugar. ¾ Cup Butter.
A Tablespoonful of Cornstarch.
1 Gill of Boiling Water.
1 Gill of White Wine or Maraschino.

Beat the butter and sugar to a cream, and blend the cornstarch with a little cold water to form a paste. Boil the gill of water and add the cornstarch, stirring constantly as it thickens; continue stirring till transparent. Then add the butter and sugar, stirring well till perfectly blended, being careful to have the vessel containing the sauce in a bain-marie, or another vessel of boiling water. Add a gill of White Wine or Maraschino, and the juice of a lemon or orange, or vanilla extract, according to taste. Serve hot with any pudding.

### White Wine Sauce.
#### Sauce au Vin Blanc.
½ Cup of Butter. 2½ Cups Powdered Sugar.
½ Cup of Boiling Water.
2 Wineglasses of White Wine.
1 Tablespoonful Grated Nutmeg.

Beat the butter and sugar to a cream, and add the boiling water. Set the vessel containing the mixture into a bain-marie or saucepan of boiling water, and stir in gradually the white wine and the grated nutmeg. Let the sauce get hot, but do not let it boil. When it forms a thick cream take off, and serve either hot or cold. Stir all the time it is on the fire. Serve with any pudding.

## CHAPTER XXXVII.

### CAKES.

#### Des Gateaux.

The Picayune has now come to one of the most interesting sections of its Cook Book—certainly a favorite section, as far as the Creole girls are concerned. There is scarcely a girl who can make a good cake who does not pride herself upon this accomplishment, and "Ma Belle Créole" is no exception to this rule. She may not be able to make a "Ratatouille à la Créole," a "Bisque d'Écrevisses," or turn a pigeon "à la Crapaudine," but if she knows how to make a "Gateau a l'Archange," or a "Gateau d'Amandes," it will not be long before she will treat you to one of these dainty Creole cakes, which her "maman" will be sure to tell you "Marguerite has made all by herself."

The mixing and baking of cakes has always been held a very important branch of cookery. The baking is the most difficult part, but good cake making depends quite as much upon the quality and quantity of the ingredients used, and the manner of putting them together. Attention to the most minute detail in mixing is required if you seek success. Careless mixing will spoil the most perfect recipe. The greatest accuracy must be followed in proportioning out the ingredients, and using just so much, and no more. Often a tablespoonful of flour above the amount specified will cause the cake to crack open. The cream, the butter, the eggs, must be of the best quality. A stale egg will spoil the best cake, as also rancid butter. No cake should be flavored with a poor, cheap extract. Care must be exercised in the choice of all the materials, care in the exact weight specified, care in the proper heat of the oven. The following

**General Directions for Making Cakes**

should be read with care and implicitly followed:

A large earthen bowl is the best for mixing and beating the cakes and for beating butter and sugar to a cream, as is required in making rich cakes, such as pound cakes, etc.

The hand is the best instrument for working the cake, although a wooden spoon will be best for stirring in the ingredients. The spoon may be used also for beating, if you do not know how to use the hand dexterously.

Measure all ingredients carefully before beginning to make the cake, and have all at hand, within reach.

The whites and the yolks of the eggs must always be beaten separately for fancy cakes.

Use the white pulverized sugar in preference to the white granulated for all cakes, except gingerbreads, as it makes a lighter cake. Sift the flour as often as the recipes specify and measure it again after sifting.

If you use cream of tartar instead of baking powder, sift the cream of tartar into the flour, and dissolve the soda that must accompany its use in a tablespoonful of boiling water, and always add it to the cake before you add the whites of the eggs.

One-half teaspoonful of soda and one teaspoonful of cream of tartar may be used instead of one teaspoonful of baking powder where the recipe calls for the latter.

Raisins should always be picked over and divested of the stems and seeded before using.

In making fruit cake, prepare the fruit the day before.

Currants should be picked over, washed and dried before using.

Always use the butter thoroughly and drain of water before making the cake, and be sure that it is fresh, sweet, and of the very best quality.

Use none but white pulverized sugar, except in making gingerbread or gingercake.

Sift your flour before weighing. All the following recipes are for sifted flour.

Be perfectly accurate in weighing and measuring.

If you use cups for measurements let them be of the same size for all ingredients for the same cake.

Sour milk will make a spongy cake and sweet milk will make a cake with a close grain.

Never mix sweet and sour milk in the same cake. Failure will be the result.

Let the eggs be sound and fresh, and beat thoroughly till light, if you wish your cake to succeed. Do not rely entirely on the baking powder or the soda for the rising. The result of such flimsy methods will be apparent in the cake.

### Rules for Mixing Ingredients.

Observe implicitly the following rules:

Always beat the yolks and the whites separately for large cakes. Beat the yolks in an earthen dish till they begin to froth and thicken. Beat the whites to a froth so stiff that you can cut through it with a knife. Beat in a shallow dish with an egg beater or silver fork, preferably the egg beater.

Beat or stir the butter and sugar to a cream, rubbing both together steadily until they form a perfect cream. Then, and not till then, mix the yolks with the butter and sugar. Beat these together till very light. Then add the milk, and mix thoroughly. Sift the baking powder with the flour, and add a little at a time, stirring in well, till all is used up. Then add the whites of the eggs, beating them in thoroughly, and lastly, add the flavoring extract.

Follow, without the least variation, the exact order given above in the mixture of ingredients. When the cake is ready to bake, line the pan with a piece of buttered paper. This will prevent the cake from scorching. Then proceed to bake immediately, following the subjoined explicit

### Directions for Baking Cake.

Have your oven ready. This is most important. The oven should be ready to bake the cake immediately after it is well mixed, as standing makes cake batter heavy.

Test the temperature of the oven before putting the cake within. If you can hold your hand in the hottest part for a quarter of an hour the temperature will be correct.

If you have a Fahrenheit thermometer, let it be your guide as to the baking heat of the oven—450 degrees is the proper heat for drop cakes, rolls, buns, tea cakes, muffins, puff paste, etc. If you have not a thermometer another good test is to throw a little cornmeal or flour in the center of the oven. If the flour smokes before you can count ten, the oven is too hot. If it smokes at ten, the oven has the proper heat for the above cakes.

As soon as these are baked the heat will be reduced to 400 degrees Fahrenheit, and then the oven is ready to bake cream puffs, sugar cakes, queen cakes, jumbles, lady fingers, jelly rolls, etc. When these cakes are baked the heat will be reduced to 350 degrees Fahrenheit, and the oven will be just at the proper temperature to bake wine cakes, cup cakes, ginger snaps, gingerbread, spice cakes, Madeira cakes, etc.

Moderate the temperature slightly, and the oven will be ready for the baking of large cakes, such as pound, citron, marble, white, raisin, currant, almond, macaroons, etc. And, after all these cakes are baked, you will have the proper temperature for wedding cake, meringue, aniseed cakes, etc.

Thermometers are so cheap that it will pay the young housekeeper to have one in the house, rather than spoil ingredients by not having the oven at the right baking heat.

It will be seen from the above that cakes made with butter will require a moderate oven; cakes without butter will require a quick oven.

In baking small cakes or cookies have a moderately quick oven.

Bake molasses cakes in a moderately quick oven, and watch carefully, as they burn easily.

A large cake will require more time to bake than a loaf of bread of the same size. From an hour and a half to two hours will be sufficient for a pound cake.

To ascertain if the cake is done, take a stiff broom straw and run it into the center of the cake. When it comes out, feel with your fingers. If it is clean and dry, the cake is done. If otherwise, the cake requires a little more baking. Never introduce the straw until you think that the cake is done.

A thick paper (brown paper is best) spread over the top of the cake after it begins to bake will prevent it from browning too much. If it begins to brown as soon as you put it in the oven, it is an indication that the oven is too hot. Cover the cake with paper, and cool the oven by lifting the lid of the stove. But this is always risky. Have the oven of the right temperature.

Never set anything else to cook in the oven while you are baking a cake. The cake will surely fall.

Never move a cake when you have once set it in the oven till the center is perfectly firm and set. If you do, it will fall. If one side seems to be browning faster than the other, have recourse to the brown paper on top.

When you set the cake in the oven shut the door very gently, and be careful not to jar the cake, or it will be heavy. Do not open the door for about ten minutes, and then as little as possible, and very gently. If the cake is browning too quickly, cover with a layer of thick paper.

Watch the cake while baking, but never leave the oven door open. When necessary to look at the cake, gently do it as quickly as possible, and then shut the door carefully, without jarring the cake.

A cake should rise to its full height before the crust begins to form. If it hardens too fast, have recourse immediately to covering with paper.

Keep the oven at a steady, regular heat, the same at the top as at the bottom.

Never take the cake out of the oven until you are sure it is done. The broom splint, clean and dry, run through the center, is the infallible test.

Let the cake cool in the pan in which it was baked, as it is apt to become heavy if turned out while hot. Never handle the cake while hot. If the cake is streaky it shows that it was not mixed properly, or that the baking was rapid and unequal, or that the oven's temperature suddenly decreased before the cake was done.

When the cake is cool, if you wish to ice, it, proceed as follows:

### How to Ice Cakes.

Take one pound of pulverized sugar and the whites of two eggs. Have the eggs set in the refrigerator for about an hour before using. Beat the eggs and the sugar and a teaspoonful of rose or orange flower water or vanilla essence together till the eggs are very light. In commencing to beat do not beat the whites separately. Break them into a cold, shallow dish, and throw in a handful of sugar at a time, beating meanwhile, and adding at short intervals, till you have used up all the sugar. Or beat the whites and sugar and essence together. When the mixture is stiff and smooth, begin to lay a thin coating of the ice over the cake, using a knife to spread it, and occasionally dipping the knife into the lemon juice, which will enable you to smooth it nicely. When it is covered with this first coat, set in a warm place to harden—or in a moderate oven, where you may let it remain about four minutes, or in the sunshine where there is no dust around. When it is hardened it will be ready for the next coat. Proceed as above. This coat will be much smoother and whiter than the first. Let the thickness of the icing always be such that it will run very slow. If the icing is well prepared this will give a smooth, glossy surface. Instead of the essence, the juice of a lemon (one tablespoonful) may be added to the icing. If you wish to use ornaments, secure a piping tube, and place the ornaments around the cake while moist, running a plain tube around the edge of the cake, and then covering the cake with a thin icing level with the rim. Let it run smooth, and dry in the sun or in the oven. The sun is always best, if you are not in a very great hurry.

The above recipe is for plain icing. It may be varied according to taste by using pineapple, strawberry, or other flavoring. In using strawberry icing, add a few drops of cochineal to color. For further particulars as to different icings for cakes, see special section on "Icings and Frostings for Cakes."

### The Picayune Cake.
#### Gateau Picayon.

For upwards of seventy years the Picayune has led the vanguard of progress in New Orleans. In all public, philanthropic, charitable and educational enterprises, and whatever has tended towards the public weal, the Picayune, old in years, but with its youth ever renewed, has always brought the movement to a triumphant issue. This gave rise to a popular saying in New Orleans that the "Picayune always takes the cake." Acting upon this fact, a New Orleans lady originated a cake, and named it, in compliment to this journal, "The Picayune Cake." It is made as follows:

1 Cup of Finely-Sifted Flour.
1 Cup of Fine White Sugar. Whites of 9 Eggs.
2 Teaspoonfuls of Baking Powder.
1 Teaspoonful of Vanilla Extract.
1 Teaspoonful Lemon.

Beat the whites of the eggs to a stiff froth, after which very little beating will be required. Add slowly a heaping cupful of fine white sugar, and one cup of flour, both of which have been sifted four times to reach this measurement. Then add one teaspoonful each of vanilla and lemon extract, and two teaspoonfuls of baking powder, just before putting into the oven. Bake in a moderate oven for twenty-five minutes, and this cake, when eaten, will give the same satisfaction that the Picayune gives to its readers, as they devour its contents daily, and never get tired, but call for "more."

### Almond Cake.
#### Gateau d'Amandes.

12 Eggs. 1 Pound of Sifted Loaf Sugar.
¾ Pound of Sifted Flour.
6 Ounces Sweet Almonds. Zest of 2 Citrons.
Zest of 1 Orange. ¼ Teaspoonful Salt.
1 Tablespoonful of Orange Flower Water.

Beat the yolks of the eggs and the whites separately, beating the latter to a stiff froth. Blanch the almonds, and peel them and pound them to a fine flour in a mortar. Grate the zest of the oranges and lemons or citrons, and mix well. Beat the sugar and the yolks of the eggs to a cream, and gradually add one-half of the flour, beating well. Then add the almonds, mixing thoroughly, and, after beating vigorously, add one-half of the whites of the eggs Beat well, add the remainder of the flour, and then add the remainder of the eggs Finally add the orange flower water, and mix lightly. Butter a paper, and put in the cake pan, and pour in the mixture, and bake for one hour in a moderate oven.

### Angel Cake.
#### Gateau d'Ange.

1½ Cups of Granulated Sugar, Sifted.
1 Cup Sifted Flour. The Whites of 11 Eggs.
1 Teaspoonful of Cream of Tartar.
1 Teaspoonful Vanilla. ¼ Teaspoonful Salt.

Sift the flour four times, and then put in the cream of tartar, mix well, and sift a fifth time. Sift the sugar four times. Have the whites of the eggs beaten to a very stiff froth, so stiff that they may be cut with a knife clearly. Then add the flour by degrees, beating all the time. Lastly, add the flavoring extract. Do not butter the pan for this cake, but turn the mixture quickly into an ungreased Turk's head pan (a pan with a tube in the middle), and bake for three-quarters of an hour in a moderate oven. Test with a broom wisp. When done, turn the cake upside down, resting on the tube of the pan, and let it cool. The cake will fall out of the pan.

### Angel's Food.
#### Biscuit d'Ange.

1½ Cups of Sifted, Powdered White Sugar.
1 Cup Sifted Flour. Whites of 11 Eggs.
1 Teaspoonful of Baking Powder.
1 Teaspoonful Vanilla. ¼ Teaspoonful Salt.

Put the baking powder and the salt (or use cream of tartar instead of baking powder) into the flour, and sift it seven times. If you use cream of tartar, add it in the last sifting. Sift the sugar seven times. Beat the whites of the eggs to a very stiff froth, and add gradually the sugar, mixing very carefully. Then add the flour, gradually beating all the while, and lastly add the flavoring extract. Pour the mixture into a Turk's head baking pan (ungreased), and bake for forty-five minutes in a moderate oven. Test with the broom wisp. When done, turn the cake upside down, resting the pan on the tube till the cake falls off.

### Archangel Cake.
#### Gateau d'Archange ou Gateau de l'Ange Gabriel.

1 Cup of Butter. 2 Cups of Sifted Flour.
1 Cup of White Pulverized Sugar.
The Whites of 8 Eggs.
1 Teaspoonful of Lemon Extract.
¼ Teaspoonful of Salt.

Beat the whites of the eggs to a stiff froth. Add the baking powder to the flour, and sift it three times. Sift the sugar three times. Beat the butter, which has been well-washed, to a cream with the sugar. Then gradually add the flour, beating all the while, and the flavoring extract. Lastly, add the whites, which must be very stiff. Mix all thoroughly, and bake for about half an hour in a moderately quick oven. Use a Turk's head tin. (Follow directions for baking cake.)

### Banana Meringue Cake.
#### Gateau de Bananes Méringués.

9 Eggs. 1 Pound of White Pulverized Sugar.
½ Pound Flour.
The Juice of 1 Lemon.
3 Bananas. 1 Cup of Cream Sauce.
Whites of 3 Eggs.

Make a Sponge Cake; slice in two across the cake; slice bananas lengthwise very nicely and lay on the bottom layer of cake; sprinkle with a little powdered sugar, and then spread over a little Cream Sauce, which you will have made to the consistency of Cream Puff filling. Put over this the second layer of cake, and then repeat the process of spreading the bananas and cream on the layer. Make a meringue with the whites of three eggs and three tablespoonfuls of sugar, and spread this over the whole. Set in a quick oven and bake to a delicate brown, and serve, either hot or cold, with a Wine Sauce, preferably Sauce au Vin de Madere. (See recipe.)

### Black Cake.
#### Gateau Noir.

1 Pound of Brown Sugar. 1 Pound of Butter.
1 Pound of Flour. 2 Pounds Currants.
2 Pounds of Seeded Raisins.
½ Pound of Citron, Cut very Thin.
½ Pound of Chipped Figs.
1 Glass of Jelly. 1 Wineglass of Brandy.
1 Pound Almonds, Blanched and Chopped.
12 Eggs.
1 Teaspoonful of Extract of Cinnamon.
1 Teaspoonful Cloves. 2 Teaspoonfuls Nutmeg.

Wash and cleanse the currants thoroughly. Seed the raisins. Beat the butter and sugar to a cream. Then add the yolks of the eggs, well beaten. Add one-half of the flour and the spices. Mix all the fruit in the remaining flour, having first sliced the citron very thin, and add to the mixture. Then add the jelly, which should be homemade and of the best quality. Otherwise, add one cup of the best Louisiana molasses. Mix thoroughly. Add the whites of the eggs and the brandy last. Divide into two tins, which must be lined with well-greased paper. Bake for four hours in a slow oven. Test with the broom wisp. If not done through cook longer, watching carefully, and using the test till the straw is dry.

### Buttermilk Cake.
### Gateau au Babeurre.

2 Cups of Buttermilk.   3 Cups of Sugar.
5 Cups of Flour.   1 Cup of Butter.   4 Eggs.
½ Teaspoonful of Soda.

Beat the butter to a cream, and then add the sugar, which has been sifted fine. Beat to a cream. Add the yolks of the eggs, and continue beating till very light. Mash the soda in the buttermilk, dissolving thoroughly, first in a half cupful, and then mixing well with the remainder of the milk. Add this to the eggs and butter. Then gradually add the sifted flour, and beat till very smooth. Lastly add the whites of the eggs, beaten to a stiff froth. Bake for forty-five minutes in a moderate oven.

### Bride's Cake.
### Gateau de Marié.

3 Cups of White Pulverized Sugar.
1 Cup of Butter.   4 Cups of Sifted Flour.
½ Cup of Cornstarch.
The Whites of 12 Eggs.
2 Teaspoonfuls of Baking Powder.
1 Cup of Sweet Milk.
1 Teaspoonful of Extract of Lemon.

Beat the whites of the eggs to a stiff froth. Sift the flour and baking powder. Sift the sugar. Beat the butter and sugar to a cream. Beat till very light. Mix the cornstarch with the sweet milk and add to the sugar and butter, beating well. Then add gradually the flour, mixing thoroughly, and beating light. Add the extract of lemon, and finally the whites of the eggs, beaten to a stiff froth. Bake one hour in a moderate oven, using the broom wisp test. If not done, bake a little longer.

### Chocolate Loaf Cake.
### Gateau au Chocolat.

1 Cup of Sugar.   1 Tablespoonful of Butter.
1½ Cups of Sifted Flour.
¾ Cup of Milk.   Yolks of 8 Eggs.
White of 1 Egg.
¼ Cake of Grated Chocolate.
2 Teaspoonfuls of Baking Powder.

Dissolve the chocolate in the cup of milk, and boil till thick. Beat the butter to a cream, and gradually add the sugar, beating constantly. Then add the yolks of the eggs, and beat till very light. Sift the flour, and add the baking powder, and sift again. Then add the flour gradually to the mixture, beating all the while. Now add the chocolate, and beat very vigorously. Beat the whites of the eggs to a stiff froth, and add to the mixture. Then add the essence, beating lightly again, and turn into a greased pan and bake in a moderate oven for three-quarters of an hour or an hour.

### Chocolate Cake à la Créole.
### Gateau au Chocolat a la Créole.

1¾ Cups of Flour.   1½ Cups of Sugar.
½ Cup of Butter.   4 Eggs.
4 Tableapoonfuls of Grated Chocolate, or 2 Ounces.
½ Cup of Milk.   1 Teaspoonful of Vanilla.
1 Heaping Teaspoonful of Baking Powder.

Beat the butter to a cream, and gradually add the sugar, beating constantly. When very light, add the yolks of the eggs, and beat till these are very light. Then add the milk and the chocolate, which you will have dissolved in four tablespoonfuls of boiling water. Mix thoroughly, and add by degrees the flour, beating all the while. Give a very vigorous beating and add the whites of the eggs, beaten to a stiff froth. Stir them very carefully into the batter, and add the vanilla, and finally the baking powder. Mix all very quickly and lightly, and set to bake in buttered pans in a moderate oven for three-quarters of an hour.

### Citron Cake.
### Gateau au Cédrat.

1 Quart of Flour.   1 Cup of Butter.
2 Cups of Sugar.   12 Eggs.
1 Cup of Cream.   1 Glass of Wine.
1 Cup of Chopped Citron.
1 Teaspoonful of Almond Extract.

Beat the butter to a cream. Add the sugar, and beat till very light. Then add the yolks of the eggs, and beat till very light. Add the cream, and mix thoroughly, and then add by degrees the citron, mixing thoroughly. Now, by degrees, add the flour, well-sifted. Beat well. Then add the wine, and lastly the whites of the eggs, beaten to a stiff froth. Mix all quickly and lightly; add the almond extract, mix lightly, and then set to bake in a buttered pan in a moderate oven for one hour.

### Cocoanut Loaf Cake.
### Gateau au Coco.

¼ Pound of Butter.   2 Cups Grated Cocoanut.
5 Eggs.   1 Cup of Milk.
½ Cup of Butter.   ½ Pound of Flour.
2 Teaspoonfuls of Baking Powder.
The Juice and Grated Zest of 1 Lemon.

Beat the butter and sugar to a rich cream. Add the yolks of the eggs, and beat till very light. Then add the milk, and the flour by degrees, beating all the while, and then add the lemon. Beat well. Add the cocoanut, and stir in carefully and well. Sift the baking powder over the whites of the eggs, which you will have beaten to a stiff froth, and add these, beating lightly and thoroughly. Have ready two loaf pans, and line them with very thin buttered paper. Now divide the batter into two even parts, filling each pan about three-quarters full. Set in a moderate oven, and bake for forty-five minutes. When done, cover the top with finely-grated cocoanut, and sift powdered sugar over it. Set it to cool. This is a famous Creole cake.

### Clove Cake.
### Gateau de Girofles.

1 Teaspoonful of Ground Cloves.
1 Cup of Sugar. 1 Cup of Sour Cream. 1 Egg.
½ Cup of Flour.
1 Teaspoonful of Soda. A Pinch of Salt.

Beat the sugar and yolk of the egg to a cream. Add the cream and soda blended. Mix thoroughly. Then add the cloves, and mix well. Sift the flour and salt together, and add gradually, beating all the while. Give several vigorous beats, and set to bake in a buttered tin in a moderate oven for forty-five minutes.

### Coffee Cake.
### Gateau de Café.

1 Cup of Cafe Noir (Black Coffee).
4 Eggs. 4 Cups of Flour.
1 Cup of Butter. 1 Cup of Molasses.
1 Cup of Sugar. 1 Cup of Seeded Raisins.
1 Cup of Currants, Washed and Dried.
1 Grated Nutmeg.
½ Teaspoonful of Ground Cinnamon.
½ Teaspoonful of Cloves.
½ Teaspoonful of Soda, Dissolved in Warm Water.

Wash and cream the butter. Add the sugar and beat till very light. Then add the yolks of the eggs. Beat them into the butter and sugar till very light. Add the molasses, and mix thoroughly. Then take the seeded currants and raisins and blend them with one-half of the flour and add gradually. Now, add by degrees the remainder of the flour, beating vigorously. Then add the coffee, and mix well. Add the soda, dissolved in hot water. Add the spices, mix well, and finally add the whites of the eggs, beaten to a stiff froth. Mix thoroughly but lightly, divide into two parts, set in two greased paper-lined tins, and bake from forty-five minutes to one hour in a moderate oven.

### Caramel Cake.
### Gateau au Caramel.

1 Cup of Butter. 2 Cups of Sugar.
1 Cup of Milk. 1½ Cups of Flour, Sifted.
1 Cup of Cornstarch.
Whites of 7 Eggs.
2 Teaspoonfuls of Baking Powder.

Cream the butter, add the sugar, and beat till very light. Then add the milk. Mix well. Sift the flour, cornstarch and baking powder together, and add gradually to the mixture, beating vigorously all the while. Then add the vanilla and the whites of the eggs, beaten to a stiff froth. Mix all quickly and lightly, turn into a long family pan, and bake for about half an hour in a moderate oven. Apply the broom wisp test. When done, take out of the oven and set to cool. When cool, take

2 Cups of Brown Sugar.
1 Cup Sweet Cream. 2 Teaspoonfuls Vanilla.
1 Tablespoonful of Butter.

Boil all together until it sugars, and spread over the top and sides. Or, if you wish something much nicer, make the following mixture:
½ Pound Brown Sugar. ½ Pound Chocolate.
½ Cup Milk. 1 Tablespoonful Butter.
2 Tablespoonfuls of Vanilla.

Grate the chocolate, and set all to boiling together until thick enough to spread over the top and sides of the cake. This is delicious.

### Cup Cake.
### Gateau Savoie.

1 Cup of Butter. 2 Cups of Sugar.
3 Cups of Flour. 4 Eggs.
2 Teaspoonfuls of Baking Powder.
1 Teaspoonful of Lemon or Rose Extract.

Beat the butter to a cream. Add the sugar gradually, beating all the while. Then beat the yolks until they are very light, and add to the mixture. Add the milk. Mix well, and add half of the flour, which you will have sifted with the baking powder. Then add the well-beaten whites of the eggs, and the remainder of the flour, and the extract of Lemon or Rose. Finally add the baking powder, mix quickly and lightly, turn into a Turk's head pan, which you will have lined with a greased paper, and bake for forty-five minutes in a moderate oven.

### One, Two, Three, Four Cup Cake.
### Un, Deux, Trois, Quatre.

1 Cup of Butter. 2 Cups of Sugar.
3 Cups of Flour. 4 Eggs.

Beat the butter to a cream. Add the sugar. Beat till very light. Beat the eggs (yolks and whites together) till very light, and add them gradually to the butter and sugar, beating all the while. Beat vigorously. Add the sifted flour, and beat thoroughly until very light. Then line a round cake pan with the buttered paper, and fill with the mixture. Set in a moderate oven, and bake for one hour and a quarter.

### Cake Without Eggs.
### Gateau Sans Oeufs.

2 Cups of Sifted Flour. 1 Cup of Milk.
1½ Cups of Sugar. 2 Tablespoonfuls Butter.
1 Teaspoonful Baking Powder.
¼ Teaspoonful of Salt.
1 Teaspoonful of Lemon Extract.

Beat the sugar and the butter to a cream, and then add the milk, stirring carefully. Add the flour, and beat well and hard. Then add the salt, flavoring extract and baking powder. Mix all thoroughly, and bake in a moderate oven for a half hour.

### Delicate Cake.
#### Délicatesse.

1½ Cups of Flour.  1½ Cups of Sugar.
½ Cup of Cornstarch, Sifted With the Flour.
½ Cup of Butter.  ¼ Cup of Milk.
Whites of 6 Eggs.
2 Teaspoonfuls Baking Powder.
½ Teaspoonful of Extract of Lemon.
¼ Teaspoonful Salt.

Cream the butter and beat it and the sugar to a cream. Add the milk, and stir carefully. Then add gradually the flour, into which has been sifted the salt and the cornstarch, and mix thoroughly. Then add the flavoring extract, and, lastly, the whites of the eggs, beaten to a stiff froth. Sift the baking powder over the whites. Mix quickly and lightly with the batter, and bake forty-five minutes in a moderate oven.

### Dried Fruit Cake.
#### Gateau de Fruits Secs.

3 Cups of Dried Apples, Peaches or any Kind of Dried Fruit.
2 Cups of Louisiana Molasses.
1 Cup of Milk.  2 Eggs.  ¾ Cup of Butter.
1 Cup of Sugar.
1 Teaspoonful of Ground Cinnamon.
½ Teaspoonful Each of Ground Cloves and Mace.
½ Pound of Stoned Raisins.
½ Grated Nutmeg.  ¼ Teaspoonful Salt.
The Juice of a Lemon.
1½ Teaspoonfuls of Baking Powder or 1 Teaspoonful of Soda.

Soak the fruit over night. Then chop very fine, and simmer in a saucepan with the molasses for two hours and a half. Let it cool. Seed the raisins. Beat the butter and sugar to a cream, until very light. Add the yolks of the eggs, and beat till light. Now add the milk and then the fruit and molasses, stirring carefully. Beat hard for five minutes. Now add the flour, which you will have sifted with the baking powder, and beat vigorously for five minutes. If you use soda, dissolve it at this point into a tablespoonful of boiling water, and add, mixing well. Then add the raisins, and beat vigorously, and the spices and salt. Add the juice of the lemon, and finally the whites of the eggs, beaten to a stiff froth. The batter must be stiff, but of sufficient elasticity to drop from the spoon. Bake in a moderate oven for two hours. Use the broom wisp to test; if it comes out clean and dry, then the cake is done. This is a very nice and economical family cake, if properly made.

### Fig Cake.
#### Gateau de Figues.

1 Cup Butter.  2 Cups Sugar.  1 Cup Milk.
3 Cups of Sneded Raisins.
1 Pound of Figs, Chopped Very Fine.
1 Egg.  2 Teaspoonfuls of Baking Powder.
3 Cups of Flour.
¼ Teaspoonful of Salt.  ¼ Grated Nutmeg.

Beat the butter to a cream and add the sugar. Then beat very light, and add the egg. Beat well and add the milk; carefully and gradually add the flour, into which you have sifted the baking powder. Add the raisins and the figs, and beat thoroughly; add the grated nutmeg, and bake for an hour in a moderate oven. Bake slowly, and use the broom wisp test. If not done, bake longer, till the straw comes out clean and dry.

### Fruit Cake.
#### Gateau de Fruits.

½ Pound of Grated Lemon and Orange Peel, Mixed,
¾ Pound of Raisins.
¼ Pound of Preserved Cherries.
¾ Pound of Sultanas.
¼ Pound of Preserved Figs.
¼ Pound of Citron.
¼ Pound of Preserved Apricots.
½ Pound of Sifted Flour.
¼ Pound of Preserved Pineapple.
½ Pound of Butter.
¼ Pound of Mashed Almonds.
1 Grated Nutmeg.
½ Pound of White Pulverized Sugar.
¼ Tablespoonful of Mace.
8 Eggs.  ¼ Tablespoonful Ground Cinnamon.
The Juice of 1 Orange.
⅛ Tablespoonful of Cloves.
The Juice of 1 Lemon.
⅛ Tablespoonful Ground Allspice.
2 Teaspoonfuls of Baking Powder.
¼ Teaspoonful of Salt.
1 Wineglassful of Good Brandy.
1 Wineglassful of Sherry Wine or Jamaica Rum.

Prepare the fruit first. Stone the raisins, picking carefully. Pick over the sultanas carefully, and wash them well. Then cut the orange and lemon zest very fine, almost grating. Cut the citron very, very fine. Cut all the remaining fruit into quarter-inch dice, or very, very small pieces. You may use the candied fruit, but the preserved is recommended as better and lighter and more digestible. Beat the butter to a rich cream, and then add the sugar, and beat all till very, very light. Beat the yolks and the whites of the eggs together till very, very light, and then add them to the sugar and butter, and then beat again very, very light. Sift the salt and baking powder and flour together, and gradually add it to the mixture, beating very vigorously till light. Then mix all the fruit together, dredging with flour, so as to keep them apart, and then add the spices to the batter. Mix well, and add the fruit. Mix thoroughly, and then add the brandy or rum. Beat all together well once more, and then line a cake pan with buttered paper, and turn the mixture into it, and bake in a very slow, steady oven for four and a half hours. Use the broom wisp test. When it comes out clean and dry the cake is done. Then let it stand over night in the pan to cool. In the morning take it out and remove the paper. Take one pint of the best French brandy, and one pint of the best champagne, and one gill of orange, raspberry or strawberry syrup, mixed with the wine. Set the cake in a stone pot of sufficient size, and pour the mixture over it. Then set the cake in a cool place and cover the top of the jar airtight with a piece of thin linen, and set the cover on top. Let the cake stand for three weeks. At the end of that time remove the cover and paper, and turn the cake, and let it stand for three weeks longer. The Creoles always let their fruit cakes stand for six weeks at least before cutting. This is an old Creole recipe for Fruit Cake, and very excellent. The above will make an eight-pound cake.

### Plain Fruit Cake.

#### Gateau de Fruits.

It is not every housewife who can afford to make the above fruit cake; those of limited means will find the following simple cake much more economical; it is very excellent:

1 Pound of Brown Sugar. 1 Pound of Butter.
10 Eggs. 2 Pounds of Seeded Raisins.
2 Pounds of Currants. 1 Pound of Citron.
¼ Pound of Almonds. 1 Nutmeg.
1 Teaspoonful Each of Ground Allspice and Cinnamon.
½ Teaspoonful Each of Ground Mace and Cloves.
½ Pound of Sifted Flour.
The Zest Each of an Orange and Lemon.
¼ Teaspoonful of Salt.
The Juice of 1 Orange and 1 Lemon.
2 Teaspoonfuls of Baking Powder.
1 Wineglassful of Good French Brandy.
1 Wineglassful of Sherry Wine or Jamaica Rum.

Prepare the fruit by seeding the raisins, washing and drying the currants, cutting the citron into shreds and dice, and mashing the almonds. Beat the butter and sugar to a cream and add the eggs, which you will first beat, without separating whites and yolks, till very light. Beat these into the sugar and butter till very light, and then add the flour gradually, and the spices. Sift the flour with the baking powder and salt, and then mix the fruit into it before adding to the cake. Beat vigorously. Then add the grated zest of the orange and lemon, and the juices of both. Stir well and add the brandy and wine or rum. Mix well. Divide the batter into two pans, which you will have lined with greased paper, and bake in a steadily moderate oven for four hours. Use the broom wisp test, and if it comes out clean and dry the cake is done. If not, let the cake bake from a quarter to a half hour longer, watching carefully. This will make a nine-pound cake, or two four-and-a-half-pound cakes. When done, put the cake into an earthenware bowl, with a flat bottom. Pour over a pint of the best brandy and half a pint of Sherry Wine. Make the vessel air tight by tying around a linen cloth, and put on the cover. Set the cake away for about three weeks, and then open and turn. Let it remain three weeks longer, and the cake is ready to cut. If you wish to use it sooner, do not add the liquor after baking, but set the cake away to cool in the pan in which it was baked. Then place in a cool place after taking out and removing the paper, and wait eight days before cutting.

### Ginger Cake.

#### Gateau au Gingembre.

3 Cups of Flour. 2 Eggs.
½ Cup of Milk or Sour Cream.
1 Teaspoonful of Soda or Baking Powder.
½ Cup of Butter or Lard.
1 Tablespoonful of Ground Ginger, or 1 Tablespoonful Each of Ground Cinnamon and Ginger.
1½ Cups of Louisiana Molasses.
1 Pint of Louisiana Molasses.

Beat the yolks of the eggs to a cream and then add the melted butter, beating till very light. Sift the baking powder and the flour together, and add the ginger, mixing well; then add the milk and the molasses to the butter and eggs, mixing thoroughly. When well blended, add the flour and ginger and baking powder (mixed) and beat vigorously. Finally add the whites of the eggs beaten to a stiff froth, turn into a well-greased tin, and bake in a moderate oven for forty-five minutes. Use the broom wisp test before taking the cake out of the oven.

### Ginger Bread.

#### Pain d'Épices.

½ Pound of Butter. ½ Pound of Sugar.
3 Pints of Flour.
2 Tablespoonfuls of Ground Ginger.
1 Teaspoonful Ground Cinnamon.
1 Pint of Sweet Milk or Sour Cream.
1 Teaspoonful of Soda or Baking Powder.

Beat the butter to a cream, and then add the sugar. Beat till very light, and then beat the yolks of the eggs till creamy and add to the butter and sugar. Beat very light. Now add the molasses and stir well, mixing thoroughly; then add the milk and mix well into the flour, with which you will have sifted the baking powder, and beat till very smooth. Then add the ground ginger and cinnamon; mix well; and finally add the whites of the eggs, beaten to a stiff froth; mix well and pour into two well-greased, shallow tins. Bake in a moderate oven for forty minutes, using the broom wisp test before taking out of the oven. Sprinkle with white sugar and serve, either hot or cold. If soda is used, dissolve it in a tablespoonful of boiling water and add to the molasses; then add to the butter and sugar before adding the flour and milk. Some beat the whites and yolks together; but the bread is much lighter and more delicate when the whites and yolks are beaten separately.

**Stage Planks or Ginger Bread Without Butter or Eggs.**

Estomac Mulâtre.

1 Cup of Molasses. 1 Cup of Sour Milk.
1 Tablespoonful of Ground Ginger.
1 Gill of Lard. 3 Cups of Flour.
1 Teaspoonful of Baking Soda.

Melt the molasses, lard and ginger together and blend well. When thoroughly melted and warmed, beat for about ten minutes. Then dissolve the soda in a tablespoonful of boiling water and add to the molasses; mix it thoroughly, and then add the flour, using good judgment and adding just enough of the three cups of sifted flour to make a stiff batter; beat thoroughly and vigorously. Have ready several greased, shallow pans; pour the mixture into them and bake for ten minutes in a quick oven. This bread makes the famous "Stage Planks," or ginger cakes, sold by the old darkies around New Orleans, in old Creole days, to those of their own race and to little white children. The ancient Creoles, fond of giving nicknames, gave to this stiff ginger cake the name of "Estomac Mulâtre," or "The Mulatto's Stomach," meaning that it was only fit for the stomach of a mulatto to digest.

**French-Creole Cake.**

Gateau Français-Créole.

1 Pound of Sifted Sugar (White Pulverized).
The Grated Peel of 1 Lemon.
1 Tablespoonful of Orange Flower Water.
12 Eggs. ½ Pound of Sifted Flour.
½ Pound of Mashed Rice (Dried).
1 Tablespoonful of Baking Powder.
4 Ounces Sweet Almonds.
1 Ounce of Bitter Almonds.

Beat the whites of the eggs to a stiff froth, after having blanched and peeled the almonds and pounded them to a fine powder in a mortar. Beat the yolks of the eggs very light, and gradually add the rice, which has been well-mashed. Mix the almonds thoroughly with the flour; then add these gradually to the sugar, beating vigorously. Add the grated zest of the lemon and the essence, and finally add the whites of the eggs and mix lightly and quickly. Butter a paper and line the bottom and sides of the pan, and bake the cake in a moderate oven for one hour.

**Fruit Ginger Bread.**

Pain d'Épices aux Fruits.

1 Pound of Flour. ½ Pound of Butter.
½ Pound of Sugar.
1 Cup of Louisiana Molasses.
¼ Pound of Raisins.
½ Pound of Currants, Washed and Dried.
½ Cup of Sour Cream. 3 Eggs.
1 Teaspoonful of Soda or Baking Powder (Level).
1 Teaspoonful of Ground Ginger.
½ Teaspoonful Each of Ground Cinnamon and Cloves.

Beat the butter and sugar to a cream, and warm the molasses and beat with the sugar and butter. Then add the well-beaten yolks of the eggs, and the milk and spices and ginger, mixing thoroughly. Add the soda, dissolved in a tablespoonful of boiling water; mix well; and mix the seeded raisins and currants well; then add the flour by degrees, beating vigorously. Finally add the whites of the eggs beaten to a stiff froth, and beat thoroughly. Put in two shallow pans in the oven for about two hours. The broom wisp test must be used before taking the cake out of the oven. Sugar ginger loaf is made in the same manner, simply omitting the fruits and spiced ginger loaf and adding a teaspoonful each of ground cloves, mace, cinnamon and allspice to the ginger.

**Gold Cake.**

Gateau d'Or.

1½ Cups of Sugar. 1 Cup of Milk.
½ Cup of Butter.
3 Cups of Flour. The Yolks of 6 Eggs.
2 Teaspoonfuls of Baking Powder.

Beat the butter to a cream; add the sugar and beat till very light. Then add the well-beaten yolks of the eggs; beat vigorously till light, and gradually add the flour, into which you will have sifted the baking powder. Bake for forty-five minutes in a moderate oven. Save the whites of the eggs for Silver Cake.

**Silver Cake.**

Gateau Argenté.

½ Cup of Butter. 1½ Cups of Sugar.
1 Cup of Milk. 3 Cups of Flour.
2 Teaspoonfuls of Baking Powder.
The Whites of 6 Eggs.

Beat the butter to a cream; then add the well-beaten sugar and beat well; add the yolks of the eggs and beat till very light. Then add the milk and mix carefully. Now sift the flour and baking powder together, and add gradually to the mixture. Turn into a buttered pan and bake in a moderate oven for forty-five minutes.

### Honey Cake.
#### Gateau de Miel.

1 Teaspoonful of Honey.
1 Teaspoonful of Sugar.
½ Teaspoonful of Melted Butter.
1 Pint of Flour. 2 Eggs.
1 Teaspoonful of Baking Powder.
1 Teaspoonful of Carraway Seeds.

This is a very popular Creole cake. Take one teacupful each of honey and sugar, and mix well. Add a half teaspoonful of melted butter and the yolks of two well-beaten eggs; sift one teaspoonful of baking powder into a pint of flour and add. Beat all together till very light, and add the whites of the eggs, beaten to a stiff froth. Finally, add a teaspoonful of carraway seed, if desired, and bake in a moderate oven from half an hour to three-quarters of an hour.

### Imperial Cake.
#### Gateau Impérial.

1 Pound of Butter. 1 Pound of Sugar.
1 Pound of Flour.
The Juice and Rind of 1 Lemon.
1 Pound of Blanched Almonds.
¼ Pound of Citron.
½ Pound of Raisins. 9 Eggs.
1 Teaspoonful of Baking Powder.

Blanch and peel and pound the almonds in a mortar. Seed the raisins, and cut the citron into shreds and quarter-inch dice, very fine. Grate the zest of the lemon. Beat the butter to a cream. Add the sugar gradually, beating till very light. Then add the yolks of the eggs beaten to a cream. Beat till very light, and mix the sifted flour and baking powder with the almonds, and add them gradually to the mixture, beating vigorously. Add the raisins, dredging with flour, and the citron. Mix well. Add the juice of the lemon, and finally the whites of the eggs, beaten to a thick froth. Turn into a buttered tin, and bake for an hour in a moderate oven. Use the broom-wisp test before taking out of the oven.

### Indian Pound Cake.
#### Gateau l'Indienne.

½ Cup of Flour. 1 Cup of Indian Meal.
½ Pound of Butter.
½ Pound Sugar. 8 Eggs. 1 Grated Nutmeg.
1 Teaspoonful of Cinnamon.
½ Glass of Sherry Wine and Brandy, Mixed.

Stir the butter and sugar to a cream, and add the well-beaten yolks of the eggs. Beat till very light, and then add the meal and flour, well blended. Beat light. Add the spices and liquor, and finally the whites of the eggs, beaten to a stiff froth. Beat thoroughly, but lightly, and turn into a buttered tin, and bake in a moderate oven for an hour and a half.

### Lady Cake (White).
#### Gateau Blanc à la Dame.

1½ Cups of Flour. 1 Cup of Sugar.
½ Cup of Butter.
The Whites of 4 Eggs. ½ Cup of Milk.
1 Teaspoonful of Baking Powder.
1 Teaspoonful of Peach Extract.

Cream the butter, add the eggs, beating the whites to a stiff froth, and mixing well. Add the milk, and gradually add the flour, blending thoroughly, and beating till very light. Add the essence, and bake in a moderate oven for one hour.

### Lunch Cake.
#### Gateau du Goûter.

4 Cups of Sugar. 3 Cups of Flour.
½ Cup of Milk. 2 Eggs.
2 Teaspoonfuls of Baking Powder.
1 Teaspoonful of Peach Extract.

Beat the sugar and eggs to a cream, and add the milk. Then add gradually the flour, into which you will have sifted the baking powder. Add one tablespoonful of Peach Extract, and bake in a moderate oven for three-quarters of an hour.

### Madame John's Cake.
#### Gateau de M'me Jean.

1 Pound of Sugar. 7 Ounces Butter.
The Whites of 16 Eggs, Whipped to a Stiff Froth.
1 Pound Sifted Flour. Juice of 1 Orange.

Cream the sugar and butter together till very light. Then add the whites of the eggs, beaten to a stiff snow, after which stir in gradually the flour and one teaspoonful of baking powder. Flavor with the juice of one orange, or with a tablespoonful of Orange Extract, and bake for from thirty to forty-five minutes in a quick oven. Use the broom-wisp test.

### Marble Cake.
#### Gateau Marbré.

The white part:
½ Cup of Butter. ½ Cup of Milk.
1½ Cups of White Pulverized Sugar.
2½ Cups of Flour. The Whites of 4 Eggs.
1 Teaspoonful Baking Powder.
1 Teaspoonful of Extract of Lemon.

Beat the butter to a cream, and gradually add the sugar, beaten thoroughly till very light. Then add the milk, and stir carefully. Add one-half of the flour, evenly divided. Beat vigorously, and add the Lemon Extract. Mix well, and add the whites of the eggs, beaten to a thick froth, and the remainder of the flour. Then stand this mixture to one side while you make the dark part of the cake.

Dark part:

¼ Cup of Butter. 1 Cup of Brown Sugar.
The Yolks of 4 Eggs.
½ Cup of Milk. 1½ Cups of Flour.
2 Ounces of Melted Chocolate.
1 Teaspoonful Vanilla.
1 Teaspoonful of Cloves (if desired).
1 Teaspoonful Baking Powder.

Beat the butter and the sugar to a cream, till very light, and then add the beaten yolks of the eggs, and beat till very light. Add the milk, and stir carefully. Then add the flour, and blend and beat till smooth. Dissolve the chocolate in a little of the milk, and add, mixing well, and then add the vanilla essence and the baking powder to tthe mixture. Add the baking powder now to the first mixture, and mix thoroughly and lightly. Then grease a piece of brown paper, and line the cake pan, and put in first a spoonful of the white mixture and then one of the dark, and continue alternating thus till all is used. Set in a moderate oven, and bake for three-quarters of an hour. Try the broom-straw test, and if it comes out clean and dry, the cake is done. If not, bake a quarter of an hour longer. The cake must cool in the pan in which it was baked. When cut you will have a beautifully marbled cake.

### Chocolate Marble Cake.

Gateau Marbré au Chocolat.

The Whites of 6 Eggs. 1 Cup of Butter.
2 Cups of Sugar. 3 Cups of Flour.
½ Cup of Sweet Milk.
2 Teaspoonfuls of Baking Powder.
½ Cake of Grated Chocolate.
1 Teaspoonful of Vanilla Extract.

Beat the butter and sugar to a cream, and then add the milk. Sift the flour and baking powder together, and stir into the cake gradually. Then add the vanilla essence and the whites of the eggs, beaten to a stiff froth. Divide the cake batter in two, and mix the grated chocolate into one half. Then put a dark layer of cake in the pan, then a light, and continue so alternating until all the batter is used. Bake in a moderate oven for three-quarters of an hour.

### Motley Cake.

Gateau Mélé.

1 Pound of Sugar. ½ Pound of Butter.
3 Cups of Flour. 12 Eggs.
1 Teaspoonful of Baking Powder.
1 Teaspoonful of Peach Extract.
1 Teaspoonful of Fruit Coloring.

Beat the butter and sugar to a cream and then add the well-beaten yolks of the eggs. Beat until very light. Then add gradually the flour, into which you will have sifted, in the second sifting, the baking powder. Mix thoroughly and beat vigorously. Then add the whites of the eggs, beaten to a stiff froth. Now divide the batter into two parts, and put one spoonful of Peach Extract into one, and one spoonful of fruit coloring into the other. Mix well, and drop by spoonfuls into the buttered cake pan, first a spoonful of the white, and then one of the pink, until all the batter is used up. Bake from forty-five minutes to one hour in a moderate oven.

### Molasses Cake.

Gateau à la Mélasse.

2 Cups of Louisiana Molasses.
1 Cup of Boiling Milk or Water.
1 Teaspoonful of Baking Powder or Soda.
3½ Cups of Flour (Sifted).
4 Eggs. 1 Cup of Butter.
1 Tablespoonful of Ground Ginger.
¼ Teaspoonful of Cloves.

Melt the butter. Dissolve the soda in the boiling water, using about one tablespoonful, and add it to the molasses. Then beat the sugar and butter to a cream, until very light, and add the well-beaten yolks of the eggs. Add these to the molasses, and then stir in the cream. Beat till smooth, and then add gradually the flour, beating till very light and smooth. Now add the ginger and cloves, or a teaspoonful of cinnamon, and the whites of the eggs, beaten to a stiff froth. Place in a shallow cake pan, buttered, and bake in a moderate oven from thirty to forty-five minutes.

### A Plain Molasses Cake.

Gateau à la Mélasse.

1 Cup of Louisiana Molasses.
3 Cups of Flour. 1 Cup of Boiling Water.
1 Teaspoonful of Soda.
2 Tablespoonfuls of Butter.
1 Tablespoonful Ginger.

Dissolve the soda in boiling water, and add it to the molasses. Then melt the butter, and add, and pour in gradually the boiling water, mixing well. Now add gradually the flour, beating well, and add the ginger. Beat until all is very smooth, and then bake for a half hour in a moderate oven.

### Manqué.

The Yolks of 8 Eggs.

The Whites of 3 Eggs, Beaten to a Froth.
½ Pound of White Pulverized Sugar.
1 Tablespoonful of Butter. 1 Cup of Flour.
The Grated Zest of 1 Lemon.
1 Teaspoonful of Baking Powder.

Beat the sugar and butter and yolks of the eggs to a very light cream, and then add the grated zest of the lemon. Gradually add the flour, which you will have mingled and sifted with the baking powder. Then add the whites of the eggs, beaten to a stiff froth. Beat lightly and quickly, and place in a buttered cake pan, and bake for thirty minutes in a moderately quick oven.

### Nut Cake.
#### Gateau aux Noix.

1 Cup of Butter. 2 Cups of Sugar.
3 Cups of Flour. 1 Cup of Milk.
4 Eggs. 1 Cup of Nut Meats, Cut Fine.
2 Teaspoonfuls Baking Powder.
½ Teaspoonful of Extract of Almond.

Beat the butter to a cream, and add the sugar, and beat till very light. Then add the well-beaten yolks of the eggs, and beat till very light. Add the milk, and mix carefully. Then sift the baking powder and flour together, and add the flour, beating till very smooth. Add half the beaten whites, which must be of a stiff froth, and mix well. Then add the nuts (pecans, mashed almonds, peanuts and Brazilian nuts, mixed, and cut or mashed very fine). Add the remainder of the whites of the eggs, the Almond Extract and the baking powder, and mix well. Pour into two square, flat pans, lined with buttered paper, and bake in a moderate oven forty-five minutes. Use the broom-straw test. If the straw comes out clean and dry, the cake is done; otherwise bake it a little longer. Keep the heat of the oven steady and moderate.

### Orange Cake.
#### Gateau d'Orange.

4 Ripe Oranges. 1 Pound Pulverized Sugar.
1 Pound of Butter.
14 Ounces of Flour. 10 Eggs.
1 Teaspoonful of Baking Powder.

Wash the oranges. Then dry and roll them under your hand on a board till very soft. Grate the zest of the oranges, and then cut up the fruit fine, and squeeze through a strainer till all the juice is extracted. Wash the butter till you extract all the salt, and then beat it to a cream. Add the sugar, and beat thoroughly, and then add the orange zest and juice, and beat till very light. Add the yolks of the eggs, well-beaten, and again beat the mixture till light. Then, by degrees, add the flour, adding alternately the whites of the eggs, beaten to a stiff froth. Beat the whole for a half hour, and then bake in a moderate oven for forty-five minutes or an hour, using the broom-wisp test. If you ice the cake, add orange juice to the icing.

### Pearl Cake.
#### Gateau à la Perle.

¾ Pound of Butter. 1 Pound of Sugar.
1 Pint of Milk. 4 Eggs.
1 Teaspoonful of Soda. 1 Pound of Flour.
½ Grated Nutmeg.
1 Tablespoonful of Vanilla Extract.

Beat the butter and the sugar to a cream. Beat the eggs, whites and yolks separately, and add the yolks. Then beat till very light. Add the soda, dissolved in a tablespoonful of boiling water, and then add the milk and beat carefully. Add the flour gradually, and beat vigorously. Then add the spices and essence, and lastly the whites of the eggs, beaten to a stiff froth. Bake for an hour in a moderate oven.

### Premium Cake.
#### Gateau Royal.

The Whites of 14 Eggs. 1 Pound of Sugar.
¾ Pound of Flour. ½ Pound Butter.
1 Wineglassful of Good Whisky.
The Juice and Grated Zest of 1 Lemon.
1 Teaspoonful of Baking Powder.

Beat the butter and sugar to a cream, and add one-half of the whites of the eggs, beaten to a stiff froth. Then add the flour gradually, beating thoroughly and well, till very light. Now add the whisky and the lemon juice, and the grated zest of the lemon, and finally add the remainder of the whites and the baking powder, beating till very light. Bake in a moderate oven from forty-five minutes to an hour.

### Pound Cake.

1 Pound of Sugar. 1 Pound of Butter.
1 Pound of Flour. 10 Eggs.
1 Teaspoonful Baking Powder.
1 Tablespoonful of Lemon or Vanilla Extract.

Wash the salt from one pound of butter. Then take a tablespoon and take out one heaping tablespoonful of butter from the pound. Experience of years in baking pound cakes has taught that a whole pound of butter will make a greasy cake, though many use a pound. If once this latter method is tried, the difference will be apparent in the superior quality of the cake. After washing the butter, beat it with the white pulverized sugar to a thick cream. Have the baking powder and the flour sifted together. Beat the yolks of the eggs well, and then add them to the sugar and butter, beating till very light. Then add a part of the flour, and beat light. Add a part of the whites of the eggs and mix thoroughly. Then alternate with the flour and the whites of the eggs until all are used up. Add the essence of lemon or vanilla and a gill of brandy, and continue beating vigorously for a half hour. Put the batter in a cake pan (a Turk's head), lined with a buttered paper, and bake for one hour in a moderate oven. Use the broom-straw test. If the cake is not quite done, bake a quarter of an hour longer. Never touch or move a pound cake in the oven till the center is set.

### Pound Cake No. 2.

1 Pound of White Pulverized Sugar.

10 Eggs. 1 Pound Sifted Flour.
1 Grated Nutmeg. 1 Wineglassful of Brandy.
1 Pound of Butter.
1 Tablespoonful of Vanilla, Lemon or Rose Water.
1 Teaspoonful of Baking Powder.

Wash the butter and drain, and take out a heaping teaspoonful. Then beat the remainder to a rich cream with the sugar, and add the well-beaten yolks of the eggs. Beat till very light, and add a part of the flour, into which you will have sifted the baking powder. Then add a part of the whites of the eggs, beaten to a stiff froth, and continue alternating with the flour and the eggs till all are used up. Then add the grated nutmeg, the brandy and the essence, and continue beating steadily for a half hour. Bake in a moderate oven for one hour. Use the broom-wisp test. If it comes out clean and dry the cake is done; otherwise continue baking for a quarter of an hour longer.

Some of the Creoles, in making pound cake, use sixteen eggs, leaving out the yolks of four, others use twelve eggs. The above measurements will be found exact, and if the cake is properly made it will be delicious.

The above measurements will make a four-pound cake.

### White Pound Cake.

1 Pound of Sugar. 1 Pound of Flour.

1 Pound of Butter. The Whites of 16 Eggs.
1 Teaspoonful Baking Powder.
1 Teaspoonful of Lemon Extract.

Wash the butter. Then beat it and the sugar to a fine cream. Add one-quarter of the flour, well-sifted with the baking powder. Then add one-quarter of the whites of the eggs, which you will have beaten to a stiff froth. Continue alternating the eggs and flour till all are used. Add the flavoring extract, and beat steadily for a half hour. Bake in a moderate oven for one hour.

### Plum Cake or Old-Fashioned Creole Wedding Cake.

Gateau de Noces Créole à l'Ancienne.

2½ Pounds Flour. 1½ Pounds Sifted Sugar.
1½ Pounds Butter.
1 Pound of Seeded and Chopped Raisins.
1 Pound Chopped and Dried Cherries.
1 Pound of Currants, Washed, Cleansed and Dried.
12 Eggs. 1 Ounce of Salt.
1½ Pounds of Shredded Orange, Lemon and Green Citron Peel, Combined.
½ Pint of French Brandy.
½ Gill of Caramel or Burnt Sugar Coloring.
8 Ounces of Ground Almonds.
The Zest of 4 Oranges.
1 Ounce of Ground Cloves.
Cinnamon, Nutmeg and Coriander Seed in Equal Proportions.

Work the butter until it becomes very creamy, using a wooden spoon. Then add the sugar, working to a thick cream, and add the yolks of the eggs, well-beaten. Beat till light, and add by degrees the flour, salt and two teaspoonfuls of baking powder, working the batter all the time. Then add the fruit, which you will have dredged slightly with flour, working them well into the batter. Add the whites of the eggs, beaten to a thick froth, and when all are well incorporated, pour the mixture into a baking pan, lined with double sheets of buttered paper, and place on top thick sheets of paper which you set in the oven. Bake in a moderate oven, and keep the heat regular and steady all the time, being careful not to increase or diminish it during the baking. Bake for two hours and a half. This is the largest wedding cake. To make a smaller one, use half the ingredients, and bake half the time.

To ice the cake, clear it of the paper when it grows cold. Place it on a baking sheet, and cover the top with a coating of Orgeat Paste (see recipe) one and a half inches thick. Let it dry for an hour and then cover with a coating of Plain Icing (see recipe) about half an inch in thickness. When this becomes hard, decorate it with a piping around the edges in tasteful designs, mingling artificial buds and blossoms in the decorations. Add a delicate wreath of blush roses. This is the old-fashioned Creole wedding cake.

### Raisin Cake.

Gateau de Raisins Secs.

1½ Pounds of Stoned Raisins.
1½ Pints of Sugar. 1½ Pints of Flour.
¾ Pound of Butter. ½ Pint of Milk. 6 Eggs.
½ Gill of White or Sherry Wine.
½ Gill of Brandy.
2½ Teaspoonfuls of Baking Powder.

Sift the flour and baking powder together. Then beat the butter and sugar to a cream, add the yolks of the eggs, and beat till very light. Beat the whites to a stiff froth, and then add alternately the whites and flour to the mixture, beating vigorously till light. Now add the wine and brandy. Flour the raisins, and shake lightly, till each becomes slightly coated on each side, and add to the cake batter, and then begin to stir lightly, stirring just sufficient to mix. Have ready a deep baking pan or two, lined with buttered paper, and bake in a slightly quick oven for from forty-five minutes to an hour. Have a thick layer of paper over the cake for the first half hour of baking.

### Spanish Cake.
#### Gateau à l'Espagnole.

1 Pound of Butter. 1 Pound of Sifted Flour.
1 Pound of Good Brown Sugar.
6 Well-Beaten Eggs.
1 Teaspoonful of Baking Powder.

Beat the butter and sugar to a cream. Add the well-beaten yolks of the eggs, and then alternately the flour, with which the baking powder has been sifted, and the whites of the eggs, beaten to a stiff froth. Bake in a buttered cake pan for about an hour in a moderate oven.

### Spice Cake.
#### Gateau d'Épices.

1 Pound of Flour.
1 Pound of White Pulverized Sugar.
¾ of a Pound of Butter. 9 Eggs.
1 Teaspoonful of Ground Cinnamon.
½ Teaspoonful Ground Allspice.
1 Teaspoonful of Grated Nutmeg.
½ Teaspoonful of Ground Mace.
1 Wineglassful Brandy.
1 Wineglassful of Sherry or Madeira.
1 Teaspoonful of Soda.
1 Cup of Sour Cream. ¼ Teaspoonful of Salt.

Beat the butter and the sugar to a cream, and then add the well-beaten yolks of the eggs. Beat till very light. Add half the flour gradually, alternating with half the whites of the eggs, which you will have beaten to a thick froth. Then add the spices, the brandy and the wine. Now add gradually the rest of the flour, and then the remainder of the whites of the eggs. Finally add the sour milk, into which you will have dissolved one teaspoonful of soda in a tablespoonful of boiling water. Stir well, and turn into a buttered Turk's head tin, and bake for one hour in a moderate oven. Use the broom-straw test.

### Spiced Molasses Cake.
#### Gateau d'Épices à la Melasse.

1 Cup of Louisiana Molasses.
1 Cup of Sugar. ½ Cup of Butter. 2 Eggs.
2 Teaspoonfuls of Vinegar.
2 Teaspoonfuls Soda.
½ Teaspoonful Each of Cloves, Allspice and Cinnamon (ground).
1 Grated Nutmeg. 3 Cups of Flour.
¼ Teaspoonful of Salt.

Warm the molasses and dilute with the vinegar. Beat the butter and the sugar to a cream, and then add the eggs, whites and yolks, well-beaten together. Then add gradually one-half of the flour and the molasses. Add the grated spices and salt. Beat well. Add the soda, dissolved in two tablespoonfuls of boiling water, and beat well. Bake in a moderate oven from thirty to forty-five minutes.

### Sponge Cake.
#### Gateau Biscuit de Savoie.

9 Eggs. 1 Pound of White Pulverized Sugar.
½ Pound Flour.
The Juice of 1 Lemon.

Beat the yolks of the eggs very light, and then add the sugar, and beat till very light. Then add the juice of the lemon, and add gradually one-half of the flour. Have the whites of the eggs beaten to a very stiff froth, so clear that they may be cut with a knife. Add one-half to the cake, and then add the remaining half of the flour. Beat well. Now add the remaining half of the whites, and beat lightly. Pour into a cake pan, lined at the bottom and around with buttered paper, and bake in a quick oven from forty-five minutes to one hour, using the broom-straw test. Cover the cake with a layer of thick brown paper when you first put it in the oven. Keep the heat of the oven steady. The Sponge Cake, next to "Lady Fingers," which are a species of sponge, is the very lightest of cakes.

### Cream Sponge Cake.
#### Biscuit de Savoie à la Crème.

2 Cups of Sugar. 1 Cup of Cream.
2 Cups of Flour. 4 Eggs.
1 Teaspoonful of Baking Powder.
1 Teaspoonful of Lemon Essence.

Beat the yolks of the eggs and the sugar to a cream. Add the cream, and gradually add the flour and baking powder, sifted. Add the whites of the eggs, beat lightly, and bake in a quick oven thirty minutes.

### Quick Sponge Cake.
#### Vitement Fait.

3 Eggs. 1½ Cups of Sugar.
2 Cups of Flour. ½ Cup of Cold Water.
1 Teaspoonful Lemon Extract.
2 Teaspoonfuls of Baking Powder.

Beat the eggs and sugar to a cream, add the water, and mix well. Then gradually add the flour, alternating with the whites of the eggs, beaten to a thick froth. Bake from thirty to forty-five minutes in a quick oven.

### White Sponge Cake.
#### Gateau Blanc.

1½ Cups of Pulverized White Sugar.
1 Cup of Flour. The Whites of 11 Eggs.
1 Teaspoonful Baking Powder.
1 Teaspoonful of Vanilla Extract.

Beat the whites of the eggs and the sugar to a thick froth. Mix the baking powder and the flour, adding the powder after the fourth sifting. Then add the flour gradually to the eggs, beating lightly and thoroughly. Add the essence, and bake for from thirty to forty-five minutes in a quick oven.

### Tutti-Frutti Cake.
#### Gateau Tutti Frutti.

1 Cup of Sugar. 1 Cup of Butter.
1 Teacup of Milk. 2½ Teacups of Flour.
2 Teaspoonfuls of Baking Powder.
1 Pound of Raisins. 1 Pound of Figs.
1 Pound of Powdered Almonds.
The Whites of 7 Eggs.

Take one teacupful of sugar and one of butter and beat to a cream. Add a teacupful of milk and two and a half teaspoonfuls of flour sifted, with two heaping teaspoonfuls of baking powder; add one pound of raisins, well-seeded, and one pound each of shredded figs and pounded almonds. After mixing all these well, and the whites of seven eggs, beaten to a stiff froth. Bake in a slow oven. When done, make a light syrup and spread over the top, and garnish with pieces of finely-cut preserved citron, oranges, preserved currants and other candies.

### White Mountain Cake.
#### Gateau à la Montagne Blanche.

1 Pound Sugar. 1½ Pounds Butter.
1 Pound of Flour. The Whites of 10 Eggs.
½ Teaspoonful of Almond Extract.

Cream the butter, add the sugar, and beat till very, very light. Add the flour alternately with the whites of the eggs, beaten to a stiff froth, and then the essence extract. Bake in a moderate oven one hour.

### White Cream Cake.
#### Gateau à la Crème.

4 Cups of Flour. 1 Cup of Butter.
1 Cup of Sweet Cream.
3 Cups of Sugar. The Whites of 10 Eggs.
2 Teaspoonfuls of Baking Powder.
1 Teaspoonful of White Rose Extract.

Proceed in exactly the same manner as for White Mountain Cake, only adding the cream just before adding the flour and the whites of the eggs.

### Twelfth Night, or King's Cake.
#### Gateau de Roi.

2 Pounds of the Best Flour.
12 Eggs. 1 Cup of Sugar.
1 Pound of the Best Butter.
½ Ounce of Yeast.
½ Ounce of Salt.
Candies to Decorate.

This is a Creole cake whose history is the history of the famous New Orleans carnivals celebrated in song and stories. The "King's Cake" or "Gateau de Roi," is inseparably connected with the origin of our now world-famed carnival balls. In fact, they owe their origin to the old Creole custom of choosing a king and queen on King's Day, or Twelfth Night. In old Creole New Orleans, after the inauguration of the Spanish domination and the amalgamation of the French settlers and the Spanish into that peculiarly chivalrous and romantic race, the Louisiana Creole, the French prettily adopted many of the customs of their Spanish relatives and vice versa. Among these was the traditional Spanish celebration of King's Day, "Le Jour des Rois," as the Creoles always term the day. King's Day falls on January 6, or the twelfth day after Christmas, and commemorates the visit of three Wise Men of the East to the lowly Bethlehem manger. This day is even in our time still the Spanish Christmas, when gifts are presented in commemoration of the King's gifts. With the Creoles it became "Le Petit Noel," or Little Christmas, and adopting the Spanish custom, there were always grand balls on Twelfth Night; a king and a queen were chosen, and there were constant rounds of festivities, night after night, till the dawn of Ash Wednesday. From January 6, or King's Day, to Mardi Gras Day became the accepted Carnival season. Each week a new king and queen were chosen, and no royal rulers ever reigned more happily that did these kings and queens of a week.

The method of first choosing the king was by cutting the "King's Cake." This famous "Gateau de Roi" was made of Brioche Batter. (See recipe.) It was an immense cake, shaped round like a great ring, and decorated with bonbons, dragees, caramels, etc. When Twelfth Night arrived there was always a flutter in old Creole New Orleans. Generally some grand mansion was chosen for the first ball, and as the evening progressed, when the clock struck twelve, the guests were all invited to be seated around the spacious dining room where the "King's Cake" was brought in. Now, hidden away somewhere in this cake was a bean, or often as not a magnificent jeweled ring. The cake was cut into as many slices as there were guests, the smiling cavaliers and the lovely Creole maidens ranged around, each of the latter cherishing the wistful hope that she might find the bean, each of the former hoping likewise that he might have the pleasure of choosing as his queen some lovely girl who held his heart. The cake, after being cut, was covered with a large linen napkin, so that one might have the opportunity of seeing if the dainty morsel had been cut near the ring or bean, for often the knife went very, very near, and the dexterous manipulator, with a smile, had to remove it an inch further from the mark. But it was generally so imbedded in the cake that it was impossible to detect the least trace. Champagne was passed with the King's Cake, for was it not a royal dish? Suddenly there would be a little flutter. Some one had found the ring or bean, and all gathered around to congratulate the fortunate finder. If a man, he was hailed as the first king of the season, and so, if it were a lady, she was saluted as the queen. If the finder of the bean were a lady, she simply chose her king by presenting him with a bouquet of violets, which was always provided with the cake. If a gentleman found the ring or bean, the uncrowned king would hold it up, and announce that the lady with whom he would make the round of the parlor, or "le tour du salon" would be his queen. Then he would take his stand near the mantel, the music would strike up, and the beautiful promenade around the room would begin, the gentlemen gracefully offering their arms to the ladies, the latter laughingly complying with the old custom of passing before the king while he choose his queen. No doubt there was much secret vexation among those bonny girls as they passed on and on, the king seemingly unable to make a choice. Suddenly, he advanced, and, taking the flower from the lapel of his coat, he presented it to the lady, and, if it happened to be a ring in the cake, often as not it was a magnificent diamond, too, that he presented to her. Then offering his arm, he led the promenade, making as he said, "le tour du salon" with her, and then passing beneath the chandeliers, he would raise his hand, the music would cease, and the king would proclaim: "Mes sujets, voici votre reine! Recevez ses commandements!" Then followed an ovation of smiles, congratulations and homage, as though she were indeed a queen succeeding to her born rights. And the honors of that night clung to her ever after, amid sunshine and clouds in the old French Quarter.

The prettiest old-time courtesies were connected with the round of balls that followed. These balls were always given at the home of the queen. The king, whether he found the bean or was simply chosen by the lady who had found it, was expected to bear the entire expense of the ball of which he was king, and to provide the next King's Cake. He was also expected, before the end of the week, to make his queen some beautiful jeweled gift. These gifts of jewels from the king were the only ones that the Creole mother ever allowed her daughters to accept from any gentleman. In this custom of presenting the queen of the week with jewels may be distinctly traced the present custom of our Carnival kings in presenting the queens with jewels.

And so, week after week, the festivities continued; a King's Cake was cut, a new king and queen chosen, and this continued till the grand culminating ball of Mardi Gras night.

A pretty superstition was also connected with the King's Cake. The lucky finder of the pecan, or bean, or ring, which was hidden within was henceforth to be favored by fortune. The queen cut the bean in two, and gave half of it to her king, and so, if a gentleman found it. The lucky bean was faithfully preserved as a talisman, and in many an old Creole family to-day there is carefully preserved a little shriveled amulet which was found in the Gateau de Roi on Twelfth Night.

To make the cake take a pound and a half of the above-mentioned quality of flour, and put it in a wooden bread trough. Make a hole in the center of the flour, and put in a half ounce of yeast, dissolved in a little warm water. Add milk or tepid water to make the dough, using milk if you want it to be very rich and delicate, and water if you have not the milk. Knead and mix the flour with one hand, while adding the milk or water with the other. Make a dough that is neither too stiff nor too soft, and when perfectly smooth set the dough to rise in a moderately warm place, covering with a cloth. Remember that if you use milk to make the dough it must be scalded, that is, must be heated to the boiling point, and then allowed to grow tepid. Let the dough rise for five or six hours, and, when increased to twice its bulk, take it and add the reserved half pound of flour, into which you will have sifted the salt. Add six eggs, beaten very light with the sugar and butter, and mix all well together, kneading lightly with your hands, and adding more eggs if the dough is a little stiff. Then knead the dough by turning it over on itself three times, and set to rise again for an hour or three-quarters of an hour. Cover with a cloth. At the end of this time take it up and work again lightly, and then form into a great ring, leaving, of course, a hole in the center. Pat gently and flatten a little. Have ready a baking pan with a buttered sheet of paper in it, and set the central roll in the middle. Cover the pan with a clean, stiff cloth, and set the cake to rise for an hour longer. When well risen, set in an oven a few degrees cooler that that used for baking bread; let bake for an hour and a half; if medium, one hour, and if very small, a half hour. Glace the Brioche lightly with a beaten egg, spread lightly over the top before placing in the oven. Decorate with dragees, caramels, etc.

## CHAPTER XXXVIII.

### LAYER CAKES.

#### General Directions.

In making layer cakes, always have ready three or four jelly tins, and bake the cake in layers in the separate tins for fifteen minutes. Then set to cool, and make the fillings and place alternately between the layers, a layer of cake always being on top, to admit of icing, if desired.

These directions for arranging the filling will hold for almost all layer cake.

#### Layer Cake.

To make the layer cake, use any good Sponge, Pound or White Cake recipes, using three-quarters of the proportions of each to make four good layers, and increasing in proportion. Bake in jelly tins for fifteen minutes, and set to cool before adding the filling.

#### Almond Cake.

#### Gateau d'Amandes.

2 Cups of Sugar. 1 Cup of Milk.
2 Tablespoonfuls of Butter.
2 Cups of Flour. The Whites of 6 Eggs.
2 Teaspoonfuls of Baking Powder.
1 Teaspoonful Lemon Extract.

Proceed to cream the butter and sugar. Add the milk, and gradually add the flour and the whites of the eggs alternately, and beat till light. Add the essence, and bake in jelly tins fifteen minutes. Make a filling as follows:

Take two pounds of almonds, blanch them, peel and pound to a flour. Beat the whites of two eggs to a froth with one-half cup of sugar, and spread on top of the bottom layer of cake as a frosting. Place over this a layer of the almonds, and then another layer of frosting. Add a layer of cake, and then go over the same process again till the top layer of cake is reached. Sprinkle with white sugar or ice neatly, according to taste.

#### Banana Layer Cake.

#### Gateau de Bananes.

9 Eggs. ½ Pound of Flour.
1½ Cups of Pulverized Sugar.
1 Teaspoonful of Lemon or Vanilla Extract.
3 Bananas.

Prepare four layers of Sponge Cake. (See recipe). Slice the bananas lengthwise very nicely and lay on the bottom layer. Sprinkle with a little powdered sugar, and then spread a little Cream Sauce which has been made to the consistency of Cream Puff Filling. (See recipe.) Over this put on the second layer of cake; cover nicely with the bananas and the Cream Sauce, and proceed thus till the top layer is placed over the bananas. Then sprinkle with white sugar or ice, according to taste.

#### Chocolate Layer Cake.

#### Gateau au Chocolat.

A Layer Cake. (See recipe). 1 Cup of Powdered Sugar.
1 Cup of Milk or Water. 4 Ounces of Chocolate.
The Whites of 2 Eggs.

Make a layer cake. Boil four ounces of chocolate in one cup of milk or water. Add one cup of sugar, and let it boil till thick. Spread between the layers of cake. Or take four ounces of chocolate, melt with a little boiling water, just sufficient to make a paste, and work till smooth. Beat the whites of two eggs to a stiff froth, add four tablespoonfuls of white sugar, and then proceed as in Almond Layer Cake, having a layer of chocolate on top.

### Cocoanut Layer Cake.

Gateau au Coco.

4 Layers of Cake. (See Layer Cake Recipe.)
The Whites of 2 Eggs.
1 Cup of Powdered Sugar. 2 Cups of Grated Cocoanut.
White Sugar to Sprinkle.

Make a good layer cake. Beat the whites of two eggs till very frothy. Add one cup of powdered sugar, and beat till very stiff. Grate the cocoanut, and then proceed as in filling the Almond Cake, having a layer of the cocoanut on top, sprinkled with white sugar. (See recipe.)

### Cream Layer Cake.

Gateau à la Crème.

4 Layers of Sponge Cake. (See recipe).
The Yolks of 2 Eggs.
1 Cup of Pulverized Sugar. 2 Teaspoonfuls of Cream.
1 Teaspoonful of Vanilla.

Make a layer sponge cake. Prepare a filling by beating together the yolks of two eggs, one cup of pulverized sugar, two tablespoonfuls of cream, and one teaspoonful of Vanilla. Beat and mix thoroughly to a thick cream, and spread between the layers, with a layer of cake on top.

### Fig Layer Cake.

Gateau aux Figues.

4 Layers of Sponge Cake. (See Recipe),
1 Pound of Chopped Figs.
1 Cup of Sugar. ½ Cup of Water.

Make a layer cake—any good white, sponge or cream. Bake in jelly tins. Boil one pound of chopped figs, one cup of sugar, and one-half cup of water, till the figs form a jelly. Spread, when cool, between the layers of cake, while they are still hot, and proceed as in Almond Layer Cake.

### Jelly Layer Cake.

Gateau à la Gelée.

4 Layers of Cake. (See Recipe Layer Cake).
1 Cup of Pineapple, Peach, Raspberry or any Jelly.

Make a layer cake, and spread, while hot, with any kind of jelly, peach, lemon, raspberry, apple, strawberry, or the like.

### Lemon Layer Cake.

Gateau au Citron.

The Grated Rind and Juice of 1 Lemon.
4 Layers of Cake. (See recipe.)
1 Cup of Sugar. 1 Egg. 1 Teaspoonful of Water.
1 Teaspoonful of Flour.

Make a good layer sponge or cup cake. Prepare a good layer filling of creamed lemon by taking one cup of sugar, one egg, the grated rind and juice of one lemon, one teaspoonful of water and one of flour. Blend the sugar, water and flour, and add the well-beaten egg. Add the rind and juice of the lemon. Boil in a bain-marie (a kettle set in a kettle of hot water), and let it thicken. Spread between the layers, and ice, or sprinkle with sugar.

### Orange Layer Cake.

Gateau à l'Orange.

4 Layers of Pound or Cup Cake. (See recipe.)
The Whites of 2 Eggs.
3 Cups of Sugar.
The Grated Rind and Juice of 1 Orange.
Juice of Half a Lemon.
1 Teaspoonful of Orange Extract.

Make a good layer, pound or cup cake. Then make a filling of the whites of two eggs, three cups of sugar, the grated rind and juice of one orange, half a lemon's juice, two teaspoonfuls of orange extract. Mix all thoroughly, and spread between the layers of the cake.

### Pecan Layer Cake.

Gateau aux Pecanes.

4 Layers of Cup or Sponge Cake.
The Whites of 3 Eggs. 1 Cup of Minced Louisiana Pecans.
3 Tablespoonfuls of Sugar. 1 Teaspoonful of Lemon Extract.

Make a good Layer Cake or Cup Cake. (See recipe.) Beat the whites of three eggs to a stiff froth. Add three tablespoonfuls of sugar, and one cup of minced and pounded pecans. Add one teaspoonful of extract of lemon, and fill the cake, leaving a layer of the filling on top. This is a typical Creole cake. Instead of mincing the pecans for the layers, some cooks shell them in halves. This is a matter of taste.

### Pineapple Layer Cake.

Gateau à l'Ananas.

½ Pound of Flour.
1½ Cups of Pulverized Sugar.
9 Eggs.
1 Teaspoonful of Lemon or Pineapple Extract.
1 Pineapple.

Prepare four layers of sponge cake. Pare the pineapple, being careful to cut out all the eyes and the core. Grate the fruit very fine. Place a layer of the fruit over the bottom layer of the cake, sprinkle with a little powdered sugar and then spread over this a little Cream Sauce, which has been made to the consistency of Cream Puff Filling. (See recipe.) Put a second layer of the cake over this, cover nicely with the grated pineapple, sugar and Cream Filling, and proceed thus till the top layer is placed over the pineapple. Then ice or sprinkle with white sugar.

### Raisin Cake.
#### Gateau aux Raisins Secs.

4 Layers of Pound or Cup Cake. (See recipe.)
¼ Pound of Raisins. ¼ Pound of Citron.
½ Teaspoonful Each of Ground Cloves, Cinnamon, Allspice and Nutmeg.
Frosting to Cover.

Make a good Pound or Cup Cake. (See recipes.) Bake in tins, taking out enough to fill three tins. Then add to the remaining batter one-half teaspoonful each of ground cloves, allspice, cinnamon and nutmeg, and one-quarter pound each of raisins, seeded, and citron, chopped very fine. Mix thoroughly, and bake in two layers. Place between the other layers, alternating with a frosting, as in Almond Layer Cake. (See recipe.)

### Rainbow Cake.
#### Gateau à l'Arc-en-Ciel.

6 Layers of Sponge or of Pound Cake.
3 Ounces of Pink Icing.
3 Ounces of Violet Icing.
3 Ounces of Chocolate Icing.
3 Ounces of Vanilla Icing.
3 Ounces of White Icing.

Make a good layer cake, either Pound or Sponge. Prepare the Cream Icings (see recipes under Chapter Icings for Cakes). Place these between the alternate layers in the order above given. Ice the cake nicely. This is a very pretty cake.

### Layer Cake of Fresh Fruits.
#### Gateau aux Fruits.

4 Layers of White or Gold Cake. (See recipes.)
3 Apples. 2-3 of a Cup of Sugar.
1 Tablespoonful of Orange or Lemon Extract.
The Whites of 2 Eggs. 4 Tablespoonfuls of Powdered Sugar.

Make a good White Cake or Gold Cake. (See recipes.) Pare and grate three apples, and cook them with two-thirds of a cup of sugar. When they come to a thick jelly, take off the stove and flavor with Lemon or Orange extract. Take the whites of two eggs, beat till very light, and then add four tablespoonfuls of white sugar, and beat till very stiff, so stiff that the whites can stand alone. Spread a layer of this on the top of the bottom layer of cake, add a layer of apples, spread another layer of frosting, cover with a layer of cake, and so continue till all is used up.

Strawberry layer cake, peach raspberry, apricot, orange, pineapple and all fresh fruit layer cakes may be made in the same manner. Only in the orange and pineapple do not cook the pineapple or orange. Simply grate four or five oranges, or one pineapple, and spread the pineapple in layers between the frosting. These cakes, properly made, are most delicious.

---

## CHAPTER XXXIX.

### DESSERT CAKES.

Patisserie Fine Pour Dessert.

**Des Bouchées, Macarons, Massepains, Meriugues, Melees, Creoles.**

Biscuits aux Amandes et aux Pistaches, Amandes Soufflés, etc.

Perhaps no cuisine can boast of such a number of delicious small cakes that may serve for desserts, both elegant and choice, as the Creole cuisine. The native ingenuity of the Creole chefs adapted many of the nuts and fruits of Louisiana to various forms of sweetened batter, and the result of their efforts, handed down from generation to generation, is given in the following carefully compiled recipes, which, perhaps, after our unique "Gumbos," "Courtbouillons," "Bouillabaise," "Ragouts" and "Jambalayas," will serve better than any other recipes to give a true idea of the infinite variety and delight of the properly conducted Creole kitchen. They will also give a glimpse into the interior life of the Creole household, some of them, especially, being associated with pleasant, simple forms of "soirées," that, alas! have almost passed away since the intercourse of the old French quarter with the American city above Canal Street has become so general.

### Advice and Instructions for Baking These Cakes.

Use the best materials. It always pays in the delicate and perfect taste of the cake.

Soda, if not properly dissolved, will give to cakes and biscuits a bad, greenish color.

Keep the cake out of the draft while beating and baking. All the following cakes, as, indeed, all cakes, should be baked in their own steam, that is, keep the door and damper shut till the cakes have finished spreading. Then, if the oven is hot enough, you may open the damper. This gives the cake a light, bright color. Remember meringues and other large cakes are not intended in these instructions. For meringues the oven must never be very hot.

If you are expert at baking, you may test the heat of the oven simply by touching the handle of the oven door, but a sure test for beginners is to throw a little cornmeal or flour in the center of the oven, count ten, and if the flour begins to smoke before you count the full number before the oven is too hot, if it smokes at ten the oven has the proper heat.

Never put flavoring extracts directly into the flour, or they will form lumps. Always put them in the wet part of the mixture.

## BOUCHÉS.

These are a delicious form of dessert cakes. and are considered both elegant and recherché. Great care must be taken to trim the cakes evenly and of equal size before attempting to finish them. Bouchés are made with batter and also with almost all our Louisiana fruits. As the name indicates Bouchées are simply "a mouthful."

### Bouchées de Dames.

9 Eggs. 1 Pound of White Pulverized Sugar.
½ Pound of Flour.
The Juice of 1 Lemon.
1 Tablespoonful of Vanilla Extract.
1 Cup of Currant or Other Jelly for Filling.
Transparent Icing to Garnish.

Prepare a sponge or cup cake batter. (See recipe under chapter "Cakes.") Have ready a baking sheet, which you will cover with white writing paper. Lay the batter out on the paper by forcing it through a biscuit cutter in rounds that will measure one inch and a half in diameter. They will spread. Dredge the surface with white sugar very lightly, and bake them for about fifteen minutes or less, until they are a light color. Then trim nicely and place them upon a wire drainer. Place circular pieces of currant or other preserves on top, and garnish with a meringue or Transparent Icing. (See recipe.) Set in the stove or the sun to dry, and in ten minutes they will be ready to serve.

### Bouchées With Oranges.

Bouchés aux Oranges.

9 Eggs. 1 Pound of Pulverized Sugar.
½ Pound of Flour.
The Juice of 1 Orange or 1 Tablespoonful of Extract.
1 Cup of Orange Marmalade.
Transparent Icing to Garnish.

Prepare the cake drops as directed above, with sponge or cup cake batter. Then place thin slices of oranges cooked in syrup on the Bouchées (see Orange Marmalade), and gloss them over with Transparent Icing. (See recipe.) Flavor the batter of these Bouchées with the zest of an orange or with Curaçoa Liqueur. (See recipe.)

### Bouchées With Peaches.

Bouchées aux Pêches.

9 Eggs. 1 Pound of White Pulverized Sugar.
½ Pound of Flour.
1 Tablespoonful of Noyau Extract.
1 Cup of Preserved Peaches.
Transparent Icing to Garnish.

Prepare the drop cakes as directed in "Bouchées de Dames." Place halves of peaches, preserved in syrup, over them (home-made preserves), and gloss over with Transparent Icing, flavored with Noyau, and slightly tinged with Carmine. (See recipe.)

In preparing all these bouchées, do not allow any excess of moisture from the preserves. The syrup should become entirely absorbed into the bouchée before you attempt to gloss is with the icing.

Bouchées with apricots or cherries are prepared in the same way, using, in the former case, a flavoring of Cedrati liqueur, and in the latter Maraschino.

In making bouchées with preserves use any kind of marmalade to stick two bouchées together, and ice the surface.

### Bouchées With Pineapples.

Bouchées aux Ananas.

9 Eggs. 1 Pound of Pulverized Sugar.
½ Pound of Flour.
1 Cup of Preserved Pineapples.
Transparent Icing to Garnish.

Prepare the drop cakes one inch and a half in diameter. Place smaller slices of thin, preserved pineapple upon each, and gloss or glacer over with Transparent Icing (see recipe), flavoring with pineapple syrup.

## MACAROONS.

Macarons.

1 Pound of Sweet Almonds.
1 Ounce of Butter.
2 Pounds of Sifted Sugar.
The Whites of 6 Eggs.

Blanch or scald the almonds by throwing them into a pan of boiling water, and letting them remain on the fire until you can take one of the almonds between your fingers and easily push off the skin by pushing it between the finger and thumb. Then drain and cool the almonds in cold water, and drain again. Rub the almond skins or hulls off with your hands in a cloth, throw the almonds in cold water with a little salt, wash clean, drain and dry them in another cloth. The almonds must be cold before you put them into a mortar. Then pound them to a pulp that will be as smooth as flour. Beat the whites of the eggs to a stiff froth. Add a little of the sugar and a little of the eggs as you pound, to prevent the almonds from becoming oily. Remember always that the paste must be kept firm as you add the remainder of the sugar and the eggs. Have ready a baking sheet, on which you will have placed a buttered piece of wafer paper. Lay the macaroons out on this, by dropping them from the spoon, in the form of a guinea fowl egg. Be very careful to place the macaroons about an inch apart, so that the balls will not touch one another. When the sheet is full, pass a wet paste brush gently over their surface. Put them in the oven, and bake at a very moderate heat till they are a light, delicate brown or fawn color. When done, take out and set to cool, and take away any excess of wafer paper that may cling to the edges. Keep in a dry place.

### Chocolate Macaroons.

Macarons au Chocolat.

12 Ounces of Ground Almonds.
1½ Pounds of Sifted White Sugar.
4 Ounces of Grated French Chocolate.
The Whites of 3 Eggs.
1 Tablespoonful of Vanilla Sugar.

Mix all the ingredients together in a bowl, and let it form a stiff paste. Then lay the macaroons out upon the wafer sheet in the form of lady fingers. Bake at a very moderate heat till a light brown.

### Creole Macaroons.

Macarons à la Créole.

12 Ounces of Shredded Almonds.
4 Ounces of Ground Almonds.
1 Pound of Sugar.
2 Eggs.    4 Ounces of Wheat Flour.
The Zest of 2 Oranges.

Blanch and wash and dry the almonds. Then grind (not pound) four ounces. Shred twelve ounces, that is, after skinning, cut the almonds lengthwise into thin shreds by dividing each almond into at least five or six long shreds, or cut them crosswise, and the shreds will be shorter. Beat the yolks of the eggs and the whites separately, and then beat them together with the sugar, rubbing till very light and smooth. Add the grated zest of two Louisiana oranges, that has been rubbed on sugar, and then incorporate all the other ingredients. Roll the paste out into balls about the size of an egg. Place them on buttered wafer paper on a baking sheet, set in a moderate oven, and bake to a light color.

### Pistachio Macaroons.

Macaroons aux Pistaches.

4 Ounces of Bitter Almonds.
6 Ounces of Shredded Pistachio Kernels or Peanuts.
12 Ounces of Sifted Sugar.
The Whites of 2 Eggs.
1 Tablespoonful of Vanilla Sugar.

Blanch the almonds and then pound them well. Mix with the whites of the eggs till thoroughly pulverized. Then mix with the shredded pistachio kernels or peanuts, and stir well. Fill a biscuit forcer with the preparation, and drop the macaroons in round balls about the size of a hickory nut upon a wafer sheet of paper, and spread upon a baking sheet. Bake in a moderate oven till very slightly colored.

### Spanish Macaroons.

Macarons à l'Espagnole.

8 Ounces of Sweet Almonds.
1 Pound of Sugar.
Yolks of 12 Eggs.
Grated Zest of 2 Oranges.
1 Teaspoonful of Vanilla.

Boil the sugar almost to a syrup, and then add the pounded almonds, and let them simmer gently for five minutes add the flavoring and let them simmer five minutes longer over a slow fire of smothered charcoal. Stir occasionally, and at the end of ten minutes add the yolks of the eggs, beaten very light. Then stir the paste over the kitchen fire with a quickened heat until it becomes firm and compact. Remove from the fire, and when it is cool roll it in your hands, which should be slightly greased with oil of sweet almonds. Lay them out in small cakes on wafer paper, spread on a baking sheet, and bake at a quick heat.

### CROQUIGNOLES.

8 Ounces of Sweet Almonds.
4 Ounces of Bitter Almonds.
Whites of 4 Eggs.
1½ Pounds of Fine Sugar.

Scald, skin and wash and dry the almonds, as directed in "Macarons," and then pound them into a pulp adding the whites of the eggs gradually, remembering always that they must be beaten to a stiff froth. Then work in the sugar, and you will have a firm paste. Drop these in small balls upon wafer paper, spread upon a baking sheet of tin or iron, in distinct and separate rows. Pass a little brush, moistened with water, lightly on their surface, and bake in a very slack oven till a very light color.

### PETITS FOURS.

1 Pound of Sweet Almonds.

1 Ounce of Butter.
2 Pounds of Sifted Flour.
The Whites of 8 Eggs.
Royal Icing to Garnish.

Prepare the paste as above directed, keeping it somewhat stiffer and firmer, however. Add two whites of eggs of Royal Icing (see recipe), and work both together till thoroughly incorporated. Fill the biscuit forcer, and push the macaroons through upon buttered wafer paper, as directed.

Petits Fours must be baked in a very moderate oven. Otherwise the excessive heat will cause the macaroons to run into one another, and produce a useless mass. The Royal Icing necessitates the moderate oven. The Petits Fours are then put in pretty plaited paper cases.

### MASSEPAINS (Plain).
Massepains (simple).

12 Ounces of Sweet Almonds.
1 Ounce of Bitter Almonds.
The Whites of 4 Eggs.
1½ Pounds of Sifted Sugar.

Scald, skin, wash and dry the almonds. Then pound them to a flour in a mortar with the whites of the eggs. When well-pulverized, beat well. Mix in the sugar by pounding it, and then take up the paste and put it in a bowl. Beat well, keeping it very firm. If soft, add sugar, to render firmer. Strew the wafer sheet, spread on a baking sheet, with white pulverized sugar. Cut the massepains into lengths of two or three inches, and twist them into fancy shapes, diamonds, hearts, rings, triangles, etc., on the wafer sheet. Then set in the oven, and bake to a very light color.

### Massepains Soufflés.

12 Ounces of Sweet Almonds.

1 Ounce of Bitter Almonds.
1½ Pounds of Sifted Sugar.
1 Ounce of Vanilla Sugar.
The Whites of 3 Eggs.
1 White of Egg Royal Icing.

Prepare the paste exactly as above, and when you take it up in the bowl add the Royal Icing, keeping the paste firm. Spread the massepains upon wafer sheets, using only the ring shape, and bake in a slack oven till a very light color.

### Strawberry Massepains.
Massepains à la Fraise.

1 Pound of Sweet Almonds.
8 Ounces of Sugar.
6 Ounces of Crushed Strawberries.

Pound the almonds, and then proceed as in plain Massepains, adding the strawberries after you will have strained them through a sieve.

Any kind of fruits or marmalades may be used in this manner for Fruit Massepains.

### SOUFFLÉS.

2 Pounds of Powdered White Sugar.

The Whites of 2 Eggs.
1 Ounce of Orange Flower Water.

To two pounds of powdered sugar add the whites of two eggs and one ounce of Orange Flower Water. Make of all a firm, consistent paste, adding more sugar, if necessary. Roll out on a sheet of paper, sprinkled with sugar, and cut into little pieces, which you will form into balls about the size of a nut. Place them on a wafer sheet on a baking sheet at a distance of two inches, so that they will not touch one another, should they run. Bake in a moderate oven.

### Almonds Soufflés.
Amandes Soufflés.

1 Pound of Sweet Almonds.
The White of 1 Egg.
12 Ounces of Powdered Sugar.

Blanch, skin, wash and dry one pound of sweet almonds, and then cut them into very small pieces. Add the white of one egg, beaten to a thick froth, and twelve ounces of powdered sugar. When well-mixed drop upon sheets of white paper, and bake to a very light color in a moderate oven.

### Pistachio Soufflés.

Soufflés aux Pistaches.

10 Ounces of Pistachio Kernels or Peanuts.
1½ Pounds of Fine Sugar.
Whites of 3 Eggs.
4 Drops Essence of Roses.
2 Whites of Eggs of Royal Icing.
(See Recipe Royal Icing.)

If you cannot procure the Pistachio Kernels, use Peanuts, which are called "Pistaches" by the Creoles.

Scald, skin, wash and dry the pistachios or peanuts. Pound them with two ounces of sugar, adding occasionally some of the whites of the eggs, until reduced to a pulp. Then add all the sugar, gradually working it into the paste on a marble slab, being careful to have the slab and the hands very clean. Roll out paste with sugar to the thickness of a quarter of an inch on the slab. Spread the icing evenly over, and cut into various fanciful shapes. Place the cakes on the sheet wafer or lay on baking sheet, and bake in a slow heat to a very light color.

### Rose Soufflés.
Soufflés à la Rose.

2 Pounds Powdered White Sugar.
The Whites of 2 Eggs.
1 Ounce of Orange Flower Water.
A Pinch of Carmine Powder.

To two pounds of powdered sugar add the whites of two eggs and one ounce of Orange Flower Water and a little pinch of Carmine Powder. Make of all a firm, consistent paste, adding more sugar, if necessary. Roll out on a sheet of paper, sprinkled with sugar, then cut the paste into little pieces, which you will form into balls about the size of a nut. Place them on a wafer sheet on a baking sheet at a distance of two inches apart, so that they will not touch one another, should they run. Bake in a moderate oven.

### Almond and Peanut Biscuit.
Biscuits aux Amandes et aux Pistaches.

4 Ounces of Sweet Almonds.
4 Ounces of Pistachio Kernels or Peanuts.
4 Eggs. 8 Ounces of Powdered Sugar.

Blanch, peel and pound the almonds and pistachio kernels or peanuts in a mortar till finely pulverized, adding the white of an egg, to keep the almonds from turning oily. Beat the whites of the eggs to a froth, and then add the yolks, beaten separately to a cream with the sugar. Beat well, and incorporate thoroughly. Add four tablespoonfuls of flour, sifted well, and mix well. Place in small cakes on wafer sheets of paper, and bake in a moderate oven till a very light color.

### Chocolate Biscuits.
Biscuits au Chocolat.

6 Fresh Creole Eggs.
1 Ounce of Powdered French Chocolate.
4 Ounces of Flour.
10 Ounces of Pulverized Sugar.

Beat the yolks of the eggs and the sugar to a cream. Add the chocolate, and mix well. Then add the flour, alternating with the whites of the eggs, beaten to a stiff froth. Add one tablespoonful of Vanilla Extract, and bake upon wafer sheets in small cakes to a light color.

### Cinnamon Biscuits.
Biscuits à la Canelle.

6 Fresh Creole Eggs.
1 Ounce of Powdered French Chocolate.
4 Ounces of Flour.
10 Ounces of Pulverized Sugar.
Ground Cinnamon.
1 Teaspoonful of Cinnamon Extract.

Beat the yolks of the eggs and the cinnamon to a cream. Add the chocolate, and mix well. Then add the flour, alternating with the whites of the eggs, beaten to a stiff froth. Add one tablespoonful of Vanilla Extract, and bake upon wafer sheets in small cakes to a light color.

### Citron Biscuits.
Biscuits au Citron.

6 Fresh Creole Eggs.
The Zest of 1 Citron.
4 Ounces of Flour.
12 Ounces of Powdered Sugar.
The Juice of 1 Lemon.

Beat the eggs and sugar to a cream, add the flour gradually, and the juice of the lemon and citron zest, and beat well. Bake on paper sheets in the form of small wafers, very thinly spread, in a moderate oven to a light color.

### Creole Biscuits.
Biscuits à la Créole.

4 Ounces of Grated Lemon.
4 Ounces of Orange Flower Marmalade.
4 Ounces of Apricot or Peach Marmalade.
The Whites of 4 Eggs.

Mix the fruits and lemon thoroughly together, and then add three ounces of white pulverized sugar and the whites of the eggs, beaten to a stiff froth. Place the mixture in small cakes on white paper, and bake lightly. Then cover with sugar beaten with the white of an egg, in meringue form, and bake to a light brown.

### Filbert Biscuits.
Biscuits aux Avelines.

4 Ounces of Sweet Almonds.
4 Ounces of Filberts.
The Whites of 4 Eggs.
8 Ounces of Powdered Sugar.

Blanch, peel and pound the almond and filbert kernels in a mortar till finely pulverized, adding the white of an egg, to keep the almonds from turning oily. Beat the whites of three eggs to a froth, and then add the yolks, beaten separately to a cream with the sugar, incorporate thoroughly, and beat well. Add four tablespoonfuls of flour, sifted well, and mix well. Place in small cakes on wafer sheets of paper, and bake in a moderate oven till a very light color.

### Lemon Biscuit.
Biscuit au Citron.

6 Fresh Creole Eggs.
The Zest of 1 Lemon.
4 Ounces of Flour.
12 Ounces of Powdered Sugar.
The Juice of 1 Lemon or 1 Tablespoonful of Lemon Extract.

Beat the eggs and sugar to a cream, add the flour gradually, and the juice and zest of a lemon, and beat well. Bake on paper sheets in the form of small wafers, very thinly spread, in a moderate oven, to a light color.

### Orange Biscuits.
Biscuits à l'Orange.

6 Fresh Creole Eggs.
The Zest of 1 Orange.
4 Ounces of Flour.
12 Ounces of Powdered Sugar.
The Juice of 1 Orange.

Beat the eggs and sugar to a cream, add the flour gradually, and the juice and zest of the orange, and beat well. Bake on paper sheets, in the form of small wafers, very thinly spread, in a moderate oven, to a light color.

### Vanilla Biscuits.
Biscuits à la Vanille.

6 Fresh Creole Eggs.
1 Ounce of Vanilla Sugar.
4 Ounces of Flour.
10 Ounces of Pulverized Sugar.
1 Tablespoonful of Vanilla Extract.

Beat the yolks of the eggs and the sugar to a cream. Add the chocolate, and mix well. Then add the flour, alternating with the whites of the eggs, beaten to a stiff froth. Add one tablespoonful of Vanilla Extract, and bake upon wafer sheets in small cakes to a light color.

### Frascati Croquantes.
Croquantes Frascati.

8 Ounces of Flour.
6 Ounces of Sugar.
2 Ounces of Ground Almonds.
2 Whole Eggs and 3 Yolks.
1 Ounce Aniseed.

Break the eggs into a bowl, and beat light, and add the sugar and beat very light; add the almonds, pounded to a powder, and the aniseed. Beat all together till well incorporated. Add the flour and beat thoroughly. Have a marble slab clean and dry. Roll the paste out on the slab in the form of a long, thick rope. Then take a knife and cut it into pieces about the size of a guinea egg. Roll each between the palms of your hands, and shape them into oval balls. Have a buttered sheet of paper on a baking sheet. Make a slight incision into each cake by pressing the back of the knife across the surface. Brush the egg over them, and sprinkle lightly with granulated sugar, and bake in a moderate heat to a light color.

### Creole Wafers.
Gaufres à la Créole.

9 Ounces of Flour.
4 Ounces of Sifted Sugar. 8 Eggs.
1 Wineglassful of Noyau.
1 Pint Whipped Cream.
1 Tablespoonful of Vanilla.
A Pinch of Salt.

Beat the sugar and yolks of the eggs to a cream. Add thé Noyau and salt. Vanilla and flour, and incorporate thoroughly till light. Then add the whites of the eggs and the cream. Mix all lightly together, taking great care that all are well-mixed. Bake very, very light in wafer irons. The irons should be heated over a clear charcoal fire, and when hot brush inside with a little clarified butter. A large spoonful of butter should be poured into the undersheet of the wafer irons, then close in, and bake to a golden brown color. Sprinkle lightly with sugar. These wafers are delicious, handed around with ices.

### Ginger Wafers.
Gaufres au Gingembre.

1 Large Spoon of Ground Ginger.
4 Ounces of Molasses.
8 Ounces of Flour.
8 Ounces of Sifted Sugar.
Whites of 4 Eggs.
½ Pint of Cream.
1 Wineglassful of Brandy.
1 Tablespoonful of Vanilla Sugar.

Beat the whites of the eggs to a cream and add it to the flour and milk, salt and sugar, molasses and ginger. Work all well together very light in a bowl, until you have a smooth batter. Add the brandy and Ginger Extract and beat vigorously ten minutes longer. Have ready the wafer irons and a clear charcoal fire. Brush the irons with butter and place the wafers within and bake on both sides to a light fawn color.

### French Wafers.
Gaufres Françaises.

8 Ounces of Flour.
8 Ounces of Sifted Sugar.
Whites of 4 Eggs.
½ Pint of Cream.
1 Wineglassful of Brandy.
1 Tablespoonful of Vanilla Sugar.

Beat the whites of the eggs to a cream and add to the flour, milk, salt and sugar. Work all together very light in a bowl, until you have a very smooth batter. Add the brandy and beat vigorously ten minutes longer. Have ready the wafer irons and a clear charcoal fire. Brush the irons with butter and place the wafers within and bake on both sides to a light brown color. If desired, the wafers may be rolled into fancy shapes.

### Spanish Wafers.
Gaufres Espagnoles

9 Ounces of Flour.
2 Ounces of Sifted Sugar.
½ Pint of Chocolate Water.
12 Drops of Essence of Vanilla. 2 Eggs.
2 Gills of Cream.

Prepare the chocolate water by dissolving well two ounces of French chocolate in a half pint of boiling water. Place the sugar, vanilla, eggs and cream in a pan, work all vigorously into a smooth, light batter, add the cold Chocolate Water, beat all together well for ten minutes longer. Then bake the wafers, as directed in recipe for French Wafers, and curl in the form of cornucopias while still warm and able to retain impressions.

### Cream Puffs.
Choux à la Crème.

1 Cup of Flour.
½ Cup of Butter.
4 Eggs. 1 Cup of Water.

Set the water to boil, and while boiling, stir in the butter. Then add the flour, and stir continually till the paste leaves the sides of the saucepan. Set the mixture to cool. When cool, stir one after another, the three eggs in, without beating them. After adding the last egg, beat very vigorously for about four minutes; then drop by tablespoonfuls on buttered tins, and set in the oven to bake from twenty to thirty minutes. Watch carefully so that they will not burn. When cold make an opening inside, through the side of the paste, with a sharp knife, and fill it with the following custard:

1 Cup of Milk.
1 Tablespoonful of Sugar.
3 Eggs. 1 Teaspoonful of Vanilla.
1 Tablespoonful of Cornstarch.

Rub the cornstarch in a little water and add it to the boiling milk. Let it boil three minutes, stirring constantly. Beat the eggs, without separating, and the sugar till light, and add to the boiling milk. Add the vanilla, stirring all well. Fill the cakes and set away to cool.

### Chocolate Eclairs.
Éclairs du Chocolat.

1 Cup of Flower. 1 Cup of Water.
4 Eggs. ½ Cup of Water.
2 Ounces of Chocolate.
4 Ounces of Powdered Sugar.

Make a Cream Puff Paste as above. Put into a tube or a pastry bag and press out upon well-buttered tins in the shape of Lady Fingers. This will give the Éclairs the right shape, making them about five inches long. Set them to bake in a quick oven twenty or thirty minutes. If the oven is of the right temperature, and the cakes are properly baked, they will be hollow within and very daintily crusted without. Fill in with a mixture made by melting two ounces of chocolate and four ounces of powdered sugar, and set away to cool. You may ice by dipping one end into the icing, and then setting away to dry. The Éclairs may be filled with preserved fruits, Orange Icing, Whipped Cream, or any marmalade.

### Pineapple Eclairs.
Éclairs à l'Ananas.

1 Cup of Flour. 1 Cup of Water.
4 Eggs. ½ Cup of Water.
2 Ounces of Preserved Pineapple or Pineapple Mousse.

Pineapple Éclairs are made in the same manner as Chocolate Éclairs (see recipe), only they are filled in with preserved pineapple or Pineapple Mousse.

### Cup Cake.
Pétits Gateaux.

1 Cup of Butter. 2 Cups of Sugar.
4 Cups of Flour. 1 Cup of Sour Cream.
3 Eggs. 1 Tablespoonful of Brandy.
1 Tablespoonful of Rose or Vanilla Extract.

Beat the butter and sugar to a cream, add the well-beaten yolks of the eggs, and then add the cream. Mix thoroughly, and sift in gradually the flour, beating thoroughly. Add the whites of the eggs, beaten to a stiff froth, and the brandy and rose water. Now dissolve a half teaspoonful of soda in a little sweet milk and add, being very careful that there are no lumps in the soda. Beat well for a few minutes and bake at once, in small tins or cups, which you will grease well with butter and only half fill with the cake batter.

### Jelly Cake.
Gateau aux Confitures.

1 Cup of Butter. 2 Cups of Sugar.
4 Cups of Flour.
1 Cup of Sour Cream.
3 Eggs. 1 Tablespoonful of Brandy.
1 Tablespoonful of Vanilla Extract.
3 Ounces of Currant, Grape or any Jelly Desired.

Prepare the batter exactly as for Cup Cake or Sponge Cake, butter the small tins and pour in the batter in such thin layers as to allow the cakes to be just a half inch thick when baked. Let them bake for a few minutes to a light brown, and as they are taken from the oven lay them on the table and spread a layer of Currant or Grape Jelly between; then add alternate layers of cake and jelly, reserving the prettiest cakes for the top layers. Do not put jelly on this. Ice or powder with sifted sugar.

### Queen Cake.
Gateau à la Reine.

1 Pound of Flour.
4 Ounces of Sugar.
1 Pound of Currants. 1 Pound of Butter.
1 Teacupful of Cream. 8 Eggs.
1 Tablespoonful of Rose Water.

Beat the sugar and butter to a cream, and then add the well-beaten yolks of the eggs. Now add the cream, and then one-half of the flour, and next one-half of the whites of the eggs, beaten to a stiff froth. Add the remainder of the flour, into which you will have dredged the currants that have been well-washed cleansed and picked and dried; mix thoroughly, and add the remainder of the whites and the rose water. Beat as you would a pound cake. Then pour into small, buttered tins and bake immediately to a light brown.

### Tea Cakes.
#### Gateau de Thé.

1 Pound of Flour.
¼ Pound of Butter.   4 Eggs.
6 Ounces of Powdered Sugar.
½ Cup of Sour Milk.

Beat the butter and sugar to a cream. Add the well-beaten eggs, and incorporate thoroughly. Add the milk, and then gradually add the flour, making a light soft dough. Mix all well together, and roll the paste out very thin. Cut into rounds or squares, and put into a slightly buttered baking pan. Bake to a bright yellow, and serve as needed. Some brush the tops of the cakes with beaten eggs, and sprinkle the tops with raisins or currants, well seeded and washed and dried.

### Cocoanut Fingers.
#### Biscuits à la Cuiller au Coco.

4 Ounces of Butter.
4 Ounces of Sugar.
3 Eggs.   2 Ounces of Flour.
4 Ounces of Grated Cocoanut.

Beat the butter, sugar and eggs together for five minutes, blending thoroughly. Then add the flour, and immediately after the grated cocoanut. Beat well, and have ready buttered tins. Divide the mixture into fingers of about four or five inches in length, bake in a moderately quick oven for thirty minutes, and when cool dust with powdered sugar.

### Lady Fingers.
#### Biscuits à la Cuiller.

½ of a Pound of Flour.
4 Ounces of Powdered White Sugar.
5 Eggs.

Put the sugar and the yolks of the eggs into a bowl and beat thoroughly till very light. Beat the whites of the eggs to a stiff froth and add the flour. Mix well and add immediately the whites of the eggs. Beat all together gently for a few minutes, and the preparation is ready for baking.

Have ready a long sheet of paper, spread on a baking tin. Take a tablespoon and drop the batter along the paper, in lengths of four or five inches, being careful to leave an empty space of an inch between each cake; set to bake in a very moderate oven. The cakes must not spread or rise. If they rise, the oven is too hot, and if they spread, you may be sure the oven is too cool. Bake to a very light brown, for twenty minutes, in a moderate oven.

### Ginger Nuts.
#### Petits Gateaux au Gingembre.

2 Pounds of Flour.   2 Eggs.
1 Pint of Molasses.
½ Pound of Brown Sugar.
½ Pound of Butter.   A Pinch of Salt.
3 Tablespoonfuls of Ginger.
½ Teaspoonful of Soda.
½ Pint of Milk or Water.

Beat the butter and sugar to a cream; work in the flour and mix well; add the molasses and mix well. Then add the milk, into which you will have dissolved the soda thoroughly, and beat well; add the ginger and continue working lightly till thoroughly mixed. Then roll out and cut in various fanciful shapes and bake to a light brown.

### Ginger Snaps.
#### Gateaux Secs au Gingembre.

2 Cups of Molasses.
1 Cup of Lard or Butter.
1 Cup of Sugar.
½ Cup of Sour Cream.
1 Tablespoonful of Ground Ginger.
2 Eggs.   2½ Teaspoonfuls of Soda.
Flour Sufficient to Roll Thick.

Mix all the ingredients as above, only making the batter slightly stiffer, and cut into fancy shapes and bake in a quick oven.

### Jumbles.
#### Melée-Créole.

1 Pound of Butter.
¾ Pound of Flour.   4 Eggs.
½ Pound of Sugar.
1 Tablespoonful of Rose Water.
½ Grated Nutmeg.

Beat the butter and sugar to a cream. Add the eggs, thoroughly beaten, and the add the Rose Water and the nutmeg. Gradually add the flour, and beat well. Beat till very light before adding the flour. Dust a paper on a baking sheet with sugar, instead of flour, and roll out the paste to about one-eighth of an inch in thickness. Then use a small cutter with a round center, and take the centers out, thus forming pretty rings. Bake in a moderate oven till a light brown. Take them out and sift powdered sugar over them.

### Madeleines.

5 Eggs. ½ Pound of Powdered Sugar.

½ Pound of Sifted Flour.
½ Pound of Butter.
Washed and Drained.
⅓ Teaspoonful of Vanilla.
Grated Rind of a Lemon.

Beat the butter and sugar to a cream and add the yolks of the eggs, the lemon rind and the vanilla, and beat till very, very light. Then add the flour, beating constantly, and the whites of the eggs, beaten to a stiff froth. Turn into buttered tins, and bake in a quick oven till a delicate brown. Serve cold. These are delicious supper cakes.

### Pop-Overs.

Vitement Fait.

1 Pint of Milk.
1 Pint of Flour. 3 Eggs.
2 Teaspoonfuls of Baking Powder.
1 Teaspoonful of Salt.

Beat the yolks of the eggs separately till very light and frothy. Stir in the unskimmed milk and the flour that has been twice sifted with the baking powder. Add the whites of the eggs, beaten to a stiff froth; pour the mixture into buttered cake tins; bake in a quick oven till a light brown, and serve either hot or cold.

### Anise Drops.

Gateau d'Anis.

3 Cups of Sugar.  6 Eggs.
1 Quart of Flour.
½ Teaspoonful of Essence of Anise.

Beat the sugar and eggs for about half an hour. Add the flour gradually, and the essence. Beat well. Have ready buttered sheets of tin, and drop the mixture from the spoon, and bake to a delicate brown.

### Spice Drops.

Biscuits d'Épices.

The Yolks of 3 Eggs.
½ Cup of Sweet Milk.
3 Cups of Flour. 1 Cup of Molasses.
3 Tablespoonfuls of Baking Powder.
1 Ground Nutmeg.

Beat the butter and sugar to a cream. Add the molasses and the milk. Blend well, add the spices, and the nutmeg and lemon extract, and then add the flour, sifted with the baking powder. Beat well for fifteen minutes, and then drop on tins lined with buttered paper. Bake in a quick oven to a delicate brown.

### Creole Cookies.

Biscuits à la Créole.

1 Teaspoonful Each of Ground Cloves and Cinnamon.
1 Teaspoonful of Lemon Extract.
2 Cups of Powdered Sugar.
1 Cup of Sweet Milk.
The Whites of 4 Eggs.
1 Teaspoonful of Lemon Extract.
2 Teaspoonfuls of Baking Powder.
Flour Sufficient to Make a Soft Batter.

Beat the butter and sugar to a cream; add the milk and the baking powder, and gradually add the whites of the eggs, beaten to a stiff froth. Beat the batter hard for ten minutes, after adding sufficient flour to make a nice soft batter. Pour into baking tins, and bake to a delicate brown. When cold ice with Plain Icing. (See recipe.) These are very dainty and nice.

### Lemon Cookies.

Biscuits au Citron.

6 Eggs.  1 Cup of Butter.
3 Cups of Sugar.
1 Teaspoonful of Lemon Extract.

Beat the yolks of the eggs and butter to a cream. Add the sugar, and beat well. Add the extract of lemon, and then the whites of the eggs, beaten to a stiff froth. Add sufficient flour to make a nice dough, just stiff enough to mold, and then roll thin, and bake in a quick oven to a very light brown.

### Molasses Cookies.

Biscuits à la Mélasse.

2 Cups of Molasses.
1 Cup of Butter.
2 Eggs.  2 Teaspoonfuls of Soda.
2 Teaspoonfuls of Ginger.
½ Teaspoonful of Cloves.
2 Teaspoonfuls of Cloves.

Melt the molasses. Beat the butter and sugar to a cream, and add, mixing in the soda, dissolved in a tablespoonful of boiling water. Add the ginger and the ground cloves. Take off the fire, and beat till cool. Then add the eggs, beaten well, and flour sufficient to make a nice, soft dough, just stiff enough to roll. Cut into small cakes, and bake in a quick oven to a delicate brown.

### MERINGUES.

In order to make meringues properly one should have a meringue board of well-seasoned hard wood. This board should be cut with rounded corners, and of a size convenient to the oven. It ought to be about one and a half inches in thickness. While baking, Meringues must always remain soft underneath. To accomplish this, dampen the board thoroughly with water before placing the bands of paper upon it. In this way the Meringues are prevented from receiving heat in sufficient volume to render them hard underneath.

### Creole Meringues.

Meringues à la Créole.

1 Pint of Sifted White Sugar.
The Whites of 12 Eggs.
1 Tablespoonful of Vanilla.

Beat the whites to a stiff, snowy froth, and then gradually add the sugar and vanilla, beating until the mixture is stiff enough to cut with a knife. Then cut some stout sheets of foolscap paper into strips measuring at least two inches in width, or, if you wish to make the meringues larger, simply place the sheet of paper, slightly buttered, on the table. Take a tablespoon and gather up the meringue mixture as nearly as possible in the shape of an egg, and working it towards the side of the bowl to give it this shape, and then drop slopingly from the spoon upon the strips of paper at a distance of at least an inch apart. Draw the edge of the spoon very sharply around the edge of the meringue, to give it a smooth, round shape, resembling an egg. When all the rows are filled, sprinkle sifted sugar over them, and let them remain in this state for about three minutes. Then take hold of the strips at either end, and shake lightly, to remove all excess of sugar. Place the strips in rows about one inch apart on the wet board or baking tin (the board is much better), and as soon as the sugar begins to dissolve slightly on their surface, push them into the oven, which must be at a very moderate heat, and bake them a very light fawn color. Watch constantly, that they may not burn. When the meringues are done, remove each one very carefully and separately from the paper. Then use a small dessert spoon, if you desire to fill the meringues, scoop out the soft white part, and, with the outer side of the bowl of the spoon, smooth the interior of the meringues. Then place them with the rounded side downward on the baking tin in the oven to dry for a few minutes. When thoroughly crisp, without browning, place them between sheets of paper in a dry place. When using meringues for desserts, etc., garnish the interior with whipped cream, beaten to a stiff froth, and flavored with vanilla, orange, lemon, orange flower water, or any kind of fancy liqueur, stick the two halves together lightly and serve. Meringues may be kept for some time in their dry shell state, and filled when ready to use. In making them for immediate family use, simply drop the mixture by spoonfuls on buttered paper, dust with the sugar, wait for three minutes, fan or blow off all excess of sugar, and then place them in a very moderate oven and bake to a light brown. When dry, carefully remove the meringue from the paper, after they have cooled, brush the bottoms slightly with the white of an egg, beaten to a froth, stick two meringues together, put away to dry, and serve when needed.

### Creamed-Iced Meringues.

Meringues à la Crème Glacée.

1 Pound of Sifted White Sugar.
The Whites of 12 Eggs.
1 Tablespoonful of Vanilla Essence.
3 Ounces of Stiff Whipped Cream.
½ Cup of Transparent Icing.

Cream-Iced Meringues should be made much smaller than the ordinary Meringues—about the size of a bird's egg. Proceed as above, and fill with stiff, whipped cream, taking great care when filling that none of the cream shall ooze from between the two halves of the Meringues after they have been stuck together. If it should, wipe it off very carefully. When well-filled, hold each Meringue separately on a silver fork, and dip them all over in "Transparent Icing" (see recipe), and let them dry. These Meringues are delicious desserts.

### Cream-Iced Meringues With Preserves.

Meringues Glacées aux Confitures.

1 Pound of Sifted White Sugar.
The Whites of 12 Eggs.
1 Tablespoonful of Vanilla Essence.
3 Ounces of Currant, Orange or Any Preserves.
½ Cup of Transparent Icing.

Prepare as in Meringues à la Créole, or as above, only spread some preserves thinly inside the Meringues before garnishing them with the cream, and then ice with Transparent Icing. (See recipe Transparent Icing.)

### Biscuits Glacés aux Confitures.

9 Eggs. 1 Pound of White Pulverized Sugar.
½ Pound Flour.
The Juice of 1 Lemon.
1 Cup of Jam of Any Kind Desired.

These are elegant cakes and enhance the most fashionable dessert. Make a sponge cake or cup cake (see recipes), and bake on a baking sheet about three-quarters of an inch in thickness. When cold, cut up into fanciful shapes, trim the edges neatly with a very sharp knife, and be careful to brush off the least particle of crumbs that may adhere; carefully spread the upper part and sides of the biscuit with apricot, peach, raspberry or any jam. Then hold one at a time on a silver fork, very carefully, and with a spoon pour over, Transparent Chocolate Icing, around the sides and over the surface of the biscuit. Then carefully lay it upon a wire tray, resting upon a baking sheet. Dry the biscuit in a very moderate oven for about five minutes.

### Marbled Glacées.

Biscuits Panachés aux Confitures.

9 Eggs. 1 Pound of White Pulverized Sugar.
½ Pound of Flour.

The Juice of 1 Lemon.
1 Cup of Mixed Preserved Fruits.

Prepare the cake as directed in the preceding recipe. Then place on the baking sheet. Drop different-sized small bits of fine preserves, orange, apricot, damson, red currant, etc., on the biscuit, and spread smoothly, so as to form a beautifully marbled pattern. Then cut out the cakes in any fanciful design. Proceed as above to cover with Transparent Icing, and dry in a moderate oven for five minutes.

---

## CHAPTER XL.

### ICINGS FOR CAKES.

Glaces pour Gateaux.

Read carefully the directions given for icing cakes in the beginning of the chapter on "Cakes." (See recipe.) Then proceed to make icings according to taste, as follows:

### Plain Icing.
Glace.

The Whites of 2 Eggs.
1 Tablespoonful of Lemon Juice.
1 Pound of White Pulverized Sugar.
Essence of Rose, Orange or Lemon.

Beat the whites of the eggs, and sift in gradually the sugar, beating all the while, using good judgment as to sufficient quantity, and adding in the beginning a tablespoonful of Rose or Lemon Essence or Orange Flower Water. Beat very, very light, till sufficient almost to stand alone. Have ready in another bowl a little lemon juice, and begin to lay on the icing in a thin coat over the cake with a knife, occasionally dipping the knife into the lemon juice, to make a nice, smooth icing. When it is covered with this coat, set in the oven or the sun to harden, when it will be ready for the next coat. Add another coating as before. This coat will be much smoother and whiter than the first. If you wish to make ornamental icing it will be necessary to have piping tubes. (See General Directions for Icing.)

### Almond Icing.
Glace aux Amandes.

3 Cups of Sugar.
1 Pound of Almonds, Blanched and Pounded to a Paste.
The Whites of 3 Eggs.

Beat the eggs, stir in the almonds and sugar, and then proceed to ice according to general directions. (See above or recipe.)

### Chocolate Icing.
Glace au Chocolat.

2 Ounces of Chocolate.
2 Cups of Sugar.
The Whites of 3 Eggs.
1 Teaspoonful of Vanilla Extract.

Melt two ounces of chocolate in a little boiling water. Add two cups sugar, and stir till smooth. Stir in the well-beaten whites of three eggs and one teaspoonful of Vanilla Extract, and proceed as in Plain Icing. (See recipe.)

### Orange or Lemon Icing.
Glace à l'Orange ou au Citron.

The Whites of 2 Eggs.
1 Pound of White Pulverized Sugar.
The Juice of 1 Lemon or Orange.

For Lemon and Orange Icings make a Plain Icing, stirring in at the start the juice of one lemon or one orange, and proceeding as in Plain Icing. (See recipe.)

### Orange Transparent Icing.
Glace Transparente à l'Orange.

½ Pound of Fine White Sugar.
Half the White of 1 Egg.
The Zest of 1 Orange.
1 Tablespoonful of Orange Essence or Orange Juice.

An Orange Transparent Icing is made by flavoring with a little orange sugar, rubbing against the zest of the orange, or tinging with Saffron and flavoring with Curaçoa.

### Colored Transparent Icing.
#### Glace Transparente à la Rose, à la Violette, Etc.

½ Pound of Fine White Sugar.
Half the White of 1 Egg.
Flavoring and Coloring According to Taste.

Green Icing is made by using the Extract of Spinach and flavoring with Cedrati; a Rose Pink by flavoring with the Essential Oil of Roses and adding a few drops of Cochineal, and a Violet Icing by flavoring with Syrup of Violet. Proceed as in Plain Icing.

### Wine Icing.
#### Glace au Vin.

The Whites of 2 Eggs.
1 Pound of White Sugar.
1 Gill of Sherry or Madeira Wine.

Proceed exactly as in Lemon or Orange Icing, only adding instead one gill of good Sherry or Madeira wine. Then proceed as in Plain Icing.

### Water Icing.
#### Glace à l'Eau.

2 Cups of Sugar.
A Pinch of Cream of Tartar.
1 Tablespoonful of Vanilla, Peach or Strawberry Extract.

Take two cups of sugar and a small pinch of Cream of Tartar. Stir with just enough water to make a thick paste, and flavor with Peach or Strawberry Extract. If Strawberry is used, add a teaspoonful of Cochineal. Beat well, and, if not stiff enough, add more sugar, and proceed as in Plain Icing.

### FROSTING.
#### Glace Neigeuse.

The Whites of 2 Eggs.
2 Cups of Pulverized Sugar.
½ Cup of Cornstarch.
4 Tablespoonfuls of Milk.

Take the whites of two eggs, two cups of pulverized sugar, and one-half a cup of cornstarch. Blend the cornstarch with a little milk, to make a thick paste, add the whites of the eggs, beaten light, and the pulverized sugar. Beat all to a stiff froth, and frost the cake while hot.

### Cream Frosting.
#### Glace Neigeuse à la Crème.

The Whites of 2 Eggs.
2 Cups of Pulverized Sugar.
4 Tablespoonfuls of Rich Cream.
1 Tablespoonful of Vanilla Extract.

For a Cream Frosting, proceed exactly as above, only omit the cornstarch, and add an equal measure of rich cream, and flavor with Vanilla Extract. Boil the cream.

### Orgeat Paste or Icing.
#### Orgeate.

1 Pound of Peeled Almonds.
1 Pound of Sugar.
1 Tablespoonful of Orange Flower Water.

To one pound of skinned almonds add one pound of sugar. Pound as directed to a pulp in a mortar, occasionally adding a few drops of water to prevent the almonds from running to oil. Use Orange Flower Water. Add fine white sifted sugar till you have sufficient to make a paste, and work till well-amalgamated and elastic. It will now be ready for any use designated in this book.

### Royal Icing.
#### Glace à la Royale.

The Whites of 2 Eggs.
1 Pound of Fine White Sugar.
1 Tablespoonful of Lemon Juice.
1 Tablespoonful of Any Kind of Essence Desired.

A Royal Icing is made of the finest possible white loaf sugar, sifted, and mixed or worked into a paste with the whites of eggs and lemon juice in the proportions given for Plain Icing, only the paste must be softer. Flavor with any kind of essence, according to fancy. This icing is used to produce fanciful effects. It is not necessary to purchase ornamental piping tubes. With a little taste and dexterity a piece of white writing paper, made into the shape of a cornet, may be utilized. Dry the paper by sticking together and rubbing with the white of an egg, to render stiff. Allow at the pointed end only a half inch opening, and with a little practice and good artistic taste, the prettiest effects in elegant ornamentation may be produced by even an amateur.

### Transparent Icing.
#### Glace Transparante.

½ Pound of Fine White Sugar.
Half of the White of 1 Egg.
The Juice of Half a Lemon.
1 Tablespoonful of Any Fancy Liqueur.

Take a half pound of the finest white clarified sugar, and clarify again by boiling it with half of the white of an egg, beaten to a stiff froth. Clear off the scum as it rises, and continue skimming till the sugar is perfectly clear. Then add to the sugar half a gill of clarified sugar, boiled to a syrup, and to which you will have added the juice of a quarter or half a lemon. Strain, and add to the sugar enough Liqueur, Curaçoa, Noyau, Cedrati or Maraschino to flavor the icing to taste, and beat or whip it to the proper consistency. Then take a silver tablespoon and stir the sugar well together, rubbing up and against the sides of the pan till it acquires an opaline appearance. Then take a silver fork, lift one of the cakes intended to be iced, dip in the sugar, or else hold it on a fork and with a spoon pour the icing over. Take another fork, lift off the cake and place it on the baking sheet, and so on till all the small cakes are iced. Then dry in the sun or in the oven for about ten minutes.

## CHAPTER XLI.

### ICE CREAMS, BISCUIT, SHERBETS.

Des Crèmes à la Glace, Biscuits Glacées, Sorbets.

In making ice creams, always use the best, fresh, sweet, rich milk or cream. Sweeten it with finely-powdered sugar, and flavor with the best quality of extracts, such as lemon, vanilla, etc., which should be procured from first-class, reliable druggists. These are the simplest means of flavoring. Sometimes, however, the old Creoles boil the Vanilla Bean until the aroma is extracted, and when cool they add it to the sweetened cream. Always avoid setting the cream near the fire, especially in warm weather, as it sours easily. Keep it in a refrigerator till ready to freeze.

There are so many improved ice cream freezers that it would almost seem superfluous to add anything in regard to freezing the cream. However, it is well to remember that the lid of the freezer must always be tight-fitting and secure, so as to preclude the possibility of any salt entering it. Directions are given with all these modern inventions as to the method of freezing the cream according to the make of the freezer.

### How to Make Ice Cream.

Some persons boil the milk and eggs, thus making a custard ice cream. This is the cream that the old Creoles prefer best. But there are others who prefer the cream unboiled. In either case it is absolutely necessary to have rich, fresh cream, and in the latter case to scald the cream, if you wish to have a good ice cream. A delicious cream, however, is made according to the old method in vogue so many years among the Creoles. The old French confectioners along Canal Street long ago found out and demonstrated that the raw frozen cream is never a smooth velvety cream, and that the flavoring is scarce apparent.

The following is the approved Creole method of making

### Ice Cream.

Crème à la Glacé.

1 Quart of Milk or Cream. 6 Eggs.
¾ Pound of Sugar.
1 Tablespoonful of Any Extract.

Put the milk or cream on to boil. If cream is used, six eggs will be sufficient; if milk, use eight. Beat the yolks of the eggs and the sugar very light, and then beat the whites to a stiff froth. Take the milk off the fire, and pour it over the sugar and yolks, stirring it all the while. Then add the whites, mixing thoroughly, and two tablespoonfuls of extract of either Lemon or Vanilla. Set to cool, and then turn into the freezer, pack and stir around in the ice for about ten minutes, and finish as in recipe for making and freezing cream. (See recipe.)

This ice cream is the basis of all ice creams used by the Creoles.

### How to Freeze the Cream.

Before putting the mixture into the freezer, see that the dasher is right side up and that everything is in proper condition and adjustment. Have the ice pounded, and a sufficient quantity of rock salt. Put a three-and-a-half inch layer of ice into the bottom of the freezer, and then a layer of salt, fully an inch and a half deep. Then put in the can, and continue to fill around it with alternate layers of ice and salt till the freezer is full. Then turn the crank slowly until it is somewhat difficult to turn it. Let off the water that has accumulated, and refill with ice, and then cover with a thick piece of bagging or carpet. Then let it stand aside in a cool place to ripen, till you are ready to serve. Then proceed as above.

Fruit puddings and custards may be frozen in the same manner.

### How to Mold Ice Cream.

When ready to serve, if you wish to take the cream out of the mold whole, have ready a dish with a flat bottom, and a pan of hot water. Then roll the tin mold for an instant only in the water, and wipe it quickly, holding the top downwards. Remove the lid, and quickly turn it right side up, setting the plate on the table and removing the mold carefully. Or you may wring out cloths in scalding water and wrap them an instant around the mold, and proceed as above. This is a very delicate way of serving the cream, and admits of it being brought to the table in all its beauty and freshness and perfection of molding.

The cream may also be molded into a single brick by having a brick-shaped mold and filling it with the cream. When well-filled, press down closely and cover the mold carefully, so that no pieces of salt or any salt water can enter it or penetrate it. Fill the bottom of a pail with ice, mingled with rock salt; lay the mold upon it, surround and cover with the broken pieces of ice and mingled rock salt; cover and let freeze for about half an hour. When frozen, set mold in luke warm water, wash off portions of ice and salt, lift the mold out gently, uncover turn into a dessert dish and serve immediately.

### Apricot Ice Cream.

Crème Glacée aux Abricots.

1 Quart of Cream.
¾ Pound of Sugar.
1 Quart of Apricots or 1 Pint Can.

Prepare the cream as in recipe Ice Cream (see recipe), and let cool for half an hour. Pare and mash the apricots, being careful to remove the stones. Then mash them into the cream, mixing thoroughly for five minutes till well dissolved in the cream. Then strain through a fine sieve into a freezer, pressing the fruit down with a wooden spoon and when well packed proceed to freeze as in the directions for Plain Ice Cream. (See directions.)

### Banana Ice Cream.

Crème Glacée aux Bananes.

6 Large Bananas.
1 Quart of Cream.
The Yolks of 3 Eggs.
¾ Pound of Sugar.

Peel the bananas and slice and mash them. Boil the milk, and add the sugar, stirring till well dissolved. Then add the yolks of the eggs, beaten very light, and let cool for an hour. Stir in the bananas, which you will have previously beaten to a smooth paste, and proceed as directed above.

### Chocolate Ice Cream.

Crème au Chocolat.

1 Quart of Milk or Cream.
½ Pound of the Best French Chocolate.
¼ Pound of Sugar.
1 Tablespoonful of Vanilla Extract.

Boil the milk, and add to it a half pound of the best French chocolate, grated. Let it boil and thicken, beating till smooth. Add a quarter of a pound of white pulverized sugar. When cool add half a quart of cream and the Vanilla Extract. Pour into the freezer, after mixing well, and proceed as in directions for making and freezing cream.

### Chocolate Ice Cream With Eggs.

Crème Glacée au Chocolat.

4 Ounces of Chocolate.
6 Ounces of Sugar. 1 Pint of Milk.
8 Yolks of Eggs.
1 Pint of Whipped Cream.
1 Tablespoonful of Vanilla.

Dissolve the chocolate in a little water, and add it to the boiling milk. Take off, and pour over the eggs and sugar, which you will have beaten to a thick cream. Add the Vanilla, and set to cool. Then add the remaining cream, and freeze as directed.

### Coffee Ice Cream.

Creme Glacee au Cafe.

1 Pint of Cream.
1 Pint of New Milk.
6 Eggs. 1 Pound of Sugar.
½ Cup of Strong Cafe Noir (Black Coffee.)

Boil the milk. Take from the fire. Whip the cream to a stiff froth. Add the sugar and yolks of eggs, thoroughly beaten, to the milk and coffee, sweetening to taste. Set aside to cool, and add the whipped cream, and proceed to freeze as directed.

### King of the Carnival Ice Cream.

Crème à la Glace au Rex.

1 Quart of Milk or Cream. 6 Eggs.
1 Pound of Sugar.
1 Tablespoonful Each of the Coloring Extracts Given Below.

This cream was originated by a famous New Orleans confisseur in honor of "Rex," the King of the world-famed New Orleans Carnivals. It was first served at a Carnival luncheon in St. Charles Avenue. The King's colors are purple, green and gold. The cream represents these colors, and is made according to the following directions:

Make a Plain Ice Cream. Divide into three distinct and equal portions. Color one with Spinach Greenery, to obtain the green effect; flavor another with Essence of Vanilla, and tinge with orange juice or a bit of saffron, to obtain the golden yellow, and the third with a deep Crème de Violettes, to obtain the royal purple. Freeze in separate molds. Then pack into one freezer, and when frozen remove, according to directions for taking ice cream whole from a mold. Cut in slices and serve. Molds now come made in the shape of tiny flags, and the effect of freezing thus is very beautiful, and suggests at once Rex and his merry reign.

### Lemon Ice Cream.

Crème Glacée au Citron.

1 Quart of Cream or Milk.
6 Eggs. ¾ Pound of Sugar.
1 Tablespoonful of Lemon Extract.

Put the milk or cream on to boil. If cream is used, six eggs will be sufficient; if milk, use eight. Beat the yolks of the eggs and the sugar very light, and then beat the whites to a stiff froth. Take the milk off the fire, and pour it over the sugar and yolks, stirring all the while. Then add the whites, mixing thoroughly, and two tablespoonfuls of extract of lemon. Set to cool, and then turn into the freezer, pack, and stir around in the ice for about ten minutes, and finish as in recipe for making and freezing Cream. (See recipe.)

### Liqueur Ice Cream.

Crème Glacée au Liqueurs.

1 Quart of Milk. 1 Pound of Sugar.
The Yolks of 8 Eggs.
A Gill of Any Kind of Liqueur.

Boil the milk and take from the fire, and add the sugar and the eggs, beaten to a thick cream. Add a gill of any kind of fancy liqueur, and then turn into a mold and freeze as above directed.

### Mandarin Ice Cream.

Creme Glacee a l'Oranges.

1 Quart of Cream or Milk.
1 Pound of Sugar.
The Yolks of 6 Eggs.
The Grated Zest of 2 Mandarins.
The Juice of 1 Dozen, With the Grated Pulp.

Peel the mandarins, grate the rind or zest of two very fine, extract the juice of twelve, and, after taking out the seeds, mash the inner fruit or pulp through a sieve. Put the milk or cream on to boil. Beat the yolks of eggs and sugar till very light, and beat the whites to a stiff froth. Take the milk from the fire and pour it over the sugar and yolks, stirring all the while. Set to cool, then add the whites of the eggs, and finally the grated mandarin pulp, zest and juice, and mix well. Turn all into a freezer and proceed as in the directions given for making Ice Cream. (See recipe.)

### Maraschino Ice Cream.

Crème Glacée au Maraschino.

1 Quart of Milk.
1 Pound of Sugar. 8 Eggs.
A Gill of Any Kind of Maraschino.
The Juice of 1 Lemon.

Boil the milk and take from the fire, and add the sugar and the yolks of the eggs, beaten to a thick cream. Set to cool. Add a gill of Maraschino and the whites of the eggs, beaten to a stiff froth, and then turn into a mold and freeze as above directed.

### Neapolitan Ice Cream.

Crème Neapolitaine.

1 Pint of Vanilla Cream.
1 Pint of Pistache Ice Cream.
1 Pint of Strawberry or Raspberry Cream.

Prepare the ice cream according to recipes. (See recipes.) Have at hand a brick form or mold that will hold three pints. Lay at the bottom of the mold Pistache Ice Cream; place over this the Vanilla Cream and on top of this the Raspberry or Strawberry Cream. Cover the mold tightly and set to freeze for two hours. Then plunge the mold into warm water, wash off all the salt and dry. Then carefully uncover, and unmold the cream in a cold dessert dish or on a piece of paper. Take a long, sharp knife, dip into warm water, cut the brick of cream through the center, and then divide the pieces into three or four parts, each being perfectly square. Arrange daintily on a cold dessert dish and serve immediately.

### Nectarine Ice Cream.

Crème Glacée aux Poires.

1 Quart of Cream or Milk.
1 Pound of Sugar.
1 Quart of Nectarines or 1 Pint Can.
6 Eggs.

Peel the nectarines, stone and mash well, with half of the sugar. Let them stand for an hour or more, and press through a sieve. Set the milk to boil; beat the yolks of the eggs and the remaining half of the sugar to a cream, and beat the whites of the eggs to a stiff froth. Take the milk off the fire and pour it over the sugar and yolks, stirring all the while. Set to cool. Then add the mashed nectarines and sugar, and mix well; mix all thoroughly, turn into a freezer and proceed as in the general directions for making Ice Cream. (See recipe.)

### Nougat Ice Cream.
#### Crème Glacée au Nougat.

1 Pint of Nougat,
8 Eggs.   ¾ Pound of Sugar.
1 Quart of Cream.
3 Drops of Essence of Peach Kernels.

Make some Nougat (see recipe), using about a pint. Bruise and mash it, and blend with one gill of orange flower water. Add to this the sugar and the yolks of the eggs, beaten to a thick cream. Set the milk to boil. Then take from the fire and add the above ingredients, stirring well, and adding at the end the Essence of Peach Kernels, and the whites of the eggs, beaten to a stiff froth. Then freeze in the manner above directed. Left-over Nougat may be utilized in this way.

### Noyau Ice Cream.
#### Crème Glacée au Noyau.

1 Quart of Milk.
1 Pound of Sugar.
The Juice of 1 Lemon.   8 Eggs.
A Gill of Noyau.

Boil the milk and take from the fire, and then add the sugar and the yolks of the eggs, beaten to a thick cream. Add a gill of Noyau Extract and the whites of the eggs, beaten to a stiff froth. Set to cool, and then turn into a mold and freeze as above directed.

### Orange Ice Cream.
#### Crème Glacée à l'Orange.

1 Quart of Cream.
1 Pound of Sugar.
The Juice of 12 Oranges.
The Grated Rind of 2 Oranges, Rubbed on Sugar.

Boil the milk or cream in a farina boiler. Take off the fire, and while hot pour this over the yolks of the eggs, which have been beaten to a thick cream, with the sugar; add orange juice and rind of the oranges. Stir till all begins to thicken. Then add the whites of the eggs beaten to a stiff froth. Set to cool. Turn into the freezer, and proceed in the manner above indicated.

### Orange Flower Ice Cream.
#### Crème Glacée à la Fleur d'Oranger.

1 Quart of Cream.   ¾ Pound of Sugar.
1 Ounce of Candied Orange Flowers.
The Yolks of 8 Eggs.

Bruise the orange flowers, and mix and stir them with the boiling milk. Then take from the fire, and add the sugar, and dissolve well, and then the beaten yolks of the eggs, mix well. Freeze in the manner above indicated.

### Peach Ice Cream.
#### Crème Glacée aux Peches.

8 Ripe Peaches or 1 Can.
6 Eggs.   1 Pound of Sugar.
1 Quart of Cream.

Put the milk to boil, and when hot take from the fire, and add the yolks of the eggs, which have been beaten to a thick cream with the powdered sugar. Then set to cool for thirty minutes. Then add the peaches, which you will have pared, stoned and mashed, and stir them quickly into the cream. Now add the whites of the eggs, beaten to a stiff froth. Mix all thoroughly together and turn into the freezer. Turn the crank rapidly for a few minutes, till thoroughly mixed, and then cover and let stand for two hours. Delicious.

### Pistachio Ice Cream.
#### Crème Glacée aux Pistaches.

1 Quart of Milk or Cream.
¾ Pound of Sugar.
¼ Pound of Shelled, Scalded and Cleaned Pistachio Nuts.
The Yolks of 8 Eggs.
2 Tablespoonfuls of Spinach Greening, or 5 Drops of Spinach Green.
1 Tablespoonful of Orange Flower Water or Almond Extract.

Wash and boil the Spinach for five minues, and then drain through a colander. Reduce it to a pulp, and then squeeze out the juice through a piece of fine muslin. One quart of Spinach will furnish the proper amount of juice when boiled and squeezed. Then wash, scald, clean and pulverize the pistachios to a pulp. Set half the milk to boil in a farina boiler. Add the sugar, and stir till well dissolved. Take off and add the yolks of the eggs, beaten very, very light. Stir and add the nuts, and stir till it thickens. Then stand away to cool. When cool, add the flavoring extract and the remaining cream, reserving a small portion to work into the Spinach, which you will add and blend smoothly. When the color is a light green, turn into a freezer and proceed as directed above.

### Pineapple Ice Cream.
#### Crème Glacée à l'Ananas.

1 Large, Ripe Pineapple.
1 Quart of Cream or Milk.   6 Eggs.
1 Pound of Sugar.
The Juice of 1 Lemon.

Peel the pineapple, and then grate and pound and mash the pulp with one-half of the sugar. Press through a sieve. Put the milk or cream on to boil. Beat the yolks of the eggs and the remaining half of the sugar very light, and then beat the whites to a stiff froth. Take the milk off the fire, and pour it over the sugar and yolks, stirring all the while. Then add the whites, mixing thoroughly. Add the pineapple and juice and mix well. Set to cool and then turn into the freezer, pack and stir around in the ice box for about ten minutes, and proceed as in the recipe for making and freezing Cream.

### Pineapple Mousse.
Mousse à l'Ananas.

1 Pineapple.
3 Teaspoonfuls of Vanilla.
3 Tablespoonfuls of Jamaica Rum.
1 Quart of Cream.
1 Pound of Powdered Sugar.

Peel the pineapple, and cut one-half into slices. Lay them in a bowl and sprinkle with powdered sugar and one-third of the rum. Cover and set aside till needed. Grate the remainder of the pineapple into an earthen vessel, and add sugar sufficient to sweeten to taste, and pour the vanilla and the rest of the rum over it. Then mix carefully with the cream, which should be at least three times the weight of the pineapple. Turn all into an ice cream mold and proceed to freeze as directed above. Serve with slices of pineapple and its syrup around the frozen composition, which should be turned out of the mold according to directions given for making and freezing cream.

### Raspberry Ice Cream.
Crème Glacée aux Framboises.

1 Quart of Cream.
1 Quart of Raspberries or 2 Tablespoonfuls of Raspberry Extract.
1 Pound of Sugar.
The Yolks of 6 Eggs.
The Juce of 1 Lemon.

Set the milk to boil, add the sugar, and when well-dissolved take from the fire, add the eggs, well beaten to a cream, and set aside to cool. Then, when cool, add the remaining half of the sugar, which you will have blended with the berries, which have been mashed well, and allowed to stand for several hours, and then press through a sieve. Mix well with the milk, add the lemon juice, turn into the freezer, and freeze as above directed. If the berries are too pale to impart a sufficient rosy tinge to the cream, add a few drops of Raspberry Extract. It is only possible to make the Raspberry Cream with the fruit when raspberries are in season. Otherwise use two tablespoonfuls of Raspberry Extract, and proceed as in recipe for Vanilla Cream.

### Rice Ice Cream.
Crème Glacée au Riz.

2½ Pints of Milk. ¾ Pound of Sugar.
The Yolks of 8 Eggs.
4 Ounces of Boiled Rice.
1 Gill of Curacoa.
½ Pint of Milk of Almonds.
A Compote of 6 Oranges.

Boil the rice in the milk till very soft. Do not mash. Set the pint and a half extra milk to boil, and add the rice and the milk of almonds and the sugar and eggs, beaten to a cream. Make a custard. Take from the fire, and add the Curacoa, and mix well. Set to freeze as above directed, and when cold turn out of the mold (see recipe), place in a dish, garnish around with the oranges (see Compote of Oranges), pour the syrup over all, and serve.

### Rose Ice Cream.
Crème Glacée à la Rose.

1 Quart of Cream.
1 Pound of Sugar.
2 Teaspoonfuls of Red Rose Extract and Vanilla.

Prepare exactly as in recipe for Ice Cream, using the same ingredients, and flavor with two tablespoonfuls of Red Rose Extract and Vanilla.

### Strawberry Ice Cream.
Crème Glacée aux Fraises.

1 Quart of Cream.
1 Quart of Strawberries or 2 Tablespoonfuls of Strawberry Extract.
1 Pound of Sugar.
6 Eggs. The Juice of 1 Lemon.

Set the milk to boil; take from the fire, add the yolks of the eggs, well beaten to a cream, with half the sugar, and set aside to cool. Then, when cool, add the remaining half of the sugar, which you will have blended with the strawberries, mashed well, and allowed to stand for several hours, and then press through a sieve. Mix well with the milk, add the lemon juice and the whites of the eggs, beaten to a stiff froth; turn into the freezer, and freeze as above directed. If the strawberries are too pale to impart a sufficiently rosy tinge to the cream add a few drops of Cochineal. When not in season flavor with the Extract.

### Tutti-Frutti.

1 Pint of Vanilla Ice Cream.
½ Pint of Strawberry Ice Cream.
½ Pint of Lemon Sherbet.
2 Ounces of Candied Cherries.
1 Ounce of Candied Orange.
2 Ounces of Candied Apricots.
1 Ounce of Candied Currants.

Prepare the Vanilla and Strawberry Ice Cream and the Lemon Sherbet according to recipes given (see recipes). Have ready six or eight tutti-frutti molds. Cut the candied cherries into halves or quarters, and the candied oranges and apricots into small pieces. Open the tutti-frutti molds and fill in the bottom with Vanilla Cream. Lay side by side in the covers of the molds a spoonful of Lemon Sherbet and a spoonful of Strawberry Cream; mix the candied fruits together and divide them into equal parts, and lay these on the Vanilla Cream in the bottom of the molds. Then press the covers tightly on each mold and after seeing that they are very firmly closed, lay the mold in a pail, the bottom of which has been filled with broken ice and rock salt. Cover the mold with more rock salt and ice and proceed to lay each mold one over the other, alternating with the ice and rock salt. When all are covered, fill in the pail with broken pieces of ice and rock salt, cover and let freeze for one hour. Have ready a vessel with warm water and six or eight very cold dessert plates on which you will have arranged dainty paper cases fancifully cut. Lift up the molds gently and wash them off very quickly with the warm water, being careful to see that no salt adheres. Then open the molds and lay the tutti-frutti in the paper cases and serve immediately.

### Tutti-Frutti à la Créole.

1 Quart of Orange Sherbet. (See recipe.)
½ Pint of Cherries, Seeded.
½ Pint of Stoned Apricots.
½ Pint of Stoned Peaches.
½ Pint of Figs. ½ Pint of Pineapple.
½ Pint of Watermelon.

Cut the watermelon and the pineapple into very small square lozenges first seeding the watermelon. Cut the rest of the fruits very fine. Then put a layer of the watermelon into the freezer, and sprinkle generously with white powdered sugar. Then put a layer of the mixed fruits, sugar abundantly, pour in a little of the sherbet, and proceed in this way until the whole form is nearly filled with the mixture in alternate layers. Then set in a double boiler just long enough for the sugar to melt. Take out, pour over the orange sherbet, close tightly, and set to freeze. This is the genuine Tutti-Frutti, and is most delicious.

### Vanilla Ice Cream.

Crème Glacée à la Vanille.

1 Quart of Milk or Cream.
6 Eggs. ¾ Pound of Sugar.
2 Teaspoonfuls of Any Extract.

Put the milk or cream on to boil. If cream is used, six eggs will be sufficient; if milk, use eight. Beat the yolks of the eggs and the sugar very light, and then beat the whites to a stiff froth. Take the milk off the fire, and pour it over the sugar and yolks, stirring all the while. Then add the whites, mixing thoroughly, and two tablespoonfuls of extract of either Lemon or Vanilla. Set to cool, and then turn into the freezer, pack, and stir around in the ice for about ten minutes, and finish as in recipe for making and freezing cream. (See recipe.)

### Variegated Ice Cream.

Crème Panachée.

1 Quart of Milk or Cream.
1 Pound of Sugar. 6 Eggs.
1 Teaspoonful of Essence of Strawberry.
1 Teaspoonful of Essence of Vanilla.
1 Teaspoonful of Chocolate.
1 Teaspoonful of Cream of Violets.
1 Teaspoonful of Spinach Greenery.

Prepare a Plain Ice Cream. (See recipe "Ice Cream.") Divide it into portions. Color one with Essence of Strawberry, another with Spinach Greenery, another with Vanilla, to obtain yellow, another with Creme de Violettes, another with Chocolate, etc. Freeze all these in separate molds, that come specially prepared for this purpose, and which may be obtained from any dealer. When frozen, take from the individual molds and pack in a large ice cream freezer in a beautiful order of arrangement, so that the colors may blend well. Freeze again, and then remove from the mold according to directions given above for unmolding. Cut into slices and serve. The effect of the various colors is very pretty.

### BISCUIT GLACÉS.

1 Quart of Cream.
The Yolks of 6 Eggs.
1 Tablespoonful of Vanilla.
¾ Pound of Sugar.
1 Gill of Maraschino or 1 Gill of Kirsch.

Set one-half the cream to boil. Beat the yolks of the eggs and the sugar till they are exceedingly light. Take the boiling milk from the fire, and stir in, while still very hot, the sugar and eggs. Then set to cool. When cool add the Maraschino or Kirsch, and set to freeze as Ice Cream. In the meantime, whip the remaining cream to a very thick froth, as in Whipped Cream à la Vanille, adding the Vanilla, and stir it into the freezing cream. Cut paper cases, or use the specially prepared molds that come for Biscuit Glacé, and fill with the mixture, and then fill the top one inch high with a little of the cream, which you will have colored with a teaspoonful of Strawberry Extract and a few drops of Cochineal. Pack these molds or cases in salt, and freeze for two hours longer, until they can be turned out whole.

### Biscuits Glacés à la Créole.

1 Pint of Milk.
The Yolks of 6 Eggs.
½ Pound of Pulverized Sugar.
1 Tableapoonful of Vanilla or Lemon Extract.

Set one pint of milk to boil. Beat the yolks of six eggs with a half pound of white pulverized sugar until light. Stir in the milk. Take from the fire, and let cool. Flavor with vanilla and freeze. Whip one pint of cream to a stiff froth, and stir in. Fill molds, or fancy paper cases with the mixture, pack in salt and ice for two hours, and serve.

### BOMBE GLACÉ.

1 Pint of Milk.
The Yolks of 6 Eggs.
½ Pound of White Pulverized Sugar..
1 Tablespoonful of Vanilla Extract.
½ Pint of Strawberry Sherbet.

For this purpose you must have Bombe Glacé molds. Line the molds about three-fourths of an inch thick with Strawberry Water Ice (see recipe), and then fill the center with the Biscuit Glacé, prepared as above. The biscuit must be freezing cold when put into the mold. Pack in salt and ice, and set to freeze several hours.

### SHERBET.
Sorbets.

Sherbets are delightful water ices, differing from ice creams in this, that no milk or eggs are used in the making, the juice of the fruit or extract of fruit or essence flavoring and sugar and water being prepared and frozen together. Sherbets are among the most pleasant of the Creole summer desserts; they are extensively served of a hot summer evening in Creole families and are both for the family and guests, who may drop in for a social half hour. The sherbet is served in glasses. Water ices are made in exactly the same manner as sherbets, only the water and sugar are not boiled; they are mixed together and the flavoring or fruit juice added and frozen, and are served immediately.

### Apple Sherbet.

Sorbet aux Pommes.

1 Pound of Sugar.
1½ Pnits of Apple Juice.
1 Quart of Water.
The Juice of 1 Lemon.

Take about a dozen apples, pare, core and quarter, and cook till very tender. Put the sugar and water to boil, add the apples, and when very tender strain all through a sieve. Add the juice of the lemon and set to freeze as in Ice Cream. (See recipe for Freezing Ice Cream.) Serve as needed.

### Apricot Sherbet.

Sorbet aux Abricots.

½ Pint of Apricot Juice.
1 Pound of Sugar.
1 Quart of Water.
The Juice of 1 Lemon.

Put the sugar and water to boil. Take about one dozen apricots, pare, press them through a sieve, and add to the boiling syrup. Let all boil for five or ten minutes. Then press through a sieve again; add the lemon juice, mix well and set to freeze as in general directions for freezing Ice Cream.

### Banana Sherbet.

Sorbet aux Bananes.

1 Dozen Bananas. 1 Pound of Sugar.
1 Quart of Water.
The Juice of 2 Oranges.

Peel and mash the bananas. Boil the sugar and water together for five minutes. Take from the fire, and let cool. Then add the bananas and the orange juice, and press all through a sieve. Set to freeze as directed. This is a favorite Creole Sherbet.

### Cherry Sherbet.

Sorbet aux Cerises.

1 Pound of Cherries. 1 Pound of Sugar.
1 Quart of Water.

Boil the sugar and water together for five minutes. Stone the cherries and add them to the syrup. Then set to cool. Press through a sieve till all the juice is extracted from the cherries. Set to freeze and serve as directed.

### Currant Sherbet.

Sorbet aux Groseilles.

1 Pint of Currant Juice.
1 Quart of Water. 1 Pound of Sugar.

Mash one quart of currants. Boil the sugar and water for five minutes. Add the currants and strain through a napkin or sieve, being careful to press very hard to extract the juice of the currants. Set to freeze as directed.

### Grape Sherbet.

Sorbet aux Raisins.

1 Pint of Malaga Grapes.
1 Pound of Sugar.
1 Quart of Water.

Boil the sugar and water five minutes. Mash the grapes and add all to the sugar and water. Set to cool. Then press through a fine cloth, pressing hard to extract all the juice of the grapes. Set to freeze and serve as directed.

### Lemon Sherbet.
#### Sorbet au Citron.

The Juice of 10 Lemons.
The Grated Zest of 3 Lemons.
1 Pint of Sugar.
1 Quart of Water.

Put the sugar and water to boil. Grate the zest or yellow rind of three lemons, and add to the syrup, and let it boil for five minutes. Then set away to cool. Extract the juice from the lemons, and grate the fruit. Mix this with the syrup, and then strain through a thin muslin cloth. Turn into the freezer, and proceed as in Ice Cream.

### Orange Sherbet.
#### Sorbet à l'Orange.

12 Large Louisiana Oranges.
1 Quart of Water.
The Juice of 2 Lemons.
The Zest of 3 Oranges.
1 Pint of Sugar.

Put the sugar and water to boil. Grate the zest or yellow rind of three oranges, and add to the syrup, and let it boil for five minutes. Then set away to cool. Extract the juice from the oranges and lemons, and grate the fruit. Mix this with the syrup, and then strain all through a thin muslin cloth. Turn into the freezer, and proceed as in Ice Cream.

### Peach Sherbet.
#### Sorbet aux Peches.

1 Dozen Fine Peaches.
1 Pound of Sugar.
The Juice of 2 Lemons.
1 Quart of Water.

Pare and cut the peaches in halves, remove the stones. Cut the peaches up very fine and sprinkle with a half pound of sugar, mash well together and set aside for an hour. Then set the water and the remaining half of the sugar to boil. After five minutes remove from the fire and let cool; add the peaches and mix well. Then press all through a fine cloth sieve, extracting all the juice from the peaches. Set to freeze and serve as directed, in glasses. This is a delicious sherbet.

### Pineapple Sherbet.
#### Sorbet à l'Ananas.

1 Pound of Grated Pineapple.
1 Quart of Water.
1 Pint of Sugar.
The Juice of 1 Lemon.

Peel and slice and pound the pineapple to a pulp. Then rub through a strainer. Put the sugar and water to boil for five minutes. Then set away to cool. Extract the juice from the lemon and mix this with the syrup, add the pineapple and juice, and then strain all through a thin muslin cloth. Turn into the freezer and proceed as in Ice cream. This sherbet is also made by using, instead of the pineapple, fruit and juice, two tablespoonfuls of Pineapple Extract.

### Pomegranate Sherbet.
#### Sorbet aux Grenades.

8 Ripe Pomegranates.
1 Quart of Water.
1 Pound of Sugar.
The Juice of 1 Lemon.
½ Teaspoonful of Essence of Vanilla.
3 Drops of Cochineal.

The pips of six or eight ripe pomegranates, pressed with a wooden spoon through a strainer, will produce a pint of juice. Make a syrup by boiling one quart of water and one pint of sugar. Add, when cooling, the pomegranate juice, a half teaspoonful of Essence of Vanilla, the juice of a lemon, and a few drops of Cochineal. Proceed to freeze as above directed.

### Raspberry Sherbet.
#### Sorbet aux Framboises.

1½ Pints of Raspberry Juice or Pulp.
1½ Pints of Picked Raspberries.
1 Pound of Sugar.
3 Drops of Cochineal.
The Juice of ¼ Lemon.

Stem the berries, and add the sugar and lemon, and stand aside in their juice for an hour and a half. Then strain through a fine sieve, and add the reserved juice. Turn into the freezer, and proceed to freeze according to directions given under heading "Ice Cream." This sherbet is also made by adding to the sugar and water two tablespoonfuls of Raspberry Extract, instead of the fruit, when not available.

### Strawberry Sherbet.
#### Sorbet aux Fraises.

1½ Pints of Strawberry Juice or Pulp.
1½ Pints of Picked Red Strawberries.
1 Pound of Sugar.
3 Drops of Cochineal.
The Juice of ¼ Lemon.

Stem the strawberries and add the sugar and lemon, and stand aside in their juice for an hour and a half. Then strain through a fine sieve, and add the reserved juice. Turn into the freezer and proceed to freeze according to directions given under the heading "Ice Cream." Strawberry Sherbet is also made by adding one tablespoonful of Strawberry Extract to the sugar and water, when the fruit is not available.

### Watermelon Sherbet.
#### Sorbet de Melon d'Eau.

1 Ripe Watermelon.
½ Pound of Pulverized Sugar.
6 Teaspoonfuls of Sherry Wine.

Split a ripe watermelon in half. Scoop out the center, rejecting the seeds. Put the scooped fruit in a bowl; take a silver fork and pick it in small pieces. Mix with a half pound of pulverized sugar; turn the mixture into a freezer and turn slowly for fifteen minutes. Serve in glasses, adding a teaspoonful of Sherry to each glass.

### WATER ICES.

Water ices are, as mentioned above, made in exactly the same manner as sherbets, only the sugar and water are not boiled. In this case always mash the fruit with the sugar and set aside to grow juicy. Then press through a fine muslin cloth, to extract all the juice, and add to the water. Mix well for a few minutes and freeze. In case peaches or apricots or cherries are used, pound the fruit, to extract all the juice, and mix well with the sugar; strain through a fine sieve or muslin cloth, and add to the cold water, and proceed to freeze.

To make Water Ices, follow the directions given for making Sherbet, with the exception of boiling the water.

### MIDDLE COURSE DRINKS.
#### Coup de Millieu.

From earliest Creole days no elegant dinner or luncheon or supper was considered complete without a "Coup de Millieu," or a middle course consisting of a form of iced sherbet or punch, into which fruit juices or fancy liqueurs were added. As the name "Coup de Millieu" indicates, these fancy punches were brought to the table in the middle of the feast, just before the roasts were served. The custom was a survival of the ancient French and Spanish usage, that in our day has been adopted by all leading northern caterers. The following are the most famous "Coup de Millieus," the recipes for which are traditional among the old Creole families of New Orleans. The "Coup de Millieu" is always frozen, but it must be remembered that it is never possible to freeze it entirely, on account of the alcohol in the liquors that enter into its composition.

### Cardinal Punch.
#### Ponche Cardinal.

4 Fine Louisiana Oranges.
1 Pint of the Best Claret or Any Fine Red Wine.
1 Pint of Old Port Wine.
1 Pint of Water.
2 Tablespoonfuls of Cloves.
1 Pint of Gelatine or the Whites of 10 Eggs, Beaten to a Froth.
2 Pounds of White Sugar.
3 Tablespoonfuls of Raspberry Juice or a Few Drops of Cochineal.

Select fine Louisiana oranges, when in season, otherwise fine, ripe oranges. Set them on a plate in the oven, and let them bake till very tender, without letting the juice exude. Make a boiling syrup of the sugar, water and the cloves. Drop the roasted oranges into the syrup, add a pint of the best Claret or any good, red wine, and set the mixture to cool, letting the oranges steep in the wine and syrup. When it grows cold, cut the oranges and press out all the juice, mashing them into the steeped syrup, and then strain all through a fine sieve into the ice cream freezer. Now add the gelatine (Calf's Foot Jelly) or the whites of ten eggs, beaten to a stiff froth. Stir well and add the raspberry juice, if raspberries are in season, otherwise color with a few drops of Cochineal, so that the punch will be of a bright cardinal color. Cover immediately and set to freeze as hard as possible for three or four minutes. Then take a wooden spoon and detach the frozen punch from the bottom, mix in with the inner liquid mixture, and cover and freeze again for three or four minutes. Repeat this four or five times. Serve in punch glasses.

A simpler and quicker way of making this punch is to prepare a Raspberry Sherbet, using half the quantity of ingredients given. (See recipe.) Strain this preparation through a sieve into a freezer, and add a half a gill of red Curaçoa and half a gill of Maraschino; cover the freezer and proceed to freeze according to general directions given above. Serve in punch glasses. This is a very pleasant middle course drink, but the first recipe given is the true Cardinal Punch, and there is no comparison between this and the latter, or more simple recipe.

Cardinal Punch is an old-time Creole punch. The French used to make a famous spiced wine, which they called "Vin de l'Eveque," or "Bishop's Wine." When the spiced wine was made of Claret, it was called "Vin de Cardinale," or "Cardinal's Wine." These wines were served during the feast. The "Coup de Millieu," or the frozen punches, are survivals of the old French custom of serving spiced wines, and "Ponche à la Cardinale" is a survival of the ancient "Vin à la Cardinale." The Creoles adapted oranges to the punch, baking them to better extract all the juices, and steeping them in wine and adding the touch of Cochineal to obtain brilliancy of coloring and still further to carry out the idea of a Cardinal's colors.

### Creole Punch.
#### Ponche à la Creole.

3 Cupfuls of Orange Juice.
1 Cupful of Water.
1 Cupful of Fine Old Port Wine.
½ Cupful of Brandy.
2 Small Cupfuls of Sugar.
2 Ripe, Delicate-Skinned Lemons.

Wash the lemons and dry, and then slice them very thin, without grating or squeezing into a bowl. Take the sugar and water and make a boiling syrup, and pour over the lemons, and let the whole mixture cool. Then add the orange juice. Take out the slices of lemon, and save them for later use. Strain the punch into an ice cream freezer, add the slices of lemon and liqueurs, and freeze as hard as possible for three or four minutes. Then take a wooden spoon and detach the frozen punch from the sides of the freezer and from the bottom, mix in with the inner liquid mixture, and cover and freeze again for three or four minutes. Repeat this four or five times. Serve in punch glasses.

### Frozen Champagne Punch.
#### Ponche Glacé au Vin de Champagne.

6 Lemons. 2 Oranges.
1 Pound of White Powdered Sugar.
1 Pint of Water.
½ Pint of Champagne.
½ Gill of Brandy.

Extract all the juice from the oranges and lemons. Dissolve the sugar in boiling water, and when cold add the juice. Freeze very hard for four or five minutes, and when firm add the liquors, turning long enough to mix well, and then proceed to freeze as in Creole Punch. (See recipe.) Serve in punch glasses. The above recipe may be varied by adding any fruit juices in season, always, as in Strawberry Punch, putting in two dozen or more whole stemmed berries for the above quantities of ingredients.

### Imperial Punch.
#### Ponche à l'Imperial.

1 Ripe Pineapple.
4 Oranges. 2 Pounds of Sugar.
The Finely-Grated Zest of 2 Lemons.
1 Pint Equal Parts of Maraschino, Noyeau, Kirsch and Curacoa.
1 Grated Nutmeg.
1 Pint of Champagne.
The Whites of 8 Eggs.
3 Pints of Water.

Make a syrup of the water and the syrup. Peel and grate the pineapple very fine. Grate the zest of two lemons very fine, and mix with the pineapple. Add the juices of the oranges and lemons. Mix thoroughly, and pour over all the boiling syrup. Let it stand till cold. Then strain through a fine sieve into the ice cream freezer, pressing out all the juice of the pineapple as you strain. Whip the whites of the eggs to a stiff froth, and add, mixing well. Add the liqueurs, stir well, and then proceed to freeze as in "Creole Punch." When you have detached the frozen punch from the sides and bottom of the freezer for the third time, add the champagne. Let it continue freezing for several turns more, and serve immediately in punch glasses.

### Kirsch Punch.
#### Ponche au Kirsch.

1 Dozen Fine Louisiana Oranges.
1 Gill of Kirsch.
2 Tablespoonfuls of Pineapple Syrup.
2 Lemons. 2 Dozen Strawberries.

Take fine, fresh Louisiana oranges, and press out all the juice, and mash the pulp and strain through a sieve. To each pint of juice allow one gill of Kirsch and two of the juice of two lemons. Sweeten to taste. Flavor with Pineapple Syrup, add whole strawberries when in season, and freeze as in Creole Punch. Serve in glasses.

### Louisiana Punch.
#### Ponche à la Louisianaise.

The Juice of 1 Large Louisiana Orange.
The Juice of 4 Lemons.
½ Pound of Pulverized Sugar.
¼ Pint of Water.
1 Gill of Kirsch. 1 Gill of Fine Rum.
1 Gill of Champagne.

Put the sugar into a bowl and squeeze over the juices of the orange and lemons. Mix well till all the sugar is impregnated with the juices. Add a half pint of cold water, and then add the Kirsch, and stir for five or six minutes. Strain all through a fine sieve into the ice cream freezer. Then remove the sieve and pour into the freezer the rum and champagne. Cover well, and let the mixture freeze for about five minutes. Then remove the cover and detach the mixture from the sides and bottom, and cover again and proceed as in "Ponche à la Créole." (See recipe.) Serve in punch glasses.

### Roman Punch.
#### Ponche à la Romaine.

1 Quart of Lemon Sherbet.
½ Pint of Champagne.
½ Pint of Jamaica Rum.
1 Gill of Maraschino.
1 Teaspoonful of Vanilla.

Make a Lemon Sherbet, and freeze it very hard. Then add the liquors slowly, and beat well. Turn into a freezer, pack and cover it well, and let it stand for four or five hours. The punch will not freeze perfectly on account of the alcohol. The correct way to serve it is in a rather liquid state, in glasses.

Or take half a pint of lemon juice, the zest of two lemons, grated on sugar, one pint of rum, one and a half pints of brandy, two quarts of water, and three pounds of sugar, and freeze as above. This is a cheaper recipe.

Still another way to make this punch is to take the juice of eight lemons and five oranges, three pints of sugar, and three pints of water. Add one wineglassful of Jamaica rum, and two of Champagne, and the whites of three eggs, beaten to a froth. Freeze and serve in glasses.

### Royal Sherbet.
#### Sorbet à la Royale.

1 Dozen Fine Louisiana Oranges.
2 Tablespoonfuls of Brandy.
2 Tablespoonfuls of Orange Syrup.

Take fine, fresh Louisiana oranges, and press out all juice, and mash the pulp and strain through a sieve. To each pint of juice allow two tablespoonfuls of brandy and two of orange syrup. Sweeten to taste and freeze and serve according to the directions given for Creole Punch.

### FROZEN FRUITS.
#### Des Fruits Glacés.

The variety of fruits always to be found in the New Orleans markets are the pleasure and surprise of visitors to the city, as well as a delight to the residents. No manner of serving fruits in summer is more acceptable than the methods of freezing them in vogue among the Creoles. Remember that in freezing fruits they must always be mashed or cut very fine, for fruit freezes more quickly than liquid. Fresh fruits are always more delicious than canned fruits. The latter are rarely used for freezing in Creole homes, as fresh fruits in season are always to be found in our markets.

The following recipe for freezing fruits will serve for almost all kinds of fruit:

### How to Freeze Fruits.

Take one pound of fruit, or one can, two cups of sugar, and one pint of water. Cut fine, and mix all the ingredients together. Then freeze in the ice cream freezer, according to directions already given for freezing.

The proportions of ingredients used in freezing fruits are generally one pint of fruit, one pint of water and half a pound of sugar. Increase in proportion. Peaches and such fruits as are watery may often be frozen without addition of water. Serve with rich cream or milk.

### Frozen Apricots.
#### Abricots Glacés.

2 Fine, Ripe Apricots.
2 Cups of Sugar.
1 Pint of Water or Cream.

Pare the apricots, cut them in two, remove the stones, and cut in small pieces. Mash the fruit and the sugar together, add the water or cream, and turn into the freezer and proceed to freeze as in Ice Cream. (See recipe Ice Cream.)

### Frozen Bananas.
#### Bananes Glacées.

1 Dozen Fine Bananas.
¾ Pound of Sugar.
1 Pint of Sugar or Cream.
The Juice of 2 Oranges.

Peel the bananas, cut them very fine and mash well; add the cream or water and the orange juice, turn into the freezer and pack away in ice and rock salt. Set to freeze according to directions given for freezing Ice Cream. (See recipe.)

### Frozen Cherries.
#### Cerises Glacées.

1 Pound of Cherries.
1 Pound of Sugar.
1 Quart of Water.

Stone the cherries, mix them with the sugar and add the water. Mix well and turn into the freezer and proceed to freeze as in directions for Ice Cream. (See recipe.) Serve with Whipped Cream or rich milk.

### Frozen Oranges.
#### Oranges Glacées.

6 Fine Oranges.
½ Pound of Sugar.
1 Pint of Water.

Pare the oranges, and grate or cut them into fine pieces. Mix well with the sugar and set aside for an hour. Add the water and mix thoroughly. Turn into a freezer and proceed to freeze as in Ice Cream. (See recipe.)

Another delightful way is to cut off the tops of the oranges, about two inches deep; then, with a small and very sharp knife, remove the orange skin whole, being careful not to break. Set the orange covers to one side. Scoop out the inside of the oranges, being careful not to break the outer skin. Take these oranges and arrange nicely in a square Biscuit Glacée mold, and set in a tub, the bottom of which has been filled with broken pieces of ice and rock salt. Prepare a Champagne Punch (see recipe), fill the interiors of the oranges with this, set the orange covers on, and place the cover on the mold, covering very tight. Cover well with broken pieces of ice and rock salt and set to freeze for an hour. Then take from the mold, place on a very cold dessert dish and serve immediately.

### Frozen Peaches.
Peches Glacées.

12 Large Peaches.
2 Cups of Sugar.
1 Pint of Water.

Take twelve large peaches or one can, two cups of sugar, and one pint of water. Cut the peaches fine, and mix all the ingredients together. Then freeze in the ice cream freezer according to directions already given.

Peaches, if very juicy, may often be frozen without addition of water. Serve with rich cream or milk.

### Frozen Pineapple.
Ananas Glacées.

1 Large Pineapple.
1 Pound of Sugar.
1 Pint of Water.

Pare the pineapples. Cut out the eyes, and then grate the fruit, or cut it very fine. Add the sugar and water and stir well. When the sugar is thoroughly dissolved, turn the mixture into a freezer, and proceed to freeze as in Ice Cream. (See recipe.)

### Frozen Strawberries.
Fraises Glacées.

1 Quart of Strawberries.
1 Pound of Sugar.
1 Pint of Water.

Mash the berries with the sugar and set aside for an hour. Add the water and mix well with the strawberries. Turn the mixture into the freezer and proceed to freeze as in Ice Cream (see recipe). Serve with rich milk or Whipped Cream.

### Macedoine of Fruits.
Macedoine de Fruits.

1 Quart of Lemon Ice Cream.
The Juice of 3 Lemons.
½ Teaspoonful of Vanilla Extract.
2 Ounces of Stoned Cherries.
2 Ounces of Pineapple, Cut in Dice.
2 Ounces of Strawberries.
2 Ounces of Grapes. 2 Ounces of Peaches.
2 Ounces of Apricots.
2 Ounces of Oranges.
1 Ounce of Candied Cherries.
1 Ounce of Angelica.
1 Ounce of Candied Pineapple.
1 Gill of Sherry Wine.

Prepare a quart of Lemon Ice Cream (see recipe.) Add to this a half teaspoonful of vanilla, 2 ounces each of stoned cherries, pineapple cut into dice shape, 2 ounces of strawberries, 2 ounces of grapes, apricots, peaches and grapes cut into small pieces, and the candied fruits in equal proportions. Add a gill of Sherry wine, mix all the fruits lightly, turn into a freezer and proceed to freeze as in Ice Cream. (See recipe.)

Again this Macedoine may be prepared by using instead of the Lemon Cream, a pint of syrup made of sugar and water, to which has been added the juice of three lemons.

A very delightful and pretty way of freezing this Macedoine is to prepare the cream, mix the candied fruits and fresh fruits together; have ready a square ice cream mold, and place one-fourth of the lemon cream at the bottom; divide the fruits into three parts, and place one portion on top of the cream. Cover this with another portion of the cream, and lay on top the fruits. Again cover with the cream, and lastly with the fruits. Fill up the mold with the remaining portion of the cream, cover closely, pack in broken ice and rock salt, and set to freeze for two hours. Just before serving have ready a vessel with warm water, lift the mold and wash off rapidly, being very careful to remove all salt and ice. Carefully take the Macedoine of Fruits from the mold, turn into a cold dessert dish and serve immediately.

CHAPTER XLII.

## FRUIT SYRUPS, CORDIALS, ETC.

Des Sirops, des Liqueurs, Etc.

No book on Creole cookery would be complete without reference to those delightful fruit syrups which, under the names of "Sirops," "Ratafias," "Granits," etc., enter so largely into the home and social life of the Creoles. Again, the ancient Creole housekeepers are famous for the delicious "Cordials" or "Liqueurs" that they put up each year. Anisette as grateful to the palate as that manufactured by the famous French distilleries is made at home by the Creoles, as also various kinds of domestic wines, than which a better quality could not be purchased from professional manufacturers.

Before entering into a discussion of these "Sirops" and "Liqueurs," the Picayune will refer to the ancient custom the Creoles have of serving sweetened water after a hearty meal, and which, under the name of

### EAU SUCRÉE,

has been handed down from generation to generation as an integral part of the life of the Creole household.

To one glass of fresh water allow one tablespoonful of sugar, or to a half glass allow a half tablespoonful stir till the sugar is dissolved, and drink after a hearty meal. Every old Creole clings to his glass of "Eau Sucré." He claims that this custom accounts for the singular freedom that the Creoles, as a rule, enjoy from that distressing complaint, becoming so common in America—Dyspepsia. It is the rarest thing in the world to hear a Creole complain of any stomachic trouble, notwithstanding heavy dinners, numbers of courses, and richest viands and wines. The Eau Sucrée is passed around the table at the close of the meal, and the children, as well as their elders, enjoy the drink.

Again "Eau Sucré" is used by all Creole mothers as a sedative for their little ones. Just before kissing her babes "Good-night," the Creole mother will give them a small glass of "Eau Sucrée." It is claimed that it insures digestion and perfect sleep.

"Eau Sucré" parties were famous in old New Orleans in those happy, innocent days when friend met friend in social gatherings for the pleasure of social intercourse, and not for the sake of the grand spread of fancy viands and wines that have become such a source of terror in our day to the housewife of limited means who wishes to entertain her friends. With that beautiful old-time courtesy so peculiar to the Creoles, the poor young woman who entertained was placed on an equal with her richer sister, for it became a kind if unwritten law that beyond a glass of lemonade and cake, or a glass of "Eau Sucrée," nothing more was expected of the household. There was no tax, no drain; the faubourg laughed and sang and danced, night after night, on iced "Eau Sucrée," or Iced Lemonade, and Orgeats, and Ice Creams, with as much zest as when grand suppers were spread and champagne flowed. There were no heartaches, no pangs, no sad thoughts, because Madame So-and-So, who lived in the Rue Esplanade or Rue Rampart, had given a grander ball than her poorer sister, who lived in the Rue de Bons Enfants or the Rue d'Amour. All this has passed away with the changing life of the old French quarter. But "Eau Sucrée" remains, and the Picayune refers to it upon the merits claimed by the Creoles, that it promotes easy digestion and insures freedom from insomnia. These claims are borne out by the longevity and good spirits for which the race is famous.

### SYRUPS.

Sirops.

Under this heading are classed those delightful beverages of fruits or nuts, served by the Creole housewives during the summer season. Of a hot, sultry day, if you enter a well-regulated Creole household, the first thing Madame will do will be to regale you with a glass of Lemonade, or "Iced Orgeat," or "Iced Pineapple," etc. The syrups are put up and bottled by Madame herself, and are always at hand. Old "Tante Zizi," in bandana and tignon, knows the customs of the household well, and does not need to be told by Madame to prepare a nice, cooling glass of "Sirop" for her guest. In a few moments you will see her enter the parlor or sitting room with a dainty silver salver, covered with a snowy napkin, and bearing, according to the number of visitors, the glasses of iced "Sirop." Of an evening, as the family sit out on the "Esplanade" or the gallery to enjoy the freshening breezes, she will come again unbidden to bring her "people" the daily refreshing summer drink. It is all these pretty little customs and touches that make life in a Creole household so pleasant and full of variety.

### General Directions for Making Syrups.

The Plain Syrup, that is the basis of all fruit syrups, is simply sugar and water boiled together in the proportion of two pounds of sugar to a pint and a half of water. Cook the sugar and water till it forms the syrup called "Le Petit Casse" (see recipe under heading "Sugar as Employed in Candy-Making"), or crack, that is, cook it till it instantly snaps asunder when placed between the fingers after dipping them in cold water to enable one to test. Then add the Fruit Syrup, and mix thoroughly. Let it boil for about five minutes; take off the fire and let it get almost cold, then bottle very tight. This is the invariable rule to be followed in making syrups of fruits.

One quart of fruit when mashed and pressed will make a pint of Fruit Syrup, to be added to the Plain Syrup given above.

### Apricot Syrup.
Sirop d'Abricots.

12 Pints of Apricot Syrup.
1 Gallon of Plain Syrup.
1 Ounce of Essence of Apricots.

Pare and stone the apricots, then cut them into pieces, pound and mash well and set them aside for thirty-six hours in a cool place. Then strain through a bag, pressing out all the juice. Cook the sugar and water till it forms the syrup called "Le Petit Casse." (See general directions for Making Syrups). Then add the apricot juice and mix thoroughly; let it boil for five minutes, take off the fire, let it get almost cold, add the essence, and then bottle for use.

### Banana Syrup.
Sirop de Bananes.

2 Pints of Banana Juice.
1 Gallon of Plain Syrup.
¼ Ounce of Banana Essence.
The Juice of a Lemon.

Peel the bananas, then cut into small pieces and pound and mash well and set aside in a cool place for thirty-six hours. Then strain through a bag and proceed in exactly the same manner as for Apricot Syrup (see recipe), and add the essence and lemon juice when about to bottle.

### Blackberry Syrup.
Sirop de Mûres.

½ Pint of Blackberry Juice.
1 Gallon of Syrup.

Pick, stem and wash the blackberries, then pound and mash them well set aside in a cool place for thirty-six hours. Then strain through a bag, pressing out all the juice, and proceed in exactly the same manner as for Apricot Syrup. (See recipe.)

### Cherry Syrup.
Sirop de Cerises.

12 Pints of Cherry Juice.
1 Gallon of Plain Syrup.

Seed the cherries, and stem, pound and mash them well, and let them stand for thirty-six hours in a cool place. Then strain through a bag. Cook the sugar and water till it forms the syrup called "Le Petit Casse," or crack (see recipe under chapter on Creole candies), that is, till it instantly snaps asunder when placed between the fingers, after dipping them in cold water to enable you to test. Then add the fruit syrups and mix thoroughly. Let it boil for about five minutes, take off the fire, let it get almost cold, and then put up in bottles.

### Cranberry Syrup.
Sirop d'Airelles.

2 Pints of Cranberry Juice.
1 Gallon of Plain Syrup.
½ Ounce of Soluble Essence of Lemon.

Proceed in exactly the same manner as for Currant Syrup (see recipe below), adding twice the quantity of sugar, and adding the essence after the syrup has somewhat cooled and you are about to bottle it.

### Currant Syrup.
Sirop de Groseilles.

2 Pints of Currant Juice.
1 Gallon of Plain Syrup.

Pick, seed, wash and dry the currants carefully. Then pound them well and set aside in a cool place for thirty-six hours. Make a Plain Syrup (see recipe), and proceed as in the General Directions for Making Fruit Syrups. (See directions.)

### Currant Syrup with Raspberries.
Sirop de Groseilles Framboisée.

1 Pint of Currant Juice.
2 Pounds of Sugar.
6 Pounds of Currants.
1 Pound of Sour Cherries.
1 Pound of Raspberries.
1½ Pints of Water.

The cherries and raspberries are not necessary, but they give the syrup a most delightful flavor and aroma. Pick, wash, seed and dry the currants carefully. Seed the cherries, and stem them and the raspberries, pound and mash them well, and let them stand for thirty-six hours in a cool place. Then strain through a bag. Cook the sugar and water till it forms the syrup called "Le Petit Cassé," or crack, that is, till it instantly snaps asunder when placed between the fingers, after dipping them in cold water, to enable you to test. Then add the fruit syrups, and mix thoroughly. Let it boil for about five minutes, take off the fire, let it get almost cold, and then put up in bottles.

### Grape Syrup.
Sirop de Raisins.

1 Gallon Plain Syrup.
2 Pints of Grape Juice.
½ Pint of Grape or Catawba Wine.

Pick, wash, stem and seed the grapes; then pound and mash well, and set aside in a cool place for thirty-six hours. Then strain through a bag, pressing out all the juice; make a Plain Syrup, and proceed in exactly the same manner as for Currant Syrup, and add the wine when you are about to bottle.

### Lemon Syrup.
Sirop de Citron.

8 Ounces of Lemon Juice.
15 Ounces of Sugar.
½ Ounce of Extract of Lemon.

Press the juice from the lemons and grate the zest of four into the syrup; set aside in a cool place for six or eight hours. Then strain carefully through a bag. Make a Plain Syrup, using the proportions of fifteen ounces of sugar to a pint and a half of water. Prepare a gallon of syrup, and then proceed as in the General Directions for Making Syrups (see directions). Add the essence when about to bottle.

### Lime Syrup.
Sirop de Limons.

2 Pints of Lime Juice.
1 Gallon of Plain Syrup.
½ Ounce of Soluble Essence of Limes.

Proceed in exactly the same manner as for Lemon Syrup, and add the essence when about to bottle.

### Orange Syrup.
Sirop d'Orange.

2 Quarts of Orange Juice.
1 Gallon of Plain Syrup.
1 Ounce of Lemon Juice.

Proceed in exactly the same manner as for Lemon Syrup, and bottle when almost cold. This is a standing Creole Syrup.

### Orgeat Syrup.
Sirop d'Orgeat.

1 Pound of Sweet Almonds.
4 Ounces of Bitter Almonds.
2 Pounds of Sugar. 1 Quart of Water.
2 Ounces of Orange Flower Water.
The Zest of a Lemon.

Do not throw the almonds into hot water and blanch them, as in other recipes for almonds, but throw them into cold water, after shelling them, until the peeling or skin comes off easily. Then mash them and pound them in a mortar till they are reduced to a fine powder, adding, from time to time, a little water and the well-grated zest of the lemon. When this paste is perfectly made, moisten it with one-half of the water, and then squeeze it hard through a linen cloth, each end of which is held by some one, when you will have drained thoroughly of all milk. Then return the paste to the mortar, throw over the rest of the water, mix thoroughly, pounding well, and then squeeze again through the towel. Put the sugar into a farina boiler, and let it boil to the degree of "Le Petit Cassé," or crack, that is, till it forms a thick syrup that will not cling to the teeth in tasting, or instantly snaps asunder between the fingers after testing in cold water. Then take the syrup off the fire and add the milk of almonds, stirring well. Return it to the fire, and let it simmer gently till it begins to boil. Let it boil for several minutes. Then take it off the fire and let it cool. When cold, add the orange flower water, and mix well. Then drain all through a cloth or bag, and fill and seal the bottles.

Orgeat, being made of the milk of almonds, easily decomposes or sours, because the oil of almonds, being lighter than the other ingredients, rises to the top. For this reason, it is well to look at the bottles frequently, and shake them daily. This will preserve the exact mingling of the mixture, and also preserve the Orgeat for use.

Orgeat is a great Creole syrup. It is not only a most delicate drink, but a healthy, popular and traditional one. In old Creole households upon the birth of a babe, the friends who call to congratulate the parents upon the new addition to the household are served with a glass of Orgeat, the mother drinking with her friends in honor of the little angel just sent from heaven. This is an ancient Creole custom, dating from earliest days in Louisiana.

Use only the finest white loaf sugar in making Orgeat Syrup.

### Peach Syrup.
#### Sirop de Peches.
2 Pints of Peach Juice.
1 Gallon of Plain Syrup.
½ Ounce of Peach Essence.

Pare and stone the peaches, then pound and mash well and set aside in a cool place for thirty-six hours. Strain through a bag, pressing out all the juice, then proceed in exactly the same manner as for Apricot Syrup, and add the essence as the syrup cools and you are about to bottle it.

### Pineapple Syrup.
#### Sirop d'Ananas.
2 Pints of Pineapple Juice.
1 Gallon of Plain Syrup.
1 Ounce of Lemon Juice.

Pare the pineapples, cutting out the eyes and the core. Then cut into very fine pieces and mash and pound well, or grate the pineapple, which is better. Set aside for thirty-six hours in a cool place. Then strain through a fine muslin bag, pressing out all the juice. Then make a Plain Syrup and proceed as in the General Directions for Making Fruit Syrups. (See directions.)

### Plum Syrup.
#### Sirop de Prunes.
2 Pints of Plum Juice.
1 Gallon of Plain Syrup.

Stone the plums, pound and mash well and set aside in a cool place for thirty-six hours. Then proceed in exactly the same manner as in the recipe for Apricot Syrup. (See recipe.)

### Strawberry Syrup.
#### Syrop de Fraises.
2 Pints of Strawberry Syrup.
1 Gallon of Plain Syrup.
1 Ounce of Raspberry Essence.

Pick, stem and wash the strawberries, then pound and mash them well, and let them stand for thirty-six hours in a cool place. Then strain through a bag. Cook the sugar and water till it forms the syrup called "Le Petit Cassé," or crack, that is, till it instantly snaps asunder when placed between the fingers, after dipping them in cold water, to enable you to test. Then add the fruit syrups, and mix thoroughly. Let it boil for about five minutes, take off the fire, let it get almost cold, and then put up in bottles.

### Raspberry Syrup.
2 Pints of Raspberry Syrup.
1 Gallon of Plain Syrup.
1 Ounce of Raspberry Esence.

Pick, stem and wash the berries and proceed in exactly the same manner as for Strawberry Syrup, adding the essence when about to bottle.

### Vanilla Syrup.
#### Sirop de Vanille.
1 Gallon of Plain Syrup.
3 Ounces of Extract of Vanilla.
¼ Ounce of Caramel.

Boil the syrup and add the Caramel. (See recipe.) Drain, and then add the essence of vanilla. Stir well and bottle.

### Blackberry Vinegar.
#### Vinaigre de Mûres.
2 Quarts of Blackberries.
1 Quart of Good French Vinegar.

Put one quart of blackberries into a jar or deep vessel, and pour over the vinegar. Let them stand for twenty-four hours longer. Strain them again, and again add the fruit, repeating this operation and letting stand twenty-four hours three times. Then strain through a muslin bag, and add one pound of white sugar to every pint of the liquor, and boil the whole in a porcelain kettle for half an hour. When cold, bottle it and keep it in a cool place. Blackberry Vinegar made after this manner will keep for years, improving with age.

Currant Vinegar and Cherry Vinegar are prepared in the same manner as above.

### Orange Vinegar.
#### Vinaigre d'Oranges.
36 Oranges.
1 Quart of Good French Cider.
Sugar in Proportion of Two-thirds of a Pound to 1 Quart of Orange Syrup.

Peel the oranges. Slice them very thin and cover with pure cider vinegar, and let them stand for three of four days. Then mash them through a cloth, straining as long as the juice runs clear. To every quart of juice allow one and two-thirds pounds of fine white sugar. Then boil all together for about ten minutes, and skim very carefully, until no scum rises upon the surface. Then take the mixture from the fire, and when it cools somewhat, bottle it. Put a tablespoonful of this extract in a glass of cold ice water in warm weather, and you will have one of the most refreshing of the Creole summer drinks.

### Pineapple Vinegar.
#### Vinaigre d'Ananas.
3 Pineapples.
1 Quart of Pure Cider Vinegar.
Sugar in the Proportion of Two-thirds of a Pound to One Quart of the Juice.

Cover the pineapples, which you will have nicely sliced, with pure cider vinegar, and let them stand for three or four days. Then mash them through a cloth, straining as long as the juice runs clear. To every quart of juice allow one and two-thirds pounds of fine white sugar. Then boil all together for about ten minutes, and skim very carefully, until no scum rises upon the surface. Then take the mixture from the fire, and when it cools somewhat bottle it. Put a tablespoonful of this extract in a glass of cold ice water in warm weather, and serve as a summer drink.

### Raspberry Vinegar.
#### Vinaigre de Framboises.
**2 Quarts of Raspberries.**
**1 Quart of Good French Vinegar.**

Put one quart of raspberries into a jar or deep vessel, and pour over the vinegar. Let them stand for twenty-four hours, and then strain through a jelly bag, and add the other quart of raspberries, and let them stand for twenty-four hours longer. Strain them again, and again add the fruit, repeating this operation of straining and letting stand twenty-four hours three times. Then strain through a muslin bag, and add one pound of white sugar to every pint of the liquor, and boil the whole in a porcelain kettle for half an hour. When cold, bottle it and keep it in a cool place. Raspberry Vinegar made ofter this manner will keep for years, improving with age. The Creoles always keep it with Strawberry Vinegar or Blackberry Vinegar on hand, simply putting a teaspoonful of it in a glass of sweetened ice water. It is a most refreshing summer beverage, and is especially grateful to the sick and delicate.

### Strawberry Vinegar.
#### Vinaigre de Fraises.
**2 Quarts of Strawberries.**
**1 Quart of Good French Vinegar.**

Put one quart of strawberries into a jar or deep vessel, and pour over the vinegar. Let them stand for twenty-four hours, and then strain through a jelly bag, and add the other quart of strawberries, and let them stand for twenty-four hours longer. Strain them again, and again add the fruit, repeating this operation of straining and letting stand twenty-four hours three times. Then strain through a muslin bag and add one pound of white sugar to every pint of the liquor, and boil the whole in a porcelain kettle for half an hour. When cold, bottle it and keep it in a cool place.

## CHAPTER XLIII.

### DOMESTIC WINES, CORDIALS AND DRINKS.
#### Vins, Liqueurs et Boissons de Ménage.

Under this heading are comprised a great variety of fruits distilled in wine, or alcohol, or brandy, and sweetened or flavored with aromatic substances. These preparations are called according to their mode of preparation, "Ratafias," "Granits," "Liqueurs," or "Fruits à l'Eau-de-Vie." The Creoles always make their own anisettes, cordials and other liqueurs.

### RATAFIAS.

These are pleasant beverages much affected by the Creoles, and are very easily prepared by the infusion of the juices of fruits or of the fruits themselves, nuts and odorous flowers, in good French brandy. To these are often added various aromatic substances capable of imparting a delightful flavor to the liqueur.

A Ratafia Liqueur is much more easily prepared than a cordial; the preparation requires far less time, and there is no necessity of a distilling apparatus. Our Louisiana fruits are very juicy, and therefore no other liquor than good French brandy is or should ever be used in preparing a fruit Ratafia. The berries should always be well-bruised, to render the Ratafia aromatic and the seeds should be well-pounded. If flowers are used, they should be just withered and steeped. Water should be used very sparingly and only in sufficient quantity to aid in the diffusion and dissolving of the sugar.

The length of time that is required for the infusion must always be in proportion to the nature of the aroma. Good judgment must be the final test. If the infusion is too short, the flavor will be weak and sometimes insipid; if too long, you will have a bitter and acrid liquor.

In order to separate the Ratafia, the liqueur must be decanted after infusion and strained. It should always, however, be allowed to stand long enough to settle well before the Ratafia is bottled, or there will be a thick deposit of sediment, or the liquor will be turbid and murky. All Ratafias must be bottled and very closely sealed. It is of the unmost importance that they be kept in cool, shady places, else the spirits will evaporate and the liqueur itself will slowly but surely decompose.

**Proportions of Ingredients for Ratafia Liqueurs.**

In making Ratafias observe the following proportions in mixing the ingredients:

To three parts of the filtered juice of any kind of rfuits or berries add one quart of good, old French Cognac, three pounds of white loaf sugar, clarified, with three pints of water, and a dessertspoonful of Essence of Cloves, Vanilla and Cinnamon.

These should be thoroughly mixed and amalgamated; then the Ratafia should be bottled and sealed and labeled. Do not use until the end of six months; twelve months' standing will produce a far finer cordial. The Creoles prepare their Christmas and New Year cordials a year in advance, and also the Ratafias, which are served with crushed ice in summer.

Use filtered Mississippi River water in making all cordials and Ratafias, and only the finest clarified white loaf sugar.

**How to Filter Cordials and Ratafias.**

The filtering is of the utmost importance. A good home-made filter may be improvised by fitting a piece of felt into a funnel, very closely. Some use flannel, but the felt is far better. Filtering paper is sold by all druggists. Put the funnel in the mouth of the bottle, fit in the paper, pour in the mixture and let it filter slowly. Again, others use the ordinary brown or white paper, but this allows the aroma to escape, and the taste of the paper clings to the cordial. If you wish the cordial to be very transparent, take very dry, clear, transparent isinglass, and cut it very, very thin. Then dissolve it with white wine until it is perfectly liquid. Put it into bottles and preserve for use. When needed, coat the inside of the strainer with this, using a light brush or sponge. It will form a glue around the funnel. Pour the cordial or liqueur through this, straining several times, again and again, until it becomes perfectly transparent. Strain it the last time into bottles, and seal very tight. You will then have a clear, limpid cordial or liqueur that will not have lost its aroma by evaporation.

This simple method may be understood by even a child, and home-made cordials are not only very delightful, but far less expensive than the imported ones. Always have the Cognac as old as possible.

**Absinthe or Wormwood Ratafia.**

Ratafia d'Absinthe.

4 Pounds of Wormwood.
8 Ounces of Juniper Berries.
2 Ounces of Ground Cinnamon.
4 Drams of Angelica Rum.
4 Pints of Good French Brandy.

Bruise and pound the wormwood and juniper berries, and steep them with four pints of brandy and the Angelica rum for twenty days. Then distill the mixture till it is reduced to three pounds, and re-distill till this is reduced to two pounds or two pints. Then add two and a half pounds of fine white powdered sugar and two pints of water, filtered, and eight ounces of doubly-distilled orange flower water. Filter and bottle.

**Aniseed Ratafia.**

Ratafia d'Anis.

4 Ounces of Aniseed.
2 Pints of Good French Cognac.
1 Pint of Water.
1½ Pounds of Sugar.

Bruise the aniseed and steep them for one month in the brandy. Then pass them through a sieve. Add a syrup made of one pint of water and one pound and a half of sugar. Filter and bottle.

If you wish to make it in larger quantities, take two ounces of green aniseed, four ounces of star aniseed, and after bruising and pounding the seeds well, steep them in seven quarts of good brandy for one month. Then strain and add a syrup made of six pounds and a half of sugar and two quarts of river water, filtered. Mix well and then filter and bottle.

**Angelica Ratafia.**

Ratafia d'Angelique.

4 Ounces of Angelica Stalk or Leaves.
1 Ounce of Angelica Seed.
1 Drachm of Nutmeg.
½ Drachm of Ceylon Cinnamon.
1 Drachm of Coriander Seed.
½ Drachm of Cloves.

Bruise the seeds and leaves well by pounding, and steep for two months in an earthen pitcher, well-covered, having added all the spices, etc. Then take out, strain and add a syrup made of four and a quarter pounds of sugar and two and a half pints of water. Filter and bottle, and keep in a cool place.

If you wish to make it in smaller quantities, to four ounces of Angelica allow one pint of good brandy, one-half pint of water, one pound of sugar, and spices in proportion.

### Orange Flower Ratafia.
Ratafia à la Fleur d'Oranger.

2 Pounds of Orange Blossoms.
10 Pints of Brandy.
4 Pounds of Sugar.
1¾ Pints of Water.

Steep two pounds of orange blossoms, well bruised and pounded, in ten and a half pints of good brandy for fifteen days, and then add a syrup made of four pounds of sugar and one and three-quarters pints of water. Filter and bottle.

Or take a half pound of orange flower blossoms, and infuse them in four pints of good brandy for five days. Strain through a sieve, add a syrup made of three pounds of sugar and two pints of water, filter and bottle.

### FRUIT RATAFIAS.
Ratafia de Fruits.

In all Fruit Ratafias, whether strawberries, raspberries, blackberries, damsons, cherries, plums, red and black currants, use the proportions given above for "Raspberry Ratafia," if large quantities are desired, and the proportions given in "Proporitons of Ingredients for Ratafia Liqueurs" if less. Always mix thoroughly and amalgamate well. Bottle in pint bottles, well-corked and sealed, and do not use for at least six months.

### Orange Ratafia.
Ratafia d'Oranges.

3 Oranges.
The Zest of 3 Oranges.
1 Piot of Brandy. 1 Pound of Sugar.

Grate the zest of three fine Louisiana oranges, very, very fine. Place this oil or zest which you will have rubbed on one pound of powdered sugar in a jar, add one pint of good brandy or alcohol, and the juice of three fine oranges, from which you will have taken out the seeds. Let the infusion stand for three days, then filter and bottle for use.

### Peach Kernel Ratafia.
Ratafia aux Noyau de Peches ou d'Abricots.

½ Pound Each of Peach or Apricot Kernels.
4 Pints of Brandy.
2½ Pounds of Sugar.
2 Pints of Water.

Pound the peach or apricot kernels—some also pound the peach stones—steep them for one whole month in four pints of brandy in an earthen jar, and at the end of that time add a syrup made of two and a half pounds of sugar and two pints of water. Mix all well together, and then filter as directed above, and bottle and seal, and keep in a cool, shady place.

Ratafia de Noyau is one of the standing Creole drinks, and is most agreeable, the taste being of a delicate vanilla and almonds combined.

### Pomegranate Ratafia.
Ratafia de Grenades.

15 Ripe Pomegranates.
4 Quarts of Good French Brandy.
3 Pounds of Sugar.

Cut the pomegranates in slices and steep them for fifteen days in the brandy. Then squeeze through a cloth, add a syrup made with three pounds of sugar, and filter and bottle for use.

### Raspberry Ratafia.
Ratafia de Framboises.

8 Pounds of Raspberries.
2 Gallons of Brandy.
7 Pounds of Sugar.
3 Quarts of Water.

Steep the berries, which you will have mashed well, for one month, or at least fifteen days, in the brandy, and then add a syrup made of the sugar and water. Filter and proceed to bottle as directed.

If smaller proportions are desired, use the quantities given in general "Proportions of Ingredients for Ratafias." The larger proportions are also given, because the longer the Ratafia stands the better it is, and it is much easier to make a quantity at a time that will last several seasons.

### Ratafia of Four Fruits.
Ratafia des Quatre Fruits.

12 Pounds of Fine, Ripe Cherries.
3 Pounds of Sour Cherries.
3 Pounds of Currants.
3 Pounds of Raspberries.
1 Pint of the Best French Brandy.
4 Ounces of Sugar to Every Pint of Fruit Liquor.

Stone the fruit and stem the berries. Put all together in a bowl, and mash well. Let the fruit stand for two hours. Then press out the juice through a cloth or sieve. Add one pint of the best French brandy and four ounces of sugar to every pint of liquor obtained. Put in a stone jar, cover tight, and let it stand for a month. At the end of the time strain and filter. Then bottle and keep in a cool place.

### Strawberry Ratafia.
Ratafia de Fraises.

8 Pounds of Strawberries.
2 Gallons of Brandy.
7 Pounds of Sugar.
3 Quarts of Water.

Steep the berries, which you will

have mashed well, for one month, or at least fifteen days, in the brandy, and then add a syrup made of the sugar and water. Filter and proceed to bottle as directed.

If smaller proportions are desired, use the quantities given in general "Proportions of Ingredients for Ratafias." The larger proportions are also given because the longer the Ratafia stands the better it is, and it is much easier to make a quantity at a time that will last several seasons.

### FRUIT WATERS.
#### Eau de Fruits Glacés.

These are famous Creole summer beverages, and are always served to friends when visiting of an evening, or at evening receptions and reunions in summer. They are made, for the most part, of fruit juices and syrups, but they are also made of different kinds of punch, and from coffee.

The Orangeade, the Orgeat and the Lemenade, with the Claret Cup, are the principal. Unlike the Ratafias, they are served soon after concoction. In freezing, the Creoles put the mixture into water bottles or earthen jugs. These are set on ice and twirled around. As the contents become frozen a wooden spatula is thrust into the jar for the purpose of scraping down the portion that is frozen into the liquid center.

#### Aromatic Water.
#### Eau Aromatique.

The Zest of 3 Limes.
The Zest of 4 Lemons.
4 Ounces of Orange Flowers.
1 Ounce of Sweet Basil.
6 Ounces of Hoarhound.
7 Pints of Brandy or Alcohol.
3 Pounds of Sugar.
1 Quart of Distilled Water.

Take the grated, macerated zests of the limes and lemons and the bruised fresh orange blossoms, Basil and White Hearhound, and steep it in seven pints of fine French Brandy or alcohol for ten days. Then distill the liquor by heating in a water bath and covering the saucepan with a piece of kid, in which you have made small holes. Add a syrup made of three pounds of sugar and one quart of distilled water; strain after mixing well, and bottle for use.

#### Cherry Water.
#### Eau de Cerises.

2 Pounds of Cherries.
1 Lemon.   8 Ounces of Sugar.

Stone the cherries and press the juice from the pulp into a porcelain vessel, and then add a little water and the juice of one lemon. Stir well, and let stand for two hours. Then wash the stones well and pound them fine, and add to the cherries, and add eight ounces of sugar. Let all stand one hour. Then strain the mixture and stir well and filter. Set on ice till ready to use. Serve in glasses with crushed ice.

### LEMONADE.
#### Limonade.

Lemonade is among the most delightful and most commonly used of all fruit waters. There are few homes in New Orleans in which it is not a standing offering for family use and for visitors during the hours of the long summer day. Lemonade is always served very cold in summer, but there is a hot lemonade, which is extensively used by the Creoles during winter days for various purposes, mostly medicinal.

#### Iced Lemonade.
#### Limonade Glacée.

1 Dozen Lemons.   1 Pound of Sugar.
2 Quarts of Water.   Cracked Ice.

Choose the finest and freshest ripe lemons. Rasp the rind with white, crushed sugar, in order to extract the fine aromatic oil that lurks in the zest. Then squeeze the juice of the lemon, and strain it, and add the sugar and the necessary quantity of water. In making lemonade never use the rinds of the lemons, except to slice one daintily and place in the glass when about to serve the lemonade. The rind simply put into the lemonade does not add to the strength, but imparts a bitter and often disagreeable flavor. Extract the fine oils in the rind by rasping, as indicated, on crushed sugar. In making cold lemonade for six persons, allow six ounces of sugar to five lemons, and one quart of water. Increase the quantity in proportion to number to be served. Serve with crushed ice.

#### Hot Lemonade.
#### Limonade Chaude.

6 Lemons.   2 Quarts of Water.
½ Pound of Sugar.

Boil the lemons whole and unpeeled till the water is reduced to one quart. Sweeten and serve. Or proceed in exactly the same manner as above, using hot water instead of cold. The Creoles sometimes boil the lemons when used for medicinal purposes.

#### Frog Lemonade.

2 Dozen Lemons.
1 Pound of Sugar.
2 Quarts of Water.   1 Pineapple.
2 Bottles of Seltzer Water.
3 Dozen Fine Strawberries.

This famous drink was originated

in honor of the Picayune Frog at a great charity festival given in New Orleans for the benefit of the Newsboys' Home. The Picayune, in common with other newspapers of the city, entered into the festival for the purpose of lifting the burden of indebtedness that rested on the home. It held a booth, presided over by the ladies of the Picayune staff and a number of the most prominent ladies of New Orleans. A prominent Creole lady kept the Picayune Frog Tent, in which lemonade only was dispensed. She concocted a delicious beverage, and named it "Frog Lemonade." The booth was the great attraction of the festival. The Picayune led the festival, outdistancing all other papers three to one as regarded the other largest English daily in New Orleans, and running far ahead of the various other newspapers five and six to one, in the total amount of over fourteen thousand dollars raised through the festival. It was all attributed to the great and unfailing popularity of the Picayune and of its famous little Weather Prophet, the Frog.

Frog Lemonade is made as follows: Take a large punch bowl. Put into it one pound of sugar, three quarts of water, the juice of two dozen lemons, the juice of one pineapple, two bottles of seltzer water. Mix all well. Add three dozen fine, large strawberries, and decorate with slices of pineapple and lemon sliced very thin. In case there is not sufficient sugar, sweeten again to taste. Put a large piece of ice in the bowl. When ready to serve, fill glasses one-quarter full of crushed ice, and fill up with the lemonade, (being careful to have several strawberries and a slice or two of lemon and pineapple in each glass. This lemonade is delicious.

### Milk of Almonds.
Orgeat.

6 Ounces of Almonds.
1 Ounce of Bitter Almonds.
8 Ounces of Loaf Sugar.
3 Pints of Filtered River Water.
½ Gill of Orange Flower Water.

Blanch and peel the almonds, and soak them in cold water for several hours. Then pound them thoroughly into a pulp, adding as you pound a half gill of orange flower water. Put this into an earthen vessel with eight ounces of the finest and whitest loaf sugar. Add three pints of clear, filtered water, and then stir all well together. Return to the mortar. Pound well and strain. Stir well and set the vessel on ice. At the end of an hour it will be ready for use. This is a delightful summer drink.

### Orange Water.
Eau d'Orange.

The Zest of 6 Louisiana Oranges.
4 Ounces of Orange Blossoms.
7 Pints of Brandy.
4 Pounds of Fine White Sugar.
3 Quarts of Water.

Macerate the zests of the oranges and orange blossoms and orange juice in the brandy for eight days. Then distill in a "bain-marie," or water bath, as indicated. Add a syrup made of four pounds of sugar and three pints of water, strain and filter, and bottle for use.

### Strawberry Water.
Eau de Fraises.

½ Pint of Strawberry Juice.
1 Quart of Water.
8 Ounces of Sugar.

Choose fine ripe strawberries, stem and bruise them in a little water, and let them stand for an hour or so. Then squeeze them in a cloth and pour the juice off clear. To half a pint of the juice add one quart of water and eight ounces of sugar. Stir well, strain, and put it on ice, and serve as needed during the sultry summer days.

Raspberry and Currant water may be made in the same way, as also pineapple and orange.

### ORANGEADE.

3 Oranges.

The Juice of 1 Lemon.
4 Ounces of Sugar.
1½ Pints of Water.

The oranges must be ripe, juicy Louisiana oranges. Peel one orange and cut it in thin slices lengthwise, and then put it into a vessel with four ounces of sugar and a pint and a half of water. Squeeze the juice of the lemon and two more oranges into another vessel, and stir well. Then pour it on the sliced orange. Let it stand for a few minutes, and it is ready to use. Strain if you desire.

### CREAM SYRUPS.
Sirops à la Crème.

Cream Syrups are distinctively French and were introduced into America by the French settlers of Louisiana. The early Creole settlers of New Orleans applied the French methods of making syrups to our fruits, flowers, herbs, etc., and thus we have distinctive Creole Cream Syrups. Cream Syrups are lighter than Ratafias.

### Absinthe Cream.
### Crème d'Absinthe.

7 Pints of Brandy.
½ Pound of Wormwood Heads.
The Zest of 2 Lemons.
2 Oranges, Thinly Sliced.
6 Pounds of Sugar.
3 Pints of Water.

Pound the wormwood and infuse it for two days in the brandy with the zest of the lemons or the sliced oranges. Then distill the liquor to one-half the quantity. Dissolve six pounds of the finest white sugar in three pints of water, let it cool, and mix thoroughly with the brandy and wormwood. Then strain it and put in tightly corked bottles.

### Bay Leaf Cream.
### Crème de Laurier.

3½ Ounces of Laurel Leaf.
2½ Ounces of Myrtle Flowers.
1 Gallon of Brandy.
6 Pounds of White Sugar.
3½ Pints of Water.
12 Cloves. ¼ of a Nutmeg.

Bruise or pound the bay leaves, the myrtle flowers, the coarsely-grated nutmeg and the cloves, and pour over them one gallon of brandy. Then reduce over a gentle fire the sugar and water till well-dissolved. Let it cool. Then mix the whole with the bay leaves and brandy, mix well, filter, put into tightly corked bottles, and preserve.

### Cacoa Cream.
### Crème de Cacoa.

1 Pound of Cacoa Beans.
2 Quarts of Brandy. 1 Pound of Sugar.
1 Quart of Water.
1 Tablespoonful of Vanilla.

The Cacao bean may be purchased from the druggists or first-class grocers. Roast the beans to a light brown and grind as you would grind coffee. Infuse in two quarts of Brandy for six days. Then make a syrup with the sugar and water; reduce to one-half and let it cool. Then add the Cacao and Brandy. Flavor with Vanilla. Strain and bottle for use.

### Cherry Water Cream.
### Crème de Cerises.

7 Pints of Cherry Water.
4 Ounces of Orange Flower Water.
4 Pounds of Sugar. 1 Quart of Water.

Take seven pints of Cherry Water and distill it to nearly one-half. Then add four ounces of Orange Flower Water. Let it stand for four or five hours. Dissolve four pounds of sugar in a quart of distilled and filtered Mississippi water, and set it over the fire till well-blended and dissolved. Take it off, and let it cool. Then add the Cherry Water, strain and bottle. This is a most delicious summer beverage, and if kept in very tightly corked bottles it will keep a very long time.

### Cream of Roses.
### Crème de Roses.

3 Pounds of Rose Leaves.
2 Quarts of Brandy.
1 Pound of Sugar.
1 Quart of Water.

Pound the rose leaves in a stone vessel, and then pour over the brandy, and infuse for six days. Distill the liquor by boiling to one-half in a "bain-marie." Then mix it thoroughly with one pound of sugar, dissolved in a quart of water or in rose water. Color with a few drops of Cochineal, and filter and bottle for use.

### Elixir of Violets.
### Elixir de Violettes.

10 Ounces of Syrup of Violets.
4 Ounces of Filtered Raspberry Juice.
4 Pounds of Sugar.
2 Quarts of the Best Brandy or Alcohol.
2 Pints of Water.

Make a syrup with the sugar and water, and let it cool. Mix the violet syrup and the Raspberry Juice, and add it to the alcohol. Add the sugar syrup, when cool, mix all thoroughly, strain and bottle tightly.

### Mint Cream.
### Crème de Menthe.

1 Pound of Freshly-Gathered Mint.
The Zests of 5 Lemons.
7 Pints of Fine Old French Cognac.
2 Drachms of Essence of Peppermint.
4 Pounds of Sugar.
2 Quarts of Water.

Gather the mint very fresh, and wash lightly in fresh water. Cut it very fine, and add the grated zests of the lemons. Pound well in a stone jar, and macerate or steep for eight days in seven pints of good brandy. Then distill it, or boil to one-half, covering the spout of the boiler with a piece of kid in which you have cut small holes. Then add a half drachm of essence of peppermint. Dissolve four pounds of sugar in three pints of water, and let it cool. Then mix it thoroughly with the mint infusion and let it stand for a half hour. Then filter and bottle it, and keep in a cool, shady place.

### Mocha Cream.
### Crème de Mocha.

1 Pound of the Best Mocha Coffee.
The Zest of 1 Orange.
7 Pints of Brandy.
4 Pounds of Sugar.
3 Pints of Water.

Roast the coffee to a light brown,

without the least trace of burning. Then grind it quickly, while it is hot, and infuse immediately in seven pints of good brandy. Add the zest of the orange, cut very fine, and let it remain thus for six days. Then place in a vessel in a "bain-marie," and distill till reduced to one-half. Dissolve the sugar and water over a slow fire, then let it cool, and mix it with the coffee mixture. Filter it, bottle and preserve in a cool, shady place.

This "Liqueur de Café" is a most wholesome and pleasant beverage, and is considered a peculiarly good antidote for dyspepsia, as it facilitates digestion.

### FRUIT GRANITS.
#### Fruit Juice Granits.
#### Des Granits.

All manner of summer fruit beverages which have been given in this chapter, or which will be given, may be served as "Granits," by simply freezing them according to the recipes given above.

A Granit is only half frozen, the thought being to make it resemble snow-frosted water; it must always be sufficiently liquid to admit of being poured out into glasses and passed around to guests. The liquid may also be frozen in a freezer, but the Creoles cling to the old-fashioned water jugs.

Granits are favorite drinks in France, the custom having been adopted from the Italians, who served them under the name of "Granitii."

The Granits which are extemporized from fruits are the most delightful of all, but they must be used at once, or they will become insipid, when not made into Ratafias or Liqueurs. The following recipe for Orange Granit will serve for almost any kind of Fruit Granit.

#### Orange Granit.
#### Granit d'Orange.

12 Oranges.
1½ Pints of Orange Juice.
1 Pound of Sugar.
1 Quart of Water.

Peel six oranges, removing every particle of pulp. Slice nicely and place in a dish, and sprinkle over them the granulated sugar. Set aside for several hours to make a syrup. Squeeze the juice from the remaining six oranges and add to the syrup formed from the other oranges, which must be carefully drained of all syrup. Add the water; mix well and strain. Then turn into a freezer and freeze till a light frosting appears. Serve in small glasses.

#### Strawberry Granit.
#### Granit de Fraises.

1 Quart of Strawberries.
1 Tablespoonful of Strawberry Extract.
1½ Pounds of Sugar.
1 Pint of Water.

Mash the berries and cover with the sugar, and set aside to form a syrup. Then drain and press through a sieve, extracting all the juice. Add the extract. Mix all with the water, and turn into a freezer and freeze till a light, snowy frosting appears. Then serve in long, thin glasses.

#### Raspberry Granit.
#### Granit de Framboises.

1 Quart of Raspberries.
1 Tablespoonful of Raspberry Extract.
1 Pound of Sugar.

Mash the berries and proceed in exactly the same manner as for Strawberry Granit.

#### Champagne Punch.
#### Ponche au Vin de Champagne.

1 Quart Bottle of Champagne.
1 Pint of Lemon Juice.
1 Quart of Rhine Wine.
¾ of a Pint of Brandy.
⅛ of a Pint of Curacoa.
2 Quarts of Seltzer Water.
1 Pound of Sugar.
1 Large Piece of Ice.

Take a large punch bowl and dissolve in it the above quantities of sugar, lemon juice, Rhine Wine, Champagne, Seltzer Water and Curaçoa. Mix well, and set to cool and serve in small punch glasses. The above quantity will serve twenty-five persons. Reduce or increase the quantity of ingredients in proportion according to the number of persons to be served.

The above punch may be served "Frappé," by putting it into a large ice cream freezer and freezing soft.

#### Champagne Punch à la Créole.
Ponche au Vin de Champagne à la Créole.

1 Pound of Sugar.
1 Pint of Lemon Juice.
1 Quart Bottle of Champagne.
1 Quart of Best White Wine.
⅛ of a Pint of Curacoa.
2 Quarts of Seltzer Water.
½ of a Grated Pineapple.
½ of a Sliced Pineapple.
3 Dozen Strawberries.
1 Large Piece of Ice.

Take a large punch bowl, and dissolve in it one pound of sugar, one pint of lemon juice, one quart of White Wine, one quart bottle of Champagne, two quarts of Seltzer Water, one-eighth of a pint of Curaçoa, and one-half of a grated pineapple. Mix well. Put in a large piece of ice, decorate with strawberries and sliced pineapple, let it cool, and serve in small cup glasses. The above quantity will serve twenty-five people.

### Champagne Frappé.

Champagne Frappe is made by putting the above mixture into an ice cream freezer and freezing it soft.

### Claret Punch.
### Ponche au Vin.

1 Quart of the Best Claret.
½ Pint of Ice Water.
½ Cup of Powdered White Sugar.
2 Lemons, Sliced Thin.

Slice the lemons and let them stand for ten minutes with the sugar. Add the water and wine. Mix well and serve in glasses with crushed ice or freeze as directed above.

### Claret Punch, Creole Style.
### Ponche au Vin à la Créole.

2½ Quarts of Claret.
1 Pound of Sugar.
1¼ Quarts of Seltzer or Appolinaris Water.
1 Pint of Lemon Juice.
1 Large Piece of Ice.
2 Lemons, Sliced Very Thin.

Slice the lemons very thin. Mix all the above ingredients together. Add the sliced lemons as a garnish, stir well, set to cool, and serve in small glass cups or punch glasses. The above quantity will serve twenty-five persons. Reduce or increase quantities in proportion to the number to be served. Claret Punch may be frapped by putting into an ice cream freezer and freezing soft.

### Hot Claret Punch.
### Ponche au Vin Chaud.

2 Quarts of Claret.
1¼ Pounds of Sugar.
6 Oranges. 3 Lemons.
½ Ounce of Cinnamon (Whole Stick).

Squeeze the juice from the oranges and lemons. Take the peeling of the oranges and lemons and boil with one quart of water and the sugar and cinnamon. Strain, and then add the claret and lemon juice and orange juice; let all come to a boil again and serve hot.

### Louisiana Punch.
### Ponche à la Louisianaise.

2 Quarts of White Burgundy Wine.
2 Quarts of Seltzer Water.
1 Pint of Brandy.
1 Pint of Good Old Cognac.
1 Pint of Curacoa.
1 Pint of Lemon Juice.
2 Dozen Cherries. 2 Dozen Strawberries.
½ of a Sliced Pineapple.
2 Lemons, Sliced Very Thin.
1¼ Pounds of Sugar.
1 Large Piece of Ice.

Mix the Seltzer Water and the sugar, add the wine, brandy, Curaçoa and lemon juice; stem and wash the strawberries and the cherries, add, and decorate the punch with thin slices of lemon and pineapple. Set to cool and serve in small punch glasses. The punch may be frapped by putting in an ice cream freezer and freezing soft.

### Milk Punch.
### Ponche au Lait.

A Glass of Good Rich Milk.
1 Tablespoonful of Sugar.
1 Tablespoonful of Brandy or Whisky.
A Small Quantity of Crushed Ice.

Dissolve the whisky or brandy and sugar together, mix well, and pour over the milk. Add a small quantity of crushed ice and serve.

### Orange Punch, New Orleans Style.
### Ponche d'Oranges à la Nouvelle Orleans.

6 Louisiana Oranges.
1 Glass of Rum.
½ Glass of Best Brandy.
2 Quarts of Boiling Water.
1 Pound of Loaf Sugar.
1 Small Glass of Cherry Bounce.
1 Large Piece of Ice.

Mix the sugar and water, and the rum and brandy. Add the juice of six oranges, and the grated peel of three, and let all infuse for one hour. Then set to cool. When ready to serve add one small glassful of Cherry Bounce. Serve in small glass cups.

### Rum Punch.
### Ponche au Rhum.

1½ Pints of Best Jamaica Rum.
¼ of a Pint of Brandy.
2 Quarts of Apollinaris or Seltzer Water.
1 Pint of Lemon Juice.
1 Pint of White Wine.
2 Lemons, Sliced Thin.
1¼ Pounds of Sugar.
1 Large Piece of Ice.

Mix the sugar and water, add the liquors, stir well, add the lemon juice and the bits of sliced lemon; set to cool and serve in small punch glasses. This quantity will serve twenty-five persons. Reduce or increase according to the number to be served. Frappée by turning into an ice cream freezer and freezing soft.

### Strawberry Punch.
### Ponche aux Fraises.

1¼ Quarts of Best Champagne or Claret.
1 Quart of Strawberry Juice.
2 Quarts of Seltzer Water.
1 Pint of Lemon Juice.
1 Pint of Pineapple Juice.
1¼ Pounds of Sugar.
1 Large Piece of Ice.
3 Dozen Fine, Ripe Strawberries.

Dissolve the sugar and water and

add the liquor, using either Claret or Champagne. Add the fruit juices and then the whole strawberries. Set to cool and serve in small punch glasses. Frappée by turning into a freezer and freezing soft. The above quantity will serve twenty-five persons. Reduce or increase quantity in proportion to guests.

### White Wine Punch.

Ponche au Sauternes.

2 Quarts of Best Sauternes.
1 Pint of Old French Cognac.
1 Pint of Lemon Juice.
1 Pint of Pineapple Juice.
1 Quart of Seltzer Water.
½ Grated Pineapple.
½ of a Sliced Pineapple.
2 Dozen Cherries.
1 Large Piece of Ice.

Mix the sugar and water, add the liquors and the fruit juices and the grated and sliced fruit. Stir well, set to cool and serve in small glass cups. The above quantity will serve twenty-five persons. Reduce or increase the quantity of ingredients in proportion to the number of persons to be served. This punch may be frapped by simply turning into an ice cream freezer and freezing soft.

### White Wine Punch, Creole Style.

Ponche au Sauternes à la Créole.

2½ Quarts of Sauterne.
1 Pound of Sugar.
1 Pint of Lemon Juice.
½ Pint of Brandy.
1 Quart of Seltzer Water.
½ of a Grated Pineapple.
½ of a Sliced Pineapple.
2 Dozen Cherries.
Sprigs of Fresh Young Mint.

Take a large punch bowl, and put one pound of sugar into it, with one pint of lemon juice, two and a half quarts of Sauterne (White Wine), half a pint of brandy, two quarts of Apollinaris or Seltzer, one-half of a grated pineapple. Decorate with sliced pineapple and whole cherries and sprigs of fresh young mint; put in a large piece of ice, and let it cool, and serve in small glass cups.

### Tea Punch.

Ponche au Thé.

1 Quart of Strong Tea.
French Brandy or Wine or Rum to Taste.
6 Lemons. 1½ Pounds of Sugar.

Squeeze the juice from the lemons and grate the zest. Add this to one quart of boiling tea, and add the sugar. Dissolve well. Let it boil up three times, take off the fire, and add rum, brandy or wine to taste. It may be served hot, or bottled, and kept for future use, in which case it is served with crushed ice.

### CUPS.

Ponches.

Cups are a form of punch that are frequently used when a smaller quantity is desired or when it is wished to make a refreshing drink for delicate members of the household. One quart cup will serve six persons. A pint cup will serve three. The Cup is served in a very delicate, thin tumbler.

### Burgundy Cup.

Ponche au Vin de Bourgogne.

1 Pint of Good Old Burgundy.
1 Sliced Lemon. 1 Orange.
A Dash of Old French Cognac.
¼ Pint of Seltzer Water.
1 Large Piece of Ice.
½ Cup of Sugar.

Dissolve the sugar and lemon and orange juice and add the liquors and water. Decorate with the sliced lemon and sprigs of green mint.

### Claret Cup.

Ponche au Vin.

1 Pint of Good Claret.
1 Pony of Curacoa. 1 Orange, Sliced.
A Dash of French Cognac.
½ Cup of Loaf Sugar.
1 Large Piece of Ice.
The Juice of 1 Lemon.

Dissolve the sugar and lemon juice. Add the Claret, Curaçoa, Brandy and sliced orange and lemon juice. Put to cool. When ready to serve pour into a thin, small tumbler and decorate the top with a sprig of fresh green mint.
This "Claret Cup" is also made by preparing one quart of "Orangeade" (see recipe), and adding one quart of Claret. Freeze as directed, or serve with crushed ice, having the glasses half full of the pounded ice.

### Champagne Cup.

Ponche au Vin de Champagne.

1 Pint of Champagne.
1 Lemon, Sliced. 1 Sliced Orange.
A Dash of Old French Cognac.
¼ Pint of Seltzer Water.
A Dash of Curacoa.
1 Large Piece of Ice.

Mix the sugar and water; add the liqueurs, and the sliced orange and lemon, and the ice. Stir well and let cool. Serve in small, thin tumblers, and decorate with a piece of fresh green mint on top.

### Moselle Cup.
#### Ponche au Vin de Moselle.

1 Pint of Moselle Wine.
1 Sliced Lemon.   1 Sliced Orange.
A Dash of Good Brandy.
A Dash of Maraschino.
¼ Pint of Seltzer Water.
The Juice of 1 Lemon.
¾ of a Grated Pineapple.
1 Large Piece of Ice.
¼ Tablespoonful of Sugar.

Mix the sugar and water, add the wine and the liqueurs, and the juice of the lemon and sliced orange and lemon, and the grated pineapple. Stir well. Let cool, and serve in small thin tumblers. Decorate the top with sprigs of fresh green mint.

### Military Cup.
#### Ponche Militaire.

1 Bottle of Claret.
2 Quarts of Water.
1 Bottle of Seltzer Water.
The Juice and Rind of 3 Lemons.
1 Cordial Glass of Benedictine.
¼ Pound of Sugar.
1 Cordial Glass of Cherry Bounce.
A Few Strawberries or French Cherries.

Take one bottle of claret and pour into a punch bowl with two quarts of water. Add one bottle of Seltzer water and a half pound of sugar and the juice and rind of three lemons. Stir all well and add a dash of old French Cognac, a cordial glass of Benedictine and of Cherry Bounce, and put sufficient ice in the bowl to make the Punch very cold. Serve with a few Strawberries or French Cherries in each glass and place a sprig of fresh young mint on top.

### White Wine Cup.
#### Ponche au Sauternes.

1 Pint of Best Sauterne.
½ of a Sliced Lemon.   ½ of a Sliced Orange.
A Dash of Old French Cognac.
A Dash of Maraschino.
1 Cup of Pineapple Juice.
1 Large Piece of Ice.
¼ Pint of Seltzer Water.
¼ Cup of Sugar.

Dissolve the sugar and the Seltzer water, add the wine and fruit juices and liquor. Add the cherries and sliced lemon and orange. Stir well. Let cool and serve in small, thin tumblers. Decorate the tops with sprigs of fresh green mint, with two or three cherries laid on top.

### Hot Whisky Punch.
#### Ponche au Whisky Chaud.

2 Tablespoonfuls of Best Old Bourbon.
3 Lumps of Loaf Sugar.
¼ of a Lemon.
Hot Water to Fill One Tumbler.

Squeeze the juice from a quarter of a lemon and dissolve with the sugar. Add the whisky and let all dissolve well. Fill with hot water; stir well, and add a little grated nutmeg, if desired, and serve hot.

### Brandy Stew.
#### Cognac Chaud à la Créole.

1 Glass of Fine Old French Cognac.
1 Tablespoonful of the Best Butter.
3 Tablespoonfuls of Sugar.
1 Teaspoonful of Ground Cloves.
¼ Teaspoonful of Grated Nutmeg.
½ Teaspoonful of Ground Cinnamon and Allspice.

Have a nice porcelain-lined saucepan. Melt the butter and sugar over a clear fire, blending well, and adding almost immediately the ground cloves, cinnamon and allspice. Let it stew slowly and add the brandy or good old Bourbon or Rye whisky very carefully, so that it will not take fire. Stir well, and let it bubble up once or twice, and then take off the fire and add the grated nutmeg.

This is a very delicate stew, and is offered to the sick and those suffering from severe cold. It is held as an infallible cure for a cold in twenty-four hours.

Hot Stews of Whisky, Rum, Gin, Claret, Sherry, Madeira or Port Wine may also be prepared according to the above ancient formula.

### Hot Spiced Port.
#### Vin d'Oporto Chaud à la Créole.

1 Lump of Sugar.
2 Cloves.   3 Allspice.
2 Tablespoonfuls of Old Port Wine.
A Dash of Grated Nutmeg.
A Bit of Lemon Peel.

Take a small mixing glass and dissolve the sugar in a little warm water. Add the Allspice and Cloves, ground well. Add the Port Wine. Fill with hot water and add a bit of lemon peel. Stir well. Grate a little nutmeg on top and serve very hot.

Hot Spiced Sherry, Madeira, Brandy, Whisky, Rum or Claret may be prepared according to the above recipe.

### Wine Cobblers.

1 Wineglassful of Sherry or Any Other Wine.
A Small Piece of Lemon Peel.
1 Tablespoonful of Sugar or Syrup.

Cobblers may be made with Port, Sherry, Rhine, Moselle, Catawba or Muscadine Wine or Vin Muscat. Take a glass, put in a tablespoonful of sugar or syrup, a small piece of cut lemon peel, one wineglass of Sherry or any other of the above wines, and then fill the glass with crushed ice. Stir well. Decorate the mixture with sprigs of fresh mint or strawberries or sliced pineapple, and serve.

### Sherry Cobbler.

1 Quart of Lemonade.

½ Bottle of Sherry or any Other Wine.
Small Bits of Lemon Peel.

To one quart of lemonade add half a bottle of Sherry and proceed to freeze as directed above, or hand around in glasses half full of crushed ice. Add a little lemon peel.

### Singaree, Hot or Cold.

Sangaree, Chaud ou Froid.

1 Cup of Claret.
1 Cup of Boiling Water.
6 Whole Cloves.
3 Tablespoonfuls of Sugar.
12 Whole Allspice.
2 Inches of Stick Cinnamon.
Grated Nutmeg to Taste.

Boil the water and spices for fifteen minutes, till the water is thoroughly flavored with the spices. Then remove from the fire and dissolve the sugar in it. Put the Claret into a pitcher. Strain the water and sugar into it. Flavor with the nutmeg, and add more sugar, if necessary, to taste. Serve hot immediately.

This is a winter drink. It is served cold in summer simply by mixing the wine and water and sugar and adding the juice of a lemon or orange, a little lemon peel and grated nutmeg.

### Mint Julep à la Créole.

1 Large Cut Glass Filled With Water.
3 Lumps of Sugar.
1 Tablespoonful of Good Brandy or Whisky.
The Juice of Half a Lemon.
A Bit of Lemon or Orange Peel.
6 Sprigs of Fresh Young Mint.
A Few Ripe Strawberries.

Take one large cut glass, half fill with water, add six sprigs of fresh mint, three lumps of sugar. Stir well, till the sugar is absorbed. Add a tablespoonful of good brandy or whisky, and stir well. Add a little lemon and orange peel, and the juice of half a lemon, if desired. Fill the glass with crushed ice, and decorate on top with sprigs of mint. Place a few ripe strawberries on top of the mint, sprinkle lightly with crushed sugar, and serve. This julep was a famous offering at the ancient plantation homes of Louisiana. Sliced orange or sliced pineapple is frequently added.

### EGG-NOG.

10 Fine, Fresh Creole Eggs.
1 Quart of Milk.
1 Pound of White Granulated Sugar.
1 Gill of Fine French Cognac.
1 Grated Nutmeg.

Beat the yolks to a cream, add the sugar, and beat to a cream. Blend all thoroughly, beating till very, very light. Now pour over the boiling milk, stirring well. When thoroughly blended add the whites of the eggs, beaten to a stiff froth, and the liquor, and serve hot. This egg-nog is also served cold by the Creoles at New Year's receptions. At the famous Christmas and New Year Reveillons it is served hot. The liquor may or may not be added, according to taste.

### Egg and Wine.

Oeuf au Vin.

1 Egg.
1 Tablespoonful of Sherry or Port Wine.
1 Tablespoonful or Teaspoonful of Sugar.

Beat the yolk of the egg to a cream in a tumbler, and add the sugar, and beat till very light. Then add the Sherry or Port, according to taste. Beat the whites to a stiff froth, and then beat it into the yolk and wine. Add a little grated nutmeg. This is excellent for invalids, and is offered to them by the Creoles as a morning or evening tonic.

### FRAPPÉES.

Any Liqueur or Beverage may be served "au Frappée" by filling a glass with crushed ice, pouring the beverage over and serving very cold, in almost a freezing state.

### Absinthe Frappée.

A Small Glass Filled With Finely-Crushed Ice and Water.
1 Tablespoonful of Absinthe.
A Dash of Anisette.

Mix the Absinthe and Anisette together, strain into small, thin glasses, with crushed ice and water; let the mixture get very cold and serve immediately. The Absinthe may be served without the Anisette. Some add the white of an egg. But this is according to taste.

The above is the recipe that used to be used in old Creole days at the famous old Absinthe House, in Bourbon Street.

### Crème de Menthe Frappée.

A Small Sherry Glass Filled With Crushed Ice.
Two Tablespoonfuls of Creme de Menthe (White or Green.)

Fill a glass with finely-crushed ice pour over the Crème de Menthe, and serve very cold.

### Crème de Noyau Frappée.

1 Claret Glass Filled With Crushed Ice.
2 Tablespoonfuls of Creme de Noyau.

Put two tablespoonfuls of Crème de Noyau in a glass of finely-crushed ice and Seltzer and serve at almost freezing point.

Crème de Violette, Crème de Cacoa, Crème de Curaçoa may all be served in the same manner.

### Coffee Frappée.
### Cafe Frappé.

2 Tablespoonfuls of Coffee (Black and Very Strong.)
A Dash of Old French Cognac.
2 Teaspoonfuls of Sugar.

Take a large glass, mix the above ingredients together, fill with finely-crushed ice, and pour into a small Burgundy glass, and serve very cold.

### Pousse Café.

1 Teaspoonful of Anisette.
1 Teaspoonful of Curacoa.
1 Teaspoonful of Benedictine or Chartreuse.
1 Teaspoonful of Good Old Bourbon or Cognac.

Mix all the above ingredients in a small glass, and serve cold, or otherwise, as preferred.

A Pousse Café is also made by putting a teaspoonful of Chartreuse, Benedictine or old Cognac or Bourbon into the after-dinner cup of Café Noir.

### Vermouth Frappé.

1 Teaspoonful of French Vermouth.
1 Dash of Orange Bitters.
A Dash of Syrup.
A Bit of Lemon Peel.
Finely Crushed Ice.

Mix all the above ingredients well together, stir well and strain into a small Punch glass, and serve very cold.

### Appetizer.

A Dash of Absinthe.
1 Teaspoonful of Vermouth.
1 Dash of Pepsin.
3 Tablespoonfuls of Seltzer Water.
Finely Crushed Ice.

Fill a glass with finely-crushed ice, and add the above ingredients; shake well together, pour into a small, delicately thin tumbler, and serve cold.

### Old-Fashioned Creole Cocktails.

1 Tablespoonful of Good Old Bourbon, Cognac, Gin, Sherry or Vermouth.
2 Lumps of Loaf Sugar.
A Piece of Ice About the Size of an Egg.
A Bit of Lemon Peel.
The Juice of 1 Orange.
1 Tablespoonful of Lemon Juice.

Take a large glass, put the lump sugar in, and mix with about three tablespoonfuls of Seltzer, dissolving the sugar well. Now add the lemon peel and the juices of the orange and lemon. Add one tablespoonful of good old Bourbon or Sherry or any of the above-mentioned liqueurs, according to the cocktail desired. Stir well, and serve with delicate sprigs of freshly-gathered mint on top. Some add a few cherries; these tend to improve the flavor.

## CORDIALS AND DOMESTIC WINES.

### Liqueurs de Ménage.

Cordials are made by distilling brandy, rum, alcohol, etc., with aromatic substances, and then diluting with water and sweetening with sugar or syrup.

Cordials should always be soft, mellow, light and transparent. Only the best white clarified loaf sugar, the best filtered river water, and the best Cognac or Brandy or alcohol should be used in making them. The sugar should always be boiled to a syrup.

The cordials should be filtered. The spirits should always be rectified in advance. It is quite possible to purchase the rectified spirits, and a great deal of trouble is saved to those who do not understand home methods of distillation.

### ANISETTE.

10 Drops of Oil of Aniseed.
3 Pints of Alcohol.
2 Pounds of the Finest White Clarified Loaf Sugar.
1½ Pints of Water.

Make a syrup with the water and sugar, and clarify. (See recipe.) When cold, add the aniseed oil, which has been well-dissolved in the alcohol. Mix all well, filter and bottle tightly.

### Anisette de Bordeaux.

10 Ounces of Green Aniseed.
4 Ounces of Star Aniseed.
1 Ounce of Coriander.
2 Ounces of Hyson Tea.
1 Ounce of Fennel.
3½ Gallons of Alcohol.
10 Pounds of Sugar.
7 Pints of Water.

The above ingredients may be purchased from first-class druggists and grocers. Take the aniseed, coriander, fennel, Hyson tea, and pound well. Then macerate or steep for fifteen days in three and a half gallons of the finest rectified alcohol. After this distill in a "bain-marie," or water bath, according to directions already given. Then make a syrup with the ten pounds of sugar and seven pints of water. Mix well with the aniseed liquor and filter. Then bottle and keep in a cool, shady place. Several large bottles of Anisette will be the result of the above quantities after distillation. The quantities may be reduced or increased in proportion to the amount it is desired to make.

### Blackberry Cordial.
### Liqueur de Mures.

2 Quarts of Blackberry Juice.
2 Pounds of Sugar.
¼ Ounce of Ground Cloves.
¼ Ounce of Allspice.
1 Pint of the Best French Brandy.

Boil eight quarts of blackberries in a porcelain-lined pot till the juice is all extracted. Then take off the fire and press out all the juice through a flannel bag. This quantity will make about two quarts. Add the sugar, allowing one glass of sugar always to two glasses of blackberries, if you wish to make larger quantities than the above measurements. Add the cloves and the allspice, and set on the fire, and let it come to a good boil. Let it boil up several times. Then take off, strain and add the brandy. Bottle while hot. Cork well and seal, and set away in a cool place, to be used after two months. The longer this excellent cordial is kept, the better it will be. It is very grateful to the sick, and can be supported by the most delicate stomachs.

### Citronelle.

The Zest of 30 Lemons.
The Zest of 4 Oranges.
3½ Quarts of Alcohol.
2½ Pounds of Sugar.
½ Drachm Each of Cloves and Nutmeg.

Grate the zests of the lemons and oranges, and grate the nutmeg and grind the cloves. Mix well. Then pour over the alcohol, and steep for fifteen days. Distill in a "bain-marie," or water bath, and add the syrup made with two and a half pounds of sugar and one quart of water. Bottle and keep in a cool, shady place.

### Curaçoa.

The Zest of 1 Dozen Fine Louisiana Oranges.
3 Fine Lemons.
3 Quarts of Fine Old French Cognac.
3⅛ Pounds of Sugar.
1 Quart of Water.

Grate the zests of the fruit as carefully as possible, so as to preserve the fine aromatic oils, and without touching the white pulp. Then put the zests in a large glass bottle or vessel that can be closed tightly, and pour over the brandy. Shake well, and let it stand for fifteen days, each day shaking the bottle well, to agitate the juices. Make a syrup with the sugar and water, first beating into the sugar the whites of two eggs, to make the infusion very clear. Then mix with the water and strain. Add it to the syrup of brandy and lemons, bottle and cork well. Shake the bottles and let them stand for fifteen days longer, agitating each day. At the end of this time filter the liquor and bottle tightly for use.

A more simple Curaçoa, but not so excellent, is made by taking the zest of one dozen oranges, three-quarters of a drachm of cinnamon and one-quarter of a drachm of mace. Blend these well together, and steep in three pints of alcohol for fifteen days. Then distill in a water bath, and add a syrup made of two and a quarter pounds of sugar and three-fourths of a quart of water. Mix well, color lightly with Caramel, and bottle for use.

### FRUIT CORDIALS.
### Liqueurs de Fruit.

2 Quarts of Juice.
2 Pounds of Sugar.
¼ Ounce of Ground Cloves.
¼ Ounce of Allspice.
1 Pint of the Best French Brandy.

Strawberry Cordial, Raspberry Cordial, Cherry and Grape Cordial, etc., are made in the same manner as Blackberry Cordial. (See recipe.)

### Kümmel.

1 Quart of the Best Rectified Alcohol.
30 Drops of Kummel Oil.
1 Quart of Boiling Water.
2 Pounds of the Finest White Loaf Sugar.

Pour the boiling water over the sugar and stir till dissolved. Bring to a boil, and let it continue boiling from fifteen to twenty minutes. Strain, and when luke warm, add the oil and the alcohol. Bottle and keep for at least two months before using. The oil is obtained from druggists.

### Nectar.
### Néctar.

4 Ounces of White Honey.
2 Ounces of Coriander.
6 Ounces of Fine White Pulverized Sugar.
3 Quarts of Water.
1 Ounce of the Fresh Zest of Lemon.
1 Ounce of Cloves.
1 Ounce of Benzoine.
1 Ounce of Storax Calamite.
½ Drachm of Tincture of Vanilla.
4 Ounces of Orange Flower Water.
5 Quarts of Highly Rectified Spirits.

Pound to a powder all the ingredients which require it, mix with the honey, benzoin, etc., pour over the alcohol, and steep for fifteen days. Then distill the liquor till it is reduced to four quarts, using a water bath, or bain-marie, for the distillation. Make a syrup of six pounds of fine white sugar, add the Vanilla, color a deep red with Cochineal, and add to the liquor. Blend and shake well, bottle and keep in a cool place.

### Parfait Amour.

2 Ounces of Zest of Lemons.
4 Ounces of Zest of Limes.
2 Drachms of Cloves.
3 Sprigs of Rosemary Leaves.
A Handful of Orange Blossoms.
2½ Gallons of Alcohol.
10 Pounds of Sugar.
5 Quarts of Water.

Grate the zests of the lemons and limes carefully, without touching the white inner pulp. Bruise the rosemary leaves and orange blossoms and steep in the alcohol fifteen days. Then make a syrup with the sugar and water, add the liqueur, distill and filter, color lightly with Cochineal, and bottle for use.

### Persicot.

10 Ounces of Bitter Almonds.
1 Ounce of Cinnamon.
2½ Gallons of Alcohol or Fine Brandy.
6 Pounds of Sugar.
3 Quarts of Water.

Peel the almonds and pound and mix with the cinnamon, and steep for fifteen days in the alcohol. Then distill in a water bath, add the syrup, color with Cochineal or Caramel, and bottle for use.

### Sassafras Mead.
#### Boisson au Sassafran.

4 Bunches of Sassafras Roots.
1½ Pints of Honey.
3½ Pints of Louisiana Molasses.
1 Tablespoonful of Cream of Tartar.
½ Teaspoonful of Carbonate of Soda.

This is a noted Creole summer drink, and is prepared as follows: Take the roots of sassafras, and make about two quarts of Sassafras Tea. Strain well. Set to boil again, and when it boils add one and one-half pints of honey, and three and one-half pints of Louisiana Syrup or Molasses. Add a tablespoonful of Cream of Tartar. Stir well and set to cool. When cool strain it. Take about a dozen clean bottles and fill with the mixture. Cork very tight, and put in a cool place. In a day it will be ready for use. When serving this Mead, take a glass and fill half full with ice water. Add a tablespoonful of the Mead and stir in a half teaspoonful of Carbonate of Soda. It will immediately foam up. Drink while effervescing. This is a cheap, pleasant and wholesome summer beverage in our clime. The above recipe has been in use in Creole homes for generations.

### Blackberry Wine.
#### Vin de Mûres.

4 Quarts of Currant Juice.
1 1-3 Quarts of Cold Water.
3 Pounds of Granulated Sugar.

Mix all the above ingredients well together, and then let them stand for twenty-four hours, having, of course, obtained the currant juice by cleanly picking, washing and drying and pressing the berries. Then let it stand for two days. After this skim well, and set in a cool place to ferment slowly for at least six days. At the end of this time remove any froth that has collected, and add a half teacupful of the best French Brandy, and close tightly. In two days, when it is well-settled, draw off, without disturbing the sediment, and bottle tightly and seal. This wine improves with age. Always have the bottles very clean and dry before bottling, and if larger proportions are used and a cask is necessary, remember that an old cask is more desirable than a new one, on account of the taste of the wood, and that the cask must be perfectly fresh and sweet-smelling, or the wine will sour.

### Currant Wine.
#### Vin de Groseilles.

4 Quarts of Currant Juice.
1 1-3 Quarts of Cold Water.
3 Pounds of Granulated Sugar.

Prepare in exactly the same manner as Blackberry Wine.

### Elderberry Wine.
#### Vin de Fleurs de Sureau.

1 Peck of Elderberries.
2½ Gallons of Water.
¼ Pound of Sugar.
¼ Pint of Hop Yeast.

Bruise the Elderberries, and then dilute with the water and boil for ten minutes. Then strain well and press out the juice from the berries. Measure the whole, and add the sugar, and while half warm the yeast. Let the whole ferment for ten days. Then cork well. After three months draw off the wine and bottle for use.

In making large quantities of this wine, which is used by the Creoles for many medicinal purposes, allow four pecks of elderberries to every ten gallons of water, and to every quart three-quarters of a pound of sugar and a half pint of yeast.

### Muscadine Wine.
#### Vin de Muscades.

4 Quarts of Muscadine Juice.
1 1-3 Quarts of Cold Water.
3 Pounds of Granulated Sugar.

Prepare in exactly the same manner as Blackberry Wine.

### Louisiana Orange Wine.
#### Vin d'Oranges de la Louisiane.

3 Pounds of Sugar to Every Gallon of Juice.
1-3 of a Gallon of Water.
The White of 1 Egg.
1 Cake of Compressed Yeast.

Take fine Louisiana oranes, and wash them well. Then dry with a cloth, and peel off the yellow outer rind very, very thin, and strain all the juice through a hair sieve. three pounds of granulated sugar, the white and shell of one egg, to clarify, and one-third of a gallon of water. Put the sugar, the crushed eggshell and white of the egg, beaten to a froth, in a porcelain-lined saucepan, and add the water, and boil to a syrup, stirring constantly to prevent the egg from hardening. Let the syrup boil till it looks clear when seen through the froth of the egg, which will rise to the surface. Then strain the syrup, and pour it over the grated orange zest, and let it stand for twenty-four hours. Then add the orange juice, and strain, and put it into a cask with a small cake of compressed yeast, allowing half a cake to five gallons of wine. Close tightly, but leave the bung out of the cask until the wine ceases to ferment. As long as fermentation is progressing there will be a hissing sound. When this ceases the fermentation has ceased. Then add a glass of good brandy for each gallon of wine, close the cask, drive in the bung, and let the wine stand for at least nine months. Then bottle it, and about four months after it has been bottled it will be ready for use. This is an excellent Louisiana wine, and can be made with litttle expense.

### Scuppernong Wine.

Vin de Muscades.

4 Quarts of Scuppernong Juice.
1 1-3 uarts of Cold Water.
3 Pounds of Granulated Sugar.

Prepare in exactly the same manner as Blackberry Wine. (See recipe.)

### Strawberry Wine.

Vin de Fraises.

4 Quarts of Strawberry Juice.
1 1-3 Quarts of Cold Water.
3 Pounds of Granulated Sugar.

Follow in every respect the recipe given for Blackberry Wine.)

### ROOT BEER.

Bière Créole.

½ Pint of Root Beer Extract (Hire's Solution).
10 Pounds of Sugar.
10 Gallons of Lukewarm. Filtered Mississippi River Water.
1 Pint of Yeast, or 1½ Cakes of Compressed Yeast.

Dissolve the sugar thoroughly in the water, and then add the Root Beer Extract and the yeast. If you use the cake yeast, dissolve it first in a little water, so that it will mix well with the beer. Stir until thoroughly mixed, and then bottle in strong bottles or in jugs, corking and tying the corks very securely, so that the gas may not escape from the solution. Then set the beer away in a place of even temperature. It will be ready for use in twenty-four hours after bottling, or even ten, but will be far more effervescing if allowed to stand three or four days. Always place the bottle on ice or in a very cool place just before opening it, if you wish it to be cool, sparkling and delicious.

### SPRUCE BEER.

Bière de Sapin.

Take sprigs of spruce and boil until you have an ounce of strong essence. Take one ounce of hops and a spoonful of ginger, and put them into a gallon of water. When well-boiled, strain the mixture, and add a pint of Louisiana Molasses or a pound of brown sugar, and then add the extract of Spruce. When cool add a teacupful of yeast (homemade), and put all into a clean, tight cask, and let it ferment for twenty-four hours or two days. Then bottle for use. Essence of Spruce may be purchased and used instead of the sprigs of spruce, or the Spruce Gum may be boiled. The Creoles always use the sprigs, or spruce bark rich with gum.

### GINGER BEER.

Bière de Gingembre.

2 Ounces of Bruised Ginger Root.
2 Ounces of Cream of Tartar.
4 Quarts of Boiling Water.
The Juice and Rind of 1 Lemon.
1½ Pounds of Granulated Sugar.
1 Tablespoonful of Yeast, or ¼ of a Cake.

Bruise and pound the ginger well, and put it into a bowl with the boiling water. Add the juice of a lemon and the well-grated zest. Add the Cream of Tartar and the sugar, mixing and stirring constantly. When it is lukewarm add the yeast, dissolved in a little water. Mix well and cover tightly, and let it stand for six hours. Then strain it and put it into bottles with patent tops and keep in a cool place. It effervesces rapidly if not kept most securely corked.

### DOMESTIC BEVERAGES.

Boissons de Ménage.

Under the heading of "Domestic Beverages" might properly be classed Coffee, Tea, Chocolate and Cocoa, daily drinks in almost every Creole household.

### TEA.

Du Thé.

Tea has a stimulating and grateful effect when not taken in excess, and promotes digestion.

The Creoles use most exclusively

the black and green tea mixed, preferring the flavor always of the Hyson, Oolong, Bohea, Gunpowder or Heno. Like Coffee, Tea should never be boiled. It should always be made from fresh boiling water, and never in any but an earthen or agate teapot. Tea made in earthen tea urns requires longer to draw than if made in bright metal pots. Tea should never be suffered to stand long, as it acquires an unpleasant taste and loses its delightful aroma and fragrance.

The spout of the teapot should always be closed by a cover, secured by a chain, to prevent the escape of the aroma, and the urn itself should be closed at the top with a tightly-fitting cover.

To make good tea, first see that the teapot is perfectly clean. Then pour boiling water into it, and let it stand for five minutes, so that the metal or earthen urn may become thoroughly heated. Then throw out this water, and drain the urn well. Allow a teaspoonful of tea for each cup of boiling water, or, if you desire stronger tea, allow two teaspoonfuls. Put this tea into the hot pot, and pour over one pint of boiling water, if you wish to make a quart, or, according to the quantity desired, one-half a cup of water to each cup. Let this solution draw for five minutes in front, not on top, the stove or range, as tea that has the least indication of boiling is condemned by the best ethics of Creole Cookery. After five minutes add the other pint of water, or water in proportion to the number of cups desired, allowing a half cup more for each person. Serve at once, very hot.

In serving the tea, put the cream or milk or sugar into the cups. The milk should be cold and unboiled, as the boiled milk destroys the flavor of the tea. Cream is far preferable to milk. Have the tea very hot, and pour over the milk, allowing two teaspoonfuls or four of milk to each person, or suiting individual tastes.

Always have a pitcher of very hot water at hand when about to serve the tea. Pour a little into each cup to warm it, and then empty before putting in the milk and tea. Pour the tea through a strainer, so as to avoid the possibility of leaves or dregs passing into the cup.

The tea leaves that have been infused in an earthen teapot may be used again, as all the aroma has not been extracted by the first infusion. The tea brewed in a metal pot must never be used a second time, as by standing it absorbs the acid of the tin. Indeed, metal teapots are condemned by the best Creole housekeepers.

## CHOCOLATE.
### Du Chocolat.

1 Cake of Grated French or German Chocolate.
1 Quart of New Milk.

Set the milk to boil; in the meantime mix the grated chocolate with a little hot water, to blend thoroughly. Stir this in the milk as it begins to simmer, and let it boil up once, and serve hot, each one sweetening to taste, or allow two tablespoonfuls of sugar to the entire mixture. Serve hot, with or without Whipped Cream.

It is a mistake to allow chocolate to boil a long time. The basis of Chocolate is sugar and cocoa, and the first gains nothing by boiling, and the second loses its fragrant perfume by evaporation.

In economical households, one-half a cup of water is sometimes allowed to three-quarters of a cup of milk in making Chocolate.

## COCOA.
### Du Cacao.

1 Quart of Milk.
4 Tablespoonfuls of Cocoa.

Set the milk to boil in a farina boiler, and moisten the Cocoa with a little milk, and pour it into the milk just as it begins to simmer, stirring all the while. Let it boil up once, and serve hot, with or without Whipped Cream.

## CHAPTER XLIV.

### JELLIES, MARMALADES, PRESERVES.

#### Des Confitures, des Marmalades et des Conserves.

In making jellies, marmalades or preserves, use only perfectly sound and fresh fruit. Do not cook them long enough to destroy their natural flavor, and seal them while boiling hot in airtight jars, and be careful to fill these even to overflowing, so as to preclude the possibility of the least air entering the bottle. Then seal quickly. Heat the jars before filling, and use a wide-mouthed funnel during the process of filling. The large-mouthed jars that now come with porcelain-lined glass tops are the best. When once the jars are filled, immediately screw on the tops, and put them in a dry, warm place, where there is not the least possibility of the air striking them. After twenty-four hours turn the tops on still more tightly, so as to be sure to exclude the entrance of all air, and set them away in a cool, dark storeroom or closet. The room must not be cold. After six days examine the jars carefully. If there is not the least sign of any air bubbles on the surface, and the liquid seems to have settled perfectly, the fruit is keeping properly. If, on the contrary, there is the least sign of an air bubble, the fruit is beginning to ferment, and if the bottle is not opened immediately, it will burst shortly. Take out the fruit, recook it, and prepare the jars again, and return the fruit to them, taking extra precautions to prevent the entrance of any particle of air. In preserving large fruits, always throw them into cold water as soon as they have been pared. Then have ready a pot of clear, boiling syrup and proceed as directed below.

Use all surplus juices that exude from berries to make jellies.

Never make preserves on a damp, rainy day, and never use fruits that are overripe, or that have been picked in wet weather. They will sour.

Always have the jars exposed several days in the air in a dry place, so that they may be perfectly dry.

In all cases the jars must be entirely full, so as to leave no room for air, and must be sealed as hot as possible.

Set the jar in warm water before filling, and let them gradually heat before introducing the hot preserves else they will crack.

Let all bubbles rise to the top, and if you see any in the lower part of the jar, insert a silver fork, which will cause them to rush to the top. Then have ready a strong piece of muslin, large enough to tie over the mouths, and with a spoon spread over a thick coat of cement made of one pound of rosin and two ounces of mutton suet, well-mixed and melted. Take up the cover quickly, place it on the jar, with the cement side downward, and press it down closely over the sides. Tie it down with twine, and finish with a good coat of cement over the whole. Set the jars in a large pan of hot water, to cool gradually, on no account attempting to cool them out of the water or they will crack. When they are cold, the tops will be found sunken in. This may be taken as an evidence that all the air has been excluded most effectually. The regular fruit jars, made for preserving do not require any muslin, as the lids are tight-fitting. But pour the cement around the groove in the top, so as to seal tightly.

If tin cans are used, it will be necessary to have a man ready at hand to solder up the can as soon as full.

If open jars are used, cover first with brandied paper, and then with white paper, fastened on with a thick flour paste. Label and set the jars away.

These directions for sealing will hold in making all preserves, marmalades and jellies. Fruit put up in this manner will rarely spoil. The one great thing to be remembered is to expel all air.

### Apple Jelly.

#### Gelée de Pommes.

1 Pound of Sugar to Every Pint of Juice.

Take pippins or other tart apples, pare them and cut into quarters, put into a preserving kettle, cover with water, and add the grated rind of a lemon, and let them boil to a marmalade. Then strain the juice, without squeezing, through a clean jelly bag made of flannel, and for every pint of juice add one pound of fine sugar. If the apples are not very tart, add the juice also.

### Apricot Jelly.
### Gelée d'Abricots.
#### To Every Pint of Fruit Juice 1 Pound of Sugar.

Choose apricots that are just ripe, and no more. Pare and cut in two, and take out the stones. Boil them in water sufficient to cover well, strain through a hair sieve, and pour the decoction into earthen dishes. To every pint of liquid add a pound of sugar. Set on the fire, let it boil twenty minutes, skimming while on the fire. Pour immediately into cups glasses or preserve jars, and proceed to seal as directed above. This jelly has a most exquisite flavor if the grated rind of an orange is added.

To make apricot juice, after pressing out the juice, put into glass bottles, and add one pound of powdered sugar to every pound of juice, and a little cinnamon. Shake the bottle well, until the sugar is melted. Let it stand eight days. Then filter the juice, pour it into bottles, fasten securely, and keep in a cool place.

Cherry juice and all fruit juices are prepared in the same manner.

### Blackberry Jelly.
### Gelée de Mûres.
#### 1 Pound of Strawberries. 1 Pound of Sugar.

To every pound of strawberries allow a half pound of sugar. Put the berries in a porcelain-lined kettle, and cover them with the sugar and let them stand for two hours. Then set over a moderate fire and bring the mixture to the boiling point. Skim while boiling; pour immediately into cups and glasses, and cover tightly and place in a cool, dry place.

For Strawberry and Blackberry Jelly combined, allow equal parts of the fruits and proceed as above.

### Blue Plum and Damson Jelly.
### Gelée de Prunes.
#### 1 Pound of Fruit. ¾ of a Pound of Sugar.

Stone the fruit, whether damsons or plums, and allow three-quarters of a pound of sugar to every pound of fruit. Proceed in exactly the same manner as for Blackberry Jelly.

### Calf's Foot Jelly.
### Gelée de Pieds de Veau.

See recipe under chapter on Compotes.

### Cherry Jelly.
### Gelée de Cerises.
#### 1 Pound of Cherries. ½ Pound of Sugar.

Stone the cherries and allow half a pound of sugar to every pound of cherries if the cherries are ripe and sour, and a quarter of a pound otherwise. Set over the fire until the heat causes the juice to flow freely, and proceed in exactly the same manner as for Strawberry or Blackberry Jelly.

### Currant Jelly.
### Gelée de Groseilles.
#### To Every Pint of Juice 1 Pound of Sugar.

Take currants that are fully ripe; clean, pick, wash and boil. To every pint of juice add one pound of fine white sugar. Let it boil for twenty minutes, always skimming it while on the fire. Do not let it remain longer than twenty minutes, or it will grow dark. Pour immediately into cups.

Some boil the currants without the sugar, and then, for every pint of juice, after taking off the fire, they add the sugar in the proportions given, stirring briskly till all is absorbed and dissolved; then the jars are filled as quickly as possible, for the preparation jellies at once. Jellies made in this way are of a much lighter color than when the sugar is boiled into them.

### Currant and Raspberry Jelly.
### Gelée de Groseilles Framboisée.
#### 1 Pound of Sugar. 1 Pint of Fruit Juice.

Take equal parts of currants and raspberries and strain the juice, and proceed as above, allowing one pound of sugar to every pint of berry juice.

To every quart of large red raspberries allow a half pint of currant juice; place in a kettle, add the sugar and bring to a boil, and proceed as directed above.

### Lemon Jelly.
### Gelée de Citron.
#### 4 Lemons. ½ Can of Gelatine. 1 Quart of Water.

Grate three or four lemons into a pound of refined sugar, and press out the juice. Then boil one-half a can of Gelatine—(see Calf's Foot Jelly)—in one quart of water, and, when reduced to one-half the quantity, add the juice and sugar; set all to boil on a very hot coal fire, and then pour immediately into a glass or porcelain dish; fill the glasses and set in a cool place.

### Orange Jelly.
Gelée de Citron.

6 Oranges.
½ Can of Gelatine.
1 Quart of Water.

Proceed in exactly the same manner as for Lemon Jelly.

### Orange Jelly, Creole Style.
Gelée à l'Orange a la Créole.

6 Louisiana Oranges.
½ Box of Gelatine.  ½ Gill of Coracoa.
Sugar to Taste.

Extract the juice of the oranges, Soak the gelatine, if prepared, and set the bowl in boiling water till the gelatine melts. Then add the juice of the orange, and add sugar to taste. Add a wineglassful of the best Curaçoa, and strain the jelly through a coarse piece of swiss. Set in a mold to harden.

The Creoles have a pretty way of making baskets out of the oranges and serving the jelly in them: Every little Creole child knows how to make these baskets. With a sharp knife they trace out a basket in the skin of the orange, and then gradually loosening the pulp, they cut out the orange, without breaking the skin. The orange meat is then used for the jelly, and the baskets are thrown into ice water for an hour. This makes them stiff. When the jelly is hard, it is cut into little squares, and gradually made to fit, like blocks, into the baskets. These baskets are placed in a dish, beautifully garnished with delicate buds and greenery, and the effect is very charming. Again, the oranges are cut open in this manner. The peel is marked off into eighths and pulled from the upper end of the stem, without separating the orange peels, which open like a beautiful flower. The jelly is piled into this when cool, whipped cream is heaped on the top, a few luscious strawberries are placed in the cream, and this is not only a most beautiful picture on the table, but a delicious dessert. Try it.

### Peach Jelly.
Gelée de Pêches.

1 Pound of Sugar to Every Pint of Fruit Juice.

Choose peaches that are just ripe, and no more. Pare and cut in two, and take out the stone. Boil them in water sufficient to cover well, strain through a hair sieve, and pour the decoction into earthen dishes. To every pint of liquid add a pound of sugar. Set on the fire, let it boil twenty minutes, skimming while on the fire. Pour immediately into cups, glasses or preserve jars, and proceed as directed above.

### Pear Jelly.
Gelée de Poires.

1 Pound of Sugar to Every Pint of Liquid.

Choose pears that are just ripe, and no more. Pare and cut in two, and take out the stones. Boil them in water sufficient to cover well, strain through a hair sieve, and pour the decoction into earthen dishes. To every pint of liquid add a pound of sugar. Set on the fire, let it boil twenty minutes, skimming while on the fire. Pour immediately into cups, glasses or preserve jars, and proceed as directed.

### Pineapple Jelly.
Gelée d'Ananas.

¾ of a Pound of White Sugar to Every Pound of Grated Pineapple.

Pare the pineapple, take out the eyes and grate carefully, or pick into fine pieces. To every pound of pineapple allow three-quarters of a pound of white sugar. Put the pineapple and the sugar to boil in a porcelain-lined kettle and cook over a moderate fire for ten or fifteen minutes, as directed above. Then proceed to pour into jelly glasses or jars, cover tightly, and set in a cool place.

### Quince Jelly.
Gelée de Coings.

1 Pound of Sugar to Every Pint of Fruit Liquid.

Pare and core the quinces, and cut into slices. Boil until well done, which may be determined by running a fork through them. Then strain the liquor through a flannel bag, and measure it, allowing one pound of white sugar to every pint of juice. Place the whole on a fire in the preserving kettle, and watch closely. Do not let it boil over. Try occasionally on a saucer. When it begins to grow solid it is done. Then proceed to bottle as directed above.

### Raspberry Jelly.
Gelée de Framboises.

To Every Pound of Berries 1 Pound of Sugar.

To every pound of raspberries allow a half of a pound of sugar. Put the berries in a porcelain-lined kettle, and cover them with the sugar and let them stand for two hours. Then set over a moderate fire and bring the mixture to a boiling point. Skim while boiling; pour immediately into cups and glasses, and cover tightly and place in a cool dry place.

### Strawberry Jelly.
### Gelée de Fraises.
#### To Every Pound of Berries a Half Pound of Sugar.

To every pound of strawberries allow a half of a pound of sugar. Put the berries in a porcelain-lined kettle, and cover them with the sugar and let them stand for two hours. Then set over a moderate fire and bring the mixture to a boiling point. Skim while boiling; pour immediately into cups and glasses, and cover tightly and place in a cool, dry place.

### JAMS.
### Des Marmelades.

Marmalades are a mixture of fruits that have been reduced to a paste of such consistency that they may be preserved. Ripe fruits, which cannot bear the process of blanching required in preserving whole fruits are used for this purpose. The beauty and the taste of a marmalade will depend on the fruits that are used and the quality of sugar, as also the care bestowed on the preparation. The Creoles, like their French ancestors, are noted for their delightful preparations of marmalades.

#### Directions for Making a Marmalade.

Always choose ripe, beautiful, luscious fruit. Cut the fruit into small pieces, and then add the sugar and fruit in alternate layers in the preserving kettle, with a layer of fruit on the bottom. Set the kettle over the fire. If the fruit is not very juicy add a small quantity of water to set it to boiling and to extract the juices. As the fruit boils, shake the kettle occasionally by lifting it from the fire, and turn the whole briskly to prevent it from burning at the bottom. Never stir with a spoon, as it will be sure to burn. When the whole mixture begins to look very clear, and you see, by testing a portion on a plate, that it is growing thick, it is done. Then take from the fire and put into jars at once. This mode of cooking distinguishes the marmalade from preserves and jellies.

Follow these directions implicitly in the subjoined recipes:

### Apple Marmalade.
### Marmelade de Pommes.
#### 3½ Pounds of Fruit to 2 Pounds of Sugar.

Peel the pears and cut them into quarters, extracting all the seeds. Then throw them into frsh water, sufficient to half cover, and set them on the fire. When they begin to grow soft, mash them with a wooden spoon; then add the sugar; add the grated rinds of several lemons; mix well, and then set all back upon the fire. Stir the mixture while boiling until it is of the proper consistency, and then pour it into jars or glasses. Allow three and a half pounds of fruit to two pounds of sugar.

### Cherry Jam.
### Marmelade de Cerises.
#### For Every Pound of Cherries ¾ of a Pound of Sugar.

Select fine, ripe cherries. Stone them, but be careful not to allow them to lose their juice. Allow three-fourths of a pound of sugar for every pound of fruit. Arrange in layers as directed above, set on the fire, and boil till the syrup is very clear and begins to form a jelly when a portion is turned upon a plate. Then bottle as directed.

### Orange Marmalade.
### Marmclade d'Oranges.
#### To Every 6 Oranges Allow 2 Lemons.
#### To Every Pound of Fruit ¾ of a Pound of Sugsr.

Select fine, ripe Louisiana oranges. Remove the rind, grate it, and grate the pulp, preserving carefully every particle of juice. Extract the seeds. To every six oranges and juice, allow the grated rind and juice of two lemons. Then weigh the whole, and allow for every pound of fruit three-fourths of a pound of sugar. Cook the whole, adding, of course, the grated rind of the oranges, and when done turn into jelly tumblers. Test by turning a portion on a plate. When it begins to jelly, which will be in about twenty-five minutes, the mixture is ready to be turned into the tumblers and sealed.

A marmalade of orange and lemon peel may be made by putting the rinds into a jar of water, and letting them stand for several days. Then drain and grate or pound soft. Allow a half pound of sugar for every pound of pulp. Mix a little water to start the boiling, and let all cook for three-quarters of an hour. Then proceed to turn into jelly glasses.

### Pear Marmalade.
### Marmelade de Poires.
#### 2 Pounds of Sugar to Every 3½ Pounds of Pears.

Peel the pears and cut them into quarters, extracting all the seeds. Then throw them into fresh water, sufficient to half cover, and set them on the fire. When they begin to grow soft, mash them with a wooden spoon; then add the sugar; add the grated rinds of several lemons; mix well, and then set all back upon the fire. Stir the mixture while boiling till it is of the proper consistency, and then pour it into jars or glasses. Allow three and a half pounds of fruit to two pounds of sugar.

### Peach Marmalade.
#### Marmelade de Pêches.
**To Every Pound of Peaches ¾ of a Pound of Sugar:**

Allow three-fourths of a pound of sugar for every pound of fruit. Take ripe fruit; pare and cut into small pieces, and place in the preserving kettle, with a layer of fruit and a layer of sugar, and so alternate till all is in. Cook over the fire as directed. Watch carefully that they do not burn. When they begin to form a jelly take off the fire and put away in stone jars or glasses. Apricot and Plum Marmalade are made in the same manner.

### Pineapple Marmalade.
#### Marmelade d'Ananas.
**To Every Pound of Pineapple ¾ of a Pound of Sugar.**

Pare the pineapple, and remove the eyes. Grate carefully, preserving the juice. Allow three-fourths of a pound of sugar to every pound of the grated fruit, and proceed as directed above.

### Quince Marmalade.
#### Marmelade de Coings.
**For Every Pound of Quinces Add ¾ of a Pound of Sugar.**

Take ripe quinces; cut them into small pieces; stem them in sufficient water to cover them, and let them cook till they can be mashed with a wooden spoon. When well-mashed in the water, pour in the sugar, allowing three-fourths of a pound for every pound of fruit. Then proceed to arrange in layers as directed above. Add the mixture; cook until it assumes a bright red color. Test by pouring on a saucer just sufficient to see if it will jelly; when it reaches this degree of consistency, proceed to run into jars or glasses. When cold it will be quite solid.

### Raspberry Jam.
#### Marmelade de Framboises.
**To Every Pound of Raspberries 1 Pound of Sugar.**

Select fine, ripe fruit, and weigh, and allow equal weights of fruit and sugar. Proceed to boil as directed. When they begin to jelly, they are ready to be turned into glasses.

Raspberry Jam is very much improved by the addition of a glass of currant juice, cooking all together.

### Strawberry Jam.
#### Marmelade de Fraises.
**To Every Pound of eBrries 1 Pound of Sugar.**

Select fine, ripe strawberries, and weigh, and allow equal weights of fruit and sugar. Proceed to boil as directed. When they begin to jelly, they are ready to be turned into the jelly glasses.

### Conserve of Grapes.
#### Marmelade de Raisins.
**To Every Pint of Fruit Juice ½ Pound of Sugar.**

Boil the grapes for one hour, and then press them through a sieve. Add a half pound of sugar to every pint of liquid, and proceed as directed above.

### Orange Flower and Rose Conserves.
#### Conserve de Fleur d'Oranger et de Roses.
**8 Ounces of Rose Water.**
**2 Ounces of Powdered Orange Petals.**
**1½ Pounds of Sugar.**

This is a delicious and recherche Creole Conserve. Take two ounces of powdered orange flower petals, one and one-half pounds of sugar, and eight ounces of rose water. Steep the petals in distilled water, and then add the sugar, and set to heat over a moderate fire. Add the rose water. When it begins to jelly turn into a jelly glass.

### Violet Conserve.
#### Conserve de Violettes.
**2 Ounces of Freshly-Gathered Violet Petals.**
**1½ Pounds of Sugar.**

This conserve is made by pounding two ounces of freshly-gathered violet petals, with great care, into a paste, after steeping in distilled water sufficient to make a paste. Then add the sugar, in proportion of one and a half pounds and boil to a flake.

## PRESERVES.
### Des Conserves.
#### General Directions for Making Preserves.

Preserving fruits is very much on the same order as the making of jellies, only in preserving equal quantities of fruit and sugar are used. Use only the best quality of sugar.

Fruits may be preserved either whole or otherwise. In preserving fruits whole, it is best to prick such fruits as pears, plums and peaches with a needle, so as to give vent to the juice, which would otherwise escape and burst the skin. This mode of preserving looks very beautiful but the best way is the old-fashioned one of paring the fruit carefully, either in halves or whole, simply removing the skins and cores. Then make a syrup of one pound of white sugar to each pound of fruit. Set the kettle on the fire, and let the syrup boil till the fruit looks:

quite clear. Or make the syrup by putting it on the fire with water, allowing a half pint of fresh water to a pound of the best white sugar. Stir well and bring to a boil. Let it boil five minutes, when it will begin to bubble and froth. As the froth rises the syrup will become clear. Skim and set to one side of the stove to settle, and it is now ready to receive the fruit.

If the former method is used, take the fruit carefully out of the syrup as soon as possible, so as to take up as little of the syrup as can be helped, and then place the fruit in the jars. Let the syrup continue to boil till it becomes very thick, and inclined to run into a jelly. Then fill the jars up with it, and when cool tie with muslin or paper around the mouth before sealing. But the new jars that come with close-fitting covers are the best, as well as the most economical finally.

Use in preference a porcelain-lined kettle. If you use a copper kettle, never allow the preserves, jams or marmalades to cool in the kettle, on account of the verdigris which will be sure to form.

Examine the preserves from time to time, and change the paper covers when they are discolored.

If the slightest sign of air bubbles is detected, open the jars immediately and boil the fruit again, but this will also destroy some of the flavor and excellent quality.

It is absolutely necessary to keep all preserves, marmalades and jellies in a cool (not cold) place, that is, perfectly free from dampness or possibility of heat. Heat will excite fermentation, and the preserves will quickly sour. Dampness will cause them to decompose and mold.

Follow implicitly the above directions, and you will be sure to succeed in making preserves, etc.

### Fig Preserves.

Take the weight in sugar of the quantity of figs to be preserved; the figs must be ripe. Cover the figs with cold water for twelve hours; then simmer in water enough to cover them until tender, and spread out upon a sieve to cool and harden. Make a syrup of the sugar, a cup of cold water being allowed for every pound. Boil until clear of scum, put in the figs, and simmer for ten minutes. Take them out and spread upon the dishes in the sun. Add the lemons and the ginger; boil the syrup thick, give the figs another boil of fifteen minutes and fill the jars three-quarters of the way up to the top. Then fill up with boiling syrup, cover, and, when cold, seal up.

### Lemon Preserves.

#### Conserve de Citron.

1 Pound of Sugar for Every Pound of Lemons.
The Juice of 1 Lemon for Every Pound of Fruit.
A Tablespoonful of Alum for Every Quart of Water.

Cut the lemon in halves, after paring, and remove the seeds. Then cut it up into a number of thin slices, and put them into a vessel with cold water, adding a tablespoonful of alum to every quart of water, or a little salt. After several hours put the lemon into cool, fresh water, and let it remain an hour, and drain. Then put it into a kettle and cover with two quarts of boiling water. Add the rinds of the lemon or citron, and a few pieces of ginger root. Let all boil till perfectly clear. Then take out the fruit and drain dry. Then prepare a syrup, allowing one pound of sugar for every pound of fruit, and add the juice of a lemon for each pound of fruit. Put the citron or lemon in without the ginger, and allow it to boil for three-quarters of an hour. It will become a beautiful, clear amber color. Proceed to bottle or seal in jars immediately.

### Peach Preserves.

#### Conserves de Pêches.

To Every Pound of Fruit One Pound of Sugar.

Prepare the syrup as above directed. Then peel the peaches and cut them into halves, removing the stones. Skim the syrup, and drop in the peaches, one at a time, and let them boil till tender, from fifteen to twenty minutes. They should be so tender that they may be pierced with a broom straw. This is the test. Then remove the kettle from the fire, carefully drain out the peaches and put them in the jars. Then boil the syrup twenty minutes longer, or until it forms a thick syrup, removing the scum as it rises. Pour off any remains of thin syrup that may have adhered to the peaches in the jar, and fill in with the syrup, and set aside to cool. When cold, screw the tops of the jars on. Label and set away.

### Fruit Preserves.

#### Conserves de Fruits.

To Every Pound of Fruit Allow 1 Pound of Sugar.

Apple, Plum, Damson, Grape, Strawberry, Raspberry, Currant, Scuppernong, Muscadine, Pumpkin, Sweet Potato and other preserves are prepared in the same manner as in the directions given for Peach Preserves, only the berries, such as Strawberries, Blackberries and

Raspberries, do not require much cooking. Preserve Cherries whole, stoning and stemming.

### Pineapple Preserves.
#### Conserves d'Ananas.
To Every Pound of Fruit One Pound of Sugar.

Pare the pineapple and remove the eyes. Then slice it nicely and weigh it. Allow equal quantities of fine, powdered sugar. Place the fruit in a deep dish and then sprinkle the sugar over it, between the slices, in alternate layers, and let it remain overnight. Drain off the syrup in the morning, and put it in a kettle, and when it gets very hot put in the fruit. Let it cook slowly till the slices look very clear, and then skim them out and put them in the jars. Fill to overflowing, and then seal.

### Quince Preserves.
#### Conserve de Coings.
To Every Pound of Fruit One Pound of Sugar.

Pare the ripe quinces, and then cut them into slices or rings. Weigh them and put them into the preserving kettle and cover with water. When they are quite tender, pour off the superfluous water, leaving about half a pint to every pound of fruit, and adding sugar, pound for pound. Let the whole boil till the fruit is tender. Then carefully drain out the fruit and lay it in the jars. Now return the kettle to the fire, and let the syrup boil to a jelly. Then fill the jars with it. The jelly will grow clearer and brighter as time goes on, and quinces preserved in this way will keep for years.

### Orange Preserves.
#### Conserve d'Orange.
To Every Pound of Oranges 1 Pound of Sugar.

Peel the oranges. Then slice nicely and weigh. Allow equal quantities of fine white powdered sugar. Place the fruit in a deep dish, and then sprinkle the sugar over it, between the slices, in alternate layers, and let it remain over night. Drain off the syrup in the morning, and put it in a kettle, and when it gets very hot put in the fruit. Let it cook slowly till the slices look very clear, and then skim them out and put them in the jars. Fill to overflowing and then seal.

### Small Oranges Preserved Whole.
#### Conserves d'Oranges.
To Every Pound of Oranges 1 Pound of Sugar.

Take small, green, sweet oranges, and pierce them several times with a penknife till very soft. Let them stand for three days in water, which must be renewed fresh every day. Put them in a dish after the third day, pour thin clarified sugar over them, and then prepare a syrup as above directed. Add the oranges when it begins to boil, cook till they are tender, and proceed in the usual way. Or the oranges may be taken out, placed on a sieve after the first ebullition of the syrup, and drained and glazed or candied, as crystallized fruit.

### Watermelon Rind Preserves.
#### Conserve d'Écorce de Melon d'Eau.
To Every Pound of Watermelon Rind 1 Pound of Sugar.

Cut the watermelon rind into thin slices, and throw into a bucket of fresh water, into which you have dissolved a teaspoonful of alum for every quart of water. Let it remain for several hours, until they grow crisp, and then proceed in exactly the same manner as in the recipe for Citron preserves.

### Brandy Peaches.
#### Pêches à l'Eau de Vie.
½ Pint of Fruit Water to 1 Pound of Granulated Sugar.

Equal Parts of Brandy and Sugar. Select fine freestone peaches, yellow or white, not overripe. Scald them with boiling water, cover well, and let them boil till tender. Then take them out, and drain on a platter, and put in the jars and cover with brandy, and let them stand one week. Then make a syrup, allowing a half pint of the water in which the peaches were boiled to one pound of granulated sugar. Take out the peaches, drain them, and put into glass jars. Let the syrup cool, and mix equal parts of this with equal parts of the brandy, in which the peaches were put up, pour over the peaches, and seal.

All brandied fruits are put up in the same manner.

## CHAPTER XLV.

### CREOLE CANDIES.

Bonbons et Sucreries Créoles.

Creole Candies occupy a unique position among confections in the United States, and it has often been said that the old French Quarter could apply for a patent for its delicious "Pacanes à la' Crème," "Rose," "Praline Blanc," "Pistaches Pralinées," "La Colle," "Maïs Tactac," "Dragées," "Guimauves," "Pastilles," "Nougâts," and other exclusive products of the Creole cuisine. The Picayune uses the term "exclusive" advisedly, especially in the use of the word "Praline," for while the term "Praline" is not of Creole origin, being a common enough word in the vocabulary of the French nation, with the mother country of Louisiana it simply means "sugared," and has no reference whatever to the delightful confections that had their origin in the old Creole homes of New Orleans. There is, indeed, a traditional recipe of the great Viart, "Homme de Bouche," as he called himself, who tickled the palate of Charles X, in the jocund days of the Bourbon restoration, and another old tradition that the Praline was a species of Dragée, which derived its name from the Marechal de Plessin-Pralin, who was very fond of almonds, and whose butler one day advised him to have them coated wuth sugar, to avoid indigestion. Again, there is an old French rhyme of Gresset's which has become incorporated in the banquette games of the little Creole children of New Orleans, and which runs thus:

"Soeur Rosalie au retour de matines,
Plus d'une fois lui porta des pralines."

But all these songs and stories simply refer to any sugar-coated nut. It was reserved for the gentle descendants of these old French ancestral homes to evolve from the suggestiveness of the word "Praline" dainty and delightful confections that have, for upwards of one hundred and fifty years, delighted the younger generations of New Orleans, and the older ones, too. The old negro cooks, quick to appreciate and apply, took up the word, and out of their own ingenuity created peculiar forms of candy, such as "La Colle," "Maïs Tactac,' 'etc., all of which are pleasant, and the delight especially of the little children of New Orleans.

Aside from these, we have our "Dragées," and "Pastilles," and "Caramels," and "Bonbons à la Crème," and "Bonbons au Liqueur," all of which are not only most agreeable to the taste, but are also elegant accessories of desserts at the most fashionable feasts.

### PRALINES.

The word "Praline" is entirely associated in New Orleans with the delicious pink and white sugar cakes made of cocoanut and sugar, or the brown ones, made of pecans and sugar, which are sold by the old Creole negro women of New Orleans. The "Pralinières," as they are called, may always be found in Canal Street, near Bourbon or Royal, or about the entrance of Jackson Square, in the dim Cathedral alley, or going about the streets of the old French Quarter, selling their wares of an evening, when the little Creole children are taking an airing with their faithful old mammies. These little ones always have a "Picayune," or five-cent pice, with which to buy a praline or a "La Colle" or a stick of "Candi Tiré à la Melasse."

### White Pralines.

Pralines Blanches de Coco.

1 Pound of Fine White Sugar (Granulated).
1 Freshly-Grated Cocoanut (Small Size).
4 Tablespoonfuls of Water.

Use a farina boiler or a porcelain-lined saucepan. Put the sugar in the saucepan with the water and let it boil well. When it begins to form a syrup, take from the fire and stir in the freshly-grated cocoanut. Mix thoroughly and return to the fire, and let it boil until you can draw it like a thread between your finger and thumb. Be careful to stir constantly from the time you add the cocoanut. When it begins to bubble, take from the stove, for it will have reached the above-mentioned state in two or three minutes. This will be sufficient if you wish the pralines to be light and flaky. Have ready a cleanly washed and somewhat wet marble slab or buttered dish. Take a kitchen spoon and drop the mixture into cakes on the slab, spreading them out with the spoon and rounding with a fork till they form a neat round cake of about a quarter of an inch in thickness and four or five inches in diameter. Let them dry; and then take a knife and gently raise them from the slab. You will have the dainty white pralines that are such peculiar Creole confections and which are also much sought after by strangers visiting New Orleans.

Increase the quantity of sugar in proportion to the size of the cocoanut, using three pounds of finest white sugar for a very large cocoanut, and never boil the cocoanut more than a few minutes in the sugar.

### Pink Pralines.

Pralines Rose de Coco.

1 Pound of Fine White Sugar (Granulated).
1 Freshly-Grated Cocoanut (Small Size).
4 Tablespoonfuls of Water.
1 Tablespoonful of Cochineal.

Proceed in exactly the same manner as above, only add about a tablespoonful of Cochineal to the pralines, just before taking off the fire. Proceed to drop on a marble slab, as above.

### Pecan Pralines.

Pralines aux Pacanes.

1 Pound of Brown Sugar.
½ Pound of Freshly-Peeled and Cut Louisiana Pecans.
1 Spoon of Butter.
4 Tablespoonfuls of Water.

Set the sugar to boil, and as it begins to boil add the pecans, which you will have divested of their shells and cut some into fine pieces, others into halves, and others again into demi-halves. Let all boil till the mixture begins to bubble, and then take off the stove and proceed to lay on a marble slab, as above, to dry. These pecan pralines are delicious.

Be careful to stir the mixture in the above recipe constantly till the syrup begins to thicken and turn to sugar. Then take from the stove and proceed to turn on the marble slab. One pound of unshelled pecans will make a half pound shelled. In using water, add just sufficient to melt the sugar.

### Cream Pecans.

Pacanes à la Crème.

1 Pound of Pecans.
The White of an Egg.
¼ Pound of Finest White Confectionery Sugar.

Under this suggestive term is known a species of confection that is much used by the Creole as an addition to the most fashionable and recherche feast. Peel the pecans in halves, being careful not to break the meat. Then take the white of an egg and beat well with its weight in water till it forms a cream. Then work in with your fingers the finest white confectionery sugar till it forms a smooth paste. Take a small piece of this paste, roll it, and put it between two halves of the pecans, and then lightly roll in the paste, flattening the pecan somewhat. The coating outside must be very, very light, so that the delicate brown of the pecan meat shows through. Set the pecans to dry, and serve on dainty china saucers, setting a saucer to each guest.

### Almond Pralines.

Amandes Pralinées.

1 Pound of Beautiful New Almonds.
1 Pound of Sugar.
½ Glass of Water.
A Pinch of Carmine.

Peel the almonds whole, and then rub them well with a linen cloth, to take off any dust. Put them into a skillet with a pound of the finest white sugar, and a dash of Carmine, if you wish to tinge them to a beautiful rose. But they are very beautiful when a snowy white. Place the skillet on the fire, stirring all the time until the almonds crackle hard. Then take off the fire and work until the sugar becomes sandy and well-detached from the almonds. Then separate one part of the sugar, and again put the almonds on the fire, stirring them lightly with a spoon as they again pick up the sugar, paying strict attention to the fire, that it be not too quick. When the almonds have taken up this part of the sugar, put in that which you have reserved, and continue to parch until they have taken up all the sugar. Then take a piece of paper and put it in a sieve, and throw the almonds upon it, shaking around so as to separate those which still cling together. Each almond must be separate and incrusted with sugar.

There used to be an old colored woman who supplied the judges and attorneys of the Civil District Court near the St. Louis Cathedral alley, with lunches. She made these ancient Creole "Amandes Pralinées" a specialty, in a little cornet of paper, just as the ancient Creole dames do when serving them at their elegant festivities.

### Peanut Pralines.
Pistaches Pralinées.

1 Pound of Peanuts.
1 Pound of Sugar.
¼ Glass of Water.
A Pinch of Carmine.

Peanuts, which have been dubbed "Pistaches" by the Creoles, may be made into delightful confections by cedure as outlined above for "Amandes Pralinées."

### Peanut Pralines.
Pralines aux Pistaches.

1 Pound of Peanuts.
1 Pound of Brown Sugar.
4 Tablespoonfuls of Water.
1 Tablespoonful of Butter.

Shell the peanuts and break into bits. Then set the sugar and water to boil, and as it begins to simmer add the peanuts and the butter. Stir constantly and as it bubbles up once take from the fire, pour from the spoon on the marble slab or a buttered plate, and set away to harden.

### Molasses Candy.
Candi Tiré à la Melassee.

Louisiana is rightly the home of Molasses Candy, for it was right here, in this old city, in the environments of which sugar was first raised in the United States, and molasses, sweet and health-giving, was first given to the world, that Molasses Candy, or "Candi Tiré," as the Creoles call it, first had birth. "Candi Tiré" parties, or Molasses Candy Pullings, were among the pleasurable incidents of life among the early New Orleans belles and beaux. Take

1 Quart of Louisiana Molasses.
1 Tablespoonful of Butter.
1 Pound of Granulated Sugar.
2 Tablespoonfuls of Vinegar.
½ Teaspoonful of Soda.
The Juice of 1 Lemon.

Boil the sugar until it becomes quite thick when dropped into water. Add the molasses and the vinegar and butter. Boil till it hardens when dropped into cold water. Then stir in a small half teaspoonful of bicarbonate of soda, and pour into buttered tins, and as soon as it begins to cool sufficiently pull till white. Moisten the hands while pulling with ice water or butter. The sticks may be single, twisted, braided or flattened, according to taste.

It was a treat to the children of this generation to see the old colored women going about with their great salvers, on which were laid snowy napkins and rows upon rows of beautiful white "Candi Tiré," or "Pulled Candy," as the name indicated. The old women used to sit in the school yards at the noon recess, and every day their stores were exhausted, whether they had "Pralines," "La Colle," or "Candi Tiré." Each school had its regular "Candy Woman," who made it her duty to be there exactly as the clock struck twelve. Many a faithful old negress helped to support her former mistress in the broken fortunes of the family after the war by her sale of Molasses Candy, Pralines, La Colle or "Maïs Tactac."

### La Colle.

2 Pounds of Brown Sugar.
Or 1 Pint of Molasses.
2 Cups of Louisiana Pecans.

"La Colle" is a delightful kind of molasses praline cake that the old negro cake and candy vendors make out of black molasses and pecans or peanuts. These cakes are placed in dainty white paper cases and dried, and sold, to the delight of the little Creole children, and older folks too, for that matter. They are made by taking two pounds of brown sugar, and boiling it down to almost one pint of syrup. To this dark syrup add two cups of pecans, cut or mashed in various irregular sizes. Then, when it becomes so thoroughly boiled that it passes like a thread between the fingers, they pour it into small white paper cases about four inches long and two inches wide, making the cake about a half or quarter of an inch in thickness. They set these to dry, and always find a ready sale for them. The cases are made out of white foolscap paper, folded neatly like the light cover of a box.

Or, take one pint of Molasses and bring to a boil. Throw in the peanuts, and then fill the little paper cases. Either way, "La Colle" is always in demand from the faithful old vendors.

### Pop-Corn Candy.
"Tac-Tac."

1 Cupful of White Sugar.
1 Tablespoonful of Butter.
3 Tablespoonfuls of Water.
3 Quarts of Nicely-Popped Corn.

Put the butter, water and sugar into a boiler, and boil till it begins to almost run to candy; then throw in the nicely popped corn; stir vigorously over the fire until the sugar is evenly distributed over the corn; then take the kettle from the fire and stir until it cools a little. In this way you will have each grain or kernel separate and coated with sugar. If you wish, pile it into mounds and roll into balls while still hot enough for the grains to adhere. These are put into dainty rolls of tissue paper and sold along the streets of New Orleans.

### Maïs "Tac-Tac."

1 Pint of Louisiana Molasses.
¾ Pound of Indian Corn (Parched).

Boil one pint of Louisiana molasses, and, as it comes to the boiling point, throw in about three-quarters of a pound of parched Indian corn, parched to a blossom; stir well, and then pour into little paper cases, about five or six inches in length, three in width and one and a half in depth. Let these cool before touching. This is another of the peculiar forms of candies sold by the old Creole negroes of New Orleans.

### CARAMELS.

Caramels.

1 Pound of Clarified Sugar.
Sufficient Water to Melt.

Take one pound of clarified sugar and add just sufficient water to melt; boil it till it is very brittle and has the slightest odor of beginning to burn; then pour it on a buttered slab or plate, and, as soon as it is cool enough to receive an impression from the finger, cut it out with a common case knife into small squares of about an inch in size, after which glace with another coating of sugar. Let them dry and keep them tightly closed, as they are easily injured and become soft by contact with the atmosphere.

### Chocolate Caramels.

Caramels au Chocolat.

½ Pound of Chocolate.   2 Cups of Sugar.
½ Cup of Milk.
1 Tablespoonful of Butter.
1 Teaspoonful of Vanilla.

Set the sugar to boil; scrape the chocolate in the milk, and add it to the boiling sugar, and stir in the butter; then boil till it forms a syrup. Take from the fire and turn upon a greased slab or upon a buttered dish or pan that is quite square. When it begins to cool sufficient to receive an impression from the finger, cut into small squares with the case-knife and set in a cool, dry place to harden. A good test as to whether the mixture is done is to drop a little from the end of a spoon into a cup of cold water. If it begins to harden instantly, it is ready to take from the stove.

The Cream Chocolate Caramel is made in the same way, only cream is used instead of milk. Again, the Chocolate Caramel may be made simply by dissolving four ounces of chocolate in a little water and adding to a syrup made of one pound of sugar.

To any of the above recipes, essence of vanilla, orange or lemon may be added, in which case you will have Vanilla or Orange or Lemon Cream Caramels. In making the Lemon Caramels, however, grate the zest of the lemon with a lump of sugar, and then add to this the lemon juice and water enough to dissolve the sugar. Stir the whole into the boiled Caramel a few minutes before taking from the fire. Orange and Lime Caramel may also be made from the fruits in this manner.

### Caramel Oranges.

Oranges au Caramel.

6 Oranges.
2 Cups of Sugar.
1 Tablespoonful of Butter.

Peel and quarter the oranges in their natural divisions, being careful not to break through the pith or allow the juice to escape. Then string them on fine wire, or take up on the point of a hatpin and dip into the Caramel. When sufficiently coated, place them in the stove for a few minutes to dry and "Glacée," or Glaze. (See recipe under Icings for Cakes, etc.)

### Caramel Chestnuts.

Marrons au Caramel.

1 Pound of Chestnuts.
2 Cups of Sugar.
1 Tablespoonful of Butter.

Take fine, large Chestnuts, and transfix them on a hatpin or on small pointed sticks. Dip them in the Caramel, and then dry and Glacée them. (See Glacée under heading Icings for Cakes, etc.)

### BONBONS.

### Candy Drops.

Pastilles.

1 Pound of Sugar.
Water to Dilute.
Flavoring Extract to Taste.

These are favorite candies with the Creoles, and very easy to make. They may be of any size, a lozenge, a tablet or a drop, and they may also be of any color. Pound and sift a pound of sugar that has been doubly refined, first through a coarse and then through a fine sieve. Put in an earthen vessel, and add the flavoring extract, whether of lemon, orange, cinnamon, cloves, rose or violet or vanilla or carmine. Dilute the sugar with a little water and the liquid. It must not be too thin, or it will run, nor too thick, or it cannot be poured easily, but a nice rather stiff paste. Set the saucepan on the fire, being careful to select a saucepan that has a spout. As soon as the mixture begins to bubble up about the sides of the saucepan, stir it once well and take from the fire, and drop it in small lumps through the spout of the saucepan upon sheets of tin, and let it stand two hours to dry. Then put in the stove a few seconds to finish drying. As they become hard and brilliant, take them out, else they will lose their flavor.

### Cream Pastilles.
Pastilles à la Crème.
1 Pound of Fine White Confectionery Sugar.
1 Tablespoonful of Vinegar.
1 Teaspoonful of Lemon Extract.
1 Teaspoonful of Cream of Tartar.
4 Tablespoonfuls of Water.

Moisten the sugar with the water and set to boil. Add vinegar and Cream of Tartar. Let it boil till brittle. Then take from the fire and add the Lemon Extract. Turn quickly on a wet slab or buttered plates. When it begins to cool, pull till very, very white, and then cut into small squares of about a half inch.

### Orange Pastilles.
Pastilles à l'Orange.
The Strained Juice of 2 Oranges.
½ Ounce of Orange Sugar.
3¼ Ounces of Coarse Sugar.

To make the orange sugar, rub the rind of the oranges on the sugar and dry. Then proceed to add the water and three and a quarter ounces of sugar and flavoring. As soon as it begins to dissolve in the pan, take a small wooden spoon and stir it for a few minutes. Then remove it from the fire, stirring continuously, and drop the pastilles upon a sheet of paper, cutting them off in drops about the size of a pea with a curved piece of wire or a hairpin. When they are quite dry, turn the paper upside down, brush the reverse side with a paste brush slightly moistened with water, and shake off the pastilles with the point of a knife upon a dry sieve. Then move the sieve to and fro over a very slow fire, so that all the moisture may be removed from the drops, and keep them in well-bottled jars.

The above recipe will serve as a guide for all Fruit and Liquor or Essence Pastilles.

### Fruit Pastilles.
Pastilles de Fruits.
3½ Ounces of Sugar.
½ Ounce of Any Fruit Juice.

All pastilles with fruit juices may be made in exactly the same manner as Orange Pastilles. Use one-half an ounce of juice and three and a half ounces of sugar, and add a little more sugar if it appears liquid after taking from the fire.

### Ginger Pastilles.
Pastilles de Gingembre.
½ Ounce of Lemon Juice.
3½ Ounces of Sugar.
1 Teaspoonful of Essence of Jamaica Ginger.

Proceed in the same manner as for Orange Pastilles.

### Health Pastilles.
Pastilles pour la Santé.
6 Grains of Saffron. 6 Grains of Musk.
6 Grains of Ambergris.
½ Drachm of Basil Seed.
½ Drachm of Orange Peel.
18 Grains of Mace.
18 Grains of Nutmeg.
½ Drachm of Storax Calamite.

Pound the Musk, Storax and Ambergis to a sugar, so as to extract all the resinous properties. Make the whole into a paste with a half pound of sugar and just enough Gum Tragacanth to give it sufficient consistency. Mix the paste thoroughly and then cut into small tablets that will weigh about a drachm each. Many of the old Creoles take these pastiles three or four times a day, as they facilitate digestion and create an excellent appetite. They are also excellent for persons suffering from debility.

### Lemon Pastilles.
Pastilles au Citron.
¼ Ounce of Water.
3½ Ounces of Sugar.
½ Ounce of Lemon Juice.

Proceed in the same manner as for Orange Pastilles.

### Liqueur Pastilles.
Pastilles à la Liqueur.
A Small Wineglassful of Any Kind of Cordial or Liqueur.
3½ Ounces of Coarse Sifted Sugar.
Cochineal or Carmine to Color, if Desired.

Proceed in the same manner as for Orange Pastilles.

### Pastilles to Relieve Thirst.
Pastilles pour la Soif.
8 Grains of Tartaric Acid.
1 Pound of Sugar.
20 Drops of Lemon Essence.
Sufficient Gum Tragacanth to Make a Paste.

Take eight grains of Tartaric Acid, one pound of sugar, twenty drops of Lemon Essence, and make a paste with all, adding a sufficient quantity of mucilage or Gum Tragacanth to make a paste. Cut out into tablets and dry in the open air. These tablets are excellent in hot summer months.

### Rose Pastilles.
Pastilles à la Rose.
1 Ounce of Water.
3½ Ounces of Sugar.
4 Drops of Essence of Roses.
3 Drops of Cochineal.

Proceed in the same manner as for Orange Pastilles.

### Marshmallow Drops.
Tablettes de Guimauve.

½ Pound of White Gum Arabic.
1 Pint of Water.
The Whites of 4 Eggs.
1 Teaspoonful of Extract of Vanilla.

Dissolve the Gum Arabic in one pint of water and strain, and add one-ahlf pound of the finest white sugar, and place over the fire, stirring constantly all the time until the syrup is dissolved. Then gradually add the whites of the eggs, beaten to a stiff froth. Stir in the mixture until it becomes thin and does not adhere to the fingers. Then flavor with the Vanilla Extract, and drop in tablets of about the size of a five-cent piece upon a sheet dusted with powdered starch. Make the shape of the tablets slightly convex, and in two hours remove from the papers, dry for a few minutes in the stove and put away for use.

### Peppermint Drops.
Pastilles à la Menthe.

1 Cupful of Sugar.
½ Teaspoonful of Essence of Peppermint.
A Pinch of Cream of Tartar.

Crush the sugar very fine, and boil for five minutes with water just sufficient to moisten. Then take from the fire, and add the Cream of Tartar, and after mixing well add the Essence of Peppermint. Beat briskly until the mixture begins to whiten well, and then drop upon white paper and dry in the open air. If it sugars before all is dropped, add a little water and boil again for two minutes.

### NOUGAT.
Nougât.

10 Ounces of Sifted Sugar.
1 Pound of Shredded Almonds, Dried.
A Few Drops of Essence of Vanilla.

Put the almonds on a baking sheet or plate at the entrance of the oven. Let them heat through and through. In the meanwhile put the sugar in a pan or porcelain-lined saucepan, and set on a moderate stove. Keep stirring with a wooden spoon until it begins to melt. Then quicken the stirring, and as soon as the sugar begins to form upon the surface in small white bubbles, like pearls, immediately throw in the almonds. Stir all gently until thoroughly mixed, and then pour out on a wet marble slab, and flatten to one-sixth of an inch in thickness. As soon as it begins to thicken, cut into pieces of about three inches long and two wide, or, better still, if you have fancy molds, line them thinly with the Nougat, having previously slightly buttered them on the inside. Cut the edges of the Nougat even and level before it becomes cold, for then it is brittle, and breaks easily.

A very charming and elegant Creole dessert is to take a dozen or so of the Nougats, form into small baskets with an ornamental Caramel handle, fill the little basket with whipped cream and one or two strawberries on top. Serve cold.

Again, the young Creole girls have a pretty way at Christmas and New Year's of making dainty boxes of Nougat and sending them to their friends, lining the boxes about the edges with fresh leaves and rosebuds or violets, or simply tying them in white tissue paper with pink or baby blue ribbon.

### Parisian Nougats.
Nougâts à la Parisienne.

8 Ounces of Scalded or Split Pistachio Kernels.
6 Ounces of Sugar.
1 Teaspoonful of Vanilla.
A Few Drops of Prepared Cochineal.

Boil the sugar till brittle, and then add the Pistachio Kernels or Peanuts and the Cochineal. Add the flavoring and mix gently. Then pour the Nougat out on a marble slab, slightly buttered. Flatten out the Nougat by means of a hard lemon slightly rubbed with butter to prevent sticking. Roll to about one-sixth of an inch in thickness, and before it cools sprinkle all over with small bits of granulated sugar, free from dust, and seeded raisins or cleaned currants. Press these lightly in with the fingers, and then divide the sheets of Nougat while hot into small diamond shapes, about two and a half inches long and one in width. This is a very graceful form of dessert, as well as an inexpensive and elegant offering to friends at the holiday season.

### DRAGÉES.

Almonds enter very largely into the composition of Dragées, as also Gum Arabic. Dissolve the Gum Arabic in a saucepan with enough water to color it, and then set the saucepan over a moderate fire. Stir in the mixture of candy a drop preparation, whether of Vanilla, Peppermint, Lemon, etc., and then mix thoroughly till the solution is complete. Strain through a sieve, and then, with a wire shaped like a hairpin, cut the candy preparation into the tiniest pieces of various sizes and shapes, and pour on a marble slab which has been oiled with butter or wet, to cool, and after an hour or so set in the oven for a few minutes. In case they are not beautifully polished, give them another light coating with the solution of Gum Arabic. The next day give them a finer polish by putting them into a basin with a little solution of sugar and rose water and a little starch, allowing one part of starch to six of sugar. Swing the basin back and forward over a very moderate fire, and continue until the Dragées are quite dry.

In making the Dragées use the proportions given for Pastilles.

### Sugar Plums.
#### Des Dragées Sucrées.

2 Pounds of Best Confectionery Sugar.
Sufficient Water to Dissolve.
1 Pound of Any Fruit.

Sugar Plums, or crystallized fruits, are among the daintiest preparations of the Creole cuisine. They are the real "Bonbons" so highly prized by the Creole girls. To crstallize fruits or candies in small quantities, take two pounds of the best sugar, and add sufficient water to dissolve it or to start it boiling. Let it boil to a syrup. Place the fruit to be crystallized in a pan, and pour over the syrup. Turn the fruit lightly by shaking the pan till every side is coated, and set to cool. When cool, drain off the syrup and set the pans on their sides, so that remaining particles may be drained off, and every side be coated with the crystallized mixture. It is always best to pour the syrup over the fruit while it is warm, as it takes a firmer hold and makes a brighter crystal, but it will not hurt the fruit if the crystal warms them enough to make them very soft, as they will be all right when the syrup and fruits cool. A small batch of crystallized fruit may be prepared at noon, and be ready for a 6 o'clock dining.

Fruits and almond paste bonbons should always be softened by the hot syrup, and it is always best to prepare the fruits two days in advance when they will be sufficiently soft for a light crystal to form on them. Chocolate and other bonbons may be crystallized in the same way.

### Crystallized Oranges.
#### Oranges Cristallisées.

6 Oranges.
2 Pounds of Sugar.
Sufficient Water to Dissolve.

Crystallize oranges in quarters, keeping the skins from being punctured. Cherries, Strawberries and other berries are crystallized whole, Peaches and Apricots in halves, and so on.

### Crystallized Orange Blossoms.
#### Fleurs d'Oranger Cristallisées.

Pick the petals one by one from the flowers, and put them into water. Drain this off, and then squeeze the flowers with your hands to bruise them, and drain on a sieve. Make a fine syrup, equal in bulk to the flowers, clarify it and add the flowers. Let the syrup boil up about seven times. Then remove it from the fire and let it stand till the sugar forms a coating all around the petals. Then drain them, separate them on a paper for an hour or so, till perfectly dry, and then put in boxes lined with white paper, and keep in a cool, dry place.

### Crystallized Violets.
#### Violettes Cristallisées.

1 Pound of Violet Petals, Freshly Gathered.
1 Pound of Sugar.

Proceed in exactly the same manner as for Orange Blossoms, only do not squeeze the petals in your hands. These are among the daintiest of confections, and while they cost very high when purchased, they may be easily prepared at home.

### Crystallized Rose Petals.
#### Feuilles de Roses Cristallisées.

Pound of Rose Petals.
1 Pound of Sugar.

Select beautiful red or pink rose petals that have been freshly gathered, and proceed in exactly the same manner as for Crystallized Violets.

### Crystallized Watermelon.
#### Melon d'Eau Cristallisé.

Take the bright red heart of the watermelon. Cut into dainty and fanciful forms, and place in a dish in the sun to dry. Make a syrup as directed above for Crystallized Fruits and with the point of a long hatpin or hairpin immerse the watermelon in it. Hang to dry from these points and you will have a beautiful crystallized fruit, the dainty pink and red of the melon showing through the transparent crystal icing. This is a beautiful confection for "red teas," "pink dinners," etc., where red or pink predominates in the decorations.

### Liqueur Bonbons.
#### Bonbons à la Liqueur.

1 Pound of Sugar.
1 Pint of Water.
Essence or Liquor to Taste.

Liqueur Bonbons are made of Boiled Sugar, flavored with some kind of liqueur. They are also flavored with the juice of fruits. Boil the sugar. Then remove the saucepan from the fire, and immerse it in a pan containing cold water, so that the sugar may cool quickly. Place a lid over the pan, to prevent the sugar forming a crust on top by contact with the air. Then roll the sugar into balls or pellets, flatten out and work the flavoring, whether of any kind of liqueur, fruit or essence, or Essence of Coffee, into them. Then set them in a box or mold and thinly cover their surface with a little starch powder to prevent forming lumps, and dry in a moderately warm closet for about fifteen hours. As you remove the bonbons place them on a dry sieve and brush off any remains of starch with a long-haired soft brush, for if any powder adheres it spoils the beauty of the bonbons.

### Cream Bonbons.

Bonbons à la Crème.

Bonbons a la Creme are famous Creole holiday candies. There is scarcely a Creole girl who does not pride herself upon her ability to make these dainty luxuries.

### Cream Bonbons.

Bonbons à la Crème.

2 Pounds of the Finest White Icing Sugar.
2 Ounces of Gum Arabic.
The Whites of 2 Eggs.
1 Gill of Any Essence Desired.

These delicious bonbons are prepared by soaking two ounces of the finest Gum Arabic in a gill of hot water, and then using two pounds of the finest icing sugar, the whites of 2 eggs, and a few drops of essence, and any cream, whether of Chocolate, Coffee, Cognac, Orange Flower, Maraschino or Lemon, which it is desired to use. The soaked gum must be strained through a piece of muslin bag into a bowl, and the essence added to it, and then it must be filled in with as much icing as it will hold, till it forms a stiff, yet elastic body. Then fill a biscuit forcer with the vanilla preparation mentioned above, and push it through upon a sheet of paper, well-dredged with sugar. As the contents are forced through, with a small knife cut off the cream, as it is pressed out, into pieces of about the size of a filbert. Place them in the baking pan in the oven for a few minutes, merely to dry their surfaces, and then dip these white balls into the chocolate icing, holding one at a time on the tip of the fork, so as to be able to turn it all around and ice each part. Then put on a wire tray, set to dry in the oven for about ten minutes.

### Chocolate Cream Bonbons.

Bonbons à la Crème de Chocolat.

2 Pounds of Finest White Icing Sugar.
2 Ounces of Gum Arabic.
The Whites of 2 Eggs.
4 Ounces of French Chocolate.

Soak two ounces of the finest Gum Arabic in a gill of hot water, and then add two pounds of the finest icing sugar, the whites of two eggs. The soaked gum must be strained through a piece of muslin bag into a bowl, and the essence added to it, and then it must be filled in with as much icing as it will hold, till it forms a stiff, elastic body. If it is desired to make Chocolate Creams, dissolve four ounces of French Chocolate with about a tablespoonful of water, and incorporate this with the whites of two eggs, of Royal Icing. (See recipe.) Then fill a biscuit forcer with the vanilla preparation mentioned above and push it through upon a sheet of paper, well-dredged with sugar. As the contents are forced through, with a small knife cut off the cream, as it is pressed out into pieces of about the size of a filbert. Place them in the baking pan in the oven for a few minutes, merely to dry their surfaces, and then dip these white balls into the Chocolate Icing, holding one at a time on the tip of the fork, so as to be able to turn it all around and ice each part. Then put on a wire tray, set to dry in the oven for about ten minutes.

### Coffee and Cognac Cream Bonbons.

Bonbons à la Crème de Café et de Cognac.

2 Pounds of Finest White Icing Sugar.
2 Pounds of Gum Arabic.
2 Ounces of Essence of Mocha Coffee.
½ Gill of Fine Old Cognac.

Coffee and Cognac Cream Bonbons are made in exactly the same manner as the above, only instead of the Chocolate a half gill of fine old Cognac and two ounces of the essence of Mocha Coffee are used. Then gum, brandy and icing sugar are worked into a paste and then covered, as in Chocolate Creams, with the Royal Icing, flavored with Essence of Coffee.

### Cherry and Noyeau Cream Bonbons.

Bonbons à la Crème de Noyau et de Cerises.

2 Ounces of Soaked Gum Arabic.
2 Pounds of Sugar.
1 Gill of Cherry Juice.
½ Gill of Noyeau.
The Whites of 2 Eggs.

Work the gum, Noyeau and sugar to an elastic paste, and use the cherry juice and whites of the eggs and some of the sugar for the Royal Icing. Then proceed as in Chocolate Cream Bonbons, the white Noyeau Cream forming the inside and the cherry-colored icing the outside.

**Lemon and Maraschino Cream Bonbons.**

Bonbons à la Créme de Citron et de Maraschino.

> 2 Ounces of Soaked Gum Arabic.
> 1 Ounce of Lemon Sugar.
> ¼ Gill of Maraschino.

Use the same amount of soaked Gum Arabic, icing sugar, whites of eggs and one ounce of lemon sugar, made by rasping the lemon on the sugar, and half a gill of Maraschino.

Follow the same directions as for Orange Bonbons, the Maraschino forming the cream for the inside, and the lemon sugar for the outside.

**Orange Cream Bonbons.**

Bonbons à la Créme d'Orange.

> 1 Ounce of Orange Sugar.
> The Whites of 2 Eggs.
> ½ Gill of Oragne Flower Water.

For Orange Flower Bonbons work the orange sugar, using one ounce, with the whites of the eggs, and make a Royal Icing. (See recipe.) Then work the gum, Orange Flower Water, using half a gill, and the icing sugar into a stiff paste, and proceed as in Chocolate Creams, finally covering with the Royal Icing, the white cream forming the interior of the Bonbons and the orange cr yellow the outside.

**Cream Peanuts.**

Pistaches à la Créme.

> 1 Pound of Fine White Sugar.
> 1 Teacupful of Water.
> 1 Teaspoonful of Extract of Vanilla.
> ½ Pound of Peanuts, Shelled.

Boil the sugar and water till it comes to a thread. Flavor highly with extract of vanilla. Then take from the fire and stir until it is a creamy white. Throw in the peanuts. Drop in a little white granulated sugar. Then put them on a table on a piece of white paper, and shake well till each stands apart. Roll again lightly in white powdered or granulated sugar, and let them dry.

**LOZENGES.**

Des Pastilles.

> 1½ Pounds of Finest White Icing Sugar.
> 2 Ounces of Any Essence Preferred.
> 1 Ounce of Gum Tragacanth.
> 2 Ounces of Tepid Water.

In making lozenges take one ounce of Gum Dragon or Gum Tragacanth, and soak it in two ounces of tepid water for about six hours. Then squeeze and wring out through a cloth, and add about a pound and a half of fine icing sugar and the desired essence and flavor the lozenges in the proportion of about two ounces of essence to the quantities above given. If peppermint flavor is desired, use one teaspoonful, Then work this prepared gum on a marble slab, as you would knead dough, until it is firm and white, yet elastic. Gradually work in the sugar and add the essence and work till smooth and very elastic. Then roll the paste out with fine sugar dredged on the slab, and cut into ten-cent size pieces, and also into diamond shapes. Place them in rows upon sugar-powdered baking sheets and dry in the oven. They must be kept in a well-stopped jar in a cool place. Orange, Clove, Lemon and Cinnamon Pastilles are all made in the same way. Every mother can thus make the candy that her children use, and know that there will be no deleterious effects.

**Cough Lozenges.**

Pastilles pour la Toux.

This book would not be complete without giving this famous old Creole Cough Lozenge. Take

> 1 Ounce of Gum Dragon.
> 2 Ounces of Orange Flower Water.
> 2 Pounds of Fine Sugar Icing.
> 50 Drops of Paregoric.
> 20 Drops of Ipecacuanha.
> 1½ Ounces Syrup of Squills.

Work the gum on the slab with about one-third of the sugar, and then work in gradually the syrup of squills After working well add the rest of the sugar and again work. Lastly add the Paregoric and the the Ipecacuanha. Then proceed to finish these old-fashioned lozenges in the manner directed in the general recipe given below.

**Sugar as Employed in Candy Making.**

Du Sucre.

As mentioned above, always select the best granulated loaf sugar for making candies. Beware of glucose. As a general rule, loaf sugar will do for all candy making without clarification. Brown or yellow sugars are used for Caramels, dark Pralines and pulled Molasses Candy generally.

Sugar is boiled more or less, according to the kind of candies one wishes to make. It is absolutely necessary to understand the proper degree of boiling if you wish to be successful in your efforts in making fine candies at home. The degrees are, respectively, "The Small Thread," "The Large Thread," "Blow," "Soft Ball," "Hard Ball," "Crack and Caramel." The following carefully prepared recipes will prove invaluable to the amateur:

### Sugar Boiling.

Le Cuisson du Sucre.

3 Pounds of Sugar.
1 Pint of Water.

To every three pounds of sugar allow a pint of water. Put to boil on a brisk fire, and skim carefully and wash on the sides with a hair brush dipped in water, to prevent the sugar from graining.

### Small Thread.

Le Petit Lissé.

3 Pounds of Sugar.
1 Pint of Water.

Dip the forefinger into iced water, and then into the boiling sugar, and instantly again into the iced water, to prevent burning the finger. Then pinch between the index finger and thumb. If a small thread forms, which breaks when the attempt is made to pull apart through the fingers, the proper degree is reached.

### Large Thread.

Le Grand Lissé.

3 Pounds of Sugar.
1 Pint of Water.

Boil the sugar a little longer, and then try as before; if a thread forms that can be pulled two inches without breaking, this degree is reached. This is the best degree for preserves, etc.

### The Pearl.

La Grande et la Petite Perle.

3 Pounds of Sugar.
1 Pint of Water.

Let the sugar boil a little longer. If you find that on drawing it out to a thread it snaps quickly, and also that while boiling the sugar presents the form of large pearls or globules on its surface, it will then have reached the small pearl degree. When the pearls become closely connected on the surface of the sugar, it will have reached the large pearl degree.

### The Blow.

Le Soufflé.

3 Pounds of Sugar.
1 Pint of Water.

Continue boiling, and after a few minutes dip the skimmer in the boiling sugar. Strike it on the edge of the boiler. Blow through the holes, and you will find that if the sugar is of the right degree, it will form into small globules or air bubbles on the other side. This is the best degree for creams, and also gives a rich flavor to Preserves.

### The Feather.

La Plume.

3 Pounds of Sugar.
1 Pint of Water.

Boil up the sugar a little longer, dip the skimmer in it, and on finding that it shivers into a thready fringe from the edge, it will have reached the degree called the "Feather." If large and elevated, the degree is the "Large Feather," or "La Grande Plume." In a few minutes more they become small and flaky, and the next degree, the "Small Feather," or "La Petite Plume," is reached.

### The Soft Ball.

Le Petit Boulet.

3 Pounds of Sugar.
1 Pint of Water.

Keep the sugar Boiling. Dip the finger into iced water and then into the boiling sugar and immediately into the water again. If the sugar has enough consistency to form a small ball when rolled between the finger and the thumb, the degree is reached.

### The Hard Ball.

Le Grand Boulet.

3 Pounds of Sugar.
1 Pint of Water.

Continue the test, and if a firmer ball is formed, this degree is reached.

### The Crack or Snap.

Le Cassé.

8 Pounds of Sugar.
1 Pint of Water.

Continue boiling, and dip the finger after a few moments in iced water and then in the boiling sugar, and instantly in the water again. The proper degree is reached when the sugar is placed between the fingers, and will not stick, or when distended it snaps hard and dry. The first degree is called "Little Crack," or "Le Petit Cassé," and the second is called "The Big Crack," or "Le Grand Cassé." This is a good degree for Fruits Glacé, etc.

### Caramel.

Caramel.

3 Pounds of Sugar.
1 Pint of Water.

Continue boiling till the sugar reaches a light brown color. Then take the vessel off immediately, or it will burn. Any degree beyond this renders the sugar calcined and barely fit for cooking purposes. On taking the vessel from the fire, insert the bottom in cold water to prevent the sugar from burning.

### To Clarify Sugar.
Du Sucre Clarifié.
8 Pounds of Sugar.
1 Pint of Water.
The White of 1 Egg.

In clarifying sugar for Candies, take the whole white of an egg for brown sugar and half the white for refined sugar. Beat to a froth in a dish with about a cupful of water, adding it by degrees. Then put about eight pounds of sugar into a kettle, and dilute it with the half of the beaten egg. Let it become very thick. Set it over the fire, and let it boil up twice before you skim it. Then skim and continue to add the egg by degrees, until the scum is perfectly white. Take the skimmer from the sugar, add another cup of cold water, to carry off any remaining scum, take it from the fire and strain. The sugar is then kept for use.

### COLORING FOR CANDIES.

Candies may be colored beautifully with such harmless preparations as Cochineal, Carmine (when properly prepared), Spinach, Indigo, Saffron or Burnt Sugar.

### Cochineal.
Cochenille.
1 Pound of Powdered Cochineal.
1 Ounce of Burnt Alum.
2 Ounces of Salts of Tartar.
2 Ounces of Cream of Tartar.
12 Ounces of Sugar.
2 Quarts of Water.

Cochineal is an extremely harmless coloring matter, which is used extensively by the Creoles. It is made from the Cocus Cacti, an insect indigenous to Mexico, and which is found on several species of fig trees. The color is crimson, and when diluted in water it has a deep reddish-brown color, and makes a beautiful coloring for Pralines and other preparations which demand it. It is sold by confectioners and druggists in preparations for the purpose of coloring candies, liqueurs and bonbons.

Take one ounce of powdered Cochineal, one ounce of salts of tartar, one ounce of burnt alum, two ounces of Cream of Tartar, twelve ounces of sugar, and two quarts of soft water. Boil the water in a porcelain-lined vessel, and add the other ingredients. Remove from the fire, and then strain at once through a sieve or cloth, and bottle for use.

### Carmine.
Carmin.
2 Gallons of Water.
3 Drachms of Powdered Alum.
2 Drachms of Bismuth.
2 Drachms of Nitro-Muriate of Tin.
2 Drachms of Nitric Acid.

Carmine is made by pulverizing Cochineal in a stone mortar and putting it into water at nearly a boiling point. One ounce of Brazil wood, obtained from the druggist, and one ounce of powdered Cochineal are put into separate vessels with one quart of water each. The Cochineal is always put in the water in a linen bag.

To make half a pound of the Carmine used so extensively in Creole homes, simply pound the Cochineal in a mortar, add two gallons of water, and let it boil for an hour and a quarter. Then add about three drachms of nitro-muriate of tin, made by taking two drachms of nitric acid, two drachms of muriatic acid and one drachm of bismuth, and dissolving under a gentle heat. Continue boiling the Cochineal ten minutes longer, and strain the mixture through a fine cloth, and let it stand for eighteen hours. Pour off the water, and add the solution of tin, in three pints of water, and let it stand for five days longer, changing the water every twenty-four hours. When free from any taste or smell the Carmine has been sufficiently washed, and is ready for use. Put into china saucers and dry in the stove.

It is exceedingly dangerous to purchase Carmine, and often it is nothing more than a red lead mixture, and poisonous. The Creoles always make their own preparations of Carmine.

### Green (Spinach.)
Vert (Epinards.)
1 Pound of Young Spinach.
A Few Grains of Powdered Alum.

Pound one pound of young Spinach to a pulp, and then carefully squeeze all the juice out of it. Set to boil, and the moment it begins to curdle remove from the fire, and strain all the juice from it. Then add to the curd the same weight in sugar, a few grains of powdered alum, and a little alcohol, and bottle for use. Keep in a cool place.

### Yellow (Saffron.)
Jaune (Saffran.)
3 Ounces of Saffron.
1 Ounce of Alum.
20 Ounces of Sugar.
1 Pint of Water.

Take three ounces of Saffron, one ounce of powdered Alum, twenty ounces of sugar, and one pint of water and boil all together. Strain and add a little alcohol, and bottle for use.

### Orange.
Orange.
1 Ounce of Yellow (Saffron.)
1 Ounce of Cochineal.

This color is obtained by mixing equal quantities of yellow and red (Cochineal.)

### Blue.
#### Bleu.
1 Pound of Sugar.
1 Pint of Water.
⅟₄ Ounce of Indigo.
1 Tablespoonful of Alcohol.

Take one pound of sugar, one pint of water and boil to a syrup. Add one ounce of Indigo, powdered very fine. Let all coil. Then add a little alcohol, and strain and bottle.

### Burnt Sugar.
#### Sucre Brûlé.
1 Pound of Granulated Sugar.
1 Quart of Water.

Take one pound of granulated sugar, and set it on the fire, and stir with a wooden spoon until thoroughly dissolved and burnt black. Add one quart of water, and let it boil until thoroughly dissolved. Reduce to half the quantity and strain and bottle for use. To make colored sugar, add a little coloring and mix thoroughly. Then dry in an oven, and keep in a jar.

### Vanilla Sugar.
#### Sucre à la Vanille.
2 Pounds of Loaf Sugar.
3 Vanilla Beans.

Take three vanilla beans and cut them into shreds. Let them dry, and then pound them with about two pounds of fine loaf sugar. When reduced to a very fine powder, sift, put in a jar and cork tight.

### Lemon Sugar.
#### Sucre au Citron.
The Zest of 3 Lemons.
1 Pound of Loaf Sugar.

Grate the zest or outer rinds of the lemons on pieces of loaf sugar, and then set to dry. When dry, pound very fine, sift, and put in a jar and cork tight. Orange Sugar is prepared in the same manner.

---

## CHAPTER XLVI.

## CANNING OR PICKLING.

#### Conservation des Substances Alimentaires et Végétales.

The best method of pickling, and the surest, is to put the substance to be pickled in a glass bottle or a tin can that has been hermetically sealed, and subject it to a temperature ranging from 80 to 100 degrees, in a water bath, or "bain-marie," always taking the previous precaution to eliminate all air from the vessel before sealing it.

The great success of canning and preserving is to exclude the air and to can while hot, filling thte vessel to the brim. Have your jars in a vessel of hot water on the stove. Roll them in the hot water, and then fill immediately to the top with the hot boiling fruit or vegetables. Have the tops of the jars ready and heated, and seal quickly, screwing down every few moments a little tighter, as the ingredients cool and the glass consequently contracts. Keep the jars in a cool, dark place.

Attention to a few rules will make it possible for each housekeeper, especially the Louisiana country housewife, to put up all her own goods, whether of vegetables or fruits or pickles.

### Canned Corn.
#### Du Maïs en Conserve.
8 Quarts of Corn.
1 Tablespoonful of Lard to Each Quart of Corn.

Boil the corn on the cob until no milk will exude if the grains are pricked with a needle. Then cut the corn off the cob, and pack into cans or stone jars, putting first a layer of salt half an inch deep, and then a layer of corn two inches deep, and continuing with these alternate layers until the jar is nearly filled. The top layer must be of salt, and about an inch thick. Pour over all this melted lard in proportion of about a tablespooful to a quart of the corn. Set on the fire, in a bain-marie, and let all the bubbles come to the surface. Take off, stick a silver fork down into the jar, to see that all bubbles have ceased to form. Seal hermetically, and then set in a bain-marie, at a temperature of from 80 to 100 degrees, and let it cool. Keep in a cool place, and use as wanted.

### Canned Tomatoes.
#### Des Tomates en Conserves.
8 Dozen Tomatoes.
A Bain Marie.

Pour boiling water over the Tomatoes to loosen the skins. Then skin the Tomatoes, and bring to a hard boil for twenty minutes. Then drain and can as quickly as possible, excluding all air. Set in a bain-marie to cool, and keep in a cool, dark place.

### Canned Mushrooms.
#### Des Champignons en Conserve.
8 Quarts of Mushrooms.

Cook the mushrooms for three-quarters of an hour in salted water, drain lightly and can them, excluding all air. Submit to the "bain-marie," letting them cool gradually. Keep in a cool place.

### Canned Green Peas.
#### Des Petits Pois en Conserve.
1 Dozen Quarts of Green Peas.

Select the youngest and most tender peas, put them in boiling water, and let them cook for about thirty minutes. Drain lightly, and can immediately, excluding all air.

Other vegetables may be canned in almost the same identical manner.

### PICKLES.
#### Des Cornichons.

Pickles should not be made in vessels of brass, copper or tin, and should always be put up in glass bottles or hard stoneware. Only the best vinegar should be used. All vinegar should be scalded before using with pickles, otherwise it will not keep well. This is a fact that must be remembered if you wish for success.

In sour pickles use only the best cider vinegar. Never boil it, but simply bring it to the boiling point, before you pour it over the pickles. Always add a small piece of alum to Cucumber or Gherkin Pickles, if you wish them to be a beautiful green and crisp.

Never use any but a wooden spoon in putting up pickles, and be careful in the use of spices, so that no one flavor will predominate, but that all will unite in a most agreeable whole.

Pickles must be kept in a cool, dark place, and always well-covered with vinegar.

The jars should be examined at frequent intervals. If white specks make their appearance in the vinegar, draw it off, scald and add, if the pickles are sweet, two tablespoonfuls of sugar and a few cloves.

### Sweet Pickles.
#### Cornichons Sucrés.
100 Small Cucumbers.
3 Dozen Black Peppers.
1 Dozen Allspice.
1 Dozen Blades of Mace.
3 Dozen Black Peppers.
3 Dozen Cloves.
1 Cup of Sugar.
1 Gallon of Boiling Vinegar.

Wash the Cucumbers, selecting nice small ones, of about a finger in length. Cover them with a strong brine, sufficiently strong to bear an egg. Put a cover on the jar, and let them stand for about three days. Then take them out and throw away the brine, rejecting all the pickles that have become soft under pressure. Put into a kettle of fresh water, and add a little powdered alum allowing about a quarter of a teaspoonful, or a piece about half the size of a bird's egg, to one gallon of liquid. Put a close lid over all the boiler, and steam, without letting them boil, for about four or five hours. To one hundred small cucumbers or a gallon, allow three dozen black peppers, one dozen blades of mace, three dozen cloves, one dozen allspice, all whole, and one cup of sugar. Boil five minutes. Place the pickles in clean jars, and pour over the boiling vinegar. These pickles must then be corked closely. Three days after take or draw off this vinegar, boil it again, and again pour over the pickles. Repeat this operation three times, at about intervals of three or four days. Then cover with a stout cloth, cork with a wooden or cork stopper, and in about two months they will be ready for use. Examine from time to time.

### Sour Pickles.
#### Cornichons au Vinaigre.
100 Small Cucumbers.
A Boiling Brine.
24 Whole Spices.
1 Ounce of Mustard Seed.
12 Small Red Peppers.
6 Blades of Mace.
8 Cloves.   2 Onions.

Take about 100 small Cucumbers, and place them in a jar. Cover them with boiling brine that will be strong enough to bear an egg. Let them stand for several days. Then take them out of the brine, wipe them well, and place them in clean jars. Add two dozen whole spices, one ounce of mustard seed, and six blades of mace, eight cloves, two chopped onions, and the red peppers. Cover them with boiling vinegar and cork. In several weeks they will be ready for use.

If you wish the pickles to be very green, put them into cold vinegar, and set on the stove, and let them heat slowly over a moderate fire till they are green; or, after the fourth day in which they have stood in the brine, pour this off, and take a porcelain-lined kettle, and line the bottom with fig and grapevine leaves, put the cucumbers in, with a small piece of alum, cover them closely with the vine leaves, and then pour cold water sufficient to almost fill the kettle. Cover closely with an inverted pan or a dish, and let them steam slowly for four or five hours, till they are green. When a beautiful green, take out of the kettle, drain, season as above, pour over boiling vinegar, boil for five minutes, and they will be ready to be bottled for future use.

### Home-Made Chow-Chow.

Variantes à la Moutarde.

1 Head of Cauliflower.
½ Head of Cabbage, Cut as for Slaw.
1 Quart of Tiny Cucumbers, the Very Smallest Kind.
1 Quart of Small Button Onions.
2 or 3 Pods of Green and Red Peppers, Chopped Fine.
½ Pound of French Mustard.
¼ Teacupful of Celery Seed.
1 Teacupful of Horseradish.
1 Whole Garlic, Minced Very Fine.
1 Pint of String Beans.
1 Gill of Salad Oil.
¾ Gallon of Vinegar.
2 Tablespoonfuls of Mustard Seed.
1 Cupful of Brown Sugar.
¼ Ounce of Tumeric.

Shred the cabbage as for cold slaw, and cover the bottom of a stone jar with the cucumbers and the cabbage. Then cover with a brine of salt and water strong enough to float an egg. Let them stand for twenty-four hours. At the end of that time boil the cauliflower, the onions and the beans in separate pots till tender. Then drain off all water. Mix them with the cucumbers and the cabbage. Put the vinegar into a porcelain-lined kettle, and let it come to a boil. Add the mustard seed, the celery seed, the grated horseradish, the minced garlic, and the pepper pods, cut fine. Let all boil for about five minutes, and stir constantly till it begins to thicken. Then add the sugar and make a paste of the Tumeric, the mustard and the salad oil, moistening with a little cold vinegar, and pour into the mixture. Stir well and pour while boiling hot over the vegetables. Put it away in stone jars, and in about ten days it will be ready for use.

### Mixed Pickles.

Variantes.

1 Head of Cauliflower.
½ Head of Cabbage, Cut as for Slaw.
1 Quart of Tiny Cucumbers, the Very Smallest Kind.
1 Quart of Small Button Onions.
2 or 3 Pods of Green and Red Peppers, Chopped Fine.
½ Pound of French Mustard.
½ teacupful of Celery Seed.
1 Teacupful of Grated Horseradish.
1 Whole Garlic, Minced Very Fine.
1 Pint of String Beans.
1 Gill of Salad Oil.
¾ Gallon of Vinegar.
2 Tablespoonfuls of Mustard Seed.
1 Cupful of Brown Sugar.
½ Ounce of Tumeric.

Take young cauliflower heads, small onions, peppers, cucumbers cut in dice, nasturtiums and string beans, in the proportions given above, and boil till tender. Drain very dry, and pack in wide-mouthed bottles. Boil in one pint of cider vinegar, one tablespoonful of sugar, half a teaspoonful of salt and two tablespoonfuls of mustard seed and spices. Pour over the pickles, mix well, and seal carefully.

### Pickled Cauliflower.

Choux-Fleurs Confits au Vinaigre.

3 Dozen Cauliflowers.
To Each Quart of Vinegar 2 Teaspoonfuls of Mustard and a Half Cup of White Sugar.

Boil the cauliflower for about twenty minutes in salt and water; then remove and drain, and break carefully, and let them get cold. Pack in a jar and pour over them hot Spiced Vinegar (see recipe), which you will have strained, having first stirred into each quart of vinegar two teaspoonfuls of French mustard and a half cup of white sugar. Cover the Cauliflower well with the mixture and bottle tight.

### Green Pepper Pickles.

Piments Verts Confits au Vinaigre.

2 Dozen Green Peppers.
1 Dozen Red Peppers.
½ Large Head of Cabbage.
3 Tablespoonfuls of Mustard Seed.
1 Teaspoonful of Ground Cloves.
1 Tablespoonful of Ground Allspice.
2 Tablespoonfuls of Salt.

Cut the tops from the peppers and remove the seeds. Then put a teaspoonful of salt into each pepper, cover with cold water, and soak for twenty-four hours. Chop the cabbage very fine, and mix well with the ground spices, mustard seed and salt. When thoroughly blended, stuff the peppers with this mixture. Then put on the tops, and stand upright in stone jars, and cover with cold vinegar. In handling the peppers use a napkin or gloves, as they will blister the hands.

### Green Tomato Pickles.
Tomates Verts Confites au Vinaigre.

1 Peck of Green Tomatoes.
1 Dozen Onions.   1 Ounce of Cloves.
1 Ounce of Mustard Seed.
1 Tablespoonful of White Mustard Seed.
1 Cupful of Salt.
½ Teaspoonful of Red Pepper, or the Pods Cut into Strips.
1 Ounce of Cloves.
1 Ounce of Black Pepper.

Slice the tomatoes and the onions. Then put a layer of tomatoes and a layer of onions, and sprinkle with salt, and continue till all are used up. Let them stand over night. In the morning drain off all the liquor that has cacumulated, and put the vegetables into a porcelain-lined pot with all the other ingredients, and cover with two quarts of vinegar. Let all simmer gently for a quarter of an hour, and then put away in stone jars, letting the vinegar cover the pickles, and boiling while hot.

This recipe is for Sour Green Tomato Pickles. The Sweet Green Tomato Pickles are made by adding one cup of sugar to the above ingredients.

### Pickled Mangoes.
Mangos Confits au Vinaigre.

24 Pepper Mangoes or Young Melon Mangoes or Muakmleons.
A Piece of Alum the Size of a Pecan.
½ Pound of Ginger.
½ Ounce Each of Black Pepper, Mace, Allspice, Tumeric.
¼ Pound of Garlic.
½ Pint of Grated Horseradish.
½ Pint Each of Black and White Mustard Seed.
½ Teacupful of the Best Olives.
¼ Head of Fine Young Cabbage.
4 Green Tomatoes.

Take two dozen Pepper Mangoes or young Muskmelons that are no larger than an orange. Let them lie for two weeks in a brine strong enough to float an egg. Then soak them in pure water for two days, changing the water every day. Remove the seed by cutting a slit down the side of the Mangoes, but do not take the meat out. Rinse in cold water. Put a layer of green grape leaves in a kettle, and lay on this a layer of Mangoes, and then a layer of leaves, and so continue till all are used up. Let the top layer be of grape leaves. Now add a piece of alum about the size of a pecan, and pour vinegar over the mixture, and let all boil for fifteen or twenty minutes. Then take out the leaves, and let the Mangoes remain in this vinegar for five or six days. Prepare a stuffing of half a pound of ginger, which has been soaked in brine for two days and which you will have cut into small dice; one-half on ounce each of black pepper, mace, allspice, Tumeric; one-quarter of a pound of garlic, which has been soaked in brine for twenty-four hours and dried; a half pint of grated horseradish, and a half pint each of black and white mustard seed. Bruise all the spices well till fine, and mix them with a half teacupful of the best olive oil. Take a half head of fine solid cabbage, and chop fine; add a half pint of finely-chopped onions, a few small cucumbers, and a few green tomatoes, which have lain in a brine overnight. Drain all well and then select any imperfectly shaped mangoes, or any that have become too soft to stuff, and chop these fine with the spices; mix all this stuffing well together, and stuff the mangoes. Tie them with pieces of twine, or sew them up, put in a stone jar, and pour over them the very best cider vinegar. Set them in a dry place and cover well. At the end of a month add a pound and a half of brown sugar, and bottle for use. This preparation will keep for two years.

### Pickled Onions.
Ognons au Vinaigre.

100 Small Onion Buttons.
1 Tablespoonful of Allspice.
1 Tablespoonful of Black Pepper and 1 Red Pepper Pod to Each Pint of Vinegar.
1 Dozen White Pepper Corns.
1 Dozen Cloves.
4 Blades of Mace.

Select the smallest white button onions. Remove the outer skin, and then remove the inner skin with a silver knife. Steel will blacken the onions. Pack them in well-washed and carefully dried jars. Then pour over the onions a strong brine, and let them stand for twenty-four hours. At the end of this time pour off this brine and add another, and let them stand twenty-four hours longer. On the fourth day make another strong brine, and let it come to a boil, and throw in the onions, and let them boil just five minutes. Then throw them into cold water for several hours. At the end of three hours drain off all water and pack closely in jars, allowing one tablespoonful of black pepper and a red pepper pod to every pint of vinegar. While packing the onions, intersperse them with white pepper corns and the spices, with an occasional piece of mace or cloves. Fill this up with the scalding vinegar, and cork or bottle while very hot.

If you desire the pickles to be slightly sweet, allow a tablespoonful of sugar to every pint of vinegar. After three weeks they will be ready.

for use, but, like all pickles, will be better if allowed to stand a month or two.

### Pickled String Beans.
Haricots Verts Confits.

To Every 7 Pounds of Beans Allow One Quart of Best Cider Vinegar.
1 Teaspoonful of Alum.
1 Ounce of Cloves.
6 Red Pepper Pods.

Take young tender beans, and cut the two extremities lightly, and string carefully. Throw them into fresh water for several hours. Wash well and drain, and put them into earthen jars. Pour over boiling vinegar, spiced as for Tomato Pickle, and allow one-quarter of a teaspoonful of powdered alum to each quart of vinegar. Cover and cork well. Three days after pour off this vinegar and boil again and pour over the pickles, and let them stand again for three days. Add a few cloves and pieces of red pepper pods, and bottle closely.

Young cauliflower, radishes, white and red; young corn and melons that have just begun to form may be pickled according to the above recipe.

### Pickled Watermelon Rind.
Ecorces de Melon d'Eau Confites au Vinaigre.

4 Pounds of Watermelon Rind.
½ Pint of Best French Vinegar.
1 Pound of Mrown Sugar.
1 Tablespoonful of Mixed Ground Cloves, Mace, Cinnamon and Allspice.

Cut the watermelon rind into strips, cook in clear water and drain. To four pounds of rind take one pound of brown sugar and half a pint of vinegar, and make a syrup, to which add the ground spices. Boil the watermelon rind in this syrup till quite tender. Put in jars while hot and seal. This is a sweet pickle.

### Pickled Fruits.
Fruits Confits au Vinaigre.

6 Pounds of Fruit.
3 Pounds of White Sugar.
1 Pint of Best Cider Vinegar.
1 Ounce Each of Cloves, Allspice, Mace and Cinnamon.
1 Nutmeg.

In pickling fruits, whether peaches, pears, plums, damsons or cherries, allow six pounds of fruit, three pounds of white sugar, and one pint of the best vinegar, and spices of mace, cinnamon, cloves, allspice and nutmeg in proportion. Put the fruit into a kettle with alternate layers of sugar and spices, and add the vinegar. Let all boil for about five minutes, and then skim out the fruit and pack in glass jars as it begins to cool. Let the syrup boil till thick, and then pour the boiling syrup over. Bottle tight, and examine from time to time. If they show signs of fermenting, open the jars or set them uncovered in a kettle of boiling water, and heat the contents till they begin to bubble and cork again.

In pickling cherries, always leave the stems on the cherries, and to every quart allow a pint of vinegar and two large teaspoonfuls of sugar, a dozen cloves and allspice, and five or six blades of mace. Let the vinegar and spices boil together for about five minutes, and then turn into an earthen jar and let them cool. Then strain and fill the pickle jars with the cherries about three-quarters full, and pour the cold vinegar over them. Bottle tight, and keep in a cool place.

Sweet Tomato Pickles are put up by using the ingredients mentioned above, allowing, however, a pint and a half of vinegar to the above quantities of sugar and fruit. Stew the tomatoes, vinegar and spices together for about three-quarters of an hour, and then bottle for use.

### Tomato Catsup.
Sauce de Tomates.

4 Pecks of Ripe Tomatoes.
2 Quarts of Vinegar.
¼ Pound of Salt.
¼ Pound of Sugar.
¾ Ounce of Black Pepper.
¾ Ounce of Allspice. 1 Ounce of Mustard.
1 Ounce of Ginger, Ground.
One-third Ounce of Cloves, Ground.
1-8 Ounce of Garlic, Minced Very Fine.
A Good Dash of Cayenne.
½ Pint of Alcohol.

Set the tomatoes to boil in a porcelain-lined pot, and, after half an hour, press them through a sieve, to remove all the seeds and skin. Then return the liquid obtained to the pot, and let it reduce to three-quarters. Now add the vinegar, and let all reduce to about one and a quarter quarts. Mix thoroughly, and add the spices, garlic, ground mustard, pepper, etc., and let all come to a boil, stirring continually. Then take from the fire, and add the alcohol. Bottle while the mixture is very hot, and seal well. This is an excellent recipe, and the above sauce is very good, served with cold boiled fish, oysters, etc. The Creoles often add a half bottle of Port Wine, instead of the vinegar.

### Chervil Vinegar.
Vinaigre au Cerfeuil.

1 Pint of Dried or Fresh Chervil Leaves.
1 Quart of Best French Vinegar.

Hake a wide-mouthed bottle, and half fill it with either fresh or dry Chervil leaves. Fill the bottle with the best vinegar, and set it in hot water till it reaches the boiling point. Then remove from the fire. When cool cork and in about two weeks it will be ready for use. The Creoles use this vinegar to add a flavoring to sauces for salads.

### Pepper Vinegar.
#### Vinaigre Pimenté.

½ Pint of Small Cherry or Chili Peppers.
½ Pint of Best French Vinegar.

Every Creole housewife keeps on hand a bottle of Pepper Vinegar. It is made by filling a pint bottle about half full of small Cherry Peppers or Chili Peppers, red and green, and then filling up with the best French vinegar or cider. Bottle well, and in about a week it will be ready for use. A peculiarity about this Pepper Vinegar is that the bottle may be filled again and again as it diminishes, without adding new peppers. It is very strong and hot, and a few drops in one's soup or salad will be found quite sufficient.

### Tarragon Vinegar.
#### Vinaigre à l'Estragon.

½ Pint of Tarragon Leaves.
1 Quart of Best Cider or White Wine.

The best French vinegar is made from the Tarragon leaves. The French gather the leaves and expose them to the heat of the sun for several days. Then they throw them into the best Cider or White Wine and steep for about two weeks. The liquor is then carefully strained, a flannel bag being generally used, and it is afterwards bottled, corked and sealed, and kept in a cool place for exportation.

Tarragon Vinegar may also be made by purchasing Tarragon leaves from any druggist, and allowing a half pint of the leaves to a quart bottle filled with the best Cider or White Wine, and follow the directions given above.

### Spiced Vinegar.
#### Vinaigre Aromatisé.

1 Pound of Sugar.
1½ Gallons of the Best Cider or White Wine.
1 Ounce Each of Cloves, Allspice, Mace, Celery and Mustard Seed.
1 1-3 Ounces Each of Black Pepper, Tumeric and White Ginger.

Mix all the spices together with the vinegar and the bits of ginger, and place in an earthen jar and cover closely.

For smaller proportions take one quart of cider vinegar, and put it into one-third of an ounce each of dried mint, dried parsley, one grated garlic, two small onions, two cloves, one teaspoonful of pepper, corns of grated nutmeg, salt to taste, and one tablespoonful of sugar and good Brandy. Put all into a jar, and let it stand for three weeks; then strain and bottle.

### Tabasco.
#### Tabasco à la Créole.

3 Dozen Large Red Peppers.
1 Clove of Garlic.
¼ Pint of Hot Spiced Vinegar.

This is one of the most famous of our Creole sauces. It is made from celebrated Louisiana Tabasco Peppers, whose flavor is unsurpassed. The hot peppers are much sought after. The following method of preparing this famous Sauce à la Créole is the one used in all the ancient Creole homes of Louisiana. Take three dozen large red Tabasco peppers or Chili peppers, and one clove of garlic, chopped very fine, and scald them until very tender. Then mash the peppers and garlic together, and press them through a sieve. Take the paste thus formed and dilute it with spiced vinegar till it reaches the consistency of rich cream. Bottle and seal for use. The garlic may be omitted.

### Red Pepper Catsup à la Créole.
#### Sauce de Poivre Rouge à la Créole.

4 Dozen Pepper Pods.
2 Quarts of Best French Vinegar.
3 Tablespoonfuls of Grated Horseradish.
5 Onions.  1 Garlic.

Take four dozen pods of ripe green peppers, two quarts of vinegar, one of water, three tablespoonfuls of grated horseradish, five onions, sliced, and one garlic. Boil all together till the onions are very soft. Then mash all together to a paste and strain, rubbing through the sieve till nothing remains but the seeds and skins. When cold, bottle and cork tightly for use.

### Maunsell-White.

This is a famous Creole preparation, and it bears the name of the family that originated it. In Maunsell-White the infusion of Cayenne is so hot that only a few drops suffice, but the taste is most pungent and stimulation to the palate, and is especially agreeable when eating oysters with Oyster Bread, or "Hard Tack."

### Creole Mustard.
#### Moutarde Creole.

1 Pound of Creole Mustard.
1 Pint of White Wine.
1 Teaspoonful of Ground Cloves.
1 Tablespoonful of Celery Seed.
1 Tablespoonful of Ground Allspice.
2 Blades of Ground Mace.
1 Clove of Garlic.
1 Teaspoonful of Salt.

Put a pint of white wine into a clean saucepan, add the mixed ground spice, crushed clove of garlic, celery seeds and salt. Steep on the rear part of the stove for one hour. Mix the mustard, ground to a flour, into a smooth paste, with equal parts of cider and Tarragon Vinegar. Strain out the spices from the wine and add to the paste while boiling hot. Mix thoroughly and bottle for use.

### Salted Almonds.

Amandes Salées.

1 Pint of Almonds.
1 Tablespoonful of Salt.

Take about a pint of almonds, shell them, and then blanch or scald them in boiling water till the skin comes off easily. Dry well, and place in a flat tin dish; add about an ounce of butter, and set the plate in a moderate oven until the almonds are a golden brown. Then take them out of the oven, add a heaping tablespoonful of salt, stir them round and round, or according to the way in which the almonds pick up the salt, dredging quickly with the salt, and turn them into a dish to cool. Pick out the almonds, and throw aside the extra salt. When cool, place in a box for use, covering tightly. The salt may be added, when the almonds are first put in the oven. Be careful to turn frequently while they are in the oven, so that they may be equally browned on all sides. Almonds prepared after this manner are delicious.

Another way to prepare Salted Almonds is to take the whole blanched almonds and put them on a baking sheet, and roast in a hot oven to a slight brown. Then make a solution of Gum Arabic and water and wet the almonds with it. Dust over them very finely powdered and sifted table salt, and stir well but gently till dry.

### Salted Peanuts.

Des Pistaches Salées.

1 Pint of Whole Peanuts.
1 Tablespoonful of Salt.

Take blanched whole peanuts, and proceed in exactly the same manner as in the last recipe given for Salted Almonds.

---

## CHAPTER XLVII.

### CREOLE BREADS.

Des Pains à la Créole.

Perhaps no branch of Creole cookery so interests visitors to New Orleans as our Creole Breads. While in breakfast relishes, such as batter cakes, flannel cakes, waffles, buckwheat cakes, biscuit, etc., we have much in common with other sections, there is a distinctiveness about our "Brioches," "Babas," "Calas," "Sacamités," "Sweet Potato Bread," French Loaves, French Rolls, etc., which are peculiar to ourselves alone. Our "Baker's Bread," or "Pain de Boulanger," of itself stands unique among the breads of the United States, and has been the subject of more than one interesting newspaper and magazine article. It has this peculiarity, that one never tires if it, as they do of other breads, and the reason for this is that it is of exquisite lightness, white and tender, of an even porous character, with a thin, crisp crust, and, best of all, is just such a bread as is required in our climate. Made into toasts, it is the most delightful of all breads, no home-made light bread or bakers' bread in any other part of the United States standing comparison with it. Bakers' Bread is the daily offering, morning, noon and night, on every New Orleans table.

Our "Calas" are famous, and have been treated on under the chapter on Louisiana Rice, while our "Brioches" are not only the joy of the natives, but the delight of visitors from all parts of the country. A cup of Café Noir in the French Market and a Brioche is one of the standing treats to which every visitor to New Orleans is invited.

**How to Make and Bake Bread.**

Bread, to be perfect, should be light and sweet, with a rich, nutty flavor of the wheat. To obtain this result, only the best flour and the best dough must be used. While the bread is rising the temperature of the oven should be at about 75 degrees Fahrenheit, and the heat of the oven in baking should be about 360 degrees, or hot enough to raise the inside of the bread to about 220 degrees. This is necessary to cook the starch, expand the carbonic gas, steam and air, and also to drive off the alcohol which is used in the yeast. The bakers in New Orleans have a way of testing the temperature of the oven by putting a piece of white paper in it. If it turns dark in five minutes the oven is of the right temperature. If it burns, the oven is too hot, and must be cooled before putting the bread in, and if the paper is only a light brown at the end of five minutes, the oven must be made hotter. Again, they sprinkle flour and if it browns or smokes before you can count ten, the oven is too hot; if it browns at ten, the oven is of the right temperature.

Brick ovens are used, and the loaves of bread are shoved into the oven generally on baking boards.

Rolls are always baked first; then the bread, and afterwards the pies and cakes. It is best to have the oven heated in time and close for one hour at least before beginning to bake.

Bread should be in the oven about ten minutes before it begins to brown. When done, remove carefully from the pan, and tip it against a bread board, just as they do in New Orleans bakeries. This allows the air to circulate freely around it. Never cover bread that has been freshly baked, if you wish it to be fresh and sweet and crisp. When cool, place in a clean bread box, without using a "bread bag," as is so common among many families. This bag absorbs the moisture from the bread, and causes it to sour quickly.

The New Orleans bakers always use Compressed Yeast for leavening bread, as it does not necessitate making a ferment or setting sponge before mixing the dough.

### Bakers' Bread.
Pain de Boulanger.

1 Ounce of Compressed Yeast.
1½ Ounces of Salt.
2 Quarts of Water.

Flour Sufficient to Make a Smooth Dough.

Allow one ounce of Compressed Yeast to one quart of lukewarm water, and mix well in a wooden bread trough. Then add flour enough to make a nice smooth dough of medium degree, not too stiff, nor yet too soft. Work it well, and then let it stand for about five hours in a warm place so as to rise well. When it drops, or begins to fall (you can tell this by watching the sides of the dough), add the same amount of water that was used in making the dough, putting two teaspoonfuls of salt into the water before adding it. Work this well, and then throw down on the table, cut and mold the dough into loaves of whatever length is desired, and take a smooth stick and press lightly down across the loaf about two inches from the edge. The bakers put the loaves into the oven without setting in a pan. Watch carefully, and see that the oven is of the temperature mentioned above. By following these directions, you will have nice, fresh, sweet New Orleans Bakers' Bread.

The above quantity will make about five loaves.

### French Bread.
Pain Français.

1 Ounce of Yeast.
1½ Ounces of Salt.
2 Quarts of Water.
1½ Ounces of Sugar.

Flour Sufficient to Make a Smooth Dough.

Dissolve the yeast, salt and sugar into the water and mix in flour sufficient to make a nice smooth dough of medium degree, not too stiff, nor yet too soft. Work until it no longer adheres to the hand or bowl, and then cover with a cloth and set to rinse until it has doubled its size. This will be in about four or five hours. When it begins to sink, work it well again and set to rise anew. When well risen divide the dough into equal pieces, and mold into round ball shapes, or into long loaves of about two inches in thickness. Lay the loaves on a board previously sprinkled with flour and at sufficient distance apart not to touch one another, and set to rise again. Let them rise to nearly double the previous size. Have the oven heated, transfer the loaves into it, wash over with eggs mixed with water, make diagonal cuts half way across on each loaf, half way through, and close the oven. When baked, brush off the flour, wipe the tops with a damp cloth and the bread is ready to serve.

### Pan Bread.
Pain de Plaque.

1 Ounce of Compressed Yeast.
¼ Pound of Lard.
2 Quarts of Water.
1½ Ounces of Salt.

Flour Sufficient to Make a Smooth Dough.
1½ Ounces of Sugar, if Desired.

This is a nice, large-loafed bread, with a dainty crust, that is somewhat glutinous, and, as the name indicates, is baked in a pan by our bakers. It is remarkable for the daintiness of grain of the bread after baking. Make the same dough as for Bakers' Bread, only work the loaves twice over; then put them in the oven and dredge lightly with flour. As they begin to rise make a light paste of flour and water or egg and water and spread very lightly over them. This is brushed lightly with lard, to keep from getting too crusty. Bake in a rather hotter oven than the other bread.

### French Loaves.
#### Des Petits Pains Francais.

1 Ounce of Compressed Yeast.
2 Quarts of Water.
1½ Ounces of Salt.
Flour Sufficient to Make a Smooth Dough.

These are the dainty little loaves so generally used in our New Orleans restaurants and hotels. Make the dough as in Bakers' Bread, and after it has risen and begins to drop, scale the dough off, and cut and mold them into little loaves of about the length of a man's hand. Mold them round and set them to rise again. When they are very light, which will be in a few minutes, take them up and work them well separately, and then mold them again and gently press in the center with a smooth stick. Lay them in a box with a stiff cloth over them, and let them lie for a few minutes. Take off the cloth and set them in the oven to brown nicely. Set to cool as above indicated.

### Twist Loaves.
#### Pain Tresse.

1 Ounce of Compressed Yeast.
2 Quarts of aWter.
1½ Ounces of Salt.
Flour Sufficient to Make a Smooth Dough.

Make the identical dough as in "Bakers' Bread." After the first rising and throwing in of water and working the bread, cut the dough, and divide each portion into three pieces of dough. Dust this dough well with parched flour and roll the pieces into lengths of about two feet, or a foot and a half, and plait them. Then lay them in a long box or on a board, and cover with a stiff cloth, as in French Loaves, and let them lie till they begin to rise. Place in the oven and bake to a nice brown.

### Rye Bread.
#### Pain de Seigle.

1 Ounce of Compressed Yeast.
2 Quarts of aWter.
1½ Ounces of Salt.
Rye and Flour Sufficient to Make a Smooth Dough.
A Few Kummel Seed.

Make the dough a little stiffer than for White Bread, allowing one-half of wheat flour and one-half rye. Allow the same amount of yeast, and add a few Kummel seeds and a little more salt than for White Bread. Set to rise. After one rising, work again as in Bakers' Bread, divide it into loaves, and set it to rise again. When about twice its original size, bake in a moderate oven.

### Home-Made Creole Light Bread.
#### Pain de Ménage à la Créole.

2 Quarts of Flour.
½ Cake of Compressed Yeast.
1½ Pints of Milk or Water.
Teaspoonful of Salt.
1 Tablespoonful of Lard.

Sift the flour. Then put into a wooden bread trough or a pan, and make a hole in the center of the flour. Add warm water or milk sufficient to make a nice, smooth, rather stiff batter. Mix the yeast with a little tepid water till well-dissolved, and add. Then set to rise over night in a warm place. In the morning take up and again make a hole in the center of the dough, and add half a tablespoonful of melted lard or butter, one and one-half teaspoonfuls of salt, and one and one-half pints of warm milk or water. Then add the flour and knead well about ten times. When it forms a smooth dough, form into a cake, and set to rise again. When risen to about twice its size, take it up and knead again about five times, that is, work one piece of dough over the other about five times, and set to rise again. Always, when setting to rise, sprinkle the bottom of the pan with a little flour. After an hour, take up the bread and knead for about ten minutes, till you have a nice dough, that can be worked without sprinkling the biscuit board with flour. Then form the dough into two loaves. Place them side by side in the baking pan, and bake in a moderate oven for about three-quarters of an hour. Serve hot or cold.

### Milk Bread.
#### Pain au Lait.

2 Quarts of Flour.
½ Teacupful of Yeast or ½ Cake of Compressed Yeast.
1 Pint of Fresh Milk.
1 Teaspoonful of Salt.
2 Ounces of Butter.

Scald the milk, and then turn it into the bread trough or pan. Add immediately the butter and the salt. When it becomes tepid add the yeast and about three-quarters of a pint or half a pint of flour, using always good judgment in adding sufficient, more or less, to make a thick batter. Then beat thoroughly till air bubbles accumulate all over the surface of the batter. Then cover and set in a warm place over night. Very early in the morning work in the rest of the flour, and take it out of the pan and put on a board and knead quickly and lightly until the dough is perfectly smooth and does not cling to the hands or the board. Then put it back in the trough or pan and cover with a cloth, and set to rise again in a warm place. When it has increased to twice its bulk, turn again upon the board, and then divide the dough into two parts. Mold these lightly and gently into small loaves, and stand away to rise for about half an hour. Then set in the oven, which should be moderately quick, and bake for three-quarters of an hour.

The famous Vienna Bread, now so much sought after, is nothing else than this ancient Milk Bread, or Creole "Pain au Lait," that has been used for generations in Creole homes.

### Buttermilk Bread.
Pain au Babeurre.

1 Quart of Flour.
1 Pint of Buttermilk.
1 Dessertspoonful of Soda.
1 Tablespoonful of Butter.
¼ Pound of Powdered Sugar.
1 Teaspoonful of Salt.

Warm the milk, add the sugar, butter and soda, the latter dissolved in a little warm water. Then add the flour and set to rise. When well risen knead lightly, place in a baking pan, let it rise again for half an hour, and bake in a moderate oven. This makes an excellent, nutritious and very white bread, and is much used by the Creoles in making French Toasts.

Buttermilk Rolls are made by simply pinching off the above dough into pieces about the size of a walnut or egg, shaping into little balls, and proceeding as above.

### Rice Bread.
Pain de Riz.

1 Cup of Cold Boiled Rice.
2 Cups of White Indian Meal. 2 Eggs.
1 Tablespoonful of Melted Butter.
2 Heaping Teaspoonfuls of Baking Powder.
1¼ Pints of Milk.
1 Teaspoonful of Salt.

Beat the yolks and whites of the eggs together until very light, and then pour in the milk, mixing gradually. Add the well-prepared meal, into which you will have mixed the salt and Baking Powder. Beat well. Then add the melted butter and the rice, which you will have pressed through a sieve. Mix all thoroughly, and beat till very light. Then grease the bottom of a shallow pan and turn the mixture in and bake half an hour in a hot oven. Serve hot, buttering the slices freely. This is a delicious breakfast bread, and, as in any of the above recipes, cold rice left over may be utilized in its making.

### Sweet Potato Bread.
Pain de Patates.

1 Quart of Mashed Sweet Potatoes.
1½ Pints of Flour.
1 Pint of Milk or Warm Water.
2 Tablespoonfuls of Butter.
1 Teaspoonful of Salt.
½ Teacup of Fresh Yeast, or Half a Cake of Compressed Yeast.

This is a delicious Creole Bread. The potatoes must be baked, peeled and mashed. Put the milk, or water, and the yeast and salt into a bowl or pan; add the butter, which must be melted. Beat thoroughly, and set over night in a warm place. In the morning add the potatoes, mashed and pressed through a sieve, and gradually add the flour, which must be sifted three times. Beat to a light sponge; then cover, and set to rise in a warm place till it doubles its size. Then turn out on a bread board and mold into loaves; put in a slightly greased pan and let rise till light. Then bake in a moderate oven 45 minutes.

### ROLLS.
Bourrelet.

1 Quart of Milk.
1 Quart of Water.
¾ Ounce of Yeast.
1 Teaspoonful of Salt.
¼ Pound of Lard.
1 Tablespoonful of Sugar (if desired.)

Dissolve the sugar (if desired), the yeast and salt, with the milk and the water. Then add flour sufficient to make a nice dough of medium firmness. Add the lard, and work the dough until smooth. Then form into a round mass and set to rise. When the dough has doubled it size, work anew and mold into small round balls and set into greased baking pans at a little distance apart from one another. Set to rise again and when they have doubled their size bake in a brisk oven.

### French Rolls.
Bourrelets à la Française.

1½ Pints of Fresh Milk.
2 Quarts of White Flour. 2 Eggs.
2 Ounces of Butter.
- Teaspoonful of Salt.
1 Teaspoonful of Sugar (which may be omitted, according to taste).
¾ Cake of Compressed Yeast, Dissolved in Warm Water.

Boil the milk, take off the stove, and add the butter, sugar and salt. Then add the well-beaten eggs. Stir in about one and a half pounds of flour, more or less, to make a stiff batter, and beat till air bubbles accumulate all over the surface. Then cover with a close cloth and set to rise oven night in a warm place. Then take up the dough and knead lightly with the remaining flour to make a nice, soft dough, and shape with your hands into nice, small rolls or balls. Set them together in the baking pan, which you will have lightly sprinkled with flour. Then set to rise for an hour longer. Set in the oven, and bake about a half hour. These rolls are delicious for breakfast, or for luncheon or supper. They may be set to rise in the early morning, and served hot at luncheon.

### Tea Rolls.
Bourrelets pour le Thé.

1 Quart of Flour.
1 Pint of Milk.
½ Cake of Compressed Yeast.
1 Teaspoonful of Salt.
1 Gill of Warm Water.

Sift the flour and salt together. Scald the milk, and when tepid add the yeast, dissolved in a little warm water, to one-half of the milk. Add one-half of the flour, and make a thin batter, stirring very smooth. Set it to rise in a warm place, and at the end of three hours make it into a dough with the remainder of the milk and flour, and knead well till the dough no longer adheres to the board or to your hands. Then shape it with your hands into small balls, set to rise for a half hour longer, or an hour, and bake in a moderate oven for a half hour.

### RUSKS.
Echaudés Secs.

1 Pint of Warm Milk.
½ Cup of Butter.
1 Cup of Sugar.   2 Eggs.
1 Teaspoonful of Salt.
1 Cake of Compressed Yeast.
Flour Sufficient to Make a Batter.

Dissolve the yeast in the warm milk, and then add flour sufficient to make a thin batter. Set to rise over night. In the morning beat the sugar and the butter to a cream, and add the eggs, well beaten. Add these to the batter, beat well, add the salt, and sufficient flour to make a soft dough. Then mold the dough into balls with your hands, or into small loaves. Set to rise until they have reached about twice their bulk. Then place in the oven and bake for thirty minutes. If sweet rusks are not desired, omit the sugar.

### TOAST.
Pain Roti.

6 Slices of Bread.
Butter to Taste.

Slice the bread, neither too thick nor too thin. Cut off the rough edges of the crust. Hold on a fork before burning coals till nicely toasted on one side. Then turn on the other, and proceed as before. If dry toast is desired, the bread is not buttered. If buttered toast, butter nicely, set in the oven a second and send to the table hot.

Some cooks toast bread by simply setting the slices in the oven and letting them brown on either side. But there is no comparison in lightness to the toast prepared in the above old-fashioned way.

### Cream or Milk Toast.
Rotis à la Crème ou au Lait.

6 Slices of Bread.
1 Pint of Hot Cream or Milk.
1 Tablespoonful of Butter.

Toast the bread nicely, and butter well on both sides. Lay in a dish, and pour over hot milk. Serve hot.

Or, heat one pint of Cream, add one large tablespoonful of butter, and pour over the hot toast. Slightly stale bread may be utilized in this way.

Soda crackers may be toasted and served in the same way. This is a great supper dish among the Creole plantation homes of Louisiana.

### Lost Bread or Egg Toast.
Pain Perdu.

5 Eggs.
2 Tablespoonfuls of Orange Flower Water.
½ Cup of Sugar.
Slices of Stale Bread.
The Finely-Grated Zest of a Lemon.
3 Tablespoonfuls of Brandy (if desired).

The Creoles utilize left-over stale bread in that delightful breakfast relish known as "Pain Perdu." Break the eggs into a bowl, beat them till very light, add the Orange Flower Water and the Brandy, if desired, and then add the sugar, and beat thoroughly. Add the grated zest of a lemon, mix well, and then cut the bread into slices or round pieces, taking off the crust, or still again into diamond shapes, and soak them well for a half hour in the mixture. Have ready a frying pan of boiling lard (see General Directions for Frying), lay in the bread, and fry to a golden brown. Lift the slices out with a skimmer, and drain on brown paper in the mouth of the oven. Then place on a hot dish, sprinkle with powdered sugar, as you would fritters, add a little grated nutmeg, if desired, and serve hot.

### Spanish Toast.
Rotis à l'Espagnole.

1 Egg.   1 Cup of Milk.
1 Gill of Brandy or Rum (if desired).
3 Tablespoonfuls of Powdered Sugar.
½ Ounce Each of Powdered Nutmeg and Cinnamon.
6 Slices of Stale Bread.
Lard for Frying.

Beat the egg and sugar well, and add the milk and the rum or brandy, if desired. Have ready the slices of stale bread, cut in diamond shapes or square, and let them soak for about a half hour in the mixture. Then lay into a pan of boiling lard, and fry to a golden brown. Skim out and drain on brown paper in the mouth of the oven, and place on a hot dish. Sprinkle with powdered sugar and grated cinnamon and nutmeg, and serve with milk or cream.

### BRIOCHES.

2 Pounds of the Best Flour.
½ Ounce of Yeast.
1 Cup of Sugar.
½ Ounce of Salt.
1 Pound of the Best Butter.
12 or 8 Eggs.

Under the name of "Brioche" is known the dainty "Roll Cake Bread" that is sold by all New Orleans bakers; that is brought to your door in the early morning by the "Bread Man," and which forms such a delightful accompaniment to the morning cup of Café Noir, whether in the exclusive homes of the old French Quarter, or at the world-famed coffee stands in the French Market.

To make "Brioches," take a pound and a half of the best quality of flour, and put it in a wooden bread trough. Make a hole in the center of the flour, and put in a half ounce of yeast, dissolved in a little warm water. Take milk or tepid water to make the dough, using milk if you want it to be very rich and delicate, and water if you have not the milk. Knead and mix the flour with one hand, while adding the milk or water with the other. Make a dough that is neither too stiff nor too soft, and when perfectly smooth set the dough to rise in a moderately warm place, covering with a cloth. Remember that if you use milk to make the dough, the milk must be scalded, that is, it must be heated to the boiling point and then allowed to grow tepid. Let the dough rise for five or six hours, and when increased to twice its bulk, take it and add the reserved half pound of flour, into which you will have sifted the salt. Add six eggs, beaten very light, with the sugar and butter, and mix all well together, kneading lightly with your hands, and adding more eggs if the dough is a little stiff. Then knead the dough by turning it over on itself three times, and set to rise again for an hour or three-quarters of an hour. Cover with a cloth. At the end of this time take it up and work again lightly, and then form into "Brioches," that is, work the dough gently with your hands, and then break it into pieces about the size of an egg. Pat these gently, forming them into neat rolls, a little flattened, and then make one roll about twice the size of the others. This roll will form the head of the Brioche. Have ready a baking pan with a buttered sheet of paper in it, and set the central roll in the middle. Arrange around the other rolls, having at least six or eight, to form a perfect-looking cake. Cover the pan with a clean, stiff cloth, and set the cake to rise for an hour longer. When well risen, set in an oven a few degrees cooler than that used for baking Bread. If the rolls are large, let them bake an hour and a half; if medium, one hour, and if very small, a half hour. Some bakers and cooks glace the Brioche lightly with a beaten egg, which is spread lightly over the top, before placing in the oven. This gives the rich, glossy surface so often seen on the Brioche Again, if you cannot afford butter, use lard, or half butter and lard, but the Brioche made with butter and milk is the most delicate and refined, and the true Creole Brioche, peculiar to New Orleans. After the Brioches are baked, set them to cool, if you do not wish to eat them hot. When serving, whether hot or cold, sprinkle lightly with powdered white sugar.

### BABA.

2 Pounds of the Best Flour.
½ Ounce of Yeast.
1 Cup of Sugar.
½ Ounce of Salt.
1 Pound of the Best Butter.
12 or 14 Eggs.
½ Pound of Seeded Raisins.
½ Pound of Currants.
½ Glass of Sweetened Water.
A Tinge of Saffron.

The dough for the "Baba" is exactly the same as that for the Brioche. Proceed in exactly the same manner, only at the moment of adding the reserved flour to the leavened add a half pound of raisins seeded, and a half pound of currants, washed, picked and dried. Add also a half glass of sweetened, tepid water, in which you will have put a little saffron. Be careful to keep this dough much softer than that for the Brioche, adding more eggs, if necessary, to insure the proper degree of consistency. The dough must rise at least six or seven hours. When it has increased to twice its volume, after the third rising, cook as you would the Brioche, in an oven a few degrees cooler than that used in baking Bread. The "Baba" is made into a round cake, just like a Pound Cake or Sponge Cake, and is formed into this round shape with the hands. After baking let cool and sprinkle with powdered white sugar. This is the cake that the Creole bakers of New Orleans send as a "Christmas" or "New Year's Offering" to their customers.

The German bakers of New Orleans took up the custom, and make the "Baba" by adding to the raisins and currants a little Aniseed, instead of the Saffron.

### BULLFROGS.
Grenouilles.

½ Pound to the Best Flour.
½ Ounce of Yeast.
¼ Cup of Sugar.   ½ Ounce of Salt.
1 Pound of the Best Butter.
12 or 8 Eggs.

Under this amusing name are sold the delicious small rolls, so dainty and fine, and which are served in all our Creole homes and restaurants. The rolls are joined together lightly in long rows of about eight inches in length and three in width. They are brought to the doors by the bakers every morning in this old French city. The dough for "Bullfrogs" is just the same as that for the Brioche, only a half pound of flour is used, instead of a pound, and a cup of butter. Bake in the same manner. They are delightful accompaniments to the most recherché breakfast.

### CHEESE CAKES.
Talmouses.

¼ Pound of Flour.
1 Glass of Water.
A Pinch of Salt.
2 Tablespoonfuls of Flour.
6 Eggs.   2 Cream Cheeses.
A Brioche or Plain Paste (see Recipe Plain Paste.)

Put the butter in a saucepan, and add the water and the salt. Let all come to a boil, stirring constantly. Then take from the fire and add the eggs, beaten well, and the cream cheese. Mix all well. Then take small molds or tins and line with the Plain Paste, or Brioche Paste, rolled very thin. Place within the preparation of cream cheese in quantity equal to an egg in size. Then cover the cakes with a piece of rolled dough, and bake in a slow oven. These are delicious breakfast cakes, and much in vogue in ancient Creole homes.

### PEILLARO.

2 Pounds of Flour.
1 Pound of Butter, or Half Butter and Lard
12 Eggs.   ½ Ounce of Yeast.
1 Gill of Brandy.
1 Tablespoonful of Orange Flower Water.
Milk or Tepid Water to Form a Dough.
1 Pound of Figs or Stoned Cherries.

Make the same dough as for the Brioche. At the moment of adding the leavened flour and the reserved flour, add the stoned cherries or peeled figs, the latter cut in halves. Then proceed as for "Brioches," and at the last kneading add the orange flower water and the brandy. Bake as you would the "Brioche."

### WINE CAKE.
Savarin.

2 Pounds of the Best Flour.
½ Ounce of Yeast.
1 Cup of Sugar.
½ Ounce of Salt.
1 Pound of the Best Butter.
12 or 8 Eggs.

Make the same dough as for the "Brioche," and at the last kneading place it in a cake pan lined with a buttered paper. Set it to rise for an hour longer. Then place it in the oven, and brush over lightly with a beaten egg. Let it bake for about an hour and a half, according to the size, and then take from the oven and soak in a syrup made of one pound of sugar and a pint of water, and boiled to a syrup, and into which you will add a wineglass of brandy or Jamaica rum.

These delicious cakes may be formed into small cakes, like the "Brioche," only they must not be joined together around a central cake. But the "Savarin" is nearly always baked in small cake tins.

### BISCUIT.
Des Biscuits.

1 Quart of Flour.
1 Heaping Teaspoonful of Lard.
1 Teaspoonful of Salt.
2 Teaspoonfuls of Yeast Powder.
1 Pint of Water or Sweet Milk.

Sift the flour well, and add the salt and yeast powder, rubbing in thoroughly with your hands. Then rub in the lard, rubbing the flour between your hands till every portion is permeated by the lard, and there are no lumps. Gradually add water or milk, using about a pint, more or less, mixing in with your hands. Then knead the dough until smooth and elastic. Form into molds, and lay on the biscuit board, and roll out till about a quarter of an inch in thickness. Cut into round cakes with the biscuit cutter. Stick lightly with a fork here and there over the surface, and bake in a quick oven for about five or six minutes. By adding four or five eggs, and, instead of the lard, one tablespoonful of butter, to the above, you will have egg biscuit.

### Beaten Biscuit.
Biscuit Battu.

This is a great Southern biscuit, and is much affected by the ancient Creoles. Take

1 Quart of Flour.
1 Teaspoonful of Salt.
1 Heaping Teaspoonful of Lard.
1 Pint of Milk or Water, or Half and Half.

Sift the flour and add the salt, mixing thoroughly. Then add the lard, and blend by rubbing through the hands till not a lump remains in the flour. Now add gradually the water or milk, or the milk and water combined, using half and half of each, and knead all the whole till the dough, which must not be too soft, but rather stiff, is formed. Then lay the dough on a biscuit board on a block, and beat for a half hour with a rolling pin. Knead lightly, and beat again for a full ten minutes, till from every portion of the surface and sides the air bubbles or "blisters" form. Then roll out and cut into round biscuits with the cutter, or square ones with a knife, and stick here and there with a fork. Bake in a moderate oven for about ten or fifteen minutes, till a delicate brown above and below.

These biscuits are delicious and are much liked by delicate people. The biscuit should be white as snow within. The sides should be slightly cracked. It was the pride of the ancient Creole cooks as to how long they could beat these biscuits without growing tired. The steady "beat-beat" would gently echo through the olden manors from the kitchen in the rear, and every one knew what to expect when Tante Zizi came in smiling with her beautiful biscuit, that had risen fresh, sweet and light without yeast powder or soda.

### Stewed Biscuits.

Biscuits Sautes.

6 Left-Over Biscuits.
½ Pound of Butter.
1½ Pints of Milk.

Left-over biscuits may be thus utilized. Take a porcelain-lined saucepan, cut the biscuit in halves, lay in the bottom of the saucepan, place a layer of butter over this, and then a layer of biscuit, and so on till all are used up. Pour milk over the whole, let it come to a boil, and serve hot.

### Soda and Milk Biscuit.

Biscuit au Lait et à la Soude.

1 Quart of Flour.
1 Heaping Teaspoonful of Lard.
2 Cups of Sour Milk.
½ Teaspoonful of Soda.
1 Teaspoonful of Salt.

Sift the flour and add the salt and lard, rubbing them in thoroughly with your hands, as above indicated. Then dissolve the soda in a little warm water and add to the milk, and work rapidly and lightly. Then lay on a biscuit board or a block of wood, and beat till the surface of the dough is full of air bubbles, or "blisters," as the old Creole cooks call them. Roll the dough out to about a quarter of an inch in thickness, cut into round biscuits with a biscuit cutter, or square ones with a knife. Stick here and there over the surface with a fork, and bake for about six minutes in a quick oven. If too much is used, it not only imparts a bitter taste, but gives the flour an ugly yellowish green color, that is neither tempting nor inviting.

The Graham Biscuit is made by using three cups of Graham flour, one cup of white flour, one teaspoonful of Baking Powder, one heaping tablespoonful of sugar or molasses, and two cups of lukewarm water, mixing the batter until it reaches the consistency of oatmeal porridge, and then pouring into buttered tins. Let it rise till light, and bake in a moderate oven. Milk may be used instead of water, if you have it.

### Sweet Potato Biscuit.

Biscuits de Patates Douces.

6 Potatoes.
4 Tablespoonfuls of Butter or Lard.
1 Pint of Milk.
½ Cake of Compressed Yeast.
1 Teaspoonful of Salt.
1 Tablespoonful of White Sugar.
Sufficient Flour to Make a Batter.

Boil the potatoes, pare and mash them very fine through a sieve. Scald the milk and add the salt and sugar. Then beat till perfectly smooth. Add these to the potatoes and mix well. Then add about half a cup of flour, well-sifted several times, so that it will be very light. When the mixture grows tepid, add the yeast, which you will have dissolved in warm water, and beat well till you have a good batter. Then cover the mixture with a thick cloth, and put to rise in a warm place. After three or four hours, when it is well-risen, add flour sufficient to make a nice, soft dough. Knead very lightly and quickly for about ten or fifteen minutes. At the end of this time take up and knead lightly several times, and roll the dough out. Cut into little biscuits, place them in a slightly-buttered or greased pan, about two inches apart, let them stand for half an hour in a warm place and then bake in a quick oven for twenty minutes.

### Tea Biscuits.

Biscuits de Thé.

1 Quart of Flour.
½ Pint of Milk. 3 Eggs.
2 Ounces of Butter or Lard.
1 Teaspoonful of Sugar.
¼ Cake of Compressed Yeast.

Scald the milk and add the butter. Set to cool, and then add the salt and the sugar and yeast. Add one-half of the flour. Mix well, and then beat rapidly for about five or ten minutes. Cover up the pan with a cloth, and set in a warm place for about two hours. Then take up, add the well-beaten eggs and the remainder of the flour. Make a soft dough, and knead lightly but constantly for about twenty minutes. If the dough is then elastic, form into loaves and set to rise in a warm place. When it has increased to twice its bulk, which will be in about two hours, pinch off into small pieces about half the size of a hen's egg, and mold into a small ball. Place all in a pan about two inches apart, and cover again for half an hour. Then bake in a moderate oven for about a quarter of an hour. They must be baked to a nice brown.

### Soda Crackers.

Biscuits de Soda.

1 Quart of Flour.
3 Tablespoonfuls of Butter.
2 Cups of Sweet Milk or Water.
½ Teaspoonful of Soda.
1 Teaspoonful of Salt.

Sift the flour several times and add the salt. Mix well. Then rub in the butter thoroughly. Add the soda, which you will have dissolved in a little boiling water, and the milk, and mix all well together. Then knead well and put upon the biscuit board and beat with a rolling pin for upwards of half an hour, frequently rolling the dough over, and beating hard until the air bubbles cover every part, above and below. Then roll out into a nice square even sheet of dough, about one-eighth of an inch in thickness, and cut into nice square cakes. Stick through and through with a fork here and there over the surface in even rows, and bake them in a moderate oven till they are hard and crisp, but not brown. Then hang in a muslin bag for about two days to thoroughly dry, and they are ready to be served.

### WAFERS.

Gaufres.

1 Pint of Flour.
1 Tablespoonful of Butter.
½ Teaspoonful of Salt.
½ Pint of Sweet Milk.

Sift the flour very, very fine, and then add the salt, and mix well. Add the milk and make into a nice, rather stiff dough. Place on a biscuit board and beat for fully a half hour, and then turn the dough over and beat for fifteen minutes more, the lightness depending upon the beating. Roll them out into cakes that are almost transparent in thinness, but which can also be handled without losing their shape. Lay them gently in the pan, or better still, roll them out on a baking sheet which has been sprinkled with flour; then they will not require handling. Bake quickly in a hot oven.

### SHORT CAKE.

Gateau de Pate au Beurre.

1 Pound of Flour.
4 Tablespoonfuls of Butter or 2 of Lard.
½ Teaspoonful of Salt.
A Pinch of Soda, or ½ Teaspoonful of Yeast Powder.

Sift the flour and yeast powder together, if you desire it instead of soda. Otherwise sift the flour, add the salt, and mix the lard or butter thoroughly together, rubbing between your hands till there is not a lump left. Then add sufficient tepid water to make a nice, rather stiff dough. Roll out into a thin sheet, about half an inch thick, and criss-cross with a knife lightly in diamond shapes. Set in the oven and bake for about fifteen minutes to a light brown. This is brought to the table split open and buttered, and eaten while hot.

The short cake for fruits is made in exactly the same manner, only a quarter of a pound of butter is used, and two eggs, well beaten, and instead of water sour milk or buttermilk is used to mix, if you use soda, and sweet milk if you use yeast powder. This dough is divided in two, one for the upper, and the other for the lower crust, and is sprinkled thickly between with such fruits as strawberries, raspberries, etc. The dough should be soft and crisp.

### CORN BREAD.

Pain de Maïs.

It has been said, and justly, that the only people who know how to make corn bread are the Southern people, and that the further you go south of Mason and Dixon's line, the better the corn bread, corn cakes, corn muffins, that will be offered you. Throughout Louisiana the dainty "Egg Breads," Corn Cakes, Muffins, "Crackling Bread," etc., are the gracious offerings that typical Creole planters place before the guests who have been invited to partake of morning hospitality. As in these ancient Southern manors, so also is the olden Creole homes of New Orleans. The Creole planters of the ancient regime had their plantation and city homes, and life gravitated between the one and the other with pleasing and infinite variety. And so the cookery of the Creole New Orleans is the cookery of Creole Louisiana, and in this cookery Corn Bread occupies, with "Potato," "Hominy," "Rice," and "Wheat Breads," its unique and interesting place.

It may be added here that the Creoles, like all true Southerners, never use the yellow corn meal for making bread, but always the whitest and best meal. In the South the yellow meal is only used to feed chickens and cattle.

### Plain Corn Bread.
#### Pain de Maïs.

1 Quart of the Finest Indian Meal.
1 Teaspoonful of Salt.
A Heaping Tablespoonful of Lard or Butter.
1 Pint of Water.

Pour just enough boiling water over the meal to scald it through and through, without making a dough or batter. Stir it well, and let it grow tepid. It will then be quite dry. Add a melted teaspoonful of lard or butter. Mix this well, and add water, and beat till the batter is very smooth. Dissolve one teaspoonful of soda in a little boiling water, and add to the mixture, and grease a baking pan. Turn the mixture in and bake in a quick oven for about thirty-five minutes, till a golden brown. Take the bread from the pan whole, and place on a hot platter, and serve, cutting it at the table into slices about two inches long and three wide, and serving with butter.

### Egg Corn Bread.
#### Pain de Maïs aux Oeufs.

1 Quart of Cornmeal. 4 Eggs.
1 Tablespoonful of Butter or Lard.
1 Pint of Milk (Buttermilk if Possible).
1 Teaspoonful of Salt.

Scald the meal with boiling water sufficient to melt. Beat the yolks of the eggs very, very light. Add the corn meal and melted butter, and the salt, and beat till very light, moistening with the milk. Then add the whites of the eggs, beaten to a stiff froth. Beat all well together. Pour into a buttered or greased pan, or into shallow tins, and bake quickly. This is the real Creole Corn Bread, so highly praised by all tourists through Louisiana. The secret of the exquisite flavor depends upon the proper beating of the eggs, as well as on the rising of the corn bread itself. If the eggs are well-beaten, the corn bread will need neither soda nor yeast to make it rise properly. Some add a tablespoonful of sugar when they wish to have sweetened corn bread. Corn bread, to be delicious, should always be served hot and generously buttered.

### Nonpareil Corn Bread.
#### Pain de Maïs Nonpareil.

2 Cups of Indian Meal.
1 Cup of Flour. 3 Eggs.
2½ Cups of Sweet Milk.
1 Tablespoonful of Lard.
2 Tablespoonfuls of Sugar (if desired).
2 Teaspoonfuls of Baking Powder.
1 Teaspoonful of Salt.

Beat the eggs very, very light, the whites and yolks separately. Melt the lard or butter, and sift the Baking Powder into the sifted meal and flour. Stir this into the yolks of the eggs and the milk. Blend thoroughly. Add the whites, beaten to a stiff froth. Beat well together, and bake quickly and steadily in a quick oven for about a half hour. Serve hot, with butter.

### Risen Corn Bread.
#### Pain de Maïs au Levain.

1 Quart of Cornmeal.
1 Pint of Milk or Water. 3 Eggs.
1 Teaspoonful of Salt.
2 Tablespoonfuls of Yeast.

Beat the eggs well, and use boiling water or milk to blend the cornmeal, eggs and salt together. Then add the yeast, which you will have dissolved in a little hot water. Set the bread to rise for three or four hours and then bake in tins or in a greased pan, like a pone of bread, or make it into loaves.

Again, the risen corn bread can be made much more quickly by simply adding two tablespoonfuls of yeast powder to the batter, or a half teaspoonful of soda, dissolved in a cup of milk. Mix thoroughly, and bake in buttered tins or a pan. Always scald the meal with boiling water first.

### Steamed Corn Bread.
#### Pain de Maïs à la Vapeur.

1 Cup of Flour.
1 Cup of Louisiana Molasses.
2 Cups of Sweet Milk.
2 Teaspoonfuls of Baking Powder.

Scald the meal. Beat the eggs very light, and beat the milk into them till very light. Add the molasses and yeast powder, and blend well. Then add the flour, mixing and beating till thoroughly blended. A half cup of sugar may be used instead of the molasses. Tie in a cloth, as you would roll a pudding, and place in a steamer, on top of a pot of boiling water, and cover first with a close cloth, and then with the steamer cover, and steam for three hours. Then turn into a hot dish, and eat as a plain dessert, with a Brandy or Hard or Cream Sauce. (See Pudding Sauces.)

### Cornmeal Pone.
#### Pain de Maïs Créole.

1 Quart of the Finest Indian Meal.
1 Teaspoonful of Salt.
A Heaping Teaspoonful of Lard or Butter.
1 Pint of Sour Milk or Buttermilk.
3 Eggs.

Pour just enough boiling water over the meal to scald it through and through, without making a dough or batter. Stir it well, and let it grow tepid. It will be then quite dry. Beat two eggs very light, and add to the meal, and add a melted tablespoonful of lard or butter. Mix this well, and add the milk or buttermilk, and beat till the batter is very smooth. Dissolve one teaspoonful of soda in a little boiling water, and add to the mixture, and grease a baking pan. Turn the mixture in and bake in a quick oven for about thirty-five minutes, till a golden brown. Take the pone from the pan whole, and place on a hot platter, and serve, cutting it at the table into slices about three inches long and two wide, and serving with butter.

A Plain Pone may be made by using hot water and lard, instead of milk and butter, making a thick dough, and form into loaves and bake. But it bears no comparison to the real Creole Pone, as made above. Nevertheless, this is a very good and nutritious white corn bread. In the rural districts of Louisiana the lard is often omitted, and the pone made simply of the hot water and cornmeal.

### Corn Dodgers.
#### Petits Pain de Maïs.

1 Quart of Indian Meal.
1 Tablespoonful of Lard.
1 Teaspoonful of Salt.

Scald the meal with boiling water. Add the melted lard and the salt. Use sufficient boiling water to make a very stiff batter or soft dough. Then take up a handful of the mixture, and mold it with your hands into oval mounds, tossing the cake of dough lightly between your hands in a dexterous manner, and leaving the impression of your fingers across. Bake the pones thus formed in a quick oven. They may be served at dinner, and are delicious when properly made.

### Ash Cake.
#### Petits Gateaux Cuits dans la Cendre.

1 Quart of Indian Meal.
1 Tablespoonful of Lard.
1 Teaspoonful of Salt.

This is a real old Southern darky cake. The ancient Creole negroes of Louisiana excelled in making and baking it, so that no ashes clung to the clean white cake. An ash cake, as the name suggests, is always baked in the ashes, on the open hearth, and wood ashes must be used. The darkies had a roaring fire and a sufficient quantity of hot ashes. They swept a clean place on the hearth and drew out a pile of hot ashes, and placed the pone of bread, shaped like the Corn Dodgers, on top of the ashes. This was covered with hot ashes, and let bake to a nice brown. Then the cake was drawn out of the ashes, wiped clean with a cloth till every particle of ashes that adhered in the crevices disappeared, and served hot with butter or molasses.

Again, the old Creole darkies wrap the cake in a layer of fig leaves, to bake more neatly, but the real Ash Cake is baked as above.

### Fried Corn Cakes.
#### Gateaux de Maïs Frits.

1 Quart of Indian Meal.
1 Tablespoonful of Lard.
1 Teaspoonful of Salt.

Make the dough as above, adding, if you wish, a well-beaten egg, and milk instead of water. Beat till very light, and drop the stiff batter in large spoonfuls on a frying pan that you will have greased well with fat bacon skin. These cakes are very delicious when properly made. They must be fried to a golden brown. After each cake is taken from the skillet, the latter must be wiped off and regreased with the fat bacon before putting the next cake upon it. Serve hot at breakfast or dinner.

### HOECAKE.
#### Gateau a la Houe.

1 Pint of Flour.
½ Teaspoonful of Salt.
Boiling Water Sufficient to Make a Batter.

These cakes may be baked on a griddle, just as you would a griddle cake, and served with butter. But the old Southern cooks, of which the Louisiana Creole plantation cooks were not the least, always baked these cakes on a hoe on hot coals in front of a wood fire, right out in the open air, before their cabin doors, or in their cabins before the roaring hearth fire. Hence the name Hoecake. The Hoecake was made of flour, with sufficient water to moisten it well. A teaspoonful of butter or lard was added.

The term Hoecake, so extensively used by the field hands, was taken up by masters and mistresses, and applied to a biscuit bread made of one pint of flour, one-half pint of milk, one teaspoonful of yeast powder, and two spoonfuls of butter or one of lard, kneaded well together, rolled out with a rolling pin, and cut criss-cross, like diamonds, with a knife, and baked in the oven.

This delightful refinement of the ancient Hoecake is served at dinner with a glass of milk or cream, as an accompaniment to Compotes of Fruits.

### JOHNNY CAKE.

1½ Pints of Indian Meal. 3 Eggs.
A Pint of Sweet Milk or Buttermilk or Hot Water.
2 Tablespoonfuls of Melted Butter, or 1 of Lard.
½ Teaspoonful of Soda (May Be Omitted.)

Beat the eggs till very light, and add the cornmeal, and beat till light. Add the melted butter and the milk or water. If buttermilk is used, you may use the soda, dissolving it in two tablespoonfuls of boiling water. Do not use the soda with the sweet milk. Make a dough or batter thick enough to be spread into cakes a half inch in thickness and about five inches in diameter, the cakes, of course, being formed round. Place in buttered tins, and bake in a moderate oven for about a half hour, frequently brushing across while baking with melted butter. Do this about four or five times.

In the olden days, Johnny Cake was baked on a clean, sweet board. before a hot coal fire. The board had to be made of oak wood. The cake was formed and placed on the board, and the board was inclined at an angle before the hot coal fire, with a piece of wood or a flatiron to hold it up, and the cake was placed at such an angle that it could harden without slipping off. When quite hard it was stood upright and baked to a nice, crisp brown on both sides, turning as needed, and frequently basting with butter. The Johnny Cake was served hot for lunch or tea, being sent to the table hot, split and buttered, or served with fresh, sweet butter and buttermilk. Hence the old Creole song, which was sung to the little children, and which, being translated, runs:

"Come, Butter Cake! Come, Butter Cake!
Two little boys are waiting at the gate
For a hot Johnny Cake.
Come, Butter Cake!"

And so on, the lines varying "Two little girls," or "Little girl and boy are waiting at the gate," according to the number of children the old mammy was tending. The old Southern darkies also sang this song while churning.

### CRACKLING BREAD.
#### Gratons.

Cracklings are the bits of fat meat left after all the lard has been rendered from the fat pork. They are eaten extensively throughout rural Creole Louisiana. The fat pork is cut into small bits, about the size of a man's hand, and then fried till every bit of grease has been extracted. This grease is then clarified and used as lard. The cracklings are saved, and eaten from time to time within the next two weeks, simply being warmed over again. Again, they may be made at any time by frying small bits of fat pork. These cracklings, to use the country parlance, "Go very well with Corn Bread," and are not only eaten with it "au naturel," but also made into that typical rural bread of the country parishes, "Crackling Bread," or "Gratons."

To make this, take one pint of meal, a half teaspoonful of salt, and cold water enough to make a thick batter. Mix the cracklings, already fried, of course, in the batter, and pour a large tablespoonful at a time on a griddle. Fry to a golden brown.

Crackling bread is very crisp, and if properly made is a very palatable bread, requiring no butter or other accompaniment to make it toothsome.

### MUFFINS.
#### Galettes.

No breakfast cake admits of greater variety than the Muffin. We have Plain Muffins, Egg Muffins, Corn meal Muffins, Rice, Hominy and Cream Muffins, besides several fancy Muffins, and that delicious breakfast accompaniment, "Muffin Bread."

#### Muffin Bread.
Pain Levé à la Pate de Galette.

3 Cups of Flour.
1 Pint of Milk.
½ Cake of Compressed Yeast.
4 Eggs.  ¼ Pound of Butter.
1 Teaspoonful of Salt.

Scald the milk and add the butter. When it grows lukewarm, add the yeast, dissolved in about three tablespoonfuls of warm water. Add the salt and flour, and beat well for about ten minutes. Then set in a warm place over night. In the morning beat the yolks of the eggs well, and then the whites to a stiff froth; add the yolks and beat well, and then add the whites, and mix all thoroughly. Beat till very light, let it stand for about a quarter of an hour, and then bake in a buttered pan for about twenty minutes in a quick oven.

#### Bread Muffins.
Galettes de Pain.

Left-over bread may be utilized in this way:

2 Pints of Stale Bread Crumbs.
1 Pint of Milk.
½ Cup of Sifted Flour.  2 Eggs.
1 Tablespoonful of Melted Butter.
2 Teaspoonfuls of Baking Powder.

Soak the stale bread crumbs in the milk for a half hour. Beat the yolks of the eggs till very light, and the whites to a stiff froth. Add a teaspoonful of salt to the bread, and then pour in the melted butter, and mix thoroughly. Add the flour, into which you will have sifted the baking powder, and beat well. Lastly, add the whites of the eggs, and put the muffins into the muffin rings or gem pans, and bake for about a half hour in a quick oven.

#### Cornmeal Muffins.
Galettes de Farine de Maïs.

2 Cups of Cornmeal.
½ Cup of Sifted Flour.  2 Eggs.
1½ Cups of Buttermilk or Sweet Milk.
2 Spoonfuls of Butter.
2 Teaspoonfuls of Baking Powder.
¼ Teaspoonful of Salt.

Scald the meal. Scald the milk,

and add the butter. When lukewarm add to the cornmeal and beat well. Add the well-beaten yolks of the eggs, and beat well. Add the flour, into which the yeast powder must previously be sifted. Mix well and add the whites of the eggs, beaten to a stiff froth. Beat steadily for about ten minutes, and then pour into greased muffin rings or gem pans, and bake for twenty minutes, in a quick oven. If buttermilk is used, add a teaspoonful of soda, dissolved in the milk.

In making Muffins, if milk is not available, use lukewarm water, or half milk and half water, if possible.

### Cream Muffins.
Galettes à la Crème.
1 Pint of Cream.
1 Pint of Flour. 3 Eggs.
1 Tablespoonful of Butter.
1½ Teaspoonfuls of Yeast Powder.

Beat the whites and yolks of the eggs separately. Then add the cream and salt, and finally the flour, into which you will have blended the yeast powder. Beat well and fill the muffin ring or gem pans one-half full. Place in a quick oven and bake for twenty minutes.

### Egg Muffins.
Galettes aux Oeufs.
3 Cups of Flour.
1 Pint of Milk.
¼ Cake of Compressed Yeast, or 2 Teaspoonfuls of Baking Powder.
1 Large Tablespoonful of Butter.
1 Teaspoonful of Salt.

Prepare the Muffin batter as above, and set to rise over night. In the morning prepare the eggs as above indicated. Blend and beat till light. Then turn the muffin batter into greased muffin rings, and bake about twenty minutes in a hot oven. The Muffins must be eaten hot.

Graham Muffins are made in exactly the same manner, only the Graham flour is used instead. Sometimes the Graham flour is mixed with the plain flour in the proportion of two cups of the former to one of the latter. In Plain Muffins the eggs are omitted.

### Hominy Muffins.
Galettes de Saccamité.
2 Cups of Fine Hominy. 3 Eggs.
½ Cup of Melted Butter.
3 Cups of Fresh Milk or Sour Milk.
2 Tablespoonfuls of White Sugar.
2 Teaspoonfuls of Salt.
1 Teaspoonful of Soda, if Sour Milk is Used.
¾ Cup of Flour.

Mash the hominy through a sieve, and then stir in the milk, salt, yeast powder and sugar. Add the yolks of the eggs, beaten very light, and then the flour, well-sifted. Lastly, add the whites of the eggs, beaten to a stiff froth, and bake in a quick oven for twenty minutes.

If buttermilk is used, add a half teaspoonful of soda, instead of the yeast powder. These Muffins may also be made out of the left-over cornmeal.

### Queen Muffins.
Galettes à la Reine.
1 Cup of Sugar.
3 Cups of Flour. 3 Eggs.
1 Pint of Sweet Milk.
1 Tablespoonful of Melted Butter.
1 Teaspoonful of Salt.
2 Teaspoonfuls of Baking Powder or ½ Cake of Compressed Yeast.

If yeast is used, set the batter to rise over night, as in Egg Muffins, and then proceed in exactly the same manner, adding the eggs in the morning. Beat the eggs separately till very light, and add to the batter, and pour into muffin rings or gem pans and let the mixture rise a half hour longer. Then bake for twenty minutes in a quick oven. If yeast powder is used, beat the yolks of the eggs to a cream, add the scalded milk and butter, and add the flour. Beat till very light, and add the yeast powder, and finally the whites of the eggs, beaten to a stiff froth. Turn into gem pans or muffin rings, and bake for twenty minutes in a hot oven.

### Quick Muffins.
Galettes à la Vitesse.
3 Cups of Flour.
1 Pint of Milk.
¼ Cake of Compressed Yeast, or 2 Teaspoonfuls of Baking Powder.
1 Large Tablespoonful of Butter.
1 Teaspoonful of Salt.

Scald the milk, and add the butter. When it grows lukewarm, add the yeast, the flour and salt, and beat all well for about ten minutes. Then set the bowl in a warm place, cover with a cloth, and let the mixture rise for about two hours. When very light, beat well again, and add two eggs well beaten. Turn into muffin rings or gem pans, and let them rise a half hour longer. At the end of that time place them in the oven and bake for about twenty minutes. If yeast powder is used, beat into the batter, and proceed to bake immediately. The Muffins may be baked in muffin rings, on a griddle, or as above indicated.

### Rice Muffins.
Galettes de Riz.
2 Cups of Boiled Rice.
1 Cup of Flour. 3 Eggs.
1½ Pints of Milk.
1 Tablespoonful of Lard or Butter.
2 Tablespoonfuls of Sugar (May be Omitted).
1 Teaspoonful of Salt.

Mash the rice through a close sieve,

and beat the yolks very light, and add. Add the milk and butter, and then sift in the flour and half a teaspoonful of baking powder. Add the sugar and the whites of the eggs, beaten to a stiff froth. Add the salt, and bake in muffin rings, in a quick oven for about fifteen or twenty minutes.

## GEMS.
### Petits Bijoux.

Prepare the same batter as for Quick Muffins. Pour into gem pans, and bake for about twenty-five minutes. Graham Gems are made by using two cups of Graham meal to one cup of boiled rice or cornmeal, or two cups of Graham flour to one of wheat flour, and the other ingredients in the same proportion as for Quick Muffins.

### Corn Gems.

Petits Bijoux à la Farine de Maïs.

2 Cups of Cornmeal.
1 Cup of Flour.
2 Tablespoonfuls of Butter.
4 Eggs.  1 Pint of Sweet Milk.
2 Tablespoonfuls of Baking Powder.

Boil one-half of the milk and pour it over the cornmeal. Add the butter instantly, and stir well. When thoroughly mixed add the cold milk and the well-beaten yolks of the eggs. Add the salt and then the flour, into which you will have sifted the baking powder. Mix thoroughly, and then add the whites of the eggs, beaten to a stiff froth. Pour into greased or buttered gem pans, and bake about a half hour in a hot oven. Always remember to fill the pans only half full, leaving room for the batter to rise.

## CRUMPETS.
### Emietes.

1 Pint of Milk.
3 Cups of Flour.
4 Tablespoonfuls of Butter.
½ Cake of Compressed Yeast.
1 Tablespoonful of Salt.

Scald the milk and set to cool. Add the salt, and gradually beat in the flour. Beat till very smooth, and add the yeast Beat continuously for ten minutes and then set in a warm place to rise. After several hours beat well again, and add the melted butter. Mix thoroughly and then turn into greased muffin rings and bake till a beautiful brown, turning first on one side and then on the other. Send to the table very hot. Break open with your fingers, and butter nicely.

## SALLY LUNN.
### Pain à la Vieille Tante Zoe.

Sally Lunn is nothing more than the old breakfast dish known to the Creoles for generations as "Pain à la Vielle de Tante Zoe." Take

1 Pint of Milk.
1½ Pints of Flour.
½ Cupful of Butter.
4 Eggs.  1 Teaspoonful of Salt.
½ Cup of Sugar.
¼ Cake of Compressed Yeast.

Warm the butter in a pint of milk till the milk reaches the boiling point. Do not let it boil. Simply scald. Then add the salt and a talbespoonful of sugar. Let it cool. When tepid add the flour, well sifted, and beat thoroughly into the mixture. Lastly, add the yeast, dissolved in a little hot milk or water. Beat it continuously for at least five minutes. Then, when the batter begins to break into blisters, cover it and set to rise for the night. In the morning add the yolks of the eggs, beaten till very light, and the whites, beaten to a stiff froth. Mix carefully, and dissolve a half teaspoonful of soda in the mixture, if it seems anyway sour. Turn the whole into a shallow buttered dish, and set to rise for fifteen minutes longer. Bake about twenty or twenty-five minutes in a moderately quick oven, till it is a light brown.

This cake, like all muffin batter, should not be cut with a knife, but torn apart with your hands. If cut, all muffin batter at once becomes heavy. The cake may be also made much more quickly by mixing in the morning, using the above ingredients, only adding three teaspoonfuls of baking powder, instead of the yeast. Beat quickly and thoroughly, and turn into a buttered tin, and set to bake at once. Send to the table hot, and eat with a generous endowment of butter.

## WAFFLES.
### Gaufres.

Waffles are delightful accompaniments of breakfast, lunch or tea, and may be made of flour, rice, hominy or cornmeal. In all recipes for Waffles, if you have not the milk, substitute lukewarm water, and if you have no butter, use instead a half spoon of lard, but certainly the taste of the Waffles is much improved by the butter and milk, especially the butter. Half milk and half water, boiled and grown tepid, may also be used in the proportions indicated in the recipes.

### Plain Waffles.
#### Gaufres de Froment.

These Waffles are made of flour, and are more especially known as "Plain Waffles." They are the Waffles most generally served. They are made as follows:

3 Cups of Flour.
2 Eggs.   2 Cups of Milk.
1½ Teaspoonfuls of Baking Powder.
1 Large Tablespoonful of Butter.
1 Teaspoonful of Salt.

Sift the flour and salt and baking powder together. Beat the yolk of the egg till very light. Add the melted butter to the milk, which should be scalded and grown lukewarm, and then mix in the whites of the eggs. Now add the flour gradually, making a nice, light batter. If it appears at all stiff, add a little more milk. Have your waffle irons ready, thoroughly heated. Have at hand a small brush or a stick with a piece of clean, fringed cloth wrapped around the end. Dip this in a little melted lard, and brush over the interior of the irons, till every part is greased. Pour the batter into a pitcher, so that you may the more easily fill the irons. Fill until the elevations are lightly covered, and then close the irons quickly and turn it over. Bake the Waffle about two minutes, or till a nice, delicate brown. Carefully remove from the irons, place in a hot plate or waffle dish in the mouth of the oven, and proceed with the baking. Send to the table very hot.

### Cornmeal Waffles.
### Gaufres de Farine de Maïs.

2 Cups of Cornmeal.
1 Cup of Flour.   3 Eggs.
1 Pint of Milk.
1 Tablespoonful of Melted Butter.
½ Teaspoonful of Soda, Dissolved in Hot Water.
1 Teaspoonful of Salt.

Scald the milk and then add the well-beaten yolks of the eggs. Add the milk and the soda, dissolved in a little hot water, and then add the melted butter and the whites of the eggs, beaten to a stiff froth. Now add the flour, gradually making a nice batter, not too thick, nor yet too thin. Beat till all is very smooth and proceed to bake as above.

Rice may be substituted for the flour, if you desire rice and cornmeal muffins; add about two tablespoonfuls of flour to bind.

Waffles of left-over grits may be prepared by adding one cup of grits to two of flour, and proceeding as above.

### Potato Waffles.
### Gaufres de Pommes de Terre.

1 Pint of Irish Potatoes.
4 Eggs.   1 Pint of Flour.
1½ Pints of Milk.
½ Cake of Compressed Yeast.

Mash the boiled, left-over potatoes through a sieve, and then add the milk and the sifted flour. Add the yeast, which you will have dissolved in a little warm water, and set the whole to rise for two hours. At the end of that time add the eggs, beaten separately, and mix well. Set to rise again for a half hour, till light, and then proceed to bake as in Plain Waffles.

### Sweet Potato Waffles.
### Gaufres de Patates Douces.

2 Cups of Mashed Sweet Potatoes.
1 Cup of Melted Butter.
½ Cup of Sugar.
1 Pint of Milk.   2 Eggs.
4 Tablespoonfuls of Flour.

Mash the potatoes through a sieve, and add the eggs, beaten separately. Mix well, and add the sugar, and beat till very light. Then add the butter and beat again, and add the milk, mixing thoroughly. Now add the flour, using sufficient to make a thin batter, that will bind the potatoes. Grease the waffle irons well, and proceed to bake as above indicated. Properly made these waffles are delicious. Left-over potatoes may be thus utilized. The eggs may be omitted.

### Rice Waffles.
### Gaufres de Riz.

1 Cup of Boiled Rice.
1½ Pints of Milk.   2 Eggs.
1 Cup of Flour or 2 Cups of Rice Flour.
2 Teaspoonfuls of Baking Powder.
1 Teaspoonful of Salt.
1 Tablespoonful of Butter.

Mash the rice through a sieve. Beat the yolks light, and add, and then add the salt, the baking powder and the milk. Beat well, and add the whites of the eggs, beaten to a stiff froth. Now add the rice flour to make a thin batter, and proceed to bake as above. Be careful to grease the irons very well, so that the rice may not adhere. If white flour, rather than the rice flour, is used, use in proportion two cups of boiled rice, instead of one.

### Risen Waffles.
### Gaufres au Levain.

1 Quart of Flour.
1½ Quarts of Milk.
½ Cake of Compressed Yeast.
3 Eggs.
2 Tablespoonfuls of Melted Butter.
1 Tablespoonful of Salt.

Scald the milk, add the butter, and let it grow tepid. Sift the flour and salt together, and add the milk and butter, and finally the yeast. Beat all continuously for five or ten minutes, and then cover well and set in a warm place for about two hours. Beat the whites and the yolks of the eggs separately, and add first the yolks to the batter, after it has risen well, and then add the whites. Beat in thoroughly, and set to rise again for about a quarter of an hour. Then beat lightly and pour into a pitcher. Prepare the waffle irons as indicated above, and proceed to bake in the same manner.

These Risen Waffles may also be made by mixing the flour, milk and salt and yeast together, and setting to rise over night. In the morning add the melted butter and the eggs, beaten separately, set to rise fifteen minutes longer, and proceed as above.

### Other Breakfast Cakes.
Autres Gateaux de Déjeuner.

In addition to Muffins, Waffles, etc., "Batter Cakes," "Flannel Cakes," "Buckwheat Cakes," "Griddle Cakes," etc., form pleasing and toothsome varieties for the morning meal, and, it might be added, not only for the morning meal, but for luncheon and tea as well.

### BATTER CAKES.
Galettes de Pâte.

2 Cups of Flour, Finely Sifted.
2 Cupfuls of Sweet Milk.
2 Tablespoonfuls of Baking Powder.
3 Eggs.

Beat the whites and the yolks of the eggs separately, the former to a stiff froth. Add the flour to the yolks, and beat till very light. Add the yeast powder and bake again. Then add the sweet milk and beat well. Now add the whites of the eggs and mix all to a very smooth, light batter, as thick as a batter that will run in a stream from the mouth of a spoon. Have ready the hot griddles, which you will grease with lard lightly, or better still, with a piece of fat bacon. Drop the cakes on the griddle from a large spoon, and bake about two minutes to a nice brown, turning first on one side and then quickly on the other. Pile the cakes on a plate in the mouth of the oven, buttering each generously as soon as baked, and send to the table almost as fast as you bake. These are the most delicate and delightful of all Griddle Cakes.

They may also be made with sour milk, instead of sweet, in which case use a half teaspoonful of soda, instead of the baking powder.

### BUCKWHEAT CAKES.
Galettes de Sarrasin.

3 Cups of Buckwheat-Flour (Perfectly Pure).
1¾ Pints of Sweet Milk or Water.
¼ Cake of Compressed Yeast.
½ Teaspoonful of Salt.

Take a small earthen crock, or a pitcher, and put the warm milk or water, or half milk and water, into it, and then add the salt and the buckwheat flour. Beat till perfectly smooth, and then, when you have a stiff batter, add the yeast, dissolved in a little water. Beat this till smooth, and then cover well and set to rise over night. In the morning add a half teaspoonful of soda or saleratus, to remove any sourness that may have accrued during the night, and this addition will also increase the lightness of the cakes. Bake on a griddle, like Batter Cakes.

Buckwheat Cakes are also often made by taking two cups of buckwheat flour, one cup of wheat flour, one and three-quarters pints of milk, one teaspoonful of salt, three teaspoonfuls of baking powder, and mixing all together till very light, and baking immediately on griddles. Many, indeed, prefer them combined with the flour. This mixture may also be made as in the above recipe, by using compressed yeast, and setting to rise over night. A tablespoonful of butter may also be added if desired. Serve with Louisiana Syrup.

### FLANNEL CAKES.
Galettes de Pâte au Levain.

1 Pint of Milk. 2 Eggs.
¼ Cake of Compressed Yeast.
3 Cups of Flour.
½ Teaspoonful of Salt.

Heat the milk, and when it grows tepid, add the yeast, dissolved in a little hot milk or water, and flour sufficient to make a stiff batter. Set to rise over night, or for at least three hours in the morning. In the morning add the yolks of the eggs, beaten light, and the melted butter, and mix well. Then add the whites beaten to a stiff froth. Beat well, and then bake on a griddle, as in the above recipe for Batter Cakes.

Be sure to make the batter stiff enough at the start to allow for the admixture of the eggs and butter in the morning. When once the cakes have risen, no flour must be added, unless the cakes are set to rise for an hour again.

Sweet Flannel Cakes are made by adding a half cup of sugar. These are nice for tea.

Again, Flannel Cakes may be made without yeast, by using one pint of buttermilk and one teaspoonful of soda. The batter is then made in the morning, without setting to rise over night, and is baked on the griddle immediately after mixing. Omit the butter in these buttermilk cakes. They will be very light and spongy without the butter.

### GRIDDLE CAKES.
Gateau à la Plaque.

3 Cups of Flour.
3 Cups of Sour Milk or Warm Water.
1 Teaspoonful of Soda.
3 Eggs, Beaten Very Light.
1 Teaspoonful of Salt.

Mix the flour and meal, and pour

on the milk or warm water. Make a batter somewhat stiffer than for Buckwheat Cakes, and add the eggs, well-beaten, the whites and yolks separately, and finally add the soda, dissolved in a little warm water. Bake on a griddle, making the cakes large and generous. Serve with Louisiana Syrup.

### Bread Griddle Cakes.

Gateau de Pain à la Plaque.

Utilize stale, left-over bread for these cakes. Take

- 1 Quart of Boiling Milk.
- 2 Cups of Fine Bread Crumbs.
- 3 Eggs.
- 1 Tablespoonful of Melted Butter.
- ½ Teaspoonful of Salt.

Soak the bread in the boiling milk, and as it cools beat it to a very smooth paste. Then add the yolks of the eggs, beaten very light, and the soda, dissolved in a little warm water. Finally add the whites of the eggs, beaten to a stiff froth, and a half cupful of sifted flour to bind well. Bake on a hot griddle, and butter, and serve with Louisiana Molasses or Syrup.

### Cornmeal Griddle Cakes.

Gateau de Farine de Maïs à la Plaque.

- ½ Teaspoonful of Soda.
- 2 Cups of Cornmeal.
- 1 Cup of Flour.
- 1 Teaspoonful of Salt.
- 3 Eggs.
- 3 Cups of Sour Milk or Warm Water.
- 1 Teaspoonful of Soda.

Scald the meal and mix with the milk. Add the flour, into which you will have mixed the salt. Beat the eggs very light and add, and when all has been beaten very light add a teaspoonful of soda, dissolved in a little warm water. Bake on a griddle to a nice brown. If sweet milk is used, be careful to use, instead of the soda, two teaspoonfuls of baking powder.

Graham flour, which is now used so much, may be made into griddle cakes, using two cups of the flour to one of wheat flour, and adding also one large tablespoonful of lard or butter. Cook as other Griddle Cakes on a hot griddle.

### Hominy Griddle Cakes.

Gateau de Saccamité à la Plaque.

- 2 Cups of Hominy.
- 1 Cup of Flour.
- 1 Teaspoonful of Salt.
- 3 Eggs.
- 3 Cups of Sour Milk or Warm Water.
- 1 Teaspoonful of Soda.

Boil and mash the hominy, or utilize left-over hominy. Add the flour, into which you will have mixed the salt. Beat the egg very light, and add, and when all has been beaten very light add a teaspoonful of soda, dissolved in a little warm water. Bake on a griddle to a nice brown. If sweet milk is used, be careful to use, instead of the soda, two teaspoonfuls of baking powder. Serve with Louisiana Molasses or Syrup.

### French Griddle Cakes.

Gateau de Plaque à la Française.

- 1½ Pints of Sifted Flour.
- 6 Eggs.
- 1 Tablespoonful of Butter.
- 1 Ounce of Sugar.
- 1 Cup of Milk.

Beat the yolks of the eggs and the sugar very light; then add the flour and melted butter, and then add the warm milk. Beat all till very light. Add a half teaspoonful of baking powder, and then add the whites of the eggs, beaten to a stiff froth. Beat all till very smooth. Drop a tablespoonful at a time upon the hot griddle; turn quickly and bake on the other side, allowing about two minutes in all; place on a hot platter, butter well and spread with jelly; then roll up, dust with powdered sugar and serve very hot.

### Green Corn Griddle Cakes.

Gateau de Maïs Tendre à la Plaque.

- 1 Quart of Finely-Grated Green Corn.
- 1 Pint of Milk. 4 Eggs.
- ½ Teaspoonful of Salt.
- 1 Cup of Flour.
- 1 Tablespoonful of Melted Butter.

Beat the eggs separately, and then add the yolks, well beaten, to the corn. Add the salt, melted butter and the milk, and mix well. Then add sufficient flour to make a thin batter, and finally the whites of the eggs, beaten to a stiff froth. Bake on a hot griddle, butter generously, and serve very hot. This is a great Creole cake, and very delicious.

### Rice Griddle Cakes.

Gateau de Riz à la Plaque.

- 2 Cups of Boiled Rice.
- 1 Cup of Flour. 2 Eggs.
- 1 Pint of Milk or Water.
- ½ Teaspoonful of Salt.
- 1½ Teaspoonfuls of Baking Powder.
- 1 Teaspoonful of Sugar.

Mash the rice through a sieve. Sift the flour, baking powder and salt together, and add the sugar to the milk. Add this to the flour and mix in the rice till free from any lumps. Then add the eggs, the whites and yolks beaten separately, and mix into a very smooth batter. Have the griddle well-heated. Bake the cakes to a nice brown, and serve with Louisiana Syrup.

## PUFFS.

### Soufflés.

1 Pint of Sweet Milk.
½ Pound of Flour.
2 Ounces of Butter.
4 Eggs.

Beat the whites and the yolks separately till very, very light. Warm the milk and add the melted butter. When cold, mix with the yolks of the eggs, and add the flour and salt, beating till very light. Now add the whites of the eggs, beaten to a stiff froth. Stir lightly, turn into buttered tins, filling each about half full, and bake to a light brown.

## CRACKNELS.

### Craquelins.

2 Cups of Rich Milk.
4 Tablespoonfuls of Butter.
1 Gill of Yeast.
1 Teaspoonful of Salt.

Scald the milk and add the butter, and let it grow tepid. Then add the yeast and dissolve well. Add the salt, and now add the flour sufficient to make a light dough. Set to rise, and when twice its bulk work lightly, and roll out very thin, and cut into pieces about two and a half inches square. Stick well with a fork through and through, and bake in a slow oven, as you would soda crackers.

## HOME-MADE YEAST.

### Levain de Ménage.

6 Large Potatoes.
A Handful of Hops.
3 Pints of Water.
½ Cup of Sugar.
½ Cup of Yeast.
Flour Sufficient to Make a Batter.
Cornmeal to Blend.

In these days of baking powders and prepared yeasts that are sold by all grocers, and that have proved such a saving of time and trouble to the housekeeper, it might seem superfluous to add a recipe for making yeast. Nevertheless, the following ancient recipe, in use for many years in Creole homes, is given as the final recipe of the Picayune's Creole Cook Book:

Take six large potatoes, and pare them, and then boil in about three pints of water. Take a handful of hops, and tie them in a muslin bag, and boil with the potatoes. When these are thoroughly cooked, drain the water on sufficient flour to make a good batter, and set the mixture on the stove for a few minutes, till the flour is well-scalded. Do not let it boil or simmer under any consideration. Take it from the fire, and let it cool. Then mash the potatoes and add them to the flour, and add a half cup of sugar and a half cup of yeast. Let it stand in a warm place till it has thoroughly risen. Then add cornmeal that has been sifted and dried, and knead well, until you have a dough thick enough to roll out, and that will crumble when dry. Cut this dough into cakes, and spread on a board and place in the shade to dry. Then keep in a box in a dry place.

This mixture may be also kept and used as a liquid by simply stopping when you have come to the point where you must add the cornmeal. Let the mixture thus stand in a warm place till it has thoroughly risen. Then scald a large jar, wipe dry, and put in the yeast. Cover tight, and keep in a cool place. One-third of a cupful of yeast will make two loaves of bread.

But as Compressed Yeast can be had at any grocer's, and is a great saving of time and trouble, it is always better to get it, and it has this advantage, that it may be procured fresh when needed.

## CHAPTER XLVIII.

## SUGGESTIONS TO HOUSEKEEPERS.

The following suggestions will be found of interest to all housekeepers, especially to the young and inexperienced. They have been carefully prepared, with especial reference to the needs of the household, and bear in every respect upon the recipes given in the Picayune's Creole Cook Book:

### Comparative Table of Weights and Measures Used in the Picayune's Creole Cook Book.

Every housekeeper should have for her own convenience and for the correct measurement of ingredients used in making any dish, where ex-measurements are absolutely necessary to success, a pair of scales, and a set of tin measures with small lips or spouts; these measures should range from one gallon to a half gill. But as so few housekeepers think of the necessity of having such measures until they set to making preparations where measurements must be exact, the following carefully prepared table may be referred to with absolute reliance upon the comparative quantities given:

Twenty-five drops of thin liquid equal half a teaspoonful.
Four tablespoonfuls of solid or liquid equal one tablespoonful of solid or liquid.
Four tablespoonfuls equal one wineglassful or one-half gill.
One wineglassful equals half a gill or a quarter of a cup.
Two wineglassfuls equal one gill, or half a cup.
Two gills equal one teacupful, or sixteen tablespoonfuls.
One teacupful or one kitchen cupful equals half a pint.
Two teacupfuls or two kitchen cupfuls equal one pint.
Two pints equal one quart.
Four quarts equal one gallon.
One tablespoonful of liquid equals half an ounce.
Two tablespoonfuls equal one ounce.
One level tablespoonful of flour equals half an ounce.
Two level tablespoonfuls solid equal one ounce liquid.
Sixteen ounces equal one pound.
One pound of solid is equal to one pint of liquid.
One quart of unsifted flour equals one pound.
Four teacupfuls of sifted flour equal one pound.
Three cups of cornmeal equal one pound.
One and one-half pints of cornmeal equal one pound. t
One pint or two cups of granulated sugar equal one pound.
One pint or two cups of brown sugar equal one pound.
Two and one-half cupfuls of white pulverized sugar equal one pound.
One well-rounded tablespoonful of butter equals one ounce.
1 Tablespoonful of salt equals one ounce.
One teacupful of cold, hard butter, pressed down, equals half a pound.
Two cups of cold butter, pressed down, equal one pound.
One pint of finely-chopped meat, solidly packed, equals one pound.
An ordinary sized tumblerful is equal to half a pint, or one teacupful.
Ten eggs equal one pound.
A dash of pepper is equal to one-eighth of a teaspoonful.

### Rules to be Observed in Mixing Ingredients.

In every recipe given in this book follow implicitly the exact order given for the mixing of ingredients. This mixing has been systematically arranged, and any deviation will fail of success. Do not think that you can put all your ingredients together pell-mell and succeed in making any Creole dish. Whether mixing the ingredients in a "Roux," preparatory to adding the ingredient which constitutes the dish proper, or whether making desserts, cakes, etc., add every ingredient, even though it be only a dash of pepper or a flavoring extract, in the exact order and proportion given. On the strict observance of these rules followed by Creole cuisinieres, depends the success of Creole Cookery.

### Cutting, Chopping, Slicing and Mincing.

Observe implicitly the directions given in regard to cutting, chopping, slicing and mincing, whether applied to vegetables, meats or seasonings.

When the Picayune Creole Cook Book says to chop an ingredient, it means to chop in the strict sense of the word. When it directs that vegetables, etc., shall be cut, it means to cut, in the proper acceptation of that term in cookery. When it says to slice, it means that the ingredient shall be sliced, and not cut or chopped; and so when the term "mince" is used, it means that the ingredient shall be minced, or hashed, or grated, as fine as possible.

### The Use of Wines and Liquors in the Picayune's Creole Cook Book.

In regard to the use of Wines and Liquors in cooking, it may be said that wine enters frequently into the preparation of Creole dishes, such as meat, stews, courtbouillons, etc. In all recipes, however, where its use is indicated in this book, it may be omitted, according to taste, without detriment to the dish, except in "Courtbouillon à la Créole," the famous "Bouilliabaisse," and in all Matelotes, in Salmi of Venison, and in certain preparations of meats and poultry and game in which the success of the dish depends greatly upon the flavoring given by a small addition of wine. But, as a general rule, wine may be used or omitted according to the taste. This explanation is given because there are many families, Creole and otherwise, who object to the use of wine, even in cooking.

As regards Wine, Brandy and Rum in Sauces for Puddings, etc., a variety of recipes that are equally recherche and in which liquors of no kind are used, are specified in this book. The intelligent housekeeper, therefore, will find a varied and pleasing selection with or without wine or liquors.

## The Use of Broth, Bouillon or Consommé in Cooking.

What has been said in regard to Wines and Liquors holds good with regard to the use of Broth, Bouillon or Consommé, indicated in many of the recipes for fish, meats, poultry, etc. While the infusion of Broth, Bouillon or Consommé, or oyster water in lieu of plain water, adds, where indicated, a delightful flavor to the dish, the use of any of these is not imperative in making the dish, and water, in the proportion given for Broth or Consommé, may always be used instead, except in special recipes. For instance, if you wish to have a real "Jambalaya à la Créole," the use of Broth or Consomme instead of water, where the Jambalaya is made of meats, and the use of oyster water where it is made of oysters, will impart a flavor that is far superior to a dish prepared with water. Nevertheless, in hundreds of households water is used almost exclusively, even in making a Jambalaya, because it is not every family that chooses to make a pot of Broth or Consomme just for the purpose of using it as an ingredient for a dish, and in our climate it is not possible to always keep a quantity of meat or fish stock on hand for culinary purposes.

Never be afraid, therefore, to undertake a dish because it calls for wine or Bouillon or Consommé. Just proceed with the cooking, using wagood, and other directions implicitly ter instead, and if your seasoning is followed in the preparation and cooking, the absence of either wine or Consomme will scarcely be detected by even the most experienced cook or epicure.

## Explanation of French Terms Used in Cooking and Serving Dishes.

In preparing the Creole Cook Book the Picayune has sought to overcome the great difficulty that the majority of people outside of Louisiana experience in understanding French terms, as applied to various dishes and orders of service. Discussions have been going on in all parts of the country of late as to the desirability of abolishing all French terms on bills of fare, one celebrated newspaper declaring: "What is the use of calling a dish 'Canard Canvasback,' when there is no French name for the famous Canvasback Duck?" All this is very amusing down here in Louisiana, where the Canvasback Duck has been always known as the "Canard de Cheval." And so with other dishes. The use of French, however, continues in bills of fare prepared for all distinguished banquets, etc., critics to the contrary notwithstanding, and will continue, because the French order of service is the one accepted the world over, in all state and official gatherings, and the pretty touch given to a dish called by a French name is one that ladies especially will be slow to give up. An air of distinction is conferred upon even a homely dish by calling it by its French name, and, as remarked above, all criticisms against the practice will not do away with the usage.

The Picayune has sought to overcome the difficulty experienced by those who are not acquainted with the French language and French terms in cooking by giving with each recipe not only the correct English name of the dish, but the French one also. It now proposes to further assist housekeepers and caterers generally by giving the definitions of a few additional French terms used in cooking and serving dishes:

Assaisonement—A Seasoning; a salad dressing.

Assaisonnement Aromatique—An aromatic seasoning, such as parsley, chervil, etc.

Aspic—This is a meat jelly or savory for cold dishes. Boned Turkey, Galantine, Calf's Foot Jelly, Cold Tongue, Cold Daube, are all termed "En Aspic."

Au Gratin—All baked or roasted dishes that are prepared with crumbs grated and sprinkled over are called "Au Gratin."

Bouchees—A Bouchee indicates a mouthful, and is from the French "Bouche," the mouth. It is applied in cooking to all very thin, small patties or cakes, as "Bouchees d'Huitres," "Bouchees a la Reine," etc.

Bonne Bouche—A good mouthful.

Baba—A peculiar Creole sweet cake, made of yeast, flour, milk and eggs.

Bisque—A soup made of shellfish. It is red in color, such as "Crawfish Bisque," the shells of which are boiled and mashed and pounded and strained and added to the soup stock. A "Lobster Bisque" may be prepared after the same manner as the "Crawfish Bisque" in latitudes where lobsters may be obtained fresh. The Bisque then becomes "Bisque d'Homard."

Bisque d'Ecrevisse—A Crawfish Bisque or soup.

Blanchair—To blanch. To blanch an article set it on the fire till it boils, and then plunge in cold water. This rule applies to vegetables, poultry, nuts, almonds, etc. The skin is thus removed and the article is blanched. Blanching also means simply to scald, as blanching oysters.

Bouillon—A bouillon is a clear soup, much stronger than broth, and yet not quite so strong as Consomme.

Boudins—A form of sausage.

Boulettes—A small ball of meat, fish, etc., hashed and formed in balls and fried.

Bouilliabaisse—A famous French-Creole way of cooking fish, the French using the Sturgeon and Perch; the Creoles the Redfish and Red Snapper. The fish is cooked to the point where it begins to boil; then you must stop on the instant. Hence the word "Bouillibaisse," from "Bouillir," to boil, and "Baisse," to stop. (See recipe for Bouillabaisse.)

Buisson d'Ecrevisse—A Crawfish Bush. This is a celebrated Creole hors d'oeuvre, as also a very handsome table garnish. The crawfish are boiled; a glass fruit or cake stand is placed in the center of the table, and a goblet is set upon it; the goblet is filled with celery tips and parsley tips, and the entire dish is beautifully garnished like a bush of greenery. The crawfish are hung around the edges of the goblet and the dish, and in amid the greenery, and the effect of the red against the green is very pretty, and for all the world like a bush of green and red. The crawfish are served from the bush.

Buisson de Chevrettes—A Shrimp Bush. This resembles the Crawfish Bush, only the shrimp are small and cannot be hung with much grace from the sides and round of the dish. They are, therefore, piled into a small, deep glass dish first, and a cover is put on top to press them down. They are then turned over, and will be found clinging together in one solid mass. This is then placed on top of a lowing orders of service are intendglass cake stand or fruit dish. Dainty bits of celery tips and asparagus are heaped around as a border; another row is formed a little lower, and again intermingled with asparagus tips and celery tops, between which the pink shrimp glimmer. The effect is very pretty. This also is arranged for a table garnish, and the shrimp are served as an hors d'oeuvre.

Braise—To smother. All meats, fish, vegetables, etc., cooked in a closely-covered stewpan, so as to retain not only their own flavor but those of all other ingredients entering into the dish, are termed "Braise," or "a la Braise."

Brioche—This is our delightful Creole breakfast cake, made of slightly sweetened egg and milk, batter and yeast, set to rise over night, and formed into a "Brioche," or cake, with a central cake for a head, and the other cakes arranged, to the number of six or eight, around, and sprinkled with sugar.

Canapes—On toast. Anything served on toast is called "sur Canapes."

Canelle—Cinnamon.

Canneton (masculine); Canette (feminine)—Duckling.

Canneton—Meat stuffed and folded up; forcemeat balls.

Charcuterie—The term for all sausages.

Civet—A stew made of hare and so called because of the flavor of chives (cives) that enters into its composition.

Consomme—A clear soup that has been boiled down to almost a jelly-broth, and wheich is very rich.

Consomme Dore—A gilded or golden yellow consomme.

A la Creme—With Cream, as "Sauce a la Creme," etc.

Creme a la Glace—Ice Cream.

Coup de Milieu—A middle drink or course served in the middle of the meal, just before the roasts, as "Ponche a la Cardinale," "Roman Punch," "Sorbet a la Royale," etc.

Crapaud—A toad; bullfrog.

A la Crapaudine—Crapaudine means like a toadstool, or stove, as "Pigeons a la Crapaudine," which means pigeons cooked and dressed to resemble little toadstools or frogs on a stove. (See recipe Pigeons a la Crapaudine.)

Courtbouillon—A fish stew, generally made of Redfish.

Courtbouillon a la Creole—A stew of Redfish, to which wine is added.

Croutons—Crusts of bread cut like dice or in any fancy shape, and toasted or fried in butter.

Croustades—Pieces of bread larger than Croutons toasted or fried in butter or lard, and used to serve minces or meats upon.

Dindonneau—A turkey chick.

Dariole—A custard pie.

Diable—The devil.

A la diable—According to the devil. Generally applied to hot, fiery preparations of meats, sauces, etc.

Entree—A side dish, served between the courses at dinner.

Entremet—A small by-dish. Entremets are sweet or otherwise.

Eau de Vie—Brandy or Whisky. Eau de Vie properly means "water of life."

Entremet Sucre—A sweet by-dish. Sweet entremets are generally served towards the close of the meal, just before the roasts.

Flan—A custard.

Fondue—To melt. Generally applied to a light preparation of melted cheese, such as "Welsh Rarebit."

Fondant—Sugar boiled and beaten to a cream paste.

Granits—Aromatized fruit waters.

Grille—Broiled.

Hors d oeuvres—A by-dish; an outwork; a digression. Under this term is classed all dishes that are regarded simply as accessories to a meal, and designed to excite the appetite, but not to satisfy. It is undoubtedly because they are placed on the table outside or apart from other dishes that they have been so called.

A la Jardiniere—According to the gardener's wife.

Matelote—A rich fish stew, made with wine.

Mayonnaise—A rich salad dressing, made with eggs, oil, vinegar, etc., and served with chicken, shrimp, fish salad generally.

Meringue—The whites of eggs beaten to a stiff froth with sugar.

Meringuees—Covered with a Meringue.

Marinade—A rich liquor of spices, vinegar or wine, etc., in which beef or fish are steeped for several hours before cooking.

A la mode—After a mode or fashion.

Mironton—Cold boiled meat; hashed and warmed over, and served in various ways.

Neige—Snow.

A la Neige—Snowy; like snow.

Pate—A batter; a pie dough.

Pates—Small pies or patties of oysters, meats, fruits, etc.

Panache—Mottled, variegated. As "Creme Panachees," or "Variegated Ice Cream."

Poulet—A chicken.

A la Poulette—As a chicken; for instance, a "Sauce a la Poulette," always has eggs added, the eggs giving the distinctive name "a la Poulette."

Praline—A distinctive Creole sugar cake made of cocoanut and sugar or pecans and sugar. (See recipes "Pralines.")

Pralinee—Sugared, or sugar-coated.

Piment—Pepper.

Pimente—Peppered.

Piquante—A sauce of piquant flavor, vinegar or acid predominating, and highly seasoned with pepper.

A la Plaque—A "Plaque" is a flat baking pan or griddle. Articles baked in it are called "a la Plaque," as Pan Bread, or "Pain a la Plaque."

Quenelles—Meat, liver, fish or potatoes chopped and highly seasoned and rolled into balls or boulettes and boiled and served as a garnish. We have also "Potato Quenelles."

Ragout—A rich stew of meat or poultry, generally made with vegetables, such as mushrooms, green peas, truffles, potatoes, etc.

Ratafia—A kind of liqueur or wine cordial.

Remoulade—A dressing for salads, somewhat like the Mayonnaise, but differing in this, that the eggs are all hard-boiled and rubbed in a mortar with mustard, vinegar, minced garlic, etc.

Releves—A side dish; a term applied when it is desired to serve another dish beside an entree.

Rissoles—Minced meat or fish, rolled in thin pastry and fried.

Roux—A mixture of flour and butter, or flour and lard, used as a foundation for sauces or as a foundation for stews, salmis, etc.

Roti—A roast.

Tarte—A pie.

Tartelette—A tartlet.

Sauter—To smother and toss meats, fowl, vegetables, etc., over the fire in butter or fat.

Savarin—A wine cake.

Salmi—A rich stew of venison, duck or other game, cut up and dressed generally with wine.

Salmigondis—A hotch-potch of game, such as venison, etc.

Saucissons de Lyons—Bologna Sausage.

Salade d'Anchois—Anchovy Salad.

Souffle—An omelet, pudding or custard, thoroughly beaten and whipped up until it becomes so light that when cooked it must be eaten immediately, or else it will fall.

Talmouse—A cheese cake.

Tartine d'Anchois—Anchovy Tartines; circles of brown bread, spread with Anchovy Paste, yolks and whites of hard-boiled eggs, chopped fine, also chopped pickles, all arranged in alternate rows.

Timbale—A pie cooked in a mold. In "Macaroni en Timbale" the macaroni is cooked in the cheese head.

Vinaigrette—A sauce or salad dressing, made of salt and pepper, vinegar predominating.

Vol-au-Vent—A chicken, meat, fish or game pie, baked in a light Puff Paste, and served as an entree.

## General Order of Service of Meals.

The manner in which meals are served is equally important as the cooking. As previously remarked, the most elegant viands badly served lose all their savor, and the pleasure of a meal is destroyed, while the simplest viands neatly and properly served give an air of distinction and elegance, not to speak of comfort, to even the humblest feast.

The spotless white tablecloth, the plainly folded napkins, the shining silverware and glassware, are important factors in good service, and should receive the most minute attention from the housekeeper. Never, especially at formal dinings, crimp or fold napkins in fancy shapes; it is inelegant and vulgar. Lay them perfectly flat and plain, and let everything present the most scrupulously clean appearance. In formal dinings the layer plate should not be less than two inches larger than the service plate, and should not be removed until the salad has been served.

In giving formal dinners or banquets a card corresponding with the name of the guest is placed on the napkin belonging to the seat to which he or she is to be assigned.

Formal banquets or dinners, or state and official banquets all over the world are served according to the French fashion. This fashion divides the meal into three distinct parts. Two are served from the kitchen, and the third from the pantry. The first part is from the oysters on shell to the Coup de Millieu or middle drinks (sherbets, punches, etc.); the second service continues through the roasts to the sweet entremets. That which is considered the dessert course is served from the pantry, and includes all ices, cakes, fruits, cheese, etc. A cup of Cafe Noir is served at the close of all dinners or suppers. It is served daily after dinner in all Creole households.

Flower decorations on the table should always be in low cut bowls, and of flat designs, so as not to obscure the view of any guests. A simple bouquet of flowers from the home garden, or a bit of greenery, should appear every day on the home table, and will brighten up a meal wonderfully. In formal feasts the corsage bouquets for ladies should not consist of more than six or eight large roses, if these flowers are used. The bouquets are tied with ribbon, and bear the name of the guests. They should be placed on the right side of the plate at the seat the lady is to occupy. A gentleman's boutonniere consists of one single rosebud, if this flower is used. Otherwise of a small "boutonniere" arrangement, and this is placed on the napkin next to the card bearing his name.

If Menus are used, they are placed on each cover.

Liqueurs, cordials, cigars, etc., are placed on a separate table, and are served after the ladies have retired to the parlors.

These suggestions will serve for all formal entertainments. The following them order and comfort will make the simplest meal a happy and pleasant one.

## BREAKFAST.

### Dejeuner.

The home breakfast is generally a modest repast consisting generally of such hors d'oeuvres as Cress, Radishes, etc., with some cereal (served with milk), beefsteak or fish, with potatoes, and numerous forms of breads or griddle cakes, waffles or muffins.

In Creole households fruits are always served first at breakfast, and generally raw.

### Cereals for Breakfast.

Grits, Hominy, Oatmeal, Cracked Wheat, Cornmeal Mush, Farina, Cerealine, Wheatena, etc. All these may be servel with cream, milk, milk and sugar, or with gravies.

### Vegetables for Breakfast,

Radishes, Cress, Sliced Cucumbers, Lettuce, Sliced Raw Tomatoes, Celery, Potatoes in any of the various forms of cooking given, Stewed Tomatoes, Fried Sweet Potatoes, are all served at breakfast, the raw vegetables as hors d'oeuvres.

### Warm Breakfast Dishes.

Broiled Tenderloin, Sirloin, Broiled Chops, Chicken, Ham, Fish, Small Fancy Game, Quail on Toast, Snipe, Woodcock, Fried Liver and Bacon, Fried Pork, Tenderloin or Chops, Fried Pigs' Feet, Grillades, Fried Soft-Shell Crabs, Veal Cutlets Breaded, Sausage, Stewed Tripe, Stewed Kidneys, all kinds of Hash (turkey, chicken, mutton, veal, beef, cornbeef, or otherwise), all kinds of Meat, Fowl and Fish Croquettes, Codfish Balls, Creamed Codfish, Creamed Chicken, Stewed Meats, Eggs in every variety of cooking (such as boiled, fried, scrambled, poached, on toast), Fried Ham and Eggs, Omelets, etc.

### Breakfast Breads and Cakes.

Any of the numberless varieties of Breads and Cakes, besides the Bakers' Bread, so generally used in New Orleans, such as Rolls, Biscuit, Muffins, Waffles, Corn Cakes, Griddle Cakes, Batter Cakes, Corn Bread, Muffin Bread, Sweet Potato Bread, Fritters, etc.

### Breakfast Beverages.

Coffee (Cafe Noir and Cafe au Lait) Chocolate, Cocoa and Tea (if preferred) may all be served as breakfast beverages.

### Hors d'Oeuvres for Breakfast.

These include Celery, Olives, Radishes, Cress, Pickles, Canapes, Sliced Cucumbers, Sliced Raw Tomatoes, Lettuce, Raw Oysters (when in season), and in general any hors doeuvres that may be served at dinner.

### LUNCHEON.

Goûter.

Perhaps no meal admits of such infinite variety as luncheon. Almost anything may be served for luncheon, from cold left-over meats, fish, etc., and all hors d'oeuvres and salads to desserts. Tea, coffee, cocoa, chocolate, iced lemonade, and almost all iced summer drinks, as well as fruits, are served acceptably at luncheon. Hot or cold bread may be served, as also forms of breakfast cakes and syrups.

The order of service varies. For instance, fruits may be served at the beginning of the meal, or as a dessert at the close, and so also with watermelons and muskmelons.

### DINNER.

Diner.

The order of service for dinner varies. In simple homes, where generally only two or three courses are served, such as soups, meats and vegetables and dessert, these should be served in their order. The hors d'oeuvres, whether one, two or many, should always be placed on the table before the dinner proper is served. Soups or Gumbos are served first.

The Creoles divide dinners into three classes: The dinner of one course, of two courses, and of three courses. The first they have appropriately named "Ambigu," because it admits of all dishes being brought to the table at the same time, from the soups to the desserts, and dishes are confounded. Among wealthy classes, the "Ambigu" is a dinner served hastily at night, after a theatre or opera party, or otherwise, coming in from a soirée, but among the poorer classes the "Ambigu" is made a very pleasant meal. Hors d'oeuvres and such desserts as cakes and fruits are placed on the table before the family is seated, and the soup is served as a "Releve," all the other dishes, from the roasts to the entrees and entremets and entremets sucres and saläd, being placed on the table at the same time. Jellies, fruits and cake compensate for the absence of elaborate desserts, and the vegetables anl sauces are few. Properly served, as is done daily in many a Creole home, an "Ambigu" may become an elegant and distinguished repast, though the viands are plain and simple.

In dinners of two courses the soup is again the "Releve," and the fish or meats and all the vegetables, entremets and entrees, and also the salad, constitute the first course. Salads, as a rule, should always be served with the roasts. The desserts constitute the second course.

In dinners of three courses, following always the French order of arrangement, which has always been observed in elegant Creole homes, the following is the order of service:

First Course—Soup or Gumbo, Hors d'Oeuvres.

Second Course—Fish (and with fish are always served potatoes in any form), Releves (where another dish is desired), Entrees, Coup de Millieu (a middle iced drink), Rotis or Roasts, Vegetables, Entremets, Salads, Entremets Sucres.

Third Course—Desserts, Compotes, Puddings, Pies, Cakes, Pieces Montees, Ices, Fruits, Petit Fours, Cheese, Coffee.

### Suitable Dishes for these Various Courses.

The following constitutes the list of suitable dishes for these various

#### Hors d'Oeuvres.
#### Relishes.

These may be either hot or cold, but ordinarily only cold hors d'oeuvres are used, and are passed as appetizers or relishes between the courses.

Cold Hors d'Oeuvres—Radishes, Celery, Olives, Cress, Lettuce, Roquette, Pickled Onions, Sliced Cucumbers, Sliced Tomatoes, Pickles, Mangoes, Melons, Anchovies, Sardines, Lyonnaise Sausage (Saucissons Lyonnaise), Bread and Butter, Crackers, Anchovy Sandwiches, Bologna Sausage cut and sliced, Cold Ham, Pigs' Feet, a Crawfish Bush (Buisson d'Ecrevisses), a Shrimp Bush (Buisson de Chevrettes), Boiled Crawfish, River Shrimp on Ice, Oysters on Half Shell, Raw Oysters, Sliced or Quartered Lemon, Salted Almonds, Salted Peanuts, Canapes of Caviar, Ham, Crab, etc.

Hot Hors d'Oeuvres—Petits Pâtes au Jus (or small hot patties of meats, etc.), Boudins Noirs et Blancs (Boudin Sausages, white and black), Rissoles, Sausages with or without Truffles, Rognons à la Brochette or Broiled Kidneys, Pigs' Feet, Bouchées d'Huitres or Oyster Patties, Fried Brains (whether of mutton or veal), Calves' Feet, Oxtail with Vinegar or Mustard Sauce.

#### Entrées.

Entrées are side dishes, and are served between the courses, immediately following the fish, and always preceding the roast. Entrees comprise all Stews, Ragoûts, Salmis, Matelotes, Vol-au-Vents, Cutlets, Sweetbreads, Rissoles, Compotes of Meats, Fowl or Fish, Filets of Veal or Beef Sauté, etc.; all Daubes, whether of Meat, Fowl or Pigeons; Poulet au Riz, Poulet Saute aux Champignons ou aux Petits Pois.

#### Relevés.

Releves are side dishes added to a course when it is desired to serve another dish. They comprise Filets of Beef or Veal, Boiled Meats served with garnish, Brochettes of Kidneys, Liver, etc.; Capons and Poulardes cooked with Rice, Poulet au Riz, Pâtes de Foies Gras, Loin of Veal, Knuckle of Veal, Sirloin Steak, etc.; Soft-Shell Crabs, Stuffed Crabs, etc.

#### Entremets.

These are of two kinds, Vegetable Entremets and Sweet Entremets. The former comprise all vegetables, and one or two are always served with an entrée, and the remainder are brought on with the roasts. Potatoes are always served with fish, and are good with all meats. With fowls they are best mashed. Sweet potatoes are served with all roasts, especially Roast Pork. Onions, Squash, Cucumbers, Asparagus, Eggplants are excellent with roast meats. Carrots, Parsnips, Turnips, Pumpkin, Greens, Cabbage, are good with boiled meats. Corn, Green Peas, Beets, Peas, Beans, may be served with either boiled or roast meats. Mashed Turnips are very appropriate to Roast Duck, Roast Pork and Mutton, and boiled meats, such as Boiled Mutton. Tomatoes and Green Peppers are served with every kind of meats. Green Peas are especially nice served with Young Spring Lamb, Sweetbreads, Filets of Veal or Beef, Spring Chicken, etc. Spinach is a very proper accompaniment to veal. Lemons cut into dice may be served with all fowls and fish.

#### Sweet Entremets.

These comprise all kinds of Fritters or Beignets, various sweet Omelets, and Fruits cooked in divers manners. (See chapter on Sweet Entremets.) Fritters, etc., are served in the middle of the course, often just before the Coup de Millieu, with the entrées. Sweet Entremets such as Omelette Souffle, Rhum Omelette, etc., always precede the dessert, being served immediately after the roasts.

#### Roasts.

These comprise all manner of Roast Meats, Poultry, Game, etc. The Salads are always brought to the table and served with the Roasts.

#### Desserts.

These comprise all manner of Compotes, Pies, Puddings, Cakes, Jellies and Marmalades, Preserves, Fruits, Ices, Petits Fours, Bonbons etc. Cheese and Nuts are brought to the table with the Desserts. Coffee is served as a finale to all dinners, banquets and suppers.

#### Important.

After having analyzed the above forms of service and the accompaniments of the various courses, a sensible woman will make her own deductions, remembering always that a good soup, a roast or entree, with one or two vegetables and a salad, and a simple dessert, is enough for any family, even when guests are expected. A well-served, simple dinner is far more satisfying to the average person than the most elaborate banquet.

**Above all devote your taste and ingenuity to devising appetizing dishes for your own loved ones at home. "To Make Home Happy"—this is the object of the Picayune Creole Cook Book.**

### How to Utilize Left-Over Food.

Never throw away scraps of bread or broken crusts or stale bread. Take all the broken pieces and brown them in the stove, and roll them on the bread board till grated fine, and sift through a coarse sieve. Again roll the crumbs that remain in the sieve, and sift as before. Put them all into a jar and cover, and keep them for use in cooking. A box of bread crumbs for dishes prepared "au Gratin" is indispensable in a kitchen.

Left-over stale bread is also used in making Bread Puddings, Bread Muffins, Queen Pudding etc.

Use all broken pieces of cakes in making puddings, such as Banana Souffle, and all Cake Puddings.

All cold left-over mashed potatoes may be used for making Croquettes or Puffs or Quenelles of Potatoes. Cold boiled potatoes left over may be utilized in preparing Lyonnaise Potatoes or French Fried Potatoes.

Left-over Greens may be used in making Salads. Left-over fish and chicken may be used in making Fish or Chicken Salad à la Mayonnaise.

Left-over meat, whether veal, mutton or beef, may be used in making Hash Croquettes of Boulettes.

Save all fat drippings and bits of fat meat and bacon skin. The former are excellent for frying fritters and doughnuts and pancakes; the latter for greasing the griddle for corn cakes, etc.

Keep all coarse, rough ends of beefsteak or sirloin, or the ends of tenderloin steaks. They make excellent stews or croquettes of meat balls.

The remains of yesterday's roast beef or mutton may be utilized in croquettes for breakfast, or cecils or cold meat for luncheon.

Remains of turkey or chicken or rabbit may be used in making Gumbos.

Save all left-over rice for Riz au Lait, griddle cakes, Calas, Jambalaya, etc.

All left-over cold boiled meat from soup may be used for Beef Hash.

When you have finished with the ham bone, do not throw it away, but after chipping all the meat off for "Frizzled Ham," boil the bone with cabbage or turnip or other vegetable greens, or with red or white beans or lentils. It gives a flavor to these dishes that they will not otherwise have.

Keep all the green parts of the Celery tips that do not make a beautiful decoration at the table when celery is served and use for flavoring for soups, salads, stews, etc.

Turnips and beans left over from yesterday may be made into a puree for dinner next day.

Keep all pieces of Plain or Puff Paste that are trimmed from the pies or patties. Roll them over again, cut into pretty squares, and serve at supper with preserves spread over them. Or simply put in the ice box and use the next day in making Rissoles with left-over meat.

When making Gold Cake, save the whites of eggs for Silver Cake. Or they may be used for making Angel Cake, Apple Snow, and all other forms of desserts in which Meringues are called for.

Finally, do not waste anything in the kitchen. Our grandmothers scrupulously saved every piece of bone or fat and these were utilized in making soft soap.

The careful housekeeper will manage to keep out of debt and set a good table, with much variety, on a small allowance, by faithfully saving and utilizing the left-overs.

### Invalid Cookery.

It has not been thought necessary to add a chapter on "Invalid Cookery" in this book, as all Creoles know how to prepare dainty articles of diet for the sick. Invalid cookery, moreover, does not differ much from the general household cookery, and all recipes given in this book for Bouillons, Oyster Soups, delicate Purées, Chicken Broth, Toasts, Broiled Chicken and Birds, Broiled Tenderloin Steak, delicate Custards, such as Milk Custards, Riz au Lait, Blanc Manger, Jellies, Gruels, Porridge, Egg Toasts, Fruit Waters, Mint Julips, Cobblers, Egg Nogg, Blackberry Cordials, etc:; delicate ways of serving oranges and other fruits—in fact, almost anything that may be ordered by a physician, from a Beef Broth or Oyster Soup to Milk Toast or Charlotte Russe may be found in the Picayune's Creole Cook Book. Reference has only to be made to the index, and with a slight reduction of quantity in all proportions, say about one-fourth, for a dish intended for one person, where Custards, etc., are indicated, the dish may be prepared.

The serving is the most important point after cooking. Never crowd a dish intended for an invalid. Spread a dainty napkin on the salver. Arrange the food in a most appetizing way, lay a rosebud or a flower fresh from the garden on the salver, and bring in the dainty, tempting morsel with a happy, cheery smile, though your heart may be sinking. The dish, in nine cases out of ten, will not fail to please, while your sunny smile will encourage the patient, and make him or her feel that recovery is certain. Then the battle is half won.

### KITCHEN HINTS.

The most important essential in regard to the economy and management of the kitchen is cleanliness—cleanliness in cooking, cleanliness in the keeping of the kitchen, from the clean floor to the pots and pans, and absolute cleanliness of person. It is to be feared that while many pay great attention to the two former requisites, the latter is too often neglected. The slovenly, untidy, unkempt cook has no place in a well-regulated kitchen, where, from earliest Creole days, the clean, tidy, old negresse, with neat guinea blue dress, white kerchief and bandana tignon, pots and pans washed so clean inside that you might pass your white gloved hand over them without a trace of soot or dirt attaching itself; brightly polished stove, and dish towels clean and spotless, is among the pleasant traditions that have, with modifications to times and events as regards domestic service, been accepted as a foundation rule in kitchen management and government.

The hands of a cook should be thoroughly washed before touching or handling anything that pertains in the least to the preparation of any dish. Never allow a number of dishpans, basins and piles of plates, spoons and other utensils to accumulate on the kitchen table or sink while you are engaged in cooking a meal. Do not let pans of dirty dish water, filled with kitchen refuse and grease so thick that it may be skimmed off, stand upon your kitchen table. By a little intelligent and careful management, a little care in cleansing and putting away a pan, dish or cup the moment that you have finished using it, a great deal of confusion and extra work may be avoided. When you finish with your rolling pin, flour pan, biscuit or paste board, go to the kitchen sink at once wash them off before the flour becomes too thick and hard to remove, and wipe dry and put them away in their proper places till wanted again. When you finish with your saucepans, gravy kettles, roasting pans, etc., fill them at once with hot water, let them stand a minute or so on the stove; then wash immediately, and dry thoroughly. Set them before the fire another minute or so, so that the interiors may be thoroughly dried before putting them away, and then put these also in their proper places. Never allow a dirty pot to remain over from one day to the next, covering it out of sight till it is again wanted. Such slovenly methods cannot be too strongly condemned.

Don't be afraid of hot water. Have your reservoir constantly filled, and your kettle always steaming when cooking. Use hot water freely in washing up all kitchen utensils, in which grease must accumulate while cooking, and all dirty, greasy dishes. Wash your cooking utensils, iron and agateware, and tin, inside and out, with hot water and soap; then rinse thoroughly in hot water, wipe them dry with a dry clean towel. Never, on any account, wipe a pot with a soapy or a greasy dish cloth.

Keep a cake of good kitchen soap in your kitchen, and use it freely in the cleansing of all pots or tins that require scouring. To remove the odor of onions from fish kettles and saucepans, put some wood ashes or soda in them, let stand on the stove a few minutes, till they boil, and wash in hot suds and rinse well.

In washing up the dishes, begin with the glasses. Wash these in clean water, using a few drops of ammonia, and you will be surprised what a beautiful clear cut-glass look will be imparted to even the cheapest glassware. Dry with a clean towel and rub lightly inside and out with a piece of paper. A beautiful, clear polish will thus be given. Nothing is so disgusting as a dingy glass. Let your crystal and glassware be as clear as a mirror.

Wash the cups and saucers next, and rinse and dry. Never let your dishes "drip," as is frequently done in many kitchens. Dishes that have been placed in a sink or pan to "drip" before being dried are always disagreeable to the touch, no matter how clean you may have washed them. An experienced housekeeper can tell in a moment, simply by touching a dish, whether it has been allowed to drip or was dried as soon as washed.

Don't be afraid of using soap, but remember, too, to rinse thoroughly after using. Cut bar soap into pieces, and keep in a dry place. Use one piece at a time, and thus avoid waste.

Wash greasy plates, dishes etc., with clean hot water and soap. Rinse thoroughly in clean hot water, and dry immediately on a clean, dry towel.

Wash silverware in clean hot water. Never put your forks and spoons into greasy, dirty water, in which you have already washed the dishes. Have a clean, fresh supply of hot water. Wash well, using soap freely where necessary, and then rinse in clean, hot water. A little salt will remove all stains from silver. Apply with a dry cloth. Dry silverware immediately after washing on a clean, dry towel.

Never throw white-handled ivory knives into water. Wash the steel part in hot water. To remove stains and also to polish, rub with a little dry wood ashes or a small quantity of baking powder, mixed with a little brickdust. Have a sufficient quantity of dish towels. It pays in the long run, not only in kitchen economy, but in the cleanliness of the kitchen and dining-room and the consequent good health of the family. Have a set of towels for the glassware, and mark these "Glass." In like manner for the cups and saucers and plates. Mark kitchen use, for pots and pans, and never use these on any account in washing or drying dishes intended for table use.

When you have finished washing the glassware, dishes, and pots and pans, wash the towels well in separate waters, using hot water and soap, and then rinse thoroughly in hot water first, and then in cold or tepid water. On no account, unless in rainy weather, hang them around the kitchen stove to dry, but hang them out in the fresh, open air, where the sun can shine upon them, and when they are thoroughly dry fold and put them away for use just as carefully as you would your toilet towels. In this way you will keep your kitchen towels clean, sweet and fresh.

Water that passes through zinc-lined iron pipes should never be used for cooking or drinking purposes, and water boiled in galvanized iron pots should never be used in cooking, as it becomes poisonous. Keep a good supply of fresh hot water in your kettles while cooking, and if taken from pipes always use that taken from hot water pipes. Never use water that has stood in a lead pipe over night for any purposes, especially a stone reservoir. There is art even in boiling water, and freshly-boiled water should always be used in cooking.

When using canned goods, never allow vegetables, fish or fruits to stand in the can when once the can is opened.

Do not keep vinegar or yeast in any but glass jars or bottles. Their acid attacks the glaze in stone crocks and jars, and becomes poisonous.

Never let meat stand in brown paper. It will absorb the taste of the paper.

Remember that salt will curdle new milk. Hence, in all dishes where new milk is used, add the salt after the dish is prepared.

Provide your kitchen with a clock. This is almost imperative. And, in addition to the regular supplies of pots which come with every stove, have a double kettle for cooking custards, grains, etc.; a double wire broiler, a wire toaster, a tin skimmer, a wooden spoon for beating cakes, a meat board, a biscuit board, a dozen patty pans and tartlet pans, a set of tin measures, two dish pans, one for washing the dishes, the other to rinse them in; a set of jelly cake tins, three or four pie pans, a can opener, a chopping knife, a wooden chopping bowl, two dippers, two funnels, one for sweets, and one for sour liquids; a lemon squeezer, a whisk brush for greasing griddles, a large flour box, a dredging box, a large-sized pepper box, a spice box in which you can put smaller spice boxes, a potato masher, a steamer, several kitchen knives, an apple corer, a set of tin pans and basins, and four or five stone jars. Do not buy low-priced earthenware, that will soon break; it pays in the end to get strong stoneware, costing a few cents more, for it will last for a lifetime.

All these conveniences purchased by the young housekeeper when setting out in life will last for years, with careful management, and will be found economical investments, as regards time, money and convenience, and kitchen comfort.

Remember to always keep your good temper in the kitchen. There is nothing like a bright, cheery, sunny-tempered housekeeper or cook. If you employ servants, never lose your temper in dealing with them. You will at once forfeit their respect. A surly, cross, ill-tempered, fault-finding mistress will make a cross, ill-tempered dissatisfied servant.

Let the Golden Rule be your guide in dealing with your servants, "Do unto others as you would have others do unto you."

CHAPTER XLIX.

## VARIETIES OF SEASONABLE FOODS FOUND IN THE NEW ORLEANS MARKET DURING THE YEAR.

How often is the complaint heard from the busy, tired housekeeper: "My husband and children are so tired of eating the same things, day in and day out; I really do not know what to give them for a change in diet!"

This is a complaint that should never be heard in the latitude of New Orleans, where nature is so prolific; where at all seasons of the year some dainty bit of game, poultry or meat is to be had at wonderfully low prices; where our rivers and lakes are stocked with the finest fish from January to December, and where our spring and autumn crops of vegetables and fruits, the former running all through the summer, the latter to the verge of the succeeding spring, make it possible for even the poorest family to enjoy variety and delicacy of viands at each daily meal.

The Creoles have an old adage that "Nature itself tells us what to eat," in the various vegetables and fruits of each season, and in the varieties of fish and flesh meat that are particularly adapted to each season. As the months wane, and a new season dawns, the good Creole housekeeper, even of unlimited means, far from trusting entirely to servants to do the marketing, makes it her duty to take a leisurely stroll through the French Market, where all the first fruits, vegetables, fish and game of the season are to be found, and she takes her own mental notes, and knows just what to order when her cook comes for the daily interview. Again, many of the most famous housekeepers do their own marketing entirely, and it is not an uncommon thing to see Madame or Mademoiselle going to market every morning, followed by some faithful old domestic who may still adhere to the fortunes of the family.

For the convenience of housekeepers generally, however, the Picayune will close this Creole Cook Book by giving for each month in the year the varieties of seasonable foods to be found in our latitude. By a simple daily reference to this list, the housewife may at once make her selections for the daily menu. With slight modifications incident to climate and productions, the list may be useful in any latitude. Again, to facilitate the choice of the housekeeper as to viands, a daily menu is given for one week, as also for great festivals, such as Christmas, New Year's, Easter and Thanksgiving Days.

**Two sets of these menus are given. The one is intended for families who are not obliged to exercise rigid economy in household management; the other for families of limited means, showing how it is quite possible for a family of six to live comfortably on a dollar a day, and at the same time enjoy as pleasing a variety, in a way, as wealthier people.**

These classifications will enable even the most inexperienced housekeeper, whether rich or poor, to make her own deductions in a clear and comprehensive manner, with benefit to herself and family.

### Seasonable Foods From January to December.

### JANUARY.

#### Meats.
Des Viandes.

Beef, Mutton, Pork, Lamb.

#### Poultry.
De la Volaille.

Turkey, Chicken, Capons, Geese, Domestic Ducks, Pigeons, Guinea Fowl.

#### Game.
Gibier.

All Game peculiar to January.

Canvasback Ducks, Mallard Ducks, Squab, Becassine or Snipe, Becasse or Woodcock, Partridge, Quail, Venison, and a variety of small birds, Rabbit, Hare, Squirrel and Poule d'Eau.

#### Fish.
Poisson.

Red Fish, Red Snapper, Flounder, Sheepshead, Spanish Mackerel, Pompano, Grouper, Green Trout, River Trout, Speckled Trout, Croakers, Bluefish, Sacalait, Patassas, Green Turtle, Diamond Back Terrapin,

Frogs, Oysters, Hard-Shell Crab, Soft-Shell Crab, Lake Shrimp, River Shrimp, Crawfish.

### Vegetables.
### Des Legumes.

Fresh Vegetables may be had as follows: Beets, Cabbage, Carrots, Chervil, Celery, Cress, Corn Salad, Cauliflower, Endive or Chicoree, Spinach, Salsify, Sorrel, Lettuce, Parsley, Parsnips, Radish, Roquette for salad, Mustard for salad, Turnips, Leeks and Rutabaga.

These are sown from August to December in the open ground, and are perfectly hardy in ordinary winters, such as we are accustomed to in Louisiana. Cucumber grown under glass, and sown in the beginning of October ripens about Christmas time, and continues to supply the home market, as well as the demands from Northern points, until about the end of April, when our open-ground Cucumbers begin to ripen and appear in the market.

### Fruits.
### Des Fruits.

Fresh fruits: Bananas, Pears, Apples, Oranges, Grapes, Lemons, Pineapples, Cherries, Cranberries.

## FEBRUARY.
### Meats.
### Des Viandes.

Beef, Mutton, Pork, Lamb.

### Poultry.
### De la Volaille.

Turkey, Capons, Chickens, Guinea Fowl, Geese, Domestic Ducks and Pigeons.

### Game.
### Gibier.

Canvasback Ducks, Mallard Ducks, Teal Duck, Squab, Becassine or Snipe, Becasse or Woodcock, Partridge, Quail, Wild Turkey, Wild Geese, Rabbit, Hare, Squirrel, Poule d'Eau, Venison.

### Fish.
### Poisson.

Red Fish, Red Snapper, Flounder, Spanish Mackerel, Sheepshead, Green Trout, Speckled Trout, Croakers, Bluefish, Green Turtle, Diamond-Back Terrapin, Frogs, Oysters, Hard-Shell Crab, Soft-Shell Crab, Lake Shrimp, River Shrimp, Crawfish.

### Vegetables.
### Des Legumes.

Beets, Carrots, Cabbage, Chervil, Celery, Cress, Cornsalad, Cauliflower, Endive or Chicoree, Spinach, Salsify, Sorrel, Lettuce, Parsley, Parsnips, Radish, Roquette, Mustard, Turnips, Leeks, Rutabaga.

### Fruits.
### Des Fruits.

Bananas Pears, Apples, Oranges, Grapes, Lemons, Pineapples, Cranberries.

## MARCH.
### Meats.
### Des Viandes.

Beef, Veal, Mutton, Lamb, Pork.

### Poultry.
### De la Volaille.

Turkeys, Ducks and Pigeons (domestic), Geese, Chickens, Capons, Young Pullets.

### Game.
### Gibier.

All the game common to February.

### Fish.
### Poisson.

The first Pompano of the season used to appear in March. It was much sought after. Of late years it has become so abundant that it is now shipped during every month of the year to every part of the Union. In February we have also Redfish, Red Snapper, Spanish Mackerel, Flounders, Trout, Croakers, Bluefish, Grouper, Saccalait, Patassas, Sheepshead, Perch, Hard-Shell Crab, Soft-Shell Crab, Oysters, Green Turtle, Terrapin, Lake and River Shrimp, Crawfish.

### Vegetables.
### Des Legumes.

All the above-mentioned Vegetables for February are to be found in the market in March, with the addition of Green Peas. The large Marrowfat Green Peas are hardy, and are planted from October to the end of March, while the little French Pea (Petit Pois) is more subject to damage from freeze, and is planted during January, and until April, ripening a crop in from forty to sixty days, according to weather and cultivation.

The vegetables for the month stand as follows: New Green Peas, Beets, Cabbage, Carrots, Chervil, Celery, Cress, Cornsalad, Cauliflower, Endive, Spinach, Salsify, Sorrel, Lettuce, Parsley, Parsnips, Roquette, Mustard, Turnips, Leeks, Rutabaga.

### Fruits.
### Des Fruits.

The first Strawberries appear early in March, and have been ripened at the end of February, when the blossom escapes the freezes that begin regularly in February. Oranges,

Bananas, Pineapples, etc., are plentiful.

## APRIL.
### Meats.
#### Des Viandes.

Beef, Veal, Mutton, Pork, Lamb, Spring Lamb. (This is Lamb born during the winter and reared under shelter, and fed almost entirely on milk. It is killed in the spring, generally at Easter time, and is a regular accompaniment to the Creole Easter dinner. It is a great delicacy, but Lamb that is not over six months old makes good eating.)

### Poultry.
#### De la Volaille.

Chicken, Young Guinea Fowl, Green Geese, Young Ducks, Capons.

### Fish.
#### Poisson.

Pompano, Spanish Mackerel, Red Snapper, Redfish, Bluefish, Grouper, Sea Trout, Brook Trout, Croakers, Perch, Sacalait, Patassas, Green Turtle, Frogs' Legs, Hard-Shell Crab, Soft-Shell Crab, Poule d'Eau.

Oysters begin to grow milky in the latter part of April, when kept standing for any length of time, and are, consequently, not eaten by the Creoles, unless they are at the lakeside, where the toothsome bivalve is taken directly from the waters. From April till September, following the old adage that Oysters are good in every month in which an "R" occurs, the Oysters will disappear from this list of seasonable fish. Nevertheless, in nearly all the large restaurants of New Orleans they are served.

### Game.
#### Gibier.

Mallard Ducks, Canvasback Ducks, Spring Teal Ducks, Squabs, Snipe, Woodcock, Partridge.

### Vegetables.
#### Des Legumes.

This is a most interesting month in the New Orleans markets. We have all the staple articles from the open ground, but. besides Green (sweet) Peppers, Tomatoes and Eggplants, sown in November, and kept under glass until late in March, make their appearance in the market. The general crop of Green Peas is now in the market, and within the range of everybody's purse. New Potatoes are quite plentiful. Snap Beans are gradually getting cheaper, and thousands of bushel boxes go by express every day to Northern points. Early Corn and Artichokes, from the Lower Coast of Louisiana, arrive with every boat. The market stands: New Potatoes, New Green Peas, Early Corn, Sweet Green Peppers, New Tomatoes, Eggplants, Hot Peppers, Snap Beans, and all the vegetables mentioned in the list for March. (See March Vegetables.

### Fruits.
#### Des Fruits.

The Japan Plum, also called the Medlar, or Loquet, and in familiar Creole Mespilus, ripens in the beginning of April, while the Mariana Plum comes in towards the 15th of April, if the weather is favorable. Strawberries are now plentiful and cheap. Dewberries and Blackberries are brought in by the negroes in large quantities, and the cry fills the streets. We have also a continued abundance of Apples, Oranges, Bananas, Pineapples, etc.

## MAY.
### Meats.
#### Des Viandes.

Beef, Veal, Mutton, Lamb, Pork.

### Poultry.
#### De la Volaille.

Spring Chickens, Young Ducks, Chickens, Capons, Green Geese, Young Turkeys (Dindonneau, considered a great delicacy).

### Fish.
#### Poisson.

The same as for the month of April.

### Vegetables.
#### Des Legumes.

During the month of May the New Orleans markets are fairly glutted with Snap Beans, Green Peas, Peas, Lentils, Cucumbers, Young Onions, Potatoes, etc. Tomatoes and Eggplants that have ripened in the open ground fill the stalls. Cabbage, which does not resist much heat or drought, grows scarce, as also celery. Otherwise the vegetables continue in abundance, the same as found in the list for March. (See March Vegetables).

Young Squash makes its appearance this month, and is plentiful. The first Muskmelons arrive in New Orleans from the parishes and gardens around the city towards the middle of May, and Watermelons come in fine and tempting at the close of May, Carloads of Creole Onions and New Potatoes are shipped North.

### Game.
#### Gibier.

The game laws now begin to be enforced, and, with the exception of Sand Snipe and Reed Birds, we have little game until the 1st of September, when the hunting season opens.

### Fruits.
#### Des Fruits.

The first peaches ripen together with the large-fruited Plums. In a week or so these fruits overrun the market. Figs begin to ripen towards the end of the month, providing the weather was warm during April. Oranges, Bananas, Pineapples, etc., continue plentiful.

## JUNE.
### Meats.
#### Des Viandes.

Beef, Veal, Mutton, Lamb. Pork is eschewed in New Orleans from June to the beginning of October and November, as, from hygienic principles, it should never be eaten in warm weather.

### Poultry.
#### De la Volaille.

Spring Chickens, Chickens, Geese, Young Turkeys, Pigeons.

### Game.
#### Gibier.

The famous Pababotte makes its appearance this month, and remains a delightful article of food till the middle of October. In the months of August and September they are very fat and excellent and a game much prized by epicures and connoisseurs. Reed Birds, Grassets, Robins, Larks, which are the terror of the rice planters, appear in abundance, and overrun the market.

### Fish.
#### Poisson.

The same as for the month of April.

### Vegetables.
#### Des Legumes.

Melons are gradually gaining the first place in the market, and are shipped to all points. Peas are beginning to get scarce. Celery is now supplied by the Northern markets and is found in abundance. Butterbeans and Lima Beans appear in the market, and are in great demand, especially the Butterbeans. The market stands: Butterbeans, Snap Beans, Green Peas, Celery, Lima Beans, Beets, Carrots, Chervil, Cress, Cornsalad, Cauliflower, Corn, Endive, Spinach, Salsify, Sorrel, Lettuce, Parsley, Parsnips, Radish, Roquette, Mustard, Turnips, Leeks and Rutabaga.

### Fruits.
#### Des Fruits.

Peaches and Plums arrive in large quantities. The Lecomte Pears and Grapes ripen quickly under the hot rays of the June sun, and are soon within reach of everyone's purse. Figs are plentiful, and are being bought up by the canning establishments, but almost all the ancient homes of New Orleans have fig trees in their gardens or yards, and the luscious tropical fruit is within the reach of all. Strawberries, Blackberries, Dewberries, Bananas, Oranges, Pineapples, Muskmelons, Cantaloupes, Watermelons, which may be properly classed under the heading of fruits, because they are eaten as such for desserts in New Orleans, are everywhere in abundance.

## JULY.
### Meats.
#### Dee Viandes.

Beef, Mutton, Lamb, Veal.

### Poultry.
#### De la Volaille.

Chickens, Young Geese, Spring Chickens, Pigeons.

### Game.
#### Gibier.

Pababotte, Reed Birds, Grassets, Robins, Larks, Quail.

### Fish.
#### Poisson.

The same supplies as for the month of April. (See April Fish.)

### Vegetables.
#### Des Legumes.

To use the familiar saying of the New Orleans dealers, "The Watermelon is now the boss of the market." It is placed on ice and eaten at any hour of the day, being most cooling and refreshing. Vegetables produced with much hard work cannot now compete with the popularity of the Watermelon, which is a favorite with all classes, and is put on the market in such enormous quantities that they are almost given away. Carloads arrive each day from the parishes and from the truck farms around New Orleans, and they are bought up as fast as offered. One famous specimen, recently called the "Triumph," weighing from ninety to one hundred pounds, was found to be as sweet as honey. Other vegetables are the same as in June. (See June.)

### Fruits.
#### Des Fruits.

Pears, Grapes and Peaches continue in abundance. The Fig is everywhere, and Strawberries, Blackberries, Oranges and Pineapples are cheap. Lemons are in great demand, the Creoles using large quantities of this cooling Iced Lemonade all during the summer months.

### AUGUST.
#### Meats.
#### Des Viandes.
Beef, Veal, Mutton, Lamb.

#### Poultry.
#### De la Volaille.
Chicken, Young Geese, Young Guinea Fowl, Pigeons.

#### Game.
#### Gibier.
Pababotte, Reed Birds, Grassets, Robins, Larks, Squab.

#### Fish.
#### Poisson.
The same supplies as for the month of June. (See June Fish.)

#### Vegetables.
#### Des Legumes.
Snap Beans, Peas, Eggplant, Squash, Cucumber, Corn, Lettuce, Carrots, Beets, Parsnips, Spinach, Potatoes, Tomatoes, Butterbeans, Lima Beans, Onions, Shallots, Green Peppers, Broccoli, Cauliflower.

August is the poorest of all months for vegetables. The Snap Beans begin to get hard and stringy; and the lettuce soft under the rays of the sun. But people are quite content. Melons continue in abundance, and the markets are stocked with fruits, so grateful in our clime, and all know that in a month there will be a new crop of autumn vegetables.

#### Fruits.
#### Des Fruits.
Peaches, Pears, Plums, Grapes, Figs, Mespilus, Oranges, Bananas, Pineapples, Lemons, Grape Fruit, are all in abundance.

### SEPTEMBER.
#### Meats.
#### Des Viandes.
Beef, Veal, Mutton, Lamb.

#### Poultry.
#### De la Volaille.
Spring Chicken, Young Turkeys, Geese, Guinea Fowl, Pigeons, Domestic Ducks.

#### Game.
#### Gibier.
Woodcock, Snipe, Larks, Wild Ducks, Canvasback Ducks. Partridges, Quail, Squab, Mallard Ducks, and Teal Ducks are rare.

#### Fish.
#### Poisson.
Pompano, Red Snapper, Redfish, Spanish Mackerel, Flounder, Grouper, Bluefish, Sheepshead, Trout, Croakers, Green Turtle, Terrapin, Frogs, Hard-Shell Crab, Soft-Shell Crab, Lake Shrimp, River Shrimp, Crawfish. The Oyster is with us again, and remains a delightful article of food till the latter part of April.

#### Vegetables.
#### Des Légumes.
Potatoes, Turnips, Artichokes, Peas, Beans, Carrots, Onions, Tomatoes, Salsify, Mushrooms, Lettuce, Sorrel, Celery, Brussels Sprouts, Cauliflower, Sweet Potatoes, Squash, Eggplant, Cucumber, Green Pepper, Parsnips, Cress.

#### Fruits.
#### Des Fruits.
Fruits throughout September continue the same as in August, with still more generous supplies of Oranges, Bananas and Pineapples.

### OCTOBER.
#### Meats.
#### Des Viandes.
Beef, Veal, Mutton, Lamb, Pork.

#### Poultry.
#### De la Volaille.
Turkey, Chicken, Spring Chicken, Geese, Guinea Fowl, Domestic Duck, Pigeons.

#### Game.
#### Gibier.
Venison, Canvasback Duck, Woodcock, Snipe, Partridge, Quail, Reed Birds, Larks, Grassets, Robins, Squab. Mallard and Teal Ducks continue to be rare till November.

#### Fish.
#### Poisson.
Pompano, Red Snapper, Redfish, Spanish Mackerel, Sheepshead, Flounder, Grouper, Bluefish, Trout, Croakers, Green Turtle, Terrapin, Poule d'Eau, Frogs, Hard-Shell Crab, Soft-Shell Crab, Lake and River Shrimp, Crawfish, Oysters.

#### Vegetables.
#### Des Legumes.
Snap Beans and Green Corn sown in the end of August and early in September, are with us again in abundance. Radishes are juicy and brittle. Turnips are young and tender, and appear on time, to serve with "Salmi of Wild Ducks." Blood Beets and Young Carrots add to the assortment of vegetables, which gradually increases and assumes the

diversity of the crops of the early spring. All the vegetables that are found under the lists for March and April are again with us in October. (See lists for March and April.)

### Fruits.
#### Des Fruits.

The first Louisiana Oranges from the spring budding appear in the market this month, the Creole and the Satsumas being the first to ripen. Other fruits are Peaches, Pears, Plums, Grapes, Oranges, Bananas, Pineapples and some late Figs.

## NOVEMBER.
### Meats.
#### Des Viandes.

Beef, Veal, Mutton, Lamb, Pork.

### Poultry.
#### De la Volaille.

Turkey, Chickens, Spring Chickens, Domestic Ducks and Pigeons, and Pigeons.

### Game.
#### Gibier.

Canvasback Ducks, Wild Ducks of many varieties, Woodcock, Snipe, Partridges, Robins, Larks, Reed Birds, Quail, Rabbits, Hares, Squirrel, Venison. Teal Ducks and Mallard Ducks are abundant. Poule d'Eau appears in November.

### Fish.
#### Poisson.

All the varieties found under the list for October hold good for November. (See list for October.)

### Vegetables.
#### Des Legumes.

The market is now splendid with a variety of vegetables, principally Snap Beans, New Corn, Butterbeans, Beets, Cabbage, Carrots, Chervil, Celery, Cress, Cornsalad, Cauliflower Endive, Spinach, Salsify, Sorrel, Lettuce, Parsley, Parsnips, Roquette, Mustard, Turnips, Leeks, Rutabaga, Brocoli.

In new vegetables we have now the second crop of New Potatoes, that were planted by the farmers in August. The Crooked-necked Pumpkin, or Cashaw, is with us, and is in demand, as also the Globe Pumpkin. The Sweet Potatoes continue to arrive in abundance. The first New Cabbage reaches the market, as also New Lettuce, Spinach, Turnips, Kohlrabi, so much eaten by the Italian population; and other vegetables are most plentiful and cheap.

### Fruits.
#### Des Fruits.

The Louisiana Orange has now conquered the fruit market, and reigns supreme over all other fruits. Thousands of trees planted since the terrible freeze of 1899, it may be incidentally mentioned, are now bearing fruit, and if spared for a few years will bring abundant returns to the Louisiana orange growers. It would seem that no fruit tree offers such inducements to the planter, and even if a freeze should kill the trees every six or eight years, it still pays to grow oranges in Louisiana. Among other fruits are Bananas, Pears, Pineapples, Cherries, Grapes, etc.

### Nuts.
#### Noix.

The Louisiana Pecan now makes its appearance in the market. Pecans are now being planted on a large scale, for the demand for Louisiana nuts has never been supplied. The owners of pecan trees have the nuts gathered up and sent to market against the great demand sure to follow in the approaching Christmas holidays.

## DECEMBER.
### Meats.
#### Des Viandes.

Beef, Veal, Mutton, Pork.

### Poultry.
#### De la Volaille.

Turkeys, Chickens, Spring Chickens, Capons, Geese, Domestic Ducks, Guinea Fowl.

### Game.
#### Gibier.

Venison, Snipe, Woodcock, Partridge, Robins, Grassets, Larks, Squab, Canvasback Ducks, Mallard Ducks, Teal Ducks, Quail, Rabbits, Hare, Squirrel, and a number of game of good varieties.

### Fish.
#### Poisson.

All fish common to the New Orleans markets in the months of January and November hold for December. Fish now has a most excellent flavor, and is found daily on our tables.

### Vegetables.
#### Des Legumes.

All vegetables common to November (see list) are plentiful in December.

### Fruits.
#### Des Fruits.

All fruits common to November (see lists) are common to December. It is the holiday season and the markets are abundantly supplied.

## In the Groceries at All Seasons.

### Meats.

Canned Beef, Corned Beef, Chipped Beef, Canned Beef and Pork Tongue, Ham, Salt Pork, Deviled Ham, Breakfast Bacon, Pigs' Feet, Sausage, Lyonnaise Sausage, Hogs' Head Cheese, Extract of Beef. Canned meats are not generally used in New Orleans in summer, but they are much used as luncheon and supper dishes in winter.

### Fowl.

Canned Turkey, Chicken, Ducks, Pigeons, Foies Gras, etc. All these are used more generally in winter.

### Fish.

Salt Codfish, Salt Mackerel, Herrings, Salt Roe, Smoked Salmon, Smoked Halibut, Canned Lobster, Canned Shrimp, Canned Salmon, Canned Oysters, Sardines, Anchovies, Anchovy Butter, Caviars.

### Game.

Dried Venison, Buffalo Tongue, Wild Meats, etc.

### Vegetables.

Canned Corn, Green Peas, Asparagus, Tomatoes, Cauliflower, Cabbage, Brocoli, Cucumbers, (pickles), Lima Beans, Dried White and Red Beans, Split Peas, Kidney Peas, Carrots, Parsnips and Horseradish.

### Fruits.

Lemons, Canned Peaches, Pears, Pineapples, Cherries, Grapes, Plums, Damsons, Grape Fruit, Cranberries, Strawberries, Raspberries, Blackberries, Currants. All the above canned fruits made into jellies, marmalades and preserves. All manner of Preserves, Confitures, Dried Apples, Dried Peaches.

### Pickles and Sauces.

Chow-chow, Mixed, Sweet Cucumber, Gherkins, Green Tomatoes, Sweet Tomato, Cauliflower, Pickled Onions, etc. All kinds of Sauces and Salad Dressings generally.

### Nuts.

Pecans, Peanuts, Filberts, Hickory Nuts, Brazilian Nuts, English Walnuts, Walnuts, Chestnuts (in season), Louisiana Pecans.

### MENUS.

The Picayune will now proceed to give several forms of daily menus, which will greatly assist the housekeeper in forming the individual "Menu" that will suit her purse and the taste of her household.

The following Menus are intended as weekly suggestions for Breakfast Luncheon and Dinner. Two sets are given—one for families whose means will permit of a more elaborate expenditure of money, the other for families of limited means. A set of Menus intervene which is intended as a special suggestion for holiday feasts. These Menus have been prepared with especial care. The most inexperienced housekeeper, following their order of arrangement, will be able to vary daily by referring to the "List of Seasonable Foods", found in the New Orleans market during each month in the year. Thus there may be infinite variety of food each day on the family table. It is particularly urged that, for the sake of the good health of the family, fish, meats, game, vegetables and fruits be eaten in their proper season. It may be incidentally mentioned that canned meats are not as wholesome in our tropical clime during the summer months as fresh meats; in regard to canned vegetables, with the exception of Truffles, Mushrooms and Asparagus, there is seldom necessity for purchasing canned goods during any season, owing to the abundance of our spring and autumn crops. Fresh vegetables, fresh fish and fresh meats are always the healthiest foods. With regard to fruits, the Creoles always begin breakfast and end dinner and luncheon (and supper, if served) with fresh fruits. They consider this a requisite of good health and powerful aids to nutrition and digestion. It is the rarest thing to hear a Creole, even though far advanced in years, complaining of dyspepsia. It is practically an unknown disease among the race, notwithstanding the richness and variety of food in which they indulge. Again, most delightful and healthful customs among the Creoles are to squeeze the juice of half a lemon in water and drink it just before retiring and to eat an orange in the early morning, shortly after rising. There is an old adage among them that "an orange is gold in the morning, and silver at noon and night," thus showing how intrinsically valuable they consider the morning orange. Often as not, when the old Creole servant carries up the morning cup of "Cafe Noir" to Monsieur or Madame, beside the Daily Picayune, which for nearly seventy years has been invariably part of the "morning portion," there will, also, be found upon the platter, in a delicate china saucer, a dainty orange, peeled and resting like a blossom in the open golden shell, gracefully petaled around.

In the garden homes of New Orleans, and often around the plantation parishes, the young folks go out in the early morning and pluck an orange from the trees and eat it, and their cheeks are the rosier, their eyes the brighter and their health and spirits the better for this pleasant indulgence. Oranges are now shipped from Louisiana to every section of the United States, and there is no reason why the people from far-off Maine, or the extreme end of the States and territories, may not adopt this healthful old Creole custom.

With modifications, as regards fish and game, especially, the following Menus may be adapted to any section:

## WEEKLY SUGGESTIONS.

### Menu for Monday.

**BREAKFAST.**

Sliced Oranges.
Boiled Grits, Milk or Cream.
Fried Croakers. Olives.
Broiled Spring Chicken. Potato Croquettes.
Radishes. Watercress.
Batter Cakes. Butter. Louisiana Syrup.
Cafe au Lait.
The Daily Picayune.

**LUNCHEON.**

Oysters on Half Shell. Oyster Crackers.
Pickles.
Thin Slices of Cold Ham.
Lettuce Salad, French Dressing.
Brie Cheese. Lemon Jelly Wafers.

**DINNER.**

Okra Gumbo.
Celery. Olives. Salted Almonds.
Boiled Sheepshead, Cream Sauce.
Mashed Potatoes.
Roast Filet of Beef, Tomato Sauce.
Boiled Rice. Green Peas.
Stuffed Tomatoes. Asparagus.
Beet Salad, French Dressing.
Queen's Pudding, Wine Sauce.
Pineapple Ice.
Roquefort. Fruit. Louisiana Nuts.
Cafe Noir.

### Menu for Tuesday.

**BREAKFAST.**

Grapes.
Small Hominy, Sugar and Cream.
Boiled Trout, Sauce a la Creme.
Broiled Tenderloin Steak.
French Fried Potatoes.
Celery. Radishes.
French Rolls. Butter. Cafe au Lait.
The Daily Picayune.

**LUNCHEON.**

River Shrimp on Ice.
Cold Roast Veal.
Tomato Salad, Mayonnaise Dressing.
Hominy Croquettes. Celery.
Cup Cake. Raspberry Jelly. Cheese.
Tea or Cocoa.

**DINNER.**

Cream of Tomato Soup, with Croutons.
Celery. Olives. Mangoes.
Oyster Patties a la Reine.
Noyau of Beef With Mushrooms.

New Potatoes a la Parisienne.
Louisiana Rice.
Roast Canvasback Duck, Mashed Turnips.
Cauliflower au Vinaigrette.
Charlotte Russe. Orange Sherbet. Wafers.
Neufchatel.
Strawberry Jam. Fruits. Nuts.
Cafe Noir.

### Menu for Wednesday.

**BREAKFAST.**

Prunes or Iced Figs (in season).
Wheatena, Milk.
Broiled Tenderloin Trout, Sauce a la Tartare.
Potato Chips. Olives.
Broiled Ham. Scrambled Eggs.
French Toast. Butter.
Cafe au Lait.
The Daily Picayune.

**LUNCHEON.**

Caviars aur Canapes.
Cold Duck. Lettuce Salad. Rice Croquettes.
White Mountain Cake.
Compote of Peaches. Cheese.
Tea. Milk.

**DINNER.**

Bayou Cook Oysters.
Spanish Olives. Celery.
Consomme de Volaille.
Broiled Sheephead, Sauce a la Maitre d Hotel.
Potatoes a la Duchesse.
Lamb Cutlets Breaded, Sauce Soubiase.
String Beans. Stuffed Cabbage.
Spinach with Hard-Boiled Eggs.
Roast Leg of Mutton, Mint Sauce.
Roquette Salad, French Dressing.
Lemon Pudding.
Roquefort.
Strawberry Ice. Fruit, Nuts.
Cafe Noir.

### Menu for Thursday.

**BREAKFAST.**

Bananas.
Oatmeal. Cream.
Broiled Patassas. Potato Croquettes.
Cress. Salt. Olives.
Fried Liver and Bacon. Small Hominy.
Poached Eggs on Toast.
Waffles. Louisiana Syrup. Butter.
Cafe au Lait.
The Daily Picayune.

**LUNCHEON.**

River Shrimp on Ice.
Fish Croquettes. Olives.
Cold Mutton. Potato Salad. French Rolls.
Brioches. Orange Marmalade. Fruit.
Tea.

**DINNER.**

Green Turtle Soup. Croutons.
Radishes. Celery. Olives. Pickles.
Vol-au-Vent of Oysters.
Veal Saute aux Champignons.
Rice. Squash.
Potatoes a la Creme.
Roman Punch.
Roast Mallard Duck. Green Peas.
Banana Fritters.
Watercress Salad. Asparagus.
Peach Pie. Roquefort.
Biscuit Glace. Assorted Cakes. Fruit.
Cafe Noir.

## Menu for Friday.
### BREAKFAST.
Strawberries and Cream.
Oatmeal, Cream.
Broiled Oysters on Toast.
Olives. Celery.
Fried Perch. Small Hominy.
Lyonnaise Potatoes.
Corn Batter Bread. Butter. Louisiana Syrup.
Cafe au Lait.
The Daily Picayune.

### LUNCHEON.
Oysters on Half Shell.
Fish Croquettes. Crackers. Pickles.
Chicoree Salad.
Apple Float. Sponge Cake. Fruit. Cheese.
Tea or Cocoa.

### DINNER.
Oysters on Ice.
Bisque d'Ecrevisse (Crawfish Bisque.)
Radishes. Cress. Celery. Olives.
Broiled Pompano, Sauce a la Maitre d'Hotel.
Julienne Potatoes.
Baked Red Snapper a la Creole.
Butterbeans. New Corn on the Cob.
Boiled Young Creole Onions.
Drawn Butter Sauce.
Macaroni or Spaghetti a la Creole.
Salad a la Louisianaise.
Riz au Lait. Angel Cake. Assorted Fruit.
Lemon Wafers. Neufchatel.
Raisins. Nuts.
Cafe Noir.

## Menu for Saturday.
### BREAKFAST.
Muskmelon on Ice.
Grits. Milk.
Stewed Tripe. Omelette a la Creole. Olives.
Snipe on Toast.
Flannel Cakes. Louisiana Syrup.
Cafe au Lait.
The Daily Picayune.

### LUNCHEON.
Anchovies.
Fish Salad, Mayonnaise Dressing.
French Bread. Deviled Ham. Crackers.
Blackberry Pie. Cheese Straws.
Watermelon on Ice.
Tea or Coffee.

### DINNER.
Cream of Asparagus Soup.
Celery. French Olives. Pickles.
Bouillabaisse (Redfish and Red Snapper).
Potatoes a la Maitre d'Hotel.
Chicken Saute aux Petits Pois. Boiled Rice.
Parsnips. Carrots a la Creole.
Roast Venison, Currant Jelly.
Baked Sweet Potatoes.
Green Pepper and Tomato Salad, French Dressing.
Peach Meringue Pie. Roquefort. Fruit.
Cafe Noir.

## Menu for Sunday.
### BREAKFAST.
Peaches and Cream.
Cracked Wheat, Milk.
Broiled Spanish Mackerel.
Sauce a la Maitre d'Hotel.
Julienne Potatoes.
Radishes. Cress. Olives.
Creamed Chicken. Small Hominy.
Beaten Biscuit.
Broiled Woodcock (Becasse) on Toast.
Rice Cakes. Butter. Louisiana Syrup.
Cafe au Lait.
The Daily Picayune.

### DINNER.
Gumbo File.
Radishes. Cress. Olives. Salted Almonds.
Courtbouillon a la Creole.
Potato Puffs.
Sweetbreads a la Creole.
Green Peas.
Ponche a la Cardinale.
Roast Turkey, Cranberry Sauce.
Broiled Tomatoes. Stuffed Artichokes.
Celery Salad, French Dressing.
Broiled Quail on Toast. Asparagus.
Nesselrode Pudding.
Almond Macaroons. Pineapple Ice.
Assorted Cakes. Fruit. Assorted Nuts.
Edam Cheese.
Cafe Noir.

### SUPPER.
Oysters on Half Shell.
Cold Turkey. Tomato Salad. French Toast.
Chocolate Cake.
Cheese. Fig Preserves. Fruit.
Tea. Milk.

## MENUS FOR HOLIDAY FEASTS AND BANQUETS.

### A New Year's Menu.
Menu Pour le Jour de l'An.

### BREAKFAST.
Oranges.
Oatmeal, Cream.
Radishes. Cress. Olives.
Broiled Trout, Sauce a la Tartare.
Potatoes a la Duchesse.
Creamed Chicken. Omelette aux Confitures.
Salade a la Creole.
Batter Cakes, Louisiana Syrup. Fresh Butter.
Cafe au Lait.

### DINNER.
Oysters on Half Shell.
Spanish Olives. Celery. Pickles.
Salted Almonds.
Green Turtle Soup, Croutons.
Broiled Spanish Mackerel,
Sauce a la Maitre d'Hotel.
Julienne Potatoes.
Lamb Cutlets Breaded, Sauce Soubise.
Green Peas.
Sweetbreads a la Creole.
Ponche a la Romaine.
Roast Turkey, Cranberry Sauce.
Baked Yams. Cauliflower au Gratin.
Asparagus a la Maitre d'Hotel.
Lettuce, Salad Dressing.
Broiled Snipe on Toast.
Pouding a la Reine, Wine Sauce. Mince Pie.
Cocoanut Custard Pie.
Biscuit Glace. Petits Fours. Fruits. Nuts.
Raisins.
Cheese. Toasted Crackers.
Cafe Noir.

### SUPPER.
Cold Turkey, Currant Jelly.
Celery Salad.
French Rolls.   Butter.   Assorted Cakes.
Fruit.   Nuts.
Tea.

### A More Economical New Year's Menu.

#### BREAKFAST.
Sliced Oranges.
Oatmeal and Cream.
Broiled Spring Chicken.   Julienne Potatoes.
Radishes.   Celery.
Egg Muffins.   Fresh Butter.   Louisiana Syrup.
Cafe au Lait.

#### DINNER.
Consomme.
Radishes.   Celery.   Olives.   Pickles.
Boiled Sheepshead, Cream Sauce.
Mashed Potatoes.
Vol-au-Vent of Chicken.
Salmi of Wild Duck.   Green Peas.
Banana Fritters.
Roast Turkey, Cranberry Sauce.
Baked Yams, Sliced and Buttered.
Green Pepper and Tomato Salad, French Dressing.
Pointes d'Asperges au Beurre.
Mince Pie.   Roquefort.
Vanilla Ice Cream.   Sponge Cake.
Assorted Fruits.   Nuts.   Raisins.
Cafe Noir.

#### SUPPER.
Cold Turkey, Cranberry Sauce.
Tomato Salad.
Cake.   Fruit.   Tea.

### A New Year's Decoration.

On New Year's Day, no matter how humble her circumstances, the Creole housewife will have freshly blooming roses on her table. In our delightful climate, where flowers bloom the year round, and where, in winter, especially, roses are in their zenith of glory, there are few homes, indeed, in which a patch of ground is not set aside for the cultivation of flowers; while in the lovely open gardens in the "Garden District of New Orleans" roses in exquisite bloom overrun the trellises and arbors and smile upon you from the fancifully laid-out garden beds. It is wonderful how a bit of green, with a few roses nestling between, will brighten up the homeliest table. With the linen spotless, the crystal shining, a few loose clusters of rosebuds, typical of the budding year, blooming on the mantels and in low, glass bowls in the center, a charm is imparted to the feast, the graceful idea of beginning anew being suggested, and a lingering fragrance thrown over memory's page that will remain as an incentive to nobler effort for many a day.

### Menu for Easter Sunday.

#### BREAKFAST.
Strawberries and Cream.
Small Hominy, Milk.
Boiled Tenderloin Trout, Sauce a la Creme.
Potatoes a la Parisienne.
Cress.   Radishes.   Olives.
Breakfast Bacon.   Scrambled Eggs.
Broiled Woodcock on Toast.
Flannel Cakes.   Louisiana Syrup.
Cafe au Lait.
The Daily Picayune.

#### DINNER.
Caviars sur Canapes.
Oyster Soup.   Crackers.
Mangoes.   Olives.   Salted Almonds.
Broiled Pompano, Sauce a la Maitre d'Hotel.
Pigeons Sautes aux Champignons.
Ponche a la Cardinale.
Roast Lamb, Mint Sauce.   Green Peas.
Cauliflower au Beurre.
Asparagus.
Salade aux Laitues et aux Cerfeuils.
Teal Duck sur Canapes.
Angel Cake.   Brandied Peaches.   Lemon Ice.
Bouchees Glacees.
Fruit.   Nuts.   Raisins.   Roquefort.
Cafe Noir.

#### SUPPER.
Warmed-over Lamb.   Currant Jelly.
Celery Salad.
Waffles.   Louisiana Syrup   Fruit.
Tea.

### An Easter Decoration.

On Easter Sunday the dinner table should always be decked with flowers, or at least some bit of green indicative not only of the resurrection of all nature, but also of the most glorious festival of the year. A beautiful decoration for those who can afford it is to arrange a cut-glass bowl on a mirror and fill it with Maiden-hair Fern and Calla Lilies. Fill the center of the Calla Lilies with sprays of Maiden-hair Fern; garnish the edges of the mirror with bits of fern and smilax, and the effect of all will be a miniature pond, with the lilies reflected within and the banks overrun with smilax.

If this decoration is beyond your means, the home gardens are filled at this season with hyacinths, and violets, and narcissus. Smilax runs wild in our Louisiana woods, especially around New Orleans, and is to be had for the gathering. A bowl of hyacinths or violets, or sprays of roses, mingled with Maiden-hair fern or even a simple bowl of smilax, young mint and rose leaf greenery, will make the table beautiful, and whisper the Easter message to the heart. It is really wonderful how a bit of green brightens up an apartment. One of the most beautiful and effective Easter decorations ever seen in New Orleans was at the home of the gentle poet, "Pearl Rivers" (Mrs. E. J. Nicholson), who so long directed the management of the Picayune. It consisted entirely of smilax. There were miles and miles of it around the rooms. Graceful sprays ran hither and thither in delicate tracery about the table, over the center of which there hung from the chandeliers beautiful clusters and sprays of smilax, which lit up with a wondrous glow, brightening the minds of guests with springtime freshness, and suggesting the green fields, the wooded forests and the beautiful spring of the year and of the heart. And all this beautiful decoration cost nothing but the gathering of the graceful smilax from the woods around New Orleans.

### A Thanksgiving Menu.

Menu Pour le Jour d'Action de Grâces.
#### BREAKFAST.
Grapes.
Oatflakes and Milk.
Oysters on Toast.
Broiled Tenderloin Steaks. Potato Chips.
Milk Biscuits. Butter.
Rice Griddle Cakes. Louisiana Syrup.
Cafe Noir.

#### DINNER.
Oysters on Half Shell.
Cream of Asparagus Soup.
Spanish Olives. Celery. Mixed Pickles.
Radishes. Salted Almonds.
Baked Red Snapper a la Creole.
Mashed Potatoes.
Lamb Chops au Petit Pois.
Chicken Saute aux Champignons.
Cauliflower, Sauce Blanche.
Pineapple Fritters au Rhum.
Pates de Foies Gras.
Stuffed Tomatoes.
Turkey Stuffed With Chestnuts, Cranberry Sauce.
Endive Salad, French Dressing.
Pababotte a la Creole.
Plum Pudding, Hard or Brandy Sauce.
Pumpkin Pie.
Lemon Sherbet. Assorted Cakes.
Assorted Fruits. Assorted Nuts. Raisins.
Neufchatel.
Quince Marmalade. Crackers.
Cafe Noir.

#### SUPPER.
Cold Turkey. Tomato Salad.
Crackers.
Cake. Fruit. Tea.

### A More Economical Thanksgiving Dinner.

#### DINNER.
Oysters on Half Shell.
Shrimp Gumbo.
Radishes. Celery. Olives. Pickles.
Soles a la Orly. Julienne Potatoes.
Chicken Croquettes with Mushrooms.
Banana Fritters.
Roast Turkey, Oyster Stuffing.
Cranberry Sauce.
Young Squash. Macaroni au Gratin.
Small Onions, Boiled Sauce a la Maitre d'Hotel.
Cauliflower au Vinaigrette.
Plum Pudding. Mince or Pumpkin Pie.
Pineapple Sherbet.
Assorted Cakes. Nuts. Raisins. Fruit.
Cheese.

### A Thanksgiving Decoration.

For the Thanksgiving table nothing is more appropriate in the way of decorations than autumn leaves and berries. The woods at this season are full of beautiful trailing vines, of bronze and red; brilliant boughs, leaves, cones and berries, all of which are most appropriate on this day, suggesting, by their wild luxuriance and freedom of growth, the spirit of American liberty which gave birth to the day. If it is cold, in lieu of the usual coal fire light a blazing fire of pine knots, and you will have a glorious American illumination.

The favors may consist of tiny American flags, resting amid a cluster of autumn leaves and Maidenhair Fern, if a formal dinner is given and the symbol of our country may also be suggested in festoons of narrow red, white and blue streamers of ribbon, gracefully dropping from the chandeliers.

### Menu for Christmas.

Menu Pour la Noel.
#### BREAKFAST.
Sliced Oranges.
Boiled Grits and Cream.
Celery. Olives. Radishes.
Fried Croakers, Sauce a la Tartare.
Potato Chips.
Broiled Lamb Chops. Small Hominy.
Corn Cakes. Butter. Louisiana Syrup.
Cafe au Lait.
The Christmas Picayune.

#### DINNER.
Bayou Cook Oysters.
Cream of Celery Soup.
Spanish Olives.
Celery. Young Onions, Pickled. Radishes.
Salted Almonds.
Bouilliabaisse (Red Snapper and Redfish).
Louisiana Rice.
Potatoes au Beurre Maitre d'Hotel.
Vol-au-Vent of Pigeons.
Green Peas, Buttered.
Souffle of Bananas au Rhum, or Maraschino Punch.
Roast Turkey, Cranberry Sauce.
Stuffed Tomatoes.
Artichokes on Beurre Maitre d'Hotel.
Sliced Cucumbers au Vinaigrette.
Asparagus.
Broiled Snipe on Toast.
Pouding a la Reine, Wine Sauce.
Mince Pie. Apple Pie.
Strawberry Ice. Bouchees. Massepains.
Petits Fours.
Assorted Fruits. Assorted Nuts. Raisins.
Bonbons a la Creole.

Edam Cheese or Roquefort. Water Crackers.
Cafe Noir.

SUPPER.

Cold Turkey. Tomato Salad.
Crackers. Cake.
Marmalade of Apricots. Cheese. Fruit.
Tea.

A More Economical Christmas Menu.

BREAKFAST.

Oranges.
Grits and Milk.
Broiled Chicken. Potatoes a la Duchesse.
Omelette a la Creole.
Batter Cakes. Louisiana Syrup.
Cafe au Lait.
The Christmas Picayune.

DINNER.

River Shrimp on Ice.
Celery.
Radishes. Spanish Olives. Salted Almonds.
Julienne Soup.
Broiled Green Trout. Sauce Remoulade.
Potatoes au Brabant.
Old-Fashioned Chicken Pie, or Vol-au-Vent of Chicken.
Green Peas.
Orange Salad or Peach Cobbler.
Roast Turkey, Cranberry Sauce.
Baked Yams, Buttered. Winter Squash.
Stuffed Tomatoes.
Lettuce Salad, French Dressing.
Plum Pudding. Mince Pie or Apple Pie.
Vanilla Ice Cream.
Pound Cake or Jelly Cake. Fruits. Nuts.
Raisins.
Roquefort. Crackers. Currant Jelly.
Cafe Noir.

SUPPER.

Cold Turkey, Cranberry Sauce.
Potato Salad.
French Toast. Cheese and Jelly. Fruit.
Tea.

A Christmas Decoration.

On Christmas Day what is more beautiful and appropriate as a decoration than the holly? The woods are full of the beautiful Christmas offering of nature at this time of the year. Fill the vases and bowls with holly; hang a wreath above the mantel, and set a great clustering bouquet in a low cut-glass bowl in the center of the table. The bright red berries against the dark green speak of the Christmas glow and cheer that fill the heart.

An Old-Fashioned Creole Suggestion for Holiday Menus.

The following old-fashioned Creole holiday menu, in vogue for generations among Creole families of moderate means, may be used by families whose means are very limited, but who, nevertheless, with all the world, wish to enjoy themselves, and give to those about them a little Christmas cheer. With a little modification, such as Roast Goose with Apple Sauce, it may be within the means of the poor, and may serve for the Christmas, New Year or Thanksgiving's Dinner. Mutton is always within the reach of the poor in our market, and those families who cannot afford the traditional "Quarties d'Agneau Roti, Sauce Menthe," at Easter can always enjoy a good piece of Roast Lamb or Mutton from the brisket or shoulder.

BREAKFAST.

Sliced Oranges.
Small Hominy and Milk.
Broiled Tenderloin Steak, Potatoes a la Creole.
Omelette a la Creole.
Rice Cakes. Louisiana Syrup.
Cafe au Lait.

DINNER.

Gumbo File.
Radishes. Cress. Pickled Onions.
Courtbouillon. Mashed Potatoes.
(This Course May Be Omitted.)
Beignets d'Oranges.
Roast Turkey, Oyster Stuffing, Cranberry Sauce.
Baked Yams, Sliced and Buttered.
Stuffed Tomatoes.
Lettuce Salad, French Dressing.
Old-Fashioned Chicken Pie (may be omitted.)
Plum Pudding.
Mince Pie or Apple Pie.
Pineapple Sherbet (may be omitted).
Home-Made Sponge, Jelly and Pound Cakes.
Apples, Oranges, Bananas, Grapes.
(Or simply one or two fruits).
An Assortment of Nuts and Raisins.
Home-Made Creole Bonbons.
Cheese. Crackers. Raspberry Marmalade.
Cafe Noir.

SUPPER.

Cold Turkey, Cranberry Sauce.
Cheese.
Jelly. Small Cakes.
Tea.

How to Vary All the Above Menus to Suit the Individual Daily or Holiday Household Allowance.

In regard to all the above menus, as mentioned in the beginning of this chapter, they are simply intended as suggestions. The intelligent housekeeper will vary them to suit her means, selecting a dish here and there, or referring to the "Order of Dinner Service" given in the preceding chapter, and thence to the various recipes in THE PICAYUNE'S CREOLE COOK BOOK, and thus make out a menu to suit her own special daily or holiday allowance. With a little judicious care she will find that she can always set an elegant and cheap dinner, and, if properly cooked, the family of modest means need not envy a millionaire's Christmas, New Year's or even daily menu.

## SPECIAL MENUS.

### Suggestions for Banquets or Formal Dinners.

In giving banquets, whether breakfasts, dinners or suppers, there is generally a tendency to overdo the menu. It should be borne in mind that to the intelligent and refined nature, there always comes the thought, "Man does not live by bread alone," and any attempt to over-feed by a too-lavish expenditure or number of dishes not only displays a lack of elegant taste, but is positively vulgar. Too many courses spoil a feast, and what is intended to be an enjoyable, delightful reunion. It is too often forgotten that all the guests are not gourmands, and that it does not require fifteen or twenty courses to satisfy all appetites.

A "long drawn-out" affair becomes a very fatiguing and often disgusting meal; the guests grow tired, and cannot repress the sluggish feeling that begins to cloud their spirits, even if only a small quantity of any course is served. Ten courses are enough for the most formal dinner. Never sacrifice quality for quantity, and when the Picayune has said this, it means not only the quality of the food, but the quality of intellectual seasoning that gives a zest to even the homeliest fare.

Again, too much wine is served, as a general rule. Where wines are served, remember that three kinds are sufficient for even the most costly and elegant menu—White Wine (Sauternes) or Sherry with the soup; Sauternes with the fish; Claret with the entrees and roasts; Champagne just before the dessert is brought to the table.

The following menus will serve as suggestions for the most elegant feasts:

#### Dinner.
Oysters on Half Shell.
Amontillado.

##### SOUPS OR POTAGES.
Soupe a la Julienne or Consomme Royale.
HORS D'OEUVRES (SIDE RELISHES).
Celery, Radishes, Queen Olives, Young Onions, Salted Almonds.

##### POISSON (FISH).
Broiled Pompano (in season) or Spanish Mackerel, Sauce a la Maitre d'Hotel.
Pommes de Terre a la Duchesse (Potatoes a la Duchesse).
Sliced Cucumbers.
Sauternes.

##### RELEVES.
Filet de Boeuf Truffee aux Perigueux, or Saute aux Champignons.
ENTREE.
Sweetbrends a la Creole.

##### LEGUMES.
Green Peas.
Stuffed Artichokes. Asparagus.

##### ROTI.
Turkey Stuffed with Oysters or Chestnuts.
Snipe on Toast, or Pnbnbotte a la Creole.
Watercress.
Champagne.

##### SALADE.
Whole Tomatoes Frappe, or Lettuce Salad.
French Dressing.

##### DESSERTS.
Nesselrode Pudding. Variegated Ice Cream.
Chocolate Layer Cake or Petits Fours.
Assorted Fruits. Assorted Nuts. Raisins.
Edam or Roquefort Cheese.
Cafe Noir.

It must be remembered right here that it is no longer elegant to give the distinctive names of courses in printed menus. They are merely suggested, as in the following:

Oysters on Half Shell.
Consomme.
Sauterne.

Soft-Shell Crabs a la Creole.
New Potatoes a la Maitre d'Hotel.

Sweetbreads a la Creole.
Petits Pois (Green Peas).
Sorbet a la Royale.
Claret.
Filet Mignon de Boeuf aux Truffes ou aux Champignons.
Artichokes a la Barigoule. Asparagus.
Whole Tomatoes Frappe.

Pigeons a la Crapaudine, or Quail or Woodcock on Toast.
Cress.

Fancy Variegated Ice Cream or Pineapple Sherbet.
Assorted Cakes. Fruits. Nuts. Bonbons.
Coffee. Tea.

### Menu for a Buffet Luncheon.

Consomme Dore en Tasse (Gilt-Edged Consomme in Cups).

Sandwiches. Caviar on Toast.
Radishes. Celery. Olives. Mixed Pickles.
Salted Almonds.

Oyster Patties.

Boned Turkey (Galantine Truffe) or Cold Roast Turkey.

Mayonnaise of Chicken or Shrimp.

Biscuit Glace or Variegated Ice Cream.
Assorted Cakes. Assorted Bonbons.
Crystallized Fruits.

Tea. Coffee. Cream. Chocolate.
Iced Lemonade.
Champagne Punch Frappe (if desired).

### Menu for Suppers.

A supper is always a more elaborate affair than a dinner. It admits of an appetizer, Oysters on Half Shell, served as an hors d'oeuvre, or Anchovies, Caviars, etc.; a Soup or Gumbo; the usual hors d'oeuvres of Celery, Radishes, Cress, Pickel Onions, Mangoes, Salted Almonds, etc.; Fish, broiled, baked, Courtbouillon or Boullliabaisse; vegetable attachments; entrees of various kinds, to suit the taste and also to correspond with the course of the feast; sweet entremets; a roast, vegetables, to be served with it, and salad; game of any variety, from Venison, Canvasback, Mallard, and Teal Ducks, to Pababottes, Snipe, Woodcock, etc., on toast; Desserts, Fruits, Jellies, Cheese, Coffee.

The Menu should always be varied according to the season, selecting always the first and most elegant fish, game, vegetables, fruits, etc., of the season to set before your guests.

As a rule, any elegant dinner menu may serve also for a supper, except in case of a state dining, and even then the rule given above should be observed.

**Do not overload your table, and, above all, do not fatigue your guests with long-drawn-out affairs of eighteen and twenty courses. Observe the happy medium, ten and even less, and you and they will be the more satisfied, the more delighted, and the more comfortable for your thoughtful and refined consideration.**

### Creole Home Dining.

The Menus given for daily use may be used at any home dining not formal. Do not have such an elaborate outlay when you invite a few friends to dine "en famille," as the Creoles say, as will make them feel, especially if your means are limited, that they have put you to a great deal of unnecessary expense, and consequently will feel a delicacy in accepting your invitation again. With the exception, perhaps, of a roast fowl or duck substituted for the everyday roast meat, and a little extra touch to the dessert, it is unnecessary to go to any greater expense than that which you have laid out for the daily menu.

Again, remember that it is not quantity, but quality, that you must set before your guests; quality in the manner in which you will have prepared the food; quality in the way of serving it; quality in the neatness, delicacy and cleanliness of all around, from the table linen to the shining glassware and silver, and, above all, tact and quality in the way that you entertain your guests. A cheerful, smiling, intelligent hostess, who offers no excuse for her simple fare because it is all that she can afford; who offers you, besides the best that she has, of good temper, cultured mind and kindly heart and cordial welcome, by the way of "seasoning" the repast—such a hostess is worth thousands of rich, would-be entertainers, who rely upon the abundance of their table supplies and rich service, and who seek to dazzle by the extravagant and costly appointments of their homes and surroundings, while the true offerings which make the simple meal in the humble cottage over the way are wanting—the intellectual fare, now grave, but never sad; the wit and repartee, bright and sparkling, but never boisterous, and never a sting or wound hidden in its merry echoes; and the heart so kind, so true and loyal that echoed through the welcome greeting, "Make yourself at home," or as the Creoles, following their Spanish ancestral traditions, so gracefully say, "My house is yours." All these are the life and heart of any feast. Moreover, you know that your hostess meant every word that she said, and this thought throws a charm over the entire feast, even though it consists of nothing more than "Grillades a la Sauce," served with Red Beans and Rice, or an old-fashioned "Gumbo Choux," or "Gumbo aux Herbes," that you are positive could not have cost any more than fifteen cents for the entire dish. But it is cooked in such a way and served with such grace that a king might not disdain to eat it and consider himself fortunate for the privilege.

There is no reason why the fact of a friend entering at dinner time should cause any unnecessary commotion at the table; no necessity for any excuses to be offered, and, above all, no reason why dinner-giving should have grown to be considered such an elaborate function that persons in moderate circumstances fear to give the good, old-fashioned, simple dinings, when friend met friend for the pleasure of their company, and a hostess could extend the invitation without fear of having to retrench for days to make up for the unusual outlay.

No homes in the South suffered more through the loss of fortunes by the war than did the Creole homes of Louisiana. But the old social customs still remain, and many a hostess who years ago could invite her friends to a superb dining, which would have gladdened the heart of even the most fastidious old Creole gourmet, now finds herself reduced to perhaps even less than a dollar a day, and she has nobly accommodated herself to circumstances. And have her friends of former days fallen away? Not at all. For the Creoles hold good birth, good breeding and education higher than wealth. The poor little Creole seamstress over the way can still go into what is considered the best society. If her birth and education are good, these are the criterions, the passports into the ancient homes where wealth and luxury still abide. And in return her friends from the great mansions visit her, and sit down with zest to her simple dining. And it may be added here that the simple fare is so well-prepared, the manner of serving so elegant, and the hostess so gracious, though she only wears a five-cent-a-yard calico dress, that you might think, as Marion Crawford said, when he went into one of these humble old-fashioned homes, that you were in the presence of a princess of the royal blood, for you met with such warmth of hospitality as made you at once feel at home, and such a courtesy and charm of manner as would have done honor to a throne.

## SOIREES.

"Soirees" are pleasant forms of entertainments that have come down from earliest Creole days in Louisiana. While elaborate entertaining was also done, the Creole character being naturally gay and happy, and inheriting a French fondness for the dance, for music and song and social intercourse, the young folks had a way of giving weekly soirees, at which their parents served simple light refreshments, such as the famous "Sirops," given in a preceding chapter, ices of various kinds, lemonades and Petits Fours, or small cakes, wafers and fruits. These refreshments were passed around by the old-time servants, decked in gay bandana tignon, guinea blue dress, and white apron, and kerchief pinned across the bosom. Later in the evening tea was served, and as the "Soiree" advanced to the wee hours, coffee, chocolate and consomme in cups.

Fathers took the greatest interest in the "Soirees" in their homes, and did the honors with distinguished courtesy, inviting the older gentlemen, who acted as escorts for their daughters, to take a glass of wine or champagne, but liquors were never offered to the young people a custom that might well be adopted in our day generally. Ice Cream, Lemonade and Cakes, with a cup of Consomme or Cafe Noir, as the evening advanced, were considered sufficient refreshment.

Again, at these "Soirees" the simple "Eau Sucre" was served (see "Eau Sucre," under chapter on Domestic Drinks, Cordials, etc.) in the homes of families of most limited means. Lack of money has never debarred a Creole to the manor born from what is called the best society. These old-time "Soirees" still continue, though the "Eau Sucre" parties have passed away with changing conditions.

The Creole "Soirees" are pleasing forms of entertainment that might be adopted with profit generally.

## ECONOMICAL MENUS.

The following economical menus are intended as suggestions, showing how a family of six may live comfortably and with variety on from a dollar to a dollar and a half a day. In all these recipes the leftover from one meal is utilized in another dainty form for the next, thus equalizing expenses from day to day.

### Menu for Monday.

BREAKFAST.
Sliced Oranges.
Small Hominy. Milk.
Broiled Beefsteak. Julienne Potatoes.
Batter Cakes. Louisiana Syrup.
Cafe au Lait.
The Daily Picayune.

LUNCHEON.
Muskmelon.
Saucissea a la Creole. Hominy Croquettes.
French Rolls. Raspberry Jam.
Tea.

DINNER.
Vegetable Soup.
Baked Red Snapper.
Potatoes a la Maitre d'Hotel.
Roast Beef, Tomato Sauce.
Boiled Rice. Butterbeans. Lettuce Salad.
Apple Dumplings a la Creole. Cheese.
Cafe Noir.

### Menu for Tuesday.

BREAKFAST.
Bananas.
Grits and Milk.
Meat Rissoles. Potato Croquettes. Biscuit.
Rice Griddle Cakes. Louisiana Syrup.
Cafe au Lait.
The Daily Picayune.

LUNCHEON.
Thin Slices of Boiled Ham.
Compote of Apples.
Tea.

DINNER.
Gumbo File.
Fish Croquettes. Hominy Fritters.
Roast Pork, Apple Sauce.
Baked Sweet Potatoes. String Bean Salad.
Banana Cake. Cheese.
Cafe Noir.

### Menu for Wednesday.
BREAKFAST.
Stewed Prunes.
Oatmeal and Milk.
Fried Ham. Scrambled Eggs.
Sweet Potato Waffles. Butter.
Cafe au Lait.
The Daily Picayune.
LUNCHEON.
Cold Roast Pork.
Oatmeal Cakes. Salade a la Jardiniere.
Ginger Snaps. Tea.
DINNER.
Vermicelli Soup.
Courtbouillon. Potatoes a la Duchesse.
Grillades a la Sauce. Red Beans. Rice.
Green Pepper and Tomato Salad.
Pumpkin Pie. Cheese. Fruit.
Cafe Noir.

### Menu for Thursday.
BREAKFAST.
Peaches and Cream (in season).
Ragout of Mutton. Small Hominy.
Cornmeal Cakes. Louisiana Syrup.
Cafe au Lait.
The Daily Picayune.
LUNCHEON.
Fish Croquettes. Potato Salad.
Fried Liver With Onions.
French Toast. Tea.
DINNER.
Cream of Tomato Soup.
Boiled Sheepshead, Sauce a la Creme.
Potato Snow.
Veal Saute aux Petits Pois, Stuffed Tomatoes.
Lettuce Salad.
Riz au Lait. Cheese.
Cafe Noir.

### Menu for Friday.
BREAKFAST.
Pears (in season).
Boiled Hominy. Milk.
Broiled Trout.
Julienne Potatoes. Pain Perdue.
Cafe au Lait.
The Daily Picayune.
LUNCHEON.
River Shrimp on Ice.
Codfish Balls.
Cheese Fondue. Dry Cakes. Orange Jelly.
Tea.
DINNER.
Puree of Red or White Beans.
Spanish Courtbouillon, Potatoes a la Duchesse.
Jambalaya au Congri.
Stewed Cashaw.
Blackberry Roll, Hard Sauce.
Cafe Noir.

### Menu for Saturday.
BREAKFAST.
Cracked Wheat, Milk.
Grillades Panees.
Apple Fritters. Milk Toast.
Cafe au Lait.
The Daily Picayune.
LUNCHEON.
Fish Croquettes.
Cold Boiled Tongue. Sliced Cucumber Salad.
Orange Short Cake. Tea.
DINNER.
Vermicelli Soup.
Daube or Beef a la Mode.
Macaroni au Gratin.
Spanish Jambalaya. Turnips a la Creme.
Lentils or Peas.
Beet Salad, French Dressing.
Sweet Potato Pudding, or Custard Pie.
Cheese.
Cafe Noir.

### Menu for Sunday.
BREAKFAST.
Strawberries (in season). Milk.
Oatmeal, Milk.
Grillades Panees. Lyonnaise Potatoes.
French Rolls.
Cafe au Lait.
The Daily Picayune.
DINNER.
Corn Soup (in season).
Radishes. Cress. Home-made Pickles.
Bouillabaisse. New Potaoes, Buttered.
Fricasseed Chicken with Dumplings, or Poulet au Riz.
Salmi of Wild Duck, With Turnips.
Green Peas, Stuffed Tomatoes.
Lettuce Salad, French Dressing.
Lemon Sherbet. Cake.
Cafe Noir.
SUPPER.
Warmed-Over Duck. Potato Salad.
Blackberry Jam. Cake.
Tea.

### How to Vary These Economical Daily Menus.

These Menus may be varied with Gumbo aux Herbes; Gumbo Choux; Shrimp Gumbo; Bisque d'Ecrevisses; all manner of Purees, when vegetables are in the height of the season; all kinds of vegetables in the height of the season; various compotes and jellies and jams put up thriftily when fruits are selling at such rates as eight peaches, or six apples or pears, or a dozen bananas for five cents, etc.; fried bananas; all manner of sweet entremets, with the exception of the expensive omelets and fritters, and nearly all kinds of puddings and pies and desserts. The chief point is for the housekeeper to watch the market carefully; never to buy green peas, new corn, artichokes, etc., when they first make their appearance and are naturally very dear; but to wait till the first two weeks are over, and then she may safely purchase any and everything, from young squash, eggplants, pumpkin, to the more elegant green peas, new corn, etc. When chickens are cheap, if she does not endeavor to raise her own family supply of poultry and eggs, even in a city yard, as hundreds of the Creoles do, she may occasionally—once or even twice a week—treat the family to a dish of Roast Chicken Saute aux Petit Pois, Roast Goose a la Chipolata, Wild Duck—not, indeed, always the famous Canvasback or Mallard or Teal, but excellent and splendid wild game the taste of which is very good. Occasionally, too, she may find Mallard Ducks selling in the French Market at 25 and 30 cents a pair, especially on rainy days, when the game does not meet such a ready sale among the wealthy who, often as not, refrain from sending directly to the large market stalls. On such days she may also have opportunities to purchase even Canvasback or Teal Duck at the same low rates, and the family at these times may also enjoy a dish of Mackerel, as well as all manner of fancy game. As to Squirrels, Rabbits and Poule d'Eau, they are always within the reach of the poor. Redfish and Red Snapper may always be bought in slices, three slices selling for 10 cents. Six slices, or three of each fish, will make the famous "Bouilliabaisse" in ample quantity for a family of six and (the "Courtbouillon a la Creole" is too expensive a dish for a family limited to a dollar a day), the Spanish Courtbouillon, so much in vogue among the Creoles of all ranks, is a most excellent dish and is preferred by many who do not like the flavor of wine in fish. From time to time the family may also have the pleasure of enjoying a Roast Turkey, and this, too, will be found a most economical venture, if properly managed for the left-over turkey from the Sunday dinner may be used for hash for breakfast the next morning, and still again the carcass and bones may be utilized at dinner in making a splendid Turkey Gumbo. When this Gumbo is properly made and served with Rice, little else will be needed for the meal. Thus, if you purchase a Turkey for $1 or $1.25 (and often a splendid fowl may be had for even less,) the outlay of one day becomes a part of the next, and what seemed at first an expensive indulgence will in reality prove a most economical investment. The same may be said in regard to buying ham. Purchase a whole ham at a time, instead of buying it by the slice. Boil it and serve cold for luncheon; fry or boil slices for breakfast, and when every part of the meat seems to have been used up, do not, under any circumstances, throw away the bone, but save it to boil with cabbage, white beans, red beans, lentils, etc. All these are very cheap dishes; they are also, with all due regard to elegant and more expensive dishes, the most healthy and nutritious tissue and life-giving foods that any mother, be she the wife of a millionaire or of an humble laborer, can set before her children. Turtle Soup may be enjoyed by even the poorest, if the turtle is purchased in slices. Keep the turtle meat from the soup to make "Quenelles" (see recipe), and these may be served for supper or breakfast.

**The intelligent housekeeper will carefully calculate her expenses. While not one of the above recipes need exceed a dollar a day, properly distributed, and using the left-over from one day or meal for the next, the expense of living may be still further decreased in families which cannot afford a dollar a day, by omitting some one or other of the dishes, according to the cost. It will often be found convenient and most agreeable in large families among the poor and those of very moderate means to make one or two large, or, as the Creoles term them, "long family dishes," varying with each day, than to serve a greater number of small dishes. What is expended above a dollar in one day is made up in the next, and so at the end of the week, in rounding up her account of expenditures—for every housekeeper should keep her account, and not go above her husband's means—it will be found that not only have the expenses been kept within the dollar-a-day limit, but often she has been able to save a dime, or even a few cents, against a rainy day.**

## CHAPTER L.

### CONCLUSION.

#### How the Creole Housewife in Reduced Circumstances Manages to Live Economically and Well.

The Creole women of Louisiana have long been the subject of song and story—their beauty, their accomplishments, their grace and dignity of character, united to singular vivasity and charm of temperament, no less than the difficulty that even the most aristocratic visitors to New Orleans encounter in receiving invitations to visit them in their homes, unless presented by some intimate mutual friend, who stands as sponsor for the stranger, have invested them with a romance and charm that attach to no other women in the United States. And these charming characteristics they will be found to have retained even when as in many instances, they have been forced into rude stations of society and employments, by reason of the misfortunes that swept over their once princely and opulent homes.

With wealthy Creole homes this chapter will not deal particularly. Taste, tact and good management the characteristic traits of the Creole woman, whether rich or poor. But, as said in the beginning of this book, its object is to teach people how to live—the rich as well as the poor, THE PICAYUNE feels that the former have exceptional advantages, whereas the latter are thrown upon their own resources of thought and ingenuity in seeking, as the old adage says, "to make both ends meet." Especially is this true in regard to household management, and the special object of this chapter is to show how the Creole housewife who is reduced in circumstances manages to successfully conduct her household, pay rent, properly clothe herself and children and yet manage to keep a good table, that is a source of good health for the family and a pride to her husband.

It is often said in New Orleans that no one dresses better and with more taste than the Creole women. Even the woman of humble means will always appear neat and nice, well-shod and well-gloved, when she is seen on the street. Her husband is often surprised at the pretty new dress, cheap and of inexpensive material, wheich she has purchased for one of the little ones, without asking him for the money. The secret lies in this: She does not stint her table—trust a good Creole mother for that, for the well-supplied table is an ancient, traditional heritage of her race, from which she will not depart—but she manages most carefully, buying her supplies of sugar and molasses and rice, grits and flour when these are "down in the market;" putting up her dainty jellies, marmalades and domestic wines when fruits are "going hegging," as the term runs, because the market is so overstocked. When the children come rushing in, telling her that the first cries of "Strawberries" are heard in the streets, she quietly tells them not to be in a hurry; that in a few weeks they will have more than they can eat; and so carefully and judiciously managing that, though her husband's salary is only fifty dollares a month and the family consists of six children, besides father and mother, she manages to pay the house rent (for she will select a pretty, neat little cottage in a respectable, but not fashionable neighborhood,) to pay for the milk and bakers' bread supplies, keep her family table spotless with linen bought when bargains are offered in the Canal Street stores, and have her household linen and children's and husband's underwear always in good repair. She faithfully watches the columns of the **Daily Picayune** for announcements of "big bargain sales" in sheeting underwear, hosiery and dress goods, purchasing the children's supplies of summer and winter clothing at the end of the season when all the finest goods are marked down to fabulously low prices, because the merchants are anxious to get rid of the surplus stock, and, above all, she strives to keep the wedding day smile on her husband's face and the old love-light in his eyes, and the old song ever singing in his heart:

"Home; home, sweet home!
There is no place like home."

because of the happiness and love and devotion that there abide.

The Creole mother eminently merits the term that was bestowed upon her long ago by a sweet Louisiana poet, and which has become a household word in the French Quarter. "Femme de l'Interieure." These words indicate her life, that beautiful, interior, hidden home life, not given to solving the many vexing questions of woman suffrage and woman's rights that agitate the minds of many of the sex in our day, for she is no agressive competitor in the ranks and callings of men; she is, indeed, the "Femme de l'Interieure," the queen of the hearth and home. She holds the home as woman's supreme sphere, her ideal realm, where Love is her throne, a throne reared in the hearts of her husband and children, and of which the attendant ministers are Purity, Truth and Fidelity. She is cultured, gracious, refined; as able to grace the parlor as she is capable of presiding in the kitchen; thoroughly conversant with all the leading topics of the day, with which she familiarizes herself, not that she may be regarded simply as a brilliant woman, not for the sake of argumentative discourse on public platforms, but for her own inner satisfaction and pleasure, and that she may be the fittnig companion of her husband, the pleasing, intelligent confidant of her children, the wise and earnest director of their moral and intellectual aspirations and ambitions. And so her husband learns to look to his home during the weary working hours of the day as to a beacon star, for he knows that within bloom the fairest flowers of modest worth; the violet and the rose are there, the crysanthemum and the lily, and those that bloom in God's own garden shed not a sweeter fragrance than do these heavenly exotics around the hearth of the true Creole home.

This is the picture of the Creole mother and home, whether in the palatial homes of the Rue Esplanade or Rue Rampart, or in the humble cottages of the Faubourg Marigny, and it is this devotion to the interests of husband, home and children, coming down as a precious inheritance through long generations of noble Creole housewives and mothers, that has given the Creole cuisine such a unique and interesting place in the world's cookery, and which has made possible this compilation of

# THE PICAYUNE'S CREOLE COOK BOOK.

# CONTENTS.

|  | Page |
|---|---|
| Title Page | 2 |
| Introduction to Fourth Edition | 3 |
| Introduction to First Edition | 5 |

| | |
|---|---|
| Chapter I | Creole Coffee |
| Chapter II | Soups |
| Chapter III | Meat Soups |
| Chapter IV | Fish Soups |
| Chapter V | Lenten Soups |
| Chapter VI | The Bouilli |
| Chapter VII | Creole Gumbo |
| Chapter VIII | Fish |
| Chapter IX | Shell Fish |
| Chapter X | Shell Fish (Continued) |
| Chapter XI | Salt and Canned Fish |
| Chapter XII | Meats—Beef |
| Chapter XIII | Veal—Sweetbreads |
| Chapter XIV | Mutton |
| Chapter XV | Pork |
| Chapter XVI | Poultry |
| Chapter XVII | Pigeons |
| Chapter XVIII | Game |
| Chapter XIX | Birds |
| Chapter XX | Stuffings and Dressings for Poultry, Game and Fish, Etc. |
| Chapter XXI | Sauces for Fish, Meats, Poultry, Game, Etc. |
| Chapter XXII | Salads |
| Chapter XXIII | Eggs |
| Chapter XXIV | Louisiana Rice |
| Chapter XXV | Cereals |
| Chapter XXVI | Macaroni |
| Chapter XXVII | Cheese |
| Chapter XXVIII | Canapes |
| Chapter XXIX | Vegetables |
| Chapter XXX | Hors d'Oeuvres (Relishes) |
| Chapter XXXI | Sweet Entremets |
| Chapter XXXII | Desserts |
| Chapter XXXIII | Pastry and Pies |
| Chapter XXXIV | Puddings |
| Chapter XXXV | Custards, Creams and Other Desserts |
| Chapter XXXVI | Pudding Sauces |
| Chapter XXXVII | Cakes |
| Chapter XXXVIII | Layer Cakes |
| Chapter XXXIX | Dessert Cakes |
| Chapter XL | Icings for Cakes |
| Chapter XLI | Ice Creams, Biscuits, Sherbets |
| Chapter XLII | Fruits, Syrups, Cordials, Etc. |
| Chapter XLIII | Domestic Wines, Cordials and Drinks |
| Chapter XLIV | Jellies, Marmalades, Preserves |
| Chapter XLV | Creole Candies |
| Chapter XLVI | Canning and Pickling |
| Chapter XLVII | Creole Breads |
| Chapter XLVIII | Suggestions to Housekeepers |
| Chapter XLIX | Varieties of Seasonable Foods |
| Chapter L | Conclusion |

## ILLUSTRATIONS.

|  | Page |
|---|---|
| A Creole Negro Cook (Tante Zoe, with Tureen of Gumbo File) | 2 |
| The Picayune Frog (For Explanation See Page 51) | 4 |

# ... INDEX ...

**BEEF—Du Boeuf** .......... 74
  Guides in Choosing Meats .... 72
  Unfailing Rules Which the Creoles follow .............. 74
  BEEF (Du Boeuf) .......... 76
    Beef a la Mode ............ 76
    Beefsteak Broiled .......... 75
    Beefsteak, Smothered ....... 75
    Beefsteak, Smothered in Onions ....................... 76
    Beef Marine ................ 77
    Beefsteak Pie .............. 80
    Bouilli .................... 29
    Corned Beef ............... 81
    Daube, Cold a la Creole .... 77
    Filet of Beef Larded ....... 74
    Filet of Beef, Larded With Mushrooms ................ 75
    Filet of Beef, Larded, With Truffles .................. 75
    Filet of Beef, Smothered, with Mushrooms or Truffles ... 76
    Filet of Beef, with Stuffed Tomatoes ................. 76
    Filet of Beef, with Tomatoes 76
    Fried Meat ................ 78
    Grillades .................. 78
    Grillades, Breaded ......... 79
    Grillades with Gravy ....... 78
    Hash ...................... 80
    Hash, Dry or Baked ........ 80
    Hash, of Corned Beef ...... 81
    Hash on Toast ............. 80
    Kidneys, Broiled ........... 81
    Kidneys, Stewed ........... 82
    Left-over Meat ............ 79
    Left-over Meat (Rissoles)... 80
    Liver, Broiled ............. 82
    Liver, Fried a la Lyonnaise.. 82
    Meat Balls (Boulettes)...... 79
    Meat Balls (Boulards) ...... 79
    Ox Tails a la Bourgeoise.... 81
    Ox Tails, Breaded ......... 81
    Potted Beef ............... 80
    Roast Beef ................ 74
    Souffle ................... 80
    Tongue, Jellied ............ 82
    Tongue, Smothered ........ 82

**BEVERAGES, CREOLE HOUSEHOLD—Boissons de Menage,** 316
  DOMESTIC CORDIALS AND DRINKS ................... 316
    General Directions and Proportions for .............. 317
    How to Filter ............. 317
  BEER, Creole (Bierre Creole). 330
    Ginger Beer ............... 330
    Root Beer ................. 330
    Spruce Beer ............... 330
  CUPS (Ponches) ............ 324
    Burgundy Cup ............. 324
    Claret Cup ................ 324
    Champagne Cup ........... 324
    Moselle Cup ............... 325
    White Wine Cup .......... 325
    Brandy Stew .............. 325
    Egg-Nogg ................. 326
    Eggs and Wine ........... 326
    Hot Spiced Port .......... 325
    Mint Julep a la Creole .... 326
    Sangaree, Hot or Cold .... 326
    Sherry Cobbler ............ 326
    Wine Cobbler ............. 325
  CORDIALS (Liqueurs) ...... 327
    Anisette .................. 327
    Anisette de Bordeaux ..... 327
    Blackberry Cordial ........ 328
    Citronelle ................ 328
    Curacoa .................. 328
    Kummel .................. 328
    Nectar ................... 328
    Orangeade ............... 329
    Parfait Amour ............ 329
    Persicot ................. 329

**BREADS—Des Pains** .......... 356
  BAKERS' BREAD ............ 357
    Bread, Buttermilk ........ 358
    Bread, French ............ 357
    Bread, French Loaves .... 358
    Bread, Light Home-Made Creole .................. 358
    Bread, Milk .............. 358
    Bread, Pan .............. 357
    Bread, Rice ............. 358
    Bread, Rye .............. 358
    Bread, Sweet Potato ...... 359
    Bread, Twist Loaves ...... 358
  BABA ...................... 361
  BISCUIT ................... 362
    Biscuit, Beaten ........... 362
    Biscuit, Soda and Milk .... 363
    Biscuits, Stewed .......... 363
    Biscuit, Sweet Potato ..... 363
    Biscuits, Tea ............. 363
  BRIOCHES ................. 361
  BULLFROGS ............... 362
  CORNBREAD .............. 364
    Corn Dodgers ............ 366
    Bread, Corn Egg ......... 365
    Corn Bread, Nonpareil .... 365
    Corn Bread, Plain ....... 365
    Cornmeal Pone ........... 365
    Corn Bread, Risen ........ 365
    Corn Bread, Steamed .... 365
    Corn, Ash Cake .......... 366
    Corn Cakes, Fried ........ 366
  CRACKLING BREAD ........ 367
    Cracknels ................ 373
    Crumpets ................ 369

**BREAKFAST CAKES—**
  BATTER CAKES (Galettes de Pate) ..................... 371
    Buckwheat Cakes ........ 371

| | |
|---|---|
| Flannel Cakes | 371 |
| GEMS (Petits Bijoux) | 369 |
| Corn Gems | 369 |
| GRIDDLE CAKES (Gateau a la Plaque) | 371 |
| Griddle Cakes, Bread | 372 |
| Griddle Cakes, Cornmeal | 372 |
| Griddle Cakes, French | 372 |
| Griddle Cakes, Hominy | 372 |
| Griddle Cakes, Green Corn | 372 |
| Griddle Cakes, Rice | 372 |
| HOECAKE | 366 |
| JOHNNY CAKE | 366 |
| MUFFINS (Galettes) | 367 |
| Muffins, Bread | 367 |
| Muffins, Cornmeal | 367 |
| Muffins, Cream | 367 |
| Muffins, Egg | 368 |
| Muffins, Hominy | 368 |
| Muffins, Queen | 368 |
| Muffins, Quick | 368 |
| Muffins, Rice | 368 |
| PUFFS | 373 |
| ROLLS (Bourrelet) | 359 |
| Rolls, French | 359 |
| Rolls, Tea | 360 |
| RUSKS | 360 |
| TOAST | 360 |
| Cream or Milk Toast | 360 |
| Lost Bread or Egg Toast | 360 |
| Spanish Toast | 360 |
| SALLY LUNN | 369 |
| SHORT CAKE | 364 |
| SODA CRACKERS | 364 |
| WAFERS | 364 |
| WAFFLES (Gaufres) | 369 |
| Waffles, Cornmeal | 370 |
| Waffles, Plain | 369 |
| Waffles, Potato | 370 |
| Waffles, Rice | 370 |
| Waffles, Risen | 370 |
| OTHER BREAKFAST CAKES | 371 |
| YEAST, HOME-MADE | 373 |

**BIRDS—Des Oiseaux—**

| | |
|---|---|
| BIRDS | 133 |
| Chaud-Froid of Birds | 142 |
| Bird Pie | 142 |
| Invariable Rule for Broiling Birds | 133 |
| Invariable Rule for Roasting Birds | 133 |
| GRASSETS, Broiled or Roasted, | 141 |
| LARKS (Alouettes, Broiled or Roasted | 134 |
| PABABOTTE | 134 |
| Pababotte a la Creole | 134 |
| Pababotte, Broiled | 134 |
| Pababotte, Roasted | 134 |
| PARTRIDGES (Perdreaux) | 135 |
| Partridge a la Creole | 136 |
| Partridge a la Financiere | 136 |
| Partridge and Cabbage | 136 |
| Partridge, Breasts of, Truffle Sauce | 137 |
| Partridge, Broiled | 135 |
| Partridge, Broiled, with Sour Orange Sauce | 135 |
| Partridge, Chartreuse of | 137 |
| Partridge, Hunters' Style | 136 |
| Partridge, Roast | 135 |
| Partridge, Roast, with Bread Sauce | 135 |

| | |
|---|---|
| PIGEONS | 122 |
| Broiled | 122 |
| Broiled a la Crapaudine | 122 |
| Compote of | 123 |
| Squab, Roasted | 122 |
| Squab, with Green Peas | 123 |
| Vol-au-Vent of | 123 |
| With Crawfish | 123 |
| POULES D'EAU | 141 |
| Poules d'Eau, Stewed | 141 |
| Poule d'Eau, with Turnips | 141 |
| QUAIL (Cailles) | 138 |
| Quail, Broiled on Toast | 139 |
| Quail, Broiled with Bacon | 139 |
| Quail, Roasted | 138 |
| Quail (Cailles de Laurier), Roasted | 138 |
| Quail, Roasted in Grape Leaves | 138 |
| Quail, Smothered | 139 |
| Quail, Smothered a la Financiere | 139 |
| Quail, Smothered, Celery Sauce | 139 |
| REED BIRDS. (Ortolans), Broiled or Roasted | 141 |
| ROBINS (Grives), Broiled or Roasted | 141 |
| SNIPE (Becassine) | 140 |
| Snipe, Broiled on Toast | 140 |
| Snipe, Roast on Toast | 140 |
| WOODCOCK (Becasse) | 139 |
| Woodcock, Broiled on Toast | 140 |
| Woodcock, Roast, on Toast | 139 |

**CAKES—Des Gateaux—**

| | |
|---|---|
| General Directions for Making | 270 |
| Directions for Baking | 271 |
| Rule for Mixing Ingredients | 271 |
| How to Ice | 272 |
| CAKES | 272 |
| Almond | 272 |
| Angel | 273 |
| Angel's Food | 273 |
| Archangel | 273 |
| Banana Meringue | 273 |
| Black | 273 |
| Buttermilk | 274 |
| Bride's | 274 |
| Chocolate Loaf | 274 |
| Chocolate a la Creole | 274 |
| Citron | 274 |
| Cocoanut Loaf | 274 |
| Clove | 275 |
| Coffee | 275 |
| Caramel | 275 |
| Cup Cake | 275 |
| One, Two, Three, Four Cup Cake | 275 |
| Cake without Eggs | 275 |
| Delicate Cake | 276 |
| Dried Fruit Cake | 276 |
| Fig Cake | 276 |
| Fruit | 276 |
| Fruit Cake, Plain | 277 |
| Ginger Cake | 277 |
| Ginger Bread | 277 |
| Ginger Bread without Butter or Eggs (Stage Planks) | 278 |
| French Creole | 278 |
| Fruit Ginger Bread | 278 |

| | |
|---|---|
| Silver Cake | 278 |
| Gold Cake | 278 |
| Honey Cake | 279 |
| Imperial Cake | 279 |
| Indian Pound | 279 |
| Lady Cake (White) | 279 |
| Lunch | 279 |
| Madame John's Cake | 279 |
| Marble Cake | 279 |
| Marble Chocolate | 280 |
| Minute Cake | 260 |
| Motley | 280 |
| Molasses, plain | 280 |
| Manque | 280 |
| Nut Cake | 281 |
| Orange | 281 |
| Pearl Cake | 281 |
| Picayune Cake | 272 |
| Premium Cake | 281 |
| Pound Cake | 281 |
| Pound Cake (No. 2) | 282 |
| Pound Cake, White | 282 |
| Plum Cake, or Old-Fashioned Wedding Cake | 282 |
| Raisin Cake | 282 |
| Spanish Cake | 283 |
| Spice Cake | 283 |
| Spiced Molasses Cake | 283 |
| Sponge Cake, Cream | 283 |
| Sponge Cake, Quick | 283 |
| Sponge Cake, White | 284 |
| Tutti-Frutti Cake | 284 |
| White Mountain | 284 |
| White Cream Cake | 284 |
| Twelfth Night, or King's Cake | 284 |

**CAKES, LAYER—Des Gateaux—**

| | |
|---|---|
| LAYER CAKES | 286 |
| Almond Cake | 286 |
| Banana Layer Cake | 286 |
| Chocolate Layer Cake | 286 |
| Cocoanut Layer | 286 |
| Cream Layer | 287 |
| Fig Layer | 287 |
| Jelly Layer Cake | 287 |
| Lemon Layer | 287 |
| Orange Layer | 287 |
| Pecan Layer | 287 |
| Pineapple Layer | 287 |
| Raisin Cake | 288 |
| Rainbow Cake | 288 |
| Layer Cake of Fresh Fruits | 288 |

**CANAPES—Canapes—**

| | |
|---|---|
| CANAPES | 183 |
| Anchovy Canapes | 183 |
| Anchovy Canapes, with Hard-Boiled Eggs | 183 |
| Anchovy Canapes, Creole Style | 183 |
| Anchovy Canapes, Cracker | 184 |
| Anchovy Canapes with Gruyere Cheese | 183 |
| Caviar Canapes | 184 |
| Canapes, Cheese | 185 |
| Canapes, Chicken | 185 |
| Canapes of Chicken Livers | 185 |
| Canapes, Codfish | 185 |
| Canapes, Creole | 185 |
| Canapes, Crab | 184 |
| Cannelons | 187 |
| Canapes, Fish | 185 |
| Canapes, Ham | 185 |
| Canapes of Potted Ham | 186 |
| Canapes, Hunter's Style | 184 |
| Canapes, Indian | 186 |
| Canapes, Louisiana | 186 |
| Canapes, Olives | 186 |
| Canapes, Oysters | 186 |
| Canapes, of Potted Tongue | 186 |
| Canapes, Sardine | 186 |
| Canapes, Spanish | 186 |

**CEREALS—**

| | |
|---|---|
| CEREALS | 174 |
| Barley | 178 |
| Buckwheat | 178 |
| Corn | 176 |
| Cornmeal Mush | 177 |
| Farina | 174 |
| Farina Gruel | 174 |
| Grits | 176 |
| Grits, Boiled | 176 |
| Grits, Baked | 176 |
| Hominy, Boiled | 177 |
| Hominy, Croquettes | 177 |
| Hominy, Fried | 177 |
| Hominy Lye, or Samp | 177 |
| Milk Porridge | 178 |
| Oats | 175 |
| Oatmeal | 175 |
| Oatmeal, Steamed | 175 |
| Oat Flakes | 175 |
| Rye | 175 |
| Rye Mush | 175 |
| Wheat | 174 |
| Wheat, Cracked | 174 |

**CHEESE— Du Fromage—**

| | |
|---|---|
| CHEESE | 181 |
| Biscuits | 182 |
| Cream | 182 |
| Fondue | 182 |
| Barebit, Welsh | 182 |
| Ramakins | 181 |
| Straws | 182 |
| Scuffle | 181 |
| Toasted | 182 |

**COMPOTES—Des Compotes—**

| | |
|---|---|
| COMPOTES | 237 |
| Apple | 237 |
| Apple, Stuffed | 238 |
| Apricot | 238 |
| Banana | 238 |
| Banana Cassa | 238 |
| Blackberries | 238 |
| Cherries | 238 |
| Cocoanut | 238 |
| Cranberries | 239 |
| Currants | 239 |
| Damsons | 239 |
| Dried Fruits | 239 |
| Figs | 239 |
| Figs a la Creole | 239 |
| Lemons | 239 |
| Malaga Grapes | 239 |
| Mespilus | 239 |
| Oranges | 240 |
| Peaches | 240 |
| Pears | 240 |
| Plums | 240 |
| Pineapple | 240 |
| Plantain, Creole Style | 240 |

| | |
|---|---|
| Plantain, Old Style | 241 |
| Pomegranates | 241 |
| Prunes | 241 |
| Raspberries | 241 |
| Strawberry | 241 |

**COFFEE, CHOCOLATE, COCOA, TEA,—Cafe, Chocolat, Cacao, du The—**

| | |
|---|---|
| CREOLE COFFEE (Cafe a la Creole) | 9 |
| Cafe au Lait | 11 |
| Cafe Noir | 10 |
| Best Ingredients for | 10 |
| How to Parch | 10 |
| How to Make | 10 |
| The Creole Rule for | 10 |
| Chocolate | 331 |
| Cocoa | 331 |
| Tea | 339 |

**COUPS DE MILIEU—Middle Course Drinks—**

| | |
|---|---|
| COUPS DE MILIEU | 308 |
| Cardinal Punch | 308 |
| Creole Punch | 309 |
| Frozen Champagne Punch | 309 |
| Imperial Punch | 309 |
| Kirsch Punch | 309 |
| Louisiana Punch | 309 |
| Roman Punch | 310 |
| Royal Sherbet | 310 |

**CREAM DESSERTS—Des Cremes—**

| | |
|---|---|
| CREAM DESSERTS | 261 |
| GENERAL DIRECTIONS FOR MAKING | 261 |
| Almond Cream, Sweet | 263 |
| Burnt Cream | 263 |
| Chestnut Cream | 263 |
| Chocolate Cream | 263 |
| Creamed Coffee | 263 |
| Foamy Cream | 262 |
| Foamy Cream, with Rum | 262 |
| Gelatine | 261 |
| Light Cream | 263 |
| Macaroon Cream | 263 |
| Peanut Cream | 264 |
| Snow Cream | 264 |
| Whipped Cream | 261 |
| White Coffee Cream | 263 |
| Whipped Cream, with Curacoa | 262 |
| Whipped Cream, with Coffee | 262 |
| Whipped Cream, with Cognac | 262 |
| Whipped Cream, with Kirsch | 262 |
| Whipped Cream, with Liquors | 262 |
| Whipped Cream, with Maraschino | 262 |
| Whipped Cream with Peaches, Cherries | 262 |
| Whipped Cream and Strawberries, Raspberries, Blackberries | 262 |
| Whipped Cream, with Vanilla, etc. | 262 |

**CREAM DESSERTS, BAVARIAN— Bavaroise—**

| | |
|---|---|
| BAVARIAN CREAMS (Bavaroise) | 264 |
| Apricot Bavarian Cream | 264 |
| Caramel Bavarian Cream | 265 |
| Chocolate Bavarian Cream | 265 |
| Coffee Bavarian Cream | 265 |
| Orange Bavarian Cream | 265 |
| Pineapple Bavarian Cream | 265 |
| Raspberry Bavarian Cream | 265 |
| Strawberry Bavarian Cream | 264 |
| Spanish Cream | 265 |
| Velvet Cream | 266 |
| Wine Cream | 266 |

**CREAM CUSTARDS AND OTHER DESSERTS—Des Flans, et Autre Desserts—**

| | |
|---|---|
| CUSTARD AND OTHER DESSERTS | 257 |
| AMBROSIA | 260 |
| Ambrosia, Pineapple and Orange | 260 |
| Apple Sago | 260 |
| Apple Sponge | 259 |
| Blanc Manger | 257 |
| Blanc Manger, Cornstarch | 257 |
| Blanc Manger, Neapolitan | 257 |
| Blanc Manger, Velvet | 257 |
| Charlotte Russe | 258 |
| Charlotte Russe, Parisian | 258 |
| Custard, Almond | 258 |
| Custard, Boiled | 257 |
| Custard, Cup | 257 |
| Custard, Souffle | 257 |
| Custard, Macaroon | 258 |
| Custard, Rice | 258 |
| Custard, Tapioca | 258 |
| Floating Island | 258 |
| Snow, Apple | 259 |
| Snow, Cream | 259 |
| Snow, Pineapple | 259 |
| Snow, Orange | 259 |
| Strawberry Short Cake | 260 |
| Strawberry Sponge | 260 |

**CREOLE CANDIES—**

| | |
|---|---|
| CREOLE CANDIES | 339 |
| Coloring for Candies | 349 |
| Carmine | 349 |
| Cochineal | 349 |
| Blue | 350 |
| Green | 349 |
| Orange | 349 |
| Yellow | 349 |
| SUGAR AS EMPLOYED IN CANDY MAKING | 347 |
| Caramel | 348 |
| Burnt Sugar | 350 |
| Lemon Sugar | 350 |
| Vanilla Sugar | 350 |
| Sugar Boiling | 348 |
| The Small Thread | 348 |
| The Large Thread | 348 |
| The Pearl | 348 |
| The Blow | 348 |
| The Feather | 348 |
| The Soft Ball | 348 |
| The Hard Ball | 348 |
| The Crack or Snap | 348 |
| To Clarify Sugar | 349 |
| BON-BONS | 342 |
| Bon-Bons, Cream | 346 |
| Bon-Bons, Chocolate Cream | 345 |
| Bon-Bons, Cherry and Noyau Cream | 346 |

| | |
|---|---|
| Bon-Bons, Coffee and Cognac Cream | 346 |
| Bon-Bons, Lemon and Maraschino Cream | 347 |
| Bon-Bons, Liqueur | 345 |
| Bon-Bons, Orange Cream | 347 |
| Candy Drops | 342 |
| Cream Peanuts | 347 |
| Crystallized Oranges | 345 |
| Crystallized Orange Blossoms | 345 |
| Crystallized Rose Petals | 345 |
| Crystallized Violets | 345 |
| Crystallized Watermelon | 345 |
| DRAGEES | 344 |
| LOZENGES | 347 |
| Lozenges, Cough | 347 |
| CARAMELS | 342 |
| Caramel, Chestnuts | 342 |
| Caramel, Chocolate | 342 |
| Caramel, Oranges | 342 |
| Cream Peanuts | 347 |
| Marshmallow | 344 |
| MOLASSES CANDY | 341 |
| La Colle | 341 |
| Pop-Corn Candy | 341 |
| Mais "Tac-Tac" | 342 |
| NOUGAT | 344 |
| Nougats, Parisian | 344 |
| PASTILLES | 343 |
| Pastilles, Cream | 343 |
| Pastilles, Fruit | 343 |
| Pastilles, Ginger | 343 |
| Pastilles, Health | 343 |
| Pastilles, Lemon | 343 |
| Pastilles, Liqueur | 343 |
| Pastilles, to Relieve Thirst | 343 |
| Pastilles, Marshmallow Drops | 344 |
| Pastilles, Peppermint Drops | 344 |
| Pastilles, Rose | 343 |
| Pastilles, Orange | 343 |
| PRALINES | 339 |
| Almond Pralines | 340 |
| Cream Pralines | 340 |
| Peanut Pralines | 341 |
| Pecan Pralines | 340 |
| Pink Pralines | 340 |
| White Pralines | 339 |
| Sugar Plums | 345 |

**EGGS—Des Oeufs—**

| | |
|---|---|
| EGGS | 162 |
| A la Poulette | 164 |
| Beauregard | 164 |
| Boiled | 162 |
| Creole Omelet | 164 |
| Fried | 163 |
| Fondue | 163 |
| Ham Omelet | 164 |
| Kidney Omelet | 165 |
| Mushroom Omelet | 165 |
| Onion Omelet | 165 |
| Omelet Souffle | 165 |
| Parsley Omelet | 165 |
| Plain Omelet | 164 |
| Poached | 163 |
| Rum Omelet | 165 |
| Scrambled | 163 |
| Scrambled, with Asparagus Tips | 164 |
| Scrambled with Ham | 163 |
| Scrambled with Preserves | 163 |
| Shirred | 164 |
| Truffle Omelet | 163 |
| With Ham | 163 |

**FRAPPES—**

| | |
|---|---|
| FRAPPES | 326 |
| Absinthe Frappe | 326 |
| Appetizer | 327 |
| Creme de Menthe Frappe | 326 |
| Creme de Noyau Frappe | 326 |
| Coffee Frappe | 327 |
| Old-Fashioned Creole Cocktails | 327 |
| Pousse Cafe | 327 |
| Vermouth Frappe | 327 |

**FISH—Du Poisson—**

| | |
|---|---|
| FISH | 36 |
| Au Gratin | 38 |
| Balls | 49 |
| Canned | 69 |
| Chowder | 49 |
| Croquettes | 48 |
| Fresh | 38 |
| General Rule for Baking | 38 |
| General Rule for Boiling | 37 |
| General Rule for Broiling | 37 |
| General Rule for Frying | 38 |
| General Rule for Stewing | 38 |
| How to Tell Good Fish | 36 |
| Methods of Cooking | 37 |
| Short Resume of Louisiana Varieties | 38 |
| Salt | 69 |
| Shell | 53, 62 |
| Soups | 19 to 23 |
| ANCHOVY (Des Anchois) | 71 |
| Anchovy Salad | 72 |
| Anchovy Canapes | 183, 184 |
| BLUEFISH (Poisson Bleu) | 47 |
| Bluefish, Broiled | 47 |
| CODFISH (De la Morue) | 69 |
| Codfish Balls | 70 |
| Codfish, Bacalao | 70 |
| Codfish, Boiled | 69 |
| Codfish, Creamed | 70 |
| Codfish, Fried | 69 |
| Codfish, Stewed | 69 |
| CRABS (Des Crabes) | 63 |
| Crabs, Hard-Shell | 64 |
| Crabs, Hard-Shell, Boiled | 64 |
| Crabs, Hard-Shell, Croquettes | 66 |
| Crabs, Hard-Shell, Deviled | 65 |
| Crabs, Hard-Shell, Fried | 64 |
| Crabs, Hard-shell, How to Eat | 64 |
| Crabs, Hard-shell, Pie of | 66 |
| Crabs, Hard-shell, Salad of | 66 |
| Crabs, Hard-shell, Salad No. 2 | 66 |
| Crabs, Hard-shell, Scalloped | 66 |
| Crabs, Hard-shell, Stewed | 64 |
| Crabs, Hard-shell, Stuffed | 65 |
| Crabs, Hard-shell, Stuffed No. 2 | 65 |
| Crabs, Soft-shell | 67 |
| Crabs, Soft-shell, Broiled | 67 |
| Crabs, Soft-shell, Fried | 67 |
| CRAWFISH (Des Ecrevisses) | 67 |
| Crawfish, Baked, a la Creole | 68 |
| Crawfish, Boiled | 67 |
| Crawfish Bush | 68 |
| CROAKERS (Des Grognards) | 49 |
| Croakers, Fried | 49 |

| | |
|---|---|
| EELS, LOUISIANA (De l'Anguille) | 49 |
| Eels, a la Maitre d'Hotel | 50 |
| Eels, a la Poulette | 50 |
| Eels, Broiled | 50 |
| Eels, Fried | 50 |
| Eels, (Stewed) en Matelote | 49 |
| FLOUNDER (Sole) | 45 |
| Flounder, a la Nouvelle Orleans | 45 |
| Flounder, a la Normande | 45 |
| Flounder, a la Orly | 45 |
| Flounder, a la Tartare | 45 |
| Flounder, Baked | 46 |
| GROUPER | 44 |
| Grouper, au Gratin | 44 |
| Grouper, Baked | 45 |
| Grouper, Boiled | 45 |
| HERRING (Des Harengs) | 71 |
| MACKEREL—Salt | 71 |
| Mackerel, Salt, Boiled | 71 |
| Mackerel, Salt, Broiled | 71 |
| OYSTERS (Huitres a la Creole) | 54 |
| Oysters, a la Poulette | 57 |
| Oysters au Parmesan | 59 |
| Oysters and Bacon | 56 |
| Oysters, en Brochette | 55 |
| Oyster Balls | 60 |
| Oysters, Baked (au Gratin) | 58 |
| Oysters, Broiled | 55 |
| Oysters, Broiled in Shells | 56 |
| Oysters, Broiled, on Toast | 55 |
| Oysters, Broiled, with Sauce Espagnole | 55 |
| Oysters, Coddled | 57 |
| Oyster Croquettes | 60 |
| Oyster Croquettes a la Creole | 60 |
| Oysters, Curried | 57 |
| Oysters, Deviled | 57 |
| Oyster Dressing | 143 |
| Oysters, Fried | 56 |
| Oysters, Fried, a la Creole | 56 |
| Oyster Fritters | 59 |
| Oyster Loaf | 61 |
| Oysters, Minced | 58 |
| Oyster Pan Roast | 59 |
| Oyster Patties | 60 |
| Oyster Pie | 60 |
| Oysters, Pickled | 61 |
| Oysters, Raw, in Block of Ice | 55 |
| Oysters, Raw, on Half Shell | 54 |
| Oysters, Roasted | 59 |
| Oyster Salad | 61 |
| Oysters, Sautees | 57 |
| Oysters Scalloped | 58 |
| Oysters, Steamed | 59 |
| Oysters, Stewed | 56 |
| Oyster Stuffing for Poultry, Fish, etc. | 143 |
| Oyster Soups | 22, 23 |
| PATASSAS | 49 |
| PERCHE (De la Perche) | 48 |
| Perch, Boiled | 48 |
| Perch, Broiled | 48 |
| POMPANO | 46 |
| Pompano, a la Maitre d'Hotel | 46 |
| REDFISH (Poisson Rouge) | 40 |
| Redfish, Baked | 44 |
| Redfish, Boiled | 42 |
| Redfish, Bouillabaisse | 41 |
| Redfish, Courtbouillon a la Creole | 40 |
| Redfish, Courtbouillon a l'Espagnole | 41 |
| Redfish, with Tomato Sauce (See Red Snapper) | 44 |
| RED SNAPPER | 40 |
| Red Snapper, Baked, a la Chambord | 43 |
| Red Snapper, a la Creole | 43 |
| Red Snapper, a la Sauce Tomates | 44 |
| Red Snapper, Baked, Simple Every Day Recipe | 43 |
| Red Snapper, Boiled | 42 |
| Red Snapper, Bouillabaisse | 41 |
| Red Snapper, Courtbouillon a la Creole | 40 |
| Red Snapper, Courtbouillon a l'Espagnole | 41 |
| ROE (Oeufs de Poisson) | 51 |
| SACALAIT | 49 |
| SALMON (Saumon) | 71 |
| Salmon, Mayonnaise of | 71 |
| Salmon Salad | 71 |
| SHEEPSHEAD (Casburgot) | 39 |
| Sheepshead a la Creole | 39 |
| Sheepshead, Baked | 39 |
| Sheepshead, Baked, a la Creole | 40 |
| Sheepshead, Boiled | 39 |
| Sheepshead, Broiled (See General Rule for Broiling Fish) | 37 |
| SHRIMP (Des Chevrettes) | 62 |
| Shrimp, Baked | 63 |
| Shrimp, Boiled | 62 |
| Shrimp, Bush | 63 |
| Shrimp, Fried | 62 |
| Shrimp Gumbos | 35 |
| Shrimp Pie | 63 |
| Shrimp, Stewed | 62 |
| Shrimp in Tomato Catsup | 63 |
| SPANISH MACKEREL (Maquereau Espagnole) | 46 |
| Spanish Mackerel, Broiled | 47 |
| STINGAREE (De la Raie) | 50 |
| Stingaree au Beurre Noir | 51 |
| Stingaree, Fried | 51 |
| Stingaree, with Caper Sauce | 51 |
| STINGARETTES (Raitons) | 51 |
| TERRAPIN (De la Tortue) | 21 |
| TROUT (De la Truite) | 47 |
| Trout, Green, Boiled | 47 |
| Trout, Green, Broiled | 47 |
| Trout, Speckled | 48 |
| Trout, Speckled, Fried | 48 |
| Trout, Tenderloin of | 48 |
| TURTLE (De la Tortue) | 68 |
| Turtle, Green, Steaks of | 68 |
| Turtle, Green, Stewed | 68 |
| Turtle, Green, Soups | 19, 20 |

**FROGS—Des Grenouilles—**

| | |
|---|---|
| FROGS | 51 |
| Frogs, a la Creole | 52 |
| Frogs, a la Poulette | 52 |
| Frogs, Broiled | 53 |
| Frogs, Fried | 53 |
| Frogs, Saute, a la Creole | 52 |
| Frogs, Stewed | 53 |
| Frogs, The Picayune's | 51 |
| Frogs, The Picayune, a la Creole | 52 |

| | |
|---|---|
| **FROZEN FRUITS—Des Fruits Glaces—** | |
| FROZEN FRUITS | 310 |
| How to Freeze Fruits | 310 |
| Apricots, Frozen | 310 |
| Cherries, Frozen | 310 |
| Bananas, Frozen | 310 |
| Macedoine of Fruits | 311 |
| Oranges, Frozen | 310 |
| Peaches, Frozen | 311 |
| Pineapple, Frozen | 311 |
| Strawberries, Frozen | 311 |
| FRUIT GRANITS | 322 |
| Orange Granit | 322 |
| Strawberry Granite | 322 |
| Raspberry Granite | 322 |
| How to Serve Fresh Fruits and Desserts | 241 |
| **GAME—Gibier—** | |
| GAME | 124 |
| Chaud-Froid of | 142 |
| Game Pie | 142 |
| Something to Remember when Cooking Game | 124 |
| DUCKS, Wild (Canards Sauvages) | 127 |
| Canvasback Duck | 127 |
| Canvasback Duck, Broiled | 127 |
| Canvasback Duck, Roasted | 127 |
| Ducks a la Bourgeoise | 128 |
| Ducks, Stewed | 128 |
| Ducks, Stewed, French Marshal Style | 129 |
| Ducks, Stewed with Mushrooms | 128 |
| Ducks, Stewed with Turnips | 128 |
| Ducks, Stewed, Peasant Style | 129 |
| Mallard Ducks, Roasted | 127 |
| Wild Ducks, Cold | 129 |
| Wild Ducks, Hunter's Style | 128 |
| Wild Ducks, with Olives | 129 |
| DUCKS—TEAL (Sarcelle) | 129 |
| Teal Duck, a la Bigarade | 130 |
| Teal Duck, Broiled | 130 |
| Teal Duck, Roasted | 129 |
| HARE (Lievre) | 131 |
| Hare, Creole Style | 132 |
| Hare, Filet of, Sauce Poivrade | 132 |
| Hare, Roasted and Stuffed | 131 |
| Hare, Stewed with Onions | 132 |
| RABBIT (Lapin) | 130 |
| Rabbit, Hunter's Style | 130 |
| Rabbit, en Matelote | 131 |
| Rabbit, Stewed | 130 |
| SQUIRREL (Ecureuil) | 132 |
| Squirrel, Hunter's Style | 133 |
| Squirrel, en Matelote | 133 |
| Squirrel, Stewed | 132 |
| VENISON (Du Chevreuil) | 124 |
| Venison, Cutlets of, Broiled | 125 |
| Venison, Hash | 126 |
| Venison, Hunter's Style | 126 |
| Venison, in a Chafing Dish | 126 |
| Venison, Roast Haunch of | 125 |
| Venison, Saddle of, Currant Jelly Sauce | 125 |
| Venison Steaks, a la Poivrade | 125 |
| Venison, Stewed, a la Creole | 125 |
| Venison, Stewed, French Style | 126 |
| WILD TURKEY (Dinde Sauvage) | 127 |

| | |
|---|---|
| **GARDEN HERBS—Des Herbes—** | |
| Anise | 225 |
| Bay Leaf | 225 |
| Bene | 225 |
| Borage | 225 |
| Caraway | 225 |
| Catnip | 225 |
| Coriander | 225 |
| Dill | 225 |
| Fennel | 225 |
| Geranium | 225 |
| Horehound | 225 |
| Laurel | 225 |
| Lavender | 225 |
| Marigold | 225 |
| Marjoram | 225 |
| Mint | 225 |
| Pennyroyal | 225 |
| Pot Marigold | 225 |
| Rosemary | 225 |
| Rue | 225 |
| Sage | 225 |
| Summer Savory | 225 |
| Sweet Basil | 225 |
| Sweet Marjoram | 225 |
| Tansy | 225 |
| Tarragon | 225 |
| Wormwood | 225 |
| The Herb Bouquet (Bouquet Garni) | 12 |
| **HORS D'OEUVRES—Relishes—** | |
| HORS D'OEUVRES | 226 |
| Anchovies in Oil | 226 |
| Cold Hors d'Oeuvres | 226 |
| Coquilles of Chicken, Creole Style | 226 |
| Creole Timbales | 227 |
| Cromesquies With Truffles | 226 |
| Hot Hors d'Oeuvres | 226 |
| Lamb Sweetbreads in Cases | 227 |
| Lyonnaise Sausage | 229 |
| Macaroni Croquettes | 227 |
| Queen of the Carnival Croustades | 227 |
| Pickled Tunny | 229 |
| Reed Bird Patties | 229 |
| Salpicon, Financiere Style | 228 |
| Salpicon a la Montglas | 228 |
| Salpicon, Creole | 228 |
| Salpicon, Hunter's Style | 228 |
| Salpicon, Louisiana | 228 |
| Salpicon, Royal | 228 |
| Sardines in Oil | 226 |
| Tamales | 229 |
| **ICE CREAMS—Des Cremes a la Glace—** | |
| BISCUITS GLACES | 305 |
| Biscuit Glaces, a la Creole | 306 |
| BOMBE GLACES | 306 |
| ICE CREAMS | 300 |
| Ice Cream, Observations on | 300 |
| How to Make Ice Cream | 300 |
| Ice Cream, Ingredients of | 300 |
| How to Freeze the Cream | 303 |
| How to Mold Ice Cream | 301 |
| Apricot Ice Cream | 301 |
| Banana | 301 |
| Chocolate | 301 |
| Chocolate Ice Cream with Eggs | 301 |

Coffee ....................... 301
King of the Carnival Ice
   Cream .................... 301
Lemon ....................... 302
Liquor Ice Cream ........... 302
Mandarin ................... 302
Maraschino ................. 302
Neapolitan ................. 302
Nectarine .................. 302
Nougat ..................... 303
Noyau ...................... 303
Orange ..................... 303
Orange Flower .............. 303
Peach ...................... 303
Pistachio .................. 303
Pineapple Mousse ........... 304
Raspberry .................. 304
Rice ....................... 304
Rose ....................... 304
Strawberry ................. 304
Tutti-Frutti ............... 304
Vanilla .................... 305
Variegated ................. 305
WATER ICES ................. 308

**ICINGS FOR CAKES—Glaces Pour Gateaux—**
Almond Icing ............... 298
Chocolate Icing ............ 298
Orange or Lemon ............ 298
Colored Transparent Icing.. 299
Orange Transparent Icing.... 298
Orgeat Paste or Icing ...... 299
Plain Icing ................ 298
Royal Icing ................ 299
Transparent Icing .......... 299
Water Icing ................ 299
Wine Icing ................. 299
FROSTING—
Cream Frosting ............. 299

**JAMS, JELLIES—Des Confitures—**
JAMS, JELLIES .............. 332
  General Directions for Making ....................... 332
Apple Jelly ................ 332
Apricot .................... 332
Blackberry Jelly ........... 333
Blue Plum and Damson Jelly . 332
Calf's Foot Jelly .......... 333
Cherry Jam ................. 333
Cherry Jelly ............... 333
Currant Jelly .............. 333
Currant and Raspberry Jelly  333
Lemon Jelly ................ 333
Orange Jelly ............... 334
Orange Jelly, Creole Style.. 334
Peach Jelly ................ 334
Pear Jelly ................. 334
Pineapple Jelly ............ 334
Quince Jelly ............... 334
Raspberry Jam .............. 335
Raspberry Jelly ............ 334
Strawberry Jam ............. 336
Strawberry Jelly ........... 335

**LAMB—Agneau—**
LAMB ....................... 99
Lamb's Brain ............... 101
Lamb's Brains a la Remoulade ..................... 101
Lamb Breast of, Smothered.. 100
Lamb Chops, Broiled ........ 100

Lamb's Feet ................ 102
Lamb's Feet a la Bourgeoise  102
Lamb's Feet, White Sauce ... 103
Lamb, Filet of, a la Bechamel .................... 100
Lamb, Filet of, Roasted and
   Larded ................... 100
Lamb, En Blanquette ........ 101
Lamb, Epigram of ........... 101
Lamb, Kidneys of, Broiled .. 102
Lamb, Mince Lamb ........... 101
Lamb Roast, a la Bearnaise.. 100
Lamb Roast, with Mint Sauce  99
Lamb Tongues, Stewed ....... 102
Lamb Tongues with Tomato
   Sauce .................... 102

**LOUISIANA RICE—Le Riz de la Louisiane—**
RICE ....................... 166
Boiled Rice, Italian Style . 168
Bread ...................... 170
Calas ...................... 168
Croquettes of, with Fruit .. 170
Croquettes of, with Parsley. 170
Curry of Crawfish .......... 168
Custard .................... 171
Custard of, Frozen ......... 172
Dumplings .................. 171
Fried ...................... 173
Fritters of ................ 173
Flour, Croquettes of ....... 170
Griddle Cakes .............. 170
How to Boil ................ 166
How to Make a Border of.... 168
How to Prepare for Cooking.. 166
Jambalaya au Congri ........ 167
Jambalaya, Creole .......... 166
Jambalaya, Crab ............ 167
Jambalaya, Shrimp .......... 167
Left Over .................. 173
Meringue ................... 171
Parched .................... 173
Pilaff of, with Chicken .... 168
Pilou, French .............. 167
Pilou au Riz (Chicken with
   Rice) .................... 168
Pudding of Cream ........... 172
Snowballs .................. 172
Souffle .................... 172
Things to Remember in Boiling ..................... 166
Waffles .................... 169
With Apples ................ 170
With Compote of Oranges.... 172

**MACARONI, SPAGHETTI—**
MACARONI ................... 178
Macaroni, How to Boil ...... 178
Macaroni Balls ............. 181
Macaroni, Boiled, Italian Style  179
Macaroni, Creole Style ..... 179
Macaroni, with Daube ....... 180
Macaroni au Gratin ......... 180
Macaroni, Milanese Style ... 179
Macaroni, Neapolitan Style.. 180
Macaroni, with Tomato Sauce  179
Macaroni, Timbales of ...... 180
Spaghetti, Boiled, Italian
   Style .................... 179
Spaghetti, with Daube ...... 180
Spaghetti, Milanese Style .. 179

## MARMALADES—Des Marmalades—

| | |
|---|---|
| Directions for Making a Marmalade | 335 |
| Apple Marmalade | 335 |
| Cherry Marmalade | 335 |
| Orange Marmalade | 335 |
| Pear Marmalade | 335 |
| Peach Marmalade | 336 |
| Pineapple Marmalade | 336 |
| Quince Marmalade | 336 |
| Raspberry Marmalade | 336 |
| Strawberry Marmalade | 336 |
| Conserve of Grapes | 336 |
| Orange Flower and Rose Conserves | 336 |
| Violet Conserve | 336 |

## MELONS—Des Melons—

| | |
|---|---|
| Cantaloup | 225 |
| Muskmelon | 225 |
| Melon on Ice | 225 |
| Watermelon | 225 |

## MENUS — 389

| | |
|---|---|
| Creole Home Dining | 396 |
| A Suggestion for Each Day in the Week | 390 |
| Suggestions for Economical Menus | 397 |
| Suggestions for Holiday Feasts and Banquets | 391 |
| Suggestion for Christmas | 393 |
| Suggestion for Easter | 392 |
| Suggestion for New Year's | 392 |
| Suggestion for Thanksgiving Day | 393 |
| Old-Fashioned Creole Holiday Menus | 394 |
| Special Menus for Luncheons, Buffet Luncheons, Dinings, Suppers, etc., for Soirees | 395 |
| Special Suggestions for Table Decorations | 390 |
| Table Decorations for Christmas | 394 |
| Table Decoration for Easter | 392 |
| Table Decoration for New Years | 392 |
| Table Decoration for Thanksgiving Day | 393 |
| The Daily Economical Menu, How to Vary | 394 |

## MUTTON—Mouton—

| | |
|---|---|
| MUTTON | 96 |
| Mutton Chops, Broiled | 97 |
| Mutton Chops a la Brasseur | 97 |
| Mutton Cutlets | 97 |
| Mutton Feet a la Lyonnaise | 98 |
| Mutton Feet a la Poulette | 98 |
| Mutton Feet, Stuffed | 98 |
| Mutton, Hash | 98 |
| Mutton, Leg of, Boiled, with Caper Sauce | 96 |
| Mutton, Leg of, Roast | 96 |
| Mutton, Loin of, Roast | 96 |
| Observations on | 96 |
| Saddle of, Smothered with Turnips | 97 |
| Sheep Brains | 99 |
| Sheep Brains, Brown Sauce | 99 |
| Sheep Kidneys | 99 |
| Sheep Tongues, Smothered | 99 |
| Shoulder of, Smothered with Turnips | 97 |
| Something to Remember in Cooking Mutton | 96 |
| Stew, with Turnips | 97 |

## PASTRY AND PIES—Patisserie—

| | |
|---|---|
| PASTRY AND PIES | 242 |
| Pastry, Points in Making | 242 |
| Paste, Foundation | 243 |
| Paste, Plain, for Dumplings | 243 |
| Paste, Puff | 242 |
| PIES | 242 |
| Pie Crust | 242 |
| Apple Pie | 244 |
| Apple Tarts | 244 |
| Apple Meringue | 244 |
| Banana | 244 |
| Banana Meringue | 244 |
| Blackberry | 244 |
| Cherry | 245 |
| Chocolate Cream | 245 |
| Cocoanut | 245 |
| Creole Cocoanut | 245 |
| Cream | 245 |
| Cranberry | 245 |
| Custard | 245 |
| Currant | 245 |
| Frangipanni | 246 |
| Gooseberry | 246 |
| Green Gage | 246 |
| Huckleberry | 246 |
| Lemon | 246 |
| Mince | 247 |
| Plain Mincemeat | 247 |
| Lenten Mince | 247 |
| Molasses | 248 |
| Orange | 248 |
| Peach | 248 |
| Peach Meringue | 248 |
| Pear | 248 |
| Pineapple | 248 |
| Plantain | 248 |
| Plantain Meringue | 248 |
| Pumpkin | 248 |
| Raspberry | 249 |
| Strawberry | 249 |
| Sweet Potato Custard | 249 |
| Vol-au-Vent | 249 |
| Oyster Patties | 250 |

## PICKLING AND CANNING—Conservation des Substances Alimentaires et Vegetales—

| | |
|---|---|
| PICKLING AND CANNING | 357 |
| Methods of | 350 |
| Canned Corn | 350 |
| Canned Green Peas | 351 |
| Canned Mushrooms | 351 |
| Canned Tomatoes | 351 |
| CATSUPS | 354 |
| Catsup, Tomato | 354 |
| Catsup, Red Pepper, a la Creole | 355 |
| CREOLE MUSTARD | 355 |
| MAUNSELL-WHITE | 355 |
| PICKLES | 351 |
| Home-Made Chow-Chow | 352 |
| Green Pepper Pickles | 352 |
| Green Tomato Pickles | 353 |
| Pickled Fruits | 354 |
| Mixed Pickles | 352 |

| | |
|---|---|
| Pickled Cauliflower | 352 |
| Pickled Mangoes | 353 |
| Pickled Onions | 353 |
| Pickled String Beans | 354 |
| Pickled Watermelon Rind | 354 |
| VINEGARS | 354 |
| Chervil Vinegar | 354 |
| Pepper Vinegar | 354 |
| Spiced Vinegar | 355 |
| Tarragon Vinegar | 355 |
| SALTED ALMONDS | 356 |
| Salted Almonds | 356 |
| Salted Peanuts | 356 |
| TABASCO | 355 |

**PORK—Du Cochon—**

| | |
|---|---|
| PORK | 103 |
| Guides in Choosing | 103 |
| BACON (Petit Sale) | 107 |
| Bacon, Boiled | 107 |
| Bacon, Fried | 107 |
| HAM (Jambon) | 106 |
| Ham, Boiled | 106 |
| Ham, Broiled | 106 |
| Ham, Broiled, with Cucumber Garnish | 106 |
| Ham, Croquettes | 107 |
| Ham, Fried | 106 |
| Ham Souffle | 107 |
| HOGSHEAD CHEESE | 105 |
| PIG (Cochon de Lait) | 103 |
| Pig, Roasted and Stuffed | 103 |
| Pigs Feet | 104 |
| Pigs' Feet, Piquant Sauce | 104 |
| Pigs' Feet, Sauce Robert | 104 |
| Pigs' Feet, St. Hubert Sauce | 105 |
| Pigs' Feet, Madeira Sauce | 105 |
| Pigs' Feet, Stuffed a la Perigueux | 105 |
| Pigs' Feet, Tartar Sauce | 104 |
| Pigs' Feet, Tomato Sauce | 104 |
| PORK (Du Cochon) | 103 |
| Pork Chops, Fried | 104 |
| Pork, Pickled | 105 |
| Pork, Roast | 103 |
| Pork, Roast, Loin of | 103 |
| Pork, Spare Ribs of | 104 |
| Pork, Tenderloin | 104 |

**POULTRY—De la Volaille—**

| | |
|---|---|
| POULTRY | 109 |
| Guides in Buying | 110 |
| How to Clean | 110 |
| CAPONS | 119 |
| CHICKEN | 113 |
| Chicken a la Reine | 117 |
| Chicken Balls, Queen's Style | 118 |
| Chicken, Boned | 118 |
| Chicken, Boiled | 113 |
| Chicken, Boulettes | 118 |
| Chicken, Broiled | 113 |
| Chicken, Croquettes of | 118 |
| Chicken, Casseroles of | 117 |
| Chicken, Devlied | 114 |
| Chicken, Fried | 117 |
| Chicken, Fried, with Cream Sauce | 117 |
| Chicken Livers | 119 |
| Chicken Patties, Queen's Style | 118 |
| Chicken Pie | 118 |
| Chicken, Roasted | 117 |
| Chicken Salad, with Mayonnaise Sauce | 119 |

| | |
|---|---|
| Chicken Saute, a la Creme | 113 |
| Chicken Saute, a la Creole | 114 |
| Chicken Saute, with Green Peas | 115 |
| Chicken Saute, a la Jardiniere | 116 |
| Chicken Saute, a la Tartare | 114 |
| Chicken, Smothered | 116 |
| Chicken Souffle | 117 |
| Chicken Supreme de Volaille a la Louisiana | 116 |
| Chicken Supreme de Volaille a la Reine | 116 |
| Chicken with Dumplings | 116 |
| Chicken with Mushrooms | 115 |
| Chicken with Rice | 115 |
| Chicken with Truffles | 115 |
| GUINEA FOWLS (Pintade) | 119 |
| GOOSE (Oie) | 119 |
| Goose a la Chipolata | 120 |
| Goose Daub | 120 |
| Goose, Roast | 119 |
| Goose, Fat Livers (Des Foies Gras) | 120 |
| FOIES GRAS, Patties of | 120 |
| Foies Gras, Loaf of | 121 |
| Foies Gras Loaf, Jellied | 121 |
| Foies Gras, Stewed | 120 |
| TURKEY (Dinde) | 111 |
| Turkey, Boned | 112 |
| Turkey, en Daube | 112 |
| Turkey, Roast | 111 |
| Turkey, Roast, with Chestnuts or Oysters | 111 |
| Turkey, Roast, with Mushrooms | 111 |
| Turkey, Roast, with Truffles | 111 |

**PRESERVES—Des Conserves—**

| | |
|---|---|
| PRESERVES | 336 |
| GENERAL DIRECTIONS FOR MAKING PRESERVES | 336 |
| Brandy Peaches | 338 |
| Fig Preserves | 337 |
| Fruit Preserves | 338 |
| Lemon Preserves | 337 |
| Orange Preserves | 338 |
| Oranges (Small) Preserved Whole | 338 |
| Peach Preserves | 338 |
| Pineapple Preserves | 338 |
| Quince Preserves | 338 |
| Watermelon Rind Preserves | 338 |

**PUDDINGS, DUMPLINGS—Des Poudings, Des Echaudes—**

| | |
|---|---|
| DUMPLINGS | 250 |
| Apple Dumplings, Old-Fashioned Creole | 251 |
| Blackberry Roll | 250 |
| Boiled Dumplings | 250 |
| Baked Dumplings | 251 |
| Rice Dumplings | 251 |
| Roly Poly | 251 |
| PUDDINGS | 251 |
| Baked Puddings and Dumplings | 252 |
| Apple | 252 |
| Apple Meringue | 252 |
| Banana | 252 |
| Birds' Nest | 252 |
| Bread | 252 |
| Brown Betty | 253 |
| Cake or Bread | 253 |

| | |
|---|---:|
| Chocolate | 253 |
| Cottage | 253 |
| Cocoanut | 253 |
| Cream | 253 |
| Creole Fig | 253 |
| Creole Summer Pudding | 259 |
| Fig | 254 |
| Indian | 254 |
| Baked Lemon | 254 |
| Molasses | 254 |
| Nesselrode | 254 |
| Old-Fashioned Creole Plum | 251 |
| Orange | 254 |
| Peach Batter | 255 |
| Plum | 251 |
| Fruit Batter | 255 |
| Pineapple | 255 |
| Raspberry | 255 |
| Sago | 255 |
| Snow | 255 |
| Strawberry | 256 |
| Sweet Potato | 256 |
| Tapioca | 256 |
| The Queen of all Puddings | 256 |
| Tipsy Squire | 256 |

**PUDDING SAUCES—Sauces des Poudings—**

| | |
|---|---:|
| PUDDING SAUCES | 266 |
| Apple | 266 |
| Apricot | 266 |
| Brandy | 266 |
| Hard Brandy | 267 |
| Caramel | 267 |
| Chaufausen | 267 |
| Cream | 267 |
| Cream of Butter | 267 |
| Cream of Vanilla | 267 |
| Custard | 267 |
| Foaming | 267 |
| Fruit | 267 |
| Golden | 268 |
| Hard | 268 |
| Hard Sauce a la Creole | 268 |
| Kirsch | 268 |
| Lemon | 268 |
| Madeira | 268 |
| Madeira Sabayon | 268 |
| Orange | 268 |
| Punch | 269 |
| Rum | 269 |
| Silvery | 269 |
| Strawberry | 269 |
| Vanilla | 269 |
| Velvet | 269 |
| White Wine | 269 |

**PUNCH—Ponche—**

| | |
|---|---:|
| PUNCH | 322 |
| Champagne Frappe | 323 |
| Punch, Champagne | 322 |
| Punch, Champagne a la Creole | 323 |
| Punch, Claret | 323 |
| Punch, Claret, Creole Style | 323 |
| Punch, Claret, Hot | 325 |
| Punch, Whisky, Hot | 323 |
| Punch, Louisiana | 323 |
| Punch, Milk | 323 |
| Punch, Orange, New Orleans Style | 323 |
| Punch, Rum | 323 |
| Punch, Strawberry | 324 |
| Punch, White Wine | 324 |
| Punch, White Wine, Creole Style | 324 |
| Punch, Tea | 324 |

**QUENELLES—Forcemeats—**

| | |
|---|---:|
| QUENELLES | 144 |
| Chicken Quenelles | 145 |
| Crab Quenelles | 145 |
| Creole Quenelles | 144 |
| Game Quenelles | 145 |
| Godiveaux Quenelles | 145 |
| Fish Quenelles | 145 |
| Sausage Quenelles | 145 |

**RATAFIAS—**

| | |
|---|---:|
| RATAFIAS | 316 |
| How to Filter | 317 |
| Proportions of Ingredients for | 317 |
| Ratafia, Absinthe or Wormwood | 317 |
| Ratafia, Angelica | 317 |
| Ratafia, Aniseed | 317 |
| Ratafia, Fruit | 318 |
| Ratafia, Of Four Fruits | 318 |
| Orange Ratafia | 318 |
| Orange Flower Ratafia | 318 |
| Peach Kernel Ratafia | 318 |
| Pomegranate Ratafia | 318 |
| Raspberry Ratafia | 318 |
| Strawberry Ratafia | 318 |

**SALADS—Des Salades—**

| | |
|---|---:|
| SALADS | 156 |
| Anchovy | 158 |
| Artichoke | 158 |
| Asparagus, Tips of | 158 |
| Bean | 158 |
| Bean (String Bean) | 161 |
| Beet | 159 |
| Cauliflower | 159 |
| Celery | 159 |
| Celery Mayonnaise | 159 |
| Chicken | 159 |
| Chervil | 159 |
| Corn | 159 |
| Crab a la Mayonnaise | 159 |
| Crawfish | 159 |
| Creole, French Dressing for | 158 |
| Cress | 159 |
| Cucumber | 159 |
| Dandelion | 160 |
| Endive | 160 |
| Fish | 160 |
| French Dressings for | 157 |
| Gardener's Wife Salad | 161 |
| Lentil | 160 |
| Lettuce | 160 |
| Louisiana | 160 |
| Mayonnaise Dressing | 158 |
| Mustard Dressing | 157 |
| Okra | 160 |
| Peppers, Green, a l'Espagnole | 161 |
| Potato | 161 |
| Remoulade Dressing | 158 |
| Russian | 162 |
| Sardine Shrimp | 162 |
| Spanish | 161 |
| Tomato Frappe | 161 |
| Tomato, Green Pepper and Onion | 161 |
| Tomato Salad | 161 |
| Vinaigrette | 158 |
| Watercress | 161 |

## SAUCES FOR FISH, MEATS, POULTRY, GAME, ETC.—Des Sauces Pour les Poissons, des Viandes, la Volaille, le Gibier, etc.—

| | |
|---|---|
| SAUCES | 146 |
| Allemande | 156 |
| Anchovy | 147 |
| Apple | 147 |
| Bearnaise | 147 |
| Bechamel | 147 |
| Bordelaise | 147 |
| Bordelaise, Creole Style | 147 |
| Bread | 148 |
| Brown | 147 |
| Brown Butter | 148 |
| Caper | 148 |
| Cauliflower | 148 |
| Celery | 149 |
| Chambord | 148 |
| Champagne | 148 |
| Chestnut | 149 |
| Chili | 149 |
| Colbert | 149 |
| Cranberry | 149 |
| Crapaudine | 150 |
| Cream | 149 |
| Creole | 150 |
| Cucumber | 150 |
| Currant Jelly | 150 |
| Demi-Glace | 150 |
| Devil's | 150 |
| Drawn Butter | 150 |
| Duxelle | 150 |
| Egg | 151 |
| Financiere | 152 |
| Genoise | 151 |
| Giblet | 151 |
| Hard Egg Sauce | 151 |
| Hollandaise | 151 |
| Horseradish | 151 |
| Hunter's Sauce | 151 |
| Italian | 151 |
| Jolie Fille | 152 |
| Lyonnaise | 152 |
| Madeira | 152 |
| Maitre d'Hotel | 152 |
| Mayonnaise | 152 |
| Mint | 153 |
| Mushroom | 153 |
| Normandy | 153 |
| Onion | 153 |
| Oyster | 153 |
| Parsley | 153 |
| Pepper | 153 |
| Pickle | 154 |
| Piquant | 154 |
| Poivrade | 153 |
| Poulette | 154 |
| Ravigote | 154 |
| Remoulade | 154 |
| Robert | 155 |
| Roux, White and Brown | 146 |
| Tartare | 155 |
| Tomato | 155 |
| Veloutee | 155 |
| Vinaigrette | 156 |
| White | 156 |

## SAUSAGE—Saucisses

| | |
|---|---|
| SAUSAGE | 107 |
| Boudins | 108 |
| Boudins Blancs | 109 |
| Creole Sausage | 107 |
| Chaurice | 107 |
| Chaurice, with Creole Sauce | 108 |
| Chaurice, with Puree of Potatoes | 108 |
| Chitterlings | 109 |
| Saucisse | 108 |
| Saucissons | 108 |
| Sausages a la Creole | 107 |

## STUFFINGS AND DRESSINGS FOR POULTRY, GAME, FISH, ETC.—Des Farces—

| | |
|---|---|
| STUFFINGS AND DRESSINGS | 143 |
| Bread | 144 |
| Egg | 143 |
| Onion | 144 |
| Oyster (For Fish or Game) | 143 |
| Oyster (For Poultry) | 142 |
| Stuffing (for Ducks) | 143 |
| Stuffing (For Ducks) | 144 |
| Stuffing (For Geese) | 144 |

## SHERBETS—Sorbets—

| | |
|---|---|
| SHERBET | 306 |
| Apple Sherbet | 306 |
| Apricot | 306 |
| Banana | 306 |
| Cherry | 306 |
| Currant | 306 |
| Grape | 306 |
| Lemon | 306 |
| Orange | 307 |
| Peach | 307 |
| Pineapple | 307 |
| Pomegranate | 307 |
| Raspberry | 307 |
| Strawberry | 307 |
| Watermelon | 308 |

## SOUPS—

| | |
|---|---|
| SOUPS | 11 |
| General Directions for Making | 11 |
| Boiling | 12 |
| Bouillon | 13 |
| Bouillon, to Clarify | 13 |
| Caramel, for Coloring | 14 |
| Colorings for | 13 |
| Consomme | 13 |
| Fish Soups | 19 |
| Herb Bouquet, for | 12 |
| Lenten Soups | 23 |
| Meat Soups | 14 |
| Pot-au-Feu a la Creole | 12 |
| Soup Meat (See "Le Bouilli") | 29 |
| SOUPS—Fish | 19 |
| Crab | 23 |
| Crawfish Bisque | 21 |
| Crawfish Soup | 22 |
| Fish | 19 |
| Oyster | 22 |
| Oyster, with Milk | 23 |
| Terrapin | 21 |
| Turtle (Green), No. 1 | 19 |
| Turtle (Green), No. 2 | 20 |
| Turtle, How to Serve | 20 |
| Turtle, Quenelles or Forcemeat Balls for | 21 |
| Turtle, Mock, Eggs for | 21 |
| SOUPS—Lenten (Potages Maigre) | 23 |
| Carrot | 26 |
| Chestnut | 29 |

| | |
|---|---|
| Cocoanut | 28 |
| Cream of Asparagus | 27 |
| Cream of Barley | 28 |
| Cream of Celery | 27 |
| Cream of Corn | 27 |
| Cream of Onion | 27 |
| Cream of Rice | 28 |
| Cream of Tomato | 27 |
| Cream of Spinach | 28 |
| Dried Pea | 25 |
| Fast Day Broth | 23 |
| Lentil | 24 |
| Lettuce | 26 |
| Okra | 26 |
| Onion | 26 |
| Potage a la Bonne Femme | 25 |
| Potato | 26 |
| Red Bean | 25 |
| Rice | 28 |
| Sorrel | 25 |
| Split Pea | 25 |
| Summer Fast Day | 24 |
| Vegetable, Without Meat | 24 |
| White Bean | 25 |
| Winter Fast Day | 24 |
| SOUPS—Meat—Consomme, Chicken | 17 |
| Consomme, Gilt-Edge | 17 |
| Consomme, with Poached Eggs | 18 |
| Chicken Broth | 17 |
| Corn | 16 |
| Giblet | 18 |
| Julienne | 14 |
| Macaroni | 16 |
| Mock Turtle | 17 |
| Mock Turtle, Forcemeat Balls for | 17 |
| Mushroom | 15 |
| Mutton Broth | 17 |
| Noodle | 15 |
| Okra | 15 |
| Oxtail | 15 |
| Pepper Pot | 19 |
| Potage Crout. au Pot | 16 |
| Queen | 18 |
| Rabbit | 18 |
| Rice | 15 |
| Sage | 15 |
| Savory | 16 |
| Squirrel | 19 |
| Tapioca | 14 |
| Tomato Consomme | 16 |
| Vermicelli | 14 |

**SOUP MEAT—Le Bouilli—**

| | |
|---|---|
| SOUP MEAT (Le Bouilli) | 29 |
| SOUP—Meat—(Bouilli) Possibilities | 29 |
| A la Bordelaise | 30 |
| A la Bruxelloise | 30 |
| A l'Indienne | 30 |
| A la Lyonnaise | 30 |
| A la Marseillaise | 31 |
| A la Paysanne | 30 |
| Au Pain Perdu | 31 |
| Aux Papillottes | 30 |
| Bouilli, Gros Sel | 32 |
| Croquettes | 32 |
| Hash, a good every day | 32 |
| Mirontons | 29 |
| Sausage | 31 |
| Saute a la Lyonnaise | 30 |
| Saute, with Onions | 31 |

| | |
|---|---|
| White Carrot Sauce | 31 |
| With Lettuce | 31 |
| With Tomatoes | 30 |

**SUGGESTIONS TO HOUSEKEEPERS—**

| | |
|---|---|
| SUGGESTIONS TO HOUSEKEEPERS | 373 |
| Cutting, Chopping, Slicing, Mincing | 374 |
| Directions for Serving Meals | 377 |
| Explanation of French Terms | 375 |
| Foods, Seasons when Procurable | 383 |
| Invalids, Cookery for | 380 |
| Left Over Food, How to Utilize | 380 |
| Rules for Mixing Ingredients | 374 |
| Use of Broth, Bouillon and Consomme in Cookery | 375 |
| Use of Wines and Liquors | 374 |

**SWEET ENTREMETS—Des Entremets Sucres—**

| | |
|---|---|
| FRITTERS (Des Beignets) | 225 |
| Apples, Baked | 234 |
| Apple Charlotte | 234 |
| Apples, Fried | 234 |
| Apples, Stewed | 234 |
| Bananas, Fried | 235 |
| Blackberry Charlotte, or Raspberry | 235 |
| Cherry Charlotte | 234 |
| Currant Charlotte | 235 |
| Doughnuts | 235 |
| Fruit Toasts, with Cherries, Apricots or Raspberries | 235 |
| Orange Salad | 235 |
| Stewed Peaches | 235 |
| Sweet Omelet Entremets | 235 |
| Wine and Liquor Entremets | 235 |
| PANCAKES (Crepes) | 236 |
| French Pancakes | 237 |
| French Pancakes, with Jelly | 237 |

**SYRUPS—Des Sirops—**

| | |
|---|---|
| SYRUPS (Des Sirops) | 312 |
| GENERAL DIRECTIONS FOR MAKING SYRUPS | 313 |
| CREAM SYRUPS (Sirops a la Creme) | 320 |
| Absinthe Cream | 321 |
| Bay Leaf Cream | 321 |
| Cocoa Cream | 321 |
| Cherry Water Cream | 321 |
| Cream of Roses | 321 |
| Elixir of Violets | 321 |
| Mint Cream | 321 |
| Mocha Cream | 321 |
| EAU SUCRE | 312 |
| FRUIT SYRUPS | 312 |
| Apricot Syrup | 313 |
| Banana Syrup | 313 |
| Blackberry | 313 |
| Cherry Syrup | 313 |
| Cranberry Syrup | 313 |
| Currant Syrup | 313 |
| Currant Syrup, with Raspberries | 313 |
| Grape Syrup | 313 |
| Lemon Syrup | 314 |
| Lime Syrup | 314 |

| | |
|---|---|
| Orange Syrup | 314 |
| Orgeat Syrup | 314 |
| Peach Syrup | 315 |
| Pineapple Syrup | 315 |
| Plum Syrup | 315 |
| Strawberry Syrup | 315 |
| Raspberry Syrup | 315 |
| Vanilla Syrup | 315 |
| Blackberry Vinegar | 315 |
| Orange Vinegar | 315 |
| Pineapple Vinegar | 315 |
| Raspberry Vinegar | 316 |
| Strawberry Vinegar | 316 |
| FRUIT WATERS (Eau de Fruits Glaces) | 319 |
| Aromatic Water | 319 |
| Cherry Water | 319 |
| Orange Water | 320 |
| Orgeat Water | 320 |
| Strawberry Water | 320 |
| LEMONADE | 319 |
| Iced Lemonade | 319 |
| Hot Lemonade | 319 |
| Frog Lemonade | 319 |
| ORANGEADE | 220 |

**SWEETBREADS—Ris de Veau—**

| | |
|---|---|
| SWEETBREADS | 90 |
| Sweetbreads a la Creme | 92 |
| Sweetbreads a la Financiere | 92 |
| Sweetbreads a la Poulette | 93 |
| Sweetbreads Broiled | 94 |
| Sweebreads Crepinettes | 93 |
| Sweetbreads, Definition of | 91 |
| Sweetbreads, Fried and Breaded | 93 |
| Sweetbreads, How to Blanch | 91 |
| Sweetbreads in Casseroles | 93 |
| Sweetbreads, Larded with Mushroom Sauce | 91 |
| Sweetbreads, Observations on | 94 |
| Sweetbreads with Green Peas | 92 |
| Sweetbreads, Smothered | 94 |
| Sweetbreads with Truffles | 92 |

**TRIPE—Double-Gras—**

| | |
|---|---|
| TRIPE (Double-Gras) | 94 |
| Tripe a la Creole | 95 |
| Tripe a la Lyonnaise | 94 |
| Tripe a la Mode de Caen | 95 |
| Tripe a la Poulette | 95 |
| Tripe, Fried | 95 |
| Tripe, Stewed | 94 |

**VEAL—Du Veau—**

| | |
|---|---|
| VEAL | 83 |
| Guides in Choosing | 72 |
| Veal, Blanquette of | 87 |
| Veal, Breast or Shoulder, Stuffed and Roasted | 84 |
| Calf's Brains, with Brown Butter Sauce | 89 |
| Calf's Brains, Fried | 89 |
| Calf's Head a la Poulette | 88 |
| Calf's Head, a la Tortue | 88 |
| Calf's Liver a la Bourgeoise | 89 |
| Calf's Liver, Fried | 89 |
| Calf's Feet, a la Poulette | 90 |
| Calf's Feet, Italian Sauce | 90 |
| Calf's Feet, Piquant Sauce | 90 |
| Calf's Feet, Plain | 90 |
| Calf's Feet, Sauce Remoulade | 90 |
| Calf's Feet, Tomato Sauce | 90 |
| Veal, Cream of | 86 |
| Veal, Croquettes of | 88 |
| Veal, Cutlets a la Milanaise | 84 |
| Veal, Cutlets, Breaded | 84 |
| Veal, Cutlets, Breaded and Broiled | 84 |
| Veal, Cutlets, en Papillottes | 84 |
| Veal, Cutlets, Smothered a la Creole | 85 |
| Veal Daube, à la Creole | 85 |
| Veal, en Ratoutille | 87 |
| Veal, Filet of, with Mushroom or Truffles | 84 |
| Veal, Fricandeau of | 85 |
| Veal, Jellied | 87 |
| Veal, Liver of, Fried with Bacon | 89 |
| Veal Loaf | 87 |
| Veal, Loin of, Roasted | 83 |
| Veal Patties | 87 |
| Veal Pot Pie | 88 |
| Veal, Roast with Fine Herbs | 83 |
| Veal, Shoulder of, Stuffed and Roasted | 84 |
| Veal, Stewed | 86 |
| Veal, Stewed with Mushrooms | 86 |
| Veal, Stewed with Potatoes | 86 |
| Veal, with Olives | 88 |

**VEGETABLES—Des Legumes—**

| | |
|---|---|
| VEGETABLES | 187 |
| ARTICHOKES | 188 |
| Artichokes a la Vinaigrette | 188 |
| Artichokes (French) Boiled | 188 |
| Artichokes (Jerusalem) Boiled | 188 |
| Artichokes (Fried) | 188 |
| Artichokes, Puree of | 188 |
| Artichokes, Sautees | 188 |
| Artichokes, Stuffed | 189 |
| ASPARAGUS | 189 |
| Asparagus, Boiled | 189 |
| Asparagus Tips, with Green Peas | 189 |
| Asparagus, Vinaigrette Sauce | 189 |
| BEANS (Des Haricots) | 189 |
| Bacon and Beans, a la Creole | 192 |
| Beans (Red) | 191 |
| Beans (Red) a la conde | 191 |
| Beans (Red) Boiled | 191 |
| Beans (Red) Burgundy Style | 191 |
| Beans (Croquettes) | 193 |
| Beans (Lima) | 192 |
| Bean Polenta | 192 |
| Beans (Red) Puree of | 191 |
| Beans (Red) and Rice | 191 |
| Beans (String) a la Poulette | 190 |
| Beans (String) Boiled with Ham | 190 |
| Beans (String) Brittainy Style | 190 |
| Beans (String) Butter Sauce | 190 |
| Beans (String), Butter Sauce | 190 |
| Beans (String), Cream Sauce | 190 |
| Beans (String), Vinaigrette Sauce | 190 |
| Beans (String), Panaches | 191 |
| Beans (White) | 192 |
| Beans (White), a la Maitre d'Hotel | 192 |
| BUTTERBEANS (Feves Plates) | 192 |
| BEETS (Des Bettraves) | 193 |
| Beets, Boiled | 193 |

| | |
|---|---|
| Beets, Buttered | 193 |
| Beets, Sauted in Butter | 193 |
| Beet Roots a la Bechamel | 193 |
| Beet Roots a la Creme | 193 |
| Beet Tops | 221 |
| BORECOLE OR CURLED KALE (Chou Vert) | 193 |
| BROCCOLI (Chou Brocoli) | 193 |
| BRUSSEL SPROUTS (Choux de Bruxelles) | 194 |
| Brussel Sprouts a la Creme | 194 |
| Brussel Sprouts, Sauted in Butter | 194 |
| CABBAGE (Du Chou) | 194 |
| Cabbage, Boiled | 194 |
| Cabbage and Corned Beef | 195 |
| Cabbage, Creamed | 195 |
| Cabbage, Sauted with Cream | 195 |
| Cabbage, Stewed | 195 |
| Cabbage, Stewed with Sausage | 195 |
| Cabbage, Stuffed | 195 |
| Cabbage, Stuffed, with Cream Sauce | 196 |
| CAULIFLOWER (Chau Fleurs) | 197 |
| Cauliflower, Boiled with Butter | 197 |
| Cauliflower, Boiled, Cream Sauce | 197 |
| Cauliflower au Gratin | 197 |
| Cauliflower a la Maitre d'Hotel | 197 |
| Cauliflower a la Vinaigrette | 197 |
| Cauliflower with White Sauce | 197 |
| CARROTS (Des Carrottes) | 198 |
| Carrots a la Creme | 198 |
| Carrots a la Lyonnaise | 198 |
| Carrots a la Maitre d'Hotel | 198 |
| Carrots Sautes a la Creole | 198 |
| Carrots, Stewed, | 198 |
| CELERY (Du Celeri) | 199 |
| Celery with Beef's Marrow | 199 |
| Celery, Creamed | 199 |
| Celery a l'Espagnole | 199 |
| Celery Fritters | 199 |
| Celery Mayonnaise | 159 |
| Celery Patties | 199 |
| Celery aux Petits Pois | 199 |
| Celery Salad | 159 |
| CEPS (Ceps) | 200 |
| Ceps, Broiled on Toast | 200 |
| Ceps, Stewed | 200 |
| Ceps on Toast | 200 |
| CHERVIL (Cherfeuil) | 200 |
| Chervil Salad | 159 |
| Chervil Vinegar | 354 |
| CHESTNUTS (Marrons) | 200 |
| Chestnuts, Boiled | 200 |
| Chestnuts with Brown Sauce | 200 |
| Chestnuts, Stewed | 200 |
| CHIVES (Cives) | 200 |
| COLLARDS | 201 |
| CORN (Du Mais) | 201 |
| Corn, Baked a la Creme | 202 |
| Corn Cakes | 202 |
| Corn, Creamed | 201 |
| Corn, on Cob | 201 |
| Corn, Fried | 202 |
| Corn, Fritters | 202 |
| Corn (Green), Planter's Style | 201 |
| Corn Pudding | 201 |
| Corn, Roasted | 201 |
| Corn Salad | 159, 202 |
| Corn, Sauted with Butter | 201 |
| Corn Soup | 202 |
| Corn and Tomatoes | 202 |
| CRESS (Cresson) | 202 |
| Cress (Salad) | 159 |
| CUCUMBER | 203 |
| Cucumber as a Garnish | 203 |
| Cucumber as a Relish | 203 |
| Cucumber Salad | 159 |
| CURRY (Kari) | 203 |
| DANDELION (Dent-de-Lion) | 203 |
| Dandelion Greens, Boiled | 203 |
| Dandelion Salad | 160 |
| EGGPLANT (Des Aubergines) | 203 |
| Eggplants, Fried | 204 |
| Eggplant Fritters | 204 |
| Eggplant, Stewed | 204 |
| Eggplant, Stuffed | 203 |
| ENDIVES (De la Chicoree) | 204 |
| Endive with Cream Sauce | 204 |
| Endive with Gravy | 204 |
| Endive Salad | 160 |
| GARLIC (De l'Ail) | 204 |
| HORSERADISH (Raifort) | 205 |
| KOHL-RABI OR TURNIP-ROOTED CABBAGE (Chou Navet) | 205 |
| LEEKS | 205 |
| LENTILS (Des Lentiles) | 205 |
| Lentil Salad | 160 |
| MANGOES (Mangos) | 218 |
| MUSHROOMS (Des Champignons) | 205 |
| Mushrooms with Cream | 205 |
| Mushrooms, Fried | 206 |
| Mushrooms, Stewed, Spanish Style | 206 |
| Mushrooms, Stewed on Toast | 205 |
| MUSTARD (Moutarde) | 206 |
| OKRA (Du Fevi) | 206 |
| Okra, Boiled | 206 |
| Okra, Stewed a la Creole | 206 |
| ONIONS (De l'Oignon) | 207 |
| Onions, Baked | 208 |
| Onions, Boiled | 207 |
| Onions, Creamed | 207 |
| Onions, Fried | 207 |
| Onions, Glazed | 207 |
| Onions, Smothered | 207 |
| Onions, Stuffed | 208 |
| PARSLEY (Persil) | 208 |
| Parsley, Chopped | 209 |
| Parsley, Fried | 209 |
| Parsley, Green | 209 |
| Parsley for Garnishing Purposes | 209 |
| PARSNIPS (Des Panais) | 209 |
| Parsnip Balls | 209 |
| Parsnips, Boiled | 209 |
| Parsnips with Cream Sauce | 209 |
| Parsnips, Fried | 209 |
| Parsnips, Fritters | 210 |
| Parsnips, Smothered | 209 |
| PEAS (Des Pois Secs) | 210 |
| Peas (Dried) | 210 |
| Peas (Kidney or Black-Eyed) | 210 |
| Peas (Split) | 210 |
| GREEN PEAS (Des Pois Verts) | 210 |
| Green Peas, Boiled | 210 |
| Green Peas, a la Bourgeoise | 210 |
| Green Peas, a la Paysanne | 210 |
| Green Peas, Canned, How to Cook | 210 |
| Green Peas, French Style | 211 |
| Green Peas, Old Creole Style | 211 |
| Green Peas, Puree of, a la | |

| | |
|---|---|
| Creole | 211 |
| Green Peas, Puree of, a la St. Germain | 211 |
| PEPPERS, Hot (Du Piments) | 218 |
| Cayenne | 218 |
| Chili | 218 |
| Pimentos | 218 |
| Tabasco | 218 |
| PEPPERS, Green (Des Piments Verts) | 218 |
| Peppers (Green), Sauted | 218 |
| Peppers (Green), Stuffed | 218 |
| POTATOES (De la Pomme de Terre) | 211 |
| Potatoes, Baked | 215 |
| Potato Balls | 215 |
| Potatoes, Brabant | 214 |
| Potatoes, Boiled | 211 |
| Potatoes a la Bourgeoise | 214 |
| Potatoes a la Creme | 212 |
| Potatoes a la Creole | 214 |
| Potatoes a la Diable | 214 |
| Potatoes a la Duchesse | 215 |
| Potatoes a la Francaise | 213 |
| Potatoes a la Lyonnaise | 213 |
| Potatoes a la Julienne | 213 |
| Potatoes a la Maitre d'Hotel | 212 |
| Potatoes a la Neige | 212 |
| Potatoes a la Parisienne | 215 |
| Potatoes au Gratin | 213 |
| Potatoes as a Garnish | 216 |
| Potatoes With Drawn Butter | 212 |
| Potato Chips | 213 |
| Potatoes, Creamed | 212 |
| Potato Croquettes | 213 |
| Potatoes, French Fried | 213 |
| Potatoes, New, With Butter | 214 |
| Potato Puffs | 212 |
| Potato Quenelles | 215 |
| Potato Snow | 212 |
| Potatoes, Souffle | 213 |
| Potatoes, Steamed | 211 |
| Potatoes, Stuffed, a la Creole | 216 |
| Potatoes, Stuffed, Lenten Style | 216 |
| Potatoes, Stuffed, Swiss Style | 216 |
| PUMPKIN (Des Citrouilles, des Giraumonts ou de Potiron) | 218 |
| Pumpkin, Baked | 219 |
| Pumpkin, Stewed | 218 |
| RADISHES (Des Radis) | 219 |
| Radish Tops | 221 |
| ROQUETTE | 219 |
| SALSIFY OR OYSTER PLANT (Salsifis) | 219 |
| Salsify or Oyster Plant a la Creme | 219 |
| Salsify or Oyster Plant a la Poulette | 219 |
| Salsify or Oyster Plant Fritters | 220 |
| Salsify or Oyster Plant, Sauted in Butter | 219 |
| SAUERKRAUT (Chou-Croute): | 196 |
| SHALLOTS (Echallottes) | 208 |
| SORREL (De l'Oseille) | 221 |
| Sorrell au Gras | 221 |
| Sorrell au Maigre | 221 |
| Puree of Sorrell | 221 |
| SPINACH (Des Epinards) | 220 |
| Spinach, Boiled | 220 |
| Spinach a la Creme | 220 |
| Spinach a la Cuisiniere | 221 |
| Spinach a la Maitre d'Hotel | 221 |
| Spinach with Hard-Boiled Eggs | 221 |
| Spinach au Jus a la Bourgeoise | 220 |
| SQUASH (Courge) | 221 |
| SWEET POTATOES (Des Patates Douces) | 216 |
| Sweet Potatoes, Baked | 217 |
| Sweet Potatoes, Boiled | 216 |
| Sweet Potatoes, au Caramel | 217 |
| Sweet Potatoes, Fried | 216 |
| Sweet Potato Fritters | 217 |
| Sweet Potato Pone | 217 |
| Sweet Potato Pudding | 217 |
| Sweet Potato Waffles | 217 |
| TOMATOES (Des Tomates) | 221 |
| Tomatoes, Broiled | 222 |
| Tomatoes, Fried | 222 |
| Tomatoes, au Gratin | 222 |
| Tomatoes, Puree of | 222 |
| Tomato Salad | 223 |
| Tomatoes, Scalloped | 222 |
| Tomatoes, Stewed | 221 |
| Tomatoes, Stuffed | 222 |
| Tomatoes, Stuffed a la Creole | 222 |
| TURNIPS (Des Navets) | 223 |
| Turnips, Baked | 223 |
| Turnips, Boiled | 223 |
| Turnips, Creamed | 223 |
| Turnips Fried in Butter | 223 |
| Turnips, Glazed | 223 |
| Turnips, Mashed | 223 |
| Turnip Tops | 221 |
| Turnip Tops a la Creole | 224 |
| TRUFFLES (Des Truffes) | 224 |
| Truffles with Champagne | 224 |
| Truffles on Minced Toast | 224 |
| Truffles, Spanish Style | 224 |
| VEGETABLE PEAR (Mirliton) | 224 |
| WATERCRESS | 202 |

**WINES—Domestic—**

| | |
|---|---|
| WINES, DOMESTIC (Liqueurs de Fruits) | 327 |
| Wine, Blackberry | 329 |
| Wine, Currant | 329 |
| Wine, Elderberry | 329 |
| Wine, Louisiana Orange | 329 |
| Wine, Muscadine | 329 |
| Wine, Sassafras Mead | 329 |
| Wine, Scuppernong | 330 |
| Wine, Strawberry | 330 |

**CONCLUSION—The Creole Home and Mother.**

# The Daily Picayune.

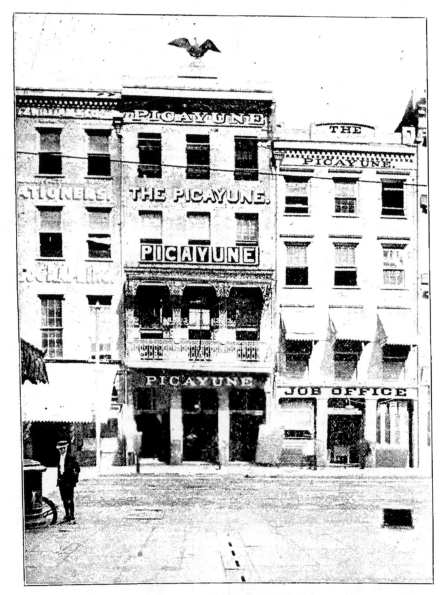

THE PICAYUNE BUILDINGS.

THE PICAYUNE is the oldest paper of the English tongue and, with the exception of the French daily, "L'Abeille de la Nouvelle Orleans," the oldest paper published in Louisiana. It was founded

January 25, 1837, in a very small way, by Francis Lumsden and George Wilkins Kendall, two practical printers and newspaper men, who have long since passed away. Its first great success was won during the war with Mexico when Mr. Kendall, acting as its war correspondent, frequently anticipated in his paper the news contained in the official dispatches. During the Civil War, and the Reconstruction Era which succeeded it, The Picayune shared the vicissitudes affecting its constituency. It was issued regularly throughout those troublous times but for a brief period in 1864, when it was seized by the United States Military authorities and its publication suspended. After the war, in 1867, the management of the paper devolved upon Mr. A. M. Holbrook, who had for some years previous been a partner in the concern, and who by deaths and withdrawals was left sole proprietor. Mr. Holbrook died in 1876 and was succeeded in the ownership and management by his widow who, as Miss E. J. Poitevent, had achieved distinction as a writer of verse and prose under the nom-de-plume of "Pearl Rivers." Her control was the first instance of the successful management of a metropolitan daily by a woman, and the progress of the paper during her regime is an eloquent tribute to her talent and her tact. In 1878, Mrs. Holbrook and Mr. George Nicholson, who had for many years been the able Business Manager of the paper, were married, and the paper was conducted under their joint management until February, 1896, when both husband and wife died within the brief period of ten days. The paper then passed, as part of their inheritance, to Leonard Kimball Nicholson and Yorke Poitevent Nicholson, sons of the preceding proprietors, and was conducted in their behalf under the title of "The Estate of Mrs. E. J. Nicholson," the wife having survived the husband, by Thos. G. Rapier, who had long been Business Manager of the paper. In 1904, the heirs having attained their majority, the Nicholson Publishing Company, Limited, was incorporated and has since conducted the paper. The spirit of progress which marked the career of the founders of the paper has continued a dominant factor in its management. In every particular The Picayune has kept abreast of the times. Its mechanical equipment comprises the latest and most valuable inventions known to the newspaper world; its news facilities are second to none, and it guards jealously its well-earned reputation of being a clean, straightforward journal, as valuable in the commercial atmosphere of the counting-room as it is welcome in the sacred precincts of the home.

ESTABLISHED 1860

# T. FITZWILLIAM & CO.,
### —LIMITED—

## Stationers, Lithographers, Printers.

## Manufacturers of Flat Opening Blank Books.

TRY ..A.. "STERLING FOUNTAIN PEN"

**GENERAL STATIONERY AND OFFICE SUPPLIES.**

=LICENSEE=
## JONES IMPROVED LOOSE LEAF LEDGERS
—AND—
## PATENT EUREKA FLAT OPENING SHEETS.

..IN.. OUR **Engraving and Lithographing Department**

We are prepared to execute promptly orders for

Wedding and Society Invitations, Bonds, Stock Certificates, Diplomas, Certificates of Deposit, Checks, Drafts, Notes, Letter, Note and Bill Heads, Labels, Show Cards, Etc.

## JOB PRINTING IN ARTISTIC STYLE

We solicit your orders for anything you may need in our line, and will give them prompt and careful attention.

# T. FITZWILLIAM & CO., LIMITED,
### 324 CAMP STREET.    321 BANK PLACE.
### TELEPHONE MAIN 993.
### NEW ORLEANS

It covers wide fields and gathers all the news.  It is attractive and enterprising without being sensational,  It is clean and impartial, reliable and progressive.

## The Paper to Read in School,

## ..Home and Mart...

ESTABLISHED JANUARY 25, 1837

*Published Daily and
Semi-Weekly*

*Is the Most Popular and Influential
Newspaper in the Southwest*

*It is an Independent
Democratic Journal*

| Gives the **Latest News** | Promotes the commercial, mechanical, agricultural and industrial interests of the Southern People :: :: :: | Cultivates Literature and commends itself as an exceptional Southern family Newspaper |

### Terms of Subscription

| Daily Picayune | Twice-a-Week Picayune |
|---|---|
| Including Sunday Issue, seven papers per week | Published Monday and Thursday Mornings, 10 pages each issue |
| 12 months...........$12.00 | 12 months, outside New Orleans.......$1 |
| 6 months........... 6.00 | 12 m'ths in New Orleans 2 |

PRINTED BY

THE PICAYUNE JOB OFFICE

330 CAMP STREET

NEW ORLEANS, U. S. A.

# ImTheStory.com

Personalized Classic Books in many genre's

Unique gift for kids, partners, friends, colleagues

Customize:

- Character Names
- Upload your own front/back cover images (optional)
- Inscribe a personal message/dedication on the inside page (optional)

Customize many titles Including
- Alice in Wonderland
- Romeo and Juliet
- The Wizard of Oz
- A Christmas Carol
- Dracula
- Dr. Jekyll & Mr. Hyde
- And more...

CPSIA information can be obtained
at www.ICGtesting.com
Printed in the USA
LVHW081528140119
603842LV00020B/1168/P